Encyclopedia of
Gothic Literature

Encyclopedia of Gothic Literature

MARY ELLEN SNODGRASS

☑® Facts On File, Inc.

Encyclopedia of Gothic Literature

Copyright © 2005 by Mary Ellen Snodgrass

Facts On File, Inc.
132 West 31st Street
New York NY 10001

Library of Congress Cataloging-in-Publication Data
Snodgrass, Mary Ellen.
Encyclopedia of Gothic Literature / by Mary Ellen Snodgrass.
p. cm.
Includes bibliographical references and index.
ISBN 0-8160-5528-9 (alk. paper)
1. Gothic revival (Literature)—Encyclopedias. I. Title: Encyclopedia of Gothic literature. II. Title.
PN3435.S58 2005
809'.911—dc22
2004046986

Text design by Joan M. Toro
Cover design by Semadar Megged

Printed in the United States of America

VB Hermitage 10 9 8 7 6 5 4 3 2

This book is printed on acid-free paper.

For my friend Diana Norman, who is ever an example to me of careful research and spirited writing

CONTENTS

Imagination is a capricious rover, fond of every object that
carries it out of the track of daily and familiar occurrences.
It loves to traverse the pathless desert and enchanted forest,
to roam amidst wild uncultivated nature, and amuse itself
with the extravagant effects of untutored passions.

—Poet Elizabeth Carter in a letter to Elizabeth Vesey, August 14, 1780

A man who does not contribute his quota of grim story nowadays,
seems hardly to be free of the republic of letters. He is bound to wear
a death's head as part of his insignia. If he does not frighten everybody,
he is nobody. If he does not shock the ladies,
what can be expected of him?

—Leigh Hunt, *Tale for a Chimney Corner* (1819)

PREFACE

Encyclopedia of Gothic Literature invites the writer, literary historian, researcher, student, teacher, librarian, and general reader to sample a wide range of works grouped under the definition of Gothic fiction. The text offers an easy-to-use source of information arranged alphabetically into more than 400 entries. Lengthy discussions of Gothic convention, horror narratives, Gothic drama, the supernatural, suspense, female victims, and the rescue motif outline the evolution of genre parameters. Enhancing the reader's understanding of genre development are details of anti-Catholic themes and subtexts and discussions of such topics as female Gothic and *The Madwoman in the Attic,* a feminist breakthrough in interpretation. Entries on writers (Joanna Baillie, Isaac Bashevis Singer, Stephen King), sources (*Blackwood's Edinburgh Magazine,* Gothic bluebooks, Kabbalism, legend), literary history (preromanticism, censorship), literary method (hyperbole, atmosphere, mood, tone), characters (Heathcliff, Bertha Rochester, Montresor, Hazel Motes), monsters (dybbuk, lycanthropy, witchcraft, vampirism), motifs (the wandering Jew, Bluebeard, Faust, otherness), conventions (Byronic hero, diabolism, flight motif), and settings (Castle Dracula, Udolpho, Manderley) contribute to an understanding of the Gothic mode.

Research materials derive from various sources beginning with a lengthy roll call of Gothic scholars: Jennifer Carnell, E. J. Clery, Jeffrey Cohen, Kate Ellis, Teresa Goddu, Claire Gorrara, Michael Hadley, Judith Halberstam, Cyndy Hendershot, Brendan Hennessy, Avril Horner, Wolfgang Kayse, Julia Kristeva, Clara McIntyre, Peter Messent, Michael Meyer, Robert Mighall, Kay Mussell, Elizabeth Napier, Margot Northey, Joyce Carol Oates, Paul Ranger, Gabriel Ronay, Victor Sage, Cannon Schmitt, Andrew Smith, Robert Spector, Jack Sullivan, Tsvetan Todorov, Yi-Fu Tuan, James Twitchell, S. L. Varnado, Andrew Webber, Susan Williams, Judith Wilt, and Leonard Wolf. Of particular merit are the analyses of Margaret Atwood, Susan Gubar, Sandra Gilbert, H. P. Lovecraft, David Punter, Montague Summers, Mary Tarr, Devendra Varma, and Anne Williams. In addition to a panoply of recovered Gothic works and facsimile editions are the handy electronic texts, including biographies from the University of Pennsylvania and Sheffield Hallam University, *The Literary Encyclopedia, Blackwood's Edinburgh Magazine,* the illustrations of George Cruikshank from Princeton University, Dickens's London, The Northanger Canon, and Chris Willis's Web sites.

Rounding out the text are additional study aids to particularize the lives of writers such as William Cullen Bryant and August Wilson; published works including *Bellefleur* and "The House of Night"; and details of Japanese Gothic, La Llorona, chiaroscuro, premature burial, and Gothic serials. Reference helps include alphabetic listings of major titles and authors, a time line of the evolution of Gothic literature, an overview of cinematic versions, and separate bibliographies of primary and secondary sources. A thorough index covers people, places, sources, motifs, literary terms, titles, publishers, and literary authorities.

In collecting primary and secondary source material, I called on numerous people for assistance and advice. I am indebted to book dealer Avis Gachet at Wonderland Books; to Beth Bradshaw and Hannah Owen at the Patrick Beaver Library in Hickory, North Carolina; to Amy Jew and Wanda Rozzelle at the Catawba County Library in Newton, North Carolina; to Susan Keller at Western Piedmont Community College in Morganton, North Carolina; and to Mark Schumacher at the Jackson Library, UNC-Greensboro. Additional thanks go to Elisabeth McRae at the Toronto Reference Library in Toronto, Canada.

INTRODUCTION

Scary stories are indigenous to human artistry. Out of curiosity about the secrets of nature, human behavior, and unexplained bumps in the night, from early times people have investigated the mystic and aberrant and shared their findings about the unknown. When literary trends fled the high-toned, artificial sanctuary of the Age of Reason, the backlash against regularity and predictability sent literature far into the murky past to retrieve traditional folksay about intriguing mysteries. The most accessible model of imaginative narrative derived from the Middle Ages, a fertile period textured with contrasts—great productivity and abominable crimes, piety and religious barbarism, admirable soldiery and the doings of witches, scientific innovation and the dabblings of alchemists, royal ritual and the danse macabre, and bold architecture to suit church and civic needs. The period thrived on a grand cultural exchange as wandering rabbis visited distant enclaves of Judaism, traders imported the wonders of Asia, and Christian crusaders tramped the long road to Jerusalem. The writings generated from the period range from saint lore and "Salve, Regina" to Reynard the Fox fables, Chinese spirit tales, troubadour love plaints, and stories of shape-shifting. Like finely stitched tapestry, the strands of medievalism held firm, lending their color and decorative meanderings to the late 1700s, when traditional Gothic literature made its formal debut.

As is often true with something new and different, analysis discloses familiar elements at the heart of originality. Thus, the 18th-century writings of Abbé Prévost, the graveyard poets, Tobias Smollett, and Horace Walpole presented oddments culled from Asian storytelling, Scheherazade's cyclic stories from *The Arabian Nights*, Charles Perrault's "Beauty and the Beast," Geoffrey Chaucer's *Canterbury Tales,* and the bloody tragedies of the Renaissance stage. With scraps of picaresque literature, episodic adventure lore, and supernatural balladry, the gothic school returned to the wilderness and the architecture of the distant past for night sounds and shadows on which to anchor tales of terror. The critic Anna Laetitia Barbauld legitimized such nerve-tingling page-turners for their stimulus to the emotions and intellect. Buoyed by the example of Johann Wolfgang von Goethe, Friedrich von Schiller, and the German romantics, the English-speaking world created its own pulse-pumping narratives, beginning with William Beckford's *Vathek*, Sophia Lee's *The Recess*, Charlotte Smith's *The Old Manor House*, and the pace-setting *The Mysteries of Udolpho* by Ann Radcliffe, matriarch of the English Gothic movement.

As with any organic matter, gothic literature flexed its tentacles in varied territory to touch the scandalous, perilous, and outré—German bandit lore, stalking in William Godwin's *Caleb Williams*, escapism in the abbey and castle novels of Francis Lathom and Regina Roche, domestic battery in Punch-and-Judy street shows, and the shocking merger of piety with sex crimes in Matthew Gregory Lewis's *The Monk*, a high point of anti-Catholic daring. For the semiliterate underclass, a new industry in Gothic bluebooks and penny shockers offered scaled-down versions of classic stories and spin-offs of bestselling bodice rippers.

Simultaneous with the flowering of popular pulp fiction were the writings of England's romantics—the nature-based odes and allegories of John Keats and Samuel Taylor Coleridge, the stirring sensibilities of Lord Byron and Percy Bysshe Shelley, and the emergence of vampire tales by John Polidori and Mary Wollstonecraft Shelley. One aspect that the era's writers had in common was the idealism of youth: Monk Lewis was 15 when he began imitating German ballads; Percy Shelley was still in school when he completed *Zastrozzi*; Mary Shelley was 21 when she published *Frankenstein*; Keats wrote *The Eve of St. Agnes* at 24.

A significant factor in the untidy burgeoning of Gothicism was the interchange of themes and styles as English writers devoured contemporary French romances, the Grimms' Teutonic tales, and German doppelgänger motifs, both in the original and English translations. Europeans thrilled to the frontier gothic of North America, beginning with Charles Brockden Brown's eerie *Wieland* and advancing to racial warfare in John Richardson's *Wacousta* and the serial murders in Robert Montgomery Bird's *Nick of the Woods*, the first overt testimony of white America's intent to eradicate Native Americans from the frontier. Decades before Sigmund Freud provided a paradigm for the human psyche, echoes of disturbing behaviors forced readers of Gothic literature to interpret subtexts of prejudice, classism, and abnormality in thought and action: in the motivation for James Hogg's *The Private Memoirs and Confessions of a Justified Sinner*, and in Caroline Lamb's *Ada Reis*, James Fenimore Cooper's *The Last of the Mohicans*, Goethe's *Faust*, Sir Walter Scott's *Ivanhoe*, and Charles Maturin's *Melmoth the Wanderer*.

Gothic literature made its way along the low road with the lengthy serial *Varney the Vampire* and Minerva Press crowd-pleasers, and the high road of fine writing by Edward Bulwer-Lytton, Théophile Gautier, Nikolai Gogol, Hans Christian Andersen, Vladimir Odoevsky, and Edgar Allan Poe, the star Gothicist of the 1830s and 1840s. At mid-century, in *The Scarlet Letter* and *The House of the Seven Gables*, Nathaniel Hawthorne turned his thoughts on New England's late 17th-century witch persecutions into soul-deep musings on the devastation wrought by secret sin and public shame. His friend

Herman Melville ventured into the perils of vengeance with *Moby-Dick*, a sea epic that peels away layers of anguish and striving to get at the core of an obsession so virulent that it wipes out all but one of a whaler's crew and sends the ship to the briny depths. As cities began to fester from the pollution and ethical rot instigated by the Industrial Revolution, Charles Dickens focused less on individual fault than on society's failings. His rage at apathy in the genteel class inspired one of Victorian literature's finest ghost stories, *A Christmas Carol*, and empowered *Oliver Twist*, *Bleak House*, *Great Expectations*, and *A Tale of Two Cities* with fictional glimpses of civil dysfunction and international chaos.

For the first time in literary history, female writers flourished along the book industry's continuum as writers, publishers, editors, adapters, and translators of gothic works. Reared among the literary elite, Christina Rossetti presented female relationships in *The Goblin Market*, a charmingly macabre fairy tale of menacing trolls and the rescue of one sister by another without the aid of a male. In 1847, two of the Brontë sisters produced a literary epiphany with a pair of trendsetters, Charlotte's *Jane Eyre* and Emily's *Wuthering Heights*. Their respective heroines, Jane Eyre and Catherine Earnshaw, escaped the shackles of patriarchy to actualize career and personal longings, both at considerable cost. In New England, Harriet Beecher Stowe examined a subset of female enslavement in *Uncle Tom's Cabin*, an abolitionist melodrama.

The second half of the 19th century advanced gothic motifs beyond the trite maiden-in-the-castle scenarios of the 1790s to mature artistry elucidating humanistic themes. Charles Baudelaire, a disciple of Poe, voiced urban terrors of death and decay in *Les Fleurs du Mal*, a symbolist verse classic. Wilkie Collins capitalized on increasing unrest at immigration and city crime in *The Woman in White*, the prototype sensation novel. Subsequent shockers abandoned medieval atrocities to divulge realistic violence, forced marriage, incest, bigamy, inheritance theft, illegitimacy, dissipation, and spousal abuse, the scenarios in domestic novels by Ellen Wood and Mary Elizabeth Braddon. Victor Hugo turned the standard crime tale to social purpose by exposing continued injustice to the underclass in *Les Misérables,* a novel that reaches its dramatic climax in the sewers of Paris.

American Gothic evolved a unique study of human guile and cruelty. In the Mississippi Delta, George Washington Cable spoke for both the Creole and the slave in "Jean-ah Poquelin" and in "Bras Coupé," a hero tale of slave coercion nested in a tormented biracial saga, *The Grandissimes.* The Atlantic Coast elite found a spokesman in Henry James, author of *The Portrait of a Lady* and a perplexing face-to-face encounter with self in "The Jolly Corner." His elegant prose stimulated the imagination of Edith Wharton, who crafted her own spectral tales as well as the domestic horrors of *Ethan Frome,* a novella replete with unrequited love amid unstinting toil and despair.

As Europe elevated literary standards with the refined storytelling of Guy de Maupassant, the short story moved far from polite society to the visceral trauma of *contes cruels* (cruel tales) by Villiers de L'Isle-Adam and the writing team of Émile Erckmann and Louis Alexandre Chatrian. Expatriate Lafcadio Hearn turned translation of Asian tales into art. The Scottish storyteller Robert Louis Stevenson fled a sickly body by writing the imaginative pirate tale *Treasure Island* and the Gothic masterpiece of the 1880s, *Dr. Jekyll and Mr. Hyde,* a psychodrama of lethal duality in the human spirit. A contemporary, the Anglo-Indian Rudyard Kipling, presented his own stark images of the split persona in his colonial short fiction. Such Kipling stories as "The Mark of the Beast," "Without Benefit of Clergy," and "The Phantom Rickshaw" question a "have" nation's right to exploit the global "have-nots." The query, posed decades earlier in Lewis's "The Anaconda," refused to disappear as Gothic writers W. W. Jacobs and Arthur Conan Doyle infused texts with disturbing hints of the evils imported from subject nations. Doyle's command of logic suited the birth of Sherlock Holmes, one of the world's most revered fictional sleuths, whose knowledge of world exotica and criminal motivation wowed a huge fan base on both sides of the Atlantic.

Late in the 1800s, the disparate strands of Gothicism remained vigorous. From the American West came the ghost and Civil War stories of Ambrose Bierce, the author of "An Occurrence at Owl Creek Bridge." Charlotte Perkins Gilman used the dungeon motif in "The Yellow Wallpaper," a diatribe against madness induced by obstacles to female freedom of movement and expression. From Oscar Wilde came cautionary fables, the allegorical novel *The Picture of Dorian Gray,* and the play *Salomé,* a resetting of the biblical tale of the princess who dances with the head of John the Baptist on a salver. George du Maurier provided the English language with an eponymous character, Svengali, the manipulator of a singer in *Trilby,* set in the modish art district of Paris. In *The Island of Dr. Moreau,* H. G. Wells used science fiction to oppose the amorality of animal experimentation, a precursor of current outrage at unethical cloning and cell manipulation. The height of fin de siècle Gothic fiction, Bram Stoker's *Dracula,* impressed on readers the ambiguous nature of evil and its victimization of innocence. Amplifying additional moral concerns were Wilde's *The Ballad of Reading Gaol,* Mark Twain's devil story "The Man That Corrupted Hadleyburg," and Henry James's *The Turn of the Screw.*

Twentieth-century Gothic stepped up the moral challenge, beginning with Joseph Conrad's *Heart of Darkness,* one of the genre's unflinching studies of human depravity. While Mary Roberts Rinehart's detective stories and Victoria Holt's romances fed the demand for cerebral puzzlers and happily-ever-after love stories, Gaston Leroux continued the search for the impetus to male-on-female cruelty in *The Phantom of the Opera,* a long-lived narrative of obsessive love. Djuna Barnes's gay Gothic ventured out of the closet once occupied by Marie Corelli and Oscar Wilde. Karel Čapek depicted out-of-control scientific quest as crime against humanity in *R.U.R.,* a dystopian play that gave the world the term *robot.* Gertrude Atherton's *Black Oxen* made a parallel foray into the pseudo-science of everlasting youth and beauty. From Edna Ferber and O. E. Rölvaag, respectively, came *Cimarron* and *Giants in the Earth,* two post-frontier novels depicting the price of westering as prairies gave way to farms and villages. Carrying the settlement of the wilderness through all its phases were William Faulkner's southern sagas, picturing racism and giving glimpses of the decline of gentility in *Absalom, Absalom!* and "A Rose for Emily."

In the past half-century, Gothic literature has continued to supply readers with escapist fiction as well as challenges to mind and heart. Neogothicism serves a variety of motifs and themes—the convoluted horror tales of H. P. Lovecraft, Daphne du Maurier's English thriller "The Birds," threats to midwestern children in Ray Bradbury's *Something Wicked This Way Comes,* the quirky human dramas in Shirley Jackson and Eudora Welty's short story collections and the plays of Marsha Norman and Beth Henley, Truman Capote's nonfiction novel *In Cold Blood,* and the love-gone-wrong plots of Carson McCullers, Iris Murdoch, and Joyce Carol Oates. Serious writers have pressed Gothic convention into exacting fields—for example, Arthur Miller's reprise of the Salem witch trials in *The Crucible,* Jean Rhys's image of Caribbean passion spurned by cold English repression in *Wide Sargasso Sea,* and Rudolfo Anaya's revelation of Old World herbalism put to use by a good witch in *Bless Me, Ultima.* Gothic settings

and situations have maintained their popularity in non-Gothic novels; examples include the Spanish Inquisition grilling innocent monks in Umberto Eco's *The Name of the Rose,* the quest for female autonomy in Margaret Atwood's *The Handmaid's Tale,* the dangers of institutional coercion in Margaret Edson's *Wit,* and the value of the occult during the Mexican Revolution in Laura Esquivel's *Like Water for Chocolate* and in Isabel Allende's *The House of the Spirits.* One of the most successful Gothicists, Toni Morrison, won a Nobel Prize in part for *Beloved,* a ghost narrative set at a safe house along the Ohio Underground Railroad. With the turn of the millennium, Gothic works showed no sign of letup as Atwood and Michel Faber reexamined patriarchal gender relationships in *The Blind Assassin* and *The Crimson Petal and the White,* Dan Brown revived the Illuminati novel with *The Da Vinci Code,* and Virginia Renfro Ellis graced the wistful longing of *The Wedding Dress* with an odyssey of homesick revenants.

A

The Abbey of Clunedale
Dr. Nathan Drake
(1804)

The Abbey of Clunedale is the work of Dr. Nathan DRAKE, a Shakespearean scholar and respected literary critic who moonlighted as a writer of GOTHIC BLUEBOOKS. The story is the outgrowth of his scholarly interest in SUPERNATURAL literature as a balance to critical, didactic, and satiric writings, which dominated the Augustan Age. Drake was influenced by the Gothic philosophy of novelist Ann RADCLIFFE, who introduced enigmas and frightening events, then produced a logical explanation of their provenance. Drake opens his story with the MELANCHOLY of Edward de Courtenay in 1587, who grieves for his dead father. On Edward's walk to the abbey of Clunedale, which Henry VIII had pillaged in 1540, Drake describes the stereotypical Gothic setting, a crumbling stone façade covered in ivy.

Drake's tale follows the Radcliffean mode of arousing fear of a Gothic scenario with the unexpected appearance of a couple at the altar, then stripping the two of their menace. Edward interviews Clifford, a fellow soldier, and learns of the accidental killing of his wife and brother-in-law. Mateless, Clifford and his sister Caroline visit the graves at evening; Caroline plays the harp to relieve his sadness. The austere couple and the ethereal strains of plucked strings are sources of a rumor of ghosts at Clunedale Abbey. Drake closes the story with Edward's tenderness and respect for Clifford's grief and with the marriage of Edward to Caroline, a common SYMBOL of restored order and harmony in Gothic novels.

Bibliography

Clery, E. J. *The Rise of Supernatural Fiction, 1762–1800.* Cambridge: Cambridge University Press, 1995.

Varma, Devendra P. *The Gothic Flame.* New York: Russell & Russell, 1966.

aberrant behavior

The peculiarities of behavior in Gothic literature derive from author intent to explain the perverse, cruel, and murderous tendencies in human nature, as found in a widower's OBSESSION with the teeth of his wife's corpse in Edgar Allan POE's "Berenice" (1835), a neurotic girl's retreat from a suffocating family in Eudora WELTY's comic story "Why I Live at the P. O." (1941), and the minister's swooning from fear of water in Australian novelist Peter Carey's *Oscar and Lucinda* (1988). Types of inexplicable behavior vary in intensity from the self-burial of Miss HAVISHAM in SATIS HOUSE in Charles DICKENS's GREAT EXPECTATIONS (1861) and the call of satanic voices in James HOGG's crime novel *The Private Memoirs and Confessions of a Justified Sinner* (1824) to the soul POSSESSION in S. Ansky's *Der Dybbuk* (ca. 1916) and the jeering sodomizer who stalks a party of hunters in James Dickey's *Deliverance* (1970), a vehicle of SOUTHERN GOTHIC. By examining dialogue, dreams, visions, and delusions, Gothic authors provide psychological insight into human perversity and the survival instincts that enable individuals to combat terrifying experiences, as in Robert Louis STEVENSON's lab scientist's suicidal ending of schizophrenic bouts in DR. JEKYLL AND MR. HYDE (1886); and the librarian's defiance of Mr. Dark, the manic carnival owner and victimizer of children in Ray BRADBURY's SOMETHING WICKED THIS WAY COMES (1962).

AMERICAN GOTHIC got its start with dismaying images of frontier mayhem and racism. Charles Brockden BROWN's seminal novel WIELAND (1798) depicts a berserk family murderer, Theodore Wieland, whose heinous crimes parallel the mania of the doomed killer Ajax in Greek mythology. Following Brown in the tradition of frontier VIOLENCE was Robert Montgomery BIRD's picture of murderous psychosis in NICK OF THE WOODS; or, The Jibbenainosay: A Tale of Kentucky (1837), a vision of Nathan/Nick, the Quaker husband and father turned savagely genocidal in the wake of his family's massacre by Indians. In a final face-off against Wenonga, a Wyandott chief, Nathan's persona is transformed: "A laugh that would have become the jaws of a hyena lighted up his visage, and sounded from his lips" (Bird, 323). The merger of Quaker speech with menace produces a chilling outburst: "Look!" he cried, "thee has thee wish! Thee sees the destroyer of thee race,—ay, murdering villain, the destroyer of thee people, and theeself!" (ibid.). A precursor of Nathaniel HAWTHORNE's guilt-obsessed protagonists and Herman MELVILLE's sick-souled Captain Ahab, Bird's Nathan Slaughter brazens a dual position in society as traumatized family man and the vengeful slayer of Shawnee.

Victorian novels thrived on breakthroughs in the treatment of melancholia and other mental ills. Charlotte BRONTË exposed her own psychological flaws by filling Gothic fiction with autobiographical details. In VILLETTE (1853), protagonist Lucy Snow develops sadomasochism complicated by anger, bitterness, exhibitionism, and voyeurism in a European setting that the author had experienced. Brontë created her misguided character to express the bleakness of human motives. Repressed, sarcastic, and haunted by inner voices, Snow is an UNRELIABLE NARRATOR who conceals her past, leaving the reader to guess the reason for her self-mutilation and the undisclosed conclusion to her life story. More complex are actual incidents of INSANITY. In Bram STOKER's DRACULA (1897), the lunatic Renfield, a pseudo-apostle of the master vampire, sinks into eccentricity that declines further into aberrance. Deranged and manic, he devours insects and sniffs out drops of blood, a characteristic of VAMPIRISM that his uninformed physician, Dr. Seward, misinterprets.

Twentieth-century Gothic perpetuated the focus on abnormal human motives and actions. An example is the Southern Gothic writings of Flannery O'CONNOR, who capped her string of peculiar characters with Hazel MOTES, a self-made apostate and martyr in WISE BLOOD (1952). Turning to nature for models of oddness, Daphne DU MAURIER's "THE BIRDS" (1952) characterizes strange behaviors in songbirds that develop the instincts of birds of prey. Toni MORRISON combined madness with haunting in BELOVED (1987), in which the spirit of a murdered child returns to whine and to demand attention from her elders as a blatant reminder that her frenzied mother slit her throat to shield her from a life of slavery and slave breeding. Playwright August WILSON examines the complexity of aberrance in Seven Guitars (1995), in which the crazed visionary Hedley slays chickens for sale, then inexplicably turns his machete on a neighbor.

Bibliography

Bird, Robert Montgomery. Nick of the Woods; or, The Jibbenainosay. New Haven, Conn.: College & University Press, 1967.

Forsyth, Beverly. "The Two Faces of Lucy Snowe: A Study in Deviant Behavior," Studies in the Novel 29, no. 1 (spring 1997): 17–25.

Griffin, Susan M. "'The Dark Stranger': Sensationalism and Anti-Catholicism in Sarah Josepha Hale's Traits of American Life," Legacy 14, no. 1 (1997): 13–24.

Paige, Linda Rohrer. "White Trash, Low Class, and No Class At All: Perverse Portraits of Phallic Power in Flannery O'Connor's 'Wise Blood,'" Papers on Language & Literature 33, no. 3 (summer 1997): 325–333.

Twitchell, James B. The Living Dead: A Study of the Vampire in Romantic Literature. Durham, N.C.: Duke University Press, 1981.

Absalom, Absalom!
William Faulkner
(1936)

Absalom, Absalom!, William FAULKNER's circuitous Gothic tragedy of the fall of the house of Sutpen, is his strongest denunciation of the South's accumulated sins of enslavement of blacks, racism and miscegenation, incest, fratricide, and land lust. The novel lacks the trappings of traditional Gothic, but adheres to the atmospheric recounting of horror. In a recasting of the FAUST LEGEND, Faulkner fills the nightmarish novel with moral depravity in the villain Thomas Sutpen. By depicting the misspent passions of the self-made frontiersman, the text reprises regional sins and self-incrimination.

The saga derives its power from the OBSESSION of Thomas Sutpen to establish a self-ennobling lineage. Willful to the point of madness, he dwells outside society in a compact diabolic realm. As Faulkner describes him, "the demon himself had grown old: with a kind of condensation, an anguished emergence of the primary indomitable ossification which the soft color and texture, the light electric aura of youth, had merely temporarily assuaged but never concealed" (151). After Sutpen realizes that Eulalia Bon, his Haitian wife, is a Creole, he replaces her with a white mate and rejects Eulalia's son Charles. Like Count DRACULA's Lucy Westenra, Ellen Coldfield caters to Sutpen's designs by producing the son and daughter who legitimize his dynasty. However, like Edgar Allan POE's HOUSE OF USHER, the Sutpen mansion, built on cruelty and bondage, collapses under the weight of despair, racism, and the repudiation of Sutpen's mixed-blood son Henry. In amazement at the complex web of sins in the Sutpen history, the OUTSIDER Shreve McCannon marvels, "No wonder you folks all outlive yourselves by years and years and years" (*ibid.*, 301).

Bibliography
Faulkner, William. *Absalom, Absalom!* New York: Vintage International, 1990.

Howe, Irving. *William Faulkner: A Critical Study.* New York: Vintage Books, 1962.

Ruland, Richard, and Malcolm Bradbury. *From Puritanism to Postmodernism: A History of American Literature.* New York: Penguin, 1991.

Williams, Anne. *Art of Darkness: A Poetics of Gothic.* Chicago: University of Chicago Press, 1995.

Ainsworth, William Harrison
(1805–1882)

A master of the GHOST STORY, crime novel, and historical romance, William Harrison Ainsworth earned his living primarily from writing for the popular press. He was born in Manchester, England, and wrote GOTHIC DRAMA in boyhood. After abandoning the study of law, he began publishing stories at age 17 under the pseudonym Cheviot Ticheburn. In 1822, he emulated Ann RADCLIFFE's style to produce his first sensational works, "The Test of Affection" for *European Magazine* and "The Spectre Bride" for *Arliss's Pocket Magazine.* After expanding to longer fiction, he invented the NEWGATE NOVEL with *Rookwood* (1834), a best-selling thriller about highwayman Dick Turpin and his horse Black Bess published anonymously and illustrated by George CRUIKSHANK, the era's most prominent illustrator of Gothic fiction. The text, based on characters and action from Sir Walter SCOTT's Gothic MELODRAMA *The Bride of Lammermoor* (1819), satisfied reader interest in dark and fearful elements—a gypsy fortune-teller, a family curse and dispossessed heir, disguises, burial vaults, and the criminal flight of the outlaw Turpin, Ainsworth's boyhood hero. The book appeared in France under the title *Gentile-hommes du Grand Chemin* (*Gentlemen of the Great Highway*).

Following Charles DICKENS into the editor's chair at *Bentley's Miscellany*, Ainsworth progressed to the composition of 39 historical novels and costume romances while encouraging the careers of American Gothicist Robert Montgomery BIRD and English freelancer Ellen WOOD. Influenced by Edward BULWER-LYTTON's *Paul Clifford* (1830), Ainsworth advanced the Newgate novel with a study of criminality, the three-volume *Jack Sheppard* (1839), which denounced the justice system for reserving the gallows primarily for the poor and underprivileged. Eight imitators rapidly emulated the juicy episodic text for London stage drama; the author Mary Elizabeth BRADDON acted in one such play at the Surrey Theatre.

Ainsworth followed with an historical romance, *The Tower of London* (1840), which depicts Lady Jane Grey's flight from captivity, a common motif in Gothic fiction.

From the proceeds of these popular novels, Ainsworth purchased *Bentley's* and the *New Monthly Magazine* and launched his own publication, *Ainsworth's Magazine,* in which he serialized the novel *Auriol; or, The Elixir of Life* (1846), depicting alchemy, a pact with Satan, and blood sacrifice during the reign of James I. Ainsworth's forthright style and careful allotment of detail within episodes influenced both Dickens and the novelist William Makepeace Thackeray. Ainsworth's graveyard poetry cropped up in an unusual reprise, Dickens's imitation of Ainsworth's Gothic verse "Mandrake" and "Churchyard Yew," which Dickens reset as "The Ivy Green" in *Pickwick Papers* (1836–37).

Though financially successful, Ainsworth never rose above derivative melodrama and ended his career writing at the low end of Gothic media, the penny dreadful or GOTHIC BLUEBOOK. With *Windsor Castle* (1848), a tale of Herne the Hunter, he exploited a universal curiosity about demonic SHAPE-SHIFTING and tapped British interest in the late Tudors, particularly the lascivious Henry VIII and the adultery of his second wife, Anne Boleyn. Ainsworth focused on DIABOLISM in *The Lancashire Witches: A Romance of Pendle Forest* (1849), England's first major witch novel and the first depiction of an historic witch trial of 1612, which sent 10 people to the gallows.

Bibliography

Carnell, Jennifer. *The Literary Lives of Mary Elizabeth Braddon.* Hastings, Sussex: Sensation Press, 2000.

Haining, Peter, ed. *Gothic Tales of Terror.* New York: Taplinger, 1972.

Hollingsworth, Keith. *The Newgate Novel, 1830–1847.* Detroit: Wayne State University Press, 1963.

Worth, George J. *William Harrison Ainsworth.* New York: Twayne, 1972.

allegory

The presentation of literal and symbolic meaning through allegory heightens meaning by imposing order on complex ideas and making themes more striking and vivid, as with the nature of class struggle in William GODWIN's CALEB WILLIAMS (1794) and in William FAULKNER's *ABSALOM, ABSALOM!* (1936), an allegory of the rise and fall of the American South in the failure of Thomas Sutpen to establish a dynasty. Gothic literature depends upon the visual imagery of allegory to supply multiple levels of significance, for example, the alienation of the wandering OUTSIDER in Samuel Taylor COLERIDGE's *THE RIME OF THE ANCIENT MARINER* (1798) and the implication of DIABOLISM in Mark Twain's "The Man Who Corrupted Hadleyburg" (1898), which fosters a SUBTEXT of greed and hypocrisy. Allegory promotes ATMOSPHERE and characterization in the DANSE MACABRE, a pictorial reminder of human mortality.

Gothic settings such as crumbling cathedrals and cloisters and colonial outposts pique the imagination with implications of institutional decay, the theme of Umberto ECO's medieval detective novel *The Name of the Rose* (1980). The phobias and visceral fears represented by MONSTERS, phantasms, and ABERRANT BEHAVIOR acquire immediacy, as in the characterization of peasant fears in vampire LEGENDS, Robert Montgomery BIRD's depiction of racial genocide in *NICK OF THE WOODS; or, The Jibbenainosay: A Tale of Kentucky* (1837), and the colonial exploitation and VIOLENCE implied in W. W. JACOBS's "THE MONKEY'S PAW" (1902). Sexual allegory in the BLUEBEARD MYTH and "BEAUTY AND THE BEAST" scenarios clarifies the misogyny and domestic horror of patriarchal marriage, which can place women in the clutches of fearsome males, the situation in Angela CARTER's *The Bloody Chamber* (1979).

Nineteenth-century allegory developed psychological aberrations through close-up images of human oddities. Matthew Gregory LEWIS's "THE ANACONDA" (1808) acts out the author's dismay at colonial totalitarianism. In "YOUNG GOODMAN BROWN" (1835), Nathaniel HAWTHORNE presented the uncompromising moral milieu of the Salem witch trials of 1692, when his ancestor, Justice John Hathorne, condemned suspected witches to death. Edgar Allan POE applied an allegorical tableau to more universal themes in "THE MASQUE OF THE RED DEATH" (1842), which creates in masque form the human flight from pestilence.

As a reflection of the human condition, allegory accommodates a wide range of individual failings and weaknesses. Hans Christian ANDERSEN portrays vanity in "The Red Shoes" (1845), a terror fable that describes the amputation of a young girl's feet to free her from demonic slippers. On a grander scale, Charles DICKENS lambastes mid-Victorian institutions and public apathy toward the poor in *BLEAK HOUSE* (1853), an extended allegory of illegitimacy and its corruption of the nuclear family. In *THE GOBLIN MARKET* (1862), poet Christina ROSSETTI characterizes the power of sibling love over worldly temptation.

Twentieth-century allegory tended toward somber Gothic pictures of humanity's struggle for survival, the controlling image of Karel ČAPEK's macabre robot play *R.U.R.* (1921) and the warnings of technological disaster in the MAD SCIENTIST plots of Ray BRADBURY, H. P. LOVECRAFT, and H. G. WELLS. The individual's powerlessness permeates Shirley JACKSON's "THE LOTTERY" (1948) and Daphne DU MAURIER's "THE BIRDS" (1952), an allegory of the human struggle against rampaging nature. Fearful images of the twisted human psyche empower Flannery O'CONNOR's Christian allegory in *WISE BLOOD* (1952) and John GARDNER's dark fable *Grendel* (1971), an allegory of the human stalker from a feral beast's point of view.

Bibliography

Johnson, Barbara E. "Allegory and Psychoanalysis," *Journal of African American History* 88, no. 1 (winter 2003): 66–70.

Ruland, Richard, and Malcolm Bradbury. *From Puritanism to Postmodernism: A History of American Literature.* New York: Penguin, 1991.

Whitt, Jan. *Allegory and the Modern Southern Novel.* Macon, Ga.: Mercer University Press, 1994.

Allende, Isabel
(1942–   )

The Latin American author and journalist Isabel Allende textures her imaginative fiction with Gothic themes and motifs. Born in Lima, Peru, and reared in gentility at a Swiss girls' school, she rebelled in girlhood against traditional Catholicism, social barriers, and gender inequities. In adulthood, she remained alert to OMENS and premonitions and considered the occult as an everyday facet of her life and family history, a philosophy shared by Gothic writers Isak DINESEN and Gabriel GARCÍA MARQUEZ. At a turning point in middle age, Allende began practicing NECROMANCY to reunite her with deceased grandparents and a daughter, Paula, a victim at age 27 of porphyria, a rare blood malady.

Allende's first novel was *La Casa de los Espíritus* (*THE HOUSE OF THE SPIRITS*, 1981), a roman à clef and international bestseller translated into 27 languages. She followed her instincts about earthly existence and the afterlife and wrote the saga as a love letter to Tata, her tyrannical 100-year-old grandfather, who lay dying in a Santiago mission. She filled the story with elements of saga, FEMALE GOTHIC, magical realism, hauntings, clairvoyance, and levitation. Some of the horrors she experienced vicariously and in person after her uncle, Chilean president Salvador Allende, was assassinated during a coup.

Allende extended her retelling of Latin American history with more fiction about the empowerment of courageous women: *Of Love and Shadows* (1987), which extols a journalist fighting government corruption and brutality, and *Eva Luna* (1987), which depicts a street urchin's survival through STORYTELLING, the ruse that saved Scheherazade from execution in *The Arabian Nights.* In "And of Clay Are We Created," collected in *The Stories of Eva Luna* (1991), Allende describes Azucena, who is buried from the neck down in mud. The horrific tragedy of inept efforts to free her changes the life of Rolf Carlé, a would-be rescuer.

In 1998, Allende turned her elegant Latin American prose to an examination of MYSTICISM and Orientalism in *Aphrodite, a Memoir of the Senses.* The book is a melange of memories, DREAMS and visions, recipes for aphrodisiacs, and commentary on passions, fetishes, and love charms. The text loads images with sexual fantasy and such culinary exotica as Eggplant to a Sheik's Taste, for-lovers-only soup, Harem Turkey, Novice's Nipples, and Odalisques' Salad, all stimuli to eroticism. Allende's technique involves incorporating unbelievable elements as though they are a normal part of reality.

Bibliography

Allende, Isabel. *The House of the Spirits*. New York: Bantam Books, 1982.

————. *Eva Luna*. New York: Bantam Books, 1989.

Roof, Maria. "Maryse Conde and Isabel Allende: Family Saga Novels," *World Literature Today* 70, no. 2 (spring 1996): 283–288.

Rosen, Marjorie, and Nancy Matsumoto. "Lady of the Spirits," *People Weekly* 41, no. 16 (May 2, 1994): 107–109.

Ambrosio

One of literature's enigmatic hero-VILLAINs, the Spanish Capuchin Ambrosio, protagonist of Matthew Gregory LEWIS's THE MONK (1796), is a genre archetype possessing the satanic extremes of Gothic romance. Under rigid piety and righteous posturing, he acquires a reputation as Madrid's saint over a 30-year immurement in forced celibacy. When evil lures him from purity, he abandons sexual powerlessness and rebels against onerous church dogma to taste forbidden pleasures. Lewis uses the emergence of instinctive iniquity as an anti-Catholic SUBTEXT expressing a belief that extremes of self-denial beget religious corruption and criminality.

A sex fiend in the making, Ambrosio displays homoerotic tendencies, but moves in the direction of heterosexual VIOLENCE. He falls under the spell of the alluring Mathilda, a necromancer who disguises herself as the cleric Rosario. Ambrosio allows her to toy with his innate passions, which celibacy has subdued like banked embers. His response to sexual release causes him to lust for 15-year-old Antonia, the NAIF and least available female, as the height of Gothic sexual conquest.

The depravity of a MONSTER on the prowl requires GOTHIC SETTINGs—notably, the reeking putrescence of three corpses interred in the abbey's burial chamber. For violating his vows and for insatiable desires, Ambrosio falls under the despotic Inquisition, an institutional menace common to formulaic sensational fiction. The motif of innocence cowed by a heartless demon carries to a horrific conclusion the terrorizing of an innocent, the type of dewy young virgin that Samuel Richardson introduced in *Pamela* (1741). Ambrosio's only escape is through Satan, to whom he sells his soul.

Lewis manipulates ILLUSION for a searing coming-to-knowledge, the revelation that Ambrosio has slain his own mother and raped and killed his sister. When Satan confronts the villain in his cell, he declares Ambrosio infamous and deluded in his hope of salvation. Satan demands, "Can such enormous sins be forgiven? Hope you to escape my power? Your fate is already pronounced. The Eternal has abandoned you; Mine you are marked in the book of destiny, and mine you must and shall be!" In a Promethean finale, the fallen monk dies a riveting death. As a suitable recompense for his monumental crimes, Lewis describes the desecration of his villain's pathetic corpse, which insects sting and eagles rip with beak and talon.

Bibliography

Brooks, Peter. "Virtue and Terror: The Monk," *English Literary History* 40 (1973): 249–263.

Fleenor, Juliann E., ed. *The Female Gothic*. Montreal: Eden Press, 1983.

Karl, Frederick R. *The Adversary Literature: The English Novel in the Eighteenth Century—A Study in Genre*. New York: Farrar, Straus & Giroux, 1974.

Lewis, Matthew Gregory. *The Monk*. Oxford: Oxford University Press, 1998.

Varma, Devendra P. *The Gothic Flame*. New York: Russell & Russell, 1966.

American Gothic

The New World expression of terror shifted Gothic literature from the dying aristocracy of old Europe to the potent and terrifying Indian of the frontier and to the sexually intimidating black slave. Emerging from conflicts between explorers and Indians, Puritans and DIABOLISM, Calvinists and freethinkers, slave owners and abolitionists, American Gothic works have traditionally incorporated hatred, SECRECY, and guilt as controlling elements. Set against the backdrop of the primeval forest, the indigenous American Gothic presents destructive forces that do not exist in European experience. It is this danger-tinged allure that brought some newcomers to American shores in search of vicarious thrills, adventure, and marvels to dispel Old World repression and ennui. These perils colored the legends and yarns of Appalachian settlers, mournful versions of British ballads such as "Barbara Allen" and "Lord Randal," and the boogey tales and adventure lore of French-Canadian *voyageurs*, who created the earliest Canadian literature.

New World Gothic literature owes its idiosyncratic beginnings to Charles Brockden BROWN, author of WIELAND; or, The Transformation: An American Tale (1798), ARTHUR MERVYN; or, Memoirs of the Year 1793 (1799), and ORMOND (1799), and to the Gothic motifs in the folkloric sketches and atmospheric stories of Washington Irving, particularly the FOOL TALE, "The Legend of Sleepy Hollow," published in *The Sketch Book* (1820). Heavy Gothic leanings also freight the FRONTIER GOTHIC of James Fenimore Cooper's *The Spy* (1821) and *The Last of the Mohicans* (1826), which introduce insidious perils and racial vengeance on the American frontier. Indigenous attitudes and frustrations found their way into the early Gothicism of John Neal's *Rachel Dyer* (1828), a novel set during the Salem witch trials; William Gilmore Simms's crime novel *Martin Faber* (1833); the antinative bigotry and serial murders of Robert Montgomery BIRD's NICK OF THE WOODS; or, The Jibbenainosay: A Tale of Kentucky (1837); and the urban terrorism of George Lippard's best-seller *The Quaker City; or, The Monks of Monk Hall* (1845), a paranoic tale of a secret religious society and pornographic scenes from a Philadelphia bordello. From the Caribbean came slave tales and occult accounts of gris-gris magic, notably, the anonymous romance, *Hamel, the Obeah Man* (1827). The novel, the first representation of African characters in Anglo-Caribbean literature, presented an erotic anti-missionary story of caste prejudice, Jamaican slave SUPERSTITION, and Santerian NATURE worship imported from West Africa. A contemplative contribution from Canada, the poet Pamphile Lemay's *Les Vengeances* (1875), contrasts the ethics and behaviors of Christians and Native American tribes of the Great Lakes region.

The first true marriage of European GOTHIC CONVENTION with American themes of persecution, sin, and guilt were the classic works of Nathaniel HAWTHORNE: THE SCARLET LETTER (1850) and THE HOUSE OF SEVEN GABLES (1851), two models of America's negative romanticism and the historical underpinnings of New World supernatural. Abraham Lincoln credited Harriet Beecher Stowe's dialect MELODRAMA *Uncle Tom's Cabin* (1851–52) as one cause of the Civil War. Filled with voodoo, cruel overseers and slave catchers, and the wails and laments of parted black families, the novel expresses the misery of female breeders: "[The master] tole me that my children were sold, but whether I ever saw their faces again, depended on him. . . . Well, you can do anything with a woman, when you've got her children" (Stowe, 366).

Other native-born and immigrant authors used the Gothic mode as a means of exploring North American varieties of greed, usurpation, intolerance, and cruelty that marked the settlement of the frontier. This manipulation of genre resulted in regional Gothic in Henry Boernstein's *The Mysteries of St. Louis* (1850), Emil Klauprecht's *Cincinnati; or, The Mysteries of the West* (1853), and Baron Ludwig von Reizenstein's *The Mysteries of New Orleans* (1854–55). Fiction master Stephen Crane published "The Monster" in the August 1898 issue of *Harper's*. The story depicts the horror of a black male's maiming in a laboratory fire by an exploding jar: "Suddenly the glass splintered, and a ruby-red snakelike thing poured its thick length out upon the top of the old desk. It coiled and hesitated, and then began to swim a languorous way down the mahogany slant" (Crane, 354). Crane extends the serpentine image with the contact of liquid on flesh: "At the angle it waved its sizzling molten head to and fro over the closed eyes of the man beneath it. Then, in a moment, with mystic impulse, it moved again, and the red snake flowed directly down into Johnson's upturned face" (*ibid.*) Through the SUBTEXT of the faceless black male, Crane effectively compares the sufferings of facial disfigurement with the community racism of Whilomville that negates Henry Johnson's humanity.

FEMALE GOTHIC made its entrance in the Civil War era. In the years following her service as a nurse in the U.S. Sanitary Commission, Louisa May Alcott helped to support her family by contributing sensationalistic potboilers anonymously to *The Flag of Our Union, Atlantic*

Monthly, and other popular journals. Thirty-three of her Gothic thrillers have been recovered since 1975. Her imitation of European Gothic convention called for FEMME FATALES and dangerous alien villains STALKING victims through darkened estates, as in *Pauline's Passion and Punishment* (1862), published under the pen name A. M. Barnard. Scribbling feverishly in her own sleep-deprived version of AUTOMATIC WRITING, Alcott produced Gothic stories, collected in *Behind a Mask* (1875), and wrote a number of adult novels, notably, *The Marble Woman* (1865), *A Long Fatal Love Chase* (1866, unpublished during her lifetime), *The Abbot's Ghost* (1867), and *A Modern Mephistopheles* (1877). Critics read into her aggressive female protagonists a repressed side of her own personality that veiled an earthy, menacing, tempestuous streak. By living out on paper unspeakable fantasies, blood-and-thunder adventure, and erotic stirrings, Alcott achieved a safe, womanly vengeance for the indignities of family life and the repressive discipline of her father, Bronson Alcott.

In a parallel to the Jack the Ripper lore contained in London's GASLIGHT THRILLER, New England Gothic took a dramatic turn with a true crime story, the legendary hatchet murder that Lizzie Borden reputedly perpetrated on her father and stepmother in 1892. To disclose New England's unique moral and psychological demons, Mary E. Wilkins Freeman applied the history of the outwardly prim Lizzie Borden, a Sunday school teacher, to *The Long Arm* (1895), a GOTHIC NOVEL serialized in *Chapman's Magazine*. Barely fictionalized from the original details, the novel speaks the self-defense of a complex woman accused of unspeakable crime. Neither guileless nor monstrous, the defendant represents a normal psychological duality in women. In Missouri, Mark Twain located similar plotting in the switching of two infants—one white, the other mulatto—in his detective thriller *Pudd'nhead Wilson* (1894), which was the first crime novel to feature the forensic art of fingerprinting. As his outlook darkened, Twain turned inward, exploring the corruption of the soul for two moralistic works, "The Man That Corrupted Hadleyburg" (1898) and *The Mysterious Stranger* (1916).

Throughout the 20th century and into the 21st, American Gothic has maintained its own motifs and conventions, including the New England witch lore of Arthur MILLER's THE CRUCIBLE (1953), Anne RICE's vampire sagas, and the portentous futurism of Ray BRADBURY and H. P. LOVECRAFT. Canadian author Margaret ATWOOD sets up a literary monument to female bravery in THE HANDMAID'S TALE (1985) with the Underground Frailroad, a women's recovery system that frees the heroine, Offred, from futuristic sexual bondage. The racist strain of American Gothic remained strong during the long struggle that black Americans faced in their rise from slavery, Jim Crow, and segregation and permeates Octavia BUTLER's speculative fiction, *Kindred* (1979), a tale of time travel to a coercive Maryland plantation. Toni MORRISON's BELOVED (1987) provides a view of black female bondage and slave breeding in a compellingly erotic GHOST STORY. Playwright August WILSON perpetuates the value of the Gothic mode in THE PIANO LESSON (1990), a domestic drama in which the exorcism of a slave owner's ghost frees a family from the grudges and misery of slavery.

Bibliography

Altink, Henrice. "Deviant and Dangerous: Pro-Slavery Representations of Slave Women's Sexuality," http://www.lea.univ-avignon.fr/slav/Altink.htm.

Bergland, Renee L. *The National Uncanny: Indian Ghosts and American Subjects.* Hanover, N.H.: Dartmouth College, 2000.

Crane, Stephen. "The Monster," *Harper's Magazine* 97 (August 1898): 343–376.

Derrickson, Teresa. "Race and the Gothic Monster: The Xenophobic Impulse of Louisa May Alcott's 'Taming a Tartar,'" *American Transcendental Quarterly* 15, no. 1 (March 2001): 43.

Fiedler, Leslie. *Love and Death in the American Novel.* Cleveland: Meridian Books, 1962.

Franklin, Rosemary. "Louisa May Alcott's Father(s) and 'The Marble Woman,'" *American Transcendental Quarterly* 13, no. 4 (December 1999): 253.

McMurray, Price. "Disabling Fictions: Race, History, and Ideology in Crane's 'The Monster,'" *Studies in American Fiction* 26, no. 1 (spring 1998): 51–72.

Northey, Margot. *The Haunted Wilderness: The Gothic and Grotesque in Canadian Fiction.* Toronto: University of Toronto Press, 1976.

Rowan, Steven. "'Smoking Myriads of Houses': German-American Novelists View 1850s St. Louis," *Gateway Heritage* 20, no. 4 (2000): 30–41.

Shaw, S. Bradley. "New England Gothic by the Light of Common Day: Lizzie Borden and Mary E. Wilkins Freeman's 'The Long Arm,'" *New England Quarterly* 70, no. 2 (1997): 211–236.

Smethurst, James. "Invented by Horror: The Gothic and African American Literary Ideology in *Native Son*," *African American Review* 35, no. 1 (2001): 29–40.

Stowe, Harriet Beecher. *Uncle Tom's Cabin; or, Life among the Lowly.* New York: Harper Classics, 1965.

Williams, A. Susan, ed. *The Lifted Veil: The Book of Fantastic Literature by Women, 1800–World War II.* New York: Carroll & Graf, 1992.

"The Anaconda"
Matthew Gregory Lewis
(1808)

Anthologized in the four-volume *Romantic Tales* (1808), Matthew Gregory LEWIS's allegory "The Anaconda" tells of Everard Brooke, who returns from the East Indies in possession of a fortune for which he cannot or will not account. Laden with elements of COLONIAL GOTHIC, the framework flashes back to Everard's melodramatic encounter in Colombo, Ceylon, with a huge snake that lurks in palm trees for weeks at a time awaiting its prey. Because the head strikes rapidly and the body is impenetrable by bullets, the creature becomes a fearful stalker of islanders. Lewis heightens terror by depicting the yellow and green pattern of scales and the quick eye alert to any movement. As a FORESHADOWING of coming death, he describes a dog that the snake crushes, leaving every bone splintered. Lewis then increases the scale of horror by describing the snake's grasp of a steer.

Lewis was one of the first Gothicists to adapt themes of imperialism with horrific details. He devises a means of communication between Everard and Seafield, his employer, who taps out his whereabouts in an outbuilding and tries to dispatch a note to the main house. The chancy methods of spreading the alarm of encroaching evil reflects on the faulty relay of the state of oppression and suffering that third-world countries endured under the British raj. In the end, the noxious breath of the anaconda kills the imperialist, but his aged servant Zadi survives capture in the anaconda's coils and lives to old age. Ironically, Zadi continues to grieve for his master, whom he could not save.

Lewis returned to the theme of colonial exploitation in *Journal of a West India Proprietor, Kept during a Residence in the Island of Jamaica* (1834), a posthumous account of his own observations during voyages to the Caribbean in 1815 and 1817. The author himself succumbed to island sickness on his second voyage. On his way home to England, he died of yellow fever and was buried at sea. To the horror of fellow passengers, the canvas sack in which his body was wrapped billowed with wind and propelled Lewis's remains across the surface like a ghost ship.

Bibliography

Haining, Peter, ed. *Gothic Tales of Terror.* New York: Taplinger, 1972.

Sandiford, Keith A. "'Monk' Lewis and the Slavery Sublime: The Agon of Romantic Desire in the 'Journal,'" *Essays in Literature* 23, no. 1 (spring 1996): 84–98.

Wright, Julia M. "Lewis's 'Anaconda': Gothic Homonyms and Sympathetic Distinctions," *Gothic Studies* 3, no. 3 (2001): 262–378.

Wyatt, Petronella. "Gothic Tales," *Spectator* 292, no. 9,119 (May 17, 2003): 85.

Andersen, Hans Christian
(1805–1875)

Danish author Hans Christian Andersen's beloved fables and wonder tales earned him a reputation for child-centered STORYTELLING, a form he respected as morally instructive. After a childhood of poverty, and spotty successes at writing plays, libretti, and autobiography, at age 30 he applied his readings of GERMAN GOTHIC to original stories, beginning with a witch tale, "The Tinder-Box" (1835), and the murder of horses in "Big Claus and Little Claus" (1835). He anthologized his stories in *Eventyr, Fortalte for Børn* (Tales told for children, 1835), followed by *Eventyr* (Tales, 1837) and *Billedbog unden Billeder* (A picturebook without pictures, 1840). Some of his later works vented his social and intellectual shortcomings, particularly "Jack the Dullard" (1855), the story of a boy ridiculed for stammering. By 1872, Andersen had issued six volumes containing 168 stories. Actor Danny Kaye honored the writer's life's work with his portrayal of Andersen in the film *Hans Christian Andersen* (1952), which contained the fable songs "The Inch Worm," "The King's New Clothes," and "Thumbelina."

Blessed with psychological insight, Andersen's typically gentle stories carried a number of Gothic themes: poverty in "The Almshouse Window" (1847), the separation and deaths of Old Preben and his wife in "The Old Grave-Stone" (1852), exclusion and harsh anti-Semitism in "The Jewish Maiden" (1856), an enveloping fen in "The Marsh King's Daughter" (1858), a wicked goblin in "The Nis and the Dame" (1868), and discrimination and menace in "The Cripple" (1872). In "The Great Sea-Serpent," published in *Scribner's* in January 1872, Andersen used a fable of social chaos to describe the laying of the Atlantic cable on the sea floor. More moving is "The Little Match-Seller" (1846), a tale of apathy toward a homeless girl who freezes to death. A second Christmas folktale, "The Fir Tree" (1845), bears tragedy in the fate of a withered Christmas tree that is chopped and burned for firewood. Andersen's works were an inspiration to Charles DICKENS, who shared his concern for suffering and his interest in social betterment. Andersen's fairy tales "The Little Mermaid" (1836), "The Ugly Duckling" (1844), "Snow White" (1845), and "The Shadow" (1847) influenced Oscar WILDE's fairy tales "The Birthday of the Infanta" (1888) and "The Fisherman and His Soul," collected in *The House of Pomegranates* (1891).

Bibliography

Nassaar, Christopher S. "Andersen's 'The Shadow' and Wilde's 'The Fisherman and His Soul': A Case of Influence," *Nineteenth-Century Literature* 50, no. 2 (September 1995): 217–224.

———. "Andersen's 'The Ugly Duckling' and Wilde's 'The Birthday of the Infanta,'" *Explicator* 55, no. 2 (winter 1997): 83–85.

Anne (Ann) of Swansea
(1764–1838)

Anne (or Ann) of Swansea was the pen name of the Welsh playwright and novelist Anne (or Ann) Julia Kemble Curtis Hatton, the sister of the actress Sarah Kemble Siddons. Lame and unattractive, Anne lived an unconventional life in a brothel, fought involvement in scandal, and supported herself by writing verse, fiction, and libretti. She was widowed at age 36, in the Welsh port town of Swansea. She began writing the first of 14 novels, most for London publisher Andrew King Newman's MINERVA PRESS, and contributed to popular SHORT GOTHIC FICTION with "The Unknown!; or, The Knight of the Blood-Red Plume," an undated tale in which a scaly MONSTER spears the fleeing murderer Erilda with a trident. After Anne published a collection, *Chronicles of an Illustrious House* (1816), a five-volume work subtitled *The Peer, the Lawyer, and the Hunchback, Embellished with Characters and Anecdotes of Well Known Persons,* she ran afoul of harsh criticism for the spite of her VILLAINs, indecency in her maidens, and indelicacy unbecoming a female writer.

Anne of Swansea battled the era's double standard toward female writers. A critique published in the *Monthly Censor* elucidated her dark leanings by identifying the obscure author as the producer of a large body of Gothic works. The critic offered a pursy summary of *Guilty; or Not Guilty; or, A Lesson for Husbands: A Tale* (1822), the story of the virginal Lady Caroline Fitzallen, the rejected lost daughter of a noble family who is kidnapped from a masquerade ball. The reviewer singled out for scorn numerous allurements, artifices, and degradations of the aristocracy and denounced Anne of Swansea for incorporating too many Gothic intrigues and debaucheries for the reading pleasure of female patrons at English CIRCULATING LIBRARIES. Undeterred, she issued a popular Gothic novel, *Deeds of Olden Times* (1826).

Bibliography

"Ann Julia Hatton," *Sheffield Hallam University: Corvey Women Writers,* http://www2.shu.ac.uk/corvey/CW3/AuthorPage.cfm?Author−AJKH, 2000.

Haining, Peter, ed. *Gothic Tales of Terror.* New York: Taplinger, 1972.

anti-Catholicism

Anti-Catholicism is a pervasive SUBTEXT of classic Gothic fiction and ILLUMINATI NOVELS. The theme derives from morbid curiosity about the sufferings of saints, church domination during the Middle Ages, and the spiritual yearnings of some Protestants for the MYSTERY and high-church ritual that Europe once embraced. Feeding the suspicions of non-Catholic authors was a body of outsized myths about flagellation and other rigorous forms of penance, repressive dogma, priestly greed and corruption, and mysterious rituals and torments of nonbelievers and dissidents. Of particular value to Gothicists were imaginative scenes of sexual depravity among the clergy, forced immurement in single-sex cloisters, secret tribunals, and the sacrifice and secret burial of infants—notably, the offspring that novices bore in convents.

Catholicism itself was an unwitting partner in grotesquely false Gothic tales. The mass and the ritual of holy sacraments were so obscure to most non-Catholic readers that they took on an air of mystery. From a pervasive misunderstanding of Catholic religious dogma and ritual emerged the aspects of character behaviors, pious terrors, dejected abbeys, and MELANCHOLY or horrific ATMOSPHERE that fostered Gothicism. George William Macarthur REYNOLDS, a Victorian Gothicist, used rumored terrors of the Spanish Inquisition for an undated horror tale, "The Tribunal of the Inquisition," in which the victim was "cut so deeply into his flesh, that the blood spurted over his shirt on the ground: and . . . the victim was covered with mingled slime and gore" (Haining, 485). He concluded that Catholic ecclesiastical courts could precede judgment with torture because they "fed upon the agonies of their victims" (ibid.).

Gothic tales of Catholic horrors ranked among the genre's most sensational fiction, notably Francis LATHOM's depiction of a penitent's sadistic self-whipping in *The Midnight Bell: A German Story, Founded on Incidents in Real Life* (1798) and Canadian novelist John RICHARDSON's proto-pornographic *The Monk Knight of St. John: A Tale of the Crusaders* (1850). William Henry Ireland's *The Abbess* (1799) vilified the all-male Catholic hierarchy in one wholesale denunciation spoken by Mother Vittoria, who claims that celibacy is a dreadful perversion of nature created to ensure wretchedness in thousands of young girls. Isabella Kelly, author of *Eva* (1799), concurred through the words of Agatha, who refuses to enter a nunnery because of its cruel oppression that deprives women of the normal blessings of home and children. The most notorious novel in this genre, Matthew Gregory LEWIS's THE MONK (1796), shocked readers for its overt carnality, incest, homoeroticism, and lust generated by enforced celibacy. The work's depiction of depravity implies that celibacy itself is perverse in preserving to age 30 the virginity of an otherwise virile male.

Late 18th-century author and essayist Anna Laetitia BARBAULD enlarged on the use of the Inquisition and its attendant horrors as the ideal hellhole in which to set Gothic fiction. During a significant period in religious history, the Inquisition became a judicial arm of the Catholic hierarchy that searched out and executed heretics in cunningly wretched style. Of particular importance to Gothic fiction was the recoil from the SADISM and tyrannic mindset of the Inquisition, which Sir Walter SCOTT summarized in *Letters on Demonology and Witchcraft* (1830) and Umberto ECO explored in *The Name of the Rose* (1980).

The perversion of ecclesiastical court justice produced horrific fears of stalking, apprehension, torture, forced testimony without counsel, judgment without appeal, and immediate public execution. The worst of unjust church tribunals erupted in Spain under Ferdinand and Isabella, when savage inquisitors operated apart from the Vatican to force converted Jews and Muslims to prove their faith before grueling autos-da-fé (literally, acts of faith). William GODWIN chose these scenes for *St. Leon* (1799), which abounds with fires stoked with dry faggots and bold-eyed voyeurs observing the burning of victims. In one scene of torment, a mob in Valladolid seizes Hector, St. Leon's black servant, and rips him limb from joint.

One exploiter of anti-Catholicism was an anti-Catholic Anglican curate and closet Gothic writer, Charles Robert MATURIN. In MELMOTH THE WANDERER (1820), the author contends through a perverse monk that saints were mentally and morally deranged egotists, self-aggrandizers, and manipulators. By presenting the stalking Satanic tormentor, Maturin condemns the inhumanity of the Inquisition and the megalomania of Catholic dogma, which extends no pity to the mortal believer. However, unlike earlier antichurch screeds, Maturin imputes all religion for a penchant for extremism and blames perversions of godliness on narrow doctrines and unnatural codes of self-discipline and withdrawal from the real world.

Maturin's admirer, the author Oscar WILDE, reprises the motif of the inhuman auto-da-fé in a melancholy FAIRY TALE, "The Birthday of the Infanta" (1888), in which the king recalls a joyous marriage to his late queen. With an ironic twist, Wilde notes the scheduling of the wedding mass along with "a more than usually solemn *auto-da-fé,* in which nearly three hundred heretics, amongst whom were many Englishmen, had been delivered over to the secular arm to be burned" (Wilde, 247). The executions foreshadow a troubled period in which the king becomes obsessed with his bride as the country falls to ruin. The OBSESSION clings to him long after her death, rumored to have been caused by his jealous brother, who presented the queen a pair of poisoned gloves, a SYMBOL of the poisonous atmosphere of Catholic Spain.

In American Gothic literature, anti-Catholicism thrived on misinformation and SENSATIONALISM. James Fenimore Cooper and Charles Brockden BROWN laced their fiction with the secret doings of the Rosicrucians and other sinister male brotherhoods. Sarah Josepha Hale promoted a New World version of cruel cloistering in "The Catholic Convert," a story anthologized in *Traits of American Life* (1835). Carrying the European tradition from a convent, the protagonist, a nun, flees a repressive order.

Such romanticized horrors were an element of the overblown best-seller *The Awful Disclosures of Maria Monk; or, The Hidden Secrets of a Nun's Life in a Convent* (1836) and its sequel, *Further Disclosures of Maria Monk* (1837). In these works, ghostwriter and Philadelphia publisher T. B. Peterson allegedly exposed the lapsed nun's experience with dark oppression and sin in Montreal's Hôtel-Dieu convent. Although discredited by New York journalist William Leete Stone as the most anti-Catholic propaganda in North American history, the controversial work originated an urban myth that fueled a cottage industry in Gothic antichurch fiction in Australia, Ireland, and the United States.

Bibliography

Blakemore, Steven. "Matthew Lewis's Black Mass: Sexual, Religious Inversion in 'The Monk,'" *Studies in the Novel* 30, no. 4 (winter 1998): 521.

Griffin, Susan M. "'The Dark Stranger': Sensationalism and Anti-Catholicism in Sarah Josepha Hale's *Traits of American Life,*" *Legacy* 14, no. 1 (1997): 13–24.

Haining, Peter, ed. *The Shilling Shockers.* New York: St. Martin's Press, 1978.

Lockwood, Robert P. "Maria Monk," *Catholic Heritage* (November/December 1996): 19–21.

Sage, Victor. *Horror Fiction in the Protestant Tradition.* New York: St. Martin's, 1988.

Schmitt, Cannon. "Techniques of Terror, Technologies of Nationality: Ann Radcliffe's 'The Italian,'" *English Literary History* 61, no. 4 (winter 1994): 853–876.

Tarr, Mary Muriel. *Catholicism in Gothic Fiction: A Study of the Nature and Function of Catholic Materials in Gothic Fiction in England, 1762–1820.* Washington, D.C.: Catholic University of America Press, 1946.

Wilde, Oscar. *The Picture of Dorian Gray and Selected Stories.* New York: New American Library, 1983.

Wilt, Judith. *Ghosts of the Gothic.* Princeton: Princeton University Press, 1980.

arabesque

Originally denoting a decorative motif in Moorish architecture, the term *arabesque* derives from the Italian *arabesco,* referring to imaginative Arabic style. For Gothic writers, arabesque suggests Eastern exotica—sensuous reptilian movements before the snake-charmer's pipe, the curl of smoke from the hookah, opium-induced DREAMS, and the muscular waves of the belly dancer's abdomen. As an adjective applied to literature, music, dance, art, and architecture from the Renaissance, the term also refers to romantic elements—imagination, supple flow, caprice, spontaneity, convolutions of wit, fanciful embroidery, and serendipity, as found in Walter DE LA MARE's haunting story "The Recluse" (1930).

The term entered ROMANTICISM in noun form as an outlandish, complicated creation that Sir

Walter SCOTT equated with the GROTESQUE. In her poem "Life and Songs of the Baroness Nairne" (1905), the early 19th-century Scottish poet Carolina Oliphant made direct connection between "Arabesque" and Gothicism:

> . . . Arabesque
> Of mental imagery, the serpent's folds
> To human body joining on fantastic.
> Here swift Apollo follows in the chase,
> And grasps a laurel branch, his only need;
> Or from a grove of shady myrtles, peeps
> A dancing satyr, spreading terror round;
> Yet would our sleeping hours alone receive
> Monstrous impossibilities.
>
> (Oliphant, 270)

In art, the Viennese painter Gustav Klimt embraced the weirdness of the arabesque for his GOTHIC illustrations, particularly the allegorical DUNGEONS he designed to confine women.

To differentiate between *arabesque* and *grotesque* as descriptives, Edgar Allan POE, America's horror expert, applied *arabesque* to wonder and *grotesque* to horror. He used the terms in his title *Tales of the Grotesque and Arabesque* (1839) and provided ample illustrations of the motifs through intricate phrasing intended to enhance both horror and Gothic detail. In "LIGEIA" (1838), undecipherable arabesque figures on tapestries contribute to MYSTERY in a grieving husband's opium dreams of a dead woman's resurrection; in "THE FALL OF THE HOUSE OF USHER" (1839), the term *arabesque* applies to the expression on the face of Rockerick USHER, a neurasthenic clinging to the rim of sanity. In "THE MASQUE OF THE RED DEATH" (1842), Poe links the term *arabesque* to the masqueraders themselves, who attempt to flee a lethal pathogen.

Echoing the distaste recorded in scenes written by Honoré de Balzac, Willa Cather, Fyodor Dostoevsky, Gustave Flaubert, and George Sand, in "THE YELLOW WALLPAPER" (1892) Charlotte Perkins GILMAN equated arabesque decor with patriarchal oppression. The unnamed narrator, a despairing middle-class wife and mother undergoing a rest cure for shattered nerves, glares at the wall covering and proclaims it artistically sinful, an intrusion of psychological noise. Her musings range from accusations of revolting uncleanliness to outrageous patterns, defiance of geometric law, visual horror, and irksomeness to the mind: "Looked at in one way, each breadth stands alone; the bloated curves and flourishes—a kind of 'debased Romanesque' with delirium tremens—go waddling up and down in isolated columns of fatuity" (Gilman, 717). As a goad to INSANITY, the grotesque paper becomes a Gothic weapon and an untranslatable form of NIGHTMARE, hallucination, and emotional VIOLENCE. As such, the wallpaper explodes into an outré visual torture device that eventually exhausts the speaker, toppling her into madness.

Bibliography

Gilman, Charlotte Perkins. "The Yellow Wallpaper," in *The Harper American Literature*, 2nd ed., ed. Donald McQuade, et al. New York: HarperCollins, 1994.

Oliphant, Carolina. *Life and Songs of the Baroness Nairne*. London: John Grant, 1905.

Roth, Marty. "Gilman's Arabesque Wallpaper," *Mosaic* 34, no. 4 (December 2001): 145–162.

Arthur Mervyn
Charles Brockden Brown
(1799)

Influenced by the widespread suffering and death from the yellow fever epidemic that overran Philadelphia in 1793, Charles Brockden BROWN's URBAN GOTHIC *Arthur Mervyn; or, Memoirs of the Year 1793*, an amorphous, discordant novel of purpose, abandons American GOTHIC CONVENTION. In its place, Brown resets the European concepts of William GODWIN's *CALEB WILLIAMS* (1794) in a New World locale. Mervyn, a NAIF and symbol of agrarianism, makes his way from rural Pennsylvania into the city, where urban deceptions morph into a perplexing American labyrinth. He faces an invisible pestilence, an autobiographical touch that fictionalizes the terrors the author faced during an epidemic that killed two of his friends.

In his inconsistent study of the milieu and motivations that drive the altruist, Brown creates a disturbing ambiguity in Mervyn's humanitarianism, his naiveté about crime and love, and his foolish abetting of a murder committed by Welbeck, a villainous employer. On unknown turf against a backdrop of pestilence, Mervyn traverses an eerie landscape fraught with stench, death, body effluvia, and the mortally ill: "A female visage, bloated with malignity and drunkenness, occasionally looked in. Dying eyes were cast upon her, invoking the boon, perhaps, of a drop of cold water, or her assistance to change a posture which compelled him to behold the ghastly writings or dreadful *smile* of his neighbor" (Brown, 173). Mervyn falls ill with fever upon contact with the stricken city, where a hearse awaits a coffin open to a not-quite-dead victim and ghostly figures wrapped in cloaks flee from human contact and sprinkle vinegar to ward off contagion. In addition to disease and paranoia, the protagonist finds the city's morals corrupt and its justice system favoring the wealthy.

In a symbolic gesture of rejection to the Republican values that create urban chaos, Mervyn chooses for a mate Achsa Fielding, a mature Jewish aristocrat, over the 15-year-old Eliza Hadwin, the ideal American wife. The pairing suggests that Brown had given over ROMANTICISM in favor of the staid bourgeois ideal. On reading the novel, Percy Bysshe SHELLEY, a devoted romantic, disdained the protagonist's choice of the middle-aged wife over the vibrant young peasant girl.

Bibliography

Brown, Charles Brockden. *Arthur Mervyn; or, Memoirs of the Year 1793*. Philadelphia: David McKay, 1889.

Eiselein, Gregory. "Humanitarianism and Uncertainty in 'Arthur Mervyn,'" *Essays in Literature* 22, no. 2 (fall 1995): 215–226.

Fiedler, Leslie. *Love and Death in the American Novel*. Cleveland: Meridian Books, 1962.

Goddu, Teresa A. *Gothic America: Narrative, History, and Nation*. New York: Columbia University Press, 1997.

Hale, Dorothy J. "Profits of Altruism: *Caleb Williams* and *Arthur Mervyn*," *Eighteenth-Century Studies* 22, no. 1 (1988): 47–69.

Ruland, Richard, and Malcolm Bradbury. *From Puritanism to Postmodernism: A History of American Literature*. New York: Penguin, 1991.

Vickers, Anita. "Social Corruption and the Subversion of the American Success Story in *Arthur Mervyn*," *Prospects* 23 (1998): 129–145.

Atherton, Gertrude
(1857–1948)

A vain, self-ennobling author of AMERICAN GOTHIC, feminist Gertrude Franklin Horn Atherton of San Francisco, like her frontier predecessor Ambrose BIERCE, wrote macabre stories of psychological torment. She launched a fiction career with a study of METEMPSYCHOSIS, *What Dreams May Come* (1888), issued under the pen name Frank Lin. A filmy, rhapsodic love tale set in a Welsh castle, it depicts Harold Dartmouth caught in a time warp that pulls him from his fiancée, the hauntingly lovely Weir Penrhyn, to the ghost of her grandmother, Lady Sionèd Penrhyn, the lover of Dartmouth's grandfather. The tension between worlds threatens Dartmouth's sanity until he confesses to Weir the peculiar dream states in which Sionèd visits him. In a gesture to more liberal times, Atherton forgives Sionèd of a burden of sin and allows Dartmouth to possess her once more.

Atherton specialized in the SUPERNATURAL in her best works: the approach of death to claim a moribund man in "Death and the Woman" (1892); *The Christmas Witch*, a novella on reincarnation published in 1893 in *Godey's Magazine*; the gruesome horror story "The Striding Place" (1896), published in the London *Speaker*; and "The Bell in the Fog" (1905), a popular tale set at the atmospheric Chillingsworth estate and laced with psychological import, patriarchy, and hints of reincarnation. That same year, Atherton published "The Dead and the Countess" (1905), a tale of an accidental PREMATURE BURIAL narrated by a superstitious parish priest.

Influenced by the writings of Bierce and Henry JAMES, Atherton brought to her Gothic a cold refinement and worldliness derived from a string of residences in Berlin, Greece, London, and the West Indies. In her early 60s, she turned to spiritualism in *The White Morning* (1918) and to stories of INSANITY and twisted memory in *The Foghorn* (1934), which pictures an awakening from a coma and recovered memory. For a MAD SCIENTIST plot in *Black Oxen* (1923), Atherton described a bizarre quest for eternal youth by Mary Ogden, a self-absorbed protagonist who travels from New York to Vienna to receive astounding results from injections of hormones extracted from ox glands. At age

60, she looks nearer 30. Upon falling in love with a much younger man, she finds herself a social pariah mocked by both old and young for her dabbling in physiological experimentation.

Bibliography

Bering-Jensen, Helle. "California's Daughter: Gertrude Atherton and Her Times," *Smithsonian* 22, no. 12 (March 1992): 117–118.

Williams, A. Susan, ed. *The Lifted Veil: The Book of Fantastic Literature by Women, 1800–World War II.* New York: Carroll & Graf, 1992.

atmosphere

Atmosphere, the pervasive feeling created by a literary work, is an intangible ambience or appeal, the outgrowth of verbal clues—obvious physical terrain, implied emotional aura, dynamic thought, and subtle FORESHADOWING, qualities of Elizabeth Gaskell's Victorian GHOST STORY "The Old Nurse's Story" (1852), Katherine Anne Porter's deathbed dreamscape in "The Jilting of Granny Weatherall" (1930), and the paintings of swimmers in a cave in Canadian author Michael Ondaatje's *The English Patient* (1996), winner of the Booker Prize. Derived from the Greek for "ball of vapor," atmosphere heightens reader expectation (for example) of romance, foreboding, mystery, or terror. Atmospheric hints prepare readers for disaster in Nathaniel HAWTHORNE's "YOUNG GOODMAN BROWN" (1835), Herman MELVILLE's *Moby Dick* (1851), and Edith WHARTON's suffocatingly tragic love story *ETHAN FROME* (1911). These hints dominate the setting and convey attitudes and feelings to the reader, as with incipient tragedy in George du Maurier's sensational MELODRAMA *Trilby*, published serially from January through August 1894 in *Harper's Monthly*, and the triumph of his granddaughter Daphne DU MAURIER's Gothic short classic "THE BIRDS" (1952), in which NATURE ranges out of control as the birds attack England.

Edgar Allan POE produced a recognizable Gothic style from his mastery of atmosphere. In 1842, he wrote in *Graham's Magazine* about the importance of a "single effect," a phrase that defines the psychological impact of his poems and stories. One of the first verse pieces taught to young adult readers is his tone poem "The Raven" (1844), which narrates an ominous visitation of a black bird to a lone mourner. Embellishing the setting are shadows outside the lamp's half-light, rustling purple curtains, and shuttered windows, all suggestions of the gloom caused by a recent death. The growing tension heightens SUSPENSE as the reader contemplates how the first-person speaker will respond to the intrusion on his self-absorption.

Late in the 19th century and into the 20th, the manipulation of Gothic aura helped to maintain the popularity of ghost stories and eerie ballads, novels, and plays. Henry JAMES expanded on the concept by acknowledging an intellectual atmosphere, a willing suspension of disbelief as the reader shares the writer's frame of mind and experiences a unique literary vision, as with the prevailing mystery and threat that permeate his ghost story, *THE TURN OF THE SCREW* (1898). A frequently anthologized poem, William Rose Benét's "The Skater of Ghost Lake" (1933), loads the atmosphere with the crisp, energetic coursing of blades on ice to complement the chilling ballad of a spectral skater. In both examples, the author partners with the reader by leaving much to the imagination.

Throughout the 20th and into the 21st century, Gothic fiction reached heights of artistry through subtleties of TONE, MOOD, and atmosphere. A master wielder of spine-chilling aura, Joyce Carol OATES creates stories set in seemingly normal surroundings in which evidence of the SUPERNATURAL perches on the reader's disbelief with a light, but insistent touch. Less subtle are the pagan touches of ghosts and spiritual rejuvenation in the 10-play cycle of August WILSON. His most insistent return to old-time Gothicism occurs in *THE PIANO LESSON* (1990), in which a Pittsburgh ghetto family exorcises the evil of the slaveholding past to rid themselves of old crimes and suffering. In 2002, Virginia Renfro Ellis's novel *The Wedding Dress* touched lightly on the supernatural by picturing a steady drift of the silent spirits of Civil War casualties down country lanes on their way home.

Bibliography

Berman, Avis. "George du Maurier's 'Trilby' Whipped Up a Worldwide Storm," *Smithsonian* 24, no. 9 (December 1993): 110–116.

Davison, Neil R. "The Jew as Homme/Femme-Fatale: Jewish (Art)ifice, Trilby, and Dreyfus," *Jewish Social Studies* (winter–spring 2002): 73–113.

Forster, Margaret. *Daphne du Maurier.* New York: Doubleday, 1993.

Grossman, Jonathan H. "The Mythic Svengali: Antiaestheticism in 'Trilby,'" *Studies in the Novel* 28, no. 4 (winter 1996): 525–543.

Atwood, Margaret

(1939–   )

Margaret Atwood, Canada's famed feminist, has carried Gothic fiction to new perspectives by examining the persecution and suppression of women in modern scenarios. A voracious reader in childhood, she was brought up on Gothic fiction—the unexpurgated *Grimm's Fairy Tales,* Sherlock HOLMES mysteries, Robert Louis Stevenson's pirate tale *Treasure Island* (1883), and the dark frontier novels of James Fenimore Cooper. Avoiding the terrors of traditional European works, she wrote a parody of classic Gothic, *Lady Oracle* (1976), her third novel. The invention of comic Gothic allowed Atwood to survey the modern female psyche more minutely than traditional GOTHIC CONVENTION, which tends to stereotype without compassion or understanding. The novel surveys the dual identity of Joan Foster, a writer of Gothic costume romances who juggles a life of invisibility and sudden notoriety. By reprising the STALKING, isolation, SADISM, and SUPERNATURAL elements from late 18th-century Gothic fiction and overlayering all with humor, Atwood produces a tough heroine who endures oppression by refusing to see herself as a victim.

At a higher level of danger, THE HANDMAID'S TALE (1985), Atwood's forceful futuristic thriller, presents a dystopian nightmare—speculative fiction set in the near future that warns of the rise of the religious right. In place of the claustrophobic castles and convents of classic Gothic works, the author places the heroine, Offred, in a private home under a fascist police regime headed by ruthless males. Often compared to Nathaniel HAWTHORNE's SCARLET LETTER (1850) and George Orwell's *1984* (1949), the novel pictures a perverted technocracy based on savage misogyny during an era when humankind is threatened with extinction. Set in the ultraconservative "Republic of Gilead" outside Boston, Massachusetts, the text characterizes coercion and rape masked as a state-mandated holy ritual reminiscent of AMBROSIO's evil distortions of religion in Matthew Gregory LEWIS's THE MONK (1796).

Gothic style suits Atwood's later works, which continued to focus on suffering women in *Cat's Eye* (1988) and *Alias Grace* (1996). *The Robber Bride* (1993), a best-selling FOOL TALE and updated version of the Grimm brothers' "Der Räuberbräutigam" (The Robber Bridegroom, 1857), tweaks the cannibalistic original with confessions of three classmates who have weathered neglect and sexual abuse. The fourth, Zenia, a sociopathic FEMME FATALE, tricks the trio by seducing and destroying their menfolk. In the exposition, the author jokingly places Zenia in a formulaic Gothic backdrop: "A European print, hand-tinted, ochre-coloured, with dusty sunlight and a lot of bushes in it—bushes with thick leaves and ancient twisted roots" (Atwood, *Robber Bride,* 1). She heightens terror with an offhand description of the bracken, "behind which, out of sight in the undergrowth and hinted at by a boot protruding, or a slack hand, something ordinary but horrifying is taking place" (*ibid.*). Atwood also deceives the reader with a cinematic ploy, implying that the villain is dead, then reanimating her for another cartoonish round of woman-on-woman menace and cruelty.

In her 10th novel, *The Blind Assassin* (2001), a nested story-within-a-story, Atwood describes Canadian sisters who grow up during the Great Depression in a monstrous home setting. Compared to the confinement motifs in Edith WHARTON's *The Age of Innocence* (1920), Atwood's Booker Prize–winning novel intrigues with a blend of MYSTERY, family SECRECY, and female powerlessness, the essential triad of traditional Gothic fiction. Paralleling the interlaced trio of narratives—a novel inset with memoir and decadent science fiction—are frequent images of doors, locks, and keys, all SYMBOLS of the restrictive marriage of Iris Griffen Chase, the aptly named protagonist. Intricately plotted, the story incorporates detective work, surprise, and the self-revelation that is the hallmark of FEMALE GOTHIC.

Bibliography

Atwood, Margaret. "Ophelia Has a Lot to Answer For," http://www.web.net/owtoad/ophelia.html, 1997.

———. *The Robber Bride.* New York: Anchor, 1998.

Bignell, Jonathan. "Lost Messages: The Handmaid's Tale, Novel and Film," *British Journal of Canadian Studies* 8, no. 1 (1993): 71–84.

Fleenor, Juliann E., ed. *The Female Gothic*. Montreal: Eden Press, 1983.

Howells, Carol Ann. *Margaret Atwood*. London: Macmillan, 1996.

Martens, Catherine. "Mother-Figures in *Surfacing* and *Lady Oracle:* An Interview with Margaret Atwood," *American Studies in Scandinavia* 16, no. 1 (1984): 45 54.

Spector, Judith Ann. "Marriage, Endings, and Art in Updike and Atwood," *Midwest Quarterly* 34, no. 4 (summer 1993): 426–445.

Sullivan, Rosemary. *The Red Shoes: Margaret Atwood Starting Out*. New York: HarperCollins, 1998.

Austen, Jane

(1775–1817)

Brought up in a novel-reading family, the English novelist Jane Austen, a contemporary of Ann RAD-CLIFFE, came of age during the flowering of GOTHIC CONVENTION but flourished in domestic satire. She received free rein to read from her father's library and had access to essays from the *Tatler* and the *Spectator*, the poems of William Cowper, and many popular novels, Radcliffe's THE MYSTERIES OF UDOLPHO (1794) among them. When family finances dwindled, Austen published anonymously *Sense and Sensibility* (1811) and *Pride and Prejudice* (1813). Immediate success encouraged her to issue two more works, *Mansfield Park* (1814) and *Emma* (1815). The latter novel earned the praise of Sir Walter SCOTT in the *Edinburgh Review*. Near the end of her career, she completed *Persuasion* (1818), which was published a year after her death.

As the classic Gothic conventions in fiction waned, Austen parodied the genre's extremes with NORTHANGER ABBEY (1818), which she had begun in 1798 and first submitted for publication in 1803. The novel's unlikely heroine is Catherine MOR-LAND, an unremarkable protagonist who violates the Gothic stereotype of the foundling or orphan by being born to a normal set of parents who bore six more offspring. Austen displayed her familiarity with Gothic fiction by engrossing her heroine in the popular Gothic works of the day, notably *The Mysteries of Udolpho* and a selection of GOTHIC BLUEBOOKS. Much of the story takes place at an unimpressive estate that Catherine is visiting and that is lacking in the scary elements she had expected. Under the influence of the perverse fiction she has been reading, Catherine creates humor and a commentary on youthful extremes by losing her perspective on reality and making serious errors of judgment.

Bibliography

Austen, Jane. *Northanger Abbey*. New York: Modern Library, 1995.

Fleenor, Juliann E., ed. *The Female Gothic*. Montreal: Eden Press, 1983.

automatic writing

A forerunner of stream-of-consciousness style, automatic writing is a method of disengaging the conscious mind from rationality to allow musings, DREAMS, unpremeditated motifs, and subconscious desires to control the production of narrative. Free-flowing, unpremeditated writing was the method that Horace WALPOLE extolled in writing THE CASTLE OF OTRANTO (1765), the fount of the GOTHIC NOVEL, which he committed to paper during eight successive nights of pushing himself toward a state of exhaustion. In the 19th century, the method impacted a second landmark Gothic work, Mary Wollstonecraft SHELLEY's FRANKENSTEIN (1818), which emerged from a dream and immediate notes on her restless night.

Some writers employed the method while under the influence of hypnosis, alcohol, or drugs as a means of tapping pure imagination from the unconscious mind and of encouraging free association through synonyms, homonyms, and puns. The poet William Butler Yeats joined his wife in communing with spirits through rapid filling of notebooks, which he incorporated in *A Vision* (1925) and in the mysterious MONSTER poem "The Second Coming" (1921) and a reference to mummies, wine-sipping ghosts, and the howling of the damned in "All Souls' Night" (1920). His interest in contacting the dead invested his allegories on the occult and spooky stories based on Irish folklore, such as "The Magi" (1914). In 1924, André Breton discussed in *Manifesto of Surrealism* the value of automatic writing, which frees the artistic mind of control, intent, or CENSORSHIP. Other practitioners of the early 20th century include the American writers Gertrude Stein and Jack Kerouac and the French poet Robert Desnos.

Bibliography

Burgess, Cheryl A., et al. "Facilitated Communication as an Ideomotor Response," *Psychological Science* 9, no. 1 (January 1998): 71–74.

Varma, Devendra P. *The Gothic Flame.* New York: Russell & Russell, 1966.

Yeats, William Butler. *The Collected Poems of W. B. Yeats.* New York: Macmillan, 1956.

B

Baillie, Joanna
(1762–1851)

Scottish poet and experimental playwright Joanna Baillie joined the critical furor over the extremes of Gothic drama and the immorality of the English stage. Well read and ably educated in girlhood, she produced private theatricals at a Glasgow boarding school. She developed a conservative conscience that reflected Scots Presbyterian values. As a means of transforming public morals, in 1798 she began writing A Series of Plays on the Passions, a suite of comedies and tragedies covering the major human emotions. She completed the project in 1812. The first play achieved instant notoriety after its anonymous publication. In her "Introductory Discourse," she agreed with Lord BYRON and William Wordsworth on the questionable nature of Gothic literature and its influence on public taste and behavior.

Baillie contributed to the public's suspicions about Gothic drama by manipulating audience reaction. For the construction of a mysterious 14th-century convent chapel for the staging at Drury Lane of De Montfort: A Tragedy on Hatred (1800), a psychological thriller tinged with incest, she relied on the designer William Capon. After lowering house lights and creating the aura of torchlight in a gale, Baillie heightened the fearful ATMOSPHERE created by a procession of nuns and by Capon's stage effects—hand-held lanterns, lightning, a raw gravesite, chapel bells, owl shrieks, moaning wind, and snake-shaped clouds overhead. The setting was so gripping that Capon preserved the flats for use in subsequent gothic dramas.

Baillie won the regard of Anna Laetitia BARBAULD, Maria Edgeworth, and Mary Wollstonecraft SHELLEY, who read several of Baillie's plays. Sir Walter SCOTT was so impressed that he assumed the playwright had to be male. Her work suffered after 1803, when Francis Jeffrey, the editor of the Edinburgh Review, criticized her sacrifice of literary quality for religious zeal. The Edinburgh debut of The Family Legend (1810), a nationalistic play featuring a highland warrior on a par with Rob Roy, succeeded because of Baillie's intricate plotting and SUSPENSE. In 1812, she issued a verse play, Orra: A Tragedy, which characterized the physical response to horror. Subsequent works tended to present feeling in the abstract to the detriment of characterization.

Bibliography

Colon, Christine. "Christianity and Colonial Discourse in Joanna Baillie's 'The Bride,'" Renascence: Essays on Values in Literature 54, no. 3 (spring 2002): 162–177.

Cox, Jeffrey N., intro. Seven Gothic Dramas, 1789–1825. Athens: Ohio University Press, 1992.

Gamer, Michael. Romanticism and the Gothic: Genre, Reception, and Canon Formation. Cambridge: Cambridge University Press, 2000.

Ranger, Paul. Terror and Pity Reign in Every Breast: Gothic Drama in the London Patent Theatres, 1750–1820. London: Society for Theatre Research, 1991.

The Ballad of the Sad Café
Carson McCullers
(1951)

In a GROTESQUE novella, *The Ballad of the Sad Café*, the American author Carson McCULLERS offers a darkly comic operatic scenario: an androgynous woman, Amelia Evans, victimized by two males, her estranged husband, the womanizing Marvin Macy, and a trickster, the weaselly hunchback Lymon, who refers to himself as Miss Amelia's cousin. Amelia is a town marvel for operating a successful medical practice and bootlegging parlor. Like the troubled bisexuals in McCullers's *Reflections in a Golden Eye* (1941) and *The Heart Is a Lonely Hunter* (1941), Amelia mismanages love. She recoils from marital relations with Macy and ousts him from her residence. Charmed by Lymon's coy mannerisms, on Groundhog Day she welcomes townspeople to her café, where she serves a partially cooked roast to her capricious pet. Like an Amazon from Homeric epics, Miss Amelia trounces Macy, but is defeated after Lymon pounces on her, rescues Macy, and destroys the dining room.

Imprisoned like the helpless females in standard Gothic fiction, Miss Amelia resides alone in the sad café, rapidly turning into a bedraggled, wizened crone. Like the reclusive Miss HAVISHAM in Charles DICKENS's GREAT EXPECTATIONS (1861), the self-martyred lone woman hires a carpenter to board up her rooms, where she lives as a hermit in a town where the "soul rots with boredom" (*McCullers*, 71). McCullers echoes the protagonist's despair in the coda, a mournful call-and-response work song chanted by the 12-man chain gang that pounds pickaxes into macadam at the edge of town, a symbol of Miss Amelia's hard, love-damaged heart.

Bibliography

Auchincloss, Louis. *Pioneers and Caretakers: A Study of Nine American Women Novelists*. Minneapolis: University of Minnesota Press, 1965.

Cook, Richard M. *Carson McCullers*. New York: Frederick Unger, 1975.

King, Richard H. *A Southern Renaissance: The Cultural Awakening of the American South, 1930–1955*. Oxford: Oxford University Press, 1980.

McCullers, Carson. *The Ballad of the Sad Café and Other Stories*. New York: Bantam, 1951.

Barbauld, Anna Laetitia
(1743–1825)

Pamphleteer and essayist Anna Laetitia Barbauld, née Aikin, one of the first female writers to produce Gothic fiction, contributed to an understanding of the psychological response to early Gothic novels. She was reared in a learned environment and received encouragement from her father to write verse and to master ancient and modern languages. She produced commentary on the Gothic phenomenon complete with a narrative fragment titled "On the Pleasure Derived from Objects of Terror, with Sir Bertrand" (1773), a landmark in Gothic criticism that legitimizes the reading of terror literature as a form of intellectual stimulus. The atmospheric piece appeared in miscellanies and, from 1773 to 1820, was reprised in nine magazine issues. Admirers and plagiarizers made frequent use of the text as a model of Gothic form.

Barbauld's succinct essay praises passion and fancy for elevating the soul and extols artificial terrors as a form of mental calisthenics that tease and expand the mind, satisfy curiosity, and stretch the imagination. In the introduction, she comments on pleasure produced by "the painful sensation immediately arising from a scene of misery" ("Anna Laetitia Aikin," n.p.). She concludes that the positive response to pain makes readers want to "[be] witnesses to such scenes, instead of flying from them with disgust and horror" (*ibid.*). Her essay recognizes a human propensity for SUSPENSE and horror and the value of Gothic fiction as a relief from boredom, minor annoyances, and the ennui attendant on serious illness. She singles out William Shakespeare's use of the ghost of King Hamlet in *Hamlet* (ca. 1599) and WITCHCRAFT in *Macbeth* (ca. 1603) as well as dark elements in Horace WALPOLE's THE CASTLE OF OTRANTO (1765) and in Tobias SMOLLETT's FERDINAND COUNT FATHOM (1753) as models of pleasurable Gothic fiction. At the end of the essay, she appends an original literary fragment that applies GOTHIC CONVENTIONs. The story tells of a knight riding on the moors who enters a fearful antique mansion and falls under the spell of an alluring woman, a typical assignment of gender roles in the motif of the FEMME FATALE.

At age 31, the author married a minister, the Reverend Rochemont Barbauld, and helped him open a boys' school in Suffolk. Because of his increasing mental derangement and violence, she was forced to manage their successful institution, where she taught English and wrote curriculum guides and hymns for children. Upon selling the school, she became more active in editing and in writing for publication; among other things, she wrote social commentary on slavery and dirges on graveyard themes.

In widowhood at age 55, Barbauld immersed herself in scholarly work with the editing of a 50-volume encyclopedia on British novelists, which contains the critical essay "On the Origin and Progress of Novel-Writing" (1810). An element of ANTI-CATHOLICISM is evident in "On Monastic Institutions" (1825), in which Barbauld delights in the ruin of Catholic structures, which she vilifies as repositories of SUPERSTITION and ignorance. An admirer of Gothic romanticists, she further clarifies the psychological nature of Gothic literature in "An Inquiry into Those Kinds of Distress Which Excite Agreeable Sensations: With a Tale" and "On Evil: A Rhapsody" (1825). In describing the best of inventive fiction, she lauded most those works that evoke feelings of affection, pity, delight, moral indignation, suffering, and transport. Her critical essays indicate a preference for pure Gothic over the subgenre of historical Gothic, such as Clara REEVE's Memoirs of Sir Roger de Clarendon (1793), which Barbauld felt obscured events with artificial details. For her erudition, she earned the respect of Samuel Taylor COLERIDGE, Maria Edgeworth, Charles Lamb, Sir Walter SCOTT, and William Wordsworth.

Bibliography

"Anna Laetitia Aiken (Later Barbauld)," http://www.english.upenn.edu/~mgamer/Etexts/barbauldessays.html#pleasure.

Grove, Allen W. "To Make a Long Story Short: Gothic Fragments and the Gender Politics of Incompleteness," Studies in Short Fiction 34, no. 1 (1997): 1–9.

Haining, Peter, ed. Gothic Tales of Terror. New York: Taplinger, 1972.

Tarr, Mary Muriel. Catholicism in Gothic Fiction: A Study of the Nature and Function of Catholic Materials in Gothic Fiction in England, 1762–1820. Washington, D.C.: Catholic University of America Press, 1946.

Thomson, Douglass H. "Terror High and Low: The Aikins' 'On the Pleasure Derived From Objects of Terror; with Sir Bertrand, A Fragment,'" Wordsworth Circle 29, no. 1 (1998): 72–75.

Barnes, Djuna
(1892–1982)

The feminist fiction writer and dramatist Djuna Barnes added a problematic symbolist novel to 20th-century URBAN GOTHIC. Born in Hudson, New York, she studied art at the Pratt Institute and, at age 21, worked as a news reporter for the Brooklyn Daily Eagle. After writing poetry and satire, she moved to Paris in 1920 and wrote Nightwood (1930; reissued, 1936), a claustrophobic, doom-laden masterwork of GAY GOTHIC. It owes its citified vision and soul-sickness to Eugène Sue's The Mysteries of Paris (1842–43) and its latent vampirism to Bram STOKER's DRACULA (1897).

Paced like a Gothic folk tale with the TONE of French roman frénétique, Barnes's story employs fantasy, masquerading, transvestism, anti-Semitism, bestiality, and lunacy, elements that prefigured the freaks and GROTESQUEs of Angela CARTER, Isak DINESEN, Carson McCULLERS, and William FAULKNER. The settings replicate traditional GOTHIC CONVENTION with the dark Viennese decor of the Volkbeins' home and the twisting lanes of Paris, where the protagonist, Robin Vote, trolls for lesbian sex. Barnes's stunning FEMME FATALE is a destructive intriguer whose lyric OTHERNESS earned the praise of such prominent writers as William Burroughs, T. S. Eliot, Graham Greene, Edwin Muir, Dylan Thomas, and Edmund Wilson. Later evaluations characterize Barnes's pessimistic text as evidence of unease with the rise of European fascism.

Bibliography

Fiedler, Leslie. Love and Death in the American Novel. Cleveland: Meridian Books, 1962.

Horner, Avril, ed. European Gothic: A Spirited Exchange, 1760–1960. Manchester: Manchester University Press, 2002.

Moers, Ellen. Literary Women. New York: Oxford University Press, 1977.

Baudelaire, Charles
(1821–1867)

The French poet, critic, and translator Charles-Pierre Baudelaire found beauty and glamour in the winding sheets and burial vaults of funeral ritual. He supported the development of American Gothic with his embrace of Edgar Allan POE as a literary brother. From his intense examination of Poe's Gothic imagery, Baudelaire recognized a tormented genius writing for an unappreciative audience. He explained in "Edgar Allan Poe, Sa Vie et Ses Ouvrages" (Edgar Allan Poe, his life and his works) in the April 1852 issue of *Revue de Paris* that the two authors shared a common temperament, family background, disease and poverty, abuse of alcohol and opium, love of EXOTICISM, and uncompromising literary standards. In 1847, Baudelaire discovered and validated Poe's Gothic works by issuing positive critical commentary. He translated Poe's poems and stories into French and, from 1848 to 1864, published them in five volumes, an effort that made them available to a wider audience and placed Poe among classic world writers.

In the introduction to *Nouvelles Histoires Extraordinaires* (New extraordinary tales, 1857), Baudelaire analyzed Poe's works from a psychological angle. With *Histoires Grotesques et Sérieuses* (Grotesque and serious tales, 1865), Baudelaire extolled Poe's depiction of DREAMS and NIGHTMARES and his understanding of fear, NEURASTHENIA, OBSESSION, and INSANITY. Some of Poe's imagery appeared in Baudelaire's writings, including the poem "Un Voyage à Cythère" (A Voyage to Cythera) and *Le Spleen de Paris* (1869), an anthology of original works detailing his literary idealism and resultant melancholia. Encouraged by Poe's bold Gothic style and startling themes and character motivations, Baudelaire adopted his belief that the job of the writer was to express creativity for its own sake.

Baudelaire established supremacy among French poets with *Les Fleurs du Mal* (*The Flowers of Evil*, 1857), a paean to dark romanticism and occultism in alexandrines and octosyllabics. In the 132 poems he anthologized, Baudelaire captured the era's DECADENCE in autumnal images and Gothic imaginings on female beauty and lesbian sex, bone piles, ghosts and damnation, the urban bizarre, nightmares, SADISM, and VAMPIRISM. His works met with public disapproval and a religious ban for obscenity and depravity that remained in effect until 1949. Weakened by syphilis, he fled to Belgium, where he died of a paralytic stroke. His death-obsessed verse inspired Arthur Rimbaud's demonic hell trip in *Une Saison en Enfer* (*A Season in Hell*, 1873) and Isak DINESEN's *Seven Gothic Tales* (1934), which focus on decadent excess and nemesis.

Bibliography

Babuts, Nicole. "Baudelaire: Les Fleurs du Mal," *Symposium* 49, no. 4 (winter 1996): 307–309.

Guest, Harry. "The Flowers of Evil: A New Translation of 'Les Fleurs du Mal,'" *Journal of European Studies* 24, no. 4 (December 1994): 413–417.

Hennessy, Brendan. *The Gothic Novel*. London: Longman, 1978.

Horner, Avril, ed. *European Gothic: A Spirited Exchange 1760–1960*. Manchester: Manchester University Press, 2002.

Porter, Laurence M. "Poetiques de Baudelaire dans 'Les Fleurs du Mal': Rythme, Parfum, Lueur," *Romantic Review* 90, no. 2 (March 1999): 263.

"Beauty and the Beast"

A FAIRY TALE collected in Charles Perrault's *Contes de Ma Mère l'Oye* (*Mother Goose Tales*, 1698), "Beauty and the Beast" is a resilient motif within FEMALE GOTHIC. The myth is a version of the Greek story of Persephone, whom Hades kidnaps and carries to the underworld. The motif pervades a number of Gothic texts of DIABOLISM and VAMPIRISM, particularly George du Maurier's best-selling MELODRAMA *Trilby* (1894), the story of the mesmerist Svengali and the singer he trains and controls through hypnotism, and Bram STOKER's ghoul novel DRACULA (1897). The tale also powers Gaston LEROUX's resilient urban GHOST STORY *Le Fantôme de l'Opéra* (THE PHANTOM OF THE OPERA, 1910), which depicts the Svengalian obsession of Erik, a crazed opera fan, with Christine Daaé, an attractive soprano. The hidden facets of the story take place in the basement of the Paris Opera House rather than in the dark forest of the "Beauty" tale.

In a late 20th-century retelling, two novels reprised the tension and sexuality of the "Beauty and the Beast" myth. The Canadian author Marian Engel's erotic *Bear* (1977) scales back the comfortable fairy tale aura by setting her GROTESQUE, surreal version in the Canadian wild. Lou, the female protagonist, and a bear carry out a polite courtship that builds to episodes of embracing, dancing, sex play, and attempted coitus. As ecstasy relieves Lou's solitude, she murmurs, "Bear, take me to the bottom of the ocean with you, bear, swim with me, bear, put your arms around me, enclose me, swim, down, down, down with me" (Engel, 112). Entranced by the animal musk that coats her skin and hair, she offers herself to the animal, heart and soul. The theme of bestiality caused some critics to regard the work as pornography.

At the other extreme of menace, Robin McKinley created a tender young-adult Gothic novel, *Beauty* (1978), a bildungsroman of honor and family loyalty. She sets the action in a never-never land where a father's financial loss mars the wedding dreams of his 12-year-old daughter, Beauty. A move to the edge of an enchanted forest places her in reach of the Beast, a humanoid MONSTER who compensates for a hirsute body with refined courtesies. For their meeting, the author sets the NAIF on the back of Greatheart, a sturdy mount, and protects her with invisible SUPERNATURAL watchers. The standard happily-ever-after transformation of the handsome prince provides Beauty with her reward for goodness and compassion.

Bibliography

David, Kathy S. "Beauty and the Beast: The 'Feminization' of Weyland in the Vampire Tapestry," *Extrapolation* 43, no. 1 (spring 2002): 62–80.

Engel, Marian. *Bear*. New York: Atheneum, 1976.

Glyn-Jones, William. "Beauty and the Beast: The Hellenic Culture Model as a Tool for Recovering the Original Human Blueprint," *Kindred Spirit*, no. 61 (winter 2002): 45–47.

Williams, Andrew P. "The Silent Threat: A (Re)viewing of the 'Sexual Other' in 'The Phantom of the Opera' and 'Nosferatu,'" *Midwest Quarterly* 38, no. 1 (autumn 1996): 90–101.

Beckford, William

(1760–1844)

Like Horace WALPOLE, the oriental romanticist and voluptuary William Thomas Beckford chose to live an amoral romantic ideal. He was the son and namesake of a wealthy investor in Caribbean slaves and sugar who was twice mayor of London. From these colonial holdings, Beckford inherited ample funds to indulge his fantasies and narcissistic dreams. He traveled to Belgium, France, Germany, Holland, and Italy, where he wrote *The Long Story* (1777), a bit of Gothic juvenilia tinged with occultism. Bored with the legislative process after he entered Parliament, he was ostracized for a scandalous affair with the 10-year-old William Courtney in the boy's bedroom at Powderham Castle and retreated from the British Isles to the Continent to read exotic Eastern texts.

At age 21, Beckford had absorbed enough detail to begin writing VATHEK (1782), an extravagant life's-work based on his Asian scholarship and knowledge of the Koran and Arabic and Persian tales, which he studied as an escape from courses in classical literature. The GROTESQUE and antireligious nature of the text is boyishly defiant, obviously in opposition to his mother's Calvinism. Drawing on Antoine Galland's translation of *The Arabian Nights* (1704–17) and French romance, he proceeded in French and teamed with Samuel Henley to translate the finished work into English.

The novel reached print in unauthorized form. While Beckford vacationed in Europe, Henley issued, against Beckford's wishes, a first edition as *An Arabian Tale, from an Unpublished Manuscript* (1786), followed that same year by the release of the original in France. Beckford's famous phantasmagoria, England's chief contribution to the ORIENTAL ROMANCE, influenced the romanticists—Lord BYRON, Mary Wollstonecraft SHELLEY, and Percy Bysshe SHELLEY—as well as American Gothic genius Edgar Allan POE. Additional tales remained unpublished and vanished, turning up in the early 1900s in Ireland in fragmented form. One of them, "The Nymph of the Fountain" (ca. 1791), describes the use of fire to extract the demonic soul of a cruel woman.

After the death of his wife, Lady Margaret Gordon, Beckford was wealthy enough to travel and indulge his whims on money pouring in from his sugar plantations in the Caribbean. He wearied of avoiding stalkers and of concealing his bisexuality, remarking, "How tired I am of keeping a mask on my countenance. How tight it sticks—it makes me sore" (Beckford, introduction, xxx). Dubbed the "fool of Fonthill," he hired the architect James Wyatt to feign medieval decline in the design of Fonthill Abbey, a park and pseudo-ruin in Wiltshire built on the Gothic model.

Beckford's eccentric lifestyle freed him from social restraint. He posed as an Asian satrap who demanded that his team of builders work by daylight and, at night, by bonfire to complete the structure. His description of their labors testifies to a mind skewed toward Gothic details at the nightly spectacle by torchlight: "The immense and endless spaces, the gulph below; above, the gigantic spider's web of scaffolding . . . amid shouts from subterranean depths, oaths from Hell itself, and chanting from Pandemonium" (Stevens, 13). The workers created groves, oversized doorways, galleries for rare art objects and books, and rooms designed for secret orgies with young boys, which rumor embroidered far beyond fact. Keeping the 35-foot portals were dwarf janissaries, who opened the way for the rare guest to enjoy a sumptuous art collection and a library containing the best in travel, magic, DECADENCE, and DIABOLISM. In 1811, Beckford reported to his lover Gregorio Franchi that Fonthill Abbey was a blessed refuge from prying eyes.

By 1822, Beckford had run through his fortune, which the abolition of slavery diminished. He had to sell his dream home, which by then had been expanded into a cross-shaped edifice topped with a massive 285-foot octagonal tower. Outside Bath, he built a new amusement, Landsdown Baghdad, a miniature playground similar in tone and extravagance to Fonthill. Although lavish in his Gothic imagination, Beckford lacked the personal warmth necessary to maintain friendships, and he withdrew into eccentricity and solitude. Stricken with a fatal influenza, he requested that upon his death he be buried in unhallowed ground.

Bibliography

Beckford, William. *Vathek*. London: Oxford University Press, 1970.

Garrett, John. "'Ending in Infinity': William Beckford's Arabian Tale," *Eighteenth-Century Fiction* 5, no. 1 (1992): 15–34.

Gemmett, Robert J. "The Caliph Vathek from England and the Continent to America," *American Book Collector* 18, no. 9 (1968): 12–19.

James, Jamie. "The Caliph of Fonthill," *American Scholar* 72, no. 1 (winter 2003): 67–79.

Scott, John. "The Rise and Fall of Fonthill Abbey," *British History Illustrated* 2, no. 3 (1975): 2–11.

Stevens, David. *The Gothic Tradition*. Cambridge: Cambridge University Press, 2000.

Bellefleur
Joyce Carol Oates
(1980)

Written shortly after Joyce Carol OATES settled in Princeton, New Jersey, her complex horror tale *Bellefleur* is the first in a series of four Gothic novels that comment on contemporary issues. She applies Gothic touches to highlight dark elements in American history, particularly the rise of wealthy families and psychological OBSESSIONs, which she symbolizes in the form of a werewolf. The Faulknerian saga, woven of connecting stories, narrates the history of the Bellefleur clan, who live in an American castle on spirit-haunted Lake Noir. At the crux of the family quandary is the search for identity, a recurrent theme in Oates's novels.

Oates presents a chaotic scenario. She fills her MELODRAMA with incidents of nightwalking, a huge bird stealing an infant, serial murder, spiritualism, vampirism, incest, and the impressions of Germaine, a freakish girl born with the bottom half of her twin brother attached to her torso. Harrowing the family are a conflagration, predictions of doom, and ghosts juxtaposed by light passages of gossip, jokes, and family stories. The author complicates nested episodes with the theme of nihilism and parallel time sequences that turn ancestors into contemporaries.

Bibliography

Couzens, Gary. "Containing Multitudes: The Fiction of Joyce Carol Oates," *Third Alternative*, no. 10 (spring 1996): 48–50.

Creighton, Joanne V. "Digging Deep into Familiar Ground," *Chicago Tribune*, November 17, 2002: 1.

Latta, Alan D. "Spinell and Connie: Joyce Carol Oates Re-Imagining Thomas Mann?" *Connotations* 9, no. 3 (1999/2000): 316–329.

Wesley, Marilyn C. *Refusal and Transgression in Joyce Carol Oates' Fiction.* Westport, Conn.: Greenwood, 1993.

Beloved
Toni Morrison
(1987)

Beloved is the nightmarish GHOST STORY by Toni Morrison, winner of the 1993 Nobel Prize in literature. She pursued a unique strand of AMERICAN GOTHIC in the rapturous SUPERNATURAL novel by depicting the legacy of racism as a literal haunting. Modernizing a tradition of slave-era horror tales that dates to the eroticism and procreative evils of slavery in Harriet Beecher Stowe's *Uncle Tom's Cabin* (1851–52) and Louisa May Alcott's short stories "M. L." (1863) and "My Contraband" (1863) and the novel *A Long Fatal Love Chase* (1866), Morrison probed the pathology of slaveholding through the genre of the ghost tale. She based the action on horrific details—the victimization, violation, and scapegoating of blacks during the African diaspora and the middle passage. The superb characterizations reach into a uniquely American heart of darkness.

The controlling image is the black woman's burden as a bearer of future slaves via cyclical conceptions and childbirths. Through a Faulknerian stream-of-consciousness blended with NIGHT-MARES and memories of a carnal union celebrated in a cornfield like a primitive fertility rite, Morrison resurrects suppressed yearnings, sufferings, and dissociations that express a Gothic horror peculiar to Southern history. In counterpoint against the story of Sethe, the protagonist, is the masculine strand, Paul D's experience with the chain gang and immurement each night at the convict camp in coffin-shaped boxes set in the ground. The symbol of Paul's internalized anguish is a tobacco tin corroded shut and secured in his shirt pocket.

Morrison's characters are crippled emotionally by plantation-style slavery and the exploitation of the slave breeder. Violent scenes picture Sethe in the power of mossy-toothed white boys who commit mammary rape by sucking out her breast milk. Slowed by the last days of pregnancy and a severe whipping with rawhide, she escapes north, gives birth in the woods, and crosses the river into Ohio. A month of freedom concludes in catastrophe as slave catchers ride into the yard of a Cincinnati safe house. The crux of Sethe's tragedy is her instinctual sacrifice of BELOVED, the female toddler she murders by one quick slash to the throat with a handsaw. An eyewitness foresees the coming battle with the child's spirit: "People who die bad don't stay in the ground" (Morrison, 188).

The woman-centered ghost story serves as a fiction of conscience and bears witness to human misery that refuses to be quieted. Guilt and pain so overshadow Sethe's Ohio home that her fellow sufferer, Paul D, senses a venomous presence as soon as he reunites with his old friend. From abuse by her Kentucky masters, Sethe bears the outlines of a chokecherry tree on her back and the ghost of Beloved all around her. Morrison exorcises the cumbrous spirit with a touch of grace, Paul D's acceptance and forgiveness of Sethe's crime. He affirms that Sethe herself—her courage and devotion to motherhood and to self—constitutes her "best thing" (*ibid*, 273). The result is a visible liberation as the ghost's footprints recede in the distance and disappear as Beloved passes from live girl into LEGEND.

Bibliography
Goldner, Ellen J. "Other(ed) Ghosts: Gothicism and the Bonds of Reason in Melville, Chesnutt, and Morrison," *MELUS* 24, no. 1 (spring 1999): 59.

Hamilton, Cynthia S. "Revisions, Rememories, and Exorcisms: Toni Morrison and the Slave Narrative," *Journal of American Studies* 30, no. 3 (1996): 30–32.

Morrison, Toni. *Beloved.* New York: Plume, 1987.

Beloved

The ambiguous title character in Toni Morrison's stunning GHOST STORY BELOVED (1987) is the spirit of a two-year-old girl killed by her mother, Sethe, a plantation runaway, before the child could be reclaimed into slavery. Beloved's spirit haunts the family home in Cincinnati three months after Sethe's jailing for infanticide. After years of unnerving the family, on the day of the local carnival Beloved takes the form of a palpable REVENANT dressed in white. The ghost, like a petulant brat, bedevils the family with sour smells, bed-wetting, topplings from shelves, and demands for attention. Morrison uses the description of her wobbly head as a reminder of the gash to the throat that ended baby Beloved's life.

Sethe develops a terrifying mother-child relationship with the ghost-girl, whose return overwhelms the parent with dire memories of "what it took to drag the teeth of that saw under the little chin; to feel the baby blood pump like oil in her hands; to hold her face so her head would stay on" (Morrison, 251). The ghost-girl rapidly outgrows childhood to develop into a seductive FEMME FATALE. By stealing Sethe's lover, Paul D, in a mystic love nest, Beloved becomes her mother's rival and tormentor. Through the concerted efforts of 30 black women, embracing both Christian faith and pagan amulets, Beloved is exorcised into LEGEND, retreating to the stream, "cutting through the woods, a naked woman with fish for hair" (ibid., 267). In grief at the parting of the noxious ghost, Sethe whimpers, "She was my best thing" (ibid., 272).

Bibliography

Goldner, Ellen J. "Other(ed) Ghosts: Gothicism and the Bonds of Reason in Melville, Chesnutt, and Morrison," *MELUS* 24, no. 1 (spring 1999): 59.

Hamilton, Cynthia S. "Revisions, Rememories, and Exorcisms: Toni Morrison and the Slave Narrative," *Journal of American Studies* 30, no. 3 (1996): 30–32.

Morrison, Toni. *Beloved*. New York: Plume, 1987.

Benito Cereno
Herman Melville
(1855)

A stark, enigmatic Gothic fable first published in *Putnam's Monthly Magazine*, Benito Cereno demonstrates author Herman MELVILLE's skill at amalgamating American history with MYSTERY, SUSPENSE, and an ATMOSPHERE of dread, essential elements of the Gothic mode. When the protagonist, Amasa Delano, captain of the American trader *Bachelor's Delight*, happens upon the Spanish slaver *San Dominick* off the coast of South America, he discovers that the ship drifts aimlessly. On the prow is the skeleton of the murdered captain, an image that sets an aura of hauntings derived from slavery. In a detailed survey of the ship, Delano pieces together evidence that the aristocratic captain, Don Benito Cereno, is the pawn of Babo, a Senegalese servant. After overthrowing the white crew, Babo took command of the ship, creating a claustrophobic atmosphere, psychological tension, and ambiguity of leadership.

In this masterful work of COLONIAL GOTHIC, Melville manipulates one of his most successful techniques, the imprisoning microcosm. In the custody of vengeful blackmen, Don Benito finds himself caged in his own ship and acting out an elaborate hoax. The shabby, ill-kept decks attest to a symbolic decline of morality in the New World brought on by slavery. Delano envisions himself in a stereotypical Gothic setting, "in some far inland country; prisoner in some deserted château, left to stare at empty grounds, and peer out at vague roads, where never wagon or wayfarer passed" (Melville, 200). A shocking splintering of a rotted balustrade is a symbol of secret corruption, but the naive Delano fails to interpret an increasing number of ominous signs. An elderly sailor, surveying the event, works a large knot, another SYMBOL of the New World's self-incrimination and a condemnation of the complex problem of black enslavement.

Complex in its structure, the dramatic novella offers a stark picture of AMERICAN GOTHIC themes based on New World sins. The story projects the limitations on Delano as central intelligence. Because of his preconceived notions of black inferiority, he is initially incapable of recognizing intelligence and rage in Babo. The tale produces an unsettling conclusion—the poetic justice of Babo's excised head gazing at the white enslavers of Africans. The riveting death scene foreshadows the conclusion of Joseph CONRAD's HEART OF DARKNESS (1902), a devastating glimpse of colonial racism.

Bibliography

Coviello, Peter. "The American in Charity: 'Benito Cereno' and Gothic Anti-sentimentality," *Studies in American Fiction* 30, no. 2 (autumn 2002): 155–180.

Goddu, Teresa A. *Gothic America: Narrative, History, and Nation*. New York: Columbia University Press, 1997.

Goldner, Ellen J. "Other(ed) Ghosts: Gothicism and the Bonds of Reason in Melville, Chesnutt, and Morrison," *MELUS* 24, no. 1 (spring 1999): 59.

Melville, Herman. *Billy Budd and Other Stories*. New York: Penguin, 1986.

Pahl, Dennis. "The Gaze of History in 'Benito Cereno,'" *Studies in Short Fiction* 32, no. 2 (spring 1995): 171–183.

Bierce, Ambrose

(1842–1914)

An eccentric American master of the tall tale and the gruesome and uncanny images of SUPERNATURAL stories, Ambrose Gwinett Bierce turned a job of writing columns and news reports for frontier newspapers into a career in adventure lore and macabre fiction. In his youth, he fled the regimented Calvinism of his parents and joined the army. He learned to respect the thin separation between life and death while fighting on the Union side in the Civil War, a source of his savage, pessimistic short fiction.

Bierce's most famous story, "An Occurrence at Owl Creek Bridge," anthologized in *Tales of Soldiers and Civilians* (1891), builds on the dream state of Peyton Farquhar, a Confederate sympathizer about to be hanged for treason. Meticulously structured to distort time while building on the impending strangulation and/or snapped neck, the plot melds present peril with past escapades and with a projected flight from the Union detail ordered to execute planters who support local rebels by burning bridges. Owl Creek Bridge, its fateful use identified by the traditional death bird, looms in the reader's consciousness as a symbol of the tenuous link between past and present, survival and extinction. The hyperreality of Farquhar's mental escape to wife and home expands to a universal consciousness of humanity's slim tether to life.

Known as Bitter Bierce because of his sardonic wit, the author had a flair for cynicism, the absurd, and free-floating misanthropy. He refined his skills by translating and adapting Richard Voss's German romance *The Monk and the Hangman's Daughter* (1892) and by collecting ghost tales in *Can Such Things Be?* (1893). One story in the anthology, "The Damned Thing," is a resetting of the Irish-American Gothicist Fitz-James O'BRIEN's "What Was It?" (1859). Bierce issued 500 mordant aphorisms in *The Devil's Dictionary* (1906) and such finely honed HORROR NARRATIVES as "A Bottomless Grave" in *Negligible Tales* (1911).

Still clinging to a reputation for daring, at age 72 Bierce disappeared in Chihuahua while observing General Pancho Villa's rebels during the Mexican civil war. Long after Bierce's demise, he dominated AMERICAN GOTHIC through frequently anthologized tall tales, keen-edged satire, and raw frontier fictions, in particular, "The Secret of Macarger's Gulch" (1874), an eerie ghost tale about a miner haunted by the wife he murdered by bashing her skull with a pickax. Bierce's refined sense of irony influenced the Gothic stories of Gertrude ATHERTON, Robert William Chambers, Emma Frances Dawson, and W. C. Morrow.

Bibliography

Habibi, Don Asher. "The Experience of a Lifetime: Philosophical Reflections on a Narrative Device of Ambrose Bierce," *Studies in the Humanities* 29, no. 2 (December 2002): 83–109.

Lovecraft, H. P. *The Annotated Supernatural Horror in Literature*. New York: Hippocampus, 2000.

Switheff, Peter. "'Something Uncanny': The Dream Structure in Ambrose Bierce's 'An Occurrence at Owl Creek Bridge,'" *Studies in Short Fiction* 30, no. 3 (summer 1993): 349–357.

Bird, Robert Montgomery

(1806–1854)

A popular romanticist and playwright, Robert Montgomery Bird, a physician interested in abnormal psychology, developed a dark subgenre of FRONTIER GOTHIC and COLONIAL GOTHIC with a bloody MYSTERY novel, *NICK OF THE WOODS; or, The Jibbenainosay: A Tale of Kentucky* (1837), a popular frontier thriller. Bird advanced from frontier lore in the plays *Oralloossa* (1832) and *The Broker of Bogota* (1834) to more lucrative conquistador novels, *Calavar* (1834) and *The Infidel* (1835), and to a tale of METEMPSYCHOSIS, *Sheppard Lee* (1836), the story of a man killed in an accident and the wanderings of his soul through six other bodies. The account of Nick derived from the author's interest in split personalities as well as from travels among the Shawnee, his research on the Indian Wars, and eyewitness accounts of native-on-white atrocities.

While editing the *Southern Literary Messenger*, Edgar Allan POE solicited Bird's work for the magazine. The resulting novel opposes the ideal of the racially inclusive frontier pictured in James Fenimore Cooper's Leatherstocking Tales. Bird presents the aptly named Nathan Slaughter as a pacifist Quaker turned bloodthirsty Indian slayer in Kentucky during the 1780s. Bird bests Cooper through the rapid development of episodes and the vivid portrayal of such horrors as a besieged cabin, escape over a flooding river, ambush and torture, and the secret entrance to an Indian village by night. For VIOLENCE and MELODRAMA, Bird adds a gruesome scalping, kidnapped infants, a missing will and contested inheritance, and a plot to force the maiden, Edith Forrester, into an unthinkable marriage.

Following Poe's positive reception of *Nick of the Woods,* the Gothic writer William Harrison AINSWORTH presented Bird's work in London as original and worthy of interest. The American historian Francis Parkman admired the text for its true portrayal of the Indian hater driven by ill fate to commit heinous serial crimes. The graphic story was so well received by Americans and Europeans that the book went through 20 English editions, two pirated versions, and a translation into German. The work's popularity sired a strain of dime novels. In 1838, Louisa Hamblin Medina adapted the character of Bloody Nathan Slaughter and his ritual killings for one of the most popular stage melodramas of its day, which shocked wide-eyed urban audiences at Boston's National Theater in 1843. A year before Bird's death from exhaustion while trying to publish the Philadelphia *North American,* he issued a revised edition of *Nick of the Woods.*

Bibliography

Review of *Nick of the Woods* by Robert Montgomery Bird. *Southern Literary Messenger* 3, no. 4 (April 1837): 254–257.

Ruland, Richard, and Malcolm Bradbury. *From Puritanism to Postmodernism: A History of American Literature.* New York: Penguin, 1991.

"The Birds"
Daphne du Maurier
(1952)

Daphne DU MAURIER's perplexing DOMESTIC GOTHIC story of an attack by birds on residents of a seaside town tentatively explores the suggestion that NATURE may hold a grudge against humankind and technology. She explains in the preface to *Classics of the Macabre* (1987) that she once heard gulls screaming as she walked along the cliffs near her Cornwall home, Menabilly. She mused, "Supposing they stop being interested in worms?" (du Maurier, 12). From her application of Gothic traits to birds came the macabre speculative fiction that spools out from the account of a crippled plowman, Nat Hocken. He prepares his soil with time-honored reliance on nature to provide. His tractor and the rest of the manufactured hardware pall beside the seemingly limitless phalanxes of birds that fling their bodies against dwellings and hurl themselves down chimneys to get at human residents.

After an unsettling autumn when a glut of birds went hungry, the restless jackdaws, rooks, and gulls precipitate avian aggression in small, usually meek songbirds—blue tits, bramblings, finches, larks, robins, and sparrows—and a lone gannet. As a contrast to the reassuring commonalities of tea in the kitchen and embers on the hearth, du Maurier establishes outdoor menace with a cutting east wind, a black December frost, and the eerie madness in small birds. She manipulates ATMOSPHERE with formulaic devices—a candle blowing out at the bedroom door, the hostile beating wings in the dark, threats to tender children, a telephone ripped out of the wall—and develops a mundane bird-in-the-house scenario into a battle: "They were not yet defeated, for again and again they returned to the assault, jabbing his hands, his head, the little stabbing beaks sharp as a pointed fork" (*ibid.,* 157).

Du Maurier stresses the value of radio to rural people seeking news about aberrant bird behaviors. Nat recognizes modernity's foolishness in the absence of ample stores, salted pilchards, and candles and tobacco to supply them during the siege. As the pantry declines, nature increases the menace as sea birds rise above the morning tide, "circling, hundreds of them, thousands of them, lifting their wings against the wind" (ibid., 167). After the British military musters airplanes to fight the birds, the author recreates the controlled panic that the English lived through during the Blitz and includes a frail hope that America will involve itself in the anti-bird war just as it came to England's aid against the Nazis. Doggedly, Nat remarks to his wife, "There isn't going to be any news. . . . We've got to depend upon ourselves" (ibid., 184).

Du Maurier withdraws from the gruesome survival struggle with sounds of splintering wood as hawks attack the farmhouse door. The narrator wonders "how many million years of memory were stored in those little brains, behind the stabbing beaks, the piercing eyes, now giving them this instinct to destroy mankind with all the deft precision of machines" (ibid., 173). Critic Nina Auerbach interpreted the dark tale as a prophecy of doom for England, which some of du Maurier's other Gothic stories depict as reaching the end of an irreversible civil and moral decline.

The popular 1963 screen version, written by Evan Hunter, was Alfred Hitchcock's first horror fantasy. To dramatize Gothic tensions, he enlarged on the apocalyptic ALLEGORY of the human struggle against nature, replacing du Maurier's domestic motif with a frail sexual attraction between actors Tippi Hedren and Rod Taylor.

Bibliography

Auerbach, Nina. Daphne du Maurier: Haunted Heiress. Philadelphia: University of Pennsylvania Press, 1999.

du Maurier, Daphne. Classics of the Macabre. Garden City, N.Y.: Doubleday, 1987.

Forster, Margaret. Daphne du Maurier. New York: Doubleday, 1993.

Halberstam, Judith. Skin Shows: Gothic Horror and the Technology of Monsters. Durham, N.C.: Duke University Press, 1995.

Kauffman, Stanley. Review of The Birds, New Republic, April 13, 1963: 26.

"The Birthmark"
Nathaniel Hawthorne
(1843)

A parable of the MAD SCIENTIST story, Nathaniel HAWTHORNE's "The Birthmark" characterizes the ruin of the romantic ideal. The story was first issued in the Pioneer in 1843, and was published that same year in a collection, Mosses from an Old Manse. The parable is an ALLEGORY of dominance through forceful personality, subverted will, and masculine superiority, with overtones of FEMALE GOTHIC. The Gothic narrative depicts the beautiful bride Georgiana in the hands of her possessive husband Aylmer, a perverter of science. Because of his longing for perfection in a mate, he is driven to expunge from Georgiana's cheek a superficial hand-shaped stain, her only unattractive feature. Passing from hurt feelings to anger, she charges, "You cannot love what shocks you!"; yet, under his influence, she gradually comes to detest the birthmark as much as Aylmer does (Hawthorne, 1,021).

The Faustian story, which parallels the manipulation of NATURE in Mary Wollstonecraft SHELLEY's FRANKENSTEIN (1818) and Robert Louis STEVENSON's DR. JEKYLL AND MR. HYDE (1886), characterizes the optimistic age of progress, with a self-centered, godlike lab experimenter who takes risks that violate bioethics as well as his marriage vows. Aylmer's OBSESSION reflects overconfidence, hubris, and a yearning for power more than concern for Georgiana's disfigurement. To create a menacing ATMOSPHERE, Hawthorne stresses hellish DREAMS, a plant blighted by Georgiana's touch, and Aylmer's admiration of medieval alchemists and a vial of "precious poison" (ibid., 1,027). Anticipating success, Aylmer expects his wife to worship him for his brilliance. A hulking, Igor-like assistant, the shaggy Aminadab, chuckles while the victim sinks to her death as the poison erases the birthmark. Symbolically, she expires from a loss of self, which her husband causes by imposing on her a subjective view of perfection.

Bibliography

Bunge, Nancy. Nathaniel Hawthorne. New York: Twayne, 1993.

Eckstein, Barbara. "Hawthorne's 'The Birthmark': Science and Romance as Belief," Studies in Short Fiction 26, no. 4 (1989): 511–515.

Hawthorne, Nathaniel. The Complete Novels and Selected Tales of Nathaniel Hawthorne. New York: Modern Library, 1937.

Ruland, Richard, and Malcolm Bradbury. *From Puritanism to Postmodernism: A History of American Literature.* New York: Penguin, 1991.

"The Black Cat"
Edgar Allan Poe
(1843)

Edgar Allan POE's compelling HORROR story of INSANITY, OBSESSION, and evil, "The Black Cat" studies the mental aberrations of a moody, unstable alcoholic. The author incorporates senseless repetition and inverted sentence elements, both testimonials to an UNRELIABLE NARRATOR. Unlike 18th- and 19th-century plots involving the STALKING of a lone female, Poe's text describes the pursuit and torment of the cat Pluto, appropriately named for a god of the underworld. The battle of wills arouses an abnormal loathing in the male speaker's psyche. After blinding and hanging Pluto, the unnamed man discovers on the premises a second cat bearing a gallows-shaped cipher on its fur.

Poe then shifts from the man-against-animal scenario as the protagonist transfers his obsessions to his wife when she becomes the cat's protector. By murdering his wife with an ax and sealing her remains behind a brick basement wall, he intends to elude a police investigation. In a twist common to GOTHIC CONVENTION, diabolical plans fail because of all-too-human flaws. To the killer's dismay, four days later he finds his plans foiled by the second cat, which he has immured with the corpse.

The allure of "The Black Cat" is the manic narrator's ability to rationalize his viciousness and to invite the wary reader's sympathy and belief. Inspired by Sir Walter SCOTT's *Letters on Demonology* (1830), Poe enlarges on congenital malice and animal cruelty. In the motif of PREMATURE BURIAL, he presents poetic justice as the direct result of the protagonist's own warped thinking. The claustrophobic setting and torture enhance Poe's images of a vulnerable animal and human victim, a pattern that draws upon the persecution and murder of women in the Middle Ages and during the Salem witch trials of 1692.

Burdened with fears for his dying wife, Virginia Clemm Poe, who suffered from tuberculosis, the author, under the influence of both drugs and alcohol, published the gruesome story in the August 1843 issue of *United States Saturday Post,* to mixed reviews. Reacting to the tale's extremes of SADISM, VIOLENCE, and gore, in 1844 Poe's friend-turned-enemy Thomas Dunn English parodied "The Black Cat" as "The Ghost of the Grey Tadpole," which appeared in the *Irish Citizen.* Nonetheless, in a letter to the poet James Russell Lowell in July of that year, Poe claimed that the story was one of his best and added it to an anthology, *Tales* (1845). In January 1847, Isabelle Meunier translated the story into French for publication in *La Democratie Pacifique.*

The compelling account of an internal battle between remorse and perversity made Poe's story a popular vehicle for film, although several adaptations loaded the spare story with Gothic cinematic embroiderings. In 1934, Universal Studios' cinema version, *The Black Cat,* paired Boris Karloff with Bela Lugosi for a story of DIABOLISM, sadism, and necrophilia. Seven years later, Universal's film MYSTERY of the same title teamed Basil Rathbone with Lugosi. For maximum shock, a ghoulish Italian version, *Il Gatto Nero* (*The Black Cat,* 1981), starring Patrick Magee, depicted a twisted psyche and multiple murders.

Bibliography
Piacentino, Ed. "Poe's 'The Black Cat' as Psychobiography: Some Reflections on the Narratological Dynamics," *Studies in Short Fiction* 35, no. 2 (spring 1998): 153–168.

Blackwood, Algernon
(1869–1951)

Algernon Henry Blackwood was a brilliant oral storyteller and the leading writer of SHORT GOTHIC FICTION. He earned renown for his interest in the occult and for his orchestration of eerie ATMOSPHERE. Born in Kent, England, to a conservative Victorian family, he later emigrated to Canada, where in turn he ran a dairy, panned for gold, and managed a hotel. He then settled in New York City to report for the New York *Times* and the *Evening Sun.* In rebellion against his father's implacable evangelism, he pursued research into Buddhism, Hinduism, Rosicrucianism, Madame Blavatsky's theosophy, KABBALISM, and mesmerism. He later tapped his knowledge to create MYSTICISM and SENSATIONALISM in his spectral stories.

At age 30, Blackwood fled the crime and insincerity of the big city and returned to England. He subsequently traveled in the Danube region of Europe and began a career writing MYSTERY, DETECTIVE STORIES, and tales of the SUPERNATURAL. He incorporated sorcery in "Smith: An Episode in a Lodging House" (1906), described the haunting spiritual remains of a leper in "The Listener" (1907), wrote about satanism and spooks in "Secret Worship" (1908), and explored LYCANTHROPY in "The Camp of the Dog" (1908). In 1907, he created a psychic detective, Dr. John Silence, whom the author later rewrote for BBC radio broadcasts of the 1930s and 1940s and for television on *Saturday Night Story* in 1947, when he told ghost stories. Unlike the exhibitionistic Sherlock HOLMES, Silence maintains a low profile while using his powers to help people in distress, as in an exorcism of fiends in "A Psychical Invasion" (1908).

Among the many tales from Blackwood's collections that eventually were adapted for British radio and television was "The Willows" (1907), an impressionistic story honored by H. P. LOVECRAFT as the finest of its type. It tells of an unseen presence that inhabits a part of Austria visited by unsuspecting campers. Grandly picturesque, the action overturns the benign outdoors of English ROMANTICISM by depicting NATURE as a sinister force. Blackwood, dubbed the "ghost man," wrote additional eerie stories of the outdoors, including "The Wendigo" (1910), a weird tale of a wind fiend of the North Woods of Canada that sweeps the setting and carries off a group of woodsmen. In 1918, Blackwood wrote of communicating with the dead in *The Garden of Survival* and of reincarnation in the GOTHIC DRAMA *Karma*. An odd duck by most standards, he lived a solitary life, spied for England during World War I, and spent his last years traveling and writing reviews. In 1949, King George VI named him a Commander of the British Empire.

Bibliography

Johnson, George. "Algernon Blackwood," *English Literature in Transition 1880–1920* 46, no. 2 (spring 2003): 195–199.

Wilson, Colin. "Starlight Man: The Extraordinary Life of Algernon Blackwood," *Spectator* 287, no. 9,043 (December 1, 2001): 46–47.

Blackwood's Edinburgh Magazine

A popular source of MYSTERY, the SUPERNATURAL, and SHORT GOTHIC FICTION, the long-lived, family-operated monthly *Blackwood's Edinburgh Magazine* had its beginnings in April 1817. It successfully competed with the *Edinburgh Review* and *London Magazine* and survived until 1980.

The Scottish book dealer William Blackwood and his sons established the firm on George Street in London. Under their leadership, the publication encouraged both Tory politics and good literature, including translations of GERMAN GOTHIC lore by E. T. A. HOFFMANN and Friedrich von SCHILLER. The magazine's office, affectionately dubbed "Maga," became a social gathering spot for writers and a publishing venue for some of the best works of British Gothic fiction, notably submissions by Felicia Hemans, James HOGG, William MUDFORD, and Sir Walter SCOTT, who weathered a troubled relationship with the opinionated elder Blackwood. The firm also cultivated such promising writers as American Gothicist Charles Brockden BROWN and presented editorials, critiques, articles, and short stories that stimulated a broad span of the reading public. Among these stories were Robert Macnish's demonic tale "The Metempsychosis," issued in May 1826; Mudford's terror story "The Iron Shroud" (1830); and Edward George BULWER-LYTTON's "The Haunted and the Haunters; or, The House and the Brain," an occult chiller published in *Blackwood's* in August 1857.

Writers found springboards to their work in *Blackwood's*, notably Hogg's classic Gothic thriller *The Private Memoirs and Confessions of a Justified Sinner* (1824), a psychological tale reflecting ironies drawn from "Confessions of an English Glutton," a story published anonymously in *Blackwood's* the previous year. One story, initially published in *Blackwood's*, the Irish writer William Maginn's "The Man in the Bell" (1821), a tale of instant INSANITY, was subsequently featured in many Gothic anthologies. In 1827, Thomas De Quincey submitted a literary jest, "On Murder

Considered as One of the Fine Arts," which he composed in the vein of the NEWGATE NOVEL. Readers like Charlotte and Emily BRONTË combed through editions of BLACKWOOD'S; the suggestion for the haunted mansion that Emily developed into the main setting in WUTHERING HEIGHTS (1847) and the name *Eyre* that Charlotte gave to her heroine in JANE EYRE (1847) both came from the magazine's pages. In the 1860s, *Blackwood's* trenchant critic Margaret OLIPHANT repaid Charlotte's devotion to the magazine by lauding *Jane Eyre* (1847) as a worthy Gothic novel.

Under the editorship of John Blackwood, the magazine continued to encourage the best fiction, publishing De Quincey's *Suspiria de Profundis* (Sighs from the depths, 1845) and the morbid tale "The Lifted Veil" (1859), the work of George Eliot, whose talents Blackwood acknowledged despite her gender. Edgar Allan POE chose to tweak *Blackwood's* with "How to Write a Blackwood Article" (1850), a droll piece issued under the pseudonym Signora Psyche Zenobia, a parody of Gothic names not far removed from some Poe gave to his own characters. In the text, Blackwood himself advised Zenobia on writing sensational fiction as a means of profiting from her publications.

William Blackwood III, who edited the magazine in the last quarter of the 19th century, published writers of the caliber of Joseph CONRAD, and Margaret Oliphant, a prolific author of the ghostly "The Open Door" (1881) and the supernatural thriller "The Library Window" (1896). The works of these and other writers provided ATMOSPHERE, mystery, adventure, and outré experiences from throughout the British Empire, drawing more middle-class readers. Probably the finest such piece of fiction to appear in *Blackwood's* was Conrad's serial HEART OF DARKNESS (1902), the tale of a pilgrimage up the Congo River to confront the white VILLAIN Kurtz.

Bibliography

Groves, David. "'Confessions of an English Glutton': A (Probable) Source for James Hogg's 'Confessions,'" *Notes and Queries* 40, no. 1 (March 1993): 46–47.

"The Haunted Library: *Blackwood's Edinburgh Magazine,*" http://www2.widener.edu/Wolfgram-Memorial-Library/facultypages/gothic/journals.htm.

Hollingsworth, Keith. *The Newgate Novel, 1830–1847.* Detroit: Wayne State University Press, 1963.

Morrison, Robert, and Chris Baldick, eds. *Tales of Terror from Blackwood's Magazine.* New York: Oxford University Press, 1995.

Bleak House
Charles Dickens
(1853)

Charles Dickens's ninth novel, *Bleak House*, provides readers a MYSTERY, DETECTIVE STORY, and an ALLEGORY of the dismal life England offered its poor and laboring classes. It was first published serially in the weekly magazine *Household Words*, appearing in 20 installments during the period from March 1, 1852, to September 20, 1853. The urban narrative intrigued reader curiosity with Gothic elements—shameful family secrets, a legendary ghost's walk, a man who dies with blood in his mouth, and the sweep of the riverbank for a potential suicide. Blanketed with fog, the decaying slum called Tom-All-Alone's is an urban nightmare: "A villainous street, undrained, unventilated, deep in black mud and corrupt water . . . and reeking with such smells and sights that [Mr. Bucket], who has lived in London all his life, can scarce believe his senses" (Dickens, 330–331). The infamous tenement incubates a contagion—street urchin Jo's smallpox, which spreads temporary blindness, disfigurement, and death. Festering blight creeps into London's fashionable district, symbolizing the social rot that threatens every household, even the lord chancellor's family.

The most astonishing event involves the demise by spontaneous combustion of the skeletal rag-and-bone dealer Krook, a dissolute alcoholic and emblem of the putrefaction that threatens England. Dickens concludes chapter 32 with horror: "It is the same death eternally—inborn, inbred, engendered in the corrupted humours of the vicious body itself, and that only—spontaneous combustion, and none other of all the deaths that can be died" (Dickens, 474, 479). At the chiming of midnight, Krook vanishes from his fireside, leaving grease stains and an odor of roasted meat as proof of his trade and as an OMEN of the implosion that awaits a fragmented society. The scene is so overcharged with theatrics that critic George Henry Lewes ridiculed Dickens for stooping to ignorant SUPERSTITION.

Characteristic of Dickens's Gothicism is the use of mystery and sleuthing to advance his social themes. A focus of Police Inspector Bucket's investigations is the past of the orphaned Esther Summerson, a servant girl who ponders a haunting face that she recalls from childhood. The face turns out to be that of Lady Honoria Dedlock, Esther's mother, who abandoned her base-born daughter in infancy. Disguised in working-class dress, Lady Dedlock dies holding to the iron grate of a graveyard while mourning Nemo—Latin for *nobody*—the nickname of Captain Hawdon, Esther's father, who died of an opium overdose. Stage versions of the novel flourished by reprising Dickens's handling of dramatic dialogue and character interaction. Four plays extracted the most poignant scenes by reprising the sufferings of Jo, the pox-ridden street urchin.

Bibliography

Dickens, Charles. *Bleak House*. Oxford: Oxford University Press, 1996.

Eagleton, Terry. "Hard Times: False, Fragmented and Unfair, Dickens's 19th-century London Offers a Grimly Prophetic Vision of the World Today," *New Statesman* 132, no. 4,632 (April 7, 2003): 40, 41.

Hall, Patsy. "Building 'Bleak House,'" *English Review* 2001, no. 3 (February 2001): 24.

Sen, Sambudha. "'Bleak House,' 'Vanity Fair,' and the Making of an Urban Aesthetic," *Nineteenth-Century Literature* 54, no. 4 (March 2000): 480.

Bluebeard myth

Bluebeard, the diabolic VILLAIN-husband who slays his brides, is a durable character. He recurs in literature as a mysterious, virile patriarch cloaked in scowls and SECRECY to conceal a cycle of VIOLENCE. The key to his OTHERNESS is his prominent blue beard, a bestial symbol in an unnatural shade that implies coldness. He was based on the arts patron and soldier Gilles de Laval, Marechal and Baron de Rais of Brittany, an historical sexual pervert and serial killer from the early 15th century. The fictional character originated in fablist Charles Perrault's "La Barbe Bleue" in *Contes de Ma Mère l'Oye* (*Mother Goose Tales*, 1697). In his version, the wife escapes at the fatal moment when her two brothers advance on the evil husband and run him through with their swords. Similar to the Breton archetype are horror and cautionary tales in Africa, Asia, and Europe that enliven the sinister plot with the allure of curiosity, which Perrault called "a charming passion . . . the most fleeting of pleasures" (Perrault, 41).

Essential to the plot, as delineated for the stage by the German Gothicist Johann Ludwig TIECK in 1797, are two players: the overbearing ogre and his fiancée/bride, a curious NAIF isolated in unfamiliar territory. He forbids her to unlock the door to a secret room, a haunted space filled with the clotted remains of former wives. When apprehended disobeying his order, the daring woman typically has her head lopped off, the symbolic penalty for using her mind to think things out for herself. The scenario is an outgrowth of the Greek myths of Psyche and Pandora, two sexual allegories of the prototypical curious female who oversteps male-dictated boundaries. In feminist philosophy, the off-limits box/doorway/closet/room represents sexual self-knowledge and awareness of the past, both of which less venturesome, housebound, uneducated females perceive through the distorted filter of male interpretation.

The fearful concept of swift and lethal punishment for infractions of men's rules migrated from FOLKLORE and FAIRY TALE to Gothic fiction, drama, art, and opera. Acquiring various scenes of mayhem in Ernst Meier's *Deutsche Volksmärchen aus Schwaben* (German folktales from Swabia, 1852), the theatrical myth blossomed in Sheridan LE FANU's *Uncle Silas* (1864), Paul Dukas's *Ariane et Barbe-Bleue* (Ariane and Bluebeard, 1907), and Bela Bartók's *Duke Bluebeard's Castle* (1911), from a play published the previous year by Bela Balázs. Le Fanu summarized the story's mystique as the lure of ambition: "Knowledge is power—and power of one sort or another is the secret lust of human souls; and here is, beside the sense of exploration, the undefinable interest of a story, and above all, something forbidden" (Le Fanu, 2). The myth pervades chapter 11 of Charlotte BRONTË's *JANE EYRE* (1847), in which the heroine tours the third story of THORNFIELD, her unseen master's manse. A row of closed doors reminds her of the terrors of Bluebeard's castle.

Daphne DU MAURIER reprised the terrors of the bride in REBECCA (1938), a Gothic masterwork that places the unnamed naif at a large estate where the dominating presence of her husband's deceased first wife terrorizes the unnamed heroine. In place of an ogre, the author substitutes a cryptic older husband; instead of locked doors, the new wife must unravel the MYSTERY of the former wife's allure and sudden death. In both the Brontë and du Maurier versions, fire cleanses evil from the house, which sinks to the ground in charred ruins. A neo-Gothic author, Angela CARTER, reset the Bluebeard motif in *The Bloody Chamber* (1979), which flourished in Kara Feely's stage version featuring a bride's snooping in a forbidden room. A posthumous collection of Shirley JACKSON's macabre SHORT FICTION, *Just an Ordinary Day* (1996), contains "The Honeymoon of Mrs. Smith," the story of a spinster who is the willing victim of a Bluebeard-style serial murderer who allegedly knifed his past six brides in the bathtub.

Bibliography

D'Eramso, Stacey. "Just an Ordinary Day," *Nation* 263, no. 21 (December 23, 1996): 25–26.

Le Fanu, Sheridan. *Uncle Silas*. London: Penguin, 2000.

Lovell-Smith, Rose. "Anti-housewives and Ogres' Housekeepers: The Roles of Bluebeard's Female Helper," *Folklore* 113, no. 2 (October 2002): 197–214.

Perrault, Charles. "Bluebeard," in *The Blue Fairy Book*. New York: Dover, 1965.

Robertson, Ritchie. "The Tale of Bluebeard in German Literature from the Eighteenth Century to the Present," *Journal of European Studies* 31, no. 2 (June 2001): 230–231.

Weinert, Laurent. "Angela Carter's 'The Bloody Chamber' at the Metal Shed at the Toy Factory," *Back Stage West* 10, no. 4 (January 23, 2003): 19.

Wolf, Leonard. *Bluebeard: The Life and Crimes of Gilles de Rais*. New York: Clarkson N. Potter, 1980.

bluebook

See GOTHIC BLUEBOOK.

Bly House

The American novelist Henry JAMES created an evocative country estate as the setting for his perplexing ghost novella THE TURN OF THE SCREW (1898). From the GOVERNESS's immature point of view during her pre-bedtime three-mile stroll about the grounds, Bly House estate reminds her of a FAIRY TALE setting in which she will meet a smiling stranger on the path. Her first viewing of a male phantasm occurs in June on one of the square crenellated towers. She admits that the grandeur of such antique touches sparks her fancy. The vision causes her to wonder, "Was there a 'secret' at Bly—a mystery of Udolpho or an insane, an unmentionable relative kept in unsuspected confinement?" (James, 29). The allusions suggest that she lets readings of Ann RADCLIFFE's novel THE MYSTERIES OF UDOLPHO (1794) and Charlotte BRONTË's JANE EYRE (1847) interfere with rational thought and mature expectations.

Unlike the outdoors, Bly House offers the governess a secure, formal setting, particularly the cocoon-like school room and the dining room, which she describes as "that cold, clean temple of mahogany and brass" (*ibid.*, 32–33). It is from the window of this room that she sees the male apparition a second time. The third episode, a glimpse of a woman, occurs at the lake edge, where the unidentified female appears to make a sailboat from two pieces of wood. The episodes reach terrifying proportions from intrusions on the family when the governess encounters the female apparition at the table writing a letter and spies the male phantasm staring directly into the window at young Miles, one of the two children in her charge. James advances the terror of the ghosts of the former governess, Miss Jessel, and the former valet, Peter Quint, by bringing them too close, breaching the periphery of the governess's outdoor imaginings and invading the internal haven, where she superintends order and discipline. The manipulation of settings establishes an ALLEGORY in which evil may flourish without harm in the outside world, but must be challenged when it enters the family living space.

Bibliography

James, Henry. *The Turn of the Screw and Daisy Miller*. New York: Laurel, 1954.

Sawyer, Richard. "What's Your Title?—'The Turn of the Screw,'" *Studies in Short Fiction* 30, no. 1 (winter 1993): 53–61.

Stipe, Stormy. "The Ghosts of Henry James," *Biblio,* September 1998: 16.

Walker, Steven F. "James's 'The Turn of the Screw,'" *Explicator* 61, no. 2 (winter 2003): 94–96.

Bradbury, Ray

(1920–)

Ray Douglas Bradbury has acquired a sizable world following for his wealth of Gothic fiction, fantasy, and futurism. He grew up in Waukegan, Illinois, a midwestern setting that dominates many of his madness and MONSTER stories published in *Flynn's Detective Fiction* and *Weird Tales* magazines. He intensified the ARABESQUE in a horror tale, "The Veldt" (1950), that, like Charlotte Perkins GILMAN's "THE YELLOW WALLPAPER" (1892), develops the emotional menace of figured paper to a telepathic threat. In "There Will Come Soft Rains" (1950), a dystopic classic, he describes a robotic house in Allendale, California, in the year 2026 that clicks through its daily routine oblivious to the apocalypse that has leveled every other residence. In token of end of the world horror, Bradbury sends the family dog into a lethal frenzy, then dispatches mechanical mice to tote the dog's carcass to the basement for incineration.

In the prologue to his popular collection *The Illustrated Man* (1951), Bradbury comments on the ambivalence of purveyors of the macabre: "Everyone wants to see the pictures, and yet nobody wants to see them" (Bradbury, *Illustrated*, 2). He stated his respect for the hard-boiled American writers Raymond Chandler, Dashiell Hammett, James M. Cain, and Ross MacDonald. With similar acknowledgment of human fears, in an autobiographical novel *Dandelion Wine* (1957), Bradbury juxtaposed a boy with terror by describing dread of "The Lonely One," a stalker of 10-year-old Tom Spaulding. The story takes place amid the evil ATMOSPHERE of a ravine, which had a "dark-sewer, rotten-foliage, thick-green odor" (Bradbury, *Dandelion*, 41). The DOMESTIC GOTHIC scenario develops a controlling theme in Bradbury's fiction—the retreat into boyhood's innocence to avoid the terrors of old age and death. A subsequent Gothic thriller, SOMETHING WICKED THIS WAY COMES (1962), was the subject of a 1983 film starring Jason Robards as the father who protects his son from the allure of Cooger & Dark's Pandemonium Shadow Show. The carnival, a model of Bradbury's antitechnology images, echoes the mechanized menace of Gothic tales by H. P. LOVECRAFT and H. G. WELLS. Bradbury spread his cautionary fiction through a televised anthology series, *The Ray Bradbury Theater*, which flourished from 1986 to 1992.

Bibliography

Bradbury, Ray. *Dandelion Wine.* New York: Bantam Books, 1959

———. *The Illustrated Man.* New York: Bantam Books, 1951.

Gottschalk, Earl C. "Ray Bradbury Achieves His Own Fantasy," *Wall Street Journal,* (October 28, 1985): 1.

Mogen, David. *Ray Bradbury.* Boston: G. K. Hall, 1986.

Braddon, Mary Elizabeth

(1835–1915)

Dubbed the Queen of the CIRCULATING LIBRARIES, the Anglo-Irish novelist and actress Mary Elizabeth Braddon Maxwell was sometimes accused of fostering immorality (Carnell, 147). She shares with her friend and colleague Wilkie COLLINS the title of inventor of the sensational novel, sometimes identified as the GASLIGHT THRILLER. In the wake of Charles Felix's *The Notting Hill Mystery* (1862–63), an early detective novel, she also contributed to an urban vein of the DETECTIVE STORY known as the yellowback railway reader, the forerunner of airport paperbacks (Pearl, 228). Braddon's extension of the genre was the intrepid female investigator Eleanor Vane in *Eleanor's Victory* (1863) and her fictional peer, Margaret Dunbar, who out-snoops Scotland Yard in *Henry Dunbar* (1864).

Reared and educated by her mother, in girlhood Braddon read the French realists, the poetry of Lord BYRON and Percy Bysshe SHELLEY, and the pulp serials of George William Macarthur REYNOLDS, which were imported into the Braddon home by the family cook. As Braddon's tastes developed, she adored and emulated the novels of Edward BULWER-LYTTON and the HISTORICAL FICTION and ballads of Sir Walter SCOTT. Under their influence, she wrote plays and short MELODRAMAs for the *Brighton Herald, Beverley Recorder,* and *Brighton Gazette* as her contribution to the family's meager finances.

Under the gender-neutral signature of M. E. Braddon, the author segued from poems, short pieces, and ballads to write a first novel, *Three Times Dead; or, The Secret of the Heath* (1860), reissued as *The Trail of the Serpent* (1861). She earned £10 for the serialized detective thriller, which features Daredevil Dick, a sleuth who is falsely incarcerated in a lunatic asylum. For *The Black Band; or, The Mysteries of Midnight* (1861), a long-running serial on a secret society of thieving Austrian anarchists, she used the uppity pen name Lady Caroline Lascelles. In stories that placed crime in middle-class neighborhoods, Braddon pursued similar intriguing scenarios—ghost stories, the SUPERNATURAL, MYSTERY, delirium tremens, poisonings, real and fake suicide, blackmail, bigamy, illegitimacy, desertion, secret marriages, train wrecks, foiled inheritances, spouses presumed dead. Ultimately, her career brought her as much as £2,000 per title and a favorable comparison to Scott.

For *Sixpenny Magazine,* Braddon emulated Collins's *The Woman in White* (1860) by creating a best-seller, *Lady Audley's Secret* (1862), a sensational Victorian mystery and domestic crime novel about a homicidal bigamist whom one critic described as a female Mephistopheles. Central to the protagonist's freedom of movement are her assumed identities, which allow her anonymity in a society that prefers its ladies either confined at home or anonymous in public. Writing on assignment, Braddock completed the first installment overnight and left it on the breakfast table of the Irish publisher John Maxwell, her future husband. She doled out the tale of the archvillain Laura Fairlie chapter by chapter in *Robin Goodfellow* and again in the *Sixpenny Magazine* and *London Journal.* While pitting the sweet-faced Lucy Graham Audley against a cache of dark secrets, Braddon's *Lady Audley* pursued feminist themes that battled patriarchy, miscegenation, hypocrisy, prudery, SADISM, and gender typing.

Braddon exploited the Victorian craving for crime, both real and fabricated. Fast-paced and fraught with danger and lawlessness, her story of Robert Audley's amateur investigations involves bigamy, arson, murder, and INSANITY. The enticing plot earned a full-page ad in the *Athenaeum* and caused a reviewer for the *Court Journal* to salivate over "the doubt as to whether the heroine has or has not been the perpetrator of a most revolting murder" (Carnell, 146). Within months, Colin Henry Hazlewood had readied a stage adaptation for the Britannia Theatre in London's East End, thrilling audiences with the red-haired protagonist's death onstage and launching a fashion in red-haired stage villains.

Within the year, three versions in London theaters and more on the road perpetuated the fame of Braddon's *Lady Audley.* In bound version, the solid moneymaker sold out overnight and went through nine editions in 12 weeks. The *Court Journal* predicted that Braddon would soon outpace Wilkie Collins in readership. On the dedicatory page of the third edition, Braddon acknowledged her debt to Bulwer-Lytton, her friend and literary idol. By 1865, the critic W. Fraser Rae, writing for the *North British Review,* exonerated Braddon for writing blood-and-thunder fiction and for elevating the questionable genre through proper grammar, simpler diction, and a style and themes appealing to the middle class.

Over a lengthy career, Braddon published work in numerous journals, including *All the Year Round, Halfpenny Journal, Reynolds' Miscellany, St. James Magazine, Temple Bar,* and *Welcome Guest.* She was still actively writing at age 80. In 1866, she founded her own magazine, the fully illustrated *Belgravia,* and, two years later, a Christmas annual, *The Mistletoe Bough,* which she edited and cowrote. Upon the publication of Bram STOKER's DRACULA (1897), she penned an ebulliently positive review. Braddon earned the regard of Henry JAMES and Oscar WILDE, the readership of Queen Victoria, and the disapproval of the critic Margaret OLIPHANT, who charged Braddon with corruption stemming from lower-class values. She reset Wilde's downfall in *The Rose of Life* (1905), a novel of character. With more than ninety novels and nine plays to her credit in a 50-year career, she influenced the writings of George Eliot, Thomas Hardy, and Sheridan LE FANU and enriched herself by issuing more titles than any of her female contemporaries. In 1915, the novelist and critic Sir Arthur Quiller-Couch was quoted in an obituary for the *Daily Mail*, "Miss Braddon and Wilkie Collins will be studied some day as respectfully as people now study the more sensational Elizabethans" (Carnell, 1).

Bibliography

Carnell, Jennifer. *The Literary Lives of Mary Elizabeth Braddon.* Hastings, Sussex: Sensation Press, 2000.

Gilbert, Sandra M., and Susan Gubar. *The Madwoman in the Attic,* 2nd ed. New Haven, Conn.: Yale University Press, 2000.

Pearl, Nancy. "Gaslight Thrillers: The Original Victorians," *Library Journal* 126, no. 3, (February 15, 2001): 228.

Willis, Chris. "Mary Elizabeth Braddon and the Literary Marketplace: A Study in Commercial Authorship," http://www.chriswillis.freeserve.co.uk/meb2.html.

"Bras Coupé"
George Washington Cable
(1879)

One of Southern Gothicist George Washington Cable's finest tales is "Bras-Coupé" (literally, "cut arm" or "lopped arm"), a story-within-a-story in *The Grandissimes: A Story of Creole Life.* It derived from a true account and appeared serially in *Scribner's Monthly* in 1879. In a novel spilling over with racist mob violence and a near-lynching, Bras-Coupé's story stands out for nefarious cruelties against a tall, noble African chief unsuited to Louisiana-style enslavement. When the overseer sends him to the fields to hoe, the former prince strikes and bites his way out of bondage. The overseer ends the rebellion with a pistol shot to the chief's head. Immediately, the episode takes on legendary proportions: "[The bullet] had struck him in the forehead, and running around the skull in search of a penetrable spot, tradition—which sometimes jests—says came out despairingly, exactly where it had entered" (Cable, 172).

The Gothic tragedy of the African royal lies in his survival of racist brutality. Yoked and chained, Bras-Coupé acclimates to confinement, but not to subservience. In retaliation, he issues a curse on all males within the house and on the plantation. Although the Code Noir (a code that Louis XIV issued in 1685 as a guideline to policing colonial slavery) demands death for striking the master, the truculent slave earns a harsh clemency—flogging, hamstringing, and lopping of ears, none of which defeats his defiant spirit. By turning Bras-Coupé into a proud, loathsome MONSTER, Cable prophesies the violent heritage of a South where slavery can be truncated and altered but not obliterated from history. The episode, rejected by the *Atlantic* and *Scribner's* in 1873 and 1875 as a stand-alone story, provided the author Lafcadio HEARN and composer Louis Gottschalk with Gothic material. The composer Frederick Delius revised the story for his opera *Koanga* (1904), and the playwright Dalt Wonk and composer Alvin Batiste reset the story for a musical drama, *A Bitter Glory* (1998), which debuted at Southeastern Louisiana University.

Bibliography

Bradbury, John. *Renaissance in the South.* Chapel Hill: University of North Carolina Press, 1963.

Cable, George Washington. *The Grandissimes.* New York: Sagamore Press, 1957.

Stephens, Robert O. *The Family Saga in the South: Generations and Destinies.* Baton Rouge: Louisiana State University Press, 1995.

Brontë, Charlotte
(1816–1855)

Perhaps the most respected author of Victorian Gothic romance, Charlotte Brontë, like Charles DICKENS, came of age at the height of the popularity of the GOTHIC BLUEBOOK and novels of the macabre. She was reared in the morally upright household of her father, the Reverend Patrick Brontë, an Anglican pastor in a rural parish at Haworth, Yorkshire, where she and her siblings lived under tight constraints in a parsonage abutting the parish cemetery. Nonetheless, Charlotte managed to read Edward Young's graveyard poems and Lord BYRON's MELANCHOLY works and revelled in Sir Walter SCOTT's *The Tales of a Grandfather* (1828).

Engulfed by grief and loss at the death of her mother, Maria Branwell Brontë, from cancer, and of two older sisters, Maria and Elizabeth, from consumption, Charlotte thrived under the care of Tabby, a benevolent domestic. In JANE EYRE (1847), the author incorporated Tabby's maternalism as an antidote to Gothic terrors in a series of tender hearth scenes superintended by the servant Bessie Lee at GATESHEAD HALL, by the teacher Maria Temple at Lowood, by Mrs. Fairfax at THORNFIELD, and by Mary and Diana Rivers on the moors.

Charlotte joined her remaining sisters Anne and Emily BRONTË and her brother, Patrick Branwell Brontë, in a homeschool in the parsonage library. While Patrick studied the classics, the girls attended lessons under their spinster aunt, Elizabeth "Bess" Branwell, a tight-lipped Calvinist. Free reading made an impression on the children, beginning with the *Arabian Nights* (1704–17). In their spare time, they perused the SHORT GOTHIC FICTION of the German author E. T. A. HOFFMANN; Jane AUSTEN's popular novel *Mansfield Park* (1814); and a Scots fiend romance, James HOGG's *The Private Memoirs and Confessions of a Justified Sinner* (1824). The girls also had access to Gothic serials in BLACKWOOD'S EDINBURGH MAGAZINE, in which Charlotte obtained an image of an iron shroud from a story by William MUDFORD. In the *Methodist Magazine,* the Brontës read apocalyptic articles, cautionary tales about the deaths of children, and such evangelical terrors as "The Absolute Eternity of the Torments of Hell." When ennui set in, the Brontë siblings entertained themselves by creating games and plays and by writing and producing their own cliffhangers, in which Charlotte mimicked the Gothic strains of MYSTERY, license, psychological forces, and EXOTICISM that she absorbed from the popular press. She produced a comic GHOST STORY, "Napoleon and the Spectre" (1833), in which an apparition leads the emperor in nightdress into a ballroom filled with courtiers.

While her brother wasted the family's resources on drink and drugs, at age 19 Charlotte Brontë took concurrent jobs as teacher and governess, a professional post that influenced her later fiction. During her work on staff at Roe Head, she heard the story of a governess who married her employer, who turned out to be a bigamist already married to a madwoman; this scenario provided the plot for *Jane Eyre.* As depression set in and Charlotte's health diminished, she abandoned thoughts of marriage and journeyed to Brussels for eight months to study French, German, and music. After her illusion of romance with the school's headmaster, Constantin Héger, evaporated, she returned to Haworth and coped with loss and frustration through constructive daydreams, an escape through which her ideal self enjoyed a wider range of opportunities and stimulus.

Charlotte Brontë joined her sisters in writing under the pen names Acton (Anne), Currer (Charlotte), and Ellis (Emily) Bell, a literary ruse to obscure their gender and ease their entry into the writer's market. While her sisters worked at their own writings, Charlotte tried to turn her heartbreak into a novel, *The Professor,* then scrapped the idea to compose *Jane Eyre,* a pilgrimage tale of a deserving girl who grows into a stout-hearted adult. The novel is a compelling story of one of English literature's most beloved heroines, who refuses to give in to obstacles to a sustained passion. Endowed with an intuitive extrasensory perception and prophetic DREAMS, she communicates with her spiritual mate and returns to rescue him from his melancholy after he is badly injured and blinded when his crazed wife torches Thornfield, his eerie mansion.

Response to the novel was immediate, including both raves from ordinary readers and harsh retorts from critics in the *Spectator,* the *Quarterly Review,* and the *Guardian.* In general, negative reviews took issue with the character Jane Eyre for being coarse, unfeminine, and blunt in an era when well-bred women made no formal declaration of their passions. In a letter issued on December 31, 1847, to William Smith Williams, a reader for the publisher, Charlotte, speaking as Currer Bell, regretted to hear complaints that *Jane Eyre* appeared godless. Charlotte took heart from more positive reviews in the *Oxford Chronicle,* the *Critic,* the *Morning Post,* and the *Berkshire and Buckinghamshire Gazette,* which appreciated her presentation of forceful characters and moral truths. Sitting on the fence was the critic George Henry Lewes of the *Westminster Review* and *Fraser's Magazine,* who proclaimed Currer Bell a prize author but regretted her frequent reliance on coincidence and MELODRAMA.

After the deaths of her two remaining sisters and her brother, Charlotte Brontë found herself alone with an aging father. She created a charismatic hero in *Shirley: A Tale* (1849), an early English regional novel, and pursued a Gothic strain in VILLETTE (1853), a ghost-ridden autobiographical account of her years in Brussels. Both works lack the emotional power of her masterpiece. She began a fourth novel, *Emma* (1860), which remained unfinished at her death. After disobeying her father by marrying an Irish curate, Arthur Bell Nicholls, in June 1854, Charlotte made a home at the parsonage for herself, her husband, and the Reverend Brontë. A photograph recovered in 1996 pictures her as a contented wife. The following March, she died from complications of pregnancy brought on by tuberculosis, exhaustion, and a tumble from a horse.

Although Charlotte Brontë died at age 39, her impact on the reading public turned into a literary phenomenon that spawned the Brontë Society, formed in 1893 to preserve Haworth as a museum and shrine. Her memorable heroine, Jane Eyre, took on a life of her own. The account of a working-class hireling who falls in love with her gruff employer, one of literature's more complex BYRONIC HEROES, the novel entranced lovers of romance and GOTHIC CONVENTION at the same time that it satisfied Victorian demands for moral behavior, a just conclusion, and a contented domestic scene. The psychological maneuvering that reduces the social and economic distance between Jane and Rochester and assures their success as a couple pleased English readers, including Queen Victoria, who read the work aloud to Prince Albert. *Jane Eyre* influenced the modern Gothic of Daphne DU MAURIER's REBECCA (1938) and served numerous revivals in stage adaptations and in Hollywood and made-for-television films.

Bibliography

Alexander, Christine. "'That Kingdom of Gloom': Charlotte Brontë, the Annuals, and the Gothic," *Nineteenth-Century Literature* 47, no. 4 (1993): 409–436.

Brontë, Charlotte. *The Letters of Charlotte Brontë: With a Selection of Letters by Family and Friends*, Vol. 2: 1848–1851. New York: Oxford University Press, 2000.

Gilbert, Sandra M., and Susan Gubar. *The Madwoman in the Attic*, 2nd ed. New Haven, Conn.: Yale University Press, 2000.

Gordon, Lyndall. *Charlotte Brontë: A Passionate Life*. New York: W. W. Norton, 1994.

Hoeveler, Diane Long. *Gothic Feminism*. University Park: Pennsylvania State University Press, 1998.

Hunt, Linda. "Charlotte Brontë and the Suffering Sisterhood," *Colby Library Quarterly* 19, no. 1 (1983): 7–17.

Schimank, Uwe. "Daydreaming and Self-Assertion: The Life of Charlotte Brontë," *Bios* 14, no. 1 (2001): 3–25.

Brontë, Emily
(1818–1848)

In her short life, Emily Jane Brontë made a significant contribution to the Gothic novel. One of the five daughters and one son born to the Reverend Patrick Brontë, an Anglican minister, and Maria Branwell Brontë, she grew up at the parsonage at Haworth, Yorkshire. After her mother died of cancer and the bearing of six children in a span of eight years, and Emily's two older sisters, Maria and Elizabeth, succumbed to tuberculosis, the remaining four children bolstered and challenged each other.

The Brontës studied at home, chose from popular Gothic works checked out of the local CIRCULATING LIBRARY, read the emerging feminism of Mary WOLLSTONECRAFT, and composed their own sagas and verse with a heavy tinge of Byronism. At age 17, Emily studied at Miss Wooler's school at Roe Head near Halifax, but returned home as symptoms of tuberculosis developed in her lungs. Two years later, she was strong enough to teach at Law Hill school, but for only six months. At age 26, she joined her sister Charlotte BRONTE in the study of French, German, and music for eight months in Brussels.

At the urging of her brother, Patrick Branwell Brontë, in 1845 Emily Brontë and sisters Charlotte and Anne began to write for publication. They submitted verse manuscripts under the pseudonyms Acton (Anne), Currer (Charlotte), and Ellis (Emily) Bell, an implied masculinity as a hedge against discrimination against female novelists. In the poem "Remembrance" (1846), Emily initiated a graveyard motif that dominated her later writing—the compulsion of a grieving lover to join a deceased mate. The year before her death, she produced a literary success, WUTHERING HEIGHTS (1847), at the same time that Anne published *Agnes Grey* (1847) and Charlotte succeeded with JANE EYRE (1847). Emily chose to stay at home when her sisters ventured to London for a face-to-face meeting with their publisher. On December 19, 1848, only weeks after Branwell's death, Emily died at home, leaving Charlotte saddened and bereft at losing her companion and writing partner.

Emily Brontë was a bright comet that flamed out rapidly. Belying her declining health and weakened state were the vigor and lyricism of her MELODRAMA, *Wuthering Heights*, a novel alive with innovation and rhythmic phrasing and pioneering disruption of chronology and altered point of view. Unlike the submissive heroine of Matthew Gregory LEWIS's THE MONK (1796), Brontë's Catherine EARNSHAW rebels against GOTHIC CONVENTIONs to live free of social restraint. In Emily's defense, in 1850 Charlotte explained in the "Biographical Notice of Ellis and Acton Bell," appended to a second edition of *Wuthering Heights*, that the author was indeed Emily and not, as some critics surmised, the same person who wrote *Jane Eyre*.

Wuthering Heights was the forerunner of Gothic ghost tales that built intensity through sensational revelation of character, fascinating details, and shifting fortunes. The novel earned the guarded praise of Sydney Dobell, a reviewer for the *Palladium*, who proclaimed Emily Brontë a giant in the making. Her novel's energy and shock value brought critical charges of GROTESQUE passion, lack of self-discipline, vice, vulgarity, cruelty, and loss of touch with love in the real world. Especially troubling to the reading public was the visceral hunger the main characters have for each other and their wildly erotic farewell, a display of unbridled passion that has influenced generations of subsequent writers, particularly Daphne DU MAURIER. Boldly erotic scenes have charged film versions of the novel that paired the acting talents of Merle Oberon and Laurence Olivier, Anna Calder-Marshall and Timothy Dalton, and Juliette Binoche and Ralph Fiennes.

Bibliography

Heywood, Christopher. "Yorkshire Landscapes in 'Wuthering Heights,'" *Essays in Criticism* 48, no. 1 (January 1998): 13–33.

Hoeveler, Diane Long. *Gothic Feminism.* University Park: Pennsylvania State University Press, 1998.

Moers, Ellen. "Female Gothic: Monsters, Goblins, Freaks," *New York Review of Books,* (April 4, 1974): 30–42.

———. "The Monster's Mother," *New York Review of Books,* (March 21, 1974): 24–33.

Smith, Lisa. "Landscape and Place in Wuthering Heights," *English Review* 11, no. 1 (September 2000): 22.

Steinitz, Rebecca. "Diaries and Displacement in *Wuthering Heights,*" *Studies in the Novel* 32, no. 4 (winter 2000): 407.

Brown, Charles Brockden
(1771–1810)

A progenitor of the DOMESTIC GOTHIC style in U.S. literature, Charles Brockden Brown was the nation's first professional author and the founder of American ROMANTICISM. Through Gothic fiction, he depicted the psychological ills and religious and social tensions of a new republic. His novels were the literary precursors of the psychological fiction of Nathaniel HAWTHORNE and Herman MELVILLE, the first-person narratives of Henry JAMES, and the detective thrillers of Edgar Allan POE.

Religion was an impetus to Brown's creative perspective. He grew up amid Philadelphia Quakerism, studied classics at the Friends Latin School, and, from age 16 to 22, read law under the supervision of attorney Alexander Wilcocks. By age 18, he was submitting philosophical essays to *Columbian Magazine*. The trauma of the city's yellow fever epidemic of May 1793 marked Brown with MELANCHOLY and religious doubt after he was unable to save his friends Elihu Hubbard Smith and Joseph Scandella from succumbing to the disease. After Brown survived the fever, the terror of fatal infection colored his journal writings as well as his composition of two graphically detailed novels, ARTHUR MERVYN; *or, Memoirs of the Year 1793* (1799) and ORMOND (1799). Driven by intellectual curiosity,

Brown hobnobbed with writers in the Belles Lettres Club and the Friendly Club and began writing nonfiction articles and sketches for the city's *Weekly Magazine* and *Columbian Magazine*.

Brown's writings are of major importance to literary history and the development of American Gothic and the genre itself. He dared to move beyond sense impressions into the realm of intuition and the GROTESQUE, which he embellished with SENSATIONALISM, including incidents of ventriloquism, hypnotism, and spontaneous combustion, which kills one of his characters with a bang and a puff of smoke. Both urban and frontier in setting, his innovative fiction derived from an immersion in extravagant Gothic elements, particularly romanticism, which he acquired from reading the Gothic novels of Ann RADCLIFFE and of his idol William GODWIN. Brown incorporated a woeful tone, morbid psychological inquiry, and MYSTERY into his six novels and in "Somnambulism, a Fragment" (1805), a DETECTIVE STORY about a sleepwalker.

Although Brown tended to mimic European genres, his works received acclaim for their redirection of classic GOTHIC CONVENTION from grim castles and helpless maidens to urban blight and the North American wilderness, which he studied during a tramp through Ohio. In the March 17, 1798, edition of the *Weekly Magazine*, he declared the new nation an untrodden land and urged writers to choose originality over slavish emulation of European models. In place of the Spanish Inquisition and the libidinous monk or marquis of Old World Gothic, Brown inserted realistic frontier terrors that remain significant to American Gothic into the 21st century: self-doubt, family anguish, religious fanaticism, conspiracy, racism, and slaughter.

In addition to writing fiction, Brown worked at a feverish pace to compose diaries, polemics and pamphlets, and essays. In 1799, he founded a literary journal, the *Monthly Magazine and American Review*, later called the *American Review and Literary Journal*. Through editorial selection, he exposed an unsettling national identity crisis as the new republic began making hard choices concerning settlement of the rapidly receding frontier. These issues permeated his most famous novel, allowing him to speak through fictional characters their rejection of European traditions, a subse-

quent loss of identity, and a mounting discontent and disillusion with republican ideals.

Gothic enlivened Brown's most important work, WIELAND; or, The Transformation (1798), a macabre narrative laced with CHIAROSCURO, madness, religious ambiguity, and multiple murders. A year later, he produced *Arthur Mervyn, Ormond*, and EDGAR HUNTLY; or, Memoirs of a Sleepwalker, which revisited his previous stratagem of using SOMNAMBULISM as a symbol of psychic unrest. At age 30, he turned from dark settings to sentimental woman-centered fiction with *Clara Howard* (1801) and *Jane Talbot* (1801), both monetary and critical failures. With the cessation of his first journal, in 1803 he launched a more successful vehicle, the *Literary Magazine and American Register*, and translated a work on soil and climate shortly before his death from tuberculosis at age 29.

Brown was the first American novelist acclaimed on the basis of merit. Acknowledging the efforts of a young genius cut down in his prime were James Fenimore Cooper, Margaret Fuller, Henry Wadsworth Longfellow, William Gilmore Simms, and John Greenleaf Whittier. On the opposite side of the Atlantic, Brown earned the respect of the romantic poets John KEATS and Percy Bysshe SHELLEY, the Gothic writer Mary Wollstonecraft SHELLEY, and the historical novelist Sir Walter SCOTT, who admired Brown's powers of imagination. Scott, however, believed that Brown wasted his talents on an unwholesome perversity that brought no benefit to author or reader.

Bibliography

Bergland, Renée L. *The National Uncanny: Indian Ghosts and American Subjects.* Hanover, N.H.: Dartmouth College, 2000.

Christophersen, Bill. *The Apparition in the Glass: Charles Brockden Brown's American Gothic.* Athens: University of Georgia Press, 1993.

Ferguson, Robert A. "Yellow Fever and Charles Brockden Brown: The Context of the Emerging Novelist," *Early American Literature* 14, no. 3 (1979–80): 293–305.

Frye, Steven. "Constructing Indigeneity: Postcolonial Dynamics in Charles Brockden Brown's *Monthly Magazine and American Review*," *American Studies* 39, no. 3 (1998): 69–88.

Gould, Philip. "Race, Commerce, and the Literature of Yellow Fever in Early National Philadelphia," *Early American Literature* 35, no. 2 (2000): 157–186.

Hedges, William L. "Charles Brockden Brown and the Culture of Contradictions," *Early American Literature* 9, no. 2 (1974): 107–142.

Kafer, Peter. "Charles Brockden Brown and Revolutionary Philadelphia: An Imagination in Context," *Pennsylvania Magazine of History and Biography* 116, no. 4 (1992): 467–498.

Winter, Douglas E. "The Man Who Invented American Gothic," *Insight on the News* 15, no. 2 (January 11, 1999): 36.

Young, Philip. "Born Decadent: The American Novel and Charles Brockden Brown," *Southern Review* 17, no. 3 (1981): 501–519.

Bryant, William Cullen
(1794–1878)

William Cullen Bryant, the first American poet to achieve international recognition, created a lasting image of death in "THANATOPSIS" (1817), his most memorable work. In youth, he was influenced by the Scots dialect ballads of Robert Burns and the ROMANTICISM and nature worship of William Wordsworth. In his mid-teens, Bryant completed "Thanatopsis," the youthful, stoic masterwork of graveyard poetry named from the Greek for "a view of death." He did not submit it to *North American Review* until six years later, when the poem became an American classic.

A co-owner and editor of the New York *Evening Post* for a half-century, Bryant used to advantage his Puritan background, Unitarianism, and legal training at Yale to further liberal ideals, especially the abolition of slavery. Images of terror and death recurred in his later work, notably, a macabre story of human remains in "The Skeleton's Cave" and the SUPERNATURAL intervention in deadly anger in "Medfield," both collected in *Tales of the Glauber Spa* (1832). In a COLONIAL GOTHIC tale, "A Story of the Island of Cuba" (1829), Bryant describes the rumors and unease among white Americans living in a heavily black population. In a multiracial theme that motivated much of 19th-century Gothic fiction, he also pictures the ghosts of Indians long killed off in the West Indies. The VIOLENCE of a white posse preserves a frontier scenario of newcomers securing their hold on the land through genocide.

Bibliography

Brickhouse, Anna. "'A Story of the Island of Cuba': William Cullen Bryant and the Hispanophone Americas," *Nineteenth-Century Literature* 56, no. 1 (June 2001): 1–22.

Ruland, Richard, and Malcolm Bradbury. *From Puritanism to Postmodernism: A History of American Literature.* New York: Penguin, 1991.

Bulwer-Lytton, Edward
(1803–1873)

The Victorian poet and critic Edward George Earle Bulwer-Lytton arrived late on the scene of the traditional English GOTHIC NOVEL and gave it new direction. Born an aristocrat to Gothic fan Elizabeth Bulwer-Lytton, he received a quality education at Cambridge in classical languages, history, and composition. He mused deeply on Gothic lore, particularly the German writings of Johann Wolfgang von GOETHE and Friedrich von SCHILLER, William GODWIN's *CALEB WILLIAMS* (1794), and James HOGG's *Private Memoirs and Confessions of a Justified Sinner* (1824). Bulwer-Lytton toured continental Europe before beginning a literary career in his late 20s with a terror novel, *Falkland* (1817), and a best-selling crime tale, *Pelham* (1828). To support his acquisition of the finer things while serving as a member of Parliament, he produced a steady stream of verse, Arthurian romance, dramas, novels, and short stories.

Bulwer-Lytton's major contribution to GOTHIC CONVENTION was a variety of intriguing elements: ORIENTAL ROMANCE, opium use, metaphysics, and the paranormal. To acquaint himself with clairvoyance, incantations, prophecy, and ritual magic, he studied KABBALISM under the French scholar and Hebrew mystic Alphonse Louis Constant, later known as Magus Eliphas Lévi, a cult figure who popularized astrology, magic, mesmerism, and divination. Through occult suggestion and subtle nuance, Bulwer-Lytton refined his spectral tales, introducing SUPERNATURAL horsemen in "Glenallan" (1826), the terrifying MONSTER in "A Manuscript Found in a Mad-House" (1829), the torment of a DOPPELGÄNGER duality in "Monos and Daimonos" (1830), and hovering villainy in "Night and Morning" (1845).

Acclaimed the founder of the English occult novel, Bulwer-Lytton was influenced by the dark malevolence of Lord BYRON's works and reached beyond the supernatural to manipulate SENSATION-ALISM and generate awe in his readers. Literary historians credit him with inventing the NEWGATE NOVEL with his true crime tale *Paul Clifford* (1830), a wildly popular social novel proposing a sympathetic view of a misanthropic highwayman. The author based his work on his wife Rosina's combings of the Newgate Calendar and opened the novel with the cliché phrase "It was a dark and stormy night," his literary legacy. The story made its way to the stage in 1832 and again in 1835 as MELODRAMA.

Bilious and disgruntled in his view of humankind, Bulwer-Lytton produced two more Newgate thrillers. In *Eugene Aram* (1832), a best-selling tale of a cerebral killer gibbeted in 1759, he set part of the action in a forest during a thunderstorm. In *Lucretia; or, The Children of the Night* (1846), in token of his problems with his feisty wife, Bulwer-Lytton touched on the popular subjects of poisoning of husbands, asylum scenes, and criminal madness in women, all elements of DOMESTIC GOTHIC. The book critic at the *Athenaeum* leaped on the novel and dismissed it as "a bad book of a bad school." Nonetheless, in *The Nigger of the "Narcissus"* (1897), the author Joseph CONRAD comments on the popularity of Bulwer-Lytton's crime novels among British sailors (Hollingsworth, 191).

Bulwer-Lytton is best known for the MYSTERY novel *Ernest Maltravers* (1837); *Alice; or, The Mysteries* (1838); the nightmarish Gothic castle and ancient Rosicrucian brotherhood in *Zanoni* (1842); and the spectral theme and disembodied eye in *A Strange Story* (1861), a plot suggested by William GODWIN's *St. Leon* (1799). Bulwer-Lytton blended Gothic aspects of mystery, flight, and CHIAROSCURO in *The Coming Race* (1871), a dystopian classic. In addition, he published an enduring short work, "The Haunted and the Haunters; or, The House and the Brain," issued in *BLACKWOOD'S EDINBURGH MAGAZINE* in August 1857. One of the most popular writers of the Victorian era who faded in subse-

quent decades, he influenced the sensation fiction of Mary Elizabeth BRADDON, Wilkie COLLINS, J. Sheridan LE FANU, Bram STOKER, and Ellen WOOD and the novels of Charles DICKENS, William Makepeace Thackeray, and Anthony Trollope.

Bibliography

Christensen, Allan C. "Bulwer, Bloch, Bussotti and the Filial Muse: Recalled and Foreseen Sources of Inspiration," *Mosaic* 26, no. 3 (summer 1993): 37–51.

Haining, Peter, ed. *Gothic Tales of Terror.* New York: Taplinger, 1972.

Hollingsworth, Keith. *The Newgate Novel, 1830–1847.* Detroit: Wayne State University Press, 1963.

Lane, Christopher. "Bulwer's Misanthropes and the Limits of Victorian Sympathy," *Victorian Studies* 44, no. 4 (summer 2002): 597–625.

Roberts, Adam. "Dickens's Jarnydyce and Lytton's Gawtrey," *Notes and Queries* 43, no. 1 (March 1996): 45–46.

Butler, Octavia
(1947–)

An award-winning author of science fiction and FEMALE GOTHIC, Octavia Estelle Butler creates speculative scenarios in which female characters face complex threats. While working odd jobs and attending evening writing classes at UCLA, she began a freelance career that saw publication of stories in such magazines as *Clarion, Chrysalis 4, Isaac Asimov's Science Fiction Magazine, Future Life,* and *Transmission.* In *Kindred* (1979), a novel about African-American time-trekkers in Maryland before the Civil War, she depicts California newlyweds Dana and Kevin Franklin in a slave milieu. At the home of the unscrupulous Tom Weylin, the owner of a plantation outside Easton, Maryland, Dana tests 20th-century courage against the terrors of lashings, mutilation, slave breeding, and concubinage faced by her grandmother Hagar's generation. Dana's rapid in-and-out visit to the past seems nonthreatening until she realizes that her time-tripping is under the control of Weylin's spoiled young son, Rufus.

Gothic scenarios loom throughout the fantasy, which depicts the protagonist and Alice, her future great-grandmother, as two halves of the same person. Dana faces night riders who try to rape her. Because literacy was a crime for blacks during the slave era, she is beaten severely when she is caught reading. She treats Alice for dog bites and emotional trauma, but cannot rescue her from sexual enslavement or save herself from the overseer's cowhide whip. From her fears and frustrations, she realizes that the brunt of slavery on individuals was "a long slow process of dulling" (Butler, 183). In the fatal departure from Maryland in 1831, Dana stabs the master to escape and loses an arm as she emerges from the wall of her living room on July 4, 1976, the nation's 200th birthday. The lost limb symbolizes the part of her emotions that she leaves behind with the slaves she befriended in Maryland and with the white oppressor who sired her grandmother.

Bibliography

Allison, Dorothy. "The Future of Females: Octavia Butler's Mother Lode," in *Reading Black, Reading Feminist.* New York: Meridian Books, 1990.

Govan, Sovan Y. "Connections, Links, and Extended Networks: Patterns in Octavia Butler's Science Fiction," *Black American Literature Forum* 18, no. 2 (1984): 82–87.

———. "Homage to Tradition: Octavia Butler Renovates the Historical Novel," *MELUS* 13, nos. 1–2 (1986): 79–96.

Salvaggio, Ruth. "Octavia Butler and the Black Science-Fiction Heroine," *Black American Literature Forum* 18 (fall 1984): 78–81.

Byron, George Gordon, Lord
(1788–1824)

The controversial English romantic poet George Gordon, Lord Byron, earned a vast cult following on both sides of the Atlantic for his literary panache while weathering public denunciation for multiple scandals. As a leading member of the romantic circle, he acted out the Gothic themes of licentiousness, seduction, cruelty to women and children, and incest. His name is connected with a streak of INSANITY in the family, emotional instability and drunken fits of temper, outrageous flirtations, and mistreatment of his two wives, Anne Isabella Milbanke and the Countess Guiccioli.

While channeling his considerable artistry into verse, he read the notable literature of the era, especially the Gothic fiction of William BECKFORD, Harriet LEE, Sophia LEE, Charles Robert MATURIN, Ann RADCLIFFE, Friedrich von SCHILLER, and Horace WALPOLE, as well as the ballads of Sir Walter SCOTT and Voltaire's *Candide* (1759).

Byron incorporated Gothic touches in his early works—elements of decay in "Lines Inscribed upon a Cup Formed from a Skull" (1808); the biblical Angel of Death, bearer of doom in "The Destruction of Sennacherib" (1815); and the protracted agony of the chained Greek hero-martyr in "Prometheus" (1816). Byron drew on SCHEDONI, the evil Capuchin in Radcliffe's classic Gothic novel THE ITALIAN (1797), for his scowling males in THE GIAOUR (1813), a patriarchal tale of a man cursed with regret and a yearning for expiation of sins. Byron reprises the characterization in "Lara" (1814), a doom-ridden psychological tale related by an UNRELIABLE NARRATOR plagued by guilt and remorse, standard sufferings of the unknowable OUTSIDER. Perhaps prophetic of the poet's own social ostracism, the poems prefaced his self-exile from England in April 1816.

Byron actively promoted GOTHIC CONVENTION, VIOLENCE, and OBSESSION in *The Giaour* and MELANCHOLY and a confinement motif in "THE PRISONER OF CHILLON" (1816). That same year, he aided Charles Robert Maturin in producing *Bertram,* an original GOTHIC DRAMA, at the Drury Lane Theatre in London. With John POLIDORI, his personal physician, and the SHELLEYs, Mary and Percy, in summer 1816, Byron formed a foursome engaged in a GHOST STORY competition. After Byron presented a vampire tale published as "A Fragment of a Novel" (1819), Polidori posed his own version, "The Vampyre" (1819), which the publisher passed off as the work of the famous Byron. The poet was appalled to be identified as the writer of an inferior work and publicly distanced himself from its authorship. His own ghoulish work was the fount from which Bram STOKER created Count DRACULA, a fatal aristocrat who displays Byronic traits.

Byron's genius made a profound impact on European literature. He crafted MANFRED (1817), a closet drama laden with Gothic elements, and

Cain (1821), a narrative pairing the grim, skeptical title figure with Lucifer, a powerful demon endowed with the magnetic personality of Satan in John Milton's *Paradise Lost* (1667). Byron's egocentric behavior and his masterful development of the antihero gave rise to the BYRONIC HERO, a complex male egotist shrouded in MYSTERY and prone to dark brooding. The poet's works became favorites for public declamation and literary citation and invested the style and TONE of a number of Gothic writings by Mary Elizabeth BRADDON, Edward BULWER-LYTTON, and Edgar Allan POE. In Edward ROCHESTER, the surly hero in JANE EYRE (1847), Charlotte BRONTË, a true Byron fan, incorporated strands of Byronism from her reading of *Cain, Childe Harold's Pilgrimage* (1812–17), *Don Juan* (1819–20), and the poet's published letters and journals.

Bibliography

Auerbach, Nina, *Our Vampires, Ourselves.* Chicago: University of Chicago Press, 1995.

Byron, Lord. *Lord Byron: The Major Works.* Oxford: Oxford University Press, 2000.

Goldberg, Leonard S. "'This Gloom . . . Which Can Avail Thee Nothing': Cain and Skepticism," *Criticism* 41, no. 2 (spring 1999): 207.

LaChance, Charles. "Naive and Knowledgeable Nihilism in Byron's Gothic Verse," *Papers on Language & Literature* 32, no. 4 (fall 1996): 339–368.

Phillipson, Mark. "Byron's Revisited Haunts," *Studies in Romanticism* 39, no. 2 (summer 2000): 303.

White, Pamela. "Two Vampires of 1828," *Opera Quarterly* 5, no. 1 (spring 1987): 22–57.

Byronic hero

A grand, charismatic, yet ambiguous male, the Byronic hero is a child of the Renaissance love of adventure. The quasi-satanic type dates back to the Greek Prometheus, a suffering god, and to the WANDERING JEW, and became a pervasive OUTSIDER in world art, dance, drama, opera, sculpture, film, and fiction. In mystic literature, the Byronic hero suffers alienation as his occluded spirit searches for some divine truth or link to a deity or supreme being. Ann RADCLIFFE created a forerunner of the stereotype in SCHEDONI, a sinister, glum-

faced monk in THE ITALIAN (1797) who is both soulless predator and doomed victim.

In the wake of Radcliffe's invention of a disturbingly enigmatic protagonist, the Byronic hero had his formal beginnings in the work of the English poet George Gordon, Lord BYRON, a notorious rake and despoiler of women and a powerhouse among the literati of the romantic era. A larger-than-life manipulator of public opinion, the Byronic hero is antisocial, in part because of self-scorn, an element of Byron's MELANCHOLY poems "Lara" (1814) and "My Soul Is Dark" (1815). The fallen romantic protagonist feels remorse for some unnamed misdeed, yet refuses to recount his wrongs or repent. Self-reliant to a fault, he is capable of chameleon-like shifts from brooding loner to celebrity, from self-mocker to strutting egocentric.

As a lover, the Byronic hero intertwines love and hate to shape a destructive, all-consuming passion, the impetus to tragedy in the love affair of HEATHCLIFF and Catherine EARNSHAW in Emily BRONTË's WUTHERING HEIGHTS (1847). Whether a heartbreaker, sexual predator, bon vivant, or reckless rogue, the stereotype accommodates extremes of behavior, often for unconscionable reasons, as is the case with Charlotte BRONTË's Edward ROCHESTER, the guilt-wracked charmer in JANE EYRE (1847) who woos Jane while immuring his insane wife in an upper story of THORNFIELD. Similarly ambiguous in behavior and outlook are the main characters in Christopher Marlowe's DR. FAUSTUS (ca. 1588), Byron's MANFRED (1817), Alexander Pushkin's *Eugene Onegin* (1831), Johann Wolfgang von GOETHE's *Faust* (1790–1832), and Algernon Swinburne's "A Ballad of François Villon" (1878). The character type emerged in AMERICAN GOTHIC in the person of Ahab, the obsessive whaling captain in Herman MELVILLE's *Moby-Dick* (1851).

For all its waywardness and sin, Byronism exudes glamour. As the literary critic Peter Haining explained in his introduction to *The Shilling Shockers* (1978), Radcliffe, Matthew Gregory LEWIS, and Horace WALPOLE emphasized villainy in an appealing form to boost reader interest. Likewise, Emily Brontë explored the elements of the ill-natured hero in Heathcliff, a proud, passionate suitor of an unattainable woman. Like the conventional heroic villain of Gothic fiction, he conceals a guilty-sad past beneath lingering melancholy. Clinging to his reputation are hints of DISSIPATION in the past and of unspecified infractions against society that include the hanging of a pet dog. Moody and willful, he both repels and fascinates in the style of Napoleon and of Milton's Satan in *Paradise Lost* (1667), a touchstone of Gothic villainy.

A lone wanderer usually endowed with an electric appeal, somber good looks, and charm, the Byronic hero of modern English novels relies on intellect and self-sufficiency, the coping devices of the suave, purposefully tight-lipped wife-slayer Maxim de Winter in Daphne DU MAURIER's *REBECCA* (1938). The unnamed female speaker, at the beginning of her relationship with Max, jumps to fearful speculation through surreptitious character study: "He had a face of one who walks in his sleep, and for a wild moment the idea came to me that perhaps he was not normal, not altogether sane" (du Maurier, 29). When Max speaks of himself at age 42 to his youthful bride-to-be, he blames bitter memories and a repressed secret. True to type, he declares, "Those days are finished. They are blotted out. I must begin living all over again" (*ibid.*, 39).

In American literature, the Byronic outsider merged with the adventuresome western hero, an ambiguous plainsman who is capable of defiance of the social code and of performing noble and courageous acts, often anonymously. The frontier-code hero, the equivalent of Europe's Byronic hero, often reveals an enigmatic glint in his eye, a clue to his attitude toward challenge, Indian savagery, injustice, and threats to women. At the root of his allure is the self-destructive outcast cursed with an instinct for VIOLENCE, as is the case with Zane Grey's battered Lassiter, a former Texas Ranger in *Riders of the Purple Sage* (1912). The pattern generated a pageant of imitations: the title character in Jack Schaefer's *Shane* (1949), Gus McCrae and Woodrow F. Call in Larry McMurtry's *Lonesome Dove* (1985), John Wayne's multiple film depictions of the Indian fighter, and the steely-eyed lone rider, a semi-SUPERNATURAL mystic avenger, played by Clint Eastwood in *High Plains Drifter* (1972).

Bibliography

du Maurier, Daphne. *Rebecca.* New York: Avon Books, 1971.

Goldberg, Leonard S. "'This Gloom . . . Which Can Avail Thee Nothing': Cain and Skepticism," *Criticism* 41, no. 2 (spring 1999): 207.

Haining, Peter, ed. *The Shilling Shockers.* New York: St. Martin's Press, 1978.

Norton, Rictor. *The Mistress of Udolpho.* London: Leicester University Press, 1999.

Phillipson, Mark. "Byron's Revisited Haunts," *Studies in Romanticism* 39, no. 2 (summer 2000): 303.

Williams, Anne. *Art of Darkness: A Poetics of Gothic.* Chicago: University of Chicago Press, 1995.

C

Cable, George Washington
(1844–1925)

A master of SUSPENSE and MYSTERY, George Washington Cable produced a virulent form of SOUTHERN GOTHIC. He was so skilled at verisimilitude that he hurt the feelings of friends and neighbors in post-Reconstruction New Orleans with his portrayal of ABERRANT BEHAVIOR, hot Cajun tempers, and family feuds and secrets. In the dialect morality tale "Jean-ah Poquelin," published in *Scribner's* in 1875 and collected in *Old Creole Days* (1879), a pseudo-detective, Little White, lurks around a Frenchman's property in search of the source of a pungent odor and a will-o'-the-wisp. The local suspicions of piracy and murder come to naught with a full explanation of old Jean's love for his brother, a depigmented leper whom Jean hides from society.

Cable later excelled at a picturesque but ominous URBAN GOTHIC, examining the deterioration of the aristocracy in *Madame Delphine* (1881). He was also adept at writing psychological thrillers and spy tales, as in *The Cavalier* (1901) and *Kincaid's Battery* (1908). Like William FAULKNER, Cable wrote of the unavoidable interdependence of whites, blacks, and Métis in a social matrix roiled by bitter antagonisms and paradoxical, often explosive relationships. He achieved a minor classic with "BRAS-COUPÉ" (literally "cut arm" or "lopped arm"), a regional LEGEND told within the novel *The Grandissimes: A Story of Creole Life* (1879). Describing the sufferings of a one-armed African prince, the tale captures lurid strands of Southern plantation life. In Cable's view, racial vengeance is not ended by brutality—it is only postponed.

Bibliography

Bradbury, John. *Renaissance in the South*. Chapel Hill: University of North Carolina Press, 1963.

Haspel, Paul. "George Washington Cable and Bonaventure: A New Orleans Author's Literary Sojourn into Acadiana," *Southern Literary Journal* 35, no. 1 (fall 2002): 108–122.

Payne, James Robert. "New South Narratives of Freedom: Rereading George Washington Cable's 'Tite Poulette' and 'Madame Delphine,'" *MELUS* 27, no. 1 (spring 2002): 3–24.

Stephens, Robert O. *The Family Saga in the South: Generations and Destinies*. Baton Rouge: Louisiana State University Press, 1995.

Caleb Williams
William Godwin
(1794)

A precursor of the DETECTIVE STORY, psychological study, and the novel of doctrine, William GODWIN's politically motivated *The Adventures of Caleb Williams; or, Things As They Are* depicts the hardships of humble peasants against a world controlled by the privileged class. Following the upheaval of the French Revolution, Godwin presents through Gothic fiction the insidious nature of tyranny and the class divisions that prohibit opportunity for the proletariat. Polemical in TONE, his novel coordinates terror, MYSTERY, STALKING, and SUSPENSE through allegorical figures depicting the ongoing power struggle between the privileged and the peon.

In his youth, the title figure investigates the corruption of Falkland, his master, who was exonerated for murdering a neighbor. Curiosity, a common element in the GOTHIC NOVEL, proves Williams's undoing after his employer casts suspicion for the crime on Williams and scorns Williams's belief in justice and the court system. An isolated loner in search of exoneration, the protagonist finds himself relentlessly pursued, imprisoned, and harried on a nightmarish flight from Falkland, a man who cloaks his cruelties with elegant manners. The VILLAIN's ominous presence builds tension as Williams, the first-person narrator, searches for release and attempts to relay details of his tormentor's crime to a callous magistrate.

Crying out for succor, Williams, the postrevolutionary hero, pictures himself as a pariah, an alien ejected from society, a victim of authoritarianism whom novelist William Hazlett called unforgettable. The powerful novel earned favor with the English romantic poets Lord BYRON, Samuel Taylor COLERIDGE, John KEATS, Percy Bysshe SHELLEY, and William Wordsworth and set an example for the title villain in Charles Brockden BROWN's *ARTHUR MERVYN* (1799). In 1796, George Colman the Younger adapted Godwin's novel as a three-act stage musical, *The Iron Chest,* a popular MELODRAMA that debuted at Covent Garden with John Philip Kemble as the hounded victim.

Bibliography

Davies, Damian Walford. "The Politics of Allusion: *Caleb Williams, The Iron Chest, Middlemarch,* and the *Armoire de Fer,*" *Review of English Studies* 53, no. 212 (November 2002): 526–543.

Karl, Frederick R. *The Adversary Literature: The English Novel in the Eighteenth Century: A Study in Genre.* New York: Farrar, Straus, 1974.

Punter, David, ed. *The Literature of Terror,* vol. 1, 2nd ed. London: Longman, 1996.

Čapek, Karel
(1890–1945)

The Czech playwright and psychological fiction writer Karel Čapek employed Gothic elements in early 20th-century romantic tales and experimental drama. Born in Bohemia and educated in Berlin, Paris, and Prague, Čapek overcame a spinal anomaly to forge a career in speculative fiction, moral fables, and mysteries, which he collected in *Wayside Crosses* (1917), *Painful Tales* (1921), *Tales from Two Pockets* (1929), *Nine Fairy Tales* (1932), and *Apocryphal Tales* (1945). For Gothic effect, he manipulated TONE and ATMOSPHERE and, during the rise of Nazism, expertly wielded CLAUSTROPHOBIA and terror as indicators of the era's mood. His play *The Makropulos Case* (1922), a savage MYSTERY, served Leos Janacek as the basis for the opera of the same title (1925), which depicts the antiheroine Emilia Marty, an opera star, menaced by an evil lover. Like the WANDERING JEW, she guards the secret that she has lived for 337 years. Čapek turned to detective fiction for "The Adventures of a Breach-of-Promise Con Man" (1929), hauntingly surreal ALLEGORY in "The Last Judgment" (1929), and magic in "The Great Cat's Tale" (1932).

Čapek is best known for the dark dystopian play *R.U.R.* (1921), an ominous allegory about servant automata. (The term *robot* was coined in this work.) By depicting artificial intelligence run amok from a MAD SCIENTIST's lab, Čapek voiced an evolving distrust of technology and its assault on traditional morals. In the characters of the atheistic entrepreneur Dr. Rossum and his engineer son, Young Dr. Rossum, Čapek develops parallel themes—the perils of arrogance and greed. The production of humanoids populates the microcosm of Rossum's Island with robots 12 feet tall who are capable of performing drudgery as well as complex tasks requiring thought and judgment.

The play advances from industrial efficiency to terror as the factory's products begin bedeviling buyers with grumbling and erratic behavior. As the robots acquire nerves, emotions, and heart movement, their evolution presages doom for humanity. Radius's revolt in act 3 and the macabre romance of robots Helena and Primus betoken a world in which engineering marvels can both defeat humankind and repopulate the Earth through mechanical reproduction. Čapek's fear of future chaos influenced Isaac Asimov's *I, Robot* (1950) and Arthur C. Clarke's *Childhood's End* (1953).

Bibliography

Simon, John, "The End of Immortality," *Opera News* 60, no. 9 (January 20, 1996): 12–16.

Capote, Truman
(1924–1984)

A multitalented southern author and screenwriter and three-time winner of the O. Henry short fiction award, Truman Streckfus Persons Capote was skilled at SOUTHERN GOTHIC components but avoided total immersion in any one genre. Born in New Orleans, he was in his youth a scamp who preferred private readings of Edgar Allan POE, Isak DINESEN, and Sarah Orne Jewett to doing his homework assignments. He came of age in the care of maiden aunts in Monroeville, Alabama, and during World War II served an apprenticeship as copyboy at the *New Yorker.* For the settings of his popular works, he alternated primarily between Alabama and New York City, a pattern he followed in two popular novels: *Other Voices, Other Rooms* (1948), featuring GROTESQUE characters and pedophilia and set at a lonely, secluded mansion at Skull's Landing, and *Breakfast at Tiffany's* (1958), a whimsical escapist novel filmed in 1961 starring Audrey Hepburn as the enigmatic waif Holly Golightly, a runaway from a possessive southern husband.

Capote's predilection for eccentricity, loneliness, and despair colored his SHORT GOTHIC FICTION for *Harper's Bazaar* and *Mademoiselle,* particularly in "Shut a Final Door" and "The Headless Hawk," which he collected in *A Tree of Night* (1949). In *The Grass Harp* (1951), an autobiographical novel about ESCAPISM and late-in-life romance, his concern with innocence and worldly corruption inspired him to pair the orphaned nephew Collin Fenwick with the boy's repressed aunt Dolly Talbo, an elderly NAIF. Capote adapted the nostalgic story for the stage in 1952 and as a musical in 1971. In 1996, a film version reprised Capote's command of southern quaintness. Lesser touches of Gothic EXOTICISM illuminate the popular "A Christmas Memory" (1956), depicting a young boy's confrontation with Mr. Haha Jones, a scarred, unsmiling Indian moonshiner, and the flying of a ghostly kite that carries away the spirit of the boy's aged friend.

Capote's raffish, ebullient youth gave way to a serious professional interest in crime fiction, beginning in 1954 with his screenplay for *Beat the Devil,* a parody of the detective novel *The Maltese Falcon.* In 1961, he completed the screenplay for *The Innocents,* an adaptation of Henry JAMES's enigmatic Gothic novella THE TURN OF THE SCREW (1898), starring Deborah Kerr as the mystified GOVERNESS. Working with the novelist Harper Lee, his cousin, Capote developed his flair for murderous plots into a voyeuristic nonfiction crime novel, *In Cold Blood* (1966), an innovative marriage of GOTHIC CONVENTION and investigative technique. This in-depth study of two psychopathic drifters who tormented and murdered the Clutters, a Kansas farm family, appeared in four installments in *The New Yorker* and on film the following year.

Bibliography

Bradbury, John. *Renaissance in the South.* Chapel Hill: University of North Carolina Press, 1963.

Pugh, William White Tison. "Boundless Hearts in a Nightmare World: Queer Sentimentalism and Southern Gothicism in Truman Capote's 'Other Voices, Other Rooms,'" *Mississippi Quarterly* 51, no. 4 (fall 1998): 663.

Carter, Angela
(1940–1992)

Angela Olive Stalker Carter, a 20th-century specialist in extreme neo-Gothicism, flourished as a writer of CONTES CRUELS (cruel tales), novels, children's stories, plays for radio and screen, and stage drama; she even authored a chapbook on the legendary American VILLAIN Lizzie Borden. Reared in Yorkshire, England, during and after World War II, Carter was fascinated with FOLKLORE and with the vulgar sideshow aspect of British life, both of which colored her wildly fantastic works. She mastered writing by turning out reviews and features for the *Croyden Advertiser* newspaper. After marriage at age 20, she studied medieval literature at Bristol University, with additional coursework in psychology and the social sciences. Simultaneously, she began publishing Gothic fiction with *Shadow Dance* (1966), featuring the hero-villain Honeybuzzard, and *The Magic*

Toyshop (1967), winner of the Rhys Prize for its magical realism.

In an inventive style blending elements of Walter DE LA MARE, the Marquis de Sade, Isak DINESEN, E. T. A. HOFFMANN, and Edgar Allan POE, Carter continued her career with scholarly work and lecturing while developing a cult following with her macabre stories. She added to the canon of FEMALE GOTHIC through resettings of the FAIRY TALE and scenarios picturing a panoply of Gothic themes—CLAUSTROPHOBIA and confinement, SOMNAMBULISM, eroticism and fetishism, SADISM, LYCANTHROPY and VAMPIRISM, occultism, occluded gender roles, urban crime, and VIOLENCE against women. In one example, "The Werewolf" (1995), she presents through a naive peasant voice a diabolic story in which the devil leads witches in a Walpurgis Night picnic on fresh corpses. The action evolves into a nightmarish version of "Little Red Riding Hood" in which ignorant SUPERSTITION leads to the beating death of an old woman.

In *Heroes and Villains* (1969), Carter employed a MAD SCIENTIST motif to describe violence against NATURE; in *The Infernal Desire Machines of Doctor Hoffman* (1972), she modernized the myth of FAUST with diabolic fascism. She produced a horror anthology, *The Bloody Chamber* (1979); reset the focus of de Sade in *The Sadeian Woman and the Ideology of Pornography* (1979); engineered the movements of a swan-woman for the critically acclaimed GASLIGHT NOVEL *Nights at the Circus* (1984); and scripted two cinema versions of her stories, *The Company of Wolves* (1984) and *The Magic Toyshop* (1986).

Bibliography

Bonca, Cornel. "In Despair of the Old Adams: Angela Carter's 'The Infernal Desire Machines of Dr. Hoffman,'" *Review of Contemporary Fiction* 14, no. 3 (fall 1994): 56–62.

Bradfield, Scott. "Remembering Angela Carter," *Review of Contemporary Fiction* 14, no. 3 (fall 1994): 90–93.

Horner, Avril, ed. *European Gothic: A Spirited Exchange 1760–1960.* Manchester: Manchester University Press, 2002.

Pearson, Jacqueline. "'These Tags of Literature': Some Uses of Allusion in the Early Novels of Angela Carter," *CRITIQUE: Studies in Contemporary Fiction* 40, no. 3 (spring 1999): 248.

Weinert, Laurent. "Angela Carter's 'The Bloody Chamber' at the Metal Shed at the Toy Factory," *Back Stage West* 10, no. 4 (January 23, 2003): 19.

"The Cask of Amontillado"
Edgar Allan Poe
(1846)

A classic tale of vengeance and PREMATURE BURIAL first printed in the November 1846 issue of *Godey's Lady's Book,* Edgar Allan POE's "The Cask of Amontillado" has been labeled his most perfect short work for its blend of irony and dark humor with horror. Aficionados of the author's work recognized in its gleeful vengeance a fictional comeuppance to Thomas Dunn English, an amateur poet who parodied "THE BLACK CAT" (1843) and circulated vicious libels in the New York *Mirror.* Later analysis connected the death madness in the story with Poe's fears for his dying wife, Virginia Clemm Poe, who suffered a five-year battle with tuberculosis. The story inspired Argentine, French, and German films, none of which captured its masterful psychological insight.

Told in flashback half a century after the event, the moody, suspenseful narrative takes place in Italy during carnival season on the eve of Lent. Poe may have heard the core of the plot in 1827 while he was stationed with the army at Fort Independence, near Boston Harbor. According to an anecdote related in Austin N. Stevens's *Mysterious New England* (1971), some soldiers waylaid a Captain Green, who had killed a Lieutenant Massie in a duel. The angry avengers treated Green liberally to wine. When he was suitably drunk, they chained him to a dungeon floor and bricked over the opening, leaving him to a GROTESQUE demise from starvation and cold in a blackened tomb.

In the fictional version, Poe blends a festival motif with the intent of the monomaniac Montresor. Montresor walls up Fortunato, a pompous adversary easily lured into a dank cellar on the pretext of tasting a rare dry sherry stored there. The plot incorporates pre-spring festivities where the costume of Arlecchino, the standard mime of the commedia dell'arte, is a common disguise. A proud member of the mystic order of Masons, a fraternal order that originated in medieval trade unions, Fortunato sheds his connection with the arcane secret society to wear carnival motley. The author elevates Fortunato's vulnerability through the irony of his name, his oblivious mental state, and the lightheartedness of his clownish dress. Proceeding down winding stairs in catacombs redolent with mold and rimed with nitre, the two characters pass through ranks of wine casks interlaid with heaps of human bones. They sample wine along the way and arrive at an inner niche the size of an upright coffin. Poe uses the descent as a MOOD-altering device as the Gothic ATMOSPHERE gradually supplants the street-level celebration.

The carefully controlled action allows the narrator gradually to immure his victim with deft strokes of a trowel. Like a corpse laid to rest in a crypt, Fortunato disappears from view until only the bells of his conical jester's cap echo in the recess. Unrepentant, the killer takes literally the family motto *Nemo me impune lacessit*, Latin for "No one provokes me with impunity" (Poe, 16). Montresor chuckles like a madman before plastering over his handiwork with the standard graveyard platitude *In pace requiescat* ["May he rest in peace"] (*ibid.*, 19).

Bibliography

Poe, Edgar Allan. "The Cask of Amontillado," in *The Complete Stories*. New York: Knopf, 1992.

Symons, Julian. *The Tell-Tale Heart: The Life and Works of Edgar Allan Poe*. New York: Harper & Row, 1978.

Castle Dracula

In Bram STOKER's DRACULA (1897), the setting looms like a medieval repository of evil. When the law clerk Jonathan HARKER falls under the power of the vampire, he experiences the duplicity of an outward elegance that cloaks an evil interior in both the VILLAIN and his domain. Conveyed by carriage, Harker, a male NAIF, sleeps fitfully, offering an unclear commentary on the howling of wolves, occluded moonlight, and a touch of the SUPERNATURAL—the queer blue flame that precedes his arrival to Castle Dracula at the crest of a slope in the Carpathian Mountains of Transylvania. When Dracula later explains the burst of blue flame as a mark of hidden treasure, Stoker adds a note on a milieu that has been "fought over for centuries by the Wallachian, the Saxon, and the Turk" (Stoker, 22). The author depicts the visitor suddenly eyeing a large ruined castle with windows offering no glints of light, an optical coming-to-knowledge of the dark hall. The approach presages Harker's intellectual awareness of the morbid soul of the vampire and his power over human victims.

Stoker continues his survey in chapter 2 with Harker's on-again, off-again architectural description that parallels later attempts to characterize the nebulous Count Dracula and his corrupt lifestyle. Harker admits that grogginess and the enveloping gloom obscure his view of the courtyard, which seems large. He recalls a huge door studded with iron nailheads and a projecting stone portal. At the bell-less, knockerless entrance, he receives a benediction suitable for the OUTSIDER arriving in Transylvania. Acting the jocular host, Dracula offers a hearty handshake and booms a country platitude: "Welcome to my house. Come freely. Go safely; and leave something of the happiness you bring!" (*ibid.*, 16).

Stoker is adept at allying good manners with terror. Like the villain's charismatic exterior, the elements of hospitality disquiet rather than welcome as the count shows Harker to a bright log fire in a great bedroom and serves a chicken dinner with Tokay wine. Too late, Harker realizes his predicament in architectural terms: "Doors, doors, doors everywhere, and all locked and bolted. In no place save from the windows in the castle walls is there an available exit. The castle is a veritable prison, and I am a prisoner!" (*ibid.*, 27).

In the last pages of the resolution, Stoker depicts an all-too-human ennui that overcomes the posse of cavaliers who stake the vampire's minions and seal DRACULA'S CRYPT. Late on a snowy November day, Mina Harker notes the fierce cold and desolation, a suitable milieu for the conquered vampire. She looks back at the castle amid the howling of wolves and perceives a grandeur that she describes as "wild and uncanny" (*ibid.*, 393). The theatrical departure replaces the supernatural menace with NATURE's threat—wolf packs and the river, "lying like a black ribbon in kinks and curls" (*ibid.*, 394). After Harker and Morris complete a terrifying exorcism, the count's faithful gypsy escort retreats, leaving Mina to look toward the grim mountain crest. In a brief afterword, Jonathan remarks on a visit seven years later to Castle Dracula, which survives on the Carpathian heights as a monument to the count's singularity and isolation.

Bibliography

Auerbach, Nina. *Our Vampires, Ourselves.* Chicago: University of Chicago Press, 1995.

Senf, Carol A. "Bram Stoker: History, Psychoanalysis and the Gothic," *Victorian Studies* 42, no. 4 (summer 2000): 675.

Stoker, Bram. *Dracula.* New York: Bantam Books, 1981.

The Castle of Otranto
Horace Walpole
(1765)

Horace WALPOLE's operatic novel *The Castle of Otranto*, the first official Gothic romance and progenitor of an enduring genre, was an immediate best-seller. Composed at the author's manse at Strawberry Hill, Twickenham, outside London, the vigorous narrative applied Gothic architectural style and aura to a groundbreaking new genre, which Walpole issued from his own press, Strawberry Hill Gothic. Beginning in June 1764, he developed his text from a vivid dream that placed him in an ancient castle. Over a period of two months, he encouraged the dreamscape to grow organically by giving full range to musings and whimsy in an exercise in AUTOMATIC WRITING. From his introduction to literature of the structural term *Gothic* came an era dominated by an initial set of GOTHIC CONVENTIONs that flourished from the 1760s to the 1820s.

In the preface, Walpole identifies the medieval tale as the impetus to imagination and fantasy and an abandonment of pure reason, the guiding principle of the neoclassicists. To set the stage, he deliberately misleads the reader with a title page claiming that the story is an antique Italian fiction related by a priest, Onuphrio Muralto, and translated by William Marshall, an English gentleman. The ruse, a familiar one to readers of the genre, implies that Gothic fiction is foreign to England and must be imported from more deca-

dent parts of Europe. In the second edition, Walpole identifies the narrative with a straightforward title, *The Castle of Otranto: A Gothic Story*, and appends a sonnet explaining his "dauntless sail" blown on the deep by "fancy's gale" (Walpole, 13). His use of the word *Gothic* in the subtitle sets the story in the medieval era.

The author chose as themes parental duties to offspring and the righting of previous wrongs that plague a family's history, which he states in the preface with a passage from the Ten Commandments (Exodus 20:5). He fills the story with characters bearing Germanic names (Conrad, Jerome, Theodore) and Italianate names (Bianca, Hippolita, Matilda, Alfonso the Good), and sets the action in a deliberately vague era near the end of the Middle Ages. Influencing the ominous interior settings were Giovanni Battista Piranesi's etchings of *Carceri d'Invenzione* (Prison caprices, ca. 1761).

Walpole initiates his story as though it were a stage tragedy. The opening scene describes the efforts of the usurper Manfred, the prince of Otranto, to circumvent an ancient prediction of doom for his family. When his son Conrad is felled on his wedding day in a bizarre accident—an outsized helmet crashes down into the castle courtyard—Manfred learns of his loss from the shouts of servants, "Oh, my lord! the prince! the prince! the helmet! the helmet!" (Walpole, 16–17). Manfred arrives too late to save his son and heir from the weight of the ominous black-feathered helmet 100 times larger than normal, a touch of HYPERBOLE that suits the author's style.

From outlandish beginnings, Walpole develops *The Castle of Otranto* into a cautionary tale based on an ancestral curse. More like a FAIRY TALE than a terror novel, the plot leans heavily toward Gothic ROMANTICISM with its story-within-a-story told through run-on dialogue punctuated with dashes and exclamation points to enhance emotional outpourings. After imprisoning an innocent peasant under the helmet on charges of NECROMANCY, Manfred dooms the man to starvation. Meanwhile, to save the house of Otranto from a dire prophecy, Manfred attempts to marry Isabella, the groomless bride-to-be. In protest, the nose of a statue sheds three drops of blood, a FORESHADOWING of the conflict to come.

With a gesture to both medieval and modern traditions, the inventive author overlays the episodes with exotic settings in Algiers and Sicily, death in the Holy Land, SUPERNATURAL rustlings and sighs, temporary INSANITY, a portrait come to life, a secret passage to a convent, enslavement, the intervention of clergy, and a mysterious friar's disclosure of Otranto's real heir. Walpole inserts the basis of a literary and cinematic cliché, a gust of wind that extinguishes the heroine's light, leaving her to flounder in total darkness. He establishes the helplessness of female characters with such theatrical outbursts as "'Ah me, I am slain!' cried Matilda sinking: 'Good heaven, receive my soul!'" and with polite references to rape, such as "'Yes,' said Isabella; "and to complete his crime, he meditates—I cannot speak it!" (Walpole, 105).

Revered as the fount of Gothic fiction, Walpole's novel went through numerous editions and intrigued notable romantic authors, including the poets Lord BYRON and Thomas Gray and the balladeer and novelist Sir Walter SCOTT. The FEMALE GOTHIC writer Clara REEVE criticized Walpole's excess of feeling, yet used the *The Castle of Otranto* as a springboard to her own Gothic novels. On November 17, 1781, Walpole's story played at Covent Garden Theatre in a stage adaptation by the Irish playwright Robert Jephson, titled *The Count of Narbonne.* A 1964 edition of the novel featured illustrations by the surrealist artist Salvador Dali.

Bibliography

Barasch, Frances K. *The Grotesque.* Paris: Mouton, 1971.

Bernstein, Stephen. "Form and Ideology in the Gothic Novel," *Essays in Literature* 18 (1991): 151–165.

Karl, Frederick R. *The Adversary Literature: The English Novel in the Eighteenth Century: A Study in Genre.* New York: Farrar, Straus & Giroux, 1974.

Porter, David. "From Chinese to Goth: Walpole and the Gothic Repudiation of Chinoiserie," *Eighteenth-Century Life* 23, no. 1 (1999): 46–58.

Punter, David, ed. *The Literature of Terror.* Vol 1, 2nd ed. London: Longman, 1996.

Stevens, David. *The Gothic Tradition.* Cambridge: Cambridge University Press, 2000.

Walpole, Horace. *The Castle of Otranto.* London: Oxford University Press, 1969.

censorship

The extremes of Gothic literature have always produced a dichotomy of public taste—fans and imitators in favor and an outraged minority against, for example, the censorship evident in the case of Christopher Marlowe's DR. FAUSTUS (ca. 1588); the mix of response to stage terrors at the GRAND GUIGNOL; and more recently, conservative pressure to suppress Lois Lowry's fable *The Giver* (1993), a Newbery Award–winning book about a child's escape from a totalitarian society and his effort to save an infant boy doomed to be euthanized. According to Samuel J. Pratt's five-volume *Family Secrets, Literary and Domestic* (1797), fears of censure for Gothic reading tastes produced some unusual means of cloaking books withdrawn from a CIRCULATING LIBRARY— "sometimes tricked between muslins, cambrics, silks, sattins, and the like, or rolled in a bundle, then thrown into a coach by some of my fair smugglers; the old ones, meanwhile, mams and dads, never the wiser" (Stevens, 27). Public censorship seemed to arise from even the covers of the Gothic shockers, which required clever masking of shocking, evocative headings. The following year, Pratt released a bowdlerized version of his commentary, presumably to spare his work excess public condemnation.

A backlash against classic Gothicism occurred in 1796 with the publication of Matthew Gregory LEWIS's THE MONK, a compelling horror novel that juxtaposes lust and murder within a Catholic setting. Expanding its ill repute was Edmon Ploërt's French translation, *Le Moine Incestueux* (The Incestuous Monk). Outcries from the *Monthly Review* and *Scots Magazine* against Lewis's affront to decency and religious faith caused Britain's attorney general to launch an injunction against the novel for blatant impiety, ANTI-CATHOLICISM, and carnality. Writing in the *Critical Review,* Samuel Taylor COLERIDGE, himself a writer of sexually charged Gothic poetry, questioned whether Lewis was a Christian or an infidel. As a result of widespread consternation and disapproval, Gothic literature acquired a stigma that it has never expunged.

The to-do in public and in print over *The Monk* forced the author to deny any political ALLEGORY in his novel and, that same year, to issue a new version, in which he toned down the eroticism and blasphemy. Still, the public debate bubbled ominously, with Lord BYRON denouncing Lewis's novel and the Marquis de Sade condoning it. Not surprisingly, de Sade himself was the next major writer of Gothic to run afoul of public sensibilities. In 1801, French police nabbed him at his publisher's office and seized copies of *Justine, ou les Malheurs de la Vertu (Justine; or, The Unhappiness of Virtue)*, which he had published a decade before. Authorities maintained the ban on *Justine* for 170 years. The hubbub elevated the author above Lewis and—eventually, even Oscar WILDE—to the tawdry status of most-despised Gothicist.

One champion of censorship, Bram STOKER, author of the vampire classic *DRACULA* (1897), became the mouthpiece of Victorian prudery with the publication of "The Censorship of Fiction," issued in *Nineteenth Century and After* in July 1908, less than four years before his death from paralytic syphilis. As though speaking for Sigmund Freud, Stoker identified lust as the most harmful of human impulses and blamed dissolute women as the most frequent offenders of public taste. To prevent harm from the unleashing of sexual evil among the innocent, he urged that England vigorously suppress any literature that would disgrace the motherland and corrupt English youth.

The zealot's perennial rooting out of evil boosted the reputation and sales of such 20th-century Gothic works as S. Ansky's Yiddish play *Der Dybbuk* (ca. 1916); Angela CARTER's *CONTES CRUELS* (Cruel Tales); Stephen KING's *Salem's Lot* (1975); and Isabel ALLENDE's *La Casa de los Espíritus* (*The House of the Spirits*, 1981), which contains graphic political detail that made it unwelcome to Chile's repressive regime. An early 21st-century outcry consisted of self-appointed activism and pulpit sermons against the Harry Potter series, J. K. Rowling's young-adult fantasy phenomenon. Charges of DIABOLISM and WITCHCRAFT colored some calls for suppression. The support of teachers, librarians, civil libertarians, readers, and parents countered these exhibitions of piety and concern for child endangerment with a suitable rejoinder—questions about the authority and motivation of the censors themselves.

Bibliography

Gamer, Michael. *Romanticism and the Gothic: Genre, Reception, and Canon Formation.* Cambridge: Cambridge University Press, 2000.

Hawkins, Joan. "Gothic Revisited," *Review of Communication* 2, no. 3 (July 2002): 327–333.

Kirk, Connie Ann. *J. K. Rowling: A Biography.* Westport, Conn., Greenwood Press, 2003.

Stevens, David. *The Gothic Tradition.* Cambridge: Cambridge University Press, 2000.

character names

Gothic authors make good use of symbolic character names as a means of divulging character traits, attitudes, or attributes—the good-natured twinkle in Mattie Silver, or the ingenue in Edith WHARTON's *ETHAN FROME* (1911), for example. Females often carry emblematic names implying some aspect of their behavior and/or value: animal traits (Moggy), blessedness (Beatrice), beauty (Annabel, Christabel, Isabella, Isadora, Rosabella), chastity (Virginia), diminution (Antoinette, Marionetta, Mina, Morella, Rosella), duty (Martha), excellence (Laurina), finality (Ultima), grief (Ulalume), innocence (Agnes, Eva, Evelena), light (Biondetta, Hester, Lucy), liveliness (Vivian), love (Aimée), nature (Fiorimunda, Flora, Lilla, Phoebe, Rosario, Stella), nobility (Alexena, Diana, Emily, Georgiana, Julia, Marcelia), EXOTICISM (Almena, Arabella, Ianthe, Ligeia, Zenobia, Zuleima), piety (Celestina, Coelina, Faith), punishment (Férula), purity (Alba, Blanche, Bianca, Clara, Ellena Rosalba, Pearl, Roselva), simplicity (Jane), strength (Leonora), truth (Vera), and vision (Avisa). From *BLACKWOOD'S EDINBURGH MAGAZINE*, Charlotte BRONTË chose the title surname of *JANE EYRE* (1847), a homonym for heir FORESHADOWING the character's inheritance from a relative in the West Indies. Even Gothic animals project meaning in their names, as with Edgar Allan POE's cat Pluto, named for the god of the underworld in "The Black Cat" (1843).

Men, too, carry evocative names, as with the Baron von Stickmeheart in the anonymous chapbook "The Black Spider" (ca. 1798) and Mary Wollstonecraft SHELLEY's MAD SCIENTIST Victor in *FRANKENSTEIN* (1818). Male characters also bear emblematic surnames: the flitting insect implied in Charles Robert MATURIN's MELMOTH THE WANDERER (1820), the tortuous Wringhim in James HOGG's murder MYSTERY *The Private Memoirs and Confessions of a Justified Sinner* (1824), the venomous Count di Venoni in the anonymous "The Astrologer's Prediction" (1826), and the serial killer Nathan Slaughter in Robert Montgomery BIRD's bloody mystery novel, NICK OF THE WOODS; or, The Jibbenainosay: A Tale of Kentucky (1837). Poe exonerates an early suspect of murder in "The Mystery of Marie Rogêt" (1842) by naming the character Adolphe le Bon (the Good). That same year, Poe turned a character name to irony with Prince Prospero, who is doomed to die of plague in "THE MASQUE OF THE RED DEATH" (1842), and with the jovial sounding Charles Goodfellow, the murderer in "Thou Art the Man" (1844) and the unlucky Fortunato, the victim buried alive in a wall in "THE CASK OF AMONTILLADO" (1846). Robert Louis STEVENSON chose a worthy image for his lurking Mr. Hyde in DR. JEKYLL AND MR. HYDE (1886). The surname becomes a pun on Jekyll's inability to conceal his evil alter ego.

In Daphne DU MAURIER's REBECCA (1938), Maxim de Winter, the widower who marries a nameless NAIF, displays a frosty exterior to his befuddled wife, who misinterprets his surliness as grief for the deceased Rebecca. In mid-20th-century Gothic fiction, Shirley JACKSON's "THE LOTTERY" (1948) alludes to American history by naming her victim Tessie Hutchinson, a reference to the New England religious leader Anne Hutchinson. Jackson packs her story with allegorical significance with the bystanders Old Man Warner and Mr. Graves, whose names allude to the stoning death awaiting Tessie. In SOUTHERN GOTHIC, William Faulkner's "A ROSE FOR EMILY" (1930) implies male dominance in the wooing of Miss EMILY by Homer Barron. In WISE BLOOD (1952), Flannery O'CONNOR adds an inkling of her protagonist's moral misperceptions by naming him Hazel "Haze" Motes.

Bibliography

Fleenor, Juliann E., ed. *The Female Gothic*. Montreal: Eden Press, 1983

Chesnutt, Charles
(1858–1932)

The innovative fiction writer Charles Waddell Chesnutt wrote SOUTHERN GOTHIC literature with an African-American slant. Born three years before the onset of the Civil War, he attended a North Carolina school operated by the Freedmen's Bureau, completed a law degree, and established a successful court reporting business in Cleveland, Ohio. He admired the plantation fiction of the abolitionist Harriet Beecher Stowe and began writing nightmarish tales and sketches of black bondage. With his issuance of an OUTSIDER's view of racism in the Carolinas in "The Goophered Grapevine" (1887), he became the first black author published in *Atlantic Monthly*.

In the seven stories collected in *The Conjure Woman* (1899), Chesnutt employs dialect repartee, FOLKLORE, and SUPERSTITION as entrees to black and mulatto lifestyles, which he refused to stereotype or sentimentalize. One story, "The Gray Wolf's Ha'nt," depicts SECRECY, sorcery, cat killing, and METEMPSYCHOSIS. Another, "Sis' Becky's Pickaninny," describes an evil master who trades a slavewoman for a race horse. With "Mars Jeems's Nightmare," Chesnutt turns to NECROMANCY to change a white plantation owner into a black slave, who suffers the lash from his own overseer.

In a surreal GHOST STORY, "Po' Sandy," Chesnutt pictures the black spirit that animates a tree, and the white invention that further torments and reshapes him. In an evocative aural image, the machine groans as it cuts its way into the trunk to produce planks. As material for the plantation owner's kitchen, the sturdy lumber imbues the construction with the resilience of slaves. Sandy's grieving wife bemuses the white residents, who fail to understand how he could continue to resist dismemberment and crafting into place as flooring or paneling. In his new guise, Sandy continues to needle and disquiet white complacency through haunting.

Bibliography

Church, Joseph. "In Black and White: The Reader's Part in Chesnutt's 'Gray Wolf's Ha'nt,'" *American Transcendental Quarterly* 13, no. 2 (June 1999): 121.

Goldner, Ellen J. "Other(ed) Ghosts: Gothicism and the Bonds of Reason in Melville, Chesnutt, and Morrison," *MELUS* 24, no. 1 (spring 1999): 59.

Petrie, Paul R. "Charles W. Chesnutt, 'The Conjure Woman,' and the Racial Limits of Literary Mediation," *Studies in American Fiction* 27, no. 2 (autumn 1999): 183.

Ramsey, William M. "Family Matters in the Fiction of Charles W. Chesnutt," *Southern Literary Journal* 33, no. 2 (spring 2001): 30.

White, Jeannette S. "Baring Slavery's Darkest Secrets: Charles Chesnutt's Conjure Tales as Masks of Truth," *Southern Literary Journal* 27, no. 1 (fall 1994): 85–103.

chiaroscuro

An art term frequently applied to Gothic literature, *chiaroscuro*, the Italian for "light-dark," accentuates the extremes of good and evil, welcome and menace in characters and MONSTERS, settings, and events, as found in the lurid passageways in William BECKFORD's *VATHEK* (1782), the fearful half-light of Charles Robert MATURIN's *MELMOTH THE WANDERER* (1820), and the nighttime martyrdom of the maiden in Alfred Noyes's rhythmic ballad *The Highwayman* (1907). The manipulation of small points of light from moon, taper, or flickering gas lamp in a profoundly dark setting is a given in GOTHIC CONVENTION, particularly for the urban GASLIGHT THRILLER. Combined with groans, creaks, and ambiguous sounds from crypt or battlement, the effect on the reader's psyche is a heightening of the senses in search of more distinguishable clues to action. The enhancement encourages imagination and MELANCHOLY and produces SUSPENSE, a hallmark of reader response to Gothic fiction.

The masters of classic Gothic style turned the play of light and shadow to artistic and symbolic purpose, as in the mystic shadings that enhance Gothic nuance in Dante Gabriel Rossetti's poem "The Portrait" (1847), the gloomy subterranean Morlock society in H. G. WELLS's *The Time Machine* (1895), and the lights of zooming futuristic vehicles that bear down on pedestrians on shadowy streets in Ray BRADBURY's *Fahrenheit 451* (1953). The use of intense contrasts showcases fearful actions and intensifies villainy and somber settings, as found in the increasing bleakness as MONTRESOR lures Fortunato to his underground doom in Edgar Allan POE's atmospheric revenge tale "THE CASK OF AMONTILLADO" (1846). Nathaniel HAWTHORNE's "YOUNG GOODMAN BROWN" (1835) deliberately depicts shadows during a plunge into the forest for what may be a satanic gathering.

Chiaroscuro retained its prominence in Gothic works into current times. In the allegorical novel *The Natural* (1952), Bernard Malamud's villainous Judge Banner muses on his preference for dark over light: "There is in the darkness a unity, if you will, that cannot be achieved in any other environment, a blending of self with what the self perceives, an exquisite mystical experience" (Malamud, 89). When adaptations of Gothic novels and stories reached the screen as FILM NOIR, cinema directors applied the light-dark word pictures to actual orchestrations of illumination and shading, highlighting extremes of darkness with bright points for uninviting castles, cathedrals, and the laboratories of MAD SCIENTISTs, a standard treatment of Frankenstein spin-offs.

Bibliography

King, Stephen. *Danse Macabre.* New York: Everest House, 1981.

Malamud, Bernard. *The Natural.* New York: Avon Books, 1952.

Varma, Devendra P. *The Gothic Flame.* New York: Russell & Russell, 1966.

"Christabel"
Samuel Taylor Coleridge
(1816)

Samuel Taylor COLERIDGE manages ATMOSPHERE and cryptic action to create a superstitious dread in "Christabel," one of the first poems about vampiric POSSESSION in the English language. Composed in 1797, the unfinished verse tale is a disturbing, incomplete HORROR NARRATIVE based on Friedrich von SCHILLER's *Schauerroman* (literally "shudder novel") *DER GEISTERSEHER* (*The Ghost-Seer*, 1786) and Johann Wolfgang von GOETHE's ballad *Die Braut von Corinth* (*The Bride of Corinth,* 1797), a seminal model of the female vampire. Coleridge toys with the SUPERNATURAL and VAMPIRISM while restraining terror in a dreamy overlay of dangerous intimacy with an alien female. The result is a teasingly truncated episode.

The narrative establishes a sinister aura by beginning in the middle of a chilly night, when occluded light obscures a distant castle. Contributing to the funereal TONE of "Christabel" are images of mistletoe and oak, both of which bear ominous druidic implications. As the title figure departs her father's castle to pray with Geraldine, their meeting under a shorn oak looms starkly autumnal because of the lack of leaves and the growth of mistletoe and moss. An alluring ghoul or wily sorceress, Geraldine, clad in white, gleams with an internal brightness as she seduces the NAIF, her would-be rescuer. From the folkloric tradition that Satan must be invited into a dwelling, the poet has Christabel welcome Geraldine into the castle. The vampire's pretense of weakness forces her hostess to carry her indoors.

The shift of setting places Christabel in peril of a reptilian lover, who mesmerizes Christabel with a snaky glance. As Christabel fails to voice her dread, the speaker, too, appears incapable of describing the seduction scene, thus producing a lapse of Gothic detail concerning the dangers that Geraldine poses toward the innocent maid. The ambiguity of Geraldine's nature and intent creates an unusual application of GOTHIC CONVENTION, leaving the reader in doubt as to the aim and degree of evil that the poet means to convey. He enhances the duality of good/evil, desire/dread, and nurture/menace by frequent references to illness and death and to sanctity and blessedness.

Coleridge's work fed England's developing ROMANTICISM. The poem's shifting images riveted Lord BYRON and Percy Bysshe SHELLEY, who read the text aloud in July 1816 during their summer residence at the Villa Diodati on Lake Geneva. The concept of vampirism had already taken root in Byron's imagination in "THE GIAOUR" (1813), in which he characterizes the entrancing doom of the undead. Another romantic poet, John KEATS, reframed the FEMME FATALE in "LA BELLE DAME SANS MERCI" (1819).

Bibliography

May, Claire B. "'Christabel' and Abjection: Coleridge's Narrative in Process on Trial," *Studies in English Literature, 1500–1900* 37, no. 4 (autumn 1997): 699–723.

Parry, Susan. "Coleridge's 'Christabel,'" *Explicator* 58, no. 3 (spring 2000): 133.

Taylor, Anya. "Coleridge and the Pleasures of Verse," *Studies in Romanticism* 40, no. 2 (winter 2001): 547–570.

———. "Coleridge's 'Christabel' and the Phantom Soul," *Studies in English Literature, 1500–1900* 42, no. 4 (autumn 2002): 707–731.

———. "Filling the Blanks: Coleridge and the Inscrutable Female Subject," *Wordsworth Circle* 33, no. 2 (spring 2002): 84–88.

A Christmas Carol
(1843)

Charles DICKENS's beloved SUPERNATURAL tale *A Christmas Carol in Prose: A Ghost Story of Christmas* is a world-favorite GHOST STORY. In October 1843, as his wife anticipated the birth of their fifth child, he wrote his holiday classic of love in action without naming the Virgin Mary, Jesus, the star of Bethlehem, shepherds, angels, mangers, or wise men. The novella was influenced by Washington Irving's *The Keeping of Christmas at Bracebridge Hall* (1820) and brought the author an advance in the sum of £250—at a time when Dickens's personal finances were at a low ebb—as part of a series of short yule fiction that he submitted to *Household Words* and *All the Year Round.*

None of Dickens's other works so moved readers to praise his humanity and greatness of heart. Within five months of the first printing, *Carol* sold 12,500 copies. Although critics lambasted Dickens for the tale's MELODRAMA, heavy-handed sentimentality and social criticism and its overapplication of caricature and coincidence, the public embraced the uplifting themes and Gothic motifs. To the end of his days in 1870, Dickens gave annual readings from *A Christmas Carol.* He exhausted himself with dramatic gesture and voicing of macabre scenes depicting a miser's dread of imminent death.

For dramatic effect in this conversion fable, in the opening scene, the image of the walking dead strikes the cold-hearted Ebenezer Scrooge. When his former partner, Jacob Marley, appears as a REVENANT seven years after his demise, Scrooge manages to remain cool and objective. As he observes Marley's "death-cold eyes" and binder swathing head and chin, "he was still incredulous, and fought against his senses" (Dickens, 842). The full import of the apparition sinks in gradually after the miser mutters a double "humbug." Dickens turns Marley into the traditional clanking Gothic horror, who "raised a frightful cry, and shook its chain with such a dismal and appalling noise, that Scrooge held on tight to his chair, to save himself from falling in a swoon" (*ibid.*, 843). A stagy specter, Marley becomes a sexless phantasm to whom the author repeatedly refers as "it."

Like an organist gradually increasing a dour pedal tone, Dickens enlarges on the Christmas haunting in three defined sequences, past, present, and future. In the second sequence, the author points to the poor, "yellow, meagre, ragged, scowling, wolfish; but prostrate, too, in their humility. . . . Where angels might have sat enthroned, devils lurked, and glared out menacing" (*ibid.*, 869). Bringing home to the hard-hearted Scrooge his limited time on earth, the third spirit speaks no words, but points relentlessly to a grave marker inscribed EBENEZER SCROOGE (*ibid.*, 878). The author pictures the old man's hands clutching at the phantom's hooded raiment, which "shrunk, collapsed, and dwindled down into a bedpost" (*ibid.*). The success of this well-modulated ghost narrative caused the author and critic G. K. Chesterton to call Dickens a quintessential mythographer.

Bibliography

Butterworth, R. D. "'A Christmas Carol' and the Masque," *Studies in Short Fiction* 30 no. 1 (winter 1993): 63–69.

Dickens, Charles. *A Christmas Carol*, in Vol. 1 of *The Annotated Dickens*, ed. by Edward Guiliano and Philip Collins. New York: Clarkson N. Potter, 1986.

Rowell, Geoffrey. "Dickens and the Construction of Christmas," *History Today* 43, no. 17 (December 1993): 17–24.

circulating libraries

William Lane, owner of the MINERVA PRESS, enlarged the demand for mysteries, tales, and Gothic romance by franchising a chain of circulating libraries. To the dismay of the sneering intelligentsia, who deplored recreational reading and the very name Minerva, Lane developed a working-class readership at a string of sites, the chief venue for his blue-and-white bound publications. He encouraged grocers, engravers, bookbinders, picture framers, perfumers, apothecaries, ticket sellers, and tobacconists to invest in the project, which supplied several thousand bound volumes to each new location for organization and display by genre. In media advertisements, he expressed the value to the nation of reading for pleasure: "Institutions of this Kind must be forcibly convenient to all Classes of People, of general Service and public Utility" (Blakey, 121).

Lane's intent paid off for both reader and writer of romances and Gothic novels and short fiction. Copies of Mary Elizabeth BRADDON's Faustian novel *Gerard; or, The World, the Flesh and the Devil* (1891) survive from the shelves of Mudie's Select Circulating Library. Library patrons had access to the shelves from 9:00 A.M. until 9:00 P.M. each day except Sundays. They paid either an annual subscription rate or left deposits for the books they checked out. The costs ranged from twopence or threepence per day for a play or quarto to fourpence for a volume. Because the rules were stringent—one book per patron at a time for no more than four days—readers had to dig in and progress rapidly through their choices.

Lane's system worked so well that lending libraries spread to Margate and other spas and throughout Ireland, Scotland, Jamaica, Bombay, and New York City. The Reverend Edward Mangin, a would-be censor and author of *An Essay on Light Reading* (1805), complained that "there is scarcely a street of the metropolis, or a village in the country, in which a circulating library may not be found" (Mangin, n. p.). For good measure, he added that circulating libraries extended throughout the English-speaking regions of the British Empire (*ibid.*). His complaint expressed the position of conservatives that hobby readers of romances and Gothic fiction wasted their time and endangered their morals. To keep patrons coming back for more, Lane advertised new titles: "The modern and valuable publications will be continually added to this Collection as they come from the Press; a written list of which is always kept at the Library for the inspection of Subscribers" (Blakey, 118). Among the fans of the 17,000 works at his circulating libraries were Ann RADCLIFFE, in Bath; Leigh Hunt, a patron of the Leadenhall Street library; and young Percy Bysshe SHELLEY, who checked out romances from the Brentford location.

Bibliography

Blakey, Dorothy. *The Minerva Press, 1790–1820.* London: Oxford University Press, 1939.

Clery, E. J. *The Rise of Supernatural Fiction, 1762–1800.* Cambridge: Cambridge University Press, 1995.

Gamer, Michael. *Romanticism and the Gothic: Genre, Reception, and Canon Formation.* Cambridge: Cambridge University Press, 2000.

Mangin, Edward. *An Essay on Light Reading.* London: Ridgway, 1805.

Stevens, David. *The Gothic Tradition.* Cambridge: Cambridge University Press, 2000.

claustrophobia

A psychological dread of confinement, DUNGEONS and PRISONS, insane asylums, PREMATURE BURIAL, patriarchal marriage, and emotional repression, claustrophobia is a recurrent motif in Gothic literature. Close quarters contribute to stories of helplessness and horror of impending doom from some unseen menace, a scenario developed in Greek myth with the heroics of Theseus, who conquered the Minotaur, a MONSTER concealed in a labyrinth on the island of Crete. William MUDFORD applied the confines of a shrinking dungeon cell in "The Iron Shroud" (1830), a story that proved popular as a GOTHIC BLUEBOOK. Edgar Allan POE thrived on claustrophobic elements, notably, enclosure and decapitation in the clock tower of a Gothic cathedral in "A Predicament" (1838), and wall burials in "THE BLACK CAT" (1843) and "THE CASK OF AMONTILLADO" (1846). In composing a too-hasty burial in "THE FALL OF THE HOUSE OF USHER" (1839), Poe refers to the Danish fantasist Baron Ludwig Holberg's *Nikolai Klimii Subterra-*neum (*The Subterranean Voyage of Nicholas Klimm,* 1741), a fictional journey from Norway to the afterlife. In a similar scenario in *Birdsong* (1997), Sebastian Faulks enhances the consuming passions of Stephen Wraysford with the suffocating tunnels and decaying remains of dead soldiers on the battlefields of World War I.

In FEMALE GOTHIC, claustrophobic elements reflect the circumscribed world of women. Protagonists tend to be trapped by patriarchy and forced into social roles that give no outlet for unfettered friendships, curiosity, adventure, or artistic expression, as is the case with the institutionalized wife in Charlotte Perkins GILMAN's "THE YELLOW WALLPAPER" (1892) and with Offred, the heroine locked in a chaste bedroom where a former captive hanged herself in Margaret ATWOOD's dystopic best-seller THE HANDMAID'S TALE (1985). In a break with woman-centered Gothic, Toni MORRISON paralleled male and female imprisonment by comparing the sufferings of slaves in BELOVED (1987). To picture the black male's nightly horror in a convict camp, she describes Paul D's immobilization in a box shut so tightly with bars that he can't raise a spoon to his lips. When rain triggers a mud slide, he communicates to the rest of the chain gang through yanks on their shackles and joins a coordinated plunge under the iron gate. Unlike the men's terror, Sethe, the protagonist, suffers the emotional suffocation of guilt for killing her baby girl to save her from life as a plantation breeder. Mirroring Paul D's chain gang cooperative, local women gather to pray in Sethe's front yard to exorcise the infantile ghost that enthralls her.

Bibliography

Gilbert, Sandra M., and Susan Gubar. *The Madwoman in the Attic,* 2nd ed. New Haven, Conn.: Yale University Press, 2000.

Williams, Anne. *Art of Darkness: A Poetics of Gothic.* Chicago: University of Chicago Press, 1995.

Coleridge, Samuel Taylor
(1772–1834)

An admirer of Friedrich von SCHILLER and a reader of William GODWIN, Charles Robert MATURIN, Ann RADCLIFFE, and Mary ROBINSON,

Samuel Taylor Coleridge was respected as both critic and poet. He was dreamy from childhood from immersion in the ORIENTAL ROMANCE of Antoine Galland's translation of *The Arabian Nights* (1704–17), filled with Sinbad's voyages to exotic locales and the magic of genies and Ali Baba, subverter of a den of thieves. In adulthood, Coleridge suffered agitation, insomnia, phantasmic DREAMS, and alcohol and opium addiction. Only through the treatment of Dr. James Gillman did he survive the ailments of his middle age to give full range to wonder, a beguiling theme in "KUBLA KHAN" (1816), a mystic, visionary fragment he produced by AUTOMATIC WRITING following profound sleep from a prescription drug.

To jolt readers into spontaneous emotional response to the gray area separating spirit and matter, Coleridge explored the far reaches of imaginative literature to include the SUPERNATURAL. Both a Gothic master and a severe critic of misapplied Gothicism, the poet pondered MELANCHOLY in "Fears in Solitude" (1798), MEDIEVALISM in "The Ballad of the Dark Ladie" (1798), and NATURE in "Frost at Midnight" (1798). He strayed more deeply into Gothicism with the DIABOLISM in "The Devil's Thoughts" (1799), the confinement motif in "This Lime-Tree Bower My Prison" (1800), and the spectral EXOTICISM in "A Tombless Epitaph" (ca. 1809) and "Limbo" (1817).

At the height of his verse powers, Coleridge produced an ALLEGORY of the wandering OUTSIDER and VAMPIRISM in an oft-quoted penance ballad, THE RIME OF THE ANCIENT MARINER (1798), and a spooky, perplexing lesbian seduction scene in "CHRISTABEL" (1816). In the former, a work similar to supernatural poems popular at the time, the poet invests a long narrative verse with inexplicable weather patterns, a bird OMEN, a curse for violating nature, and haunting by the walking dead. The life-in-death scenario is similar to the legend of the WANDERING JEW, which the poet read in Friedrich von Schiller's psychological novel DER GEISTERSEHER (*The Ghost-Seer*, 1786) and Matthew Gregory LEWIS's THE MONK (1796). Coleridge's guilt-ridden mariner, who is doomed to a cycle of telling his tale, encounters spirits from a snowy landscape and a trance state similar to traditional vampiric tales of animated corpses and automata. Both poems influenced Bram STOKER's DRACULA (1897), particularly in the count's ability to turn Lucy Westenra into a specter-woman.

Coleridge's exploration of the human psyche and his literary theories and verse inspired such contemporaries as the English essayist Charles Lamb and the poet Robert Southey. The American Gothic master Edgar Allan POE was an admirer of "Christabel" and "Kubla Khan" and student of *Biographia Literaria* (1817), the acme of romantic criticism. In a review of Coleridge's letters in June 1836 for the *Southern Literary Messenger*, Poe acknowledged his peer's greatheartedness and towering intellect, two qualities that American critics typically discounted. Sir Walter SCOTT, on the conservative side of Gothicism, found Coleridge too opaque and unwholesome; Scott believed these qualities negated the benefits of ROMANTICISM. A late 20th-century fan, the American poet and novelist James Dickey, applied Coleridge's style in *Deliverance* (1970), a stalker novel set in the southern Appalachians.

Bibliography

Bidney, Martin. "Spirit-bird, Bowshot, Water-snake, Corpses, Cosmic Love: Reshaping the Coleridge Legacy in Dickey's 'Deliverance,'" *Papers on Language & Literature* 31, no. 4 (fall 1995): 389–405.

Stevens, David. *The Gothic Tradition.* Cambridge: Cambridge University Press, 2000.

Twitchell, James B. *The Living Dead: A Study of the Vampire in Romantic Literature.* Durham, N.C.: Duke University Press, 1981.

Collins, Wilkie
(1824–1889)

A master of urban MELODRAMA, VIOLENCE, and MYSTERY, William Wilkie Collins was a prize storyteller and a major contributor to the DETECTIVE STORY genre and to URBAN GOTHIC. With Mary Elizabeth BRADDON, he shares the title of inventor of the sensational novel. A native Londoner well read in the NEWGATE NOVELS and occultism of Edward BULWER-LYTTON, Collins trained in the tea trade and read law at Lincoln's Inn. Out of preference for a more raffish, less constrictive life than the import-export business or the English courts, he began publishing at age 19, with a piece in the August 1843 issue of *Illuminated Magazine*.

Collins became a collaborator and traveling companion of the novelist Charles DICKENS, with whom Collins served on the staff of *Household Words*. In the Christmas 1855 issue, he published "The Ostler," a tale about a REVENANT or specter returned from the dead. He reissued the story as "The Dream Woman," a horrific narrative of a succubus who menaces the genitals of her male victim with a knife. The story marked his decision to become a full-time writer and prefaced frequent submissions to the *Atlantic*, *Cornhill Magazine*, *Harper's Weekly*, and *National Magazine*.

At his height, Collins produced *The Woman in White* (1860), the touchstone GASLIGHT THRILLER, a tale of lunacy and asylums set at a dark Elizabethan estate and reported by a series of narrators. The novel appeared serially in *All the Year Round* beginning in November 1859 and was so popular that crowds mobbed the magazine office for the next installment. Essential to the novel's appeal are the DISGUISE MOTIF and sequential narrations of core events, a layering technique that encloses a secret, an impetus to the imitative best-seller *Lady Audley's Secret* (1862) by his admirer Braddon. Collins's novel was translated into French and German and was a smash hit with Russian readers. In a review in 1865, the American novelist Henry JAMES characterized Collins's success in reshaping the GOTHIC NOVEL from a labored tale of castles and vampires to "those most mysterious of mysteries, the mysteries that are at our own doors" (Carnell, 159).

Collins followed his best-seller with *Armadale* (1866), a sensational action story of the adulterous Lydia Gwilt. The complex plot was so salacious that the *Westminster Review* presumed that Collins had stolen the criminal element from Braddon. The reviewer trashed the subject matter as a virus spreading "from the penny journal to the shilling magazine to the thirty shillings volume" (*ibid.*, 201). Collins reached greater popular success with a famous detective, the knowledgeable Sergeant Cuff, hero of the Gothic detective novel *THE MOONSTONE* (1868), which Collins produced under the influence of the opium he was taking as a treatment for his gout, and which was serialized in *All the Year Round*. The novel influenced the plotting

of Bram STOKER's *DRACULA* (1897) and was much admired by the poet and critic T. S. Eliot, the mystery romance writer Victoria HOLT, and the Gothic novelist Sheridan LE FANU. Five years later, Collins returned to SENSATIONALISM in *The New Magdalen* (1873), followed by *The Law and the Lady* (1875) and the GHOST STORY "Miss Jéromette and the Clergyman" (1875), a tale of guilt and SUPERSTITION. He made a late success with *The Black Robe* (1880), an anti-Catholic psychological novel serialized in the *Canadian Monthly*.

Bibliography

Beetz, Kirk H. *Wilkie Collins: An Annotated Bibliography.* Metuchen, N.J.: Scarecrow, 1978.

Carnell, Jennifer. *The Literary Lives of Mary Elizabeth Braddon.* Hastings, Sussex: Sensation Press, 2000.

Pearl, Nancy. "Gaslight Thrillers: The Original Victorians," *Library Journal* 126, no. 3 (February 15, 2001): 228.

Schmitt, Cannon. *Alien Nation: Nineteenth-Century Gothic Fictions and English Nationality.* Philadelphia: University of Pennsylvania Press, 1997.

colonial Gothic

Oriental settings, ARABESQUE motifs, and the barbarism inflicted on primitive societies generated a vast wing of GOTHIC FICTION and pervaded a range of writings. English Gothic works—such as Wilkie COLLINS's *THE MOONSTONE* (1868), "The Phantom Rickshaw" (1888) and other Indian horror stories by Rudyard KIPLING, and Arthur Conan DOYLE's SHERLOCK HOLMES stories—bear the menace of horrific NIGHTMARES, curses and vendettas, bizarre weapons, and exotic poisons imported from less civilized realms. In the early 20th century, the horrors of genocide and the ill-gotten assets of colonial entrepreneurs filled Joseph CONRAD's *HEART OF DARKNESS* (1902), the story of the OUTSIDER Kurtz's deterioration from greedy ivory merchant to brutalizer of black Africans. W. W. JACOBS's classic HORROR NARRATIVE "THE MONKEY'S PAW" (1902) examines the effects of a SUPERNATURAL artifact imported to England from the Empire. Late in the century, Sam Watson, an Australian aborigine, depicted VIOLENCE and SHAPESHIFTING in *The Kadaitcha Sung* (1990), a tale of

Terror (1926). Angela CARTER and Joyce Carol OATES reprised the *contes cruels* in late 20th-century FEMALE GOTHIC works with plots highlighting society's cruelties against women. Toni MORRISON particularized the barbarities of slaving vessels and plantation servitude in the novel BELOVED (1987).

Bibliography
Villiers de L'Isle-Adam. *Cruel Tales.* London: Oxford University Press, 1963.
Voltaire. *Candide.* New York: Signet, 1961.

Corelli, Marie
(1855–1924)

A popularizer of ghost stories, EXOTICISM, and the occult, Marie Corelli was one of England's most lauded novelists of the 1890s. Born Marie Mills Mackay in London of Anglo-Scots parentage, she grew up in a liberal household and displayed a talent for music before venturing into freelance writing under her Italian pen name, which means "little heart." From *The Romance of Two Worlds* (1886), she progressed immediately to a horror novel, *Vendetta!; or, The Story of One Forgotten* (1886) and *Ardath: The Story of a Dead Self* (1889), a baroque novel on astral projection that achieved popular notoriety and earned the praise of William Ewart Gladstone, a prime minister during the reign of Queen Victoria.

Corelli was adept at glamour, SECRECY, and vendettas. Her next novel, *The Soul of Lilith* (1892), is a Faustian plot questioning the meaning of psychic and spiritual phenomena. Corelli turned to historical MELODRAMA with *Barabbas: A Dream of the World's Tragedy* (1893), a decadent Gothic masterwork that proposed her own vision of Christianity and DIABOLISM. She issued a sequel, *The Sorrows of Satan; or, The Strange Experience of One Geoffrey Tempest, Millionaire* (1895), a mystical study of drawing-room vice that became England's first runaway best-seller. Its popularity boosted her earnings to the star range of £10,000 per book.

Late in her career, Corelli produced ghost stories for *Strand* magazine and pursued occultism with a study of METEMPSYCHOSIS in Egypt in *Ziska: The Problem of a Wicked Soul* (1897). In 1906, she published *The Treasures of Heaven*, which sold 100,000 copies within hours of its distribution to bookshops. Her fan base included the actresses Lillie Langtry and Ellen Terry; Queen Victoria, who ordered a complete set of Corelli's books; Czarina Alexandria of Russia; and King Edward VII, who invited the popular Gothicist to his coronation.

Bibliography
Forward, Stephanie. "Idol of Suburbia: Marie Corelli and Late-Victorian Culture," *Critical Survey* 13, no. 2 (May 2001): 141–144.
Moers, Ellen. *Literary Women.* New York: Oxford University Press, 1977.

Crane, Ichabod

In Washington Irving's atmospheric FOOL TALE "The Legend of Sleepy Hollow," published in *The Sketch Book of Geoffrey Crayon, Gent.* (1820), Ichabod Crane is a victim of a rival's SADISM. As a result, the hapless, well-meaning schoolmaster suffers a breakdown and vanishes. In happier times, Ichabod displays the heightened suggestibility of a listener who quails at ghostly STORYTELLING. His naiveté gives his rival, "Brom Bones" Van Brunt, an easy method of removing an obstacle to romance with Katrina van Tassel without committing any more VIOLENCE than tossing a jack-o-lantern in fun.

To heighten emotional response in reader and victim, Irving sets the Gothic scene "under the sway of some witching power that holds a spell over the minds of the good people," leaving them open to belief in SUPERNATURAL visions and sounds of a famed headless Hessian rider (Irving, 3–4). Ichabod, who is by nature inward and moody, goes to the woods on a peaceful mission to gather grapes and entertain himself by singing hymns and writing verses about Katrina. The author stresses that his protagonist's surname describes his gangly body and loose, stork-like frame. The imagery foreshadows the spooking of a softy by the local bully, whom Irving describes as a Tartar. Assailed by horror lodged in his overactive imagination, the gentle, well-intentioned Ichabod becomes a victim of ROMANTICISM. His name passes into community LEGEND as the innocent quarry of the "galloping Hessian" (*ibid.*, 66).

Bibliography

Benoit, Raymond. "Irving's 'The Legend of Sleepy Hollow,'" *Explicator* 55, no. 1 (fall 1996): 15–17.

Irving, Washington. *The Legend of Sleepy Hollow.* New York: Tor, 1990.

Piacentino, Ed. "'Sleepy Hollow' Comes South: Washington Irving's Influence on Old Southwestern Humor," *Southern Literary Journal* 30, no. 1 (fall 1997): 27–42.

Smith, Greg. "Supernatural Ambiguity and Possibility in Irving's 'The Legend of Sleepy Hollow,'" *Midwest Quarterly* 42, no. 2 (winter 2001): 174.

Crimes of the Heart
Beth Henley
(1979)

Deceptive in its amiable ATMOSPHERE, Beth Henley's play *Crimes of the Heart* explores a family's off-kilter past, a source of SOUTHERN GOTHIC commentary on dysfunctional parenting. A reunion of the three McGrath sisters precedes a discussion of the jailing of the youngest, Babe Botrelle, for shooting her husband Zackery, a lowlife county politician. Meg, a would-be singer, and Lenny, the dotty, still-at-home spinster, huddle with Babe, who exits jail and defends herself from an arbitrary decision to have her "put away" (Henley, 31).

Henley distributes Gothic touches in pinches and dabs. The ensuing comic MELODRAMA reveals grim scenarios in the girls' troubled past—their child-abusing father deserted the family and their despairing mother hanged herself and the family cat. More recently, their horse Billy Boy was killed by lightning and their grandfather lies moribund from stroke. Babe summarizes the author's philosophy: "Life sure can be miserable" (*ibid.*, 97). In the estimation of Chick Boyle, a snoopy, intrusive cousin, the family tendency toward catastrophe derives from innate character flaws: "You trashy McGraths and your trashy ways: hanging yourselves in cellars; carrying on with married men; shooting your own husbands" (*ibid.*, 112). Henley's deft handling of tragedy and an upbeat ending assure audiences that Southern Gothic need not go to extremes to express a range of human emotion. The 1986 film version featured an all-star cast of Jessica Lange, Diane Keaton, and Sissy Spacek as the three McGraths.

Bibliography

Hargrove, Nancy D. "The Tragicomic Vision of Beth Henley's Drama," *Southern Quarterly* 22, no. 4 (summer 1984): 54–70.

Henley, Beth. *Crimes of the Heart.* New York: Penguin, 1981.

Laughlin, Karen L. "Criminality, Desire, and Community: A Feminist Approach to Beth Henley's *Crimes of the Heart*," *Women and Performance*, no. 5 (1986): 35–51.

The Crimson Petal and the White
Michel Faber
(2003)

Dutch-Australian writer Michel Faber, a resident of Scotland, revisited the Victorian domestic novel to fashion *The Crimson Petal and the White*, an escapist fiction set in London's Gothic underworld in 1874 and 1875. In foul slums and amid seamy characters lives Sugar, the clever, energetic prostitute who becomes mistress of the perfume and soap manufacturer William Rackham. Faber addresses the reader and introduces an ominous Gothic maze, the mucky, foul-odored backstreets of the metropolis, where the procuress Mrs. Castaway introduced the 13-year-old Sugar to whoring: "Watch your step. Keep your wits about you; you will need them. This city I am bringing you to is vast and intricate, and you have not been here before" (Faber, 5). The warning precedes repeated character journeys on dangerous thoroughfares that suggest the degenerate underside of the good life.

Heavy on irony, the text follows the MELANCHOLY musings of a feminist writer-prostitute from a gritty, ill-lit bawdyhouse at Church Lane, St. Giles, to elevation as a kept woman. Using sexual guile as bait, she obtains permanent residence with the wealthy Rackham, a smarmy industrialist who deserts the economic prestige and social prominence of his family's sweet-smelling cosmetics line to prowl rank urban stews. While bettering herself, Sugar mentors her dunderheaded lover on ways to improve cosmetic sales by upgrading his factory's lackluster soap wrappers. Her FOIL or alternate "petal," Rackham's neurasthenic wife Agnes, is a cyclical hysteric who poses as the respectable Victorian lady of the house. Monthly, she raves over the appearance of her menses, which throw her into despair and withdrawal to a darkened bedroom. Her suicide by drowning reaches a peak of MELODRAMA when William ogles the frail breasts of her corpse and suffers brief pangs of remorse for neglecting a woman he once loved.

Critics find in the neo-Victorian plot echoes of William Makepeace Thackeray's satire, Charles DICKENS's hatred of hypocrisy, and character parallels to Charlotte BRONTË's governess JANE EYRE, womanizer Edward ROCHESTER, and Bertha ROCHESTER, the madwoman in the attic. Just as Jane retrieves herself from a dire situation on the moors, Sugar relies on inner strength to empower her flight from London with a stash of capital and Rackham's neglected daughter Sophie in tow. Faber colors the story with laudanum binges, hallucinations of angels, chemical birth control, and a protracted home abortion accomplished in a bathtub. Richly satisfying in its comeuppance to the smug, brothel-crawling elite, Faber's novel successfully applies GOTHIC CONVENTION, elements of the GASLIGHT THRILLER, and the FLIGHT MOTIF to social criticism.

Bibliography

Abrams, Rebecca. Review of *The Crimson Petal and the White*, by Michael Faber, *New Statesman* 131, no. 4,609 (October 14, 2002): 55.

Review of *The Crimson Petal and the White*, by Michael Faber, *Kirkus Reviews* 70, no. 15 (August 1, 2002): 1,059.

Faber, Michael. *The Crimson Petal and the White*. Orlando, Fla.: Harvest Books, 2003.

Kincaid, James R. "*The Crimson Petal and the White*: The Victorian Nanny Diaries," *New York Times*, (September 15, 2002): 7, 14.

Lyall, Sarah. "A Writer's Tale Is Victorian; His Past, Gothic," *New York Times*, (October 28, 2002): E1.

The Crucible
Arthur Miller
(1953)

Arthur Miller's anti-Puritan stage parable *The Crucible*, his only history play, is a stellar contribution to AMERICAN GOTHIC. After developing an admiration of Fyodor Dostoyevsky's novels and earning a degree in journalism, Miller became one of the nation's prime playwrights and a two-time Pulitzer Prize winner. He wrote the play during the communist witch-hunt, red-baiting, and blacklisting of suspected subversives of the 1950s. For analogy, the text returns to a source of New England Gothic, the mass executions of suspected sorcerers of 1692 that had intrigued Nathaniel HAWTHORNE. At the heart of Miller's play is his concern for ambiguous morality, conscience, and individual responsibility, three themes he shared with Hawthorne.

Miller builds drama by recreating an era when sanity gives way to mass hysteria among the ultra-righteous zealots of the Massachusetts theocracy. Domestic unrest in the home of Elizabeth and John Proctor takes on community meaning after the authorities of Salem enter the residence and arrest Elizabeth. Miller depicts the "barbaric frontier inhabited by a sect of fanatics" as the source of an illogic that escalates to a national incident of terror (Miller, 2). He blends FRONTIER GOTHIC with COLONIAL GOTHIC by citing claims of "reddish work" committed by marauding Indians and the persecution of the slave Tituba for teaching young girls the incantations common to West Indies voodoo (*ibid.*, 17). Exacerbating Salem's disapproval are the pseudo-learned sources of the Reverend John Hale, who legitimizes SUPERSTITIONs about incubi, succubi, and wizards with a stout claim: "We cannot look to superstition in this. The Devil is precise; the marks of his presence are definite as stone" (*ibid.*, 35).

The themes of *The Crucible* are well interwoven, beginning with public hysteria and moving into the Proctor household to reveal marital unhappiness, jealousy, and betrayal. Injustice arises from Abigail Williams's spite at her former lover, Judge Hathorne's unrelenting evil, and unsubstantiated claims that a midwife killed Ann and Thomas Putnam's seven infants. The community's clutch of adolescent girls who have rebelled against public morality box themselves in with lies and mad playacting at demonic POSSESSION. The moral contretemps leads Abigail to claim that Tituba made her drink blood. Abigail sticks her abdomen with a long needle, a sadistic act that is intended to prove her charges of witchcraft in Salem.

Miller relies heavily on SYMBOLs to express his Gothic intent. Beginning with the title, an image of an earthenware vessel in which smithies melt metal, he creates irony with a suggestion of America as the melting pot of immigrants. The term *crucible* also connects with crucifixion. The author stresses the frontier forest, a Gothic setting suited to conjurations with Satan, and concludes at the gallows by sunrise, where John chooses martyrdom over dishonor for himself and his family. Tested in a public crucible, John rises above colonial ignorance, moral rigidity, and controversy over nonexistent OCCULTISM.

Bibliography

Budick, E. Miller. "History and Other Spectres in *The Crucible*," *Modern Drama* 28, no. 4 (December 1985): 535–552.

Griffin, Caroline. *Understanding Arthur Miller.* Columbia: University of South Carolina Press, 1996.

Miller, Arthur. *The Crucible.* New York: Bantam Books, 1959.

Martine, James J. *The Crucible: Politics, Property, and Pretense.* New York: Twayne, 1993.

Cruikshank, George
(1792–1878)

A producer of popular caricatures and a major contributor to Victorian Gothic lore, the Scottish artist George Cruikshank illustrated classic works as well as pamphlets and prints, playing cards, GOTHIC BLUEBOOKs, and crime novels. He was born into an artistic family and chose a career in publishing in his teens. He quickly outpaced a grandfather as well as his father Isaac and brother Isaac Robert by impacting mass culture with mildly humorous satire that focused on GROTESQUE beings, ATMOSPHERE, and MOOD.

Cruikshank's graphic denunciation of alcohol abuse and political corruption connected with the popular imagination and furthered his social reform agenda. After issuing an 1827 edition of *Grimms' Fairy Tales*, which he rewrote and adorned with sepia copperplate engravings of Rumplestiltskin, witches, and goblins, he suffered the reproof of Charles DICKENS, who demanded in a review for *Household Words* that FAIRY TALES not be altered. Nonetheless, for his skill in adorning some 900 works, and the pages of *Ainsworth's, Satirist, Scourge,* and *Town Talk* magazines, Cruikshank earned the admiration of the art critic John Ruskin and the novelist William Makepeace Thackeray and acquired the sobriquet "the Venerable George" (Goldern, 680).

Cruikshank partnered with writer Payne Collier to issue a volume of Gothic puppet episodes titled *The Tragic Comedy or Comical Tragedy of Punch and Judy* (1828), featuring steel etchings that capture the SUBTEXT of treachery, VIOLENCE, and misogyny. After meeting novelist and fellow social reformer Dickens in 1836, the artist began illustrating *Bentley's Miscellany.* He provided provocative line art for Dickens's *Sketches by Boz* (1836) and OLIVER TWIST (1838), for which he produced a sketch of the VILLAIN Bill Sikes trying to murder his dog. A specialist in Gothic scenarios, Cruikshank also adorned William Harrison AINSWORTH's NEWGATE NOVEL *Rookwood* (1834) and *The Tower of London* (1840) and illustrated Sir Walter SCOTT's Waverley series.

Bibliography

"Cruikshank Artwork at Princeton University Library," http://libweb5.princeton.edu/Visual_Materials/cruikshank/.

Goldern, Catherine J. "George Cruikshank's Life, Times, and Art, vol. 2: 1835–1878," *Victorian Studies* 40, no. 4 (summer 1997): 680–682.

Jackson, Trevor. "Demon Drink: George Cruikshank's 'The Worship of Bacchus' in Focus," *British Medical Journal* 322, no. 7,300 (June 16, 2001): 1,494.

D

Dacre, Charlotte
(ca. 1782–ca. 1841)

A poet, satirist, and contributor to GOTHIC BLUE-BOOKs, Charlotte King Dacre Byrne populated her GOTHIC NOVELs with FEMME FATALEs capable of STALKING, aggression and violence, sexual rivalry, and physical desires. Dacre was fatherless from the age of six after John King, a bankrupt Jewish financier and blackmailer, went to debtor's prison. Out of love for him, she and her sister, Sophia King, composed a juvenile Gothic miscellany, *Trifles from Helicon* (1798). At age 23, Dacre produced *Hours in Solitude* (1805) and, in imitation of Matthew Gregory LEWIS's THE MONK (1796), she wrote *The Confessions of the Nun of St. Omer* (1805), a three-volume Gothic novel issued under the pseudonym Rosa Matilda Charlotte and dedicated to Lewis. In her introduction, "Apostrophe to the Critics," she comments on reviewers' tendency to denounce Gothic works as obscure and senseless.

Lewis's descriptions of sexual pleasures permeated Dacre's next work, *Zofloya; or, The Moor* (1806), a cautionary novel based on spine-chilling Jacobean stage plays and featuring crude psychology and the occult through alchemy, hypnotism, and telepathy. She exploits the titillating fear-of-rape plot by pitting a virile satanic tempter against Lilla, a sexually repressed female whom he murders by pushing her over a cliff. More shocking for the times was the female VILLAIN Laurina, the miscreant daughter of the Marchese di Loredania. Haughty and willful, Laurina outdistances male villains in guile and iniquity with her sexual depravity and knowledge of poison and potions.

In chapbook form, the abridged *Zofloya* appeared as *The Daemon of Venice* (1810); it influenced ZASTROZZI (1810) and *St. Irvyne* (1810), two experimental Gothic novels by Percy Bysshe SHELLEY, who read Dacre's Gothic works at the Brentford location of William Lane's popular CIRCULATING LIBRARIES. Dacre followed with a DOMESTIC GOTHIC tale, *The School for Friends* (ca. 1800), and a Gothic erotic novel, *The Libertine* (1807), a wildly speculative exposé of upper-class debauchery. Popular with middle-class readers, it went through three English versions and, in 1816, a French translation.

Bibliography

Dunn, James A. "Charlotte Dacre and the Feminization of Violence," *Nineteenth-Century Literature* 53, no. 3 (December 1998): 307.

Gamer, Michael. *Romanticism and the Gothic: Genre, Reception, and Canon Formation.* Cambridge: Cambridge University Press, 2000.

Hoeveler, Diane Long. *Gothic Feminism.* University Park: Pennsylvania State University Press, 1998.

Horner, Avril, ed. *European Gothic: A Spirited Exchange 1760–1960.* Manchester: Manchester University Press, 2002.

danse macabre

In medieval and Renaissance art and writing, the danse macabre ("dance of death") was a morbid motif portraying skeletons and ghoulish phantasms leading victims in an allegorical jig to their graves. The doomed formed a montage of humanity—a procession of male and female, old and young, and a variety of professions and social classes, from pope to beggar. Graphic details of the dance of death motif feature skulls and bones, mournful expressions, and a fascination with death as the great equalizer. In some depictions, the grand parade leads directly to Hellmouth, a depiction of damnation.

The danse macabre suited the eyewitness art and literature emerging from the Black Death, a world epidemic of plague that began in 1345. One of the renowned writers of ghoulish death imagery was Florentine fabulist Giovanni Boccaccio, author of the *Decamerone* (*The Decameron*, 1353), a compendium of fabliaux and short stories. In *The Canterbury Tales* (ca. 1385), Geoffrey Chaucer applied the hellish procession to *The Pardoner's Tale*, in which three seekers go on a quest for death.

The spectral dance emerged anew in the 19th-century GOTHIC NOVEL and GOTHIC BLUEBOOK. One story, "The Dance of the Dead" (ca. 1810), reprises a Silesian legend that reads like a hellish version of "The Pied Piper of Hamlin": At the tolling of midnight, "Corpses and skeletons, shrouded and bare, tall and small, men and women, all running to and fro, dancing and turning, wheeling and whirling round the player, quicker and more slow according to the measure he played" (Haining, 233). In Bram STOKER's vampire classic DRACULA (1897), the cerebral Dutchman, Dr. Van Helsing, suffers a fit of hysteria at the funeral of Lucy Westenra. He envisions "Bleeding hearts, and dry bones of the churchyard, and tears that burn as they fall—all dance together to the music that he make with that smileless mouth of him" (Stoker, 183–184). Acknowledging a perversion of the Christian concept of resurrection and the GROTESQUE, his frenetic words spiel on. The scholarly physician and folklorist chuckles in horror at the burial of the un-dead Lucy, whom he knows will return to earth to stalk and suck the blood of her victims.

Bibliography

Haining, Peter, ed. *Gothic Tales of Terror*. New York: Taplinger Publishing, 1972.

Stoker, Bram. *Dracula*. New York: Bantam Books, 1981.

Turner, Alice K. *The History of Hell*. New York: Harcourt Brace & Co., 1993.

Danvers, Mrs.

The unofficial chatelaine of MANDERLEY in Daphne DU MAURIER's REBECCA (1938), Mrs. Danvers is one of the more sinister female VILLAINs in Gothic literature. A twisted emblem standing lone and silent like a crag on the shore, she is both nurse and firebrand, the adoring duenna of the master's first wife and the arsonist who destroys Manderley, the de Winter ancestral estate. In the first role, she so spoiled and catered to Rebecca DE WINTER that the housekeeper condoned the girl's illicit love for a cousin, Jack Favell, and, after her death, delights at Rebecca's audacity and deceit. In nightly brushings of Rebecca's hair, the beloved "Danny" stroked away her mistress's tensions while sharing in her ridicule of husband, lover, and other men who fawned over the silky smooth beauty.

Du Maurier portrays the housekeeper as the coach and cheerleader in a Gothic tug-of-war. Through the earthly agency of Mrs. Danvers, Rebecca's presence refuses to relinquish Manderley to Maxim's unnamed second wife, the story's narrator. The gaunt, disapproving housekeeper goads the NAIF, whose efforts to take charge of home and husband fall short of the heroine's image of her predecessor. As though voicing the discontent of a peevish REVENANT, Mrs. Danvers scorns and undermines the new wife by promoting domestic dissension and by emphasizing unflattering differences in the two women, particularly Rebecca's poise and strength versus her successor's awkwardness and dependence. The author shapes Rebecca's spirit as that of a boy, a hint at an androgynous character for whom the housekeeper may have harbored a homoerotic lust. Du Maurier further complicates the characterization with descriptions of INSANITY, picturing Rebecca "raving like a mad-woman, a fanatic, her long fingers twisting and tearing the black stuff of her dress" (du Maurier, 243).

In the plot resolution, du Maurier shifts much of the evil away from Rebecca to her devoted

Danny by revealing the first wife's intentional provocation of the shooting to end her life before cancer could kill her. As flames devour Manderley, the evil housekeeper slips away through the woods like Grendel, the elusive beast that stalks the night. Ironically, it is the jeopardizing of the second marriage and the midnight cleansing of the estate with fire that inadvertently exorcises Rebecca's ghost. The loss of their grand home equalizes the de Winters by ridding Max of a guilty conscience and his new wife of illogical fears and balances their lives with mutual love and dependence.

Bibliography

du Maurier, Daphne. *Rebecca*. New York: Avon Books, 1971.

Fleenor, Juliann E., ed. *The Female Gothic*. Montreal: Eden Press, 1983.

Nigro, Kathleen Butterly. "Rebecca as Desdemona: 'A Maid That Paragons Description and Wild Fame,'" *College Literature* 27, no. 3 (fall 2000): 144.

The Da Vinci Code
Dan Brown
(2003)

Based on histories of the Priory of Sion and the Knights Templar, Dan Brown's *The Da Vinci Code* is a critical and commercial blockbuster that sold 4.3 million copies in nine months. A 21st-century ILLUMINATI NOVEL plotted like a murder mystery, it depicts an occult society formed in 1099 at the end of the First Crusade to protect the Holy Grail, an object of intrigue and a source of ROMANTICISM since the Middle Ages. In a prefatory scene, Brown details the cruelty of a "horribly drawn-out death" in the Louvre's Grand Gallery: "For fifteen minutes, [curator Jacques Saunier] would survive as his stomach acids seeped into his chest cavity, slowly poisoning him from within" (Brown, 5). The perpetrators are assassins dispatched by the Opus Dei, a secret society whose operation launches stalkings across Europe to protect a mystic heritage, the children of the clandestine marriage of Mary Magdalene and Jesus Christ.

Brown builds suspense from medieval SUPER-STITION, the DISGUISE MOTIF, ESCAPISM, a SUBTEXT of anti-Catholicism, and a series of cliffhangers that lead to the identity of protectors of religious patriarchy. These woman-hating males suppress the history of female involvement during the formative years of Christianity, thus creating an all-male bastion of religiosity and social and economic power. The brilliant mind that unravels the Gothic plot is, ironically, a woman—Saunier's granddaughter, Sophie Nevue, a turncoat Paris cop and cryptographer who leads symbologist Robert Langdon through a maze of real and false clues. Implications of a corrupt Catholic hierarchy derive from the unscrambling of word, number, and tarot puzzles and from bizarre interpretations of Leonardo da Vinci's *Mona Lisa* and *The Last Supper*. Grim in TONE and replete with SENSATIONALISM, including ritual self-torment and the struggles of a dying man to encode a message to his survivors, the novel succeeds by interweaving traditional GOTHIC CONVENTION with the breakneck pacing of a spy thriller.

Bibliography

Kantrowitz, Barbara, et al. "The Bible's Lost Stories," *Newsweek* 142, no. 23 (December 8, 2003): 48–56.

Klinghoffer, David. "Religious Fiction," *National Review* 55, no. 23 (December 8, 2003): 48–49.

McCormick, Patrick. "Painted Out of the Picture," *U.S. Catholic* 68, no. 11 (November 2003): 36–38.

Miesel, Sandra. "Dismantling *The Da Vinci Code*," *Crisis*, September 1, 2003.

Reidy, Maurice Timothy. "Breaking the Code," *Commonweal* 130, no. 15 (September 12, 2003): 46.

decadence

A marked stylistic shift in a significant literary period, decadence typically takes shape through overdevelopment, self-conscious attention to detail, and relaxing of more conservative standards. As a result, spiritual confusion, deliberate perversity, nostalgia for youth and innocence, and artificiality creep in, altering genres with deviations from the original form. Decadence redirected classic Gothic art by emphasizing SENSATIONALISM, EXOTICISM, and extremes of ornamentation. The lapse from purity of neoclassic principles reached a liberal extreme in the Marquis de Sade's *Les Crimes de l'Amour* (*The Crimes of Love*, 1788), a compendium of sadomasochism, torture, and gratuitous eroticism that met with public censure. Essentially pessimistic and antiromantic in its thrust, decadent art of the 19th century portrayed destruction, urban deterioration, satanic heroes, and escapism through vice and alcohol and opium consumption, the focus of Thomas De Quincey's *Confessions of an English Opium Eater*, which he published in *London Magazine* in 1821, and his *Suspiria de Profundis* (Sighs from the Depths), issued in 1845 in BLACKWOOD'S EDINBURGH MAGAZINE. The popular press capitalized on working-class taste for HORROR FICTION and sensationalism by issuing the GOTHIC BLUEBOOK, the NEWGATE NOVEL, CONTES CRUELS, and the GASLIGHT THRILLER, and by serializing slasher crime and potboilers in popular magazines.

A period of mounting indolence, hopelessness, and compromised morality reached its height with Charles BAUDELAIRE's darkly romantic verse collection *Les Fleurs du Mal* (*The Flowers of Evil*, 1857) and the short stories of Théophile GAUTIER anthologized in *La Morte Amoreuse* (The dead lover, 1836), a forerunner of Bram STOKER's classic vampire novel DRACULA (1897). In the late 1880s, VILLIERS DE L'ISLE-ADAM pursued a narrow subgenre of VIOLENCE and sadism in his *contes cruels* ("cruel tales"), which overemphasized suffering, despair, and the anticipation of death. During the 1890s, languor, HYPERBOLE, theatricality, and bizarre themes infiltrated Gothic literature throughout Europe as artists extolled a self-indulgent philosophy of *l'art pour l'art* ("art for art's sake"). In France, disenchantment and libertinism overcame influential writers, notably the poets Stéphane Mallarmé and Paul Verlaine; Flanders produced its own Gothic specialist, Joris-Karl Huysmans, author of the black mass exposé in *Là-Bas* (*Down There*, 1891) and *Against the Grain* (1884), a novel chronicling an immersion in arcana that caught the attention of Oscar WILDE and H. P. LOVECRAFT.

The last stage of European decadence produced some of its most controversial Gothic works. In England's fin de siècle ("end of the century") period, the short fiction and verse of Ernest Dowson and the writings of Arthur Llewellyn Jones-Machen and Wilde epitomized flamboyant decadence and a fashionable despair. Heavily castigated for un-

wholesomeness were Machen's *The Great God Pan* (1894) and *The Three Imposters* (1895) as well as Wilde's novel THE PICTURE OF DORIAN GRAY (1891) and the historical play SALOMÉ (1893), which Wilde published with evocative illustrations by Aubrey Beardsley. In Italy, the novelist Gabriele D'Annunzio explored passion, sensuality, and murder in *L'Innocente* (The Innocent, 1892), a tale of betrayal, adultery, and debauchery among Rome's aristocracy. In Germany, the depraved SADISM and VAMPIRISM of Hanns Heinz EWERS resulted in vulgar extremes that presaged the barbaric and inhuman medical experiments launched by Adolf Hitler's Nazi regime.

Bibliography
Hanson, Ellis. *Decadence and Catholicism*. Cambridge, Mass.: Harvard University Press, 1998.

de la Mare, Walter
(1873–1956)
An influence on the ghostly STORYTELLING of Edith WHARTON, the English poet and writer Walter de la Mare produced dreamy verse, FAIRY TALES, and stories of magic. He tinged his fearful narratives with fantasy, REVENANTs, graveyards, and evil spirits. Gothic elements lurk in his titles, as with "Out of the Deep" (1923), "All Hallows" (1926), "The Lost Track" (1926), "Hodmadod" (1933), and "What Dreams May Come" (1936), a title taken from William Shakespeare's *Hamlet* (ca. 1599). Strands of menace and the SUPERNATURAL in common settings produced tension in works intended for young readers and adults, as found in the frequently anthologized poem "The Listeners" (1912).

In prose, de la Mare departed from the graceful lyricism of his verse to sketch weird plots—for example, the cat practicing sorcery with his paws in "Broomsticks" (1925), an enchanting Oriental setting in "The Recluse" (1930), and a shy fairy wishing to remain anonymous in "The Scarecrow" (1945). His placement of evil within family dominates "Seaton's Aunt" (1923), a DOMESTIC GOTHIC tale that focuses on a murderous blind woman. He incorporated psychological examinations of motivation in "Miss Jemima" (1925), in which an evil presence poses as a child's rescuer, and in "Alice's Godmother" (1925), in which the title character promises Alice a life without death. De la Mare created a panoply of macabre character behavior: a child's recognition of an alter ego in the haunting tale "The Looking Glass" (1923); a spirit's search for his burial plot in "Strangers Pilgrims" (1926); and the soul of French pirate Nicholas Sabathier inhabiting the body of a visitor to a cemetery in *The Return* (1910), his most famous novel. In one of his juxtapositions of VIOLENCE and innocence, he describes a child's death at the hands of a demon in "The Guardian" (1955). De la Mare's verses and fiction earned the praise of the poets W. H. Auden and T. S. Eliot, the novelist Graham Greene, and the fantasist H. P. LOVECRAFT.

Bibliography

Hecht, Anthony. "Walter de la Mare," *Wilson Quarterly* 21, no. 3 (summer 1997): 108–109.

Manwaring, Randle. "Memories of Walter de la Mare," *Contemporary Review* 264, no. 1,538 (March 1994): 149–152.

Der Geisterseher
(The Ghost-Seer)
Friedrich von Schiller
(1786)

The German playwright and critic Friedrich von SCHILLER composed a significant contribution to the psychological novel in *Der Geisterseher (The Ghost-Seer)*, which he narrated through letters and nested stories. He set the unfinished story in Venice, a venal society where a MELANCHOLY prince, living in penury, encounters a masked Armenian stranger who prophesies serious incidents to come. The boldly anti-Catholic plot develops Oriental touches from the mysterious movements of the Armenian, and SECRECY through the intrigues of a secret body of Venetian males who murder as a means of establishing justice.

Schiller builds MYSTERY and SUSPENSE at a fair where a phony conjurer pretends to summon the ghost of the Marquis of Lanoy, the prince's friend. Schiller debunks the mechanics of NECROMANCY, which require a black circle on the floor, a Chaldee bible, skull, silver crucifix on an altar, burning wine, frankincense, and an amulet suspended from a chain of human hair. A convoluted DISGUISE MOTIF heightens the story, which presents the unnamed Armenian also as a Russian and a Franciscan friar, identities adopted as well by the WANDERING JEW. The intent of the tale is a moral and spiritual change in the prince, a theme that Schiller explored as the purpose of didactic sensational writings.

Bibliography

Anderson, George K. *The Legend of the Wandering Jew.* Providence, R.I.: Brown University Press, 1965.

Chaitkin, Gabriel. "'For He Was One of Us': Friedrich Schiller, the Poet of America," *American Almanac,* October 1996.

Horner, Avril, ed. *European Gothic: A Spirited Exchange, 1760–1960.* Manchester: Manchester University Press, 2002.

detective story

A subset of the MYSTERY genre, and an outgrowth of and successor to the GASLIGHT THRILLER, detective fiction allies the Gothic elements of SUSPENSE, intrigue, terror, and VIOLENCE with keen deductive logic, such as the precision of the fingerprinter in Mark Twain's *Pudd'nhead Wilson* (1894). Key to the detective plot is the STALKING of criminals or phantasms. Similar in characterization and events to medieval romances, the detective story is a domesticated Gothic genre that offers an accepted outlet for human curiosity about crime and violence. In the words of the literary historian C. A. Brady, the plot "allows the reader to run with the hounds at the same time as he doubles with the hare" (*New Catholic* 4, 809). The result is a satisfying immersion in puzzle solutions amid moral disorder and often romantic ATMOSPHERE. Critics of the genre note the importance of action and shocking incident to the detriment of character development, a quality the detective story shares with the sensational novel.

Essential to detective fiction is a triad of characterizations: one or more innocent suspects toward whom evidence seems to point; unimaginative police who bungle the investigation; and a detective, usually a freelancing agent or amateur problem-solver, a divergent thinker who is keener of eye and wit than the officials of the civil bureaucracy. Frequently, a lesser intellect, a junior investigator or partner, accompanies the star detective—a classic pairing that Sir Arthur Conan DOYLE originated with Sherlock HOLMES and his friend and aide Dr. Watson. Investigations typically focus on crimes motivated by middle-class greed and selfishness and conclude with a surprising denouement—the refutation of too-obvious clues and red herrings by arcane, superficial evidence that establishes the innocence of the original suspect. The Italian medieval scholar Umberto ECO advanced Doyle's prototypes with Brother William of Baskerville and his apprentice Adso in a detective murder mystery, *The Name of the Rose* (1980), set in a northern Italian monastery in 1327.

The detective genre has many forerunners, beginning with German *Kriminalgeschichte* ("criminal history"), a series of true crime stories from the mid-18th century that publishers collected and issued in volumes. Fictional sleuthing evolved through such NEWGATE NOVELS, as Voltaire's *Zadig* (1747), Charles Brockden BROWN's amateur sleuth novel *EDGAR HUNTLY; or, Memoirs of a Sleepwalker* (1799), and E. T. A. HOFFMANN's "Mademoiselle De Scudéry" (1819). The fictional detective story flourished in the hands of Edgar Allan POE, who was adept at ratiocination plots. He may have developed true crime into Gothic fiction after reading the ghost-written memoirs of Paris criminologist François-Eugène Vidocq, a crook-turned-informer who, in 1811, organized and headed the Sûreté, the world's first detective bureau. Excerpts appeared in America in a serial published in *Burton's Gentleman's Quarterly* from September 1838 to May 1839.

In "THE MURDERS IN THE RUE MORGUE" (1841), Poe's energetic protagonist, C. Auguste DUPIN, objectively collects and analyzes clues to a hideous double murder and precipitates the capture of a mysterious, elusive killer. Amid bafflingly grotesque details, the detective applies a detached reconnection of clues to reach a novel conclusion— that the killer was beast rather than human. Poe observed the same conventions of logic for "The Mystery of Marie Rogêt" (1842) and "The Purloined Letter" (1844). In the former, the first detective story composed about a real crime, Poe chose a

symbolic character name in Adolphe Le Bon ("the Good"), the bank clerk whom the police first suspect of murder and whom Dupin exonerates.

Without employing Dupin, Poe composed a fourth detective story, "Thou Art the Man" (1844), which he published in the November issue of *Godey's Lady's Book*. Based on reasoned investigation, the case seems clear to the unnamed narrator, who creates a dramatic but GROTESQUE terror device to force the killer to confess. By sealing the corpse in a wine crate like a jack-in-the-box, the detective causes the remains to spring forth. With a bit of ventriloquism, the narrator cites a line from 2 Samuel 12:7, "Thou art the man!," the words of the prophet Nathan to the guilty King David. To increase the irony of a best friend as murderer, Poe names the culprit Charles Goodfellow.

In Poe's wake came four crime specialists: Charles Felix, author of the first true detective novel, *The Notting Hill Mystery* (1862–63); gaslight thriller master Mary Elizabeth BRADDON, author of *Eleanor's Victory* (1863), featuring Eleanor Vane, one of England's first fictional female detectives; French novelist Victor Hugo, whose romantic classic *Les Misérables* (1862) showcases the stalkings of obsessed police inspector Javert; and French author Émile Gaboriau, who wrote *Le Crime d'Orcival* (*The Crime at Orcival*, 1867), which introduces the clever investigations of Paris Sûreté investigator Monsieur Lecoq in the first *roman policier* ("police novel"). The following year, the English thriller author Wilkie COLLINS published *THE MOONSTONE*, a much-admired model of novel-length detective fiction that incorporates such Gothic details as a valuable but cursed yellow diamond belonging to an heiress and coveted by sinister Hindu priests.

A half-century after Poe's invention of detective fiction, the genre flourished with the creation of Doyle's star analyst, Sherlock Holmes, whose cases also offered outlandish, often grotesque enigmas requiring keen observation and logic. A Doyle admirer, Gaston LEROUX, created his own memorable detective, cub reporter Joseph Rouletabille, featured in *Le Mystère de la Chambre Jaune* (*The Mystery of the Yellow Room*, 1907) and its sequel, *Le Parfum de la Dame en Noir* (*The Fragrance of the Lady in Black*, 1909). Doyle's stories were so popular in America that his imitators flourished in popular magazines—

Black Mask, Collier's, Cosmopolitan, Detective Fiction Weekly, Dime Detective, Ellery Queen's Mystery Magazine, Ladies' Home Journal, and *Saturday Evening Post.* As the detective story grew into novel length, its Gothic qualities lapsed as SENSATIONALISM, eroticism, and hard-edged realism took over.

Subsequent adaptations of the detective story generated police crime novels, urban gaslight thrillers, dime Westerns, and collections of whodunits as well as the serials of the so-called Golden Age writers Margery Allingham, Agatha Christie, Ngaio Marsh, Dorothy L. Sayers, and Michael Innes in Britain and Raymond Chandler, Ellery Queen, Mary Roberts RINEHART, and Ross Macdonald in the United States, all of whom produced varying combinations of mystery, inventive murders, exotic settings, and deranged characters as foils of the clever detective. Another twist, the inverted whodunit, originated by the English mystery writer Richard Austin Freeman in "The Case of Oscar Brodsky" (1912), revealed a felon's identity to the reader, but not to the detective. Gilbert Keith Chesterton took the detective story into a smaller subset with his creation of Father Brown, the ecclesiastical detective, protagonist of a five-book series that began with *The Innocence of Father Brown* (1911).

Detective stories adapted easily to radio plays, such as the adventures of Nick and Nora Charles in Dashiell Hammett's *The Thin Man* (1932). Sound engineers enhanced suspense with creaking doors, footsteps in gravel, muffled cries, gunshots, and other Gothic clichés. Under the influence of such writers as Mickey Spillane, the genre strayed from its original focus on mental challenge and Gothic decorum and began to emphasize violence and darker themes, though more traditional detective stories, such as those by P. D. James and Ruth Rendell, continue to be popular.

Bibliography

Carnell, Jennifer. *The Literary Lives of Mary Elizabeth Braddon.* Hastings, Sussex: Sensation Press, 2000.

New Catholic Encyclopedia. Washington, D.C.: Catholic University of America, 1967.

Willis, Chris. "The Female Sherlock: 'Lady Detectives' in Victorian and Edwardian Fiction," http://www.chriswillis.freeserve.co.uk/femsherlock.htm.

de Winter, Rebecca

A psychological phantom and unrelenting source of conflict in Daphne DU MAURIER's *REBECCA* (1938), the first Mrs. Maxim de Winter—the Rebecca of the title—haunts the unnamed heroine in myriad ways—a presence like a cold draft, in the fragrance on her handkerchief tucked into a raincoat pocket, in the art objects and decor of MANDERLEY estate, in the monogrammed stationery, and in the mesmerizing effect her loveliness had on everyone who encountered her. Although deceased, the adulterous, deceitful Rebecca permeates the text at every turn with evidence of her reptilian beauty and aggressive immorality. Even the name of her sailboat, *Je Reviens* ("I Return"), haunts with its presence and with the recovery of her skeleton from the sunken boat's cabin.

Du Maurier recounts Rebecca's story through flashback, memories, and evocative reports from major and minor characters. Like Catherine EARNSHAW in Emily BRONTË's *WUTHERING HEIGHTS* (1847), Rebecca, according to a hired man, drew life from the challenge of NATURE by sailing her sloop into a wild sea in defiance of a storm. The author puts in the mouth of Ben, a tremulous retardate, a picture of her bestial presence: "She gave you the feeling of a snake" (du Maurier, 154). The image suggests the presence of evil in Eden and the insidious nature of Rebecca's foul adulteries.

Du Maurier works at a verbal portrait of the deceased former mistress, who stalks Manderley in every scene. A willful, corrupt sexual predator, Rebecca mocked her husband, Maxim de Winter, terrifying him with false news of a child and potential heir obviously sired by one of her lovers. She goaded Max with challenges to prove her adulteries. To Rebecca's rival, he bursts out, "I hated her, I tell you, our marriage was a farce from the very first. She was vicious, damnable, rotten through and through. We never loved each other, never had one moment of happiness together" (ibid., 271).

To separate the first Mrs. de Winter from her replacement, the author strips the title figure of humanity. In her husband's estimation, "Rebecca was incapable of love, of tenderness, of decency. She was not even normal" (ibid.). Fittingly, the cuckolded husband admits that he ended her taunts with a bullet through the heart, a symbolic touch common to Gothic crime fiction. Nonetheless, the housekeeper, Mrs. DANVERS, insists on a spectral presence—a quick, light footfall in the corridor, a ghost leaning from the minstrels' gallery, a disembodied voice calling to the dogs. To spook the new Mrs. de Winter, Mrs. Danvers asks, "Do you think she can see us, talking to one another now? . . . Do you think the dead come back and watch the living" (*ibid.*, 172). In a later outburst, Mrs. Danvers warns of a malevolence from beyond the grave, "And she doesn't come kindly, not she, not my lady" (*ibid.*, 242).

Bibliography

du Maurier, Daphne. *Rebecca*. New York: Avon Books, 1971.

Fleenor, Juliann E., ed. *The Female Gothic*. Montreal: Eden Press, 1983.

Nigro, Kathleen Butterly. "Rebecca as Desdemona: 'A Maid That Paragons Description and Wild Fame,'" *College Literature* 27, no. 3 (fall 2000): 144.

de Winter, the new Mrs.

A powerful version of the shy, unassuming NAIF, Daphne DU MAURIER's unnamed speaker in RE-BECCA (1938) is a study in self-denigration worsened by solitude. An orphan working as a traveling companion to an odious social climber, the girl is so uncertain of herself that she fails to respond when the housekeeper, Mrs. DANVERS, calls her "Mrs. de Winter" on the house phone. Crucial to the psychological motivation of the story is the new wife's self-punishment. She castigates herself bitterly: "My faux-pas was so palpably obvious, so idiotic and unpardonable that to ignore it would show me to be an even greater fool if possible, than I was already" (du Maurier, 84). The author uses the telephone incident to express a crucial weakness in the Gothic heroine, a vulnerability to ridicule from others and to an even more cutting self-criticism. She persists in the hurtful contrasts by contrasting the sweeping *R* of Rebecca DE WINTER's signature with her own cramped script and finds it "without individuality, without style, uneducated even, the writing of an indifferent pupil in a second-rate school" (*ibid.*, 87).

At the novel's climax, the costume ball that is the speaker's only social gathering at MANDERLEY, the author heightens the unflattering contrast between the two wives of Max de Winter. Ironically, by analyzing the DISGUISE MOTIF of guests, the speaker sums up the galling contrast between Max's wives. Rebecca, like Marie Antoinette, was assassinated for her outrages; the second wife, like the orange seller who became the mistress of Charles II, feels forever tagged as a parvenu. As a former member of the servant class who feels more kinship with the maid Clarice than with tony guests, the speaker is elevated out of her sphere to become the mate of an aristocrat and mistress of his haunted country estate.

Bibliography

du Maurier, Daphne. *Rebecca*. New York: Avon Books, 1971.

Fleenor, Juliann E., ed. *The Female Gothic*. Montreal: Eden Press, 1983.

Nigro, Kathleen Butterly. "Rebecca as Desdemona: 'A Maid That Paragons Description and Wild Fame,'" *College Literature* 27, no. 3 (fall 2000): 144.

diabolism

The depiction of Satan as a character originated in profound Judaeo-Christian fear of hell and damnation and permeated ALLEGORY, morality plays, German FOLKLORE, and modern works. Like the bestial werewolf, the supreme demon, humankind's oldest adversary, often possessed untold powers of SHAPE-SHIFTING and instant travel to any point of the globe.

One explanation for the diabolic mode in literature came from the Marquis de Sade, creator of erotic Gothicism in such works as *Justine; or, Good Conduct Well Chastised* (1791). He equated the market for demonic plots with the fear of Europeans following the American and French Revolutions. He expressed the demand for Satan as a hero-VILLAIN as the result of oppressive miseries encountered during the decline and downfall of nations. Representing the collapse of the old order were Gothic settings in the ruins of ecclesiastical and secular institutions, SYMBOLS of obsolete seats of power and control.

In the romantic era, Matthew Gregory LEWIS's THE MONK (1796) introduced an appealing demon: the title character AMBROSIO, a fallen religious figure who consorts with Satan. The character's excesses of menace, coercion, rape, and murder scandalized the conservative reader and brought a literary reply from Ann RADCLIFFE, who softened her own fiction with SCHEDONI, the debauched hero-villain in THE ITALIAN (1797). Despite her example, lethal diabolism emerged in literary form as an element of the psychological study or of horror, for example, the keen-eyed tempter in William GODWIN's *St. Leon* (1799), the powerful subverter in Prussian novelist E. T. A. HOFFMANN's *Die Elixiere des Teufels* (The Devil's Elixir, 1815–16), and the relentless pursuer in Irish Gothic author Charles Robert MATURIN's MELMOTH THE WANDERER (1820). Drawing on Melmoth is the avenger in English writer and journalist James HOGG's *The Private Memoirs and Confessions of a Justified Sinner* (1824), a horror novel set in 17th-century Scotland containing a handwritten confession supposedly located in the grave of Robert Wringhim, a deranged Calvinist. The killer listens to voices that urge him to murder a minister, a brother, and his own mother before he realizes that the heavenly voice he obeys is the call of Satan, not of God.

In AMERICAN GOTHIC, satanic musings derived from confrontations with fierce NATURE and Indians and from New England Puritanism and its obsessions with evil in human form, a pervasive subject in Nathaniel HAWTHORNE's fiction. In 1832, Edgar Allan POE explored the malicious persona in "Bon-Bon," a story issued in the Philadelphia *Saturday Courier*. The tale depicts Satan as a vampirish human who takes an interest in Pierre Bon-Bon, a lively conversationalist and chef who readily discusses recipes for cooking human remains. Six years later, Poe published "Silence: A Fable," an enigmatic tale of a less engaging encounter between a lone man and a demon. Late in his career, Poe followed with "Never Bet the Devil Your Head: A Tale with a Moral" (1841), a blend of humor and diabolism that follows the classic pattern of a hasty bet with Satan and the bizarre death of the hero, Toby Dammit, who accidentally decapitates himself. With the publication of "The Imp of the Perverse" (1845), Poe turned allegory to

self-castigation by depicting the devil as the incarnation of the author's self-destructive urges and habits, notably alcoholism, belligerence, and mistreatment of colleagues and companions.

The diversion of New World Gothic from European folktale to frontier racism added immediacy to the prototypical devil. A stark Quaker-turned-demon motif, Robert Montgomery BIRD's NICK OF THE WOODS; or, The Jibbenainosay: A Tale of Kentucky (1837), depicts a DOPPELGÄNGER's diabolic serial killings of Shawnee in outback Kentucky. It is not surprising that Poe, the master of American macabre, encouraged Bird's career by soliciting the manuscript for the *Southern Literary Messenger*. From there, the gory devil tale thrived on the American stage as MELODRAMA suited to the unwary audiences of the more settled Atlantic seaboard.

North American texts emulated diabolic elements from European Gothic. Canadian author William Kirby's *Chien d'Or* (The Golden Dog, 1859) reprised the crumbling castle as a setting for the actions of two villains, Intendant Bigot and Angélique, a bold sinner who makes a pact with Satan. At a dire moment in the action, La Corriveau's body is left in a cage to rot. Similarly adept at SENSATIONALISM, Canadian author Joseph Étienne Eugène Marmette, influenced by the historical novels of Sir Walter SCOTT and the frontier romances of James Fenimore Cooper, developed the Indian Dent-de-Loup—literally "Wolf Tooth"—into a fierce, satanic antichrist in *François de Bienville: Scenes of Seventeenth-Century Canadian Life* (1870), a novel frequently dramatized on the Canadian stage.

In later European fiction, diabolism was gentled in classic novels as writers pushed GOTHIC CONVENTION from sensational extremes toward melodrama. Simultaneously, the strand remained potent in popular fiction, particularly in the short story "The Devil in the Belfry" (1839), which Désiré-Emile Inghelbrecht turned into a ballet and French composer Claude Debussy reset as an opera, *Le Diable dans le Beffroi*, left unfinished at his death. Romantic poet and journalist Théophile GAUTIER published a charmingly tender study, "Une Larme du Diable" (The devil's tear, 1839), which was composed in a serene home setting at the Place Royale in Paris and adapted for radio in 1951.

Diabolism continued its metamorphosis from focal theme to side issue as literary demons took on more human behaviors. Overt devilry gave place to the accusation of satanism that Catherine EARNSHAW hurls at HEATHCLIFF in Emily BRONTË's *WUTHERING HEIGHTS* (1847). English romancer William Harrison AINSWORTH achieved a bestseller with fictionalized history, *The Lancashire Witches: A Romance of Pendle Forest* (1849), a diabolic tale of a curse set in England in 1612. In pulp fiction, horror specialist George William Macarthur REYNOLDS blended overt diabolism with LYCANTHROPY for his popular serial and GOTHIC BLUEBOOK "Wagner the Wehr-Wolf" (1847). A subtle SUBTEXT of diabolism fueled Oscar WILDE's cautionary tale *THE PICTURE OF DORIAN GRAY* (1891) and the heavily nuanced *The Mysterious Stranger* (1916), which Mark Twain wrote during a dark period in his career.

Joseph CONRAD energized the malevolence of *HEART OF DARKNESS* (1902) with implications of compacts with Satan. In descriptions of the villain Kurtz, the protagonist Charlie Marlow describes how imperialistic sin reduces the colonial entrepreneur to a demon: "The wilderness had patted him on the head, and, behold, it was like a ball—an ivory ball; it had caressed him, and—lo! he had withered; it had taken him, loved him, embraced him, got into his veins, consumed his flesh, and sealed his soul to its own by the inconceivable ceremonies of some devilish initiation" (Conrad, 121). Devil fiction enjoyed a resurgence in the later 20th century with Ira Levin's *Rosemary's Baby* (1967), Fred Mustard Stewart's *The Mephisto Waltz* (1968), and Stephen KING's *Carrie* (1974), a prom-night twist on the Cinderella myth. John Updike turned to Gothic comedy in *The Witches of Eastwick* (1984), the vehicle for a 1987 film starring Jack Nicholson as Satan.

Bibliography
Conrad, Joseph. *Heart of Darkness and The Secret Sharer.* New York: Signet, 1983.
Corsbie, Ken. *Theatre in the Caribbean.* London: Hodder & Stoughton, 1984.
Northey, Margot. *The Haunted Wilderness: The Gothic and Grotesque in Canadian Fiction.* Toronto: University of Toronto Press, 1976.
Worth, George J. *William Harrison Ainsworth.* New York: Twayne, 1972.

Dickens, Charles
(1812–1870)

Charles John Huffam Dickens, who was a youth when the classic GOTHIC NOVEL and chapbook were at their height, blended the genre with social commentary to challenge England's self-absorption. He developed the English social novel with MELODRAMA and a ragtag cast of characters ranging from cranks, misers, and GROTESQUEs to MONSTERS. At age 22, he was befriended by a giant of the popular press, the Gothic writer and editor William Harrison AINSWORTH, the editor of *Bentley's Miscellany.* Dickens studied Ainsworth's bestseller, *Rookwood* (1834), a crime thriller. At the Ainsworth residence and at meetings of the Trio Club, the budding novelist met other writers, who helped to groom him for literary stardom.

Dickens had a lifelong love affair with theater. For maximum social protest, he infused his novels with quick episodic action, terrifying ATMOSPHERE, VIOLENCE, leering criminals, and the trappings of the Gothic thriller, beginning with "A Madman's Manuscript," an interpolated terror story in *Pickwick Papers* (1837). In his recreation of moral and social ills in *OLIVER TWIST* (1838), he staged Gothic themes and situations like a master dramatist, picturing the hero's job leading funeral corteges from the undertaker's parlor to the cemetery. Alongside the innocence of his consummate NAIF, little Oliver, a defenseless orphan rescued from a den of child pickpockets, the author touched up the falling action with the wages of villainy—Bill Sikes's throttling of Nancy, Sikes's unforeseen death by hanging, and Fagin's execution. Almost immediately, adapters produced a stage version, the first of many, which condensed the action to its most sensational moments.

Dickens kept the underworld and Gothic modes as essentials to his varied canon. In 1841, he contributed criminal scenes to *Barnaby Rudge: A Tale of the Riots of Eighty,* the grim story of a murderer on the loose, which the author serialized weekly in *Master Humphrey's Clock.* Reigniting Dickens's interest in the macabre was a literary friendship with the American Gothic master Edgar Allan POE, who reviewed three of the eminent author's novels and interviewed him in 1842 during an American tour. Dickens displayed an interest in Poe's work and sympathy for his unfortunate demise in 1849 at age 40.

In later works, Dickens returned frequently to the Gothic mode. He shaped BLEAK HOUSE (1853) into melodrama and employed SUSPENSE, cliffhangers, and a STALKING motif in macabre stories that display the Victorian shift from Gothicism to psychological fiction. For Christmas issues of *All the Year Round,* he solicited supernatural tales from such competent writers as Elizabeth Gaskell and composed a first-person narrative of childhood, "The Haunted House" (1859), which recast the hauntings in A CHRISTMAS CAROL (1843). Six years later, he wrote "The Trial for Murder" (1865), depicting a victim's ghost standing in the courtroom; the next year, he published "The Signalman" (1866), a doom-laden story of apparitions along a rail line.

In *A Tale of Two Cities* (1859), an outgrowth of the NEWGATE NOVEL, the author centered on a Gothic specialty, the DOPPELGÄNGER motif, picturing mirror images and rivals for the same woman who are FOILS in character and behavior. Six years before he pictured the nihilistic cynic, barrister Sydney Carton, replacing a condemned family man, alter ego Charles Darnay, in the Bastille, Dickens defamed the English penal system in "Where We Stopped Growing," an essay in the January 1853 issue of *Household Words.* He portrayed prisons as arched and rheumy, laced with spider webs, dimly lighted by the jailer's lamp, and hellishly convoluted, fanning out to "a maze of low vaulted passages with small black doors" (Dickens, 581). Of the horrors of incarceration, Dickens wrote: "We have never outgrown the rugged walls of Newgate, or any other prison on the outside. All within, is still the same blank of remorse and misery" (*ibid.*). His diatribe lambasted sentried bastions as a perpetual Gothic misery, a blot on civilization. From the author's revulsion at subterranean lockups came his fictional resurrection of the elderly prisoner Dr. Manette in the section titled "Recalled to Life." The carefully honed novel was one of Dickens's finest applications of Gothic terrors to the historical novel.

Bibliography

Dickens, Charles. *A Tale of Two Cities,* in vol. 2 of *The Annotated Dickens,* ed. by Edward Guiliano and Philip Collins. New York: Clarkson N. Potter, 1986.

Petch, Simon. "The Business of the Barrister in 'A Tale of Two Cities,'" *Criticism* 44, no. 1 (winter 2002): 27–43.

Tytler, Graeme. "Dickens's 'The Signalman,'" *Explicator* 53, no. 1 (fall 1994): 26–29.

Dinesen, Isak
(1885–1962)

A writer of disturbing short fiction, under the pen name of Isak Dinesen, Karen Christence Dinesen, Baroness Blixen, applied Gothicism to stories that feature women freed of social restriction. Born in Denmark, Dinesen gained the vision of the raconteur only after successive losses of her coffee farm in Kenya, her lover Denys Finch Hatton to a plane crash, her health from syphilis, and her residence in Africa to debt. In the mold of Robert Louis STEVENSON's *New Arabian Nights* (1882), she enlarged simple romantic tales with VIOLENCE, horror, and passion and with CHIAROSCURO and pictorial imagery drawn from her early training in visual arts at the Royal Academy of Art in Copenhagen. Her most popular work, *Seven Gothic Tales* (1934), a Book-of-the-Month Club selection, places her in the role of Scheherazade, the Arabian storyteller, spinning imaginative plots in the transcultural style that dates back into prehistory.

To express a mix of outrage and sorrow before departing Africa in 1931, Dinesen began writing a series of carefully crafted Gothic tales with "The Dreamers" and followed with "The Old Chevalier" and "The Supper at Elsinore," the story of a REVENANT pirate who visits his spinster sisters. Driving her weakened body through excesses of activity and dependence on amphetamines, she refused to give in to illness after she returned to Rungstedlund, Denmark, and launched a career in fiction to replace anticipated income from the failed coffee plantation in Kenya. She remarked to a friend, "I promised the Devil my soul, and in return he promised me that everything I was going to experience hereafter would be turned into tales" (Thurman, 285). To achieve that goal, she abandoned the hard reality of Europe during the 1930s and retreated into motifs of piracy, SHAPE-SHIFTING, and DISGUISE. Unifying the seven tales are myths of desire, sin, and guilt, themes that she read in Mary SHELLEY's FRANKENSTEIN (1818), in the stories of German masters Johann von GOETHE and E. T. A. HOFFMANN, and in the decadent poems of Charles BAUDELAIRE and the French symbolist poets.

Contributing to unreality in Dinesen's stories was her own confusion resulting from leaving Africa and reorienting herself in Scandinavia. To retain the freedom she knew as a coffee planter in the Ngong Hills, she chose the name Isak as a masculine persona that liberated her from constraints on female writers. At the same time, the name connected her with laughter, the Hebrew meaning of Isak. For the framework story "The Deluge at Norderney," she introduced aristocratic characters marooned by a rising river. In composing the remaining five tales, she focused on Europe's aristocratic decline and the triumph of materialism. The characters, a series of GROTESQUEs entranced by a wide range of obsessions, take shape in the imagination of a refined, mature narrator, who sets each in a striking tableau like a puppet on a painted stage.

By filling the stories with magic, MONSTERS, forebodings, ghosts and witches, and fantasy, the author was able to examine unique tragedies with psychological insight into human fate. One of the tales, "The Monkey," pictures a female survivor, Athena Hopballehus, whom a man chooses to marry in order to clear his reputation for homosexual activity. Their courtship takes place at a convent under the supervision of the suitor's aunt, a conniving prioress, a standard character from the tradition of Ann RADCLIFFE. A foiled rape scene takes place in Athena's chamber, where the maiden bites her attacker and knocks out two of his teeth. The story ends with a surprising plot twist in which the mother superior's monkey shape-shifts into the mother superior. The revelation of evil in the monstrous prioress provides a coming-to-knowledge for both Athena and her suitor. The remaining tales express additional human challenges and their resolutions through similarly strange and SUPERNATURAL interventions. Their subtle plot twists inspired the Gothicism of American authors Truman CAPOTE and Carson MCCULLERS and earned the praise of the American poet Louise Bogan and the American SOUTHERN GOTHIC writer Eudora WELTY. Near the end of her life, Dinesen added *Babette's Feast* (1959) to her canon. She based the dark religious fable on the sufferings of a Jutland syphilis epidemic, which spread over Denmark for 65 years before officials acknowledged it.

Bibliography

Mussari, Mark. "L'Heure Bleue," *Scandinavian Studies* 73, no. 1 (spring 2001): 43.

Thurman, Judith. *Isak Dinesen: The Life of a Storyteller.* New York: St. Martin's Press, 1982.

Trousdale, Rachel. "Self-invention in Isak Dinesen's 'The Deluge at Norderney,'" *Scandinavian Studies* 74, no. 2 (summer 2002): 205–222.

Williams, A. Susan, ed. *The Lifted Veil: The Book of Fantastic Literature by Women, 1800–World War II.* New York: Carroll & Graf, 1992.

disguise motif

The disguise motif is a given of GOTHIC CONVENTION. The purpose of shifting identities is implicit in the FAIRY TALE "Snow White," in which an evil enchantress greets the unsuspecting heroine in the form of an aged apple seller, and in "BEAUTY AND THE BEAST," in which the beast's true identity must remain concealed until Beauty proves her worth as a potential mate. SECRECY through costume serves numerous purposes in classic Gothic works—masking royalty in Thomas Leland's historical novel *Longsword, Earl of Salisbury* (1762), concealing the trickery of a seducer in Charles Brockden BROWN's ORMOND (1799), providing means to rescue a Venetian maiden in Matthew Gregory LEWIS's stage MELODRAMA *Rugantino, the Bravo of Venice* (1805), and enabling slaves to flee on the Underground Railroad in Harriet Beecher Stowe's melodrama *Uncle Tom's Cabin* (1851–52).

Through concealment, Gothic characters obtain both good and bad ends, as in the instance of the men's clothes worn by the protagonists in Abbé PRÉVOST's MANON LESCAUT (1731) and Friedrich von SCHILLER's DER GEISTERSEHER (The

Ghost-Seer, 1786). In Schiller's novel, the shifting identities of a mysterious Armenian OUTSIDER contribute to MYSTERY and inject an image of the WANDERING JEW, a nameless, stateless nomad whose presence generates tension in a suspenseful psychological novel. Wilkie COLLINS, developer of the GASLIGHT THRILLER, heightened tensions by disguising Laura Fairlie as Anne Catherick in *The Woman in White* (1860). His imitator Mary Elizabeth BRADDON enhanced SUSPENSE with the title character's numerous disguises in the sensational *Lady Audley's Secret* (1862). In the former, both Laura and Anne end up in a madhouse; in the latter, new identities allow freedom in a society that restrains and confines women.

Disguise enhances the romance and titillation of Gothic fiction, which beguiles readers through the blurring of character traits, places, and motives, particularly in examples of METEMPSYCHOSIS, demonic POSSESSION, VAMPIRISM, DIABOLISM, and LYCANTHROPY. Matthew Gregory Lewis's *THE MONK* (1796) presents a perversion of religious celibacy in the deceitful Mathilda, an evil necromancer disguised as the male cleric Rosario, who enchants the celibate monk AMBROSIO. Sir Walter SCOTT employs masking in his historical novel *Ivanhoe* (1819), in which King Richard must conceal his royal status in order to aid Ivanhoe at the pivotal tournament that saves the innocent Rebecca from burning at the stake for WITCHCRAFT. In Sutherland Menzies's magazine story "Hughes, the Wehr-Wolf" (1838), the main character, mistreated by local gossips, dons a dyed sheepskin and immediately feels the urge to run, bite, and howl like a wolf to terrorize his tormentors. In Edgar Allan POE's "THE MASQUE OF THE RED DEATH" (1842), masking contributes to the ALLEGORY of the elite deceiving themselves by withdrawing from peasant society to hide from pestilence. In "THE CASK OF AMONTILLADO" (1846), Poe used harmless carnival dress to another purpose, the luring to a PREMATURE BURIAL of Fortunato, who goes to his death in a clown suit complete with jingling bells.

Both Charlotte BRONTË and Emily BRONTË employed disguise in their landmark novels. A misrepresentation of identity occurs in Charlotte Brontë's fortune-telling episode in *JANE EYRE* (1847), in which Edward ROCHESTER, the would-be bigamist, decks himself out as a gypsy. His failure to fool the protagonist is a clue to her intelligence and cool-headedness. In contrast, in Emily Brontë's *WUTHERING HEIGHTS* (1847), housekeeper Nellie Dean uplifts the orphaned HEATHCLIFF's self-image by suggesting that he may be a prince in disguise.

In the last half of the Victorian era, scenes of camouflaged identities and subsequent disclosure contributed to FREUDIAN THEMES of submerged evil and the cloaking or suppression of perverse sexual desires. The psychological disguise motif permeates Robert Louis STEVENSON's *DR. JEKYLL AND MR. HYDE* (1886), in which the demonism of Hyde refuses to stay submerged beneath the conservative exterior of a respected laboratory scientist. Five years later, Oscar WILDE followed the same line of thought by revealing the hidden paganism in the murderous title character of *THE PICTURE OF DORIAN GRAY* (1891). The novel, based on a SUBTEXT of homoeroticism, depicts actress Sibyl Vane concealing her feminine curves in men's clothes. In Japan, the tricking out of an all-male cast of Kabuki performers with padded garments and stark-white makeup contributed to the drama in stories of scheming, poisoning, and suicide. One plot involving the interaction of upper- and lower-class people is *Ningen Ganji Kane Yo No Naka* (1879), which was adapted from Edward BULWER-LYTTON's satiric comedy *Money* (1840). Stylized posturing and gestures mask the insincerity of a guardian who must shift his attitude toward a poor boy who comes into a legacy.

In 20th-century Gothic works, disguises are evident, but less dramatic or pivotal to themes and ATMOSPHERE. Sir Arthur Conan DOYLE's famed detective Sherlock HOLMES flourishes in disguise in *THE HOUND OF THE BASKERVILLES* (1902), in which he gathers clues and information without revealing his connection with an ongoing investigation. In Daphne DU MAURIER's *REBECCA* (1938), the unnamed protagonist's selection of a costume for a formal ball at MANDERLEY is less a disguise than an attempt to fit in with genteel society as the estate's new mistress. In current times, Dan Brown retreated to traditional Gothic mystery with a series of false identities for the complex secrecies of *THE DA VINCI CODE* (2003).

Bibliography

Fleenor, Juliann E., ed. *The Female Gothic*. Montreal: Eden Press, 1983.

Gilbert, Sandra M., and Susan Gubar. *The Madwoman in the Attic*, 2nd ed. New Haven, Conn.: Yale University Press, 2000.

Turner, Alice K. *The History of Hell*. New York: Harcourt Brace, 1993.

dissipation

Gothic literature depicts spiritual bankruptcy and behavioral dissipation as keys to character decline. Dissipation is a controlling theme in the sexual addiction of des Grieux in Abbé PRÉVOST's *MANON LESCAUT* (1731). It is seen in the isolation and intemperance of the laboratory scientist in Mary Wollstonecraft SHELLEY's *FRANKENSTEIN* (1818), the spending sprees of Pip and his roommate Herbert Pocket in Charles DICKENS's *GREAT EXPECTATIONS* (1861), the addiction to a drug that precipitates time travel in Daphne DU MAURIER's *The House on the Strand* (1969), and the crimes and addictions in August WILSON's 10-play cycle based on African-American history. Ray BRADBURY commented on the insidious nature of bad habits in "The Veldt," a story collected in *The Illustrated Man* (1951): "You didn't know what to do with yourself. . . . You smoke a little more every morning and drink a little more every afternoon and need a little more sedative every night. You're beginning to feel unnecessary, too" (Bradbury, 10). In Gothic extremes, the creeping demands of ESCAPISM gradually consume the personality, reducing a normal being into a derelict, addict, psychotic, or MONSTER.

Typically licentious in regard to drugs, alcohol, money, narcissism, and/or criminal and sexual urges, wastrels and VILLAINs abandon self-control, a pattern that the classic Gothic author stressed to distance Gothic fiction from the coldly disciplined writings of their Augustan forebears. A forerunner of the Gothic rake, the title character in Tobias SMOLLETT's dramatic *FERDINAND COUNT FATHOM* (1753), yields to selfish whims, allowing nocturnal carouses to grow into cruelty and murder. Like the staged decline of the famed sinner in Christopher Marlowe's *DR. FAUSTUS* (ca. 1588), the count's demise reprised a stereotypical Gothic denoue-ment, the deathbed regrets of the debauchée. A similar death-house recompense awaits Charles Robert MATURIN's title figure in *MELMOTH THE WANDERER* (1820), who knows that Satan will hurl him into a black abyss for a host of sins.

William BECKFORD depicted dissipation at society's highest level. His *VATHEK, an Arabian Tale* (1782) set a villainous prototype by characterizing a sybaritic caliph who damns himself through an orgy of gluttony and sexual self-gratification. The height of excess in classic Gothic novels was Matthew Gregory LEWIS's AMBROSIO, protagonist of *THE MONK* (1796). Ambrosio dooms himself through ungoverned appetites and ends lifelong celibacy after the wily Mathilda draws him into vice and carnal depravity. Similarly dissolute but less violent is Ann RADCLIFFE's SCHEDONI, protagonist of *THE ITALIAN* (1797). He exemplifies a two-sided prodigality, his retreat from holy vows and the unleashing of murderous inclinations that bring him to the brink of parricide. Radcliffe intended her treatment of extreme immorality to prove that Gothic villainy need not depend on orgies or bloodbaths to make an impact. Mary WOLLSTONECRAFT emulated Radcliffe's novel with *MARIA; OR, THE WRONGS OF WOMEN* (1798), a contribution to FEMALE GOTHIC in which the title character suffers at the hands of her husband George Venables, a drunken spendthrift and womanizer.

In the 19th and 20th centuries, debauchery took a number of more complex forms—for example, the dream visions of Thomas De Quincey, author of an unusual Gothic autobiography, *Confessions of an English Opium Eater* (1822, 1856), and the drug-induced self-pity of the widower in Edgar Allan POE's "LIGEIA" (1838). In reference to Poe's reliance on alcohol for creativity, Hanns Heinz EWERS, a writer of barbaric Gothic fiction during the time of Hitler's rise to power, exonerated the artist who needs intoxication as a stimulus. A prelude to modern dissipations derives from the materialism of Jacob Marley and Ebenezer Scrooge in Charles DICKENS's *A CHRISTMAS CAROL* (1843). In the opening confrontation, Marley's ghost reveals that he, like his former partner Scrooge, allowed the stockpiling of wealth to subsume his soul to the exclusion of friends, family, and compassion for London's poor. Dickens produced a theatrical display of the evils of addiction in BLEAK HOUSE (1853), in which the alcoholic Krook, a dealer in rags and bones, dies of spontaneous combustion, a symbolic demise implying that effects of dissipation reach so destructive a level that they consume the addict body and soul.

Oscar WILDE showcased extreme narcissism in the title character of his play SALOMÉ (1893), a pseudohistorical stage event so revolting for the use of a severed head as a prop for an exotic dance that English authorities banned performances. The era's memorable voluptuary, the Transylvanian count in Bram STOKER's DRACULA (1897), sates a never-ending lust for fresh blood by piercing the necks of victims with his fangs, which spread the evil of VAMPIRISM like a disease. Gaston LEROUX injected more romance into immoderation in a variation of the GHOST STORY, *Le Fantôme de l'Opéra* (THE PHANTOM OF THE OPERA, 1910), which depicts the villain Erik overpowering an opera star as a soul sickness drives him to shape and glory in his puppet singer. Victoria HOLT resurrected the extremes of the GOTHIC BLUEBOOK by characterizing a lust for social prominence in MISTRESS OF MELLYN (1960), in which the FEMME FATALE Celestine Nansellock commits serial murders to secure for herself the title of lady of the manor. In 1988, the Australian Gothicist Peter Carey used gambling as the shared weakness of an unlikely pair, an heiress and a failed Anglican minister, in *OSCAR AND LUCINDA*, winner of the Booker Prize.

Bibliography

Bradbury, Ray. *The Illustrated Man*. New York: Bantam Books, 1951.

Hennessy, Brendan. *The Gothic Novel*. London: Longman, 1978.

Hoeveler, Diane Long. *Gothic Feminism*. University Park: Pennsylvania State University Press, 1998.

Schmitt, Cannon. *Alien Nation: Nineteenth-Century Gothic Fictions and English Nationality*. Philadelphia: University of Pennsylvania Press, 1997.

domestic Gothic

Domestic Gothic is a woman-centered hybrid of Gothic terror novels that blends SENSATIONALISM with the epistolary novel, the novel of manners, and sentimental fiction, such as Ray BRADBURY's autobiographical work *Dandelion Wine* (1957), which depicts evil stalking a midwestern family; Marsha Norman's two-actor psychodrama *'night, Mother* (1982), a tit-for-tat mother-against-daughter harangue that concludes in the daughter's suicide; and Larry Larson, Levi Lee, and Rebecca Wackler's darkly humorous play *Tent Meeting* (1987), in which incest forces a young mother to flee a corrosive home environment. In *Lives of Girls and Women* (1971), the Canadian writer Alice Munro describes the settings of her characters as linoleum caves. (The Canadian author and critic Margaret ATWOOD popularized the term in her 1991 Clarendon Lectures in English Literature and in *Strange Things: The Malevolent North in Canadian Literature* [1995] as an apt description of home-grown barbarism.)

Influenced by the refinement of Ann RADCLIFFE's terror novels, authors of domestic Gothic incorporate seduction of the NAIF, often a young woman, whose inexperience with evil males exposes her to kidnap, fear, and NIGHTMARES. The genre contributed to FEMALE GOTHIC elements of the brave heroine searching for her identity, locating and/or protecting an inheritance, and liberating herself from coercion and VIOLENCE, the controlling motifs of the anonymous GOTHIC BLUEBOOK *The Victim of Seduction* (1790) and Charlotte DACRE's novel *The School for Friends* (ca. 1800). Masters of domestic Gothic include Charles Brockden BROWN, Lady Caroline LAMB, Francis LATHOM, Eliza PARSONS, and Regina Maria ROCHE, who applied the domestic model in *The Children of the Abbey: A Tale* (1796), an episodic story of the dispossessed heirs of Dunreath Abbey in Scotland. She characterized perils to females with scenes of separated lovers, dueling and forgery, confinement in an estate, convent, and debtors' prison, and an arranged marriage.

The subgenre of domestic Gothic took a remarkably violent turn in the 1860s with the rise of sensational scenarios of middle-class crime and domestic abuse. In England, Mary Elizabeth BRADDON examined the plight of women tricked into matrimony with *The Lady's Mile* (1866) and *Dead Sea Fruit* (1868), the life-in-death drama of a wife separated from her husband. W. W. JACOBS characterized a homey, Dickensian setting beleaguered by the walking dead in "THE MONKEY'S PAW" (1902), sometimes selected as a model of short Gothic fiction. A surprising psychological shocker in the United States was the work of feminist author Charlotte Perkins GILMAN, who spoke for the physically and emotionally constrained and silenced wife in the classic autobiographical story "THE YELLOW WALLPAPER" (1892), a domestic horror tale of madness precipitated by confinement to a single room and restriction to rest without intellectual or creative outlets.

Into the 20th and 21st centuries, domestic anguish pervaded literature as women reached for independence and self-fulfillment, the controlling theme in Margaret Atwood's *The Blind Assassin* (2001) and Michel Faber's *The Crimson Petal and the White* (2002), a prostitute-earns-respect story set in the style of a Victorian novel. American short story master Shirley JACKSON produced a lengthy canon of domestic terror that juxtaposed evil with humor. Christina Stead updated the domestic Gothic novel *The Man Who Loved Children* (1940) with realism, stressing the commonalities of keeping house, shopping, and serving meals. A sleeper that found audiences late in the 1960s, this novel characterizes the dysfunctional family at Gothic extremes of parental dominance and hysterical tirades. Under Stead's guidance, the Gothic introduces the neuroses of parents Henny and Sam Pollit at the height of their destructiveness. The distorted personalities result in Dickensian GROTESQUEs whose minds overflow with a psychological sludge of ridicule, jealousy, revulsion, and outrage.

Similarly focused on family favoritism and cruelty, Laura Esquivel's bestselling first novel *Like Water for Chocolate* (1989) is a complex FAIRY TALE that depicts a mother's cruelty to her daughter Tita, who compensates for lovelessness through magical cookery. After brutalizing Tita's face with a wooden spoon, the mother immures her in a dovecote and sends for a doctor to remand her to an asylum. Doctor Brown finds her "naked, her nose broken, her whole body covered with pigeon droppings . . . and curled up in a fetal position" (Esquivel, 97). Esquivel pictures Tita's release from a life of torment in a late-in-life coupling with her lover Pedro, who dies in her embrace. To rescue their love, Tita devours candles, which burn and spark, igniting the family ranch. The fable-like ending depicts a SUPERNATURAL love as enduring in explosive form in the afterlife.

Bibliography

Atwood, Margaret. *Strange Things: The Malevolent North in Canadian Literature.* Oxford: Clarendon Press, 1995.

Carnell, Jennifer. *The Literary Lives of Mary Elizabeth Braddon.* Hastings, Sussex: Sensation Press, 2000.

Ellis, Kate Ferguson. *The Contested Castle: Gothic Novels and the Subversion of Domestic Ideology.* Urbana: University of Illinois Press, 1989.

Esquivel, Laura. *Like Water for Chocolate.* New York: Anchor Books, 1992.

Fee, Margery. "Strange Things: The Malevolent North in Canadian Literature," *University of Toronto Quarterly* 67, no. 1 (winter 1997–98): 335–337.

Hume, Beverly A. "Managing Madness in Gilman's 'The Yellow Wall-Paper,'" *Studies in American Fiction* 30, no. 1 (spring 2002): 3–30.

doppelgänger

A mirroring or duality of a character's persona, the concept of the doppelgänger refers to the twin, shadow double, demon double, and split personality, all common characterizations in world folklore. Dating back to playwright Plautus in Republican Rome and his separated twins in *Menaechmi* (186 B.C.) and to possession by a DYBBUK in Jewish KABBALISM, the concept of paired characters evolved into a psychological study of duality in a single person. The term *doppelgänger* derives from the German "double goer" or "double walker," a complex characterization that novelist Jean Paul Richter coined in *Siebenkäs* (1796), a novel depicting a bisected persona. The story was the beginning of a subset of Gothic psychological fiction in which characters gaze inward at warring dichotomies through shadowscapes, look-alikes, sexual doubles, mirror images, portraits and statues, and DREAMS and NIGHTMARES.

Literary models of the doppelgänger flourished in German fantasy with the tales and novels of the Prussian horror specialist E. T. A. HOFFMANN, author of the Gothic horror thriller *Die Elixiere des*

Teufels (*The Devil's Elixir,* 1815–16) and in the short Gothic story "Die Doppelgänger" (1821). In England, less obvious examples of the double permeate GOTHIC NOVELs of conflicted personality, the motivating force in the pairing of Catherine EARNSHAW's disparate loves in Emily BRONTË's *WUTHERING HEIGHTS* (1847) and in the story of physically identical men of opposite character and disposition who love the same woman in Charles DICKENS's classic historical novel *A Tale of Two Cities* (1859), a protest of injustice, prisons, and capital punishment. In the former, as a means of expressing her love for a foundling gypsy boy and for the wild moors that reflect their undisciplined roamings, Catherine asserts, "My love for Heathcliff resembles the eternal rocks beneath—a source of little visible delight, but necessary. . . . I am Heathcliff" (Brontë, 84). In the latter novel, the debauched barrister Sydney Carton redeems himself by supplanting the hero, the husband and father Charles Darnay, and by riding the fateful tumbrel through jeering Paris mobs to the guillotine.

The doppelgänger motif typically depicts a double who is both duplicate and antithesis of the original, as is the case with Charlotte BRONTË's Jane EYRE and Bertha ROCHESTER, William GODWIN's Caleb Williams and the stalker Falkland, Mary Wollstonecraft SHELLEY's Victor FRANKENSTEIN and FRANKENSTEIN'S MONSTER, the female patient and the phantasmagoric image in the wall design in Charlotte Perkins GILMAN's "THE YELLOW WALLPAPER" (1892), the ship's captain and the stowaway in Joseph CONRAD's "The Secret Sharer" (1912), and the slave and the rescuer in Octavia BUTLER's *Kindred* (1979). In MYSTERY stories and crime novels, the pairing of opposites, similar to the ancient Egyptian alliance of a human with a *ka* or spiritual double, usually pits a normal character against a demonic alter ego or a mysterious harbinger of death. The former example invigorates the wrathful Nathan Slaughter in Robert Montgomery BIRD's *NICK OF THE WOODS; or, The Jibbenainosay: A Tale of Kentucky* (1837) and Mark Twain's *Pudd'nhead Wilson* (1894) and dooms Robert Wringhim, the tool of Satan in James HOGG's *The Memoirs and Confession of a Justified Sinner* (1824). Wringhim feels so enveloped by Gil-Martin, the embodiment of Satan, that he re-

marks, "I feel wedded to you so closely that I feel as if I were the same person. Our essences are one, our bodies and spirits being united" (Hogg, 229).

The latter form of the double fuels Edgar Allan POE's macabre tale "THE FALL OF THE HOUSE OF USHER" (1839), in which Madeline USHER's escape from PREMATURE BURIAL in the family crypt results in the death of her twin brother Roderick USHER, whom the author hints is also her lover. The appearance of a phantom self also controls psychological fiction—Poe's "William Wilson" (1839), an autobiographical tale of a man who stalks and overpowers his double during carnival season in Venice; the overpowering of the self by a wraith in Fyodor Dostoyevsky's *Dvoynik* (*The Double,* 1846); the fierce good-versus-evil struggle in Robert Louis STEVENSON's *DR. JEKYLL AND MR. HYDE* (1886); Frisian poet and novelist Theodor Storm's depiction of the doomed ex-convict in *Ein Doppelgänger* (A double-goer, 1887); and Oscar WILDE's regret-filled novel *THE PICTURE OF DORIAN GRAY* (1891), the story of a doomed sybarite who witnesses his decline in a portrait.

AMERICAN GOTHIC produced a unique twist on the motif of the double with examinations of white and mixed-race children in the antebellum South. A dramatic example, George Washington CABLE's colonial plantation saga *The Grandissimes* (1880), injects the themes of social class and miscegenation into a confrontation between the Creole and mulatto sons of a powerful Louisiana Delta landowner. The novel elucidates the dilemma of mirror-image brothers who share names—Honoré Grandissime the Creole and Honoré Grandissime the free man of color, the former destined to inherit all and the latter doomed to frustration and VIOLENCE. Cable heightens the MELODRAMA of failed ambitions and near-suicide by depicting a murder, flight to France, and the quadroon's drowning after he leaps from the brig *Américain* in a symbolic abandonment of his alter ego and an unloving motherland.

The 20th century offered more heavily nuanced versions of the doppelgänger motif. American novelist Henry JAMES created a subtle form of duality in the yearnings of Spencer Brydon, the protagonist of "The Jolly Corner" (1908), a suspenseful tale published in *English Review.* The story depicts a man obsessed with STALKING his alter ego through the dark passages of a house he inherited in New York City. A confrontation with the monstrous phantasm gives Brydon a chance to study himself. Critics view Brydon's double identity from two perspectives—as a psychological reclamation of self and as a tentative gesture toward homoeroticism in a straitlaced American male. A significant contribution to FEMALE GOTHIC is Quebec author Anne Hébert's *Kamouraska* (1970), a tale of the duality of murderer Elisabeth Rolland. The novel was translated into English and filmed in 1973 by Claude Jutra.

Bibliography

Brontë, Emily. *Wuthering Heights*. New York: New American Library, 1959.

Herdman, John. *The Double in Nineteenth-Century Fiction*. New York: Macmillan Press, 1990.

Hogg, James. *The Memoirs and Confession of a Justified Sinner*. New York: W. W. Norton, 1970.

Ivkovi, Milaca. "The Double as the 'Unseen' of Culture: Toward a Definition of Doppelgänger," *Linguistics and Literature* 2, no. 7 (2000): 121–128.

Northey, Margot. *The Haunted Wilderness: The Gothic and Grotesque in Canadian Fiction*. Toronto: University of Toronto Press, 1976.

Webber, Andrew J. *The Doppelgänger: Double Visions in German Literature*. Oxford: Clarendon Press, 1997.

Doyle, Sir Arthur Conan
(1859–1930)

The consummate Scottish MYSTERY and DETECTIVE STORY writer, Sir Arthur Ignatius Conan Doyle gave the world the archetypal sleuth, Sherlock HOLMES, a master of observation and deductive reasoning based on subtle clues. Educated in ophthalmology in Vienna, Doyle earned professional renown and a knighthood for his contribution to field medicine during the Boer War, but he is better known for fiction dealing with fairies, magic, spiritualism, the SUPERNATURAL, psychic research, and crime. He sold his first work, "The Mystery of Sassassa Valley," to *Chambers's Journal* in 1879, and contributed a decade later to the paranormal genre with a novel, *The Mystery of Cloomber* (1889), a macabre story of magic from the Indian subcontinent.

Doyle attributed his entry into the detective genre to two forerunners: Edgar Allan POE, the American father of the detective genre, and Émile Gaboriau, the French inventor of the *roman policier* ("police novel"). Doyle saluted Poe formally as the life's breath of detective fiction. From Gaboriau, the author of *Monsieur Lecoq* (1869) and *Les Esclaves de Paris* (The keys of Paris, 1869), Doyle reshaped his protagonist, the prototypical disguise artist and crime solver, into Holmes, the world-renowned detective. A historical figure, Dr. Joseph Bell, an instructor at the University of Edinburgh Medical School, provided models of inference, ingenuity, and incisive diagnosis. The stories, available at book shops and railway stations, appealed primarily to men who read for pleasure.

As a vehicle for Holmes, Doyle initiated an intricately plotted story, "A Study in Scarlet" (1887), based on the actual disappearance of a London baker. Doyle published the tale in a sellout edition of *Beeton's Christmas Annual* and in a bound volume the next year. The story turned Gothic detail into evidence of a grotesque murder, which left the corpse in pitiable disarray: "On his rigid face there stood an expression of horror, and, as it seemed to me, of hatred, such as I have never seen upon human features" (Doyle, vol. I, 168). The clinical study of contorted face and writhing limbs precedes a panoply of the unexpected—the pathetic corpse of a terrier, the Mormon Prophet of Utah, a Trichinopoly cigar, a romantic feud—and the famed wrap-up, in which Holmes explicates his reasoning that demystifies Gothic touches and ties all neatly together.

Doyle followed with "The Sign of the Four; or, The Problem of the Sholtos" in the February 1890 issue of *Lippincott's Monthly Magazine* in both England and the United States. He began writing more episodes in *Strand* magazine, notably, "A Scandal in Bohemia" (1891), "The Bascombe Valley Mystery" (1891), "The Blue Carbuncle" (1892), and "The Adventure of the Speckled Band" (1892), four favorites of Holmes fans. Doyle considered the latter, a "locked room" mystery influenced by Poe's "THE MURDERS IN THE RUE MORGUE" (1841), his best effort. It incorporates a favorite ploy, the pitiable female imploring Holmes's aid, which the author juxtaposes against a GROTESQUE evil, a swamp adder, India's deadliest snake, wrapped around a victim's upper skull. Doyle extended the series with a pair of collections, *The Adventures of Sherlock Holmes* (1894), dedicated to Dr. Bell, and *The Memoirs of Sherlock Holmes* (1894). Doyle's most anthologized novella, THE HOUND OF THE BASKERVILLES (1902), draws on macabre evidence and a range of Gothic techniques. The remoteness of a grand mansion overlooking a deserted moor foreshadows the sudden death of an elderly gentleman terrorized by a phantom hound flashing phosphorescent teeth. Doyle's one-act play, *The Crown Diamond: An Evening with Sherlock Holmes* (1921), is a second-rate effort. Simultaneous with a stage version of "The Speckled Band," it enjoyed a three-month run and has had no revivals. He adapted the text into a short story, "The Adventure of the Mazarin Stone" (1921).

As a whole, Sherlockiana was popular because it stressed such outré elements as rare poisons, unusual tobacco, cryptic messages, fake beards, a family curse, baritsu wrestling, tiger-hunting stratagems, an opium den, tattooing, sudden death, and grisly murders invested with exotic guile. Settings adorned with Moorish and Turkish decor and memorabilia—hookahs, pillows, divans, ARABESQUE hangings—bear the flavor of British colonialism, since returnees carried such objects home with them from the field. Like details in Wilkie COLLINS's THE MOONSTONE (1868), the exotic clues in Holmes mysteries imply that England was tainted by colonial sins that spawned crime.

Bibliography

Doyle, Arthur Conan. *The Annotated Sherlock Holmes*, 2 vols. New York: Wings Books, 1967.

Hodgson, John A., ed. *Sherlock Holmes: The Major Stories with Contemporary Critical Essays.* Boston: Bedford/St. Martin's, 1994.

Knight, Stephen. "The Case of the Great Detective," *Meanjin* 40, no. 2 (1981): 175–185.

Priestman, Martin. *Detective Fiction and Literature: The Figure on the Carpet.* London: Macmillan, 1990.

Dracula
Bram Stoker
(1897)

Epitomizing the primordial clash between light and dark, Bram STOKER's ghoul novel popularized one of the world's most fearful and erotic culture hero-VILLAINs. The riveting story and its complex conclusion so impressed Sir Arthur Conan DOYLE that he exclaimed, "I think it is the very best story of diablerie which I have read for many years. It is really wonderful how with so much exciting interest over so long a book there is never an anticlimax" (Belford, 275). Another adventure writer, Anthony Hope Hawkins, author of *The Prisoner of Zenda* (1894), commended the viciousness of Stoker's vampires, which kept him awake nights.

On another level, Stoker's book raised to a new height Victorian anxieties about fluid gender roles and spread the xenophobic terror of the foreign OUTSIDER while introducing hints of modernism with references to the phonograph, telegraph, and typewriter. Inspired by the LEGEND of Nosferatu the vampire, the serial narrators in Wilkie COLLINS's *The Woman in White* (1860), and the bold predations of the female vampire in Sheridan LE FANU's lesbian thriller *Carmilla* (1872), Stoker's terror romance created a whole category of OTHERNESS and a new subgenre of Gothic tradition. In the estimation of critic Anne Williams, author of *Art of Darkness: A Poetics of Gothic* (1995), Stoker empowered his vampire as a sexual threat to Western civilization and world order.

Through a series of diaries, journals, letters, and notes, Stoker reveals the ultimate outlaw, the Transylvanian count, who attacks his prey with fangs that leave paired holes on the neck. Because of Dracula's preference for virgins, his menace sullies females through an ambiguous transfer of impurity more terrifying than pestilential disease. In spontaneous outcry against the corruption of English womanhood, Professor Abraham Van Helsing, Dracula's FOIL, exclaims, "How are all the powers of the devils against us!" (Stoker, 142).

The monstrosity of Dracula's degeneracy is the seduction of English womanhood, embodied in literary opposites, Lucy Westenra and Mina Murray Harker. For his prime victim, Stoker chose not only to threaten the sweet-natured Mina, but also to sacrifice Lucy, the anti-Victorian female rebel, whom the vampire's lethal bite alters into a female ghoul. Thus, the Gothic menace perverts normal human procreation by reproducing itself asexually from a mateless male progenitor. The result—a

STALKING nightmare—destroys innocence. As the Bloofer Lady, Lucy the vampire shape-shifts into a growling, doglike heath wanderer of Hampstead Hill who entices children to their doom. An unsanctified form of maternity, instead of suckling young like a normal woman, she preys on them and drains their life forces.

At a central scene in chapter 15, Stoker enlarges on female culpability through CHIAROSCURO, which dramatizes the horrors of Lucy's tomb via contrast of the site by day and night. Funeral wreaths turned brown with age overhang the sordid monument amid "time-discoloured stone, and dust-encrusted mortar, and rusty, dank iron, and tarnished brass, and clouded silver-plating [which] gave back the feeble glimmer of a candle" (Stoker, 206–207). The saturation of detail suggests human putrefaction, a horrid transformation of living tissue in death to discoloration, decay, and ravishment by flesh-eating insects. Stoker pits the monstrous image against a small, but sturdy nemesis, the minute candle flame, a symbol of the faith and experience with the occult offered by Professor Van Helsing. The author ennobles the wise magus, whose given name, Abraham, recalls the author's first name and the Old Testament patriarch and originator of monotheism in the Western world. Courageously, the master problem-solver attacks insidious corruption by sawing open Lucy's tomb and revealing an empty coffin.

The return of Lucy's remains, which extends SUSPENSE and the horror of a body corrupting over a week's time, bears out Van Helsing's insistence that she has fallen under occult powers that have flourished in Greece and Rome, Germany, France, India, the Chersonese, and China. Like an attending physician, he lifts her eyelids and raises the dead lips to expose sharp doglike teeth, the emblem of vampire menace that permeates Dracula fiction into the 21st century. For Stoker, who depicts her as an offensively aggressive feminist, the grotesque death of the un-dead Lucy in chapter 16 suits the crime—staking, decapitation, and stuffed like a piglet for a banquet with garlic, an herb connected in folklore with clear thinking as an antidote to SUPERSTITION. Wielding the phallic stake in a manly plunge is the Thor-like arm of her fiancé Arthur Holmwood, who strikes decisively while Van Helsing reads from his missal. Feminist interpretation describes the act as exorcism of an evil spirit. The SUBTEXT implies that patriarchal religion exonerates an earth-purifying rape.

By convening the thinker-folklorist Van Helsing, the aristocratic Holmwood, the husband Jonathan HARKER, and the wealthy Quincey P. Morris, Stoker creates an international consortium, a miniature Round Table of cavaliers that produces multiple victories with Gothic finesse. After the quartet rescues Mina from vampire taint, the destruction of Dracula and his lurid consorts ends the novel with a promise that the world—at least Transylvania and England—will remain free of evil. In the afterword, the birth of Quincey Harker to Mina and Jonathan restores order through the heterosexual production of normal offspring.

A perpetual source of interest to the Western world, *Dracula* has passed through numerous analyses, which have treated the text as allegories of capitalism, the crumbling aristocracy, the advance of urban crime, the spread of syphilis through degraded sex, and immigration of the outsider—dark-skinned slaves, gypsies, Italians—from lesser nations into northwestern Europe and England, thus introducing a corrupting ethnicity into purer stock. In the estimation of post-Victorian Freudians, the story expresses the era's repression of normal carnal urges at the same time that it vents the author's repressed homosexuality and his aversion to women, the theme of his second most popular work, *The Lair of the White Worm* (1911). Later literary historians point to the perversion of blood, a trinity of female wraiths, and communion wafers as proof of an anti-Catholic bias. In a more recent view, critic Judith Halberstam, author of *Skin Shows: Gothic Horror and the Technology of Monsters* (1995), proposes that the novel's hidden agenda is latent anti-Semitism revealed through the demonization of typical Jewish features and behaviors, particularly a purported lust for money and blood.

Bibliography

Auerbach, Nina. *Our Vampires, Ourselves.* Chicago: University of Chicago Press, 1995.

Belford, Barbara. *Bram Stoker.* New York: Alfred A. Knopf, 1996.

Cohen, Jeffrey Jerome, ed. *Monster Theory*. Minneapolis: University of Minnesota Press, 1996.

Croley, Laura Sagolla. "The Rhetoric of Reform in Stoker's 'Dracula': Depravity, Decline, and the Fin-de-siecle 'Residuum,'" *Criticism* 37, no. 1 (winter 1995): 85–108.

Halberstam, Judith. *Skin Shows: Gothic Horror and the Technology of Monsters*. Durham, N.C.: Duke University Press, 1995.

Ronay, Gabriel. *The Dracula Myth*. London: W. H. Allen, 1972.

Scandura, Jani. "Deadly Professions: Dracula, Undertakers, and the Embalmed Corpse," *Victorian Studies* 40, no. 1 (autumn 1996): 1–31.

Signorotti, Elizabeth. "Repossessing the Body: Transgressive Desire in 'Carmilla' and 'Dracula,'" *Criticism* 38, no. 4 (fall 1996): 607–632.

Stoker, Bram. *Dracula*. New York: Bantam Books, 1981.

Taylor, Susan B. "Stoker's 'Dracula,'" *Explicator* 55, no. 1 (fall 1996): 29–31.

Wolf, Leonard. *A Dream of Dracula: In Search of the Living Dead*. New York: Popular Library, 1977.

Dracula, Count

A pinnacle of Gothic characterization, Count Dracula, Bram STOKER's parasitic Boyar vampire, and his loathsome appetites have generated extreme terror among readers and movie fans. A prototypical loner, he is an exotic patrician in the medieval lineage of Attila the Hun and is endowed with magical powers of SHAPE-SHIFTING. Suitably, the count resides among subservient plebeian Transylvanians in Castle Dracula in the Carpathian Mountains. With its hairy palms, pointed ears, gleaming red eyes, bushy brows, pale skin, and knife-blade nose, his physique is a perversion of manhood. Because his appearance, like that of all vampires, is not reflected, he hangs no mirrors in Castle Dracula. When he opens his cruel mouth, beneath a long white mustache are sharp protruding teeth and breath fetid with a charnel stench. In explanation of his repellent mouth, Stoker has him utter scripture from the Christian communion ritual, which identifies the vampire's sustenance as a demonic reverse of bread and wine that the faithful partake of as symbols of Christ's body and blood.

In an extended parody of Christ, the count displays his anathema through a mastery of easily cowed peasants and by a veiled warning of OTHERNESS to Jonathan HARKER, the OUTSIDER: "Our ways are not your ways, and there shall be to you many strange things," a warning that he enlarges with a prediction of bad dreams for any who wander his castle (Stoker, 22). He explains away his strangeness as an aspect of an old and prestigious family: "We transylvanian nobles love not to think that our bones may lie amongst the common dead" (*ibid.*, 24). He piles on additional peculiarities: a lack of mirth, an avoidance of sunshine and sparkling water, and a love of shadow and solitude, qualities that he shares with the dour BYRONIC HERO. Boasting ends on a biblical note. Like the apostle Peter denying Christ for the third time, Dracula hears the cock crow and recedes from advancing sunrise to rest up for the next night's prowl for blood.

Dracula gives evidence of sexual predations and DIABOLISM, particularly an aversion to communion wafers and crucifixes, both embodiments of Christian sanctity that derail the vampire's satisfaction of primitive hungers. As proof of shape-shifting, Stoker pictures the count arriving at Whitby in the form of a dog that plunders the graves of drowned sailors and suicides. In London, he visits Lucy Westenra's quarters in the form of a large black bat or bird, which the madman R. M. Renfield views through the window of his cell in an asylum. After Dracula's nightly bloodsucking from Lucy's throat, an unspeakable sex act producing a morbid version of orgasm, the attending physician Dr. Seward looks out and catches sight of the dark creature. Escaping dawn, Dracula resembles a silent ghost flapping determinedly toward the west, the source of night and everlasting death.

A sexual triad forms with the vampire at one apex opposite the normal male characters and their women at the other two points. Like a boastful seducer, the demon brags to his pursuers that he offers a satanic form of *eros,* a bestial lust for blood that paradoxically invigorates and dooms the women he has lured away from their impotent male protectors. Concerning the gender split in Stoker's novel, Bela Lugosi, the actor who turned the sensational vampire into a cinema idol, remarked on his fan mail, 91 percent of which came from females who admire terror for its own sake. He concluded: "For generations [women] have been the subject sex. This seems to have bred a masochistic interest—an enjoyment of, or at least a keen interest in, suffering experienced vicariously on the screen" (Wolf, vii). A subsequent matinee Dracula, Christopher Lee, concurred with Lugosi that men admire the hero-villain for his power; women swoon at the female victim's complete surrender to a male tormentor.

Imbued with the sin of hubris, the downfall of doomed protagonists from ancient Greek literature, in chapter 3, the count boasts of ancestry dating far earlier than the Prussian Hapsburgs and the Russian Romanovs, whom he dismisses as newly sprung like mushrooms. As an antichrist seeking to overthrow both decent womanhood and religiosity, he plots to create a race of vampires in England by purchasing Carfax, an estate at Purfleet named after the French Quatre Face, a suggestion of his range to the four points of the compass. Unlike his stay-at-home vampire predecessors, who preyed on their families, Stoker's fiend is an itinerant who replenishes his supply of home soil by carrying earth from his grave like luggage. As the invader's menace grows, in chapter 8, his insane apostle Renfield, like a Christ-crazed religious fanatic longing for the apocalypse, looks forward to the approach of the "Master" (Stoker, 106).

Symbolically, Stoker kills off his lurid count with a reduction of evil to dust, a reference to the Book of Common Prayer, which commits the dead to earth—the Hebrew *adamah*—to return to the common element—Adam—from which they sprang. As the cavalier stalkers—Harker, the appropriately named Arthur Holmwood, and Lucy's former suitor Quincey P. Morris—corner Dracula's 50th box of Transylvanian soil in the hands of gypsy sentries, they ward off female vampires and guards. With touches of the American West, two of the posse brandish Winchester rifles. At the coup de grâce, the Texan Morris wields a bowie knife to the throat, applying the savage invention of frontier warrior Jim Bowie, who died at the Alamo. The act is not without sacrifice. Stoker, employing the Arthurian death of the chivalric hero, salutes the English in the war against VAM-

PIRISM as Morris dies with a smile on his face. The onlookers, like knights of the Round Table, kneel to offer a benediction to the martyred gallant, a self-sacrificing gentleman who saves the orphan Mina Murray from the vampire's curse.

Bibliography

Auerbach, Nina. *Our Vampires, Ourselves*. Chicago: University of Chicago Press, 1995.

Barber, Paul. *Vampires, Burial, and Death: Folklore and Reality*. New Haven, Conn.: Yale University Press, 1988.

Hustis, Harriet. "Black and White and Read All Over: Performative Textuality in Bram Stoker's 'Dracula,'" *Studies in the Novel* 33, no. 1 (spring 2001): 18.

Ronay, Gabriel. *The Dracula Myth*. London: W. H. Allen, 1972.

Senf, Carol A. "Bram Stoker: History, Psychoanalysis and the Gothic," *Victorian Studies* 42, no. 4 (summer 2000): 675.

———. "Dracula: The Unseen Face in the Mirror," *Journal of Narrative Technique* 9 (1979): 170.

Stoker, Bram. *The Annotated Dracula*. New York: Clarkson N. Potter, 1975.

———. *Dracula*. New York: Bantam Books, 1981.

Twitchell, James B. *The Living Dead: A Study of the Vampire in Romantic Literature*. Durham, N.C.: Duke University Press, 1981.

Wolf, Leonard. Introduction to *The Annotated Dracula*. New York: Clarkson N. Potter, 1975.

Dracula's crypt

In DRACULA (1897), Bram STOKER marks the way to the vampire's crypt with cold, darkness, decay, and a foul odor as FORESHADOWINGs of the unpleasant task of killing a member of the un-dead. When the dutiful clerk Jonathan HARKER eludes the locked wing of the castle, he follows a circular stone staircase down to a tunnel redolent with newly dug earth. Trailing after the smell like a hunting dog after grouse, he reaches Stoker's perverse religious setting, a crumbling chapel, burial ground, and a series of large wooden boxes. In the dim light, Harker encounters "dread to my very soul," a suitable response to a vile literary Antichrist (Stoker, 50). In one of the boxes is the count, an open-eyed life-in-death apparition with so fierce a glare that Harker flees in terror. On a second foray to the crypt, Harker finds the count much rejuvenated from clotted blood that satiates abysmal longings, a perversion of communion wine, the sacramental blood of Christ. The vision of a leechlike MONSTER inspires nationalistic fervor in Harker, who fears for millions of Londoners threatened by a vampire who plans to settle at Carfax Estate.

In the falling action, the evil spreading from a vampire's crypt precipitates the formation of a cavalier brotherhood and a quest that takes the members from England through the Dardanelles, a dividing line between West and East, back to Transylvania, Dracula's ancestral grounds. On the way to facing consummate horror, the group locates Dracula's boxes of soil, a nationalistic emblem of a Hungarian homeland nurtured with blood. They sterilize 49 containers with the sanctified Host, leaving the 50th still virulent. In a symbolic act, the ever-faithful Szgany gypsies, an historically homeless tribe, bear it home to Dracula's lair, the home of the doomed wanderer.

In the last pages, the final confrontation with Dracula's crypt extends SUSPENSE. The final face-off pits the irrational with the rational, the horrific with the objectivity of the scientist, Dutch physician Abraham Van Helsing, the count's alter ego, who is strategist and leader of the posse. Like a chivalric knight in the lists, Van Helsing approaches the last unsanitized tomb in the count's chapel. Fighting an abnormal lethargy, the doctor locates a lordly monument marked with the single word *Dracula,* a name so imbued with terror that the three syllables are adequate to maintain Stoker's focus. In halting English, Van Helsing remarks with appropriate respect: "This then was the Un-Dead home of the King-vampire, to whom so many more were due. Its emptiness spoke eloquent to make certain what I knew" (*ibid.,* 392).

Stoker ends the quest with Van Helsing's "butcher work," which requires nerve over a paralyzing fear, a counter-balance that infuses his hand with strength (*ibid.*). The staking of Dracula's company of monsters summons screeching, a muscular spasm, and bloody foam from the un-dead lips. To assure that the count and his loathsome minions never walk earth again, the meticulous physician

"fixed [the crypt's] entrances" (*ibid.,* 393). As the sun sets, Jonathan Harker and Arthur Holmwood complete the banishment of vampirism from Transylvania by beheading and staking the chief vampire, a task that martyrs Quincey P. Morris, himself an outlander from Texas.

Bibliography

Auerbach, Nina. *Our Vampires, Ourselves.* Chicago: University of Chicago Press, 1995.

Hustis, Harriet. "Black and White and Read All Over: Performative Textuality in Bram Stoker's 'Dracula,'" *Studies in the Novel* 33, no. 1 (spring 2001): 18.

Ronay, Gabriel. *The Dracula Myth.* London: W. H. Allen, 1972.

Stoker, Bram. *Dracula.* New York: Bantam Books, 1981.

Wolf, Leonard. *A Dream of Dracula: In Search of the Living Dead.* New York: Popular Library, 1977.

Drake, Nathan
(1766–1836)

Physician, essayist, and fiction writer Dr. Nathan Drake is one of Gothic fiction's many multitalented moonlighters. A practicing medical doctor for 40 years, Drake was also an expert on Shakespeare and author of *Shakspeare* [sic] *and His Times* (1817), published in *Gentleman's Magazine,* and *Memorials of Shakspeare* [sic] (1828). After graduating from Edinburgh University, he opened an office in Sudbury and, two years later, resettled at Hadleigh, Suffolk. At age 62, his health declined from his extensive research-of-a-century overview of essays that Joseph Addison, Sir Richard Steele, and Dr. Samuel Johnson published in the *Guardian, Tatler,* and *Spectator.*

On the side, Drake wrote GOTHIC BLUEBOOKS during the heyday of English Gothic. He issued "Montmorenci, a Fragment" (1798), a short piece that followed the overworked conceit that the text derived from scraps of early manuscripts revealing Gothic terrors. He completed the atmospheric THE ABBEY OF CLUNEDALE (1804) and two undated works, *Captive of the Banditti* and the story "Henry Fitzowen: A Gothic Tale." He also published criticism on the literary mode in "On Gothic Superstition" and "On Objects of Terror," both contained in the three-volume miscellany *Literary Hours; or,*

Sketches Critical, Narrative, and Poetical (1798). In the former, he ties the Gothic genre to Geoffrey Chaucer and Edmund Spenser. The text notes the delight in Gothic at all levels of reading proficiency: "All were alive to the solemn and terrible graces of the appalling spectre . . . even the most enlightened mind, the mind free from all taint of superstition, involuntarily acknowledges its power" (Haining, 1).

In exacting references to style, Drake helped to set the parameters of Gothic estheticism when he used the term *Gothic* to refer to the SUPERNATURAL and to unfettered, macabre flights of imagination that included "the awful ministrations of the Spectre, or the innocent gambols of the Fairy." (Tarr, 5). A fan of Irish and Welsh lore, he urged poets of his own time to emulate the Celts by pursuing "the sublime, the terrible, and the fanciful" (McNutt, 34). In "On Objects of Terror," he advised that Gothic authors avoid unpleasant repercussions by writing of picturesque scenes and pathetic sentiment to stimulate curiosity and produce pleasurable emotions. In admiration of Gothic progenitor Ann RADCLIFFE, who met these criteria, Drake dubbed her "the Shakespeare of romance" (Clery, 1995, 53).

Bibliography

Chandler, David. "William Taylor and Some Traditions of Shakespeare Biography," *Notes and Queries* 42, no. 3 (September 1995): 338–340.

Clery, E. J. *The Rise of Supernatural Fiction, 1762–1800.* Cambridge: Cambridge University Press, 1995.

———. *Women's Gothic from Clara Reeve to Mary Shelley.* Tavistock, Devon: Northcote House, 2000.

Grove, Allen W. "To Make a Long Story Short: Gothic Fragments and the Gender Politics of Incompleteness," *Studies in Short Fiction* 34, no. 1 (winter 1997): 1–10.

Haining, Peter, ed. *Gothic Tales of Terror.* New York: Taplinger Publishing, 1972.

McNutt, Dan J. *The Eighteenth-Century Gothic Novel: An Annotated Bibliography of Criticism and Selected Texts.* New York: Garland, 1975.

Tarr, Mary Muriel. *Catholicism in Gothic Fiction: A Study of the Nature and Function of Catholic Materials in Gothic Fiction in England (1762–1820).* Washington, D.C.: Catholic University of America Press, 1946.

dreams and nightmares

Nighttime phantasms are realistic landscapes on which the psyche combats terrifying threats. In childhood, the battles are so real that young dreamers have difficulty separating dreamscape from the waking world. Because children hear FOLKLORE and FAIRY TALES involving ogres and great flying beasts, in their early years, they begin to connect fiction with darkness and Gothic horrors—pursuit, suffocation, dismemberment, devouring, and the unidentified MONSTER that lurks in the shadows. Into adulthood, Gothic literature taps the uncertainties that lurk in the mind when the body stretches out for rest and surrenders thoughts to the fantasies of sleep, the scenario in Katherine Anne Porter's deathbed dreamscape in "The Jilting of Granny Weatherall" (1930). Granny misidentifies the people around her as she relives unsettled problems from the past and seeks relief from old resentments.

Because of their significance to the subconscious mind, dreams, visions, and nightmares impinge on Gothic literature in two forms. The first group are writings prompted by dreams—for example, Horace WALPOLE's dreams and subsequent AUTOMATIC WRITING that generated THE CASTLE OF OTRANTO (1765), the drug-induced sleep that preceded Samuel Taylor COLERIDGE's "KUBLA KHAN" (1816), a friend's dream related in James HOGG's posthumous tale "The Expedition to Hell" (1836), and Bram STOKER's vampire classic DRACULA (1897), which he evolved from a phantasm resulting from a heavy seafood meal. Other nightly phantasms that inspired creative plots include Louisa May Alcott's typhus-generated hallucinations that impacted her short stories "M. L." (1863) and "My Contraband" (1863) and her novel *A Long Fatal Love Chase* (1866), Robert Louis STEVENSON's nighttime horror that inspired DR. JEKYLL AND MR. HYDE (1886), and the skillfully wrought visions of the Irish-American Gothicist Fitz-James O'BRIEN that inspired his influential story "What Was It?" (1859).

In recent times, critic Anne Williams, author of *Art of Darkness: A Poetics of Gothic* (1995), questioned these claims of fiction arising from dream. She suspects the method of dream-turned-into-gothic as a rationalization of a literary mode lacking in respectability. For the serious writer, a claim of an overnight phantasm excuses the legitimate author of slumming in a bad neighborhood.

The second application of phantasms to Gothic mode is a body of writings in which dreams influence character action, as with AMBROSIO's dreams that misidentify the alluring Mathilda as the Virgin Mary in Matthew Gregory LEWIS's THE MONK (1796) and Clara WIELAND's warning dream in Charles Brockden BROWN's WIELAND; or, The Transformation (1798). Throughout 18th-century fiction, dreams were a gendered phenomenon, typically the province of desexed clerics and women, whose inward, repressed lives were conducive to daydreams, fantasies and visions, and night phantasms. With THE ITALIAN (1797), Ann RADCLIFFE, the progenitor of FEMALE GOTHIC, presented an horrific nightmare of the murderous monk Vivaldi as normal. She justifies his late-night trauma as the outgrowth of his questioning by the Spanish Inquisition. Lacking a background in militarism and self-defense, Vicentio di Vivaldi, the heroine's suitor, compensates by challenging torments intellectually rather than physically.

Dreams were integral to the plots of 19th-century fiction, as seen in Lord BYRON's "Darkness" (1816), a lengthy apocalypse that concludes with the eclipse of the universe; Victor FRANKENSTEIN's nightmare about his mother's corpse in Mary SHELLEY's FRANKENSTEIN (1818); the visionary dream state in George Eliot's "The Lifted Veil" (1859); and VILLIERS DE L'ISLE-ADAM's morbid nightmares in Contes Cruels (Cruel Tales, 1883) and Nouveaux Contes Cruels (New Cruel Tales, 1888). American Gothicist Gertrude ATHERTON depicted dreamscapes and METEMPSYCHOSIS in What Dreams May Come (1888), in which lovers fluctuate between their own times and those of their grandparents, who shared an illicit affair. In sleep, the protagonist teeters on the brink of a time warp: "Why was he falling—falling?—What was that terror-stricken cry? that wild, white face of an old man above him? Where had this water come from that was boiling and thundering in his ears? What was that tossed aloft by the wave beyond? If he could but reach her!—She had gone!" (Atherton, 192).

In these instances, retreats into the subconscious are gender-neutral probings that illuminate universal realities—the curiosities, impulses, and sexual urges that drive the conscious mind to strange actions. Authors use such gray areas as liminal states between reason and fantasy or dream and doom, the situation that Isadora faces in Charles Robert MATURIN's MELMOTH THE WANDERER (1820). As she characterizes the approach of her demon-husband Melmoth to the Inquisition's torturers, she struggles to explain how hellish dreams take on reality. Nikolai GOGOL further blurred the separation between dream and hallucination in "The Diary of a Madman" and "Nevsky Prospect," two stories anthologized in Arabeski (Arabesques) (1835).

Edgar Allan POE began studying the overlap between reality and dream states in an early poem, "A Dream," which he developed from a reading of Lord Byron's "I Would I Were a Careless Child" (1807) and published in Tamerlane and Other Poems (1827). That same year, Poe composed "Dreams," a salute to mental creations as escapes from reality. Two months later, he wrote "In Youth I Have Known One" (1827), a dream overview of Philadelphia's battle with the great yellow fever epidemic of 1793. At his creative height, he composed the ghoulish MYSTERY lyric "Dream-Land" (1844), a blend of beauty and horror. Two months later, he followed with "Mesmeric Revelation" (1844), a tale of a hypnotic trance during which the dying subject, Vankirk, experiences death and speaks from the world beyond his observations on the afterlife. Still obsessed by the overlay of dreams in the waking world, Poe issued "A Dream within a Dream" (1849), a tormented outcry revealing his troubled mental state following the death of his wife, Virginia Clemm Poe.

Dream-states reflect the psychological underpinnings of mid-19th-century Gothic fiction. In JANE EYRE (1847), Charlotte BRONTË turns dreams into prescient visions of the festering SECRECY at THORNFIELD. During the four weeks preceding the protagonist's wedding to Edward ROCHESTER, Jane experiences prophetic visions of the hall in ruins and inhabited by bats and owls, images that she may have derived from reading the Gothic fiction popular in her day. Carrying an unidentified child, a SYMBOL of the nascent love that she hopes to nurture into a home, Jane anticipates separation as her fiancé departs for a lengthy sojourn in a distant land. Her hold on the estate proves insufficient to endure a strange upheaval, during which the babe nearly strangles her. The dream spools out in mock narrative of her eventual loss of Thornfield, future husband, and family.

Jane Eyre's night vision turns to confrontation with a true evil, the insane wife who dwells in the third floor of Rochester's mansion. The phantasm rustles near the wedding dress and veil, lifting a candle to reveal a dark-haired woman with savage, discolored face set with red eyes and blackened features. Brontë increases meaning with damage to only one part of the nuptial costume, the veil, which conceals the truth from the bride-to-be. Jane continues the litany of ghoulish details, "the lips were swelled and dark; the brow furrowed: the black eyebrows widely raised over the bloodshot eyes" (Brontë, 270). Jane identifies the woman as a German vampire. The approach of evil shocks Jane into unconsciousness, but does not jolt Rochester into a confession of wrongdoing in keeping his crazed wife locked away.

Brontë balanced spectral visitations with more hopeful visions. On the night before Jane's departure from Thornfield, she experiences a beneficent dream. Seeing herself lying in the red-room of GATESHEAD HALL, her childhood foster home, she envisions a heavenly light and the gradual appearance of her dead mother. The advice to "flee temptation" guides Jane's thinking and strengthens her resolve to leave her trousseau behind and take to the moors, even if flight ends at the workhouse and a pauper's grave (ibid., 304). The dreams, taken as a whole, inform the heroine's subconscious with a knowledge far beyond her experience.

Late-Victorian and modern Gothic retained the dreamscape as an enduring internal setting for hauntings and psychological terror. In *Dracula* (1897), after the shipwreck of the schooner *Demeter* (an allusion to the loss of a daughter of the Greek goddess Demeter to Hades, the master of the underworld), Stoker depicts Lucy Westenra as a female victim named from the Latin *lux* for *light*, a glow that blazes into a lurid flame under Dracula's power. When her friend Mina Murray finds Lucy sleepwalking at a graveyard, Lucy shivers with cold and pain from the recent bite of the vampire. His fangs leave the tell-tale twin punctures and a bloodstain on her nightgown as though a serpent had struck in the night. Lucy is overwhelmed by anemia, fitful sleep and excitability, languor, pallor and deteriorating gums, strange dreams, and fixation on an ominous male figure with red eyes, a foreboding of Count Dracula's menace to the Whitby shore.

Within decades, ominous symbolic dreams gave place to realistic phantasms. With seeming innocence, Daphne DU MAURIER opens her mystery classic REBECCA (1938) with the rueful, MELANCHOLY line, "Last night I dreamt I went to MANDERLEY again" (du Maurier, 1). In one of Richard Wright's Gothic poems, "Between the World and Me," published in *Partisan Review* in 1935, the unidentified speaker is devastated by the cooling detritus of a lynching and the burning of the black victim, the haunted ground of AMERICAN GOTHIC. In a state of trauma, he experiences a daylight nightmare of himself in the hands of white racists: "The dry bones stirred, rattled, lifted, melting themselves into my bones" (Wright, 437). The speaker envisions himself captured, tormented, and burned alive as he "clutched to the hot sides of death" (ibid.). Later in the century, Caribbean author Jean RHYS applied dreams to COLONIAL GOTHIC and its insistent terrors. As tokens of displacement, she depicts Antoinette, the troubled bride in *Wide Sargasso Sea* (1966), experiencing prophetic visions of life far from the Caribbean pleasures of Jamaica in a cold, unfeeling English household. In each instance, the dream-state increases the Gothic terror by extending trauma through mental images.

Bibliography

Atherton, Gertrude. *What Dreams May Come*. Chicago: Belford, Clarke, 1888.

Brontë, Charlotte. *Jane Eyre*. New York: Bantam Books, 1981.

Doody, Margaret Anne. "Deserts, Ruins, and Troubled Waters: Female Dreams in Fiction and the Development of the Gothic Novel," *Genre* 10 (1977): 529–573.

du Maurier, Daphne. *Rebecca*. New York: Avon Books, 1971.

Klimasmith, Betsy. "Slave, Master, Mistress, Slave: Genre and Interracial Desire in Louisa May Alcott's Fiction," *ATQ* 11, no. 2 (1997): 115–135.

Stewart, Charles. "Erotic Dreams and Nightmares from Antiquity to the Present," *Journal of the Royal Anthropological Institute* 8, no. 1 (June 2002): 1.

Tuan, Yi-Fu. *Landscapes of Fear.* New York: Pantheon Books, 1979.

Williams, Anne. *Art of Darkness: A Poetics of Gothic.* Chicago: University of Chicago Press, 1995.

Wright, Richard. "Between the World and Me," in *Black Voices.* New York: Mentor Books, 1968.

Dr. Faustus
Christopher Marlowe
(ca. 1588)

Christopher Marlowe's popular play *The Tragicall Historie of Doctor Faustus* provided Gothic fiction with a durable vision of the MAD SCIENTIST doomed by egomania and DIABOLISM. At a time when witchery and human culpability for sin were serious concerns, Marlowe tempted fate by placing both topics center stage. He based his superhuman character on *Historia von Dr. Johan Fausten* (The story of Dr. John Fausten, 1587), an anonymous German work drawn from the legend of the necromancer Simon Magus of Samaria. Although Marlowe's controversial play was acted 23 times from 1594 to 1597, outcries of "monstrous" and "sacrilegious" arose, even among his fellow playwrights. The English Parliament decreed that no one restage the play's hellish motifs.

The Gothic shadows of satanism derive from Marlowe's Mephistophilis, the earthly agent of evil and a forerunner of the MELANCHOLY, self-seeking BYRONIC HERO. Through the equivocation of right and righteousness, he leads Faustus astray, causing him to deny the real world and Christian dogma in his scramble to embrace a fantasy. By negotiating a pact with the devil, Faustus commands the black arts and cloaks himself in a foolish self-delusion that he has surpassed human limitations on knowledge and power. By play's end, Mephistophilis, Beelzebub, and Lucifer superintend the deathbed watch that precedes the disclosure of Hellmouth and Faustus's eternal damnation. In his plunge, the self-destroyer falls into the hands of devils that rend him in pieces. His rise and fall generated a lengthy Gothic canon of egotistical sinners: Jacques Cazotte's *Le Diable Amoreux* (*The Devil in Love*, 1772), Matthew Gregory LEWIS's THE MONK (1796), the anonymous GOTHIC BLUEBOOK titled *The Life and Horrid Adventures of the Celebrated Dr. Faustus* (1810), Lord BYRON's closet drama MANFRED (1817), Charles Robert MATURIN's terror novel MELMOTH THE WANDERER (1820), Johann von GOETHE's *Faust* (1790–1832), George William Macarthur REYNOLDS's *Faust: A Romance of the Secret Tribunals* (1845–46), Oscar WILDE's MELODRAMA THE PICTURE OF DORIAN GRAY (1891), and Angela CARTER's *The Infernal Desire Machines of Doctor Hoffman* (1972).

Bibliography
Hamlin, William M. "Casting Doubt in Marlowe's Doctor Faustus," *Studies in English Literature, 1500–1900* 41, no. 2 (spring 2001): 257.

McMurtry, Jo. *Understanding Shakespeare's England.* Hamden, Conn.: Archon Books, 1989.

Sullivan, Ceri. "Faustus and the Apple," *Review of English Studies* 47, no. 185 (February 1996): 47–50.

Turner, Alice K. *The History of Hell.* New York: Harcourt Brace & Co., 1993.

Dr. Jekyll and Mr. Hyde
Robert Louis Stevenson
(1886)

The Scottish romancer Robert Louis STEVENSON focused on fictional studies of moral ambiguity, crime, and villainy. Writing rapidly to earn money from the "shilling shocker" market, he produced a classic application of the DOPPELGÄNGER motif in *The Strange Case of Dr. Jekyll and Mr. Hyde,* a complex novella influenced by the serial narrators in Wilkie COLLINS's *The Woman in White* (1860). Stevenson builds his story on elements of SUSPENSE that imply a shocking, deadly outcome. Through a perversion of science, Dr. Henry Jekyll, a variation on the MAD SCIENTIST stereotype, concocts a chemical salt to free the bestial elements of his personality. Jekyll represents the curious man of science; his double and FOIL, Mr. Edward Hyde, whose name implies the act of hiding and the hide that covers a beast, acts out the primitive, murderous, STALKING urges of the MONSTER. After a series of experiments on himself, the seriously fragmented Dr. Henry Jekyll speaks of himself both as "I" and as "Jekyll." His descent into evil appears to have wrenched his original self from its psychological moorings and turned him at intervals into a brute.

As an enhancement of character duality, Stevenson places his protagonist in an aggressively sinister GOTHIC SETTING at a home laboratory and former dissecting theater protected from prying eyes by a foggy cupola, closed windows, heavy doors, and a courtyard. Staying apart from the handsome, respectable home of Dr. Jekyll, the troglodytic Hyde resides to the rear of the block in a windowless residence behind a discolored wall lacking bell and knocker, a suitable dwelling for a man with the evocative name of Hyde. Because Hyde is given to puerile tricks of scrawling blasphemies in books, burning letters, and marring a portrait of Jekyll's father, the scientist acquires a flat for Hyde in Soho. The area is known for lowlife pubs, cabarets, cheap eateries, and brothels "with its muddy ways, and slatternly passengers . . . like a district of some city in a nightmare" (Stevenson, 22–23). In the CHIAROSCURO common to his late hours, Hyde can prowl Soho's disreputable streets, then disappear for months when Jekyll consumes him by SHAPE-SHIFTING back into his normal self.

Stevenson's Gothic crime story reaches its climax when the overconfident Jekyll realizes that he has no control of Hyde, who emerges uncensored in Regent's Park. Hyde drubs an old man to death and harms a child who is selling matches; the latter act is a SYMBOL of darkness in the soul that costs Jekyll his life and reputation. Critics have formulated PSYCHOLOGICAL INTERPRETATIONs of the duality as a study of Victorian principles—the individual's outward respectability and the hidden chaos and VIOLENCE within. Another interpretation describes the novella as an ALLEGORY depicting the rash scientist fleeing less challenging, less dramatic inquiry to dabble in occult secrets of life.

Bibliography

Arata, Stephen D. "The Sedulous Ape: Atavism, Professionalism, and Stevenson's 'Jekyll and Hyde,'" *Criticism* 37, no. 2 (spring 1995): 233–259.

Halberstam, Judith. *Skin Shows: Gothic Horror and the Technology of Monsters*. Durham, N.C.: Duke University Press, 1995.

Stevenson, Robert Louis. *Dr. Jekyll and Mr. Hyde*. New York: Bantam Books, 1981.

Wright, Daniel L. "'The Prisonhouse of My Disposition': A Study of the Psychology of Addiction in 'Dr. Jekyll and Mr. Hyde,'" *Studies in the Novel* 26, no. 3 (fall 1994): 254–267.

du Maurier, Daphne
(1907–1989)

The prime source of modern FEMALE GOTHIC, MYSTERY writer Daphne du Maurier produced REBECCA (1938), one of the enduring Gothic novels of the 20th century. Born to a refined literary household, she was the granddaughter of George du Maurier, author of the best-selling MELODRAMA *Trilby* (1894). She began writing short fiction at age 21 and composed her first period romance, *The Loving Spirit* (1931), as a form of escape from family pressures. As her command of fiction increased, she set her blockbusters—*Jamaica Inn* (1936), *Rebecca,* and *Frenchman's Creek* (1941)—in Cornwall, a part of England that inflamed her imagination with LEGENDs of pirates, smugglers, and hauntings.

Du Maurier reflected over her motivation for *Rebecca* in *The Rebecca Notebook* (1980), which expresses her surprise at the novel's success and its influence on her later life and publications. While living in Alexandria, Egypt, where her husband was on military assignment with the Grenadier Guards, she plotted the atmospheric master thriller. During the war years, interspersed with the rest of her career in Gothic fiction, were encouraging personal observations that the author submitted to the *Edinburgh Evening News* and provincial papers, including "A Mother and Her Faith, Comforting Words by Daphne du Maurier," published in March 1940. The proceeds from her sixpenny booklet "Come Wind, Come Weather" went to the Soldiers, Sailors and Air Force Association.

In the aftermath of World War II, the Gothic short story became du Maurier's next triumph after she turned to SUPERNATURAL motifs. In the October 1952 issue of *Good Housekeeping*, she published a classic short story, "THE BIRDS." It later appeared in *Kiss Me Again Stranger* (1953), a collection named for her tale of a demure young woman who turns out to be the killer of a Nazi. For the anthology *Not After Midnight* (1970), she produced another thriller, "Don't Look Now," a tale of the GROTESQUE and occultism set on an eerie night in Saint Mark's Square in Venice, featuring psychic twins and a dwarf. She loaded the story with Gothic elements by stressing hallucination, mistaken identity, and transvestism.

A precursor of the contemporary Gothic of Victoria HOLT and Shirley JACKSON, du Maurier was a successful storyteller and creator of memorable characterization. She displayed appreciation for Radcliffean Gothic and Victorian forerunners, especially the novels of Charlotte BRONTË and Emily BRONTË. *Rebecca,* du Maurier's most acclaimed Gothic page-turner, earned mixed critical response. Although millions of readers adored the story, critics carped about the author's reliance on coincidence and melodrama. Nonetheless, the novel earned du Maurier a National Book Award and a citation from the American Literary Society. At age 62, she was appointed Dame Commander in the Order of the British Empire.

Bibliography

du Maurier, Daphne. *The Rebecca Notebook and Other Memories.* Garden City, N.Y.: Doubleday, 1980.

Fleenor, Juliann E., ed. *The Female Gothic.* Montreal: Eden Press, 1983.

Forster, Margaret. *Daphne du Maurier.* New York: Doubleday, 1993.

dungeons and prisons

Confinement, particularly of an innocent female character, is a major motif in Gothic lore. It derives in part from FOLKLORE—the Greek myth of Persephone's imprisonment in the underworld; the GRIMM brothers' FAIRY TALE of Rapunzel in the tower; and the wife-and-master tale "Peter, Peter Pumpkin Eater," an undated Gothic NURSERY RHYME about a dominating husband who secures his wife in a pumpkin shell. After the formation of Gothic conventions in the late 18th century, authors used cells, murder holes, and oubliettes to accentuate CLAUSTROPHOBIA, mental torment, and

terror. These settings typically produced a living death in some forgotten cell, as with the male inmate in the Sicilian dungeon in Scottish storyteller William MUDFORD's "The Iron Shroud" (1830), the walled-up female corpse found in a priest hole in Victoria HOLT's MISTRESS OF MELLYN (1960), the underground warrens in Richard Adams's *Watership Down* (1972), and the torture of an injured man in Stephen KING's *Misery* (1987). The motif was often aimed at women as a metaphor of suffocating social roles that paralyzed them and robbed them of self-actualization. Feminist critics point out that the standard motifs of Gothic literature tend toward a confining space—the castle, tower room, abbey, or dungeon, such as the iron and wood lockup in which Hester Prynne waits out pregnancy and childbirth in Nathaniel HAWTHORNE's THE SCARLET LETTER (1850). Freudian interpretation of these cells points to the intricate subterranean passageways, trapdoors, vaults, and sliding panels as psychological code for entrances to the female body. The heroine's preservation of life, sanity, and virtue from physical overpowering or sexual mastery often hinges on ingenious means of warding off intruders to the passages, a symbolic prolonging of virginity or postponement of response to normal sexual awareness and arousal.

The matriarch of the GOTHIC NOVEL, Ann RADCLIFFE, introduced the fair damsel trapped in compromising situations with an evil count's enclosure of Emily ST. AUBERT in the castle of the title in THE MYSTERIES OF UDOLPHO (1794), a dismal setting in the Apennines. Matthew Gregory LEWIS augmented the menace of a male confining a female with atrocities committed in a crypt by the ominous AMBROSIO in THE MONK (1796). In retort to Lewis's SENSATIONALISM, Radcliffe augmented the enclosure motif in THE ITALIAN (1797), which imprisons both male and female, the ingenue and her lover. For menace, Radcliffe turned to ANTI-CATHOLICISM by placing Vivaldi, Ellena's suitor, in the torture chambers of the Spanish Inquisition, a favorite GOTHIC SETTING. The author left heroine Ellena Rosalba to languish at the convent of San Stefano, an abbey named for Stephen, the first Christian martyr.

The link between confinement and female cloistering recurred in reams of Radcliffean imitations, many published by William Lane's MINERVA PRESS. In the pulp novel *Bungay Castle* (1796), author Elizabeth Bonhote, one of the Minerva stable, exploited the notion that convents imprisoned unwilling novices. In the first volume, Edwin, the rescuer, plans to access the convent chapel from a nearby castle to end Madeline's coercion by a high-church conspiracy. His promise to sneak into her cell balloons into a diatribe against nunneries as the equivalent of dungeons that seclude women from society and amusement while they spin out their days in solitude and friendlessness. Mary WOLLSTONECRAFT, a Radcliffe admirer, reset her own novel, *MARIA; OR, THE WRONGS OF WOMEN* (1798), in an asylum rather than in the imaginative castle, tower, or prison cell. Her choice reflects a real menace to women, who were more frequently incarcerated as lunatics than men.

In more deadly form, the entrapment motif thrilled readers of HORROR FICTION, including Philip FRENEAU's post–Revolutionary War diatribe *The British Prison-Ship* (1781), a reflection of personal experience while confined in New York harbor in the enemy ship *Scorpion*. Imitative writers such as Anne YEARSLEY, author of the historical novel *The Royal Captives* (1795), chilled the reader with fearful lockups, chambers of horror, and unspeakable props—the pit, rack, and iron maiden, a mummy case equipped with daggers that riddled the victim with stab wounds as the lid closed. Authors of GOTHIC BLUEBOOKs enlarged on jailing and claustrophobia—as, for example, in C. F. Barrett's "Douglas Castle; or, The Cell of Mystery, a Scottish Tale" (1803), in which the villain locks his wife and daughter in an iron tower. Such fairy tale scenarios encouraged the image of ineffectual womanhood as easy prey for fortune hunters, incestuous fathers and uncles, killers, and sadists, who removed their quarry from normal society to remote locales and walled them up to quell rebellion against patriarchy.

The motif of incarceration amid unimaginable torments matured along with GOTHIC CONVENTION, which branched out toward psychological study and realism. In the unrelieved terror of Edgar Allan POE's "THE PIT AND THE PENDULUM" (1843), the author probes the instincts and logic of a male detainee of a grotesquely repressive regime.

In Emily BRONTË's *WUTHERING HEIGHTS* (1847), a subtle image of the restraints imposed on women by marriage takes shape in the implied restriction of Catherine EARNSHAW at Thrushcross Grange, her husband's splendid home from which she looks out on the moors through latticed windows, metaphoric bars. In Charlotte Perkins GILMAN's AMERICAN GOTHIC story "THE YELLOW WALLPAPER" (1892), imprisonment is more overt in an asylum, a male-governed institution that awaits the restless wife or too-ambitious female. Further internalization of captivity in the 20th century pointed the motif toward existential significance, as with the casual commitment of a local woman to a home for the feeble-minded in Eudora WELTY's SOUTHERN GOTHIC story "Lily Daw and the Three Ladies" (1941). Jean-Paul Sartre's "The Wall" (1939) identifies walls with fascism, lack of human beneficence, and death; overt class warfare in Isabel ALLENDE's Argentine novel *THE HOUSE OF THE SPIRITS* (1981) parallels social strictures with Gothic lockups. A symbolic terror of water and drowning suffocates a failed minister in Australian Gothicist Peter Carey's *OSCAR AND LUCINDA* (1988).

Bibliography

Gilbert, Sandra M., and Susan Gubar. *The Madwoman in the Attic*, 2nd ed. New Haven, Conn.: Yale University Press, 2000.

Roth, Marty. "Gilman's Arabesque Wallpaper," *Mosaic* 34, no. 4 (December 2001): 145–162.

Tarr, Mary Muriel. *Catholicism in Gothic Fiction: A Study of the Nature and Function of Catholic Materials in Gothic Fiction in England (1762–1820)*. Washington, D.C.: Catholic University of America Press, 1946.

Wolff, Cynthia. "The Radcliffean Gothic Model," in *The Female Gothic*. Montreal: Eden Press, 1983: 207–223.

Dupin, C. Auguste

The intuitive sleuth in three of Edgar Allan POE's detective stories, Le Chevalier C. Auguste Dupin, the prefect of Paris police, is adept not only at investigation but also at scholarship. The author may have named his detective in honor of the French attorney and legislator Andre Marie Jean-Jacques

Dupin, a revered orator. Born to a noble family and living at a fashionable address in the Faubourg St. Germain, the fictional Dupin merges brilliance and personal eccentricities to advantage, particularly his yen for solitude and for retracing the thought patterns of criminals. In "The Purloined Letter" (1844), his musing over the phrase *facilis descensus Averni* [easy is the descent into Hell] not only links him to Virgil's *Aeneid* (19 B.C.), but also embellishes the logical explanation of a minister's fall (Poe, 219).

Dupin exemplifies the importance of emotional detachment and high levels of concentration in the solving of baffling crimes. The most arcane of his solutions occurs in a famous locked-room MYSTERY, "THE MURDERS IN THE RUE MORGUE" (1841), and involves the discounting of red herrings. In ascertaining the language of a bizarre killer and mutilator of Madame L'Espanaye and her daughter, Henry Duval identifies the suspect as Italian, the undertaker Alfonzo Garcio attests that the voices arising from the death chamber argued in French and English, and the confectioner Alberto Montani describes the voice as Russian. In deriving the truth, Dupin dismisses the views of Monsieur G——, the inept prefect of police that Poe may have drawn from Henri-Joseph Gisquet, the prefect of the Parisian police in the 1830s.

Dupin's lone-wolf method of detection set a pattern among the detectives of fiction, whom subsequent authors tended to pair with ineffectual, less cerebral colleagues. At a crime scene in the Rue Morgue, without help from the authorities, Dupin reaches an horrendous conclusion: He identifies an orangutan from Borneo as the possessor of a straight razor, with which it decapitated a human victim. The ingenuity of Dupin's keen assembly of data presaged later detectives, notably Sir Arthur Conan DOYLE's Sherlock HOLMES and Agatha Christie's Belgian sleuth Hercule Poirot.

Bibliography

Eco, Umberto, and Thomas A. Sebeok, eds. *The Sign of Three: Dupin, Holmes, Peirce.* Bloomington: Indiana University Press, 1983.

Poe, Edgar Allan. *Selected Stories and Poems.* New York: Airmont, 1962.

dybbuk

A MONSTER from Jewish peasant FOLKLORE in Germany, Poland, and Russia, the dybbuk (also spelled *dibbuk*) is a displaced soul that expiates former sins by wandering until it can locate a living body in which to dwell. The term derives from the Yiddish word for "cling" or "attach." A form of METEMPSYCHOSIS or transmigration of souls, the dybbuk's wicked infiltration of an unsuspecting soul was the source of horror tales in the 1500s describing INSANITY and multiple personalities. In Hasidic communities, spiritual disturbance in a victim often required exorcism through incantation and ritual to rid the individual of ABERRANT BEHAVIOR.

Based on KABBALISM, the Gothic concept of dybbuk POSSESSION emerged from the writings of the mystic Isaac Luria, who characterized the demon's intrusion on living humans as a striving for self-improvement. Gothic stagecraft pictured the restless spirit in the moody, evocative *Der Dybbuk* (1916), a stylized Yiddish play based on a distillation of peasant lore. The play was written by the Ukrainian-American playwright and ethnographer Solomon Rappaport, who published under the pseudonym S. Ansky. He filled his version with undying passion, MYSTICISM, sacrilege, numerology, and the SUPERNATURAL as the dybbuk attempts to escape entrapment between earth and heaven.

In front of a synagogue in the 1860s, the terrifying stage set presents a pair of graves in the middle of the street, where eastern Europeans interred victims of a pogrom inflicted by Russian Cossacks in 1648. Leah, a young bride, feels herself overpowered by a hovering spirit that forces her into a trance. A messenger states the nature of a dybbuk: "Sinful souls return to earth in animals, in birds, in fish, and even at times in plants" (Ansky, 25). Only through the act of a holy man can they attain purification and release. The male dybbuk claims Leah, causing her to faint after she rejects Frade, her groom. She cries out in the spirit's voice, "There is a heaven and there is an earth and there are worlds upon worlds in the universe, but nowhere is there a place for me" (*ibid.*, 36). Frequently banned because of its fearful scenes of a corrupt soul invading a tender bride, the play concludes with a failed exorcism and Leah's merger with the dybbuk.

Ansky's play debuted in Moscow before its run in New York, San Francisco, and Vilna, Poland. It gained world stature in Bulgarian, English, French, German, Polish, Russian, Swedish, and Ukrainian translations. In addition to presentation in puppet theaters and as a ballet, the long-lived play evolved into an Italian opera by the composer Ludovico Rocca, Israeli and Polish screenplays, a New York musical by Renato Simoni and David Temkin, and dramatic versions that ran on Broadway in 1925, 1926, 1948, and 1964.

Bibliography

Ansky, S. *The Dybbuk and Other Writings*. New York: Schocken Books, 1992.

Serper, Zvika. "'Between Two Worlds': The Dybbuk and the Japanese Noh and Kabuki Ghost Plays," *Comparative Drama* 35, no. 3 (fall 2001): 345–376.

E

Earnshaw, Catherine

The uninhibited, driven protagonist in Emily BRONTË's ghost novel *WUTHERING HEIGHTS* (1847), Catherine Earnshaw is one of the first Gothic protagonists to embrace her darker side. She represents the soul's fierce battle between immersion in NATURE and society's demand for domestication and acceptable womanly conduct. Unlike most nubile heroines, she is the rare Gothic protagonist who enters fiction as a little girl, when desire emerges in the form of wayward behavior and petulance.

From early childhood, Catherine expresses an unfulfilled passion for adventure sated through friendship with HEATHCLIFF, her gypsy foster brother. From their mutual rovings on the English moors, she later determines that "he's more myself than I am," an acknowledgment of the DOPPELGÄNGER motif, which binds the two immutably and tragically as one (Brontë, 82). By internalizing Heathcliff's longings and anguish, she attempts to breathe freedom and acceptance into a pathetically rejected OUTSIDER. Her fantasies of playing the rescuer prove her undoing.

The author develops the troubled female protagonist through spurts of change and reversions to type. Headstrong and domineering, Catherine matures from moorland hoyden into a conflicted young woman following a five-week visit to Thrushcross Grange, the home of genteel neighbors. After viewing its scarlet carpets and chairs, gold-edge ceiling, and limpid crystal chandelier through the window, she recognizes a passion for refinement that competes with girlish wildness. The internal conflict threatens her long-term relationship with Heathcliff.

Catherine's shift toward the Lintons' way of life is a gesture toward pragmatism. Arrogant and self-seeking, she chooses union with a stable, wealthy husband as a social niche more likely to reward her with material comfort than would endless tramps on the moors with a swarthy nobody. She rationalizes the split of her persona into pragmatic and willful halves by telling herself that she can elevate Heathcliff from boorishness by marrying a gentle, thoughtful husband. Unlike the typical Gothic story, marriage does not resolve her discontent or rid her of overidealization or pagan intensity.

As both Catherine and Heathcliff reach sexual maturity, Brontë builds desire and conflict to a peak. After Catherine betrays her inner yearnings by marrying the passive, overrefined Edgar Linton, she tries to settle into a prim, but lackluster domesticity. Catherine's love for Edgar proves transitory. In her double life, she manages to grace Edgar's home while escaping for jaunts with Heathcliff. Their tenuous alliance fractures after Heathcliff romances Isabella Linton, a tender NAIF. Catherine's defense of the younger girl releases some hidden truths. She admits that Heathcliff harbors potential for evil and proclaims him "fierce, pitiless, wolfish" (*ibid.*, 103). Disgusted with extremes—the weak-willed Edgar vs. the potentially dangerous Heathcliff—Catherine considers her dilemma "stupid to absurdity" (*ibid.*, 114).

Brontë's heroine pays for risk-taking with an early death, one of the more melodramatic leave-takings in English Gothic fiction. The author advances the SUBTEXT of Catherine's emotions through her mad babblings during a postpartum illness, when she confesses to "a paroxysm of despair" after separation from Heathcliff (*ibid.*, 124). Like Shakespeare's mad Ophelia and Lady Macbeth, she becomes death-haunted and expresses internal torments that distort reason, causing her to threaten housekeeper Nelly Dean: "You witch! So you do seek elf-bolts to hurt us! Let me go, and I'll make her rue! I'll make her howl a recantation!" (*ibid.*, 127). After Catherine's suffering and death from premature childbirth, the Gothic heightening continues through the PATHETIC FALLACY with a period of driving sleet and snow after her funeral and through the SUPERNATURAL by her return to Wuthering Heights as a weeping wraith. Her grave, dug at the extreme of the kirkyard, mingles her remains with heath and bilberry vines, elements of the moor that force its wildness across a sanctified perimeter to grace the lonely spot.

Bibliography

Brontë, Emily. *Wuthering Heights*. New York: New American Library, 1959.

Goodlett, Debra. "Love and Addiction in 'Wuthering Heights,'" *Midwest Quarterly* 37, no. 3 (spring 1996): 316–327.

Hoeveler, Diane Long. *Gothic Feminism*. University Park: Pennsylvania State University Press, 1998.

Stoneman, Patsy. "Catherine Earnshaw's Journey to Her Home among the Dead: Fresh Thoughts on 'Wuthering Heights' and 'Epipsychidion,'" *Review of English Studies* 47, no. 188 (November 1996): 521–533.

Thormahlen, Marianne. "The Lunatic and the Devil's Disciple: The 'Lovers' in 'Wuthering Heights,'" *Review of English Studies* 48, no. 190 (May 1997): 183–197.

Eco, Umberto

(1932–   )

Umberto Eco, a linguist and lecturer at the University of Bologna, applies his expertise in semiotics— the explanation of signs and SYMBOLs—to allegorical fiction. With the publication of *Il Nome della Rosa* (*The Name of the Rose*, 1980), an international best-seller, Eco revived a number of classic Gothic traditions by merging MEDIEVALISM and heresy with occultism and the detective thriller. Set in a Benedictine monastery in 1327 during the Inquisition, the text features macabre murders, homosexuality among monks, a lone female in an ascetic population, mysterious passages through a vast library, and an historic master torturer, Bernard Gui of Toulouse. By sending the protagonist, the learned Franciscan brother William of Baskerville, with his apprentice Adso on a dizzying dash through a tower confused with multiple stairways and switchbacks, Eco implies the abbey's moral chaos and the challenge to rationality posed by multiple killings committed by ostensibly Christian clerics.

Eco positions his novel on the cusp of the Renaissance, when enlightenment was beginning to permeate the eccentricities of religious dogma and refute peasant SUPERSTITIONs about sex, sin, and Satan. In conflict with an abbot who blames heretics for jeopardizing order in the civilized world, the detective William refuses to accept SUPERNATURAL causes of the abbey's interlocking crimes. During the investigation, Eco provides comic relief in an addled GROTESQUE, Salvatore, speaker of mangled English mixed with Latin, French, and Italian. Salvatore tells Adso how to dig out a cat's eyes, place them in hen's eggs, season them in horse manure, and reap two little imps who would run errands at his command.

Eco's novel concludes in conflagration. In the final view of the abbey, a cleansing fire has performed a "divine chastisement" (Eco, 605). On a return to the abbey years later, Adso finds ruins symbolic of the collapse of religious authority in the late Middle Ages: "I still glimpsed there, dilated by the elements and dulled by lichens, the left eye of the enthroned Christ, and something of the lion's face" (*ibid.*, 608). Within the dismembered rubble of the labyrinthine scriptorium lie fragments of burned, water-damaged pages, the stumps and ghosts of books, symbols of the imperfect transfer of medieval learning to the modern world.

Bibliography

Birkerts, Sven. "The Name of the Rose," *New Republic* 189 (September 5, 1983): 36–38.

Eco, Umberto. *The Name of the Rose*. New York: Warner Books, 1983.

Hallissy, Margaret. "Reading the Plans: The Architectural Drawings in Umberto Eco's 'The Name of the Rose,'" *CRITIQUE: Studies in Contemporary Fiction* 42, no. 3 (spring 2001): 271.

Langer, Adam. "Italian Hero: Umberto Eco," *Book,* September–October 2002, 62–63.

Edgar Huntly
Charles Brockden Brown
(1799)

At the height of 18th-century ROMANTICISM, the American innovator Charles Brockden BROWN completed *Edgar Huntly; or, Memoirs of a Sleepwalker,* a blend of MYSTERY novel and bildungsroman or formation novel. The nation's first work depicting the Indian and the American frontier, it toys with the DOPPELGÄNGER motif and presents the first American flight-and-pursuit theme in a prototype of detective fiction. In the introduction, Brown states a prospectus for American fiction—a transfer of European GOTHIC CONVENTIONs into an American form based on New World imagination and experiences. Abandoning castles, crypts, and phantasms, he looked to hostile Indians and the woods, caverns, and cliffs of the perilous western edge of civilization for new sources of danger and excitement. His setting replaced such passé Gothic stereotypes as feudalism, crumbling aristocracy, and the Spanish Inquisition.

In addition to the rough wilderness setting outside Norwalk, Pennsylvania, Brown emphasizes the title character's internal chaos, a psychological OBSESSION over the killing of his friend Waldegrave, who collapses mysteriously under an elm tree. Wracked by guilt and psychosis, the moody Irish OUTSIDER Clithero Edny sleepwalks, a useful motif in Gothic fiction illustrating a dissociative mental state brought on by ambivalence and self-doubt. The protagonist watches Edny in silence while Edny digs a hole with a spade, fills it, then breaks into vehement sighs and weeping. In the ensuing action, Brown echoes the psychological pitfalls of Huntly's unrest through vigorous outdoor scenarios filled with CHIAROSCURO—a chase motif over Norwalk's cataracts and rocky caves, a tumble into a pitch-dark pit, and the callous murder of five Indians with hatchet, musket, and bayonet. As though yearning

for a redemptive baptism, the hero takes refuge in NATURE—he gulps from the waterfall while cleansing his head and torso of blood guilt.

Brown characterizes the decline of his protagonist into barbarism by Huntly's killing and eating the raw flesh of a panther and his implacement of a rifle as a totem to VIOLENCE. A SYMBOL of the American tendency to settle racial, social, and economic matters with murder, the upraised firearm embodies a SUBTEXT, the white settler's dependence on the enslavement and coercion of black Africans and the displacement and mass murder of Indians. Brown's theme of the no-good redskin recurs in Robert Montgomery BIRD's *NICK OF THE WOODS* (1837), an outré racist fiction about a crazed Quaker who abandons pacifism to slay Indians with relish and to slash their remains with crosses, an eerie precursor to the horrific slaughter of Native Americans that followed the Civil War.

Bibliography
Hamelman, Steve. "Rhapsodist in the Wilderness: Brown's Romantic Quest in 'Edgar Huntly,'" *Studies in American Fiction* 21, no. 2 (autumn 1993): 171–190.

Levine, Paul. "The American Novel Begins," *American Scholar* 35, no. 1 (1965): 134–148.

Mackenthun, Gesa. "Captives and Sleepwalkers: The Ideological Revolutions of Post-Revolutionary Colonial Discourse," *European Review of Native American Studies* 11, no. 1 (1997): 19–26.

"Elegy Written in a Country Churchyard"
Thomas Gray
(1751)

A dignified model of GRAVEYARD VERSE, Thomas Gray's famed pastoral elegy applies the sobriety and control of Greek and Roman lyrics to a panorama of rural lives. A meticulous craftsman of private musings, this preromantic poet seeks a picturesque backdrop for serious consideration of mortality and eases into the subject with the metaphor of an evening curfew. Out of sympathy with the universal terror of death, he elevates humankind with a serene MELANCHOLY at commonplace losses and disappointments from lives cut short. By leaving unresolved the matter of death's inevitability, the graceful narrative anticipates the extremes of Gothic fiction that Gray's friend Horace WALPOLE introduced in 1765.

In consoling the reader for an inevitable human demise, Gray sets his lyrics in the comforts of NATURE and selects mild images—a knell, fading, drowsiness, and moping—rather than the extremes of Gothic horror and grotesquerie that later authors popularized. He invests his scenario with England's beauty and, as a sentinel, inserts an ivied tower, the podium of an owl, a traditional symbol of death. By the fourth stanza, the poet works his way through the sheltering yews to gravesites, where he gentles the concept of death as sleep. Crucial to his commentary on evanescence is its evenhandedness to high and low, humble and proud. He concludes with a hypothetical death and pictures the newly deceased in the dreaded grave, but portrays his soul as received by God. The scenic quality of Gray's mournful verse inspired the scene-setting of Gothic novelist Ann RADCLIFFE.

Bibliography

Mack, Robert L. *Thomas Gray: A Life.* New Haven, Conn.: Yale University Press, 2000.

Sharp, Michele Turner. "Elegy unto Epitaph: Print Culture and Commemorative Practice in Gray's 'Elegy Written in a Country Churchyard,'" *Papers on Language & Literature* 38, no. 1 (winter 2002): 3.

Emily, Miss

Emily Grierson in William FAULKNER's short story "A ROSE FOR EMILY" (1930) is a masterpiece of SOUTHERN GOTHIC characterization, not only of the protagonist, but also of the gossips who speculate on her life. She emerges from the short story on the day of her death at age 74, when males respect her as "a fallen monument" (Faulkner, 119). One of Faulkner's famed elderly female bulwarks, she lives a reclusive life in Jefferson, the seat of his fictional Yoknapatawpha County, Mississippi. When visiting aldermen make fruitless demands that she pay county taxes, she receives them with cold courtesy and, fleshy and pale like a bloated drowning victim, stands defiant before them until instructing her butler to show them out.

SECRECY is paramount in Faulkner's development. He divulges the revolting truth about Emily's self-confinement through rumors and a series of hints about the family, beginning with an aunt who went crazy. After Miss Emily's father dies, she refuses for three days to acknowledge the loss or allow his burial. When her sweetheart, Homer Barron, vanishes, she says nothing. In the ensuing 30 years, no life is visible at her forbidding house except for Tobe, her Negro factotum. The town's hostility focuses less on Emily than on the odor that arises from her property. Faulkner describes her as oblivious to gossip, a stiff silhouette peering out of a window "like the carven torso of an idol in a niche"—a FORESHADOWING of the funereal scene to come (*ibid.*, 128). When she demands arsenic from the druggist, citizens fear she is contemplating suicide out of isolation and despair. Faulkner emphasizes how far their suppositions stray from the truth.

The revelation of Miss Emily as the murderer of Homer Barron solves the loose ends of Faulkner's MYSTERY story at the same time that it enlarges the Gothic interpretation of her love life. After Miss Emily's funeral, citizens force open the upstairs room and discover her secret, the decaying remains of Barron laid out like a lover on her bed. Amid the stink and dust of the in-house mausoleum, a strand of Miss Emily's hair is a frail testimony to her fantasized marital relationship with a rotting corpse. The story deflates the concept of delicate Southern ladies riding in buggies on Sundays and giving china-painting lessons to refined girls. In place of the stereotype, Faulkner forces the reader to accept Emily Grierson as a willful, territorial tyrant who gets what she wants with poison.

Bibliography

Faulkner, William. *Collected Stories of William Faulkner.* New York: Vintage Books, 1950.

Howe, Irving. *William Faulkner: A Critical Study.* New York: Vintage Books, 1962.

Erckmann, Émile

(1822–1899) and

Alexandre Chatrian

(1826–1890)

At the height of French romanticism, the successful Alsatian duo of Émile Erckmann and Louis Alexandre Chatrian wrote historical novels and atmospheric SUPERNATURAL tales and mysteries. Influenced by a strain of German Gothicism, they began publishing novels, drama, and short fiction in their early 20s, right out of college. Their subjects reached back to classic Gothic themes: metaphysics, haunted forests, curses, WITCHCRAFT, MONSTERS, and fearful incantations. In 1847, they issued an anthology, *Contes Fantastiques* (Fantastic stories), which the public ignored. They followed two years later with "The Invisible Eye," the story of multiple suicides caused by a sorceress who charms mannequins, which the authors published with the novella *The Wild Huntsman.*

Under the pen name Erckmann-Chatrian, their writings enjoyed a brief flourish in the mid-19th century as the pair succeeded with historical novels set in the French revolution and the Napoleonic wars, including *The Conscript: A Tale of the French War of 1813* (1865). That same year, their horror stories were available in translation in England, where Victorian readers of Gothic thrillers enjoyed their straightforward style; in 1880, a collection, *Strange Stories*, was issued in the United States. The pair contributed a significant work to LYCANTHROPY with "The Man-Wolf" (1876) and a favorite ghost story, "The Murderer's Violin," published in September 1876 in *Dublin University Magazine.*

In 1889, after a legal battle over money ended their partnership, Chatrian usurped their works and died within months of a favorable court judgment. Erckmann retired. One of their most spectacular monster tales, "The Crab Spider," appeared three years after Chatrian's death in the October 1893 issue of *Romance Magazine.* Set in a cave on the French border, the story describes a spider that threatens the countryside by devouring human flesh. These tidy, unrelenting tales of the uncanny influenced the well plotted works of the British antiquary and GHOST STORY writer M. R. James.

Bibliography

Lovecraft, H. P. *The Annotated Supernatural Horror in Literature.* New York: Hippocampus, 2000.

escapism

Escapism is a mainstay of Gothic fiction, cropping up in the flight from mortality in the MAD SCIEN-TIST and FAUST motifs and permeating tales of SOMNAMBULISM, flight, runaway lovers, and DREAMS AND NIGHTMARES. Escapism lightens the cares and trials of fictional characters, authors, and readers. Some characters flee for their lives, as is the case with the creator of the MONSTER in Mary Wollstonecraft SHELLEY's *FRANKENSTEIN* (1818); the unnamed visitor in Edgar Allan POE's "THE FALL OF THE HOUSE OF USHER" (1839), who gallops away as the manse self-destructs and slides into the tarn; the farmer beset by nature in Daphne DU MAURIER's "THE BIRDS" (1953); and the medievalist fleeing a secret brotherhood in Dan Brown's MYSTERY novel *THE DA VINCI CODE* (2003). In more recent times, Isabel ALLENDE, Margaret ATWOOD, and Toni MORRISON have described protagonists running away from tyranny, as is the case with the Trueba family eluding revolutionary chaos and reprisals in Argentina in Allende's *THE HOUSE OF THE SPIRITS* (1981), the women escaping a misogynistic society in Atwood's *THE HANDMAID'S TALE* (1985), and the blacks fleeing slavery on the Underground Railroad in Morrison's *BELOVED* (1987).

Writers such as H. P. LOVECRAFT, Carson McCULLERS, Flannery O'CONNOR, and Edith WHARTON valued Gothic fiction as an emotional release from ill health. At a turning point in his political maturity, Horace WALPOLE retreated to his quiet lair at Strawberry Hill to compose *THE CASTLE OF OTRANTO* (1765). Structuring a "truant fantasy" furthered his escape from the tensions of the day (Varma, 46). AUTOMATIC WRITING allowed him to sublimate his own aggressions through the atrocities of the usurper Manfred, his hero-VILLAIN. By retreating into MEDIEVALISM, the author manipulated the horrific details of a Gothic setting and visionary tale. After acquiring a suit of armor equivalent to his fictional helmet, he wrote, "If this is not realising one's dreams, I don't know what is" (*ibid.*).

Readers value Gothic escape plots as entertainment, a diversion that buoyed the GOTHIC BLUEBOOK to success in the early 1800s. Publishers such as William Lane of MINERVA PRESS wooed the poorly educated and unrefined working class with thrillers offering vicarious shock value. For those readers who could not afford to buy books, copies were available at alehouses and in CIRCU-

LATING LIBRARIES. One reader, the fictional Catherine MORLAND, expects amusement from her volume of Ann RADCLIFFE's THE MYSTERIES OF UDOLPHO (1794) in Jane AUSTEN's Gothic parody NORTHANGER ABBEY (1818).

Bibliography

Hodgson, John A., ed. *Sherlock Holmes: The Major Stories with Contemporary Critical Essays.* Boston: Bedford/St. Martin's, 1994.

Varma, Devendra P. *The Gothic Flame.* New York: Russell & Russell, 1966.

Ethan Frome
Edith Wharton
(1911)

Speaking from experience, novelist Edith Wharton denounced social repression and loveless marriage in *Ethan Frome,* a claustrophobic novella set on the rocky hillsides of New England in winter. Laced with private cruelties, latent eroticism, and personal anguish, the story develops a love triangle involving a failing farmer and Mattie Silver, the live-in nurse-housekeeper who cooks, cleans, and tends the farmer's hate-mongering wife, Zeena Pierce Frome. Unlike the confrontational FEMME FATALE, Zeena is a venomous passive-aggressive whose maiden name speaks volumes about her emasculating attacks on Ethan's pride. In close quarters, their moribund marriage acts out in small gestures and measured phrases the corrosive hatred that builds from lack of intimacy and mutual love.

ESCAPISM fuels the Gothic scenario with hope that Ethan can abandon a cheerless emotional landscape to seek a new start with Mattie. At the end of a pleasant evening escorting Mattie home from a town social, Ethan encounters a dead cucumber vine and a missing door key, SYMBOLS of the withered relationship and lost opportunities of Ethan's everyday life. The glass by the bed holds Zeena's dentures, reminders of her verbal lacerations. Ethan reminisces about his one trip to Florida, stares at constellations in the twinkly night sky, and studies magazine ads in the *Bettsbridge Eagle* enticing malcontents from the East with ILLUSIONS of prosperity in the far West, where new settlements offer land for homes, businesses, and ranches. The title of the newspaper bears Wharton's ironic antithesis—the image of the free-flying eagle and the wager that Ethan makes on future happiness. Turning back to his wretched home, he declares from a scientific standpoint, "It's like being in an exhausted receiver," referring to an early name for the vacuum in a bell jar (Wharton, 28).

Wharton fills her story with elements of loss, poor health, and inadequate income. She names five widows, Zeena's trip to an appointment with Dr. Burke, Ethan's halting gait, and the sudden death of Mattie's father, whose penury forces her to sell the family piano. A bit of graveyard drollery notes that the wife of a Frome ancestor was named Endurance. The story builds to crashing irony with the failed double suicide of Ethan and Mattie, who slide down School House Hill toward sudden death at a landmark elm. Her genial sparkle twists into a "witch-like stare" and her lilting voice to the same whine that Zeena directs at Ethan (*ibid.*, 85). Still poor, hopeless, and bowed with recriminations he trudges on to field, barn, and sawmill as he ekes out a living for himself and two bitter invalids. In a neighbor's estimation, "I don't see's there's much difference between the Fromes up at the farm and the Fromes down in the graveyard" (*ibid.*, 88).

Bibliography

Fedorko, Kathy Anne. *Gender and Gothic in the Fiction of Edith Wharton.* Tuscaloosa: Alabama University Press, 1995.

Lewis, R. W. B. *Edith Wharton: A Biography.* New York: Fromm International, 1985.

Wharton, Edith. *Ethan Frome.* New York: Charles Scribner's Sons, 1970.

The Eve of St. Agnes
John Keats
(1819)

John KEATS's most successful venture into Gothic verse, *The Eve of St. Agnes* is a Gothic prothalamion or hymn preceding an elopement scenario illustrating the interrelation of ROMANTICISM and Gothicism. The poem contains an acute interweaving of subtle textures, STORYTELLING, and hints of NECROMANCY that Keats also used in his demon lover poem "LA BELLE DAME SANS MERCI"

(1819). Building on William Shakespeare's *Romeo and Juliet* (ca. 1593), the Spenserian stanza, and the romanticism of Sir Walter SCOTT, Ann RAD-CLIFFE, Matthew Gregory LEWIS, and Samuel Taylor COLERIDGE, the visionary poem heaps psychic impressions. Its GOTHIC ARCHITECTURE and sensuous erotic images contribute to a MOOD rich in anticipation of sexual surrender. The virginal protagonist, Madeline, shut away in a patriarchal prison, dreams of rescue by a lover.

The poem begins with a tactile sense of cold that then gives way to the warming of visual and aural senses. The ballad opens on January 21 in numbing cold that chills the fragile limping hare and the owl, a pervasive symbol of night watchfulness and death. Against the muttering of prayers from the Beadsman, whom the family hires to say rosaries for their salvation, the setting takes shape in a chapel where funeral effigies of knights and ladies and carved angels mark the holy interior. The exoticism of Catholic ritual in the Beadsman's penance precedes a retreat to rough ash, where he sits through the night. With a deft touch of drama, Keats segues from mortal prayers for salvation to a colorful prewedding pageant.

FOLKLORE undergirds the story of Madeline, a maiden curious to know her future. She embraces the tradition of the vision of St. Agnes' Eve, when Porphyro hurries to her. He is noble and daring despite the likelihood that "a hundred swords will storm his heart" in response to Hildebrand's curse (Keats, 173). With the help of the aged Angela, the bold lover approaches his sleeping lady and plays on her lute a Provençal tune, "La belle dame sans merci" (*ibid.*, 177). The two elope amid the murderous dangers of "sleeping dragons all around at glaring watch, perhaps, with ready spears" (*ibid.*, 182). Stealing away through groaning hinges, they flee into a wintry storm, a SYMBOL of youthful idealism facing reality.

In sharp deviation from the voyeurism and manipulation of male Gothic, Keats turns a violation of patriarchy into a positive experience for both Madeline and Porphyro. The deflowering complete amid complicated food imagery, Porphyro goes Romeo one better. Rather than leave his lady at daybreak, he awakens her both consciously and carnally and carries her away. In the wake of the lovers' flight lies the cold corpse of the Beadsman, an ascetic figure discarded at the patriarchal castle contrasting the jubilant passion of young love. The forbidding surroundings of cold, old age, and death heighten the joy and promise of their escape.

Bibliography

Edgecombe, Rodney Stenning. "Keats's 'The Eve of St. Agnes,'" *Explicator* 52, no. 2 (winter 1994): 77–79.

Gamer, Michael. *Romanticism and the Gothic: Genre, Reception, and Canon Formation.* Cambridge: Cambridge University Press, 2000.

Keats, John. *The Complete Poems of John Keats.* New York: Modern Library, 1994.

Perry, Seamus. "Reading 'The Eve of St. Agnes': The Multiples of Complex Literary Transaction," *Modern Philology* 100, no. 1 (August 2002): 130–133.

Thomson, Heidi. "Eavesdropping on 'The Eve of St. Agnes': Madeline's Sensual Ear and Porphyro's Ancient Ditty," *Journal of English and Germanic Philology* 97, no. 3 (July 1998): 337.

Ewers, Hanns Heinz
(1872–1943)

A specialist in semiautobiographical SENSATION-ALISM, DIABOLISM, and barbarism, Hanns Heinz Ewers of Düsseldorf, Germany, gave up law to write verse, cabaret skits and libretti, and skillful but vulgar horror fiction, dramas, and CONTES CRUELS ("cruel tales"). Well read and well traveled, he was a student of modern psychology. His tastes ran to the extremes of GROTESQUE, eroticism, VAMPIRISM, and a type of SUPERNATURAL called German black romanticism. He applied his inventiveness to a long-lived folktale, *Der Zauberlehrling* (*The Sorcerer's Apprentice; or, The Devil Hunters*, 1907), a demonic tale that Johann von GOETHE had pioneered in 1797 from a Syrian original. In Ewers's hands, the motif alters from a lab boy working for a sorcerer to a male hypnotist manipulating his young mistress, whom fearful peasants crucify.

Ewers's decadent masterwork, *Alraune* (The mandrakes, 1911), describes a perverted scientific project: the creation of an unnatural being, a soulless female vampire named for the poisonous mandragora or mandrake plant. He creates a hopelessly degraded lineage: conception from the recovered sperm of a depraved murderer hanged on the gallows implanted in the womb of a Berlin prostitute. The blood-mad novel, which a Hungarian company filmed in 1918, anticipated the worst of Nazi medical experimentation on concentration camp inmates. Ewers turned to sadistic fantasy and MYSTICISM with *Vampir* (1921), the story of a German in New York who incites public sympathies for Germany during World War I. He replenishes his energies with the blood of his Jewish mistress, whom he attacks during intercourse.

Ewers broached the extremes of Gothic DECADENCE with short pieces in *Nachtmahr* (Nightmare, 1922), focusing on pornography, blood sport, torture, and execution. He outraged Germans with *DER GEISTERSEHER* (*The Ghost-Seer*, 1922), an occult story begun by Friedrich von SCHILLER in 1786. Ewers also updated ERCKMANN-CHATRIAN's "The Crab Spider" (1893) with a FEMME FATALE's coercion of her lover into suicide. With the rise of Nazi *Blut und Boden* ("blood and soil") philosophy during the 1930s, Ewers produced Nazi propagandist fiction in *Reiter in Deutscher Nacht* (*Rider of the Night*, 1932) and a biography of Horst Wessel, but enraged Adolf Hitler by straying from strict Third Reich dogma sanctifying the Teutonic master race. By the time of Ewers's death from tuberculosis, he was a forgotten writer whose "degenerate" books were reduced to ash on Hitler's bonfires.

Bibliography

Mangione, Jerre. "Vampire," *New Republic* 81, no. 1,043 (November 28, 1934): 82–83.

Ronay, Gabriel. *The Dracula Myth*. London: W. H. Allen, 1972.

Wolf, Leonard. *A Dream of Dracula: In Search of the Living Dead*. New York: Popular Library, 1977.

exoticism

Exoticism refers to the inclusion of foreign customs, ethnic groups, religious practices, and settings in art and literature. Critics today often find exoticism subjective, judgmental, and even racist. Exoticism satisfies curiosity and voyeurism, as found in the ORIENTAL ROMANCEs of Lord BYRON and Thomas Moore, the colonial horror stories of Rudyard KIPLING, Lafcadio HEARN's translations of Chinese and Japanese ghost stories, and the outré tales of French journalist and poet Théophile GAUTIER. One classic adventure tale, Jules Verne's *Around the World in 80 Days* (1873), includes a string of shocking scenarios: escape on an elephant, pursuit by Sioux Indians, and the rescue of Aouda, an Indian female terrified of burning to death at a suttee, the custom of immolating a living wife during the cremation of her dead husband. In the same vein are SUPERSTITIONs connected with the title image in W. W. JACOBS's horror story "THE MONKEY'S PAW" (1902), primitive gestures in Congo natives in Joseph CONRAD's *HEART OF DARKNESS* (1902), the eerie demon ritual in SAKI's revenge tale "SREDNI VASHTAR" (1911), and African shrine imagery in the Scottish author John Buchan's "The Grove of Ashtoreth" (1912).

Authors dress up Gothic literature with exotic detail as an intensification of weirdness and a heightening of ESCAPISM from the ordinary, a characteristic of Alfred McLelland Burrage's "Between the Minute and the Hour" (1927), which depicts a gypsy curse that transcends the bounds of time to toss the victim about in the historical continuum. As the British developed their world empire during the 19th century, Sir Arthur Conan DOYLE and Oscar WILDE embroidered their writings with outlandish furnishings, dress, foods, and behavior—for example, a deadly Indian snake trained to kill in Doyle's "A Study in Scarlet" (1887) and the erotic dance in Wilde's biblical play *SALOMÉ* (1893), which the title character performs with a salver containing the severed head of Jokanaan (John the Baptist). In AMERICAN GOTHIC, the poet and fiction writer Edgar Allan POE made a fetish of the unheard-of setting with place names and allusions, such as Astarte, Belphegor, Gilead, Lethe, Nicaea, Porphyrogene, and Samarkand, which he chose or made up for their evocative sound and rhyme. Following Poe's examples was the author and critic H. P. LOVECRAFT, who added strangeness to his stories with such titles as "Azathoth" (1922) and "The Call of Cthulhu" (1928).

Bibliography

Tarr, Mary Muriel. *Catholicism in Gothic Fiction: A Study of the Nature and Function of Catholic Materials in*

Gothic Fiction in England (1762–1820). Washington, D.C.: Catholic University of America Press, 1946.

"The Eyes"
Edith Wharton
(1910)

Edith WHARTON's psychological GHOST STORY "The Eyes" is considered her finest SUPERNATURAL short piece. She published the story in the June 1910 issue of *Scribner's* and anthologized it in *Tales of Men and Ghosts* (1911), which earned mixed reviews. Set at a private residence among friends who tell ghost stories, the tale discloses the cruelties of a lone doubter, Andrew Culwin, a dilettante who disbelieves the supernatural. After the other guests depart, in a one-to-one narrative, Phillip Frenham relates a tale of disembodied eyes that come to haunt Culwin. Wharton develops irony from Culwin's suggestibility, which he claims to lack.

The evil of Wharton's story echoes the greed and personal gain that invests AMERICAN GOTHIC. The first appearance of the specter coincides with Culwin's manipulation of his cousin Alice Nowell, to whom he disingenuously proposes marriage. A later appearance involves the gulling of Gilbert, a would-be writer whom the protagonist pretends to mentor. Wharton reveals the eyes to be a manifestation of Culwin's power over the unsuspecting, a SYMBOL of the powers of art that he next focuses on Frenham. The tale echoes the study of inner evil, inflated ego, and psychological control that empowers the fiction of Wharton's forerunners, Nathaniel HAWTHORNE, Henry JAMES, and Edgar Allan POE.

Bibliography

Fedorko, Kathy Anne. *Gender and Gothic in the Fiction of Edith Wharton*. Tuscaloosa: University of Alabama Press, 1995.

Lewis, R. W. B. *Edith Wharton: A Biography*. New York: Fromm International, 1985.

Eyre, Jane

Jane Eyre, the protagonist of Charlotte BRONTË's *JANE EYRE* (1847), is Gothic literature's most famous NAIF and stirring liberated woman. Orphaned in childhood and educated through grit and determination, she represents the new self-empowered woman emerging from the economic and social ferment of the Industrial Revolution. For the author, the character was a bold departure from the MELANCHOLY, recessive victims who dominated the novels of the first half of the 19th century. For her rebellion and staunch individualism, Jane Eyre has earned the label of Byronic heroine, the female counterpart to the dashing, moody Edward ROCHESTER.

Jane escapes confining Cinderella stereotypes by making her own way in the world. She relates her story from a decade's perspective, looking back from age 29 to her marriage at age 19 and farther back to her orphaned childhood. Even then, she refuses to be coerced by older, more powerful people. Unrepentant in the home of her sour-tempered aunt Sarah Reed, Jane remains locked in the redroom at Gateshead Hall with a phantasm of her imagination until she faints. In an allegorical romantic quest, she journeys from childhood at GATESHEAD HALL to Lowood school, employment at THORNFIELD HALL, and marriage and family at Ferndean. Along the way, she expresses thoughts and ambitions through conversation and sketches. She acts intelligently on her intuition that alliance with a married man would cost her self-respect.

Brontë guides her heroine over a series of settings rich with Gothic terrors and hints of the occult from DREAMS, telepathy, and fitful visions. While studying at Lowood, a girl's school, Jane endures a wretched experience with unappetizing food and cold walks on the grounds, harpy-like staff members, and an outbreak of typhus. She eases the passage of a dying schoolmate and spiritual sister, Helen Burns, a tender FOIL who lacks the fire and determination that help Jane survive. As though infusing her departed friend with resolve, Jane returns to the cemetery 15 years after Helen's death to place a triumphant gray marble tablet inscribed with *Resurgam*, the Latin for "I shall rise again" (Brontë, 75).

At her first job, governess at Thornfield, the absence of background information about her employer again plunges Jane into apprehension about her place in a privileged household. Derailing her growth as a competent teacher is detrimental speculation about disjointed clues to Edward Rochester, the man who wins her heart. Brontë applies the familiar motif of animal magnetism in describing his firm mouth and jetty eyebrows that draw Jane into hero-worship and, eventually, love for a capricious, ill-tempered master. She disclaims fault by stating, "I had not intended to love him" and by declaring the attraction spontaneous and unforeseen (*ibid.*, 163). When she recognizes an attraction between Rochester and Blanche Ingram, Jane regrets, "I could not unlove him now" (*ibid.*, 174).

When Rochester chooses Jane over Blanche, Brontë renders the master's wooing as vigorous and commanding as his other attributes, all of which suit Jane's restlessness and overt appetites. Although he makes dizzying claims of love and desire for her, he toys with her affections by playing the role of the gypsy fortune-teller and by pretending that he will send her away to a new post in Ireland after he marries Blanche, a beautiful, elegant woman more suited to his status. His spontaneous rejection of Blanche and proposal of marriage to Jane surprise her, but do not deflect her caution. She demands an explanation of why he pretended to court Blanche Ingram. The prospect of taking a place by her beloved's side does not tempt Jane to dress and live the part of lady of Thornfield and the mate of the cultured, well-traveled Rochester. Symbolically, when presented with fabrics for new dresses, she chooses a subdued gray over more vivid colors.

Brontë creates foils in Rochester's first and second wives. Speaking through the visceral counter-world of illogic and madness, Jane's alter ego, Bertha Mason ROCHESTER, vents the pent-up fury of the era's female professionals and artists who prospered at the whim of male overseers. In contrast, Jane uses art as an outlet for her feelings and manages to make her way in the world through willful behaviors and choices. Morally, she obeys the Victorian dictates of modesty and purity in its maidens and acts out a chaste gender role through a thinly veiled sexual yearning couched in sighings and moonings over Rochester.

Lacking carnality as a dramatic tool, Brontë plots the liaison between passion-charged maid and suitor by transferring the story's deep emotions to NATURE, to Jane's enigmatic dreams, and to the ravings of Bertha, the "maniac upstairs" (*ibid.*, 301). Upon witnessing Rochester's fearful secret, Jane retreats to unconsciousness, fainting like the dead, and frames a prayer that she has no energy to utter. Like the fair maid beset by the ravenous VILLAIN in Radcliffean Gothic scenarios, she prays, "Be not far from me, for trouble is near: there is none to help" (*ibid.*, 282). To her credit, she does not wait for God's intervention. To Rochester's ardent rationalization of bigamy, she listens sympathetically, but refuses an offer of intimacy before marriage or, worse yet, the role of mistress, even though he tempts her with a Mediterranean villa.

Brontë allows ESCAPISM to create a beneficial separation of lovers, a time for Rochester to cool down and for Jane to reflect on ideals and realities. She hears his piteous description of her as "my better self my good angel," yet chooses to abandon him and save herself (*ibid.*, 300). Against emotional battery of her principles, she flees to the moors, a romantic setting common to English literature, where her virtue remains intact. Like Christ in soulful solitude, Jane wanders the wilderness, which threatens her survival. Bolstering her at the extremes of low self-esteem and despair is a mysterious extrasensory perception that beams in messages from Rochester. This SUPERNATURAL touch is subdued, appearing only at melodramatic moments when she requires rescue and spiritual sustenance. More realistic are her success at opening a school and her part in a real family, one of whom leaves a bequest that makes her financially independent.

On Jane's return to Rochester, Brontë overturns the classic setting for the plot resolution, deflating the Gothic elements one by one. First, the author shifts from the massive, looming Thornfield to the symbolic inn the Rochester Arms and on to a bucolic cottage at Ferndean, an unpretentious, workable home that suits Jane's status and homemaking talents. Before reuniting with her demanding lover, she quickly takes charge of the house staff, John and Mary, and gives polite, but firm instructions about her bag and accommodations for the night. On return to Rochester, Jane finds a broken man who needs a loyal, industrious helpmeet. Still gloomy and tormented, he so misdoubts his fortune that he thinks her a delusion or dream rather than his flesh-and-blood Jane.

Brontë gives Jane a forthright statement of the change in her status from dependent household employee to teacher and heiress. She announces, "I am an independent woman now. . . . I am my own mistress," a reflection both of monetary worth and self-assessment (*ibid.*, 416). Nonetheless, verbally subservient out of habit, she continues calling Rochester "sir," even in reply to his proposal of marriage, thus maintaining a socially motivated respect well-suited to Gothic distancing of a young working-class woman from an older, more prominent male suitor. Rid of the Gothic excesses of an estate and an unsettled past, he thrives from the leveling of marital roles with a wife who is more nearly his equal. As a domestic gesture, she presents a tray bearing candles and a half-filled glass of water, which the dog Pilot upsets in his generous welcome to Jane. Rochester, fully repentant of his dissipated youth, bestows on her a watch to fasten to her belt, the emblem of the lady of the house. The triumph of Jane Eyre inspired other Gothic heroines—in particular, the unnamed new Mrs. DE WINTER in Daphne DU MAURIER's REBECCA (1938) and Victoria HOLT's Martha Leigh, the plain but proper governess in MISTRESS OF MELLYN (1960).

Bibliography

Brontë, Charlotte. *Jane Eyre*. New York: Bantam Books, 1981.

Chen, Chih-Ping. "'Am I a Monster?': Jane Eyre among the Shadows of Freaks," *Studies in the Novel* 34, no. 4 (winter 2002): 367–384.

Deiter, Kristen. "Cultural Expressions of the Victorian Age: The New Woman, *Jane Eyre*, and Interior Design," *Lamar Journal of the Humanities* 25, no. 2 (2000): 27–42.

Lamonaca, Maria. "Jane's Crown of Thorns: Feminism and Christianity in Jane Eyre," *Studies in the Novel* 34, no. 3 (fall 2002): 245–263.

Oates, Joyce Carol. "Romance and Anti-Romance: From Brontë's *Jane Eyre* to Rhys's *Wide Sargasso Sea*," *Virginia Quarterly Review* 61, no. 6 (winter 1985): 44–58.

Starzyk, Lawrence J. "The Gallery of Memory: The Pictorial in *Jane Eyre*," *Papers on Language & Literature* 33, no. 3 (summer 1997): 288–309.

F

fairy tale

A deceptively simple, moralistic fantasy, the fairy tale speaks of charms and dizzying raptures while harboring a variety of SUPERNATURAL evildoers—giants, trolls, elves, dragons, dwarves, ogres, magicians, enchanters, and witches and their familiars—as well as fantastic and disguised creatures. Examples range from the glowering wizard in Johann Wolfgang von GOETHE's whimsical *Der Zauberlehrling* (*The Sorcerer's Apprentice,* 1797) to the soulless sprite in Friedrich de la Motte Fouqué's *Undine* (1811), a tale of a nymph's loss of her beloved knight Huldbrand that earned the praise of H. P. LOVECRAFT and Edgar Allan POE. In oral folklore and storybooks, malefic beings are prompted to evil through jealousy, a yearning for tyranny and control, and delight in wickedness, as found in the wolf that swallows the grandmother in "Little Red Riding Hood." The lurking evildoers of folklore produce Gothic effects when they interact with innocent children, often a foundling or wandering NAIF from rural areas, such as Hansel and Gretel, Snow White, and the little mermaid, a character in the Danish storyteller Hans Christian ANDERSEN's *Eventyr, Fortalte for Børn* (Tales told for children, 1835). In 1862, the English poet Christina ROSSETTI applied a RESCUE THEME in THE GOBLIN MARKET, a cautionary tale of sister love and the retrieval of one sister by the other from fearful goblins who tempt the unwary with lush, ripe fruit.

An amazing Gothic convention in fairy tales is the creation of beings that take multiple shapes, rendering them faster, stronger, invisible, or uncatchable, as with the primate that turns into an abbess in Isak DINESEN's story "The Monkey" (1934) and the flying Africans in American slave narratives that Nobel Prize–winning novelist Toni MORRISON incorporates into the falling action of *Song of Solomon* (1977). Enhancing the menace of unpredictable and improbable attackers and spell-casters are the abilities of supernatural disappearances at will or SHAPE-SHIFTING, two dramatic plot twists in "Cinderella" and "Rumplestiltskin," the story of a predator menacing a blameless maiden in Jacob and Wilhelm GRIMM's *Kinder- und Hausmärchen* (Children's and household tales, 1812, 1815, 1822). In Angolan animal fables, Yoruba trickster tales, and Native American *pourquoi* stories or "why" stories told by the Blackfoot, Cheyenne, Comanche, Micmac, Winnebago, Zuñi, and other tribes, jungle and forest animals alter at will from bird to beast to fish. The same disconcerting and at times terrorizing characteristic dominates the fantasy and pilgrimage motifs in Lewis Carroll's *Alice in Wonderland* (1865) and terrorizes a grieving couple in W. W. JACOBS's sinister colonial tale "THE MONKEY'S PAW" (1902).

In creating fearful confrontations, authors of the fairy tale model good-triumphs-over-evil plots, as in the foiling of an evil enchantress in "Sleeping Beauty" and the erotically charged gentling of a MONSTER in "BEAUTY AND THE BEAST." Fairy stories also aim to balance threat with flight or miracles, as in the escape from the tower in "Rapunzel" and the resurrection of "Snow White" from a living death. In Charlotte BRONTË's Gothic novel JANE EYRE (1847), Edward ROCHESTER uses an impromptu fairy tale as a cautionary fable, a means of informing his ward, Adèle Varens, of a more believable miracle, his love for her governess Jane Eyre. He elevates Jane to a being "come from Elfland" who promises that "we shall leave earth, and make our own heaven yonder" (Brontë, 254). The child, expressing Gallic skepticism, dismisses his *"contes de fée"* ("fairy stories") as a lie about beings that never existed (*ibid.*).

When the fictional motifs of the fairy tale appear as adult Gothic, they represent a psychological triumph over nightmares, SUPERSTITION, confinement, domination, and lethal menace. These elements are the hallmark of Anne RICE's perusal of SADISM in a trilogy consisting of *The Claiming of Sleeping Beauty* (1983), *Beauty's Punishment* (1984), and *Beauty's Release* (1985), which she published under the pen name A. N. Roquelaure. In the words of Margaret ATWOOD, feminist author of the mythic *The Robber Bride* (1993), "Fairy tales have sometimes been faulted for the Handsome Prince Syndrome—for showing women as weak and witless and in need of rescue—but only some of them actually display this pattern" (Talese, 14). As Atwood implies, the survival of a tender, untried female NAIF from modern Gothic tradition boosts her to a new status as achiever and completer of the quest. Unlike the shrinking violets of the GOTHIC BLUEBOOK, the new heroine blossoms into a mature adult capable of living in a world where the variance between male and female power and control has moved closer to a balance.

Examples emerge early in FEMALE GOTHIC from Ann RADCLIFFE's THE MYSTERIES OF UDOLPHO (1794), in which Emily ST. AUBERT regains control of her life and patrimony, and from *Jane Eyre*, in which the youthful heroine survives loss, challenge, threat, and wandering in the wilderness to create a professional and domestic niche for herself. Self-confident and loyal, she returns to Edward Rochester as a fully realized adult female who is capable of marrying, starting a family, and supporting a handicapped husband. Like the happily-ever-after conclusions of fairy stories, Jane's example comes close to complete contentment as a result of self-empowerment, not through the intervention of a fairy godmother. In an adaptation of the Jane Eyre mode, Daphne DU MAU-

RIER's classic MYSTERY novel REBECCA (1938) develops a similarly retiring female into a true wife and helpmeet through her completion of the quest and her understanding of hints of the supernatural that formerly terrorized and paralyzed her. Victoria HOLT produced a paler mid-20th-century version of the story in MISTRESS OF MELLYN (1960).

Bibliography

Brontë, Charlotte. *Jane Eyre.* New York: Bantam Books, 1981.

Lüth, Max. *European Folktale: Form and Nature.* Bloomington: Indiana University Press, 1982.

McGlathey, James M., ed. *The Brothers Grimm and Folktales.* Urbana: University of Illinois Press, 1992.

Radin, Paul. *The Trickster: A Study in American Indian Mythology.* New York: Schocken Books, 1972.

Talese, Nan A. *Book Group Companion to Margaret Atwood's "The Robber Bride."* New York: Doubleday, 1993.

Tatar, Maria. *The Hard Facts of the Grimms' Fairy Tales.* Princeton, N.J.: Princeton University Press, 1987.

"The Fall of the House of Usher"
Edgar Allan Poe
(1839)

First published in *Burton's Gentleman's Magazine* before its collection in *Tales of the Grotesque and Arabesque* (1839), Edgar Allan POE's "The Fall of the House of Usher," one of his most powerful stories, derives its impact from the motif of the ancestral curse. Animated by a looming death madness that Poe experienced as his young wife, Virginia Clemm Poe, declined from tuberculosis, the story offers a classic example of claustrophobic ATMOSPHERE, EXOTICISM, somber MOOD, and a mounting fear of PREMATURE BURIAL. Some literary historians interpret the auditory and visual images as models of the effects of opium on the protagonist, Roderick USHER, and advance the theory that he is an autobiographical portrait of Poe. An alternate analysis pictures Usher as the epitome of ROMANTICISM run amok and the victim of a human effort to transgress rational boundaries for a dangerous exploration of INSANITY.

Gripping with SUSPENSE, the SUPERNATURAL, and revelation of a diseased mind, the story begins with an epigraph, a French image of sensibility—the human heart vibrating like a lute. The text sets an unsuspecting traveler in a bleak, deteriorating manse along a forbidding lake. To the unnamed visitor, Usher, his host and boyhood friend, dwells on hypochondriacal symptoms and the approaching terminus of his family's lineage. Amplifying his obsession are the decline and death of Roderick's twin, Madeline USHER, a female DOPPELGÄNGER with whom he appears to share an incestuous relationship.

Poe enhances the Gothic setting and characterization with a stormy night, mention of a copy of procedures for torture during the Spanish Inquisition, a copy of Pomponius Mela's *Geography* (ca. A.D. 100), and Roderick's immersion in a story-within-a-story—the religious text "Vigiliae Mortuorum Secundum Chorum Ecclesiae Maguntinae" (Watches of the Dead According to the Choir of the Maguntian Church). The handbook of ritual for mourning or grave vigils provides commentary suited to the approaching collapse of Madeline in a cataleptic seizure. In counterpoint during Roderick's reading of "The Mad Trist," Poe creates a verbal duet of Ethelred's pounding in the story with a rising tempest, cracking, and ripping coming from Madeline's burial vault. The shrieking of the dragon that Ethelred arouses parallels screaming and grating from Usher's departed sister. The coincidence terrifies the narrator at the same time that it identifies Poe's Gothic intent. The author depicts the unnamed visitor as wise in fleeing a cumulative evil in the HOUSE OF USHER, which NATURE reclaims as it slides into the dark tarn.

Within the story, Poe incorporates "The Haunted Palace" (1839), a 48-line poem he introduced in the *Baltimore Museum* magazine. Described as Roderick's original fantasy, the poem poses an ALLEGORY of a royal dwelling threatened by an undesignated evil. As the menace besets the king, it echoes the onset of mental disorder that precipitates insanity, a mirror image of Usher's advancing dementia. The story's atmosphere engaged the fancy of VILLIERS DE L'ISLE-ADAM, who used the motif in "The Sign," one of his stories in *CONTES CRUELS* (*Cruel Tales*, 1883), a French cult classic.

Poe's mastery of GOTHIC CONVENTIONS of MYSTERY, hypersensitivity, madness, and death OB-SESSION earned the respect of subsequent masters of the macabre, notably, Isabel ALLENDE, Ambrose BIERCE, George Washington CABLE, Angela CARTER, Arthur Conan DOYLE, William FAULKNER, Charlotte Perkins GILMAN, Nathaniel HAWTHORNE, Joyce Carol OATES, and Eudora WELTY. One admirer, H. P. LOVECRAFT, considered Poe the premiere fictional miniaturist. Poe's canon influenced artists on both sides of the Atlantic, including the composer Claude Debussy, who failed in the attempt to turn the Usher tragedy into an opera, and Luis Bunuel and Jean Epstein, creators of a French film retelling, *La Chute de la Maison Usher* (1928), in which Roderick drains the life from his wife Madeline by painting her portrait.

Bibliography

Dougherty, Stephen. "Foucault in the House of Usher: Some Historical Permutations in Poe's Gothic," *Papers on Language & Literature* 37, no. 1 (winter 2001): 3.

Hustis, Harriet. "'Reading Encrypted but Persistent': The Gothic of Reading and Poe's 'The Fall of the House of Usher,'" *Studies in American Fiction* 27, no. 1 (spring 1999): 3.

Faulkner, William
(1897–1962)

America's most important fiction writer of the 1900s, William Cuthbert Faulkner contributed an interconnected series of short and long fiction that is a cornerstone of southern literature. Imbued with a Gothic view of Mississippi history, he set events in the fictional Yoknapatawpha County, a manageable microcosm in which succeeding generations of southerners live out their predilections for gentility and VIOLENCE. He was a raw genius blessed with an ear for regional and racial dialect, which he used to create the interrelated genealogies of the Carothers, Compsons, De Spains, McCaslins, Snopeses, and Sutpens. As evidence of miscegenation, incest, and degeneracy, the families spawned blueblood aristocrats and slaves, including a number of mulattos and octoroons, all with varying degrees of vice, criminality, INSANITY, and mental retardation to their credit.

Faulkner placed his characters in the southern milieu as witnesses to the displacement of Native

Americans and the resulting rise of antebellum aristocracy, agrarianism, and slavery. Interaction between social classes and races amplifies incidents fraught with Gothic elements, notably, adultery and illegitimacy in *As I Lay Dying* (1930), vengeance in "A ROSE FOR EMILY" (1930) and "THAT EVENING SUN" (1931), lynching in "Dry September" (1931), perverse violence in *Sanctuary* (1931) and *Light in August* (1932), fratricide in the Gothic saga ABSALOM, ABSALOM! (1936), and arson in "Barn Burning" (1939). For their uniqueness and truth to life, Faulkner's writings won an O. Henry Prize and the 1950 National Book Award for Fiction.

Faulkner was in his element with the lurid humor of the Snopeses, the demonic spite of the stalker, and the terrors of the gloom-ridden southern family in its final decades of decline. He employed mock Gothic in the novel *As I Lay Dying* (1930), in which an agrarian family transports the remains of its matriarch, Addie Bundren, to her family's burial plot. In *Sanctuary* (1931), Faulkner's most sadistic Gothic novel, he created a true VILLAIN, Popeye, who directs frustration with sexual impotence at Temple Drake, whom he rapes with a corncob. In a moment of dark humor, a ghastly mishap causes a coffin to tumble forward, causing the corpse to land face-down on a floral wreath and the hidden wire to lodge in the deceased's cheek. With *Intruder in the Dust* (1948), Faulkner retreated to a less tense coming-of-age plot to extol Chick Mallison, a moral youth who defeats the would-be lynchers of an innocent black man. To delay mob violence, Chick exhumes the victim's body and conceals it, "laying (the body) face down and only the back of the crushed skull visible," until the sheriff can straighten out an obvious miscarriage of justice (Faulkner, 1948, 175).

In 1994, the recovery of an unpublished short story presented Faulkner fans with a compelling twist on psychological FEMALE GOTHIC. "Rose of Lebanon," issued in the *Oxford American* in 1995, depicts the release of tension and rage after 65 years of suppression. The main character, the elderly Lewis Randolph Gordon, conceals her terror during the Civil War when Yankee marauders attack her kitchen. At a formal banquet in 1930, she finds herself reliving the trauma of solitude, help-

lessness, and fear for her infant son, whose milk she warmed at the stove. In a rush of foul language, the elderly Lewis vents her anger over a half-century later. She hurls soup across the table and grabs a fruit knife to ward off the mental phantasms that have stalked her since 1865. As sleep eludes her that night, "the sound was there, the long rushing surges dying away like a sudden rush of horsemen" (Faulkner, 1996, 22).

The story reprises one of Faulkner's familiar character types, the indomitable elderly woman who refuses to give in to terror and intimidation—a figure found in *Intruder in the Dust*, "A Rose for Emily," "The Odor of Verbena," and *The Sound and the Fury*. More energized than "That Evening Sun," the story lauds a young mother whose character and determination equal that of her husband and male contemporaries who fight for the Confederacy. Just as gray-uniformed soldiers faced advancing phalanxes many times stronger than their own forces, so Lewis countered with words and derringer the five brigands who assailed her privacy. Her courage typifies the strength of character in the Old South that readers admire in Faulkner's works.

Bibliography

Faulkner, William. *Intruder in the Dust*. New York: Vintage Books, 1948.

———. "Rose of Lebanon," in *New Stories from the South: The Year's Best of 1996*. Chapel Hill, N.C.: Algonquin Books, 1996.

Howe, Irving. *William Faulkner: A Critical Study*. New York: Vintage Books, 1962.

Ruland, Richard, and Malcolm Bradbury. *From Puritanism to Postmodernism: A History of American Literature*. New York: Penguin, 1991.

Faust legend

A phenomenon of DIABOLISM, the damnation of Faust has survived centuries of redactions, revisions, retellings in chapbooks, versification, filming, and settings to music. Most notably, the Faust legend was recounted in Christopher Marlowe's play *The Tragicall Historie of* DOCTOR FAUSTUS (ca. 1588), Jacques Cazotte's prototypical SUPERNATURAL novel *Le Diable Amoreux* (*The Devil in Love*, 1772), the anonymous GOTHIC BLUEBOOK "The

Black Spider" (ca. 1798), Ivan Turgenev's *Faust* (1856), and Thomas Mann's *Doctor Faustus* (1947). At the heart of the demonic story lie alchemy, blasphemy, and NECROMANCY, a forbidden communion with the dead that doomed Georgius Faust, an early 16th-century conjurer. The more ornate plots advance the tale into a pageant of famous figures returning from the nether world to interact with Faust. The blood pact that the great egotist signs with Mephistopheles introduces him to WITCHCRAFT, but ultimately demands a GROTESQUE surrender to eternity in hell. Johann von GOETHE made a life's work of reprising the MONSTER myth, beginning in 1790 and finishing in 1832. Critics consider Goethe's *Faust* the pinnacle of his multifaceted career.

The Faust myth invests much of English Gothic fiction. Matthew Gregory LEWIS built into THE MONK (1796) some of the menace of Faust in the VILLAIN AMBROSIO's bargaining with the devil. The legend appealed to the popular reader of early 19th-century England, who purchased an anonymous Gothic bluebook entitled *The Life and Horrid Adventures of the Celebrated Dr. Faustus*, which Orlando Hodgson published in London around 1810. The Faust legend also provided motivation for Lord BYRON's closet drama MANFRED (1817), aided Mary Wollstonecraft SHELLEY in framing the motivation of the proud scientist Victor FRANKENSTEIN, and provided the psychological basis for Charles Robert MATURIN's MELMOTH THE WANDERER (1820). For *London Magazine*, translator Thomas De Quincey produced "The Dice" (1823), a Gothic tale in the German style, which describes diablerie as the doom of Rudolph, the last of his lineage. In William Child GREEN's *The Abbot of Montserrat; or, The Pool of Blood* (1826), the doomed monk Obando finds himself trapped between the Inquisition and the demon Zatanai, who offers "the scorching, fiery pile—the bright, curled flames around thee, hissing—crackling—mounting" (Green, vol. 2, 210). The character Faust speaks the philosophy of the Russian romanticist Vladimir ODOEVSKY in the epilogue of *Russkiye Notchi* (*Russian Nights*, 1844), a study of the effects of science and technology on Western culture. Mary Elizabeth BRADDON, a writer of GASLIGHT THRILLERS, applied the Faust motif to the three-volume novel *Gerard; or, The World, the Flesh and the Devil*, issued in the *Saturday Review* in November 1891.

Bibliography

Green, William Child. *The Abbot of Montserrat; or, The Pool of Blood*, 2 vols. New York: Arno Press, 1977.

Haining, Peter, ed. *Gothic Tales of Terror*. New York: Taplinger Publishing, 1972.

Hamlin, William M. "Casting Doubt in Marlowe's Doctor Faustus," *Studies in English Literature, 1500–1900* 41, no. 2 (spring 2001): 257.

Horner, Avril, ed. *European Gothic: A Spirited Exchange 1760–1960*. Manchester: Manchester University Press, 2002.

female Gothic

Female Gothic romance is a major strand of Gothic literature that expresses sympathy for a female protagonist who is oppressed by a VILLAIN or patriarchal authority figure through STALKING, abusive relationships, or outright persecution. In an overview of the literary subgenre in *Literary Women* (1977), the feminist critic Ellen Moers coined the term *female Gothic* to characterize uniquely woman-liberating Gothic literature, which offered a new avenue of exploration of women's place in society. She stated three focal elements of female Gothic: the gendered behavior and attitudes of the heroine and hero, the importance of the female protagonist's virginity and sexuality, and the impact of social, racial, and economic status on the action, a controlling theme in Jean RHYS's *Wide Sargasso Sea* (1966) and Michel Faber's neo-Victorian domestic novel THE CRIMSON PETAL AND THE WHITE (2002). Moers set the historical and critical parameters of the subgenre as the work of female authors following Ann RADCLIFFE's landmark Gothic mode, notably Charlotte BRONTË, Emily BRONTË, Charlotte DACRE, Jane PORTER, Sarah PORTER, Clara REEVE, Regina Maria ROCHE, Christina ROSSETTI, Mary Wollstonecraft SHELLEY, Charlotte SMITH, Sarah WILKINSON, and Mary WOLLSTONECRAFT. Moers selected as the pinnacle of female Gothic Mary Shelley's FRANKENSTEIN (1818), a creative blend of Gothic elements that critics originally categorized as a creation myth. Moers replaced traditional interpretations of

Mary Shelley's vision with a new female Gothic explanation of the story—a unique birth myth picturing a perversion of conception and childbirth. The resulting MONSTER-child, which remains unnamed, becomes a repository for scientist Victor Frankenstein's dread of birth trauma and for his guilt at rejecting the newborn.

Female Gothic stories develop ATMOSPHERE by setting action within intricate architecture or over perplexing terrain, as found in the haunting and coercion of Chinese peasant women in Maxine Hong KINGSTON's *The Woman Warrior* (1976), the reliving of slave women's nightmares in Octavia BUTLER's *Kindred* (1979), and the sexual exploitation of Mestizo women in Isabel ALLENDE's ghostly colonial saga *La Casa de los Espíritus* (THE HOUSE OF THE SPIRITS, 1981). As Kate Ferguson Ellis explains in *The Contested Castle* (1989), male Gothic turns domestic space into a prison or banishes the disobedient or threatening female from her rightful place in the home; female gothic reclaims the home from the usurping male. The critic Margaret Anne Doody, author of *The True Story of the Novel* (1996), lauded the female version of Gothicism for supplying a literary venue for women to express their frustrations. "It is in the Gothic novel that women writers could first accuse the 'real world' of falsehood and deep disorder" (Fleenor, 13). This realistic view of the womanly domain became the standard scenario of stories published in the *Lady's Magazine,* the mass-produced pulp fiction hawked by MINERVA PRESS, and the classic novels of Ann Radcliffe, Charlotte Brontë, Daphne DU MAURIER, and Victoria HOLT, as well as texts of open-minded men, notably Charles Brockden BROWN, Charles DICKENS, William FAULKNER, Nathaniel HAWTHORNE, and Sheridan LE FANU.

The division betweem male and female Gothic is evident in the author's choice of TONE. Male Gothic often victimizes and graphically brutalizes heroines as a source of titillation and voyeuristic fascination. William Child GREEN's "Secrets of Cabalism; or, Ravenstone and Alice of Huntingdon" (ca. 1819) is a case in point. He describes the beguiling demon as gazing with the eyes of a wild leopard while the female victim disrobes: "She loosened her bright hair till it fell to her feet, and [waved] round her uncovered shoulder, and amongst the thin blue silk that clung to her shape, like wreaths of gold" (Haining, 198). In contrast to the male preference for wantonness, female Gothic reflects concern for the powerlessness and male domination of heroines within the rigid gender restrictions of society and church, a source of plots in Charlotte Dacre's DOMESTIC GOTHIC novel *The School for Friends* (ca. 1800), Harriet Beecher Stowe's MELODRAMA *Uncle Tom's Cabin* (1851–52), and Eudora WELTY's *The Robber Bridegroom* (1942).

Crucial to writers of female Gothic are motifs castigating patriarchal control of wives and daughters, the marginalization of women and devaluation of their concerns, the isolation of female artists and trivialization of their work, and the denial of women's sexual autonomy, as found in the ghost's chastisement of the homebound Tita in Laura Esquivel's Mexican melodrama *Like Water for Chocolate* (1989). To circumvent Tita's love for Pedro, the evil spirit of Mama Elena appears to Tita to scold her for immorality: "You are worthless, a good-for-nothing who doesn't respect even yourself. You have blackened the name of my entire family" (Esquivel, 169). In addition to serious treatments of the historical diminution of women, particularly Nobel Prize–winning author Toni MORRISON's *The Bluest Eye* (1969) and BELOVED (1987), the theme also pervades Margaret ATWOOD's comic Gothic in her bestseller FOOL TALE *The Robber Bride* (1993), a subversive novel that hones parody and ridicule as abstract weapons to demoralize and weaken patriarchy.

Female Gothic legitimizes classic GOTHIC CONVENTIONS as means of redress of women's plight. The heroines tend to be powerless, either motherless or orphaned, sometimes low-born, and usually penniless. They frequently bear emblematic CHARACTER NAMES that imply purity, goodness, nobility, and innocence. Their stories are comparable to standard female dilemmas of FAIRY TALE and FOLKLORE—the demon lover of "BEAUTY AND THE BEAST," the threatened fiancée/wife in the BLUEBEARD MYTH, or the incarcerated princess in "Rapunzel" or "Snow White." Facing imprecise threats to body, sanity, and/or life, heroines of female Gothic works suffer extremes of cruelty and menace or enclosure in fetters, traps, slave quarters, prisons, towers, asylums, cloisters, or premature burial. Typically, the weaklings cower and survive until they can be rescued from confinement. More motivated females seize the initiative to explore their cells and work out ways of freeing themselves. A significant difference in the views of female Gothic writers is the commendation of the heroine's new understanding of her tribulations and of the society in which she functions. The female Gothic allows her to assert both independence and sexual autonomy, two qualities found in Charlotte Brontë's doughty governess Jane EYRE and Emily Brontë's willful Catherine EARNSHAW.

Ann Radcliffe introduced the rational, art-loving survivor in Julia de Razzini, the heroine of THE SICILIAN ROMANCE (1790), and set the pattern for the stable, intelligent Gothic heroine in Emily ST. AUBERT in THE MYSTERIES OF UDOLPHO (1794), a melodrama in which the coddled female experiences thrilling, picaresque adventures usually denied to women. Emily proves her ability to reason out the disappearance of her mother and to combat a villainous team, the heroine's father and second wife. To equalize the gender differences between heroine and hero, Radcliffe introduces the wounded hero, Hippolitus, whose sufferings lessen his value as a rescuer. As Julia de Mazzini, the heroine, gains strength, the simultaneous rise of the heroine and disabling of the hero bring the two closer in strength and ability to overcome wrongdoing.

In response to Radcliffe's admirable female characters, traditional male writers—notably Matthew Gregory LEWIS and Francis LATHOM—mocked the stout-hearted Julias and Emilys. To lure male readers, they produced tremulous fantasy victims who are weak, weepy, and delectably defenseless. In Lewis's THE MONK (1796), a sensational Gothic tale of a cloistered fiend who murders Elvira and rapes her helpless daughter Antonia, he blames the female victims for their sufferings. The exception to his stereotyping is the voluptuous Mathilda, an evil seductress endowed with SUPERNATURAL strength, a FEMME FATALE who corrupts the monk and sets him on his path to depravity and crime. The contrast is illuminating: For Lewis, good girls, by nature and upbringing, are natural victims; bad girls, by virtue of their sins, prevail by emulating the vice of men.

In the 1860s, when the English began to liberalize divorce law, the female Gothic took a new turn away from terror toward everyday crime against the middle class as depicted in the domestic Gothic novel. In 1866, unattributed male criticism in the article "Homicidal Heroines" for *Saturday Review* assured readers that female writers could not flourish in a seamy milieu. However, such views discounting the experience of female authors were obviously shortsighted.

London's smash success Mary Elizabeth BRADDON used the sensational novel to reveal the plight of women tricked and despoiled by ordinary English evildoers. In 1866, she exposed the marriage market with *The Lady's Mile*, a tale of a wife framed by a conniving mate for the crime of adultery, which gave him grounds for divorce. Two years later, Braddon moved in another direction in *Dead Sea Fruit* (1868), a dilemma novel about a woman's legal separation from an adulterous husband and the limbo that limited her choices, a titillating scenario that shocked critics. Through a parody, *Lucretia; or, The Heroine of the Nineteenth Century* (1868), the Reverend F. E. Paget voiced his disapproval of women writing about willfulness, unbridled passion, profligacy, and licentious behavior. He based his charge on Victorian extremes of gender stereotyping: "No *man* would have dared to write and publish such books as some of these are: no *man could* have written such delineations of female passion" (Carnell, 167). He piously concluded that such examples of female Gothic abused women's literary gifts and prostituted their skills.

Bibliography

Carnell, Jennifer. *The Literary Lives of Mary Elizabeth Braddon*. Hastings, Sussex: Sensation Press, 2000.

Doody, Margaret Anne. "Deserts, Ruins, and Troubled Waters: Female Dreams in Fiction and the Development of the Gothic Novel," *Genre* 10 (1977): 529–573.

Ellis, Kate Ferguson. *The Contested Castle: Gothic Novels and the Subversion of Domestic Ideology*. Urbana: University of Illinois Press, 1989.

Esquivel, Laura. *Like Water for Chocolate*. New York: Anchor Books, 1992.

Fleenor, Juliann E., ed. *The Female Gothic*. Montreal: Eden Press, 1983.

Haining, Peter, ed. *Gothic Tales of Terror.* New York: Taplinger Publishing, 1972.

Ibsen, Kristine. *The Other Mirror: Women's Narrative in Mexico, 1980–1995.* Westport, Conn.: Greenwood, 1997.

Moers, Ellen. "Female Gothic: Monsters, Goblins, Freaks," *New York Review of Books,* (April 4, 1974): 30–42.

———. "The Monster's Mother," *New York Review of Books,* (March 21, 1974): 24–33.

Mussell, Kay. *Women's Gothic and Romantic Fiction: A Reference Guide.* Westport, Conn.: Greenwood, 1981.

female victims

The victimization of tender, vulnerable young women is the heart-thumping stuff of Gothic lore. The figure dominates LEGEND and folktales—for example, *LA LLORONA* ("the weeping woman"), a pitiable phantom of Central American lore, and Alfred Noyes's early 20th-century bandit ballad "The Highwayman" (1907), in which the captive woman shoots herself to warn her lover of danger.

In 1769, Elizabeth Robinson Montagu composed "Essay on the Praeternatural Beings in Shakespeare," which summarized the relegation of women to gender-specific roles in Gothic motifs, an acknowledgment of a pattern set in FOLKLORE and FAIRY TALE. From the Middle Ages, literature portrayed saintly females in a number of unbearable dilemmas: daughters refusing incestuous relationships, the choice offered the Irishwoman St. Dympna; women suffering rape and dishonor, the fate of Florinda of Tangiers; alleged witches facing persecution and torment, the sentence of Jehenna de Brigue of Meaux and Alice Kyteler of Ireland; and victims of barbarism, the cause of the murders of St. Winifred of Wales and St. Ursula and her company of virgins in Cologne. Most common of these misogynistic scenarios was the plight of maidens rejecting the betrothals arranged by their fathers, the choice of St. Grimonia of Ireland. In subsequent martyrdoms, the anti-brides chose torture and death over union with odious, sometimes murderous husbands, a motif reminiscent of the BLUEBEARD MYTH and a common basis for ballads and cautionary tales.

From these beginnings, Horace WALPOLE, a student of MEDIEVALISM and inventor of the GOTHIC NOVEL, set the genre's pattern of male stalkers and pursuers of females. In *THE CASTLE OF OTRANTO* (1765), he describes the plight of Isabella, who suffers the strange death of her fiancé, Conrad, cries to the saints for succor, and flees Manfred, her father-in-law-to-be: "For a considerable time she remained in an agony of despair. At last, as softly as was possible, she felt for the door, and, having found it, entered trembling into the vault" (Walpole, 26). Walpole's depiction forms the prototype from which male-oriented Gothic fiction achieves its appeal— the terror of a pious, tremulous virgin who traverses unknown terrain or the passageways of convoluted architecture to escape apprehension, rape, cloistering, forced marriage, torture, or death.

In the flowering of GOTHIC CONVENTION, scared women served as FOILS to ominous villains, as with the mysterious female victim of an unexplained duel of knights in feminist writer Mary Hays's "A Fragment: In the Manner of the Old Romances" (1793), a perplexing scrap of a story that implies victimization by senseless woman-haters. The motif flourished in Regina ROCHE's imprisoned wife in *The Children of the Abbey: A Tale* (1796), the innocent rape victim Antonia in Matthew Gregory LEWIS's sensational thriller *THE MONK* (1796), and Eleanor Sleath's menaced maiden in the four-volume *The Orphan of the Rhine: A Romance* (1798), a best-selling pulp work for MINERVA PRESS. In these novels, heiresses and other sex objects are recurrent pawns, the chattel of male action figures who woo, manipulate, defraud, and coerce at their whim. Upon release or escape from villains, these protagonists tend to throw themselves into the power of husbands, in whom they entrust all hope for safety and contentment.

Ann RADCLIFFE, the fount of FEMALE GOTHIC, made an impact on the genre with a deviation from type. She describes in her four-volume *THE MYSTERIES OF UDOLPHO* (1794) a new kind of heroine, a woman capable of overcoming terror to think her way out of peril. The visionary, conflicted Emily ST. AUBERT is capable of sizing up her tormentor, Montoni, by recognizing shifts in his emotions, as when "[his] eyes lost their sullenness, and seemed instantaneously to gleam with fire; yet they still retained somewhat of a lurking cunning" (Radcliffe, 171). At moments when her courage withers, she reflects on her lover, rereads his letters, and "[weighs], with intense anxiety, the force of every word, that spoke of his attachment; and dried her tears, as she trusted in his truth" (ibid., 295). To emphasize a positive outlook in Emily, Radcliffe rewards her heroine with the restoration of her inheritance and a wedding at Chateau-le-Blanc, literally "the white castle," a color-coded SYMBOL of unclouded joy to come.

Despite Radcliffe's inroads against voyeuristic fiction, the old ploys flourished. The delicious malevolence of romantic plots served self-supporting hacks of the Gothic potboiler and GOTHIC BLUEBOOK genres, many of whom were female. At the heart of their fictional conflicts were male ogres, often priests and monks, who forced untenable choices on women too weak or outnumbered to rebel. The anti-Catholic SUBTEXT flourished in Sarah Lansdell's *The Tower; or, The Romance of Ruthyne* (1798), a title projecting phallic imagery. In the heroine's recounting of a forced marriage to a count, she blames a chaplain for hurrying her through the wedding ritual. More coercive is a scene in John Palmer's *The Haunted Cavern: A Caledonian Tale* (1796), in which a priest absolves the evil groom-to-be of his sins, then abets him in a dead-of-night assault on the unsuspecting maiden. In Martha Harley's fanciful *Priory of St. Bernard* (1789), the complicity of a bishop compounds the forced nuptial scenario, in which an unwilling virgin invokes heaven's law to no avail.

In contrast to the cardboard female characters of such Gothic fiction, Charles Brockden BROWN advanced the heroine toward realism in *WIELAND* (1798), the prototype of AMERICAN GOTHIC. Characterizing Clara WIELAND as the victim of her brother, Theodore WIELAND, a deluded monomaniac, Brown offers more introspection in the depiction of female terror. She blames lack of learning and experience and admits, "I was powerless because I was again assaulted by surprise and had not fortified my mind by foresight and previous reflection against a scene like this" (Brown, 171). Fleshed out by an emergent American feminism, Clara is more in touch with her humanity and less willing to pose as the retiring, modest pawn of males than her counterparts in English Gothic novels. She admits to weakness, but blames "perverse and vicious education," which keeps Clara and her peers enthralled under patriarchy (ibid., 90).

In the 19th century, prurience dominated sensational novels with images of the palpitating heroine in fearful clutches. In Charles Robert MATURIN's *MELMOTH THE WANDERER* (1820), the title character, a vindictive agent of Satan, gloats at his power over his trembling bride Immalee (later called Isadora): "Me, the single, pulseless, eyeless, heartless embracer of an unfertile bride,—the brooder over the dark and unproductive nest of eternal sterility" (Maturin, 354). In a class-conscious depiction of the aristocracy preying on the working class, Mary Elizabeth BRADDON produced *The Black Band; or, The Mysteries of Midnight* (1861–62), a tale of a thieving band of Austrian anarchists that counters the frailty of dancer Clara Melville with the villainy of Sir Frederick Beaumorris. In formulaic Victorian logic, the author rewards Clara's durable virginity with an appropriate marriage and happy ending.

Similarly denigrating to women is Svengali, the demonic Jewish hypnotizer of diva Trilby O'Ferrall in bohemian Paris in George du Maurier's MELODRAMA *Trilby*, published serially from January through August 1894 in *Harper's Monthly*. The height of the manipulative relationship depicts the singer appearing on stage like an automaton to be directed by a demonic master: "[She] made a slight inclination of her head and body towards the imperial box, and then to right and left. . . . Her face was thin, and had a rather haggard expression in spite of its artificial freshness" (du Maurier, 316–317). At his death, Trilby loses the hypnotic tether to her master and sinks into artistic oblivion. Less controlling of his puppet woman is Jonathan HARKER, the intended of the redoubtable Mina Murray, an orphan whom he patronizes as a frail helpmeet and victim of a vampire in Bram STOKER's *DRACULA* (1897). Maintaining the Victorian tradition that women require constant protection from grim sights, hard labor, and emotional shock, he overlooks her past aid in nursing Lucy Westenra and her journey to a Budapest hospital to aid Harker himself. Ironically, she produces evidence of Dracula's demise and the restoration of order by giving birth to a child, a male.

Bibliography

Berman, Avis. "George du Maurier's 'Trilby' Whipped Up a Worldwide Storm," *Smithsonian* 24, no. 9 (December 1993): 110–116.

Brown, Charles Brockden. *Wieland; or, The Transformation.* New York: Harcourt Brace, 1926.

Carnell, Jennifer. *The Literary Lives of Mary Elizabeth Braddon.* Hastings, Sussex: Sensation Press, 2000.

Davison, Neil R. "The Jew as Homme/Femme-Fatale: Jewish (Art)ifice, Trilby, and Dreyfus," *Jewish Social Studies* (winter–spring 2002): 73–113.

du Maurier, George. *Trilby.* New York: Harper & Brothers, 1894.

Grossman, Jonathan H. "The Mythic Svengali: Antiaestheticism in 'Trilby,'" *Studies in the Novel* 28, no. 4 (winter 1996): 525–543.

Grove, Allen W. "To Make a Long Story Short: Gothic Fragments and the Gender Politics of Incompleteness," *Studies in Short Fiction* 34, no. 1 (winter 1997): 1–10.

Maturin, Charles Robert. *Melmoth the Wanderer.* Oxford: Oxford University Press, 1968.

Radcliffe, Ann. *The Mysteries of Udolpho.* London: Oxford University Press, 1966.

Walpole, Horace. *The Castle of Otranto.* London: Oxford University Press, 1969.

femme fatale

A womanly FOIL of the frail, lovely, and good-hearted Gothic heroine is her fictional counterpart, the imperious, darkly emotional femme fatale, or fatal female. The character type is as old as Lilith in the Garden of Eden and the entrancing Medusa and Medea in Greek mythology. The fatal female takes numerous guises and poses: the inconstant mistress in Abbé PRÉVOST's MANON LESCAUT (1731); the diabolical transdresser Mathilda, the abettor of AMBROSIO's sex crimes and murders in Matthew Gregory LEWIS's THE MONK (1796); the heartless Mother Superior and vindictive Marchesa de Vivaldi in Ann RADCLIFFE's THE ITALIAN (1797); and the disturbingly androgynous Geraldine in Samuel Taylor COLERIDGE's "CHRISTABEL" (1816). The killer female may emerge from a normal girlhood, then turn into a vibrant flirt, smoldering succubus, or GROTESQUE predator. Years of thwarted aims alter

her striving into venom and her sweet nature into guile, a motivation Johann von GOETHE stresses in "The New Melusina" (1826). The positive drive toward liberation can take a negative turn toward dominance, the overt trait in the title character of Edgar Allan POE's "LIGEIA" (1838) and in the allure of the siren protagonists of John KEATS's LA BELLE DAME SANS MERCI (1819) and Oscar WILDE's Gothic history play SALOMÉ (1893). In all three women, female charm, like the threat of the black widow spider, has deadly results for the male who succumbs to her seduction.

Late Victorian literature anticipated the emergence of the liberated woman, but depicted female boldness as costly, even deadly. In Bram STOKER's DRACULA (1897), unlike the sweet, maidenly girlhood friend Mina Murray, the wanton Lucy Westenra despoils her fiancé Arthur Holmwood and lusts hungrily for Count Dracula. As she sinks toward death from a fatal bite to the neck, she produces large canine teeth and threatens Dracula's foil, Dr. Van Helsing, a man of reason and restraint who diagnoses her ailment as VAMPIRISM. After her demise, he sets about autopsying her remains by lopping off the head and staking the heart, SYMBOLs of Dracula's mastery of the FEMALE VICTIM's thoughts and soul. The return to the crypt of an alluring wraith carrying a child victim to drain of its blood convinces Lucy's male admirers that the only antidote to evil is to exorcise the vampire Dracula and exterminate all his minions.

Modern Gothic fiction exploits the wickedness and mercilessness of its black-widow female, such as William FAULKNER's poisoner in "A ROSE FOR EMILY" (1930) and his taunting slut Temple Drake in *Sanctuary* (1931), the destructive Robin Vote in Djuna BARNES's *Nightwood* (1930), and the first Mrs. Max DE WINTER, the amoral mantrap shot through the heart in Daphne DU MAURIER's classic novel REBECCA (1938). Morally fallible, Faulkner's prim Miss EMILY manages to ensnare and detain her only beau with arsenic while maintaining a discreet distance from snoopy townspeople. On the other hand, du Maurier's dark lady gains strength only through loss, as with the bullet through the heart served up by her long-suffering husband. In some Gothic works from the last half of the 20th century, the emergence of intellect and logic in liberated women soured into deception and connivance—the qualities of the villainess Celestine Nansellock in Victoria HOLT's MISTRESS OF MELLYN (1960); Zenia, the dastardly siren in Margaret ATWOOD's *The Robber Bride* (1993); the vindictive sister-in-law in Joyce Carol OATES's "The Premonition" (1994); and the fleeing mistress in Michel Faber's THE CRIMSON PETAL AND THE WHITE (2002).

Bibliography

Bucknell, Brad. "On 'Seeing' Salome," *English Literary History* 60, no. 2 (summer 1993): 503–526.

Davison, Neil R. "The Jew as Homme/Femme-Fatale: Jewish (Art)ifice, Trilby, and Dreyfus," *Jewish Social Studies* (winter–spring 2002): 73–113.

Yarbrough, Scott. "The Dark Lady: Temple Drake as Femme Fatale," *Southern Literary Journal* 31, no. 2 (spring 1999): 50.

Ferdinand Count Fathom
Tobias Smollett
(1753)

Tobias SMOLLETT's dramatic *The Adventures of Ferdinand Count Fathom* (1753), a sleeper novel that gradually acquired a literary following, initiated the scrutiny of innate criminality in English literature. He based his study of the title VILLAIN on the trans-European life of a peripatetic con artist devoid of remorse for a life dedicated to vice and cruelty. At the same time that Smollett explored new fictional venues, he pioneered gloom, OMENS, and MYSTERY as adjuncts to the GOTHIC NOVEL. In the introduction, he justifies terror fiction as suited to the most memorable of human passions. He anchored his text in contemporary life and, like Charlotte SMITH and Ann RADCLIFFE, preferred the SUPERNATURAL explained to outré spectral elements or extravagant Gothic SENSATIONALISM.

In darkly picaresque episodes, the satanic rogue, Count Fathom, is capable of extremes of depravity, as when he robs a man he had seen stabbed by attackers but had made no effort to rescue. Fathom systematically fleeces members of elegant society, including the ladylike Monimia, and fools the girl's beloved, Melvile, into believing her dead. In the dark of midnight, within earshot of a screeching owl, Melvile follows the sexton to the gravesite, where the sexton, "by the light of a glimmering taper, conducted the despairing lover to a dreary isle, and stamped upon the ground with his foot, saying, 'Here the young lady lies interred'" (Smollett, 312). The height of the lover's grief and his devotion to her grave add a touch of dark humor to his OBSESSION with an outward show of mourning.

Under an enveloping physical and moral CHIAROSCURO, Smollett concocts a fiercely cruel tale. Parallel to Melvile's immersion in suffering is the despair of Don Diego the Castilian, a remorseful husband and father who torments himself in the erroneous belief that he murdered his family. With a deft bit of poetic justice, Smollett conjures up an ominous graveyard ATMOSPHERE and suitable comeuppance to Fathom, who withers away on his sickbed crying to heaven for succor and displaying the blackened lips and marbled pallor of a corpse. The deathbed confession of the dissipated carouser was the forerunner of similar last-minute pleadings of villains, including the sybaritic caliph in William BECKFORD's VATHEK: *An Arabian Tale* (1782), the lustful AMBROSIO in Matthew Gregory LEWIS's THE MONK (1796), the avenger in Lord BYRON's THE GIAOUR (1813), and the title character in Charles Robert MATURIN's MELMOTH THE WANDERER (1820).

Bibliography

Goode, Okey. "Tobias Smollett: Novelist," *ANQ* 13, no. 3 (summer 2000): 61.

Punter, David, ed. *The Literature of Terror*, vol. 1, 2nd ed. London: Longman, 1996.

Smollett, Tobias. *The Adventures of Ferdinand Count Fathom*. Athens: University of Georgia Press, 1988.

film noir

An offshoot of the French ROMAN NOIR ("black story") and German black romanticism, film noir is a self-conscious dark cinema based on gothic HORROR NARRATIVES and manipulations of CHIAROSCURO, the play of light against shadow. The cultural mythology of middle-class pessimism began in France in the 1920s with movies overstocked with cruelty and fatalism, for example, Henri Desfontaines's *Le Puits et le Pendule* (*The Pit and the*

Pendulum, 1910), Luis Buñuel and Jean Epstein's surreal classic *La Chute de la Maison Usher* (*The Fall of the House of Usher,* 1928), and Marcel Carné's *Le Jour Se Lève* (*The Day Awakens,* 1939). American film noir got its start at Warner Brothers Studio in Hollywood with *Little Caesar* (1930) and *I Am a Fugitive from a Chain Gang* (1932), cinematic shockers that stressed neurotic killers and VIOLENCE against hopeless victims in nightmarish settings—often ordinary places, such as neon-lit cafés, hotels, bars, and pool rooms, made dangerous by the lowlifes and their bleached-blonde molls who frequent them.

With the evolution of gangster films following the Prohibition and Great Depression eras and the onset of World War II, a new wave of brutal Gothic screenplays exploited a pervasive unease with tales of sleazy eroticism, betrayal, and doom. Underworld settings fueled the best in grainy black-and-white crime stories—film versions of Dashiell Hammett's *The Maltese Falcon* (1941), Vera Caspary's *Laura* (1944), James M. Cain's *Mildred Pierce* (1945), James M. Cain's *The Postman Always Rings Twice* (1946), an adaptation of Ernest Hemingway's *The Killers* (1946), William FAULKNER's screenplay of Raymond Chandler's *The Big Sleep* (1946), Ben Hecht's *Kiss of Death* (1947), Malvin Walk's *The Naked City* (1948), and W. R. Burnett's *The Asphalt Jungle* (1950), a cautionary tale exposing the rise of urban crime. Climaxing with Orson Welles's Kafkaesque version of Whit Masterson's *Touch of Evil* (1958), the genre comprised some 300 titles. Many found their way into the dossiers of McCarthyites and fueled the mid-century paranoid witchhunt of the House Un-American Activities Committee.

Still viable in the 21st century, late-stage film noir turned brooding and decadent with nostalgic recreations of early detective and crime stories, con games, and sordid whodunits, as in *Chinatown* (1974), *Body Heat* (1981), *Prizzi's Honor* (1985), *The Grifters* (1990), *Pulp Fiction* (1994), *The Usual Suspects* (1995), *L.A. Confidential* (1997), and *Mystic River* (2003). Crucial to retro tastes was the revival of sour jazz background music, the cynical detective, corrupt ward-heeler, forlorn loner, and street-corner punks. Contributing to an aura of self-defeat were the amoral habitués of smoky night-clubs, flophouses, and urban alleys, including the obligatory cripples, such as Ratso in *Midnight Cowboy* (1969), and a variety of GROTESQUEs, often survivors of torture, knife fights, and shootouts. The tone projected disillusion, particularly about the intent of police and the court system to prosecute crime and return justice to ordinary people.

Bibliography

Adams, Jeffrey. "Orson Welles's 'The Trial': *Film Noir* and the Kafkaesque," *College Literature* 29, no. 3 (summer 2002): 140–157.

Covey, William B. "More Than Night: *Film Noir* in its Contexts," *Film Criticism* 24, no. 2 (winter 1999): 66.

Naremore, James. "American *Film Noir:* The History of an Idea," *Film Quarterly* 49, no. 2 (winter 1995): 12–28.

Okon, Christine M. "Dark City: The Lost World of *Film Noir,*" *Journal of Popular Film and Television* 29, no. 4 (winter 2002): 190–191.

Sharrett, Christopher. "The Endurance of *Film Noir,*" *USA Today* 127, no. 2,638 (July 1998): 79.

Welsch, Tricia. "Yoked Together by Violence," *Film Criticism* 22, no. 1 (fall 1997): 62–73.

flight motif

In traditional GOTHIC CONVENTION, flight is the flip side of STALKING and confinement. Vulnerable characters who find themselves in the clutches of MONSTERS or menaced by psychopaths retreat to the bestial logic of the hunted and instinctively search out safe haven, as depicted in Michel Faber's neo-Victorian novel THE CRIMSON PETAL AND THE WHITE (2002). In the FOOL TALE "The Legend of Sleepy Hollow" (1820), Washington Irving pictures Ichabod CRANE fleeing a phantasm of the imagination, Brom Bones in the Halloween guise of a headless Hessian horseman. Set against a backdrop of CHIAROSCURO at "the very witching time of night," Ichabod's departure occurs immediately after a STORYTELLING session stressing ghosts and goblins (Irving, 53). Whistling in a display of fake courage, he trudges into the dismal dell amid shifting shadows that trigger a psychological terror. Ultimately, his vivid imagination defeats him. Bested by Brom, whose only weapon is a pumpkin, Ichabod not only loses the lovely Katrina Van Tassel to his rival, but disappears entirely from the region, leaving behind folk explanations of his flight.

The path of the runner typically fills Gothic romance with unusual settings and modes of escape, as with the retreat of a royal court to a rural abbey to elude an epidemic in Edgar Allan POE's "THE MASQUE OF THE RED DEATH" (1842) and the dash by canoe into a waterfall in James Fenimore Cooper's *The Last of the Mohicans* (1826), a classic of American FRONTIER GOTHIC. More poignant is the flight from harm of an elderly character, cripple, hapless female, or child, the motif in Charles DICKENS's child crime novel *OLIVER TWIST* (1838) and in Henry JAMES's ghostly *THE TURN OF THE SCREW* (1898). In *Bless Me, Ultima* (1972), Rudolfo Anaya pairs a child and his aged grandmother, the title *curandera* ("healer") accused of WITCHCRAFT. Anaya sacrifices the older character for the younger, leaving the boy Antonio to mourn Ultima and bury her pet owl. The episode rids the town and family of evil at the same time that it proves the mettle of Antonio, who combats the sinister men who intimidate a blameless herbalist.

The failure of the hunted to outrun the hunter dominates suspenseful Gothic works, particularly Mary Wollstonecraft SHELLEY's *FRANKENSTEIN* (1818), in which the nameless monster ranges over Europe into the Arctic realm in pursuit of experimenter Victor FRANKENSTEIN. A failed escape also colors the opening chapter of *VARNEY THE VAMPIRE* (1847), a popular continued story. Because the tapping of the huge vampire at the window freezes Flora in her boudoir, Varney seizes and pierces her throat with his sharp fangs and sucks her blood. A symbolic failure to escape forms the crux of Oscar WILDE's *THE PICTURE OF DORIAN GRAY* (1891), in which the protagonist attempts to elude inner corruption, which his SUPERNATURAL portrait displays in sequential views of his moral decline. In "The Final Problem" (1893), Sir Arthur Conan DOYLE uses a failed flight as a means of rounding out the Sherlock HOLMES series with the detective's death in the Alps caused by the relentless VILLAIN Moriarty.

Bibliography

Doyle, Arthur Conan. *The Annotated Sherlock Holmes*, 2 vols. New York: Wings Books, 1967.

Irving, Washington. *The Legend of Sleepy Hollow*. New York: Tor, 1990.

Punter, David, ed. *The Literature of Terror*, vol. 1, 2nd ed. London: Longman, 1996.

Varney, the Vampire; or, The Feast of Blood, 3 vols. New York: Arno Press, 1970.

foil

The foil is usually a secondary or minor character who reflects personal traits, beliefs, philosophies, and behavior opposing those of the protagonist—for example, the crippled Tiny Tim and the genial Mr. Fezziwig as diametric opposites of the ogreish miser Ebenezer Scrooge in Charles DICKENS's holiday ghost classic *A CHRISTMAS CAROL* (1843); the maidenly orphan Mina Murray and wanton heiress Lucy Westenra in Bram STOKER's *DRACULA* (1897); the demonic pairing in Stephen Vincent Benét's AMERICAN GOTHIC story "The Devil and Daniel Webster" (1939); and the sweet-natured, companionable Mattie Silver and the grim hypochondriac Zeena, the wife of the title character in Edith WHARTON's dark novella *ETHAN FROME* (1911). The use of polar opposites is a revealing strategy in Gothic fiction; for example, the amenable "good child" Helen Burns versus the stubborn, rebellious title "bad girl" in Charlotte BRONTË's *JANE EYRE* (1847). In adulthood, Jane outpaces two foils, the charmingly upperclass Blanche Ingram and a more destructive opposite in Bertha Mason ROCHESTER, the criminally insane first wife of Jane's intended. Daphne DU MAURIER's *REBECCA* (1938) and Victoria HOLT's *MISTRESS OF MELLYN* (1960) stick to the foil motif to present fictional opposites—du Maurier's Rebecca and the anonymous second Mrs. de Winter; Holt's governess Martha Leigh and rival Celestine Nansellock, who commits murder and plots against Leigh to prevent her taking over Mount Mellyn.

The literary purpose of an opposite or alter ego is an accentuation of paired characters' distinctive traits, as with the vivid black mistress and subdued, black-draped fiancée in Joseph CONRAD's *HEART OF DARKNESS* (1902). An enduring example is the stodgy, conventional Dr. Watson and the brilliant Sherlock HOLMES in the detective fiction of Sir Arthur Conan DOYLE. Providing contrast in Robert Louis STEVENSON's MAD SCIENTIST novella *DR. JEKYLL AND MR. HYDE* (1886) is the demonic Hyde, who underscores the depraved nature repressed in Dr. Henry Jekyll, a gentleman scholar who inadvertently unleashes murderous intent during his alter ego's rampages through London. Stevenson carries the foil motif to psychological ends by presenting his famed opposites as two sides of the human personality. In his parting words, Dr. Jekyll admits that, "as I lay down the pen and proceed to seal up my confession, I bring the life of that unhappy Henry Jekyll to an end" (Stevenson, 103).

Bibliography

Hennessy, Brendan. *The Gothic Novel.* London: Longman, 1978.

Herdman, John. *The Double in Nineteenth-Century Fiction.* New York: Macmillan, 1990.

Stevenson, Robert Louis. *Dr. Jekyll and Mr. Hyde.* New York: Bantam Books, 1981.

folklore

Folklore is a vast body of creative expression encompassing adages, animal and plant lore, LEGENDs, myths, riddles and proverbs, fabliaux and FOOL TALEs, rituals, ceremonial pantomime and mummery, NURSERY RHYMES, work and wooing songs, and STORYTELLING of preliterate and semiliterate people. Gothic versions of these highly fluid works of peasant culture survive through oral and artistic telling and retelling, as with devil and witch stories, Irish banshee tales, and Hispanic *corridos* (ballads) of injustice turned to ambush and murder, such as "The Ballad of Gregorio Cortez." The latter is the undated story of a young Mexican who kills a white sheriff, T. T. Morris, in 1901, for attempting to arrest him unjustly for horse stealing. To preserve the wrongs and lessons of the past, Gothic folklore reiterates traditional beliefs and world views, such as SUPERSTITION regarding the WANDERING JEW and vampires and gender archetypes in the legends of Bluebeard's wives and of *LA LLORONA* ("The Weeping Woman"), a complex female nomad in Mexican lore.

Of unknown authorship, true folklore arises from spontaneous oral narrative or song about community events and challenges to shared values, as exemplified by the endangerment of Maid Marion as a pawn of the villainous sheriff of Nottingham in episodes of Robin Hood. These literary treasures follow folk on journeys and diasporas, as in the mournful love plaint "Barbara Allen," which accompanied settlers from the British Isles to New World colonies in the Carolinas, and the rollicking trickster tales of Anansi the spider, which black slaves brought from West Africa as cautionary and wonder tales. Warning stories replete with Gothic details alert common folk to danger; among such stories are the Appalachian ghost tales compiled in Eliot Wigginton's series of Foxfire books and the woman-controlling Chinese talk-story and the hero tale of Fa Mu Lan related in Maxine Hong KINGSTON's *The Woman Warrior* (1975).

Folklore depends on a unique body of Gothic conventions, as found in the enchanters and shape-shifters of FAIRY TALEs (wicked witches in L. Frank Baum's *The Wizard of Oz*), the villains of cowboy lore (the legend of rhyming bandit Black Bart and outlaws in Larry McMurtry's *Lonesome Dove*), the seducers and murderers of African-American fiction and blues lyrics (Du Bose Heyward's folk novel *Porgy* and the folk song "Frankie and Johnny"), and the looming phantasm of GHOST STORIES (the hovering girl-ghost in Toni MORRISON's *BELOVED* and Stovall's haunting of a Pittsburgh apartment in August WILSON's play *THE PIANO LESSON*). Folk narrative frequently anticipates the Gothic traditions of the hunted and persecuted female, a motif that empowers the cruel STALKING of women in hagiography (legends of St. Bee of Cumbria and St. Osith of Chichester), the harmful deities and spirits of myth (Hades, god of the underworld and captor of Persephone in Greek mythology), and demoralizing genealogy in sagas and love plaints (the ancestor forbidden to marry in Laura Esquivel's *Like Water for Chocolate*). In raw form, folklore often supplies the kernel story of Gothic literature, as is the case with superstitions about DREAMS in John KEATS's narrative poem *THE EVE OF ST. AGNES* (1819) and the SOUTHERN GOTHIC themes of slave punishments in George Washington CABLE's "BRAS-COUPÉ" (1879).

Bibliography

Thompson, Stith. *The Folktale.* Berkeley: University of California Press, 1977.

fool tale

The fool tale, the clever trickster's blend of humor and horror to victimize a rube, often overturns the stereotypical Gothic stalker-and-virgin scenario by substituting a sissy or effeminate male for the maiden, as is the case with SAKI's "The Open Window" (1911), anthologized in *Toys of Peace* (1919), and Isaac Bashevis SINGER's "Gimpel the Fool" (1957). A favorite American tale, Washington Irving's "The Legend of Sleepy Hollow," published in *The Sketch Book of Geoffrey Crayon, Gent.* (1820), skewers the easily gulled Yankee schoolmaster Ichabod CRANE, rival of "Brom Bones" Van Brunt for the delectable Katrina Van Tassel, a ripe partridge of a girl who stands to inherit her father's farm. Ichabod's heightened sensibilities, abraded by terror of the SUPERNATURAL as described in the story of the headless horseman, panic him as he gallops through the wooded dell on a tenebrous autumn night in flight from a ghost he identifies with a deceased Hessian trooper. Irving enhances the inevitable face-off between Ichabod and Brom, his rural FOIL, by setting the story at midnight under a darkened sky. The trick of the ambiguous headless ghost muffled in a cloak, groaning, and hurling a pumpkin head produces the desired effect of scaring Ichabod out of the county.

Critics read into the conventions of the fool tale a parallel to the frontier test of manhood. A common motif in the Western literature of Ambrose BIERCE and Mark Twain, folly literature pits the awkward, inexperienced dude against the proud, self-assured man's man. Their clash, typically a bout of machismo, ambush, and fire power rather than a war of words, exposes the wimp and Eastern dilettante and banishes from the Wild West the would-be frontiersman. In *THE BALLAD OF THE SAD CAFE* (1951), author Carson Mc-CULLERS overturns the paradigm by pitting an androgynous female protagonist, Miss Amelia Evans, against Cousin Lyman, a devious hunchback. Canadian novelist Margaret ATWOOD carries the motif further afield from the original male-on-male

set-to in *The Robber Bride* (1993), a best-selling novel about a clever FEMME FATALE who bests her female rivals.

Bibliography

Benoit, Raymond. "Irving's 'The Legend of Sleepy Hollow,'" *Explicator* 55, no. 1 (fall 1996): 15–17.

Piacentino, Ed. "'Sleepy Hollow' Comes South: Washington Irving's Influence on Old Southwestern Humor," *Southern Literary Journal* 30, no. 1 (fall 1997): 27–42.

Smith, Greg. "Supernatural Ambiguity and Possibility in Irving's 'The Legend of Sleepy Hollow,'" *Midwest Quarterly* 42, no. 2 (winter 2001): 174.

foreshadowing

Writers of Gothic literature rely on ATMOSPHERE and foreshadowing of significant events and revelations to come, especially horrific surprise endings, such as the collapse of a mansion in Edgar Allan POE's "THE FALL OF THE HOUSE OF USHER" (1839), the purchase of rat poison in William FAULKNER's "A ROSE FOR EMILY" (1930), the ominous mad dog shooting and surreptitious contacts with a handicapped neighbor in Harper Lee's *To Kill a Mockingbird* (1960), and perilous behind-the-scenes plotting in Dan Brown's *THE DA VINCI CODE* (2003). In Joseph CONRAD's *HEART OF DARKNESS* (1902), a voyage upriver into the Congo introduces a seminal thought to Charlie Marlow, who considers colonialism "the merry dance of death and trade" (Conrad, 78–79). By the end of the novel, the VILLAIN Kurtz reposes in a dark cabin and declares to Marlow, "I am lying here in the dark waiting for death" (*ibid.*, 147). In his last words, Kurtz cries out a crazed foretaste of his well-deserved hell, "The horror! The horror!" (*ibid.*). In this way, the Gothic author's orchestrated SYMBOLS, hints, suggestions, MYSTERY, and evocative names of people and places become tools in the elevation of anxiety, expectation, and uncertainty, the hallmarks of SUSPENSE in Gothic tales.

The Gothic writer arranges data and episodes as a means of preparing the reader for climactic events—for example, the title character's first meeting with Edward ROCHESTER and her subsequent DREAMS AND NIGHTMARES in Charlotte

BRONTË's *JANE EYRE* (1847), ominous extrasensory impressions that precede the protagonist Latimer's death in George Eliot's Gothic tale "The Lifted Veil" (1859), and hints of the SUPERNATURAL in William Rose Benét's spooky poem "The Skater of Ghost Lake" (1933). At a pivotal moment in THE PICTURE OF DORIAN GRAY (1891), Oscar WILDE makes use of visual foreshadowing. At the climax, the protagonist-killer retreats from a murder scene and looks over the balustrade "down into the black seething well of darkness" (Wilde, 171). The unseeable bottom of the stairwell haunts Dorian until his last day, when he commits a second knifing, freeing his demonic soul from his portrait and engulfing his pretty-boy face in the ghoulish evil that he bears inside. A more chilling revelation of self-destruction occurs in Mariano Azuela's *The Underdogs* (1914), a minimalist glimpse of the Mexican Revolution serialized in the *El Paso del Norte* during Pancho Villa's self-exile in Texas. At a turning point in the army's carousing, Blondie aims his pistol at a mirror, fires a bullet at his own image, and shatters the glass. The telling act recurs in the emotional and moral letdown that follows victory, when Blondie shoots himself.

Foreshadowing is an organic device of the DETECTIVE STORY and FILM NOIR, particularly in the presentation of details, witnesses, and clues that later turn out to be either red herrings or significant components of the solution, as with the family resemblance between the villain and a portrait at Baskerville Hall in Sir Arthur Conan DOYLE's novella "THE HOUND OF THE BASKERVILLES" (1902) and the confusing relationship between the protagonist and her child/sister in the dark incest plot of the film *Chinatown* (1974). These narrative enhancements affirm unity by allying early information with the conclusion, gradually controlling and shaping reader response, and justifying the shock and surprise of the outcome, for example, the psychotic escapee's murder of an unsuspecting family in Flannery O'CONNOR's SOUTHERN GOTHIC story "A Good Man Is Hard to Find" (1955), the walling up of an innocent woman in a priest's hole in Victoria HOLT's *MISTRESS OF MELYN* (1960), and the painful revelation of a female masquerader in Donna Cross's historical novel *Pope Joan* (1996).

Bibliography

Conrad, Joseph. *Heart of Darkness and The Secret Sharer.* New York: Signet, 1983.

Rashkin, Esther. "Art as Symptom: A Portrait of Child Abuse in 'The Picture of Dorian Gray,'" *Modern Philology* 95, no. 1 (August 1997): 68–80.

Wilde, Oscar. *The Picture of Dorian Gray and Selected Stories.* New York: New American Library, 1983.

Frankenstein
Mary Shelley
(1818)

Mary Wollstonecraft SHELLEY's *Frankenstein; or, The Modern Prometheus* is sometimes identified as the world's first science fiction novel and one of the most influential works written by a woman. Unlike transitory GOTHIC BLUEBOOKs and popular thrillers issued by MINERVA PRESS, *Frankenstein* is the only horror novel of the classic Gothic era to have remained popular into the 21st century. Influenced by the myth of Prometheus, the Greek fire-stealer and man-maker, and by Ann RADCLIFFE's terror novel THE MYSTERIES OF UDOLPHO (1794), Shelley created a cultural icon in Victor FRANKENSTEIN, an obsessive laboratory scientist eager to create life from necrotic tissue. The idealistic project implodes when the MONSTER returns to the experimenter to kill first his family, then his best friend, and the scientist himself. Despite literary frailties and inconsistencies, the compelling image so impressed readers that the name Frankenstein has, illogically, become a synonym for a monstrosity.

The novel blends didacticism and science fiction with GOTHIC CONVENTIONs, beginning with the nascent career of the Swiss medical student, who is still in training at the University of Ingolstadt when he resolves to make a humanoid from the spare parts of corpses. Shelley chose this source of materials as a commentary on early 19th-century grave-robbing, a social and economic problem much ballyhooed in the popular press and discussed by lawmakers. The resulting fictional creature, confused as to its place on earth, receives only revulsion for its yearning and retreats into an involuntary banishment. The unnamed ghoul becomes a pariah like the WANDERING JEW and stalks Europe and the British Isles, leaving in its wake terror and horrific murders.

Emotions engulf Mary Shelley's Gothic text. She enhances MELODRAMA with Victor's sensibilities and MELANCHOLY, flirtations with INSANITY, and neurasthenic faints when reality overwhelms him. The doom-laden TONE derives from such details as isolation on an ice floe, the menacing yellow-hued face at the window, and a series of unsolved strangulations. In punishment for having cobbled together a lone being, Victor retreats from society to duplicate the lurid laboratory experiment in an attempt to make a female version as the monster's companion. In recompense for the scientist's destruction of the second body, the monster murders a young girl in her bridal chamber, flees to the Arctic, and orchestrates the inevitable death that awaits Victor, the ill-advised seeker of NATURE's secrets.

For its daring, Shelley's novel was destined to be a classic. Within five years of publication, it was the subject of a stage adaptation, Richard Brinsley Peake's three-act opera *Presumption; or, The Fate of Frankenstein* (1823), which the *London Morning Post* found appealing. Beginning in 1910, the novel went through a series of adaptations to cinema. Thomas Edison made the first film, which preceded German versions, *The Golem* (1914) and *Homunculus* (1916), and was followed by an American movie, *Frankenstein* (1931). Knockoffs of the original plot turned the story into bathos, satire, and humor, as with Mel Brooks's *Young Frankenstein* (1974).

Bibliography

Cohen, Jeffrey Jerome, ed. *Monster Theory*. Minneapolis: University of Minnesota Press, 1996.

Levine, George, and U. C. Knoepflmacher, eds. *The Endurance of Frankenstein: Essays on Mary Shelley's Novel*. Berkeley: University of California Press, 1979.

Rosenberg, Samuel. *The Come As You Are Masquerade Party*. Englewood Cliffs, N.J.: Prentice-Hall, 1970.

Yousef, Nancy. "The Monster in a Dark Room: Frankenstein, Feminism, and Philosophy," *Modern Language Quarterly* 63, no. 2 (June 2002): 197–226.

Frankenstein, Victor

Frankenstein, an enduring Gothic figure, derived from Mary Wollstonecraft SHELLEY's readings in popular French and German ghost tales. Around 1810, the publication of *Fantasmagoria* in Germany preceded translated editions in English and French, notably, *Fantasmagoriana; ou Recueil d'Histoires d'Apparitions, de Spectres, Revenans, Fantomes, Etc.* (*Fantasmagoriana; or An Anthology of Stories of Ghosts, Specters, Revenants, Phantoms, Etc.*, 1812), which the author named in her diary. After immersing herself in thriller fiction in Geneva in summer 1816, Shelley reshaped the classic Gothic stalker in an original horror novel, *FRANKENSTEIN; or The Modern Prometheus* (1818). Influencing her creation of a MAD SCIENTIST were her husband, Percy SHELLEY; Lord BYRON; and John POLIDORI; and a contemporary interest in bodysnatching and in galvanism, a study of the medical application of electricity conducted by Scottish physician James Lind. The intriguing story of Frankenstein recurred in such GOTHIC BLUEBOOKs, as the anonymous *The Old Tower of Frankenstein* (n.d.) and *Fantasmagoria* (ca. 1812), issued in Cheapside, London, by Thomas Tegg.

Shelley's Frankenstein projects a unique focus: the study of a willful, temperamental Swiss lab researcher at the University of Ingolstadt who is interested in metaphysics and inadvertently embraces doom by violating NATURE. To heighten the irony of the experimenter's failure, Shelley names her introspective hero Victor. While pursuing the synthesis of a living being in the laboratory through credible scientific methodology, he ignores the advice of his mentor, Monsieur Krempe, and the warning in M. Waldman's lecture: "The ancient teachers of this science . . . promised impossibilities and performed nothing. The modern masters promise very little; they know that metals cannot be transmuted and that the elixir of life is a chimera" (Shelley, 46). Enveloped in grief for his recently deceased mother and sunk in constant solitude, the foolhardy Victor presses into dangerous territory, pushing himself without rest until he compromises his mental and physical health, a common element in extreme Gothic scenarios. His manic involvement in anatomy is oddly erotic in that his workaholism far outpaces any interest in Elizabeth, his bride-to-be.

Shelley depicts her tragic protagonist as incapable of containing his curiosity, another common trait among Gothic figures. His profane fingers a-twitch to get back to work, Victor voices his intent to know the secrets of heaven and earth, a longing for metaphysical skills that places him in a doomed category with Adam and Eve and FAUST. Victor's obsession robs him of intimacy with colleagues and family and forces him into a half-crazed state as he plunges into the shadowy mechanism by which death ends life. For material, he combs unwholesome climes—mortuaries and graveyards— which further distance him from normality as he busies himself in ghoulish investigation.

In a parallel to self-confinement in the lab, Shelley subjects her manic scientist to the debilitating effects of prison. During the police investigation of Henry Clerval's death, Victor remains for three months in an Irish lockup and regains freedom in a state of spiritual torpor. Although reunion with his father triggers feelings of homesickness, the malaise overwhelms Victor's spirit, a reprise of the final scene in Lord Byron's poem "The Prisoner of Chillon" (1816), in which the prisoner no longer feels at home with freedom. Victor's loss of vitality coincides with the monster's invigoration from jealousy and a lust for vengeance as Shelley weakens the monster-maker to balance forces for a final clash.

In the final scenes, Frankenstein's coming-to-knowledge is painful and swift. In grief over his brother William's inexplicable murder, the monster-builder gazes into a copse and glimpses his creature illuminated by a flash of lightning. The MELODRAMA suggests the heavenly retort of an irate deity whom the scientist has mocked by dabbling in black arts. The vision informs Frankenstein of the creature's strength at the same time that horror saps the scientist of the power to stand. Leaning against a tree as his teeth chatter, he totters under a burden of guilt. Symbolically, the story concludes in the frozen north, a vast reflection of Victor's soullessness and violation of nature.

Bibliography

Green, Andrew. "Location and the Journey in 'Frankenstein,'" *English Review* 11, no. 1 (November 2000): 20.

Halberstam, Judith. *Skin Shows: Gothic Horror and the Technology of Monsters*. Durham, N.C.: Duke University Press, 1995.

Shelley, Mary. *Frankenstein*. New York: New American Library, 1963.

Frankenstein's laboratory

Mary Wollstonecraft SHELLEY sets the work sessions of FRANKENSTEIN (1818) in a laboratory in Ingolstadt, Germany, a spot she may have adapted from Burg Frankenstein, a castle built in 1250 near Darmstadt, Germany, and the home of Johann Konrad Dippel, a legendary early 18th-century alchemist and body snatcher. The writing took place before dissection and surgery gained respectability, the absence of which forces Victor Frankenstein to conceal his endeavors. Against advice to stick to pure science, he labors for two years to discover a method of passing the spark of life into a shape assembled from oddments culled from numerous corpses. He describes his solitary work station as "a cell, at the top of the house, and separated from all the other apartments by a gallery and staircase" (Shelley, 53). Applying Gothic forebodings to the story, Shelley emphasizes the severe isolation by which Victor pursues his hellish inquiry and the increasing agitation that drives him to create life.

Concealment takes on major significance in the final stage of Victor's experiments, which feminist critics have defined as a rape of NATURE. Into his workplace, he brings observations of mortuaries and vaults, where he spends days studying decaying tissue, the material that paradoxically advances his knowledge of life. To protect the secret experiments, he indicates that experimental body parts come from dissecting rooms and abattoirs, but he conceals how he animates rotting organs and torsos. Mary Shelley omits the details for a practical reason, her inexperience with laboratory equipment and procedures. Her focus remains on solitude, the separation from friends and family that pushes Victor to near nervous collapse. In this mental miasma, he usurps the role of human procreation and, lacking a female parent, produces his doom-dealing ghoul

In a parallel effort to provide the monster with a mate, Victor once more postpones his wedding, withdraws from loved ones, and traverses the Rhine to view ruined castles before taking up residence in Scotland. A SYMBOL of the pursuit of scientific breakthroughs, the researcher cannot free himself from the monster or halt the fiendish experiments that the monster demands. With a collection of unnamed body parts, Victor separates from his friend Henry Clerval at Edinburgh to set up a new laboratory in the Orkney Islands at a site he describes as a rock battered by waves. In a tumbledown hut with thatch falling in and walls unplastered, he installs needed furnishings and sets to work. Again, lacking details of equipment and method, Mary Shelley describes a task that "became every day more horrible and irksome" (*ibid.*, 156). She later avoids describing the dismembered parts of the second monster, which Victor collects in a basket, weights with stones, and drops into the sea.

Bibliography

Liggins, Emma. "The Medical Gaze and the Female Corpse: Looking at Bodies in Mary Shelley's 'Frankenstein,'" *Studies in the Novel* 32, no. 2 (summer 2000): 129.

Marcus, Steven. "Frankenstein: Myths of Scientific and Medical Knowledge and Stories of Human Relations," *Southern Review* 38, no. 1 (winter 2002): 188–202.

Nickell, Joe. "Germany: Monsters, Myths, and Mysteries," *Skeptical Inquirer* 27, no. 2 (March–April 2003): 24–28.

Seabury, Marcia Bundy. "The Monsters We Create: Woman on the Edge of Time and Frankenstein," *Critique: Studies in Contemporary Fiction* 42, no. 2 (winter 2001): 131–143.

Shelley, Mary. *Frankenstein*. New York: New American Library, 1963.

Frankenstein's monster

The result of arcane, unprincipled research, Frankenstein's monster, the focus of Mary Wollstonecraft SHELLEY's *FRANKENSTEIN* (1818), poses a model of the relentless pursuer and the DOPPELGÄNGER motif. He is capable of good, but mirrors the base, egotistical instincts of his creator, Victor Frankenstein, whom he honors in conversation with the formal "thou." On a rainy November night, the monster comes to life an hour after midnight. At his creation, a perversion of human birth that negates women and normal childbirth, the monster opens a yellow eye, gasps, and convulses with a full-body muscular spasm. The author enlarges on terror by describing yellow flesh that "scarcely covered the work of muscles and arteries beneath; his hair was of a lustrous black, and flowing; his teeth of a pearly whiteness; but these luxuriances only formed a more horrid contrast with his watery eyes, that seemed almost of the same colour as the dun white sockets in which they were set" (Shelley, 56). Victor responds not with glee at his success but with disappointment, disgust, and horror that force him to vacate the lab and pace his quarters. Mary Shelley increases the protagonist's terrors with a SHAPE-SHIFTING dream of his fiancée, whom he appears to embrace only to witness her body dissolve into the worm-eaten corpse of his mother. The author returns to the fearful visage by depicting the monster lifting Victor's bed curtains, opening its jaws, and grinning while uttering unintelligible sounds.

Unnamed and shunned by all, the monster shelters in caves in the northern mountains and, like its maker, lives outside the realm of human habitation. Lonely and frightened on an uninviting landscape, he desires a female companion to relieve his depression. In a bizarre reversal of Christ's parable of the prodigal son, the monster takes the tone of a petulant son chastising a recalcitrant father: "Do your duty towards me, and I will do mine towards you and the rest of mankind. . . . If you refuse, I will glut the maw of death, until it be satiated with the blood of your remaining friends" (*ibid.*, 95). The monster's battle with self-loathing and self-pity exemplifies the quandary of the pariah, an unsalvageable OUTSIDER too GROTESQUE, too freakish to reside in human society.

Mary Shelley's tale returns at the end to the image of perverted procreation. Central to the monster's demands on his maker is the pining for a mate who shares his anomalies of size and shape. Without a companion, the monster's propensity for VIOLENCE increases with each rejection, each shudder at his unwelcome visage. The nature of his repulsive shape and inhumanity has served cinema as a touchstone of screen horror. Each film remake restructures the visual effect to produce a new form of revulsion.

Bibliography

Ozolins, Aija. "Dreams and Doctrines: Dual Strands in Frankenstein," *Science-Fiction Studies* 2 (July 1975): 103–110.

Shelley, Mary. *Frankenstein.* New York: New American Library, 1963.

Thompson, Terry W. "Shelley's 'Frankenstein,'" *Explicator* 58, no. 4 (summer 2000): 191.

Yousef, Nancy. "The Monster in a Dark Room: Frankenstein, Feminism, and Philosophy," *Modern Language Quarterly* 63, no. 2 (June 2002): 197–226.

French Gothic

French Gothic literature earned a place in world fiction for its imagination and flair and for a frank acceptance of human sexuality. Like other European Gothicists, the French drew on a body of medieval folk *romans* (narratives) and created a French version of MONSTERS, as with the werewolf in French *contes de fées* (FAIRY TALEs) of Madame Gabrielle-Suzanne Barbot de Gallon de Villeneuve in *La Jeune Ameriquaine, et les Contes Marins* (The young American and the sea stories, 1740). Short fiction by French authors enlivened the European and North American popular press, as with Baculard D'Arnaud's sensational novels published in *Ladies' Magazine* in the 1780s. The cross-fertilization of Continental and British Gothic influenced the writings of Jane AUSTEN, Mary Elizabeth BRADDON, the BRONTË sisters, Harriet and Sophia LEE, Sheridan LE FANU, Edward BULWER-LYTTON, Toni MORRISON, Iris MURDOCH, Eliza PARSONS, and Edgar Allan POE. Ann RADCLIFFE, Clara REEVE, and Charlotte SMITH gained insight into romantic crime scenarios from *MANON LESCAUT* (1731), an enduring MELODRAMA written by Abbé PRÉVOST and preserved in stage versions and operas. Authors of English crime fiction and GASLIGHT THRILLERS took as models the *roman noir* (black novel) or *littérature noire* (black literature) of the early 1800s—works such as Reveroni Saint-Cyr's *Pauliska, ou La Perversité Moderne* (Pauliska, or modern perversity, 1796) and J. F. Regnault-Warin's *Le Cimetière de la Madeleine* (The Graveyard of the Church of the Madeleine, 1800). Resettings of the WANDERING JEW story replicated the intensity of French novelist Eugène Sue's *Le Juif Errant* (*The Wandering Jew,* 1844).

At the same time, shared techniques and themes carried English Gothicism to France—the VIOLENCE of Matthew Gregory LEWIS's THE MONK (1796), the FEMALE GOTHIC of Radcliffe's THE MYSTERIES OF UDOLPHO (1794) and THE ITALIAN (1797), Charlotte DACRE's erotic novel *The Libertine* (1807), and Wilkie COLLINS's gaslight thriller *The Woman in White* (1860). Inspired by Mary Wollstonecraft SHELLEY's MAD SCIENTIST motif in *FRANKENSTEIN* (1818), Jean Charles Nodier created the first stage vampire in the three-act melodrama *Le Vampire* (1820). Victor Hugo imported German terror into *frénétique* fiction and English MEDIEVALISM into his historical novel *Notre-Dame de Paris* (*The Hunchback of Notre-Dame,* 1831). Honoré de Balzac prefigured the symbolist movement with *Le Peau de Chagrin* (*The Fatal Skin,* 1831), a powerful shocker. Jules JANIN added his own version of German horror to *La Confession* (1830), *Contes Fantastiques* (Fantastic tales, 1832), and *Les Catacombes* (1839), which he dedicated to French sensational novelist the Marquis de Sade. Vladimir ODOEVSKY incorporated French romantic REVENANTS, magic, and MYSTICISM into his fiction. To Europe's growing body of Gothicism, Odoevsky contributed *Variegated Tales* (1833) and his most respected work, *Russkiye Notchi* (*Russian Nights,* 1844), which returned to France in translation. Sir Arthur Conan DOYLE acknowledged his debt to Émile Gaboriau, French inventor of the *roman policier* (police novel). Théophile GAUTIER and the Alsatian duo of Émile ERCKMANN and Louis Alexandre CHATRIAN made similar gestures toward the English vampire motif and the German SUPERNATURAL tales and *Schauerroman* ("shudder stories") that inspired their fantastic stories.

During the age of DECADENCE, the French produced significant deviations from classic Gothicism. Poet Charles BAUDELAIRE incorporated the style and TONE of Poe's writings in the classic verse anthologies *Les Fleurs du Mal* (*The Flowers of Evil,* 1857) and *Le Spleen de Paris* (*Paris Spleen,* 1869), both replete with urban unease. Poe's insights into insanity impacted the writings of VILLIERS DE L'ISLE-ADAM, author of the cult classic *Contes Cruels* (*Cruel Tales,* 1883), an overdeveloped sinister genre packed with HYPERBOLE and SENSATIONALISM. Poe's detective stories influenced the crime novels of Paris journalist Gaston LEROUX, creator of the classic GHOST STORY *Le Fantôme de l'Opéra* (*THE PHANTOM OF THE OPERA*, 1910), a long-lived story popularized on stage and screen. In this same era, French poets Guillaume Apollinaire and André Breton carried Gothicism into the surreal by developing fresh insights and events out of chronological order to mirror human thought patterns, a forerunner of stream-of-consciousness in the novels of Southern Gothicist William FAULKNER.

Bibliography

Browne, Julius Henri. "A Few French Critics," *Harper's* 47 (June–November 1873).

Gamer, Michael. *Romanticism and the Gothic: Genre, Reception, and Canon Formation.* Cambridge: Cambridge University Press, 2000.

Gorrara, Claire. *The Roman Noir in Post-War French Culture.* Oxford: Oxford University Press, 2003.

Horner, Avril, ed. *European Gothic: A Spirited Exchange, 1760–1960.* Manchester: Manchester University Press, 2002.

Freneau, Philip
(1752–1832)

Partisan writer and journalist Philip Morin Freneau, the poet of the American Revolution, captured the beauties of NATURE as well as frontier and prison horrors. From personal observation, he composed *The British Prison-Ship* (1781), a powerful diatribe against the British for inhumane treatment of prisoners of war in the hulk of the *Scorpion,* a makeshift jail anchored in New York Harbor. Like inmates of a Gothic DUNGEON, despairing men in this jail die in large numbers in claustrophobic compartments from hunger, damp, disease, and poor sanitation.

Unlike novelists Robert Montgomery BIRD and Charles Brockden BROWN, Freneau detested racism and avoided colonial demonizing of Native Americans in his poems "The Dying Indian" (1784) and "Lines Occasioned by a Visit to an Old Indian Burying Ground" (1788). The former depicts Tomo-Chequi's dread of the long journey of death, where he travels a cheerless path without companion or guide. The latter poem contrasts Freneau's dark philosophy of death with that of

American Indian philosophies, which anticipate feasting and hunting in the afterlife. At poem's end, he returns to the popular view of Indians as vengeful and sexually depraved.

Freneau is best known for his composition of two romantic graveyard poems: "Pestilence" (1793), a response to Philadelphia's yellow fever epidemic, and "*THE HOUSE OF NIGHT*" (1799), an extended personification of Death as the driver of a black chariot attended by specters. He also composed a Gothic abolitionist poem, "To Sir Toby" (1792), which depicts snakes and scorpions, hellish lashings, slow starvation, and the dark slave pens on a Jamaican sugar plantation, in which many slave laborers died. His lyric works earned him the regard of Sir Walter SCOTT, who committed Freneau's verses to memory.

Bibliography

Bergland, Renee L. *The National Uncanny: Indian Ghosts and American Subjects.* Hanover, N.H.: Dartmouth College, 2000.

Goddu, Teresa A. *Gothic America: Narrative, History, and Nation.* New York: Columbia University Press, 1997.

Freudian themes

The writings of the Viennese neurologist Sigmund Freud provided later literary historians and critics with numerous insights into the motifs and psychological SUBTEXTs of Gothic fiction. From his commentary on primitivism, anxiety, and vulnerability in *The Interpretation of Dreams* (1899) come explanations for the literary use of DREAMS AND NIGHTMARES as psychological insight into characters, a strategy used by Clara REEVE, Mary Wollstonecraft SHELLEY, and Marion Zimmer Bradley. Freud described the symbolic displacement of sexual fears in nightmares, which Gothic writers translate into STALKINGs and hauntings by demon lovers, and into pursuit by werewolves, vampires, the DYBBUK, golem, and other MONSTERS, as in the erotic dreamworld of Charles Nodier's *Smarra; or, The Demons of the Night* (1821), the fruit sellers in Christina ROSSETTI's *THE GOBLIN MARKET* (1862), and the night prowler in John GARDNER's *Grendel* (1971). An understanding of human fears offers a logical explanation for the extravagant imaginings in Horace WALPOLE's THE CASTLE OF OTRANTO (1765), which pits the sexually virile father Manfred against his weak and incompetent son Conrad. The same male assault on an unworthy challenger informs William BECKFORD's *Vathek* (1782), the tale of an unsuitable caliph who inherits the throne of his grandfather, and Emily BRONTË's *WUTHERING HEIGHTS* (1847), in which HEATHCLIFF manipulates his impotent son as an agent to secure the father's outsized desires.

While mapping the workings of the conscious and subconscious regions of the mind, Freud found in the uncanny a release of the unspeakable, the thought or deed that should remain hidden. Such dark themes of VIOLENCE, sorcery, and DIABOLISM pervade the slave rebellion in Herman MELVILLE's *BENITO CERENO* (1855), Joseph CONRAD's hellish voyage in *HEART OF DARKNESS* (1902), and the ghastly stories of H. P. LOVECRAFT and Joyce Carol OATES. Freud's summation of repressed energies explains the release of the primitive id in Robert Louis STEVENSON's *DR. JEKYLL AND MR. HYDE* (1886), in which the apelike Hyde can club to death an elderly member of Parliament with no remorse. Another manifestation of repression is the demon child, a recurrent figure in modern Gothic—particularly, Henry JAMES's ambiguous brother and sister pair, Miles and Flora, in *THE TURN OF THE SCREW* (1898) and the vengeful boy in SAKI's "SREDNI VASHTAR" (1911), the macabre story of imaginary powers that the repressed child unleashes against a powerful adult.

In much of classic Gothic fiction, sexual assault creates an undercurrent of dread, an unnamed emotion that Freud explained through the workings of the subconscious mind. Female victims fear imprisonment, molestation, and death at the hands of male VILLAINs, such as Ann RADCLIFFE's female dominators Montoni and SCHEDONI. Exploiting eroticism and fears of the unspeakable were also devices of such classic male Gothicists as Matthew Gregory LEWIS and Edgar Allan POE, and of Bram STOKER, who turns the demon lover into a serial killer in *DRACULA* (1897). In similar fashion, threats of perverse or homosexual menace and violation pervade the Gothicism of Lord BYRON, Samuel Taylor COLERIDGE, Sheridan LE FANU, and Oscar WILDE.

Bibliography

Karl, Frederick R. *The Adversary Literature: The English Novel in the Eighteenth Century—A Study in Genre.* New York: Farrar, Straus & Giroux, 1974.

Mighall, Robert. *A Geography of Victorian Gothic Fiction: Mapping History's Nightmares.* Oxford: Oxford University Press, 1999.

O'Neill, John. "Freud and the Passions," *Canadian Journal of Sociology* 24, no. 1 (December–February 1998): 158–162.

Paglia, Camille. *Sexual Personae.* New York: Vintage Books, 1990.

Smith, Andrew. *Gothic Radicalism: Literature, Philosophy and Psychoanalysis in the Nineteenth Century.* New York: St. Martin's Press, 2000.

frontier gothic

Lacking the architectural ruins and medieval backdrop of European Gothic, American Gothic derived its own conventions of terror from the motifs of law and order and survival of the fittest, both of which dominate such enduring works as Walter Van Tilburg Clark's *The Ox-Bow Incident* (1940), Jack Warner Schaefer's *Shane* (1949), Larry McMurtry's *Lonesome Dove* (1990), and Laura Esquivel's Mexican tale of a family curse, invading army, and accusing witch in *Like Water for Chocolate* (1989), which is set on the Tex-Mex border during the Mexican Revolution of 1910. From the wilderness came the elements of frontier Gothic, particularly the wonder of explorers at geological formations and stampeding bison, reprisals of displaced Native Americans against immigrants, the walk-down on a town street that pitted brigand against sheriff, and the pioneer experience of living isolated on the untamed land amid claim jumpers, rustlers, Comancheros, Mexican revolutionaries, and such outlaws as the James and Younger gangs and Quantrill's Raiders. Readers eager for information on the wilderness devoured nonfiction accounts of whites captured by Indians and thrilled to sexual innuendo in the stories based on real-life rescued females such as Mary White Rowlandson and Mary Ann and Olive Ann Oatman. More terrifying are Ole Edvart Rölvaag's picture of the soul sickness and lethal rage of Beret Hansa on the desolate prairie in *Giants in the Earth* (1927) and the threat of genocide for the Sioux in Mari Sandoz's *Crazy Horse* (1942).

The fount of frontier fiction, James Fenimore Cooper, began supplying romance to New World readers with the nation's first historical fiction, *The Spy* (1821), a suspenseful Revolutionary War thriller. In 1840 he initiated the Leatherstocking Tales, a frontier series of five novels beginning with *The Pathfinder* (1840) and continuing the next year with *The Deerslayer* (1841). He set the action during the French and Indian wars and, for a hero, featured an outback loner, Natty "Hawkeye" Bumppo, whose yearnings and ambitions typify the conflicted Easterner acquiring rapport with the North American forest.

Cooper's most popular book is *The Last of the Mohicans* (1826), a hard-hitting adventure tale of unrequited love and vengeance that concludes with the VILLAIN Magua spinning into the air as his body hurtles over a cliff. Cooper pairs Natty, a chivalric hero, with Chingachgook, whose shaved head and scalp lock adorned with an eagle feather provided armchair readers with the romance of the Mohicans. The clash of European and forest customs, along with New World terms such as "Dutchers," "fire-water," and "Yengeese," the Indian pronunciation of "English," energized the text.

Added zest derives from Cooper's handling of graphic VIOLENCE. The slaughter of a deer and colt, the scalping of an Oneida and a French sentinel, and Uncas's running of the Huron gauntlet express the perils of living in the wild among hostile factions. At a high point of fighting in *The Last of the Mohicans*, the author comments, "The shrieks of the wounded and the yells of their murderers grew less frequent, until, finally, the cries of horror were lost to their ear, or were drowned in the loud, long, and piercing whoops of the triumphant savages" (Cooper, 185). In the resolution, Uncas's funeral supplies a MELANCHOLY touch and an opportunity for Cooper to extol the red man's virtues.

Frontier Gothic influenced other venues, including the English poet Felicia Hemans's graphic narrative "Indian Woman's Death-Song" (1828), a lament for a suicidal mother and her babe, and Peter Carey's Australian Gothic in OSCAR AND LUCINDA (1988), in which the murder of aborigines parallels the genocide of the American Indian. Key additions to the American frontier canon include Joaquin Miller's dialect play *Danites of the Sierras* (1876), a MELODRAMA that features a haunted house and a murderous Mormon cult; the impressionistic psychological study of a farmer-turned-warrior in Mariano Azuela's *Los de Abajo* (*The Underdogs*, 1914), fraught with violence and exploitation of ignorant Mexican peasants; and Paul Green's grudge matches among mountain outlaws in the dialect play *The Last of the Lowries* (1920). Characterizing the appeal of frontier Gothic is the historical fiction of Edna Ferber's *Cimarron* (1929), which celebrates a "brand-new, two-fisted, rip-snorting country, full of Injuns and rattlesnakes and two-gun toters and gyp water and desper-*ah*-does!" (Ferber, 322). In *The Ox-Bow Incident*, Clark exploited the familiar scenario of the lynch mob with a psychological study of vigilantism and scapegoating. This atmospheric quest novel concludes with remorse over the hasty Western-style execution of three innocent men and an anticlimactic suicide Roman fashion by falling on a sword, a SYMBOL of the faulty logic of the European mindset.

Bibliography

Cooper, James Fenimore. *The Last of the Mohicans*. New York: Bantam Books, 1989.

Vause, Mikel. "Frontier Gothic: Terror and Wonder at the Frontier in American Literature," *Weber Studies* 11, no. 2 (fall 1994): 141–142.

G

García Márquez, Gabriel
(1928–   )

The Colombian novelist Gabriel García Márquez rose to worldwide fame for his folkloric fiction. He learned COLONIAL GOTHIC traditions from the STORYTELLING of his maternal grandmother, who specialized in horror tales. Invigorated by the fiction of North American authors William FAULKNER and Ernest Hemingway, García Márquez writes short fiction and novels filled with myth, absurdity, and innovative Gothic motifs and settings—notably, *Leaf Storm* (1955), a dreamlike novella; *Big Mama's Funeral* (1962), a comic GROTESQUE narrative; *Chronicle of a Death Foretold* (1982); and *Love in the Time of Cholera* (1988). His short pieces, collected in *Innocent Eréndira and Other Stories* (1972), focus on bizarre evil, violent death, SOMNAMBULISM, and reincarnation. In 1982, he won a Nobel Prize.

García Márquez is famous for ALLEGORY marked by satire, HYPERBOLE, morbid humor, fable, fantasy, and magical realism. His blockbuster saga *Cien Años de Soledad* (*One Hundred Years of Solitude*, 1967) is a repository of timeless narrative picturing the patriarch José Arcadio Buendía in flight from capture for spearing a man to death. With his wife, Ursula, he sets his course for the unknown, the other side of a mountain chain to a swamp where Sir Francis Drake once shot crocodiles with cannon balls. The swamp is home to "soft-skinned cetaceans that had the head and torso of a woman, causing the ruination of sailors with the charm of their extraordinary breasts" (García Márquez, 19).

In a style reminiscent of Rabelais's *Pantagruel* (1562), the author pursues the bizarre with ghosts of the Spanish conquest, random deaths, a gypsy prophecy, and a family curse that results in the birth of a relative bearing a vestigial pig's tail. At a dramatic moment in the Buendía saga, the author pictures the death of an Italian musician and tinkerer named Pietro Crespi, who coordinates music boxes and clock chimes to mark his suicide with a discordant symphony. García Márquez's novel influenced the Gothicism of Isabel ALLENDE, author of the saga THE HOUSE OF THE SPIRITS (1981).

Bibliography

García Márquez, Gabriel. *One Hundred Years of Solitude.* New York: Avon Books, 1970.

Solomon, Irving D. "Latin American Women in Literature and Reality: García Márquez's 'One Hundred Years of Solitude,'" *Midwest Quarterly* 34, no. 2 (winter 1993): 192–205.

Spiller, Elizabeth A. "'Searching for the Route of Inventions': Retracing the Renaissance Discovery Narrative in Gabriel García Márquez," *CLIO* 28, no. 4 (summer 1999): 375.

Gardner, John
(1933–1982)

An American scholar, critic, and author of moral novels, John Champlin Gardner applied GOTHIC CONVENTION to his psychological study of conflicted characters. While teaching English at several colleges in the United States, he produced seven novels and numerous short pieces, including "The Ravages of Spring" (1974), which updates Edgar Allan POE's "THE FALL OF THE HOUSE OF USHER" (1839). Gardner's third novel, *Grendel* (1971), is a dark fable that revisits the Anglo-Saxon epic *Beowulf* (ca. A.D. 600) from the MONSTER's perspective. The text is a tour de force of language tricks and literary echoes that examine the mindset of a stalker obsessed with an apocalyptic vision of human oppressors.

Gardner penetrates the murky consciousness of the beast to create a Gothic scenario prickly with perils, yet illuminated by epiphanies. The ALLEGORY of good and evil pictures Grendel as a sensitive, contemplative beast who snoops on nightly gatherings of thanes and comments on human folly. On his first view of humankind, he recognizes the difference between bulls and men and characterizes local people, the Geats, as "thinking creatures, pattern makers, the most dangerous things I'd ever met" (Gardner, 21). Over a 12-year period, the allure of human society draws the monster repeatedly to the mead hall of Hrothgar. At length, Grendel advances from Peeping Tom to informed philosopher.

Gardner creates a Gothic milieu in which the monster develops humanity in tandem with his killer's evolving guile. The author depicts Grendel as an OUTSIDER and a MELANCHOLY loner, "as solitary as one live tree in a vast landscape of coal" (*ibid.*, 65). His humanistic mentor, the in-house moralist known as the Shaper, uplifts the terrified Geats with STORYTELLING that the eavesdropper absorbs like nourishment. In reference to Geat savagery, Grendel muses, "If the Shaper's vision of goodness and peace was a part of himself, not idle rhymes, then no one understood him at all" (*ibid.*, 45).

Gardner builds SUSPENSE as the lengthy cat-and-mouse game pits Grendel against the unnamed human champion. On a night when "darkness lay over the world like a coffin lid," Grendel realizes too late that he has met his match (*ibid.*, 139). In a terrifying clash in the dark, the challenger rips off the monster's arm: "I scream, facing him, grotesquely shaking hands—dear long-lost brother. . . . I feel the bones go, ground from their sockets, and I scream again" (*ibid.*, 148). As stalker becomes victim, he retreats into the bestial environment to die among beasts.

Bibliography

Fenlon, Katherine Feeney. "John Gardner's 'The Ravages of Spring' as Re-creation of 'The Fall of the House of Usher,'" *Studies in Short Fiction* 31, no. 3 (summer 1994): 481–486.

Gardner, John. *Grendel*. New York: Ballantine Books, 1971.

Parks, Ward. "Prey Tell: How Heroes Perceive Monsters in Beowulf," *Journal of English and Germanic Philology* 92, no. 1 (January 1993): 1–16.

gaslight thriller

An urban phenomenon preceded by stage MELODRAMA and the NEWGATE NOVEL, the Victorian gaslight thriller generated city-bred terrors and graphic VIOLENCE. By flickering street lamps, crime flourished along foggy thoroughfares, misty wharves, and dim alleyways, where hansom cabs rattled away in the dark and boat whistles sounded along the waterways. The emergence of citified dread reminded smug Victorians that industrial progress and global imperialism did not free them from vestiges of paganism lurking at their own doorsteps. The genre, a creation of Wilkie COLLINS, thrived on CHIAROSCURO, MYSTERY, STALKING, psychological twists, xenophobia, and SUSPENSE. Manipulators of these elements, including Mary Elizabeth BRADDON, Sir Arthur Conan DOYLE, George du Maurier, J. Sheridan LE FANU, Edgar Allan POE, and George William Macarthur REYNOLDS, applied melodrama to horrific crime plots and placed their investigators in murky locales where witnesses were suspect and seedy, clues scanty, and crime scenes difficult to reconstruct.

The typical gaslight novel avoided MEDIEVALISM, MONSTERS, and phantasms and showcased realistic terrors, as is the case with Robert Louis STEVENSON's re-creation of a lurid cemetery invasion in "The Body Snatcher" (1881). Contributing to the outré genre were imported poisons, weapons, and vendettas stemming from British colonialism. Authors featured the jaded aristocrat, tawdry streetwalker, shopgirl, Asian immigrant, and lame beggar as standard characters and played up class differences in major cities where the value of a life depended in part on color of skin, quality in the bloodlines, and money in the bank. In Poe's

C. Auguste DUPIN adventures and Doyle's Sherlock HOLMES detective stories, the invincible inspectors maneuver side streets and residential scandals and crimes to unmask the criminal and restore justice.

Bolstering reader interest in the late gaslight mystery were media features on the hunt for Jack the Ripper. The unidentified serial killer terrorized London's East End for 13 weeks in 1888 and left brutally flayed victims. The details of male-on-female cruelties recurred in stories, novels, stage music, and dramas offering plausible identifications and motives for the Ripper's crimes against women. Books treating the Ripper theme included the anonymously written Canadian *Chronicles of Crime and Criminals* (ca. 1890), Felix Burns's *The Albert Victor Waltz* (1890), Detective Warren's *The Whitechapel Murders; or, On the Track of the Fiend* (1898), and crime fiction writer Marie Adelaide Belloc Lowndes's *Studies in Love and Terror* (1913) and *The Lodger* (1913), the latter a fearful tale about a suspect OUTSIDER that sold more than 1 million copies and, in 1926, served as impetus for an Alfred Hitchcock film. In Gaston LEROUX's THE PHANTOM OF THE OPERA (1910), a knowledge of art increases the reader's sympathy with Erik, the stalker who manipulates a stage diva to his own perverted ends.

In 2002, novelist Michel Faber rejuvenated the gaslight mode with a neo-Victorian social novel, THE CRIMSON PETAL AND THE WHITE. He cloaks London's brothel district with a familiar haze: "Apart from the pale gas-light of the streetlamps at the far corners, you can't see any light in Church Lane, but that's because your eyes are accustomed to stronger signs of human wakefulness than the feeble glow of two candles behind a smutty windowpane" (Faber, 5). In his introduction to the tale of a prostitute's life, he shepherds the modern visitor to Mrs. Castaway's whorehouse through soggy, foul-smelling carpet, pox odors, and musty linens and looks beyond the seamy neighborhood to opium sellers and the gibbet, the final recompense for criminals.

Bibliography

"East End Horror: Two More Women Murdered," *Woodford Times*, October 5, 1888.

Faber, Michel. *The Crimson Petal and the White*. New York: Harcourt, 2002.

Mighall, Robert. *A Geography of Victorian Gothic Fiction: Mapping History's Nightmares*. Oxford: Oxford University Press, 1999.

Morley, Sheridan. "Dusting Off the Gaslight Thriller," *International Herald Tribune*, August 20, 1997.

Pearl, Nancy. "Gaslight Thrillers: The Original Victorians," *Library Journal* 126, no. 3 (February 15, 2001): 228.

Gateshead Hall

The initial setting in Charlotte BRONTË's JANE EYRE (1847), Gateshead Hall is the site of a short period of confinement that depicts the harsh cruelties faced by an orphaned NAIF. Lacking family, wealth, and social status, the title character must learn to fend for herself at Sarah Reed's forbidding home. The author sets the manse against a backdrop of cold winter wind and leafless shrubbery. Sarah torments her niece, 10-year-old Jane EYRE, by blaming her for family discontent and squabbles with her three cousins, particularly John Reed, a 14-year-old snitch and VILLAIN in the making. The tongue-lashing is instructive in that it suggests to Jane that she, too, may empower herself against her harpy aunt through hostile words.

Interestingly, Brontë characterizes the sadistic domination of the young heroine as the work of other females. The author omits the architectural grotesqueries common to Gothic fiction and heightens Jane's terror of the manor by describing her late-night imaginings after Reed's servants lock Jane in the chill, silent redroom. Miss Abbot, a pursy, self-ingratiating toady, distorts deity into demon by suggesting that God may punish Jane by striking her down for throwing tantrums. The verbal threat of eternal damnation is a standard Gothic misapplication of Christian dogma favored by cruel fanatics and religious poseurs.

The hostile environment grows more frightening after Jane experiences a SUPERNATURAL visitation from her uncle, John Reed, who died nine years before in the redroom, where his corpse lay in state. Brontë enhances dreariness with a marble chimneypiece, dark wood, muffled windows, and a mirror that displays to Jane the face of terror. The author intensifies the psychological landscape by describing Jane as overwrought by SUPERSTITION, with a mind churning like sludge at the bottom of a murky well. The text indicates that misgivings and apparitions are common to people suffering mental unrest, particularly during a predawn rainstorm, which increases Jane's misery. Feverish and agitated, she imagines the rustle of wings, an aural clue to an otherworldly presence. Brontë extends the effect by distancing a potential source of comfort when Mr. Lloyd comes to render a medical opinion. He calls Jane a baby for believing in ghosts.

In chapter four, the setting alters from Gothic haunting to MELODRAMA over Christmas, when the house returns to normal. Shut out of yuletide fun, Jane experiences rejection from the family and must accept comfort from Bessie Lee, the nursemaid. Inadvertently, Bessie has fed Jane's overactive imagination during evenings when Bessie ironed lace frills and borders at the nursery hearth while narrating scary FAIRY TALEs, ballads, and passages from Samuel Richardson's *Pamela* (1740) and Henry Brooke's five-volume *The Fool of Quality; or, the History of Henry Earl of Moreland* (1782). Increasing Jane's despair is an interview with a child-tormenting educator-villain, the sable-clad Mr. Brocklehurst, a ministerial hypocrite who implies that Jane is wicked of heart and doomed to hell. To prolong her discomfort, he leaves a book of meditation containing "an account of the awfully sudden death of Martha G——," a Gothic touch that borders on the comic (Brontë, 28).

Brontë puts steel in Jane's spine in her last days at Gateshead Hall. For the first time, the unwanted foster child learns to fight back by transferring charges of deceitful behavior from herself to the real deceiver, Sarah Reed. No longer in the grip of the unwelcoming estate and its daily pummelings, Jane exults that she has won a first victory over adult intimidation. It is significant that she withdraws from the manor at the depth of winter, after rising at 4:30 in the predawn darkness to dress and complete her packing. She remarks that she is "whirled away to unknown . . . remote and mysterious regions," but she harbors less fear of the future than she did of Sarah Reed and the redroom (ibid., 35).

Brontë establishes the value of experience as an antidote to terror. After Jane Eyre's departure from Gateshead Hall, she matures, completes her education, and gains employment as a governess at

THORNFIELD. A summons back to Sarah Reed's domain after nine years' absence finds Jane prepared for the chill discourtesy of the family and their estate. Luckily for Jane, the villainous John Reed had previously died violently at age 21, perhaps by suicide. Jane's first view of the lodge on May 1 is filled with tokens of cheer: "The ornamental windows were hung with little white curtains; the floor was spotless; the grate and fire-irons were burnished bright, and the fire burnt clear" (ibid., 214). To Bessie, Jane admits that self-confidence and a "less withering dread of oppression" enable her to function well at a professional post (ibid., 215).

Brontë pits Jane once more against death, which hangs over the manor and Sarah Reed, who is dying from the effects of a stroke. Jane's resilience against sneering cousins works wonders during a one-month visit with the family. No longer beset by mental hobgoblins or fears of ghosts, she is unafraid to clasp the hand of the dying aunt, who inhabits her darkened room like an evil spider, and to confront her once more for deceit and cruelty. Brontë turns the cowed aunt into a scolding but eviscerated harpy who wishes aloud that Jane had died. For 10 days, Jane survives the visit by sketching portraits of her cousins and sheds no tear at her aunt's demise.

Bibliography

Brontë, Charlotte. *Jane Eyre*. New York: Bantam Books, 1981.

Fleenor, Juliann E., ed. *The Female Gothic*. Montreal: Eden Press, 1983.

Hoeveler, Diane Long. *Gothic Feminism*. University Park: Pennsylvania State University Press, 1998.

Gautier, Théophile
(1811–1872)

A respected poet, dramatist, journalist, and critic, Théophile Gautier gave up painting to contribute to French ROMANTICISM. He was a vigorous traveler and travel writer who frequented gatherings of European romantic poets and read the German *Schauerroman* ("shudder stories") of Johann von GOETHE and E. T. A. HOFFMANN, the decadent verse of Charles BAUDELAIRE, and Victor Hugo's *frénétique* fiction. At age 20, Gautier developed his own style for tales of DIABOLISM and the GROTESQUE, notably, the phantasmagoric "La Cafétière" (The coffee machine, 1831), his first publication, which presaged his success at skillful imagery. An experimenter with form and theme, he turned to the macabre with the long narrative *Albertus* (1833), EXOTICISM in "Omphale" (1834), sensuality and lesbianism in *Mademoiselle de Maupin* (1835), fantasy in *Fortunio* (1837), graveyard verse in *La Comédie de la Mort* (The comedy of death, 1838), satanic fiction with "Une Larme du Diable" (The devil's tear, 1839), and freakishness in *Les Grotesques* (1844). Simultaneously, he supported himself by editing and writing art and drama criticism for *Le Moniteur Universel*, *La Presse*, and *Revue de Paris*.

A proponent of *l'art pour l'art* ("art for art's sake"), Gautier developed the formulaic vampire story in *La Morte Amoreuse* (The dead lover, 1836), which Lafcadio HEARN translated into English as the erotic ghost story "Clarimonde: A Supernatural Passion" (1888). The dreamy, wistful tale describes a SHAPE-SHIFTING priest who is obsessed by a FEMME FATALE. Gautier developed the siren's amorality in "One of Cleopatra's Nights" (1845). Late in his career, he mused on METEMPSYCHOSIS, the evil eye, and dichotomies of love and death with "Arria Marcella" (1852), *Avatar* (1856), *Jettature* (1857), "The Mummy's Foot" (1863), and *Spirite* (1866), the story of a pining lover's breach of the afterlife to find the perfect woman. Gautier's interest in horror, fantasy, allure, and desire influenced Gustave Flaubert and inspired translator Hearn, a specialist in Chinese, French, and JAPANESE GOTHIC.

Bibliography

Lovecraft, H. P. *The Annotated Supernatural Horror in Literature*. New York: Hippocampus, 2000.

Rivers, Christopher. "Inintelligibles pour Une Femme Honnete: Sexuality, Textuality and Knowledge in Diderot's 'La Religieuse' and Gautier's 'Mademoiselle de Maupin,'" *Romantic Review* 86, no. 1 (January 1995): 1–29.

gay Gothic

Homosexual characterizations and motifs permeate much of Gothic literature and its SUBTEXTs, particularly Sophia LEE's historical romance *The Recess; or, A Tale of Other Times* (1783–85), Matthew Gregory LEWIS's THE MONK (1796), Samuel Taylor COLERIDGE's mesmerizing she-demon in CHRISTABEL (1816), Sheridan LE FANU's lesbian VAMPIRISM in *Carmilla* (1872), Karl Heinrich Ulrichs's German gay vampire in *Matrosengeschichten* (Sailor stories, 1884), and Oscar WILDE's THE PICTURE OF DORIAN GRAY (1891). However, straightforward gay Gothic literature is a 20th-century phenomenon—for example, the silky-smooth evil of the lesbian FEMME FATALE in Djuna BARNES's *Nightwood* (1930). Unlike eras that reduced homoeroticism to meager hints, current gay Gothic is a subset of NEO-GOTHIC writings that focus on a frank eroticism shared by people of the same sex, a quality found in Quebec-based writer Marie-Claire Blais, author of *Une Saison dans la Vie d'Emmanuel* (*A Season in the Life of Emmanuel*, 1965) and *Soifs* (Thirsts, 1995). In previous decades, gay writers such as Estonian-Swedish Gothicist Count Stanislaus Eric Stenbock, author of *The True Story of the Vampire* (1894) and *Studies of Death* (1894), and Marie CORELLI, England's best-selling writer of OCCULT FICTION, chose to remain closeted. Corelli lived out of the mainstream with her mate and biographer Bertha Vyver at Mason Croft, Stratford, but ventured onto the Avon River in a unique gondola. Corelli's exotic fiction referred to sexuality with ambiguous phrasing, a method she introduced in her first novel, *The Romance of Two Worlds* (1886). More seriously closeted was Bram STOKER, author of DRACULA (1897), a lustful depiction of the charismatic Transylvania male shut for eternity in a crypt, and *The Lair of the White Worm* (1911), a woman-fearing horror story.

Echoing the stereotypical predator and quailing female, the winsome, delicate librarian Robert Whyte and secretive sophisticate Donough Gaylord in Vincent Virga's *Gaywyck* (2000) present a homoerotic version of standard themes: INSANITY, rejection, monstrous intimacies, and deflowering of a virgin. Lauded as a groundbreaking gay Gothic romance, this symbol-laden MELODRAMA earned comparison to Charlotte BRONTË's JANE EYRE (1847) and Daphne DU MAURIER's REBECCA (1938) for its themes of narcissism and concealed crimes and for employment of the DOPPELGÄNGER motif and a remote setting with secret passage-

ways. More adept at MELANCHOLY and the SUPER-
NATURAL are Gregory L. Norris's story anthology
Ghost Kisses (1994) and Byrd Roberts's *The Duskouri Tales* (2000). A revered gay horror novel,
Looking Glass Lives (1998), by Felice Picano, explores duality and the tragic results of concealed
sin, durable themes that empowered AMERICAN
GOTHIC, particularly Nathaniel HAWTHORNE's
story "YOUNG GOODMAN BROWN" (1835) and
novel *THE SCARLET LETTER* (1850).

Bibliography

Isaac, Megan Lynn. "Sophia Lee and the Gothic of Fe-
    male Community," *Studies in the Novel* 28, no. 2
    (summer 1996): 200–217.
Sedgwick, Eve Kosofsky. *Between Men: English Literature
    and Male Homosocial Desire.* New York: Columbia
    University Press, 1985.
———. *Epistemology of the Closet.* Los Angeles: Univer-
    sity of California Press, 1992.
Zabus, Chantal. "Soifs," *World Literature Today* 71, no. 4
    (autumn 1997): 745–746.

German Gothic

German FOLKLORE, *Volksbücher* ("people's books"),
and the *gotischer Roman* (German "Gothic novel")
made a major impact on English and French Gothic
and fueled a demand for German works in translation. Elements of English Gothic owe some of their
creativity to German originals, which display the
national traditions of Teutonic tribalism, medieval
knight tales, feudal robber stories, FAIRY TALEs, and
mysteries. Dramatist and poet Andreas Gryphius's
Kirch-hof Gedanchen (Graveyard thoughts, ca. 1650)
contributed to the preromantic trend in funereal
verse. In the mid-1700s, the German *Kriminalgeschichte* ("criminal history"), a series of true
crime stories, prefaced the development of the DE-
TECTIVE STORY, GASLIGHT THRILLER, and NEWGATE
NOVEL. Playwright Friedrich Gottlieb Klopstock
produced the grand satanic VILLAIN Adramelech for
his verse epic *Messiah* (1773), which influenced
Friedrich von SCHILLER, one of the insightful European Gothicists of the late 18th century. Balladeer
Gottfried August Bürger developed the demon lover
motif in the compelling chivalric ballad *Lenore*
(1774), an archetypal romance that influenced

Percy Bysshe SHELLEY and 19th-century Russian
Gothic works by Alexander Pushkin, Mikhail Lermontov, and Vasily Zhukovsky.

German strands were present in English
Gothic at the birth of the GOTHIC NOVEL and during the surge in Gothic drama. Horace WALPOLE
hinted at the strength of the Teutonic literary strain
with the Germanic names Conrad, Jerome, and
Theodore in the prototypical *THE CASTLE OF
OTRANTO* (1765). Johann von GOETHE's *Götz von
Berlichingen* (*Goetz with the Iron Hand,* 1773) exhibits the medievalism that powered later Gothic
fiction. The treatment of NECROMANCY in a translation of Lawrence Flammenberg's *Der Geisterbanner* (The ghost banner, 1792) provided Peter
Teuthold with a German setting and the secretive
magician Volkert, the title character in *The Necromancer; or, The Tale of the Black Forest* (1794). The
story, one of the popular fictions issued by MINERVA
PRESS, is one that Catherine MORLAND reads in
Jane AUSTEN's *Northanger Abbey* (1818). Offering
critical direction for developing Gothicism was
Schiller's essay "Über Naive und Sentimentalische
Dichtung" (On naive and sentimental poetry, 1795).

German tendencies and motifs made a significant impression on European drama. Heinrich
Wilhelm von Geistenberg's violent tragedy *Ugolino*
(1768) and Heinrich Leopold Wagner's *The Child
Murderess* (1776) developed Gothic stage conventions that became the vogue in England and
France and nourished the *Schicksalstragödie* ("fate
tragedy") of the mid-19th century. Exploiting their
vivid plots for audience appeal was Matthew Gregory LEWIS, a passionate reader of German literature, particularly the folktales of Johann Karl
August Musäus and collaborators Johann Mathias
Müller and Benedikte Naubert. Lewis translated
the works of Schiller and August Friedrich von
Kotzebue for the English stage and developed
Heinrich Zschokke's *Aballino, der Grosse Bandit*
(Aballino, the great bandit, 1793) into *The Bravo
of Venice* (1805). A conservative minority castigated Lewis for his own shocking novel *THE MONK*
(1796) and for his translations of sinister German
fiction, which critics denounced as morally offensive and dangerous to public morals.

The flowering of European Gothic derived
from the best in German literature, which English-

speaking readers enjoyed in translation in BLACK-WOOD'S EDINBURGH MAGAZINE. The first major GHOST STORY to impact English writers was Schiller's *Der Geisterseher* (*The Ghost-Seer*, 1786), from which Samuel Taylor COLERIDGE borrowed elements for THE RIME OF THE ANCIENT MARINER (1798) and "CHRISTABEL" (1816). From Jean Paul Richter's *Siebenkäs* (1796) came the term DOPPEL-GÄNGER for a split persona, a concept investing Prussian horror specialist E. T. A. HOFFMANN's horror thriller *Die Elixiere des Teufels* (*The Devil's Elixir*, 1815–16) and his short story "Die Doppel-gänger" (The double-goer, 1821). From German spectral tales and bandit lore such as Christian August Vulpius's *Rinaldo Rinaldini* (1798), Minerva Press novelist Eleanor Sleath derived the kernel story of *The Orphan of the Rhine: A Romance* (1798), Sir Walter SCOTT took elements of the SUPERNATU-RAL for his play *House of Aspen* (1799), Mary Woll-stonecraft SHELLEY acquired the setting and tone of FRANKENSTEIN; or, The Modern Prometheus (1818), John POLIDORI developed "The Vampyre" (1819), and Charles Robert MATURIN evolved the demonic stalker for MELMOTH THE WANDERER (1820). The GRIMM brothers' publication of *Kinder- und Haus-märchen* (Children's and household tales), later known as *Grimm's Fairy Tales* (1812, 1815, 1822), became a major force in children's literature and a source for Gaston LEROUX's complex opera tale *Le Fantôme de l'Opéra* (THE PHANTOM OF THE OPERA, 1910), a perennial favorite on stage and film.

German-style terrors from the *Schauerroman* ("shudder tales"), fantasies by Johann Ludwig TIECK, Joseph Alois Gleich's 300 ghost tales, and the writings of Goethe and Schiller influenced a wide span of western European works, particularly Edward BULWER-LYTTON's novels, Jules-Gabriel JANIN's *frénétique* Gothicism in "Le Dernier Jour d'un Condamné" (The Last Day of a Con-demned Man, 1829), George William Macarthur REYNOLDS's popular serial and GOTHIC BLUEBOOK "Wagner the Wehr-Wolf" (1847), Alsatian duo Émile ERCKMANN and Louis Alexandre CHATRIAN's *Contes Fantastiques* (Fantastic stories, 1847), and Count VILLIERS DE L'ISLE-ADAM's *contes cruels* (cruel tales). In the waning of classic Gothic fiction, the SADISM, killer instincts, and VAMPIRISM of Hanns Heinz EWERS pushed European Gothicism to un-

pleasant extremes with the perverse vampire novel *Alraune* (The mandrakes, 1911), *Vampir* (1921), and his own version of Schiller's psychological novel DER GEISTERSEHER (*The Ghost-Seer*, 1786), which Ewers published in 1922. In the 20th century, Ger-manic imagery remained strong in Danish Gothicist Isak DINESEN's collection *Seven Gothic Tales* (1934). In the 1940s, critics saw in the German vampire a Teutonic superman obsessed with a mounting blood-madness that sought the destruction of Old Europe to make way for Hitler's New Order.

AMERICAN GOTHIC also owes a debt to Ger-many for TONE and ATMOSPHERE as well as sub-ject matter. Edgar Allan POE devoured German and French horror literature and adopted Euro-pean settings for his most famous stories. Cajetan Tschink's *Der Geisterseher* (*The Ghost Seer*, 1797) influenced the Gothic novels of Charles Brockden BROWN, America's first novelist. Frontier journal-ist and Gothicist Ambrose BIERCE emulated Euro-pean authors by translating and resetting a German romance, *The Monk and the Hangman's Daughter* (1892).

Bibliography

Blackall, Eric A. *The Novels of the German Romantics.* Ithaca, N.Y.: Cornell University Press, 1983.

Hadley, Michael. *The Undiscovered Genre: A Search for the German Gothic Novel.* Berne, Switzerland: Peter Lang, 1978.

Nickell, Joe. "Germany: Monsters, Myths, and Myster-ies," *Skeptical Inquirer* 27, no. 2 (March–April 2003): 24–28.

Robertson, Ritchie. "The Tale of Bluebeard in German Literature from the Eighteenth Century to the Pre-sent," *Journal of European Studies* 31, no. 2 (June 2001): 230–231.

Thum, Maureen. "Feminist or Anti-feminist? Gender-coded Role Models in the Tales Contributed by Dorothea Viehmann to the Grimm Brothers' 'Kinder- und Hausmärchen,'" *Germanic Review* 68, no. 1 (winter 1993): 11–31.

Webber, Andrew J. *The Doppelgänger: Double Visions in German Literature.* Oxford: Clarendon Press, 1997.

ghost story

Based on fears of the dark and SUPERSTITIONS about death, the ghost story is a pervasive folk genre in world culture from earliest times, for example, Japanese oral *kaidan* tales of horror and revenge. More modern examples include Teutonic spectral lore in Johann von GOETHE's ballad *Der Erlkönig* (The elf king, 1782), the ghostly presence in Ivan Turgenev's "Phantoms" (1864), Mexican author Juan Rulfo's return to the ghosts of the Mexican Revolution in *Pedro Páramo* (1955), Kwakiutl spirit masks in Margaret Craven's *I Heard the Owl Call My Name* (1973), and the power of Chinese specter aversion in Amy Tan's semiautobiographical novel *The Kitchen God's Wife* (1991). Gothic trappings color suspenseful tales of SUPERNATURAL beings that return from death to wreak vengeance, expose a crime, or enlighten or harry victims, particularly former lovers and the sin-laden—for example, Jacob Marley in Charles DICKENS's Christmas classic *A CHRISTMAS CAROL* (1843), a ghost child visiting his guilty father in Nobel laureate Kenzaburo Oe's *Sora No Kaibutsu Aguii* (Agwhee the sky monster, 1964), and protagonist Eva Galli's vengeance on the rapists who slew her in Peter Straub's *Ghost Story* (1979). In *WUTHERING HEIGHTS* (1847), author Emily BRONTË expresses through HEATHCLIFF the torment of the ghost-ridden lover: "Be with me always—take any form—drive me mad! only do not leave me in this abyss, where I cannot find you! Oh God! it is unutterable! I cannot live without my life! I cannot live without my soul!" (Brontë, 163–164). The destructive love Heathcliff bears for Catherine EARNSHAW is distilled through death to the shared passion of two effulgent ghosts on the moor, an afterglow of an ill-starred love that could not survive in human society.

Derived from powerful GOTHIC NOVELs, brief HORROR NARRATIVES achieved popularity at the birth of the novella and short story by satisfying cravings to know about the afterlife, a facet of Elizabeth Gaskell's "The Old Nurse's Story" (1852). George Lucas noted in his specter-ridden *The Castle of Saint Donats* (1798): "A castle without a ghost is fit for nothing but—to live in; and, were it generally the case, the poor novelist might starve and the book-seller publish sermons" (Tarr, 103). In the 19th century, the ghost story was a standard feature of the GOTHIC BLUEBOOK—for example, the anonymous thriller *The Spectre Mother; or, The Haunted Tower* (1864), published by Ann Lemoine of Lon-don, an adventuresome female entrepreneur in a male-dominated business. With the issuance of "Tale for a Chimney Corner" (1819), Leigh Hunt expressed through a preface the need for stories that elevate the spirit as well as shock the mind with puerile specters. In the hands of Rudyard KIPLING, a reporter and editor for the colonial media in India, ghost tales such as "The Phantom Rickshaw" (1888) accommodated a SUBTEXT on the fearful results of colonial oppression, which he warned would backfire on the British like the female wraith who besets and harries her false lover to death.

Settings and time frames vary the impact of ghosts on the living. Examples include a frontier ghost of a wife murdered by her husband in Ambrose Bierce's "The Haunted Valley" (1871), the murder of a medium in Agatha Christie's *The Hound of Death* (1933), the specter that emerges from ritual hara-kiri beneath a cherry tree in Lafcadio HEARN's "Jiu-Roku-Zakura" (1904), Elizabeth Bowen's reunion of a living woman with a suitor killed a quarter-century before in "Demon Lover" (1945), and the accusing REVENANT on the night of her death in Isabel ALLENDE's *THE HOUSE OF THE SPIRITS* (1981). In Edith WHARTON's fluent hauntings, ghosts compel the living to rekindle old loves, the motif of "Afterward" (1911) and "Pomegranate Seed" (1912). Symbolic ghosts haunt Chinese women in Maxine Hong KINGSTON's autobiographical heroine novel *The Woman Warrior* (1976) and in Tan's *The Hundred Secret Senses* (1995), in which storyteller Kwan Li looks at the world of past and present through "yin eyes" (Tan, 3). Similarly, the poltergeist Sutter, the slavemaster of the great-grandparents of Boy Willie Charles and his sister, Berniece Charles Crawley, inhabits a piano and cows family members in August WILSON's cycle play *THE PIANO LESSON* (1990). Susan Hill's carefully plotted novel *The Woman in Black* (1983) takes as its setting the stereotypical isolated stretch at Eel Marsh House, where attorney Arthur Kipps braves salt marshes to settle the estate of Alice Drabow, a reclusive widow. Hill conceals behind shuttered windows an eerie black-robed female ghost of Jennet Humfrye, who wreaks havoc on the living for depriving her of an infant son. The spectral Jennet enjoyed a lengthy haunting of theatergoers in Stephen Mallatratt's 1989 stage adaptation.

Ghost stories abound in SENSATIONALISM, as with the pounding on the door in W. W. JACOBS's riveting tale "THE MONKEY'S PAW" (1902) and the cliche of hair turned instantly white, an overstated touch in Alfred McLelland Burrage's "One Who Saw" (1931), the story of a traveler who refuses to be warned about a terrifying courtyard ghost. For their excesses of action and emotion, ghost stories suit oral transmission by offering the storyteller opportunities to dramatize spooky voices and eerie noises, both of which empower Ellen Glasgow's "The Shadowy Third" (1916), which tells of a vengeful ghost child. Expanding the ghost tale is the tale-within-a-tale, the storyteller who dismays or alarms a vulnerable audience—a device that Washington Irving employs in "The Spectre Bridegroom," which he anthologized in *The Sketch Book* (1820). Less fearful is the gentle drift of dead soldiers home along country roads in the aftermath of the Civil War in Virginia Renfro Ellis's *The Wedding Dress* (2002), a graceful tale of melancholy widows coping with loss.

In the 20th century, Lady Cynthia Charteris Asquith compiled the best of ghost lore in a series of compendia, beginning with *The Ghost Book* (1926), which appealed to people seeking a short, engrossing read. Canadian writer Robertson Davies disburdened stories of their grimness in his ghostly anthology *High Spirits* (1982), a parody of weightier Gothicism that Davies intended for reading aloud. Latina novelist Laura Esquivel turned a guilty conscience into the ghost of Mama Elena scolding her unmarried pregnant daughter in the Mexican MELODRAMA *Like Water for Chocolate* (1989). Successful early 21st-century raconteurs of the supernatural narrative include the Jewish ghost tale-teller Joel Ben Izzy, author of *The Green Hand and Other Ghostly Tales from Around the World* (1996); Brenda Wong Aoki, the Japanese-American dancer-storyteller and author of *Obake! Tales of Spirits Past and Present* (1991); and two Southern specialists, Kathryn Windham, collector of Southern campfire spook tales, and Roberta Brown, performer of "Skin Crawlers," a creepy yarn anthologized in *The Queen of the Cold-Blooded Tales* (1993).

ATMOSPHERE, MYSTERY, and SUSPENSE are essentials to novel-length ghost stories for their heightening of imagination and dread, as seen in William Harrison AINSWORTH's *Windsor Castle* (1843), a disturbing tale of the demon Herne the Hunter who leads a horde of the recent dead on gallops through the countryside; Kingsley Amis's *The Green Man* (1969), the tale of Dr. Underhill, a practitioner of black magic, and his return from the grave; and Richard George Adams's speculative story-within-a-story of child murder in *The Girl in a Swing* (1980). A Pulitzer Prize winner, Toni MORRISON's ghost novel BELOVED (1987) is a sustained reflection on the enslaved black woman's persecutions as the white slavemaster's concubine and breeder. The text stresses the burden of loss and suffering that haunts subsequent generations. Through protracted description of settings, episodes, and SYMBOLs surrounding the title character, Morrison draws out the mystery of a wandering young woman who eats, speaks, and behaves like a toddler. The response to Beloved's eerie presence contributed to Morrison's being awarded the 1993 Nobel Prize in literature—the first time a black female has received this honor.

Bibliography

Brontë, Emily. *Wuthering Heights.* New York: New American Library, 1959.

Cox, Donna. "'I Have No Story to Tell!': Maternal Rage in Susan Hill's 'The Woman in Black,'" *Intertexts* 4, no. 1 (spring 2000): 74–89.

Goldner, Ellen J. "Other(ed) Ghosts: Gothicism and the Bonds of Reason in Melville, Chesnutt, and Morrison," *MELUS* 24, no. 1 (spring 1999): 59.

Isherwood, Charles. "The Woman in Black," *Variety* 383, no. 5 (June 18, 2001): 26.

Reider, Noriko T. "The Emergence of Kaidan-shu: The Collection of Tales of the Strange and Mysterious in the Edo Period," *Asian Folklore Studies* 60, no. 1 (April 2001): 79.

Tan, Amy. *The Hundred Secret Senses.* New York: Ivy Books, 1996.

Tarr, Mary Muriel. *Catholicism in Gothic Fiction: A Study of the Nature and Function of Catholic Materials in Gothic Fiction in England, 1762–1820.* Washington, D.C.: Catholic University of America Press, 1946.

The Giaour
Lord Byron
(1813)

The BYRONIC HERO, an outgrowth of male heroes of 18th-century Gothic fiction, dominates *The Giaour:*

A *Fragment of a Turkish Tale*, a narrative MYSTERY laced with daring, SECRECY, and VAMPIRISM. A vivid ORIENTAL ROMANCE, it is set outside Athens in the 17th century and based on a real incident that Lord Byron observed in 1811. The narrative is what critic Northrop Fry characterizes as good STORYTELLING based on personal experience with a love-will-find-a-way motif. The poem recounts the enslavement of Leila in the seraglio of Caliph Hassan, who executes her for adultery with an infidel. The EXOTICISM of archaic terms and Islamic customs creates SUSPENSE in readers from Judaeo-Christian backgrounds who have no inkling of the motivation for ritual murder of a disloyal concubine.

The tale, the first of Byron's four Oriental narrative poems, blends adventure and a love motif with a gendered curse. The *giaour* (infidel) of the title, a young Venetian warrior, fails to stop Hassan from sewing Leila into a sack and hurling her into the sea. The would-be rescuer condemns himself to vengeance and penance, opposing themes aptly suited to ROMANTICISM's love of MELODRAMA and paradox. After grappling with the evil despot and killing him, the hero withdraws to an abbey to become the OUTSIDER atheist among monks to atone for murder and for his failure to save his beloved Leila. In a deathbed confession, he continues to cleanse himself of guilt for overreaching. His lengthy atonement becomes an obsessive, yet ineffective act that reveals his humanity, passion, and basic decency.

Because of its dark ATMOSPHERE, swift and decisive action, and beguiling failed rescue motif, *The Giaour* had a lasting effect on the poet's reputation. The work directed Byron's strongly masculine romanticism toward disillusion and an enigmatic MELANCHOLY, which the text describes as a "dreary voice, the leafless desert of the mind, the waste of feelings unemployed" (ll. 958–960). The reading public castigated, yet adored the dangerously willful Byron and popularized the poem, which went through 14 editions in two years and earned the admiration of novelist Jane AUSTEN. The work boosted the prominence of the fascinating, reckless BYRONIC HERO, the conflicted cavalier who rejects consolation and retreats to a cell to contemplate and mourn the indelible sins that mar his soul.

In the most frequently excerpted segment, Byron intensifies the images of male dominance and cruelty toward women with his description of the vampire, the first depicted in English literature. In lines 755 to 786, the poet contributes to GOTHIC CONVENTION by delineating the ABERRANT BEHAVIOR of a hellish phantasm from Turkish folklore, the undead whom fate forces from the tomb to commit an incestuous male-on-female violation—sucking blood from wife, daughter, and sister. The sadistic acts derive energy from an insane lust at the same time that they generate a twofold self-loathing for sustaining life on human blood and for befouling normal women with a corrupting OTHERNESS. In Byron's description, the vampire repeats the cycle as a form of survival that carries a double life-in-death punishment, self-banishment from human society and daily solitude in the grave.

According to critic Anne Williams, author of *Art of Darkness: A Poetics of Gothic* (1995), Byron's transformation of the standard FEMME FATALE from the myths of Eve, Lilith, Medusa, and the lamia to a male vampire constituted a major shift in gendering evil. Thus, *The Giaour* is a testimony to a lessening of misogyny and the rigidity of sex roles in early 19th-century England. Later in the 1800s came a deluge of vampires, including the popular chapbook serial of *VARNEY THE VAMPYRE; or, The Feast of Blood* (1847), written by either James Malcolm Rymer or Thomas Preskett PREST. To classic vampire lore, Sheridan LE FANU added *Carmilla* (1872), a forerunner of Bram STOKER's masterly DRACULA (1897).

Bibliography

Southgate, M. Therese. "The Combat of the Giaour and Hassan," *JAMA* 285, no. 13 (April 4, 2001): 1,677.

Williams, Anne. *Art of Darkness: A Poetics of Gothic.* Chicago: University of Chicago Press, 1995.

Gilman, Charlotte Perkins
(1860–1935)

A respected American feminist, intellectual, and Gothicist, Charlotte Perkins Gilman explored rampant demons within the despairing female psyche. In the autobiographical short story "THE YELLOW WALLPAPER," a work with a haunted-house and captivity motif published in the January 1892 issue of *New England Magazine*, she protests male domination and entrapment of females. Rather than attack all forms of patriarchy, she focuses on the treatment of female mental patients, whom she represents as victims silenced by incarceration for gender-biased "rest cures." Gilman knew the scenario from her own postpartum emotional collapse and treatment in 1887. Neurologist Silas Weir Mitchell, a recognized expert on NEURASTHENIA in women, advised her to forego scholarly ambitions and to devote herself to home and hearth, a disastrous course that preceded her divorce and a move from New England to California.

In the October 1913 issue of *Forerunner*, Gilman stated her reasons for writing "The Yellow Wallpaper," which a Kansas physician lauded for its true depiction of incipient madness. She acknowledged her own bout with melancholia and nervous collapse and the devastation wrought by Mitchell's rest cure. After recovering self and mind through work, she tried to save other female patients, by sending a copy of the story to Mitchell, who offered no reply. In private, Mitchell admitted that Gilman's grimly impressionistic story caused him to alter his method of treating female depression. In 1993, the Metropolitan Opera Guild performed the debut of Ronald Perera's opera *The Yellow Wallpaper*, which features Charlotte Gilman as a character.

Bibliography

Bak, John S. "Escaping the Jaundiced Eye: Foucauldian Panopticism in Charlotte Perkins Gilman's 'The Yellow Wallpaper,'" *Studies in Short Fiction* 31, no. 1 (winter 1994): 39–46.

Hume, Beverly A. "Managing Madness in Gilman's 'The Yellow Wall-Paper,'" *Studies in American Fiction* 30, no. 1 (spring 2002): 3–30.

Lane, Ann J. *To Herland and Beyond.* New York: Meridian, 1991.

Roth, Marty. "Gilman's Arabesque Wallpaper," *Mosaic* 34, no. 4 (December 2001): 145–162.

Weales, Gerald. "Perera: The Yellow Wallpaper," *Commonweal* 120, no. 3 (February 12, 1993): 16–17.

The Goblin Market
Christina Rossetti
(1862)

Christina ROSSETTI's rhythmic FAIRY TALE *The Goblin Market* has intrigued readers with its paired

SUBTEXTs of innocence/sexuality and sin/redemption. The mystic narrative pictures sisters Laura and Lizzie separated by duplicitous, stunted male humanoids, SYMBOLs of Victorian patriarchy, worldly temptation, and bestial rapists. The poem progresses from a dizzying list of NATURE's fruits for sale to Edenic disobedience and recompense for Laura's sin of gorging herself on forbidden fruit.

Rossetti stresses the wages of sin by depicting Laura's witchlike frame, a duplicate of the stereotypical consumptives of romantic fiction, whom a lethal evil corrupts from within. The long misadventure concludes with a deathbed watch:

> Life out of death.
> That night long Lizzie watched by her,
> Counted her pulse's flagging stir,
> Felt for her breath,
> Held water to her lips, and cooled her face
> With tears and fanning leaves.
>
> (Rossetti, 14)

To save Laura, Lizzie visits the goblins, who pelt her with fruit, and returns to her sister in a new form, a walking eucharist that Laura must devour to survive. The feast is bitter, a symbol of the unpalatable suppression of Victorian women by a bitter truth: ladies do not indulge their appetites. A fantasy for adult females drawn to illicit embrace and forbidden sensuality, the poem suggests the dangers of hedonism and lesbian love and salutes redeeming, sisterly affection. The ballad winds down to a safe, sanitized ending suggesting that young girls' tendencies toward chaotic Gothic fantasy and fear of ravishment decline with adulthood, marriage, and motherhood.

Bibliography

Coelsch-Foisner, Sabine. "Rossetti's 'Goblin Market,'" *Explicator* 61, no. 1 (fall 2002): 28–30.

Grass, Sean C. "Nature's Perilous Variety in Rossetti's 'Goblin Market,'" *Nineteenth-Century Literature* 51, no. 3 (December 1996): 356–376.

McSweeney, Kerry. "'What's the Import?': Indefinitiveness of Meaning in Nineteenth-century Parabolic Poems," *Style* 36, no. 1 (spring 2002): 36–55.

Rossetti, Christina. *The Goblin Market.* New York: Dover, 1994.

Godwin, William
(1756–1836)

In the years following the French Revolution and preceding the romantic movement, the English social idealist and novelist William Godwin preached the gospel of reform and individual liberty, a philosophy he explored through Gothic fiction. In 1793, he published unconventional tenets in *An Enquiry Concerning Political Justice and Its Influence on General Virtue and Happiness* (1793), which proposed utopian communes as an antidote to government corruption. The text introduced sinister imagery with his description of false feudal titles as "a ferocious monster, devouring, wherever it came, all that the friend of humanity regards with attachment and love" (Cohen, 121).

The following year, Godwin completed a novel of the OUTSIDER, *The Adventures of CALEB WILLIAMS; or, Things As They Are* (1794), one of England's first crime and detection novels and a precursor of the novel of doctrine. It abandoned the dreary medieval settings common to previous Gothic works to stress intense MYSTERY, incarceration, and the gruesome details derived from realistic terrors and oppression. Godwin used fearful moments as soapboxes from which he delivered tirades against classism and the English prison system.

At age 42, Godwin married Mary WOLLSTONECRAFT, a radical feminist and mother of their daughter Mary Wollstonecraft SHELLEY. A reader of American novelist Charles Brockden BROWN, Godwin came under the influence of WIELAND (1798), a novel of purpose he strongly applauded. A year later, after his wife died in childbirth, he concentrated on earning a living from novels and composed *St. Leon* (1799), an original but ornate Gothic perusal of DIABOLISM, the Spanish Inquisition, and Rosicrucianism. The sin-haunted protagonist, Reginald St. Leon, pursues the dark secrets of alchemy by selling his soul to Satan in exchange for the elixir of life. As a result, he suffers confinement at a dungeon at Constance, Germany, and becomes an outcast, a parallel of the WANDERING JEW.

In the December 1835 issue of the *Southern Literary Messenger*, American Gothic author and critic Edgar Allan POE reviewed Godwin's *Lives of the Necromancers* (1834), a study of practitioners of magic in search of the elusive elixir of life. Poe lauded his contemporary for maturity, diction, and broad-based imagination and regretted that Godwin intended to retire from writing. Godwin's work exposed the inequities in English society and contributed to the Gothic innovations of Percy Bysshe SHELLEY's ZASTROZZI (1810) and *St. Irvyne* (1811), Charles Robert MATURIN's MELMOTH THE WANDERER (1820), William Gilmore Simms's *Martin Faber* (1833), Edward BULWER-LYTTON's *A Strange Story* (1861), and Sir Arthur Conan DOYLE's SHERLOCK HOLMES series. Godwin's opinions influenced those of his daughter, the romantic poets, and Charles DICKENS as well as leaders of the incipient anarchic and communist movements in England.

Bibliography
Cohen, Jeffrey Jerome, ed. *Monster Theory*. Minneapolis: University of Minnesota Press, 1996.

Karl, Frederick R. *The Adversary Literature: The English Novel in the Eighteenth Century—A Study in Genre*. New York: Farrar, 1974.

Punter, David, ed. *The Literature of Terror*, vol. 1, 2nd ed. London: Longman, 1996.

Stevens, David. *The Gothic Tradition*. Cambridge: Cambridge University Press, 2000.

Goethe, Johann Wolfgang von
(1749–1832)

A major contributor to European ROMANTICISM, Johann Wolfgang von Goethe flourished as dramatist, poet, folklorist, and philosopher during Germany's intellectual golden age. He grew up in a cultured environment, received home-schooling in modern foreign languages, and enjoyed after-hours STORYTELLING. When disgust drove him from formal education, he taught himself more interesting subjects: occultism, astrology, alchemy, and MYSTICISM. At age 21, he read *Volkslied* (German folklore), accounts of the Irish hero Ossian, the verse of Homer and Pindar, and William Shakespeare's plays. He discussed his readings with a mentor, the Prussian romanticist Johann Gottfried von Herder, who also instructed the younger poet on the beauties of GOTHIC ARCHITECTURE.

Goethe achieved fame in a number of genres. He resurrected MEDIEVALISM and knighthood with the tragedy *Götz von Berlichingen* (*Goetz with the*

Iron Hand, 1773), which historical novelist Sir Walter SCOTT read with interest. Goethe produced a classic personal novel, *Die Leiden des Jungen Werthers* (*The Sorrows of Young Werther,* 1774), a study of subjectivity and emotion that brought the author fame throughout Europe. Goethe's musical *Claudine von Villa Bella* (1775) introduced the crime lore of German banditti, a strand furthered by Friedrich von SCHILLER. Goethe turned to the GHOST STORY in his ballad *Der Erlkönig* (The elf king, 1782), which the composer Franz Schubert set as a stirring art song in 1815. In writing the play *Egmont* (1787), Goethe incorporated SOMNAMBULISM, a powerful image of conflicted emotions and dissociative thought in subsequent psychological Gothic novels. His picaresque beast epic, *Reineke Fuchs* (*Reynard the Fox,* 1794), examined the motivation of the born scamp, a forerunner of the conscience-less VILLAIN. In *Die Braut von Corinth* (*The Bride of Corinth,* 1797), he set the parameters of the female vampire.

At age 28, Goethe turned the stereotypical golem motif into a whimsical fable, *Der Zauberlehrling* (*The Sorcerer's Apprentice,* 1797), a cautionary tale based on a fantasy by the Syrian fabulist Lucian (or Lycinus) of Samosata. The story pits a disobedient upstart against his master, a sinister Merlinesque magus whom the author retained and eventually reshaped as the protagonist of *Faust* (1790–1832). At the climax of the fable, the ominous workings of an enchanted besom produce a flood of water in the master's lab after the apprentice demands that the broomstick ferry water from the river. The author tempers Gothic possibilities with a gentle humor to show the boy crying out in a panic:

> Stop, now stop!
> You have granted
> All I wanted.
> Stop! Od rot it!
> Running still? I'm like to drop!
> What's the word? I've clean forgot it.
> (Goethe, 99–100)

Reaching for a hatchet, the apprentice tries to control a relentless automaton he calls the devil's child. The story subsides into a FAIRY TALE ending as the magus seizes control and chastises his wayward lab boy.

After forming a lifelong friendship with Karl August, Duke of Saxe-Weimar-Eisenbach, Goethe traveled the Mediterranean, studied Renaissance history, and returned to Germany to embrace his homeland and its pagan traditions. He wrote "The New Melusina" (1826), a wonder tale about a traveler entranced by a demon temptress. Goethe's publication of *Faust,* a profound masterpiece written over a lifetime, contributed to Europe's obsessions with the SUPERNATURAL, the DOPPELGÄNGER motif, and the complex BYRONIC HERO. Goethe's model *Schauerroman* ("shudder stories") developed romantic convention through his application of crime and terror. His skillful writing impressed the romantic poets, especially Percy Bysshe SHELLEY, and inspired a generation of English Gothic masters: Edward BULWER-LYTTON, Matthew Gregory LEWIS, and Charles Robert MATURIN.

Bibliography

Goethe, Johann. *Poems and Ballads of Goethe.* New York: Holt & Williams, 1871.

Graham, Ilse. *Goethe and Lessing: The Wellsprings of Creation.* New York: Harper & Row, 1973.

Haining, Peter, ed. *Gothic Tales of Terror.* New York: Taplinger Publishing, 1972.

Hume, Robert. "Gothic Versus Romantic: A Revaluation of the Gothic Novel," *Publication of the Modern Language Association* 84 (1969): 282–290.

Kohlschmidt, Werner. *A History of German Literature, 1760–1805.* New York: Holmes & Meier, 1975.

Rexroth, Kenneth. "Goethe," *Saturday Review,* April 19, 1969: 21.

Gogol, Nikolai
(1809–1852)

A major contributor to 19th-century Gothic style, fabulist Nikolai Vasilyevich Gogol created realistic views of mental illness and ABERRANT BEHAVIOR. He came of age in the Ukraine, where he absorbed rich folklore about DIABOLISM, hauntings, and WITCHCRAFT. From his early teens, he read the fantasies of E. T. A. HOFFMANN and produced a substantial corpus of satiric verse and absurdist stories that became his life's work. He revealed a nightmarish glimpse of Russian peasant life in *Evenings on a Farm near Dakanka* (1831), a sheaf of earthy sketches that earned the praise of Alexander Pushkin. After a brief tenure teaching medieval history at St. Petersburg University, Gogol published escapist stories in *Mirgorod* (1835), which anthologized "Viy," a harrowing tale of witchery and SHAPE-SHIFTING by a Medusa-like demon. That same year, he issued *Arabeski* (*Arabesques*, 1835), which contains "The Diary of a Madman," the story of a schizophrenic clerk who flees boredom in delusions and declines into lunacy. In another tale, "The Portrait" (1835), a VILLAIN's malevolence survives after his death in a lurid painting, a forerunner of the portrait in Oscar WILDE's THE PICTURE OF DORIAN GRAY (1891).

During a lengthy sojourn in Rome, Gogol wrote *Dead Souls* (1842), a success that preceded his own literary decline and slide into madness. The satiric story tells of the schemer Pavel Chichikov, who profits by claiming the corpses of Russian serfs. Upon his arrival in the village, he displays an alarming interest "whether there were any diseases in the province—epidemics of fever, some deadly plagues, smallpox, and the like, and all this so thoroughly and with such precision that it showed more than mere curiosity alone" (Gogol, 6). Gogol develops the skillful sharper into a ghoulish villain eager to build a business on other people's misery. Conservative Russians condemned the dark drollery as immoral. The author attempted a sequel, but burned his manuscript shortly before his death by deliberate starvation. His work influenced a generation of Russian writers as well as the Yiddish storyteller Isaac Bashevis SINGER.

Bibliography

Altschuler, Eric Lewin. "One of the Oldest Cases of Schizophrenia in Gogol's 'Diary of a Madman,'" *British Medical Journal* 323, no. 7,327 (December 22, 2001): 1,475–1,477.

Kaplan, Robert D. "Euphorias of Hatred: The Grim Lessons of a Novel by Gogol," *Atlantic Monthly* 291, no. 4 (May 2003): 44–45.

Maus, Derek. "The Devils in the Details: The Role of Evil in the Short Fiction of Nikolai Vasilievich Gogol and Nathaniel Hawthorne," *Papers on Language & Literature* 38, no. 1 (winter 2002): 76.

Nabokov, Vladimir. *Lectures on Russian Literature*. New York: Harcourt Brace, 1981.

Gothic architecture and art

Gothic architecture and art had their beginnings in the latter half of the Middle Ages and blossomed into more creative and energetic forms from the focused drive of the Renaissance, ending in the 1500s. As the movement matured, it celebrated the Gothic or pointed arch as its most overt stylistic embellishment. The structural importance of the ribbed groin vault, mullioned windows and tracery, long stained-glass panels, monstrous carved gargoyles on the upper eaves, and the flying buttress in cathedral design gave the impression of mastery and lift. The upward thrust depicted a fervid salvation anxiety among Christians terrorized by the possibility of hell and damnation.

Echoing verticality were towers, narrow spires, and turrets, notable details that mark the cathedrals of Amiens, Chartres, Mont-Saint-Michel, Notre-Dame, and Rheims, the era's French masterworks in stone. Of their sinister images, H. P. LOVECRAFT noted: "The prevalence and depth of the mediaeval horror-spirit in Europe, intensified by the dark despair which waves of pestilence brought, may be fairly gauged by the grotesque carvings" (Lovecraft, 24). In England, similar innovations in ecclesiastical architecture typified grand houses of worship at Canterbury, Gloucester, Lincoln, and Salisbury; Westminster Abbey in London is also an example of this style. Germany and Spain, influenced by the French, produced a like flamboyance at Cologne, León, St. Elizabeth's, and Ulm cathedrals; Italy created its own stone marvels in the cathedrals at Florence and Milan. Taken as a whole, these structures impressed at the same time that they evoked solemnity and a hint of intimidation.

Interior art featured inescapable images of gaping hell-mouths, apocalypses, French *diableries*, fiery cauldrons, and serpentine horrors, such as those inscribed in the "Jaws of Hell," a phantasmagoric illumination sketched in the Winchester Psalter (ca. 1150), and the quaking damned in French Romanesque sculptor Gislebertus's *The Last Judgment* (ca. 1130), a frieze carved in stone on the west tympanum of Autun cathedral. Gisle-bertus's expressionistic piece was a literal interpre-tation of judgment based on classical weighing of souls with a balance-beam scale, a motif dating back to ancient Egyptian tomb art. To stress the grim eternity of Satan's realm, the sculptor shaped devils with yawning mouths, furry flanks, pointed ears and tails, and spidery legs. The motif of souls anticipating eternal torment set the tone and style of the next five centuries of Christian art, particu-larly in Burgundy. Writers of Gothic, most far re-moved from the religious fervor of previous centuries, interpreted these images with subjective reactions that produced faulty notions of Catholi-cism and impacted fiction with multiple theologi-cal and historical errors.

In nonarchitectural efforts, fresco, painted panels, mosaic, and illuminated manuscripts high-lighted in gold leaf contributed to the artistic tone with a delight in profuse detail, as found in the bone-thin hell-bound creatures fending off clawing demons in sculptor Lorenzo Maitani's *The Last Judgment* (ca. 1320), a detail from the façade of Orvieto Cathedral in Italy. Of major significance to the Gothic mentality was Florentine artist An-tonio del Pollaiuolo's engraving *Battle of the Ten Naked Men* (ca. 1465), a grim overlay of flailing arms and legs and slashing scimitars. The theme of suffering, terror, and damnation flourished in northern Europe, particularly in brothers Hubert and Jan van Eyck's *The Last Judgment* (ca. 1420), an oil-and-tempera panel picturing a tangle of human torsos and extremities tumbling down from a jubilant skeleton with limbs outstretched. The dominant colors of red, brown, sepia, and black enhance a dismal scenario filled with unspeakable horrors caused by winged monsters and ravenous four-legged beasts.

In the high Renaissance, Hieronymus Bosch, a Dutch painter and member of a conservative Catholic brotherhood, overwhelmed viewers with a riot of bestial humanoid shapes and demons that represented evil and temptation, themes of *The Temptation of St. Anthony* (ca. 1485), a canvas de-picted in glowing colors. Bosch filled other panels with turbulent clutches of symbolic beings guilty of folly and greed and suffering intolerable punish-ments appropriate to their sins. His contemporary,

the Alsatian artist Martin Schongauer, engraved his own interpretation of *The Temptation of St. An-thony* (ca. 1485), featuring prickly beings with long tails and snouts and ravenous jaws plucking away at the holy man's face, beard, and robes. The Nuremberg engraver Albrecht Dürer turned from such otherworldly spectacle to earthly slayers in *The Four Horsemen of the Apocalypse* (ca. 1497), a gruesome, energetic portrait of the galloping rav-agers—war, famine, pestilence, and death—tram-pling male and female figures as their steeds plunge onward toward new fields of conquest. In Italy, Michelangelo contributed his version of judgment day in fresco covering the high back wall of the Sistine Chapel, completed in 1541. Huddled in fear of Satan's minions are pathetic naked figures, the unrepentant and unchurched, who register in face and gesture varying degrees of guilt, agony, and terror. For models, the artist grouped like-nesses of bishops and popes and added his own portrait as the apostle Bartholomew.

In the British Isles, the overthrow of Catholi-cism produced new sources of Gothic detail. The establishment of the Church of England triggered an onslaught of anti-Catholic art and architecture in Gothic literature. After King Henry VIII or-dered the looting, dismantling, and razing of Roman Catholic abbeys in the 1530s, their ivied stone heaps and skeletal remains produced a ro-mantic disorder patinaed with moss and sur-rounded by murky, tenebrous gardens, lone towers, and ruined crypts and oratories. From the evoca-tive nature of crumbling architecture, the Scottish romanticist Lady Margaret Maclean Compton Northampton created a Gothic scenario in "The Idiot Boy" (1830):

> On this drear shore a Gothic castle stands,
> The work of period rude, and ruder hands:
> Misshapen turrets, neither round nor
>   square,
> Hang midway 'twixt the island and the air,
> And crooked walls, from level rule so free,
> They seem to stand alone through courtesy;
> And here, a donjon's huge and dismal pile
> Served to enclose the wretched of the isle,
> Who forfeited, by actions much amiss.
>   (Northampton, 158)

The overall effect of primitive grandeur, destruction, and neglect served Northampton and other authors as MELANCHOLY touchstones for Gothic literature that tended to create MELODRAMA, MYSTERY, and disturbing passions or VIOLENCE.

Contemplation of ruins evolved into the warp and woof of literary Gothicism. In 1794, Eliza PARSONS, author of DOMESTIC GOTHIC novels, speaks through a character in *Lucy* her feelings for dilapidated structures: "I dote on ruins, there is something sublime and awful in the sight of decayed grandeur, and large edifices tumbling to pieces" (Varma, 218). Regina Maria ROCHE pictured the heroine of *The Maid of the Hamlet* (1821) as overwhelmed by the terrors of a ruined chapel, which is both sinister and grand when viewed by moonlight. In "On Monastic Institutions" (1825), the critic and Gothic writer Anna Laetitia BARBAULD applauded the collapse of Catholicism, a religious institution that, in her view, enslaved the mind with coercive legends and dreadful tales.

Gothic details enhanced fictional settings with the somber, distorted, and sometimes overwhelming dimensions of real feudal halls or ruins, as in the backdrop of Horace WALPOLE's THE CASTLE OF OTRANTO (1765). Ann RADCLIFFE depicted *The Romance of the Forest* (1791) in gloomy woods and ruins where a VILLAIN lurks. In THE MYSTERIES OF UDOLPHO (1794), she places the heroine, Emily ST. AUBERT, at the castle of UDOLPHO, a grand Gothic structure rendered unappealing for its overpowering stone walls. In a first view, the author emphasizes strength and drear in the massive ramparts and in the overwhelming size of the gateway, courts, curtain wall, pointed arches, pillars, and paired towers—structures so outdated that they support grasses, briony, and poisonous nightshade growing in the moldering stone. Radcliffe commiserates with her heroine's isolation: "As the carriage-wheels rolled heavily under the portcullis, Emily's heart sunk, and she seemed, as if she was going into her prison" (Radcliffe, *Mysteries*, 227).

More intense use of CHIAROSCURO amid ruined architecture colors the drive through a Roman carnival to the Inquisition prison in Radcliffe's THE ITALIAN (1797). The author notes that "Not even the shadow of a human being crossed the waste, nor any building appeared which might

be supposed to shelter one" (Radcliffe, *The Italian*, 195). Thus, the fearful prisoner Vivaldi passes beyond "innumerable massy bulwarks, [which] exhibited neither window or grate, but a vast and dreary blank" (*ibid.*, 196). Topped by towers and strongly barricaded, the fortified walls remind him of a line from verse, "Grim-visaged comfortless Despair" (*ibid.*).

Contemporaneous with these graphic narratives were drawings by aficionados of Gothic art, including illustrators of GOTHIC BLUEBOOKs and creators of original paintings. The Swiss-English romanticist John Henry Fuseli explored the phantasm in an oil painting entitled *The Nightmare* (ca. 1782), a source of Gothic detail and MELODRAMA in Edgar Allan Poe's "THE FALL OF THE HOUSE OF USHER" (1839). A master of subtly ominous art was Venetian etcher Giovanni Battista Piranesi, creator of *Carceri d'Invenzione* (Prison caprices, ca. 1761); noteworthy in particular was his hellish maze of dark staircases leading nowhere in *Tower with Bridges*, a work that probed both physical and psychological torments. Piranesi's punitive cells and looming dungeons colored the imaginations of Europeans, inspiring a master of Gothic fiction, William BECKFORD, the author of VATHEK (1782). Beckford said in a letter, "I drew chasms, and subterranean hollows, the domain of fear and torture, with chains, racks, wheels, and dreadful engines in the style of Piranesi" (Beckford, 104).

In England, nonconformist poet and painter William Blake, a reclusive visionary and student of medieval art, drew compelling images of *Elijah in the Chariot of Fire, Nebuchadnezzar, Hecate,* and *Good and Evil Angels* (1795). He completed 102 engravings for Dante's *Inferno* (1321), which he began adorning in 1825. Blake's layered *Last Judgment,* one of the last views of the Christian apocalypse painted by a major artist, contrasted the upward glide of the saved with the falling beings bound for a nether region tipped with flames. With little hope of mercy, the unsaved huddle in a mass of gesturing arms and pleading eyes. He left the series unfinished at his death two years later.

Nineteenth-century art made a thorough study of Gothicism. Contemporaneous with Blake's pensive art were the evocative images of hell that English mezzotint engraver John "Mad"

Martin created for an edition of John Milton's *Paradise Lost* in the early 1800s. In Martin's huge painted melodramas, among them *Destruction of Herculaneum* (1822) and *The Great Day of His Wrath* (ca. 1853), he dwarfed small human figures with immense architectural shapes and forbidding skies. Best known for the bizarre and grotesque were woodcuts of the WANDERING JEW and the popular illustrations that the French engraver and printmaker Paul-Gustave Doré applied to the *Oeuvres de Rabelais* (*Works of Rabelais*, 1854), John Milton's *Paradise Lost* (1865), a folio Bible (1866), and an edition of Samuel Taylor COLERIDGE's *THE RIME OF THE ANCIENT MARINER* (1875). In a celebrated reproduction of Dante's *Inferno* issued in 1861, Doré pictured a titanic winged Satan presiding over minuscule figures of the damned, who languish in various postures of misery in shadowed settings reminiscent of "the valley of the shadow of death" from Psalm 23. A subsequent new talent known for imagination and hedonism was English artist Aubrey Beardsley, who, in his early 20s, illustrated *The Works of Edgar Allan Poe* (1894–95).

The English art critic John Ruskin provided a retrospect of the universal Gothic ideal in *Stones of Venice* (1851, 1853), a pinnacle of Victorian prose. In reference to the PRE-RAPHAELITE BROTHERHOOD's rediscovery of Gothic themes and motifs in 1848, Ruskin's social polemic legitimized the clashing elements that Gothic architecture mingled and unified, and he lauded the resultant expression of fancy, variety, and richness. From his assessment of the English Gothic revival's recreation of the Italian Gothic mindset, he extracted six definitive Gothic elements: savagery, changefulness, naturalism, grotesqueness, rigidity, and redundance. All six defied the regularity, decorum, and predictability of neoclassicism that predominated from 1660 to 1798 and in the dreary industrial capitalism of his own time. In a paean to imagination and humanism, Ruskin exalted Gothic style for its outpouring of human roughness, oddity, ineptitude, shame, failure, and majesty.

In Ruskin's view, the massive tensions of Gothic design energized a society that had fallen into a perilous monotony. The human imagination, yearning for fulfillment, expressed its fondness of nature and passion by reaching out for rough-edged beauty and the disarrangement of a too-confining order. From his perspective, Gothic art echoed subconscious tendencies toward egocentrism and depravity through the psychological impact of massive architectural shapes that left undefined their startling, irreligious underpinnings. Restless and vain, the Gothic principle abandoned the prim tidiness and artificiality of neoclassic rules of decorum to embrace the vulgar, enslaved, and iconoclastic as valid, nurturing impulses.

Bibliography

Beckford, William. *Dreams, Waking Thoughts and Incidents*. Madison, N.J.: Fairleigh Dickinson University Press, 1971.

Lovecraft, H. P. *The Annotated Supernatural Horror in Literature*. New York: Hippocampus, 2000.

Northampton, Lady Margaret Maclean Compton. *Irene: A poem, In Six Cantos: Miscellaneous Poems*. London: Mills, Jowett, & Mills, 1833.

Radcliffe, Ann. *The Italian*. London: Oxford University Press, 1968.

———. *The Mysteries of Udolpho*. London: Oxford University Press, 1966.

Stevens, David. *The Gothic Tradition*. Cambridge: Cambridge University Press, 2000.

Varma, Devendra P. *The Gothic Flame*. New York: Russell & Russell, 1966.

Gothic bluebook

A controversial element of Gothic fiction, particularly during the Victorian era, was the bluebook or chapbook (cheapbook), a low-cost, quasi-literary miscellany characterized by poor quality paper, gaudy illustrations, and printing on quartos stitched down the center. The genre was called "literature of the kitchen" because of its low-class appeal. It capitalized on Gothic SENSATIONALISM and artistic DECADENCE both in literary style and layout. Examples of the Gothic bluebook include C. F. Barrett's *Douglas Castle; or, The Cell of Mystery* (1803), published in London by A. Neil and sold for sixpence each; moonlighter Dr. Nathan DRAKE's atmospheric THE ABBEY OF CLUNEDALE (1804); hack writer Sarah WILKINSON's eerie *The Child of Mystery* (1808); and *Mary, Maid of the Inn* (1820), an anonymous tale about sequential crises, robbery, assault, murder, and concealment of a corpse in an abbey.

Bluebook publishers targeted an underserved stratum of society. The texts appealed to poorly educated and unrefined members of the working class, who could not afford better quality novels and fiction anthologies. Buyers, ranging from students and apprentices to valets and pot girls, counted out the bluebook's cost in pennies, depending on size, slipped them into their pockets, and shared the thrilling reads with others eager for their vicarious shock value. Alehouses kept a stock of dogeared chapbooks for drinkers to peruse.

The prototype pamphlet appeared in France in the late 1400s, soon after the application of the printing press to needs and tastes of general readers. In Germany, chapbook printers issued the *Volks-bücher* ("people's books"), a similar pamphlet that tended toward romance and imported fictions showcasing exotica. In England, where the popular press gained readership during the 16th century, the bluebook developed into a fad, which reached its height in the 1800s. Each blue-bound pamphlet ranged from 36 to 72 pages, measured 4.25 by 5.5 inches, and featured dismaying, horrific, and romantic texts illustrated by amateurish woodcuts, for example, images of vampires and werewolves and sketches of witches and demons. Usually unattributed, these low-level Gothic thrillers also interspersed accounts of sensational crimes and beheadings, tall tales, crude farce, vice and wicked deeds, vulgar jests, and exaggerated biographies of royalty (Henry VIII, Anne Boleyn, Lady Jane Grey, Mary Queen of Scots, and Elizabeth I) or of pseudohistorical figures, as indicated in the title of the anonymous *Fatal Jealousy; or, Blood Will Have Blood! Containing the History of Count Almagro and Duke Alphonso* (1807).

Women flourished in the role of redactors and authors of bluebooks. Catherine Cuthbertson, Charlotte DACRE, Sarah Griffith, Sophia LEE, Sydney Owenson, Clara REEVE, Regina Maria ROCHE, and Lucy Watkins issued corrupt versions of tales that exploited, mimicked, extracted, shortened, or plagiarized from better-quality Gothic stories and novels, such as the anonymous *The Life and Horrid Adventures of the Celebrated Dr. Faustus* (1810), *Robinson Crusoe* (ca. 1830), and *The Old Tower of Frankenstein* (n.d.). Females tended toward antipa-triarchal situations and themes, as with Cuthbertson's *Santo Sebastiano; or, The Young Protector* (1806) and *Adelaide; or, The Countercharm* (1813).

Gothic fanciers bought bluebooks for their hair-raising, often titillating plots emphasizing VIOLENCE (*The Ruins of Rigonda; or, The Homicidal Father; The Iron Shroud; or, Italian Revenge*), the macabre (*The Black Forest; or, The Cavern of Horrors*), ghosts (*The Spectre of Landmere Abbey*), SUPERNATURAL events (*The Necromancer; or, The Tale of the Black Forest*), medieval Catholic arcana (*The Phantoms of the Cloister* and *The Mysterious Novice; or, Convent of the Grey Penitents*), depraved nobility (*Mysteries of the Courts of London*), erotic situations (*The Champion of Virtue*), science fiction (*Five Hundred Years Hence*), LYCANTHROPY (*The Severed Arm; or, The Wehr-Wolf of Limousin* and *Wagner the Wehr-Wolf*), and VAMPIRISM (*VARNEY THE VAMPYRE; or, The Feast of Blood* and *The Vampire; or, The Bride of the Isles*). For their overemphasis on perverse sex, crime, and mayhem, bluebooks earned the street names "penny bloods," "penny dreadfuls," and "shilling shockers." The more enterprising variety of bluebook hooked its audience with serials that ended with cliffhangers to keep buyers coming back for more, as with *The Midnight Assassin; or, The Confessions of the Monk Rinaldi* (1802), issued anonymously by *Marvellous Magazine and Compendium of Prodigies*. As a result of their popularity, publishers began allotting space to Gothic fiction in popular magazines.

One journeyman freelancer, Thomas Preskett PREST, established a following for a crime shocker, *Sweeney Todd, the Demon Barber of Fleet Street* (1848), that spooled out with an episodic plot issued at regular intervals in *The People's Periodical and Family Library*. Beginning in 1846 and continuing for two years, the story described an enterprising barber who slaughtered patrons and passed the remains to his wife to chop as filling for meat pies. George Dibdin Pitt reset the couple's macabre business as a stage MELODRAMA, *The String of Pearls: The Fiend of Fleet Street* (1847). In 1979, Stephen Sondheim reprised the tale as a Broadway musical containing the songs "The Worst Pies in London" and "God, That's Good!"

At its height in the first half of the 19th century, the bluebook mania resulted in the publication of some one thousand titles, which influenced the writings of Mary Wollstonecraft SHELLEY and Percy Bysshe SHELLEY. Issues were readily available at low cost from small lending libraries or from street stalls and itinerant hawkers called chapmen, who bellowed out one-line teasers to pedestrians to intrigue their interest. As the popular genre declined in reputation, author Mary Elizabeth BRADDON characterized the mercantile aspect of bluebook authorship with her description of Sigismund Smith, a character in *The Doctor's Wife* (1864) who writes popular pulp fiction for a pound per page. He summarizes his work for the "penny public" as "plot, and plenty of it; surprises, and plenty of 'em; mystery, as thick as a November fog" (Carnell, 208). Two years after creating her pay-per-page writer, Braddon recast him as Sigismund Smythe in *The Lady's Mile* (1866) in the new guise of a respectable novelist.

Braddon felt it necessary to apologize for her own authorship of bluebooks as a source of quick funds. In a letter to her literary idol Edward BULWER-LYTTON, she confided, "This work is most piratical stuff, & would make your hair stand on end, if you were to see it. The amount of crime, treachery, murder, slow poisoning, & general infamy required by the Half penny reader is something terrible" (*ibid.*, 200). She added that her next submission was on parricide.

The penny storypaper reached a nadir with Edwin J. Brett's publication of the anonymous *The Wild Boys of London; or, The Children of the Night* (1866), a smarmy appeal to juvenile readers. The sensational story depicts a gang of teen street nomads residing in the London sewer system. Their crimes range from minor mischief and mocking Asians to dodging and fighting "peelies" (police) and dealing in stolen goods and corpses for medical research. The text sold so well that it returned to print a decade later, when it was suppressed by police. Social investigator James Greenwood, an alarmist critic of the growing juvenile menace in *Unsentimental Journeys; or, Byways of the Modern Babylon* (1867) and *The Seven Curses of London* (1869), protested unsavory teen fiction in *The Wilds of London* (1874), a diatribe in which he referred to bluebooks as a pernicious social plague and nasty and vulgar muck retailed by the most reprehensible of shopkeepers.

In the United States, the first chapbook was available from a New York publisher at the beginning of the 1800s. One anonymous work, *The Lunatic and His Turkey: A Tale of Witchcraft* (n.d.), exploited the supernatural and historic connections to the Salem witch trials of 1692. The bluebook concept evolved into the dime novel, a venue for the Western, crime thriller, DETECTIVE STORY, and fictionalized accounts of such historic outlaws as Billy the Kid, Belle Starr, the Dalton Gang, and Butch Cassidy. The first dime novel, Anne Sophia Stephens's *Malaeska: The Indian Wife of the White Hunter* (1860), which began as a magazine serial, sold 300,000 stand-alone copies as well as five sequels, which she published over the next four years.

Bibliography

Carnell, Jennifer. *The Literary Lives of Mary Elizabeth Braddon*. Hastings, Sussex: Sensation Press, 2000.

Clery, E. J. *The Rise of Supernatural Fiction, 1762–1800.* Cambridge: Cambridge University Press, 1995.

Greenwood, James. *The Wilds of London*. London: Chatto & Windus, 1874.

Haining, Peter, ed. *The Shilling Shockers*. New York: St. Martin's Press, 1978.

Gothic convention

Gothic conventions emerged through a long and complex literary and philosophical evolution. The ornate elements that invest Gothic literature with its unique energy range from chivalry, piety, MYSTERY, vendettas, and medieval magic to the GROTESQUE, ILLUSION, terror, repression, SENSATIONALISM, DISSIPATION, and perversity that flourished during the romantic era and continue to color fiction and film today. The term *Gothic* originally pertained to the Goths, a Germanic people comprised of the Ostrogoths and Visigoths, who invaded Roman lands in the second century A.D. and spread over the Roman Empire for the next four centuries. The literary application of the term gradually shifted from the original straightforward synonym for Teutonic or Germanic into a general descriptive for the pagan vigor, profusion, and embellishment of medieval art and lore.

The traditional Gothic romance was a conscious rebellion against cold, sterile rationalism, which dismayed readers with its precise regularities, artificial control, and banishment of emotion. During the neoclassic era (1660–1798), fastidious writers and critics held resurgences of fancy at bay and brandished the term "Gothic" contemptuously as a pejorative meaning crude, barbaric, unlettered, disorderly, and licentious. Undeterred, detractors of stiff neoclassic decorum embraced a fashionable MELANCHOLY, the result of immersion in the heroic monuments and events of the Middle Ages. As Thomas Warton explained in *The Pleasures of Melancholy* (1745), the soul profits from daydreams and a contemplation of the ruins of past ages by allowing intellect free play with insight.

The extremes of plotting, TONE, and characterization in Gothic writings were an outgrowth of anomalies and phantasms in Edmund Spenser's *The Faerie Queene* (1590), sensational Jacobean tragedies of blood, and extravagant French and German novels and verse. In an era infatuated with freedom, Gothicism liberated period literature from the neoclassic drive toward simplicity and restraint of fancy. The emerging Gothic genre relieved the boredom aroused by neoclassicism's lack of heroism and danger, the hallmarks of the Crusades. From a psychoanalytic stance, an embrace of Gothicism freed the staid, materialistic, overly ebullient Augustan age from its unspeakable SUBTEXT, the avoidance of death and decay through an artificial aura of control of the unexpected. Far from the sparkling salon and witty conversants, the graveyard poets and preromantics revelled in solitude, the irregular contours of the medieval ruin, and the somber beauty of the gaping crypt. From England's haunted ballads grew a tradition that empowered 20th-century American ballads, bluegrass, and country music with haunted loves and vengeful jealousies.

Unlike the self-controlled, intellectual neoclassics, Gothic writers gave full reign to intuition, exuberance, variety, improbability, rough behaviors, and morbid fantasies. To create the stark, sometimes shocking contrast that fuels Gothic romance, they often focused on the control, torment, and/or murder of an inexperienced female NAIF. The early Gothic masters ornamented verse and fiction with outrage, the SUPERNATURAL, mystery, PATHETIC FALLACY, CHIAROSCURO, and a foreign EXOTICISM against a backdrop of dim, stormy nights and characters peering through the mist from massy battlements at dismaying rogues, stalkers, or MONSTERS. Contributing to a terror of obscure phantasms and entrapment was a collection of sinister paraphernalia, the hidden passageways, sliding panels, and trapdoors that allowed VILLAINS access to hapless maidens. Heightening reader response were ominous sense impressions, as found in the auditory stimuli of Ann RADCLIFFE's *THE MYSTERIES OF UDOLPHO* (1794).

Although stereotyped by barbaric, tempestuous scenarios of the guileless virgin fleeing a lustful predator, rabid monster, or madman, the Gothic genre is vastly more inclusive. Recurrent motifs of Gothic fiction consist of the vulnerable female naif, heartless villains, physical and emotional confinement and liberation, sexual awakenings, and an expansive play of light on dark, all archetypal essentials of psychological fiction. In 1765, British author Horace WALPOLE established the basics of Gothic convention with *THE CASTLE OF OTRANTO*, a deliberately scary novel filled with the creaking trap doors, shadowed stairs, subterranean passages, and mysterious sounds and OMENS that generate the standard ATMOSPHERE of the GOTHIC NOVEL. Grandiose but bleak settings redolent with decay tended toward rambling estates and cloisters in remote locales, where unexplained disappearances and deaths or eerie portents and manifestations contributed to SUSPENSE, dark tone, and a disturbingly vague foreboding and dread.

A literary phenomenon, Gothic convention flourished as a subset of ROMANTICISM, a popular philosophy anchored in Germany and extending across western Europe to North America. Beginning in 1790 in England in the wake of horrific upheaval during the French Revolution, William Lane's MINERVA PRESS catered to readers of Gothic fiction with a variety of titles written by specialists. With the publication of *FRANKENSTEIN* in 1818, novelist Mary Wollstonecraft SHELLEY added dimensions of horror and the pursuing ghoul. Charlotte BRONTË produced a literary gem of feminine sensibilities, *JANE EYRE* (1847), which set high standards for plot and character development within a passionate, yet destructive love match. The author incorporated Gothic clichés of a ghostly country estate, a fierce watchdog, unexplained comings and goings, the male protagonist disguised like a gypsy fortune teller, the heroine's fitful DREAMS AND NIGHTMARES, and a wedding disrupted by a madwoman locked away on an upper story. Unlike lesser writers, the author turned convention into art by maintaining the humanity and plausibility of her protagonists.

The Victorians looked back on a century of Gothic literature with sophistication and understanding of the psychological basis of horror fiction. The art critic Walter Horatio Pater extrapolated from analyses of Gothic art the Gothic ideal. In *Studies in the History of the Renaissance* (1873), he characterized the Gothic esthetic with an offbeat description of Leonardo da Vinci's *La Gioconda (Mona Lisa)*, whom he described as a vampire posed in the tradition of the undead. He envisioned her as a fanciful embodiment—a mysterious, dreamlike repository of wisdom, extravagant sins, and burial secrets. He characterized her beauty as the physical representation of strangeness, fantasy, reverie, and passion. Unlike the objective art commentators of the period, he allowed the diction and obscurity of Gothicism to rechannel his perceptions into imaginative, intuitive appreciation. In the estimation of critic Robert Mighall, author of *A Geography of Victorian Gothic Fiction* (1999), the indulgence in the paganism of the past was a visible congratulation that Victorians heaped on themselves and the era's progressivism.

In the United States, the fiction of Robert Montgomery BIRD, Charles Brockden BROWN, and Ambrose BIERCE and, to a lesser degree, the verse and short tales of Edgar Allan POE exemplified the New World version of European Gothic. Essential to Poe's skill at turning out sensational, largely Eurocentric poems and stories was his command of literary embellishments—self-consciously ornate sentence structure, obsolete and outlandish diction, controlling metaphors and SYMBOLs, irony, surprise endings, and repetition and onomatopoeia for effect. Bird, Brown, and Bierce cut their ties with European settings and social situations to tap the energy of the frontier and the menace of a lawless society.

In the 1900s, a shift from the castle settings and medieval trappings of formulaic Gothicism preceded a focus on mystery, eeriness, surreality, subconscious impulses, and terror, as found in a classic example from the American South, the novel *Their Eyes Were Watching God* (1937). Florida-born folklorist Zora Neale Hurston uses Gothic convention to establish the double betrayal of Janie, the protagonist who not only must elude and murder her husband Tea Cake in the throes of rabies, but also must face down black accusers at her trial for murder. AMERICAN GOTHIC produced an enduring set of conventions in the ghost tales of Henry JAMES and Edith WHARTON, the sensational adventures of Louisa May Alcott, Tennessee Williams's plays, the science fiction and fantasy of Ray BRADBURY and H. P. LOVECRAFT, the Southern novels of Harper LEE and Carson McCULLERS, the short and long fiction of Flannery O'CONNOR and William FAULKNER, feminist writings of Charlotte Perkins GILMAN, and popular bodice rippers, Kathleen Woodiwiss's *The Flame and the Flower* (1974) and *The Wolf and the Dove* (1974) and Rosemary Rogers's *Sweet Savage Love* (1974).

Bibliography

Curren, Erik D. "Should Their Eyes Have Been Watching God?: Hurston's Use of Religious Experience and Gothic Horror," *African American Review* 29, no. 1 (spring 1995): 17–25.

Eisenger, Chester E., ed. *Fiction of the Forties*. Chicago: University of Chicago Press, 1963.

Goddu, Teresa A. "Blood Daggers and Lonesome Graveyards: The Gothic and Country Music," *South Atlantic Quarterly* 94, no. 1 (1995): 57–80.

Greeson, Jennifer Rae. "The 'Mysteries and Miseries' of North Carolina: New York City, Urban Gothic Fiction, and *Incidents in the Life of a Slave Girl*," *American Literature* 73, no. 2 (2001): 277–309.

Longueil, Alfred. "The Word 'Gothic' in Eighteenth Century Criticism," *Modern Language Notes* 38 (1923): 459–461.

Mighall, Robert. *A Geography of Victorian Gothic Fiction: Mapping History's Nightmares*. Oxford: Oxford University Press, 1999.

Miller, Robin Feuer. "The Castle in the Gothic Novel," *Nineteenth Century* 9, nos. 1–2 (1984): 3–5, 48.

Sedgwick, Eve Kosofsky. "The Character in the Veil: Imagery of the Surface in the Gothic Novel," *Publica-

tion of the Modern Language Association 96, no. 2 (1981): 255–270.

Smith, A. G. Lloyd. "Gothic Reception," *European Contributions to American Studies* 14, no. 1 (1988): 184–190.

Gothic drama

Less successful than Gothic tales and novels, the Gothic play achieved its moment of glory from excessive staging of horror and the SUPERNATURAL. Gothic theater works displayed reverberations of the Elizabethan and Jacobean tragedy of blood—William Shakespeare's *Titus Andronicus* (ca. 1588) and *Hamlet* (ca. 1599) and John Webster's *The Duchess of Malfi* (ca. 1613), plays laced with murder, INSANITY, and ILLUSION. Gothic dramatists were further influenced by the colonial grotesqueries in Aphra Behn's *Oroonoko* (1688), the German *Sturm und Drang* (storm and stress) movement, and translations of such French successes as J. C. Cross's *Julia of Louvain; or, Monkish Cruelty* (1797) and Thomas Holcroft's MELODRAMA *The Child of Mystery* (1801). Playwrights manipulated settings in charnel houses and feudal halls as adjuncts to SENSATIONALISM, as with Heinrich Wilhelm von Gerstenberg's *Ugolino* (1768), a hellishly violent tragedy based on an episode in Dante's *Inferno* (1321), and the rape and child-killing in Heinrich Leopold Wagner's *The Child Murderess* (1776). Fans thronged theaters expecting to quail at shocking action and rhapsodic emotions, the typical responses to François Baculard d'Arnaud's *Le Comte de Comminges* (The count de Comminges, 1764), which he set at a crypt in a Trappist abbey. D'Arnaud's horror tale was the source of *La Favorite*, a popular opera that Gaetano Donizetti launched in Paris in 1840.

In the dialect play *The Gentle Shepherd* (1790) by the Scottish poet Margaret Turner, the powers of DIABOLISM and sorcery are integral to the pastoral drama, which describes a suspected crone who casts fortunes for a pittance:

> She can o'ercast the night, and cloud the
>   moon,
> And mak the devils obedient to her crune:

> At midnight hours, o'er the kirkyard she
>   raves,
> And howks unchristen'd weans out of their
>   graves;
> Boils up their livers in a warlock's pow:
> Rins withershins about the hemlock low.
>
>   (Turner, 28)

Like the litany of witches' powers in William Shakespeare's *Macbeth* (ca. 1603), the fearful verse drama characterizes sacrilege in uttering prayers seven times backwards, mixing snake and black toad venom, and making voodoo pictures to stick full of pins and cast in the fire.

Along with original plays by recognized Gothic authors, such as Matthew Gregory LEWIS's *The Castle Spectre* (1798), Charles Robert MATURIN's *Bertram* (1816), and playwright Jean Charles Nodier's *Le Vampire* (1820), and with the doom-laden *Schicksalstragödie* (fate tragedy) of the German stage, adaptations of long Gothic fiction were common. Among these were Robert Jephson's *The Count of Narbonne* (1781), based on Horace WALPOLE's THE CASTLE OF OTRANTO, and James Boaden's *The Italian Monk* (1796), taken from Ann RADCLIFFE's THE ITALIAN. Gothic dramas retained a fan base over the next 60 years, a period in which GROTESQUE plays featuring gruesome spectacle gave place to the more genteel, less nerve-wracking melodrama. One example, Joanna BAILLIE's psychological thriller *De Montfort* (1800), a successful tragedy of hate, was a Drury Lane vehicle for actors John Kemble and Sarah Siddons; Siddons played the magnetic but distant beauty Jane de Montfort. That same year, a critical journal, the *Dramatic Censor*, declared the era a crisis in stage history, marked by venality, darkness, and barbarism.

From 1815 to 1840, a raffish lowbrow trend at penny theaters toward extolling such criminal-heroes as Dick Turpin and Jack Sheppard milked the popularity of the NEWGATE NOVEL and the penny dreadful. In 1829, the magazine mogul Douglas William Jerrold composed a working-class hit, *Black-Eyed Susan*, commissioned for the Surrey Theatre in Blackfriars. The scurrilous plot featured a stabbing and condemnation to the gallows. George Dibdin pressed stage horror to extremes with *The String of Pearls; or, The Fiend of Fleet Street* (1847), a staging at the Britannia Theatre of the story of the cannibal barber Sweeney Todd and his trade in human meat pies.

More cerebral fare favored the intellectual playgoer. Within a year of Charlotte BRONTË's publication of JANE EYRE (1847), John Courtney began producing the stage version, *Jane Eyre; or, The Secrets of Thornfield Hall* (1849), the first of nine dramatizations of the novel in England and the United States. The trend toward true-crime drama expanded to include the villainy, emotion, and SUSPENSE of the sensational novel. The French moved away from gentility by developing a unique theater of fear known as the GRAND GUIGNOL. Oscar WILDE blended eroticism, DISSIPATION, and terror in his play SALOMÉ (1893), which sparked controversy in England over the representation of Bible characters in a text featuring necrophilia, suggestions of incest, and murder.

Gothic stage works thrived into the 21st century through subtle recasting of traditional terrors. In 1999, Margaret Edson reprised the MAD SCIENTIST motif by setting her play *Wit* in a sterile, neon-lighted oncology ward. The keen musings and epiphanies of Dr. Vivian Bearing reflect a humanism lacking in Dr. Harvey Kelekian, the staff physician who demeans and discounts her as a guinea pig for tests on a powerful tumor-shrinking drug. His hubris and cold-heartedness allies him with earlier stage villains whom playgoers despised and hissed out of sympathy with their victims.

Bibliography

Anthony, M. Susan. "'Some Deed of Dreadful Note': Productions of Gothic Dramas in the United States, 1790 to 1830," *DAI* (1998): 58–66.

Auerbach, Nina. *Our Vampires, Ourselves.* Chicago: University of Chicago Press, 1995.

Clery, E. J. *Women's Gothic from Clara Reeve to Mary Shelley.* Tavistock, Devon: Northcote House, 2000.

Gamer, Michael. *Romanticism and the Gothic: Genre, Reception, and Canon Formation.* Cambridge: Cambridge University Press, 2000.

Hollingsworth, Keith. *The Newgate Novel, 1830–1847.* Detroit: Wayne State University Press, 1963.

Turner, Margaret. *The Gentle Shepherd: A Scotch Pastoral.* London: T. Bensley, 1790.

Gothic novel

An outgrowth of Jacobean tragedies of blood, such as John Webster's *The Duchess of Malfi* (ca. 1613), and Samuel Richardson's sentimental virgin-testing novel *Pamela* (1740), Gothic fiction depicts through story the deepest human dread. The genre grew into a phenomenon of reader demand for SUPERSTITION and the macabre. The sinister novel profited from a marriage of high ROMANTICISM to pseudo-MEDIEVALISM, a dizzying, at times voluptuous union. From 1765, with Horace WALPOLE's THE CASTLE OF OTRANTO, until 1806, one-third of Britain's published novels were Gothic in style and contained recognizable formulae and predictable elements, notably menace and fear, according to critic Elizabeth R. Napier's *The Failure of the Gothic* (1987).

The early Gothic strain thrived for three decades on a murky, terror-ridden ATMOSPHERE, ominous TONE and MOOD, and vague geographical settings among Gothic structures and ruins, particularly caves, abbeys, towers, castles, crypts, and oratories. Implying duplicity and danger to innocent or naive characters were formulaic elements: grim battlements, sliding panels, underground passageways, shuttered windows, and trapdoors. Readers also enjoyed the vicarious experience of a well-crafted FEMALE GOTHIC story that let women join in adventures and solve mysteries. The plot moved deliberately and without digression, usually to a "happily ever after" conclusion. The passage of a series of suspenseful events toward the rescue of a heroine and/or the redemption of a hero proved more satisfying than did an ordinary uneventful life.

A conservative element in society rejected thrillers by defaming them as prefaces to personal ruin. In June 1797 in an article for *Scots Magazine*, an anonymous opponent of Gothicism alerted society to the dangers of Gothic novels to impressionable, susceptible women, whose "tender emotions, which, not to speak of other possible effects, have been known to betray women into a sudden attachment to persons unworthy of their affection, and thus to hurry them into marriages terminating in their unhappiness" (Stevens, 23). Taken as a left-handed compliment to Gothic novels, the warning suggests that male readers are unimperiled by reading them, but that women, weakened by a predilection for tenderness, lack the emotional strength to withstand a dangerous allure.

The Gothic genre was intricately self-nourishing. As appealing as an adult FAIRY TALE, the style became a fad after Walpole's beginnings. He influenced Gothic master Ann RADCLIFFE, author of *The Romance of the Forest* (1791), the best-selling THE MYSTERIES OF UDOLPHO (1794), and THE ITALIAN (1797). The last, a villainous tale, draws characterization from the evil title figure in Matthew Gregory LEWIS's THE MONK (1796). From Radcliffe and Lewis came new strains of Gothic-permeating romanticism in William Wordsworth's narrative poem *Guilt and Sorrow* (1794), Samuel Taylor COLERIDGE's atmospheric narrative poems "CHRISTABEL" (1816) and the fragmentary vision poem "KUBLA KHAN" (1816), Sir Walter SCOTT's historical novel *Ivanhoe* (1819), John KEATS's "THE EVE OF ST AGNES" (1819), and Lord BYRON's THE GIAOUR (1813) and MANFRED (1817). These reverberations of Gothic style echoed throughout Europe, particularly among French and German imitators. Likewise, the devils, ghosts, and witches of the late 18th-century German *Schauerroman* ("shudder novel") piqued English authors' interest in manipulating terror and the SUPERNATURAL in more inventive ways.

The Gothic novel branched out into ORIENTAL ROMANCE, a direction launched by William BECKFORD's VATHEK (1782) and advanced by the Faustian motif of Charles Robert MATURIN's terror novel MELMOTH THE WANDERER (1820). In 1818, Mary Wollstonecraft SHELLEY took a philosophical approach with the tour-de-force novel FRANKENSTEIN (1818), a horrific study of a MAD SCIENTIST's urge to rival God by creating a life through a patchwork of body parts scavenged from graves and mortuaries. Bram STOKER further developed the MONSTER motif with DRACULA (1897), the quintessential English vampire novel based on an eastern European folk tradition of the living dead. DECADENCE in Gothic art and literature led to extravagance and SENSATIONALISM, the beginning of the end for the original genre as authors Wilkie COLLINS and Mary Elizabeth BRADDON relocated scandal, crime, and horror from distant castles to middle-class homes.

Gothic conventions marked serious literature, notably, Charlotte BRONTË's JANE EYRE (1847),

Emily BRONTË's WUTHERING HEIGHTS (1847), and several of the social novels of Charles DICKENS: OLIVER TWIST (1838), *Barnaby Rudge* (1841), A CHRISTMAS CAROL (1843), BLEAK HOUSE (1853), and GREAT EXPECTATIONS (1861), a coming-of-age novel featuring a spurned bride and her immolation in a tattered wedding dress long after she retreats from the world to ponder a decaying wedding cake. In the United States, the innovative fiction of Robert Montgomery BIRD and Charles Brockden BROWN, the verse stories and novellas of Edgar Allan POE, the novels and tales of Nathaniel HAWTHORNE, the sea romances of Herman MELVILLE, and Western dime novels and paperback romances set AMERICAN GOTHIC in new directions. When examined through the lens of Freudian psychology, the Gothic novel cast light on the relationship between men and women in an ongoing power struggle over patriarchy and oppressive gender roles, an element explored in the ghost stories and novels *The House of Mirth* (1905) and ETHAN FROME (1911) by Edith WHARTON. In the 21st century, Virginia Renfro Ellis recast Gothic conventions in *The Wedding Dress* (2002), a post–Civil War love story tinged with grace and the haunting presence of combat casualties drifting home down country lanes. More robust Gothicism emerged from Michel Faber's neo-Victorian THE CRIMSON PETAL AND THE WHITE (2002) and Dan Brown's reprise of ILLUMINATI NOVELS in THE DA VINCI CODE (2003).

Bibliography

Napier, Elizabeth R. *The Failure of the Gothic.* Oxford: Oxford University Press, 1987.

Punter, David, ed. *The Literature of Terror,* vol. 1, 2nd ed. London: Longman, 1996.

Stevens, David. *The Gothic Tradition.* Cambridge: Cambridge University Press, 2000.

Gothic revival

Literary historians refer to various Gothic revivals, an inexact term applied to waves of Gothicism in philosophy, art, architecture, and literature. Late 17th-century and early 18th-century writers who stressed the value of vision and imagination set the stage for a Gothic upsurge in literature. Joseph

Addison's essay series in the *Spectator*, titled *On the Pleasures of the Imagination* (1712), popularized the concept of mental stimulation through the picturesque; from the philosopher George Berkeley came *An Essay Towards a New Theory of Vision* (1732), a summation of the effects of color and shape on the senses. Simultaneously, antiquarian interests encouraged the display of burnished armor, illuminated texts, tapestry, religious artifacts, carved wood, and coin collections on particular historic eras and subjects, particularly classical Greece and Rome, Byzantium, and the European Middle Ages. The artists Claude Lorrain, Nicolas Poussin, and Salvator Rosa chose MELANCHOLY ruins and landscapes as subjects for their paintings. In architecture, a Gothic revival took shape in medieval ornamentation on mid-18th-century buildings, particularly in the United States. Fiction produced rumblings of Gothicism in Tobias SMOLLETT's crime MELODRAMA, *The Adventures of FERDINAND COUNT FATHOM* (1753).

By the 1760s, Gothicism spilled full-force into literature with a renewed interest in MEDIEVALISM. Fiction writer Horace WALPOLE, author of the classic THE CASTLE OF OTRANTO (1765), created his own Gothic getaway at Strawberry Hill, Twickenham, which he had begun building in 1753. In literature, the Gothic mode influenced four divisions: A period of artificial ruins and derivative medievalism dominated by Thomas Percy's *Reliques of English Poetry* (1765), a collection of medieval verse that he revised. The initial interest preceded the second stage, a romantic revival, marked by the chivalric ballads of Sir Walter SCOTT and an outpouring of popular sensational fiction exploited by the MINERVA PRESS, which pirated the Jacobean tragedy of blood, German romances and the German *Kriminalgeschichte* (criminal history), translations of Abbé PRÉVOST's *MANON LESCAUT* (1731), and the *frénétique* French novels of Baculard d'Arnaud. Contributing original English fiction were Sophia LEE, author of *The Recess* (1785), and Charlotte SMITH's *The Old Manor House* (1793).

After peaking in 1810 and collapsing a decade later, the demand for Gothic literature resurged in a third stage of Gothic revival. It was an English national Gothic, an impetus to historian Thomas Carlyle's *Past and Present* (1843). The last stage was an eclectic period that saw the paintings and writings of the PRE-RAPHAELITE BROTHERHOOD, an English translation of Victor Hugo's *Notre-Dame de Paris* (1831; *The Hunchback of Notre-Dame*, 1834), the art criticism of John Ruskin in *Stones of Venice* (1851, 1853), and the architectural triumphs of Sir Charles Barry, chief architect of the British Houses of Parliament, and of George Gilbert Scott, builder of the churches of St. Agnes, Kennington, and All Hallows, Southwark.

Bibliography

Hennelly, Mark M. "Framing the Gothic: From Pillar to Post-Structuralism," *College Literature* 28, no. 3 (fall 2001): 68.

Norton, Rictor, ed. *Gothic Readings: The First Wave, 1764–1840*. London: Leicester University Press, 2000.

Whyte, William. "An Architect of Promise: George Gilbert Scott (1839–1897) and the Late Gothic Revival," *English Historical Review* 118, no. 476 (April 2003): 542–543.

Gothic setting

Gothic settings provide an allegorical and psychological extension to the human character and behavior in Gothic literature, as displayed in the hold of a prison hulk in New York Harbor in Philip FRENEAU's poem *The British Prison-Ship* (1781), the surgical suite of the MAD SCIENTIST in Arthur Lewellyn Jones-Machen's *The Great God Pan* (1894), the ARABESQUE tracery and lichened walls of Baskerville Hall in Sir Arthur Conan DOYLE's *THE HOUND OF THE BASKERVILLES* (1902), the trapdoors and subterranean retreats of master and slave in Edward Sorensen's Australian Gothic novel *The Squatter's Ward* (1919), the ravenous house in Robert Marasco's neo-Gothic novel *Burnt Offerings* (1973), and the intriguing floor plan and mirrored passages in Umberto ECO's *The Name of the Rose* (1980). As the critic Anne Williams explains in *Art of Darkness: A Poetics of Gothic* (1995), Gothic draws on "the (fantasy) epitome of that distant time and place, a vast, mysterious structure built at a time benighted as well as 'beknighted,' when the population believed in ghosts and witches and superstitions of all kinds" (Williams, 20). Intersecting past with present, dark and sinister dwellings and edifices surrounded by ivy, shrubbery, or encroaching wolds contribute to SECRECY, MYSTERY, CLAUSTROPHOBIA, and the medieval appeal of lapsed care, default, or ruin of buildings that once were well kept and serviceable, as with the dusty museum in H. G. WELLS's *The Time Machine* (1895) and the monstrous castle in Mervyn PEAKE's Gormenghast trilogy. In Nathaniel HAWTHORNE's AMERICAN GOTHIC, trees reach inward to cloak forest scenes and windows and doors, implying a need to conceal a terrible sin or to screen an unspoken evil. In urban Gothic, cold steel girders and glass replace the 18th-century castle with an updated authoritarian menace, as found in Margaret Edson's Pulitzer Prize–winning play *Wit* (1999), which takes place in the boxed-in oncology ward of a modern hospital.

The creator of the first Gothic setting was Horace WALPOLE, who placed *THE CASTLE OF OTRANTO* (1765) in an evocative medieval edifice equipped with rusted hinges, a trapdoor, a walking portrait, and lamps that flicker out at tense moments in the action. Ann RADCLIFFE, the fount of Gothic romanticism, exploited the Gothic mode in the setting of her classic novel *THE MYSTERIES OF UDOLPHO* (1794). As a NAIF from the Pyrenees, Emily ST. AUBERT, approaches the prison her uncle has in store for her, she witnesses an engulfing MELANCHOLY in decrepit gray stone shadowed in purple and in the mist rising from Italy's Apennine Mountains. The building is so dominating that it appears to suck in light from the setting sun and issue a somber duskiness to the whole exterior. In Emily's view, the personified building greets her with a frown.

Radcliffe's influence took hold of the Gothic market within months, spawning a host of imitations. Five years later, novelist Mary Charlton, a bestselling author for MINERVA PRESS, summarized the predictability of Radcliffean Gothic settings. In commentary in *Rosella; or, Modern Occurrences* (1799), the author states the importance of "pale moons, blue mists, gliding figures, hollow sighs, shaking tapestry, reverberating voices, nodding pictures, long corridors, deserted west towers, north towers, and south towers, ruined chapels, suspicious vaults, damp charnel-houses, great clocks

striking twelve, wood embers expiring, dying lamps, and total darkness" (Tarr, 6). Her poetic summary blends two essentials of evocative place: human architecture and the embellishments of NATURE.

In Charles Robert MATURIN's terror novel *Melmoth the Wanderer* (1820), darkness and foul weather combine with a deteriorated structure to create Gothic ATMOSPHERE. Melmoth, looking out the window at the cheerless garden of his uncle's home in Wicklow, allies the deceased miser with dwarfed and leafless greenery and a profusion of nettles and weeds that spreads over the graveyard. Indoors, the view is no more uplifting in the rust, dirt, and cracked plaster that surround him and the rump-sprung chairs with drooping stuffing and the smoky mantle that offer little comfort.

Later Gothic fiction increased the importance of setting, notably, Emily BRONTË's cheerless manse in *WUTHERING HEIGHTS* (1847), in which the moors and children reared in the wild outdoors refuse to be compatible with society. When the OUTSIDER Lockwood arrives, he glimpses "atmospheric tumult": "Indeed one may guess the power of the north wind blowing over the edge, by the excessive slant of a few stunted firs at the edge of the house; and by a range of gaunt thorns all stretching their limbs one way, as if craving alms of the sun" (Brontë, 10). In the interior, he finds a family room overwhelmed by an immense fireplace ranked by pewter dishes. Drinking vessels fill a dresser that reaches to the roof, where the staff stores legs of beef, ham, and mutton. Along the chimney, Lockwood detects menace in old rifles and pistols.

In *DRACULA* (1897), Bram STOKER further embroidered Gothic setting by taking his lordly vampire, Count DRACULA, from a castle in Transylvania and the hospital of St. Joseph and Ste. Mary in Budapest to a London insane asylum and a bucolic Yorkshire landscape outside Whitby. The shift in locales offers readers inferences about the nature of innocence hunted by an evil needing new sources of nourishment from human blood. For the guest's bedchamber, the author appears to have reset the boudoir from John KEATS's "THE EVE OF ST. AGNES" (1819). In introducing the old monastery, Stoker pays tribute to claustrophobic atmosphere in the work of the Scottish historical novelist Sir Walter SCOTT: "Right over the town is the ruin of Whitby

Abbey, which was sacked by the Danes, and which is the scene of part of *Marmion,* where the girl was built up in the wall" (Stoker, 66). The parallel allusions to violence reflect the vampire's sacking of Englishwomen and the demise of Lucy Westenra, the maiden whom Dracula despoils with his fiendish bite.

Bibliography

Brontë, Emily. *Wuthering Heights.* New York: New American Library, 1959.

Stoker, Bram. *Dracula.* New York: Bantam Books, 1981.

Tarr, Mary Muriel. *Catholicism in Gothic Fiction: A Study of the Nature and Function of Catholic Materials in Gothic Fiction in England (1762–1820).* Washington, D.C.: Catholic University of America Press, 1946.

Tuan, Yi-Fu. *Landscapes of Fear.* New York: Pantheon Books, 1979.

Williams, Anne. *Art of Darkness: A Poetics of Gothic.* Chicago: University of Chicago Press, 1995.

governess

The naive daughter of a rural vicar, the unnamed governess in Henry JAMES's ghost novella THE TURN OF THE SCREW (1898) leads herself into an emotional cataclysm by letting imagination control reason. From the time she is hired to educate the children at BLY HOUSE, she describes impressions of people and setting in glowing extremes. She envisions "a castle of romance inhabited by a rosy sprite, such a place as would somehow, for diversion of the young idea, take all colour out of storybooks and fairy-tales. Wasn't it just a storybook over which I had fallen a-doze and a-dream?" (James, 19). The absence of mature reflection leaves her vulnerable to letdowns, particularly in her evaluation of the housekeeper and children, Flora and Miles. After the governess encounters the ghosts of the valet Peter Quint and Miss Jessel, the previous governess, she concludes that the house is clouded by SECRECY. Overconfident of her ability to counter the fleeting visions, she presumes that evil stalks her charges. Further confusing the governess is a surmise that the children are less innocent of corruption than she initially presumed.

James engineers alienation in his self-deceptive protagonist, an UNRELIABLE NARRATOR who begins to see herself as the OUTSIDER at Bly. With a familiar Gothic strategy, a chill wind and extinguished candle, the author removes external aid from the governess, leaving her literally in the dark. The concluding scene, in which the governess shields Miles from the phantom valet at the window, results in the boy's death from heart failure. The lack of closure to James's story leaves the reader to decide whether the governess has seen the apparitions or whether her lack-logic investigation of events has triggered hysterical delusions. Evidence points equally to two conclusions: that her smothering and terrifying of a 10-year-old leads to the stilling of his heart or that her exorcism of the spectral Peter Quint costs Miles his life.

Bibliography

Sawyer, Richard. "What's Your Title?—'The Turn of the Screw,'" *Studies in Short Fiction* 30, no. 1 (winter 1993): 53–61.

Stipe, Stormy. "The Ghosts of Henry James," *Biblio* (September 1998): 16.

Walker, Steven F. "James's 'The Turn of the Screw,'" *Explicator* 61, no. 2 (winter 2003): 94–96.

Grand Guignol

In late 19th-century France, GOTHIC DRAMA took bizarre turns with puppet shows of the Théâtre du Grand Guignol, a Parisian venue for brief horrific plays and cabaret shows focusing on titillating barbarism, rape, suicide, SADISM, and murder. Named for a marionette created in Lyons, the subset of Gothic theater got its start in 1897 when Oscar Méténier, secretary to the police commissioner of Paris, opened the first adult puppet theater in Montmartre. Presentations featured MAD SCIENTISTS, excessive vengeance tales, decapitations, throttlings, and hyperbolic DELUSION and madness. Playwrights selected materials for the earliest stage works from police files and from the best of Gothic writings, including the works of André de Lorde, Guy de MAUPASSANT, and Oscar WILDE. The worst of stage SENSATIONALISM caused some playgoers to hyperventilate, vomit, and flee the premises.

The theater of fear was contemporaneous with the surreal tendencies and buffoonish grotesquery of Alfred Jarry's stage farce *Ubu Roi* (*King*

Ubu, 1896), a travesty of traditional tragedy. By 1908, public obsession with Jack the Ripper preceded the importation of the Grand Guignol to England, where it survived for over a half-century. A later theatrical development, Antonin Artaud's theatre of cruelty of the 1930s, gave performances of shocking spectacles, including Artaud's *Les Cenci* (1935) and Peter Weiss's *The Persecution and Assassination of Marat as Performed by the Inmates of the Asylum of Charenton under the Direction of the Marquis de Sade* (1964). Flourishing in North America and, to a lesser degree, in Britain, the Grand Guignol remained in vogue into the 1960s and influenced later works, including Joyce Carol OATES's short story "Madison at Guignol" (2002), which concludes with slashings and the rape of a woman with the stiletto heel of a shoe.

Bibliography

Gordon, Mel, ed. *The Grand Guignol: Theatre of Fear and Terror*. New York: DaCapo, 1997.

Oates, Joyce Carol. "Madison at Guignol," *Kenyon Review* 24, no. 1 (winter 2002): 43–50.

graveyard verse

A morbid literary phenomenon of the early 1700s, graveyard poetry was a precursor to the bitter prophecies, ghostly visitations, dark charnel houses, sepulchral settings, bereavement, and nocturnal death obsessions of Gothic literature, particularly the works of Ann RADCLIFFE and Matthew Gregory LEWIS. By exalting obscurity, MYSTERY, mutability, and free-flowing emotion and passion, the high ROMANTICISM of funereal verse provided a cathartic release to normal human stirrings of marvel, longing and curiosity, and dread. These meditative, introspective works posed a therapeutic easing of tension that Anna Laetitia BARBAULD exalts in "On the Pleasure Derived from Objects of Terror" (1773).

Developing apart from neoclassicism with its artificial predictability and control, the graveyard school of funereal elegies was a disparate movement that delighted in the themes of mortality and evanescence and a subjective contemplation of funerary ritual and grave processionals. The writers' self-indulgent obsessions with solitude, MELANCHOLY, and mortality reproached neoclassic rationalism, the formal strictures that bound imagination and innovation. Preceded by John Donne's holy sonnets of the early 17th century and translations of German dramatist and poet Andreas Gryphius's *Kirch-hof Gedanchen* (Graveyard thoughts, ca. 1650), British graveyard poets produced a recognizable canon: Irish poet Thomas Parnell's "A Night Piece on Death" (1721), Scottish poet Robert Blair's "The Grave" (1743), and Edward Young's rhapsodic "Night-Thoughts" (1742) and "Welcome Death!" (1743), two favorites of Charlotte BRONTË and Ann YEARSLEY. The latter poem exercises the PATHETIC FALLACY with its morbid self-absorption in the speaker's release from earthly fetters and disease. These poems, along with James Hervey's *Meditations among the Tombs* (1745–47), William Taylor Collins's "Ode to Fear" (1741) and "Ode to Evening" (1746), and Thomas Warton's *On the Pleasures of Melancholy* (1747), anticipate the pinnacle of the genre, Thomas Gray's gently pensive "ELEGY WRITTEN IN A COUNTRY CHURCHYARD" (1751). A controlled masterpiece of reflection on social status, Gray's "Elegy" initiated a sheaf of imitative poems on mortality. Additional contributions to the canon include the Reverend Beilby Porteus's "Death: A Poetical Essay" (1759) and William Dodd's multistage *Thoughts in Prison* (1777).

In the late 18th century, the graveyard vogue spread to France, Holland, Germany, Sweden, and the Americas. Beginning in the United States, the graveyard branch of Gothic literature fueled a uniquely American view of death. The Huguenot poet Philip FRENEAU, a veteran of the American Revolution, produced two original romantic works, "THE HOUSE OF NIGHT" (1799) and "To the Memory" (1781), an ode to the fallen of a battle fought at Eutaw Springs, South Carolina. He pursued the harsh elements of slavery in "To Sir Toby" (1792) and pondered the demise of Native Americans in two elegies, "The Dying Indian" (1784) and "The Indian Burying Ground" (1788). The former, dedicated to Tomo-Chequi, draws on the pathetic fallacy for NATURE's response to loss:

> No spongy fruits from verdant trees depend,
>   But sickly orchards there
>   Do fruits as sickly bear,

And apples a consumptive visage shew,
And withered hangs the hurtle-berry blue.
                                    (Freneau, 244)

Freneau looked inward for "The British Prison Ship" (1781), a Gothic text filled with his bitterness and horror at his inhumane treatment in the Tory hulks. The journalist and poet William Cullen BRYANT brought the American graveyard movement to its height in "THANATOPSIS" (1817), a beloved and oft-cited death poem. At its heart lies the seriousness and tight-lipped resolution of New England Puritanism.

Graveyard elements did not wither with the waning of romanticism, but gravitated to more personal musings on death-bound humanity, such as Felicia Hemans's reflective poems "England's Dead" (1826) and "A Spirit's Return" (1830). In England, Dante Gabriel Rossetti, a leader of the PRE-RAPHAELITE BROTHERHOOD in the mid-19th century, followed the tenets of graveyard verse in "My Sister's Sleep" (1847), a childhood memory of a deathbed watch. His sister, Christina ROSSETTI, produced a dreamy, nonthreatening vision of tomb existence in "Song" (1848). American poetaster Julia Ann Davis Moore, the Sweet Singer of Michigan, pushed mourners' verse to sentimental extremes with maudlin elegies collected in *The Sentimental Song Book* (1876), an anthology so weepy, so filled with apostrophes to death and eulogies of young victims, that it churned the bile of Mark Twain. In token of her obituary ditties on seizures and choking, terminal ailments, fires and drownings, train wrecks, and epidemic disease, he used Moore as the model for Emmeline Grangerford, the caricatured occasional poet who cranks out dolorous funeral poems in *Huckleberry Finn* (1884). Still peeved at her ludicrous verse 13 years later, Twain ridiculed Moore by name in *Following the Equator* (1897).

In 1874, the English poet James Thomson used graveyard style for personal ends when he composed *The City of Dreadful Night*, a dreary paean to his seven years of depression, alcoholism, and supporting himself with hack writing. Bereft of hope, he pictures a diseased outlook in settings that offer neither light nor uplift:

What men are they who haunt these fatal
    glooms,
And fill their living mouths with dust of
    death,
And make their habitations in the tombs,
And breathe eternal sighs with mortal
    breath,
And pierce life's pleasant veil of various
    error
To reach that void of darkness and old terror
Wherein expire the lamps of hope and faith?
                                    (Thomson, 10)

He collected this and other of his sepulchral verse in *The City of Dreadful Night, and Other Poems* (1880), published two years before his death from extensive DISSIPATION.

Early in the 20th century, Thomas Henry MacDermot, Jamaica's poet laureate and editor of the *Jamaica Times*, perpetuated the Gothic dimensions of graveyard verse. Apart from his journalistic career, he published under his pen name Tom Redcam—his last name spelled backwards. In Columbus's soliloquy from the narrative folk play *San Gloria* (1920), the poet describes the "dark foreboding" of the Genoan navigator's arrival in San Gloria Bay, Jamaica, in 1503. The melancholy air captures Columbus's fear that he will die on Jamaica and lie entombed beneath an island surface teeming with life. More than death, he fears that his voyages will sink into oblivion. The moody obsessions of graveyard verse found a new voice in Sylvia Plath, who contemplated the decay and reek of the corpse in "Lady Lazarus" (1963) and death's relentless search for new prey in "Fever 103°" (1965), published two years after her suicide. To honor Plath, her friend and contemporary Anne Sexton composed a funereal ode, "Sylvia's Death" (1963), which echoes the modes and voicing of traditional graveyard verse.

Bibliography

Colvin, Sarah. "Andreas Gryphius: A Modern Perspective," *Journal of European Studies* 24, no. 94 (June 1994): 191–192.

Freneau, Philip. *The Poems of Philip Freneau*, vol. 2. Princeton, N.J.: The University Library, 1903.

Ramchand, Kenneth. *The West Indian Novel and Its Background*. New York: Barnes & Noble, 1970.

Stevens, David. *The Gothic Tradition*. Cambridge: Cambridge University Press, 2000.

Thomson, James. *The City of Dreadful Night and Other Poems*. London: Watts, 1934.

Great Expectations
Charles Dickens
(1861)

Influenced by the NEWGATE NOVEL, fiction writer Charles DICKENS produced an enduring bildungsroman with his 13th novel, *Great Expectations*. As England developed into the world's richest and most progressive nation, he refused to overlook its accumulated human failings. For verisimilitude, he set the fictional story in a real place and period in history, the London of the mid-1800s, when the empire projected great expectations for investors. He introduced the novel on December 1, 1860, in the first of 36 installments in the weekly *All the Year Round*, carrying readers into graphic scenes in a lapsed mansion, a grimy blacksmithy, a limekiln, a rowboat on the Thames, and a deathbed scene in a prison infirmary. The story spun out to its conclusion on August 3, 1861, rapidly reviving the magazine's readership.

To establish a menacing atmosphere, Dickens opens his novel in sinister Gothic surroundings—a mist-hung cemetery overgrown with nettles at Woolwich Marsh, an ague-ridden fen at the estuary of Gravesend, England. The unpromising setting suits young Pip's visit to the graves of his parents and five of their six sons, who lie grouped in a family plot. Pip, a NAIF cast as a vulnerable seedling and survivor, looks over the leaden river at an ominous evening sky and back to the boggy turf surrounded by dikes, a ditch, mounds, and the battery at Cliffe Creek. Dickens introduces the controlling motif of VIOLENCE and criminality by having the churchyard face a scaffold on which authorities hanged a pirate. In period style, they left the executed man to rot in chains as a warning of the fate awaiting budding criminals.

Within his realistic study of education and career in Victorian England, Dickens introduces a number of Gothic elements, including the reclamation of a fleeing convict, Abel Magwitch, to the hulks, derelict ships anchored offshore as floating prisons. During a rise in the police war on crime, the hulks served England's hard-pressed penitentiaries as makeshift cell space. Within the merciless legal system, the chains that bind Abel and other prisoners in place suggest the implacable ties between felons and their former lives. Dickens used this same motif in the opening scene of A CHRISTMAS CAROL (1843), in which Jacob Marley drags the SYMBOLs of his misspent life on chains attached to his ghostly form. Upon Abel's apprehension on Christmas Day for escaping the hulks, Pip looks toward the cheerless prison ship with no inkling of how the links that fetter the convict will reach out and connect Pip irrevocably to the escapee he feeds on Christmas Eve.

Dickens's alliance with popular magazines disposed him toward manipulating reader reaction to serialized fiction through harsh ATMOSPHERE, grim TONE, and mounting SUSPENSE. From the opening scene, bleakness of weather on the foggy morn anticipates Pip's clouded hopes for the future, the harrowing life of the convict, and the moral ambiguity of requiring payment of a debt to society in the crudely inadequate hulks. Contributing to Gothic intensity is the convict's mock-serious threat that if Pip disobeys, "your heart and your liver shall be tore out, roasted and ate" (Dickens, 836).

The author indicates that despair is not limited to country or city. After Pip ventures to London to be educated, he encounters the worst of the city's Gothic reality—Newgate Prison in Cheapside, the gallows, public whipping post, and the debtors' door, through which the condemned pass to their executions. In a depressing street suited to the impersonal mechanics of Victorian law and justice, Pip glimpses the attorney Jaggers's office, outfitted with a chair of black horsehair tacked with brass nailheads like a coffin, a rusted pistol, scabbarded sword, and odd-shaped parcels containing two death masks of deceased clients, "faces peculiarly swollen and twitchy about the nose" (*ibid.*, 928). Dickens populates the outer office with suspicious clients fidgeting as they await legal advice. Despite a forbidding demeanor, Jaggers accepts felons and the dregs of society as clients. An ambiguous shadow figure who conceals his motives and intent, the attorney possesses courtroom secrets that he confides in small bits to Pip.

By fooling both Pip and the reader into believing that the opportunity to achieve great expectations comes from Miss HAVISHAM, a Gravesend brewery heiress, Dickens readies his audience for a grand unveiling of the convict in new form—Abel Magwitch, returned from New South Wales as a successful stockman. The author's love of showmanship is evident in the theatrical stormy-night meeting between Pip and the stranger in chapter 39, which Dickens orchestrates with a fleeting mental image of Pip's sister as a ghost. By lifted lamp, Pip peers over a stair rail toward the sound of footsteps. In the small circle of light, reality yanks him out of boyish dreams by revealing the grizzled sea voyager, who enters the apartment and impacts Pip's adult life and fortunes.

Beginning with Abel's faults, the novel surveys the nature of criminality in a panoply of felons. Molly, the 40-year-old housekeeper at Jaggers's Soho residence, is the silent servant with strong hands and scarred wrists whom the author compares to the witches in the opening scene of Shakespeare's *Macbeth* (ca. 1603). Jaggers saved her from execution for strangling a woman by convincing the court that Molly was too weak to throttle so large a victim. Hidden in Molly's past is the abandonment of her child, Estella, sired by Abel and adopted by Miss Havisham during Molly's trial, the new mother intended to protect Estella from the unsavory elements in her birth parents' lives.

Dickens extends the Gothic collection of rogues with a variety of crimes and misdemeanors. A more devious manipulator and blackmailer, Compeyson, is a handsome, glib con artist who abuses his wife, Sally; ridicules his dying boarder, Arthur Havisham, for visions of a ghost; and defrauds Arthur's sister, Miss Havisham, whom Compeyson falsely promised to marry with a cold indifference to her sufferings and humiliation. The least attractive of felons is Dolge Orlick, a strong, but morose shophand who suits the element of SECRECY that enfolds the plot. Slouching and envious, he nurses spite toward Pip and assaults Uncle Pumblechook and Pip's sister, Mrs. Joe. As an accomplice of Compeyson, Orlick lures Pip to the lime kiln in a foiled murder plot, one of the novel's many startling moments.

On the domestic level, Dickens depicts another form of criminality in Bentley Drummle, an odd-looking, glowering malcontent cheated of a baronetcy. He represents the stereotypical English second-rater who is doomed to live on the edge of the aristocracy while another relative inherits money and title. For obvious reasons, Drummle seems perpetually out of sorts. After winning a trophy bride, he mistreats her and dies ignobly by abusing a horse that kicks him to death. The demise is typical of Dickens's assignment of appropriate deaths to VILLAINs.

The reception of *Great Expectations* was voluminous and ongoing as it quickly rose to a world classic. In 1871, playwright W. S. Gilbert adapted it for the London stage and cast actress Adah Isaacs Menken in a breeches role as Pip. In 1939, Barbara Field collaborated with Alec Guinness in a version in which Guinness played Herbert Pocket. A 1917 silent movie version preceded Gladys Unger's 1935 screenplay for Universal Pictures, which featured Jane Wyatt as Estella and Phillips Holmes as Pip. In 1946, a popular British cinema version succeeded over past attempts at filming, largely through David Lean's direction and the acting talents of John Mills as Pip and Jean Simmons as the austere and distant Estella. A musical MELODRAMA, Dominick Argento's *Miss Havisham's Fire* (1979), opened at the New York City Opera as a vehicle for diva Beverly Sills, who, at the height of her career, relished a Gothic mad scene.

Bibliography

Braun, William R. "Rekindling Miss Havisham's Fire," *Opera News* 65, no. 12 (June 2001): 30.

Craig, Amanda. "On Charles Dickens's Great Expectations," *New Statesman*, 131, no. 4,616 (December 2, 2002): 51–52.

Dickens, Charles. *Great Expectations*, in vol. 2 of *The Annotated Dickens*, ed. by Edward Guiliano and Philip Collins. New York: Clarkson N. Potter, 1986.

Green, William Child
(fl. 1820s–1830s)

A minor 19th-century British writer, William Child Green acquired a fan base for his brand of

STORYTELLING in a series of Gothic thrillers, one of which invigorated the English Gothic market during a downturn in reader interest. Little is known of his background; some clues suggest that he was born in Scotland. A reader of Lord BYRON, Charles Robert MATURIN, Matthew Gregory LEWIS, Sir Walter SCOTT, and Ann RADCLIFFE, he began writing Gothic lore with "Secrets of Cabalism; or, Ravenstone and Alice of Huntingdon" (ca. 1819), a tale of a voluptuous witch that Green published in a Christmas journal. His early novels, *The Maniac of the Desert* (1821) and *The Prophecy of Duncannon; or, The Dwarf and the Seer* (1824), display his study of LEGEND and FOLKLORE. He is best known for *The Abbot of Montserrat; or, The Pool of Blood* (1826), a sister MYSTERY and rape tale in which a gang of banditti besiege a Catalonian abbey. A pair of NAIFs, Fernandez de Leon and Isabel de Gracey, elope to the monastery, where monks yield to the extortion of Roldan, a robber chief. Green's focus on institutional corruption and outlawry created a demand at CIRCULATING LIBRARIES.

Influenced by the frenzied pacing of the German *Schaurroman* ("shudder novel") and the extreme VIOLENCE in a religious setting found in Lewis's THE MONK (1796), Green created a story exploiting an unlikely tangle of Gothic motifs. His plot juggles the lustful monk Obando's selling his soul to the demon Zatanai, the rescue of Isabel from potential rape, a hand-to-hand knife fight, and a catastrophic convent fire. Green invokes the Inquisition as Obando's accuser and reprises the familiar Faustian death scene in which Obando tumbles to his doom, leaving the happy couple to marry with the blessings of Fernandez's parents. In 1832, Green published *The Algerines; or, The Twins of Naples*, a vigorous Oriental tale based on piracy headquartered in Algiers.

Bibliography

Blakey, Dorothy. *The Minerva Press, 1790–1820.* London: Oxford University Press, 1939.

Green, William Child. *The Abbot of Montserrat; or, The Pool of Blood,* 2 vols. New York: Arno Press, 1977.

Summers, Montague. *The Gothic Quest: A History of the Gothic Novel.* London: Fortune Press, 1969.

Grimm, Jakob
(1785–1863) and
Grimm, Wilhelm
(1786–1859)

The scholarly brothers Jacob and Wilhelm Grimm teamed to collect and compose a hallmark of world FOLKLORE, the three-volume *Kinder- und Hausmärchen* (Children's and household tales), later known as *Grimms' Fairy Tales* (1812, 1815, 1822). Incidents of confinement, ostracism and verbal abuse, evil spells and enchantments, misogyny, cannibalism, and other gruesome perils to life and happiness permeate the most memorable of their Germanic fantasies—"Cinderella," "The Bremen Town Musicians," "The Elves and the Shoemaker," "Rapunzel," and the dark, menacing tales "Hansel and Gretel," "Snow White," "The Juniper Tree," and "Rumplestiltskin." The Grimm brothers made no effort to spare young readers excessive horror. In one of their most Gothic fables, "The Mouse, the Bird, and the Sausage," VIOLENCE claims the lives of two of the triad, the mouse and sausage, leaving the bird forlorn and fearful until its sudden death. In a *pourquoi* story, "The Straw, the Coal, and the Bean," the authors kill off two of the trio by burning and drowning. In 1853, Gothic artist and redactor George CRUIKSHANK earned a scolding from critic Charles DICKENS with "Frauds on the Fairies," an essay in *Household Words,* for revisions to the original stories in a new edition of *Grimms' Fairy Tales.*

The influence of Gothic scenarios from Grimms' FAIRY TALEs received the opprobrium of 20th-century children's reading specialists and extensive reevaluation by feminist critics, who recognize folkloric strands in GOTHIC FICTION. An understanding of the Cinderella figure aids in the analysis of Charlotte BRONTË's JANE EYRE (1847), in which an underprivileged orphan throws off the social and domestic shackles of her Aunt Sarah Reed at GATESHEAD HALL. After departing, Jane actualizes self and talents. Allusions to "BEAUTY AND THE BEAST" and "Bluebeard's Castle" color Jane's escape from the MELANCHOLY and beastliness of her chastened lover, Edward ROCHESTER, and from the bigamous marriage that he offers. The Grimms' German stories also inspired the image of the powerless female in French author Gaston LEROUX's complex opera tale *Le Fantôme de l'Opéra*

(*THE PHANTOM OF THE OPERA*, 1910). In 1993, Canadian Gothic novelist Margaret ATWOOD reset the Grimm brothers' cannibalistic tale "The Robber Bridegroom" as *The Robber Bride*, a reexamination of women's plight to reveal self-rescue as an option.

Bibliography

Clarke, Michael M. "Brontë's Jane Eyre and the Grimms' Cinderella," *Studies in English Literature, 1500–1900* 40, no. 4 (autumn 2000): 695.

Hempen, Daniela. "Bluebeard's Female Helper: The Ambiguous Role of the Strange Old Woman in the Grimms' 'Castle of Murder' and 'The Robber Bridegroom,'" *Folklore* 108 (1997): 45–48.

Lüth, Max. *European Folktale: Form and Nature*. Bloomington: Indiana University Press, 1982.

Tatar, Maria. *The Hard Facts of the Grimms' Fairy Tales*. Princeton, N.J.: Princeton University Press, 1987.

Thum, Maureen. "Feminist or Anti-feminist? Gender-coded Role Models in the Tales Contributed by Dorothea Viehmann to the Grimm Brothers' 'Kinder- und Hausmärchen,'" *Germanic Review* 68, no. 1 (winter 1993): 11–31.

grotesque

A stylistic enhancement of Gothic literature, the term names a perverse intertwining of ludicrous, estranged beings or comic events and their tragic outcomes, as with the pervasive mythic figure of LA LLORONA from Central American FOLKLORE and incongruities in the post–World War II fiction of Mervyn PEAKE, the drama of Swiss playwright Friedrich Dürrenmatt, and in the rural tales of English Gothic master Alfred Edgar Coppard, particularly the story of multiple amputations in a rodent and a woman in "Arabesque: The Mouse" (1920). With similar motifs, Dürrenmatt describes a multiple amputee in the absurd drama *Der Besuch der Alten Dame* (*The Visit*, 1956). Set in a German-speaking hamlet, the play covers the visit of the wealthy Madame Zachanassian, who suffered numerous losses in a plane crash in Afghanistan. The Gothic twists of her prostheses and bearers of her sedan chair, whom she ordered castrated and blinded, precede the sacrifice of her former lover, Alfred, whom she wants executed for abandoning her unborn child. Like a tourist packing souvenirs, the matron ends the play by collecting Alfred's corpse in a coffin and pressing on to the seacoast spa at Capri.

A stirring application of the tragic grotesque occurs in children's literature—the entrapment and display of a pathetic dwarf child removed from a feral setting and forced to entertain royalty in Oscar WILDE's sad FAIRY TALE "The Birthday of the Infanta" (1888). Unaware of his ugliness, the hunchbacked dwarf witnesses his monstrous body and wry limbs in a mirror, collapses, and dies. The peevish princess, annoyed that her fantastic live toy will never return, demands that future royal playmates "have no hearts," a portentous command that reveals the twisted, unloving heart within her (Wilde, 263).

The term *grotesque* derives from the Italian *grotte* (caves) and entered English as a descriptor of imaginative and incongruous human and animal shapes and unnatural physical and sexual images in sculpture. Horace WALPOLE drew on the grotesque characters from William Shakespeare's plays for his Gothic vision in THE CASTLE OF OTRANTO (1765), the first Gothic romance. Introduced as a literary term in the 1700s, the grotesque involves the elevation or obsessive mention of lurid, unwholesome, estranged, aberrant, or terrifying details, such as caricatures of ogreish schoolmasters and pulpit ministers in Charles DICKENS's novels, the misshapen herbalist and failed husband Roger Chillingworth in Nathaniel HAWTHORNE's THE SCARLET LETTER (1850), and the oddities in the Titus Groan series by the English writer Mervyn PEAKE. In a mid-19th-century English model, Christina ROSSETTI's dark narrative poem THE GOBLIN MARKET (1862), diminutive creatures display "wry faces, demure grimaces, cat-like and rat-like, ratel and wombat-like" as they peer into the eyes of Laura, the hapless protagonist (Rossetti, 3).

Of particular repugnance are Edgar Allan POE's fetid plague victims in the puzzling "King Pest the First: A Tale Containing an Allegory" (1835), the victim's offensive eyeball in "THE TELL-TALE HEART" (1843), and the crippled, murderous jester and his diminutive mate Trippetta in "Hop-Frog" (1849), a medieval tale of revenge and death by immolation set at the court of Charles VI of France. The durable streak of grotesquerie remained strong in fiction into the late 1800s with the reconstructed animals created in H. G. WELLS's *THE ISLAND OF DR. MOREAU* (1896), a caution to progressives that technology and living tissue experiments could someday doom them. Charles Grandison Finney organized his grotesques into a bizarre sideshow in *The Circus of Dr. Lao* (1935). He describes reactions to peepshows, curiosities, and freaks as a condemnation of the unimaginative middle-class residents of Abalone, Arizona, during the Great Depression. In 1920, Sherwood Anderson reflected on freaks of NATURE in the short story "The Egg," which depicts chickens born with an abnormal number of heads, wings, or legs. Anderson characterizes as barbaric the human urge to preserve these pathetic anomalies in alcohol-filled glass vials for display to the curious.

Dismaying, dehumanizing, or shocking imagery of distortions of nature, ugliness, the bizarre, and deformity dominate the writings of Southern Gothicists—for example, Erskine Caldwell's *Poor Fool* (1930), Carson MCCULLERS's *Reflections in a Golden Eye* (1941), and Eudora WELTY's short fiction. A worthy example of obsession with freaks is the weak, one-legged, and spiritually bereft Joy-Hulga of Flannery O'CONNOR's short story "Good Country People" (1955). Mississippi novelist William FAULKNER created an entire first-person narrative, *As I Lay Dying* (1930), from the reflections and pinings of a mother looking through the window at her family engaged in making her coffin. Of the transportation of the decaying mother's corpse for nine days to her burial place, her son Cash remarks, "But I aint so sho that ere a man has the right to say what is crazy and what aint" (Faulkner, 228). His logic, stated in Delta dialect, bears wisdom: "It's like there was a fellow in every man that's done a-past the sanity or the insanity, that watches the sane and the insane doings of that man with the same horror and the same astonishment" (*ibid.*).

The prominence of such grotesque details and behavior in Southern works prompted the identification of SOUTHERN GOTHIC as a subset of the Gothic canon. Reflecting a comic view of the same social milieu, Larry Larson, Levi Lee, and Rebecca Wackler's sick humor in the play *Tent Meeting* (1987) brings to the stage Becky, a girl crazed by incest who stuffs cotton in her ears to distract her from thoughts of her profoundly handicapped child, Arlene Marie, sired by Becky's father, the jake-leg revivalist Reverend Ed. The tense drama builds up to a Satan-bashing, breath-sucking pulpit sermon preceding a murderous baptismal scene, where the father/grandfather attempts to drown Arlene. To rescue the freakish babe, Becky leaves in its place a swaddled eggplant. The play was a featured performance at the 1985 Spoleto Festival in Charleston, South Carolina.

Bibliography

Barasch, Frances K. *The Grotesque.* Paris: Mouton, 1971.

Faulkner, William. *As I Lay Dying.* New York: Vintage Books, 1964.

Kayser, Wolfgang. *The Grotesque in Art and Literature.* Bloomington: Indiana University Press, 1963.

Meyer, Michael J., ed. *Literature and the Grotesque.* Amsterdam: Rodopi, 1995.

Rossetti, Christina. *The Goblin Market.* New York: Dover, 1994.

Wilde, Oscar. *The Picture of Dorian Gray.* New York: New American Library, 1983.

H

The Handmaid's Tale
Margaret Atwood
(1985)

Margaret Atwood contributed a milestone to FE-MALE GOTHIC with an ominous dystopian novel, *The Handmaid's Tale*. By setting a nightmare society in her own time and merging Gothic tradition with fable and dystopian literature, she generates fearful perspectives on the immurement and coercion of women in a gender-polarized totalitarian state polluted by radioactivity and toxic chemicals. *The Handmaid's Tale* disturbs the reader by the distortion of normal female roles through onerous uniforms that religious extremists assign for daily wear. Thus, the hierarchy of women allots places for state-controlled prostitutes dressed in sequins and feathers, subservient Marthas in veils, and the anonymous breeders, called handmaids, arrayed in red habits and veils with white winged wimples that obscure the face. The costume disempowers at the same time that it stains with the color of menstrual discharge and the ill savor of the scarlet woman.

Like the evil prioresses of convents in GOTHIC BLUEBOOKS, Atwood's women are capable of intimidation and torture. The author sets a female patrol over the subdued handmaids in the form of wives and aunts, the repressive supervisors of public executions and the indoctrinators of the Rachel and Leah Re-education Center, a female concentration camp. Silenced by cattle-prod-wielding guards, the inmates "learned to whisper almost without sound. In the semidarkness we could stretch out our arms, when the aunts weren't looking, and touch each other's hands across space. We learned to lip-read, our heads flat on the beds" (Atwood, *Handmaid*, 4). Fearful of the least infraction, the handmaids exchange names that restore their identities as free women. The irrepressible Moira, the old friend of Offred, the protagonist, sneers at the system and suffers the consequences: "It was the feet they'd do, for a first offense. They used steel cables, frayed at the ends. After that the hands. They didn't care what they did to your feet or your hands, even if it was permanent" (*ibid.*, 91).

A modernist twist on the Gothic VILLAIN is Frederick Waterford, the middle-aged Commander of the Faithful for whom his state-allotted concubine Offred—"of Fred"—is renamed, producing a snide alternate reading of "off red." Waterford follows the official policy of ritualized copulation in order to supply an infertile society with another child; but he also enjoys covert forays to Jezebel's, the state-run brothel, where he squires Offred in tarty night-out attire. On these jaunts into the hierarchy's demimonde, she bargains for information on the fate of her young daughter. In his own fantasy, Fred pretends to be a sporty roué and acts out the part of Offred's short-term liberator and rescuer. To the OUTSIDER Offred, "It's like a masquerade party; they are like oversize children, dressed up in togs they've rummaged from trunks" (*ibid.*, 235). The rapid switch of identities worsens her despair in a world where dehumanized women must suit the whims and fantasies of their male incarcerators.

Atwood extends Gothic overtones with subtle imagery and ambiguity. In the familiar rescue motif led by the good male or lesser of two evils, her text comes to a sudden close after Offred submits to sex with Nick, the Commander's chauffeur, and agrees to a daring jailbreak. Under a cloud of paranoia worsened by fears of a spy ring called the Eyes, she flees in the custody of unidentified male goons, who thrust her into a police van in a KGB-style arrest. A flash forward to June 25, 2195, supplies bits of data suggesting that Offred escaped fascist concubinage to Bangor, Maine, on the Underground Frailroad, Atwood's literary acknowledgment of AMERICAN GOTHIC traditions.

Bibliography

Atwood, Margaret. "Ophelia Has a Lot to Answer For," http://www.web.net/owtoad/ophelia.html, 1997.

———. *The Handmaid's Tale.* Toronto: O. W. Toad, 1986.

Cavalcanti, Ildney. "Utopias of/f Language in Contemporary Feminist Literary Dystopias," *Utopian Studies* 11, no. 2 (spring 2000): 152.

Coad, David. "Hymens, Lips and Masks: The Veil in Margaret Atwood's 'The Handmaid's Tale,'" *Literature and Psychology* (spring–summer 2001): 54.

Hogsette, David S. "Margaret Atwood's Rhetorical Epilogue in 'The Handmaid's Tale': The Reader's Role in Empowering Offred's Speech Act," *Critique: Studies in Contemporary Fiction* 38, no. 4 (summer 1997): 262.

Spector, Judith Ann. "Marriage, Endings, and Art in Updike and Atwood," *Midwest Quarterly* 34, no. 4 (summer 1993): 426–445.

Harker, Jonathan

Bram STOKER engages an UNRELIABLE NARRATOR to tell part of the story in DRACULA (1897), world literature's enduring model of VAMPIRISM. Harker is the appropriate male for Gothic romance—a wimpish, overly punctilious stenographer and law clerk dispatched by Exeter solicitor Peter Hawkins to Transylvania to serve a client. Obviously not a typical man of action, Harker is the dutiful Englishman and sexually nonthreatening rescuer who marries the sensitive, well-bred heroine and defends the nuclear family. In descriptions by his wife, he comes off as weak, supine, and ineffectual in protecting her from a blood-sucking ghoul.

In chapter 1, Harker arrives on a routine assignment, the transfer of ownership of Carfax Estate to Dracula, a sinister Boyar nobleman. As literary FOILS, the two men illustrate national extremes—Harker, the office habitué on a business mission, and Dracula, the exotic OUTSIDER who relies on Harker for lessons in English pronunciation and advice on how to ship goods to London. For his role in the novel, Harker bears a meaningful name that points to his centrality. His given name reflects the Old Testament friend of David, the patriarch who depended on Jonathan to protect him from Saul, the old-guard king. Harker's surname carries a gospel significance, the messenger who points out the mounting menace of the foreigner Dracula, a satanic Antichrist.

The author stresses the GROTESQUE in his creation of character and action. Harker receives immediate clues to his host's bizarre traits. When the count notices the razor cut on Harker's throat, a rosary protects the Englishman from a host who is obviously mentally disturbed. Nonetheless, Harker's immurement in Castle Dracula comes as a surprise. His host inflicts house arrest by confining his guest to one area of the edifice, locking doors, and visiting only after dark, a gender twist on the immured females in the BLUE-BEARD MYTH.

During the incarceration, Harker encounters a more fearful threat, a SUPERNATURAL visitation of ghostly women, who immobilize him with their tongues and lips, a fiendish sexual dominance that reduces him to languor and sadomasochistic delight. Upon righting himself and fleeing his cell, Harker, a pale version of the English detective, discovers a crypt and the earth-filled box where the count spends his daylight hours. The odor of human blood attests to a horror—a humanoid who sustains himself by killing and draining blood from victims. Stoker carefully depicts Harker as weak and antiheroic as a contrast to the monstrous power and range of Dracula.

Bibliography

Auerbach, Nina. *Our Vampires, Ourselves.* Chicago: University of Chicago Press, 1995.

Boone, Troy. "He Is English and Therefore Adventurous: Politics, Decadence, and 'Dracula,'" *Studies in the Novel* 25, no. 1 (spring 1993): 76–91.

Havisham, Miss

One of the GROTESQUE figures in the social novels of Charles DICKENS, Miss Havisham dominates the Gothicism of *GREAT EXPECTATIONS* (1861) as an expression of ABERRANT BEHAVIOR. Within the metaphoric PREMATURE BURIAL of Satis House, dark hallways and curtained chambers obscure from Pip the true state of the dilapidated lair of a corpse-like old lady, whom Dickens compares to a figure in a lurid waxworks museum. Clad in tattered bridal gown and veil and protected from daylight, the recluse lives among moldering splendors, where an épergne hung with cobwebs and the remains of her wedding cake decline on a dusty banquet table. Pip remarks, "I saw that the bride within the bridal dress had withered like the dress, and like the flowers, and had no brightness left but the brightness of sunken eyes" (Dickens, 867).

As punishment to the antibride, whom Carlos Fuentes has called a "supernatural virgin," Dickens condemns her to a ruined existence symbolized by endless circles (Horner, 120). She relies on her adopted daughter Estella and Pip to stage amusements as she spends her days touring the bridal table with its wax candles and decaying edibles. Like a spider lurking in a web, she stokes her anger at all males while the clocks point unceasingly at 8:40, the moment she was jilted. In her own defense she understates a self-diagnosis: "I sometimes have sick fancies" (*ibid.*, 867). The effect of her monomania is a psychological battery that marks Estella, deforming her personality with old hates transferred from mentor to child.

Although Dickens depicts the psychological torment in Miss Havisham as self-willed, Pip offers a child's pity for her wretchedness: "Her chest had dropped, so that she stooped, and her voice had dropped, so that she spoke low, and with a dead lull upon her; altogether, she had the appearance of having dropped, body and soul, within and without, under the weight of a crushing blow" (Dickens, 870). Her masochistic intent is to live out the ruin of her life and to be stretched on the table, a FORESHADOWING of her actual death. In Gothic style, the author accords her a suitably chivalric end by fire on her own hearth. Swept up by the heroic Pip, she lies severely burned and wrapped in cotton wool under a white sheet in the light of windows that her rescuer has ripped open. Her body is cruelly burned clean of the rotted wedding dress, sending her to her death muttering on unforgiven sins. Pip pictures her as "the phantom air of something that had been and was changed" (*ibid.*, 1,068). Symbolically, Dickens pierces her Gothic lair with the light of reality, which reveals a victim rather than the fairy godmother Pip had originally envisioned.

Bibliography

Craig, Amanda. "On Charles Dickens's Great Expectations," *New Statesman* 131, no. 4,616 (December 2, 2002): 51–52.

Dickens, Charles. *Great Expectations*, in vol. 2 of *The Annotated Dickens*, ed. by Edward Guiliano and Philip Collins. New York: Clarkson N. Potter, 1986.

Horner, Avril, ed. *European Gothic: A Spirited Exchange, 1760–1960.* Manchester: Manchester University Press, 2002.

Morgentaler, Goldie. "Meditating on the Low: A Darwinian Reading of 'Great Expectations,'" *Studies in English Literature, 1500–1900* 38, no. 4 (autumn 1998): 707.

Walsh, Susan. "Bodies of Capital: 'Great Expectations' and the Climacteric Economy," *Victorian Studies* 37, no. 1 (autumn 1993): 73–98.

Hawthorne, Nathaniel
(1804–1864)

Nathaniel Hawthorne, the dominant American fiction writer of the mid-19th century, excelled at DOMESTIC GOTHIC. A reader of Johann von GOETHE's *Faust* (1790–1832) and New World history, Hawthorne was the first major author to examine America's inherited guilt from New England's sinful, materialistic founders and to explore the themes of psychological motivation and atonement. For personal reasons, he tackled moral ambiguity as his focal theme. His selection was an outgrowth of birth and rearing amid the tight-lipped Puritans of Salem, Massachusetts, where his great-grandfather, Justice John Hathorne, condemned alleged witches in 1692.

In the early years of Hawthorne's writing, he turned a flair for short stories into a career spanning the publication of *Twice-Told Tales* (1837) and *Mosses from an Old Manse* (1846), both laden with colonial and postcolonial Gothicism, as displayed in the titles "Roger Malvin's Burial" (1832) and "The Minister's Black Veil" (1837). A master of tormented characters and Gothic SYMBOLs, Hawthorne used his literary gift to probe the effects of religious fanaticism, disillusion, guilt, and isolation. In an early story, "The Hollow of the Three Hills" (1830), NATURE seems complicit in human evil as the author freights the demonic ATMOSPHERE with mold, decay, and sluggish water. Resurrecting the fearful history of Salem's WITCHCRAFT hysteria, he pictures a withered crone lifting an irreligious prayer, shrieking and groaning, and intoning funeral hymns while a female supplicant kneels for a satanic initiation. Hawthorne concludes with a surreal funeral train led by a priest and his followers mouthing anathemas that "faded away like a thin vapor, and the wind, that just before had seemed to shake the coffin, moaned sadly round the verge of the Hollow between three Hills" (Hawthorne, 944).

Images of youthful naiveté and goodness subverted by a monstrous Faustian evil dominate Hawthorne's best stories: "YOUNG GOODMAN BROWN" (1835), "THE BIRTHMARK" (1843), and "Rappaccini's Daughter" (1844), all of which he published in popular magazines before anthologizing them in *Mosses from an Old Manse*. In a limited lineup of characters, the female protagonists—Faith, Georgiana, and Beatrice—share a dewy freshness quickly withered by contact with evil in the form of Satan and two daring MAD SCIENTISTs, Georgiana's husband Aylmer and Beatrice's father, herbalist Giacomo Rappaccini. In "My Kinsman, Major Molineux," anthologized in *The Snow Image* (1851), Hawthorne turns to a common scenario of frontier America, mob VIOLENCE resulting in the tar-and-feathering of the title character, a self-important Tory. In reference to the hellish sport conducted late at night by flickering torchlight, the author concludes, "On they went, in counterfeited pomp, in senseless uproar, in frenzied merri-

ment, trampling all on an old man's heart" (Hawthorne, 1,222).

Although typically nonviolent and free of decadent Gothic extremes, Hawthorne was an admirer of the romantic innovator Edgar Allan POE, with whom he corresponded. In a review published in *Graham's Magazine*, Poe extolled his contemporary as an American genius who outpaced Washington Irving in originality, control, refinement, and imagination. With uncanny accuracy, Poe predicted Hawthorne's value to American fiction five years before publication of one of the nation's indigenous fictions, THE SCARLET LETTER (1850), a poignant tale of social ostracism and misogyny.

Hawthorne's most prominent theme is the effect of secret sin on the individual and on a whole lineage, the focus of THE HOUSE OF THE SEVEN GABLES: A Romance (1851). The novel, a model of American-style supernaturalism, is the tale of a curse that causes victims to choke on blood. In the opening chapter, the author sets the TONE of his story with a glimpse of past evil taken from cloth merchant Robert Calef's *More Wonders of the Invisible World* (1700). Hawthorne recasts the persecution of witches in Colonel Pyncheon's fictional martyrdom of old Matthew Maule.

The Gothic theme of earthly punishment for wrongdoing remained strong in Hawthorne's next novel. In the search for an earthly utopia in *The Blithedale Romance* (1852), he represented the Puritan's lifelong salvation anxiety in the death of Zenobia, a corpse frozen in prayer as though repenting in the moments before she drowned herself in a pond. "Her arms! They were bent before her, as if she struggled against Providence in neverending hostility" (*ibid.*, 578). Hawthorne returned to moral corruption when he began *Doctor Grimshawe's Secret* (1861), left incomplete and issued posthumously in 1883 by Julian Hawthorne, the author's son.

Critics in the mid-19th century, focused on the surface aspect of Hawthorne's writings and characterized him as a moral allegorist obsessed by the blackness of doomed souls and their deeds. In *The Marble Faun; or, The Romance of Monte Beni* (1860), Hawthorne represented evil and OTHERNESS through social and psychological conflict and through ANTI-CATHOLIC scenarios denigrating the religious practices of Italians. Details such as the replication of a human skull and the violent death of a monk increase morbid overtones. Through Donatello, a MELANCHOLY Italian said to be a descendant of a mythic faun, the author depicts an unhealthy preoccupation with violent death, a "perilous fascination which haunts the brow of precipices, tempting the unwary one to fling himself over, for the very horrour of the thing; for, after drawing hastily back, he again looked down, thrusting himself out farther than before" (Hawthorne, 687). Subsequent critiques of Hawthorne's dark fiction produced broader-based analyses of fable, ambiguous symbolism, metaphysical romance, and psychological realism. Literary historians concluded that his fiction disclosed the disillusion of newcomers failed by the ephemeral promises of the New World. His skill earned the praise of William Gilmore Simms and Walt Whitman; Henry JAMES named Hawthorne an "American genius" (Cowie, 361).

Bibliography

Hawthorne, Nathaniel. *The Complete Novels and Selected Tales of Nathaniel Hawthorne*. New York: Modern Library, 1937.

Nattermann, Udo. "Dread and Desire: 'Europe' in Hawthorne's 'The Marble Faun,'" *Essays in Literature* 21, no. 1 (spring 1994): 54–66.

Hearn, Lafcadio
(1850–1904)

The expatriate Anglo-Irish fiction writer and translator Lafcadio Hearn introduced Western readers to the OTHERNESS of Japanese Gothic stories. After working in a New Orleans publishing house, he fled American materialism and, in 1890, sought peace in Asian philosophy and Orientalism. He obtained Japanese citizenship and married a Japanese woman, Setsu Koizumi. Taking the name Yakumo Koizumi, he lectured at the Imperial University of Tokyo and translated the stories of the French Gothicist Theophile GAUTIER.

Hearn generated a unique style of musings and MYSTERY stories published in *Atlantic Monthly and Harper's*. With Setsu's help, he translated macabre tales in *Some Chinese Ghosts* (1887) and Japanese FAIRY TALES and thoughts on the afterlife for *In Ghostly Japan* (1899) and collected from FOLKLORE 17 naturalistic Asian ghost cameos in *Kwaidan* (Weird tales, 1904). In the latter, he began with "Mimi-Nashi-Hoichi," the story of a blind performer who plucks a lute while reciting for a noble court the events of a Samurai battle. After discovering that he is seated in a cemetery reciting to ghosts, the blind man feels iron-sheathed hands ripping off his ears. In "Oshidori," a female spirit emerges from a duck to accost Sonjo for shooting her mate. When she uses her beak to rip open her own body, her pathetic death causes Sonjo to repent and to become a priest. In a more romantic tale, "O-Tei," a man reunites with his dead lover, who appears in the form of an earthly double and speaks with the voice of a REVENANT.

Bibliography

Bordewich, Fergus M. "Wandering Ghost: The Odyssey of Lafcadio Hearn," *Smithsonian* 22, no. 5 (August 1991): 120–122.

Johannsen, Kristin L. "In Search of Lost Japan," *World and I* 17, no. 5 (May 2002): 106–113.

Heart of Darkness
Joseph Conrad
(1902)

Basing fiction on a real journey into the Belgian Congo in June 1890, Joseph Conrad addressed the hellish legacy of colonialism in *Heart of Darkness*, a moody, complex novella that sparked a century of debate. To demonstrate the chasm lying between romance and realism, he deliberately chose the Gothic mode for one of the first fictional works to castigate exploitation of third world countries. Charlie Marlow, Conrad's protagonist, remarks: "There were no colonists; their administration was merely a squeeze. . . . They were conquerors, and for that you want only brute force. . . . They grabbed what they could get for the sake of what was to be got" (Conrad, 69). Marlow feels justified in his condemnation: "It was just robbery with violence, aggravated murder on a grand scale, and men going at it blind—as is very proper for those who tackle a darkness" (*ibid.*). To establish the innocence of the newcomer Marlow, the novelist gives his yawl the girlish name *Nellie*. By the novel's end, Marlow is no longer the NAIF in a strange country.

The title suggests the harrowing truth that Marlow encounters when he reaches the heart of Africa and the inner malevolence in a VILLAIN's heart. Consumed by anguish, Marlow pursues his hypnotic tale of ambition turned to monstrous evil with frequent FORESHADOWING of the savagery that lies ahead. To exorcise Europe's past sins, Conrad develops his demonization of colonialism through a painstakingly slow narrative. The boat gradually penetrates the inner Congo with two symbolic characters on board, an accountant and a lawyer, SYMBOLs of greed and legal corruption during the era's rape of colonial empires.

The crux of Conrad's condemnation of the racist imperialism of the Belgian king Leopold II is the deterioration of Kurtz, a demonic white FAUST who declines from his pact with colonial moneymakers into pure evil. He delights in savagery by decorating a fence with the skulls of his black victims and joins in "midnight dances ending with unspeakable rites" (*ibid.,* 123). Parallel to his deteriorating morality, his handwriting declines into a scrawl urging extermination of black Africans. At the end of his predations along the Congo River, Kurtz is doomed to resemble a death's head carved from ivory, the commodity he has forced locals to extort from NATURE. The terror of Conrad's novel provided the basis for Orson Welles's radio play and for the United Artists film *Apocalypse Now* (1979), which replaced African colonialism with the atrocities of the Vietnam War.

Bibliography

Conrad, Joseph. *Heart of Darkness* and *The Secret Sharer.* New York: Signet, 1983.

Hoffman, Tod. "Dark Heart Beating: Conrad's Classic at 100," *Queen's Quarterly* 109, no. 1 (spring 2002): 73–84.

Mitchell, Angus. "New Light on the 'Heart of Darkness,'" *History Today* 49, no. 12 (December 1999): 20–27.

Moore, Gene M. "Art of Darkness," *Book,* May–June 2003: 22–23.

Thompson, Terry W. "Conrad's 'Heart of Darkness,'" *Explicator* 60, no. 1 (fall 2001): 27–30.

Heathcliff

The gypsy lad Heathcliff, whom Mr. Earnshaw rescues from a Liverpool slum in Emily BRONTË's *WUTHERING HEIGHTS* (1847), suits the GOTHIC CONVENTIONs of the demon lover and the smoldering, sexually energized VILLAIN. Heathcliff is a creature molded by the economic extremes between England's privileged haves and coarse havenots. The author garners sympathy for him in childhood, when deprivation and rejection trigger dark moods and shape his destructive tendencies. As would-be son and a harum-scarum playmate for Catherine EARNSHAW, he resides on a tenuous tether between family member and outcast. Catherine's father's return with the foundling boy in 1769 provokes grinning and spitting from Catherine and envy and resentment in her brother, Hindley Earnshaw. To the spiteful foster brother, Heathcliff is a "beggarly interloper" and "imp of Satan" (Brontë, 43). The mounting hatred between the two boys bodes ill for a time when Mr. Earnshaw can no longer mediate their quarrels.

Brontë creates a set of secondary characters as commentators and facilitators of the action. Worsening the uproar at Wuthering Heights is the tedious, self-appointed bible thumper Joseph, a rustic servant who oversteps social bounds and ennobles himself as snitch by revealing the waywardness of Catherine and Heathcliff. As a balance to Joseph's meddling, Brontë turns Ellen "Nelly" Dean, the maternal housekeeper, into Heathcliff's protector. She bolsters his self-image with a touch of EXOTICISM: "You're fit for a prince in disguise. Who knows but your father was Emperor of China, and your mother an Indian queen, each of them able to buy, with one week's income, Wuthering Heights and Thrushcross Grange together?" (*ibid.,* 60). To enhance the fantasy, she suggests that sailors kidnapped the boy and transported him to England. Ironically, her vision of the purchase of contrasting houses comes true at the climax of Heathcliff's depravity, when he makes himself lord of the Earnshaw and Linton mansions.

Early on, Heathcliff displays monstrous emotions. At the height of mutual loathings between the competing sons, the author cites a verbal vendetta, a Gothic technique expressing motivation at the same time that it builds SUSPENSE. At the extreme of desperation and madness after being exiled from Christmas dinner, the crazed stable boy vows, "I'm trying to settle how I shall pay Hindley back. I don't care how long I wait, if I can only do it at last. I hope he will not die before I do!" (ibid., 63–64). Thus begins his unrelenting STALKING of an enemy.

In adolescence, Heathcliff mirrors Catherine's abandonment of childish behavior after she snubs and ridicules him for uncleanliness. He is so willing to retain her friendship that he begs Nelly to make him presentable. He turns from self-improvement to ESCAPISM after hearing Catherine declare him too lowly for marriage. He flees on a stolen horse and, for three years, supports himself on some mysterious source of wealth. On return, his handsome face and upright posture reinflame passion in Catherine and launch the consuming love affair that pushes the two toward their tragic end.

In maturity, Heathcliff displays complexity in his blend of dark skin, genteel dress and courtesies, and a tinge of morbidity and slovenliness. On the edge of racism, the author dooms the character's evolution into an immaculately groomed country gentleman as though the tastes and longings of a nonwhite Englishman can never escape heredity. Grim and sour of temper, Heathcliff ranges from sullenness to vibrant love, elemental passion, perpetual persecution, and, at times, vicious SADISM, as displayed by his seizure of Isabella's springer spaniel Fanny at two o'clock in the morning to hang it from a tree limb in the garden of Thrushcross Grange. From a childhood lacking in normal friendships and love, he advances to a manipulator, using his charm to lead Hindley into financial ruin from carousing and gambling. Heathcliff asserts his malice by subjugating Hareton, Hindley's son, and hanging a litter of pups. In a flashover of spite, Heathcliff exults in fervid malice: "I have no pity! I have no pity! The more the worms writhe, the more I yearn to crush out their entrails! It's a moral teething; and I grind with greater energy, in proportion to the increase of pain" (ibid., 150).

Brontë retains command of the one element over which Heathcliff has no control. For all his manipulations of others and cruelty to children and animals, Heathcliff is never able to rid himself of yearning for Catherine. As he grasps her frail body on her deathbed, he acknowledges the DOPPELGÄNGER motif that links their being: "You know you lie to say I have killed you, and, Catherine, you know that I could as soon forget you as my existence" (ibid., 156). Destructive of self and of his beloved, he is incapable of separating love from hate, a dilemma shared by both the demonic lover and the BYRONIC HERO. From a life of machinations against his victims, he manages to relive Catherine's illness and death and to kill off not only his body, but also his intended dynasty.

By interposing Gothic elements, the author dramatizes a ghoulish graveyard scene to express Heathcliff's uncivilized extremes, which some critics label diabolic. After Catherine's burial, he tears at her coffin and hears her sigh, a visitation that leaves him "unspeakably consoled" (ibid., 275). He experiences a calm night of sleep and a dream of lying against her cheek to cheek. This glimpse of Heathcliff's OTHERNESS attests to a merger of lovers whom even death cannot part.

Brontë allows her clever villain to attain vengeance through plots and schemes, but denies him the will to persist in destroying the families of Earnshaw and Linton once he obtains control of both Wuthering Heights and Thrushcross Grange. Given to surly outbursts and episodes of barbarism, he castigates his tender son Linton with roaring insults: "God! what a beauty! what a lovely, charming thing! . . . Haven't they reared it on snails and sour milk?" (ibid., 200). As the boy nears death, Heathcliff works rapidly to assure a marriage with Linton's cousin Cathy, Catherine and Edgar's daughter, by recklessly kidnapping the girl and Nelly.

The duality of the Byronic hero forces the author to extend both distaste for an unredeemable rebel and compassion for a morose soul wracked by OBSESSION and INSANITY. Bereaved by Catherine's death, for nearly two decades, he vents grief and unrequited love, a powerful melodramatic pairing. In bouts of wretchedness, he longs to love Hareton, Catherine's nephew, for bearing her eyes and features and pleads with his beloved's spirit to return as a ghost to end the ache that threatens his sanity. To Nelly Dean, he admits that he could have total revenge, "But where is the use? I don't care for striking, I can't take the trouble to raise my hand!" (*ibid.*, 306). Spiritually whipped, he courses the heath, forcing himself to go on functioning. To Nelly, he is no longer a living man, but a ghastly goblin pacing the floors and addressing Catherine's unseen presence. The author hints that Heathcliff's love is requited in death: after he dies of despair, he lies buried alongside her.

Bibliography

Brontë, Emily. *Wuthering Heights*. New York: New American Library, 1959.

Goodlett, Debra. "Love and Addiction in 'Wuthering Heights,'" *Midwest Quarterly* 37, no. 3 (spring 1996): 316–327.

Thormahlen, Marianne. "The Lunatic and the Devil's Disciple: The 'Lovers' in 'Wuthering Heights,'" *Review of English Studies* 48, no. 190 (May 1997): 183–197.

Henley, Beth
(1952–   )

Playwright Beth Henley successfully blends black humor with crime and family dysfunction to produce unpredictable, character-rich SOUTHERN GOTHIC drama. A native of Jackson, Mississippi, she inherited her mother's love of community theater and came of age among set builders and scene blockers. In the works of Carson McCULLERS, Flannery O'CONNOR, Eudora WELTY, and Tennessee Williams, Henley studied the craft of picturing lost souls and refined her skills while studying for a degree from Southern Methodist University. She produced an irreverent satire of a beauty OBSESSION and womanly strivings in *The Miss Firecracker Contest* (1980), the beginning of her depictions of heart misery generously coated with whimsy and humor.

Henley reveals the effect of family trauma on the ditzy, off-center McGrath sisters in CRIMES OF THE HEART (1979). The zany Gothic plot features the trio working through years of grief and shame resulting from their mother's hanging of a cat and herself in the family basement. Forcing her daughters to release pent-up tensions and animosities is the crime of Babe, the youngest sister, who languishes in a jail cell for shooting her husband after he mistreated her black teenaged lover. For the dark-edged stage comedy's debut Off-Broadway,

Henley earned a Pulitzer Prize and a Tony. The award-winning 1986 film version starred Jessica Lange, Diane Keaton, and Sissy Spacek as the three loopy McGrath sisters. Henley followed with *Signature* (1990), an offbeat comedy about the pseudoscience of graphology, or handwriting analysis.

Bibliography

Hargrove, Nancy D. "The Tragicomic Vision of Beth Henley's Drama," *Southern Quarterly* 22, no. 4 (summer 1984): 54–70.

Laughlin, Karen L. "Criminality, Desire, and Community: A Feminist Approach to Beth Henley's *Crimes of the Heart*," *Women and Performance* (1986): 35–51.

historical fiction

Sinister elements often emerge in the dark focuses of historical fiction, generating a subset of GOTHIC FICTION. Writers redirect GOTHIC CONVENTION to fact-filled stories, as with the MEDIEVALISM and DISGUISE MOTIF in Thomas Leland's two-volume depiction of the era of Henry II and Rosamond in *Longsword, Earl of Salisbury* (1762) and the quasi-royal underpinnings of Sophia LEE's suspenseful *The Recess; or, A Tale of Other Times* (1785), an early blending of romance with real events. The concept of enlarging on history with the picturesque influenced a number of Gothic works—for example, the presentation of miracles in James White's *Earl Strongbow; or, The History of Richard de Clare and the Beautiful Geralda* (1789) and the medieval setting and burning of witches in Sir Walter SCOTT's *Ivanhoe* (1819). In the popular vein, pulp fiction produced its own versions of history, as seen in the dramatist John Frederick Smith's serialized GOTHIC BLUEBOOK *Black Bess; or, The Knight of the Road* (1863–68), which ladled out the misadventures of the highwayman Dick Turpin in a record-setting 254 weekly episodes. Historical fiction perpetuated Gothic scenarios and characterizations during the 19th century and well into the 20th; examples include the diseased shape and ABERRANT BEHAVIOR of Roger Chillingworth in Nathaniel HAWTHORNE's novel THE SCARLET LETTER (1850), the telepathic and magic-laden retelling of the Salem witch trials of 1692 from the point of view of a Barbadian slave in Ann Petry's novella *Tituba of Salem Village* (1964), and telekinesis and the walking dead during Chile's economic upheaval in Isabel ALLENDE's *THE HOUSE OF THE SPIRITS* (1982).

Historical fiction from North America applied racial stereotypes and animosities to starkly Gothic scenarios. Two vivid Canadian classics, John RICHARDSON's colonial romances *Wacousta; or, The Prophecy: A Tale of the Canadas* (1832) and its sequel, *The Canadian Brothers; or, The Prophecy Fulfilled* (1840), focus on predations of the Ottawa chief Pontiac against the British. Richardson, a Canadian-Odawa veteran of the War of 1812 and the region's first novelist, incorporates looming NATURE scenes in the Detroit area, FORESHADOW-ING, betrayed love, and savagery in *Wacousta*, a MELODRAMA about Reginald Morton, a Cornish soldier robbed of his bride. By adopting the belligerence and name of an Indian, Chief Wacousta, Morton seeks vengeance against Captain De Haldimar and curses all English troops. At a tense frontier confrontation in chapter 2, Indians raise a fierce outcry similar to an Indian's triumphant shriek after scalping a victim. Modeled on James Fenimore Cooper's Natty Bumppo, hero of *The Last of the Mohicans* (1826), Wacousta earns for himself the sobriquet "the warrior of the Fleur de Lis" (Baker, 138). The verisimilitude of Richardson's characterization and the incorporation of actual events of the 1763 siege at Fort Detroit made him the most successful Canadian novelist writing about North American Indians and an early contributor to New World Gothic.

In the late 18th century, the critic and author Anna Laetitia BARBAULD protested the coloring of history with artificial musings and blamed Sophia Lee and Clara REEVE for violating truth. Nonetheless, the melding of Gothic fiction with history proved appealing to readers, many of whom were drawn to the ghost lore and tournament trappings in Ann RADCLIFFE's *Gaston de Blondeville* (1802) and to the border tales of Scott. The latter author stripped the Gothic historical romance of DECADENCE and replaced extremism with realistic detail by revealing prophecy and a curse in *Guy Mannering* (1815) and impending doom in *The Bride of Lammermoor* (1819), the story of death in quicksand, forced marriage, and a bride driven to insanity after

stabbing the groom. Subsequent writers who recreate history concentrate on evocative details similar to those that enliven Scott's fiction, particularly pageantry and spectacle as well as heinous murders, plottings, and schemes. There is, for example, the hallmark of court intrigues in William Makepeace Thackeray's *Barry Lyndon* (1844); poisonings in the Roman imperial household in Robert Graves's *I, Claudius* (1934); enslavement and concubinage in Octavia BUTLER's *Kindred* (1979); forbidden lust and torture in a monastery in Umberto ECO's medieval DETECTIVE STORY *The Name of the Rose* (1980); the predations of the great plague on London's poor in Diana Norman's *The Vizard Mask* (1994); and misogyny and religious oppression in Donna Cross's *Pope Joan* (1996).

Bibliography

Atwood, Margaret. *Strange Things: The Malevolent North in Canadian Literature.* Oxford: Clarendon Press, 1995.

Baker, Ray Palmer. *The History of English-Canadian Literature to the Confederation.* New York: Russell & Russell, 1968.

Chandler, James. "Scott and the Scene of Explanation: Framing Contextuality in 'The Bride of Lammermoor,'" *Studies in the Novel* 26, no. 2 (summer 1994): 69–98.

Monkman, Leslie G. "A World under Sentence: Richardson and the Interior," *University of Toronto Quarterly* 67, no. 1 (winter 1997–98): 244–245.

Morillo, John, and Wade Newhouse. "History, Romance, and the Sublime Sound of Truth in 'Ivanhoe,'" *Studies in the Novel* 32, no. 3 (fall 2000): 267.

Parkinson, Edward, "'That 'ere Ingian's One of Us!': Orality and Literacy in 'Wacousta,'" *Studies in the Novel* 29, no. 4 (winter 1997): 453–475.

Richardson, John. *Wacousta; or, The Prophecy.* Plattsburgh, N.Y.: McClelland & Stewart, 1996.

Hoffmann, E. T. A.
(1776–1822)

A Prussian contributor to SUPERNATURAL lore, the ultraromantic artist and writer Ernst Theodor Amadeus Hoffmann excelled at the sinister, hallucinatory, and GROTESQUE. His penchant for weird and aberrant plots appealed to a variety of contemporary readers, including the BRONTË sisters, Guy de MAUPASSANT, Charles Nodier, Fitz-James O'BRIEN, Vladimir ODOEVSKY, and Auguste VILLIERS DE L'ISLE-ADAM. An attorney by profession, at age 30, Hoffmann gave up his bureaucratic post and began composing ballets, operas, and theatrical music. To relieve frustration with civil service, he abandoned his former interests in the justice system and took up ESCAPISM, FAIRY TALES, and automata, fantastic machines that spring to life.

In his late 30s, Hoffmann's venture into writing began with the four-volume *Phantasiestücke in Callots Manier* (Fantasy pieces in the style of Callot, 1814–15). Inspired by Matthew Gregory LEWIS's THE MONK (1796), Hoffmann advanced to a diabolical novel of sexual repression, *Die Elixiere des Teufels* (*The Devil's Elixir*, 1815–16). His story "The Sand-Man" and other wildly imaginative horror tales collected in *Nachtstücke* (*Strange Stories*, 1817) were forerunners of the DETECTIVE STORY. He composed the short story "Die Doppelgänger" (The double-goer, 1821), which he published in the journal *Feierstunden*. Sir Walter SCOTT denounced Hoffmann's style as mordant and emotionally unsettling, like the hallucinations of an opium user. Literary historians find enough similarity between his works and those of Edgar Allan POE to pose Hoffmann's writings as one of the American Gothic master's major sources. Further comparisons indicate that the Russian surrealist Nikolai GOGOL adapted Hoffmann's fantasy mode; neo-Gothicist Angela CARTER drew on Hoffmann's *Nussknacker und Mausekönig* (*Nutcracker and Mouse-king*, 1816) for her Faustian *The Infernal Desire Machines of Doctor Hoffmann* (1972).

Hoffmann's literary ARABESQUEs have survived largely through music. In 1868, composer Richard Wagner reset Hoffmann's tales as *Die Meistersinger von Nürnberg* (The Guild Singer of Nuremberg). Léo Delibes captured the menace of a Hoffmann story in the engaging ballet *Coppélia* (1870), in which a doll turns into a human maiden. Jacques Offenbach developed musical strains to mimic Hoffmann's macabre imagination for *The Tales of Hoffmann* (1881), a popular orchestral suite. Peter Ilyich Tchaikovsky recast *Nussknacker und Mausekönig* as the classic Christmas dream-fantasy ballet *The Nutcracker* (1892).

Bibliography

Heller, Terry. *The Delights of Terror: An Aesthetics of the Tale of Terror.* Urbana: University of Illinois Press, 1987.

Horner, Avril, ed. *European Gothic: A Spirited Exchange, 1760–1960.* Manchester: Manchester University Press, 2002.

Labriola, Patrick. "Edgar Allan Poe and E. T. A. Hoffmann: The Double in 'William Wilson' and The Devil's Elixirs," *International Fiction Review* 29, nos. 1–2 (January 2002): 69–77.

Wain, Marianne. "The Double in Romantic Narrative: A Preliminary Study," *Germanic Review* 36, no. 4 (December 1961): 257–268.

Hogg, James
(1770–1835)

A minor Gothic poet, lyricist, and novelist, James Hogg made his mark on fiction with a single novel. He produced a psychological thriller and murder MYSTERY, *The Private Memoirs and Confessions of a Justified Sinner* (1824), which he published anonymously in BLACKWOOD'S EDINBURGH MAGAZINE, a widely read popularizer of Gothic literature. A Scottish romanticist, Hogg learned Scots lore from his mother, a renowned storyteller. He was poorly educated and lived most of his career in the Ettrick Forest, where he herded sheep for smallholders. He played folk tunes on the fiddle, studied the local idiom from readings of Robert Burns's poetry, and submitted verse and regional tales to periodicals. His friendship with Sir Walter SCOTT earned him minor acclaim and the nickname "the Ettrick shepherd." At age 40, Hogg ventured to Edinburgh to edit the *Spy*, a failed satiric journal.

Upon return to rural Scotland, Hogg issued the occult ballad *The Witch of Fife* (1813) and worked on an allegorical masterpiece, *Private Memoirs*, a revealing pseudo-autobiography of a psychotic Calvinist fanatic, Robert Wringhim, told through parallel UNRELIABLE NARRATORs. Influenced by an English translation of E. T. A. HOFFMANN's *Die Elixiere des Teufels* (*The Devil's Elixir*, 1815–16), Hogg created the character Gil-Martin, a Satanic DOPPELGÄNGER who leads Wringhim into evil by twisting the doctrine of the elect, whom God redeems regardless of their earthly misdeeds. The plot entwines religious mania with traditional Gothic elements—alcohol abuse, the SUPERNATURAL, STALKING, VIOLENCE, and INSANITY. Hogg enlarges the role of the ironically named Wringhim, a self-righteous VILLAIN, with powers to haunt, terrify, and shape-shift as he rids the world of reprobates and heretics. Although the novel earned a rebuff in the *Westminster Review,* it won the regard of the BRONTË sisters and Edward BULWER-LYTTON and inspired elements of Robert Louis STEVENSON's *DR. JEKYLL AND MR. HYDE* (1886) and Oscar WILDE's *THE PICTURE OF DORIAN GRAY* (1891). In the 1920s, the French novelist André Gide rediscovered Hogg's novel and lauded its genius at depicting megalomania.

Bibliography

Groves, David. "'Confessions of an English Glutton': A (Probable) Source for James Hogg's 'Confessions,'" *Notes and Queries* 40, no. 1 (March 1993): 46–47.

MacKenzie, Scott. "Confessions of a Gentrified Sinner: Secrets in Scott and Hogg," *Studies in Romanticism* 41, no. 1 (spring 2002): 3–33.

Holmes, Sherlock

Western literature's enduring London sleuth, Sherlock Holmes, the hero of Sir Arthur Conan DOYLE's 56 detective stories, is both a hyperanalytic investigative genius and a shrewdly inventive hypothesizer. As an early consulting private eye, he epitomizes the mental acuity that pervades modern detective and crime fiction. He is an eccentric in dress, mien, and compulsions who relishes the chase; his cases present bizarre characters and macabre, seemingly insoluble crimes and clues, which he analyzes by drawing upon arcane bits of encyclopedic knowledge in his mental store. A citified, world-weary BYRONIC HERO, Holmes is, by turns, manic-depressive, dramatic, and self-adulating and is given to relieving stress by playing his violin, smoking a pipe, and indulging in cocaine injections in the privacy of his quarters at 221B Baker Street. His conclusions impress the narrator, his friend and sidekick Dr. Watson, who aids Holmes through manipulations of anatomy, chemistry, and physics without arriving at the summations of his mentor.

A brilliant and divergent thinker, Holmes is more intellectual than sensational. His cases demand a wide range of psychological and technological knowledge, prefiguring forensic police work; he is often required to identify various types of tobacco, disguises, and poisons from the outer limits of the British Empire. For example, in "The Adventure of the Sussex Vampire" (1924), Holmes has to unravel the strange behavior of Robert Ferguson's Peruvian wife, who sucked blood from her stepson and her own infant. Detection requires the concerted efforts of Watson and a clutch of sidewalk arabs known as the Baker Street Irregulars. Their streetwise data collection outpaces the pedestrian investigation of Scotland Yard's Inspector Lestrade in foiling the consummate felon, Professor James Moriarty, an antagonist whom Holmes identifies as "the Napoleon of crime" (Hodgson, 229).

Significant to Holmes's complex personality is the chivalric code of honor toward women and personal integrity. In "A Scandal in Bohemia" (1891), Doyle begins the tale with the introduction of Irene Adler, who "eclipses and predominates the whole of her sex" (Doyle, vol. 1, 346). Holmes's response to romantic allure is compartmentalization, the shutting out of tenderness to admit only elements of cold, unrelenting rationality. Watson explains: "[Holmes] never spoke of the softer passions, save with a gibe and a sneer. They were admirable things for the observer—excellent for drawing the veil from men's motives and actions" (Doyle, vol. 1, 346). Thus, controlled subjectivity enables Holmes to admire Irene only as the rare female capable of thinking logically about criminality. The chivalric demands of personal behavior catch Holmes at odd moments concerning himself less with victimized women than with society's problems with minor legal infractions that precipitate serious crime, as in his musings in "A Case of Identity" (1892) about a scoundrel who is likely to find himself a candidate for the gibbet.

Doyle admits duality in Holmes, who allows himself to mimic the criminal's debased life in "The Adventure of Charles Augustus Milverton" (1905), a case that reverses his role as detective. Earlier, in "The Sign of the Four" (1890), Watson ponders his friend's choice of profession: "So swift, silent, and furtive were his movements, like those of a trained bloodhound picking out a scent, that I could not but think what a terrible criminal he would have made" (Doyle, vol. 1, 639). In reference to a long-term involvement in freeing England of the criminal element, in "The Final Problem" (1893), Holmes leaves a note for Watson attesting "I am pleased to think that I shall be able to free society from any further effects of [Moriarty's] presence" (Doyle, vol. 2, 316).

In "The Final Problem," a stopping point in the series, Doyle turns VIOLENCE and STALKING to his own purposes by killing off Holmes in the grasp of Moriarty in Switzerland, where the two tumble from the Reichenbach Falls. The premature farewell to Holmes allows Doyle to speak through Watson his regard for "the best and the wisest man whom I have ever known" (ibid., 317). English fans of the Strand and those reading the series in McClure's in America wept in disbelief. So great a protest arose from 20,000 Holmesians, including Queen Victoria and her family, that Doyle revived the character in THE HOUND OF THE BASKERVILLES (1902), "The Adventure of the Empty House" (1903), and "The Adventure of the Second Stain" (1904).

Doyle's detective made an indelible mark on English Gothic fiction. At the end of her long career in sensational novels, Mary Elizabeth BRADDON, a fan of Doyle's stories, remarked in Beyond These Voices (1910) on the English enjoyment of crime fiction. She observed, "Every man is at heart a Sherlock Holmes," a tribute to the dominance of Doyle's detective over the genre (Carnell, 126). In imitation of Holmes's scholarly approach to crime solving, subsequent detectives such as Gaston LEROUX's Joseph Rouletabille and G. K. Chesterton's Father Brown stressed science and logic over intuition as a basis for apprehending criminals. Screen and stage versions of Doyle's detective have been vehicles for many actors, including John Barrymore, Jeremy Brett, Peter Cushing, William Gillette, Frank Langella, Roger Moore, Eille Norwood, Christopher Plummer, Fritz Weaver, Nicol Williamson, and John Wood. Basil Rathbone was one of the most successful of the lot.

Bibliography

Eco, Umberto, and Thomas A. Sebeok, eds. The Sign of Three: Dupin, Holmes, Peirce. Bloomington: Indiana University Press, 1983.

Doyle, Arthur Conan. The Annotated Sherlock Holmes, 2 vols. New York: Wings Books, 1967.

Hodgson, John A., ed. Sherlock Holmes: The Major Stories with Contemporary Critical Essays. Boston: Bedford/St. Martin's, 1994.

Knight, Stephen. "The Case of the Great Detective," Meanjin 40, no. 2 (1981): 175–185.

Priestman, Martin. Detective Fiction and Literature: The Figure on the Carpet. London: Macmillan, 1990.

Holt, Victoria
(1906–1993)

Eleanor Alice Burford Hibbert, a London-born novelist, earned the title of queen of romantic SUSPENSE for her command of MYSTERY, HISTORICAL FICTION, and the GOTHIC NOVEL; Victoria Holt was the most familiar of her several pseudonyms. An early reader of the BRONTËs, Wilkie COLLINS, Charles DICKENS, Victor Hugo, and Leo Tolstoy, she attended class irregularly because of poor health and read independently at home. She quit school at age 17 to wait tables, clerk in a jewelry store, and write novels. After succeeding with short fiction submitted to the London Daily Mail and the Evening News, she accepted an editor's challenge to publish novels and, writing under her maiden name and the pseudonyms Philippa Carr, Elbur Ford, Victoria Holt, Kathleen Kellow, Jean Plaidy, and Ellalice Tate, quickly rose to an impressive position in the field of women's fiction.

Holt plotted at a furious rate of two novels annually, gradually increasing to three per year. In 1960, she achieved stardom by reviving the Gothic MELODRAMA in the form of a suspenseful romance, MISTRESS OF MELLYN, a bestselling bildungsroman based on Charlotte BRONTË's JANE EYRE (1847) and Daphne DU MAURIER's REBECCA (1938). The novel exploited fears of CLAUSTROPHOBIA and PREMATURE BURIAL, and woman-on-woman VIOLENCE, in the plotting of Celestine Nansellock against her rival, Martha Leigh. First serialized in the Ladies' Home Journal, the novel was chosen as a Readers' Digest selection and issued in a treasury volume that allied Holt's masterwork with Gothic thrillers by Evelyn Anthony, Madeleine Brent, Du Maurier, Jessica North, and Phyllis A. WHITNEY. Holt's first triumph preceded an outpouring of 30 more imitation

Victorian novels snapped up by faithful fans, particularly *Kirkland Revels* (1962), a chilling tale of the adventuresome bride soon widowed and left to weather the horrific secrets of a Yorkshire mansion.

As Jean Plaidy, Holt became England's most respected author of historical fiction. She deliberately toned down the historical backgrounds of her Gothic novels to free them of the ponderous period underpinnings of her Plaidy works. With 80 titles, she covered the Norman Conquest, the Plantagenets and Tudors, Mary Queen of Scots, the Stuarts and Georgians, Queen Victoria, Ferdinand and Isabella, Lucrezia Borgia, the Medici, Henri of Navarre, and the French Revolution. Holt's canon is available in 20 foreign translations of some 200 titles.

Bibliography

Fleenor, Juliann E., ed. *The Female Gothic*. Montreal: Eden Press, 1983.

Williams, Anne. *Art of Darkness: A Poetics of Gothic*. Chicago: University of Chicago Press, 1995.

horror narratives

The horror narrative, whether novel, GOTHIC BLUE-BOOK, German *Schauerroman* ("shudder novel"), or graveyard verse, is a staple of the Gothic canon. Unlike terror fiction, which heightens the senses and unleashes the imagination, horror sickens the mind, congeals the blood, and stymies the faculties with repulsive evidence of VIOLENCE, contact with ghastly SUPERNATURAL beings and presences, and a dread of impending doom. The genre, named for the Latin *horrere* (meaning, "to cause hair to stand on end"), dates to early folklore, when oral stories cultivated episodes in which human characters encounter ghosts and ghouls, poltergeists, vampires, voodoo, werewolves, and WITCHCRAFT. In one example collected in Roald Dahl's *Someone Like You* (1953), paralyzing dread lies at the core of "Poison," the tale of Harry Pope's immobility while a venomous krait crawls across his stomach. As a dramatic vehicle for both radio and television, the reptilian contact with skin horrified audiences. By emphasizing fearful scenes, such tales touch on psychological fears and on curiosity about the unspoken terrors that color DREAMS AND NIGHTMARES, a sinister element in Jean RHYS's psychological novel *Wide Sargasso Sea* (1966). However, the psychological examination of character and motivation as well as probability take second place to action and the visual elements of setting.

In the Middle Ages, horrific accounts permeated Dante's *Inferno* (1321) and Geoffrey Chaucer's *The Pardoner's Tale*, a segment of *The Canterbury Tales* (ca. 1385). During the Renaissance, Christopher Marlowe built on a tradition of bargainers with the devil for his play DR. FAUSTUS (ca. 1588). Horror was the focal emotion in Horace WALPOLE's THE CASTLE OF OTRANTO (1765), generally considered the first GOTHIC NOVEL, and in William BECKFORD's VATHEK (1782). In "On the Pleasure Derived from Objects of Terror, with Sir Bertrand" (1773), the critic and author Anna Laetitia BARBAULD acknowledged the pleasure that readers received from suspenseful, stupefying literature, particularly that of Walpole and Tobias SMOLLETT. Harriet Jones, author of *The Family of Santraile; or, The Heir of Montault* (1809), concurred that horror symbolized the depravity and corruption of society. The horror motif dominated Mary Wollstonecraft SHELLEY's seminal MAD SCIENTIST novel FRANKENSTEIN (1818), in which an innovative researcher unleashes a humanoid MONSTER that stalks the creator and his family. Charles Robert MATURIN produced the last of the traditional Gothic horror novels with MELMOTH THE WANDERER (1820), a convoluted tale of DIABOLISM and Faustian tragedy.

Of literary importance in the United States as well as Europe, the horror narrative remained popular throughout the 1800s. The height of innovation and ATMOSPHERE occurred in the macabre stories of Edgar Allan POE, who investigated human responses to horror ranging from curiosity to insanity. His fatalistic thriller "Metzengerstein: A Tale in Imitation of the German" (1832) preceded later masterworks of dread—the ghost tales of Irish writer and journalist Sheridan LE FANU's *The House by the Churchyard* (1861–62) and *In a Glass Darkly* (1872), English sensation writer Wilkie COLLINS's THE MOONSTONE (1868), and Bram STOKER's long-lived vampire novel DRACULA (1897). In German lore, E. T. A. HOFFMANN excelled as the creator of *Die Elixiere des Teufels* (*The Devil's Elixir*, 1815–16) and the Gothic anthology *Nachtstücke* (*Strange Stories*, 1817). A distinct branch of horror writing features the DOPPELGÄNGER motif, a German creation that probed the diabolical side of the human psyche, exemplified by Robert Louis STEVENSON's *DR. JEKYLL AND MR. HYDE* (1886) and the Frisian poet and novelist Hans Theodor Woldsen Storm's monstrous *Ein Golem* (A Golem, 1851) and *Ein Doppelgänger* (A double-goer, 1887).

The conventions of horror fiction permeate other genres, for example, PUNCH AND JUDY puppet plays, which began in London in 1785; the anonymous Gothic bluebook *The Black Forest; or, the Cavern of Horrors* (1802); the GRIMM brothers' folklore in *Kinder- und Hausmärchen* (Children's and household tales), later known as *Grimm's Fairy Tales* (1812, 1815, 1822); "Le Horla; or, Modern Ghosts" (1887), a diary of madness in Guy de MAUPASSANT's canon of short fiction; and "SREDNI VASHTAR" (1911), SAKI's psychological revenge tale. Saki also spoofed horror lore with a tongue-in-cheek story, "The Open Window" (1911), the fabricated terrors of a skillful liar with the improbable name of Vera. In frontier literature, the journalist Ambrose BIERCE established a reputation for the macabre, violence, black humor, and misanthropy, beginning with his first ghost story, "The Haunted Valley" (1871), which Bierce published in the *Overland Monthly*.

With the adaptation of horror narrative to film, a new genre was born, the male-dominated horror movie—a venue for such actors as Boris Karloff, Bela Lugosi, Vincent Price, and John Carradine and for directors like Alfred Hitchcock and Roman Polanski. In the 1950s, horror narrative invested another popular venue, horror comics—notably, the American pulp thrillers bearing such titles as *Horror Tales, Tales from the Tomb, Tales of Voodoo, Weird,* and *Witches Tales.* Though suppressed by censorious laws and community and religious activism, sensational films, comics, and computer simulation games appear to have caused none of the corruption of young minds that pulpit ministers and crusaders predicted.

Bibliography

Hume, Robert. "Gothic Versus Romantic: A Revaluation of the Gothic Novel," *Publication of the Modern Language Association* 84 (1969): 282–290.

Kristeva, Julia. *Powers of Horror: An Essay on Abjection.* New York: Columbia University Press, 1982.

Oates, Joyce Carol. *Telling Stories.* New York: W. W. Norton, 1998.

Sringhall, John. "Horror Comics: The Nasties of the 1950s," *History Today* 44, no. 7 (July 1994): 10–13.

The Hound of the Baskervilles
Sir Arthur Conan Doyle
(1902)

Sir Arthur Conan DOYLE's revival of the Sherlock HOLMES series was so welcome to Holmesians that the editors of *Strand* magazine made an additional press run of 30,000 copies for the appearance of *The Hound of the Baskervilles,* a serial begun in August 1901 and completed in 1902. The demand reached such fervor that fans stood at the pressroom door on Southampton Street, London, to buy copies before they could be transported to dealers. Publisher Sidney Paget issued 15,000 copies for India and the British colonies and 70,000 for sale in the United States. Publication of a bound version in England and the United States in 1902 assured readers of quality shelf editions of the popular DETECTIVE STORY.

By suggesting LYCANTHROPY, the plot perpetuates the standard pitting of ROMANTICISM against reason in Gothic fiction by explaining bizarre events and details through scientific fact. Set on the Devon moors, the baffling case of a vengeful hound and a family curse offers Holmes an opportunity to refute SUPERSTITION with rational evidence. The tale incorporates familiar Gothic machinery—an old manuscript telling a story-within-a-story, greed for a family estate, and a portrait bearing a tell-tale family resemblance. To the macabre tradition of a great black hound that pursues a despoiler of women over the moors, Doyle grafts poetic justice, the disappearance of a VILLAIN in a bog, and the downgrading of a werewolf into an ordinary dog.

For ATMOSPHERE, Doyle speaks through Dr. Watson, Holmes's associate, who relays reports on an initial survey of the terrain. In awe of prehistory, Watson notes evidence of the prehistoric settlers of England: "On all sides of you as you walk are the houses of these forgotten folk with their graves and the huge monoliths which are supposed to have marked their temples" (Doyle, vol. 2, 52). From his dramatic visions of "skin-clad, hairy men," Watson moves on to the crime itself, a primeval attack in Yew Alley that caused an elderly gentleman to drop dead of fright. Watson presents his imperfect understanding of the crime through open-ended questions about the silent, spectral MONSTER that reputedly roams the area.

From classic GOTHIC CONVENTION, Doyle retains the "crumbling mansion" aspect of the main setting, Baskerville Hall, which lies beyond more fertile country in a cup-shaped depression surrounded by bleak boulders and stunted firs. Gradually, he tightens the claustrophobic element by sending his OUTSIDERs through gates and pillars and beyond a ruined lodge to a hushed avenue. Like the Radcliffean confinements of early Gothic fiction, the lane turns into a somber tunnel formed of tree branches. Doyle reverses the process in the falling action a month later as Holmes, seated in his cozy London flat, deconstructs the MYSTERY of the huge hound, which the villain transported to Grimpen Mire as a means of terrorizing the rightful owners of the estate. In commentary on the intersection between Gothic details and detective fiction, Holmes speaks his philosophy of weirdness in criminal investigations: "The more *outré* and grotesque an incident is, the more carefully it deserves to be examined" (*ibid.*, 109).

Bibliography

Cavendish, Richard. "Publication of 'The Hound of the Baskervilles': March 25th, 1902," *History Today* 52, no. 3 (March 2002): 57.

Cook, William. "The Dog That Barked in the Night," *New Statesman* 130, no. 4,568 (December 17, 2001): 118–119.

Doyle, Arthur Conan. "The Hound of the Baskervilles," in vol. 2 of *The Annotated Sherlock Holmes.* New York: Wings Books, 1967.

Hodgson, John A., ed. *Sherlock Holmes: The Major Stories with Contemporary Critical Essays.* Boston: Bedford/St. Martin's, 1994.

"The House of Night"
Philip Freneau
(1799)

A contribution to American GRAVEYARD VERSE, Philip Morin FRENEAU's *The House of Night* (1799)

is an extended personification of Death. The poem, anticipated by dire imagery in his short meditation "The Vanity of Existence" (1781), pictures midnight gloom amid the howls of dogs and wolves and the plaintive call of the whippoorwill. Leaning over a corpse, the speaker fancies a host of ghosts, imps, and a hellish assembly of the damned. He passes by sad inscriptions on tombstones that remark the dismal state of the lamented down below. He extends his description of a skeleton with lipless grin and hairless skull.

Unlike Thomas Gray in his contemplative "ELEGY WRITTEN IN A COUNTRY CHURCHYARD" (1751), Freneau avoids romanticizing the topic and sees no reason to exalt the dead. The poem's action sinks contentedly into horror to describe the chivalric image of Death, whom specters attend while he drives his inky chariot. Like a hero from the nether world, Death claims sway over humankind and boasts fame twice that of Alexander the Great. Even princes dread Death's advance. Freneau offers one shred of hope to the living—to live decorous lives and to hope for more than decay and neglect in the tomb.

Bibliography

Bergland, Renee L. *The National Uncanny: Indian Ghosts and American Subjects.* Hanover, N.H.: Dartmouth College, 2000.

Goddu, Teresa A. *Gothic America: Narrative, History, and Nation.* New York: Columbia University Press, 1997.

House of the Seven Gables

In his grim Gothic romance THE HOUSE OF THE SEVEN GABLES (1851), Nathaniel HAWTHORNE depicts the famous elm-shaded edifice as a SYMBOL of New England's crime-ridden past, marked by displacement and murder of Indians and persecution of Quakers and suspected witches. The author based his novel on a real structure completed in Salem, Massachusetts, in 1668. The once-grand white-oak frame house, raised at the edge of virgin forest, stands near a pleasant spring, which suggests the blessings of NATURE on the original site. Like Adam in Eden, a Puritan settler, Matthew Maule, erected a humble log hut, roofed it with thatch, and planted a garden. The building of the manse followed Maule's hanging for WITCHCRAFT and his curse on a greedy enemy, Colonel Pyncheon. Hawthorne notes that the death "blasted with strange horror the humble name of the dweller in the cottage, and made it seem almost a religious act to drive the plough over the little area of his habitation, and obliterate his place and memory from among men" (Hawthorne, 246).

Romantic detail establishes the centrality of the House of the Seven Gables in the lives of characters and the community. Some 160 years after Pyncheon's construction, the GROTESQUE homeplace takes on an antique air as shabbiness replaces former grandeur. At the novel's opening, the exterior is marked by rusted shingles and a seven-stage roof, a suggestion of the seven deadly sins. The moss-tufted siding, crumbling plaster and chimney, and broken lattice lapse further into ruin, and the spring loses its freshness. In unrelenting CHIAROSCURO, the current residents wither from isolation. Hawthorne relieves the doomed surroundings with a quaint Edenic touch—Alice's crimson posies, which a former relative, Alice Pyncheon, sowed by strewing a handful of seeds from Italy.

Like the fearful castles in GOTHIC CONVENTION, the House of the Seven Gables develops menace from its lack of grace. The ugly dwelling represents moral depravity, authoritarianism, and ethical bankruptcy, all of which overshadow the promise of the New World. The text remarks that the intricate old manse with its projecting second story was produced over time by a series of builders and blueprints. Inside, Colonel Pyncheon's portrait holds a commanding view of the dark parlor in which he succumbed to sudden death from apoplexy the day he first occupied his home. Outside stands a sundial, a marker of time the family has spent on ill-gotten land.

In a Gothic atmosphere shrouded in curtains, shut away by doors, and surrounded by oversized weeds, visitors experience a tenebrous tour of rooms suggesting an occluded search for truth. The author depicts the house as a MELANCHOLY place that misleads outsiders with its shadowy passageways and outdated stairs: "The very timbers were oozy, as with the moisture of a heart. It was itself like a great human heart, with a life of its own, and full of rich and sombre reminiscences"

(*ibid.*, 258). After Phoebe Pyncheon marries Holgrave, a scion of the Maule line, the birth of love leads the couple away from the barren house and leaves it untenanted.

Bibliography
Hawthorne, Nathaniel. *The Complete Novels and Selected Tales of Nathaniel Hawthorne.* New York: Modern Library, 1937.

The House of the Seven Gables
Nathaniel Hawthorne
(1851)

Nathaniel HAWTHORNE composed *The House of the Seven Gables,* a picturesque family history of the Maules and Pyncheons, with more leisure and less moral compunction than the intensely sin-revealing mindset that shaped his composition of *THE SCARLET LETTER* (1850). He based the work on familiar Gothic motifs of NECROMANCY, feuding families, greed, inherited guilt, a crumbling portrait and hidden deed, and an ancestral curse. His moody, finely plotted Gothic romance focuses on an architectural pattern, the peaked, multi-gabled homes common to the New England colonies. As a SYMBOL of the convoluted consciences of early European settlers, the house and its ill-fated provenance represent the diseased thinking and tinges of horror that marked the Puritan occupancy of New England.

Hawthorne builds his novel on a Puritan myth of a historical victim, Thomas Maule, a blameless man whom bigots persecuted for his Quaker beliefs. The fictional event that set *The House of Seven Gables* in motion was the lawlessness of Colonel Pyncheon, an early robber baron who usurped the property of Matthew Maule and condemned him to the noose for alleged sorcery. On the way to execution, Maule hexed his tormentor from the scaffold with a chilling prophecy: "'God,' said the dying man, pointing his finger, with a ghastly look, at the undismayed countenance of his enemy,—'God will give him blood to drink!'" (Hawthorne, 247). After Pyncheon employed Maule's son to raise a commanding manse on the property, the house reached completion on the day of Maule's inexplicable death. The colonel's sudden demise is poetic justice to a materialistic despoiler of a humble settler. The coincidence generates rumors of the curse and a blight on the Pyncheon line.

Rather than conjure up ghosts and apparitions as avengers, Hawthorne pursues his joyless drama through intimation and irony. He focuses on the withered remains of the family, which dwindles down to the sour shopkeeper Hepzibah and her befuddled brother Clifford Pyncheon. Like the Genesis account of Joseph and his brothers, Clifford, reviled as "Old Maid Pyncheon's bloody brother," is an injured soul whom his kinsman, Judge Pyncheon, diminishes through wrongful imprisonment for allegedly murdering an uncle (*ibid.*, 419). As the photographer Holgrave, a scion of the Maule family, admires the sunny beauty of a country cousin, Phoebe Pyncheon, a potential seduction suggests that opportunism still stalks the property. Transforming himself by repudiating evil, Holgrave ponders history's stern lessons and remarks, "In this age, more than ever before, the moss-grown and rotten Past is to be torn down, and lifeless institutions to be thrust out of the way and their dead corpses buried, and everything to begin anew" (*ibid.*, 350).

The comment is prophetic. Hawthorne chooses sentiment over tragedy and ends his tale with the death of the villainous Judge Pyncheon, whose demise releases "a hidden stream of private talk, such as it would have shocked all decency to speak loudly at the street-corners" (*ibid.*, 430). His end precipitates a release from festering guilt, exorcism of the curse, and the wedding of sweet-natured Phoebe to Holgrave. The photographer's metamorphosis from Puritanism to Yankee commercialism presages the robustness of the American republic. In the concluding scene, Hawthorne dispels the Gothic aura overshadowing the seven-gabled house. As the wedded pair mounts a barouche to depart, the Pyncheon Elm "whispered unintelligible prophecies" and the ghost of Alice Pyncheon, relieved of past woe, floats upward (*ibid.*, 436).

Bibliography

Hawthorne, Nathaniel. *The Complete Novels and Selected Tales of Nathaniel Hawthorne.* New York: Modern Library, 1937.

The House of the Spirits
Isabel Allende
(1981)

The Latin American Gothicist Isabel ALLENDE created an international sensation with her best-selling HISTORICAL NOVEL *La Casa de los Espíritus* (*The House of the Spirits*, 1981), a saga of VIOLENCE and REVENGE set in 1973 during the military takeover of Chile. The focus of the story is the life of Clara del Valle, a kindhearted clairvoyant who is capable of trances, telekinesis, necromancy, and magic. In childhood, she is fearless amid "the sudden appearance of the most livid and undernourished monsters in her room, or by the knock of devils and vampires at her bedroom window" (Allende, 74).

To communicate the cruelties of life under tyranny, Allende parcels out evocative images of COLONIAL GOTHIC, particularly a graphic rape scene in which Esteban Trueba, the fictional version of the author's grandfather, manhandles an Indian woman, siring a demon son. Pedro García, a folkteller, relates to village children a beast fable about a fox robbing a henhouse each night to steal eggs and devour chicks. The story characterizes the sufferings of the agrarian class, who endure centuries of exploitation at the hands of Hispanic overlords. Pedro's story empowers the hens with a Marxist solution to tyranny: they encircle the fox and peck him until he runs away. For its verisimilitude to real class struggles, the book was banned in Chile and launched an underground phenomenon in black market editions.

Allende's handling of the SUPERNATURAL mirrors the realistic detail of the fiction of the Colombian novelist Gabriel GARCÍA MÁRQUEZ. In a grave-robbing scene, Trueba unites the corpse of his wife Clara with that of her sister Rosa, his former fiancée who died when Clara was a small child. As he places a kiss on Clara's cold lips, "a breeze crept through the cypresses, slipped through a crack in the coffin, which until that instant had remained hermetically sealed, and in a flash the unchanged bride dissolved like a spell, disintegrating into a fine gray powder" (*ibid.*, 305). The scene captures the high drama that unites FAIRY TALE scenarios and superstitious dread with passion and believable incidents.

Allende describes the retribution for Esteban's racist cruelties and sexism through the appearance of his sister Férula, a REVENANT who appears in the dining room of the family hacienda, Tres Marias. Her name, which refers to the metal ferule at the tip of a rod, is symbolic of her role as punisher. After her banishment six years earlier, she dies alone and sends her silent spirit to accuse her brother of greed. In a GROTESQUE scenario, Clara visits her body and finds "that she must have been dead for many hours, because the mice were already beginning to nibble her feet and eat her fingers" (*ibid.*, 151). Bille August's screen version, filmed in 1994, captures the creepy quality of leave-taking between Clara, played by Meryl Streep, and her deceased sister-in-law, acted by Glenn Close.

Bibliography

Allende, Isabel. *The House of the Spirits.* New York: Bantam Books, 1982.

Jenkins, Ruth Y. "Authorizing Female Voice and Experience: Ghosts and Spirits in Kingston's 'The Woman Warrior' and Allende's 'The House of the Spirits,'" *MELUS* 19, no. 3 (fall 1994): 61–73.

Tayko, Gail. "Teaching Isabel Allende's 'La Casa de los Espiritus,'" *College Literature* 19, no. 3 (October–February 1992): 228–232.

House of Usher

The blighted manse of a declining family, Edgar Allan POE's famed setting in "THE FALL OF THE HOUSE OF USHER" (1839) cracks and literally crumbles to dust upon the death of its last two inmates, Roderick USHER and Madeline, his twin sister and possible lover. To the OUTSIDER, a visitor who arrives on horseback in autumn, the house is a holdover from feudal times—an unspeakably gloomy and monochromatic residence amid rank gray weeds and decaying trees. The author heightens the vision by describing both the manse and its reflection in a nearby tarn, a liquid horror overhung with mist and pestilential stagnation. Thus, twin manses, like the Usher twins, vanish inexplicably into corruption as the family line comes to a sudden horrific end.

Poe focuses on the extreme age of the house, which has resulted in discoloration, fungal growth, fissures, and cobwebbed eaves. To the observer, the building is an ILLUSION—it seems likely compromised by decay, but gives no evidence of structural weakness. Inside, the visitor passes through intricate hallways and staircases to get to his friend Roderick's studio. Poe persists in funereal appointments with the room's black oak flooring, profuse antique furniture, dark drapes, and trellised windows. The action reaches its climax with the entombment of Madeline USHER in the light-bereft vault under the house in a former dungeon and copper-sheathed powder magazine.

Upon Madeline's clawing herself free from PREMATURE BURIAL, the house, as though in recompense for Roderick's haste in burying her, quakes in the path of a mystic whirlwind. Poe depicts the outsider fleeing over an old causeway, a slim tether to normality. He turns back toward Usher's madness to glimpse a terrifying landscape illumined by a blood-red moon. In a brief dissolution, the house cracks from roof to baseline before collapsing. Critical interpretations of the fallen House of Usher suggest a number of possibilities, notably the demise of an effete artist from self-absorption and self-confinement and the end of a family line from an incestuous relationship between brother and sister.

Bibliography

Benoit, Raymond. "Poe's 'The Fall of the House of Usher,'" *Explicator* 58, no. 2 (winter 2000): 79.

Dougherty, Stephen. "Foucault in the House of Usher: Some Historical Permutations in Poe's Gothic," *Papers on Language & Literature* 37, no. 1 (winter 2001): 3.

hyperbole

A vital element of Gothic writing, hyperbole is a common figure of speech derived from the Greek for *overshoot.* Hyperbole clarifies author intent through exaggerated SUPERNATURAL encounters or extremes of ILLUSION, terror, and ABERRANT BEHAVIOR. Overstated scenarios generate a heightened emotional response in characters and readers, as found in Daphne DU MAURIER's perplexing DOMESTIC GOTHIC story "THE BIRDS" (1952). Anna Laetitia BARBAULD, the author of "On the Pleasure

Derived from Objects of Terror, with Sir Bertrand" 1773, concurred on the reader's craving for startling details, such as the monstrous helmet that crushes the groom Conrad on his wedding day in Horace WALPOLE's classic novel *THE CASTLE OF OTRANTO* (1765). The improbability of such a death is the author's introduction to a series of outlandish episodes suited to the story's MEDIEVALISM.

Through overstatement, Gothic writers achieve an intensity that raises curiosity to SUSPENSE, the enduring appeal of the animaloids in H. G. WELLS's *THE ISLAND OF DOCTOR MOREAU* (1896), a REVENANT at the door in W. W. JACOBS's horror tale "THE MONKEY'S PAW" (1902), and the otherworldly fantasies of H. P. LOVECRAFT. Hyperbole empowered the late 18th-century German *Schauerroman* ("shudder novel"), which English writers read in translation, and contributed to the appeal of the GOTHIC BLUEBOOK, the publications of MINERVA PRESS, American dime novels, stage MELODRAMA, and the French *CONTES CRUELS* (cruel tales) and the *frénétique* school of Gothic writing. In the end-

stage of Gothic DECADENCE, some authors overstepped hyperbole, thus creating ludicrous scenarios too charged with danger for belief, a fault that mars the heroine's confinement in a priest's hole in Victoria HOLT's overworked terror novel *MISTRESS OF MELLYN* (1960) and the prognostications in Amy Tan's *The Hundred Secret Senses* (1995). Other writers—particularly Isabel ALLENDE, Louise Erdrich, and Gabrel GARCÍA MARQUEZ— channeled hyperbole into morbid humor, fable, fantasy, and magical realism. Dramatist Tony Kushner balanced hyperbole with pathos in *Angels in America* (1991, 1992), a two-part stage spectacle that humanizes the gay AIDS victim.

Bibliography

Grove, Allen W. "To Make a Long Story Short: Gothic Fragments and the Gender Politics of Incompleteness," *Studies in Short Fiction* 34, no. 1 (1997): 1–9.

Thomson, Douglass H. "Terror High and Low: The Aikins' 'On the Pleasure Derived From Objects of Terror; with Sir Bertrand, A Fragment,'" *Wordsworth Circle* 29, no. 1 (1998): 72–75.

I

Illuminati novels

An ·impetus to English Gothic fiction, the *Volks·bücher* (people's books) and *bundesroman* (novels of secret societies) of 18th-century Germany focused on the Illuminati, or enlightened ones, as well as on members of the Freemasons, Rosicrucians, and other secret mystic or utopian societies supposedly involved in paganism, occultism, heresy, DECADENCE, political subversion, and international plots. The Illuminati, similar in organization to Freemasons, were the creation of Bavarian law professor Adam Weishaupt, who in 1776 applied the group leadership of his brotherhood to further enlightenment and republicanism. The activities of males in such secret societies survived political suppression in 1785 from rumors and legends that ranged far afield with charges that individual cells practiced Satanism.

Friedrich von SCHILLER set the standards for secret society literature with DER GEISTERSEHER (*The Ghost-Seer,* 1786), a psychological novel that generated a body of imitations, including works by Samuel Taylor COLERIDGE (*Osorio*) and Hanns Heinz EWERS. The MINERVA PRESS exploited the public perception of clandestine male groups with Peter Will's four-volume *The Horrid Mysteries: A Story from the German of the Marquis of Grosse* (1796), a tale of VAMPIRISM and an anarchic secret cabal, adapted from *Horrid Mysteries* (1757) by Karl, marquis of Grosse. An illustration on the title page of Will's novel expresses at a glance the author's SENSATIONALISM in the figure's rounded eyes and hair standing on end alongside a chain,

dagger, and flambeau, all symbols from the action. The text builds SUSPENSE with STALKING, macabre deaths, ghosts, and eroticism.

The themes and ATMOSPHERE of Illuminati novels remained viable into the 1800s in European and New World Gothic. The concept of arcane ritual and regalia, rebellion against an established order, and group activity under heavy SECRECY pervades the anonymous GOTHIC BLUEBOOKs *The Secret Tribunal; or, The Court of Wincelaus* (1803) and *The Mysterious Spaniard; or, The Ruins of St. Luke's Abbey* (1807). Another, *The Astrologer's Prediction; or, The Maniac's Fate* (1826), maintains the stereotype of Italian surnames and a castle in Germany's Black Forest, where contact with an evil astrologer precipitates insanity and murder. Additional versions of secret brotherhoods appeared in Percy Bysshe SHELLEY's second Gothic novel, *St. Irvyne; or, The Rosicrucian* (1811), Jan Potocki's Gothic arabesque *The Manuscript Found In Saragossa* (1815), Edward BULWER-LYTTON's view of Rosicrucianism in *Zanoni* (1842), George Lippard's seamy *The Quaker City; or, The Monks of Monk Hall* (1845), Mary Elizabeth BRADDON's *The Black Band: or, The Mysteries of Midnight* (1861), and Joris Karl Huysmans's novel *Là-bas* (*Down There,* 1891).

AMERICAN GOTHIC seized on secret sects as a vehicle for MYSTERY, as found in Charles Brockden BROWN's ORMOND (1799) and Edgar Allan POE's "THE CASK OF AMONTILLADO" (1846), which describes the PREMATURE BURIAL of a Mason with the unlikely name of Fortunato. A conservative

Kentucky expatriate, Jules-Paul Tardivel, writing in Montreal, Canada, produced *Pour la Patrie* (*For My Country*, 1895), a futuristic novel replete with the diabolic plots of Freemasons to undermine French colonial efforts in the Western Hemisphere. Illuminati plots continued to flourish early in the 21st century, notably in Dan Brown's best-selling murder mystery, THE DA VINCI CODE (2003), which employs an ultrasecret sect as the repository for proof that Jesus sired a royal lineage with his wife, Mary Magdalene.

Bibliography

Horner, Avril, ed. *European Gothic: A Spirited Exchange 1760–1960*. Manchester: Manchester University Press, 2002.

Lagree, Michel. "De Veuillot a Tardivel, ou les Ambiguites de la Haine de la Modernité," *Historical Studies* annual (2001): 251.

Northey, Margot. *The Haunted Wilderness: The Gothic and Grotesque in Canadian Fiction*. Toronto: University of Toronto Press, 1976.

illusion

Illusion is a core motif that connects readers of Gothic fiction with the human frailties of fictional characters, such as the gulling of intelligent men at a phony séance in Friedrich von SCHILLER's psychological novel DER GEISTERSEHER (*The Ghost-Seer*, 1786), the baptism of converts at a witches' coven in Nathaniel HAWTHORNE's "YOUNG GOODMAN BROWN" (1835), and the magical carnival owner whose calling card changes color and whose wrist crawls with a tattooed snake in Ray BRADBURY's SOMETHING WICKED THIS WAY COMES (1962). Central to fearful stories is the blurring of differences between godly and godless, licit and illicit, and real and SUPERNATURAL. The prototypical self-deception dominates Christopher Marlowe's *The Tragicall Historie of DR. FAUSTUS* (ca. 1588), a touchstone for subsequent Gothic applications of the FAUST LEGEND. By deceiving himself into believing that true power derives from heresy, Dr. Faustus abandons Christianity to ally with the powers of Satan. The defeat of Faustus's misbeliefs provides the MELODRAMA of the final act, in which he screams for Christ's salvation as demons pull the sinner limb from limb during his tumble into eternal hellfire.

As a GOTHIC CONVENTION, distorted beliefs trigger audience identification with suffering, as for the tender, inexperienced title hero in Voltaire's *Candide* (1759) and the fallen cleric in Matthew Gregory LEWIS's THE MONK (1796). Unlike Candide, Lewis's VILLAIN cleric AMBROSIO is a mature adult who has no excuse for choosing evil as his guiding principle. He attains quasi-tragic status while lying on his deathbed contemplating how he inadvertently murdered his mother and raped and slew his sister. Unlike Marlowe's Faustus, whom imps escort to retribution, the former monk suffers the recompense of NATURE in the stinging of insects and clawing of eagles, a gory demise suggesting the Greek myth of Prometheus.

During the romantic period, false beliefs lay at the heart of the BYRONIC HERO, a fictional stereotype who chooses to feed egotism and wallow in MELANCHOLY rather than disencumber the spirit of erroneous and ill-conceived tenets. Ann RADCLIFFE created the mirage of omniscience in the craggy face of the monk SCHEDONI, the alluring evildoer in THE ITALIAN (1797). His trust in self and narcissistic wrongs crumbles in a deathbed scene in which he chooses a quick end from poison rather than an ecclesiastical trial and punishment for myriad crimes. The motif recurs in Lord BYRON's MANFRED (1817), in which the debauched title character engages in a lengthy rumination on character faults before he faces the same damnation that doomed Faustus.

A landmark in the contemplation of Gothic illusions, Jane AUSTEN's NORTHANGER ABBEY (1818) depicts protagonist Catherine MORLAND as a young, vulnerable reader who is susceptible to the graphic romanticism of Gothic novels. Despite Austen's debunking of Gothic plots, illusion continued to buoy AMERICAN GOTHIC—notably, an elite court's attempt to escape from plague in Edgar Allan POE's "THE MASQUE OF THE RED DEATH" (1842), the stream-of-consciousness hallucinations of the title character in Katherine Anne Porter's "The Jilting of Granny Weatherall" (1930), the floating dreamscapes in Eudora WELTY's SOUTHERN GOTHIC stories "A Worn Path" (1941) and "Livvie Is Back" (1943), and the dramatic response to an invisible bird during a trial scene of Arthur Miller's THE CRUCIBLE (1953). URBAN GOTHIC further explored the illusory state, as in the surface appearance of democracy in Shirley JACKSON's "THE LOTTERY" (1948), the humorous denial of death in Evelyn WAUGH's droll novel THE LOVED ONE (1948), and the trust in a religious setting in H. P. LOVECRAFT's "The Rats in the Walls" (1924).

Bibliography

Delcourt, Denyse. "Magie, Fiction, et Phantasme dans le 'Roman de Perceforest': Pour une Poetique de l'Illusion au Moyen Age," *Romanic Review* 85, no. 2 (March 1994): 167–178.

Heller, Terry. *The Delights of Terror: An Aesthetics of the Tale of Terror.* Urbana: University of Illinois Press, 1987.

insanity

Insanity is a pivotal theme in Gothic literature, in part as a retreat of the mind from sensational or macabre events and apparitions that overthrow reason. The emotion-charged ATMOSPHERE of mental disorder rivets the reader in Sir Walter SCOTT's terror novel *The Bride of Lammermoor* (1819), in the trauma-induced savagery of Robert Montgomery BIRD's *NICK OF THE WOODS; or, The Jibbenainosay: A Tale of Kentucky* (1837), in a series of symptoms investing "A Madman's Manuscript" in Charles DICKENS's *Pickwick Papers* (1837), and in the psychotic love OBSESSION in Emily BRONTË's ghost novel *WUTHERING HEIGHTS* (1847). Interest in the peculiarites of the insane are focal elements in a number of works: J. Sheridan LE FANU's *Uncle Silas* (1864), H. G. WELLS's *THE ISLAND OF DR. MOREAU* (1896), Gertrude ATHERTON's *The Foghorn* (1934), and Marge Piercy's *Woman on the Edge of Time* (1979). Unlike more shocking revelations in Gothic lore, the identification of characters as unstable or psychotic creates an OTHERNESS that elicits pity and compassion and elevates the humanity of the social situation, as is the case with the delusional schizophrenic in Nikolai GOGOL's "The Diary of a Madman" (1835) and the manic Captain Ahab and the gibbering cabin boy Pip in Herman MELVILLE's *MOBY DICK* (1851).

The application to human terror of madness, inner weakness, and susceptibility to evil is pronounced in Charles Robert MATURIN's *MELMOTH THE WANDERER* (1820). Maturin produced a masterful description of the collapse of mental faculties in a speech by the diabolic wanderer: "You will echo the scream of every delirious wretch that harbours near you; then you will pause, clasp your hands on your throbbing head, and listen with horrible anxiety whether the scream proceeded from *you* or *them*" (Maturin, 56). With complete assurance, he insists, "All humanity will be extinguished in you" (*ibid.*). Diametrically opposite of Maturin's depiction of inner susceptibilities are encounters with random external events that derange and terrify—notably, the SHORT GOTHIC FICTION about a bizarre case of instant insanity that William Maginn proposes in "The Man in the Bell" for the November 1821 issue of *BLACKWOOD'S EDINBURGH MAGAZINE*. The story describes a man unintentionally overwhelmed by the clangor in a church bell tower during a funeral. The bleak scenario suggests that anyone is likely to lapse into madness if the senses are overwhelmed.

Insanity also afflicted some Gothic writers. Edgar Allan POE, the master of American Gothic literature, immersed himself in the overlay of dream states with reality and in the clouded reasoning and uncontrolled perversions of insane protagonists. He focused on obsession, particularly freakish aspirations, death madness, mortal decay, and PREMATURE BURIAL, the subjects of his masterly "THE FALL OF THE HOUSE OF USHER" (1839). At age 22, he published "Lenore" (1831), a dirge that describes a mournful widower, Guy de Vere, who channels his grief into exaggerated claims of adoration for his dead Lenore and behaves as though his mind is unhinged. In "Berenice" (1835), Poe depicts Egaeus's monomania toward teeth and the mutilation of his dead wife's mouth; in "LIGEIA" (1838), Poe created another mournful widower overwrought from the decay of his second wife's corpse and the powers of his first wife to defeat death. Public curiosity about the poet's mental stability reached print on May 26, 1846, when author and editor Charles F. Briggs published an unsigned article implying that Poe's vengeful Gothic imagery proved that he was mentally ill. An episode of public drunkenness, hallucination, and attempted suicide in July 1849 corroborated the role of alcohol in producing Poe's delirium tremens. Rufus Wilmot Griswold produced a derogatory obituary for the New York *Daily Tribune* that confirmed Briggs's diagnosis of insanity.

States of depression, DISSIPATION, and psychosis also permeate lesser Gothic works, as in James Thomson's hopeless vision in his poem *The City of Dreadful Night* (1874). Thomson wrote in the subgenre of GRAVEYARD VERSE, the result of "seven songless years" in fleabag inns (Thomson, 18). Wracked by sleeplessness, dejection, and binge drinking, he wrote hack verse to keep from starving. The stirrings of madness and the loss of contact with reason permeate his musings:

> Some say that phantoms haunt those
>   shadowy streets,
> And mingle freely there with sparse
>   mankind;
> And tell of ancient woes and black defeats,
>   And murmur mysteries in the grave
>   enshrined:
> But others think them vision of illusion,
> Or even men gone far in self-confusion;
>   No man there being wholly sane in mind.
>   (*Ibid.*, 19)

By the time that he collected poems for an anthology, *The City of Dreadful Night, and Other Poems* (1880), he had declined into irrationality, but continued to write horror verse, including *Insomnia* (1882), completed months before his death at age 48.

Victorian Gothic works introduced studies of gendered diagnoses of mental illness and unusual treatment of female patients. In 1892, Charlotte Perkins GILMAN published from personal experience a classic FEMALE GOTHIC tale of madness, "THE YELLOW WALLPAPER." The rapid decline of a wife-patient under the care of John, her knowledgeable but patronizing husband-doctor, takes place in a step-by-step descent into obsession and derangement. Gilman's feminist intent intrudes on the telling through obvious autobiographical statements. John, according to the speaker, charged that, "with my imaginative power and habit of story-making, a nervous weakness like mine is sure to lead to all manner of excited fancies, and that I ought to use my will and good sense to check the tendency. So I try" (Gilman, 715). To the detriment of the speaker, pretending to be the bland, unimaginative woman John wants forces her under a suffocating heap of dormant rage. By story's end, she can only creep around the room like a persistent ghost.

In the 20th century, more sophisticated glimpses of psychosis and its causes permeated fiction, for example, the mental decline of the VILLAIN Steerpike in the post–World War II Gormenghast trilogy of Mervyn PEAKE. H. P. LOVECRAFT, one of the most significant American Gothicists since Poe, turned horrific settings into atmospheric mind-wrenching hells. In "The Rats in the Wall," collected in *The Best of H. P. Lovecraft* (1987), an investigator of horrific burial tumuli at Exham Priory accidentally tumbles into a pit overrun by rodents. Presented with evidence of centuries of his ancestors' brutality, he begins to lose touch with reality: "It's voodoo, I tell you . . . that spotted snake. . . . Curse you, Thornton, I'll teach you to faint at what my family do!" (Lovecraft, 35). His language declines from refinement to working-class dialect, Latin, and Gaelic: "'Sblood, thou stinkard, I'll learn ye not to gust . . . wolde ye swynke me thilke wys? . . . *Magna Mater! Magna Mater! . . . Atys . . . Dia ad aghaidh's ad oadaun*" (ibid.). The retreat into gabble and a neurasthenic sensitivity to rat-like sounds reflects a degeneracy and inborn weakness over which the protagonist has no control.

Bibliography

Gilman, Charlotte Perkins. "The Yellow Wallpaper," in *The Harper American Literature*. 2nd ed. Donald McQuade, et al. New York: HarperCollins, 1994.

Lovecraft, H. P. *The Best of H. P. Lovecraft: Bloodcurdling Tales of Horror and the Macabre*. New York: Del Rey, 1987.

Maturin, Charles Robert. *Melmoth the Wanderer*. Oxford: Oxford University Press, 1968.

Thomson, James. *The City of Dreadful Night and Other Poems*. London: Watts, 1934.

Winchester, Simon. *The Professor and the Madman*. New York: Harper Perennial, 1999.

Interview with the Vampire
Anne Rice
(1976)

Anne RICE's blockbuster *Interview with the Vampire* turns Southern antebellum DECADENCE into a powerful source of MYSTICISM, haunting, and ESCAPISM from grief. She approaches the narrative from a masculine point of view as the young interviewer begins taping a question-and-answer encounter with the vampire Louis. The reporter looks first at Louis's physical exterior, which was "utterly white and smooth, as if he were sculpted from bleached bone, and his face was as seemingly inanimate as a statue, except for two brilliant green eyes that looked down at the boy intently like flames in a skull" (Rice, 4). As though tricked out for Mardi Gras, Louis dresses the part of monstrosity in glossy black curls, black cape, immaculate white collar, and black silk tie. The fanciful biography begins at Pointe du Lac, a Louisiana indigo plantation, in 1791 with his entry into a life of the undead at age 25, when the narcissistic Lestat le Lioncourt drained his blood.

Rice's version of Louis's introduction to blood thirst reads like a stereotypical cynic's exploitation of the NAIF—the neophyte male's homosexual deflowering by the older, more experienced roué. A dreamy aura enshrouds Louis's weakening from blood loss, during which Lestat insists that he keep his eyes open. When Lestat offers his own punctured wrist to Louis, the first sip of human blood produces an overpowering aural sensation as Louis's heartbeat roars in his ears. As though advising a young man on his first carouse, Lestat orders him not to "fall so madly in love with the night that you lose your way" (*ibid.*, 21).

Rice's brooding cult classic deviates from traditional vampire lore by depicting the moral conflict in Louis, who must first die as a mortal before entering the realm of the undead as the ultimate OUTSIDER. In recounting two centuries of depravity, alienation, and despair, he debunks misconceptions of vampirism and reveals a deeply ingrained humanism as he acquires the quirks and nighttime habits of the vampire. In subsequent segments of her Vampire Chronicles, Rice abandons the conscience-ridden Louis and returns to Lestat, whose amorality suits the SADISM and self-indulgence of postmodern Gothic. In 1994, she wrote the screenplay for the film version, which stars Brad Pitt as Louis and Tom Cruise as Lestat.

Bibliography

Novak, Ralph. "The Vampire Lestat," *People Weekly* (November 24–25, 1985): 21–22.

Ramsland, Katherine. "Eloquent Fantasies," *Biblio* (October 1998): 30.

Rice, Anne. *Interview with the Vampire.* New York: Ballantine Books, 1993.

Rout, Kathleen. "Who Do You Love? Anne Rice's Vampires and Their Moral Transition," *Journal of Popular Culture* 36, no. 3 (winter 2003): 473–479.

The Island of Doctor Moreau
H. G. Wells
(1896)

A model of the MAD SCIENTIST motif, H. G. WELLS's *The Island of Doctor Moreau* creates tragedy out of failed ethics and lapsed decency. The tense, moody story takes place in a fictional microcosm, a tropical South Sea island a three-day sail from Apia, Samoa. To enhance horror, Wells features a lifestyle and code of conduct that evolve apart from social and moral constraints. The doctor's inhumane surgeries and brainwashing of imported animals come to the attention of a marooned OUTSIDER, Edward Prendick, who judges the results of sadistic experimentation as violations of NATURE. In the House of Pain, lab specimens live in a limbo of OTHERNESS, neither human nor bestial, and regress to their original state as the island society crumbles. The unforeseeable catastrophe is the author's prophecy of a world gone mad from reckless technology and scientific meddling.

Wells dispenses the horror of his fiction through contrast. In a palm-shaded paradise, Moreau, a renowned physiologist, becomes an in-house god who manipulates life forms in a fearful hell of cringing, howling mutants. In his research suite, fetid with feral odors, the conflict between man and beast reflects a subconscious battle between civilization and brutality, instinct and morality, good and evil. Prendick, on facing one of the hairy simians, asks the pivotal question, "What on earth was he—man or animal?" (Wells, 57).

By extracting truth from SECRECY, the outsider exposes Moreau's breach of boundaries between the natural and unnatural. The revelation of secret sin plunges the protagonist into a milieu made sinister by the CHIAROSCURO of tangled jungle, a symbol of the murky ethical issues that enshroud the lab. Prendick's heroism comes at a steep price, beginning with jailing and a calm lecture by an obviously insane Moreau on the mechanics of grafting bone and skin and transfusing blood to create a leopard-man, hyena-swine, mare-rhinoceros, ape-man, fox-bear, and Saint Bernard dog–man. Serenely self-confident, Moreau exults in his hunt "to find out the extreme limit of plasticity in a living shape" (*ibid.*, 102).

Wells paces his horror classic like a tumbling avalanche. After finding the doctor's corpse, "calm even after his terrible death, and with the hard eyes open, staring at the dead white moon above," Prendick must save himself from the onslaught of angry, terrified, and confused animaloids (*ibid.*, 152). Ironically, salvation comes in the form of a ghost ship bearing the decayed carcasses of the ship's company that had originally abandoned Prendick. Wells returns his protagonist to civilization in a fragile state, his mind seriously unbalanced by terror. Prendick lives out his years in seclusion, gazing at the stars in search of peace.

Bibliography

Batchelor, John. "The Island of Dr. Moreau," *Review of English Studies* 47, no. 186 (May 1996): 286–288.

Ribalow, M. Z. "Script Doctors," *The Sciences* 38, no. 6 (November–December 1998): 26–31.

Wells, H. G. *The Island of Dr. Moreau*. New York: Modern Library, 1996.

The Italian
Ann Radcliffe
(1797)

Ann RADCLIFFE's fourth romance, *The Italian; or, The Confessional of the Black Penitents*, demonstrates her marked disapproval of the SENSATIONALISM and DECADENCE in Matthew Gregory LEWIS's THE MONK (1796). A tale of duplicity, SECRECY, and conspiracy, Radcliffe's novel contrasts the beauties of Naples with the characters' grim retreat at an abbey in the Abruzzi Apennines, a manifestation of the author's anti-Catholic sentiments. The novel opens around 1764 at Santa Maria del Pianto, a convent church outside Naples. Radcliffe introduces MYSTERY and potential terror by revealing an assassin claiming sanctuary, a medieval right accorded by the church to fugitives from the law. The critic and author Anna Laetitia BARBAULD lauded the aura by comparing it to the tuning of a musical instrument to enhance a TONE that suited the entire work.

The story details the foiled love match of Vicentio di Vivaldi and heroine Ellena Rosalba, a sensitive 18-year-old orphan drawn to music and the beauties of NATURE. After learning of a death in the Villa Altieri, Vivaldi exhibits the keen, but misguided analysis common to Gothic characterization. Immediately fearing for Ellena, he leaps to an extreme conclusion that she lies wounded and bleeding. He envisions "her ashy countenance, and her wasting eyes, from which the spirit of life was fast departing, turned piteously on himself, as if imploring him to save her from the fate that was dragging her to the grave" (Radcliffe, 41). This romantic failing in Vivaldi proves his undoing after a dark and mysterious religious tribunal of the Inquisition orders the couple apprehended.

Radcliffe indulges in HYPERBOLE with the imaginings of Vivaldi and Ellena, who make hideous associations between their captors and murderous rumors about the judicial arm of the Vatican. Ellena, no less given to heightened suggestability than Vivaldi, looks at a fearful chamber and vents her terrors, "On this very spot! in this very chamber! O what sufferings have these walls witnessed! what are they yet to witness!" (*ibid.*, 143). Vivaldi recoils from the Inquisitor, an ominous figure cloaked in black, who precedes doomed prisoners into a closed room, from which issue piteous groans.

Radcliffe's MELODRAMA draws on the plot of William Shakespeare's *Winter's Tale* (ca. 1610) and on the Spanish cleric AMBROSIO from *The Monk* for characterization of the proud, sinister cleric SCHEDONI, who arranges for the immurement of the gentle Ellena at the convent of San Stefano and for a subsequent incarceration overlooking the Adriatic before being slain. To hint at evil, the author characterizes his pale, unsmiling face glimpsed within a shadowy cowl, from which Ellena can see large, penetrating eyes and detect an aura of guilt and malignant power. To the heroine, his manly physique suggests superhuman strength and treachery; his dark features foreshadow unseemly introspection and a capacity for hideous crimes and violations of his religious vows.

Against the negative panorama of the monk's persona, Radcliffe contrasts the sweet, artistically inclined nature of the NAIF. The last-minute reprieve as Schedoni raises his weapon to stab Ellena derives from a literary device as old as classic Greek drama—the miniature portrait she wears in a necklace that pictures her father as the image of Schedoni. The blood kinship between heroine and VILLAIN arouses ambiguous feelings, both in the suitor and the reader. Vivaldi can only shudder that "his Ellena was the daughter of a murderer, that the father of Ellena should be brought to ignominious death, and that he himself, however unintentionally, should have assisted to this event" (*ibid.*, 367).

Radcliffe's command of Gothic mode in *The Italian* graced her finest fiction and earned the praise of critic Mary WOLLSTONECRAFT, who applauded the author's genius. The novel influenced later efforts, notably, Mary Gay's French translation of the novel as *Elénore de Rosalba, L'Italian, ou le Confessionnal des Pénitents Noirs* (Eleanor of Rosalba, the Italian; or, the confession of the black penitents, 1797) and James Boaden's bowdlerized three-act stage version, *The Italian Monk* (1797), which opened at London's Haymarket Theatre on August 15 of that year. The play moves directly to Schedoni's realization that he is Ellena's father. While retaining Radcliffe's mystery and the elements of the kidnapping, separated lovers, un-

known parents, hired assassins, evil clerics, and the Inquisition, Boaden's play adds songs by the composer Samuel Arnold and removes the harsher elements to reward a chastened Schedoni in a family reunion with wife and daughter. The critic Steven Cohan remarked that Boaden tried to correct the emotional limitations of the genre. The play, an ambitious project, attempted "to move his audience to tears as well as screams" (Cohan, xxvi). The reviewer described the stage script as Boaden's "most imaginatively coherent rendering of Gothic fiction on stage" (*ibid.*). Five years later, an abridger serialized a version of the novel entitled *The Midnight Assassin; or, The Confessions of the Monk Rinaldi* (1802), issued by *Marvellous Magazine and Compendium of Prodigies*. The Gothic attributes of Radcliffe's novel influenced the writing of Wollstonecraft's novel MARIA; OR, THE WRONGS OF WOMEN (1798), Percy Bysshe SHELLEY's first novel, ZASTROZZI (1810), and Lord BYRON's title figure in MANFRED (1817).

Bibliography
Cohan, Steven. Introduction to *The Plays of James Boaden*. New York: Garland, 1980.

McIntyre, Clara Frances. *Ann Radcliffe in Relation to Her Time*. New Haven, Conn.: Yale Studies in English, 1970.

Radcliffe, Ann. *The Italian*. London: Oxford University Press, 1968.

Saglia, Diego. "Looking at the Other: Cultural Difference and the Traveller's Gaze in 'The Italian,'" *Studies in the Novel* 28, no. 1 (spring 1996): 12–37.

Schmitt, Cannon. "Techniques of Terror, Technologies of Nationality: Ann Radcliffe's 'The Italian,'" *English Literary History* 61, no. 4 (winter 1994): 853–876.

Wilt, Judith. *Ghosts of the Gothic*. Princeton: Princeton University Press, 1980.

J

Jackson, Shirley

(1919–1965)

Shirley Hardie Jackson was a skilled SHORT GOTHIC FICTION writer, the author of some 100 disturbingly sinister and violent psychological stories. A proponent of FEMALE GOTHIC, she was known for her tender handling of the domestic horrors common to post–World War II family life. Her stories returned repeatedly to a creepy set piece, a killing blow against a lone beleaguered female. Often, her casual murder scenarios juxtapose smugness or boring normality with an unforeseen attack. The impetus to her version of Gothic horror tales were medieval devil stories and folk tales retold during the so-called age of anxiety with an updated slant on WITCHCRAFT, magic, and occultism (Bellman, 282).

Jackson's themes of intrusive evil expose real hazards that modern women risk from dominating lovers and husbands and from social misogyny. Kafkaesque terrors arise from unexpected sources, as found in an old woman's recoil from familiar toys during a surreal visit to her childhood home in "The Bus" (1949) and a leg washed ashore near a middle-class Long Island neighborhood in "The Pillar of Salt" (1949). Best known for "The Daemon Lover," "The Tooth," and the frequently anthologized "THE LOTTERY," all collected in *The Lottery and Other Stories* (1949), Jackson also published *The Haunting of Hill House* (1959), an atmospheric masterpiece, and *We Have Always Lived in the Castle* (1962), a unique melding of humor with Gothic horror. Published the year after she won

the Mystery Writers of America Edgar Allan Poe Award, the latter novel applies drollery to a witty psychological horror novel about family murders. The story is set at Blackwood House and involves talk of arsenic, talismans, eccentricity, and an insular life on the remote family estate disturbed by the arrival of an ominous OUTSIDER, Cousin Charles.

Jackson's skill at GOTHIC CONVENTION derives from the deft way she links hauntings, outrageous crimes, and psychopaths with New England's culture and history, notably, the Salem witch trials of 1692, an event connected with a barbaric antifemale backlash against innocent townswomen charged with sorcery. She enjoyed a career as a writer of popular fiction for *Charm, Harper's Bazaar, Redbook, Saturday Evening Post,* and *Woman's Home Companion* but made no significant impact on the public consciousness until 1948, when "The Lottery" appeared in the *New Yorker.* At the time, she lived with her husband and four children in North Bennington, a suffocatingly sedate Vermont community sharing traits with the town described in the story. She escaped domestic CLAUSTROPHOBIA, depression, and a womanizing husband through tranquilizers, alcohol, and a steady outpouring of Gothic fiction.

Jackson was a master of ATMOSPHERE, which she established through visual details drawn from quirks of New England architecture and homelife. At the time of her sudden death from a heart attack at age 47, she was completing *Come Along with Me,* a novel about NECROMANCY practiced by a New England woman. From a carton of manuscripts turned up in the barn, her children, Laurence and Sarah Jackson, issued 54 of their mother's previously uncollected stories in *Just an Ordinary Day* (1996), which contains her characteristic take on small-town ghosts, immured FEMALE VICTIMS, and DIABOLISM. Two of Jackson's works were adapted for cinema: *The Lottery* (1950), filmed by Encyclopaedia Britannica for classroom use, a made-for-television version of "The Lottery" in 1996, and *The Haunting* (1963), a shortening of *The Haunting of Hill House*, a suspense-filled melodrama set in a decrepit New England manse and starring Julie Harris, Claire Bloom, and Russ Tamblyn. In 1999, a Dreamworks remake cast Liam Neeson, Catherine Zeta-Jones, and Bruce Dern in the lead roles, but failed to capture Jackson's signature aura of evil.

Bibliography

Bellman, Samuel Irving. "Shirley Jackson: A Study of the Short Fiction," *Studies in Short Fiction* 31, no. 2 (spring 1994): 282–293.

Griffin, Amy A. "Jackson's 'The Lottery,'" *Explicator* 58, no. 1 (fall 1999): 44.

Hall, Joan Wylie. *Shirley Jackson: A Study of the Short Fiction*. New York: Twayne, 1993.

Schneider, Steven Jay. "Thrice-told Tales: The Haunting, from Novel to Film . . . to Film," *Journal of Popular Film and Television* 30, no. 3 (fall 2002): 166–176.

Willingham-Sirmans, Karen, and Mary Lowe-Evans. "Jackson's 'The Tooth,'" *Explicator* 55, no. 2 (winter 1997): 96–98.

Jacobs, W. W.

(1863–1943)

The Edwardian horror and crime story writer, playwright, and humorist William Wymark Jacobs made his mark on SHORT GOTHIC FICTION with a single story, "THE MONKEY'S PAW," published in *Harper's* and collected in *The Lady of the Barge* (1902). The background derives from the author's youth along the River Thames and his encounters with nightwatchmen, the shrewish wives of stevedores, bargees and roughnecks, and Londoners returning from the British colonies. While working for the post office and savings bank, Jacobs began writing fiction, sometimes producing only one sentence in a half-day's work. At the rate of one story per month, he published 12 volumes of over 150 ghost yarns, cautionary tales, mysteries, and dialect sea stories in the *Idler, Pearson's, Strand, Today,* and *Windsor* magazines and collected his works in *Many Cargoes* (1896), *The Skipper's Wooing* (1897), *Sea Urchins* (1898), *Captains All* (1905), and *Sailor's Knots* (1909).

The novelist Evelyn WAUGH lauded Jacobs's verbal precision, an element that furthered ATMOSPHERE and TONE. Jacobs produced unrelieved terror in "Jerry Bundler," the story of a haunted inn published in the Christmas 1897 issue of *Windsor.* Two years later, Jacobs adapted the story for the stage as *The Ghost of Jerry Bundler* (1899), but toned down the ghastly conclusion to suit delicate playgoers. The play ran at the Haymarket Theatre for 100 performances and, in 1913, flourished on Broadway, as had his plays *Beauty and the Barge* (1905) and *The Flag Station* (1907).

As a follower of the humorist P. G. Wodehouse and keen observer of human behavior and speech, Jacobs successfully blended Gothic lore with bumbling rural antics, as in the sea-serpent yarn "The Rival Beauties" (1896). Jacobs manages both dread and delight at the story's climax: "Joe had 'ad another fit while at the wheel, and, *not knowing what he was doing,* had clutched the line of the foghorn, and was holding on to it like grim death, and kicking right and left. The skipper was in his bedclothes, raving worse than Joe" (Jacobs, 20). The author turned to straight village comedy with "A Tiger's Skin" (1902), in which a rumored pig-eating beast turns out to be a human poacher. Wodehouse remarked: "I could see how good he was and how simply and unerringly he got his effects" (Jacobs, back cover).

In his version of DOMESTIC GOTHIC, Jacobs interspersed homey settings with world exotica, SUSPENSE, MYSTERY, and menace—for example, the Burmese killer and his pet cobra in "The Brown Man's Servant" (1897). Jacobs filled "The Toll House" (1909) with delicious working-class repartee as a party of drinking buddies tries to figure out what causes a string of deaths in an otherwise ordinary residence. He refined his storytelling for a carefully nuanced tale of a REVENANT in a crumbling manse, "The Three Sisters," collected in *Night*

Watches (1914). His skill at the macabre earned respect from the authors G. K. Chesterton, Henry JAMES, Christopher Morley, J. B. Priestley, and H. G. WELLS as well as from the British royal family.

Bibliography

Fusco, Richard. "Pensive Jester: The Literary Career of W. W. Jacobs," *Studies in Short Fiction* 35, no. 1 (winter 1998): 110.

Jacobs, W. W. *Selected Short Stories*. London: Bodley Head, 1975.

Jascoll, John. "Crowning a Literary Landmark," *Biblio* 4, no. 4 (April 1999): 36.

Kirby, Kathleen M. "Resurrection and Murder: An Analysis of Mourning," *American Imago* 50, no. 1 (spring 1993): 55–68.

James, Henry
(1843–1916)

A giant of punctilious literary style and master technician of Gothic, Henry James contributed to the development of the psychological novel and the atmospheric short story. He was educated in New York and England and developed sophistication and a dual perspective of Western culture. Through mannered dialogue and controlled TONE and diction, he managed to beguile readers. From age 21, he worked at a rapid pace to produce succinct, subtle, and carefully controlled novellas and short fiction that balanced realism with romance.

Gothic was one of the many modes that intrigued James. At the end of a 46-year career, he had published 112 short works, including "De Grey" (1868), a tale of a family curse; "The Last of the Valerii" (1874) and "The Beast in the Jungle" (1903), two troubling stories of OBSESSION; "Sir Dominick Ferrand" (1892), which turns on clairvoyance; and *The Other Room* (1896), a GASLIGHT THRILLER set in aristocratic homes. James produced a Gothic masterpiece of naiveté and hovering evil, *THE TURN OF THE SCREW* (1898), and such understated ghost stories as "The Ghostly Rental" (1874) and "The Friends of the Friends" (1896). He employed the DOPPELGÄNGER motif in "The Private Life" (1892) and "The Jolly Corner" (1908), a fable of the haunted self that suggests the author's despair at returning from Europe to find himself a stranger in his old neighborhood. His realistic spin on DOMESTIC GOTHIC through metaphor and MOOD in the fragmentary ARABESQUE novel *The Sense of the Past* (1900), and in *The Portrait of a Lady* (1881), *The Wings of the Dove* (1902), and *The Golden Bowl* (1904), influenced Gertrude ATHERTON. Other literary admirers of James include Joseph CONRAD, Violet Hunt, Joyce Carol OATES, Edith WHARTON, and Virginia Woolf.

Bibliography

Metzcher-Smith, Marilyn K. "James's 'The Beast in the Jungle,'" *Explicator* 53, no. 3 (spring 1995): 147–148.

Thompson, Terry. "James's 'The Jolly Corner,'" *Explicator* 56, no. 3 (summer 1998): 192–195.

James, M. R.
(1862–1936)

A master of SUPERNATURAL fiction, Montague Rhodes "Monty" James titillated readers with understated scenes of irrational fear and malice ranging beyond the grave. A native of Goodnestone, Kent, the author was a child prodigy who learned to love ghost lore from experiencing nightmares and from seeing a PUNCH-AND-JUDY performance. An affable scholar, he developed into an expert on the Bible and medieval manuscripts and an author of learned nonfiction. To relax from his job as provost of Eton College, he wrote short fiction that displays the influence of Charles DICKENS, ERCKMANN-CHATRIAN, and Sheridan LE FANU. On successive Christmas Eves, James read his stories aloud by candlelight to colleagues at King's College, Cambridge, delighting them with mimicry of voices. In 2000, BBC-TV revived the tradition by presenting actor Christopher Lee reading four of the stories.

James set fearful scenes in ordinary surroundings—train stations, gardens, libraries, coastal guesthouses, and country estates. One of his best tales, "Canon Alberic's Scrap-Book" (1904), takes place at a cathedral near Toulouse, France, where an English visitor makes notes on the historic site. James introduces a not-quite-right atmosphere in a meeting between the outsider and the verger, a wizened old man bearing a "curious furtive, or rather hunted and oppressed air" (James, 9). The Englishman builds SUSPENSE while meticulously studying the grounds and perusing an antique scrapbook.

James's stories earned a following for their patient telling, painstaking details, and decorum. He achieved fame in 1904 with the publication of *Ghost Stories of an Antiquary*, which some critics credit as the beginning of the modern horror story. His 1931 anthology, *The Collected Ghost Stories of M. R. James*, contains some of the most revered tales, which he originally published in *Ghosts and Scholars* magazine. The collection has been reprinted more often than any other in the subgenre. In 1957, Jacques Tourneur directed the film *The Curse of the Demon*, a loose retelling of James's "Casting the Runes" (1904).

Bibliography

Fielding, Penny. "Reading Rooms: M. R. James and the Library of Modernity," *Modern Fiction Studies* 46, no. 3 (fall 2000): 749–771.

James, M. R. *Ghost Stories of an Antiquary*. New York: Dover, 1971.

Simpson, Jacqueline. "The Rules of Folklore in the Ghost Stories of M. R. James," *Folklore* 108 (Annual 1997): 9–18.

Jane Eyre
Charlotte Brontë
(1847)

Jane Eyre is a milestone in the history of the English novel. Gothic in TONE and ATMOSPHERE, Charlotte BRONTË's seminal work seems at war with the classic GOTHIC CONVENTIONS, producing a style that some critics have labeled "anti-Gothic." She embroiders the story of a motivated NAIF with romantic touches—visions and portents, flight from a pending marriage to a bigamist, retreat to the moors, rescue from near-death by cousins she has never met, telepathic messages to her true love, and the unforeseen bestowal of an inheritance from an uncle in Madeira. A monument to Victorian fiction and to the rise of women in English society, the novel blends Gothic SUSPENSE and settings with a feminist *Pilgrim's Progress* motif, a romantic search for justice and the domestication of a near-VILLAIN, Edward ROCHESTER, whom Jane rescues from a MELANCHOLY invalidism.

Brontë had an inborn sense of character balance. For MYSTERY and romance, she created Edward Rochester and his milieu as the antithesis of all that Brontë's restrictive home at Haworth parsonage represented. Jane EYRE, the protagonist, exemplifies the author's strongest traits—artistry, scholarship, self-reliance, and the pluck to breach the male-dominated world. The eventual pairing of Edward and Jane bespeaks a writer who is the obedient parson's daughter, decent, tidy, and true to Victorian family mores. In the resolution, Brontë sorts out the relationships of good and bad—the blameless Adèle Varens, who becomes Jane Eyre's confidante, and the worthy Diana and Mary Rivers, who wed suitable husbands. The rejected suitor, St. John Rivers, slinks away to the mission field to find the self-ennobling toil that he deserves. In fairness to her model of poetic justice, Brontë tediously rights the flaws in Rochester by depriving him of one hand and one eye before rewarding him with a loving wife, a son, the restoration of some of his vision, and a home at Ferndean, a pared-down property that replaces the overblown grandeur of THORNFIELD HALL. The supreme sacrifice in Brontë's cast is Bertha Mason ROCHESTER, the insane wife-MONSTER who must die if the main characters are to live in peace as lawful man and wife.

Jane Eyre was an immediate success. Queen Victoria noted in her diary that she read the novel to her husband Albert until nearly midnight. The novel met with thunderous approval from William Makepeace Thackeray, the era's leading novelist, who halted his concluding work on a manuscript to read Brontë's finely honed prose. Characterizing the novel as a scene stealer was the author Margaret OLIPHANT, who wrote in *BLACKWOOD'S EDINBURGH MAGAZINE* that Brontë's book was a revolution in novel-making. Postmodern criticism concurs with Oliphant, elevating Brontë's book to a pinnacle of Victorian Gothic.

Imitations acknowledge the novel's place among English Gothic works. Numerous similar plots flooded the Victorian popular market, including John Brougham's 1856 adaptation for the New York stage and Ellen WOOD's orphan tale *Anne Hereford*, serialized in *Argosy* in 1867. In 1938, popular novelist Daphne DU MAURIER reset similar characters, the

Gothic mansion, and the cleansing fire as elements of REBECCA, a modern blockbuster novel; Victoria HOLT made a similar gesture of honor to *Jane Eyre* in the plotting of MISTRESS OF MELLYN (1960), a pale reflection of Brontë's work. During the coalescing of American feminism in the late 1960s, critics once more embraced *Jane Eyre* for its staunch individualism and depiction of personal emancipation and moral courage in the face of caste restrictions on a governess betrothed to her employer.

Bibliography

Franklin, J. Jeffrey. "The Merging of Spiritualities: Jane Eyre as Missionary of Love," *Nineteenth-Century Literature* 49, no. 4 (March 1995): 456–482.

Frost, Robert. "The Fable of the Poor Orphan Child," *English Review* 10, no. 2 (November 1999): 10.

Gilbert, Sandra M., and Susan Gubar. *The Madwoman in the Attic*, 2nd ed. New Haven, Conn.: Yale University Press, 2000.

Janin, Jules
(1804–1874)

A sometime follower of the German SCHAUER-ROMANTIK, the historical novelist, columnist, and literary historian Jules-Gabriel Janin was a major player of the French school of *frénétique* Gothic fiction, which translators made available in English. Egotistical and opinionated, he dominated French theatrical review. He founded the *Revue de Paris* and contributed drama commentary to *Revue des Deux Mondes* and *Figaro*. For 40 years, he was the prime critic for the *Journal des Débats* and defender of classicism over an encroaching romanticism.

Janin's beginnings belie his later devotion to classical style. On February 3, 1829, in his mid-20s, he published in *Quotidienne* the article "Le Dernier Jour d'un Condamné" (The Last Day of a Condemned Man). Three months later, he issued a two-volume expansion on the article, *L'Ane Mort et la Femme Guillotinée* (The dead donkey and the guillotined woman), a promising contribution to French Gothic that appeared in a handsomely illustrated edition featuring macabre poses. Critical opinion was divided over whether he meant to write serious Gothic literature or whether he intended his book as a parody or satire. He followed

with *La Confession* (1830), *Contes Fantastiques* (Fantastic tales, 1832), and *Les Catacombes* (1839), which he dedicated to the Marquis de Sade.

Bibliography

Browne, Julius Henri. "A Few French Critics," *Harper's* 47 (June–November 1873).

Gamma. "History of a Critic," *Scribner's* 11, no. 6 (April 1876).

Japanese Gothic

A departure from the barbarity and cruelty of European GOTHIC CONVENTION, Japanese literary Gothic leans strongly toward ROMANTICISM, aestheticism, and subdued eroticism. Gothic elements permeate five types of Noh plays: stories about gods, the ghosts of male soldiers, spirits of grieving female lovers, raving women, and demonic tales. At the Kabuki theater, a popular Japanese entertainment that emerged from *odori* folk dance in 1600, an all-male cast presents semirealistic ghost drama. Increasing Gothic effects are masklike makeup, exaggerated gestures and voices, vivid costumes and sets, and accompaniment by drum, flute, three-string samisen, and wooden *batabata* (clappers). Heightening terror are scary animal noises, gushes of fake blood, and trapdoors that facilitate the emergence of ghosts. One popular crime play, *Nemuru Ga Rakuda Monogatari* (1929), describes the poisoning of a village ogre with a dish of blowfish, which instantly paralyzes and suffocates.

Introducing the stirrings of SHORT GOTHIC FICTION in Asia during the Heian Period is *Konjaku Monogatari* (*Tales of Times Now Past*, ca. 1130), a master compendium of more than 1,000 short, extraordinary medieval stories from India, China, and Japan that range from secular fiction and Samurai yarns to Buddhist cautionary tales. Within these lie Chinese demonology, Indian METEMPSYCHOSIS, and Japanese Shintoism and FOLKLORE. These stories ground modern Gothic fiction, notably Lafcadio HEARN's naturalistic Asian ghost miniatures in *Kwaidan* (Weird tales, 1904) and the murderous fury in Ryunosuke Akutagawa's "Rashomon" (1915), the kernel story of Akira Kurosawa's classic film drama *Rashomon* (1950). In 1776, the founder of the Japanese

GHOST STORY, Ueda Akinari, issued the first true Gothic text, which Hamada Kenji translated as *Tales of Moonlight and Rain* (1971), a monument to atmospheric literature of the late Edo period.

Although Japanese pulp fiction has its own Edgar Allan POE, H. P. LOVECRAFT, and Stephen KING in the person of Edogawa Rampo (a Japanese approximation of Poe's full name), the artistic Japanese Gothic lacks the extremes of the Western war on evil and anti-Catholic motifs, mainly because of the absence of Christian concepts of sin and hell. Japanese Gothic avoids male-on-female SADISM because of respect for female ghosts, who can return to avenge cruelty and abuse through fearful hauntings. In 1996, Charles Shiro Inouye translated into English Izumi Kyoka's *Japanese Gothic Tales,* a compendium of MYSTERY stories, fantasy, and romance that introduced English readers to a refined Asian version of Gothic tradition.

More delicate than violent, "One Day in Spring" describes a horrific double drowning with aesthetic dignity, decorum, and a touch of allure. Lacking the romanticist's drive to defend individuality, Japanese Gothic tends toward intrinsic suffering. The cause derives from Buddhist philosophy, which characterizes psychic pain as a craving for the material world. In describing a loss of self-control, the genre captures a uniquely Eastern DOPPELGÄNGER motif—the split of the personality between its duty to religion and its suppressed desires.

Bibliography

Hughes, Henry J. "Familiarity of the Strange: Japan's Gothic Tradition," *Criticism* 42, no. 1 (winter 2000): 59.

Serper, Zvika. "'Between Two Worlds': The Dybbuk and the Japanese Noh and Kabuki Ghost Plays," *Comparative Drama* 35, no. 3 (fall 2001): 345–376.

K

Kabbalism

Jewish MYSTICISM, drawn from the Kabbala, is a source of Gothic motifs. An obscure facet of Judaism, Kabbalism began in Egypt and Babylon and grew out of oral folklore. Early Kabbalists deviated from the standard two-dimensional doctrine of law and obedience and sought to know more about NATURE, the infinite, and the divine. Through twists of logic, Kabbalists speculated on terror by seeking ways to breach the bounds of the visible world to experience God face to face. The canon of Kabbalistic wisdom incorporates MYSTERY, forbidden knowledge, marvels, magic spells, and the scientific pursuit of the secrets of the universe.

In the second century A.D., the first formal Kabbalist, Saadiah ben-Joseph, traveled from eastern Palestine to Syria and Babylonia to head a school. He composed compelling works on mysticism that legitimized questionable folklore with firm scholarship. From unwritten traditions, Kabbalism expanded with research into intellectualism, dreams, penitence, extreme forms of prayer, amulets, cryptic incantations, and asceticism. In this same era, from the experience of Rabbi Akiba (or Akiva) ben-Joseph of Jerusalem came a major treatise, *Hékhalot Zutarté* (The Smaller Book of Celestial Palaces, ca. A.D. 100), a guide to the beginning Kabbalist. Perhaps the most important text of Kabbalism is the *Zohar* or *Sefer ha-zohar* (Book of Splendour or Illumination, ca. 1286), a Spanish text composed in Aramaic and Hebrew. It enlarges on the source and nature of evil, goodness, and the soul through exegesis, commentary, and parables that are so revered that they approach the sanctity of scripture. An earlier handbook, *Sefer Yetzira* (Book of Creation, A.D. 200–500), took shape over three centuries and posed a means of applying sacred numbers and letters to create psychic paths by which seekers could know God and sacred mystery. The motif of the magic formula spawned a tradition that continued into current times with literary examples of demonic cybernetics.

In the early Middle Ages, German Hasidic pietists feared that such magic formulae could summon the golem, a mythic MONSTER or zombie, a soulless phantasm comprised of an angel's physique and a mortal's instincts. In Austria, Bohemia, Moravia, and Germany, Yiddish storytellers transmuted the golem into an artificial man—a quasi-human robot or automaton not unlike Mary SHELLEY's laboratory monster in *FRANKENSTEIN* (1818) and the sinister personality of HAL in Arthur C. Clarke's *2001: A Space Odyssey* (1968). According to a 16th-century myth, Rabbi Loew of Prague formed a huge shape from river clay as a protector of the poor from the pogroms against Jews launched by fanatic Christians. To give life to his mud man, he inscribed God's holy name on the face and limbs and sanctified the mute, inert being with holy words.

The flaw in the project was human error, the fatal overreaching of a mortal creator, which caused the monster to long for freedom. Like the hexed broom in Johann Wolfgang von GOETHE's fable *Der Zauberlehrling* (The Sorcerer's Apprentice, 1797) and Mary Shelley's monster, the golem went berserk and threatened the very lives he was intended to save. By the early 1500s, *golem* was a household word that Yiddish storytellers used to terrify naughty children. To adults, the story empowered lowly Jews against centuries of anti-Semitic disenfranchisement and abuse.

Late in the medieval era, poets and philosophers of western Europe pursued ecstatic worship, intuitive study, and numerology as means to know God's duality as the creator and the wrathful punisher. Their interest in two-sided divinity resulted in literary and stage applications of the golem motif and of the DOPPELGÄNGER, a study of the dual nature of a single personality, the theme of Robert Louis STEVENSON's *DR. JEKYLL AND MR. HYDE* (1886) and Oscar WILDE's *THE PICTURE OF DORIAN GRAY* (1891). The Gothic stalker, a long-lived golem sometimes affectionately dubbed Igor, permeated Gothic stories, drama, film, opera, ballet, and symphonies, invigorating Paul Dukas's symphonic poem *L'Apprenti Sorcier* (*The Sorcerer's Apprentice*, 1897), Rabbi Yudl Rosenberg's tale *The Maharal of Prague* (1909), Gustav Meyrink's novel *Der Golem* (1915), Paul Wegener's film *Der Golem* (1920), Joseph Achron's orchestral *Golem Suite* (1932), Walt Disney's animated feature *Fantasia* (1940), Francis Burt's ballet *Der Golem* (1962), Nobel Prize–winner Isaac Bashevis SINGER's cautionary tale "The Golem" (1982), and John Casken's opera *The Golem* (1989). The Italian writer Primo Levi, author of a series of autobiographical stories in *The Periodic Table* (1987), compared the golem to the modern-day computer.

Bibliography

Glinert, Lewis. "Golem! the Making of a Modern Myth," *Symposium* 55, no. 2 (summer 2001): 78–94.

Koven, Mikel J. "'Have I Got a Monster for You!': Some Thoughts on the Golem, the X-Files, and the Jewish Horror Movie," *Folklore* 111, no. 2 (October 2000): 217.

Sherwin, Byron L. "The Golem, Zevi Ashkenazi, and Reproductive Biology," *Judaism: A Quarterly Journal of Jewish Life and Thought* 44, no. 3 (summer 1995): 314–322.

Keats, John
(1795–1821)

In his short life, the influential English romantic poet John Keats made a tremendous impact on Gothic literature. From reading William BECKFORD's *VATHEK* (1782), William GODWIN's *CALEB WILLIAMS* (1794), Ann RADCLIFFE's terror novel *THE MYSTERIES OF UDOLPHO* (1794), Friedrich von SCHILLER's psychological novel *DER GEISTERSEHER* (*The Ghost-Seer*, 1786), and Charles Brockden BROWN's *WIELAND* (1798), Keats gained respect for GOTHIC CONVENTIONs, which he incorporated in such melodious verse as "O Solitude!" (1816), which describes murky edifices and heaps of structural ruins. Like his fellow poets, he developed medieval themes in atmospheric works resplendent with illusory touches, the hallmark of "Sleep and Poetry" (1817). Overall, however, he preferred more sublime musings on NATURE, mortality, and death, which mark "After Dark Vapors" (1817), "When I Have Fears" (1818), *Endymion* (1818), and "The Human Seasons" (1819).

As literary historian Michael Gamer attests in *Romanticism and the Gothic: Genre, Reception, and Canon Formation* (2000), Keats's most Gothic works derive from his most productive period. Already fatally ill with tuberculosis, he built into the woeful courtship ballad "LAMIA" (1819) the terrors of a beguiling serpentine woman who leads a young NAIF to his doom. In the sensuous, erotic "THE EVE OF ST. AGNES" (1819), the poet incorporated the traditional scenario of a lone damsel in a picturesque feudal setting. Amid gorgeously worked tapestries, she leans from a casement window lighted by moonbeams and expresses a virginal MELANCHOLY and Gothic dream state. Edgar Allan POE admired Keats for an unerring sense of beauty and for skillful portrayal of sound and MOOD.

Bibliography

Gamer, Michael. *Romanticism and the Gothic: Genre, Reception, and Canon Formation.* Cambridge: Cambridge University Press, 2000.

Motion, Andrew. *Keats.* Chicago: University of Chicago Press, 1999.

King, Stephen
(1947–   )

A one-man literary juggernaut of the late 20th century, Stephen King has inherited Edgar Allan POE's title of master of fantasy and Gothic horror. Born and reared in Maine and educated at the state

with Mark Twain and established his genius in North America with the publication of tamer children's fare in *The Jungle Book* (1894) and *Just-So Stories for Little Children* (1902). He returned to ghost fiction with the comic piece "The Haunted Subaltern" (1897) and, in 1905, with "They," in which he merged his interest in youth with a phantom story of ghost children.

Bibliography

Bauer, Helen. *Rudyard Kipling: A Study of the Short Fiction.* New York: Twayne, 1994.

Orel, Harold. *Critical Essays on Rudyard Kipling.* New York: G. K. Hall, 1989.

Paffard, Mark. *Kipling's Indian Fiction.* New York: St. Martin's Press, 1989.

"Kubla Khan"
Samuel Taylor Coleridge
(1816)

A mystic, evocative poem, Samuel Taylor COLE-RIDGE's "Kubla Khan; or, A Vision in a Dream. A Fragment" incorporates in a filmy ILLUSION the Gothic terrors of the demon lover. The poet creates romantic ATMOSPHERE with a sensual setting lighted by an occluded moon and haunted by prophecies of war and the keenings of a lovelorn woman. Contributing to the mesmerizing flow of verse was a prescription of morphia the poet was taking for dysentery in summer 1797. The dosage produced a three-hour sleep and filled his consciousness with edenic imagery, which he was able to transcribe into verse. According to Coleridge,

he was unfortunately interrupted, and when he returned to the task, he found his mind clear of the vision and incapable of the AUTOMATIC WRITING that produced the original 54 lines. Nonetheless, he enjoyed repeating his verse aloud and captivated Lord BYRON with a recitation.

Reviewers for the *Academic, Augustan Review,* and *Edinburgh Review* dismissed the MYSTERY and SUPERNATURAL in "Kubla Khan" and favored "CHRISTABEL" (1816) as Coleridge's most important Gothic poem. One reason for their lack of enthusiasm for the former may have been the poet's preface, which describes the poem as the result of a dream. Because he exploited an ethereal aura, critics misread the misty flow as lackadaisical and devoid of serious craftsmanship. Subsequent criticism characterizes the compact Gothic poem as a celebration of the imagination, which can accommodate extremes of sunny pleasure domes and icy caves. Another possibility is a dreamscape on which the poet pictures a cataclysmic sexual adventure depicted in NATURE through references to fertile earth, a "deep romantic chasm," and the ceaseless seething of coitus (Coleridge, 297). The erupting fountain, a dynamic image of male sexual climax, and the subterranean caverns, a corresponding image of the mysterious womb, precede the call to war, which ends a profane dalliance.

Bibliography

Ball, Stefan. "Coleridge's Ancestral Voices," *Contemporary Review* 278, no. 1,624 (May 2001): 298.

Coleridge, Samuel Taylor. *Samuel Taylor Coleridge: The Major Works.* Oxford: Oxford University Press, 2000.

L

"La Belle Dame sans Merci"
John Keats
(1819)

A notoriously ambiguous ballad, John KEATS's "La Belle Dame sans Merci" uses medieval trappings and chivalric setting and conventions to create a haunting FAIRY TALE of duplicitous or illusory love. The cautionary story reprises age-old FOLKLORE of the treacherous, dominating FEMME FATALE. A recounting of a sexual union, the poem violates convention by connecting grief and regret to the man's loss of love. The players in the scenario, the lady and the knight, are medieval archetypes of an underworld journey, where the knight finds himself displaced amid the otherworldly conventions of fairyland. Like the Greek singer Orpheus, who fails to retrieve his wife Eurydice from the underworld, the knight is unable to hold on to his "belle dame," who slips back into the dream world that gave her being and magic.

Setting the action in autumn, a SYMBOL of the declining years of human life, Keats manipulates NATURE to characterize a despairing spirit and the failure of courtly love. Like the victim in the woeful ballad "Lord Randal," Keats's knight suffers recompense for venturing beyond human bounds to court a fairy maid. Surrounded by withered sedge devoid of birdsong, the miserable knight recalls his encounter with the wild-eyed temptess, who elicits a prophetic nightmare of the undead, men whom the fair lady has enchanted. Having experienced his spring years, the knight declines into bitterness and regret, becoming a figurative REVENANT devoid of hope.

Bibliography
Finlayson, J. Caitlin. "Medieval Sources for Keatsian Creation in 'La Belle Dame sans Merci,'" *Philological Quarterly* 79, no. 2 (spring 2000): 225–247.
Williams, Anne. *Art of Darkness: A Poetics of Gothic.* Chicago: University of Chicago Press, 1995.

La Llorona

A gender archetype in Latino literature, music, dance, and art, *La Llorona* (the Weeping Woman) is a maternal legend recurring in Central American FOLKLORE over three centuries. She takes the form of a sorrowing banshee howling in the night for her little ones. The kernel story depicts her as an abandoned Azteca-Mexica sex slave who slays her children and tosses their remains into a river. One explanation for her deed is that the slayings, like the mercy killing in Toni MORRISON's BELOVED (1987), are an act of love to spare the children enslavement and concubinage by Spanish *conquistadores*.

The child murders take fearful shape in a variety of ballads, stories, and verse. In Yxta Maya Murray's short story "La Llorona" (1996): "They asked no questions, only smiling up at me until the very end, the sounds of the water rushing and their raised cheeks, letting me fold them into the murk, into the cold water like the sky in the dark night" (Murray, 24). As described in Mary McArthur's eerie poem "La Llorona" (2000), the mother drowned her children so long ago that she can't relocate the site or find "where she waded out in all her skirts / and let the water pull her down" (McArthur, 42). Driven mad by vengeance, the legendary killer suffers the fate of the WANDERING JEW—a female MONSTER in perpetual torment as she combs towns and waysides for her little ones. Variances on her appearance indicate shifts in point of view concerning guilt. In some settings, she is a beautiful maiden clad in white; in the more prevalent opposing versions, she is a deformed hag or witch dressed in dusky tatters.

The resilience of La Llorona from as far back as Aztec oral lore places the Gothic tale in the pre-Columbian Native American canon and as recently as *The La Llorona Legend* (1984), a novella by Southwestern folklorist and fiction writer Rudolfo A. Anaya; Southwestern storyteller Joe Hayes's performances of "La Llorona" (1987); and the short fiction of Helena Maria Viramontes anthologized in *The Moth and Other Stories* (1995). Evolved without reference to European Gothic convention, the original sobbing woman appeared as a manifestation of Cihuacoatl or Snake Woman, patron of fertility and of women who die in childbirth. An omen of death to innocent mothers and infants, she appears in the late 16th-century chronicles of the mestizo historian Diego Muñoz Camargo and in biographies of the exploiter Hernán Cortés, who abandoned his slave mistress/interpreter, Doña Marina, called La Malinche (the captain's woman). In despair, she reputedly stabbed their illegitimate son; Cortés passed her to a Castilian knight, Don Juan Xamarillo, who displayed her as his trophy wife. The tale abounds with standard Gothic motifs of the underclass woman abused by an aristocrat or of a mestiza despoiled by a pure-blood hidalgo rapist. Her penalty is transformation into the forbidding witch-woman, a GROTESQUE hag capable of flaunting her evil appearance to terrorize the unwary.

A complex figure, La Llorona is both warning and solace, betrayer and betrayed. She displays the duality of the seductress/maiden trapped by the strictures of a male-dominated society. In an historical context, she is a casualty of racism and wartime lust, the Aztec female ravished and discarded by Spanish *conquistadores*. Rapidly reduced from youthful beauty to bedraggled crone, she cries out for lost children, the SYMBOLs of her former charm and grace. In Catholic interpretation, she is deprived of her promise, either through willing fornication or rape, and embodies the soul's scouring of Purgatory in search of redemption. A mirror image of the serpent-haired gorgon Medusa in Greek mythology, the forbidding weeper undergoes punishment that extends to any foolhardy enough to follow her. All who chance too close die from one glance of the evil eyes and sob-contorted face. In a version of the 20th-century FEMALE VICTIM, the weeping woman was the impetus for Sandra Cisneros's complex culture study in *Woman Hollering Creek and Other Stories* (1991), a Gothic-tinged escapist story in which an abused wife flees her marriage and shrieks with joy in independence and anger at her sufferings.

Bibliography

Carbonell, Ana Maria. "From Llorona to Gritona: Coatlicue in Feminist Tales by Viramontes and Cisneros," *MELUS* 24, no. 2 (summer 1999): 53.

Domecq, Alcina Lubitch. "La Llorona," *Literary Review* 43, no. 1 (fall 1999): 17.

McArthur, Mary. "La Llorona," *Midwest Quarterly* 42, no. 1 (autumn 2000): 42.

Murray, Yxta Maya. "La Llorona," *North American Review* 281, no. 6 (November–December 1996): 24–27.

Lamb, Lady Caroline

(1785–1828)

Poet, novelist, and purveyor of exotica, Lady Caroline "Caro" Ponsonby Lamb was a popular writer of DOMESTIC GOTHIC fiction. From childhood, she bore traces of an innate excitability and neurosis. After marriage at age 17 to the statesman William Lamb, the future Lord Melbourne and prime minister of England, she weathered an emotionally unsettled existence complicated by the birth of a retarded child. Her close relationship with Lamb altered in 1806, when he became a member of Parliament and spent time away from home. Witty and artistic, she devoted her solitude to writing verse and letters and drawing portraits.

In 1812, Lamb entered into a passionate affair with Lord BYRON, whose scandalous reputation intrigued her. Following their breakup and a threat to her marriage, she was still obsessed with his wayward but engaging personality. She composed her most popular work, the three-volume Gothic MELODRAMA *Glenarvon* (1816), a satiric tale of implied VAMPIRISM and an imbroglio of two aristocratic houses, including the Lamb family. She completed the text at night while her family slept and published it anonymously. The plot is a transparent roman à clef of her affair with Byron, who expressed amusement that she depicted him as the antihero Ruthven, literally "in-joke," a name that John POLIDORI reused for the hero of his tale "The Vampyre" (1819). Lamb's work enjoyed a long life in English and Italian and was reissued in 1865 with a more titillating title, *The Fatal Passion*.

Lamb's writing career continued with *Graham Hamilton* (1822), a crime novel about gambling and theft in fashionable London, and an exotic tour of hell in the three-volume novel *Ada Reis* (1823), the fitful ORIENTAL ROMANCE of a promiscuous pirate who stabs his mistress in the heart. He carries his daughter Fiormunda away to Egypt to be reared by a witch in unorthodox luxuries, a scenario based in part on Byron's treatment of his own daughter, Ada Lovelace. When Fiormunda passes to the underworld, through a Faustian pact, she is allowed to return to earth to repent and live a pure life. Lamb's hysterical response to Byron's death in 1824 ended her marriage. With the reemergence of Gothic novels in the 1930s, her writings enjoyed a resurgence.

Bibliography

Review of *Caroline Lamb, This Infernal Woman*, by Susan Normington, *Contemporary Review* 279, no. 1627 (August 2001): 126.

"Lamia"
John Keats
(1819)

English romanticist John KEATS produced his sensuous "Lamia" near the end of his life. He derived the subject from a Greek myth of the lamia, a female serpent-demon who ate infants and children. The lamia was an exotic shape-shifter and FEMME FATALE who could function as a reptile or as a voluptuous siren who seduced and devoured males. The concept of Keats's female vampiric monster had forerunners in the Gothic era: Johann von GOETHE's ballad *Die Braut von Corinth* (*The Bride of Corinth*, 1797), Samuel Taylor COLERIDGE's "CHRISTABEL" (1816), and Thomas Love PEACOCK's "Rhododaphne" (1818).

In Keats's vividly dramatic version, the female vampire is a sinuous, snaky ghoul enamored of Lycius, a young Corinthian scholar. Keats describes her mystique in medieval images tinged with bright reds, gold, blue, and green. From a tangle of coils with lifted head like a cobra, she observes Lycius in secret, then woos him with sweet song. The poet gradually increases the Gothic menace of a lethally mismatched pair. The day of her wedding, she wears a wreath of willow and adder's tongue, symbols of grief and guile; Lycius bears the thyrsus, a classic phallic emblem. She is empowered with a blended animal body and magic stare, which she fixes on the philosopher Apollonius, who cries to Lycius, "Shall I see thee made a serpent's prey?" (Keats, 156). To counter her menace, Apollonius outstares her at the wedding feast, causing her to vanish and Lycius to die of grief. Ironically, he expires out of longing for his ILLUSION.

Bibliography

Endo, Paul. "Seeing Romantically in 'Lamia,'" *English Literary History* 66, no. 1 (spring 1999): 111.

Martin, Tony. "Transformations and Ambiguities in Keats's 'Lamia,'" *English Review* 13, no. 3 (February 2003): 6–9.

Parry, Susan. "Keat's 'Lamia,'" *Explicator* 59, no. 4 (summer 2001): 178.

Lathom, Francis
(1777–1832)

A dramatist and novelist published by MINERVA PRESS, Francis Lathom contributed to DOMESTIC GOTHIC lore with classic tales of jealousy, greed, confinement, VIOLENCE, and uncontrolled passions. The bastard son of a noble, he was born to precarious social circumstance. By age 18, he had read examples of the *Schauerroman* (shudder novel) of Friedrich von SCHILLER, the Marquis de Sade's *Les Crimes de l'Amour* (*The Crimes of Love*, 1788), and Ann RADCLIFFE's *THE MYSTERIES OF*

UDOLPHO (1794) and had written a comedy staged at the Theatre Royal in his hometown of Norwich. Lathom turned to Gothic fiction with *The Castle of Ollada* (1795), which earned critical rejection for its failure to turn up anything new in terror.

Mentioned in Jane AUSTEN's NORTHANGER ABBEY (1818), Lathom's chief domestic MELODRAMA, *The Midnight Bell: A German Story, Founded on Incidents in Real Life* (1798), is a Gothic quest tale set at a ruined castle. The plot exhibits ANTI-CATHOLICISM and the influence of de Sade with its excessive bloodshed in the self-flagellation of a penitent. After 11 years' imprisonment, the main character, Count Byroff, is condemned to death by drinking a phial of thick black liquid. Shortly, his eyes grow weary as he sinks into a deathlike sleep. Revival and a fierce struggle with a swordsman conclude with the ladylike swoon of Lauretta, the wooden female protagonist whom Lathom turns into a Gothic caricature.

During an era that saw Gothic fiction become a fad, Lathom followed with a variety of thrillers, crime stories, MYSTICISM, and romance: *Mystery* (1800), *Astonishment* (1802), *Very Strange, But True* (1803), *The Impenetrable Secret* (1805), *The Mysterious Freebooter* (1806), *The Fatal Vow* (1807), *The Unknown* (1808), *The One-Pound Note and Other Tales* (1820), *Italian Mysteries* (1820), *The Polish Bandit* (1824), *Fashionable Mysteries* (1829), and *Mystic Events* (1830). In "The Water Spectre" (1809), he tricked out three apparitions to look and speak like the witches in William Shakespeare's *Macbeth* (ca. 1603). Lathom's most enduring work appeared anonymously in GOTHIC BLUEBOOK redaction as *The Midnight Bell; or, The Abbey of St. Francis* (1811), a gem of sinister ATMOSPHERE. Generally ignored by critics, Lathom retreated to Aberdeenshire, Scotland, late in life and lived in seclusion.

Bibliography

Haining, Peter, ed. *Gothic Tales of Terror.* New York: Taplinger, 1972.

Lathom, Francis. *The Midnight Bell.* London: Skoob Books, 1989.

Summers, Montague. *The Gothic Quest: A History of the Gothic Novel.* London: Fortune Press, 1969.

Lee, Harriet
(1757–1851) and
Lee, Sophia
(1750–1824)

Two of the early English experimenters in historical fiction were Harriet and Sophia Lee, London-born sisters. The daughters of actors, they were free to read the contemporary French writers Baculard d'Arnaud and Abbé PRÉVOST, and the English Gothic novels of Clara REEVE and Horace WALPOLE. In 1781, on the proceeds of Sophia Lee's three-act opera, *The Chapter of Accidents* (1780), based on Denis Diderot's *La Père de Famille* (The father of the family, 1758), the Lee sisters supported their younger siblings and opened a girls' school at Belvidere House at Bath before pursuing careers in drama and fiction. An unusual coincidence brought the Lees into friendships with the founders of traditional English Gothic—William GODWIN, Jane PORTER, and Ann RADCLIFFE.

Harriet Lee was the lesser of the two writers. She composed the three-act stage play *The Mysterious Marriage; or, The Heirship of Roselva* (1798) and "Kruitzner, the German's Tale" (1797), the story of an evil son's cruelties to his mother. An influence on Lord BYRON's *Werner* (1821), the story was a successful segment of Lee's *The Canterbury Tales* (1797–1805), an original 12-part series to which Sophia Lee contributed the frame story and two additional tales, one the story of a kidnapped child who grows into a hero and the other "The Old Woman's Tale—'Lothaire: A Legend,'" a symbolic scenario of ruin and distortions of history.

Best known for escapist fiction, Sophia Lee has been called the founder of historical Gothic. In addition to transcribing the French works of d'Arnaud, she produced a landmark novel, *The Recess; or, A Tale of Other Times* (1783–85), a three-volume pseudohistorical text that won critical praise for its depiction of a female community within a patriarchal system. Unlike authors choosing a nebulous period in the Middle Ages, Sophia Lee based the epistolary romance on gross exaggerations of the lives of Ellinor and Matilda, the twins who supposedly resulted from a secret marriage between the duke of Norfolk and Mary, Queen of Scots in the late 16th century. Salted with details drawn from D'Arnaud's novels, which Lee translated for *Ladies' Magazine,* the story of the royal girls takes shape around MYSTERY, SECRECY, and hardships suffered in migrations to North America and St. Helena. Lee depicts the sisters as growing up concealed from public notice in a recess beneath a ruined abbey, a standard labyrinthine enclosure that mimics a setting from Prévost's *Histoire de Cleveland* (1731–39).

Sophia Lee assigns her two protagonists fictitious shadow roles in British history, which she substantiates through mention of the queen's visit to Kenilworth Castle in 1575, the execution of Mary Stuart at Fotheringhay Castle in 1587, the defeat of the Spanish Armada in 1588, and the revolt of Lord Essex in 1601. In one of Lee's more inspired Gothic touches, she uses lightning to reveal a trapdoor that allows the secretly wed lovers Matilda and Leicester to escape a DUNGEON. The orchestration of remote voices, dreams and visions, confinement with lunatics, and ghostly music segues neatly into a realistic gimmick of explained SUPERNATURAL, the substitution of the body of a dead servant for Ellinor and the general assumption that Ellinor has died. When she confronts Queen Elizabeth, the visit paralyzes the monarch, who believes she is viewing a ghost. Lee followed with a ROMAN NOIR (black novel), *Warbeck: A Pathetic Tale* (1786), a reworking of d'Arnaud's *Varbeck* (1774).

Sophia Lee's imaginative work earned the disapproval of Anna Laetitia BARBAULD, an author and critic who disdained the subgenre of historical Gothic for misrepresenting real events. Nonetheless, Lee's handling of dread and SUSPENSE was an influence on the writings of Lord BYRON and Sir Walter SCOTT and on Anne Fuller's *Alan Fitz-Osborne* (1786) and *The Son of Ethelwolf* (1789), the latter of which details a Druidic human sacrifice in a fictional setting during Alfred the Great's war against the Danes. Ann Radcliffe's *Castles of Athlin and Dunbayne* (1789) also bears a striking resemblance to Lee's historical Gothic. Elements of the ill-fated marriage and news from Jamaica in Lee's *Recess* may have colored Charlotte BRONTË's halting of Edward ROCHESTER's bigamous union with his governess in *JANE EYRE* (1847).

Bibliography

Grove, Allen W. "To Make a Long Story Short: Gothic Fragments and the Gender Politics of Incompleteness," *Studies in Short Fiction* 34, no. 1 (winter 1997): 1–10.

Isaac, Megan Lynn. "Sophia Lee and the Gothic of Female Community," *Studies in the Novel* 28, no. 2 (summer 1996): 200–217.

Nordius, Janina. "A Tale of Other Places: Sophia Lee's 'The Recess' and Colonial Gothic," *Studies in the Novel* 34, no. 2 (summer 2002): 162–176.

Le Fanu, Sheridan
(1814–1873)

A daringly innovative Anglo-Irish Gothic writer, Joseph Thomas Sheridan Le Fanu was a master of GROTESQUE actions and black humor and the creator of the first female vampire in English literature. In childhood, he took an interest in demonology, occultism, and psychic phenomena, subjects contained in the books found in his father's library. Le Fanu studied classics and law at Trinity College, Dublin, and cultivated literary tastes. He abandoned law to edit *Dublin University Magazine* and the *Protestant Guardian* and, in the style of Sir Walter SCOTT, to write Gothic tales for *All the Year Round.* At age 24, Le Fanu issued his first SUPERNATURAL tale, "The Ghost and the Bone-Setter" (1838), a dialect story about a tippler who pulls a leg off the devil. Le Fanu next produced a revolutionary erotic occult tale, "Schalken the Painter" (1839), an eerie plot featuring the lurking apparition of the suicide victim Rose Velderkaust, a specter bride who summons the painter from a burial crypt.

Publishing anonymously, Le Fanu incorporated the lore of Ireland into his atmospheric, subtly paced ghost stories and contributed to SENSATIONALISM in the style of Mary Elizabeth BRADDON, Edward BULWER-LYTTON, and Wilkie COLLINS. Le Fanu advanced a number of Gothic themes—notably, VIOLENCE in *The House by the Churchyard* (1861–62), the BLUEBEARD motif and anti-Catholic SUPERSTITION in *Uncle Silas* (1864), INSANITY and confinement to asylums in *Wylder's Hand* (1864) and *The Rose and the Key* (1871), phantoms in *The Haunted Baronet* (1870), and the

MAD SCIENTIST motif in *Checkmate* (1870). In "Green Tea" (1869), a quirky occult story issued in *All the Year Round,* the author created a spectral presence that takes a surprising form: "I soon saw, with tolerable distinctness, the outline of a small black monkey, pushing its face forward in mimicry to meet mine" (Messent, 121). The curious observer is startled when he pokes the monkey with an umbrella and pierces the ghostly shape.

Influenced by Samuel Taylor COLERIDGE's "CHRISTABEL" (1816) and by French supernatural tales, Le Fanu's venture into lesbian VAMPIRISM the year before his death resulted in *Carmilla* (1872). The tale, serialized in *The Dark Blue* over four installments, treats a perennial ghoul alternately known by the anagrams Carmilla, Millarca, and Mircalla. The author breaches Victorian proscriptions against homosexuality by probing the passionate, sadistic attachment between Laura and the title character. Chapter 4, in which Carmilla claims her love object, merges self with self and introduces Laura to rapturous cruelty. Carmilla murmurs seductively that Laura will die, a pun on sexual climax. Critic Nina Auerbach, author of *Our Vampires, Ourselves* (1995), characterized Carmilla as "one of the few self-accepting homosexuals in Victorian or any literature" (Auerbach, 41). After a period of neglect, Le Fanu returned to vogue through the editorship of Gothicist and GHOST STORY writer M. R. JAMES, who collected original tales in *Madam Crowl's Ghost and Other Tales of Mystery* (1923).

Bibliography

Auerbach, Nina. *Our Vampires, Ourselves.* Chicago: University of Chicago Press, 1995.

Le Fanu, Sheridan. *The Best Horror Stories.* London: Sphere, 1970.

Messent, Peter B. *Literature of the Occult.* Englewood Cliffs, N.J.: Prentice-Hall, 1981.

Signorotti, Elizabeth. "Repossessing the Body: Transgressive Desire in 'Carmilla' and 'Dracula,'" *Criticism* 38, no. 4 (fall 1996): 607–632.

legend

Legend forms a branch of traditional FOLKLORE that includes traditional oral tales, plaints, love songs, and ballads of WITCHCRAFT, DIABOLISM, and heroic deeds and accomplishments, as with the extremes of menace, grief, and heroism in English grail lore and the MAD SCIENTIST motif in medieval tales of alchemists and sorcerers. The purpose of the legend is the transmission of a community's identification and belief system, the theme that motivates Thomas Love PEACOCK's chivalric romance *Maid Marion* (1818) and American author August WILSON's urban ghost play THE PIANO LESSON (1990). Legend presents a personal encounter or event that is unverifiable by historical fact, for example, the dark, elusive vice of the Faustian motif, an integral part of German ROMANTICISM; the terrors of LA LLORONA, the mystic weeping woman of Central American literature that has survived since the first encounters of the Aztec with Spanish conquistadors; and east European vampire legends that inspired Bram STOKER's DRACULA (1897).

Legend conveys a cultural truth or national spirit, as found in the titillation of early 19th-century voyeurs in G. Creed's gruesome MONSTER tales in *Legends of Terror! And Tales of the Wonderful and Wild* (1840) and the winnowing out of the weak in Washington Irving's eerie American frontier FOOL TALE "The Legend of Sleepy Hollow," published in *The Sketch Book* (1820). Literary convention allows the legend to exaggerate biographies and events for maximum impact, as with the unauthenticated kidnap of children in the medieval tale "The Pied Piper of Hamelin" (or Hameln), an established motif that fabulists Jacob and Wilhelm GRIMM developed in 1816. Robert Browning reset the story in narrative verse in 1888 with sinister details of dogs attacked, cats killed, and babes bitten in their cradles by a deluge of vermin. For its tendency toward such intriguing facets and character voicing, legend is a frequent vehicle of STORYTELLING.

Bibliography

Benoit, Raymond. "Irving's 'The Legend of Sleepy Hollow,'" *Explicator* 55, no. 1 (fall 1996): 15–17.

Hoffman, Daniel. *Form and Fable in American Fiction.* New York: Oxford University Press, 1965.

Leroux, Gaston
(1868–1927)

The Paris-born dramatist, film scenarist, journalist, and writer of the MYSTERY novel, DETECTIVE STORY, GASLIGHT THRILLER, and Gothic SERIAL, Gaston

Louis Alfred Leroux was educated in law but made his name in pulp fiction. After squandering an inheritance on foolish investments, gambling, and drink, in 1888, he began working as a court reporter, foreign correspondent during the Russian Revolution, and theater critic for *L'Echo de Paris* and *Le Matin*. Field work took him to Scandinavia, Korea, Egypt, Morocco, and the Middle East.

From his work as a media reporter, Leroux stored up incidents from the Belle Epoque, notably, oriental exotica, brilliant stage performances, and the fall of a chandelier's counterweight in the Paris Opera House in 1896, which he inserted into a fictional episode. During the phenomenal growth of public libraries, he gave up journalism to craft intricate mysteries, writing about the detective work of cub reporter Joseph Rouletabille in *Le Mystère de la Chambre Jaune* (*The Mystery of the Yellow Room*, 1907) and its sequel, *Le Parfum de la Dame en Noir* (The fragrance of the lady in black, 1909), classic stories that mimic the style and tone of Sir Arthur Conan DOYLE's SHERLOCK HOLMES series. Under the influence of Edgar Allan POE and the novelists Alexandre Dumas and Victor Hugo, Leroux produced horror novels *Baloo* (1912) and *The Man with the Black Feather* (1912), a tale of a REVENANT in *The Man Who Came Back from the Dead* (1916), and CONTES CRUELS (cruel tales) and mysteries published in French newspapers and *Weird Tales* magazine. Generally relegated to the second tier of fiction writers, Leroux survives in literary history primarily for one haunting GHOST STORY, *Le Fantôme de l'Opéra* (THE PHANTOM OF THE OPERA, 1910), a work that has been adapted memorably for stage and screen.

Bibliography

Sauvage, Leo. "Phantom of the Opera," *New Leader* 71, no. 3 (February 22, 1908): 21–22.

Wildgen, Katherine E. "Making the Shadow Conscious: The Enduring Legacy of Gaston Leroux," *Symposium* 55, no. 3 (fall 2001): 155–167.

Lewis, Matthew Gregory
(1775–1818)

A compatriot of the romantic poets Percy Bysshe SHELLEY and Lord BYRON, Matthew Gregory Lewis was a major contributor to the growing popularity of Gothic literature. He grew up in Essex at Stanstead Hall, a partially abandoned mansion that the staff insisted was haunted. In childhood, he enjoyed Joseph Glanville's compendium of demonology, *Sedducismus Triumphatus; or, A Full and Plain Evidence Concerning Witches and Apparitions* (1681). In 1790, Lewis emulated Gottfried August Bürger's German Gothic verse in the ballad *Alonzo the Brave and the Fair Imogene*. At age 17, Lewis advanced to reading Johann von GOETHE and Friedrich von SCHILLER's contemporary crime fiction, Teutonic SCHAUER-ROMANTIK, versions of the WANDERING JEW, and GROTESQUE stories by German authors, particularly Johann Karl August Musäus's *Volksmaerchen der Deutschen* (German folk tales, 1782–87), Christian Friedrich Schubart's *Der Ewige Jude: Eine Lyrische Rhapsodie* (The wandering Jew: a lyric rhapsody, 1783), and Benedikte Naubert and Johann Mathias Müller's *Neue Volksmärchen der Deutschen* (New German folk tales, 1789–93). Freed from school to travel to Weimar, Germany, on his own, Lewis attended stage productions in the *Sturm und Drang* (storm and-stress) style. (*Sturm und Drang* was a dramatic movement based on SENSATIONALISM.)

During his study of modern foreign languages at Oxford, Lewis started writing his own versions of German Gothic. While on staff at the British embassy at The Hague in 1794, he began reading Ann RADCLIFFE's restrained terror novel THE MYSTERIES OF UDOLPHO (1794). He wrote a letter to his mother declaring Radcliffe's GOTHIC NOVEL the most interesting ever published. The reading came at a crucial point in his life, when the diplomatic career he had chosen palled, leaving him with excess energy to apply to his own projects.

While under the novel's evocative power, over 10 weeks during the summer of 1795, Lewis, at age 20, wrote a romance, THE MONK (1796), the most notorious Gothic shocker of the age. His extravagantly nightmarish anti-Catholic plot set during the Spanish Inquisition ventured from Radcliffe's fearful tales into genuine horror narrative, comprised of sensationalism, the SUPERNATURAL, SADISM, sensuality, and unbridled evil. Unlike Radcliffe's implicit sexuality, Lewis preferred explicit, even pornographic carnality. The publication produced such a frisson that the author was forever dubbed "Monk" Lewis. Because of court action against his extreme license, blasphemy, and threat to public virtue, that same year he reissued a bowdlerized version. Although he considered the text cleansed, it earned a reproof from Byron, who, in the satiric *English Bards and Scotch Reviewers* (1809), lambasted the novel for its satanic thrust.

Completely dedicated to a career in literature, Lewis earned a nod from George III and entered Parliament, but gave only cursory attention to pursuing politics. He followed *The Monk* with a GOTHIC DRAMA, *The Castle Spectre* (1798), a bustling musical romance cobbled together from borrowed elements. It enjoyed a run of 60 nights at Drury Lane. The poet William Wordsworth admired it after attending a performance in Bristol on May 21 at the Theatre Royal. Lewis completed ballads for *Tales of Wonder* (1801) and returned to stage works with *Alfonso, King of Castile* (1801) and *The Captive* (1803), two impressive MELODRAMAs. Feeling less public censure of his plays, he published 15 additional stage scripts, including original dramas and an opera and translations from Schiller's and August Friedrich von Kotzebue's German texts.

In 1804, while residing at Inveraray Castle, Lewis translated Heinrich Zschokke's *Abällino, der Grosse Bandit* (Aballino, the great bandit, 1793) for his second most popular work, *The Bravo of Venice: A Romance* (1805), an outlaw tale bearing elements of Schiller's *Die Räuber* (*The Robbers*, 1781). Lewis reset it the following year as the stage melodrama *Rugantino, the Bravo of Venice* (1805), which featured the charming bandit Abellino, rescuer of the lovely Rosabella, daughter of a Venetian doge. Lewis moved in the direction of the ORIENTAL ROMANCE with Eastern stories in *Romantic Tales* (1808), a collection permeated with exoticism, SUSPENSE, and poetic justice. One of the most chilling short works from the anthology is "THE ANACONDA," a COLONIAL GOTHIC story describing the demise of an entrepreneur from the venomous breath of a snake.

Lewis had a profound effect on the readers of his day, notably, the Marquis de Sade, Mary Wollstonecraft SHELLEY, and the poet Samuel Taylor COLERIDGE, who in a review in the February 1797 issue of the *Critical Review* took Lewis to task for writing horrific prose that would terrify children. The critic Leigh Hunt attacked Lewis for his

Gothic excesses: "When his spectral nuns go about bleeding, we think they ought in decency to have applied to some ghost of a surgeon. His little Grey Men, who sit munching hearts, are of a piece with fellows who eat cats for a wager" (Hunt, 254–255).

Lewis died suddenly at sea of fever after a trip to his Caribbean holdings in Jamaica. In his lifetime, imitators produced a clutch of Monkish novels, notably, H. J. Sarratt's *Koenigsmark the Robber; or, The Terror of Bohemia* (1801), Charlotte DACRE's *Zofloya; or, The Moor* (1806), and Edmund Montague's *The Demon of Sicily* (1807).

Bibliography

Gamer, Michael. "Authors in Effect: Lewis, Scott, and the Gothic Drama," *English Literary History* 66, no. 4 (1999): 831–861.

Hunt, Leigh. *Essay by Leigh Hunt*. London: Walter Scott, 1900.

Trott, Nicola. "A Life of Licence and Gothic Literature," *National Post* 2, no. 257 (August 19, 2000): B10.

"Ligeia"
Edgar Allan Poe
(1838)

A gloomy, SENSATIONAL short story by Edgar Allan POE, "Ligeia" models metamorphosis or transformation as an element of the SUPERNATURAL. He wrote the story during the five-year decline of his child-bride, Virginia Clemm Poe, from tuberculosis, and published it in the September 1838 issue of *Baltimore American Museum* magazine. The complex plot anticipates the doom-laden female decline of Madeline USHER in "THE FALL OF THE HOUSE OF USHER" (1839), another in a series of writings filled with MELANCHOLY and regret over the death of a beautiful woman in a phantasmic residence.

"Ligeia" takes shape from interlocking love matches resulting in METEMPSYCHOSIS, the migration of a soul from one body to another. The author names the title figure from a character mentioned in John Milton's *Comus* (1634). Because the name also occurs in the epic verse of Homer and Virgil, Poe suggests scholarliness in his REVENANT. Poe applies to Ligeia's story a range of Gothic conventions—a decrepit castle on the

Rhine, a harem-like setting heightened by rich decor in a remote English abbey, and tapestries covered with twining ARABESQUEs—along with an UNRELIABLE NARRATOR, the unnamed speaker who successively weds women completely different in nature. Like Poe's typical female characters, the women never advance from sex objects to palpable, multifaceted beings.

Poe's Gothic settings contribute to the otherworldliness of the story. The first couple settle in the Rhineland and inhabit dark rooms suited to phantasms of the imagination. Visual images of oversized ottomans, arcane arrases, and wispy, wind-ruffled curtains increase the ATMOSPHERE essential to Gothic romance. For unspecified reasons, the ailing Lady Ligeia dwindles and dies. After the widower marries a vivacious blonde, the Lady Rowena Trevanion of Tremaine, the couple live in an English abbey, which contains a bridal chamber furnished with an oversized granite sarcophagus, where hallucinations consume the excitable bride.

Poe centers his plot on power struggles of mind and volition over body, life over death, a dark FEMME FATALE over a Teutonic beauty, and a strong-willed wife over an unsuitable successor. Upon Rowena's death, the twice-widowed husband discovers that Ligeia has overpowered Rowena's mummied remains, a show of conquest that critics have compared to the overthrow of a controlled English Gothicism by a more muscular, intrusive GERMAN GOTHIC style. Manic, clouded by opium, and probably raving after three days of keeping vigil by the rigid corpse, the watcher relives his delight in the first wife, who embodied more sensuality and physical appeal than the cold remains of Rowena, whose tomb wrappings suggest the corseting and silencing of Victorian women. He discovers evidence of reanimation and the ultimate reincarnation of the black-eyed, raven-haired Ligeia, a virago too independent to submit to husbandly stifling.

Poe leaves unexplained the MYSTERY, metaphysical nature, and purpose of Ligeia's reanimation, but suggests that the husband may have willed Ligeia's return to Rowena's inanimate form. Alternate analyses characterize her as a vampire, ghost, or supernatural force and propose that he, too, has fallen under the power of hallucination. Feminists characterize the husband as the murderer of Ligeia out of frustration with her voluptuous beauty, self-possession, and intellect. One explanation for the wifely FOILs is the strength of Ligeia to defy death and to overcome her rival by robbing their mutual love of his preferred mate. Like Madeline Usher, Ligeia represents the overtly passionate, strong-willed female who refuses to be suppressed by a male lover. The feminist take on the husband's collapse and hysteria ponders a wry overturning of a female stereotype—a man in tears over the loss of his woman.

In January 1843, Poe enlarged on "Ligeia" with a poem, "The Conqueror Worm," that he had previously issued in *Graham's Magazine*. The poem appeared as a component of the story in a February 1845 issue of *New York World*. The deathbed confessional of Ligeia cleared up misinterpretations of her reanimation as proof of resurrection. Poe's text insists on the victory of death over life and on the role of morbid thoughts as elements of insanity and horror. In his depressed state, he saw heavenly forces as feeble and ineffectual in their support of mortals, whom he described as doomed to die and decay in the grave. The beauty of Poe's seminal story earned the regard of the Irish-born playwright and critic George Bernard Shaw and a host of Gothic imitations.

Bibliography

Frushell, Richard C. "Poe's Name 'Ligeia' and Milton," *ANQ* 11, no. 1 (winter 1998): 18–20.

Schueller, Malini Johar. "Harems, Orientalist Subversions and the Crisis of Nationalism: The Case of Edgar Allan Poe and 'Ligeia,'" *Criticism* 37, no. 4 (fall 1995): 601–623.

Von Mucke, Dorothea. "The Imaginary Materiality of Writing in Poe's 'Ligeia,'" *Differences: A Journal of Feminist Cultural Studies* 11, no. 2 (summer 1999): 53.

"The Lottery"
Shirley Jackson
(1948)

The prize story of author Shirley JACKSON's lengthy canon of 100 titles, "The Lottery" took her only two hours to write. It was first published in *The New Yorker* on June 28, 1948, and later anchored an anthology, *The Lottery; or, The Adventures of James Harris* (1949). The story generated a storm of protest, mostly from New Englanders denying any part in a barbaric annual execution. The author replied that her story exposed the senseless VIOLENCE and inhumanity that permeate all of human history.

In a village setting tense from the outset, the depiction of a sacrificial lamb at an atavistic ritual focuses on a male-dominated town. Citizens of both genders maintain social order through the ILLUSION of a democratic process—the random selection of a citizen to be killed on the spot by a community stoning, an execution method bearing biblical significance. The practice dates to Old Testament times and is mentioned in I Samuel 30:6 as a threat against David. It recurs in the New Testament in John 8:7 when Jesus intervenes before a mob can stone an adulteress and challenges, "He that is without sin, let him cast a first stone at her."

Jackson's story emerges from Gothic tradition. The bizarre midsummer ritual murder occurs in a rural setting where citizens annually allot a lethal penalty to whatever luckless family draws the losing slip of paper. A second drawing among family members pits mate against mate, child against child, and parent against offspring. Jackson emphasizes the alienation of the victim, who progresses from beloved wife, mother, and townswoman to a targeted OUTSIDER as her killers mass into a mob. Character names identify standard American Joneses and Martins and suggest village professions in Baxter (bakester), the time of year in Summers, alarm in Old Man Warner, and lethal intent in Mr. Graves. The name of the communal victim, Tessie Hutchinson, points to a real victim, Anne Hutchinson, an English herbalist and midwife whom male religious authorities ousted from the Massachusetts Bay Colony in 1637 for her performance of the male-dominated role of Bible teacher to local women. Tessie's first name alludes to Tess of the d'Urbervilles, Thomas Hardy's hapless farm girl who faces execution for murdering a male stalker.

The TONE is deliberately casual as townspeople arrive to take part. They seem eager to finish the work quickly as though ridding themselves of a noxious, but necessary chore. Most menacing is Mrs. Delacroix (literally, "of the cross"), a name recalling New England's historical penchant for Christian fanaticism, who needs two hands to lift a huge stone. At the crucial moment, encircling friends, neighbors, and family withdraw their loyalty and humanity to dissociate themselves from the martyr-to-be as they reach for stones to crush out her life. Mr. Warner's recitation of a common adage implies that the death assures a good harvest of corn, a crucial grain crop linked to Native American agrarianism.

Critics respond with various analyses of Jackson's modern HORROR NARRATIVE, one of the most anthologized in literature. Some point to the illogical embrace of terrible traditions. Others interpret the grim lottery as a condemnation of sexism, capitalism, material gain, and the victimizing of marginalized citizens—women and children, the homeless, the handicapped, Jews and Muslims, Gypsies, and nonwhites. In existential criticism, the story describes an impersonal process by which a community pinpoints a scapegoat, the bearer of everyone's sins.

Bibliography

Griffin, Amy A. "Jackson's 'The Lottery,'" *Explicator* 58, no. 1 (fall 1999): 44.

Hall, Joan Wylie. *Shirley Jackson: A Study of the Short Fiction.* New York: Twayne, 1993.

Kosenko, Peter. "A Marxist/Feminist Reading of Shirley Jackson's 'The Lottery,'" *New Orleans Review* 12, no. 1 (spring 1985): 27–32.

Lovecraft, H. P.
(1890–1937)

Virtually unknown during his lifetime, the writer and critic Howard Phillips Lovecraft attracted a huge readership for cult science fiction, fantasy, and Gothic terror. According to the author and critic Joyce Carol OATES, the posthumous publication of his collected stories made the greatest impact on HORROR NARRATIVE since the writings of Edgar Allan POE. Born in Providence, Rhode Island, to a deranged mother and syphilitic father, Lovecraft developed verbal acumen in childhood and retreated into a fictive world of terror and extraterrestrial phantasms inspired by the fantastic Pegana tales of Edward Plunkett, Lord Dunsany.

Lovecraft created his own mythic cycle populated with MONSTERS such as those that permeate "The Call of Cthulhu" (1928), a murky nether world where titans speak an unknown language. Emphasizing perverse science, NECROMANCY, occultism, LYCANTHROPY, cannibalism, and demonology, he wrote a distinctive brand of horror for the pulp magazines *Weird Tales* and *Astounding Stories*. He took the time to admire a peer, poet Walter DE LA MARE, and to lavish encouragement and advice on a field of young, promising Gothic writers, including a contemporary, Clark Ashton Smith, author of "The Hashish-Eater" (1922). Lovecraft was also quick to single out the fakes and flakes, including the American horror writer Robert William Chambers, author of the play *The King in Yellow* (1895), which Lovecraft castigated for its lack of thought.

Like Poe, Lovecraft expressed his debt to ATMOSPHERE. In the critical volume *Supernatural Horror in Literature* (1945), he extolled the worth of surroundings above plot mechanics as the source of a sensation, a concept introduced by the Gothic master Ann RADCLIFFE in 1794. As a result of Lovecraft's control of setting and TONE, he produced unrelentingly pessimistic views of humankind in a world in which evil and savagery prevail, both in reality and nightmares, as found in "The Beast in the Cave" (1905), an early tale in which a tourist in Mammoth Cave kills an albino being resembling a prehistoric human. In a posthumous collection, *The Dream Cycle of H. P. Lovecraft: Dreams of Terror and Death* (1995), his tales of urban dread fuse midnight phantasms with waking horror. In "Azathoth" (1922) and "The Descendent" (1926), his doomed characters cringe before threatening worlds where fearful, whirling phantasms reach beyond land into sky and sea.

In "The Rats in the Wall," one of the tales collected in *The Best of H. P. Lovecraft* (1987), the author exploits the oldest human dread, fear of the unknown. His hapless protagonist digs into the tiled floor of Exham Priory to discover a horror— the remains of people who died in a state of panic: "and over all were the marks of rodent gnawing. The skulls denoted nothing short of utter idiocy, cretinism, or primitive semi-apedom" (Lovecraft,

The Best, 33). The revelation suits a prevalent theme in Lovecraft sagas—the degeneracy of a family into crime, immorality, and madness. Underlying this and other nihilist views is Lovecraft's atheism and the hopelessness for humanity, themes replicated in Fred Chappell's *Dagon* (1968) and in the pessimistic urban Gothic of Leonard Lanson Cline's *The Dark Chamber* (1927) and John Ramsey Campbell's *To Wake the Dead* (1980) and *New Tales of the Cthulhu Mythos* (1980).

Bibliography

Clements, Nicholaus. "Lovecraft's 'The Haunter of the Dark,'" *Explicator* 57, no. 2 (winter 1999): 98–100.

Heller, Terry. *The Delights of Terror: An Aesthetics of the Tale of Terror.* Urbana: University of Illinois Press, 1987.

Lovecraft, H. P. *The Best of H. P. Lovecraft: Bloodcurdling Tales of Horror and the Macabre.* New York: Del Rey, 1987.

Oates, Joyce Carol. *Telling Stories.* New York: W. W. Norton, 1998.

Price, Robert M. "H. P. Lovecraft: Prophet of Humanism," *Humanist* 61, no. 4 (July 2001): 26.

Wohleber, Curt. "The Man Who Can Scare Stephen King," *American Heritage* 46, no. 8 (December 1995): 82–90.

The Loved One
Evelyn Waugh
(1948)

Set in Hollywood, California, Evelyn Waugh's absurd Anglo-American satire *The Loved One* employs unsettling details of death, corpse preparation and viewing, and burial to expose American commercialism and shallow Pacific Coast society. The story involves a love triangle, that of funerary cosmetician Aimée Thanatogenos of Whispering Glades Memorial Park and two men—her boss Mr. Joyboy and Dennis Barlow, an English OUTSIDER and employee of a pet burial service at the Happier Hunting Ground. To maintain a soothing ILLUSION, a series of euphemisms—"Waiting Ones" for dressers of the "Loved One," a human body on view in the "Slumber Room"—spares clients from the harsh realities of death. To uphold the company's reputation for discretion, Joyboy quickly relieves of his duties the crass embalmer from Texas who referred to bodies as "the meat."

Waugh's "little nightmare" manipulates contrast to good purpose. Descriptions of mortuary arrangements at Barlow's place of employment are darkly humorous. Waugh ridicules the solemnity of the dog Arthur's interment with the release of a white dove to symbolize a departing soul and the mailing of annual remembrance cards on the anniversary of the funeral. Parallel to Arthur's funeral are preparation of a dead baby and a hanging victim at the human mortuary. Because of Aimée's suicide and the threat to Joyboy's job, Dennis accommodates his rival by incinerating the girl's remains in a gas-fired brick oven. He estimates, "I reckon she'll take an hour and a half" (*ibid.*, 162). The accompanying sympathy card promises Joyboy that Aimée is wagging her tail in heaven.

Bibliography

Beaty, Frederick L. *The Ironic World of Evelyn Waugh.* Dekalb: Northern Illinois University Press, 1992.

Patey, Douglas Lane. *The Life of Evelyn Waugh: A Critical Biography.* Oxford: Blackwell, 1998.

Waugh, Evelyn. *The Loved One.* Boston: Little, Brown, 1948.

lycanthropy

Lycanthropy (from the Greek for "wolf man") is a belief either in the reincarnation of deceased humans as fearful beasts, instant SHAPE-SHIFTING of demonic powers, or METEMPSYCHOSIS, the transmigration of souls from humans to the bodies of other humans or other species, particularly bears, hyenas, jaguars, leopards, tigers, and wolves. Growing out of the folk SUPERSTITION is a subset of horror fiction, a type of creature literature in the vein of VAMPIRISM. The werewolf motif is based on the emotional and psychological exploitation of the innocent, the motivating factor that causes Robert Louis STEVENSON's Mr. Hyde to harass and destroy Dr. Jekyll. The pattern existed in Irish and English FOLKLORE and Norse mythology, and in Roman lore as the tale of the *versipellis* (turnskin), a form of shape-shifting that altered a normal human into a fierce monster.

In northern Europe, stories about werewolves described them as normal by day and changed into STALKING beasts by the light of a full moon. Medieval stories featured the corpse-eating werewolf, which the French called a *loup-garou*, source of the nursery tale "Little Red Riding Hood." In a 16th-century Gothic version, the werewolf was a form chosen by a sorcerer, a motif that found its way into testimony at WITCHCRAFT trials. Those hapless people who believed themselves changed into beasts were tried like alien OUTSIDERS and condemned to immolation, the only antidote to what was surely a psychological delusion. In death, werewolves reputedly changed into vampires. In the mid-1600s, Calvinist authorities on the islands of Guernsey and Jersey connected lycanthropy with VIOLENCE and outlawry as a means of condemning nighttime dances, masquerades and mumming, and social activities called *vueilles* (vigils). The whispered tales of encounters with werewolves invested the folklore of Canada imported from the British Isles and preserved along the St. Lawrence River valley.

Lycanthropy influenced the "BEAUTY AND THE BEAST" motif, a version of which appeared in the French *contes de fées* (FAIRY TALEs) of Madame Gabrielle-Suzanne Barbot de Gallon de Villeneuve in *La Jeune Ameriquaine, et les Contes Marins* (The young American and the sea stories, 1740). In the 19th century, an avid readership welcomed literary versions of folklore—for example, the anonymous GOTHIC BLUEBOOK *The Severed Arm; or, The Wehr-Wolf of Limousin* (ca. 1820), the story of Gaspar de Marcanville, the Limousin werewolf, set in Poitou, France; English seaman Frederick Marryat's "The White Wolf of the Hartz Mountains," published in *New Monthly Magazine* in July 1839; and George William MacArthur REYNOLDS's popular serial and Gothic bluebook *Wagner the Wehr-Wolf* (1847), a story linked to the FEMME FATALE Nisida and to a German peasant who makes a deal with Satan. In Sutherland Menzies's magazine story "Hughes, the Wehr-Wolf" (1838), a vengeance tale about a man harmed by vicious gossip, the protagonist finds a werewolf disguise in an old chest and decides to punish his accusers. As he dons the dyed sheep skin, "he felt his very teeth on edge with an avidity for biting; he experienced an inconceivable desire to run: he set himself to howl" (Haining, 897). More literary models of lycanthropy fed a growing fan base; among these works were Alexandre Dumas père's *Le Meneur des Loups* (*The Wolf-Leader*, 1857), Prosper Mérimée's sexually charged "Lokis" (1869), Stevenson's "Olalla" (1887), and Rudyard KIPLING's "The Mark of the Beast" (1891). In a gesture toward werewolf folklore, Bram STOKER's *DRACULA* (1897) refers to the Norse berserker, a warrior capable of shapeshifting into a bear or wolf.

Bibliography

Chase, Richard, and David Teasley. "Little Red Riding Hood: Werewolf and Prostitute," *Historian* 57, no. 4 (summer 1995): 769–776.

Haining, Peter, ed. *Gothic Tales of Terror.* New York: Taplinger, 1972.

Ogier, Darryl. "Night Revels and Werewolfery in Calvinist Guernsey," *Folklore* 109 (1998): 53–62.

Lytton, Edward Bulwer

See BULWER-LYTTON, EDWARD.

M

The Madwoman in the Attic
Sandra Gilbert and Susan Gubar
(1981)

Sandra M. Gilbert, professor of English at the University of California at Davis, and Susan Gubar, professor of English and women's studies at Indiana University, produced groundbreaking feminist criticism in *The Madwoman in the Attic: The Woman Writer and the Nineteenth-Century Literary Imagination*, an academic-publishing best-seller of 70,000 copies and a nominee for the National Book Award and the Pulitzer Prize. The vigorous and highly readable text, issued by Yale University Press, created new paradigms for examining fiction, particularly Victorian fiction and the Gothic novel. From the authors' reshaping of critical point of view came a controversial canon of women's writing and a rejuvenation of women's studies and seminars on university campuses. In 2001, a 20th-anniversary edition of *The Madwoman in the Attic* celebrated a major breakthrough in feminist criticism.

By way of establishing a women's literary tradition, Gilbert and Gubar connected female writing directly to the GOTHIC NOVEL. They generated feminist examinations of Charlotte BRONTË's JANE EYRE (1847), focusing on the tie between Edward ROCHESTER's two wives. Enlightening and uplifting to readers of worn-out, one-sided, male-generated critiques of Gothic writing, Gilbert and Gubar's text proposes that the famed governess is the alter ego of Bertha Mason ROCHESTER, the raving wife whom Edward sequesters in the upper floor of THORNFIELD HALL. Like Bertha, Jane is the perennial OUTSIDER, unwelcome at GATESHEAD HALL, shunned and taunted at Lowood school, and relegated to the background as governess at Thornfield.

From Gilbert and Gubar's feminist perspective, Brontë needed the deranged version of Jane as a means of venting outrage at a repressive society that suppressed the voices of career women, particularly authors. To establish a marriage based on equality, Jane's negative alter ego runs amok in the manse, setting a fire and creating chaos that leaves Rochester blind and crippled. The rampage costs Bertha her life and robs Jane and Edward of their beloved home but levels the economic and social differences between them before they reunite. According to *The Madwoman in the Attic*, Jane is able to play rescuer to Edward's helpless, MELANCHOLY male. Eventually, he regains partial vision, a SYMBOL of his more enlightened view of Jane as a life partner.

Bibliography

Donaldson, Elizabeth J. "The Corpus of the Madwoman: Toward a Feminist Disability Studies Theory of Embodiment and Mental Illness," *NWSA Journal* 14, no. 3 (fall 2002): 99–119.

Heller, Scott. "The Book That Created a Canon: 'Madwoman in the Attic' Turns 20," *Chronicle of Higher Education* 46, no. 17 (December 17, 1999): 20–21.

"The Madwoman in the Attic: The Woman Writer and the 19th Century Literary Imagination," *Women and Language* 24, no. 1 (spring 2001): 39.

Peters, John G. "Inside and Outside 'Jane Eyre' and Marginalization through Labeling," *Studies in the Novel* 28, no. 1 (spring 1996): 57–75.

mad scientist

The depiction of a decline in medical standards, unwise experimentation, dissection of living tissue, and meddling with NATURE permeates a subset of Gothic horror, based on the motif of the mad scientist. Such works as the anonymous GOTHIC BLUEBOOK "The Black Spider" (ca. 1798) and Wilkie COLLINS's *Heart and Science* (1883) feature mad researchers whose evil curiosity, inhumanity, and dabblings in fearful concoctions parallel the guile of the Gothic VILLAIN. Key to the ATMOSPHERE and TONE are eerie GOTHIC SETTINGs presented in CHIAROSCURO of bizarre operations and potions, details that derive from KABBALISM and the alchemy lore of the Middle Ages. From the FAUST LEGEND, writers developed the notion that intrusion on universal knowledge was tantamount to propitiating Satan. These unholy acts fell under the Christian church's condemnation of mortals practicing black magic, performing autopsies, speculating on the nature and purpose of the divine, or playing God. The primary sin of the mad doctor is older than medieval probings, dating to the Greek horror of hubris, the inborn pride that precipitates the downfall of the great.

The height of European laboratory lore and unethical medical practice occurs in Mary Wollstonecraft SHELLEY's FRANKENSTEIN (1818), a touchstone for later explorations of perverse science. Mary Shelley reprised the motif in "The Mortal Immortal: A Tale" (1833), which depicts the alchemist Cornelius Agrippa obsessed by his probings into the MYSTERY of life. In his dying hour, Agrippa speaks of doom: "Behold . . . the vanity of human wishes" (Williams, 26). The motif of ill-advised research serves Nathaniel HAWTHORNE's "THE BIRTHMARK" (1843) and "Rappaccini's Daughter" (1844), Fitz-James O'BRIEN's fantasy on telescopy in "The Diamond Lens" (1858), Sheridan LE FANU's *Wylder's Hand* (1864) and *The Rose and the Key* (1871), VILLIERS DE L'ISLE-ADAM's "The Doctor's Heroism" (1883), and Robert Louis STEVENSON's DR. JEKYLL AND MR. HYDE (1886), the tragic tale of a scientist's discovery of savagery in his own personality. Stevenson's interest in multiple views of the human psyche informed Arthur Lewellyn Jones-Machen's *The Great God Pan* (1894), a decadent tale of

atavism elicited from a curious scientist's operation on a girl's brain to locate the beginnings of humankind. The surgeon releases despair and suicide on London in the form of a FEMME FATALE, the child borne by the altered patient.

The mad scientist remained a staple of Gothic fiction and the French GRAND GUIGNOL in the late 1800s and 1900s, touching on vivisection in H. G. Wells's *The Island of Dr. Moreau* (1896). The motif developed into new horrors with early 21st-century manipulation of cloning, gene replication, and biotechnology. Gertrude ATHERTON applied the theme of perennial youth to *Black Oxen* (1923), the story of a woman rejuvenated by injections of hormones from oxen. Angela CARTER enhanced horror with her mad scientists in *Heroes and Villains* (1969) and *The Infernal Desire Machines of Doctor Hoffman* (1972), a resetting of the Faust myth amid fascism. Michael Crichton pressed insane research toward apocalypse with *The Andromeda Strain* (1969). More devious is Robin Cook's novel *Coma* (1978), which locates evil in the heart of the medical practitioner who keeps bodies in a moribund state as sources of harvestable organs for transplant. Simultaneous with 20th-century delvings in laboratory Gothic are dark medical horror films that exploit bubbling concoctions, unexplained explosions, retrieval of horrific beings from outer space, and incidents of engineered SHAPE-SHIFTING of humans into ominous insects and beasts.

In 1999, the American playwright Margaret Edson earned a Pulitzer Prize for her philosophic play *Wit* (1999), a resetting of the mad scientist motif within the confines of an isolated oncology ward in a modern research hospital. Complicating the female patient's horror of death from ovarian cancer is the presumption of Dr. Harvey Kelekian in using her to test a powerful drug. Hubris precludes him from sympathizing with his patient, Dr. Vivian Bearing, who suffers from intense pain and his rudeness and impersonal treatment. In a brief comment to Vivian, he remarks: "Dr. Bearing. Full dose. Excellent. Keep pushing the fluids" (Edson, 40). Only days from death, the patient recognizes that her treatment is more lethal than the tumor itself in destroying both her body and self-worth. Following the example set by his superior, Dr. Jason Posner, mad-scientist-in-training, is equally brusque:

"Professor Bearing. How are you feeling today? Three p.m. IV hydration totals. Two thousand in. Thirty out. Uh-oh. That's it. Kidneys gone" (*ibid.*, 81). In a moment of dark humor, Posner realizes that he is addressing Vivian's corpse.

Bibliography

Cohen, Jeffrey Jerome, ed. *Monster Theory*. Minneapolis: University of Minnesota Press, 1996.

Eads, Martha Greene. "Unwitting Redemption in Margaret Edson's 'Wit,'" *Christianity and Literature* 51, no. 2 (winter 2002): 241–255.

Edson, Margaret. *Wit*. New York: Faber & Faber, 1999.

Levine, George, and U. C. Knoepflmacher, eds. *The Endurance of Frankenstein: Essays on Mary Shelley's Novel*. Berkeley: University of California Press, 1979.

Williams, A. Susan, ed. *The Lifted Veil: The Book of Fantastic Literature by Women, 1800—World War II*. New York: Carroll & Graf, 1992.

Manderley

A standard setting for Gothic romance, lavish estates such as Daphne DU MAURIER's Manderley bear serious emotional significance to the heroine and VILLAIN. In her classic MYSTERY novel REBECCA (1938), the ancestral home by the sea creates an evocative sense of place. It is an unsatisfactory residence to the owner, Maxim de Winter, who remarks, "An empty house can be as lonely as a full hotel" (du Maurier, 25). On the speaker's first view of the residence, she compares it to a picture-postcard view. Edenic in May with rhododendrons in bloom, the house is a "thing of grace and beauty, exquisite and faultless, lovelier even than I had ever dreamed, built in its hollow of smooth grassland and mossy lawns, the terraces sloping to the gardens and the gardens to the sea" (*ibid.*, 65). Du Maurier based its seaside appeal on her own home, Menabilly, a 17th-century mansion in Cornwall, and equipped it with a maze of hallways and servants' quarters.

Unlike the stereotypical castles and abbeys of classic GOTHIC NOVELs, the mansion that once was the domain of the former Rebecca DE WINTER is more psychological challenge than prison to the unnamed heroine, who becomes the second Mrs. DE WINTER. Rather than search the sinister environs of a castle in the style of an Ann RADCLIFFE heroine, du Maurier's protagonist acquaints herself with the first wife, whose perfection overawes at every turn with tasteful decor, azaleas and rhododendrons on the expansive grounds, even a costume based on the portrait of Caroline de Winter for a grand dress ball. The protagonist feels hunted by a ghost: "A board creaked in the gallery. I swung round, looking at the gallery behind me. There was nobody there. . . . I wondered why the board creaked when I had not moved at all" (*ibid.*, 222). The effect is claustrophobic, isolating the protagonist and pushing her to morbid thoughts and despair that her marriage is a failure.

Du Maurier elevates the setting to a theme, a physical and emotional challenge to the NAIF. To exorcise the ghost of Manderley, the mousy protagonist must conquer her fears of house, staff, furnishings, and grounds. Out of sight of the manse, she can relax in nature by walking through Happy Valley with her husband and his dog Jasper. On her return, however, the edifice exudes the menace of a Gothic castle, closing over the speaker like the seawater that shrouds Rebecca's corpse. At the heart of the structure, du Maurier turns the stereotypical locked room into a shrine to Rebecca, a constant reminder of the beauty who once made Manderley her home.

In a twist on the BLUEBEARD MYTH, the villain is a female, the overbearing Mrs. DANVERS, the housekeeper whose loyalty to Rebecca smacks of an obsessive lesbianism. As the speaker enters the well-tended boudoir, the feminine belongings overwhelm her with the first wife's self-assurance. As though facing a rival, the speaker feels an urge to commit suicide by leaping from the window of Rebecca's old room as though sacrificing herself to a demanding goddess. Turning to Charlotte BRONTË's JANE EYRE (1847) for closure, the author has the housekeeper burn Manderley, thus releasing the protagonist from confinement in a stifling milieu that threatens her marriage and well-being. With a parting Gothic touch, du Maurier describes the flames as "shot with crimson, like a splash of blood," a suggestion that the house dies a human death (*ibid.*, 380).

Bibliography

du Maurier, Daphne. *Rebecca*. New York: Avon Books, 1971.

Fleenor, Juliann E., ed. *The Female Gothic.* Montreal: Eden Press, 1983.

Forster, Margaret. *Daphne du Maurier.* New York: Doubleday, 1993.

Manfred
Lord Byron
(1817)

Layered with death and debased sensuality, Lord BYRON's closet drama *Manfred* showcases a man who kills the thing he loves. The plot is a Faustian motif set on the Jungfrau and in the Bernese Alps and featuring SUPERNATURAL beings—a witch, the ghost of Nemesis, and Destinies. An example of the BYRONIC HERO, the tyrannic title character, sunk in MELANCHOLY, expresses a dour, funereal mood: "My own soul's sepulchre, for I have ceased to justify my deeds unto myself—the last infirmity of evil" (Byron, 591). On the brink of suicide from guilt over the despoliation and death of Astarte, the sister with whom he had an incestuous relationship, he is rescued by a chamois hunter who believes Prince Manfred is insane. In act 2, the hunter names the cause of Manfred's disquiet, a cankering sin that requires the assistance of a holy confessor. Like the wayward poet himself, Manfred acknowledges that he has brought woe to the people he most loves.

Byron intended his nihilistic, brink-of-the-abyss death scene to shock the conventional reading public. Details of *Manfred* link the fatalistic romantic drama with dark GOTHIC CONVENTIONs: the title character's hermitage at his castle and tower, the exotic throne of Arimanes, social and spiritual displacement, and a raging cataract, which echoes the disintegration and emotional chaos within a tortured mortal. In act 3, when a spirit comes to fetch Manfred's soul, the protagonist, like Prometheus, describes himself as alone, yet finds a ministering abbot willing to ward off demonic powers. The conclusion sinks to MELODRAMA with the abbot's despair that the rebellious Manfred died unrepentent and cold of heart.

Bibliography

Byron, Lord. *Lord Byron: The Major Works.* Oxford: Oxford University Press, 2000.

Neff, D. S. "'Manfred' and the Mac-Ivors," *ANQ* 10, no. 4 (fall 1997): 24–29.

Manon Lescaut
Abbé Prévost
(1731)

Abbé PRÉVOST's sensational novel *Manon Lescaut* draws on the author's shady lifestyle as priest-turned-writer, forger, and con artist. Set in France and Louisiana, the story tells of the knight Des Grieux's sexual awakening upon discovering the sensual charms of Manon, a FEMME FATALE who appeals to male fantasies of the voluptuous siren chained in a coffle of female inmates. Spared deportation in shackles to America, she develops into a demanding sybarite and liar. In desperation at his love's prostitution, Des Grieux confesses his sexual addiction: "It is love, you know it, that has caused all my errors. Fatal passion!" (Prévost, 235).

The author fills the dark romance with Dickensian settings, from roadhouses and Grub Street to prison and a vessel of deportation. As he degenerates from obsessed love of Manon, Des Grieux lapses into dueling, cardsharping, felony, and exile. In a melodramatic burial scene along the Mississippi River delta, he breaks his sword and uses the stub end to dig Manon's grave in the sand. He relinquishes his clothes to enshroud her body and lies naked upon the grave in abject torment. Charlotte SMITH's translation of the novel as *Manon L'Escault; or, The Fatal Attachment* (1785)—later titled *The Romance of Real Life* (1787)—helped introduce French Gothicism into England. The composers Daniel-François Auber, Hans Werner Henze, Jules Massenet, and Giacomo Puccini have all used the MELODRAMA of the worldly, inconstant Manon as a basis for opera.

Bibliography

Brady, Valentini Papadopoulou. "'Manon Lescaut, C'est Lui': A Study of Point of View in Prévost's 'Manon Lescaut,'" *Intertexts* 5, no. 2 (fall 2001): 156–168.

Prévost, Abbé. *Manon Lescaut,* in *Great French Romances.* New York: Duell, Sloan & Pearce, 1946.

Maria; or, The Wrongs of Women
Mary Wollstonecraft
(1798)

With *Maria; or, The Wrongs of Women* (1798), a MELANCHOLY psychological novel published posthumously by her husband, William GODWIN, feminist writer Mary Wollstonecraft became the first female novelist to set fictional action in an asylum. She crafted a series of nested stories as a podium from which to denounce narrow and/or false Gothic stereotypes. The story replaces MELO-DRAMA with a mother's trauma and sorrow at the alleged death of her child, a trial for adultery, abandonment by her lover, and an attempt at sui-cide with an overdose of laudanum. Maria deserts reality to embrace hallucinations of an all-female society devoid of brutalizing males.

Basing the work on Gothic elements in Ann RADCLIFFE's THE ITALIAN (1797), Wollstonecraft supplanted confinement in Gothic castles and DUNGEONS with the horrors of mental institutions. Maria Venables, the heroine, is the victim of her husband George, a despotic drunkard and woman-izer who drugs and imprisons her and refuses her any visitors except a physician. In seclusion with the matron Jemima, Maria survives gloomy sur-roundings and restraints along with the shrieks and sorrowful singing of madwomen. Through a small grated window, she gazes at blue sky and de-caying buildings. She reads the fables of Dryden, Jean-Jacques Rousseau's *Heloise,* and John Milton's *Paradise Lost* and learns the sufferings of Jemima and inmate Henry Darnford. The accounts of child abuse, rape, abortion, forced labor, homeless-ness, prostitution, drugged sleep, and a masked ab-ductor establish the author's intent to use Gothic fiction as a vehicle of female protest.

Bibliography

Cosslett, Tess. "Maria, or the Wrongs of Woman," *Notes and Queries* 42, no. 4 (December 1995): 502.

Hoeveler, Diane Long. "Reading the Wound: Woll-stonecraft's 'Wrongs of Women; or, Maria' and Trauma Theory," *Studies in the Novel* 31, no. 4 (win-ter 1999): 387.

"The Masque of the Red Death"
Edgar Allan Poe
(1842)

Edgar Allan POE's macabre ALLEGORY "The Masque of the Red Death" was first published in the May 1842 issue of *Graham's Magazine.* The story employs the motif of STALKING as a SYMBOL of mortality, which Poe adapted from Giovanni Boccaccio's *De-cameron* (1353). The Renaissance Italian storyteller prefaced his classic anthology of fabliaux and short cautionary tales with a description of four reactions to the advance of the bubonic plague over Europe. One group gave themselves to street revelry and drinking in taverns. A second group hid away in seclusion. A third maintained normal activities. A fourth fled into rural areas where contagion had not yet penetrated.

Poe merges the first two of Boccaccio's groups by depicting 1,000 nobles avoiding a contagion that kills off half a realm. Self-absorbed to the point of apathy toward the peasantry, they with-draw to a remote abbey to indulge themselves in pleasure. Invigorating the plot is the virulence of the unseen epidemic and a jocular host, ironically named Prince Prospero from the Duke of Milan, a castaway in William Shakespeare's *The Tempest* (ca. 1610). Amid a profusion of clowns, dancers, and musicians, guests lose themselves in wine, an illusory pleasure that allows them to feel light-hearted, as though dancing on their own coffins.

In a morbid reflection, Poe describes the pow-ers of the Red Death to inflict pain, disorienta-tion, and profuse hemorrhaging. Heightening the failure of flight from contagion are the seven boldly colored rooms at the abbey and the cos-tumes of masqueraders, a surface covering that does nothing to prevent the pestilence from in-vading and destroying the revellers' bodies. Mak-ing its way through ARABESQUE figures from the blue to the purple, green, orange, white, and vio-let rooms to the black chamber at the western ex-treme, the disease takes the form of an intruder dressed in Halloween garb and armed with a dag-ger. The pursuer completes a tour of the party rooms at the chiming of an ebony clock, the signal for instant death among the maskers.

The ominous wraith, a silent and relentless grim reaper, symbolizes the unavoidable doom of mortals, who delude themselves that wealth, privi-lege, and an isolated dalliance can save them from death. By referring to the epidemic as an "Avatar," Poe links the menace to the Hindu being that is reincarnated in every age, for either good or ill (Poe, 604). He introduced the stalking motif in

"Shadow: A Parable" (1835), in which a hellish death from the underworld rises along the Nile River at Ptolemais to engulf the host Oinos and his dinner guests. Poe reprised the image in "The Sphinx" (1850), a tale of overblown fear of cholera along the Hudson Valley. In each case, the height of human dread results from the realization that no earthly refuge can stave off death.

Bibliography

Dudley, David R. "Dead or Alive: The Booby-trapped Narrator of Poe's 'Masque of the Red Death,'" *Studies in Short Fiction* 30, no. 2 (spring 1993): 169–173.

Tuan, Yi-Fu. *Landscapes of Fear.* New York: Pantheon Books, 1979.

Maturin, Charles Robert
(1782–1824)

A follower of Ann RADCLIFFE and reader of William GODWIN, Matthew Gregory LEWIS, and Friedrich von SCHILLER, the Irish novelist Charles Robert Maturin produced the last of the great traditional GOTHIC NOVELs. His work fused the romantic terror strand of Radcliffe with the lurid horror fiction of Lewis for a subgenre that H. P. LOVECRAFT calls "spiritual fright" (Lovecraft, 31). An Anglican clergyman and curate of St. Peter's parish in Dublin and the great-uncle of Oscar WILDE, Maturin was descended from persecuted Huguenots who fled France to live in Ireland. He entered the ministry in 1804. Perpetually torn between his flare for pulpit ministry and his talent for Gothic fiction, in *Sermons* (1819) he defended SUPERNATURAL tales as a normal interest of childhood. He established his professional expertise and anti-Catholic point of view by delivering a series of six sermons issued in a pamphlet entitled "On the Errors of the Roman Catholic Church" (1824).

To preserve his clerical reputation, Maturin concealed a yen to write and the need for extra cash by publishing his first novel, *The Fatal Revenge* (1807), under the pen name Dennis Jasper Murphy. Influenced by the popular fiction of William Lane's MINERVA PRESS, Maturin wrote two Irish nationalistic works, a romance, *The Wild Irish Boy* (1808), in imitation of Sydney Owenson's *Wild Irish Girl* (1805), and the bleak, savage *The Milesian Chief* (1812), a derivative HISTORICAL NOVEL drawn from Jane PORTER's *The Scottish Chiefs* (1810). His success in the marketplace earned him the disdain of the church hierarchy, which denied him promotion above the job of parish curate, which paid only £80 per year.

Maturin first wrote original Gothic fiction in the romance *The Fatal Revenge; or, The Family of Montorio* (1807). The novel owes much to the myths of FAUST and the WANDERING JEW; to Radcliffe's decorum and subdued style; and to her hero-villain SCHEDONI, the model for Maturin's priest Schemoli. Maturin's powerful, but flawed work earned the regard of Sir Walter SCOTT, who aided the parson in establishing himself as a serious writer. Maturin contributed to the growth of GOTHIC DRAMA with *Bertram; or, The Castle of Aldobrand* (1816), a blasphemous five-act tragedy reviled by Samuel Taylor COLERIDGE for blatant Jacobinism and gross stage atrocities. Nonetheless, the play flourished under the direction of Edmund Kean at Drury Lane Theatre. When Maturin's next two dramas—*Manuel* (1817) and *Fredolfo* (1819)—failed as a source of income, he returned to long fiction, his specialty.

Maturin felt compelled to write about the paradox of Christian love, cruel sectarianism, and perversions of faith. His perceptions of dark impulses within the human heart colored a sermon in which he toyed with the Faustian model. He asked if any in the congregation would take "all that man could bestow, or earth afford, to resign the hope of salvation?—No, there is not one—not such a fool on earth, were the enemy of mankind to traverse it with the offer!" (Maturin, xiv). Maturin reached the height of popularity with his three-volume terror masterpiece MELMOTH THE WANDERER (1820), a complex anti-Catholic horror novel that reflects the influence of Christopher Marlowe's tragedy DR. FAUSTUS (ca. 1588), Schiller's diabolical *Schauerroman* ("shudder novel"), and Mary Wollstonecraft SHELLEY's FRANKENSTEIN (1818).

Tentatively, the author opened his controversial novel with a disclaimer. He filled it with personal regret at the need to moonlight: "Did my profession furnish me with the means of subsistence, I should hold myself culpable indeed in having recourse to any other, but—am I allowed the choice?" (Oost, 291). Obviously, he chose Gothic fiction as a solution to his increasing family responsibilities, as his financial situation had been worsened by the failure of the church to award him a living wage.

Maturin depicts in six episodes and a series of nested tales the perversion of Christian love, DIABOLISM, and the motif of self-damnation. The author delineates the inner misery of his protagonist so sensitively that he forces the reader to sympathize with Melmoth's guilt while recoiling from his villainy. A review in *New Monthly Magazine and Universal Register* admired Maturin's plotting and expression. *BLACKWOOD'S EDINBURGH MAGAZINE* compared the author's handling of dark, cerebral romance favorably with the masterworks of Radcliffe and William Godwin and ranked the Irish newcomer above the GERMAN GOTHIC masters of his day. On the down side, an evaluation in *London Magazine* declared the author a misanthrope and warned that keen Gothic writing against religion and society could cause malcontents to turn vague grumblings into crime.

Melmoth the Wanderer broke new ground in the genre by abandoning extremes of lust and fantastic supernatural elements for a more realistic examination of the dark corners of the human psyche. Maturin's text alleged that the Catholic Church was guilty of sins ranging from tyranny and hypocrisy to outright murder of dissidents. The psychological novel prefigured the decadent verse of Charles BAUDELAIRE and Dante Gabriel Rossetti; the macabre tales of Edgar Allan POE and Robert Louis STEVENSON; the Scottish folkpieces of Sir Walter SCOTT; and two French novels, Victor Hugo's *Han d'Islande* (1823) and Honoré de Balzac's sequel *Melmoth Reconcilié à l'Eglise* (Melmoth reconciled to the church, 1892). Maturin's inventive writing extended to the short story "Leixlip Castle: An Irish Family Legend," a witch tale set at a real castle at the confluence of the Liffey and Rye Rivers and published posthumously in 1825. Lord BYRON, John KEATS, and Percy Bysshe SHELLEY gained psychological insight from Melmoth's characterization.

Bibliography

Lew, Joseph W. "'Unprepared for Sudden Transformations': Identity and Politics in 'Melmoth the Wan-
derer,'" *Studies in the Novel* 26, no. 2 (summer 1994): 173–195.
Lovecraft, H. P. *The Annotated Supernatural Horror in Literature.* New York: Hippocampus, 2000.
Maturin, Charles Robert. *Melmoth the Wanderer.* Lincoln: University of Nebraska Press, 1961.
Oost, Regina B. "'Servility and Command': Authorship in 'Melmoth the Wanderer,'" *Papers on Language & Literature* 31, no. 3 (summer 1995): 291–312.

Maupassant, Guy de
(1850–1893)

In rapid succession, Henri René Albert Guy de Maupassant produced the best in French stories of exotica, MONSTERS, and the macabre. Influenced by the French romantics, Gustave Flaubert, and the decadent verse of Charles BAUDELAIRE, Stéphane Mallarmé, and Paul Verlaine, Maupassant was educated by the clergy until he deliberately antagonized seminary authorities to end his connection with Catholicism. He interrupted his study at law school to enlist in the army and fight in the Franco-Prussian War. While working in subsequent bureaucratic posts, he read the Gothic tales of E. T. A. HOFFMANN and Baudelaire's translations of the works of Edgar Allan POE. Maupassant sought the mentorship of Flaubert and cultivated friendships with a variety of writers—Alphonse Daudet, Edmond de Goncourt, Henry JAMES, Ivan Turgenev, VILLIERS DE L'ISLE-ADAM, and Émile Zola. From their examples, Maupassant developed a precision and clarity in the short story unequaled by his peers.

At age 30, Maupassant quit his job at the ministry of education and began earning his living by reporting for *Gil Blas, Le Figaro,* and *Le Gaulois,* and by penning tales for French magazines specializing in intrigue, CONTES CRUELS (cruel tales), and psychological studies. He pursued an eerie dismemberment in "La Main d'Ecorche" (The flayed hand, 1875), which accords the hand a life of its own. His first success was "Boule de Suif" (Butterball, 1880), an ironic story about a women who agrees to sex with an enemy for the sake of ungrateful strangers. A notorious prankster, drug abuser, and sex addict, Maupassant often wrote of the prostitutes who were his favorite companions and probable contributors of the venereal disease that, along with migraines, hallucinations, and NEURASTHENIA, sapped his energies. His stories ranged from comic macabre in "La Main" (The hand, 1883) to the erotic obsessive in "La Chevelure" (The gold braid, 1884) and moral derangement in "Moiron" (1887), the story of a teacher who punishes God by murdering students.

From the author's decline in the final stages of syphilis came more chilling stories of INSANITY and OBSESSION—the graveyard tale "La Morte" (The dead, 1887), and "La Nuit" (The night, 1887), the horror story of the last human left alive on earth. Maupassant is best known for the destructive and haunting hallucination in "Le Horla, or Modern Ghosts" (1887), a masterpiece that he evolved from the phantasm in the Irish-American author Fitz-James O'BRIEN's "What Was It?" (1859). Maupassant's story presents a first-person fixation on a phantasm, which the speaker tries to kill through arson. The story ends with a realization that suicide is the only escape from the macabre. Ironically, the author himself attempted suicide, but failed and spent the final 19 months of his 43 years in an asylum.

Bibliography

Barrow, Susan M. "East/West: Appropriation of Aspects of the Orient in Maupassant's Bel-Ami," *Nineteenth-Century French Studies* 30, nos. 3–4 (spring–summer 2002): 315–329.

Hadlock, Philip G. "(Per)versions of Masculinity in Maupassant's 'La Mere aux Monstres,'" *French Forum* 27, no. 1 (winter 2002): 59–79.

Heller, Terry. *The Delights of Terror: An Aesthetics of the Tale of Terror.* Urbana: University of Illinois Press, 1987.

Hiner, Susan. "Hand Writing: Dismembering and Remembering in Nodier, Nerval and Maupassant," *Nineteenth-Century French Studies* 30, nos. 3–4 (spring–summer 2002): 300–315.

McCullers, Carson

(1917–1967)

Lula Carson Smith McCullers produced a remarkable canon of Gothic stories about GROTESQUE, alienated, and freakish characters who botch repeated attempts at intimacy. A native of Columbus, Georgia, she grew up in the South, but settled in New York City, where she refined short and long fiction replete with SOUTHERN GOTHIC. Her strengths were rich dialogue, motivation, and ATMOSPHERE. Her favorite themes of misfit females and mismanaged love, derived from her own ill health and her failed marriage to Reeves McCullers, dominate 20 short stories, the novels *Reflections in a Golden Eye* (1941), *The Heart Is a Lonely Hunter* (1941), and *Clock without Hands* (1961), and two novellas, *Member of the Wedding* (1946) and THE BALLAD OF THE SAD CAFE (1951), a bizarrely comic love triangle.

Influenced by Isak DINESEN's Gothic tales, McCullers applied GOTHIC CONVENTION to complex characters to produce poignant, often ridiculously perverse behaviors and situations. She described androgyny, isolation, and explosive rage and VIOLENCE in *The Heart Is a Lonely Hunter*, a circular narrative of angry people in a small Southern mill town. The NAIF, Mick Kelly, finds the corpse of her deaf-mute friend John Singer, who shoots himself in despair because of his inability to communicate. In *Reflections in a Golden Eye*, McCullers expands on hostility and masochism arising from disjointed loves. In both novels, she builds a pervasive unease from loneliness, fights, body dismemberment, and social and sexual displacement.

Bibliography

Auchincloss, Louis. *Pioneers and Caretakers: A Study of Nine American Women Novelists.* Minneapolis: University of Minnesota Press, 1965.

Cook, Richard M. *Carson McCullers.* New York: Frederick Unger, 1975.

King, Richard H. *A Southern Renaissance: The Cultural Awakening of the American South, 1930–1955.* Oxford: Oxford University Press, 1980.

Whitt, Jan. *Allegory and the Modern Southern Novel.* Macon, Ga.: Mercer University Press, 1994.

medievalism

The themes and motifs of the Middle Ages influenced the formation of GOTHIC CONVENTIONS, which draw on LEGENDS, art, and architecture. From these beginnings came stories of chivalry and pageantry, settings in castles and abbeys, old documents and wills, Catholic ritual and MYSTICISM, DIABOLISM, archaic diction, and the skewed vision of women as either hags or idealized damsels to be protected from harm and rescued from MONSTERS and VILLAINs. The complete scenario proposes intriguing oppositions: mannered elegance versus barbarism, pageantry versus dark cells, and religious faith versus terror of sudden violence, all elements of Horace WALPOLE's THE CASTLE OF OTRANTO (1765), Clara REEVE's THE OLD ENGLISH BARON (1778), Thomas Love PEACOCK's Arthurian lore in *The Misfortunes of Elphin* (1829), and John RICHARDSON's *The Monk Knight of St. John: A Tale of the Crusaders* (1850).

Based on inherent contradictions, medievalism provided Gothicism with a variety of theatrical scenarios, such as the training of a Celtic sisterhood in the Arthurian novels of Marion Zimmer Bradley and a secret vendetta of a murderous Catholic brotherhood in Dan Brown's THE DA VINCI CODE (2003). As characterized by H. P. LOVECRAFT, these settings derived from early oral literature, part of a humanistic legacy—"the shade which appears and demands the burial of its bones, the daemon lover who comes to bear away his still living bride, the death-fiend or psychopomp riding the night-wind, the man-wolf, the sealed chamber, the deathless sorcerer" (Lovecraft, 25). Fed on Scandinavian saga, GERMAN GOTHIC forerunners set the tone of the feudal era, with its tyrannic barons and cringing peasantry, an element of Johann von GOETHE's *Götz von Berlichingen* (*Goetz with the Iron Hand*, 1773), a prerevolutionary study of an oppressive social order. When an anonymous medieval romance, *The Castle of St. Vallery* (1792), was published in England, a critic for *Monthly Review* denounced the style as infantile for its belief in the miraculous. However, the reviewer's antiromantic stance voiced the beliefs of a shrinking minority.

In a gesture to medieval touchstones, bestselling Gothicist Ann RADCLIFFE emulated a growing vogue in the picturesque in the opening scene of THE ITALIAN (1797), an early classic. At the outset, she introduces the concept of sanctuary to criminals who seek shelter on hallowed ground. The intrusion of an unnamed assassin in an Italian convent church injects a mysterious, hostile AT-MOSPHERE and a faint note of post-Reformation ANTI-CATHOLICISM. Radcliffe expresses her era's shudder at peripheral menace in the reaction of her characters: "[The Englishman] perceived the figure of the assassin stealing from the confessional across the choir, and, shocked, on again beholding him, he turned his eyes, and hastily quitted the church" (Radcliffe, 4).

To entice the reader of the GOTHIC BLUE-BOOK, such titles as *Idlefonzo and Alberoni; or, Tales of Horror* (1803) and the anonymous *The Life and Horrid Adventures of the Celebrated Dr. Faustus* (1810) capitalized on medieval legends, notably the phantom horseman, ghost ship, demon hunter, and the alchemist willing to sell his soul to Satan in exchange for power and knowledge. The first wave of Gothicism preceded a GOTHIC REVIVAL, in which romanticists reached into the past for imagery that merged beauty with MELANCHOLY, magic, and sinister forces—all elements of Samuel Taylor COLERIDGE's atmospheric poem "CHRISTABEL" (1816) and John KEATS's "THE EVE OF ST. AGNES" (1819), a dreamy elopement poem based on SUPERSTITIONs about the revelation of the perfect mate. Sir Walter SCOTT added his own style of medievalism to the STORYTELLING element of *The Lay of the Last Minstrel* (1805) and chivalric history and gallantry to *Ivanhoe* (1819), his classic HISTORICAL NOVEL. The term *medievalism* entered the language in the mid-19th century with the poems and paintings of the PRE-RAPHAELITE BROTHERHOOD, which revived the medieval concept of NATURE as God's creative agent and the setting for human perversions and wrongdoings.

Medieval customs and sensibilities were an impetus to significant critical works, notably Thomas Carlyle's *Past and Present* (1843) and John Ruskin's *The Stones of Venice* (1851–53), and to the GROTESQUE barbarisms of Hanns Heinz EWERS's *Alraune* (The mandrakes, 1911), a repository of extreme German Gothicism. J. R. R. Tolkien harnessed the Gothic conventions of monsters, STALKING, and the rescue of the NAIF in his book *The Hobbit* (1937) and trilogy *The Lord of the Rings* (1954–55), for which he applied his considerable expertise in Old English and Middle English literature. The film version of part two of the latter, completed in 2003, contains a grim marshaling of troops and the immurement of the innocent in a medieval fortress as a handful of heroes face dire forces during a cataclysmic battle. The controlling theme is an apocalyptic clash between good and evil, a seminal topic in medieval art, ALLEGORY, and tales.

Bibliography

Chambers, E. K. *The Mediaeval Stage*. Mineola, N.Y.: Dover, 1996.

Longueil, Alfred. "The Word 'Gothic' in Eighteenth Century Criticism," *Modern Language Notes* 38 (1923): 459–461.

Lovecraft, H. P. *The Annotated Supernatural Horror in Literature*. New York: Hippocampus, 2000.

Madoff, Mark. "The Useful Myth of Gothic Ancestry," *Studies in Eighteenth-Century Culture* 8 (1979): 337–350.

Radcliffe, Ann. *The Italian*. London: Oxford University Press, 1968.

Terwilliger, Thomas. *Root of Evil*. New York: Herald Tribune Books, 1929.

melancholy

The emotions of sad longing and regret tinge much of Gothic and romantic literature, particularly the willful moodiness of the GRAVEYARD POETS, who chose shadowed cemeteries and doleful grieving as their focus. Author Robert Burton probed the subject thoroughly in *The Anatomy of Melancholy* (1621), a study of psychic despair and its antidote. The text influenced readers and scholars and promoted interest in the subject among the romantic poets in later years. Thomas Warton's *On the Pleasures of Melancholy* (1747) relieved the term *melancholy* of negativity by connecting it with a pleasurable emotional state. Horace WALPOLE, originator of the GOTHIC NOVEL, identified sorrow as a proof of true love in the conclusion of *THE CASTLE OF OTRANTO* (1765), a terror tale about a family curse that causes the death of Manfred's son and daughter. Before Theodore, a surviving suitor, can accept Isabella as a bride, he converses at length with her and concludes that "he could know no happiness but in the society of one with whom he could forever indulge the melancholy that had taken possession of his soul" (Walpole,

110). The concept of melancholia gained strength and permeated late 18th-century German Gothicism—notably, the lackluster outlook of the prince in Friedrich von SCHILLER's psychological novel *DER GEISTERSEHER* (*The Ghost-Seer*, 1786). Because of his aimlessness and eagerness for diversion, the prince lapses into an amorality that dominates the author's examination of the causes of crime.

During the initial wave of English Gothicism, novelist Ann RADCLIFFE described sad thoughts as a normal reaction to loss. In *THE MYSTERIES OF UDOLPHO* (1794), she introduces the St. Aubert family and notes that the father enjoys an active family life but retreats into solitude at twilight and mourns the deaths of his two sons, who expired in infancy. The propensity for a sweet sadness becomes an emotional bulwark to his daughter, Emily ST. AUBERT, the heroine of the novel, whom the VILLAIN Montoni locks in a tower room. She looks out over the Pyrenées, strums her lute, and sings "To Melancholy." The 10 stanzas typify a "spirit of love and sorrow" as a springboard to fancy, romantic dreams, and walks in NATURE (Radcliffe, 665–666). Unlike depressing lyrics, the song leads Emily to an affirmation of the FEMALE GOTHIC, the upbeat, spunky attitude of women who refuse to be victims.

As European Gothic fiction evolved, its melancholy varied in scope and direction. Early 19th-century ROMANTICISM produced a gentle malaise that precedes the clash of dueling knights and a woman's mysterious death in Mary Hays's "A Fragment: In the Manner of the Old Romances" (1793), the deepening disillusion and skepticism that mark Lord BYRON's narrative poems *Childe Harold's Pilgrimage* (1812) and "THE PRISONER OF CHILLON" (1816), a morbid solitude in Mary SHELLEY's MAD SCIENTIST novel *FRANKENSTEIN* (1818), a dreamy meditation in John KEATS's ballad "THE EVE OF ST. AGNES" (1819), and a reflection on military losses in Felicia Hemans's poem "England's Dead" (1826) and on a friendship enduring beyond death in "A Spirit's Return" (1830). In his youth, the Russian romantic Mikhail Lermontov reflected a preoccupation with yearning and doomed, bittersweet romance. At age 14, he wrote the first draft of *The Demon* (1840), the quaint story of a fallen angel who views earth as a prison.

In a narrative marked by exotica, the wanderer, banished from heaven, woos Tamara, a bride-to-be, with worshipful, rhapsodic love. The dramatic scenario, set at a remote convent in the rugged Caucasus Mountains of Georgia, concludes with a fiery kiss, which kills the earthling and sends her straight to heaven for her martyrdom by intimate contact with the soulful demon. The melancholy ballad inspired sketches, paintings, stage drama, and, in 1875, *The Demon and Tamara*, a three-act opera by Anton Rubinstein.

At the height of Victorian Gothicism, Charlotte BRONTË followed the Radcliffean example in picturing melancholy as a normal psychological response to loss. In the falling action of JANE EYRE (1847), Edward ROCHESTER attempts to save his crazed wife Bertha and suffers serious impairments as his allegorical punishment for multiple sins. Reduced in grasp and vision from the loss of a hand and eye, he recedes into a woeful cloud, a self-punishing funk that destroys his peaceful contemplation of the lawn at Ferndean. The author applies ESP as a SUPERNATURAL means of communication between Edward and his lost Jane, who speeds to his rescue and relieves his inward probing with a rejuvenating love, marriage, and normal home life far from the lunacy and torment of THORNFIELD HALL.

The deliberate creation of similar sad scenes infused mid- to late 19th-century literature, coloring Edgar Allan POE's "The Raven" (1845); Christina ROSSETTI's wistful contemplation of death in "Song" (1848); and Nathaniel HAWTHORNE's Gothic tales and novels, particularly THE SCARLET LETTER (1850), THE HOUSE OF SEVEN GABLES (1851), and *The Marble Faun* (1860). Oscar WILDE allowed depression to infuse the TONE of his FAIRY TALEs "The Happy Prince" and "The Birthday of the Infanta" (1888). In the 20th century, the novelist Daphne DU MAURIER reprised the languor and self-absorption of melancholy Gothic fiction in REBECCA (1938), in which the first months of the unnamed protagonist's marriage are overlaid with self-doubt, lonely walks, and secret longings. In the current century, Virginia Renfro Ellis built on post–Civil War melancholy in *The Wedding Dress* (2002), the story of Southern widows coping with loss and witnessing the return of ghost soldiers along country roads. Michel Faber balanced a believable and normal melancholy in a London mistress with the lunacy and suicidal urges in her lover's wife in his neo-Victorian novel THE CRIMSON PETAL AND THE WHITE (2002).

Bibliography

Golstein, Vladimir B. *Heroes of Their Times: Lermontov's Representation of the Heroic Self.* New Haven, Conn.: Yale University Press, 1992.

Grove, Allen W. "To Make a Long Story Short: Gothic Fragments and the Gender Politics of Incompleteness," *Studies in Short Fiction* 34, no. 1 (winter 1997): 1–10.

Radcliffe, Ann. *The Mysteries of Udolpho.* London: Oxford University Press, 1966.

Walpole, Horace. *The Castle of Otranto.* London: Oxford University Press, 1969.

Melmoth the Wanderer
Charles Robert Maturin
(1820)

A theatrical Faustian terror novel, *Melmoth the Wanderer* is the work of bold Gothic moonlighter Charles Robert MATURIN, an Anglican minister born into a family of anti-Catholic Huguenot lineage and educated in Dublin. The novel's sustained action is a marvel of tight interpolation of ancient tales and elements drawn from Dante's *Inferno* (1321) and Miguel de Cervantes's *Don Quixote* (1615). Maturin loosely based his plot on Sydney Owenson's *The Missionary* (1811), a popular novel published by William Lane's MINERVA PRESS. Maturin shaped the protagonist after the antiheroic title character in Percy Bysshe SHELLEY's closet drama *Prometheus Unbound* (1819). *Melmoth the Wanderer* influenced an impressive list of writers: Honoré de Balzac, Charles BAUDELAIRE, Lord BYRON, Johann von GOETHE, Nathaniel HAWTHORNE, Edgar Allan POE, and Sir Walter SCOTT. In his last years, Oscar WILDE, after release from imprisonment for sodomy, went into exile in Paris and wrote under the pseudonym Sebastian Melmoth, an indication of Wilde's unending torment.

Maturin violated the GOTHIC CONVENTION of placing horrific fiction in the mystic Orient or in the Catholic realms of the Mediterranean. Instead, his autobiographical plot opens in Dublin, in the fall of 1816. The MYSTERY takes shape from a situation common to Gothic novels—a young title character obsesses over a compelling manuscript about a relative (in this case, someone named Stanton). To avoid the medieval claptrap of earlier Gothic models, Maturin connects the document to an historic era of religious fanaticism, the English Puritans' execution of King Charles I on January 30, 1649. From this ominous springboard, a complex series of embedded side plots—"The Tale of the Indians," "The Tale of Guzman's Family," and "The Tale of the Lovers"—varies the narrative with motifs of alienation, temptation, fanaticism, cannibalism, and confinement to an asylum, a suggestion of the INSANITY wrought by obsessive sectarianism.

Maturin employs the anticlerical text as an ALLEGORY on Ireland's relationship with England and as a commentary on morality, ILLUSION, imprisonment and CLAUSTROPHOBIA, psychological torment, SADISM, and legalistic religion. At the heart of the story is the wretched bitterness of Melmoth, a VILLAIN who owes much to Ann RADCLIFFE's Montoni and SCHEDONI. Of melmoth's twisted personality, Maturin muses that sarcasm derived from despair: "A mirth which is not gaiety is often the mask which hides the convulsed and distorted features of agony—and laughter which never yet was the expression of rapture, has often been the only intelligible language of madness and misery" (Maturin, 270). The pervasive savagery of the wanderer symbolizes the evils and corruption that haunt humankind, both on the geographical landscape and the inner terrain of the mind. In the estimation of critic Leonard Wolf, the wanderer's plunge into primordial iniquity "becomes an apparently accurate chart of the cost to mankind of original sin" (Maturin, Introduction, xi).

One of the most gripping of Maturin's digressive tales is the involvement of a shipwrecked Spaniard named Monçada, whose story expresses the author's ANTI-CATHOLICISM. Forced into celibacy by the Inquisition, he relates his seduction by a Satanic SUPERNATURAL loner, who entices him from a restrictive monastery. Paralleling diabolic stories and tales of the WANDERING JEW, the novel reaches its high point with a confrontation between Stanton and the unnamed demon, who has extended his victim's life to 150 years. In an ATMOSPHERE of moral vacuum and theological despair, the victim resigns himself to reclamation by the devil.

On his return to Ireland, Melmoth, the agent of Satan, meets his end. The demon demands a terrible, unavoidable punishment for overreaching human boundaries, first in the sea, then in the nether reaches. In a fearful vision, the wanderer sees himself on the lip of a precipice where an unseen force flings him to perdition. Maturin expands on damnation with powerful imagery: "The upper air (for there was no heaven) showed only blackness unshadowed and impenetrable—but, blacker than that blackness, he could distinguish a gigantic outstretched arm, that held him as in sport on the ridge of that infernal precipice" (Maturin, 409). The descent ends with a succession of stop-motion images: "He fell—he sunk—he blazed—he shrieked!" (ibid., 410). As a warning to the reader, Maturin indicates that Melmoth's death does not rid the world of persecution. French readers thrilled to Émile Bégin's translation, *L'Homme du Mystère, ou Histoire de Melmoth le Voyageur* (The man of mystery; or, the story of Melmoth the traveler, 1820) and Jean Cohen's *Melmoth, ou l'Homme Errant* (Melmoth; or, the wandering man, 1820).

Bibliography

Horner, Avril, ed. *European Gothic: A Spirited Exchange, 1760–1960*. Manchester: Manchester University Press, 2002.

Lew, Joseph W. "'Unprepared for Sudden Transformations': Identity and Politics in 'Melmoth the Wanderer,'" *Studies in the Novel* 26, no. 2 (summer 1994): 173–195.

Maturin, Charles Robert. *Melmoth the Wanderer*. Lincoln: University of Nebraska Press, 1961.

melodrama

A literary term referring to sentimental romantic fiction based on shallow characterization, *melodrama* originally was a French term, *mélodrame*, which described a stage play set to music—that is, melody + drama. The genre avoids explanations of motivation and logic to focus on inflated pathos, thrills, wickedness, violence, and Gothic horror. Two examples, in John RICHARDSON's prototypical Canadian romance *Wacousta; or, The Prophecy: A Tale of the Canadas* (1832) and its sequel, *The Canadian Brothers* (1840), depict horrific clashes between English forces and the warriors of Chief Pontiac. Rich in HYPERBOLE, melodrama's characters, confined by the emphasis on action over motive, rarely stray from typecasting as the virtuous, the villainous, or cardboard bystanders. Because melodrama stresses the triumph of good over evil, the critic Northrop Fry, author of *Anatomy of Criticism* (1957), quipped that melodrama approaches "as close as it is normally possible for art to come to the pure self-righteousness of the lynching mob" (Fry, 47).

Nineteenth-century melodrama provided relief for pent-up Victorian emotions by its lack of restraint, both in word and deed. At a telling point in the action, the forceful players of stage melodrama enhanced theatricality by freezing in place for a tableau and maintaining exaggerated gestures and expressions of terror or disbelief to impress on the audience the MOOD of potential cataclysm. Typically extreme in SENSATIONALISM, disillusion, and resignation to circumstance, the melodrama utters the unspeakable in an outpouring of suppressed truths, however inappropriate or unmannerly—for example, a welter of grief in Horace WALPOLE's seminal Gothic novel THE CASTLE OF OTRANTO (1765), in which Manfred, bereft of both his children, "dashed himself on the ground, and cursed the day he was born" (Walpole, 106).

Melodrama came of age on a wave of popular demand for the GOTHIC NOVEL as well as the serialized NEWGATE NOVEL and bluebooks, publications of MINERVA PRESS, AMERICAN GOTHIC and FRONTIER GOTHIC from the colonies, and Gothic stage thrillers and verse. English strolling actor and playwright Thomas Holcroft introduced melodrama in Britain by translating and adapting René-Charles Guilbert de Pixerécourt's *Coelina; ou, L'Enfant du Mystere* (Coelina; or, the mysterious child, 1800) as *A Tale of Mystery,* which debuted at Covent Garden Theatre in November 1802. Holcroft set the story at a decaying castle, a standard backdrop for Gothic staging. He presented his VILLAIN, the malicious Malvoglio—an allegorical

name meaning "wishing evil"—before others in the garden at a moment of shock and dismay as the characters remain motionless to ponder what will happen next. The audience responded with a gasp and an involuntary shiver of terror.

For the popular market, publishers of the GOTHIC BLUEBOOK issued original tales or redactions of popular stories and novels in small sixpenny chapbooks. One anonymous thriller, *Secret Tribunal; or, The Court of Wincelaus* (1803), allied a sensational story with Gothic illustration. Perverting religious icons by picturing a phantasm threatening the guileless NAIF clinging to a cross, the cover hooked new readers intrigued by distortions of Catholic ritual and secret societies. A later issue, *Fatal Jealousy; or, Blood Will Have Blood! Containing the History of Count Almagro and Duke Alphonso* (1807), intrigued the reader with implications of villainy and crime within the aristocracy. An undated bluebook, *The Old Tower of Frankenstein,* plucked from Mary SHELLEY's FRANKENSTEIN (1818) the most ghastly scenarios for maximum shock value.

To appeal to the bored middle class, Gothic melodrama depicted women as helpless victims of evil villains. One felon, William Corder, a killer executed in 1828 for predations on a pregnant girl, became the focus of a popular stage melodrama, *Maria Marten; or, The Murder in the Red Barn* (1830). Another violator of women, Svengali, is a Jewish manipulator who hypnotizes the singer Trilby, the title character in George du Maurier's novel *Trilby,* serialized in *Harper's* in 1894. As in spectacle, puppet shows, dioramas, and waxworks, Victorian melodrama depended on stereotyping the good and the bad rather than developing psychological insight. The heroes of melodrama were the strong, brave, respectful males who released from potential harm the endangered female, who was often an orphan or otherwise defenseless girl like Trilby. Naive, theatrical plots based on a rigid form of poetic justice tended to incorporate narrow escapes and to award the good and punish the bad. Ideally, the female rewarded the rescuer with thanks, love, even marriage.

In 1852, the Dublin-born playwright and playhouse manager Dionysius Boucicault advanced melodrama with popular thrillers, *The Corsican*

Brothers and *The Vampire*, which he adapted from French originals. The next year, he brought British melodrama to the United States and dominated the American stage with *The Poor of New York* (1857) and *After Dark* (1858). For *The Shaughraun* (1875), an Irish melodrama, Boucicault stressed Gothic settings—a hovel, prison, cliffside, and ruined abbey—for a thrilling rogue tale set during a Fenian rebellion.

Boucicault is best known for *The Octoroon, or Life in Louisiana* (1859), a race-based melodrama on miscegenation and arson that opened in New York City at the Winter Garden Theater in December 1859. Told through Southern dialect, the abolitionist plot centers on the hapless slave Zoe, the victim of M'Closky, who sets fire to a riverboat. The action incorporates a tomahawk murder, auctioning of slaves, lynching, and flight from an alligator. The play was the source of a sensational novelization, Mary Elizabeth BRADDON's *The Octoroon; or, The Lily of Louisiana* (1861–62), serialized in *Halfpenny Journal*.

Reflecting Gothic literary strands from France and Germany, North Carolina–born drama critic and playwright Augustin Daly, an innovator on the American stage, created a Gothic stereotype, the tying of the victim to railroad tracks, for *Under the Gaslight* (1867), a well-received melodrama that opened in August 1867 at the New York Theater. The text romanticized Eastern notions of frontier perils and sold out performances to viewers eager to see realistic stage machinery. A steam whistle indicates the approach of the engine that threatens the life of Snorkey, a wounded veteran, before the eyes of the heroine, Laura Cortlandt, whom the villain tied in a tool shed. As the headlights near, she manages to wield an ax and free Snorkey. For her role as Laura, the jilted lover, the star of the show, Rose Eytinge, amassed a large fan base, including Secretary of State William Henry Seward and President Abraham Lincoln. Daly further developed American melodrama by inventing for *Horizon* (1871) the stage version of the savage Indian, a staple character in late 19th-century productions.

More recent Gothic writers employ melodrama as a literary means of depicting ABERRANT BEHAVIOR and examining character motivation, for example, the family tradition requiring the youngest daughter to remain unmarried in Laura Esquivel's novel *Like Water for Chocolate* (1989) and the impending unmasking of a cross-dressing prelate in Donna Cross's historical novel *Pope Joan* (1996). Toni MORRISON orchestrates a stirring falling action in BELOVED (1987), in which a powerful community of black females converges on a haunted house to drive out the offending spirit and set free the protagonist, Sethe, a survivor of enslavement and lashing who despairs from her crime of infanticide. In August WILSON's domestic ghost play THE PIANO LESSON (1990), a grand finale depicting the pianist playing, singing, and summoning family spirits gives a double meaning to the title. The piano offers the Charles family not only a lesson in how to value the past, but also a reason for jubilation as they join in an exorcism of the sufferings of slave times.

Bibliography

Fry, Northrop. *Anatomy of Criticism.* Princeton, N.J.: Princeton University Press, 1957.

Stoneman, Patsy. *Brontë Transformations: The Cultural Dissemination of "Wuthering Heights" and "Jane Eyre."* Upper Saddle River, N.J.: Prentice-Hall, 1996.

Walpole, Horace. *The Castle of Otranto.* London: Oxford University Press, 1969.

Melville, Herman
(1819–1891)

Herman Melville, an obsessive writer of verse and short and long fiction, earned few readers and less acclaim for his monumental novel *Moby-Dick* (1851) or his insightful shorter works "Bartleby the Scrivener" (1853), BENITO CERENO (1855), and *Billy Budd,* issued posthumously in 1924. Well read in youth, Melville held in high esteem Horace WALPOLE's THE CASTLE OF OTRANTO (1765), the fount of English Gothic. Because of the Melville family's failed finances, Herman clerked and taught school before finding his life's love, the sea. As cabin boy on the whaler *Acushnet,* at age 20, he sailed from New Bedford, Massachusetts, beginning a three-year sea-going adventure that took him over much of the South Pacific and into the navy for service on the frigate *United States.* From his observations on cannibalism, tattooing, and life in the islands, he wrote two sensational autobiographical novels, *Typee* (1846) and *Omoo* (1847). In the former, he built SUSPENSE through a scene featuring spherical packages wrapped in tapa cloth and suspended from the ridgepole of a native house. At length, Tommo, the main character, discerns "a glimpse of three human heads, which others of the party were hurriedly enveloping in the coverings from which they had been taken" (Melville, *Typee*, 258). The thought of murder at the hands of head hunters sends the protagonist on a mad dash back to civilization.

Melville married, settled in New York, and produced three more works in the semifictional genre: *Mardi* (1849), *Redburn* (1849), and *White Jacket* (1850). From his friendship with Nathaniel HAWTHORNE and close reading of THE SCARLET LETTER (1850), in 1851, Melville gained the courage to attempt heavily symbolic moralism. The dark, troubling novel *Moby-Dick* narrated a seaman's Gothic nightmare, the haunting of Captain Ahab by his nemesis, Moby Dick, the infernal white sperm whale. Melville told the demonic tale through the eyes of Ishmael, the OUTSIDER. Near the final matchup between whale and whaler, Ahab mutters: "The madness, the frenzy, the boiling blood and the smoking brow, with which, for a thousand lowerings old Ahab has furiously, foamingly chased his prey—more a demon than a man!—aye, aye! what a forty year's fool—fool—old fool, has old Ahab been!" (Melville, *Moby-Dick*, 507). With a cry to the almighty, Ahab pleads, "God! God! God!—crack my heart!—stave my brain!—mockery! mockery! bitter, biting mockery of gray hairs, have I lived enough joy to wear ye" (*ibid.*). Because the text carries ambition and manic obsession to theatrical extremes, the author's contemporaries found the work morbid and morally ambiguous. His next project, *Pierre; or, The Ambiguities* (1852), an even darker psychological novel on incest, involved the expiation of a father's sexual depravity by the son's marriage to his half-sister Isabel while he keeps a pledge to Lucy, his fiancée. The novel shocked the reading public and failed to boost the author's income to a level of self-sufficiency.

As a means of addressing urban depersonalization, Melville applied the logic of the GHOST STORY to Bartleby, the dehumanized copyist who haunts an attorney's office on Wall Street in "Bartleby the Scrivener" (1856). While continuing to submit stories to *Harper's and Putnam's*, the author accepted a bureaucratic post as customs inspector in New York harbor and, at the end of the Civil War, published a sheaf of reflective poems, *Battle Pieces and Aspects of War* (1866). In "The Paradise of Bachelors and the Tartarus of Maids," issued in *Harper's Weekly* in 1855, he created a uniquely American urban Gothic castle out of a sepulchral paper mill. In constant discomfort, young female drones perform at the whim of male demons and their hellish machines, which drain the life's blood from workers like a mechanized vampire. At Melville's death, he left in his drawer the text of *Billy Budd*, a fable of villainy and victimization, one of his best received literary endeavors.

Bibliography

Goldner, Ellen J. "Other(ed) Ghosts: Gothicism and the Bonds of Reason in Melville, Chesnutt, and Morrison," *MELUS* 24, no. 1 (spring 1999): 59.

Melville, Herman. *Moby-Dick; or, The White Whale*. New York: New American Library, 1961.

———. *Typee*. New York: Signet, 1964.

metempsychosis

Metempsychosis, the concept of human metamorphosis into beasts, is a subset of LYCANTHROPY and a persistent motif in world myth. Unlike willful SHAPE-SHIFTING, a form of magic, metempsychosis is a permanent transfer of a soul to another body or species. The shift poses a particular sort of horror—the resumption of a human life in another living form, as in "Aura" (1962), one of the macabre novellas of Mexican novelist Carlos Fuentes in which a young man avoids the oblivion of death. The ancient Greek philosopher Pythagoras was so certain that souls took other living shapes that he used metempsychosis as justification for vegetarianism. The concept of the return of spirits as animals was a common strand in the lore of India that infused a classic JAPANESE GOTHIC collection, *Tales of Times Now Past* (ca. 1130).

The transmigration concept recurred with regularity in 19th-century Gothic fiction. The transmigration of a human soul was the driving force of Robert Macnish's demonic tale "The Metempsychosis," published in BLACKWOOD'S EDINBURGH MAGAZINE for May 1826. It powered Edgar Allan POE's first published short story, "Metzengerstein" (1832), a tale about a human soul transposed into a great horse. Poe applied the concept more skillfully in "LIGEIA" (1838), a dreamy, ambiguous tale of domestic jealousy. The dead wife engages the second wife, who is newly deceased, in a power struggle to possess the grieving widower. In his collection *Life's Handicap* (1891), Rudyard KIPLING depicted transmutation as nemesis in "The Mark of the Beast," a powerful COLONIAL GOTHIC story about an English desecrater of an Indian temple and his transformation into a wolf as punishment for sacrilege.

The subject of soul transport suited Gertrude ATHERTON's inclination toward MYSTERY and the SUPERNATURAL in her novel *What Dreams May Come* (1888), whose title is taken from William Shakespeare's *Hamlet* (ca. 1599). The story focuses on a beautiful Welsh noblewoman, Weir Penrhyn, whose form and figure so overwhelm Harold Dartmouth that he collapses in her alluring presence. She divulges a memory of a cataleptic trance in which she believes herself interred in a vault. Atherton advances terror with a dead-of-stormy-night meeting between Dartmouth and the ghost of Lady Sionèd Penrhyn, the love of his grandfather, who complains that she floated for millions of miles in search of Dartmouth. By morning, the ghost retreats into the lovely Weir Penrhyn, its earthly form. In accounting for metempsychosis, Atherton muses, "Their souls must be the same as when the great ocean of Force had tossed them up, and evolution work no essential change" (Atherton, 150).

Bibliography

Atherton, Gertrude. *What Dreams May Come.* Chicago: Belford, Clarke, 1888.

Baring-Gould, Sabine. *Book of Were-Wolves.* London: Smith, Elder, 1865.

Hammond, Alexander. "A Reconstruction of Poe's 1833 *Tales of the Folio Club*, Preliminary Notes," *Poe Studies* 5, no. 2 (December 1972): 25–32.

Robinson, E. Arthur. "'New Approaches' in Poe Criticism," *Poe Studies* 4, no. 2 (December 1971): 48–50.

Minerva Press

The forerunner of modern pulp publishers, Minerva Press flourished in London under the hand of William Lane, an astute businessman and newspaper publisher. The company published popular romances, sentimental novels, MELODRAMA, ORIENTAL ROMANCE, cautionary tales, and Gothic literature. As the equivalent of the 21st-century pulp publishing house, the firm's output was an impetus to popular reading. Minerva Press opened in 1787 and was relocated three years later to Leadenhall Street. The business was highly successful, issuing 26 titles in 1790, publishing 14 titles in 1810, and remaining in operation for over a quarter-century.

A vanity press and purveyor of reprints, Lane's publishing house appealed to tastes in GOTHIC NOVELS with intriguing settings and titles—religious implications in the anonymous *Phantoms of the Cloister; or, The Mysterious Manuscript* (1795) and Elizabeth Helme's *St. Margaret's Cave; or, The Nun's Story* (1801); REVENANTs in the anonymous *The Animated Skeleton* (1798); and the romance of the remote in John Palmer's *The Mystery of the Black Tower* (1796). Mary Charlton's *Rosella; or, Modern Occurrences* (1799) established the importance of Gothic architecture and surrounding NATURE in producing dramatic effect. A character in Mary Darby ROBINSON's *The Natural Daughter* (1799) comments: "Mind the title. Nothing in these times will sell so highly as the title" (Tarr, 4).

To emphasize startling rhetoric, Minerva writers employed a demonstrative style that called for typesetters to italicize significant words. Inaccuracies, typos, erroneous translations of foreign terms, and errors in time and place abounded, including faulty rendering of print dates into Roman numerals. The thrill-hungry public, which cared little for grammar, spelling, and correctness, demanded baroque Germanic fiction—for example, Lawrence Flammenberg's *Der Geisterbanner* (The ghost banner, 1792), a tale of the magician Volkert translated by Peter Teuthold as *The Necromancer; or, The Tale of the Black Forest* (1794), and Peter Will's four-volume *The Horrid Mysteries: A Story from the German of the Marquis of Grosse* (1796), a novel exploiting the SECRECY of the ILLUMINATI, a clandestine brotherhood.

Lane created his own audience by franchising a chain of CIRCULATING LIBRARIES. At their height, he supplied fans by employing a stable of writers of potboilers, at least two-thirds of whom were female. Some authors knew nothing about contract negotiation and were easily persuaded to sign away their royalties. Among the most famous of Lane's freelancers were Fanny Burney, Francis LATHOM, Eliza PARSONS, Ann RADCLIFFE, Regina Maria ROCHE, Louisa Sidney Stanhope, and ANNE OF SWANSEA, plus a number who wrote anonymously or under assumed names. Anonymity protected them and their families from the lurid reputation of sensational literature, in particular, the trick-marriage plot involving an innocent NAIF in the machinations of a villainous despoiler of women. Of the female dominance of Lane's circulating library, novelist Charles Reade complained, "They will only take in ladies' novels. Mrs. Henry Wood, 'Ouida,' Miss Braddon— these are their gods" (Carnell, 169).

A rarity in FEMALE GOTHIC was Eleanor Sleath, a Catholic writer in a genre typified by anti-Catholic sentiment. Minerva Press published her four-volume *The Orphan of the Rhine: A Romance* (1798), a Gothic novel that Jane AUSTEN lists among choice works in *NORTHANGER ABBEY* (1818). Like Peter Will, Sleath based the orphan's story on popular Germanic lore, which remained in vogue in the late 18th and early 19th centuries. Lane prepared the reader for ominous action with a melodramatic frontispiece—a male figure glowering from the forest at a tender, fearful maiden, who appeals to a holy man for succor. The illustration perpetuated the Gothic stereotype of women as frail and helpless.

At Lane's death in 1814, Anthony King Newman bought out Minerva Press, boosted the number of book runs, and followed the advertising style of his predecessor. That same year, poet George Daniel paid tribute to Lane's public success in the satiric poem *The Modern Dunciad* (1814). He teased Lane for manipulating ghosts, demons, and hobgoblins in "loose novels" (Daniel, 100). More critical were the next lines:

> For pious Lane, who knows his readers well,
> Can suit all palates with their diff'rent food,
> Love for the hoyden, morals for the prude!

> Behold! with reams of nonsense newly born,
> Th'industrious pack who scribble night and
>   morn;
> Five pounds per volume! an enormous bribe,
> Enough, methinks to tempt a hungry scribe.
>   (*Ibid.*)

In 1820, Newman altered the firm's logo to A. K. Newman & Company and shifted his marketing efforts from Gothic to children's literature.

Bibliography

Blakey, Dorothy. *The Minerva Press, 1790–1820.* London: Oxford University Press, 1939.

Carnell, Jennifer. *The Literary Lives of Mary Elizabeth Braddon.* Hastings, Sussex: Sensation Press, 2000.

Daniel, George. *The Modern Dunciad: Virgil in London and Other Poems.* London: William Pickering, 1835.

Stevens, David. *The Gothic Tradition.* Cambridge: Cambridge University Press, 2000.

Tarr, Mary Muriel. *Catholicism in Gothic Fiction: A Study of the Nature and Function of Catholic Materials in Gothic Fiction in England, 1762–1820.* Washington, D.C.: Catholic University of America Press, 1946.

Mistress of Mellyn
Victoria Holt
(1960)

Victoria HOLT's classic terror novel *Mistress of Mellyn* remains faithful to the BLUEBEARD MYTH and Gothic traditions, which Holt imported from Charlotte BRONTË's *JANE EYRE* (1847) and from Daphne DU MAURIER's *REBECCA* (1938). Holt's plot places the typically poor, homeless, but proper governess Martha Leigh at a Cornish estate, Mount Mellyn, where she tends a harridan, Alvean TreMellyn. Martha's employer, Connan TreMellyn, a mildly BYRONIC HERO, bears a clouded visage similar to the scowl of Brontë's Edward ROCHESTER. In an early encounter, Connan locks eyes with the heroine: "There was a violent temper there, and I could see that he was fighting to control it. He still looked at me and I could not read the expression in those light eyes. I believed it was contemptuous" (Holt, 90).

Holt modulates the GOTHIC SETTING with a seaside plateau that is as inviting and well groomed as MANDERLEY, the de Winter estate in *Rebecca.* After Holt's heroine becomes the love object of the irresistable Connan, she enters a Cinderella phase of her advancement with receipt of a gown and jewelry to wear to a ball, another borrowing from du Maurier's Gothic classic. As it was for the unnamed Mrs. de Winter in *Rebecca,* the occasion becomes an initiation rite and quintessential test of Martha's worthiness to rise from working-class status to gentrification. FORE-SHADOWINGS of conflict and death emerge from tapestries that line the gallery, presenting images of the English Civil War and the execution of King Charles I. At first, Martha anticipates the greatest conflict from tradition. Of the household of Mellyn, she declares, "Such and such was done because it always had been done, and often for no other reason. Well, that was the way in great houses" (*ibid.,* 177).

Balancing Martha's goodness and character, Holt counters with the FEMME FATALE, the raven-haired Celestine Nansellock, a jealous neighbor and serial murderer who lets nothing stand in the way of her becoming mistress at the cold, brooding mount. Like the NAIF in Bluebeard's Castle, the heroine is beset by nameless terrors in a manse haunted by fearful deaths, which servants and neighbors are eager to divulge. Following the Gothic pattern, endangerment brings out the best traits in Martha, who applies logic and gumption to threats from a crashing boulder, and the exhumation and autopsy of Sir Thomas Treslyn, who died by suspicious means. Martha remains true to the domestic wholeness of the Mellyn household, her reward for virtue and persistence. In keeping with the conventions of FEMALE GOTHIC, the love she feels for Connan is returned and rewarded with children, grandchildren, and great-grandchildren, the author's evidence that quality parents strengthen lineage.

Bibliography

Fleenor, Juliann E., ed. *The Female Gothic.* Montreal: Eden Press, 1983.

Holt, Victoria. *Mistress of Mellyn.* Leicester: Ulverscroft, 1960.

Williams, Anne. *Art of Darkness: A Poetics of Gothic.* Chicago: University of Chicago Press, 1995.

The Monk
Matthew Gregory Lewis
(1797)

Composed three years after Ann RADCLIFFE's novel THE MYSTERIES OF UDOLPHO (1794) and William GODWIN's CALEB WILLIAMS (1794), Matthew Gregory LEWIS's *The Monk* became a cause célèbre among Gothic works. He wrote during an historic period that saw the fall of the French Republic and the rise of Robespierre and the guillotine and completed his novel in 10 weeks. The text probes the interplay between imagination and reason and between religious repression and sexual desire. The most sensational, sexually explicit HORROR FICTION of its day, *The Monk* reflected both ANTI-CATHOLICISM and public tensions over the horrors in France. The plot produced waves of disapproval among conservative readers and outrage from the pulpit at scenes of blatant savagery. The concept of a fallen cleric negotiating with Satan explored new ground, turning DIABOLISM into a vibrant subgenre of GOTHIC CONVENTION. Within months, Ann Radcliffe riposted with THE ITALIAN; *or, The Confessional of the Black Penitents* (1797), which supplants Lewis's lurid extremes with MELODRAMA.

For his scandalous fiction, Lewis built on the traditional themes of FAUST and the WANDERING JEW. Against the backdrop of the Spanish Inquisition, a chain of stories within stories embroidered his antirealist romance with barbaric torments and cruelties of the narcissistic Spanish monk AMBROSIO, a fascinating but power-mad schemer. The narrative returned to Radcliffe the favor of a model for her own diabolical monk SCHEDONI in *The Italian,* which also takes place in Madrid during the Spanish Inquisition. Lewis's story, adapted from an original plot by the 13th-century Persian poet Saadi, also influenced a French devotional story called "De l'Hermite Que le Diable Trompa" (The ascetic whom the devil fools), which the *Guardian* summarized in English.

Lewis describes the subversion of the religious man as the work of Satan, who persuades the powerful sermonizer Ambrosio, a 30-year-old virginal friar, to abandon church-mandated celibacy and commit sensual atrocities. As a FOIL to the monk's towering faith, the author places the guile of the succubus Mathilda, a cross-dresser posing as the monk Rosario, who convinces Ambrosio that sexual abstinence is unnatural. She introduces him to debauchery with explicit carnal embraces previously unknown to him. From one sexual conquest, the formerly chaste monk moves on to a second, Antonia, a fetching NAIF, whom he approaches with a magic myrtle bough intended to keep her from awakening.

Lewis allows his protagonist to advance from sin to felony to unspeakable vice. To conceal his plunge from righteousness, Ambrosio throttles Antonia's mother, Elvira, who interrupts the rape scenario to protect her daughter. Upon Antonia's catatonic lapse from a powerful soporific, Ambrosio enshrouds her inert form, conceals her in the vaults of St. Clare, and rapes her, an act bordering on necrophilia. Lewis rapidly escalates the Gothicism of his plot: To the crime of devaluing Antonia, the depraved monk adds her murder and the imprisonment of the abbess Agnes, which coincides with the looting of a convent and the savage dismemberment of the nun.

Lewis embellished the original text with a confrontation between Ambrosio and Satan and a bartering session to spare the monk torture and execution by an auto-da-fé. To impress on readers Satan's control, Lewis embroiders on John Milton's model from book 1 of *Paradise Lost* (1667) to depict God's alter ego as swarthy, titanic in size, furious of gaze, and bristling with talons and the snaky hair of a Medusa. The signing of an infernal contract requires a parchment scroll and an iron pen, a SYMBOL of the unavoidable doom that Ambrosio agrees to. In the final flight to damnation, Satan sinks his claws into the monk's shaved scalp and carries him shrieking to a great height to drop among cruel precipices, which mar Ambrosio's corpse.

The visual detail in Lewis's initial manuscript was so horrific that the *Monthly Review* accused him of writing an obscene novel unfit for the public. Lewis published a modified version stripped of some erotic passages and a blasphemous reference to the Bible. Publishers offered to bind the cover with the title "British Butterflies" as a concealment of the scandalous work. The new edition received acclaim from the historical novelist Sir Walter

SCOTT and the poet Robert Southey, earned the regard of English romantic writers Lord BYRON, Samuel Taylor COLERIDGE, John KEATS, and William Wordsworth, and won the applause of the Marquis de Sade, who preferred Lewis's heavy-handed Gothic to the refinements of Ann Radcliffe. De Sade commented in the preface to *Les Crimes de l'Amour* (*The Crimes of Love*, 1800) that Lewis's fiction was "the fruit of the revolution of which all Europe felt the shock" (Varma, 217).

Lewis's shocker prefaced a variety of imitations and spin-offs, including the satanic Biondetta, modeled on Mathilda, in Jacques Cazotte's *Le Diable Amoureux* (*The Devil in Love*, 1772). In 1802, abridger Isaac Crookenden published a GOTHIC BLUEBOOK version of *The Monk* titled *The Vindictive Monk; or, The Fatal Ring*. Two more chapbook spin-offs appeared anonymously the next year: *Almagro and Claude; or, Monastic Murder* and *The Monk; or, Father Innocent, Abbot of the Capuchins*. Charlotte DACRE not only stole Lewis's plot, but also dedicated to him the popular thriller *The Confessions of the Nun of St. Omer* (1805), a three-volume Gothic novel. In 1819, Keats reprised Ambrosio's languorous seduction scene in his medieval ballad "THE EVE OF ST. AGNES."

Bibliography

Blakemore, Steven. "Matthew Lewis's Black Mass: Sexual, Religious Inversion in 'The Monk,'" *Studies in the Novel* 30, no. 4 (winter 1998): 521.

Brooks, Peter. "Virtue and Terror: The Monk," *English Literary History* 40 (1973): 249–263.

Paulson, Ronald. "Gothic Fiction and the French Revolution," *English Literary History* 48 (1981): 532–553.

The Monk of Horror
Anonymous
(1798)

Within weeks of Matthew Gregory LEWIS's publication of THE MONK (1797), a cadre of imitators began flooding the English book market with horror tales. Unscrupulous publishers appended Lewis's name and the title of his sensational novel to generate demand for their derivative works. An anonymously written GOTHIC BLUEBOOK titled *Tales from the Crypt* included *The Monk of Horror;*

or, *The Conclave of Corpses*. The story produced a fearful, but truncated scenario intended to arouse salvation anxiety and the horror of death, damnation, and a dismal afterlife of regret for wrongdoing. The text describes an unnamed monk engaged in NECROMANCY. His encounter with the doomed souls of three monks at the convent of Kreutzberg causes him to swoon in terror and ever after devote himself to sanctity. The brief story, which exhibits some literary merit, illustrates the shortcomings of Lewis's amateurish imitators who lacked the boldness of his novel and the ability to create sustained horror fiction.

Bibliography

Haining, Peter, ed. *Gothic Tales of Terror*. New York: Taplinger, 1972.

Summers, Montague. *A Gothic Bibliography*. New York: Russell & Russell, 1964.

"The Monkey's Paw"
W. W. Jacobs
(1902)

W. W. JACOBS's classic HORROR NARRATIVE "The Monkey's Paw" is a standard feature of classroom anthologies. A masterful example of controlled STORYTELLING and heightened SUSPENSE, the tale was issued in *Strand* magazine and collected in *The Lady of the Barge* (1902). The plot, set in 1870 at the height of Victorian imperialism, develops the concept of resurrection within a recurrent theme from the colonial era, the presence of sinister elements that follow colonials home to the motherland. As is often true of a nation's crimes against humanity, punishment falls on the unsuspecting peasantry, the people least capable of warding off doom.

Jacobs developed his tale from staple FOLKLORE, the three wishes, and increased its impact with a skillful measuring of action, ATMOSPHERE, and detail. The crux of the story is an Indian talisman, which a fakir endowed with SUPERNATURAL powers. Jacobs inserts foreshadowing from a visitor, Sergeant-Major Morris, a British noncom who divulges without elaboration that the first man to wish on the paw chose death as his third request. His hostess, Mrs. White, wisely remarks on the terror of the paw, which reminds her of *The Arabian Nights* (1704–17). The results of the first wish astound the Whites, a rural family of cottagers bereft of their son Herbert. Contributing to the horror of Herbert's mangling in machinery is the name of the company, Maw and Meggins, which suggests a voracious device like a medieval hellmouth that is capable of gobbling human flesh.

An effective quality of Jacobs's story is the absence of the actual being outside the Whites' front door. The author elongates suspense with Mrs. White's retrieval of a chair to enable her to remove the chain lock and loosen the bolt. In the interim, with the last wish, her husband hurriedly dispatches the thing at the door, which fills the house with "a perfect fusillade of knocks" (Jacobs, 42). In a critique of the story, H. P. LOVECRAFT called "The Monkey's Paw" a model of melodramatic fear literature, which Jacobs based solely on coincidence and the reader's imagination. In 1903, dramatist Louis Napoleon Parker reset the story as a one-act play that debuted at the London Haymarket Theatre.

Bibliography

Jacobs, W. W. *Selected Short Stories*. London: Bodley Head, 1975.

Jascoll, John. "Crowning a Literary Landmark," *Biblio* 4, no. 4 (April 1999): 36.

monsters

Gothic monsters are a creative rebellion of ROMANTICISM against the regularity and predictability of 18th-century neoclassic conventions. Expressing NATURE's penchant for freakishness and grotesquerie, monsters disturb universal harmony by appearing gnarled, deformed, and oversized or out of proportion, as is the case with the snaky-headed gorgon Medusa and the Minotaur, the man-beast immured in a claustrophobic labyrinth in Cretan mythology. As an allegorical facet of phobias, VIOLENCE, and horror, monstrosity invests FOLKLORE with boogeymen, banshees, werewolves, lamias, vampires, and dragons. In Harriet Elizabeth Prescott Spofford's description of the latter in "Circumstance" (1863), the dragon carries his victim aloft in sharp talons and "commenced licking her bare arm with his rasping tongue and pouring over her the wide streams of his hot, foetid breath," a terrifying threat compounded by fiery red eyes and gnashing tusks that tear off her arm and strip it of flesh (Williams, 99). In many instances, the monster looms by night, as with the predations of Grendel in *Beowulf* (ca. A.D. 600). The psychological connection between darkness and danger colors STORYTELLING, tingeing episodes of the shrieking LA LLORONA of Central American myth and the DYBBUK and golem of Jewish Hasidic lore with the implied menace in CHIAROSCURO and the counterbalance of safety in daylight.

From classic Gothic fiction, one of the most memorable of monsters is Victor FRANKENSTEIN's experimental man in Mary Wollstonecraft SHELLEY's *FRANKENSTEIN* (1818). Repulsed by his handiwork, Victor declares the patchwork body unspeakably grotesque: "A mummy again endued with animation could not be so hideous as that wretch. . . . When those muscles and joints were rendered capable of motion, it became a thing such as even Dante could not have conceived" (Shelley, 57). Varied eyesores from Gothic works developed Shelley's imaginative terrors, including the misshapen stalker in John KEATS's vampire poem "LA BELLE DAME SANS MERCI" (1819), the reptilian brute Zatanai in William Child GREEN's *The Abbot of Montserrat; or, The Pool of Blood* (1826), the German terrors of Émile ERCKMANN and Louis Alexandre CHATRIAN's *Contes Fantastiques* (Fantastic stories, 1847) and "The Crab Spider" (1893), Robert Louis STEVENSON's shape-shifter in *DR. JEKYLL AND MR. HYDE* (1886), the hunchback dwarf in Oscar WILDE's sad FAIRY TALE "The Birthday of the Infanta" (1888), and the coterie of vampires in Bram STOKER's *DRACULA* (1897). H. G. WELLS turned his MAD SCIENTIST novel *THE ISLAND OF DR. MOREAU* (1896) into a warning to the future that the creation of monsters in scientific laboratories was the worst of sins, an act of godlike meddling into the mysteries of nature.

In the 20th century, Gothic literature featured the strange shapes in the stories of Isak DINESEN, a corpse-eating specter in Lafcadio HEARN's "Jikininki" (1904), and the phantasm in Henry JAMES's "The Jolly Corner" (1908). Monsters gradually divested themselves of any semblance of humanity in the ominous robots of Karel ČAPEK's dystopian play *R.U.R.* (1920), the alien titans in H. P. LOVECRAFT's "The Call of Cthulhu" (1928), and J. R. R. Tolkien's imaginative orcs in *The Lord of the Rings* (1954–55). Sam Watson, an Australian aborigine and first-time novelist, carried the macabre into magical realism with the creation lore and SHAPE-SHIFTING of *The Kadaitcha Sung* (1990), turning monsters into allegories of colonial racism and violence.

A less visually detestable form of Gothic OTHERNESS is the morally repugnant human, notably, the shape-shifting man in the BEAUTY AND THE BEAST myth, the frontier Indian-killer in Robert Montgomery BIRD's *NICK OF THE WOODS* (1837), the madwoman Bertha ROCHESTER in Charlotte BRONTË's *JANE EYRE* (1847), and the raging HEATHCLIFF, the bereaved lover in Emily BRONTË's *WUTHERING HEIGHTS* (1847). Especially terrifying is monstrosity in a typically nurturing figure, as with the cleric AMBROSIO in Matthew Gregory LEWIS's *THE MONK* (1796) and the baby-killing mother in Joyce Carol OATES's "Family" (1991). A borderline monster is the phantasm of the imagination, for example, the headless ghost pursuing Ichabod CRANE in Washington Irving's classic FOOL TALE "The Legend of Sleepy Hollow" (1820), the misperception of evil in an ARABESQUE pattern in Charlotte Perkins GILMAN's "THE YELLOW WALLPAPER" (1892), and the dog covered in phosphorescent paint in Sir Arthur Conan DOYLE's "THE HOUND OF THE BASKERVILLES" (1902).

Bibliography

Chen, Chih-Ping. "'Am I a Monster?': Jane Eyre among the Shadows of Freaks," *Studies in the Novel* 34, no. 4 (winter 2002): 367–384.

Cohen, Jeffrey Jerome, ed. *Monster Theory.* Minneapolis: University of Minnesota Press, 1996.

Halberstam, Judith. *Skin Shows: Gothic Horror and the Technology of Monsters.* Durham, N.C.: Duke University Press, 1995.

Nickell, Joe. "Germany: Monsters, Myths, and Mysteries," *Skeptical Inquirer* 27, no. 2 (March–April 2003): 24–28.

Shelley, Mary. *Frankenstein.* New York: New American Library, 1963.

Tuan, Yi-Fu. *Landscapes of Fear.* New York: Pantheon Books, 1979.

Williams, A. Susan, ed. *The Lifted Veil: The Book of Fantastic Literature by Women, 1800–World War II*. New York: Carroll & Graf, 1992.

Montresor

The central character of Edgar Allan POE's classic revenge tale "THE CASK OF AMONTILLADO" (1846), Montresor is a murderous trickster and monomaniac. His target is Fortunato, a shallow, egotistical dilettante and self-acclaimed wine connoisseur whom Montresor easily manipulates to his doom. To exact his revenge, Montresor tempts Fortunato with a promise of a taste of Amontillado, a fragrant dry sherry. Montresor then leads his inebriated companion into a richly Gothic setting, an underground vault in the catacombs near the river, and seals him in a coffin-sized niche. By turning the poseur's field of expertise into a lure to a death chamber, the killer creates a satisfying poetic justice. The act elicits an echo of his victim's fruitless plea for God's love.

The controlling theme of Poe's story is Montresor's lethal OBSESSION. Poe embellishes the plot with layers of symbolism that depict the pipe of wine as a taste of the grape bottled for aging much as Fortunato is bricked into the subterranean niche to molder in secret. By cutting short the narration, the author leaves in doubt his own concerns for Montresor as unrepentant sinner and madman, who is still able to exult in unpunished evil a half-century after its commission.

Bibliography

Punter, David, ed. *The Literature of Terror*, vol. 1, 2nd ed. London: Longman, 1996.

Symons, Julian. *The Tell-Tale Heart: The Life and Works of Edgar Allan Poe*. New York: Harper & Row, 1978.

mood

Control of mood, the author's attitude toward a literary work, is an essential of Gothic writing. Gothic novelists create useful points of view in the female NAIF and the BYRONIC HERO, and typically set the interplay between the two against a wild, bleak natural setting, as in John KEATS's "LA BELLE DAME SANS MERCI" (1819). The skillful writer enhances the effects with a soft, alluring MELANCHOLY, as found in the free-floating gloom of Lord BYRON's MANFRED (1817), the engaging aura of Keats's "THE EVE OF ST. AGNES" (1819), and the somber falling action of Charlotte BRONTË's *JANE EYRE* (1847). The extremes of mood range from tender authorial views of romantic attachments to grim depictions of VIOLENCE, hallucination, and mental torment generated by SUPERNATURAL manifestations or the fear of imprisonment and sadistic torture, the scenarios in Edgar Allan POE's "The Black Cat" (1843) and "THE PIT AND THE PENDULUM" (1843) and Joseph CONRAD's *HEART OF DARKNESS* (1902).

Controlling mood dominated 20th-century Gothic literature, which distanced itself from the sentimentality and MELODRAMA of earlier Gothic novels and plays. To parody the conventions of Gothic mystery, American writer Shirley JACKSON orchestrated mood expectations in her satiric novel *We Have Always Lived in the Castle* (1948). Daphne DU MAURIER built an entire story, "THE BIRDS" (1952), on mood and ATMOSPHERE, which Alfred Hitchcock failed to reproduce in the 1963 film version. In the 21st century, Virginia Renfro Ellis controlled a wistful mood in her post–Civil War ghost romance *The Wedding Dress* (2002), which is haunted by the phantasms of dead Confederate soldiers returning to the South. More dramatically, Michel Faber shifted moods between alternating chapters in his neo-Victorian novel *THE CRIMSON PETAL AND THE WHITE* (2002) by contrasting the total dependence of an insane wife with the wit and guile of her husband's mistress.

Bibliography

Halberstam, Judith. *Skin Shows: Gothic Horror and the Technology of Monsters*. Durham, N.C.: Duke University Press, 1995.

Kauffman, Stanley. Review of *The Birds*, *New Republic*, April 13, 1963: 26.

The Moonstone
Wilkie Collins
(1868)

An English detective thriller by Wilkie Collins, *The Moonstone* rode the crest of SENSATIONALISM and set the conventions of novel-length detective fiction. Collins laced the story with ORIENTAL ROMANCE—an opium dream, Hinduism, coded messages, laudanum slipped into a drink, concealed clues, somnambulism, and a setting called Shivering Sand. Along with Gothic touches is the standard antipathy between municipal police and the quirky Sergeant Cuff, England's first great detective, whom Collins based on a pairing invented by Edgar Allan POE. The plot details the theft of a yellow diamond from an Indian temple and its presentation to young Rachel Verinder on her birthday. Collins deviated from the stereotypical girl character to make Rachel a strong, determined, closed-mouthed, and intuitive detective, a character more common in FEMALE GOTHIC. In his estimation, "She was unlike most other girls of her age, in this—that she had ideas of her own, and was stiff-necked enough to set the fashions themselves at defiance, if the fashions didn't suit her views" (Collins, 65).

Like Sir Conan DOYLE's Sherlock HOLMES series, Collins's MYSTERY of the moonstone's disappearance expresses Victorian interest in crime and punishment. He exploited a pervasive middle-class apprehension about established families being victimized by felons, particularly the criminal class of nonwhite emigrants from the British Empire. The diamond itself, based on the 105-carat Koh-I-Noor diamond, symbolizes the international thievery exonerated as British colonialism. Collins turns the epilogue into an anti-imperialist screed by commenting on the return of the Moonstone to the sacred city where it was first lodged eight centuries earlier. He adds, "You have lost sight of it in England, and (if I know anything of this people) you have lost sight of it for ever" (Collins, 472). Spin-offs of the novel include Anthony Trollope's parody The Eustace Diamonds (1872) and two works partially derived from Collins's story, Charles DICKENS's The Mystery of Edwin Drood (1870) and Doyle's "The Sign of Four" (1890).

Bibliography

Carnell, Jennifer. The Literary Lives of Mary Elizabeth Braddon. Hastings, Sussex: Sensation Press, 2000.

Collins, Wilkie. The Moonstone. London: Penguin Books, 1998.

Pearl, Nancy. "Gaslight Thrillers: The Original Victorians," Library Journal 126, no. 3 (February 15, 2001): 228.

Morland, Catherine

Seventeen-year-old Catherine Morland is the antiheroine of NORTHANGER ABBEY (1818), Jane AUSTEN's lighthearted counternovel and parody of Gothic fiction. She serves the author as a model of an emerging womanhood endowed with self-assurance and false impressions. Giddy with silly notions, she aids Isabella Thorpe in flirting with James Morland and clings to Ann RADCLIFFE's Gothic classic THE MYSTERIES OF UDOLPHO (1794), which provides ESCAPISM from boredom. From the novel, Catherine forms an impression of southern France. Her suitor, Henry Tilney, surprises her by admitting that he read the same book in two days in a state of terror. By mocking the Gothic courtship ritual with such exchanges, the gentle cautionary tale satirizes miseducation through fiction and exposes a need in the NAIF to expect romantic trappings as she engages a suitor in a prenuptial scenario.

The author gleefully exposes her heroine's lack-logic ILLUSIONs of romantic adventure based on inappropriate application of Gothic themes. After Catherine arrives at Blaize Castle, she searches her room for mysterious secret passages and hidden clues. In a japanned cabinet, she locates an old manuscript, a cliché detail in a host of Gothic works. Austen trivializes the discovery by downgrading the text from mystic writing to a mundane laundry list, a tongue-in-cheek SYMBOL of the domestic tedium that lies in store for Catherine after she marries. The novel's SUBTEXT was intended as instruction to ingenuous young women to rid themselves of FAIRY TALE expectations before readying themselves for powerlessness, female drudgery, and disappointment as adults.

Bibliography

Hudson, John. "Gothic, Romance and Satire in Northanger Abbey," English Review 12, no. 1 (September 2001): 21.

Karl, Frederick R. The Adversary Literature: The English Novel in the Eighteenth Century—A Study in Genre. New York: Farrar, Straus & Giroux, 1974.

Neill, Edward. "The Secret of 'Northanger Abbey,'" *Essays in Criticism* 47, no. 1 (January 1997): 13–32.

Morrison, Toni
(1931–   )

The revered American novelist Chloe Anthony "Toni" Morrison applies OBSESSION, INSANITY, alienation, and the SUPERNATURAL in novels depicting the challenges faced by black Americans. She grew up in a nurturing family of storytellers who passed along a reverence for the oral tradition. Before enrolling at Howard University, she read English, French, and Russian fiction. After a stint teaching at Texas Southern University, she developed the story of Pecola Breedlove, an abused black girl, into *The Bluest Eye* (1969), a novel that emerged during a black renaissance in American fiction. The MELANCHOLY story follows Pecola from prayers for blue eyes into alienation, hallucinations of a second self, and madness brought on by incest. In the afterword, Morrison accounts for the horrors suffered by a child impregnated by her father: "I focused, therefore, on how something as grotesque as the demonization of an entire race could take root inside the most delicate member of society: a child" (Morrison, *Bluest*, 210).

Morrison followed with *Sula* (1973), a mystic tale clouded by SECRECY, and *Song of Solomon* (1977), a murderous story of a boyhood friendship distorted by STALKING and concluded with a myth of flying men. In the latter, the author amasses bizarre details: a man who was buried in two halves, a woman born without a navel, a naked woman caressing her father's corpse, and a secret society of assassins called the Seven Days. Morrison, the first black female to appear on the cover of *Newsweek*, emulated the humanity and style of William FAULKNER and continued to explore Gothic themes. Her masterpiece, BELOVED (1987), stages through dreamscape and hauntings the story of Margaret Garner, a plantation laborer who, in 1855, slew her infant daughter to rescue her from enslavement. Interspersed are recovered memories of the voyage from Africa in the hold of a slaving vessel, a surreal impression made hellish with heat and airlessness. Through the efforts of the cream of African-American intelligentsia, Morrison won the 1988 Pulitzer Prize for fiction and the 1993 Nobel Prize in literature. She returned to Gothic themes in 2003 with *Love*, the story of a hotelier possessed by a woman named Celestial.

Bibliography
Gillan, Jennifer. "Focusing on the Wrong Front: Historical Displacement, the Maginot Line, and 'The Bluest Eye,'" *African American Review* 36, no. 2 (summer 2002): 283–298.

Morrison, Toni. *The Bluest Eye*. New York: Plume, 1994.

Motes, Hazel

The obsessed Tennessee bigot in Flannery O'CONNOR's SOUTHERN GOTHIC novel WISE BLOOD (1952), Hazel "Haze" Motes is one of the author's most debated Gothic antiheroes. One of the rural ignorant poor obsessed by fundamentalist doctrines, he makes a pilgrimage of fleeing Christianity by taking up at Leora Watts's bordello and committing senseless acts of VIOLENCE, including throwing rocks at an admirer and destroying a mummy. Through a series of missteps, he exhibits the inexperience of the NAIF alongside the world-weariness of the lifelong sinner.

Motes's route to understanding is paradoxically violent and unenlightened, a fact suggested by the nickname "Haze" and his surname as sources of spiritual blindness. Along the way to salvation, he achieves knowledge of sin and redemption through attempted rape and uses his beloved car as a murder weapon to kill his competition, street preacher Solace Mayfield. Ironically, Motes returns to righteousness in a GROTESQUE recreation of Christ's passion—wrapped in barbed wire like the crown of thorns and tormented with gravel and glass shards in his shoes and eye sockets burned out with quicklime. In the end, Motes, who epitomizes the Southern Gothic paradox of aberrant religious fervor, develops into a "pin point of light" through martyrdom (O'Connor, 120).

Bibliography
Edmunds, Susan. "Through a Glass Darkly: Visions of Integrated Community in Flannery O'Connor's 'Wise Blood,'" *Contemporary Literature* 37, no. 4 (winter 1996): 559–584.

O'Connor, Flannery. *Three by Flannery O'Connor.* New York: Signet, 1983.

Paige, Linda Rohrer. "White Trash, Low Class, and No Class At All: Perverse Portraits of Phallic Power in Flannery O'Connor's 'Wise Blood,'" *Papers on Language & Literature* 33, no. 3 (summer 1997): 325–333.

Sweeney, Gerald M. "O'Connor's 'Wise Blood,'" *Explicator* 56, no. 2 (winter 1998): 108–109.

Mudford, William
(1782–1848)

The Scottish translator, editor, and Gothicist William Mudford was renowned for his suspenseful, measured STORYTELLING. As a critic of Gothic trends in literature, he held writers to exacting standards of logic and charged novelist Tobias SMOLLETT with violating the reader's credulity. Like W. W. JACOBS, Mudford is usually remembered for a single terror story—"The Iron Shroud," which he published anonymously in *BLACKWOOD'S EDINBURGH MAGAZINE* in August 1830. An intriguing revenge tale, it relates the slow death of the ironically named Vivenzio, a condemned inmate at the Sicilian castle of his enemy, the prince of Tolfi. In a bizarre DUNGEON, Vivenzio escapes from hopelessness through DREAMS and awakens each day to discover his cell shrinking. A note on the wall from engineer Ludovico Sforza confirms the torment of the diabolical device, which crushes a prisoner within seven days. After Sforza invented the contracting walls, Tolfi made him its first victim.

Because "The Iron Shroud" allows the reader to experience danger and eminent death vicariously, the sensational hysteria plot proved lucrative to Mudford as a GOTHIC BLUEBOOK printed in 1839 and 1840 under the title *The Iron Shroud; or, Italian Revenge.* The term "iron shroud" recurred in Charlotte BRONTË's *JANE EYRE* (1847) as a metaphor for Edward ROCHESTER's marriage proposal and in Elizabeth Gaskell's novel *Mary Barton* (1848) as an image of slow torture and crushing death. Mudford's story influenced Edgar Allan POE's "THE PIT AND THE PENDULUM" (1843), which carries CLAUSTROPHOBIA and advancing menace to a bizarre extreme. Mudford's posthu-

mous anthology, *Tales and Trifles* (1849), contains a wicked ghost tale, "The Forsaken of God."

Bibliography

Derry, Stephen. "Mrs. Gaskell's Reference to Italian Punishment in 'Mary Barton,'" *Notes and Queries* 40, no. 4 (December 1993): 481–482.

Heller, Terry. *The Delights of Terror: An Aesthetics of the Tale of Terror.* Urbana: University of Illinois Press, 1987.

"The Murders in the Rue Morgue"
Edgar Allan Poe
(1841)

After establishing himself as a master of horror poems and short fiction, at age 32, Edgar Allan POE published in *Graham's Magazine* what some literary historians consider the first DETECTIVE STORY, "The Murders in the Rue Morgue." While comparing police work to a game of skill like checkers and whist, the text defines the conventions and codes of detective fiction, a subset of the MYSTERY story. Its Gothic detail and careful plotting earned the regard of Sir Arthur Conan DOYLE as one of the great short works in the English language for its balance of weirdness with cool rationality.

Poe depicts the prototypically incisive sleuth, inspector C. Auguste DUPIN, working objectively through a repulsive murder scene, a locked chamber, the standard Gothic setting for the "perfect crime." After noting a medical opinion from Paul Dumas and Alexandre Etienne as to the causes of injury, the author advances the horror several degrees by describing how a super-strong primate so mutilated a first victim, Madame L'Espanaye, that her head fell off during the investigation. The perpetrator then strangled the woman's daughter Camille and stuffed her corpse head-first up the chimney before tossing the remains of the mother out the window.

To prove the interrelation between imagination and logic, Poe counters the SENSATIONALISM of the double murder with Dupin's mental acuity. In epitomizing the job of the observer, Poe refers to "the rules of Hoyle," the 18th-century master of board and card games (Poe, 474). The image likens the cat-and-mouse job of criminal investigation to the strategy of chess. Dupin thrives at the chase, records no actual words spoken by the killer, locates a sample of an unusual bestial hair, and begins to think of the perpetrator as an animal rather than a human murderer. To locate the beast, Dupin posts a newspaper advertisement that receives a reply from a sailor who owns the killer primate. Because the animal is an orangutan lacking both motive and logical method, Poe equates the brutal slayer with murder itself, a crime not only targeting individual victims but also violating the social order.

Bibliography

Eco, Umberto, and Thomas A. Sebeok, eds. *The Sign of Three: Dupin, Holmes, Peirce.* Bloomington: Indiana University Press, 1983.

Poe, Edgar Allan. "The Murders in the Rue Morgue," in *The Complete Stories.* New York: Knopf, 1992.

Priestman, Martin. *Detective Fiction and Literature: The Figure on the Carpet.* London: Macmillan, 1990.

Murdoch, Iris
(1919–1999)

The prize-winning Anglo-Irish author Jean Iris Murdoch wrote in numerous modes, including philosophical treatise, libretto, fable, fantasy, and historical, picaresque, and GOTHIC NOVELs. Born in Dublin, she was educated in England, taking her undergraduate degree at Oxford, and later studying at Cambridge with the Viennese philosopher Ludwig Wittgenstein. In 1953, she summarized the importance of Jean Paul Sartre to French existentialism in *Sartre, Romantic Rationalist.* Venturing into fiction, she produced intellectual works permeated by sensuality, visionary characters, and enigmatic dialogue. Her intriguing but obscure philosophical SUBTEXTs probe the meaning of love and faith in the late 20th century.

Murdoch mastered a variety of GOTHIC CONVENTIONs and motifs, beginning with MYSTERY, homosexuality, and amateur sleuthing in *The Bell* (1958), the story of a quirky mix of characters at Imber Abbey. Ambiguity dominates *The Unicorn* (1963), the tale of a recluse who seems both crazed victim and witch. In *The Time of Angels* (1966), Murdoch describes Carel Fisher, an Anglican priest, and his involvement in black magic and DIABOLISM. *The Black Prince* (1973) tells of obsessive love complicated by murder and suicide. In a melodramatic moment, the speaker, author Bradley Pearson, summarizes in Gothic terms the passion that inflames him while kissing Julian Belling: "Phantoms were bred from this touch. I felt like a grotesque condemned excluded monster. How could it be that I had actually kissed her cheek without enveloping her, without becoming her?" (Murdoch, *Prince,* 208).

At the height of her career, Murdoch wrote the Booker Prize–winning novel *The Sea, the Sea* (1978), which incorporates ESCAPISM, ghosts, ILLUSION, and outsized human passions. She created an ALLEGORY of good and evil in *The Good Apprentice* (1985), the story of a psychoanalyst, and examined the theme of personal ethics in the nonfiction *Metaphysics as a Guide to Morals* (1992). Murdoch incorporated MEDIEVALISM and a haunting REVENANT in *The Green Knight* (1993), a contemporary narrative of nighttime violence. Before her mental decline from Alzheimer's disease, she wrote a psychological thriller, *Jackson's Dilemma* (1995).

Bibliography

Colley, Mary. "Iris Murdoch—the 'Good Novelist,'" *Contemporary Review* 261, no. 1,523 (December 1992): 319 322.

Murdoch, Iris. *The Black Prince.* New York: Viking 1973.

Rice, Thomas Jackson. "Death and Love in Iris Murdoch's 'The Time of the Angels,'" *CRITIQUE: Studies in Contemporary Fiction* 36, no. 2 (winter 1995): 130–144.

Sikorska, Liliana. "Constructing the Middle Ages in Contemporary Literature and Culture: The Reading of Iris Murdoch's 'The Green Knight,'" *Studia Anglica Posnaniensia* (Annual 2000): 259–271.

The Mysteries of Udolpho
Ann Radcliffe
(1794)

At the height of her artistic flowering, Ann RADCLIFFE set both the TONE and theme of the FEMALE GOTHIC with *The Mysteries of Udolpho,* a revered genre classic. In keeping with her view of limited opportunities for women in a patriarchal society, she draws on Lady Mary Walker's novel *Munster Village* (1778) to characterize a heroine's worsening situation. Emily ST. AUBERT, Radcliffe's protagonist, declines rapidly through reductions in family connections, choice of mate, and property ownership, the three social options empowering 18th-century women. In the end, she restores all three and prevails over villainy. The author's gesture toward gender emancipation took shape during the dramatic social upheaval that followed the French Revolution, a war of liberation that encouraged hopes of *Liberté, Egalité, Fraternité* within marriages as well as nations.

Beginning in 1584, the story focuses on a worthy NAIF, an orphaned and penniless heiress residing in the Pyrenées. After the death of her well-rounded, sensitive father, Emily falls under the control of Signor Montoni, her scheming, fearfully attractive uncle by marriage, a forerunner of the BYRONIC HERO who is more insidious and tyrannic than previous literary VILLAINs. To foreshadow his menace, in chapter 11, Radcliffe develops his position as foreign OUTSIDER from the southern Mediterranean. At a postnuptial entertainment, he stands apart from the merrymakers, exhibiting boredom and disapproval of frivolity.

Radcliffe applies a gender power struggle as the precipitating factor of the plot complication. After Emily's aunt, the newly married Madame Montoni, abdicates her own domestic control, Montoni begins making decisions and setting the tone of the couple's union. The aunt justifies the shift to male domination: "I am determined, that you shall submit to those, who know how to guide you better than yourself—I am determined, that you shall be conformable" (Radcliffe, 144). Rather than collapse in tears like her weepy fictional predecessor in Horace WALPOLE's THE CASTLE OF OTRANTO (1765), Emily retreats to her quarters to reflect on her family's new chain of command.

In volume 2, Radcliffe begins separating Emily from home, familiar surroundings, and her beau Valancourt as Montoni's carriage rolls east, crossing the plain of Languedoc on the way into the Italian Alps, which become geographic SYMBOLs of treachery. A typically tough, contemplative, and uncomplaining heroine, Emily remains calm as she soaks up the scenery, embraces NATURE's grandeur, and accepts its chaotic splendors—a mountain torrent, snow-capped cliffs, and dark stands of pine—as elements of rapture to be absorbed and admired. The Gothic dangers that the heroine survives are sequential cliffhangers: attempts at forced marriage and rape, loss of her inheritance, murderous banditti, and ghosts. At the peak of her struggles, she displays courage in the presence of apparitions and welcomes a battle of wits with Montoni over his theft of her estate, an issue greater than the bodily harm he or his castle's specter threaten.

As Radcliffe directs the conflict from peril to triumph, she avoids the happily-ever-after syndrome that depicts women as safe and fullfilled as soon as they say "I do." By fleeing confinement in the malignant environs of the Castle of Udolpho, Emily survives as an unsullied virgin, reclaims her patrimony, and reunites with her lover, Valancourt. Before she marries him, however, she upbraids him for causing her grief. That settled, the two become one. Radcliffe carefully words the balance in their relationship as "restored to each other . . . in domestic blessedness" (*ibid.,* 672).

Ann Radcliffe's lengthy masterwork boosted her from obscure housewife to the most read and admired writer of her day by both men and women. Her memorable contributions to fiction include the Gascon setting in the Pyrenees, wild and engaging glimpses of the outdoors, and the charmingly chatty servants Teresa, Annette, and Ludovico. Literary figures, caught up in the innovative narrative, critiqued the novel in the media. Anna Laetitia BARBAULD, author of "On the Pleasure Derived from Objects of Terror" (1773), felt let down by Radcliffe's plausible explanations for seemingly SUPERNATURAL events. In Barbauld's words, "The mind experiences a sort of disappointment and shame at having felt so much from appearances that had nothing in them beyond 'this visible diurnal sphere'" (Varma, 97).

Alive with sexual menace and psychological intensity, Radcliffe's suspenseful novel went through two printings the first year, numerous subsequent editions, a French translation in 1808, three stage adaptations, and additional press runs into the 1890s. In addition, in 1802, an anonymous GOTHIC BLUEBOOK excerpted one episode under the title *The Veiled Picture*. In 1817, MINERVA PRESS published an adaptation under the title *Alexena; or, The Castle of Santa Marco*, a confinement plot that features Count Baretto, a Montoni-esque villain with an Italianate name, and the kidnapping and threatening of three NAIFS—Alexena, Ellena, and Evelene. In 1840, the Victorian novelist William Makepeace Thackeray remarked that Radcliffe's thriller was one of England's most famous romances. Her novel still retains its value as a window on female Gothic literature.

Bibliography

Hume, Robert. "Gothic Versus Romantic: A Revaluation of the Gothic Novel," *Publication of the Modern Language Association* 84 (1969): 282–290.

Kozlowski, Lisa. "A Source for Ann Radcliffe's 'The Mysteries of Udolpho,'" *Notes and Queries* 44, no. 2 (June 1997): 228–229.

Poovey, Mary. "Ideology and the Mysteries of Udolpho," *Criticism. A Quarterly for Literature and the Arts* 21 (1979): 307–330.

Radcliffe, Ann. *The Mysteries of Udolpho*. London: Oxford University Press, 1966.

Varma, Devendra P. *The Gothic Flame*. New York: Russell & Russell, 1966.

mystery

The term *mystery* denotes both a Gothic ATMOSPHERE as well as a subgenre, the mystery story or novel. As an aura, mystery imbues the HORROR NARRATIVE, PSYCHOLOGICAL NOVEL, crime story, spy tale, and DETECTIVE STORY with SUSPENSE, fear of the unknowable, intrigue, and horror or terror. Mystery often surrounds the motif of pursuit or STALKING.

A successful venue for female authors, the mystery plot was a vehicle for Ann RADCLIFFE, who achieved a landmark place in literary history with THE MYSTERIES OF UDOLPHO (1794). Edgar Allan POE applied Gothic details in his short tale "The Gold Bug" (1843), a puzzle story that requires a searcher for lost treasure, William Legrand, to decode a cryptograph and to drop an insect through the eye hole of a skull. Mystery also fueled a literary phenomenon, the GOTHIC BLUEBOOK, a popular series of short works intended to please the working-class reader. Among examples of unknown authorship were *The Mysterious Bride; or, The Statue Spectre* (ca. 1800); *The Sicilian Pirates; or, The Pillar of Mystery* (ca. 1800); and *The Round Tower; or, A Tale of Mystery* (1803).

From the mysterious settings of classic GOTHIC NOVELS at remote mansions and abbeys, more recent authors have continued to find sources of the macabre and material for a variety of Gothic subgenres. Victoria HOLT developed a 20th-century classic, MISTRESS OF MELLYN (1960), a cautionary tale of the governess Martha Leigh, who falls under the strange powers of Connan TreMellyn, the fetchingly handsome lord of the estate.

Bibliography

Hichens, Robert. *Tongues of Conscience*. London: Methuen, 1900.

mysticism

Mysticism infuses Gothic literature with serious considerations of the search for truth, a divine being, and the secrets of NATURE, a controlling element in ILLUMINATI NOVELS. Often obscure and heavily symbolic, mystic fiction depicts the seeker during periods of alienation and self-doubt. These elements are common to the BYRONIC HERO, who may be searching for cleansing of blood guilt or redemption by a deity or supreme being, the theme of Lord BYRON's THE GIAOUR (1813), the tale of the infidel who seeks redemption for precipitating a woman's execution for adultery.

Aiding the search for expiation and salvation are intuitive and extrasensory clues or feelings that guide and instruct, a force in Christina ROSSETTI's THE GOBLIN MARKET and Other Tales (1862). In the title ballad, a cautionary tale for young girls, Laura, the protagonist, succumbs to grotesque little men, who charm her with luscious grapes. The Edenic mystique of their "fruit call" and their cooing voices lure her beyond the innate warning to avoid danger (Rossetti, 4). The enticing fruits overpower her reason until she returns home not knowing day from night. Rossetti warns the reader of the mystic perverters of Eden, the "quaint fruit-merchant men" who peddle evil in the form of honeyed fruit (*ibid.*, 1,046).

The 20th century produced an English specialist in spiritual SENSATIONALISM. The Christian Gothicist Charles Williams, a member (along with C. S. Lewis and J. R. R. Tolkien) of the group of Oxford writers known as the Inklings, incorporated mystic occultism in the eerie Grail lore of *War in Heaven* (1930), metaphysical incantation in *The Place of the Lion* (1931), and the investment of objects with mystic force in *Many Dimensions* (1931) and *The Greater Trumps* (1932). At the core of his thrillers are four theological basics—creation, the fall, damnation, and redemption—and the soul's battle against tempting earthly shadows such as music, food, drugs, alcohol, gambling, romantic love, and sex. More primitive is the frontier herbalism of an elderly *curandera* (healer) in Rudolfo Anaya's *Bless Me,*
Ultima (1972). Marion Zimmer Bradley applied medieval mysticism to a series of arcane feminist novels set in the Arthurian era: *The Mists of Avalon* (1982), *The Forest House* (1994), *Return to Avalon* (1996), *The Lady of Avalon* (1997), and *The Firebrand* (2003). Playwright Tony Kushner invests the two parts of *Angels in America* (1991, 1992) with mystic aura and angelic visitations to AIDS victims.

Bibliography

Howard, Thomas. *The Novels of Charles Williams.* Fort Collins, Colo.: Ignatius Press, 1991.

Rossetti, Christina. *The Goblin Market.* New York: Dover, 1994.

Williams, Charles. *War in Heaven.* Grand Rapids, Mich.: Eerdmans, 1981.

N

naif

A common protagonist in such menacing FAIRY TALES as the GRIMM brothers' "Der Räuberbräutigam" ("The Robber Bridegroom," 1857) and Letitia Elizabeth Landon's "The Story of Hester Malpas" (1833), the naif is standard to Gothic lore as a FOIL to innate evil. As explained by the German dramatist and literary theorist Friedrich von SCHILLER in his essay "Über Naive und Sentimentalische Dichtung" (On naive and sentimental poetry, 1795), the innocent typically display spontaneous goodness and thrive in harmony with NATURE. By misinterpreting or misjudging the power of evil, the ingenuous FEMALE VICTIM loses innocence after straying into unnatural settings, a Gothic scenario found in such naughty-little-girl FOLKLORE as "Little Red Riding Hood" and "Goldilocks," the assault of the male vampire on his bride in John POLIDORI's "The Vampyre" (1819), the temptation of Faith Brown in Nathaniel HAWTHORNE's ambiguous NECROMANCY story "YOUNG GOODMAN BROWN" (1835), and the subversion of a neurasthenic governess in Henry JAMES's THE TURN OF THE SCREW (1898).

An admired naif in FEMALE GOTHIC literature is the title character of Charlotte BRONTË's JANE EYRE (1847). At the outskirts of womanhood, Jane EYRE, an intelligent but subdued governess at THORNFIELD, allows herself to accept a marriage proposal from her employer, Edward ROCHESTER, a complex and, at times, mystifying "man with a past." Because of her lack of sophistication, Jane makes incorrect assumptions about his strange go-

ings and comings, his flirtation with a fetching aristocrat, and the hidden terrors in an upstairs room. Brontë's story follows the cautious heroine through perils on the moors, a doomed proposal of marriage to a missionary, and back to Edward. By story's end, Jane has shed naiveté and acquired both experience and sophistication about managing her personal life.

The naive point of view increases the complexity of Gothic fiction. By placing the job of storyteller under the authority of a fallible, gullible, often UNRELIABLE NARRATOR, the author increases SUSPENSE and sympathy for a potential victim. A notable example is the peripatetic title character in Voltaire's *Candide* (1759), who misinterprets sinister forces that sequentially gull, perplex, and threaten him. Charles DICKENS creates MELODRAMA in *BLEAK HOUSE* (1853) through the pathetic life story of Esther Summerson, a foster child who longs to reunite with her birth mother. A model from classic Gothic fiction is the business-minded Jonathan HARKER, an agent for an English law office who finds himself immured in Transylvania in Bram STOKER's *DRACULA* (1897) and who ventures to DRACULA'S CRYPT to gaze on the epitome of iniquity. The use of the unnamed second wife of Max de Winter in Daphne DU MAURIER's *REBECCA* (1938) allows the author to develop an enveloping evil orchestrated by the housekeeper, Mrs. DANVERS, whose manipulations escape the speaker's initial perceptions. MYSTERY grows as the intimidated, untried second mistress of

MANDERLEY attempts to learn her place in the household while discovering dismaying secrets and ambiguities that obsess and terrify her.

Bibliography

Gilbert, Sandra M., and Susan Gubar. *The Madwoman in the Attic,* 2nd ed. New Haven, Conn.: Yale University Press, 2000.

Hoeveler, Diane Long. *Gothic Feminism.* University Park: Pennsylvania State University Press, 1998.

The Narrative of Arthur Gordon Pym
Edgar Allan Poe
(1838)

The only novel of the American Gothic writer Edgar Allan POE, *The Narrative of Arthur Gordon Pym* is based on the familiar romantic motif of a shipwreck. Poe issued this sensational unsigned story about a purported June 1827 South Seas shipwreck as a hoax in two installments of the *Southern Literary Messenger* in 1836 and 1837. The plot explores the sea quest, a romantic motif that Herman MELVILLE exploited in the 1850s, and features the untried male NAIF battling extreme perils.

Focused on OBSESSION, ABERRANT BEHAVIOR, alienation, and MELANCHOLY, the symbolic voyage thrusts its title character into the mysteries of the Antarctic and the approach of death. The title character, who stows away on the whaler *Grampus,* matures through his introduction to mutiny, barbarism, stranding on a raft, starvation and survival by cannibalism, and PREMATURE BURIAL. The novel, obscure and troubling, turns the journey motif into a convoluted adventure tale covering Pym's five voyages, during which he encounters polar bears, natural MONSTERS, and monsters of the supernatural on a ghost vessel littered with rotting corpses. In a review issued in an 1838 issue of *Knickerbocker Magazine,* editor Lewis Gaylord Clark attacked Poe for careless writing and for his dependence on gore and VIOLENCE.

Bibliography

Nadal, Marita. "Beyond the Gothic Sublime: Poe's Pym or the Journey of Equivocal (E)motion," *Mississippi Quarterly* 53, no. 3 (summer 2000): 373.

nature

Nature is an essential presence in Gothic literature. Its importance is stressed in a variety of Gothic contexts: the violation of an innocent bird in Samuel Taylor COLERIDGE's THE RIME OF THE ANCIENT MARINER (1798), a crime that curses a man with a life-in-death pilgrimage similar to the punishment of the WANDERING JEW; the immersion in virgin Southern wilderness in William FAULKNER's "The Bear" (1942); and the awkward lovemaking between woman and beast in Marian Engel's erotic novel *Bear* (1976). Similarly perverse are the otherworldly people, fearful landscape, and MONSTERs in Canadian author James de Mille's *A Strange Manuscript Found in a Copper Cylinder* (1880) and the gray wolf Berserker that escapes a zoo and leaps through a window in Bram STOKER's DRACULA (1897). Other Gothic applications of nature are less fearful. In the Grimm brothers' "Der Räuberbräutigam" ("The Robber Bridegroom"), the unnamed NAIF leaves peas and lentils to mark her trail to the robbers' den. On her flight from witnessing their cannibalistic orgy, she flees into the dark forest, where moonlight reveals not only that the peas and lentils are still there, but that they have sprouted to ease her passage home. The folktale indicates that nature offers aid and solace to the terror-stricken and blossoms as a gift to the innocent.

In the 18th century, the shift from the trimmed hedges, geometric plantings, and labyrinthine herb bed paths to clashing branches and shadowy lawn alleyways signaled an end to neoclassical regularity and a delight in profusion. As literature ranged toward ROMANTICISM, the appreciation of nature in fictional characters became a virtue. Through GOTHIC CONVENTIONs, authors indicated that people who respond wholeheartedly to nature reveal an innate inclination toward artistic temperament and SENSIBILITY, as is the case with Ann RADCLIFFE's heroine Emily ST. AUBERT in THE MYSTERIES OF UDOLPHO (1794). Through layered digressions that extenuate action, Radcliffe projects on nature a welter of the protagonist's fears. In the Apennines, Emily perceives that the wild landscape obtains its charm from a chaotic surge of dangerous impulses. Looking out at the horizon, she witnesses a fearful sight—a "torrent, whose astounding roar had never failed, rumbling down the rocky chasms, huge cliffs white with snow, or the dark summits of the pine forests, that stretched mid-way down the mountains" (Radcliffe, 165). To the heroine, the menace of the terrain contrasts the peaceful repose of the Italian piedmont and the Lombardy plains. In the resolution, the final view of the newlyweds Emily and Valancourt restores them to Gascony, where "the bowers of La Vallée became, once more, the retreat of goodness, wisdom and domestic blessedness!" (ibid., 672).

For sensational effect, early Gothic writers like Radcliffe manipulated weather and terrain as vehicles for the PATHETIC FALLACY and heightened descriptions of the unemotional outdoors for its contrast to emotional disorder and suppressed character faults and evils. Among the preromantics of the late 1700s, external nature mirrored disturbing glimpses of human nature, particularly the graveyard poet's fear of death and the grave. Gothic settings and plots often perverted the natural into the preternatural, for example, the survivor's white hair resulting from a tumble down a hellish whirlpool in Edgar Allan POE's "A Descent into the Maelström" (1841), the creeping heather that carpets Catherine's burial plot and the raw earth atop HEATHCLIFF's grave in Emily BRONTË's WUTHERING HEIGHTS (1847), and the terror of greenery and green worshippers in Kingsley Amis's The Green Man (1969) and Thomas Tryon's Harvest Home (1973).

One of the most disturbing perversions of nature in short fiction is Daphne DU MAURIER's moody story "THE BIRDS" (1952). She conceived the plot of a fiendish assault by seagulls from the view of a plowman at work near her Cornwall home, Menabilly. The house-of-cards effect begins with famine after a harsh winter, which incites the seagulls to an ominous circling. She blames nature for "the restless urge of autumn, unsatisfying, sad, [that] had put a spell upon them and they must flock, and wheel, and cry; they must spill themselves of motion before winter came" (du Maurier, 154). Their aggression encourages songbirds to join a growing phalanx and inflict a full-scale war on humankind. Alfred Hitchcock directed a 1963 film classic adapted from du Maurier's story. The Gothic motif of both story and film is a savagery in nature that overwhelms and destroys.

The duality of nature as setting and theme reached a sinister height in North American FRONTIER GOTHIC. In the words of Margaret ATWOOD, "Where there is a David in Canadian literature, there is usually a Goliath, a giant Goliath, the evil giant (or giantess) is, of course Nature herself" (Atwood, 58). Atwood mentions as a prime example the first Canadian novel, John RICHARDSON's historical romance Wacousta; or, The Prophecy: A Tale of the Canadas (1830), a fierce vengeance tale set during the predations of the War of 1812. Another example of Gothic elements within nature is Canadian poet William Kirby's Chien d'Or [The Golden Dog]: A Legend of Quebec (1859), a diabolic epic set in the Niagara district that balances terror with the lusty canoeing songs of French voyageurs who keep time to the thrusts of oars.

Chicano author Rudolfo Anaya pursued the role of nature in mystic healing in his landmark novel Bless Me, Ultima (1972). A mythic tale of benign powers, the story depicts the curandera's respect for earthly magic. The beloved grandmother Ultima, whom her grandson Tony calls "la Grande," takes him into the New Mexico desert in search of orégano, oshá, and "la yerba del manso," a cure-all (Anaya, 36). In addition to applying it to respiratory and joint ills, indigestion, and cuts and bruises, after Tony witnesses a shooting death, the herbalist washes his face and limbs with the herb to protect him from bad dreams. To cure his uncle Lucas of a wasting disease brought on by a curse, Ultima doses him with herbs and roots mixed with kerosene. To Tony, she transmits her philosophy of natural healing: "Good is always stronger than evil. Always remember that, Antonio. The smallest bit of good can stand against all the powers of evil in the world and it will emerge triumphant" (ibid., 91).

Bibliography

Anaya, Rudolfo A. Bless Me, Ultima. Berkeley, Calif.: Tonitiuh International, 1972.

Atwood, Margaret. Survival: A Thematic Guide to Canadian Literature. Toronto: Anansi, 1972.

du Maurier, Daphne. Classics of the Macabre. Garden City, N.Y.: Doubleday, 1987.

Northey, Margot. The Haunted Wilderness: The Gothic and Grotesque in Canadian Fiction. Toronto: University of Toronto Press, 1976.

Radcliffe, Ann. *The Mysteries of Udolpho.* London: Oxford University Press, 1966.

necromancy

The ability to exert black magic, forecast the future, or cast spells by consorting with the dead is a standard feature of world folklore—for example, the protective magic circle outlined around Mina Harker to protect her from VAMPIRISM in Bram STOKER's DRACULA (1897) and the eating of candles to convert inner power to a union with the divine in Laura Esquivel's MELODRAMA *Like Water for Chocolate* (1989). In ancient literature, necromancy provides direction for two prototypical heroes—Odysseus in Homer's *Odyssey* (ca. 850 B.C.) and Aeneas in Virgil's *The Aeneid* (19 B.C.), both of whom risk all to journey to the underworld to seek advice from the wraiths of people they once knew. In the Middle Ages, the extremes of curiosity about the future fuel the FAUST LEGEND, a pervasive power motif of the thirst for knowledge and resultant selling of the soul to Satan. The motif of the diabolic quest energizes Matthew Gregory LEWIS's THE MONK (1796), in which the formerly pious, virginal monk AMBROSIO falls under the manipulative powers of the necromancer Mathilda. Demonic and lascivious in the extreme, she advances from lover to user, turning Ambrosio into a sybaritic doer of evil. John KEATS's romantic ballad "THE EVE OF ST. AGNES" (1819) makes a gentler use of divination by which Madeline, a susceptible audience, expresses her will to foresee the man she will marry.

In reaction against the church's damnation of fortune-tellers and spiritualists, and against the English Witchcraft Act of 1604, Charles Robert MATURIN portrayed the act of reading OMENS as a charade perpetrated on the gullible by an elderly peasant in his Gothic novel MELMOTH THE WANDERER (1820). He describes Biddy Brannigan, the stereotypical crone with grizzled hair and wizened features, as a neighborhood sybil skilled at "practising on the fears, the ignorance, and the sufferings of beings as miserable as herself" (Maturin, 7). As manipulative devices, she mutters mysteriously and offers herbal cures and advice on avoidance of the evil eye, a death-dealing SUPERNATURAL manifestation in many world cultures. At a dramatic moment

in her performance, the author notes, "No one twined so well as she the mystic yarn to be dropt into the lime-kiln pit, on the edge of which stood the shivering inquirer into futurity" (*ibid.*, 8). Maturin turns her tale into a beneficial rendering of family lore, the historical background of the Melmoths that the protagonist needs to know.

In 1920, the Swedish humanist and Nobel Prize–winning writer Pär Lagerkvist overturned the concept of necromancy with an allegorical novella, *The Eternal Smile*, a cosmic fantasy. He sets the action in the antechambers of eternity, where newly dead peasants seek God, whom they discover is an aged forester. When they demand an explanation for the human condition, the elderly deity claims that he did not intend to harm humanity. The dark theme is consistent with the author's disaffection for organized religion and his search for spiritual comfort and peace with earthly suffering, mortality, and an inscrutable God.

Bibliography

Fleenor, Juliann E., ed. *The Female Gothic.* Montreal: Eden Press, 1983.

Maturin, Charles Robert. *Melmoth the Wanderer.* Lincoln: University of Nebraska Press, 1961.

Polet, Jeff. "A Blackened Sea: Religion and Crisis in the Work of Pär Lagerkvist," *Renascence: Essays on Values in Literature* 54, no. 1 (fall 2001): 47–66.

neo-Gothic

A revised version of GOTHIC ARCHITECTURE emerged in England in the mid-19th century, influencing the design of new churches and stately mansions. Syncretized with elements of Victorianism, the style influenced massive furnishings, such as wrought-iron light fixtures and huge carved bedsteads with oversized bed drapes. The term also characterizes a body of self-conscious contemporary literature that displays a deliberate attempt at recreating traditional Gothic traits from the romantic era, for example, the infantile ghost in Toni MORRISON's BELOVED (1987), the comic Gothic MYSTERY of Margaret ATWOOD's *Lady Oracle* (1976) and *Alias Grace* (1996), Victorian garments and eccentricities in Peter Carey's OSCAR AND LUCINDA (1988), the seduction of the NAIF in the vampire novels of Anne RICE, and the homoerotic twist to traditional VILLAIN and naif in Vincent Virga's GAY GOTHIC novel *Gaywyck* (2000).

Neo-Gothic elements invigorate contemporary forms of Gothic cinema and STORYTELLING, particularly modern GHOST STORIES and HORROR NARRATIVES, such as varied retellings of the Central American legend of LA LLORONA and the parody of romance novels in Laura Esquivel's Mexican FAIRY TALE *Like Water for Chocolate* (1989). Instead of the castles and torture chambers of the original set of GOTHIC CONVENTIONS, a psychological approach replaces physical setting with distorted mindsets, OBSESSION, SADISM, INSANITY, and self-imposed hells, the literary playground of such writers as Iris MURDOCH, Joyce Carol OATES, and Flannery O'CONNOR. Typically, these 20th-century versions of Gothic speak through a first-person narrator of social and moral decline. Michel Faber applied mid-19th-century conventions in his neo-Victorian novel THE CRIMSON PETAL AND THE WHITE (2002), which contrasts the lives of the wife and the mistress who share the same house and the same man.

Bibliography

Fleenor, Juliann E., ed. *The Female Gothic*. Montreal: Eden Press, 1983.

Punter, David, ed. *The Literature of Terror*, vol. 1, 2nd ed. London: Longman, 1996.

neurasthenia

The term *neurasthenia* has been traced to 1856; but the condition, which is marked by the sufferer's hypersensitivity to light, sound, taste, smell, and touch, is a standard Gothic trait of characters in the MYSTERY, GHOST STORY, sensational fiction, and psychological thrillers. In FRANKENSTEIN (1818), Mary Wollstonecraft SHELLEY heightened the vulnerability of lab experimenter Victor FRANKENSTEIN with swoons and nervous exhaustion. Edgar Allan POE developed the neurasthenic personality in Roderick USHER, the self-diagnosed narcissist of "THE FALL OF THE HOUSE OF USHER" (1839), who is easily spooked by most stimuli. Poe's clinical assessment is accurate: "a morbid acuteness of the senses" that rules out spicy food, rough-textured garments, fragrant flowers, and strong light and sound (Poe, 42). Admirer Charles BAUDELAIRE imitated Poe's quavering character in

his verse anthology *Le Spleen de Paris* (*Paris Spleen*, 1869), which focuses on similar artistic sensibilities.

As interest in psychology increased in the late 19th century, weak-willed, apathetic characters gained more attention in Gothic fiction—for example, the male hysteric in Wilkie COLLINS's *Heart and Science* (1883), a tale of Dr. Benjulia's vivisection and cruelty. Collins employs an effete hypersensitivity to ridicule the protagonist and denigrate his masculinity. Less physically marked by neurosis is the unnamed governess in Henry JAMES's ghost novella THE TURN OF THE SCREW (1898), the tale of an ambiguous evil that emanates either from apparitions or from the protagonist's overcharged imagination. She admits to jumpiness and concludes that shock "sharpened all my senses" (James, 30). Later examples of hypersensitivity developed realistic psychological characterization, as with the incipient madness of an incarcerated woman in Charlotte Perkins GILMAN's short story "THE YELLOW WALLPAPER" (1892), the mental haunting and timidity of the unnamed protagonist in Daphne DU MAURIER's novel REBECCA (1938), H. P. LOVECRAFT's depiction of a gibbering male's lapsed hold on sanity in "The Rats in the Walls" (1924), a high-strung minister who fears drowning in Peter Carey's OSCAR AND LUCINDA (1988), and a female lunatic's terror of menstrual flow in Michel Faber's THE CRIMSON PETAL AND THE WHITE (2002).

Bibliography

Bynum, Bill. "Neurasthenia," *Lancet* 361, no. 9,370 (May 17, 2003): 1,753.

James, Henry. *The Turn of the Screw* and *Daisy Miller*. New York: Laurel, 1954.

Poe, Edgar Allan. "The Fall of the House of Usher" in *The Complete Stories*. New York: Knopf, 1992.

Thompson, G. R. "The Face in the Pool: Reflections on the Doppelgänger Motif in 'The Fall of the House of Usher,'" *Poe Studies* 5, no. 1 (June 1972): 16–21.

Newgate novels

In the 1830s, England's reading public generated a demand for the Newgate novel, a subgenre of Gothic pulp fiction, MELODRAMA, and historical novel and a forerunner of the sensational novel and GASLIGHT THRILLER. Unlike the DETECTIVE STORY or novel, which featured middle-class sleuths and police officers, the Newgate narrative showcased real thugs, pirates, and scamps as criminal-hero protagonists, often brought down by bad company rather than immorality. The source of criminality, by implication, was poverty. Named for London's infamous central prison, the Newgate novel competed with ghost and witch stories, NECROMANCY, and DIABOLISM as a realistic and immediate form of terror.

Early Victorian writers derived material from 130 years' worth of fact from purported biographies of real prisoners and from grisly woodcuts that had been in circulation since 1700. Executions prompted a demand for broadsheets listing gruesome details; these broadsheets later provided plot and characters for Newgate fiction. Those who were free to attend executions jockeyed for space on the street or rented windows above the road to the gibbet and collected souvenirs. Public engrossment in hangings boosted tavern business and encouraged a night-before revelry and an apres-execution breakfast. Hawkers peddled ballads like the anonymous 18th-century Irish ditty "The Night before Larry Was Stretched" and profited from broadsides of true confessions and glorified retellings of misspent lives, gypsy beggars, rogues, and general outlawry. Newspaper editors like Thomas De Quincey reported events from the assize along with repulsive episodes, foiled escapes, and mysterious disappearances.

Publisher John Applebee, compiler of *Applebee's Original Weekly Journal*, contributed macabre SENSATIONALISM with outrageous articles about victims hanged at Tyburn Prison, a site of public executions from the 12th century onward. Some of the descriptions were the work of the prison ordinary or chaplain, the minister to inmates who escorted condemned prisoners to execution sites—for example, *The Ordinary of Newgate, his account of the behavior, confession, and dying words of the pyrates, who were executed at execution-dock on Monday, the fourteenth of this instant March, 1736-7* (1737). Others were the scribblings of the criminals themselves. These texts, which were popular with the working class, glamorized observations on foundlings and orphans, poverty, sex crimes, and injustice perpetrated by the privileged on the have-nots. Scurrilous, overblown narratives ranged from biographies of rapists, robbers, smugglers, forgers, and scapegraces—*The Narrative of All the Robberies,*

Escapes etc. of John Sheppard (1724), *The History of the Remarkable Life of John Sheppard* (1724), *The True and Genuine Account of the Late Jonathan Wild* (1725)—to romantic sea tales of pirates, such as *An Account of the Conduct and Proceedings of the Late John Gow, Captain of the Late Pirates Executed for Murther and Piracy* (1725). The last is a revolting eyewitness account concluding with his friends yanking on his legs to hurry his demise in the noose. Because they broke the rope, the hangman had to make a second try to complete the deed.

The blood and thunder of Newgate novels reprised the factual compilations of Charles Johnson, who issued the classic two-volume sourcebook *A General History of the Robberies and Murders of the Most Notorious Pyrates* (1724, 1728). Applebee's chief agent, Daniel Defoe, author of *The Life, Adventures, and Pyracies of the Famous Captain Singleton, Alias Smith* (1720) and *The Four Years Voyages of Capt. George Roberts* (1726), stored up details from prison interviews for the picaresque classic *Moll Flanders* (1722) and "Essay on the History and Reality of Apparitions" (1727). The novelist Henry Fielding saw promise in the picaresque motif and the dash of the picaro, which he incorporated into his novel *Jonathan Wild* (1743), the story of a ringleader of thieves and frequenter of prostitutes.

A collection, *The Newgate Calendar; or, Malefactors' Bloody Register* (1773), created a useful source of information for writers. The list was the work of the prison's deputy keeper, who compiled names of new inmates and recorded details of crimes, executions, and the final statements of the condemned. A subsequent work, the Reverend John Villette's four-volume *Annals of Newgate* (1776), contributed more details to the mix. Because of the instant popularity of crime lists, a number of publishing houses began issuing crime compendia. The calendars impressed on the public that English law doled out death sentences for 160 types of crime, which included not only murder, rape, treason, conspiracy, arson, mail theft, piracy, smuggling, burglary, highway robbery, breaking and entering, shoplifting, picking pockets, animal theft, counterfeiting, and forgery but also such minor offenses as marring a riverbank, violating a pond, chopping down a tree belonging to someone else, and appearing at night in disguise. The episodes so appealed to the lowbrow reader that the calendars outsold other journals and magazines twice and three times over. They also influenced the sketches of artist William Hogarth and Gothic illustrator George CRUIKSHANK and the writings of Charles DICKENS and William Makepeace Thackeray. William GODWIN explored the criminal personality through Falkland, the fictional hero-VILLAIN of the Gothic novel CALEB WILLIAMS (1794). A quarter-century later, the popularity of pseudohistory survived in Pierce Egan's *Account of the Trial of John Thurtell and Joseph Hunt* (1824), a current-events thriller about a murderer hanged at Hertford that found its way into broadside, ballad, and GOTHIC DRAMA.

At the forefront of a wave of interest in lawlessness were the episodic true-crime tales of novelists Edward BULWER-LYTTON and William Harrison AINSWORTH. Bulwer-Lytton produced a jewel of crime fiction, *Paul Clifford* (1830), which features a criminal as the mannerly, but dishonest hero. Ainsworth vivified the predations of the highwayman Dick Turpin in *Rookwood* (1834). The author borrowed ATMOSPHERE and criminal characterization from John Gay's *The Beggar's Opera* (1728) and from Charles Dickens's serialized social novel OLIVER TWIST (1837–39) to use in *Jack Sheppard* (1840), which Ainsworth began issuing in monthly installments in *Bentley's Magazine* in January 1839. Readers thrilled to the capture of Jack at his mother's grave and to his stoic march to the gibbet. Contributing to the Newgate subgenre were Thackeray's *Catherine* (1840), a satire on the Newgate novel serialized in *Frazer's Magazine* under a pen name, Ikey Solomons Jr., and the ghost-written memoirs of François-Eugène Vidocq, a renowned criminal-turned-Paris detective, whose autobiographical crime stories appeared in installments in *Burton's Gentleman's Quarterly* from September 1838 to May 1839.

Because such works sympathized with wrongdoers and turned urban crime into titillating romance, particularly for budding juvenile delinquents, irate Londoners lashed out at the authors of the unsavory penny dreadful, the Newgate novel, and its stage equivalent, which hacks interlaced with gutter slang and the sexual escapades of lowlife folk heroes. Articles in the *Athenaeum* and the *Examiner* credited crime fiction for endangering public morality and instigating copycat crimes.

The public mused over the valet François Courvoisier, who slew his master, Lord William Russell, on May 4, 1850, reputedly inspired by Ainsworth's descriptive murder plot in *Jack Sheppard*.

Responding to attacks on Newgate novels as inspirations to criminals, Dickens, the fount of 19th-century socio-historical fiction, defended true-crime novels as models of good triumphing over evil. He depicts the response to crime narratives from impressionable children in *Oliver Twist* with a scene of Oliver turning the pages of a soiled, well-thumbed edition: "Here, he read of dreadful crimes that made the blood run cold; of secret murders that had been committed by the lonely wayside; of bodies hidden from the eye of man in deep pits and wells" (Dickens, 649). The author acknowledges that, when the bodies surfaced, they "so maddened the murderers with the sight, that in their horror they had confessed their guilt, and yelled for the gibbet to end their agony" (*ibid*). The scene concludes with little Oliver terrified and alone amid such crime and wickedness. Dickens turns the episode into an impetus for salvation after the boy sinks to the floor in prayer. In private, however, Dickens distanced himself from lurid crime fiction. He carefully expunged his praise of Ainsworth's *Rookwood* from a second edition of *Oliver Twist* and ended a relationship with his old friend.

Bibliography

Dickens, Charles. *Oliver Twist*, vol. 1 of *The Annotated Dickens*, ed. by Edward Guiliano and Philip Collins. New York: Clarkson N. Potter, 1986.

Diyen, H. "The Narrativity of Jonathan Wild in Defoe's Account of Jonathan Wild and Fielding's 'The Life of Jonathan Wild the Great,'" *Forum for Modern Language Studies* 34, no. 1 (January 1998): 16–28.

Furbank, P. N., and W. R. Owen. "The Myth of Defoe as 'Applebee's Man,'" *Review of English Studies* 48, no. 190 (May 1997): 198–204.

Hollingsworth, Keith. *The Newgate Novel, 1830–1847*. Detroit: Wayne State University Press, 1963.

Nick of the Woods
Robert Montgomery Bird
(1837)

The Philadelphia physician, historian, and dramatist Robert Montgomery BIRD contributed to

AMERICAN GOTHIC a blood-chilling study of ABERRANT BEHAVIOR in *Nick of the Woods*. Related in Kentucky dialect, the novel tells of a Quaker frontiersman named Nathan who is struck on the head, scalped, and left for dead after the Shawnee massacre his family. He develops a demonic DOPPELGÄNGER who bears a separate, secret identity as Nick or Nathan the Jibbenainosay (literally, "The Spirit That Walks"). In extremes of trauma-induced psychosis, Nick/Nathan wanders the wild swinging a hatchet and brutalizing Indians for what he maintains is a debased and ignorant way of life.

Horrific scenes of scalping, clots of blood, and skulls and torsos cloven with axes contribute to the notoriety of Bird's view of frontier life as embodied in the demonic serial killings of Nick/Nathan. One of the most appalling death scenes is "the horrible spectacle of the old Piankeshaw warrior, the lower part of his face shot entirely away, and his eyes rolling hideously, and, as it seems, sightlessly, in the pangs of death" (Bird, 218). The killing is so sudden and savage that Roland, the character Nick is rescuing, faints and awakens to the ministrations of Nick's alter ego Nathan, the kindly Quaker.

In the preface, Bird admits his racism, which he justifies as necessary to end Indian treachery against unwary white settlers, especially the native assaults and scalpings of women and children. His contribution to Kentuckiana depicts the Shawnee and Wyandott as MONSTERS, savages, and fiends who sully the American Eden and wound the character Slaughter beyond human endurance. In one scene, a Wyandott chief speaks a laborious and self-incriminating declaration: "'Me Injunman!' said the chief, addressing his words to the prisoner, and therefore in a prisoner's language,— 'Me kill all white-man! Me Wenonga: me drink white-man blood; me no heart!'" (*ibid.*, 298).

Bird enhances the Gothic ATMOSPHERE of his work with images of Nick/Nathan painting birds and lizards on his skull, setting wigwams aflame, and faking an epileptic seizure as a means of terrifying Indians. Whereas Jack, his contemporary, shoots the Shawnee through one eye, Nick/Nathan marks his handiwork by excising a cross on his victims' torsos. From Wenonga, he re-

trieves the scalps of his own children. Bird rounds out the tale in legend style, with Jibbenainosay, the phantom killer, retreating into the forest, never to be seen again.

Bibliography

Bird, Robert Montgomery. *Nick of the Woods; or, The Jibbenainosay*. New Haven, Conn.: College & University Press, 1967.

"Review: Nick of the Woods," *Southern Literary Messenger* 3, no. 4 (April 1837): 254–257.

Norman, Marsha
(1947–)

Kentuckian Marsha Norman has won awards for Gothic scenarios and eccentric and GROTESQUE characterization in her satiric plays about tormented people. She got her start with *Getting Out* (1977), a stage drama about a schizoid prostitute in an asylum. Norman's most successful work, the two-character psychodrama *'night, Mother* (1982), follows suicidal daughter Jessie Cates and her undercutting mother Thelma Cates through an evening of lacerating exchanges. The harpy-like mother badgers and berates while Jessie moves unrelentingly toward bedtime and suicide, giving as her excuse that she is not having a good time.

Norman's interlocking female characters contribute to each other's diseased views of life. In a final bit of unloving repartee, Thelma refuses Jessie compassion with a parting snipe:

Jessie: I'm through talking, Mama . . .

Thelma: You'll miss. You'll wind up a vegetable. How would you like that? Shoot your ear off?

(Norman, 17)

Norman carries the bizarre two-woman play to the final shot that concludes Jessie's complaints and leaves Thelma to inform the family and plan a funeral. A serious contribution to SOUTHERN GOTHIC, the play won a Tony and a Pulitzer Prize for drama and succeeded on film from the pairing of Anne Bancroft and Sissy Spacek as despotic mother and desperate daughter, respectively.

Bibliography

Brustein, Robert, "'night, Mother," *New Republic* 188 (May 2, 1983): 25–27.

Kauffmann, Stanley, "'night, Mother," *New Republic* 195 (October 13, 1986): 26.

Norman, Marsha. *'night, Mother*. New York: Hill & Wang, 1983.

Northanger Abbey

A stay at a GOTHIC SETTING engages the silly, immature imagination of Catherine MORLAND, the anti-heroine of Jane AUSTEN's satiric novel *NORTHANGER ABBEY* (1818). Upon hearing her father refer to the abbey, Catherine invests too much anticipation in "everything honourable and soothing, every present enjoyment and every future hope" (Austen, 95). Immediately, she envisions the type of edifice found in her Gothic reading material, comprised of "long, damp passages, its narrow cells and ruined chapel," which conjure up "the hope of some traditional legends, some awful memorials of an injured and ill-fated nun" (ibid., 96).

Austen builds SUSPENSE in both reader and heroine over three chapters until the coach rolls over the 30 miles from Bath to the abbey itself. Built low and unadorned by an antique chimney, the unassuming structure passes so quickly before her eyes that Catherine cannot enjoy the lengthy savoring that she had fantasized. From porch to hall, she enters a building that is lacking even a hint of a murderer in residence. The comfortable drawing room is common and the furniture modern; the fireplace is plain marble ornamented with English china. Although the windows rise to pointed Gothic arches, they contain large, clear panes devoid of "painted glass, dirt, and cobwebs"—a far cry from GOTHIC CONVENTION (ibid., 111).

In her room, Catherine allows an overcharged curiosity to play on the one appointment—a cedar chest embellished with a tarnished silver lock and broken handles. Before she can dig into its interior, Miss Tilney interrupts and explains that she kept the relic as storage for bonnets and hats. Although initially deflated, Catherine clings to more possibilities of terror and gloom, delighting in a dark, rainy night—"a countless variety of dreadful situations

and horrid scenes which such buildings had witnessed" (ibid., 114–115). Because of the absence of resident horrors, Catherine terrifies herself by snuffing her candle, producing a thick darkness that amplifies evocative sensations from gusty wind outdoors and footsteps and door-closings in the hall.

Austen orders the narrative around Catherine's gradual exploration of the rest of the abbey, including the cloistered garden and an unidentified portrait of a woman. To the girl's annoyance, the kitchen is equipped with modern conveniences, and additional guest chambers are equally well fitted in contemporary style. Upon learning that someone expired in one of the rooms, Catherine makes immediate connections with Montoni, the villain in Ann RADCLIFFE's classic Gothic novel *THE MYSTERIES OF UDOLPHO* (1794). The contretemps that results from Catherine's insult to the general precedes a weepy departure from the abbey by a girl too silly for her own good.

Bibliography

Austen, Jane. *Northanger Abbey*. New York: Modern Library, 1995.

Hoeveler, Diane Long. *Gothic Feminism*. University Park: Pennsylvania State University Press, 1998.

Hudson, John. "Gothic, Romance and Satire in Northanger Abbey," *English Review* 12, no. 1 (September 2001): 21.

Northanger Abbey
Jane Austen
(1818)

Northanger Abbey, Jane Austen's witty parody of Ann RADCLIFFE's Gothic classic *THE MYSTERIES OF UDOLPHO* (1794), offers a riposte to the DECADENCE of Gothicism and the pessimism of the French *ROMAN NOIR*. Austen began writing in 1798, but did not complete the text until 1803, earning only £10 for her trouble. In a resetting of the BLUEBEARD MYTH, the protagonist, Catherine MORLAND, loses touch with reality by becoming too engrossed in popular Gothic literature, particularly works from MINERVA PRESS—Eliza PARSONS's *The Castle of Wolfenbach* (1793) and *Mysterious Warnings* (1796), Peter Teuthold's *The Necromancer of the Black Forest* (1794), Eleanor Sleath's *Orphan of the Rhine* (1796),

Peter Will's *Horrid Mysteries* (1796), Francis LATHOM's *The Midnight Bell* (1798), and Regina Maria ROCHE's *Clermont* (1798) (Austen, 24).

Like other recreational readers of the author's day, Catherine prefers escapist fiction during her leisure moments at Bath. Guided by Isabella Thorpe, Catherine begins on *The Mysteries of Udolpho* and looks forward to unending fright from a stack of works. To heighten satire, Austen stresses the normality of Catherine, who bears no resemblance to the quavering, neurasthenic maidens of GOTHIC CONVENTION and who resides in a milieu devoid of SECRECY, intimidation, and MYSTERY. At length, she must admit that she has developed a neurotic craving to be frightened, the result of pernicious Gothic settings and horrifying scenes.

Austen impresses on the reader the absurdity of SENSATIONALISM and oversensitivity. To an infantile, romantic mind like Catherine's, imagination is destructive, imprisoning women's minds as surely as castle walls immure Gothic heroines. Catherine's discussion with Eleanor concerning the difference between reality and fiction is so belabored that Henry Tilney, a superior, patronizing male, concludes that women may lack the mental acuity for so fine a distinction. Ironically, Catherine's enlightenment further alienates her, leaving her to kill time until marriage supplies an arbitrary future as Henry's wife.

Bibliography

Austen, Jane. *Northanger Abbey.* New York: Modern Library, 1995.

Gilbert, Sandra M., and Susan Gubar. *The Madwoman in the Attic,* 2nd ed. New Haven, Conn.: Yale University Press, 2000.

Neill, Edward. "The Secret of 'Northanger Abbey,'" *Essays in Criticism* 47, no. 1 (January 1997): 13–32.

nursery rhymes

A longlived source of Gothic situations and conventions, the nursery rhyme bears the wisdom of the cautionary tale in its warnings to small children of danger from unforeseen sources. The term first classified children's ditties in an 1824 issue of BLACKWOOD'S EDINBURGH MAGAZINE. In 1952,

English literary historian and author-biographer Geoffrey Handley-Taylor surveyed nursery jingles and summarized dire events: 23 cases of VIOLENCE, 21 deaths, 16 episodes of sorrow, 15 maimings, 12 torturings of people or animals, 9 abandonments, 9 examples of poverty, 8 murders, 8 lashings, 7 amputations, 4 animal murders, 4 broken limbs, 2 self-inflicted injuries, 2 chokings, 2 burning houses, 2 imprisonments, and 2 graves. Gothic detail supplies the canon with decapitation, drawing and quartering, biting, starvation, drowning, bleeding to death, INSANITY, squeezing and boiling to death, shriveling, body snatching, hanging, and cannibalism plus frequent references to fear, hysteria, and pleas for mercy.

Familiar rhymes, when interpreted in the light of history, reveal ominous scenarios. "Oh! Cruel Was the Press Gang" (pre-1850) is a mournful tale of a woman forced into beggary after her husband was shanghaied into service and lost his leg; "Sing a Song of Sixpence," a quick take from *Tommy Thumb's Pretty Song Book* (ca. 1744) on the beheading of Anne Boleyn, second wife of Henry VIII; "The Rats and the Mice" (ca. 1744), a domestic scene from *Tommy Thumb* in which a husband dumps his mate after she falls from a wheelbarrow and leaves her to the "duce," a Celtic name for Satan; and "Who Killed Cock Robin?" (ca. 1744), a morbidly protracted 14-stanza narrative from *Tommy Thumb* about the shooting of a bird, an ALLEGORY on the 1742 downfall of Sir Robert Walpole's ministry. A murderous quatrain, "The Old Woman Who Lived in a Shoe," which was published in *Gammer Gurton's Garland* (1740), is a common children's rhyme that links child abuse and poverty. One of the most resilient of domestic pairs, PUNCH AND JUDY, derived from the commedia dell'arte and records a universal scenario of spousal abuse.

Bibliography

Baring-Gould, William S., and Ceil Baring-Gould. *The Annotated Mother Goose.* New York: Clarkson N. Potter, 1962.

Daniel, Anne Margaret. "Kipling's Use of Verse and Prose in 'Baa Baa, Black Sheep,'" *Studies in English Literature, 1500–1900* 37, no. 4 (autumn 1997): 857–876.

O

Oates, Joyce Carol
(1938–)

The American novelist Joyce Carol Oates has turned out a wide variety of plays, essays, and short and long fiction, including a respectable shelf of Gothic writings. A brilliant literary scholar from New York State, she joins characters at turning points in their lives, as in a complex point in the rise of an American entrepreneurial family in BELLEFLEUR (1980), and introduces modern MONSTERS—for example, the freakish assaults and killings in the bizarre fable "Family" (1991) and the bold serial killer in *Zombie* (1995). She specializes in misfits, ABERRANT BEHAVIOR, and the walking wounded on a par with the oddballs of AMERICAN GOTHIC created by William FAULKNER, Carson MCCULLERS, and Flannery O'CONNOR. In "Lethal" (1992), a tour de force of 19 lines, Oates explores the mania of an attacker who advances from wanting to touch and caress a victim to rape, biting, bloodsucking, and murder. In another story, "The Accursed Inhabitants of the House of Bly" (1992), she answers questions left unaddressed in Henry JAMES's Gothic novella THE TURN OF THE SCREW (1898) by depicting the two apparitions and the two children engaged in group sex.

Oates's works, particularly the frequently anthologized "Where Are You Going, Where Have You Been?" (1970) and the starkly violent "Secret, Silent" and "The Vampire," collected in *Faithless: Tales of Transgression* (2001), reject outdated GOTHIC CONVENTIONs. She chooses to place fear and horror in normal American venues rather than relegate them to the classic settings of remote locales, Gothic buildings, and distant anomalies. She characterizes the forbidden, lawless impulse as a given in the human psyche, which frees victims, particularly woman, to retaliate against people and situations that threaten. The impulse permeates "The Premonition" (1994), in which a man's fear for his sister-in-law turns on end when he notices the smell of blood at her house and her insistence that the family is leaving for Europe to join her husband, an abusive drinker who has allegedly gone ahead.

In addition to original modern Gothic fiction, Oates edited *American Gothic Tales* (1996), a collection drawn from two centuries of Gothic literature, including one of her stories, "The Temple." Her introduction expresses the pervasiveness of gothic convention among all writers. She describes the Puritans' initial view of New England's vast forests and their zealotry for inflicting a narrow definition of rightness on the frontier. From their unbending outlook grew the paranoia and OBSESSIONs that produced historic episodes of Gothic proportions, notably, the Salem witch trials of 1692.

Bibliography

Hoeveler, Diane Long. "Postgothic Fiction: Joyce Carol Oates Turns the Screw on Henry James," *Studies in Short Fiction* 35, no. 4 (fall 1998): 355–372.

Johnson, Greg. "Blonde Ambition: An Interview with Joyce Carol Oates," *Prairie Schooner* 75, no. 3 (fall 2001): 15.

Wesley, Marilyn C. "Reverence, Rape, Resistance: Joyce Carol Oates and Feminist Film Theory," *Mosaic* 32, no. 3 (September 1999): 75.

White, Terry. "Allegorical Evil, Existentialist Choice in O'Connor, Oates and Styron," *Midwest Quarterly* 34, no. 4 (summer 1993): 383–397.

O'Brien, Fitz-James
(1828–1862)

A promising writer who was killed while fighting for the Union during the American Civil War, the Irish-American Gothicist Fitz-James O'Brien produced elements of the macabre approaching the power of Edgar Allan POE. A native of Limerick, Ireland, O'Brien studied at Trinity College in Dublin and frittered away a sizable inheritance in London while developing into a respectable writer. Before immigrating to the United States, he submitted one anonymous horror story, "An Arabian Nightmare," to editor Charles DICKENS for publication in the November 1851 issue of *Household Words*.

At age 24, O'Brien arrived in Washington, D.C., and fell in with bohemian writers in New York. His bipolar personality caused him to sleep for long periods and to dream outlandish scenarios that he turned into stories. While editing for the *New York Times*, he wrote stage plays and libretti and witty sketches, stories, and serials for the *American Whig Review*, *Atlantic*, *Evening Post*, *Harper's*, *Home Journal*, *Lantern*, *New York Picayune*, *Putnam's*, *Saturday Press*, *Saturday Review*, and *Vanity Fair*. Later literary histories of Gothic short fiction disclosed that he also lifted translations of two stories by Prince Vladimir ODOEVSKY—"The Sylph" (1837) and "The Improvisor" from *Russian Nights* (1844)—and issued them under his own name.

O'Brien began to receive critical notice with the publication of a ghost tale, "The Pot of Tulips" (1855), and a subdued MAD SCIENTIST motif in "The Diamond Lens" (1858), an outlandish fantasy of unrequited love between a lab worker and a minuscule female living in a droplet viewed through his microscope, an instrument just gaining interest in America. O'Brien presaged the robots of Karel ČAPEK's *R.U.R.* (1920) with "The Wondersmith" (1859), a tale of demonic mechanical killer dolls that reprises the mobile toys in E. T. A. HOFFMANN's fantasies. O'Brien's evocative short piece "What Was It?" (1859) was the impetus for fiction by frontier Gothicist Ambrose BIERCE and for Guy de MAUPASSANT's masterwork, "Le Horla; or, Modern Ghosts" (1887).

Bibliography

Lovecraft, H. P. *The Annotated Supernatural Horror in Literature*. New York: Hippocampus, 2000.

Thomson, Douglass H., et al., eds. *Gothic Writers: A Critical and Bibliographical Guide*. Westport, Conn.: Greenwood, 2001.

obsession

As a motivator of the GOTHIC NOVEL and SHORT FICTION, obsession becomes a controlling form of ABERRANT BEHAVIOR in characters, as in Théophile GAUTIER's "La Morte Amoureuse" (The dead lover, 1836), translated into English as the erotic ghost story "Clarimonde," the story of a priest ensnared by a FEMME FATALE. Obsession ventures beyond romantic attachments to a number of engulfing thoughts and impulses—for example, a repetitive criminality in Tobias SMOLLETT's *FERDINAND COUNT FATHOM* (1753), the illogical guilt of the title character in Charles Brockden BROWN's *EDGAR HUNTLY; or, Memoirs of a Sleepwalker* (1799), the MAD SCIENTIST Victor FRANKENSTEIN's drive to succeed in Mary Wollstonecraft SHELLEY's *FRANKENSTEIN* (1818), the inhumanity of religious fanatics in Charles Robert MATURIN's *MELMOTH THE WANDERER* (1820), the murderer MONTRESOR's overweening pride and elitism in Edgar Allan Poe's "THE CASK OF AMONTILLADO" (1846), and the self-assurance of unethical lab experimenters in Nathaniel HAWTHORNE's "THE BIRTHMARK" (1843) and "Rappaccini's Daughter" (1844). One Russian story, Alexander Pushkin's "The Queen of Spades" (1834), the basis for a successful opera by Peter Ilyich Tchaikovsky, is a finely plotted tale of frenetic gambling and uncontrolled passion. A height of AMERICAN GOTHIC fixation, Herman MELVILLE's *Moby-Dick* (1851) dissects monumental spite in Captain Ahab's hunt for the title figure, a white whale. French short fiction specialist Guy de MAUPASSANT employed similarly diseased personalities in many of his stories, notably, "La Chevelure" (The gold braid, 1884), "La Morte" (The dead, 1887), "La Nuit" (The night, 1887), and his masterpiece, "Le Horla; or, Modern Ghosts" (1887).

Compelling, haunting actions frequently motivate faulty logic and precipitate disastrous ends, the crux of Emily BRONTË's *WUTHERING HEIGHTS* (1847), a vivid model of psychological monomania and love-wrecked lives. Obsessions precipitate twisted hopes, as with the king's MELANCHOLY adoration of his deceased queen in Oscar WILDE's wistful FAIRY TALE "The Birthday of the Infanta" (1888) and dreams of high art in George du Maurier's best-selling MELODRAMA *Trilby* (1894) and Gaston LEROUX's GHOST STORY *Le Fantôme de l'Opéra* (*THE PHANTOM OF THE OPERA*, 1910), both narratives of male manipulators enthralled with dreams of turning female singers into stage stars. Obsessions also empower 20th-century psychological fiction—notably, STALKING and persecution by the ominous housekeeper Mrs. DANVERS in Daphne DU MAURIER's novel REBECCA (1938), Mrs. Freeman's constant talk about illness and physical impairment in Flannery O'CONNOR's short story "Good Country People" (1955), and a minister's pursuit of redemption in Peter Carey's *OSCAR AND LUCINDA* (1988). In Isabel ALLENDE's *THE HOUSE OF THE SPIRITS*, 1981), Senator Esteban Trueba's insistence on his right to land and power over Chile's mestizos symbolizes ruling-class exploitation. In Allende's words, Trueba's one obsession is destroying socialists, radicals, and "the Marxist cancer," which he fights in the senate and in public with senile rants and gestures with his cane (Allende, *House*, 306).

Bibliography

Allende, Isabel. *The House of the Spirits*. New York: Bantam Books, 1982.

———. "Pinochet's Ghost," *New Perspectives Quarterly* 16, no. 3 (spring 1999): 22–26.

Goodlett, Debra. "Love and Addiction in 'Wuthering Heights,'" *Midwest Quarterly* 37, no. 3 (spring 1996): 316–327.

occult fiction

Occult fiction stresses the abstruse and mysterious as vehicles for Gothicism, as found in an invasive ghost and the rape of a corpse in Sheridan LE FANU's classic "Schalken the Painter" (1839), ritual slaughter and orgiastic voodoo practices in Hanns Heinz EWERS's "Die Mamaloi" (Mamaloi, ca. 1925), and Beth HENLEY's SOUTHERN GOTHIC comedy *Signature* (1990), which features a handwriting analyst as an offbeat psychic. The purpose of occult themes is the revelation of veiled knowledge and beliefs, such as the mystic dealings of sorcerers like the Arthurian mage Merlin, the pseudoscience of alchemists such as FAUST, METEMPSYCHOSIS in JAPANESE GOTHIC, and the secret belief systems of arcane fellowships that feature in ILLUMINATI NOVELS. The occult plot is typically suspenseful and tense with anticipation.

The fount of English occult fiction, Edward George BULWER-LYTTON, followed inklings of macabre Gothic fiction introduced by such writers as William BECKFORD, Charlotte DACRE, Johann von GOETHE, and James HOGG, as well as by Friedrich von SCHILLER, author of the influential German tale *DER GEISTERSEHER* (*The Ghost-Seer*, 1786), a story of phony NECROMANCY. Bulwer-Lytton joined a cultic society to discuss the SUPERNATURAL, KABBALISM, MYSTICISM, divination, and other paranormal occurrences and ideologies not explained by science or logic. He developed quasi-scientific schemes as vehicles for the sensational thriller "The Haunted and the Haunters; or, The House and the Brain," published in *BLACKWOOD'S EDINBURGH MAGAZINE* in August 1857, and for four novels, *Godolphin* (1833), *Zanoni* (1842), *A Strange Story* (1861), and *The Coming Race* (1871), a dystopian fantasy of human corruption and doom caused by a mysterious fluid called Vril. Bulwer-Lytton's influence on a growing fiction market is apparent in the popular COLONIAL GOTHIC in occult stories of Indian LYCANTHROPY by Rudyard KIPLING, creepy tales by Le Fanu and H. G. WELLS, and the novels of Ellen WOOD and Marie CORELLI, England's best-selling author of *The Sorrows of Satan; or, The Strange Experience of One Geoffrey Tempest, Millionaire* (1895). Simultaneous with the blossoming of occult fiction in England was decadent verse in French poet Charles BAUDELAIRE's classic collection *Les Fleurs du Mal* (*The Flowers of Evil*, 1857), which influenced a cruel streak of occultism in VILLIERS DE L'ISLE-ADAM's short fiction.

Oscar WILDE mixed occultism with commentary on art and self-indulgence in his chilling psychological novel *THE PICTURE OF DORIAN GRAY* (1891).

The 20th and 21st centuries produced their own brand of occultism, often orchestrated with other GOTHIC CONVENTIONs and blended with science fiction as answers to global problems, particularly in the weird stories of H. P. LOVECRAFT. The English short story specialist Algernon BLACKWOOD specialized in occult elements, including satanism in "Secret Worship" (1908) and eerie forces of NATURE in "The Wendigo" (1910). Saki characterized a child seeking bestial power to overcome adult tyranny in "SREDNI VASHTAR" (1911). The Irish poet William Butler Yeats turned hobby seances into vehicles for a story of mummies and damnation, "All Souls' Night" (1920), and his mystical *A Vision* (1925), which describes Vedic and Buddhist conjurings. Paul Busson, an Austrian fantasist and writer of weird stories, extended occultism in *The Man Who Was Born Again* (1921) with a panoply of hauntings, OMENS, and spiritualism. In 1942, British GHOST STORY writer Alfred McLelland Burrage ventured into the medieval theme of black magic with the novel *Seeker to the Dead*, a thriller about Garrow, a MAD SCIENTIST who attempts to resurrect corpses.

During the late 20th-century rise of multicultural and New Age literature, the occult was a means to an end rather than an end in itself. Jean RHYS used West Indian voodoo to establish a Caribbean milieu and animistic belief system in *Wide Sargasso Sea* (1966), a prequel to Charlotte BRONTË's *JANE EYRE* (1847). New Orleans superstar Anne RICE applied the same logic to her vampire tales, an outgrowth of the LEGEND-rich multiracial history of the Mississippi Delta. The occult proved useful for Daphne DU MAURIER's "Don't Look Now" (1970), Angela CARTER's *The Infernal Desire Machines of Doctor Hoffman* (1972), and Isabel ALLENDE's Latin American saga *THE HOUSE OF THE SPIRITS* (1981), which features ESP, a REVENANT, dreams and trances, and levitation as enhancements to a Chilean revolution saga.

Bibliography

Messent, Peter B. *Literature of the Occult.* Englewood Cliffs, N.J.: Prentice-Hall, 1981.

Viswanathan, Guari. "The Ordinary Business of Occultism," *Critical Inquiry* 27, no. 1 (autumn 2000): 1.

O'Connor, Flannery
(1925–1964)

A brilliant ironist and major contributor to SOUTHERN GOTHIC, Mary Flannery O'Connor focused on everyday miracles and mysteries. Born and educated in Georgia, she spent much time alone wrapped in fantasy and chose the works of Edgar Allan POE as her favorite recreational reading. After graduation from the Women's College of Georgia, she forged a career in the full knowledge that lupus, which had confined her to a wheelchair by age 25, was the end of her mobility in the world. The progressive disease killed her 14 years later.

Perhaps because of her physical handicap, O'Connor applied keen observation of the familial and religious disjunctures in local people to a series of fictional obsessives, tricksters, lunatics, and self-absorbed cranks in her Christian allegories. She examined evil among simple country folk in the story "A Good Man Is Hard to Find" (1953) and contributed to the Gothic novella with *WISE BLOOD* (1952) and *THE VIOLENT BEAR IT AWAY* (1960). For her command of black humor, symbolism, gratuitous VIOLENCE, and insightful GROTESQUEs, she won a National Book Award. A posthumous collection, *The Complete Stories of Flannery O'Connor* (1971), established her reputation for macabre short fiction.

Throughout O'Connor's quirky stories are eerie, often laughable characters who defy stereotypes: the wanderer Tom Shiftlet, the venal Mrs. Crater, the impressionable former sailor O. E. Parker, the charlatan's daughter Sabbath Lily, the seducer Manley Pointer, the self-deluding Mrs. Cope, and the tattoo artist Parker with an owl sketched on his forehead and Christ on his back. In the seduction tale "Good Country People" (1955), Mrs. Freeman, the busybody and maid of Mrs. Hopewell, demonstrates an OBSESSION with illness, limb amputation, and deformities, which she imparts in oral stories to Carramae and Glynese, her daughters. In one of her most anthologized Gothic stories, "The Displaced Person" (1953), mean-minded locals murder a blameless European refugee. O'Connor's keen-edged suffering and dark drollery influenced a generation of Southern Gothicists, including Clyde Edgerton, Cormac McCarthy, Reynolds Price, Lee Smith, and Alice Walker.

Bibliography

Boren, Mark. "Flannery O'Connor, Laughter, and the Word Made Flesh," *Studies in American Fiction* 26, no. 1 (spring 1998): 115–128.

Cheaney, J. B. "Radical Orthodoxy: The Fiction of Flannery O'Connor," *World and I* 16, no. 5 (May 2001): 255.

Ketchin, Susan. *The Christ-Haunted Landscape: Faith and Doubt in Southern Fiction.* Jackson: University Press of Mississippi, 1994.

Schaum, Melita. "'Erasing Angel': The Lucifer-Trickster Figure in Flannery O'Connor's Short Fiction," *Southern Literary Journal* 33, no. 1 (fall 2000): 1.

Odoevsky, Vladimir
(1804–1869)

The Russian musician, philosopher, and romanticist Prince Vladimir Fyodorovich Odoevsky produced a range of Gothic, occult, and fantastic fictions. He entered the literary world at age 20 by editing *Mnemosyne*, a poetic miscellany. A leading literary figure in Moscow and Petersburg in the mid-1800s and a forerunner of the symbolist movement, he was well versed in FOLKLORE, German romanticism, the French *frénétique* school, and English GOTHIC NOVELs. His success in the Gothic mode earned him the nickname "the Russian Hoffmann" (Horner, 117).

From Odoevsky's imaginative works came medieval alchemy lore, anti-Utopias, futurism, satire, prototypical science fiction, ghost stories, REVENANTs, magic, and MYSTICISM. To Europe's growing body of Gothicism he added *Variegated Tales* (1833), *The Cosmorama* (1839), *The Salamander* (1841), and his most revered work, *Russkiye Notchi* (*Russian Nights*, 1844), a collection of nested stories. Written between 1830 and 1842, the latter is the lodestone of Russian romanticism. The core theme of his Faustian work predicts that science and technology will generate the rot that will destroy Western culture. He warns that technology will rob the world of its mystery and deplete the impetus for art.

At his death, Odoevsky left unfinished a futuristic novel *4338 God* (The year 4338). The Irish Gothicist Fitz-James O'BRIEN appropriated from French translations of *Russian Nights* two stories, "The Sylph" (1837)—the basis for O'Brien's "The Diamond Lens" (1858)—and "The Improvisor." Fyodor Dostoevsky reset Odoevsky's story "The Living Corpse" in "The Gambler Bobok" (1873) and "The Dream of Ridiculous Man" (1877). Odoevsky's work was reclaimed in the late 20th century and added to the canon of world Gothic literature.

Bibliography

Horner, Avril, ed. *European Gothic: A Spirited Exchange, 1760–1960.* Manchester: Manchester University Press, 2002.

Rancour-Laferriere, Daniel. *Russian Nationalism from an Interdisciplinary Perspective: Imagining Russia.* Lewiston, N.Y.: Edwin Mellen Press, 2001.

Thomson, Douglass H., et al., eds. *Gothic Writers: A Critical and Bibliographical Guide.* Westport, Conn.: Greenwood, 2001.

Tosi, Alessandra. "Vladimir Odoevsky and Romantic Poetics," *Journal of European Studies* 29, no. 2 (June 1999): 226.

The Old English Baron
Clara Reeve
(1778)

Clara REEVE's pivotal GOTHIC NOVEL *The Old English Baron* was originally published under the title *The Champion of Virtue: A Gothic Story* (1777). Set in feudal times at Lovel Castle during the rule of King Henry II, the plot turns on the cliché of parted lovers who must overcome differences in social class. The main character, Edmund, displays the traits of the medieval chivalric hero: modesty, courage, gentleness, courtesy, discretion, generosity, compassion, and humility. Employing a ghostly visitation in a dream as a means of guiding her hero, Reeve restructured the ghost-ridden castle motif by introducing the haunted chamber, a refined Gothic touch that developed into a literary and cinematic cliché. She laced the text with images of bloody armor and a fearful cavern as enhancements of terror. The novel ends following the revelation of the true heir, the victim of a cruel, ambitious uncle.

Reeve made her stand against extreme Gothicism by replacing the actual SUPERNATURAL with DREAMS, fearful clanks and groans, inexplicable lights and swinging doors, and local legends and SUPERSTITION as wellsprings of terror. As a source of the hero's education, she applied the motif of the WANDERING JEW in the person of an aged pilgrim who serves as the protagonist's mentor. Despite the novel's popularity, the author and literary critic Anna Laetitia BARBAULD dismissed Reeve's innovative work as predictable and lacking in surprise. Gothic novelist Horace WALPOLE sniffed at Reeve's imitative efforts, which he described as weak and insipid. He used stronger language in declaring the work unimaginative, uninteresting, and contradictory to her claim of avoiding the supernatural.

Bibliography

Casler, Jeanine. "The Primacy of the 'Rougher' Version: Neo-Conservative Editorial Practices and Clara Reeve's 'Old English Baron,'" *Papers on Language & Literature* 37, no. 4 (fall 2001): 404.

Williams, A. Susan, ed. *The Lifted Veil: The Book of Fantastic Literature by Women, 1800–World War II.* New York: Carroll & Graf, 1992.

Oliphant, Margaret
(1828–1897)

One of the stable of writers for William Blackwood III, editor of BLACKWOOD'S EDINBURGH MAGAZINE, Scottish author Margaret Oliphant Wilson was a prolific producer of 100 Victorian novels and nonfiction works and 200 weird stories, including compelling examples of SHORT GOTHIC FICTION. Reared outside Edinburgh, she grew up amid fascinating family storytellers in an era of religious wrangling, a subject for her debut novel, *Passages in the Life of Mrs. Margaret Maitland* (1849). After marrying stained-glass artisan Francis Wilson Oliphant, the author lived in London and, during the remaining 45 years of her life, submitted popular works to *Cornhill* and *London Magazine*.

After her husband's death from tuberculosis, at age 31 Oliphant faced a financial crisis. She supported and educated her children and her brother's family with profits from a stream of magazine serials, literary histories, travelogues, and bi-

ographies. Independent and pragmatic, she wrote DOMESTIC GOTHIC works that ennobled female martyrs to domestication by depicting their unheralded toils. At the same time, she enriched herself by catering to the late 19th-century Gothic strand with tales about castle hauntings, REVENANTs, and occultism: *The Secret Chamber* (1876), *A Beleaguered City* (1880), *A Little Pilgrim of the Unseen* (1882), and *Stories of the Seen and Unseen* (1885). Typically, in a gesture to Victorian ethics, her specters harry the living to improve their morals.

As a critic, Oliphant denounced SENSATIONALISM and the GASLIGHT THRILLERs of Mary Elizabeth BRADDON. In the September 1867 issue of *Blackwood's*, Oliphant disdained the fattened purses of female authors pandering to the lowest in popular taste: "It is a shame to women so to write; and it is a shame to the women who read and accept as a true representation of themselves and their ways the equivocal talk and fleshly inclination herein attributed to them" (Carnell, 169). She blamed the rush of female authors to debase their work as "that mere desire for something startling which the monotony of ordinary life is apt to produce; but it is debasing to everybody concerned" (ibid.). Against a wave of mid-19th-century shocker novels and pulp serials, Oliphant championed higher standards and helped to establish the importance of Charlotte BRONTË's novel *JANE EYRE* (1847) as a pinnacle of Gothic literature.

Bibliography

Carnell, Jennifer. *The Literary Lives of Mary Elizabeth Braddon.* Hastings, Sussex: Sensation Press, 2000.

D'Albertis, Deirdre. "The Domestic Drone: Margaret Oliphant and a Political History of the Novel," *Studies in English Literature, 1500–1900* 37, no. 4 (autumn 1997): 805–830.

Michie, Elsie B. "Buying Brains: Trollope, Oliphant, and Vulgar Victorian Commerce," *Victorian Studies* 44, no. 1 (autumn 2001): 77–99.

Oliver Twist
Charles Dickens
(1838)

An enormously popular model of serial publication and the NEWGATE NOVEL, Charles DICKENS's urban MELODRAMA *Oliver Twist; or, The Parish Boy's Progress,* his first original novel, applied Gothic underpinnings to a protest text exposing underworld crime, juvenile gangs, and the organized picking of pockets by young children. Added to the motif of corrupting youth are scenes of kidnap, homelessness and hunger, confinement, anti-Semitism, theft, STALKING, and murder. From February 1837 to April 1839, the author, then aged 24, serialized the long-running story in *Bentley's Miscellany* for an avid readership. His working pen name was Boz; his pay, £21 per 16 printed pages. The bound novel, which featured drawings by Gothic specialist George CRUIKSHANK, required extra printings in 1840 and 1841.

Before Dickens completed the parceling out of installments, J. S. Coyne was already milking the popular story with a stage adaptation at the St. James Theatre that opened in May 1838. George Almar followed in November 1838 with his own version at the Surrey. In January 1869, Dickens himself added to his farewell tour *Sikes and Nancy,* a violent outtake that a London gynecologist warned might reduce female playgoers to hysteria. The author confessed that "it was madness ever to have given the 'Murder' reading, under the conditions of a travelling life, and worse than madness to have given it with such frequency" (Dickens, 545). Nonetheless, he continued staging the GROTESQUE scene until the day before his death in 1870, brought on by the exhausting stage readings.

The appeal of the story derives from Dickens's realistic representation of London's criminal element, prostitution, workhouses, law courts, and injustice against the poor. The author overworks the threats to the orphaned Oliver, aged nine, by depicting him training to rifle gentlemen's waistcoats, going along on a house robbery, wounded with a bullet, and stalked by a cruelly sinister thug named Monks. In the falling action, Dickens restores Oliver to the kindly Mr. Brownlow, his foster father, while killing off Nancy with a drubbing by Bill Sikes, a VILLAIN who scatters so much blood that it speckles his body and clothes and a dog's feet. The author rids himself of the burglar Sikes through an accidental hanging in full sight of pursuers: "The noose . . . ran up with his weight, tight as a bowstring, and swift as the arrow it speeds. He fell for five-and-

thirty feet. There was a sudden jerk, a terrific convulsion of the limbs, and there he hung" (Dickens, 806). As a Gothic fillip, Dickens describes the howling dog as springing toward Sikes, falling to the ditch, and "[dashing] out his brains" (*ibid.*).

In the melodramatic chapter titled "Fagin's Last Night Alive," Dickens depicts the stealthy child corrupter Fagin sitting in terror on his bunk, rocking side to side, and pondering his doom at a public execution. Dickens augments the public delight in the villain's demise with a commentary on the eagerness of observers for vengeance: "The windows were filled with people, smoking and playing cards to beguile the time; the crowd were pushing, quarrelling, joking. Everything told of life and animation" (*ibid.,* 820). Contrasting the merrymaking is "one dark cluster of objects in the centre of all—the black stage, the cross-beam, the rope, and all the hideous apparatus of death," the author's literary gesture against capital punishment (*ibid.*).

Bibliography

Bennett, Rachel. "Oliver Twist," *Review of English Studies* 46, no. 181 (February 1995): 138–139.

Dickens, Charles. *Oliver Twist,* in vol. 1 of *The Annotated Dickens,* ed. by Edward Guiliano and Philip Collins. New York: Clarkson N. Potter, 1986.

Hollingsworth, Keith. *The Newgate Novel, 1830–1847.* Detroit: Wayne State University Press, 1963.

Howe, Irving. "The Spell of Fagin—Reconsideration: 'Oliver Twist,'" *New Republic* 188 (June 20, 1983): 27–32.

Melada, Ivan. "Oliver Twist: Whole Heart and Soul," *Studies in the Novel* 27, no. 2 (summer 1995): 218–230.

omens

The use of omens in Gothic fiction is a natural outgrowth of pagan SUPERSTITION permeating LEGEND, FAIRY TALE, and FOLKLORE, such as the Central American figure LA LLORONA, the weeping female phantasm who foretokens death. The early French Gothicist Abbé PRÉVOST applied omens, prophetic DREAMS, and MELANCHOLY to literary purpose in the evolving *ROMAN NOIR* (black novel). In his stories, portents precede evil and terror rather than good. Tobias SMOLLETT pioneered the use of MYSTERY and omens in English Gothic lore in the dramatic *FERDINAND COUNT FATHOM* (1753), the story of a picaresque con artist who wastes his life achieving selfish desires and amusements.

As writers shaped the Gothic genre, omens were integral in the building of ATMOSPHERE. An ominous motif served British author Horace WALPOLE, who established the basics of GOTHIC CONVENTION in *THE CASTLE OF OTRANTO* (1765). Romantic poet Samuel Taylor COLERIDGE turned the mariner's shooting of an albatross, a bird of good omen, into a sign of doom in *THE RIME OF THE ANCIENT MARINER* (1798). Doomed to a terrible penance, the mariner expiates his violation of NATURE to free himself from a ghost ship. In a prosaic setting, novelist Charles Robert MATURIN portrays the peasant con artist Biddy Brannigan as a reader of signs in *MELMOTH THE WANDERER* (1820).

Omens serve multiple purposes in Victorian Gothic fiction. In *JANE EYRE* (1847), Charlotte BRONTË, like a protective mother, warns her heroine through prophetic dreams of the dangers of marrying her enigmatic employer, Edward ROCHESTER. As a SUBTEXT, Charles DICKENS inserts criticism of social decay into *BLEAK HOUSE* (1853), which depicts the indifference of London snobs and their apathy toward the poor. At a climactic moment, Krook, a dissolute rag-and-bone dealer, dies of spontaneous combustion. The author meant for readers to interpret the macabre implosion as a prophecy of urban self-destruction.

Gothic novels of the 20th century perpetuated the centrality of SUPERNATURAL warnings. Omens of doom for humanity in Karel ČAPEK's robot play *R.U.R.* (1920) alert readers to a pervasive theme, the unwise applications of science and technology to human lives. As Rossum's Universal Robots begin thinking and acting like humans, Alquist, the company engineer, grieves over the schematics of artificial intelligence and looks to the stars for comfort as robots overrun the earth. In similar fashion, Latin American author Isabel ALLENDE produced the epic novel *THE HOUSE OF THE SPIRITS* (1981) as a warning of social collapse. Preceding a revolt of the laboring classes is a series of agrarian and urban omens warning of chaos to come: "Drought, snails, and hoof-and-mouth dis-

ease. There was unemployment in the North. . . . It was a year of poverty, a year in which the only thing missing to complete the sense of disaster was an earthquake" (Allende, 67). The upheaval, along with prophetic dreams and visions and an episode of the walking dead, signals the end of the Hispanic overlord's control of land and profit.

Bibliography
Allende, Isabel. *The House of the Spirits.* New York: Bantam Books, 1982.
Messent, Peter B. *Literature of the Occult.* Englewood Cliffs, N.J.: Prentice-Hall, 1981.

Oriental romance

Like the GOTHIC NOVEL, the Oriental romance offered 18th-century readers a break from the stilted confines of neoclassic literature through imaginative, erotic Asian lore and Eastern fantasy based on ethnically stereotyped myth and imagery. To escape the primly fastidious workings of cold, unappealing fiction, writers began concocting popular tales and idylls—for example, Clara REEVE's *The History of Charoba, Queen of Egypt* (1785) and Samuel Taylor COLERIDGE's MYSTERY poem "KUBLA KHAN" (1816). As a subset of Gothic literature, the flexible, atmospheric genre made up in intricacy, intimidation, and peculiarity what it lacked of what H. P. LOVECRAFT called "sheer panic fright" (Lovecraft, 34).

The increase in demand for exotic lore paralleled a revolt against restrictions in garden layout, architecture, and home furnishings and decor, in particular, the chinoiserie, pagodas, dragons, and Chinese MONSTERS that the English imported for ornamenting their homes. In a preface to *Les Mille et Une Nuits* (*The Arabian Nights*, 1704–17), Orientalist and translator Antoine Galland set arbitrary parameters of Orientalism as inclusive of Turks, Tartars, Chinese, pagan Muslims, and idolators. Devoid of terror and violence, his 12-volume collection of Persian and Turkish tales appealed to ordinary readers and was available in cheap editions for home libraries and in bowdlerized editions for children.

Nearly a half-century later, a comment in the journal *World* noted that British tastes were moving toward a blend of Asian and Gothic styles such as that modeled by Joseph Addison's dreamy allegory *The Vision of Mirza* (1711), which he issued in the *Spectator* and the *Guardian*. Popular reading material reflected the broadening of English experience with Asia through publication of sailor lore and the journals and tales of clerks and colonials returned from posts in India. Among the journalists was Lady Mary Wortley Pierrepont Montagu, an aristocratic poet and correspondent who published essays in the *Spectator* and who, in 1715, popularized the Turkish method of variolation against smallpox. Her incisive commentary on life in France and Italy appeared posthumously as *Embassy Letters* (1763).

More literary works joined the Oriental canon in the mid-18th century. A notable contribution was Dr. Samuel Johnson's Oriental stories in the *Idler* and the *Rambler* and his utopian fable *The History of Rasselas, Prince of Abissinia* (1759), which describes a royal prince and princess who flee their home in Happy Valley, Ethiopia, to search Egypt for true happiness. Their roaming concludes at the catacombs in Cairo, where they depart a dreary Gothic setting for a more contemplative life in their native land. That same year, Voltaire produced *Candide* (1759), a similar episodic search for happiness that forces a likeable NAIF into an extensive global adventure that leads him through STALKING, violence, religious fanaticism, sexual temptation, betrayal, and disillusion before settling him in a small garden, a harbinger of domestic contentment.

Foreign settings and exotic trappings were a major influence on Horace WALPOLE's *THE CASTLE OF OTRANTO* (1765) and also marked less familiar Oriental literature. John Hawkesworth published *Almoran and Hamet* (1761), a lengthy DOPPELGÄNGER tale about the tyrannic Almoran and his alter ego, his moral brother Hamet. The next year, John Langhorne set his sentimental story *Solyman and Almena* (1762) in Mesopotamia, where a fictional journeyman seeks an understanding of God and humankind. Frances Chamberlaine Sheridan, an Irish dramatist and romanticist, produced another view of worldliness and trickery in *The History of Nourjahad* (1767), a fashionable romance issued the year after her death.

Oriental experimentation peaked in the 1780s when William BECKFORD completed a Gothic blockbuster, VATHEK: *An Arabian Tale* (1782), which draws on the rhapsodic exoticism of William Jones's *The Seven Fountains: An Eastern Allegory* (1772). Three years later, Walpole effectively capped the era of Oriental romance with a satire, *Hieroglyphic Tales* (1785), seven opaque folk narratives composed over a six-year period that include "The Dice-Box," "Mi Li," "The Peach in Brandy: A Milesian Tale," and "The King and His Three Daughters." Through exaggeration of improbability, absurdity, and the GROTESQUE, Walpole grounded his mannered narratives on the principles of oral STORYTELLING to the exclusion of intellectualism.

In the 19th century, a stylistic mode known as Orientalism emerged parallel to the growth of English imperialism. Unlike the MEDIEVALISM of classic Gothicism, Orientalism supplanted a distant time with a geographical distance. A more scholarly interest in Asian language, religions, and customs provided an explanation of unfamiliar terms and approaches to artistic expression along with a viable vehicle for romantic ideals. The stylistic mode intrigued the working-class reader of the GOTHIC BLUEBOOK and enriched chapbooks by Sarah WILKINSON, author of *The Sorcerer's Palace; or, The Princess of Sinadone* (1805). Irish freelancer Sydney Owenson exploited public curiosities with *The Missionary* (1811), in which she characterized the frontiers of India. Lord BYRON capitalized on England's view of Easternism in the narrative poem *Childe Harold's Pilgrimage* (1812), *THE GIAOUR* (1813), *The Bride of Abydos* (1813), and *The Corsair* (1814). Dubliner Thomas Moore's four-part framework tale *Lalla Rookh* (1817) combined standard Gothic elements with Orientalism, notably, the delicate naif, lurking dangers, and the exploitation of NATURE through the PATHETIC FALLACY. The popular English prose market for Eastern lore came to an end with Thomas Hope's *Anastatius; or, Memoirs of a Greek* (1819), Lady Caroline LAMB's pirate tale *Ada Reis* (1823), and James Morier's Islamic settings in *Adventures of Hajji Baba of Ispahan* (1824). American Gothic master Edgar Allan POE pursued unusual character names and settings, particularly in his mysterious REVENANT story "LIGEIA" (1838); a generation later, Louisa May Alcott depicted an Oriental menace in the recovered story "Taming a Tartar" (1988).

Notably, in mid-century, English novelist Charlotte BRONTË dismissed the need for Orientalism in female characters and Gothic plots. In chapter 24 of JANE EYRE (1847), an experiment in new woman-centered Gothicism, she inserts in the courtship of Edward ROCHESTER an admiration for his plain Jane. Declaring her an "original," he vows, "I would not exchange this one little English girl for the grand Turk's whole seraglio—gazelle-eyes, houri forms, and all!" (Brontë, 255). Rochester's declaration echoed a shift in literature toward URBAN GOTHIC and more realistic settings and characters.

Late in the 20th century, Columbia University professor Edward W. Said, a Jerusalem-born culture critic and author of *Orientalism* (1978), revisited definitions of Orientalism in a postcolonial era. His reevaluation stresses the imperialism of Western political forces that originally defined Asia. An ethnocentric term, *Orient* reflects the Westerner's generalized view and the deep-seated mistrust, hatred, and SUPERSTITIONs that were the SUBTEXTS of Gothic fiction. Faulty views of Asia and Asian OTHERNESS generated stereotypes—child brides, harem dancers, women repressed by purdah, eunuch servants, shifty traders and merchants, pirates, pagan religious fanatics, rapacious sheiks, and self-aggrandizing caliphs. Said refuted the false image of the passive, effeminate Asian villains who lurked among Westerners with harmful, even murderous intent, an element of Gothic bluebooks, Sir Arthur Conan DOYLE's Sherlock HOLMES mysteries, and the novels of Wilkie COLLINS.

Bibliography

Abu-Lughod, Lila. "Orientalism and Middle East Feminist Studies," *Feminist Studies* 27, no. 1 (spring 2001): 101.

Brontë, Charlotte. *Jane Eyre.* New York: Bantam Books, 1981.

Lovecraft, H. P. *The Annotated Supernatural Horror in Literature.* New York: Hippocampus, 2000.

Marrouchi, Mustapha. "Exile Runes," *College Literature* 28, no. 3 (fall 2001): 88.

Porter, David. "From Chinese to Goth: Walpole and the Gothic Repudiation of Chinoiserie," *Eighteenth-Century Life* 23, no. 1 (1999): 46–58.

Said, Edward W. *Orientalism.* New York: Vintage, 1979.

Windschuttle, Keith. "Edward Said's 'Orientalism' Revisited," *New Criterion* 17, no. 5 (January 1999): 30.

Ormond
Charles Brockden Brown
(1799)

One of the novels that Charles Brockden BROWN composed out of an American set of GOTHIC CONVENTIONs, *Ormond; or, The Secret Witness* is a poorly conceived and executed example of the emerging AMERICAN GOTHIC. A tale of virtue under pressure, the plot depicts a tormented NAIF, 16-year-old Constantia Dudley, as the FOIL to, and victim of, a wily seducer, the title character, who employs eavesdropping, mime, DISGUISE, and murder in his pursuit of the heroine. For a model, Brown based his VILLAIN on the character Falkland in William GODWIN's novel CALEB WILLIAMS (1794). To enhance urban elements, Brown evolves the fearful backdrop from his own realistic experience with Philadelphia's yellow fever epidemic of 1793. Ormond, who belongs to a secret society called the Illuminati, dulled his humanity through barbaric acts committed against the Turks while he fought as a volunteer with the Russian army, in particular, the collection of skulls as war trophies.

Returning to civilian life, Ormond symbolizes a peril that perverts innocence for some nefarious purpose. He is brilliant and charming, but incapable of tenderness toward his flirtatious mistress, Helena Cleves, and openly hostile toward marriage to Constantia, a rational, educated woman whom he passionately desires. In addition to the villain's plot to kill Constantia's father and to seduce and rape the blameless heroine, he further disgraces himself by rejecting Helena, who despairs and commits suicide. The author builds the GOTHIC NOVEL to an allegorical triumph—at a gloomy rural estate, the New World woman Constantia stabs the evil, woman-hating Ormond with her penknife, thus symbolically negating Old World DECADENCE.

Bibliography

Fiedler, Leslie. *Love and Death in the American Novel.* Cleveland: Meridian Books, 1962.

Monahan, Kathleen Nolan. "Brown's 'Arthur Mervyn' and 'Ormond,'" *Explicator* 45, no. 3 (spring 1987): 18–20.

Oscar and Lucinda
Peter Carey
(1988)

The Australian novelist Peter Carey won the Booker Prize for *Oscar and Lucinda,* an inventive COLONIAL GOTHIC novel detailing an unlikely romance between two gamblers, the heiress and industrialist Lucinda Leplastrier and the Reverend Oscar Hopkins, an ascetic Victorian minister. Told in retrospect by a grandson of the seriously conflicted Anglican, the plot describes Oscar's yearning for redemption by means of a cockeyed plan to ferry a 12-ton glass church to the frontier outpost of Bellinger, New South Wales. The narrator visits Oscar's early home in Devon, England, and discovers reasons for the minister's warped outlook: "Ignorance and poverty, and cold, always the cold" (Carey, 28). The unpromising background justifies Oscar's ABERRANT BEHAVIOR, which inhibits normal growth toward self-confidence, service, and love.

Gothic DISSIPATION, Dickensian eccentricities, and suggestive CHARACTER NAMES, such as Mr. Smudge and the ogreish religious fanatic Theophilus Hopkins, contribute to the Gothic MOOD of Carey's novel. The heavy symbolism of a bluestocking manufacturer allied with a prissy missionary suggests an unholy union of capitalism and orthodox religion, the two forces that beset Australia during its formative years. Armed with his Bible, Oscar "drifted up the Bellinger River like a blind man up the central isle of Notre Dame. He saw nothing. The country was thick with sacred stories more ancient than the ones he carried in his sweat-slippery leather Bible" (ibid., 492). Oblivious to Australia's uniqueness, he drifts through the aboriginal setting where "every rock had a name, and most names had spirits, ghosts, meanings" (ibid.). Sunk in self, he struggles to uplift his career while passing up myriad chances to aid the country's natives.

Overlaying native STORYTELLING, character PRESCIENCE, and FORESHADOWING of doom is Oscar's fear of drowning, a claustrophobic anticipation of the death that Carey eventually inflicts on the minister. The death scenario, an exotic distortion of baptism, takes shape as the glittering glass church, like the Anglican missions of colonial times, slips its tether and sinks. Barehanded, Oscar batters the iron mullions, but he lacks the physical force or ingenuity to free himself in time. His OBSESSION with drowning adds pathos to his failure to achieve redemption, a subtextual yearning for forgiveness for the white colonist's exploitation and violent slaughter of aboriginal Australians.

Bibliography

Brown, Ruth. "English Heritage and Australian Culture: The Church and Literature of England in *Oscar and Lucinda,*" *Australian Literary Studies* 17, no. 2 (October 1995): 135–140.

Carey, Peter. *Oscar and Lucinda.* New York: Vintage, 1997.

Koval, Ramona. "The Unexamined Life," *Meanjin* 46, no. 3/4 (1997): 666–672.

Petersen, Kirsten Holst. "Gambling on Reality," *Australian Literary Studies* 15, no. 2 (1991): 107–116.

otherness

The concept of otherness underlies Gothicism as a structural myth, in which the SUPERNATURAL or alien OUTSIDER menaces the patriarchal family. Examples are numerous: the Peruvian child abuser in Sir Arthur Conan DOYLE's Sherlock HOLMES story "The Adventure of the Sussex Vampire" (1924), the prowling lesbian protagonist in Djuna BARNES's *Nightwood* (1930), and the immigrant Miss Eckhart in Eudora WELTY's SOUTHERN GOTHIC story "The Golden Apples" (1949). The fear of the stranger forms the SUBTEXT of the BLUEBEARD MYTH, GOTHIC BLUEBOOKs, and the more threatening ORIENTAL ROMANCEs. In classic works by Ann RADCLIFFE and her imitators, the alien's threat to maidenhood requires concerted effort against fearful forms of villainy—rape, torture, murder, and unnamed barbarisms. In the resolution of Radcliffe's novel THE MYSTERIES OF UDOLPHO (1794), marriage and formation of a new family rewards the rescuer and rescued, Emily ST. AUBERT, with the reestablishment of order, rejection of the outsider Montoni, reaffirmation of cultural standards, and hope for the future.

Otherness is the controlling element of the terror of LYCANTHROPY and VAMPIRISM and the MONSTER lore of Karel ČAPEK, H. P. LOVECRAFT, and H. G. WELLS. A strong testimony to the alien nature of the vampire emerges in Bram STOKER's *DRACULA* (1897) in the log of the *Varna*, in which the captain records the fearful secret in the ship's hold. He attempts to "battle this fiend or monster" and remarks on the experience of his crazed and haggard mate: "*It* is here; I know it, now. On the watch last night I saw IT, like a man, tall and thin, and ghastly pale. It was in the bows, and looking out. I crept behind It, and gave It my knife; but the knife went through It, empty as the air" (Stoker, 90). The repetition of the neuter pronoun *it* and the physical act of stabbing the air accounts for the weirdness of a visible adversary that appears to be disembodied. Onshore at Whitby, the otherness takes a new form, a nebulous black shadow hovering over its victim, Lucy Westenra, and the approach of a red-eyed phantasm near East Cliff.

New Englander Robert Cormier pursued an occult version of otherness in *Fade* (1988). The MYSTERY novel describes a family curse, an innate tendency to disappear, that strikes one family member per generation. In the opening chapter, Cormier typifies otherness as a nonbeing depicted in a group photo: "In the space that was supposed to have been occupied by my uncle Adelard, at the end of the top row, next to my father, there is simply a blank space. Nothing. My uncle Adelard had disappeared" (Cormier, 4). As Paul, the protagonist, recognizes the telltale dematerialization of his own body, he realizes that otherness has taken hold, separating him from normal life.

Bibliography

Cormier, Robert. *Fade*. New York: Dell, 1988.

Madoff, Mark. "The Useful Myth of Gothic Ancestry," *Studies in Eighteenth-Century Culture* 8 (1979): 337–350.

Schmitt, Cannon. *Alien Nation: Nineteenth Century Gothic Fictions and English Nationality*. Philadelphia: University of Pennsylvania Press, 1997.

Stoker, Bram. *Dracula*. New York: Bantam Books, 1981.

Twitchell, James B. *The Living Dead: A Study of the Vampire in Romantic Literature*. Durham, N.C.: Duke University Press, 1981.

Otranto

The environs of Horace WALPOLE's slim Gothic tale *THE CASTLE OF OTRANTO* (1765) set the course for over two centuries of Gothic fiction. The grim edifice elicits familiarity for its likeness to the castles in FAIRY TALES and in the BLUEBEARD MYTH. The social arrangement provides for separations by gender, with the heroine Isabella and other ladies withdrawing to their quarters in fear and grief, while the usurper Manfred and his male servants scurry out to the courtyard to retrieve the remains of Conrad, the groom-to-be who dies under a massive helmet that falls from the sky. Contributing to the spooky interior are the torches that light the way to the gallery, echoing footsteps on stone floors, and the sigh emitted by a portrait on the wall.

In addition to creating a Gothic MOOD, architecture poses a problem to the heroine. To flee a forced marriage to Manfred, Isabella descends flights of stairs, a standard obstacle to escape in Gothic settings. Beyond the castle, she finds the way blocked by locked gates and guards. Walpole offers hope from the lower level, where the castle is "hollowed into several intricate cloisters," a subterranean maze that his novel established as a GOTHIC CONVENTION (Walpole, 25). The region bears its own Gothic terrors in blasts of wind shaking the doors and destroying the silence and the grating of rusted hinges that "re-echoed through that long labyrinth of darkness" (*ibid.*). With a deft touch, the author creates another Gothic cliché by having a gust of wind extinguish Isabella's lamp.

Bibliography

Barasch, Frances K. *The Grotesque*. Paris: Mouton, 1971.

Frank, Marcie. "Horace Walpole's Family Romances," *Modern Philology* 100, no. 3 (February 2003): 417–435.

Walpole, Horace. *The Castle of Otranto*. London: Oxford University Press, 1969.

outsider

The outsider, a standard character in Gothic lore, takes a number of roles: the criminal stalker in William GODWIN's *CALEB WILLIAMS* (1794); the bifurcated voices of the ventriloquist Carwin in

Charles Brockden BROWN's WIELAND (1798); the implacable VILLAIN-hero in Lord BYRON's THE GIAOUR (1813); the rootless, homeless MONSTER in Mary Wollstonecraft SHELLEY's FRANKENSTEIN (1818); the despised Jew Svengali in George du Maurier's MELODRAMA Trilby (1894); and a stoning victim in Shirley JACKSON's "THE LOTTERY" (1949). Emphasizing the separation between reader and outsider is often a construct of physical characteristics, as with those of the villain in Louisa May Alcott's recovered story "Taming a Tartar" (1988): "Swarthy, black-eyed, scarlet-lipped, heavy-browed and beardless, except a thick mustache. . . . A strange face, for even in repose the indescribable difference of race was visible; the contour of the head, molding of features, hue of hair and skin" (Alcott, 201). She moves from physical description to heritage by declaring that "All betrayed a trace of the savage strength and spirit of one in whose veins flowed the blood of men reared in tents, and born to lead wild lives in a wild land" (ibid.). The description echoes a classic example of exclusion of dark-skinned males in Emily BRONTË's WUTHERING HEIGHTS (1847). The gypsy boy HEATHCLIFF seems always on the outside looking in, whether among the Earnshaws with whom he lives or with the Lintons in the elegant neighboring manse. Alienation embitters him, generating jealousy and barbaric urges that bring tragedy to both families.

The outsider is frequently the bearer of an off-putting OTHERNESS. In Bram STOKER's DRACULA (1897), strangeness clings to the SHAPE-SHIFTING vampire and his victims, who succumb to his evil bite and lose their humanity in the perpetual hunger for blood meals. Clustered around Dracula are packs of wolves, his Slovak drivers, and an honor guard, the Szgany gypsies who camp in the courtyard of his castle and shoulder his square box of Transylvanian soil. Stoker describes them as outlanders living beyond the pale of law and clan-nishly attaching themselves to a Boyar aristocrat, whose surname they assume. To increase their threat, the author describes them as "fearless and without religion, save superstition" and speaking the Romanic tongue, a lingual form of otherness (Stoker, 43).

Another form of alienation derives from differences in social status, the main issue separating the governess from her employer Edward ROCHESTER in Charlotte BRONTË's JANE EYRE (1847). In Daphne DU MAURIER's REBECCA (1938), a resetting of the Brontë novel, the outsider is the unnamed heroine, an orphan and working-class companion who is unable to acclimate to life as the wife of Maxim de Winter and as the lady of the house at MANDERLEY. The workings of solitude on her self-esteem push her further into feelings of unworthiness and rejection, robbing her of joy in marriage and rescue from a lackluster existence. In 1991, playwright Tony Kushner won a Pulitzer Prize and a Tony Award for the first installment of Angels in America. The controversial drama investigates the national homophobia that turned gay AIDS victims into pariahs.

Bibliography

Alcott, Louisa May. "Taming a Tartar," in A Double Life: Newly Discovered Thrillers of Louisa May Alcott. Boston: Little, Brown, 1988.

Cohen, Jeffrey Jerome, ed. Monster Theory. Minneapolis: University of Minnesota Press, 1996.

Derrickson, Teresa. "Race and the Gothic Monster: The Xenophobic Impulse of Louisa May Alcott's 'Taming a Tartar,'" American Transcendental Quarterly 15, no. 1 (March 2001): 43.

Karl, Frederick R. The Adversary Literature: The English Novel in the Eighteenth Century—A Study in Genre. New York: Farrar, Straus & Giroux, 1974.

King, Stephen. Danse Macabre. New York: Everest House, 1981.

Stoker, Bram. Dracula. New York: Bantam Books, 1981.

P

Parsons, Eliza
(ca. 1748–1811)

A prolific female writer of DOMESTIC GOTHIC novels, Eliza Phelps Parsons flourished as translator, playwright, and author of some 60 works. Married to a Plymouth turpentine distilller for the British navy, she incurred investment losses during the American Revolution and a catastrophic fire that destroyed her husband's London storehouses. For eight years, she clerked in the Lord Chamberlain's office. In widowhood at age 40 after her eldest son's death and her husband's long decline from stroke, she needed a larger income to support the eight surviving children. In addition to sewing for the royal wardrobe, she joined the emerging Gothic school and published novels, which paid tuition for the three youngest children and underwrote two sons' entrance into the navy and three daughters' set-up in business and classroom work.

Writing under the influence of Matthew Gregory LEWIS for MINERVA PRESS, Longman, and Norbury's Brentford Press, Parsons gave a worthy picture of the laboring and servant classes. She began with *The History of Miss Meridith* (1790), a favorite of the novelist Horace WALPOLE and the Prince of Wales. Two of her works—the two-volume *The Castle of Wolfenbach; or, The Horrid Machinations of the Count Berniti* (1793) and *The Mysterious Warning* (1796), a four-volume tale of incest, seduction, SADISM, and the SUPERNATURAL—were cataloged in NORTHANGER ABBEY (1818), Jane AUSTEN's spoof of the lurid, sensational fictions that inflamed young readers' minds. The illustration for *Castle of Wolfenbach* depicts a charged moment when a man and woman open the door of a bedchamber to find a woman's torso draped like a corpse on her bed coverings. The CHIAROSCURO of the print parallels the shifts of light and dark in the thrilling plot. Similarly ominous is the engraved frontispiece for *The Mysterious Warning*, which pictures a cloaked VILLAIN abusing victims locked in a dungeon, a setting that may have influenced Francis LATHOM's melodramatic *The Midnight Bell* (1798).

In addition to sensational novels popular in CIRCULATING LIBRARIES, Parsons also translated from the French the works of Augustus La Fontaine and Molière's *Monsieur de Pourceaugnac* (1669), which opened in 1792 at Covent Garden under the title *The Intrigues of a Morning; or, An Hour in Paris*. In poor health from a shattered leg, she made enough money and received enough financial aid from the Royal Literary Fund to keep herself out of debtors' prison. Her titles remained in circulation into the mid–1800s.

Bibliography

Blakey, Dorothy. *The Minerva Press, 1790–1820.* London: Oxford University Press, 1939.

Tarr, Mary Muriel. *Catholicism in Gothic Fiction: A Study of the Nature and Function of Catholic Materials in Gothic Fiction in England, 1762–1820.* Washington, D.C.: Catholic University of America Press, 1946.

pathetic fallacy

Common to GOTHIC NARRATIVE is the pathetic fallacy, a perversion of NATURE through the imputation of human motives and emotions in weather and inanimate settings—as, for example, in the turbulent winter storm that stunts firs and forces Mr. Lockwood indoors in Emily BRONTË's WUTHERING HEIGHTS (1847) and the midnight storm and the lightning bolt that shatters the horse chestnut tree at THORNFIELD, a SYMBOL of family solidarity in Charlotte BRONTË's JANE EYRE (1847). The loss curses the betrothal of a governess and her employer, Edward ROCHESTER. The English art critic John Ruskin coined the term *pathetic fallacy* in *Modern Painters* (1856) to describe a subjectivity of MOOD that personifies some part of external nature. Ruskin used the term pejoratively to castigate weak writers for distorting natural phenomena by filtering them through personal opinion, producing hostile winds, brooding cliffs, clashing branches, and gloomy nights. In Ruskin's view, such depiction of attitude or emotion in nature constituted conceits both false and morbid.

In the romantic era, poet Percy Bysshe SHELLEY charged nature with complicity in the death of John KEATS in *Adonais* (1821). Shelley creates a Gothic scenario in stanza 28 when he complains of herds of wolves, clamoring ravens, and vultures "Who feed where Desolation first has fed, / And whose wings rain contagion" (Shelley, 488). The narrator depicts death as a stalker and despoiler of beauty and rejoices that Keats outdistanced the ominous shadows of night and earthly contagion.

Bibliography

Ruskin, John. *Modern Painters*. Boston: Dana Estes, 1873.

Shelley, Percy Bysshe. *Complete Poems of Percy Bysshe Shelley*. New York: Modern Library, 1994.

Peacock, Thomas Love
(1785–1866)

In a series of inventive conversational novels, Thomas Love Peacock produced incisive studies of characters engaged in friendly debate. After composing dark-edged verse in "The Monks of St. Mark" (1804) and the exotic "Palmyra" (1812), he abandoned Gothic and Oriental poetry to write romances. He began with *Headlong Hall* (1815) and *Melincourt* (1817), both filled with eccentrics given to alcohol abuse and self-important posturing. In his satiric roman à clef *Nightmare Abbey* (1818), he

skewers Lord BYRON, Samuel Taylor COLERIDGE, Percy Bysshe SHELLEY, and Shelley's relationships with his first and second wives. The text ridicules the conventions and motifs common to traditional Gothic romance with glimpses of a mermaid, threats of suicide by poison, GERMAN GOTHIC extremes of terror and tragedy, and the mysterious doings of the Illuminati. In a send-up of standard English mating rituals, the author mocks Gothic paganism with a morbid blood ritual, which the MELANCHOLY Scythrop Glowry proposes to Marionetta Celestina O'Carroll: "Let us each open a vein in the other's arm, mix our blood in a bowl, and drink it as a sacrament of love" (Peacock, 101). He declares that the bizarre pledge will summon transcendent visions of illumination. The suggestion causes Marionetta to flee from the tower room in a spasm of nausea.

Peacock's novel strays from the vivid action of classic Gothicism into talky scenarios in which GOTHIC CONVENTION is a frequent discussion topic. Secondary characters bear allegorical names: Mr. Lackwit, Mr. Listless, Fatout, the Reverend Mr. Larynx, the ichthyologist Mr. Asterias, and Mr. Toobad, a pious pessimist who warns that the devil stalks the abbey. In an intellectual exchange, residents at the abbey discuss the dire settings of Dante's poetry; Marionetta proposes singing the finale from Mozart's opera *Don Giovanni* (1787). In a farcical conclusion, Scythrop loses the women he pursues. Peacock's witty, frivolous writings influenced Byron, John KEATS, and Shelley, but remain marginalized from the best in romantic fiction.

Bibliography

Behrendt, Stephen C. "Questioning the Romantic Novel," *Studies in the Novel* 26, no. 2 (summer 1994): 5–25.

Mulvihill, James. "A Periodical Source for Peacock's 'Headlong Hall,'" *Notes and Queries* 44, no. 3 (September 1997): 334–335.

Peacock, Thomas Love. *The Novels of Thomas Love Peacock*. London: George Newnes, 1903.

Peake, Mervyn
(1911–1968)

A virtuoso fantasist and illustrator, Mervyn Laurence Peake developed wildly Gothic settings and characters into a depiction of the monstrous evil of World War II. Born to medical missionary parents in Kuling, China, he learned to draw by sketching deformations in patients treated at a Christian clinic. Contributing to his offbeat view of the human condition were the poverty and cruelties suffered by Chinese peasants during the collapse of the imperial dynasty. As a result of his early experiences, he remained an OUTSIDER among the English and settled on the Channel Isle of Sark, where he devoted his art to the GROTESQUE. Ironically, his life ended after a decade of tremors and crippling from encephalitis and Parkinson's disease.

After surveying the human wreckage at the liberation of Bergen-Belsen, a death camp in northern Germany, in the summer of 1945, Peake entered a morbid phase when he set about fictionalizing Nazi atrocities. He produced a darkly comic horror trilogy—*Titus Groan* (1946), *Gormenghast* (1950), and *Titus Alone* (1959)—filled with nightmarish episodes, CLAUSTROPHOBIA, eroticism, complex rituals, and fierce OBSESSIONs. Interacting with a vast gallery of cartoonish allegorical characters—Flay, Fuchsia Groan and Lady Fuchsia, Irma Prunesquallor, Lord Sepulchrave, Pentecost, Rottcodd, Sourdust, and Swelter—is the power-mongering VILLAIN Steerpike, whose eyes are the color of dried blood. For sustained horror fiction, Peake acquired a cult following, including novelist Graham Greene and poet Dylan Thomas. In 1999, the BBC adapted *Gormenghast* for television.

Bibliography

Gray, John. "Draughtman's Contract," *New Statesman* 129, no. 4,473 (February 14, 2000): 54.

Heffern, Rich. "The Real Miracle: To Walk on Earth," *National Catholic Reporter* 38, no. 6 (December 7, 2001): 37–40.

The Phantom of the Opera
Gaston Leroux
(1910)

Gaston LEROUX based his long-lived Gothic romance *The Phantom of the Opera* on resilient motifs—the Greek myths of Pygmalion and Persephone and the FAIRY TALEs "The Frog Prince," "Rumplestiltskin," and "BEAUTY AND THE BEAST." In the prologue, Leroux strives to give his story a basis in fact by outlining his method of researching the story as though it were a media article rather than fiction. Filled with MELODRAMA, the plot focuses on the Svengalian scheme of a masked psychopath named Erik, a GROTESQUE, skull-faced outlander and wanderer from Rouen. He resides in the Paris Opera House and learns the layout of its seven-story subterranean passages, a suggestion of Dante's multilevel hell. After snatching Christine Daaé, an attractive soprano, from her dressing room and removing her through a passage behind the mirror to his den in the cellar, the opera ghost satisfies his sexual longings and executes multiple killings to push her to stardom.

Leroux carefully develops psychological motivation for his VILLAIN's deviance. In the final chapter, the obsessive music master, reeking of death, utters a jerky, emotional summation of his courtship of Christine, who is "waiting for me erect and alive, a real, living bride . . . as she hoped to be saved. . . . And, when I . . . came forward, more timid than . . . a little child, she did not run away . . . no, no . . . she stayed . . . she waited for me" (Leroux, 252–253). Adaptations, beginning with translations in England and America in 1911, include ballets and a 1925 silent film version starring Lon Chaney. After a half-century of neglect, the macabre story of Erik spawned a popularized screen reprise, *The Phantom of the Paradise* (1974); a fictional romance, Susan Kay's *Phantom* (1990); and, in 1986, Andrew Lloyd Webber's romantic musical, one of Broadway's most popular shows.

Bibliography

Leroux, Gaston. *The Phantom of the Opera*. Cutchogue, N.Y.: Buccaneer Books, 1976.

"An Opera House Phantom," *New York Times*, February 19, 1911: 90.

Sauvage, Leo. "Phantom of the Opera," *New Leader* 71, no. 3 (February 22, 1988): 21–22.

Williams, Andrew P. "The Silent Threat: A (Re)viewing of the 'Sexual Other' in 'The Phantom of the Opera' and 'Nosferatu,'" *Midwest Quarterly* 38, no. 1 (autumn 1996): 90–101.

The Piano Lesson
August Wilson
(1990)

Named for Romare Bearden's painting, August WILSON's domestic drama *The Piano Lesson* pictures black family life in Pittsburgh during the Great Depression. Long after slave times, the Charles clan continues to fight plantation cruelties vicariously through a family heirloom, a piano carved with a montage of images from their lineage. Because of its tie to suffering and heinous crimes, it becomes a repository of black history and pride.

Because ownership of the piano once raised a serious controversy between the Charles ancestors and their master, Robert Sutter, VIOLENCE erupted. Guilty of theft and the burning of the carver, plantation carpenter Boy Charles was a curse on his white pursuers. The drowning deaths of the racist Sutter and Ed Saunders released racial animosity in the form of a ghost, which still haunts the piano in 1936. Contributing to hostility is Boy Willie's incarceration and service on the notorious Parchman farm, where white overseers force black convicts to toil in the fields as their ancestors did during slave times.

By depicting historic evils as a pervasive burden, Wilson uses his Gothic scenario as a commentary on how families respond to hard times and old grudges. In the words of wise Uncle Doaker Charles, the piano carries a great personal value: "It was the story of our whole family and as long as Sutter had it . . . he had us . . . we was still in slavery" (Wilson, 45). When a fierce squabble erupts over whether to keep the piano or sell it and invest the cash in farmland, the resolution requires an exorcism. Berniece, the current matriarch and possessor of the heirloom, pounds out a melody and summons ancestral spirits to restore peace and harmony. Her brother warns of the insidious nature of ghosts: "If you . . . don't keep playing on that piano . . . ain't no telling . . . me and Sutter both liable to be back" (*ibid.*, 108).

Bibliography
Boan, Devon. "Call-and-Response: Parallel 'Slave Narrative' in August Wilson's 'The Piano Lesson,'" *African American Review* 32, no. 2 (summer 1998): 263–272.

Brustein, Robert. "The Piano Lesson," *New Republic* 202, no. 21 (May 21, 1990): 28–30.

Wilson, August. *The Piano Lesson.* New York: Plume Books, 1990.

Wolfe, Peter. *August Wilson.* New York: Twayne, 1999.

The Picture of Dorian Gray
Oscar Wilde
(1891)

The Irish-born satirist and wit Oscar WILDE captured the essence of European DECADENCE in a serious Faustian MELODRAMA, *The Picture of Dorian Gray*, serialized in *Lippincott's Magazine*. The text is a haunting cautionary fable of immoderate passion based on the DOPPELGÄNGER motif. In the preface, Wilde expresses his belief that art is blameless, whether it replicates vice or virtue. As though anticipating a firestorm of disapproval, he charges the reader and critic to refrain from delving too deeply beyond the surface, lest they reveal too much about themselves.

The story of Dorian Gray, an immature narcissist drawn toward sensuality and luxury, contrasts his self-absorption with the compassion of the artist, Basil Hallward, who fears for the soul of his frivolous model. Basil warns that a false front can never conceal the vice that always emerges in facial expression and hand gestures. Hidden in an attic room, Dorian's enchanted portrait, which epitomizes an unnatural self-interest, gradually reveals its secret—the eyes of a demon, which drive the model to VIOLENCE. Wilde dresses Dorian's knifing of Basil in gruesome detail—choking sounds, arms outstretched convulsively, and blood dripping onto the carpet. As though envisioning his own doom, the killer peers down the stairwell into darkness.

The murder scene, which unmasks a heinous duality in the self-absorbed Dorian, pictures him as a shallow pleasure-seeker calmly resuming his daily activities after the savage dispatch of Basil. In a startling falling action, the model attacks the loathsome portrait with the knife he used to slay the painter: "It would kill the past, and when that was dead, he would be free. It would kill this monstrous soul-life, and without its hideous warnings, he would be at peace" (Wilde, 234). In the final throes,

Wilde reveals the twisted inner being of the hypocritical Dorian, whose corpse reverts to withered old age after he stabs his alter ego in the portrait.

Bibliography

Haslam, Richard. "Wilde's 'The Picture of Dorian Gray,'" *Explicator* 61, no. 2 (winter 2003): 96–98.

Nunokawa, Jeff. "The Importance of Being Bored: The Dividends of Ennui in 'The Picture of Dorian Gray,'" *Studies in the Novel* 28, no. 3 (fall 1996): 357–371.

Rashkin, Esther. "Art as Symptom: A Portrait of Child Abuse in 'The Picture of Dorian Gray,'" *Modern Philology* 95, no. 1 (August 1997): 68–80.

Wilde, Oscar. *The Picture of Dorian Gray and Selected Stories.* New York: New American Library, 1983.

"The Pit and the Pendulum"
Edgar Allan Poe
(1843)

Anthologized in *The Gift: A Christmas and New Year's Present*, Edgar Allan POE's suspenseful dungeon lore depicts the helplessness and psychological torment of a political prisoner suffering a doom-laden enclosure in a dark chamber. Influenced by William MUDFORD's "The Iron Shroud" (1830), which Poe read in BLACKWOOD'S EDINBURGH MAGAZINE, "The Pit and the Pendulum" takes place in Toledo during the Spanish Inquisition and reprises the terrors of an era when the Roman Catholic Church victimized Jews, Muslims, and accused heretics. The persecution was a true horror story from history that permeated many anti-Catholic Gothic novels and chapbooks.

For a fictional glimpse of the era's horrors, Poe offers no personal or place names, but builds on sensational details—the protagonist's immobility amid multiple perils, a tomb-like cell, fungal smell, drugged food and water, a pit full of rats, hot iron walls, and the ultimate horror, a swinging metal arm that inch-by-inch arcs a honed edge over the victim's torso. Worsening the man's sufferings are the rumors he has heard of arcane miseries dreamed up by fanatical monks to punish apostates and those who scoff at Catholicism. Poe applies irony to the prisoner's escape after rats gnaw through the bindings that he has smeared with his prison rations. A subsequent hell awaits as the prison walls grow hot. At the last moment, the author releases his protagonist through an unforeseen deus ex machina, the arrival of General Lasalle and the French army.

Bibliography

Heller, Terry. *The Delights of Terror: An Aesthetics of the Tale of Terror.* Urbana: University of Illinois Press, 1987.

Symons, Julian. *The Tell-Tale Heart: The Life and Works of Edgar Allan Poe.* New York: Harper & Row, 1978.

Poe, Edgar Allan
(1809–1849)

A genius of macabre operatic plots and suspenseful pacing, Edgar Allan Poe earned the title of father of modern horror literature. He lived a life replete with some of the Gothic elements of his stories and poems. An orphan at age two, he survived a pinch-mouthed godfather and barely tolerant foster mother and sank into gambling, dissipation, alcohol and laudanum abuse, and financial and social profligacy. He read voraciously and came under the influence of Gothic romance, particularly the Teutonic terror tales of E. T. A. HOFFMANN, William BECKFORD's VATHEK (1782), frontier INSANITY in John Neal's Gothic *Logan* (1822) and *Rachel Dyer* (1828), a story of religious bigotry based on the Salem witch trials of 1692. In his late teens, Poe anonymously published *Tamerlane and Other Poems* (1827), a preface to his failure as a soldier at West Point and the rise of his career as a writer for the *Baltimore Saturday Visitor* and editor of the *Southern Literary Messenger*. His marriage at age 26 to Virginia Clemm, a cousin half his age, precipitated in his writings a series of unrequited loves, heartsick lovers, and frail, sinking damsels.

Poorly housed and fed in Lower Manhattan and Philadelphia, Poe read widely and came under the influence of the English poet and critic Samuel Taylor COLERIDGE, author of "CHRISTABEL" (1816), "KUBLA KHAN" (1816), and *Biographia Literaria* (1817), a seminal work that shaped Poe's literary standards and philosophy. Poe also absorbed the subjective power of Thomas De Quincey's dreamy *Confessions of an English Opium Eater* (1821). Poe had already set his course toward Gothic themes with the poem "The Lake" (1827), a wistful study of NATURE, solitude, and mortality. He continued editing and writing for *Godey's Magazine and Lady's Book* and the *Philadelphia Saturday Courier*, explored his interest in cryptography and decoding, and interviewed the British novelist Charles DICKENS in 1842, whose crime novel *OLIVER TWIST* (1838) Poe greatly admired.

As his literary skills developed, Poe applied them almost exclusively to writing Gothic poems and stories. His early poem "The Sleeper" (1831) is a sensational death lyric that focuses on worms riddling a corpse. One of his horror stories, *Berenice* (1835), which features grave robbing and a morbid obsession with the teeth and odor of a corpse, bore an implication of VAMPIRISM, a subject that had enjoyed popularity in England since the publication of John POLIDORI's *The Vampyre* (1819). Poe showcased ghasty details in the poem "Bridal Ballad" (1837) and in *Tales of the Grotesque and Arabesque* (1839), which included an apocalyptic dialogue, "The Conversation of Eiros and Charmion." A later story, "The Colloquy of Monos and Una" (1841), published in *Graham's Magazine*, described the reunion of dead lovers who share the physical symptoms of dying. With his wife's physical decline from tuberculosis in 1842, the author became fixated on mortality and clung to shreds of reason. One tale of a doomed beauty, "Eleonora" (1842), describes the fears of the dying and the widower's travels in search of emotional release. The story proved prophetic of Poe's misery and creative ESCAPISM through Gothic fiction and verse.

At the height of his MELANCHOLY, Poe coordinated the disparate elements of his genius— beauty, loss, death, and horror, all set in European or exotic settings. While editing *Graham's Magazine* and writing columns for the New York City *Evening Mirror*, in 1844, he published an AMERICAN GOTHIC masterwork, "The Raven," the anchor of *The Raven and Other Poems* (1845). He may have developed the poem from an image in Dickens's *Barnaby Rudge* (1841), which Poe reviewed. He pondered a new element of SENSATIONALISM in "Some Words with a Mummy" (1845), a far-fetched adventure tale. In the poem "Eulalie: A Song" (1845), he expressed a longing for release from fears through union with a radiant, other-worldly soulmate.

Virginia's death from throat hemorrhage on January 29, 1847, preceded her husband's downward slide into alcoholism and neurotic self-absorption. During the worst of his mental and physical torments, he produced his last four poems—the ghoulish "ULALUME" (1847), the ominous "The Bells" (1848), the tender love poem "For Annie" (1849), and the mournful "Annabel Lee" (1849), a tribute to the poet's dead wife, which the New York *Tribune* published along with the author's obituary on October 9, 1849. His last lyric verse was a source for composers, including Irish musician William Charles Levey's art song "Many a Year Ago" (1866), English musician Henry Leslie's somber concert piece, "Annabelle Lee: The Beautiful Classic Ballad" (1891), and German pianist George Liebling's song "Annabel Lee" (1934).

Poe was a master of the technical elements of verse, including caesura, inversion, repetition, and rhetorical question; equally, in prose, he had consummate skill in manipulating the drama of character duality, SUSPENSE, morbidity, intimidating ATMOSPHERE, unresolved conflict, and escalating psychotic obsession, the motivation in "THE TELL-TALE HEART" and "THE BLACK CAT," both written in 1843. He set the parameters for numerous Gothic subgenres, notably, the DETECTIVE STORY ("THE MURDERS IN THE RUE MORGUE"), Gothic escapism ("THE MASQUE OF THE RED DEATH" and "THE PIT AND THE PENDULUM"), the prison of the self ("Descent into the Maelstrom"), and the sustained poetic lament ("Ulalume" and "Annabel Lee"). In his landmark essay on criticism, "The Philosophy of Composition," issued in the April 1846 edition of *Graham's Magazine*, Poe set forth an ideal of the most engaging elements of melancholy. To attain an elegiac height, he advised the author to link ephemeral loveliness and death by presenting the demise of a beautiful woman. He applied this motif in "The Raven," his most cited poem, and in his widely acclaimed short fiction, notably, "LIGEIA" (1838) and "THE FALL OF THE HOUSE OF USHER" (1839). His compelling motifs influenced other 19th-century art, particularly, Nathaniel HAWTHORNE's "The Birthmark" (1843) and Anglo-Italian poet Dante Gabriel Rossetti's paintings and sonnet sequence honoring his dead wife, Elizabeth Siddal.

Poe masterminded evocative works in which he juxtaposed looming evils against pallid, alluring young maidens, usually noble and unattainable, like chivalric models from the Middle Ages. Some are disordered and enervated by vague maladies and the approach of death. In the words of Angela CARTER, author of *Fireworks* (1974), Poe's Gothicism "grandly ignores the value systems of our institutions; it deals entirely with the profane. Its great themes are incest and cannibalism. Character and events are exaggerated beyond reality, to become symbols, ideas, passions" (Carter, 122). She characterized his style as "ornate, unnatural. . . . Its only humour is black humour. It retains a singular moral function—that of provoking unease" (*ibid.*). To detach himself from urban life on the Atlantic seaboard, Poe set events in such romantic locales and milieus as Batavia, the Faubourg St. Germain in Paris, Europe during the Black Death and the Spanish Inquisition, and Venice during Carnival. He enhanced his depiction of fearful terrain with such lyric terms as *crag, parterre, tarn,* and *vortex.* Over his failing women, he placed egotistical, often lethal males like the jangled Roderick USHER, the frenzied husband of Ligeia, and the wife-slayer in "The Black Cat."

Poe's influence and reputation soared posthumously in France, where he was hailed by the novelist André Gide, critics Paul Claudel and Paul Valéry, short story writer VILLIERS DE L'ISLE-ADAM, and the romantic poet Charles BAUDELAIRE. Stéphane Mallarmé immortalized his hero in the sonnet "Le Tombeau d'Edgar Poe" (Edgar Poe's Tomb, 1876), which extols the love of beauty. Enthusiasm for Poe's works spread to the Swedish writer Ola Hansson, the Irish novelist James Joyce, the English poets Ernest Dowson and Algernon Swinburne, the Irish-born wit and playwright Oscar WILDE, and the short fiction writers Ambrose BIERCE, Hart Crane, and Robert Louis STEVENSON, all of whom imitated Poe's command of Gothic stylistic detail and motifs. From Europe's embrace of Poe's peculiar genius came American literary success among critics who recognized the insight of his literary criticism and the lyric command of language, rhythm, tone, and atmosphere in his brooding verse and psychological thrillers.

As realism began supplanting Gothic literature, a growing tide of anti-Poe feeling arose in the 20th century. In 1930, Aldous Huxley refuted early acclaim of Poe in *Vulgarity in Literature,* a critique that accused him of producing mechanical rhythms and writing in egregiously bad taste. H. P. LOVECRAFT negated Huxley's remarks in *Supernatural Horror in Literature* (1945), in which he named Poe as the fount of Gothic artistry. Films of *The Fall of the House of Usher* (1960), *The Pit and the Pendulum* (1961), *The Premature Burial* (1962), *The Raven* (1963), *The Haunted Palace* (1963), *The Masque of the Red Death* (1964), *Ligeia* (1965), *The City under the Sea* (1965), *The Conqueror Worm* (1968), *The Oblong Box* (1969), and *The Murders in the Rue Morgue* (1971) established in cinema some of the Gothic techniques that Poe pioneered in literature.

Bibliography

Carter, Angela. *Fireworks: Nine Profane Pieces.* New York: Harper & Row, 1974.

Labriola, Patrick. "Edgar Allan Poe and E. T. A. Hoffmann: The Double in 'William Wilson' and 'The Devil's Elixirs,'" *International Fiction Review* 29, nos. 1–2 (January 2002): 69–77.

Symons, Julian. *The Tell-Tale Heart: The Life and Works of Edgar Allan Poe.* New York: Harper & Row, 1978.

Polidori, John
(1795–1821)

John William Polidori, Lord BYRON's secretary and personal physician, initiated English vampire lore. He published a vampire thriller in *Colburn's New Monthly Magazine* in April 1819 for a fee of £30. "The Vampyre" had its beginning in a brainstorming session among some of England's most influential romanticists. During the rainy summer of 1816, Polidori shared the Villa Diodati on Lake Geneva with four giants of the romantic age—Byron, Matthew Gregory LEWIS, Mary Wollstonecraft SHELLEY, and Percy Bysshe SHELLEY. To pass the time until the weather brightened, the company engaged in a competition to decide who could compose the best GHOST STORY in the tradition of the German *Schauerroman* ("shudder novel").

Influenced by European legends and late 18th-century German horror literature, Polidori apparently performed after Byron's "A Fragment of a Novel" (1819), the story of the vampire Darvell preying on a Turkish graveyard. Polidori incorporated the TONE and style as well as elements of Byron's THE GIAOUR (1813) in his own morbid tale. He departed from the stereotypical automaton to create the first peripatetic vampire and the first described as an individual nobleman. To further distance the wicked from the innocent and exploit an erotic SUBTEXT, Polidori dwelled on the wedding-night predation of the sinister vampire on his bride, a tender, unsuspecting NAIF. When Polidori's carnal version reached print, the publisher at first boosted sales by claiming that the author was Byron, who distanced himself from a work less polished than his own.

Unlike tales of previous folk vampires, Polidori's sex-charged narrative features a Gothic prototype, Lord Ruthven, a name the author took from Lady Caroline LAMB's tell-all Gothic MELODRAMA *Glenarvon* (1816), a confessional account of her affair with Byron. Polidori's Ruthven is a refined and charismatic roué who set the style of enlightened vampire stories. Mannered, aristocratic, and as appealing as the BYRONIC HERO, the vampire entranced an educated company before despoiling the maiden Ianthe. Critics believe that the author's subconscious motivation for the attack was a pervasive fear that Victorians had of handsome, unscrupulous exploiters who might overpower their daughters, then abandon them to moral and social ruin. Of particular danger was the fortune-hunting OUTSIDER who disrespected bourgeois British values.

However brief Polidori's Ruthven was in the original composition, he proved to be a long-lived character in literature. Contemporaneous with Mary Wollstonecraft Shelley's FRANKENSTEIN (1818), Polidori's story was translated into French, German, Spanish, and Swedish. The suave Ruthven was a forerunner of opera and stage versions, such as the French playwrights Pierre Adrien Carmouche, Achile de Jouffroy, and Jean Charles Nodier's three-act melodrama *Le Vampire* (1820), the first stage vampire, which debuted at the Theatre de la Porte Saint-Martin; the Scots vampire bridegroom in James Robinson Planché's stage musical *The Vampire; or, The Bride of the Isles* (1820); Ukrainian author Nikolai GOGOL's short story "Viy" (1835), a terror tale of a priest's prayers in a crypt beside the corpse of a beautiful female ghoul; and another French version, Théophile GAUTIER's *La Morte Amoureuse* (The dead lover, 1836). Polidori also influenced the work that was the apex of Europe's literary vampirism, Bram STOKER's DRACULA (1897), and its numerous literary, cinematic, television, and computer game spin-offs.

Bibliography

Auerbach, Nina. *Our Vampires, Ourselves.* Chicago: University of Chicago Press, 1995.

Twitchell, James B. *The Living Dead: A Study of the Vampire in Romantic Literature.* Durham, N.C.: Duke University Press, 1981.

White, Pamela C. "Two Vampires of 1828," *Opera Quarterly* 5 (spring 1987): 22–57.

Porter, Jane
(1776–1850)

Jane Porter was one of the early Gothic writers of romanticized historical fiction and GOTHIC BLUE-BOOK thrillers. She grew up in Scotland and read widely in chivalric romance, a genre that also captured the imagination of her sister, the novelist Anna Maria Porter. For William Lane's MINERVA PRESS, Jane issued a popular story of Poland's General Tadeusz Kosciusko as *Thaddeus of Warsaw* (1803), in which she overwhelmed historical data with rhapsodic ROMANTICISM. Fascinated with heroism, she followed with *The Campaigns of Count Alexander Suwarrow Rymnikski* (1804) and the two-volume *The Scottish Chiefs* (1810), an imaginative 13th-century story about the martyred rebel William Wallace, who died a gory death. His friend Gloucester cried, "there broke the noblest heart, that ever beat in the breast of man!" (Porter, cover). The grandly melodramatic death scene prefaces additional grief over Wallace's execution and his loss to Scotland.

In 1828 and again in 1840, Porter reissued the popular melodramatic work, with its emblazoned arras, hermit's cell, and ominous prison and tower as settings. The novel fueled a rage for Scottish lore and culture. It was a source for Charles Robert

MATURIN's *The Milesian Chief* (1812) and influenced the historical novels of Sir Walter SCOTT and the film *Braveheart* (1995). Porter continued her resettings of history with three plays: *The Pastor's Fireside* (1817) about the Stuart dynasty; *Duke Christian of Luneberg: or, Traditions of the Harz* (1824), on the ancestry of George IV; and *Sir Edward Seaward's Narrative of His Shipwreck* (1831), a Caribbean fiction that mimicked the conventions of a diary. Shortly before her death, the translation of *The Scottish Chiefs* into German earned Porter the Cross of Lady of the Teutonic Order of Saint Joachim.

Bibliography

Blakey, Dorothy. *The Minerva Press, 1790–1820.* London: Oxford University Press, 1939.

Porter, Jane. *The Scottish Chiefs.* New York: Athenaeum, 1991.

possession

Possession by demons, DYBBUKs, ghosts, or evil spirits permeates diabolic stories and psychological novels and plays, seizing the minds and souls of such memorable characters as the wicked cleric SCHEDONI in Ann RADCLIFFE's THE ITALIAN (1797), the title character in Robert Louis STEVENSON's dialect tale "Thrawn Janet" (1887), the ill-fated lover in S. Ansky's Hebrew drama *Der Dybbuk* (1916), and the hotelier in Toni MORRISON's *Love* (2003). In 1911, Bram STOKER allied the theme of possession with MONSTER lore in *The Lair of the White Worm.* In 1935, Isaac Bashevis SINGER advanced the concept by describing a whole community in satanic bondage in *Der Sotn in Gorey* (*Satan in Goray*). Aldous Huxley sharpened the face-to-face conflict between good and evil with nuns thrown into frenetic writhing in *The Devils of Loudun* (1952).

Seizure of fictional characters results in mental and emotional stress, bizarre personality traits, speaking in tongues or with a devil's voice, ecstatic trances, and other forms of ABERRANT BEHAVIOR, such as the fits suffered by Edmund Bezant and relieved by the mystic inscription of Ptolemy Horoscope in the anonymous "The Possessed One" (1831) and the hysteria of teenage girls in Arthur MILLER's play THE CRUCIBLE (1953). Control by a malevolent spirit is a useful SYMBOL of the authoritarianism and governmental control people face in their everyday lives. By identifying with the victim in a Gothic tale of possession, the audience or reader finds an outlet for the frustrations and fears of big business, patriarchal and fundamental religion, the police or military, and more powerful forms of tyranny and brainwashing.

The exorcism of a demonic power is often the most dramatic element of a text on possession. The Danish storyteller Hans Christian ANDERSEN wrote a fearful tale about the vindictive power controlling an enthusiastic young dancer in "The Red Shoes" (1845). The ALLEGORY describes the girl's punishment for vanity and self-indulgence in refusing to remove her dance shoes when she attends mass. When her shoes take on a life of their own and dance across fields and through churchyards, she earns an angel's scolding for lack of piety. In the end, the only cure for frantic dancing feet is the headsman's ax, which chops off the girl's feet, leaving the shoes to trip away on their own. With publication of William Peter Blatty's bestseller *The Exorcist* (1971), controversy arose over depiction of actual Catholic exorcism ritual, which consumes the plot of the terrifying Gothic novel. In 1973, a film version depicting Max von Sydow in combat with Satan contributed to the notoriety of Blatty's novel.

Bibliography

Nickell, Joe. "Exorcism! Driving Out the Nonsense," *Skeptical Inquirer* 25, no. 1 (January 2001): 20.

Serper, Zvika. "'Between Two Worlds': The Dybbuk and the Japanese Noh and Kabuki Ghost Plays," *Comparative Drama* 2001, no. 3 (fall 2001): 345–376.

premature burial

A morbid focus of HORROR NARRATIVES is the subject of premature burial, a popular concern in detective magazines and GOTHIC BLUEBOOKS before the advent of death certificates, professional mortuaries, and embalming. Because of the amplification of public fears from spurious articles about people buried alive, various inventions—breathing tubes, bell cords, and banners—offered some reassurance that any living person immured in a coffin or vault could signal for help. Authors exploited the issue of hasty interment, which enhanced claustrophobic elements to Gothic fiction. Sir Walter SCOTT wrote of deliberate immurement in *Marmion, a Tale of Flodden Field* (1807), a romantic narrative about the love of the nun Constance for the disloyal knight Marmion, for whom she renounces the veil. In punishment for violating her vows, in canto 2, Benedictine judges order her bricked into the wall of a dungeon at Whitby Abbey.

Untimely burial is a pervasive motif in the poems and stories of Gothic horror narratives. The master of the concept was Edgar Allan POE, who may have become fascinated by slow suffocation from reading, at age 10, a review of John Snart's gruesome "Thesaurus of Horror: or, The Charnel House Explored!" in the June 1819 issue of BLACK-WOOD'S EDINBURGH MAGAZINE. Snart remarked in his text, "If dramatic writers want a transcendent figure for their future fictions, to harrow up the soul! let them find the motive to it in the untimely grave!!" (Brown, 14). Poe took Snart's advice and developed fear of live burial and slow suffocation in "Berenice" (1835), THE NARRATIVE OF ARTHUR GORDON PYM (1838), "LIGEIA" (1838), "THE FALL OF THE HOUSE OF USHER" (1839), "The Black Cat" (1843), "THE CASK OF AMONTILLADO" (1846), and "The Premature Burial" (1844), a story issued in the July issue of the *Philadelphia Dollar Newspaper*.

Poe based his versions of premature interment on the burial of an attractive Frenchwoman, Victorine Lafourcade, whose lover retrieved her body from burial and restored her to health. A 1961 film version and *Buried Alive*, a 1990 television horror movie, offered only token nods to Poe's originals. The subject also appealed to Ellen WOOD for the GHOST STORY "The Punishment of Gina Montani" (1852), to Charlotte BRONTË for an anti-Catholic story-within-a-story ghost legend in VILLETTE (1853), and to Gertrude ATHERTON for use in the macabre tale "The Dead and the Countess" (1905), a story of a priest's accidental interment of a living person. Victoria HOLT's best-seller MISTRESS OF MELLYN (1960) depicts the heroine, Martha Leigh, temporarily walled up in a priest's hole at a Cornish estate along with the corpse of a VILLAIN's previous victim.

Bibliography

Brown, Byron K. "John Snart's 'Thesaurus of Horror': An Indirect Source of Poe's 'The Premature Burial'?," *ANQ* 8, no. 3 (summer 1995): 11–14.

"Premature Burial," *Journal of the American Medical Association* 279, no. 3 (January 21, 1998): 182.

Scandura, Jani. "Deadly Professions: Dracula, Undertakers, and the Embalmed Corpse," *Victorian Studies* 40, no. 1 (autumn 1996): 1–31.

Pre-Raphaelite Brotherhood

In 1848, the Pre-Raphaelite Brotherhood, a coterie of young writers and painters, formed an influential philosophical movement that inserted MEDIEVALISM into ROMANTICISM. Their intent was to dislodge the fine arts from their rut by injecting more vibrant themes, settings, and characters. Among the idealistic poets and artists protesting the predictability and conventionality of the Victorian era were Dante Gabriel Rossetti, William Holman Hunt, Edward Burne-Jones, Algernon Charles Swinburne, Ford Madox Brown, John Everett Millais, and William Morris, all of whom wanted to rescue painting and verse from artificiality and corruption. They took their cues from FOLKLORE, medieval art and romance, and the symbolic poems and drawings of William Blake. At the forefront of the Pre-Raphaelite rebellion was a desire to return to untrammeled NATURE, an honest expression that the English critic John Ruskin praised in *Modern Painters* (1856).

Essential to Pre-Raphaelite tenets were freshness, thematic sincerity, pictorial integrity, arcane Catholic symbolism, sensuous detail, archaic diction, and attention to medievalism, intuition, metaphysical states, magic, and the SUPERNATURAL. The men were well read, particularly in the Gothic innovations of Edgar Allan POE, whose poem "The City in the Sea" (1845) charmed and pleased Swinburne. The brotherhood's Gothic tendencies influenced the mystic sensuality and CHIAROSCURO shadings of Rossetti's "The Portrait" (1847), the primitive fight to the death in William Morris's poem "Riding Together" (1856) and the FAIRY TALE essence of female confinement in his poem "Rapunzel" (1858), and romantic brigandage in Swinburne's "A Ballad of François Villon" (1878), a salute to a BYRONIC

HERO praising "our sad bad glad mad brother's name" (Swinburne, 88). The Pre-Raphaelite focus prefigured the extremes of DECADENCE that crept into the arts late in the 19th century.

Bibliography

Bullen, J. B. "An Anthology of Pre-Raphaelite Writings," *Notes and Queries* 45, no. 3 (September 1998): 399–400.

Canaday, John. "The Rise and Fall and Rise Again of the Pre-Raphaelite Brotherhood," *Smithsonian* 14 (November 1983): 72–81.

Cervo, Nathan. "Morris's 'Rapunzel,'" *Explicator* 51, no. 3 (spring 1993): 167–169.

preromanticism

The preromantic tendencies of the mid- to late 1700s prefigured the full flowering of ROMANTICISM in 1798. The preromantics were writers eager to escape the artificial grandeur, elitism, austerity, and confining ideals of neoclassicism to confer sincerity and freedom of expression on their art. The movement reflected a shift from aristocratic elegance to the beliefs, tastes, and interests of an emerging industrial class. More primitive and less refined, preromantic literature promoted the admiration of natural beauty, preservation of FOLKLORE, and the free flow of spontaneous emotion, including the terror, MYSTERY, savagery, and OBSESSIONs of the GOTHIC NARRATIVE.

Among the loosely organized tenets of the movement was an embrace of primitivism, sentimentality, SENSATIONALISM, and picturesque outdoor settings, a return to NATURE found in GOTHIC NOVELS and ballads. A contributing factor to Gothic sensibilities, preromanticism stressed the lament or dirge as an essential form of spiritual release. In Edward Young's *Night Thoughts* (1743), the MELANCHOLY and morbidity of graveyard poesy suffuses the speaker's welcome to death, "the crown of life," recognized by "dreaded harbingers, age and disease; disease, though long my guest; that plucks my nerves, those tender strings of life" (Young, 4, 5). In 1762, James Macpherson forged a sensational romance, the Ossian manuscripts—purportedly translations of epic poems by an ancient Gaelic poet, Ossian—in emulation of Irish

sagas. His popular work incorporates an eerie death cry in "Colma's Lament": "Cold, cold are their breasts of clay. Oh! from the rock on the hill; from the top of the windy steep, speak ye ghosts of the dead! speak, I will not be afraid!" (Macpherson, 55). Macpherson's embrace of the SUPERNATURAL presaged the birth of European Gothicism.

Bibliography

Macpherson, James. *The Poems of Ossian and Related Works.* Edinburgh: Edinburgh University Press, 1996.

Young, Edward. *Night Thoughts or the Complaint and the Consolation.* New York: Dover, 1996.

prescience

Found in the works of Ray BRADBURY, Samuel Taylor COLERIDGE, Joyce Carol OATES, Maria Regina ROCHE, and Bram STOKER, prescience, or foreknowledge of events to come, is a common facet of Gothic fiction. Unlike FORESHADOWING, which readies the reader for danger, prescience alerts the characters themselves, as with the minister's fear of the drowning death that awaits him in Australian novelist Peter Carey's COLONIAL GOTHIC novel OSCAR AND LUCINDA (1988). In a classic example, "THE FALL OF THE HOUSE OF USHER" (1839), Edgar Allan POE equips Roderick USHER with a foretaste of his family's eradication, a creepy terror of collapse that haunts him and unnerves his unnamed guest. Similarly, Charlotte BRONTË builds into the action of *JANE EYRE* (1847) a series of portents. Through dreams, the title character anticipates her future. She recognizes from the lightning bolt that destroys a horse chestnut tree after Edward ROCHESTER's garden proposal that their relationship will be plagued by serious obstacles and suffering. When Jean RHYS revisited the novel with her own work, *Wide Sargasso Sea* (1966), she preserved the prescience of Brontë's novel in Antoinette's foreknowledge that England would be cold and unwelcoming and her marriage doomed. In each of these examples, however, prescience offers the characters no power to elude or stave off catastrophe.

A less fearful model of foreknowledge invests Isabel ALLENDE's Latin American saga *THE HOUSE*

OF THE SPIRITS (1981). She heightens suspense through the visions and foreknowledge of Clara, the protagonist, whom her granddaughter Alba describes as "the soul of the big house" (Allende, 283). The warning of chaos to come encourages Clara to rely on extrasensory perception, DREAMS, and foresight to weather hardships, including the earthquake that destroys Tres Marias, the Trueba hacienda. In childhood, Clara awakens screaming and anticipates an unspecified family death, the poisoning of her sister Rosa, which occurs within days. Clara also envisions the beheading of her mother Nívea in a train-car collision and communes with the REVENANT spirit of Férula, Clara's sister-in-law, before learning of her demise. When Clara's death approaches, she uses the remaining time to good purpose, distributing her belongings, organizing her papers, and tying her notebooks in ribbons as a gift to her daughter Blanca as guideposts to the future. During preparations for death, Clara seems "to be detaching herself from the world, growing ever lighter, more transparent, more winged" as she retreats fearlessly into the dark world beyond (*ibid., 289*).

Bibliography

Allende, Isabel. *The House of the Spirits.* New York: Bantam Books, 1982.

Hustis, Harriet. "'Reading Encrypted But Persistent'· The Gothic of Reading and Poe's 'The Fall of the House of Usher,'" *Studies in American Fiction* 27, no. 1 (spring 1999): 3.

Prest, Thomas Preskett

(1810–1879)

Thomas Preskett (or Peckett) Prest was a prolific storyteller popular during the Victorian era. He started his career writing songs for the popular stage and translating French MELODRAMA for London's Britannia Theatre. By 1835, he found his metier in Gothic horror. One of the energetic hacks for the popular press, he flourished at GOTHIC BLUEBOOKS, parodies of the novels of Charles DICKENS, and short fiction collected in *The Calendar of Horrors* (1839) and published by Fleet Street horror entrepreneur Edward Lloyd under a string of pen names. In the latter anthology, Prest compiled "The Demon of the Hartz," a MONSTER tale of a giant laughing demon set in Germany's Hartz Mountains, a locale connected with witchcraft and diablerie.

Prest attained fame for two horror novels, *The Skeleton Clutch; or, The Goblet of Gore* (1842) and *The Black Monk; or, The Street of the Grey Turret* (1844), which he cribbed from works by Matthew Gregory LEWIS and Ann RADCLIFFE. From Prest's *The String of Pearls* (1846) derived a melodrama that Stephen Sondheim evolved into the musical *Sweeney Todd* (1979), based on a quasi-historical story of a demonic barber who turns corpses into meat pies. Prest may also have authored VARNEY THE VAMPIRE; *or, The Feast of Blood* (1847), a long-running serial also identified as the work of James Malcolm Rymer.

Bibliography

Barber, Paul. *Vampires, Burial, and Death: Folklore and Reality.* New Haven, Conn.: Yale University Press, 1988.

Cohen, Jeffrey Jerome, ed. *Monster Theory.* Minneapolis: University of Minnesota Press, 1996.

Gates, Barbara T. *Victorian Suicide: Mad Crimes and Sad Histories.* Princeton, N.J.: Princeton University Press, 1988.

Prévost, Abbé

(1697–1763)

A major source of the Gothic movement stems from France and the writings of Abbé Antoine-François Prévost d'Exiles, a prolific Flemish scholar, author, translator, and master storyteller. His picaresque works became a preromantic touchstone by importing MELANCHOLY, the SUPERNATURAL, tragedy, and terror into a subgenre of Gothic fiction called ROMAN NOIR (black novel). Much of his past is a mystery complicated by picaresque brushes with the law. He was educated by Jesuits and volunteered in the French army before taking orders with the Benedictines of St. Maur. In rebellion against oppressive religious dogma, he gave up his priestly duties and turned to writing.

A brief stay in Paris and a two-year sojourn in Holland gave Prévost the privacy to write in secret a seven-volume romance, *Mémoires d'un Homme de Qualité* (Memoirs of a man of quality, 1728–31), which he intended to encourage religious tolerance. At age 30, he abandoned religion to live in London and write *Histoire de Cleveland* (The story of Cleveland, 1731–39), a tale of New World settings and swashbuckling heroics by an alleged son of Oliver Cromwell. The episodic plot, which carries the protagonist to a native tribe in South America, appealed to the curiosity of English readers. Prévost filled his stories with OMENs and DREAMs, tyrannic VILLAINs, BYRONIC HEROes, and the ruins and DUNGEONS AND PRISONs that anchored the GOTHIC NOVEL to a chilling ATMOSPHERE. His notion of rearing children in a cave provided Sophia LEE with a primitive motif for *The Recess* (1783–85).

English writers imitated subsequent works by Prévost, particularly the resilient novel *L'Histoire du Chevalier des Grieux et de Manon Lescaut* (The story of Chevalier des Grieux and of Manon Lescaut, 1731), a segment of *Mémoires d'un Homme de Qualité*, a tale of obsessive love. It was the first official French novel of passion and one of the great romances of the century. Prévost edited a London periodical, *Le Pour et Contre* (For and Against, 1733–40), and translated into French the sentimental novels of Samuel Richardson and the plays of John Dryden. At age 37, Prévost fled mounting debt, retreated once more to the French Benedictines in Chantilly, and served as the chaplain and historiographer of the Prince de Conti. The demand for more of Prévost's engaging tales inspired the novels of French imitator Baculard d'Arnaud and of English Gothic writers Clara REEVE, Ann RADCLIFFE, and Charlotte SMITH, the chief replicator of French sensibilities and the translator of Prévost's *Manon Lascaut* as *The Romance of Real Life* (1787), a summation of French criminal activities.

Bibliography

Brady, Valentini Papadopoulou. "'Manon Lescaut, C'est Lui': A Study of Point of View in Prévost's 'Manon Lescaut,'" *Intertexts* 5, no. 2 (fall 2001): 156–168.

Horner, Avril, ed. *European Gothic: A Spirited Exchange, 1760–1960*. Manchester: Manchester University Press, 2002.

"The Prisoner of Chillon"
George Gordon, Lord Byron
(1816)

To give psychological insight into a prisoner's mindset, the romantic poet Lord BYRON turned to a confinement motif in "The Prisoner of Chillon" (1816), a picturesque narrative set in a gloomy dungeon among family graves. The poem, based on the immurement of the 16th-century Swiss freedom fighter François Bonivard at Lake Geneva, depicts an intimidating ATMOSPHERE and MELANCHOLY yearnings as elements of the theme of liberty, which religious chaos denies the unnamed political prisoner. The horrors of war, which cost him all six of his family members, reduce him to mental torment worsened by inactivity. As the only survivor out of seven, he half-heartedly endures the sounds of waves above his subterranean cell as he hardens into a stone among stones.

Byron stresses the prison staff's role in perpetuating horror and notes the emergence of their humanity. Early in his captivity, the speaker pleads with cruel captors for a burial in sunshine for his brothers, but the unidentified jailers smirk and inter the last of the prisoner's siblings in hard-packed earth topped by empty fetters—a grim, unyielding monument. When compassion leads them to unchain the last prisoner, freedom of movement allows him to peer at the mountains beyond the Rhône and take comfort in NATURE. The poet ends his intuitive work with the hopelessness and melancholy of a liberated man whose suffering is unrelieved by his release from Chillon's walls.

Bibliography

LaChance, Charles. "Naive and Knowledgeable Nihilism in Byron's Gothic Verse," *Papers on Language & Literature* 32, no. 4 (fall 1996): 339–368.

Phillipson, Mark. "Byron's Revisited Haunts," *Studies in Romanticism* 39, no. 2 (summer 2000): 303.

psychological interpretation

Since the late 19th century, the advance of analytic psychology provided literature with a vocabulary and frame of reference for interpreting Gothic writings from a humanistic point of view. As the original Gothic novel evolved from implied and actual wickedness, romancers developed the VILLAIN-hero, a satanic figure who personified dark unconscious drives toward cruelty and revenge, as demonstrated in the demonic side of the human personality in Robert Louis STEVENSON's *DR. JEKYLL AND MR. HYDE* (1886), the repressed homoeroticism in Bram STOKER's *DRACULA* (1897), the need to control a sex object in Gaston LEROUX's *THE PHANTOM OF THE OPERA* (1910), and jealousy in Daphne DU MAURIER's *REBECCA* (1938). Through symbolic threats and violent acts, depraved and superhuman Gothic creations performed deeds that represent to the reader such unconventional or taboo subjects as sex between mates of differing social rank, rape, sodomy, bestiality, and necrophilia. The thrill that readers obtained from Gothic fiction provided an opportunity for a private and diminutive rebellion against social strictures.

At the height of traditional Gothic writing, Joanna BAILLIE's writings offered a progression of psychological studies in Gothic drama. In 1798, she introduced *A Series of Plays on the Passions*, in which she examined facets of human emotions over a 14-year period. In *De Montfort: A Tragedy on Hatred* (1800), a psychological thriller, she heightened audience involvement with blatantly terrifying settings and sound effects. Like the ancient Greeks, who revered emotional catharsis as a religious purging of negative impulses, she believed that the theatrical experience was enlightening and uplifting for playgoers.

Psychologists referred to classic fiction for examples of human failings, such as the cruelty of Medea and the madness of Ajax in Greek mythology and the mental deterioration of the queen in William Shakespeare's *Macbeth* (ca. 1603). Favorites of clinicians were characters and behaviors in the Gothic works of Truman CAPOTE, Lewis Carroll, Arthur MILLER, Edgar Allan POE, Jean RHYS, Mary Wollstonecraft SHELLEY, and Oscar WILDE. In 1965, psychoanalyst Eustace Chesser published *Shelley and Zastrozzi: Self-Revelation of a Neurotic*. Judging young Percy Bysshe Shelley's adolescent novel *ZASTROZZI* (1810) as a glimpse into the boy's subconscious, Chesser determined that the rebellious, murderous novel revealed disturbing strands of psychoneurosis that raged in the poet's mind during his late teens.

Bibliography

Chesser, Eustace. *Shelley & Zastrozzi: Self-Revelation of a Neurotic*. London: Gregg/Archive, 1965.

Gamer, Michael. *Romanticism and the Gothic: Genre, Reception, and Canon Formation*. Cambridge: Cambridge University Press, 2000.

Senf, Carol A. "Bram Stoker: History, Psychoanalysis and the Gothic," *Victorian Studies* 42, no. 4 (summer 2000): 675.

Punch and Judy

Europe's popular streetside and park entertainment, the noisy Punch and Judy glove-puppet shows presented an unending cycle of domestic VIOLENCE. Beginning in London in 1785, creators of the emotive plays pictured a long-nosed husband bludgeoning his wife to death and clubbing and tossing their infant, and sometimes the dog Toby, out the window. Puppeteers called Punchmen trained in a time-honored family business and forced their voices through a squeaker compressed by the lips. From small puppet booths, they presented original scenarios that they bequeathed to their own sons like family jewels. The roguish main character, a reprise of Pulcinello or Punchinello from the Italian commedia dell'arte, was a GROTESQUE married to a shrew. The feuding couple's indiscreet behavior and the workings of the law called for a number of secondary characters—a servant, beggar, doctor, beadle, policeman, and a hangman called Jack Ketch.

Crowds at spas, country fairs, wayside markets and festivals, and private gatherings thrilled to the marital mayhem, anticipating with glee the couple's knockabout assaults, accompanied by shrill shrieks and groans. Like the NEWGATE NOVEL, the puppet show colored criminality and justice with wide swaths of gallows humor, such as Jack Ketch's misunderstanding of the noose, which Punch uses to garrot the hangman. Like medieval mystery plays, the scripts sometimes called for Satan to haul the woebegone soul to hell.

Punch and Judy's soap opera lives inspired episodes of Gothic fiction. Ann RADCLIFFE incorporated the vicious puppet show at a pivotal moment in *THE ITALIAN* (1797) as a commentary on vice. In 1828, popular Gothic illustrator George

CRUIKSHANK teamed with Payne Collier to issue a volume of the puppet episodes entitled *The Tragic Comedy or Comical Tragedy of Punch and Judy*. The motif of streetside puppetry recurred in English writer. M. R. JAMES's "The Story of a Disappearance and an Appearance" (1919), in which a dream of the stalking of Punch precedes the death of two puppeteers the next day. In 1938, Frederick Ignatius Cowles depicted a traveling puppet show and angry canine and human REVENANTS pursuing a killer in the story "Punch and Judy."

Bibliography
Hollingsworth, Keith. *The Newgate Novel, 1830–1847.* Detroit: Wayne State University Press, 1963.

Speaight, George. "The Origin of Punch and Judy: A New Clue?," *Theatre Research International* 20, no. 3 (autumn 1995): 200–206.

R

Radcliffe, Ann
(1764–1823)

The chief shaper of a restrained branch of TERROR FICTION, Ann Ward Radcliffe channeled a flair for lyricism into the most influential GOTHIC NOVELs of the romantic era. Born the year that Horace WALPOLE began inventing the genre with THE CASTLE OF OTRANTO, Ann Ward grew up in Bath in a middle-class Protestant household and read from a wide range of books: ballads and romantic lore, criminal cases compiled in Gayot de Pitavel's *Causes Célèbres* (Notorious cases, 1734), Sophia LEE's chivalric mode in *The Recess; or, A Tale of Other Times* (1785), and the French novels of Abbé PRÉVOST and Jean-Jacques Rousseau. She entered a domestic phase by marrying William Radcliffe, editor of the *English Chronicle*, with whom she hiked and attended the operas of Handel and Paesiello, from which she extracted melodramatic motifs for her novels.

Childless, and reclusive by nature, Radcliffe found evenings long and boring while her husband worked. She wrote to pass the time, reprising glamorous European settings she knew only from Shakespeare's plays and the French and German books of François Baculard d'Arnaud, Karl Grosse, Friedrich August Naubert, and Friedrich von SCHILLER, one of her favorite authors. Of her historical underpinnings, English critic Julia Kavanagh, author of *English Women of Letters* (1863), warned that Radcliffe was vague about GOTHIC SETTINGS and that she "threw the date of her stories only so far back as to give them romantic interest" (Tarr, 9).

Under the influence of Sophia Lee's *The Recess*, Radcliffe began penning terror fiction with the tentative novella *The Castles of Athlin and Dunbayne: A Highland Story* (1789) and the two-volume *A SICILIAN ROMANCE* (1790), two stilted romances issued anonymously. The former, which she set in the wild Scottish highlands, earned a personal reproof from the critic of the *Monthly Review* for being childishly amusing and tasteless. The latter, with a VILLAIN motif, is set among Catholics in Sicily and pictures a confined wife and an innocent daughter, the stereotypical NAIF.

Radcliffe mirrored the dreary sylvan setting of Charlotte SMITH's fiction in *The Romance of the Forest* (1791), a popular, three-volume Gothic novel that was the first published under Radcliffe's name and the first offering slivers of autobiography. The story exploits imagination amid the ruins of a Gothic abbey in 17th-century France, where the orphaned heroine, Adeline, flees her duplicitous uncle, Philippe de Montalt, a marquis. The villain is both a voluptuary and ruthless killer, a step beyond the menace of the Marquis of Mazzini in *A Sicilian Romance*. The growth of Radcliffe's command of illusion earned the regard of *Critical Review* and *Monthly Review* and the sincerest form of flattery, dramatist James Boaden's adaptation of *The Romance of the Forest* under the title *Fountainville Forest* (1794), to which he added a ghost for the play's debut at Covent Garden's Theatre Royale. The mystic Joanna Southcott was so stricken by the villain's evil that she considered Radcliffe a prophet inspired by God.

Radcliffe achieved Gothic mastery in the four-volume THE MYSTERIES OF UDOLPHO (1794), a work that relies on improbable characters, garrulous servants, evocative locales and episodes, and extremes of emotion, but only hints of the SUPERNATURAL. As adjuncts to ATMOSPHERE, SUSPENSE, and dread, she enhanced the effect with suggestive terrors triggered by amplified auditory sense impressions. The novel, which earned her an unprecedented £500, influenced Matthew Gregory LEWIS, who, in THE MONK (1796), produced a higher degree of carnality and lurid Gothicism.

In turn, Lewis's sensational horror tale provided an impetus to Radcliffe's next work, the three-volume THE ITALIAN; or, The Confessional of the Black Penitents (1797), a somber anti-Catholic novel set in the Apennines during the Inquisition. The plot rejects Lewis's blatant sexuality, but takes from Schiller's DER GEISTERSEHER (The Ghost-Seer, 1786) the technique of building suspense and speculation on mysteries, and then providing natural explanations that defeat the supernatural. In the novel's depiction of religion, clerics, and ritual, Radcliffe stresses the dangers of corruption by depicting a powerful tribunal that forces a priest to break the seal of confession. Critic Judith Wilt, author of Ghosts of the Gothic (1980), comments that in Radcliffe's hands, "The great God rules, even as His Church is purged of its villain, its evil fathers" (Wilt, 32).

Radcliffe's genius at building atmosphere results in carefully crafted irony as prisoners of the Inquisition plod down darkened side streets to the Corso, the inner-city site of the Roman carnival. She orchestrates an ominous montage of "gay carriages and masks, with procession of musicians, monks, and mountebanks . . . lighted up with flambeaux, and resounded with the heterogeneous rattling of wheels, the music of serenaders, and the jokes and laughter of the revellers" (Radcliffe, Italian, 194). Such evocative scenarios of CHIAROSCURO amid Roman ruins and MELANCHOLY saints' images assured Radcliffe's place as most-read and most influential novelist until Sir Walter SCOTT challenged her supremacy with his Waverley novels.

Radcliffe's genteel classical background—particularly her knowledge of Shakespeare, Samuel Richardson's sentimental novels, and the GRAVEYARD POETS as well as English translations of the French Gothic novelist Abbé Prévost—served her well in the writing of her second most influential work. For a villain, she borrowed from John Milton's glamorous characterization of Satan in book 1 of Paradise Lost (1667) to create the evil, scowling monk SCHEDONI, who anticipates the BYRONIC HERO of the romantic era. Her previous work was so well received that the publisher paid her an unprecedented advance of £800 for The Italian, a jump of 60 percent over her earnings from the previous novel. Samuel Taylor COLERIDGE reviewed the work favorably in the June 1798 issue of Critical Review and praised her command of passion and image.

In five Gothic novels written over an eight-year span during the era of revolution in America and France, Radcliffe manipulated terrifying contrasts of sound and silence and light and dark without presenting actual VIOLENCE. Through the suggestion of the supernatural, she produced MYSTERY plots flawed by insubstantial characterization, anachronism, and inattention to motivation. To extend the effects of suspense, she applied the PATHETIC FALLACY in melodramatic scenes embroidered with heightened elements of nature, which the overcharged imaginations of her delicate heroines interpret as hostile or menacing. In the estimation of the critic and author Anna Laetitia BARBAULD, Radcliffe's successful depiction of sensations, "alarms with terror; agitates with suspense, prolonged and wrought up to the most intense feeling; by mysterious hints and obscure intimations of unseen danger" (Varma, 102). Radcliffe concluded each mystery with plausible explanations of seeming preternatural occurrences, a technique emulated by the American Gothic novelist Charles Brockden BROWN. Her works were so clearly stated that they served GOTHIC BLUEBOOK writers like Dr. Nathan DRAKE and Sarah WILKINSON as fodder for several decades of redactions, abridgments, and imitations.

Radcliffe next produced a travelogue of her journey to Holland and the Rhineland and a less successful sixth novel, Gaston de Blondeville (1802), for which she drew on traditional ghost lore for a specter haunting Kenilworth Castle. She chose to suppress the work, which remained unpublished for nearly a quarter-century. Her retreat into domesticity and depression was so complete that she was rumored to be dead or to have gone insane from allowing her imagination full play of Gothic horror.

In 1826, three years after Radcliffe's sudden death during an asthma attack, *New Monthly Magazine* extracted the frame story of her last novel, which turns on the discovery of an antique manuscript describing King Henry III. Imitators published 20 works under her name, all of which flaunted a panache out of proportion to the subdued quality of her fiction. Much praised by Sir Walter Scott, Radcliffe's works were widely read in translation and earned the admiration of Thomas De Quincey and William Wordsworth, Gothicist William Harrison AINSWORTH, playwright Francis LATHOM, polemicist Mary WOLLSTONECRAFT, novelists Jane AUSTEN, Charlotte BRONTË, Emily BRONTË, Charles Brockden BROWN, Edward BULWER-LYTTON, James Fenimore Cooper, the Marquis de Sade, Charles DICKENS, Maria Edgeworth, Henry JAMES, Sheridan LE FANU, Charles Robert MATURIN, and Mary Wollstonecraft SHELLEY. Another admirer, the Victorian poet Christina ROSSETTI, abandoned attempts to write a biography of her elusive idol for an Eminent Women series.

Bibliography

Clery, E. J. *Women's Gothic from Clara Reeve to Mary Shelley.* Tavistock, Devon: Northcote House, 2000.

Mackenzie, Scott. "Ann Radcliffe's Gothic Narrative and the Readers at Home," *Studies in the Novel* 31, no. 4 (winter 1999): 409.

Norton, Rictor. *The Mistress of Udolpho.* London: Leicester University Press, 1999.

Tarr, Mary Muriel. *Catholicism in Gothic Fiction: A Study of the Nature and Function of Catholic Materials in Gothic Fiction in England, 1762–1820.* Washington, D.C.: Catholic University of America Press, 1946.

Varma, Devendra P. *The Gothic Flame.* New York: Russell & Russell, 1966.

Wilt, Judith. *Ghosts of the Gothic.* Princeton, N.J.: Princeton University Press, 1980.

Rebecca
Daphne du Maurier
(1938)

Daphne DU MAURIER's MYSTERY classic *Rebecca* reprises the plot and characters of Charlotte BRONTË's *JANE EYRE* (1847). Du Maurier's work separates medievalism from Gothic convention to concentrate on MELODRAMA set at a brooding English manor. Freighted with unspoken terrors, the story anchors SUSPENSE to the observations and behaviors of a NAIF, a quavering, unnamed heroine who daydreams in her new post as mistress of MANDERLEY, an isolated seaside estate. Rather than take charge, she allows her imagination to stalk her in the form of the previous Mrs. Max DE WINTER, whose belongings and monogram deck the house and its environs with ambiguous memories. The work avoids the excesses of sex and VIOLENCE common to Gothic novels to dwell on mystery, undisclosed crime, and a SUBTEXT of class differences.

To create the story of the mismatched de Winters, du Maurier updated a familiar Gothic paradigm—the story of the lonely, self-negating, but sincere heroine who marries a superior male and who must fend off the invasive presence of the worldly, glamorous other woman. At the heart of the conflict lies an air of unease resulting from an oppressive secret, which du Maurier expands into an investigation of Rebecca's apparent drowning when her sailboat capsized. The author replaces Brontë's governess, BYRONIC HERO, and aristocratic rival with a modern trio: the unnamed heroine, the dashing Maxim de Winter, and the wraith of the enigmatic Rebecca, who baited her husband into providing a quick, violent death. Thus, murder/suicide reduces her from dying wife to an overpowering evil presence. The heroine's new domain lies under the power of Mrs. DANVERS, the ominous housekeeper and jealous, witchlike VILLAIN. In the end, evil consumes the mansion in fire, just as Brontë's THORNFIELD burns at the hand of the monstrous Bertha Mason ROCHESTER, an in-house repository of anger and vengeance. Rather than kill off the arsonist, as Brontë does, du Maurier allows Mrs. Danvers to skulk away in the night like the MONSTER Grendel retreating over the moors after a night of marauding.

The novel is a major contribution to FEMALE GOTHIC for its empowerment of the timid, self-reproaching heroine. She cringes on the window seat out of a false belief that she has failed her husband, the tight-lipped Max, whose SECRECY worsens his young wife's self-doubt. For a climactic costume ball, the housekeeper convinces the heroine to wear a dress similar to the outfit that the beautiful Rebecca had worn. After a dramatic scolding from Max, the heroine experiences a coming-to-knowledge that boosts her from tagalong bride to mistress of Manderley. Instead of looking out the window for rescue, the liberated heroine rescues herself.

Rebecca flourishes from suspense. Tension increases from the author's manipulation of Gothic terrors, wildness, and the uncanny presence that refuses to quit Manderley and leave its control to the new lady of the manor. In her oddly unerotic relationship with Max, the new Mrs. DE WINTER suffers a neurotic self-castigation, a form of self-stalking that gives her no peace. In the falling action, the revelation of the first Mrs. de Winter as a corrupt, mocking adulterer eases the self-imposed impression of inadequacy that belittles the heroine.

Du Maurier concludes the psychological mystery with a murder investigation and a house fire that reveal to the heroine both the real Rebecca and her own strengths. No longer outclassed by the brainy, beautiful, and well-bred Rebecca, the heroine is not only able to retrieve herself from the sulks, but also she can begin to support her husband emotionally until he is exonerated of a murder charge. Just as Brontë levels the social and economic differences between Edward ROCHESTER and his governess in *Jane Eyre* with a conflagration, du Maurier levels Manderley and equalizes the balance of power between the de Winters, who draw closer in loyalty and affection as Max recedes into a semi-invalid cared for by his competent wife.

Lauded by the *Times of London*, du Maurier's novel sold 45,000 copies in its first month and earned critical acclaim. It connected instantly with North American audiences for its psychological study of jealousy. After *Rebecca* swept Europe and North America's best-seller lists, the author began adapting the novel for the stage. The work encountered additional success in Orson Welles's 1938 radio play for *The Campbell Playhouse*, starring Welles as Max de Winter. In 1940, Alfred Hitchcock filmed the novel with an all-star cast—Laurence Olivier as Max, Joan Fontaine as his self-effacing wife, George Sanders as the cad Favell, and Judith Anderson as the sinister Mrs. Danvers.

The screen version netted eight Oscar nominations and two Oscars, for photography and best picture, in part because of the handwritten directions that the author passed to director Hitchcock. Victoria HOLT honored du Maurier's Gothic setting, characterization, and plotting with considerable borrowings for her novel MISTRESS OF MELLYN (1960).

Bibliography

du Maurier, Daphne. *The Rebecca Notebook and Other Memories*. Garden City, N.Y.: Doubleday, 1980.

Forster, Margaret. *Daphne du Maurier*. New York: Doubleday, 1993.

Nigro, Kathleen Butterly. "Rebecca as Desdemona: 'A Maid That Paragons Description and Wild Fame,'" *College Literature* 27, no. 3 (fall 2000): 144.

Reeve, Clara
(1729–1807)

One of the popular writers of the late 18th century, Clara Reeve provided escapist Gothic literature for the entertainment of adults longing for something more interesting and imaginative than neoclassic philosophy and verse. She was a minister's daughter born in Suffolk, England, and home-schooled in the classics before establishing a career as a writer of verse and libretti, and as a translator. A follower of a disparate pair, sentimentalist Samuel Richardson and Horace WALPOLE, creator of Gothic terrors in THE CASTLE OF OTRANTO (1765), she set out to write her own style of Gothic built around MEDIEVALISM and Oriental exotica. Like her predecessor Ann RADCLIFFE, Reeve avoided unnecessary VIOLENCE and excessive emotion and accused Walpole of improbable plotting.

Reeve admired Thomas Leland's *Longsword, Earl of Salisbury* (1762), a two-volume historical Gothic romance exemplifying love and religion in the chivalric era. In imitation, she published a famous GOTHIC NOVEL, *The Champion of Virtue: A Gothic Story* (1777), which she reissued as THE OLD ENGLISH BARON (1778), a genteel didactic text later translated into French and German. She defended her choice of the Gothic romance as more instructive to the young than novels and history. Distancing herself further from incredible extravagances of HORROR FICTION, Reeve composed

The History of Charoba, Queen of Egypt (1785), an ORIENTAL ROMANCE, and ably defended the art of Gothic fiction with the critical treatise *The Progress of Romance* (1785), which differentiates between medieval fable and the realistic novel.

Three years later, Reeve created a romantic hero for *The Exiles; or, Memories of Count de Cronstadt* (1788), a MELANCHOLY novel based on a ROMAN NOIR by François Baculard d'Arnaud. She balanced the dominant male image with a resourceful female protagonist and antimarriage theme in *The School for Widows* (1791). In her last major work, she applied a medieval motif to *Memoirs of Sir Roger de Clarendon, a Natural Son of Edward the Black Prince, with Anecdotes of Many Other Eminent Persons of the Fourteenth Century* (1793), a historical Gothic novel that reflects on the era of King Richard II. The latter earned the disapproval of the novelist and critic Anna Laetitia BARBAULD, a purist who objected to Reeve's coloring real events with imaginary details.

Bibliography

Clery, E. J. *Women's Gothic from Clara Reeve to Mary Shelley.* Tavistock, Devon: Northcote House, 2000.

Gamer, Michael. *Romanticism and the Gothic: Genre, Reception, and Canon Formation.* Cambridge: Cambridge University Press, 2000.

Stevens, David. *The Gothic Tradition.* Cambridge: Cambridge University Press, 2000.

rescue theme

Early Gothic literature tends to feature a stereotypical maiden, the unassertive, shilly-shallying female whose faint heart sets the stage for the entrance of the bold male rescuer. Authors of both genders built rescue plots around female protagonists who were emotionally passive, personally inexperienced, and intellectually under-schooled for asserting self or combating danger. Exacerbating the image of the frail darling are signs of excess SENSIBILITY and imagination running wild. Lack of self-control heightens the typical heroine's excitability and renders her as quavering and helpless as a rabbit beneath the cobra's eye. One classic example is the work of Matthew Gregory LEWIS. Lewis copied the TONE and ATMOSPHERE of Heinrich Zschokke's *Aballino, der Grosse Bandit* (Aballino, the great bandit, 1793) for a stage MELODRAMA, *Rugantino, the Bravo of Venice* (1805). The plot develops an androcentric protection theme and rescue motif that place the noble banditto Abellino in disguise as beggar or bandit at the right moment to save the Venetian beauty Rosabella, the daughter of a doge.

Toward the mid-19th century, heroines began to stand on their own feet. Charlotte BRONTË overturned the standard gender roles of the rescue motif in *JANE EYRE* (1847), in which the NAIF develops into an independent, outspoken educator. At novel's end, Jane dominates the falling action by rescuing Edward ROCHESTER, her impaired employer, who lost his mansion and the use of his eye and hand while attempting to save his crazed wife. Brontë returns Jane to her former fiancé to become his source of hope and comfort. With admirable poise, Jane confides, "Reader, I married him" (Brontë, 429). Through union with Jane, Edward regains partial vision and welcomes their infant son. Without gloating, Jane rejoices in an equal domestic partnership: "All my confidence is bestowed on him, all his confidence is devoted to me; we are precisely suited in character—perfect concord is the result" (*ibid.*, 432).

In a later overthrow of the male rescue plot, the English poet Christina ROSSETTI applied the motif to two females in *THE GOBLIN MARKET* (1862), a perplexing Gothic FAIRY TALE involving entrapment and the retrieval of one sister by the other. At a fearful point in Laura's enchantment by the goblins, Lizzie wonders:

> Gone deaf and blind?
> Her tree of life drooped from the root:
> She said not one word in her heart's sore ache,
> But peering thro' the dimness, naught discerning,
> Trudged home, her pitcher dripping all the way.
>
> (Rossetti, 10)

An enigmatic narrative, the poem earned respect as one of Rossetti's finest, yet explication of its fearful story has generated a list of possible meanings.

A variety of critics interpret the narrative poem as a cautionary tale to little girls, a literary rebellion against restrictions on female artists, an anti-fantasy on female freedom, an ALLEGORY on Victorian patriarchy and materialism, a Christian parable of redemptive love, and a dark satire on the relentless flesh-peddling in the marriage market.

Bibliography

Brontë, Charlotte. *Jane Eyre.* New York: Bantam Books, 1981.

Coelsch-Foisner, Sabine. "Rossetti's 'Goblin Market,'" *Explicator* 61, no. 1 (fall 2002): 28–30.

Grass, Sean C. "Nature's Perilous Variety in Rossetti's 'Goblin Market,'" *Nineteenth-Century Literature* 51, no. 3 (December 1996): 356–376.

Rossetti, Christina. *The Goblin Market.* New York: Dover, 1994.

revenant

Interest in the revenant or walking dead dates from antiquity into more recent times, as with the return of a dead lover in Lafcadio HEARN's *Kwaidan* (Weird tales, 1904), a spirit's search for his grave in Walter DE LA MARE's "Strangers Pilgrims" (1926), the chastising spirit of Mama Elena in Laura Esquivel's *Like Water for Chocolate* (1989), and the drifting phantasms of dead Confederate soldiers returning south from the Civil War in Virginia Renfro Ellis's *The Wedding Dress* (2002). The spirit returned from the nether world first entered literature in *Book of the Dead*, which derives from pyramid texts from Egypt's Old Kingdom (2575–2130 B.C.) found on coffins and sarcophagi, stelae, and papyri. A theatrical element of the SUPERNATURAL, revenants link the living with an unknown nether world by returning to familiar places and appearing to or greeting people they once knew, a common confrontation in JAPANESE GOTHIC. Familiar from Elizabethan stagecraft is the ghost scene in William Shakespeare's tragedy *Hamlet* (ca. 1599), in which the Danish king Hamlet charges his son and namesake with the task of wreaking revenge on Claudius, a regicide and wife-stealer.

Gothic novelist Mary Wollstonecraft SHELLEY immersed herself in the walking dead while reading *Fantasmagoriana; ou Recueil d'Histoires d'Appari-*

tions, de Spectres, Revenans, Fantomes, Etc. (*Fantasmagoriana; or An Anthology of Stories of Ghosts, Specters, Revenants, Phantoms, Etc.,* 1812). The motif fueled encounters with the dead in Edgar Allan POE's story "THE FALL OF THE HOUSE OF USHER" (1839) and the poem "LIGEIA" (1838), the summons of a dead woman to the title character in Sheridan LE FANU's "Schalken the Painter" (1839), the return of Jacob Marley in novelist Charles DICKENS's *A CHRISTMAS CAROL* (1843), and the haunting by a deceased nun in Charlotte BRONTË's *VILLETTE* (1853). A specialist in fearful Victorian spirit lore was Wilkie COLLINS, who crafted the appearance of a ghostly FEMME FATALE in "The Ostler," a tale in the 1855 Christmas issue of *Household Words,* reissued as "The Dream Woman." He published another powerful tale of the revived corpse in "The Double-Bedded Room" (1859), which expresses terror through the eyes of the lone sleeper.

Novelist George Eliot gave a name to the phenomenon of life returned to the dead in "The Lifted Veil" (1859). As the title metaphor suggests, a supernatural force returns voice to a dead woman, who charges a female character with plotting to poison her husband. In terror of the incident, the protagonist declares: "Great God! Is this what it is to live again . . . to wake up with our unstilled thirst upon us, with our unuttered curses rising to our lips, with our muscles ready to act out their half-committed sins?" (Williams, 95). Later in the 19th century, Rudyard KIPLING produced a revenant from the British colonies in "The Phantom Rickshaw" (1888), one of his finest models of Gothic SHORT FICTION. In *THE TURN OF THE SCREW* (1898), Henry JAMES allows his naive governess to muse, "Forbidden ground was the question of the return of the dead" (James, 74).

Twentieth-century readers maintained their demand for stories of the walking dead, the source of terror in W. W. JACOBS's story "THE MONKEY'S PAW," issued in the *Strand* magazine in 1902; Joseph CONRAD's graveyard escape in "The Idiot," anthologized in *Tales of Unrest* (1908); and Gaston LEROUX's novel *The Man Who Came Back from the Dead* (1916). Anne RICE developed a New Orleans-based series on the undead, beginning with *INTERVIEW WITH A VAMPIRE* (1976).

Bibliography

James, Henry. *The Turn of the Screw and Daisy Miller*. New York: Laurel, 1954.

Stevens, David. *The Gothic Tradition*. Cambridge: Cambridge University Press, 2000.

Twitchell, James B. *The Living Dead: A Study of the Vampire in Romantic Literature*. Durham, N.C.: Duke University Press, 1981.

Williams, A. Susan, ed. *The Lifted Veil: The Book of Fantastic Literature by Women, 1800–World War II*. New York: Carroll & Graf, 1992.

revenge

A prime motivating force in Gothic literature and dramatic STORYTELLING, revenge is a precipitating element of ABERRANT BEHAVIOR and OBSESSION narratives, as found in Charles Robert MATURIN's suspenseful *The Fatal Revenge; or, The Family of Montorio* (1807), the MONSTER's grudge in Mary Wollstonecraft SHELLEY's *FRANKENSTEIN* (1818), and the fierce love triangle in John RICHARDSON's colonial romances *Wacousta; or, The Prophecy: A Tale of the Canadas* (1832) and its sequel, *The Canadian Brothers; or, The Prophecy Fulfilled* (1840). Revenge topples logic in works in which reprisal turns into mania, as with the predations of the towering villain HEATHCLIFF in Emily BRONTË's *WUTHERING HEIGHTS* (1847), Captain Ahab's unrelenting scouting of the great white whale in Herman MELVILLE's *Moby-Dick* (1851), and the avenger's self-destruction in Guy de MAUPASSANT's "Le Horla; or, Modern Ghosts" (1887). In COLONIAL GOTHIC, dark-heartedness cankers at the core of violent stories—Robert Montgomery BIRD's MYSTERY novel *NICK OF THE WOODS; or, The Jibbenainosay: A Tale of Kentucky* (1837), Melville's slave era rebellion in *BENITO CERENO* (1855), and Isabel ALLENDE's story of mestizo hatred of Hispanic overlords in *THE HOUSE OF THE SPIRITS* (1981). In British colonial Gothic, Rudyard KIPLING expands on vengeance in "The Phantom Rickshaw" (1888); SAKI depicts a child's harnessing of occult powers to avenge his powerlessness against adults in "SREDNI VASHTAR" (1911).

The urge for vengeance is often the outgrowth of misogyny, repression, threats, and violence against women—a theme in Percy Bysshe SHELLEY's stalking assassin in ZASTROZZI: *A Romance* (1810), Friedrich de la Motte Fouqué's story of a water spirit's reprisal in *Undine* (1811), the madwoman Bertha ROCHESTER's burning of THORNFIELD in Charlotte BRONTË's *JANE EYRE* (1847), and Miss HAVISHAM's perverse rearing of Estella at SATIS HOUSE in Charles DICKENS's *GREAT EXPECTATIONS* (1861). The wreaking of havoc against oppressors, torturers, and rapists provides the satisfying comeuppance in such vengeance lore as the VILLAIN's hatred in Edgar Allan POE's "THE CASK OF AMONTILLADO" (1846), in which the unsuspecting Fortunato meets his doom in a PREMATURE BURIAL, and Louisa May Alcott's picture of the manipulation of Gladys in *A Modern Mephistopheles* (1877). In the 20th century, requital for past wrongs against women powered William FAULKNER's stories "A ROSE FOR EMILY" (1930) and "THAT EVENING SUN" (1931) and Louise Erdrich's "Fleur" (1986), the tale of Fleur Pillager, a Chippewa shape-shifter who retaliates against white male rapists by summoning a tornado to sweep them away.

Bibliography

Hoeveler, Diane Long. *Gothic Feminism*. University Park: Pennsylvania State University Press, 1998.

Wesley, Marilyn C. "Reverence, Rape, Resistance: Joyce Carol Oates and Feminist Film Theory," *Mosaic* 32, no. 3 (September 1999): 75.

Reynolds, George William
(1814–1879)

A prime Victorian Gothicist, George William Macarthur Reynolds was a smash hit on both sides of the Atlantic. He failed at a Continental publishing scheme before finding his metier in SENSATIONALISM. His GASLIGHT THRILLERs, dubbed "yellowback railway readers," appealed to the literate lower-class reader with scenes of prostitution, cross-dressing and soft-core pornography, body snatching, suicide, ghastly urban crime scenes, and SADISM. British and American readers thrilled to his two most popular serials, *Mysteries of London* (1844–48), which sold 40,000 copies per week, and its sequel, *The Mysteries of the Court of London* (1848–53), which brought Reynolds's total to a million copies sold of his 10-year serials.

For a penny, readers could keep up with the lowlife characters in Reynolds's literary soap opera, an idea he borrowed from Eugène Sue's *Les Mystères de Paris* (*Paris Mysteries*, 1842–43). The pairing of a melodramatic line drawing with the gory suicide of Lady Cecilia was a gratuitous crowd pleaser: "Terrific screams burst from her lips as she rolled over and over in her precipitate whirl. Down she fell! Her head dashed against the pavement, at a distance of three yards from the base of the Monument. Her brains were scattered upon the stones" (Reynolds, 69). For material, Reynolds drew on broadsides of the era, "Dreadful Suicide of a Young Woman by Throwing Herself off the Monument" (1839) and "Another Dreadful Suicide at the Monument, by a Young Woman" (1842). From the magazine *Reynolds's Miscellany*, the works moved into hardback sold in European markets as far east as Russia in four languages. Simultaneously, the enterprising Reynolds also issued in popular magazines shocking crimes and riveting sketches in *Faust: A Romance of the Secret Tribunals* (1845–46), published in the *London Journal.*

Reynolds achieved an influential pulp depiction of LYCANTHROPY in *Wagner the Wehr-Wolf* (1846–47), a scary story set at the edge of Germany's Black Forest on Halloween night. The protagonist, Johan Wagner, curses God and bargains with Satan for power and eternal youth in exchange for his soul. Satan grants the wish, but forces Wagner to spend each night of the full moon as a werewolf. The ill-fated man-beast pays for his satanic gifts with fearful murders of his family, the suicide of the woman he seduces and marries, and involvement in piracy and Rosicrucianism, a common link between Catholicism and GOTHIC CONVENTION. Reynolds followed with *The Necromancer: A Romance* (1851–52), set in Tudor England and emulating the DIABOLISM of Charles Robert MATURIN's *MELMOTH THE WANDERER* (1820). Reynolds's frank URBAN GOTHIC influenced the works of Mary Elizabeth BRADDON and the best-selling novel *The Quaker City; or, The Monks of Monk Hall* (1844) by the American writer George Lippard.

Bibliography

Gates, Barbara T. *Victorian Suicide: Mad Crimes and Sad Histories.* Princeton, N.J.: Princeton University Press, 1988.

Reynolds, George W. M. *Mysteries of London.* Edinburgh: Edinburgh University Press, 1998.

Rosenman, Ellen Bayuk. "Spectacular Women: The Mysteries of London and the Female Body," *Victorian Studies* 40, no. 1 (autumn 1996): 31–64.

Terry, Reginald. *Victorian Popular Fiction, 1860–80.* London: Macmillan, 1983.

Rhys, Jean

(1890–1979)

A Caribbean star of neo-Gothic fiction, Jean Rhys, the pen name of Dominican-Welsh writer Ellen Gwendolen Rees Williams, incorporated West Indian strains of the occult in her novels. In girlhood, she absorbed an invigorating mix of island motifs from a Catholic convent education and observations of miscegenation and racism, gender politics, and the remnants of British colonialism. After raffish teenage employment as a stage dancer in musical comedy, she progressed from kept woman of a rich stockbroker to marriage and motherhood. She settled in Vienna, where the novelist Ford Madox Ford encouraged her first sketches, issued as *The Left Bank and Other Stories* (1927), and suggested her nom de plume.

During World War II, Rhys began a masterful psychological novel, *Wide Sargasso Sea* (1966), a prequel to Charlotte BRONTË's *JANE EYRE* (1847) from the point of view of Antoinette Cosway, a sensual Jamaican Creole. A signal contribution to FEMALE GOTHIC, the novel offers the future madwoman Bertha Mason ROCHESTER ample reason for repressed rage against her family and patriarchal husband, Edward ROCHESTER. Without realizing the danger, Antoinette submits to the inevitability of marriage and possession by the unnamed OUTSIDER, whom she barely knows: "I am wearing a long dress and thin slippers, so I walk with difficulty, following the man who is with me and holding up the skirt of my dress. It is white and beautiful and I don't wish to get it soiled" (Rhys, 59–60). The symbolism of surface soiling is a FORESHADOWING of unavoidable spiritual degradation: "I follow him, sick with fear but I make no effort to save myself; if anyone were to try to save me, I would refuse. This must happen" (*ibid.*).

Rhys confronts the reader with the protagonist's helplessness. Debased for her vibrant carnality, plagued by ghostly premonitions of death in a fire, and locked away in a remote house on England's moors, where she is socially and personally displaced from normal life, Antoinette, the racial other, is trapped between disparate cultures. Her punishment stems from nativist passion, an unfettered response to marital embraces denied to proper English-women. As Antoinette slips into INSANITY, nostalgia becomes her solace as she becomes entangled in the title image, a rich tuft of sea grass, a SYMBOL of the past that beckons her home to the islands.

Bibliography

Blais, Joline. "Qui est La?: Displaced Subjects in 'Wide Sargasso Sea' and 'Le Ravissement de Lol V. Stein,'" *College Literature* 20, no. 2 (June 1993): 98–118.

Nixon, Nicola. "'Wide Sargasso Sea' and Jean Rhys's Interrogation of the 'Nature Wholly Alien' in 'Jane Eyre,'" *Essays in Literature* 21, no. 2 (fall 1994): 267–284.

Rhys, Jean. *Wide Sargasso Sea.* New York: Norton, 1967.

Su, John J. "'Once I Would Have Gone Back . . . But Not Any Longer': Nostalgia and Narrative Ethics in 'Wide Sargasso Sea,'" *CRITIQUE: Studies in Contemporary Fiction* 44, no. 2 (winter 2003): 157–174.

Uraizee, Joy. "'She Walked Away without Looking Back': Christophine and the Enigma of History in Jean Rhys's 'Wide Sargasso Sea,'" *CLIO* 38, no. 3 (spring 1999): 261.

Rice, Anne
(1941–)

Anne Rice is one of the success stories of postmodern Gothic fiction. Educated in a convent, she grew up in New Orleans and absorbed the Gothic lore of gender politics, racism, voodoo, and Catholic MYSTICISM. She made up ghost stories and revelled in the child vampirism in Richard Matheson's "Dress of White Silk" (1951), a tale of evil's corruption of innocence. After earning a creative writing degree from San Francisco State University, she embraced atheism, married the atheist poet Stan Rice, and began writing Gothic and pornographic novels that have sold over 100 million copies.

Rice achieved stardom with INTERVIEW WITH A VAMPIRE (1976), a blend of Gothic MONSTER lore, androgyny, SADISM, and DECADENCE. Over a five-week period, she wrote the novel by night to combat sleeplessness and grief for her daughter Michelle, who died of leukemia at age six. Rice developed her protagonist, Lestat le Lioncourt, and variant views of predation through a series of vampire tales: *The Vampire Lestat* (1985), *Queen of the Damned* (1988), *Tale of the Body Thief* (1992), *Memnoch the Devil* (1995), *Merrick* (2000), *The Vampire Armand* (2000), *Blood and Gold* (2001), and *Blackwood Farm* (2002). Interspersed with her Vampire Chronicles, she produced works about WITCHCRAFT—*The Witching Hour* (1990) and *Taltos: Lives of the Mayfair Witches* (1994)—as well as terror in *The Mummy* (1989), and VIOLENCE against women in *Cry to Heaven* (1982), *The Claiming of Sleeping Beauty* (1983), *Beauty's Punishment* (1984), and *Beauty's Release* (1985). She turned to OCCULT FICTION and exotica in *Lasher* (1994), *Servant of the Bones* (1996), and *Violin* (1997), her most autobiographical work.

Bibliography

Cohen, Jeffrey Jerome, ed. *Monster Theory.* Minneapolis: University of Minnesota Press, 1996.

Ramsland, Katherine. *The Witches' Companion: The Official Guide to Anne Rice's Lives of the Mayfair Witches.* New York: Ballantine Books, 1996.

Rice, Anne. "How I Write," *Writer* 114, no. 2 (February 2001): 66.

Richardson, John
(1796–1852)

Considered Canada's first novelist, Major John Richardson, a Canadian-Odawan, developed his experiences during the War of 1812 into historical romance and Gothic fiction. After education in Detroit and Amherstburg, enlistment in the army, and a term in a military prisoner-of-war camp, he served in the British Legion and wrote combat dispatches for the London *Times*. His contribution to New World fiction includes narrative verse in *Tecumseh; or, The Warrior of the*

West (1828) and SENSATIONALISM in *Ecarté; or, The Salons of Paris* (1829).

Richardson advanced American and COLONIAL GOTHIC with two historical MELODRAMAs, *Wacousta; or, The Prophecy: A Tale of the Canadas* (1832) and its sequel, *The Canadian Brothers; or, The Prophecy Fulfilled* (1840), both set during clashes in the Detroit area between English troops and the warriors of Chief Pontiac. To dramatize Wacousta's pseudo–Indian chief with face painted black, Richardson reprised the rampant sexuality and intimidation of AMBROSIO, the Spanish Capuchin VILLAIN of Matthew Gregory LEWIS's controversial novel THE MONK (1796). In addition to dungeon scenes, fearful glimpses of NATURE's power, and sieges at frontier forts in *Waunangee; or, The Massacre at Chicago* (1852) and *Hard-scrabble; or, The Fall of Chicago, a Tale of Indian Warfare* (1856), Richardson turned to European-style Gothic with the sensual *The Monk Knight of St. John: A Tale of the Crusaders* (1850). In the latter, he set the action in Palestine at the battle of Tiberias on July 4, 1187, two years before the Third Crusade, and embroidered the plot with child kidnap, decapitation, cannibalism, incest, rape of the Saracen woman Zuleima, ANTI-CATHOLICISM, and the thunder and dash of the Muslim hero Saladin.

Bibliography

Atwood, Margaret. *Strange Things: The Malevolent North in Canadian Literature*. Oxford: Clarendon Press, 1995.

Duffy, Dennis. "The Monk Knight of St. John," *American Review of Canadian Studies* 32, no. 4 (winter 2002): 722–724.

Northey, Margot. *The Haunted Wilderness: The Gothic and Grotesque in Canadian Fiction*. Toronto: University of Toronto Press, 1976.

Parkinson, Edward. "'That 'ere Ingian's One of Us!': Orality and Literacy in 'Wacousta,'" *Studies in the Novel* 29, no. 4 (winter 1997): 453–475.

The Rime of the Ancient Mariner
Samuel Taylor Coleridge
(1798)

Samuel Taylor COLERIDGE's Gothic fantasy ballad, *The Rime of the Ancient Mariner*, became a favorite poem of both the intellectual and the ordinary reader. The text reflects the romance of sea tales, the timeless memories of the wanderer, and the STORYTELLING of an old salt who has plied the waters of the Pacific and the Antarctic and survived a voyage on a ghost ship. The lyrical poem ventures into the SUPERNATURAL with the sailor's recall of horrific events that follow his shooting of an albatross, an OMEN prophesying salvation from an enveloping sea mist. The killing of the bird with a crossbow, an image suggesting crucifixion, is a symbolic act of pride that breaches NATURE's wholeness and creates an extended isolation from humanity. Like the WANDERING JEW, the unnamed speaker survives a hellish voyage wracked by divine vengeance and recounts its fearful episodes to an absorbed wedding guest.

In a Gothic tableau, the text spools out in mystic scenarios lighted by marine phosphorescence and streaks of lightning. To stress the seriousness of the sailor's error in judgment, the poet depicts him in the agony of sin and layers his response with remorse and repentence. A skeleton ship appears crewed by the male Death and the female Life-in-Death, who cast dice for the sinner's soul; Life-in-Death wins. One by one, fellow crew members accuse the bowman with their eyes, then drop dead from thirst. The victim, who survives along with the slimy creatures of the deep, becomes the epitome of solitude.

Throughout the allegorical drama, the grizzled storyteller, as though bearing the mark of Cain, makes no effort to return to normal life. The poet pictures him as surviving like a soulless specter amid the corpses of his fellow sailors. The ship, powered by an uncanny force, glides on amid phantasms that terrify the survivor until beneficent spirits take charge of his fate. At a climactic point, he blesses water snakes without realizing that the selfless act will save him from doom. His prayer breaks the curse. The sailor's punishment for violating a sacred trust is a perpetual curse that separates him from human society by forcing his retelling of the penitential sea tale to the person most in need of hearing it.

Bibliography

Bidney, Martin. "Spirit-bird, Bowshot, Water-snake, Corpses, Cosmic Love: Reshaping the Coleridge

Legacy in Dickey's 'Deliverance,'" *Papers on Language & Literature* 31, no. 4 (fall 1995): 389–405.

Perkins, David. "The 'Ancient Mariner' and Its Interpreters: Some Versions of Coleridge," *Modern Language Quarterly* 57, no. 3 (September 1996): 425–448.

Rinehart, Mary Roberts
(1876–1958)

A professional nurse, Mary Roberts Rinehart developed a second career as master of the GASLIGHT THRILLER and MYSTERY novel. Born in Allegheny, Pennsylvania, she married a doctor and worked in his Pittsburgh dispensary. At age 28, she increased the family's income by writing macabre stories for *All-Story*, *Lippincott's*, and *Munsey's* and by serializing *The Man in Lower Ten* (1906). Two years later, she published a genre classic, *The Circular Staircase*, the atmospheric story of amateur detective Rachel Innes, which *All-Story* published in installments from November 1907 to March 1908. Heroine Innes fights dread and a vivid imagination at an isolated summer cottage in the Adirondacks, where sinuous shadows and a hidden passageway imply a spectral haunting. The best-seller, which satirized pompous male-centered investigative fare, relieved Rinehart of debt while establishing her competence at the DETECTIVE STORY.

One of America's top female financial successes, Rinehart thrived at romance and sleuthing, but failed to develop a readership for her feminist works. From 1910 until 1940, she wrote for the *Saturday Evening Post* while continuing to produce ghost stories and Gothic fiction. Treachery and vengeance are themes in *The Window at the White Cat* (1910); OMENs riddle *The Case of Jennie Brice* (1913), and a stash of money and mysterious killer feature in *The Bat* (1920). Rinehart halted her writing career during World War I to cover the Allied advance in France. In 1952, she completed a final mystery, *The Swimming Pool*. In spring 1989, the *Saturday Evening Post* published Rinehart's "The Young Visitor," a tense two-part murder thriller.

Bibliography
Fleenor, Juliann E., ed. *The Female Gothic*. Montreal: Eden Press, 1983.

Pearl, Nancy. "Gaslight Thrillers: The Original Victorians," *Library Journal* 126, no. 3 (February 15, 2001): 228.

Robinson, Mary
(1758–1800)

Shakespearian actor, Gothic horror novelist, and outspoken feminist, Mary Darby Robinson produced popular titles and translations. Her works impacted the tastes of late 18th-century readers and writers, including the poet Samuel Taylor COLERIDGE, the novelists Charlotte DACRE and Mary Wollstonecraft SHELLEY, and the philosopher William GODWIN. Robinson, the daughter of a Bristol whaler, taught at a dame school before marrying a law clerk. While the family lodged in debtor's prison in the mid-1770s, she began writing and preparing for a stage career; in the theater, she excelled in breeches roles. After a brief fling as the paramour of the Prince of Wales (later, King George IV), she gained an annuity that guaranteed solvency and ended her dependence on affairs with wealthy men.

When paralysis from rheumatic fever ended her acting career, at age 25, Robinson was forced to support herself through freelance writing. She drew on the spirit of liberty that followed the French Revolution for odes, columns for the *Morning Post*, a Gothic verse tragedy, and historical novels describing the oppression of slaves and women. In 1792, she published a popular Gothic novel, *Vancenza; or, The Dangers of Credulity*, which required a second press run 24 hours after its debut and a third two weeks later and was translated into French and German to meet the demands of European readers. She issued *Picture of Palermo* (1799), a translation of a German work that features the EXOTICISM of a Catholic procession bearing the coffin and relics of St. Rosalia for a five-day festival.

Robinson presented to readers the impressions of Gothic fiction from an industry insider. Months before her death, her last novel, *The Natural Daughter: With Portraits of the Leadenhead Family* (1799), painted word portraits of the guillotine and of Jacobin leaders Jean-Paul Marat and Maximilien Robespierre. The text tweaked her chosen profession with a tongue-in-cheek depiction of

Mrs. Morley, author of a MELANCHOLY novel, which she cautiously places in the hands of the publisher, Mr. Index. Morley warns that he must not neglect a worthy title, which "will cover a multitude of faults: a kind of compendious errata, which sets to rights all the errors of a work, and makes it popular, however incorrect and illiterate it may appear in the eyes of fastidious criticizers" (Tarr, 4). Despite appealing touches of poetry, the novel failed to earn even moderate critical reviews.

More important to literary history is Robinson's epigraph, *Letter to the Women of England, on the Cruelties of Mental Subordination* (1799), which states the themes and issues that delineate FEMALE GOTHIC fiction. Robinson's subsequent Gothic ballad, "The Haunted Beach" (1800), is an atmospheric seascape featuring the ghost of a sailor murdered by shipmates for a pouch of Spanish gold. In 1804, the author's daughter, Maria Elizabeth Robinson, honored her mother by anthologizing Gothic poems in *The Wild Wreath*, which also contained pieces by Samuel Taylor Coleridge and Matthew Gregory LEWIS.

Bibliography

McGann, Jerome. "Mary Robinson and the Myth of Sappho," *Modern Language Quarterly* 56, no. 1 (March 1995): 55–76.

Setzer, Sharon. "Mary Robinson's Sylphid Self: The End of Feminine Self-fashioning," *Philological Quarterly* 75, no. 4 (fall 1996): 501–520.

———. "Romancing the Reign of Terror: Sexual Politics in Mary Robinson's 'Natural Daughter,'" *Criticism* 39, no. 4 (fall 1997): 531–550.

Tarr, Mary Muriel. *Catholicism in Gothic Fiction: A Study of the Nature and Function of Catholic Materials in Gothic Fiction in England, 1762–1820.* Washington, D.C.: Catholic University of America Press, 1946.

Roche, Regina
(1764–1845)

Best-selling English novelist Regina Maria Dalton Roche advanced sentimental fiction and late 18th-century FEMALE GOTHIC. Under the name of her father, Captain Blundell Dalton of the Royal Army, she wrote the first of 16 novels at age 25. Married at 30, she settled in England in 1794 and issued a blockbuster, *The Children of the Abbey: A Tale* (1796), a model of DOMESTIC GOTHIC tinged with the elements of the FAIRY TALE and GHOST STORY and displaying her debt to Samuel Richardson and Gothic specialist Ann RADCLIFFE. From Horace WALPOLE's THE CASTLE OF OTRANTO (1765), Roche took the motif of the imprisoned wife, a metaphor for men's abuse of women that had also influenced Radcliffe's THE SICILIAN ROMANCE (1790).

Roche's best known Gothic novel is *Clermont* (1798), the horror tale of Madeline, a beautiful maiden reared in a ruined castle and driven to discover her true parentage. The book earned dubious regard for its inclusion among the works listed in Jane AUSTEN's satiric NORTHANGER ABBEY (1818). Roche's plot perpetuates the stereotype of the FEMALE VICTIM with the secret wedding motif. Heavily tinged with ANTI-CATHOLICISM, the story portrays Madeline rescuing a servant from self-flagellation and rebuking her for failing to be merciful to herself. Roche cloaks the funeral of the countess de Merville in decay and dread as owls hoot and ravens croak over the human remains lowered into a chapel floor. Pursuing classic female Gothic themes, Roche enlarges on the powerless anti-bride forced into a marriage ceremony performed by an unknown priest. The VILLAIN exults that Madeline can never prove the marriage took place because she lacks corroborating evidence.

Roche had her own difficulties with scoundrels. After a disreputable financier stole the family's Irish property, she made her living as a writer for William Lane's MINERVA PRESS, producing sensational fiction—including *Nocturnal Visit; or, The Mysterious Husband* (ca. 1800), *The Discarded Son; or, Haunt of the Banditti* (1807), *The Houses of Osma and Almeria; or, Convent of St. Ildefonso* (1810), *The Monastery of St. Colomb; or, The Atonement: A Novel* (1813), *The Tradition of the Castle; or, Scenes in the Emerald Isle* (1824), and *The Nun's Picture* (1834)—and an anthology, *London Tales; or, Reflective Portraits* (1814), which was issued in French. Through serious illness, the decline of her husband, and his death in 1829, Roche suffered bouts of depression and petitioned the Royal Literary Fund for financial aid. Critics relegated her to the clutch of female would-be writers of imitative Radcliffean novels. Despite a lack of originality, Roche's works remained in demand in several editions at CIRCULATING LIBRARIES in English, French, and Spanish and remained in print for a century.

Bibliography

Blakey, Dorothy. *The Minerva Press, 1790–1820.* London: Oxford University Press, 1939.

Horner, Avril, ed. *European Gothic: A Spirited Exchange, 1760–1960.* Manchester: Manchester University Press, 2002.

Rochester, Bertha Mason

In JANE EYRE (1847), novelist Charlotte BRONTË creates one of the most intriguing, capricious, and pathetic of Gothic MONSTERS in Bertha Antoinetta Mason Rochester, the daughter of a drunkard and madwoman. A majestic Creole heiress and fabled beauty of Spanish Town, Jamaica, she bears a New World mystique comprised of alluring beauty, retardation, vice, and raging INSANITY. As her personality crumbles into a coarse dementia after the first four years of marriage to Edward ROCHESTER, her husband learns too late that she "came of a mad family; idiots and maniacs through three generations!" (Brontë, 277). At night, she screeches hate-filled curses reminiscent of a streetwalker's foul argot. As her heritage dictates, she declines from appealing planter's daughter to frothing hag, whom Rochester locks away for 11 years on the third floor of THORNFIELD, his remote manse on the English moors. Like a Victorian ghost, Bertha loses first her prestige as wife, her place in her own home, and the substance of her humanity.

Brontë depicts Bertha's mental derangement as beyond the bounds of sympathy. Imprisonment far from the gentle air of the Caribbean distills Bertha's hatred into the lethal venom of a genderless, reptilian nighttime stalker. Clever and tricky after years of incarceration, she eludes her keeper, Grace Poole, and creeps to the room of her husband's intended, who sleeps fitfully on the night before the bigamous wedding. Significantly, Bertha harms only one piece of the nuptial attire, Jane's expensive London-made veil, the covering that conceals his "plebeian bride" at the same time that it prevents her from seeing the truth of Rochester's ignoble past (*ibid.,* 267). By rending the veil, Bertha discloses the truth about Rochester's moodiness and the shrieks in the night that disrupt Jane's contentment.

Brontë turns Bertha into an avenging nemesis by orchestrating her appearance at the novel's climax. In chapter 26, the source of strange noises and hauntings greets Jane on her wedding day like the snarl of a caged demon in the GOTHIC NOVEL's most terrifying confrontation: "What it was, whether beast or human being, one could not, at first sight, tell: it grovelled, seemingly, on all fours; it snatched and growled like some strange wild animal" (*ibid.,* 278). The author dignifies Bertha with nondescript clothing and "a quantity of dark, grizzled hair, wild as a mane, [that] hid its head and face" (*ibid.*).

When Brontë completes her use of Bertha as the truth that will not die, she kills off the demon woman in a fire that cleanses, then consumes Rochester's patrimony. According to an eyewitness at the Rochester Arms, Bertha is the aggressive phantasm who set the blaze and then leaped from the roof to her death on the pavement below. He adds for good measure, "dead as the stones on which her brains and blood were scattered" (*ibid.,* 410). The image suggests that Bertha chooses to end her confinement and to die on her own terms, a self-sacrifice that feminists alternately interpret as the Victorian female refusing to suffer in silence and the Gothic heroine expunging the cruelties of colonialism.

Bibliography

Beattie, Valerie. "The Mystery at Thornfield: Representations of Madness in 'Jane Eyre,'" *Studies in the Novel* 28, no. 4 (winter 1996): 493–505.

Brontë, Charlotte. *Jane Eyre.* New York: Bantam Books, 1981.

Chen, Chih-Ping. "'Am I a Monster?': Jane Eyre among the Shadows of Freaks," *Studies in the Novel* 34, no. 4 (winter 2002): 367–384.

Donaldson, Elizabeth J. "The Corpus of the Madwoman: Toward a Feminist Disability Studies Theory of Embodiment and Mental Illness," *NWSA Journal* 14, no. 3 (fall 2002): 99–119.

Meyer, Susan. "Colonialism and the Figurative Strategy of *Jane Eyre*," *Victorian Studies* 33, no. 2 (1990): 247–268.

Rochester, Edward

For maximum effect, author Charlotte BRONTË delays the reader's first view of Edward Fairfax Rochester, the strong-willed, thrillingly dangerous master of THORNFIELD in the classic Gothic novel JANE EYRE (1847). SUSPENSE builds in the title character from fall to January as she accustoms herself to a first job as tutor to his foster child, Adèle Varens. The introduction of master to governess occurs on a routine morning as Jane walks two miles to Hay to mail the housekeeper's letter. The setting is a stile halfway from Thornfield, a SYMBOL of Jane's passage into new territory. Rochester, a sour, darkly appealing BYRONIC HERO, rides up on his horse Mesrour and slips on ice. The author pictures Jane as frightened of the pawing horse and great black dog Pilot as she ponders tales of the Gytrash, a sinister animal spirit. Nonetheless, she is eager to aid the unidentified man, who remounts and gallops on. Their brief encounter foreshadows the brusque, selfish wooing that employer offers employee as Rochester begins to see in Jane a future helpmeet.

For historical background, the author draws on a 17th-century misanthrope, atheist, pornographer, and womanizer, John Wilmot, the second earl of Rochester, as the source of Thornfield's master. From the beginning, Jane's uncertain relationship with her employer stumbles over gaps in his explanation of the household. He describes his guardianship of Adèle as founded "on the Roman Catholic principle of expiating numerous sins, great or small, by one good work" and adds, "I'll explain all this some day" (Brontë, 130–131). As becomes a Byronic hero, he worsens Jane's imaginings by maintaining the dark secret of his past infractions and by refusing to account for the cankering guilt for which he must atone. Jane knows that he has led a profligate life abroad—the stereotypical background of Victorian novels that characterize foreign settings, particularly France, as lures to human license and depravity. Jane must wait to learn about the two women in Rochester's past before comprehending Rochester's discontent and his bitter torment.

A significant Gothic feature of Rochester's relationship with Jane is the chasm between their two social levels. On the day that house guests arrive, Jane, like a dowdy parsonage mouse, dresses in simple finery, creeps about in the background, and peers briefly at an elegant entourage in full evening dress. Most daunting is the hauteur of Blanche Ingram, which overawes and belittles Jane after Rochester insists that she join the gathering. The plot device of Mother Bunches, the pipe-smoking gypsy teller of fortunes as an evening amusement, serves two purposes. The bizarre cross-dressing episode adds a new note of SUPERSTITION and doubt in Jane, then buoys her to first place in Rochester's esteem when she conquers her hesitance, surveys his disguise, and unmasks him.

Ill fortune in the past as well as a distance in age raise obstacles to Rochester's wooing of Jane, who at 19 is 20 years his junior. As a suitor, he blends superiority with paternalism, angry outbursts, and a touch of SADISM. Beneath the horse chestnut tree, an idyllic setting in the Thornfield orchard, his shadow elongates ominously. He taunts Jane with projections of a new family order after his intended marriage to Blanche. Brontë overstates the threat to Jane with verbal OMENS, a new position for an Irish mistress, Mrs. Dionysius O'Gall of Bitternutt Lodge. The possibility of leaving Thornfield for a post that is bitter as gall brings Jane to the brink of tears.

Brontë challenges the notion that women lessen their stature by weeping. Jane's honest emotion counterbalances Rochester's eccentricities. Her forthright dismay elicits a candor in him that supplants the Gothic gruffness and forbidding pose as manipulator of her future. He admits that he is tied to her, rib to rib, by an invisible string—a distant allusion to Adam and Eve in the Garden of Eden. Still posturing as lord of the domain, he proposes marriage, even though she is inferior, obscure, and plain-featured. He launches into an unintelligible internal debate about self-will versus moral law. Without clarifying his emotion to Jane, he insists "It will atone—it will atone," an ambiguous expiation of bigamy (*ibid.*, 243). Like Pontius Pilate, he grandly concludes, "For the world's judgment—I wash my hands thereof. For man's opinion—I defy it" (*ibid.*).

Brontë takes Rochester within reach of true villainy at the wedding, one of the more Gothic of altar scenes in English literature. At breakfast, he appears "bent up to a purpose," a resolution punctuated by flashes of the eyes under sturdy brows (*ibid.*, 273). The author cloaks a sexual impetuosity beneath his hurried steps to the church, which leave Jane out of breath. Gothic details foreshadow doom at the entrance, where a rook encircles the steeple and two strangers read epitaphs from gravestones. An additional portent places the unidentified men at the Rochester vault with backs turned to the ceremony.

The confrontation between past and present brings out the worst and best in Edward Rochester. In the presence of an unnamed witness contesting the union, Rochester grows stubborn and rigid, his eyes "both spark and flint," a FORESHADOWING of the fire that ruins his life and destroys his fortune (*ibid.*, 275). Brontë presents him as so enraged by the dilemma that he utters retorts improper for a holy place. Scorning well-wishers at the church door, he drags Jane to Thornfield and up the stairs to the den of his rabid wife Bertha, who grapples wolflike at his throat and cheek. With a dramatic contrast before witnesses, he pictures Jane as standing "at the mouth of hell" (*ibid.*, 279).

Through Rochester's extreme behavior, Brontë offers a warning to Jane. At the peak of his ravings, she realizes that, after 15 years of keeping secret his marriage to a murderous lunatic, he could easily "plunge headlong into wild licence" (*ibid.*, 287). He admits to being a hot-tempered scoundrel and warns, "I am not cool and dispassionate. Out of pity to me and yourself, put your finger on my pulse, feel how it throbs, and—beware!" (*ibid.*, 289). After losing Jane, he grows savage, dispatching Thornfield's faithful housekeeper to retirement and retreating into anguished solitude to mourn his confinement and to prowl the charred grounds by night like a phantom.

The author engineers the emergence of the lunatic Bertha Mason Rochester from the attic and her destruction of Rochester's estate as a great leveling device. In the denouement, Brontë enlarges on the first meeting between Rochester and Jane, when neither knows the other. On her final meeting with him at the edge of the forest, architectural clues—a simple home with no flower beds and no structural pretensions—indicate his diminished stature. Rochester's blindness and loss of vigor that resulted when he was struck by a falling beam in the sensational fire that consumed Thornfield obscures his identification of Jane as she approaches and, once more, lends her strength. In assessing the change in him, Jane discerns a rough justice, the amputation of left hand and eye as a divine moral awakening to an aging roué, a comeuppance that Rochester shares with the historical John Wilmot.

While humbling the hero with a symbolic woman-inflicted wound, Brontë is careful to leave enough of the original manly, self-willed Rochester to maintain his sexual appeal. The irascible, resolute master grows maudlin with self-pity and suffering and describes himself as "no better than the old lightning-struck chestnut-tree in Thornfield orchard" (*ibid.*, 425). Jane refuses to accept his image of human ruin. Her willingness to reclaim him becomes a signal strength. From his diminution from master to semi-invalid and from Jane's rise through a small inheritance and success in the classroom, the standard Gothic separation of classes brings them into a new and more promising relationship that bodes well for marriage.

Bibliography

Brontë, Charlotte. *Jane Eyre*. New York: Bantam Books, 1981.

Kendrik, Robert. "Edward Rochester and the Margins of Masculinity in 'Jane Eyre' and 'Wide Sargasso Sea,'" *Papers on Language & Literature* 30, no. 3 (summer 1994): 235–256.

Pittock, Murray G. H. "John Wilmot and Mr. Rochester," *Nineteenth-Century Literature* 41, no. 4 (1987): 462–469.

roman noir

A Gothic thriller novel, the *roman noir*—literally, "black novel" in French—stresses crime or corruption, the gathering of clues, and a pronouncement of judgment on criminals. Derived from fictional tales of the Middle Ages, in the early 1800s, the *roman noir* or *litterature noire* developed into a popular phenomenon. A forerunner, Reveroni Saint-Cyr's *Pauliska, ou La Perversité Moderne* (Pauliska; or, modern perversity, 1796), which preceded J. F. Regnault-Warin's *Le Cimetière de la Madeleine* (The graveyard of the Church of the Madeleine, 1800), resurrects ghosts of the French Revolution, which haunt a pedestrian passing through the heart of Paris. The genre was pessimistic by nature. Mass-marketed Gothic dime novels such as VARNEY THE VAMPIRE (1847) focused on outsized passions, melodramatic flights from stalkers, gory clashes with villains, bizarre plot twists, and other unrefined elements of pulp fiction that set it apart from legitimate literature. The French dark novel was an impetus to FILM NOIR, a screen parallel of fatalism, gritty urban settings, underworld figures, and doomed protagonists.

An American version of the *roman noir* took shape during the social and economic upheaval of the Jazz Age, the Great Depression, and Prohibition with absorbing, hard-boiled crime and detective novels. The most popular works in this genre were Dashiell Hammett's *The Maltese Falcon* (1930), James M. Cain's *The Postman Always Rings Twice* (1934), and Raymond Chandler's *The Big Sleep* (1939)—all subsequent vehicles for cinematic adaptations. These authors and the screenplays they inspired captured in fiction the nagging anxieties of Americans over shifts in sexual mores, the rise of female independence, and the rampant corruption in industry and law that threatened the American dream.

Bibliography

Gorrara, Claire. *The Roman Noir in Post-War French Culture.* Oxford: Oxford University Press, 2003.

Marling, William. *The American Roman Noir: Hammett, Cain, and Chandler.* Athens: University of Georgia Press, 1995.

romanticism

A style dominating Western literature in the latter half of the 1700s and the early 1800s, high romanticism developed into a refined literary and artistic expression of MYSTICISM, imagination, individuality, love of NATURE, and freedom from the constraints of neoclassicism. These elements also formed the rudiments of Gothicism, a dark strand of romanticism that incorporates some but not all of its traits. Although disdained and ridiculed by the neoclassicists for their lack of grace and dignity, early Gothic narratives prevailed as the incubator of the romantic period and earned the regard of the romanticists for their immersion in primitivism and MEDIEVALISM and for their validation of authentic feelings and variety of expression.

Romantic poetry and fiction flourished with a resurgence of emotion and human response to solitude and to encounters with the wild. Emphasis on subjectivity and the individual allowed the Gothic subset to inveigh against traditional values and to locate dire plots within the ruins of castles and abbeys, the remains of lapsed institutions from past eras. As though released from the dominance of rationalism, readers and theater-goers welcomed the stalker tale, GHOST STORY, MONSTERS and goblins, DIABOLISM, POSSESSION and WITCHCRAFT, and other metaphysical and preternatural elements. Gothic romanticism stressed the pain, barbarity, torment, and murder suffered by human victims. Expressing the harm of authoritarianism to society, Gothic authors obliged the public with stories of entrapment, fettering, CLAUSTROPHOBIA, PREMATURE BURIAL, and confinement in DUNGEONS AND PRISONS where escape routes were small, obscure, and fraught with peril.

Beginning with the stirrings of PREROMANTICISM and the GRAVEYARD POETS, dark elements of romanticism in art, music, and literature freed writers from the rules and preconceptions of neoclassicists to reflect bourgeois tastes for fantasy, spontaneity, the SUPERNATURAL, and the macabre. The first romantic writer to frame the Gothic ideal in novel form was Horace WALPOLE, author of THE CASTLE OF OTRANTO (1765). Nineteenth- and 20th-century Gothic conventions evolving from romanticism include eccentric or GROTESQUE characters (Flannery O'CONNOR's Hazel Motes and Nathaniel HAWTHORNE's Roger Chillingworth), OBSESSION with mortality (William Cullen Bryant's "THANATOPSIS"), the FEMME FATALE or woman of mystery (Edgar Allan POE's Ligeia and Abbé PRÉVOST's Manon Lescaut), uncontrollable passion (Emily BRONTË's HEATHCLIFF and Daphne DU

MAURIER's Rebecca DE WINTER), psychological torment (Hawthorne's *THE HOUSE OF SEVEN GABLES* and Herman MELVILLE's *Moby-Dick*), brash heroics (Sir Walter Scott's HISTORICAL NOVELs and Jonathan HARKER's face-off against Count DRACULA in Bram STOKER's *DRACULA*), and inscrutable dark powers (Central American tales of *LA LLORONA* and Jewish fables of the DYBBUK).

From their reading of established folk elements—the WANDERING JEW, the knight and his lady, FAUST, and vampires and werewolves—the romantic poets helped to define the Gothic ideal. With their command of poetic devices, they shaped nightmare and terror imagery and outlined the romantic hero, often a loner, outcast, or rebel, who bore an air of MYSTERY and egocentrism, a provocative blend that reached its height in such BYRONIC HEROes as Charlotte BRONTË's Edward ROCHESTER and Algernon Swinburne's François Villon. The romantic sympathy for MELANCHOLY and loss, an evolution of graveyard verse, set the literary stage for the victim novels of Ann RADCLIFFE, a transitional preromantic. The elements came to fruition in the writings of Matthew Gregory LEWIS, who depicted the standard triad of willowy young NAIF who must flee the clutches of the lustful and/or lethal VILLAIN to find happiness with a potential mate, a lesser male lacking both the heroine's sensibilities and the stalker's dark allure. Outdistancing Gothic authors in sophistication and control, the giants of English romanticism—Lord BYRON, Samuel Taylor COLERIDGE, John KEATS, Percy Bysshe SHELLEY, and William Wordsworth—rid literature of overstatement.

The growth of subjectivity, eerie grotesque images, ORIENTAL ROMANCE, exotic subjects and themes, and translations of imaginative literature from Germany and France boosted the range of the GOTHIC NOVEL to daring extremes lacking in romantic fiction. In Russia, Vladimir ODOEVSKY directed inquiry into the impact of science and technology on art in a masterwork, *Russkiye Notchi* (*Russian Nights*, 1844). In England and the United States, the era saw publication of the best in the Gothic tradition: Charles Brockden BROWN's perusal of madness in *WIELAND* (1798), Mary Wollstonecraft SHELLEY's noble savage in *FRANKENSTEIN* (1818), Charlotte Brontë's madwoman in the attic

in *JANE EYRE* (1847), Emily Brontë's primitivism in *WUTHERING HEIGHTS* (1847), Hawthorne's study of secret sin in *THE SCARLET LETTER* (1850), and Bram Stoker's monster lore in *Dracula* (1897). Short fiction came to fruition in America and Europe with the escapist fantasies of E. T. A. HOFFMANN, the horror and detective tales of Edgar Allan Poe, the diabolic moral tales of Hawthorne, the DOPPELGÄNGER motif in Robert Louis STEVENSON's *DR. JEKYLL AND MR. HYDE* (1886), and the frontier ghost story perfected by Ambrose BIERCE.

Bibliography

Gamer, Michael. "Authors in Effect: Lewis, Scott, and the Gothic Drama," *English Literary History* 66, no. 4 (1999): 831–861.

———. *Romanticism and the Gothic: Genre, Reception, and Canon Formation.* Cambridge: Cambridge University Press, 2000.

Punter, David, ed. *The Literature of Terror*, vol. 1, 2nd ed. London: Longman, 1996.

"A Rose for Emily"
William Faulkner
(1930)

One of William FAULKNER's frequently anthologized short works, "A Rose for Emily" has intrigued readers ever since its initial publication in the April 30, 1930, edition of *Forum*. The story functions on a number of levels, from Southern ALLEGORY and metaphor for the Reconstruction era to a Gothic HORROR tale and feminist theme of the lone woman's victory over male dominance. Set in Faulkner's microcosm of Jefferson, Mississippi, seat of the fictional Yoknapatawpha County, the story tells in flashback the spinsterhood of Miss EMILY, a butt of town jokes because of her father's tyranny, and her failed love match with Homer Barron, a Northern beau. Building interest through SUSPENSE, Faulkner describes the townsfolk as puzzled by a foul odor issuing from the homeplace, yet they are too respectful of Miss Emily's privacy to question her directly about the source.

A succinct list of clues builds tension. FORESHADOWING the grim resolution are ample evidence of Emily's sufferings under a dominant father and a hint at the cause of the odor after she purchases arsenic to kill rodents, SYMBOLs of the human vermin who courts her. The concluding scene, a surprise revelation, pictures her corpse sharing a bridal bed with Barron, whose mummified remains attest to his death by poisoning. In Faulkner's words: "What was left of him, rotted beneath what was left of the nightshirt, had become inextricable from the bed in which he lay; and upon him and upon the pillow beside him lay that even coating of the patient and biding dust" (Faulkner, 130).

Critics respond to a SUBTEXT of sexual repression, madness, and necrophilia by labeling Faulkner's story a Gothic horror tale. The title gesture implies the author's pity for a victimized Southern female constrained by aristocratic elitism and stilted expectations that entrapped genteel aristocratic women. In terms of the strictures, Miss Emily is a modern version of the virgin sequestered in the castle high above the common folk, where her captor denies her normal activities, pleasures, and aims. The title also implies that she "rose" from patriarchy in her own way, by beguiling and murdering the man who toyed with her affections.

Bibliography

Faulkner, William. *Collected Stories of William Faulkner.* New York: Vintage Books, 1950.

Howe, Irving. *William Faulkner: A Critical Study.* New York: Vintage Books, 1962.

Rossetti, Christina

(1830–1894)

A prolific versifier of Gothic narratives and wistful sonnets, poet Christina Georgina Rossetti came from a complex lineage of romanticists. Her older brother, Dante Gabriel Rossetti, was a leader of the PRE-RAPHAELITE BROTHERHOOD; an older sister, Maria Francesca Rossetti, published essays and devotional treatises; a younger brother, William Michael Rossetti, was an editor, critic, and translator; an uncle, Dr. John William POLIDORI, authored "The Vampyre" (1819). Christina Rossetti, an author of poetry collections in English and Italian, began exploring versification in girlhood and was a published author by age 17. Under the pseudonym

Ellen Alleyne, she submitted poems to her brother's journal, the *Germ,* the first of one thousand poems in her career. In December 1848, she wrote "Song," a gentle, MELANCHOLY dirge permeated with a funereal rhapsody popularized by the graveyard poets.

Because she was deeply devoted to Anglicanism, Rossetti rejected two suitors and committed herself to writing. At age 32, she gained permanent fame for the RESCUE THEME of a narrative poem, *THE GOBLIN MARKET* (1862), a whimsical tale of sisterly love. After doctors diagnosed her with Graves' disease, Rossetti pressed on with her verse and devotional writing, which became a solace after the deaths of her mother, sister, and brother Dante Gabriel. She created dreamscapes, plaints, and ballads on themes of lost love, isolation, sorrow and remorse, and the allure of death.

A gifted storyteller, Rossetti explored the hellish nature of unsupervised children among ghoulish shape-shifters in *Speaking Likenesses* (1874), a beguiling cautionary tale for venturesome little girls. In sadistic episodes based on Lewis Carroll's *Alice in Wonderland* (1865), Flora, one of the heroines, involves herself in fiendish children's games, the worst being "Hunt the Pincushion," during which players stick her with pins. Arthur Hughes's illustrations for the text depict Maggie, in the guise of Little Red Riding Hood, being pulled into play by a host of ghostly cloud children and their phantom dog. Rossetti leads Maggie along a dark forest road where "The sky had turned leaden, the wind blew bleaker than ever, the bare boughs creaked and rattled drearily" (Rossetti, *Speaking,* 87). Rossetti's use of GOTHIC CONVENTION and the dark messages of the fairy tale express the Victorian woman's fearful path amid social pitfalls and personal temptations.

Bibliography

Gilbert, Sandra M., and Susan Gubar. *The Madwoman in the Attic,* 2nd ed. New Haven, Conn.: Yale University Press, 2000.

Rossetti, Christina. *Speaking Likenesses.* London: Macmillan, 1874.

Wiesenthal, Christine. "Regarding Christina Rossetti's 'Reflection,'" *Victorian Poetry* 39, no. 3 (fall 2001): 389–407.

S

sadism

The term *sadism* denotes a sexual perversion through which a twisted personality obtains pleasure and satisfaction from harming, tormenting, maiming, even killing innocent victims, an element dominating VILLIERS DE L'ISLE-ADAM's *Contes Cruels* (Cruel tales, 1883) and *Nouveaux Contes Cruels* (New cruel tales, 1888) and Hanns Heinz EWERS's twisted novel *Alraune* (The Mandrakes, 1911) and "Die Hinrichtung des Damiens" (The Execution of Damien, ca. 1925). An example from American Gothic literature, the GROTESQUE torment of Pluto, the title animal in Edgar Allan POE's "THE BLACK CAT" (1843), begins with the speaker excising the animal's eyes with a penknife. The gruesome torment concludes with hanging, a common execution method of witches' familiars during the Middle Ages.

Inextricably connected with sadism are the post–French Revolution behavior and writings of Donatien Alphonse François, Marquis de Sade, a sexual libertine and violator of prostitutes. Influenced by the writings of Matthew Gregory LEWIS and Ann RADCLIFFE, he wrote stories filled with abominable sexual acts and the villainous abuse of maidens. The psychological malady called *sadism* appeared in his *129 Days of Sodom* (1785), in which he justified the degradation and commission of violent acts on a loved one as a source of carnal excitation. In his essay "Idée sur le Roman" (Reflections on the novel, 1800), he blamed the trauma inflicted by the French Revolution for catapulting normal human beings into wicked, hellish behavior, including bondage, rape, torture, and dismemberment.

A knowledgeable commentator on Gothicism, de Sade wrote from the point of view of the apostate. In GROTESQUE pornographies and gratuitous sexual analyses of Gothic literature, he expressed belief in the dark nature of humanity. In reference to English Gothic fiction, he admired Lewis's THE MONK (1796), which de Sade characterized as a response to the VIOLENCE and human abuses engendered by the Jacobin leader Maximilien Robespierre and the guillotine. Through prurient novels—*Justine; or, Good Conduct Well Chastised* (1791), *Juliette* (1796), and *Aline and Valcour* (1795)—de Sade demonstrated that the formulaic heroine expressed an ambivalence toward male family members and menacing seducers. In his subversion of GOTHIC CONVENTION, he established that, through stagy acts of malevolence, subjugation, and humiliation, the sadist produced delight and amusement. Thus, the sexual libertine, by orchestrating hell on earth, became the heir of the doomed, self-gratifying BYRONIC HERO.

Bibliography

Brontë, Emily. *Wuthering Heights*. New York: New American Library, 1959.

Orlans, Harold. "Canonizing the Marquis de Sade," *Change* 28, no. 4 (July–August 1996): 6–7.

Moers, Ellen. "The Monster's Mother," *New York Review of Books* March 21, 1974: 24–33.

Paulson, Ronald. "Gothic Fiction and the French Revolution," *English Literary History* 48 (1981): 532–553.

Saki
H. H. Munro
(1870–1916)

The Scottish writer Hector Hugh "Hugo" Munro was one of Edwardian England's wittiest, least sentimental storytellers. He produced elegant, concise fiction under the pseudonym Saki, the name of the cupbearer in the *Rubáiyát* (1859). His specialties, according to admirer Christopher Morley, were aunts and werewolves, a reference to Saki's boyhood spent with child-hating maiden aunts while his father was posted in Burma with the Bengal Staff Corps. Saki followed the family tradition by volunteering with the Burmese Imperial Police, but suffered such severe malaria that he had to return to England.

Saki honed his writing talent as a journalist and mordant cartoonist for the *Bystander* and the *Daily Express*. While traveling the Balkans, France, Poland, and Russia as a war correspondent for the *Morning Post*, he submitted his first story to *St. Paul's Magazine* and published potent fiction in the *Westminster Gazette*. Choosing the paganism and snobbery of his age as themes, he issued *Not So Stories* (1902), the first of a string of collections tinged with hilarious weirdness. His life came to a dismal end during his service as lance sergeant in World War I, when he died from a sniper's bullet in a foxhole on the western front in France.

Saki had a penchant for absurdism. His stories glorified the savagery of animals, ranging from a fox terrier, hedgehogs, and polecats to pariah dogs, goblins, and mystic beasts, which often lurk unseen. His predations advanced to LYCANTHROPY in "Gabriel-Ernest" (1909), in which the killer is a werewolf. His allegorical fables and FAIRY TALEs produced a quirky blend of satire, horror, and acerbic Gothic humor, featuring creatures that deliver an appropriate comeuppance to nasty-nice humans, as in the title beasts in "The She-Wolf" (1912) and "The Boar-Pig" (1914). In "Esmé" (1911), a hyena delivers the death blow; in "The Story-Teller" (1914), a wolf devours a too-good little girl; in "The Guests" (1923), the coup de grâce comes from a leopard. His most famous story, "SREDNI VASHTAR," published in *The Chronicles of Clovis* (1911), features a pet ferret as a killer. Saki wrote another frequently anthologized piece of fiction, "The Open Window" (1911), in the form of a droll pseudo–GHOST STORY, which he collected in *Beasts and Super-Beasts* (1914). His succinct style, erotic touches, and vitriolic black comedy earned the kudos of G. K. Chesterton, Noel Coward, Graham Greene, and Evelyn WAUGH.

Bibliography

Birden, Lorene M. "Saki's 'A Matter of Sentiment,'" *Explicator* 56, no. 3 (summer 1998): 201–204.

Frost, Adam. "A Hundred Years of Saki," *Contemporary Review* 275, no. 1,607 (December 1999): 302.

Salomé
Oscar Wilde
(1893)

In his most Gothic play, Oscar WILDE overlays beauty, Byzantine DISSIPATION, and terror in the quasi-biblical drama *Salomé* (1893). He chose to write the portentous, stagy rendering in French, for which Aubrey Beardsley provided evocative cover art. Set under an ominous moon, the action begins with observations of onlookers and guards at Herod's palace in Palestine. To free herself from an oppressive court ATMOSPHERE, Salomé appears onstage to enjoy the night air and describes the menace of barbaric OUTSIDERs—vicious Jerusalem Jews, drunken barbarians, "Greeks from Smyrna with painted eyes and painted cheeks, and frizzed hair curled in twisted coils, and silent, subtle Egyptians, with long nails of jade and russet cloaks, and Romans brutal and coarse, with their uncouth jargon" (Wilde, 322). Her complaints precede a seductive gesture toward the prisoner Jokanaan (John the Baptist), who turns away. The rejection generates a murderous boldness in Salomé, who evolves into a Gothic FEMME FATALE.

Wilde mirrors the interplay of good and evil with a stark CHIAROSCURO that frames hints of incest in Herod's marriage to his sister-in-law, the suicide of a guard, and immurement of the wonder-worker Jokanaan in a dark cistern. After Jokanaan's decapitation, the vampirish Salomé fondles his head in a bizarre display of necrophilia, then dances with her gory trophy perched on a silver shield. Herod stifles his daring stepdaughter by ordering his body guard to crush her with their shields. The audacious play outraged the Lord Chamberlain, who banned it in London, but the drama suited the worldly tastes of French and German audiences. Richard Strauss reset the play as an opera; Theda Bara appeared in a 1913 film version.

Bibliography

Bucknell, Brad. "On 'Seeing' Salomé," *English Literary History* 60, no. 2 (summer 1993): 503–526.

Nassaar, Christopher S., and Nataly Shaheen. "Wilde's 'Salomé,'" *Explicator* 59, no. 3 (spring 2001): 132.

Thomas, David Wayne. "The 'Strange Music' of Salomé: Oscar Wilde's Rhetoric of Verbal Musicality," *Mosaic* 33, no. 1 (March 2000): 15.

Wilde, Oscar. *Plays.* London: Penguin, 1954.

Satis House

In Satis House, Charles DICKENS produced a worthy home for one of his most Gothic characters, Miss HAVISHAM, the nihilistic recluse in the Victorian social novel GREAT EXPECTATIONS (1861). The height of the novel's Gothicism is an unsettling timelessness at her hermitage, a crumbling red-brick mansion that sits behind a locked gate alongside the sour, rotting barrels of an abandoned brewery, the source of the Havisham fortune. Dickens pictures the house as forlorn and unused in chill weather: "The cold wind seemed to blow colder there, than outside the gate; and it made a shrill noise in howling in and out at the open sides of the brewery, like the noise of wind in the rigging of a ship at sea" (Dickens, 866). Pip, Miss Havisham's hired boy, notes an insidious quality about the blocked windows and ivy grasping the chimney stacks.

The inhospitable property, a Gothic wasteland, takes its name from the Latin for "enough." Dickens builds the image into a metaphoric cage that offers the owner "enough" opportunities to avenge herself on the fraud who ruined her hopes for marriage. Dark passages and staircases, lit by a single candle, lead to a decaying banquet table readied years before for a wedding that never took place. In Pip's childish description, "It was then I began to understand that everything in the room had stopped, like the watch and the clock, a long time ago" (*ibid.*, 869). Outside, Pip revisits the yard among the broken-down pigeon-house, maltless storehouses, and rank garden. At the novel's end, Dickens returns a mature Pip to Satis House, now reduced to rubble with greening ivy creeping over the mound, suggesting NATURE reclaiming a grave. To further erase the unwelcoming house from Pip's past, Dickens describes shining stars and a moon casting its light over the mansion's remains.

Bibliography

Dickens, Charles. *Great Expectations,* in vol. 2 of *The Annotated Dickens,* ed. by Edward Guiliano and Philip Collins. New York: Clarkson N. Potter, 1986.

Walsh, Susan. "Bodies of Capital: 'Great Expectations' and the Climacteric Economy," *Victorian Studies* 37, no. 1 (autumn 1993): 73–98.

The Scarlet Letter
Nathaniel Hawthorne
(1850)

A symbolist romance drawn from the ancestral history of author Nathaniel HAWTHORNE, *The Scarlet Letter* addresses the dual themes of OBSESSION with secret sin and the denial of forgiveness. The prologue, "The Custom House," introduces the story with a standard Gothic ploy, the discovery of a mysterious yellow parchment. Allegedly composed by a civic clerk responsible for measuring and weighing commodities, the prologue establishes the theme of arbitrary, male-dominated judgments, a controlling idea in the story of the punishment of Hester Prynne, a Puritan woman condemned for adultery. Among the novel's Gothic elements are a misshapen herbalist, the dosing of a crying infant with unknown medicaments, a prying witch, and a meteor that sketches an A in the sky.

Hawthorne manipulates ATMOSPHERE in his classic revelation of the despised adulterer with the swinging open of the prison door, the emotion-freighted image that begins the novel. An accusing overtone enshrouds the pious village, where one wild rose epitomizes the sweetness and goodness in Hester, who departs the iron and wood lockup with her newborn daughter, Pearl. Upon their emergence in the village, a social dungeon awaits the pair and fetters their lives with constant staring, speculation, inhospitality, and rejection: "Every gesture, every word, and even the silence of those with whom she came in contact, implied, and often expressed, that she was banished, and as much alone as if she inhabited another sphere" (Hawthorne, 133). Thus, a former citizen finds herself transformed into a despised OUTSIDER.

Hawthorne confers near sainthood upon Hester, who displays self-respect and loyalty by complying with her sentence. Out of loyalty to her own version of morality, she refuses to divulge the name of Pearl's father. Fellow Bostonians retaliate with gossip, sneers at Pearl, and social ostracism. Hester rewards scorn with good deeds by comforting the dying and gathering fallen women around her to confer acceptance and forgiveness on their damaged hearts.

Hawthorne uses Hester's dilemma as an opportunity to comment on solitude and NATURE. She chooses to retreat to the nearby seashore and rear her elf-child in a pure environment rather than in the hypocrisy and stony-heartedness of a Puritan village. The reunion of Hester, Pearl, and the Reverend Arthur Dimmesdale, Pearl's father, in the forest links their formal disunion with the wildness and savagery of the frontier, where Satan allegedly holds witches' covens. In the estimation of proper Boston Puritans, the forest equates with ungodliness and threatens the order and sanctity of a pious community. In actuality, the meeting takes place by a cleansing brook amid sparse sunbeams near the habitat of pigeons and partridges, symbols of modesty. Reared outside Puritan stodginess, Pearl plays without parental direction and feels free to question her mother about legends of the bogeyman.

Drawing on Charles Robert MATURIN's MELMOTH THE WANDERER (1820) and Edgar Allan POE's *William Wilson* (1839), Hawthorne creates a provincial stalker in Roger Chillingworth, who uses his influence as a doctor to torment his wife's lover. The novel sets the falling action on election day at a public stage, the village scaffold, where the unsanctified family stands together. A string of revelations spills over in public to satisfy scorn of Hester's adultery and speculation about Pearl's sire, the demonic leech's control of Dimmesdale, and the minister's failing health, emaciation, and emotional burden. In the shadow of the meeting house, an emblem of a fanatical theocracy that tyrannizes village life, the story reaches its somber conclusion with the minister's collapse, Hester's failed hope of escape from her tormentor, and the villainous leech's shriveling like a noxious weed. Hawthorne's ALLEGORY has maintained its ascendancy over less philosophical Gothic works. *The Scarlet Letter* influenced a number of subsequent novels, such as Herman MELVILLE's *Moby-Dick* (1851), John Updike's *The Witches of Eastwick* (1984), and Margaret ATWOOD's THE HANDMAID'S TALE (1985).

Bibliography

Hawthorne, Nathaniel. *The Complete Novels and Selected Tales of Nathaniel Hawthorne*. New York: Modern Library, 1937.

Reiss, John. "Hawthorne's 'The Scarlet Letter,'" *Explicator* 53, no. 4 (summer 1995): 200–201.

Ringe, Donald A. "The Critical Response to Nathaniel Hawthorne's 'The Scarlet Letter,'" *ANQ* 7, no. 1 (January 1994): 61–62.

Schauer-Romantik

The German tradition of horror romance, *Schauer-Romantik*, displays the Teutonic interest in demons, apparitions, and devils. The genre began in the late 18th-century as the *Schauerroman* ("shudder novel") with such violent narratives as Friedrich von SCHILLER's play *Die Räuber* (*The Robbers*, 1781) and the spectral implications of DER GEISTERSEHER (*The Ghost-Seer*, 1786). Essential to the dynamic literary trend were a fascination with evil, graphic VIOLENCE and details of sex crimes, and the SUPERNATURAL, a thrill-packed trio of elements. The TONE and ATMOSPHERE influenced Victor Hugo, Jules JANIN, Charles Lassailly, Jean Charles Nodier, and other French writers of the *frénétique* school, which inspired the Gothic works of Théophile GAUTIER. In the words of the critic and author Anna Laetitia BARBAULD, "Solitude, darkness, low-whispered sounds, obscure glimpses of objects, flitting forms, tend to raise in the mind that thrilling, mysterious terror, which has for its object the 'powers unseen and mightier far than we'" (Varma, 130). The German masters of the genre include Gottfried August Bürger, Joseph Alois Gleich, Johann Wolfgang von GOETHE, E. T. A. HOFFMANN, Franz Kafka, Ernst August Klingemann, Heinrich von Kleist, Johann Karl Musäus, Schiller, and Johann Ludwig TIECK.

At a turning point in English Gothic literature, German horror writings invigorated the imagination of a Gothic prose innovator, Matthew Gregory LEWIS, author of the horror classic THE MONK (1796). Lewis's aggressive stance on horror posed a distinct deviation from the more refined, restrained terror novels of his contemporary, Ann RADCLIFFE. In the wake of Lewis's innovation came his imitators—notably, Charlotte DACRE, Karl Grosse, Ann Julia Hatton, Francis LATHOM, Charles Robert MATURIN, Eliza PARSONS, and Regina Maria ROCHE. In the evolving AMERICAN GOTHIC, Cajetan Tschink's *Der Geisterseher* (*The Ghost Seer*, 1797) influenced Charles Brockden BROWN, who produced WIELAND (1798), the New World's first Gothic novel.

In the 19th century, English readers created a demand for translations of German horror tales, some rendered by Thomas De Quincey and Sir Walter SCOTT. The two Gothic works by the English romanticists that owe the most to German shudder novels are Mary Wollstonecraft SHELLEY's FRANKENSTEIN (1818) and Dr. John POLIDORI's "The Vampyre" (1819), which spawned their own imitations. German critics referred to this growing list of shockers as "Der Englische *Schauerroman*"; Maturin brought this subgenre to high art in his psychological novel MELMOTH THE WANDERER (1820). The imprint of German Gothicism remained strong at the end of the century, when novelist Bram STOKER drew on the anonymous tale *The Mysterious Stranger*, translated into English in 1860, for the physical description and exorcism of the vampire in DRACULA (1897).

Bibliography

Frank, Frederick S. "Gothic Gold: The Sadleir-Black Collection of Gothic Fiction," *Studies in Eighteenth-Century Culture* 26 (1998): 287–312.

Haining, Peter, ed. *Gothic Tales of Terror*. New York: Taplinger, 1972.

Schedoni

The monk Schedoni, the dissipated hero-VILLAIN of Ann RADCLIFFE's THE ITALIAN (1797), is the looming OUTSIDER, the man of unknown character and lineage for whom rumor and innuendo serve in place of fact. Far more reprehensible than Montoni, the author's first villain in THE MYSTERIES OF UDOLPHO (1794), Schedoni exhibits alien traits through the ambiguous status of the evil Italian cleric, the product of the author's twisted notions of Italy and Catholicism from readings of history, drama, and popular fiction. Approaching tragedy, the story characterizes him as a tormented BYRONIC HERO, a protagonist of psychological fiction whose very nature prohibits goodness and decency.

On the title page of her three-volume novel, the author pre-exonerates Schedoni of devious impulses and defends him from calumny. She pictures him enshrouded in mystery, brooding and silent and unfathomable. To offset too much sympathy, however, she reveals that the monk approaches the superhuman in his ferocious gloom and SECRECY. From his feral eyes, which the heroine, Ellena Rosalba, glimpses within the folds of his cowl, gleam potential cruelties. Concealed in his vest is a cache of poison, a SYMBOL of human venom, the demonic nature that leads Schedoni to murder his brother and wife and plot the stabbing of Ellena and the ruin of Vivaldi by the Inquisition.

Schedoni's reptilian guile and secretiveness suit Radcliffe as a means to heighten MYSTERY and generate dread. At the climactic moment in volume 2, chapter 10, the monk approaches with weapon drawn to impale the heroine. The author explains his inborn malevolence: "He had a dagger concealed beneath his Monk's habit; as he had also an assassin's heart shrouded by his garments" (*ibid.*, 224). Ironically, in the moments preceding the intended killing, Ellena refers to him as "father." Retreating in a welter of contradictions and inconsistent emotions, he realizes that the miniature portrait she wears of her father is his own image.

Radcliffe spares Schedoni his daughter's hatred and provides instead an indirect accusation of guilt. At an unforeseen moment along the street, a peasant points to a public PUNCH AND JUDY show and calls out to Schedoni, "Look! Signor, see! Signor, what a scoundrel! what a villain! See! he has murdered his own daughter!" (*ibid.*, 274). The announcement before people in the street causes Ellena to look deep into his face and find "the changing emotions of his soul, and the inexplicable character of his countenance" (*ibid.,* 275). That night, sleep eludes the monk, who is tormented with remorse, blunted pride, and apprehension. At this unintentionally dramatic contretemps, Radcliffe perpetuates the view of Schedoni as more than a mere villain, yet too wicked for redemption.

At the novel's moral crux, Radcliffe generates complex judgments. In custody of the grand inquisitor, the monk, the author's acknowledged "masterhand" of evil and former confessor to parish sinners, gradually is revealed as the stalker and brother- and wife-slayer Fernando Count di Bruno. After a witness links him to capital offenses, the charge dismays Vivaldi, Ellena's suitor, who realizes that he can't despise a condemned killer who is also Ellena's father.

The author juggles the positive emotion of the courtroom scene by picturing the villain flashing "an horrible smile of triumph and derision" (*ibid.,* 365). Lodged in a cell and fed on bread and water, as he lapses toward death, Schedoni redeems himself by exonerating Ellena of misconduct. Radcliffe extends his writhings, giving Vivaldi an opportunity to acknowledge Schedoni in the dual role of slanderer and rescuer. In the end, Schedoni suffers inhuman torments and dies like a demon possessed: "[He] uttered a sound so strange and horrible, so convulsed, yet so loud, so exulting, yet so unlike any human voice, that every person in the chamber . . . endeavoured to make their way out of it" (*ibid.,* 402). The horror of Radcliffe's Italian villain inspired Charles Robert MATURIN to create a copy, Schemoli, a victim of the Inquisition in his first novel, *The Fatal Revenge; or, The Family of Montorio* (1807).

Bibliography

Norton, Rictor. *The Mistress of Udolpho.* London: Leicester University Press, 1999.

Radcliffe, Ann. *The Italian.* London: Oxford University Press, 1968.

Schiller, Friedrich von
(1759–1805)

The prominent German Gothic author and critic Johann Christoph Friedrich von Schiller con-

tributed original SUPERNATURAL and occult elements to an evolving literary genre. While studying at a Stuttgart military academy, at age 19, he wrote his first play, in which he inserted dramatic facets of German opera. Impressed by Johann Wolfgang von GOETHE's light comedy *Claudine von Villa Bella* (1775), Schiller developed the German banditti mythos, a form of rogue novel, which he defended to critics for its moral instruction.

Schiller's impact on English and French authors and crime fiction was considerable. For his sensational play *Die Räuber* (*The Robbers,* 1781), depicting the sneering VILLAIN Franz Moor and his outlawry in the forests of Bohemia, the author earned honorary citizenship in the French Republic. Actors vied for the lead role, an action part that concludes with the robber's abandonment of crime. In the introduction, Schiller states the purpose of the drama is to "[trace] out the innermost workings of the soul" and to "unveil crime in all its deformity, and place it before the eyes of men in its colossal magnitude" (Dukore, 437). In 1791, he developed his theory of Gothic villainy in the essay "On the Cause of the Pleasure We Derive from Tragic Objects," in which he claims that the change of heart in a criminal is a valuable lesson: "Repentance and regret at past crimes show us some of the sublimest pictures of morality in action" (*ibid.,* 447).

In 1786, Schiller began serializing in *Thalia* magazine a classic Gothic romance, DER GEISTERSEHER (*The Ghost-Seer*). The novel features a mysterious Polish character who takes on the qualities and history of the WANDERING JEW and presages the BYRONIC HERO. The text develops the man's mystique: "He is nothing of what he appears to be. There are few conditions or countries of which he has not worn the mask. No person knows who he is, whence he comes, or whither he goes. . . . Here we know him only by the name of the *Incomprehensible*" (Anderson, 176). The mystery man is impervious to sword, poison, fire, and shipwreck. He does not age, eat, sleep, labor, or indulge in sexual activity. At the stroke of midnight, he quits his residence and moves on. The plot and character entranced Lord BYRON and influenced Cajetan Tschink's *Der Geisterseher* (1797) and

Samuel Taylor COLERIDGE's *THE RIME OF THE ANCIENT MARINER* (1798).

Schiller's didactic models penetrated the mind of the fictional OUTSIDER and provided insight into human wickedness. These traits affected the writing of Ann RADCLIFFE's novel *THE ITALIAN* (1794), Coleridge's crime play *Osorio* (1797), Matthew Gregory LEWIS's Gothic drama *The Castle Spectre* (1798) and outlaw tale *The Bravo of Venice: A Romance* (1804), and the novels of Edward BULWER-LYTTON, Fyodor Dostoyevsky, and Francis LATHOM. In the 1840s, translations (by Bulwer-Lytton, among others) of Schiller's romantic verse and Gothic tales appeared frequently in *BLACKWOOD'S EDINBURGH MAGAZINE*. In 1922, Hanns Heinz EWERS, a specialist in the supernatural and SADISM, completed Schiller's *Der Geisterseher* as *Der Geisterseher Oder die Teufelsjäger* (*The Ghost-Seer; or, The Devil Hunters*), outraging Germans with his audacity at tampering with the work of a master.

Bibliography

Anderson, George K. *The Legend of the Wandering Jew.* Providence, R.I.: Brown University Press, 1965.

Dukore, Bernard F., ed. *Dramatic Theory and Criticism.* Boston: Heinle & Heinle, 1974.

Hodgson, Moira. "Die Räuber," *Nation* 243 (August 30, 1986): 155.

Scott, Sir Walter
(1771–1832)

An innovative Scottish master of verse romance and a major influence on the writers who followed him, Sir Walter Scott flourished in the genres of the ballad and the historical novel. Born in Edinburgh to affluent parents, he had the leisure in boyhood to wander the braes, absorb Scottish border stories, and read FAIRY TALEs, verse, drama, and history, much of which he committed to memory. While studying law with his father, at age 15, the poet strayed from court cases into Scots tales, European romances, and GOTHIC NOVELs, notably Horace WALPOLE's *THE CASTLE OF OTRANTO* (1765) and Sophia LEE's *The Recess* (1783–85). Scott translated two German ballads by Gottfried August Bürger and the verse of Johann Wolfgang von GOETHE, whose tragedy *Götz von Berlichingen* (*Goetz the Iron Hand*, 1773) inspired Scott's interest in knights and chivalry.

At the beginning of his publishing career, Scott composed a GOTHIC DRAMA, *House of Aspen* (1799), and anthologized a ballad in *Tales of Wonder* (1801), edited by Matthew Gregory LEWIS. In 1803, Scott introduced himself formally as a writer with the publication of *Minstrelsy of the Scottish Border*, a polished work that established his literary reputation. Unlike Gothicists who combed the past for the evils of feudalism and the wrongs of Catholicism, in *The Lay of the Last Minstrel* (1805) he explored the conventions of STORYTELLING. A regional favorite that displays Scott's love of country and appreciation of the countryside, its scholarly footnotes explained away the SUPERNATURAL elements in the text. After serving Selkirkshire as sheriff, in 1806 he became Edinburgh's clerk of court and cofounded a printshop with James and John Ballantyne. To support the floundering firm and to underwrite his own taste in antiquarian collecting, in 1813, he turned from poetry to romantic fiction, beginning with *Waverley* (1814), a novel set during the Jacobite rebellion and issued anonymously.

Scott's command of dialect, customs, and nationalistic sentiment struck a respondent chord in readers, who made best-sellers out of two sequels, *Guy Mannering* (1815) and *The Antiquary* (1816). He fed the public's demand for thrilling details with *Old Mortality* (1816), *Rob Roy* (1818), *The Bride of Lammermoor* (1819), and his most popular work, *Ivanhoe* (1819), a tale of courage and devotion based on medieval chivalry. Tinged with Gothic elements were *The Monastery* (1820), *The Abbot* (1820), *The Pirate* (1822), and *The Talisman* (1825), a romance of the Third Crusade. In *Tales of a Traveller* (1824), the author incorporated a macabre dead-bride motif in "The German Student," developed a surreal ATMOSPHERE at a banquet in hell in "Wandering Willie's Gale," and pursued pirates' ghosts in "The Money-Diggers." Ironically, although he was a major influence on Gothicist Sheridan LE FANU, Scott's critical commentary denounced pure Gothic as a symptom of degraded taste, a regression to nursery-level pap.

In debt because of a business bankruptcy, Scott remained active into his last years. In his late 50s, he returned to SHORT GOTHIC FICTION with

"The Tale of the Mysterious Mirror" (1828), a story about his own great-grandmother, and "The Tapestried Chamber" (1828). He plotted a Gothic novel on the mythic Thomas the Rhymer or True Thomas, a youth entrapped by the queen of the fairies. To avoid the public notoriety incurred by Lewis after writing the sensational Gothic horror novel THE MONK (1796), Scott stuck scrupulously to history and FOLKLORE as sources for his novels, and maintained his anonymity when he issued a Gothic MELODRAMA, *The Doom of Devorgoil* (1830), and *Auchindrane* (1830), a crime story drawn from Robert Pitcairn's three-volume compendium *Ancient Criminal Trials in Scotland from the Original Records* (1829–33). After suffering a stroke two years before his death, he researched *Letters on Demonology and Witchcraft* (1830), a compilation of supernatural traditions, motifs, and imagery from GOTHIC CONVENTION along with scraps of tales and legends on sorcery from the author's considerable collection. The work was a scholarly source for the Argentine supernaturalist and magical realist Enrique Anderson Imbert, author of *The Other Side of the Mirror* (1961) and *Woven on the Loom of Time* (1990).

The work that caught the attention of American Gothic giant Edgar Allan POE was Scott's melodrama *The Bride of Lammermoor,* a mannered work of TERROR FICTION about the Ravenswood family, Stuart supporters reduced to a ruined residence, Wolf's Crag Castle. Scott's only true Gothic horror novel, it features the bride's madness and her spurned lover's death in quicksand. Poe saw the story onstage as the opera *Lucia di Lammermoor* (1835), composed by Gaetano Donizetti. In a late self-evaluation, Scott declared that he preferred his wholesome historical fiction to Gothic strands. He rejected his horror novel as monstrous and overly GROTESQUE and declared it murky and unhealthy. He compared its excesses to those of Charles Brockden BROWN and Samuel Taylor COLERIDGE.

Bibliography

Gamer, Michael. "Authors in Effect: Lewis, Scott, and the Gothic Drama," *English Literary History* 66, no. 4 (1999): 831–861.

Lockhart, John Gibson. *The Life of Sir Walter Scott, Bart.* Edinburgh: Adam & Charles Black, 1884.

secrecy

Bolstering the CLAUSTROPHOBIA and dread common to TERROR FICTION are examples of secret passages, unspeakable sins, disguises, and hidden identities and relationships. Secrecy is the essence of Nathaniel HAWTHORNE's tragic novel THE SCARLET LETTER (1850); of Wilkie COLLINS's anti-Jesuit Gothic MYSTERY *The Black Robe* (1881), a tale of a duel that settles a contest between scholarship and lust; and of the scientific subversions of NATURE in H. G. WELLS's THE ISLAND OF DR. MOREAU (1896). In Ann RADCLIFFE's classic THE ITALIAN (1797), quasi-religious motives, clandestine acts, and veils contribute to the SUBTEXT of ANTI-CATHOLICISM, a common strand in Gothic fiction. As critic Victor Sage, author of *Horror Fiction and the Protestant Tradition* (1988), explains, the novel employs "the habit of the monk [as] a symbol of deviousness and secrecy, which has a directly theological meaning" (Sage, 34). Secrecy, melancholia, and repressed hysteria so permeated Radcliffe's writing that her biographer, Rictor Norton, suggests in *The Mistress of Udolpho* (1999) that these Gothic aspects shed light on her personality, which has eluded previous literary historians.

In the Victorian era, secrecy was a dominant theme on multiple levels. Charles DICKENS characterized the accumulated sins resulting from an abandoned illegitimate child in BLEAK HOUSE (1853). Mary Elizabeth BRADDON wrote of an ominous cabal in *The Black Band; or, The Mysteries of Midnight* (1861), the tale of a secret London brotherhood that she issued under the pseudonym Lady Caroline Lascelles. She followed with *Lady Audley's Secret* (1862), a best-selling Gothic masterwork based on Collins's groundbreaking sensational novel *The Woman in White* (1860). An element of SUSPENSE, the aura of unspeakable vice, conspiracy, and sins, kept readers glued to installments of *Lady Audley,* issued first in *Robin Goodfellow* and reprised in *Sixpenny Magazine.* In her mastery of secrecy, Braddon outpaced Collins by layering hidden sins and violations of the respectability and order of Victorian society, especially fornication, adultery, and secret marriage. In 1863, a critic writing for *Saturday Review* differentiated between the two writers of sensation in terms of their handling of secrets and preferred

Braddon over Collins for her graceful style and ease of progression.

The critic Judith Halberstam, author of *Skin Shows* (1995), declared that the Gothic mode tends to cloak sexual secrets, typically homosexuality and illegitimacy, for example, the family secret of an illegitimate birth that triggers an aunt's suicide in Maxine Hong KINGSTON's *The Woman Warrior* (1976). Halberstam describes Robert Louis STEVENSON's *DR. JEKYLL AND MR. HYDE* (1886) and Oscar WILDE's *THE PICTURE OF DORIAN GRAY* (1891) as tales of disguise and duplicity bearing a subtext of illicit carnality. She explains that "each figure creates secrecy as a precondition for sexual perversity" (Halberstam, 71). Stevenson's dwarfish villain Hyde satisfies his loathsome desires in a dark alley at the rear of Jekyll's home and in private quarters far from London's respectable side. Wilde's Dorian Gray, a poorly masked homosexual, maintains a public persona of heterosexuality by pursuing the actress Sibyl Vane, a parallel DOPPELGÄNGER who flourishes onstage in the role of Rosalind, a maiden disguised as a boy. Following Dorian's murder of a portrait artist, the killer acknowledges that his soul has indeed been transferred to canvas and that it looks down in judgment over the crime. In the hidden selves of both Hyde and Gray, secret sin devours like a cancer, consuming the humanity of Jekyll and the serenity of Gray, an aptly named character who tries and fails to live in the shadows of candor.

Bibliography

Carnell, Jennifer. *The Literary Lives of Mary Elizabeth Braddon*. Hastings, Sussex: Sensation Press, 2000.

Halberstam, Judith. *Skin Shows: Gothic Horror and the Technology of Monsters*. Durham, N.C.: Duke University Press, 1995.

Sage, Victor. *Horror Fiction in the Protestant Tradition*. New York: St. Martin's, 1988.

sensationalism

Sensationalism as a literary term originated around 1860, and describes fiction in which characters gain through hearing, seeing, tasting, touching, and smelling. Typically, Gothic sensationalism tends toward the improbable and the melodramatic and builds reader involvement and SUSPENSE through the cumulative effect of ABERRANT BEHAVIOR, gruesome crimes, salacious details, SECRECY, MELODRAMA, NEURASTHENIA, and mounting tension. These emotional elements invest a variety of memorable Gothic scenarios—the hamstringing of an African slave in George Washington CABLE's "BRAS COUPÉ" (1879), fluttering wings and lethal peckings in Daphne DU MAURIER's story "THE BIRDS" (1952), a ritual copulation to the reading of Bible verses in Margaret ATWOOD's dystopic *THE HANDMAID'S TALE* (1985), and the self-torture of a fanatic monk in Dan Brown's MYSTERY thriller *THE DA VINCI CODE* (2003). Preceding sensationalism was a variety of sense-based writing: true-crime tales in the NEWGATE NOVEL, stage and print melodrama, GOTHIC DRAMA, Eugène Sue's *The Mysteries of Paris* (1845), and George William Macarthur REYNOLDS's *Mysteries of London* (1844–48) and the five-year spin-off serial *Mysteries of the Court of London* (1848–53). Female writers—Sarah WILKINSON, author of the anti-Catholic *The Mysterious Novice; or, Convent of the Grey Penitents* (1809) and *The Convent of the Grey Penitents; or, The Apostate Nun* (1810), and Charlotte Cowan Riddell, co-owner of *St. James Magazine* and author of the best-selling *George Geith of Fen Court* (1864)—capitalized on the GOTHIC BLUEBOOK and magazine serials by condensing and eroticizing established Gothic crime fiction. For *The Midnight Assassin; or, the Confessions of the Monk Rinaldi* (1802), an extrapolation from Ann RADCLIFFE's *THE ITALIAN* (1797), the anonymous adapter cut a three-volume terror novel down to 30,000 words. The illustrator appealed to working-class patrons by depicting an incubus with upraised dagger leaning over the bed of a distressed virgin. In addition to terror fiction, the chapbook exaggerated events from history, as with the French atrocities against the Turks in the anonymous *The Life and Exploits of Napoleon Bonaparte* (ca. 1810).

Often drawn from newspaper accounts of bigamy, drugs and poison, disguises, romantic triangles and infidelity, divorce, misdirected or purloined letters, scandal, theft, and crime sprees, the minutiae of sensationalism suited female writers—notably, the English novelist Caroline Meysey-Wigley Clive, a handicapped late-in-life wife of a Warwickshire parson. Writing for *BLACKWOOD'S*

EDINBURGH MAGAZINE under the pseudonym V, she pioneered the novel of sensation, a subset of the GOTHIC NOVEL, with *Paul Ferroll* (1855), issued in *Putnam's Magazine* the following year. The plot of a cleverly concealed crime exonerates a wife-murderer, who thrust a small instrument into her skull, and describes the complications of his escape to Boston. To explain the novel's motivation, Clive followed with a moralistic sequel, *Why Paul Ferroll Killed His Wife* (1860), issued in the *Continental Monthly* in 1862.

The emerging genre of sensational fiction owes its formal beginning to reader and critical responses to Gothic classics, Wilkie COLLINS's *The Woman in White* (1860) and Mary Elizabeth BRADDON's *The Trail of the Serpent; or, Three Times Dead* (1861). In both examples, the authors stressed action and engrossing incidents above the development of character or logic. The complex actions and motivations of the cast move beyond the cardboard predictability of the NAIFs and VILLAINs of domestic melodrama. At the crest of the wave rode Braddon, the author who continued to shape the genre and reap its rewards. She parried charges that her texts armed nascent murderers with the mechanics of macabre assassinations and poisonings, the method of dispatch in *The Black Band; or, The Mysteries of Midnight* (1861). In response to the sweeping popularity of sensationalism in the early 1860s, an unnamed critic for the *Edinburgh Review* commented that the term is "the regular commercial name for a particular product of industry for which there is just now a brisk demand" (Carnell, 142). In 1866, a critic writing for *Saturday Review* referred to the sensational novel as "crime and crinoline" and declared it "enough to take away the breath of any quiet middle-aged gentleman" (*ibid.*, 161).

The controlled unraveling of mystery in the sensational novel continued to thrive with Ellen Price WOOD's *East Lynne* (1861), a detailed account of adultery, and with Braddon's three-volume *Lady Audley's Secret* (1862), an intricate antipatriarchal tale of bigamy, arson, attempted murder, and madness serialized in John Maxwell's Irish journal *Robin Goodfellow* (1861–62) and in *Sixpenny Magazine* (1862). Braddon was so success-

ful at sensationalism that, within months, she produced *Aurora Floyd* (1863), an account of bigamy and murder, and *John Marchmont's Legacy* (1863), another shocker showcasing secret marriage, a train accident, suicide, and a missing wife presumed dead. A typically pious *tsk-tsk* in the *Christian Remembrancer* noted that these topics were elements of the times and proof that Victorians were shrugging off the restraint of principle in search of a new social ethos.

In 1864, Braddon recast Gustave Flaubert's *Madame Bovary* (1857) as *The Doctor's Wife* (1864), in which the author offered a brief commentary on the newness and faddishness of sensationalism: "That bitter term of reproach, 'sensation' had not been invented for the terror of romancers in the fifty-second year of this present century; but the thing existed nevertheless in divers forms" (*ibid.*, 151). Because of her dedication to the novel of sensation, Braddon was irrevocably linked to controversial elements and scandalous revelations. She was much reviled as a debaser of society by the Scottish novelist Margaret OLIPHANT, a critic for *Blackwood's*. Nonetheless, Braddon's canon of 90 novels flourished and impacted the detective novel and crime fiction of the modern era.

Bibliography

Braddon, M. E. *Lady Audley's Secret*. London: Tinsley Brothers, 1862.

Carnell, Jennifer. *The Literary Lives of Mary Elizabeth Braddon*. Hastings, Sussex: Sensation Press, 2000.

Gates, Barbara T. *Victorian Suicide: Mad Crimes and Sad Histories*. Princeton, N.J.: Princeton University Press, 1988.

sensibility

Referring to a susceptibility to tenderness, the term *sensibility* denotes the quality that allows an individual to identify with suffering and respond to human sorrow. The tendency marks the novels of Samuel Richardson and GRAVEYARD VERSE, both of which encouraged reader escapism through sighs and tears. Abbé PRÉVOST's translations of Richardson's *Pamela* (1740) and *Clarissa* (1748) spread the popularity of sentimental fiction to

France, resulting in a body of imitations that encouraged unrestrained feelings. Against the neoclassic tide flowing toward stoicism, logic, and reason, the encouragement of sensibility in novels and drama indicated a reaction to dehumanization in literature through the elevation of intellect and wit over instinctive emotion. More than a counterbalance to neoclassicism, the literary rebellion against the tyranny of rationality was a forerunner of ROMANTICISM, with its stress on aesthetics, NATURE, liberty, and individuality. The tender heroines of sentimental fiction also presaged the tremulous NAIFs of Gothic literature.

A strong defense of compassion and reliance on feeling as an introit to understanding truth and appreciating beauty derived from the refined Gothic fiction of Ann RADCLIFFE. In THE MYSTERIES OF UDOLPHO (1794), she describes Emily ST. AUBERT's dying father in the act of lecturing his intelligent, arty daughter on the dangers of letting sensibility take control. The sermonette is obviously the concealed voice of Radcliffe, who sets up a model of unbridled emotion in the tragedy of Signorina Laurentini/Sister Agnes, a victim of her own passions, which become sources of vice. Two years after the publication of her novel, Radcliffe rejected the coarse extremes and DECADENCE of her contemporary Matthew Gregory LEWIS, author of THE MONK (1796). With the decline of the traditional GOTHIC NOVEL and the eclipse of romanticism emerged sentimentalism, an abundance of mawkish emotion common to popular fiction and stage MELODRAMA.

Late 19th-century fiction began to redirect sensibility from positive emotions to a complex mix influenced by realism. Gertrude ATHERTON originated an AMERICAN GOTHIC strand blended of terror and grief in "Death and the Woman" (1892). In the brief story, a woman awaits widowhood as her moribund husband slips gradually from life. The sound of the personified Death approaching up the stairs and rapping on the door halt her ministrations and catapult her into lethal terror, producing two corpses as the couple lie together in death. In the late 20th century, sensibility mirrored television soap operas by coloring tearjerker films, sometimes denigrated as "women's films," "weepies," or "chick flicks."

Bibliography

Bering-Jensen, Helle. "California's Daughter: Gertrude Atherton and Her Times," *Smithsonian* 22, no. 12 (March 1992): 117–118.

Kozlowski, Lisa. "A Source for Ann Radcliffe's 'The Mysteries of Udolpho,'" *Notes and Queries* 44, no. 2 (June 1997): 228–229.

serials

In the 19th century, serial publication boosted the readership of magazines and journals. Magazine publishing was a highly competitive business in the British Isles, Europe, and North America. To maintain interest in their periodicals, publishers sought Gothic horror fiction, NEWGATE NOVELs, crime and detective stories, sensational tales, and the more decadent Gothic fiction to issue in installments or excerpts, as was the case with portions of Charles Brockden BROWN's *ARTHUR MERVYN; or, Memoirs of the Year 1793* (1799), which Philadelphia's new *Weekly Magazine* began running in June 1799. In England, Elizabeth Gaskell serialized a Gothic novella, *The Grey Woman* (1861), in Charles DICKENS's magazine *All the Year Round*. Edgar Allan POE discovered significant serialized nonfiction and a fount of crime stories in the memoir of Paris criminologist François-Eugène Vidocq, which Poe read in *Burton's Gentleman's Quarterly* from September 1838 to May 1839. At the beginning of the 20th century, pulp fiction master Gaston LEROUX colored his serialized potboilers with MELODRAMA, MYSTERY, and Orientalism, notably, *The Seeking of the Morning Treasures* (1903), featured in issues of *Le Matin*.

To increase readers' interest, authors tended to end each segment with a cliffhanger, the slang term for a high point of interest, surprise, sensation, or SUSPENSE. This method of division was the hallmark of Margaret OLIPHANT's serialized ghost novels and stories of the occult. Some writers submitted complete works for the publisher to break into segments. Others composed in a month-by-month or week-by-week work schedule, the method that Dickens introduced with the publication of *Pickwick Papers* (1836–37) and perpetuated with his horror-tinged social novel *OLIVER TWIST* (1837–39), published in *Bentley's Miscellany*. Dickens fleshed out the plot with seamy details gained from his observations while working as a crime reporter. As a working style generated by the economic demands of his growing family, the installments thrived on Dickens's knowledge and artistry. However, the method required strictly outlining the plot and lessened opportunities for him to strengthen or refine the text or remove errors. He continued parceling out chapters with his prison tale *Barnaby Rudge* (1841), serialized weekly in *Master Humphrey's Clock*, and with GREAT EXPECTATIONS (1860), a weekly publication in *All the Year Round* during 1860–61.

Examples of serialized Gothic fiction cover the gamut of Victorian and Edwardian popular prose: Sarah WILKINSON's GOTHIC BLUEBOOK *The Midnight Assassin; or, the Confessions of the Monk Rinaldi* (1802), an abridgement of Ann RADCLIFFE's THE ITALIAN (1797), issued by *Marvellous Magazine and Compendium of Prodigies*; Dr. John POLIDORI's "The Vampyre," printed in *Colburn's New Monthly Magazine* in 1819; William Makepeace Thackeray's Newgate novel *Catherine* (1840), serialized in *Frazer's Magazine*; William Harrison AINSWORTH's satanic *Auriol*, issued in *Ainsworth's Magazine* from 1844 to 1846; Mary Elizabeth BRADDON's detective thriller *The Trail of the Serpent; or, Three Times Dead* (1861), and her sensational mystery *Lady Audley's Secret* (1862); Oscar WILDE's fable THE PICTURE OF DORIAN GRAY (1891), which appeared in *Lippincott's Magazine*; and Joseph CONRAD's HEART OF DARKNESS (1902), a coup for BLACKWOOD'S EDINBURGH MAGAZINE. The issuance of these works in the popular media spread reading material to people in rural areas, as was the case with Charlotte BRONTË and Emily BRONTË, who took turns reading aloud from their favorites. In France, a similar demand for *roman feuilleton* or serialized Gothic literature netted Frédéric Soulié's *Les Mémoires du Diable* (The Devil's Memoirs, 1837–38) and Eugène Sue's *Les Mystères de Paris* (Paris Mysteries, 1842–43). The popularity of serialized Gothic literature inspired VILLIERS DE L'ISLE-ADAM, master of CONTES CRUELS (cruel tales), to issue *L'Eve Future* (The future Eve), his story of mesmerism, beginning in the March 1886 issue of *La Vie Moderne*.

In the United States, readers shared European enthusiasm for periodical serials. Edgar Allan POE popularized *The Narrative of Arthur Gordon Pym* in two installments of the *Southern Literary Messenger* dated 1836 and 1837. The Irish-American Gothicist Fitz-James O'BRIEN, a regular contributor to the New York media, serialized a surrealistic fantasy, *From Hand to Mouth*, in the *New York Picayune* in spring 1858. Anne Sophia Stephens's serialized FRONTIER GOTHIC *Malaeska: The Indian Wife of the White Hunter* (1860) became the nation's first dime novel. Another American, Mary E. Wilkins Freeman, serialized a fictional version of Lizzie Borden's trial for ax murders in *The Long Arm* (1895), which *Chapman's Magazine* published in segments. Mary Roberts RINEHART got her start in detective novels with installments of the whodunit *The Man in Lower Ten* (1906). She issued *The Circular Staircase* (1908) in *All-Story Magazine* from November 1907 to March 1908 and negotiated with the *Saturday Evening Post* to serialize *The Wall* (1938) for $65,000. A boost for the *Ladies' Home Journal* was the installment version of Victoria HOLT's best-selling melodrama MISTRESS OF MELLYN (1960).

Bibliography

Hollingsworth, Keith. *The Newgate Novel, 1830 1847.* Detroit: Wayne State University Press, 1963.

shape-shifting

To express the elusive omnipresence of evil in folk tales and Gothic literature, authors depict demonic characters as possessors of shape-shifting powers, as with Scythian wolf-men in the histories of Herodotus, the wizard Merlin in Arthurian lore, change-at-will animals in eastern European folklore and in native American and Japanese myth, and the human-into-fish tales of the Chinese SUPERNATURAL. The concept of self-transformation at will to another body or species for a brief or long-term occupation fueled much of the 15th-century hysteria that the Roman Catholic Church launched against witches and demons, SYMBOLs of disorder in a world that the papacy sought to control. By depicting Satan as a shape-shifter who roamed at large in an infinite number of forms, clerics terrified gullible parishioners into fighting any destabilizing element in their midst. In the Renaissance, the reviled image of an agile shape-altering demon arose from powerful propaganda, *Malleus Maleficarum* (The hammer of evildoers, 1486), the chief text of anti-Satanists. Enlarging on the definition of satanic powers was Francesco Maria Guazzo's *Compendium Maleficarum* (Compendium of evildoers, 1620), which characterized sorcerers as manipulators of the power of flight and of magic vanishing creams that rendered them invisible. AMERICAN GOTHIC reflects the extension of European OBSESSIONs with witchery to the New World, where male authorities persecuted the humble women of Salem, Massachusetts, in 1692 during a misogynist panic later characterized in Nathaniel HAWTHORNE's "YOUNG GOODMAN BROWN" (1835) and Arthur MILLER's history play *THE CRUCIBLE* (1953).

As a mode of Gothic fiction, shape-shifting permeated various subsets, including works concerning DIABOLISM, VAMPIRISM, and MONSTER lore, such as George William MacArthur REYNOLDS's popular GOTHIC BLUEBOOK *Wagner the Wehr-Wolf* (1847) and Robert Louis STEVENSON's psychological novella *DR. JEKYLL AND MR. HYDE* (1886) as well as his "Isle of Voices" (1893), the tale of a warlock morphing into a giant on the Hawaiian island of Molokai. By altering physical states and traveling through time and space, a propensity of the character Robert Wringhim, the Calvinist tormentor in the Scots Gothic novelist James HOGG's *The Private Memoirs and Confessions of a Justified Sinner* (1824), and of Herne the Hunter in William Harrison AINSWORTH's *Windsor Castle* (1843), the shape-shifter gained a sinister otherworldliness that defeated the earthly constraints that limit mortals. In eastern Europe, a similar localized evil plagued Transylvania in the form of the flying vampire, a folk being that Bram STOKER used as the basis of *DRACULA* (1897). To the amazement of Jonathan Harker, a British clerk, Count DRACULA, an elderly noble, can change himself into a bat, dog, or wolf and can slither lizard-fashion down the castle wall to bag living creatures for his unhallowed nourishment. Journalist Richard Marsh set a flexible insect in Egypt for *The Beetle* (1897), a Victorian thriller about a vengeful female that the author describes as "a creature born neither of God nor man" (Marsh,

364). In the DETECTIVE STORY, a modern version of shape-shifting occurs in quick-change artistry and DISGUISE MOTIFs, a talent of Sir Arthur Conan DOYLE's Sherlock HOLMES that he applies in "THE HOUND OF THE BASKERVILLES" (1902). Late in the 20th century, Peter Straub imagined incarnations of evil as a bird, lynx, and wasp in *Ghost Story* (1979), the story of Eva Galli's return from the dead to avenge her murder.

Bibliography

King, Stephen. *Danse Macabre.* New York: Everest House, 1981.

Marsh, Richard. *The Beetle.* New York: IndyPublish, 2003.

Shelley, Mary
(1797–1851)

Mary Wollstonecraft Godwin Shelley departed from the traditional Gothic narrative by composing an innovative terror MELODRAMA, *FRANKENSTEIN; or, The Modern Prometheus* (1818). As a cultural icon, the text spawned its own subgenre of horror fiction, drama—and, later—films and computer games. Born in London to the radical philosopher William GODWIN and the polemicist Mary WOLLSTONECRAFT, Mary Shelley grew up in a liberal household and read the GOTHIC BLUE-BOOKs of Harriet and Sophia LEE, Mary ROBINSON, and Charlotte SMITH. Shelley first encountered classic Gothic fiction in Ann RADCLIFFE's terror novel *THE MYSTERIES OF UDOLPHO* (1794) and Charles Brockden BROWN's *WIELAND* (1798). She was well read in the best of Gothic lore, including the Greek myth of Prometheus and the FAUST LEGEND, and in works by her father, the German romantics, William BECKFORD, and Matthew Gregory LEWIS.

Deeply troubled by her mother's death and by a strict stepmother and Godwin's lack of interest in child-rearing, Mary Shelley retreated to her mother's gravesite at St. Pancras Church to read and write over her remains in the hopes of pleasing the spirit of the famous feminist. Ironically, Mary shocked her open-minded father by eloping at age 17 with a married man, the poet Percy Bysshe SHELLEY, a young radical whom Godwin cultivated for his potential inheritance, genius, and rejection of bourgeois morals. The couple lived in France until the suicide of his wife, Harriet Westbrook Shelley. Mary wrote of the couple's Continental adventures in a travelogue, *History of a Six Weeks' Tour* (1817), which describes a summer spent at Geneva, where she read the Chevalier d'Allemand's translation of Jean Baptiste Benoît Eyriès's volume of French ghost tales, *Fantasmagoriana; ou Recueil d'Histoires d'Apparitions, de Spectres, Revenans, Fantomes, Etc.* (*Fantasmagoriana; or An Anthology of Stories of Ghosts, Specters, Revenants, Phantoms, Etc.*, 1812).

Mary Shelley joined a learned male company—Percy Shelley, Lord BYRON, and John POLIDORI—in a ghost story–writing competition. Inspired by a dream and by Erasmus Darwin's commentary on artificial life forms, she blended Gothic imagery and the settings and landmarks from her European tour in the novel *Frankenstein*, the terrifying tale of a young Swiss scientist, Victor FRANKENSTEIN, who experiments at the University of Ingolstadt with the creation of an antihero, a monstrous humanoid. In place of the haunted castle and rambling abbey of formulaic Gothic fiction, she created an original setting—the laboratory of the MAD SCIENTIST, derived from tales of KABBALISM and alchemy of the Middle Ages. Her contribution to Gothic lore was the relocation of horror from the setting to the body of the MONSTER itself. Thus, in a modernized form of portable horror, human dread grips his victims wherever he roams.

A blend of sentimental scenes and humanitarian philosophy, the novel theorizes that vitalism created the GROTESQUE life in Frankenstein's laboratory. The plot is filled with strange logic: the scientist's recoil from a being that he himself put together, the immense size of a monster made from normal body parts, the availability of clothing to fit an 8-foot body, the monster's rapid acquisition of literacy and his later ability to track Victor over large expanses of terrain, and the failure of local people to notice the monster or to have authorities pursue him. A SUBTEXT links the biblical creation myth to the novel's themes, which broach the dismaying subjects of dissection, surgery, and the galvanic re-animation of formerly dead tissue. Shelley may have intended her work as an ALLEGORY on

parents like her own who pursue their hearts' desires while ignoring their children. She also expressed some of her disappointment in marriage to a man who preferred to talk with male friends to the exclusion of his wife.

After Percy Shelley's death in 1822, Mary Shelley returned his heart to England, issued his *Posthumous Poems* (1824), and cultivated piety, a rare virtue in her early years. Literary historians muse that she may have felt the need to atone for her role in home wrecking and in Harriet Shelley's drowning. Mary Shelley completed *Valperga* (1823) and *The Last Man* (1826), her most successful novel, a fanciful account of an epidemic that wipes out humanity. In between issuing the last two of Percy Shelley's titles, she published her own *Lodore* (1835), an autobiographical fiction on her association with Shelley and Byron. She followed with *Falkner* (1837), an adventure novel set in Europe, and edited her husband's *Poetical Works* (1839). Nothing in her late literary exertions compares with *Frankenstein*, the brainchild of her late teens, which influenced a devout admirer, sensational novelist Mary Elizabeth BRADDON.

Bibliography

Halberstam, Judith. *Skin Shows: Gothic Horror and the Technology of Monsters.* Durham, N.C.: Duke University Press, 1995.

Lew, Joseph W. "The Deceptive Other: Mary Shelley's Critique of Orientalism in Frankenstein," *Studies in Romanticism* 30 (1991): 255–283.

White, Pamela. "Two Vampires of 1828," *Opera Quarterly* 5, no. 1 (spring 1987): 22–57.

Shelley, Percy Bysshe
(1792–1822)

Amid a confederacy of romantic poets and writers, Percy Bysshe Shelley developed a unique strand of Gothicism. In boyhood, he read little poetry, but he later admired Friedrich von SCHILLER's chilling murder play *Die Räuber* (*The Robbers*, 1781), Gottfried August Bürger's stirring chivalric ballad *Lenore* (1796), the first segment of Johann Wolfgang von GOETHE's *Faust* (1790–1832), and the AMERICAN GOTHIC novels of Charles Brockden BROWN. Shelley regularly borrowed romances at the Brentford circulating library. (CIRCULATING LIBRARIES were the innovation of William Lane, the publisher at MINERVA PRESS.) Giving full range to his genius, Shelley espoused atheism and plunged into medieval occultism by reading the works of Albertus Magnus, Theophrast Paracelsus, and Henricus Cornelius Agrippa, the scholar and writer of the occult who searched for the secret of eternal life.

In his juvenilia, Shelley displayed a fascination with clashing passions, vengeance, and VIOLENCE, themes and motifs drawn from Matthew Gregory LEWIS's THE MONK (1796), Ann RADCLIFFE's THE ITALIAN (1797), and Charlotte DACRE's chilling cautionary novel *Zofloya; or The Moor* (1806). In his last term at Eton, Shelley cultivated a host of Gothic beliefs in devils, spirits, and MONSTERS. Gothic atmosphere permeated his first novel, ZASTROZZI: *A Romance* (1810), a tale of rebellion and the vengeance of a spurned lover, Contessa Matilda, who hires Zastrozzi as a paid assassin. The next year, while Shelley studied at Oxford, he produced a second Gothic novel, *St. Irvyne; or, The Rosicrucian* (1811), a story of perverted science and undisciplined human yearnings for perpetual youth, literary themes taken from German *Kriminalgeschichte* (criminal histories) and from William GODWIN's CALEB WILLIAMS (1794). In the short story "The Assassins" (1814), Shelley drew on tales of the WANDERING JEW and on Crusader lore about Islamic Lebanese. In *The Revolt of Islam* (1817), he concluded a violent Oriental scenario with victims chained and immolated. His romantic plots may have inspired his wife Mary SHELLEY, author of FRANKENSTEIN (1818), and may have influenced Charles Robert MATURIN's MELMOTH THE WANDERER (1820).

Shelley's verse probes the MELANCHOLY and fearful aspects of life that haunted him in his late teens. In "Hymn to Intellectual Beauty" (1816), one of his most Gothic poems, he describes a boyhood interest in claustrophobic graves and grottoes, MYSTERY, and ghost lore. He reaches a state of Gothic ecstasy at the invisible presence of an "awful shadow of some unseen Power" (Shelley, 290). In that same period, he filled "Mont Blanc" (1816), a nature paean, with elements of solitude and death set in chill ice caverns threatened by a stalking wolf, snakes, and a ravaging eagle that grips a bone from a hunter's skeleton. The blend of beauty with fearful images prefaces his advance into high romanticism in subsequent poems.

Bibliography

Frosch, Thomas. "Passive Resistance in Shelley: A Psychological View," *Journal of English and Germanic Philology* 98, no. 3 (July 1999): 373.

Murphy, John Patrick Michael. "An Early Advocate of Freedom of the Press," *Free Inquiry* 20, no. 3 (summer 2000): 54.

Shelley, Percy Bysshe. *Complete Poems of Percy Bysshe Shelley.* New York: Modern Library, 1994.

short Gothic fiction

Called the *conte* in French and the *novelle* in German, the short story came of age at the height of Gothic ROMANTICISM. Through MELODRAMA and protracted scene-setting, these period pieces aroused apprehension in readers and a shiver of terror. The German version of the HORROR NARRATIVE, the *Schauerroman* (shudder story), expressed one view of *Sturm und Drang* (storm and stress), an 18th-century literary movement that freed German theatricals from the strictures of French classicism by encouraging FOLKLORE, nationalism, spiritual struggle, and a free expression of passion. A master of German Gothic fantasy, Johann Ludwig TIECK, wrote the FAIRY TALE "Der Gestiefelte Kater" (Puss in Boots, 1796) and "Wake Not the Dead" (1800), a story of evil sorcery that appealed to the American Gothicist Edgar Allan POE.

English readers created a demand for translations of German Gothic lore and for original fiction. At the forefront of the English movement toward tightly honed thrillers were Anne Laetitia BARBAULD's "Sir Bertrand" (1773); Francis LATHOM's "The Midnight Bell" (1798); Nathan DRAKE's THE ABBEY OF CLUNEDALE (1804), a GOTHIC BLUEBOOK; Matthew Gregory LEWIS's "THE ANACONDA" (1808); Percy Bysshe SHELLEY's "The Assassins" (1814); and numerous other works with intriguing titles—"The Astrologer's Prediction," "The Black Spider," "The Iron Shroud," "THE MONK OF HORROR," and "The

Water Spectre." The genre was an outlet for female writers, including ANNE OF SWANSEA, who wrote Gothic tales for MINERVA PRESS in London. Short tales were an impetus to ballet, particularly Léo Delibes's winsome tale of a doll come to life in *Coppélia* (1870) and Peter Ilyich Tchaikovsky's popular dreamscape with images of dancing soldier and sugar plum fairy in *The Nutcracker* (1892), both adaptations of short stories by the German writer E. T. A. HOFFMANN. From 1817 into the late 20th century, BLACKWOOD'S EDINBURGH MAGAZINE showcased thrillers and stories of the macabre, a genre mastered by the Scottish writer Margaret OLIPHANT in "The Open Door" (1881) and "The Library Window" (1896).

The United States market for short Gothic fiction proved strong for the romanticism and diabolic menace of Nathaniel HAWTHORNE's "YOUNG GOODMAN BROWN" (1835), "THE BIRTHMARK" (1843), and "Rappaccini's Daughter" (1844). The genre reached its height in the one-of-a-kind horror stories of Poe, who established the literary parameters of the short narrative in 1842 while reviewing Hawthorne's *Twice-Told Tales* (1837). Long acknowledged as a master of MYSTERY and SUSPENSE, Poe originated not only his own style of horror literature but also the DETECTIVE STORY, revenge tales, stories of PREMATURE BURIAL and REVENANTS, and Gothic ballads and laments. Throughout the Western canon, the Gothic short story remained creative and flexible, as demonstrated by Mary Noailles Murfree's Appalachian GHOST STORY "The Harnt That Walks Chilhowee" (1884), Guy de MAUPASSANT's "Le Horla; or, Modern Ghosts" (1887), Ambrose BIERCE's frontier suspense tale "An Occurrence at Owl Creek Bridge" (1891), Henry JAMES's "The Jolly Corner" (1898), Edith WHARTON's "THE EYES" (1910) and the melodramatic "Afterward" (1911), and Katherine Anne Porter's stream-of-consciousness confessional in "The Jilting of Granny Weatherall" (1930). In Cornwall, England, Daphne DU MAURIER created a classic, "THE BIRDS" (1952), which helped revive reader interest in short eerie tales.

Bibliography

Punter, David, ed. *The Literature of Terror,* vol. 1, 2nd ed. London: Longman, 1996.

Stevens, David. *The Gothic Tradition.* Cambridge: Cambridge University Press, 2000.

The Sicilian Romance
Ann Radcliffe
(1790)

The first terror MELODRAMA Ann RADCLIFFE wrote, *The Sicilian Romance* advances the husband-turned-VILLAIN scenario by depicting both his wife and daughter as prey. The thriller followed the author's first stirrings of original fiction and developed her timid beginnings with bolder revelations of fancy at a time when English concepts of womanhood were changing. For her plot, she applied the escape-from-forced-marriage motif in the story of Julia, Marchioness de Mazzini, the sensitive, art-loving daughter of the overbearing Ferdinand, Marquis of Mazzini, owner of the decrepit castle of Mazzini on the Straits of Messina and manipulator of women to suit his whim. Reflecting his menace is the setting itself, which offers a treacherous winding stairway. The lower portion collapses into a chasm, leaving Ferdinand shaken and terrified on the last remaining step. The author's implication is that men as well as women suffer terror.

Enhanced by MYSTERY, the intriguing psychological tale bears Radcliffe's commentary on the power of SUPERSTITION. In an ode embedded in the text between chapters 9 and 10, she writes of impending evil in rocks and clouds and warns that superstition violates nature. Paired with this innocuous description is a series of comeuppances to evil: the decline of the villain in the falling action and the abandonment of the castle. Ferdinand revives guile by supplying poisoned food to the imprisoned Julia, whom he incarcerated because he wanted to wed the licentious, artful Maria de Vellorno. Most startling is Maria's death from a self-inflicted dagger wound and the revelation that she has poisoned Ferdinand. In the resolution, all hints of the SUPERNATURAL come to naught in the light of investigation of ominous elements and a logical explanation of strange lights and noises, a hallmark of Radcliffean Gothic.

Radcliffe uses literary FOILs to contrast the positive sensibilities and the purer love that the virtuous Julia has for Hippolitus with the duplicity of the villainess Maria, a younger woman and the object of lust and attempted bigamy by the marquis. By contrasting an interest in the lute and in singing with a baser instinct for illicit sex, Radcliffe stakes out separate territory for sweet Julia and disreputable Maria. On her own, in chapter 2, Julia locates a likeness of her mother, Louisa de Bernini, which causes Julia to weep. The heroine thrills to the painted portrait, which generates reader sympathy with Julia's quest for the face in the miniature.

Although burdened with overwriting, an absurd plot, an anti-Catholic SUBTEXT, belabored poetic justice, and tedious strings of adjectives, the thriller held readers' interest with rapid action and retribution for the two villains. In the end, the castle lies abandoned as a SYMBOL of cruel plots against decency. Some critics laud the novel's elegance, imagination, and vigor; others complain of improbable escapes and a ghoulish pre-death funeral ceremony, an element reprised in Helen Martin's three-volume *Reginald; or, The House of Mirandola* (1799), a solid seller for MINERVA PRESS. Among the harshest of the critics of Radcliffe's romance was the Scottish novelist Sir Walter SCOTT, who noted the author's clumsy artifice and undeveloped characters—two faults that she overcame in subsequent novels.

Despite these criticisms of literary weaknesses, the popular novel spawned librettist Henry Siddons's operatic adaptation, *The Sicilian Romance; or, The Apparition of the Cliff* (1794), with music by William Reeve, which played to a standing-room-only house at Covent Garden's Theatre Royale. Playgoers witnessed the sight of a spurned wife chained to a cavern in the forest and melodramatic scenarios set in a convent, crumbling castles, tombs, towers, and a Gothic hall. Two years later, after a successful run in Philadelphia, the same opera opened at the John Street Theatre in New York City under the title *The Sicilian Romance; or, The Spectre of the Cliffs*, with music by Alexander Reinagle.

Bibliography

Hoeveler, Diane Long. "Gothic Drama as Nationalistic Catharsis," *Wordsworth Circle* 31, no. 3 (2000): 169–172.

———. *Gothic Feminism*. University Park: Pennsylvania State University Press, 1998.

Radcliffe, Ann. *A Sicilian Romance*. Oxford: Oxford University Press, 1993.

Singer, Isaac Bashevis
(1904–1991)

The Nobel Prize–winning author Isaac Bashevis Singer had a gift for writing fiction about MYSTICISM, DIABOLISM, and macabre FOLKLORE. He was born to Hasidic Jews in Leonczyn, Poland, and grew up in Warsaw amid storytellers who embraced KABBALISM and fantastic DYBBUK and golem tales as the stuff of everyday life. Influenced by the detective fiction of Sir Arthur Conan DOYLE and the surrealism of Nikolai GOGOL and Franz Kafka, Singer began composing his own off-beat tales. He immigrated to the United States at age 31 and, while working as a translator for the Yiddish press in New York City, struggled to find the appropriate literary voice and motifs in a land markedly different from the shtetls he knew in eastern Europe. In addition to epic novels, he wrote SUPERNATURAL scenarios and spectral yarns that earned him a unique place in Gothic lore.

Singer pictured a demonic underworld populated by amoral gangsters, alluring she-devils, demons, and soulless tarts. Permeating *Der Sotn in Gorey* (*Satan in Goray*, 1935), which he serialized in Poland, is a festive air that belies the novel's GROTESQUE characters and rituals in a community possessed by the devil, a motif he reprised in the parable "The Destruction of Kreshev" (1942). A more mature work, *The Magician of Lublin* (1960), features ABERRANT BEHAVIOR in the protagonist's final self-confinement and restriction of worldly temptations. Like Shirley JACKSON and SAKI, Singer seasoned some of his Gothic narratives with humor. In "A Crown of Feathers" (1973), he pictures squabbling ghosts; in the fable "Gimpel the Fool" (1957), deceivers tease, "Gimpel, your father and mother have stood up from the grave. They're looking for you" (Singer, 5). In "The Séance" (1968), the character Mrs. Kopitzky speaks for Singer's good-natured view of phantasms: "There *are* ghosts, there are! Don't be so cynical. They watch over us from above, they lead us by the hand, they measure our steps" (*ibid.*, 215).

Bibliography

Guzlowski, John. "Isaac Bashevis Singer's 'Satan in Goray' and Bakhtin's Vision of the Carnivalesque," *CRITIQUE: Studies in Contemporary Fiction* 39, no. 2 (winter 1998): 167–175.

———. "Isaac Singer and the Threat of America," *Shofar* 20, no. 1 (fall 2001): 21.

Singer, Isaac Bashevis. *An Isaac Bashevis Singer Reader.* New York: Farrar, Straus & Giroux, 1960.

Sundel, Al. "Heartaches and Limitations: Isaac Bashevis Singer," *Partisan Review* 69, no. 2 (spring 2002): 272–282.

Smith, Charlotte

(1749–1806)

An elegant romanticist, sonneteer, children's author, and domestic novelist, Charlotte Turner Smith of London developed her version of French sensibilities into MELANCHOLY works that presaged full-fledged English GOTHIC CONVENTIONs. Because of the fecklessness of her husband, Benjamin Smith, a violent abuser who wasted his inheritance and went to jail for debt in 1783, Charlotte fled to France before ending her marriage. She supported their 12 children by establishing a career in freelance translating and the writing of history, verse, and 10 novels.

Smith had an affinity for real-life struggles for justice. She learned to write by translating Abbé PRÉVOST's French Gothic novel MANON LESCAUT (1731) as *Manon L'Escault; or, The Fatal Attachment* (1785) and later as *The Romance of Real Life* (1787). She based the text on criminal trials in France and altered sexual allure by resetting the work as FEMALE GOTHIC, which stresses compassion for the title character. She defended the sensational novel as employing enough realism to convey history's human truths.

Smith next published the first of three sentimental novels, the four-volume *Emmeline, the Orphan of the Castle* (1788), a best-selling dramatic fiction that sold 15,000 copies in six weeks. It struck a responsive note in Englishwomen for championing a heroine struggling to establish her claim to Mowbray estate while shunning Delamere, a fortune-hunting predator who seeks both marriage and a claim to her patrimony. The novel earned the praise of Ann RADCLIFFE, but netted a sharp-edged critique from Mary WOLLSTONECRAFT, writing for the *Analytical Review,* who objected to sexual improprieties in the secondary plot. For the work's refutation of old notions of womanhood, critic Diane Long Hoeveler, author of *Gothic Feminism* (1998), declared the work "the forgotten ur-text for the female Gothic novel tradition" (Hoeveler, 37).

Four years after publishing *Emmeline,* Smith produced the five-volume *Ethelinde; or, The Recluse of the Lake* (1790), followed by *Celestina* (1791). The latter was a direct influence on Radcliffe's *The Romance of the Forest,* issued later that same year and featuring Louis La Motte, the foiled suitor based on Smith's Montague Thorold. In each setting, she stuck close to home by capitalizing on definite locales—England's haunted castles—rather than the exotic sites of ORIENTAL ROMANCE.

While residing at an artists' colony with William Cowper, William Hayley, and George Romney, Smith completed a masterwork, *The Old Manor House* (1793), an artful four-volume tale of Orlando Somerive, a frustrated heir, and his controlling love for Monimia, the grandniece of a domestic servant. Amid MYSTERY, a band of smugglers, a recovered will, and hidden passages, the novel develops the stereotypical decrepit estate as a setting, with the PATHETIC FALLACY of wild Canadian landscapes, ominous Iroquois Indians, soughing wind, shadowed moonlight, and lightning illuminating Monimia's cell in a turret room. The implied SUPERNATURAL element in the ATMOSPHERE spawned an anonymous GOTHIC BLUEBOOK version, *Rayland Hall* (ca. 1810).

Smith issued two more thrillers, *The Wanderings of Warwick* (1794) and *Montalbert* (1795), the latter of which describes a secret marriage, an earthquake, and capture of the heroine by Italian banditti for imprisonment in Sicily. In the five-volume *The Letters of a Solitary Wanderer* (1800–02), she enlarged on ANTI-CATHOLICISM, a common Gothic motif that casts the heroine Edouarda as a rebel against religious austerity, hypocrisy, and meaningless ritual. Smith's writings, which were bedside reading for the feminist writer Mary Wollstonecraft SHELLEY, characterized female powerlessness in an era of patriarchal property law. In addition to Shelley's admiration, Smith earned the respect of Samuel Taylor COLERIDGE, William GODWIN, Leigh Hunt, Robert Southey, and William Wordsworth.

Bibliography

Bartolomeo, Joseph F. "Subversion of Romance in 'The Old Manor House,'" *Studies in English Literature, 1500–1900* 33, no. 3 (summer 1993): 645–657.

Harries, Elizabeth W. "'Out in Left Field': Charlotte Smith's Prefaces, Bourdieu's Categories, and the Public Sphere," *Modern Language Quarterly* 58, no. 4 (December 1997): 457–473.

Smollett, Tobias
(1721–1771)

The satirical novelist, translator, and dramatist Tobias George Smollett developed the realistic novel in the Gothic direction of terror fiction. Well educated in the classics, philosophy, and mathematics, he was a respected London surgeon and a medical officer in the Royal Navy. He developed into an inventive storyteller who achieved literary fame for two picaresque classics—*The Adventures of Roderick Random* (1748), an exposé of shipboard life in the West Indies, and *The Adventures of Peregrine Pickle* (1751), a longer novel about a shameless scoundrel. In this same period, Smollett earned additional cash by translating Alain Rene Lesage's *Gil Blas* (1748) and possibly also Lesage's *Le Diable Boiteux* (The devil on crutches, 1750), and labored at length over an English edition of Miguel de Cervantes's *Don Quixote*, completed in 1755.

In 1753, Smollett presaged Gothic literature with an experiment—the two-volume MELODRAMA *The Adventures of Ferdinand Count Fathom* (1753), a mock-heroic Continental crime novel set in a thorny forest and cemetery and rife with barbarism, gang-style banditry, SUSPENSE, and treachery. The motifs carry the criminal HERO from the picaresque to the DISSIPATION and true villainy of Gothic crime fiction. The work received only one published critique, in the *Monthly Review,* which panned the protagonist as a literary impropriety. Nonetheless, the book delighted William Wordsworth and influenced the Gothic novels of Horace WALPOLE and Ann RADCLIFFE, but failed to reward the author enough to support a career in fiction.

After contracting tuberculosis, Smollett edited the *Critical Review* and settled into compiling a 58-volume history of England. He also wrote a stage farce, *The Reprisal; or, The Tars of Old England* (1757), which was performed at Drury Lane. In the last years of his career, while he edited the *British Magazine* and *The Briton* and completed *Humphrey Clinker* (1771), his final and most revered novel, *Ferdinand Count Fathom* enjoyed a modest success in CIRCULATING LIBRARIES. The novel was frequently pirated and was translated into Dutch, French, German, and Italian. In 1782, it appeared in installments in *Novelist's Magazine*.

Bibliography

Chilton, Leslie A. "Not Quite Proven: Tobias Smollett's 'The Devil on Crutches,'" *Notes and Queries* 41, no. 2 (June 1994): 206–207.

Cope, Kevin L. "The Adventures of Ferdinand Count Fathom," *Studies in the Novel* 21, no. 4 (winter 1989): 442–444.

Something Wicked This Way Comes
Ray Bradbury
(1962)

The futurist and Gothic fiction writer Ray BRADBURY enlarged on a dominant theme of innocence menaced by old age and death in *Something Wicked This Way Comes*, whose title is taken from the three witches' occult examination of the main character in William Shakespeare's *Macbeth* (ca. 1603). A semiautobiographical thriller, Bradbury's story describes the relationship of Will and his father, the librarian Charles William Halloway, who at age 54 feels too old to be rearing a rambunctious 13-year-old. Against the familiar motif of American home life in Green Town, Illinois, the arrival of a demonic carnival, Cooger & Dark's Pandemonium Shadow Show, puts their mutual trust to the test.

Through deft use of ATMOSPHERE, TONE, and CHIAROSCURO, Bradbury transforms the terrifying magic of the carnival into an allegorical warning of technology's lethal allure. In defiance of mortality, Mr. Electrico can withstand huge power jolts; the carousel can add or subtract years from life. At the height of tension, Bradbury pits Will's frail but determined father against the traveling show's freaks and terrors, which threaten the life of Will's friend, Jim Nightshade. With a flash of insight, the librarian glimpses the carnival's sorcery as "a mortuary junkpile, rust-flakes and dying coals that no wind could blow alight again" (Bradbury, 196). In the falling action, Will and his father laugh and sing to harmonica tunes to counter Mr. Dark's death hold on Jim. Bradbury turned the story into a screenplay for a 1983 film, which starred Jason Robards as Will's father.

Bibliography

Bradbury, Ray. *Something Wicked This Way Comes.* New York: Bantam Books, 1962.

Gottschalk, Earl C. "Ray Bradbury Achieves His Own Fantasy," *Wall Street Journal,* October 28, 1985.

Mogen, David. *Ray Bradbury.* Boston: G. K. Hall, 1986.

somnambulism

Somnambulism, or sleepwalking, is a dependable psychological element in Gothic thrillers—a picturesque enhancement of pervasive unrest and post-traumatic night terrors. Night walks suggest control by inscrutable psychic forces, particularly mesmerism, spiritual POSSESSION, and hallucinations. As a literary device, sleepwalking is a facet of the vengeance motif of Guy de MAUPASSANT's "Le Horla; or, Modern Ghosts" (1887). The sleepwalking of the FEMME FATALE Lucy Westenra in Bram STOKER's DRACULA (1897) reveals new powers of VAMPIRISM that allow her to visualize earth from the point of view of a bird. Stoker uses the night walk as a means of exonerating Lucy of a willful demonic alliance with Count DRACULA.

Authors influenced by Lady Macbeth's sleepwalking scene in William Shakespeare's *Macbeth* (ca. 1603) offered proof of internal stress, dread, or evil through the unconscious night strolls of disturbed characters. Johann Wolfgang von GOETHE used sleepwalking as evidence of dissociative thought in his play *Egmont* (1787), a stirring scenario of national terror sweeping Holland. Ludwig van Beethoven captured the atmospheric drama of Goethe's work in his *Egmont* Overture (1810). Wandering females also intensify Edgar Allan POE's "LIGEIA" (1838), a poem of the walking dead, and the Gothic terror story "THE FALL OF THE HOUSE OF USHER" (1839), in which Madeline USHER wordlessly confronts her tremulous twin Roderick. Feminists interpret her speechlessness as a SYMBOL of the patriarchal silencing of women.

The American Gothic progenitor, Charles Brockden BROWN, advanced character traits in *EDGAR HUNTLY; or, Memoirs of a Sleepwalker* (1799) through double somnambulism as evidence of psychic unrest in the OUTSIDER Clithero Edny and in the title character, who unintentionally profits from the mysterious death of his friend Waldegrave. In an explanation of Brown's interest in sleepwalking, the critic Leslie Fiedler enlarged the concept to a form of ESCAPISM: "Life is a nightmare through which we pursue or are pursued in a wilderness where the unexpected and the absurd, the irrelevance of what comes before to what comes after are the basic facts of existence" (Fiedler, 145). Subsequent authors perpetuated the ploy of somnambulism to reveal character traits, as in Wilkie COLLINS's *The Moonstone* (1868), which adds sleepwalking to opium use, magic, and Hinduism to enhance an eerie sense of OTHERNESS to character behaviors.

More recent applications of sleepwalking bear out earlier beliefs that restlessness indicates severe emotional stress. The American Gothic master Stephen KING developed the image of the sleepwalker as a demonstration of character psyche and as a prediction of future events in the Gothic novel *Bag of Bones* (1998), winner of the Bram Stoker Award.

Bibliography

Fiedler, Leslie. *Love and Death in the American Novel.* Cleveland: Meridian Books, 1962.

Hartman, D., et al. "Is There a Dissociative Process in Sleepwalking and Night Terrors?" *Postgraduate Medical Journal* 77, no. 906 (April 2001): 244.

Vincent, Deirdre. "Images of Goethe through Schiller's 'Egmont,'" *University of Toronto Quarterly* 69, no. 1 (winter 1999–2000).

Southern Gothic

Southern Gothic, a genre of the American South, retreats from the dark castles and clanking chains of 19th-century European literature to embrace the moody romance, MYSTERY, terror, and grotesqueries of Mark Twain's fables, Kaye Gibbons and Carson McCULLERS's novels, racial VIOLENCE in works by William Gilmore Simms and George Washington CABLE, black humor in Marsha NORMAN's plays, the voodoo and FOLKLORE of Zora Neale Hurston, and the eerie short fiction of Truman CAPOTE, William FAULKNER, Mary Noailles Murfree, and Flannery O'CONNOR. Simms narrated the horrors of frontier conflicts with Indians in *The Yemassee* (1835), a cultural MELODRAMA set in South Carolina during the Indian uprising of 1715. In 1884, Murfree published "The Harnt That Walks Chilhowee," a regional tale of a tenderhearted mountain girl who pities a ghost and feeds it with tidbits from her own plate. Local colorist Cable, a student of Creole New Orleans, sketched multicultural vignettes and stories overlayed with psychological insight and exoticism, the dominant elements of "Jean-ah Poquelin" (1879), a short story about the advance of urbanism into the life of a crusty French colonial who conceals his brother's leprosy. Contributing to the mystery of Poquelin's residence are rumors of piracy, the presence of a giant mute servant, and public outrage at a repulsive odor emanating from the exterior of Poquelin's house.

Introduced by Cable's Creole fiction, the theme of aristocratic decline permeated the works of Faulkner and his followers—notably, William Styron's *Lie Down in Darkness* (1951), featuring an elite Virginia family, and *The Confessions of Nat Turner* (1967), a brooding historical novel describing doomed blacks attempting to overturn plantation slavery. The playwright Tennessee Williams, who began writing at age 15 and submitted "The Vengeance of Nitocris" (1928) to *Weird Tales*, set his stage works in a South that ceded its colonial values in exchange for vulgar materialism. The theme dominates his carnal melodrama *Cat on a Hot Tin Roof* (1955), in which a family copes with sexual misalignment and the looming death of the patriarch, Big Daddy. Williams orchestrates melodrama, horror, and late 18th-century GOTHIC CONVENTION in *Suddenly Last Summer* (1958) by setting in the tropical gardens of a Victorian estate the theme of rivalry and the motif of lobotomizing a female witness and salvaging a dead man's repu-

tation. The torment and confinement of Catharine Holly, who witnessed the death, results in mental ravishment through multiple injections to suppress her compulsive revelations about occurrences at Cabeza de Lobo, literally "wolf's head."

A beloved Southern novel, Harper Lee's *To Kill a Mockingbird* (1960), won a Pulitzer Prize for its depiction of small-town horror. As a backdrop on which to build the admirable humanism of idealistic attorney Atticus Finch, Lee paints a dismaying picture of racial injustice and white trash violence during the Great Depression. The scenarios spool out in counterpoint—the adult quandary over a crippled black man accused of raping a white girl and children's concern over a mysterious ghost-neighbor, Arthur "Boo" Radley. Jem and Scout, Atticus's son and daughter, rescue Boo from gossip and innuendo that he is a crazed murderer. Scenes where the two actions coincide offer an unusual glimpse of humor, drama, and Gothic convention. As a lynch mob converges on the jail, Scout, with quiet courtesy, defuses potential tragedy by questioning Walter Cunningham about a legal entailment, a subject she understands only through discussions with Atticus. A second near-tragedy concludes on Halloween night, 1935, when the vindictive Robert E. Lee Ewell stalks Jem and Scout, who is dressed as a ham for a school pageant. In a dark outdoor setting, a shadowy rescuer intervenes and accosts Ewell with a kitchen knife. Like a FAIRY TALE, the novel segues from terror to normality with explanations of Boo's retreat from seclusion to save the children.

The Virginia-born writer Ellen Glasgow applied images and themes from Edgar Allan POE's "THE FALL OF THE HOUSE OF USHER" (1839) to "Jordan's End," an eerie tale in the collection *The Shadowy Third and Other Stories* (1923). Told by an outsider, the story takes place in a Gothic estate similar to the Usher mansion and features the declining Jordan family, which is plagued by a long heritage of INSANITY. Glasgow uses Mr. Jordan's physical and mental deterioration as a SYMBOL of the decline of the Southern male aristocrat. From a post-suffrage perspective, Glasgow introduces the vigorous, self-motivated female protagonist, Mrs. Jordan, who murders her weakling spouse with impunity. The shift indicates Glasgow's faith that the stereotypical wraiths like Madeline USHER had met their match in an emerging liberated American woman.

Bibliography

Donaldson, Susan V. "Making a Spectacle: Welty, Faulkner, and Southern Gothic," *Mississippi Quarterly* 50, no. 4 (fall 1997): 567–584.

Gross, Robert F. "Consuming Hart: Sublimity and Gay Poetics in 'Suddenly Last Summer,'" *Theatre Journal* 47, no. 2 (May 1995): 229–251.

Rafailovich, Pnina. "Tennessee Williams's South," *Southern Studies* 23, no. 2 (1984): 191–197.

"Sredni Vashtar"
Saki
(1911)

"Sredni Vashtar," which SAKI collected in *The Chronicles of Clovis* (1911), unleashed pent-up hostility that the author had stored from early boyhood. To repay his cruel maiden aunts for denying him normal activities, he produced an autobiographical character, 10-year-old Conradin, who cloaks his hatred of his cousin and guardian, Mrs. De Ropp. In Conradin's opinion, she "represented those three-fifths of the world that are necessary and disagreeable and real" (Munro, 136). Saki channels the boy's frustration with boredom and loneliness into withdrawal into a tool shed, the Gothic retreat in which Conradin works out a bizarre REVENGE plot.

Crucial to the horror of the story is the protagonist's use of fantasy as an escape from childhood misery. Conradin's elevation of his brown ferret into a religious icon supplies the story with a compelling OTHERNESS and a source of violent requital. In retaliation for the aunt's sale of Conradin's hen, he requests an unspecified deed from his ferret. The brief story, in typical Saki style, juxtaposes polite manners of a boy taking buttered toast and tea with a SUBTEXT of rage and rebellion, but offers no grotesque view of the victim. Thus, the reader's imagination supplies the horrors that the author implies.

Bibliography

Frost, Adam. "A Hundred Years of Saki," *Contemporary Review* 275, no. 1,607 (December 1999): 302.

Munro, H. H. *Saki: The Complete Saki*. London: Penguin, 1998.

stalking

Stalking is a pervasive element in a wide range of Gothic venues—the Renaissance DANSE MACABRE, GOTHIC BLUEBOOK, DETECTIVE STORY, FOOL TALE, vampire and MONSTER lore, golem and werewolf story, and GASLIGHT THRILLER. Through flight from a pursuer, William GODWIN sets a chilling ATMOSPHERE in his politically motivated *The Adventures of CALEB WILLIAMS; or, Things As They Are* (1794). The VILLAIN, FALKLAND, a member of the privileged class, profits from crime and tyrannizes his secretary, Caleb Williams, who knows Falkland's secret sin. In a shift from dominant male villainy, Charlotte DACRE contributed female stalkers to Gothic novels and chapbooks with *Zofloya; or, The Moor* (1806), a novel that inspired Percy Bysshe SHELLEY's ZASTROZZI (1810), a dire tale of the villainous plotter Matilda La Contessa di Laurentini.

Stalker fiction grew more terrifying with the addition of diabolic and psychological elements. In *MELMOTH THE WANDERER* (1820), Charles Robert MATURIN portrays the prevalence of evil in Satan's agent, who mercilessly persecutes a progression of victims. Washington Irving turned a late-night prank into lethal stalking in "The Legend of Sleepy Hollow" (1820), which created a male milquetoast in the gangly misfit Ichabod CRANE. Edgar Allan POE allied pursuit with an epidemic in the ALLEGORY "THE MASQUE OF THE RED DEATH" (1842) and interwove stalking and the DOPPELGÄNGER motif in "William Wilson" (1839), set in the fearfully festive streets of Venice during a pre-Lenten carnival. Henry JAMES reprised the stalking of an alter ego in "The Jolly Corner" (1908), a search for self in a large New York residence. Sir Arthur Conan DOYLE concluded the second round of Sherlock HOLMES episodes with the victory of the stalker Moriarty over England's most famous fictional detective in "The Final Problem" (1893). Sheridan LE FANU departed from the usual male-on-female VIOLENCE in *Carmilla* (1872), a terror novel about a female villain who pursues only women.

Stalking tends to pair the relentless villain with the NAIF or powerless female, cripple, or child, the scenario in Charles DICKENS's child crime novel OLIVER TWIST (1838) and in James's THE TURN OF THE SCREW (1898), in which an ambiguous evil threatens the safety of a governess's two charges. Davis Alexander Grubb created an outstanding pursuer motif in *The Night of the Hunter* (1953), which became a 1955 cult film adapted by scenarist James Agee and starring Robert Mitchum as the sinister, sweet-talking Reverend Harry. Rudolfo Anaya merged pursuit of a child with rescue by a suspected witch and her owl in the Southwestern best-seller *Bless Me, Ultima* (1972).

By enlarging on the flight of a victim through a misty CHIAROSCURO in Gothic buildings or over rough terrain, the author controls a suspenseful terror, as found in Victor Hugo's *Les Misérables* (1862) and John GARDNER's *Grendel* (1971) and in the FEMALE GOTHIC tales of Louisa May Alcott, Isabel ALLENDE, Emily BRONTÉ, Joyce Carol OATES, and Mary Wollstonecraft SHELLEY. Hugo's famed stalker, Inspector Javert, discovers an impenetrable fog in his own soul as he realizes the worth in the man he has hounded. As he contemplates suicide, he looks into the chill waters of the Seine, "then sprang up, and fell straight into the darkness; . . . and the shadow alone was in the secret of the convulsions of that obscure form which has disappeared under the water" (Hugo, 284). In SOUTHERN GOTHIC, William FAULKNER portrayed the hopeless Nancy Mannigoe, the quarry of Jesus, a crazed razor wielder in the atmospheric story "THAT EVENING SUN" (1931). Nancy recognizes a voodoo sign lying on her table: "It was a hogbone, with blood meat still on it, lying by the lamp. He's out there. When yawl walk out that door, I gone" (Faulkner, 307).

James Dickey developed an unusual male-on-male pursuit motif in *Deliverance* (1970), a Southern Gothic novel of perverse mountaineers pursuing a hunting party of OUTSIDERs. Trapped at Cahulawassee near the Georgia rapids by a knife-wielding sodomizer, Ed Gentry, the narrator, remarks on a gratuitous test of manhood: "I had never felt such brutality and carelessness of touch, or such disregard for another person's body. It was not the steel or the edge of the steel that was frightening; the man's fingernail, used in any gesture of his, would have been just as brutal" (Dickey, 98). The river generates a primordial terror as the party paddles their canoes away from a faceless, lethal bloodlust that follows them along the leafy embankment. To the medic who asks what happened, Ed replies, "The river happened to me" (*ibid.*, 197).

Bibliography

Butterworth, Keen. "The Savage Mind: James Dickey's 'Deliverance,'" *Southern Literary Journal* 28, no. 2 (spring 1996): 69–78.

Dickey, James. *Deliverance*. New York: Dell Books, 1970.

Dunn, James A. "Charlotte Dacre and the Feminization of Violence," *Nineteenth-Century Literature* 53 (December 1998): 307.

Hugo, Victor. *Les Misérables*. New York: Fawcett, 1961.

St. Aubert, Emily

The protagonist of THE MYSTERIES OF UDOLPHO (1794), Ann RADCLIFFE's masterpiece of terror, Emily St. Aubert is a literary prototype of the individual who protects the self by warding off evil. In the exposition, the author depicts her as living in a loving household and thriving on books, music, art, and the beauties of her home in Gascony. A stereotypical NAIF and the only living child of the family, she is blue-eyed, uniformly lovely, sweet, graceful, and tenderhearted, particularly in memories of her deceased father, who haunts her DREAMS. The author accords Emily home tutoring in Latin and English poetry and a suitable industriousness that shields her from "the contagion of folly and of vice" (Radcliffe, 6). Balancing her intellectual skills are a love of God and the outdoors, which sustain her after the deaths of her parents.

A model of FEMALE GOTHIC, Emily is a forthright heroine—girlish, but stable, intelligent, sensible, and chaste. When unnerved by perils in her uncle's lockup at UDOLPHO, she turns to books and sketch pads as sources of comfort. Because her aunt, Madame Montoni, is in danger, Emily risks the terrors of the castle by night to rescue her. In the face of the VILLAIN, her refusal to be cowed generates resentment in her captor, Signor Montoni, an authoritarian ogre some years her senior. When her maid Annette reports the sighting of a ghost, the ever-buoyant Emily immediately deduces that the specter is really her love Valancourt.

Rather than tremble at a specter, she rejoices that he is alive and approaching her cell. After the author clarifies the ambiguity of what has transpired outside Emily's frame of reference, the heroine welcomes an explanation of supposed SUPERNATURAL happenings and returns to her home better equipped to deal with deceit and fear. The male Gothic writers who took their cues from Radcliffe's spunky girl survivor chose to shape their heroines in a more erotic male Gothic by overturning Emily's firmness of mind and replacing it with swoons, tears, and dependence on men for succor.

Bibliography

Hoeveler, Diane Long. *Gothic Feminism.* University Park: Pennsylvania State University Press, 1998.

Radcliffe, Ann. *The Mysteries of Udolpho.* London: Oxford University Press, 1966.

Todorov, Tsvetan. *The Fantastic.* Ithaca, N.Y.: Cornell University Press, 1975.

Stevenson, Robert Louis
(1850–1894)

A multidimensioned Scottish storyteller and writer of psychological novels and travelogues, Robert Louis Balfour Stevenson mastered the elements and motifs of romantic and Gothic fiction. He suffered chronic bronchitis and possibly tuberculosis, but managed to travel the world and absorb macabre tales and sensational episodes to incorporate in his writings. After settling in California, he contributed stories to the *Californian* and sailed a schooner on the Pacific to improve his stamina. In his last years, he serialized murderous pirate lore in *Treasure Island* (1883), a GASLIGHT THRILLER in *The Body Snatcher* (1881), Eastern tales in *The New Arabian Nights* (1882), localized danger in *Kidnapped* (1886), and MYSTERY and duality in *The Master of Ballantrae* (1889). At Stevenson's death at his Samoan home, islanders buried him on Mount Vaea and honored him as "Tusitala" (Teller of Tales). He left unfinished *Weir of Hermiston* (1896), a novel promising alienation and family VIOLENCE.

Stevenson attained literary stature with DR. JEKYLL AND MR. HYDE (1886), a novella he labeled a "Gothic gnome" for its distortion of character identity (Halberstam, 12). Much admired by a contemporary, Sir Arthur Conan DOYLE, Stevenson is also known for WITCHCRAFT and demonic POSSESSION in the dialect tale "Thrawn Janet" (1887), satanic dualism in "Markheim" (1887), LYCANTHROPY in "Olalla" (1887), the SUPERNATURAL in "The Bottle Imp" (1888), and SECRECY and a SUBTEXT of cannibalism in "Isle of Voices" (1893), which pictures a warlock SHAPE-SHIFTING into a giant on the Hawaiian island of Molokai. A posthumous collection, *Fables* (1896), contains "The Devil and the Innkeeper," a diabolic folk narrative in which the title figures discuss the source of evil.

Bibliography

Buckton, Oliver S. "Reanimating Stevenson's Corpus," *Nineteenth-Century Literature* 55, no. 1 (June 2000): 22.

Calder, Jenni. *Robert Louis Stevenson: A Critical Celebration.* New York: Barnes & Noble Imports, 1980.

Halberstam, Judith. *Skin Shows: Gothic Horror and the Technology of Monsters.* Durham, N.C.: Duke University Press, 1995.

Livesey, Margot. "The Double Life of Robert Louis Stevenson," *Atlantic Monthly* 274, no. 5 (November 1994): 140–146.

Stoker, Bram
(1847–1912)

The creator of Count DRACULA, Anglo-Irish author Abraham "Bram" Stoker produced one of the longest-lived MONSTERS in Gothic art. Stoker was bedridden in childhood; his mother, Charlotte Stoker, eased his leg pain with stories of Irish banshees, fairies, and ghosts and accounts of PREMATURE BURIALs during the cholera epidemic that spread through the British Isles in 1831. After obtaining a math and science degree from Trinity College in Dublin, he worked as a government bureaucrat and married the beautiful Florence "Florrie" Balcombe, the former sweetheart of Oscar WILDE. Stoker wrote for the *Warder,* a newspaper edited by Sheridan LE FANU, and penned a drama column for the Dublin *Evening Mail* while collecting children's short fiction for an anthology, *Under the Sunset* (1882), when his son Noel was three years old.

Depicted by biographers as the consummate social climber, Stoker left Ireland to seek glory in England, where he read the Gothic fiction of Edward BULWER-LYTTON and involved himself in occultism, seances, and secret societies. He managed the Lyceum Theatre in London, from which he retrieved the character surname for Englishman Jonathan HARKER from a stagehand named Joseph Harker. Stoker's early Gothic romance *The Snake's Pass* (1890) was a mundane horror novel anticipating the development of DRACULA (1897). In addition, Stoker wrote Gothic short works for publication in *Black and White, Holly Leaves,* and *Sketch.*

Inspired by a dream brought on by gorging on crab and furthered by the SUPERSTITIONS of Irish peasants, in 1895 Stoker began writing *The Undead,* an epistolary vampire story he eventually titled *Dracula.* As background material, the author researched Hungarian vampire folklore at the British Museum and drew on the campy, 220-chapter GOTHIC BLUEBOOK serial VARNEY THE VAMPYRE; or, The Feast of Blood (1847) by James Malcolm Rymer or Thomas Preskett Prest, and on Sheridan Le Fanu's *Carmilla* (1872), a tale of lesbian VAMPIRISM. For the villainous Dracula, Stoker claimed the flowing mustache of the poet Walt Whitman and the stage mannerisms of Stoker's idol, the actor Sir Henry Irving, whose career the author managed for 27 years in a surprisingly submissive role to a vampirish manipulator.

Critics have identified Stoker's Gothic novel as a commentary on adolescent idol worship and repressed homoeroticism influenced by the imprisonment of the author's friend Wilde for sodomy only weeks before the manuscript was completed. The tale applies satanic traditions to the ultimate fiend, a ghastly night-prowler and drinker of blood based on eastern European legends of Vlad Tepes, the Impaler of Wallachia, a Transylvanian tyrant of the 1400s notorious for creative torture. To the usual traits of the vampire, Stoker added hypnotism, SHAPE-SHIFTING, predatory sex, and the SUPERNATURAL. His work earned the praise of two peers, the thriller novelist and critic Mary Elizabeth BRADDON and the short fiction master Sir Arthur Conan DOYLE.

In the estimation of the critic Nina Auerbach, author of *Our Vampires, Ourselves* (1995), Stoker's take on the vampire deviated from less formidable ghouls in earlier works to produce "animal rather than phantom, mesmerist rather than intimate, tyrant rather than fiend" (Auerbach, 7). The keen eyes and lethal ambition of the fatal aristocrat emerged from a Gothic literary tradition begun by Ann RADCLIFFE's villainous monk SCHEDONI in THE ITALIAN (1797) and refined into a conflicted BYRONIC HERO introduced by Lord BYRON's THE GIAOUR (1813). On the publication of *Dracula,* a critic for the *Athenaeum* credited the story with imagination and Gothic details, but declared it lacking in literary art and cohesion. Taking an opposing view, Stoker's mother complimented him for outpacing Mary SHELLEY's FRANKENSTEIN (1818) and for besting the works of Edgar Allan POE.

In a career that produced 18 long works and numerous short stories, Stoker added to Gothic literature *The Jewel of Seven Stars* (1904), a romance set in Egypt; *The Lady of the Shroud* (1909), which returns to the subject of the undead; and, in the last lucid months before his death from tertiary paralytic syphilis or Bright's disease, *The Lair of the White Worm* (1911), his second most popular work. The latter is a horror story based on the legendary Laidley Worm, created from a woman transformed into a ravaging vermin near Bamburgh Castle, Northumberland, in the late 13th century. Stoker's version tells of a reptilian shape-shifter living in a hole near Diana's Grove, a clumsy Gothic setting. In normal life, the she-villain is the winsome Lady Arabella March, a symbol of the aggressive FEMME FATALE, whom Stoker depicts as a man-gobbler. An alluring lamia on a par with the serpent of Eden and John KEATS's temptress in "LA BELLE DAME SANS MERCI" (1819), Arabella transforms herself into a monster capable of dragging an unwary male servant to her underground lair.

Revisiting his fascination with Lucy Westenra, the dual maiden-monster in *Dracula,* Stoker protracts his snake-woman's death from a divine thunderbolt, which boils her dismembered body. The electric charge produces a foul stench and bubbling corruption, the same residue that issued from the exorcised remains of Lucy. As a gesture toward restoring NATURE to a pristine wholeness, the author leaves as the snake-woman's monument a vein of China clay freshened by sea breezes.

Bibliography

Auerbach, Nina. *Our Vampires, Ourselves.* Chicago: University of Chicago Press, 1995.

Belford, Barbara. *Bram Stoker.* New York: Knopf, 1996.

Schaffer, Talia. "'A Wilde Desire Took Me': The Homoerotic History of Dracula," *English Literary History* 61, no. 1 (summer 1994): 381–435.

Senf, Carol A. "Bram Stoker: History, Psychoanalysis and the Gothic," *Victorian Studies* 42, no. 4 (summer 2000): 675.

storytelling

Storytelling, the transmission of narrative to a live audience, is a blend of inventive gesture, TONE, and immediacy, sometimes enhanced by a noisemaker, rhythm instrument, lute, or guitar. One example, the performance of ghostly *kaidan* tales of mystery, horror, and revenge, is a significant element of the Japanese oral Gothic tradition. An example from New World tradition, the audio version of Southwestern teller Joe Hayes's "La Llorona" (1987), probes a resilient legend that permeates Central American Gothic. Such stories relate cultural norms while interpreting apprehensions and dread experienced individually and collectively. Through the teller's skillful transmission, a fearful tale creates an internal landscape on which the listener can safely and gainfully live out the hero's role as queller of an extraordinary danger. Gothic writers often emulate the poems, dialect, and suspense of oral lore in their print tales.

To invite the listener into the world of horror, the storyteller draws on SYMBOLs and visual images. Narrative relieves unspoken anxieties in an audience by relating a universal facet of culture—for example, fear of economic or governmental change or other abstract terrors, a subterfuge that Isak DINESEN employs in the feudal stories in *Seven Gothic Tales* (1934), in which the author plays the part of Scheherazade. By visualizing poverty, pestilence, or war as a phantom or masked stalker, the audience satisfies the promptings of what critic G. Richard Thompson calls a "radiant darkness," a natural curiosity about an alluring unknown (Thompson, 43). From narrative truths, the audience develops confidence and empowerment in dealing with everyday terrors. Conversely, a study of recurrent community narratives offers social scientists a window on the underlying unrest and self-doubts that permeate culture, as with the Native American stalker called Wendigo. The icy-hearted cannibal monster and shape-shifter, found in Cree and Ojibwa lore of the Canadian northlands, can both devour humans or turn their victims into cannibals.

Storytelling is often an internal element in longer Gothic works, in which characters relate ghostly and horrific tales and anecdotes that either unintentionally or deliberately terrify other characters, as with the flaming hacienda and accusing ghost in Laura Esquivel's *Like Water for Chocolate* (1989). One example, "Tales of the Indians," one of the nested episodes in Charles Robert MATURIN's *MELMOTH THE WANDERER* (1820), advances a subtle SUBTEXT to enhance the author's Faustian plot. Other fluent tellers of intriguing stories include the German romanticist Johann Wolfgang von GOETHE, the French writer Guy de MAUPASSANT, and the Prussian author E. T. A. HOFFMANN. Hoffmann's crafting of horror narratives influenced the writing of Edgar Allan POE, America's first major horror teller.

Bibliography

Atwood, Margaret. "Cannibal Lecture: How Could a Culture So Apparently Boring As Ours Have Embraced the Flesh-devouring Wendigo?" *Saturday Night* 110, no. 9 (November 1995): 81–86.

Carroll, Noel. "Enjoying Horror Fictions: A Reply to Gaut," *British Journal of Aesthetics* 35, no. 1 (January 1995): 67–72.

Gaut, Berys. "The Paradox of Horror," *British Journal of Aesthetics* 33, no. 4 (October 1993): 333–345.

Hughes, Henry J. "Familiarity of the Strange: Japan's Gothic Tradition," *Criticism* 42, no. 1 (winter 2000): 59–89.

Reider, Noriko T. "The Emergence of Kaidan-shu: The Collection of Tales of the Strange and Mysterious in the Edo Period," *Asian Folklore Studies* 60, no. 1 (April 2001): 79.

subtext

Typically, Gothic writers are exploiters of the subtext, an author's half-statement, implication, or private intent beyond the stated text, as found in a doctor's torment of his wife in Charlotte Perkins GILMAN's "THE YELLOW WALLPAPER" (1892), implied cannibalism in Robert Louis STEVENSON's "Isle of Voices" (1893), misogyny in Shirley JACKSON's execution fable "THE LOTTERY" (1948), and misguided love and religious fervor in Australian novelist Peter Carey's OSCAR AND LUCINDA (1988). In general, the subtext derives from hints in imagery and ambiguous characterization, particularly of the BYRONIC HERO, as with the coolly aristocratic Maxim de Winter, the unintentional tormentor of his working-class bride in Daphne DU MAURIER's status-conscious novel REBECCA (1938). The unnamed new Mrs. DE WINTER recognizes her déclassé position at MANDERLEY, the de Winter ancestral mansion, by comparing herself to the dog: "I'm being like Jasper now, leaning against [Maxim]. He pats me now and again, when he remembers, and I'm pleased, I get close to him for a moment. He likes me in the way I like Jasper" (du Maurier, 101). The subtext indicates a servant mentality in the speaker that causes her to cringe before her husband-master and to accept whatever crumbs of attention and affection he cares to bestow.

Subtexts are unlimited in style and theme. One common subtextual element in horror literature is the embedded tale, a story-within-a-story that poses events and characters as interpretations of the frame story, a narrative device that Charles Robert MATURIN employs in MELMOTH THE WANDERER (1820), the last of the traditional GOTHIC NOVELS. Another form of subtext is the suggestion of VILLAINY, WITCHCRAFT, or DIABOLISM, the controlling theme in Nathaniel HAWTHORNE's subtle short story "YOUNG GOODMAN BROWN" (1835). By evading direct evidence of a demon in the story, the author skewers the mindset of New England that caused communities to persecute the innocent out of folk belief in manifest satanism. Arthur Miller returned to the motifs of Hawthorne's fiction in the stage parable THE CRUCIBLE (1953), which opened on Broadway during the McCarthy witch-hunts as a subtle diatribe against red-baiting and scapegoating.

Bibliography

du Maurier, Daphne. *Rebecca*. New York: Avon Books, 1971.

Ellis, Kate Ferguson. *The Contested Castle: Gothic Novels and the Subversion of Domestic Ideology*. Urbana: University of Illinois Press, 1989.

supernatural

A pervasive aspect of FOLKLORE and traditional narrative, the supernatural may vary from kindly spirits, talismans, and an eerie ATMOSPHERE to ghouls and ghosts, apparitions, poltergeists, witches, spooks, preternatural powers, and demonstrations of sorcery, as found in the fearful demons that flash their fangs in Charles Pigault-Lebrun's "The Unholy Compact Abjured" (1825) and the spirit of Mama Elena berating her daughter Tita for fornication in Laura Esquivel's Mexican MELODRAMA *Like Water for Chocolate* (1989). Supranormal entities have permeated most of world literature, particularly the Gothic canon—for example, Horace WALPOLE's THE CASTLE OF OTRANTO (1765), Japanese legends in Ueda Akinari's *Tales of Moonlight and Rain* (1776), Samuel Taylor COLERIDGE's vampire narrative "CHRISTABEL" (1816), John KEATS's poem "LA BELLE DAME SANS MERCI" (1819), and Jacob and Wilhelm GRIMM's FAIRY TALES anthologized as *Kinder- und Hausmärchen* (Children's and household tales, 1812, 1815, 1822). The lure of the unreal colored the GOTHIC BLUEBOOK market by appealing to the uneducated and superstitious members of the working class, as with the anonymous chapbook *The History of Mr. Fantom* (ca. 1795). Whether as characters—the monster in Mary Wollstonecraft SHELLEY's FRANKENSTEIN (1818)—or merely an elusive presence—the cold hand that reaches out to Lockwood in Emily BRONTE's WUTHERING HEIGHTS (1847), an air of MYSTERY in NATURE in Herman MELVILLE's *Moby-Dick* (1851), or a curse on a wicked family in Irish author Charlotte Cowan Riddell's *The Nun's Curse* (1888)—supernatural elements generate a tense aura and enhance TONE and MOOD, all essentials to TERROR FICTION and mystery stories.

Edgar Allan POE, the AMERICAN GOTHIC touchstone, was adept at supernatural elements. He employed a ghoul aura in the ghost ship story "MS. Found in a Bottle" (1833) and in "Morella" (1835), the tale of an evil spirit that passes from Morella, a student of forbidden arts, into the child she delivers at the moment of her death. At baptism, the unnamed daughter, who receives her mother's name from the attendant priest, dies upon the pronouncement of "Morella." To stress the supernatural elements of the story, Poe refers to Pressburg, Hungary, a town connected with black magic. In a later story. "The Oval Portrait" (1842), Poe develops an account of a painter who drains his wife of life as he paints her picture, a supernatural concept that Oscar WILDE may have used in THE PICTURE OF DORIAN GRAY (1891).

Representation of the supernatural, both as theme and image, influenced the realism of modern Gothic fiction. One of the best by American fantasist Ray BRADBURY, SOMETHING WICKED THIS WAY COMES (1962), exploits the adventures of energetic pals Will and Jim by directing them to a fortune-telling booth at a carnival, a mechanized vestige of the macabre that travels through small midwestern communities to lure the curious. The author, who favors the theme of danger in a technological universe, skillfully builds imagery and CHIAROSCURO for a terrifying revelation on a merry-go-round: "Lightning unraveled itself over the sweated outflung boys, delivered flame to the silent horse stampede to light their way around, around with the figure lying on the platform" (Bradbury, 74). The author turns dizzying motion into a whirling metamorphosis: "No longer a boy but a man no longer a man but more than a man and even more and even more, much more than that, around, around" (ibid.). The tale concludes in a happily-ever-after montage of father-son love, resurrection, leapfrogging, and laughter pushed to hysteria and back as the inanimate friend Jim returns to life.

Bibliography

Bradbury, Ray. *Something Wicked This Way Comes*. New York: Bantam Books, 1962.

Haining, Peter, ed. *Gothic Tales of Terror*. New York: Taplinger, 1972.

superstition

As ROMANTICISM challenged the rigid confines of neoclassicism, authors began reclaiming the startling and irregular lore of the heathen past, from herbalism, alchemy, and astrology to ogres, witches, demons, and vampires. Bishop Thomas Percy's *Essay on the Ancient Minstrels* (1765) speaks reverently of ancient artistry as a source of vitality, joy, and delight. For material, 18th-century writers reconnected with vivid tapestry and balladry and mined the chivalric romance for its rich mythos, splendid songs, MELANCHOLY landscapes, and barbarous rituals. From early narratives came the tragic passions, DREAMS, OMENS, oracles, sorcery, and enchantments that echoed with human truths, both positive and negative, as found in Charlotte SMITH's *The Romance of the Forest* (1791).

As Percy indicated, old traditions supplied the texture, nuance, universality, and EXOTICISM for Gothic literature, empowering the GHOST STORY and occultism, resurrecting the wisdom of the FOOL TALE and cautionary tale, and placing in new locales the flying Dutchman, the WANDERING JEW, the FEMME FATALE, werewolves, the DYBBUK, and Faust. Folk beliefs in NECROMANCY and DIABOLISM colored preromantic verse and the GOTHIC BLUEBOOK—for example, the anonymous *Tawny Rachel; or, The Fortune Teller* (ca. 1795), *The Wandering Spirit* (1802), and *Tales of Superstition* (ca. 1820). Countering a capitulation to baseless beliefs were Ann RADCLIFFE's novels, which presented superstition as faulty logic easily eradicated with a practical explanation, the plot direction in the resolution of THE MYSTERIES OF UDOLPHO (1794).

In the hands of later masters, superstition became an evocative force. Bram STOKER, an Anglo-Irish writer who learned Irish folklore in childhood from his mother Charlotte, opens DRACULA (1897) on St. George's Eve, a European holiday when dragons, ghosts, phantasms, vampires, and witches were thought to reach heights of power and boldness in confronting virtuous Christians. Stoker depicts the peasantry brandishing chaplets, crosses, crowns of thorns, and talismans and sprinkling holy water before bonfires to protect themselves from evil. To ward off harm from farmsteads, peasants invoke the powers of NATURE through flower garlands, herbal simples, and garlic strands.

In the 20th century, superstitions persisted, even among the educated, fueling a number of successful Gothic works, including Algernon BLACKWOOD's "The Wendigo" (1910), S. Ansky's supernatural play *Der Dybbuk* (ca. 1916), Flannery O'CONNOR's novel *Wise Blood* (1952), and Jean RHYS's Caribbean novel *Wide Sargasso Sea* (1966). Pearl Buck stressed the fears and beliefs of Chinese peasants in *The Good Earth* (1931), which won her a Pulitzer Prize. After O-lan's protracted illness and death, her husband chooses a geomancer to name a propitious time for her burial and vacates their marriage bed to avoid thoughts of her purple-lipped corpse. In 2003, Dan Brown resurrected medieval rumors for his secret brotherhood tale THE DA VINCI CODE, in which members of a multinational coterie vie for possession of proof that Christ fathered children with his wife, Mary Magdalene.

Bibliography

Kozlowski, Lisa. "A Source for Ann Radcliffe's 'The Mysteries of Udolpho,'" *Notes and Queries* 44, no. 2 (June 1997): 228–229.

Varma, Devendra P. *The Gothic Flame.* New York: Russell & Russell, 1966.

suspense

Sharpened through skillful HYPERBOLE, MELODRAMA, and controlled STORYTELLING, suspense derives from reader anticipation of the outcome of threats and dangers and the resolution of ambiguity, MYSTERY, enigmas, and uncertainty. In a classic example, THE MYSTERIES OF UDOLPHO (1794), Ann RADCLIFFE draws out protagonist Emily ST. AUBERT's recoil and collapse at the sight of a corpse-like figure with worm-chewed face, which she unveils in a recess in the wall. Much later in the text, Radcliffe returns to the image to explain that the shape is really a wax model. Her diminution of terror produced a literary descriptive, the Radcliffean conclusion, characterizing an ending that explains away the terrors of the SUPERNATURAL either historically or scientifically.

Suspense derives from both controlled narrative and serialization, a popular form of publication that enhanced the readership of English, French, and American magazines during the 19th and early 20th centuries. Charles DICKENS made his name by stretching out installments of OLIVER TWIST (1838) over two years in *Bentley's Magazine,* leaving readers to wonder if his undersized orphan could flee

the clutches of a coterie of criminals from London's underworld. For a more mature Victorian audience, Mary Elizabeth BRADDON's controversial serial *Lady Audley's Secret* (1862) promoted mystery by highlighting SECRECY concerning shocking vices—bigamy, SADISM, and miscegenation. In both cases, the authors parceled out information that both fed and explained unknown elements that remained unresolved until story's end.

Suspense also serves both short and long fiction as a means of building reader awareness. George Washington CABLE uses an external point of view to tighten his exposition of the title character of "Jean-ah Poquelin" (1875), whom urban Louisianians suspect of piracy, murder, and the black arts. As a civil servant creeps up on Jean's isolated house, he realizes that rumors have missed the pathos of the old man's circumstances. Cable withholds to the last sentence an accounting for the disappearance of Jean's brother: Jean keeps his sibling close to home to conceal leprous lesions. The revelation dispels reader suspicions of crime or the supernatural at the same time that it enhances the humanism of the fiery old Creole.

In a long novel, the moody thriller REBECCA (1938), Daphne DU MAURIER uses the same style of implication to depict the estrangement of a young wife from her husband, Maxim de Winter. For three months, he appears to yearn for his first wife, the beautiful Rebecca, thus earning the reader's distrust and disapproval. The recovery of Rebecca's sailboat *Je Reviens* (I return) informs both the reader and the protagonist of the first Mrs. DE WINTER's guile. TONE and ATMOSPHERE take an immediate turn toward an upbeat solution to crime as an investigation reveals that Rebecca did not die of accidental drowning. Suspense peaks a second time with a blackmail attempt to accuse Maxim of murder. As the trail leads to a London physician's office, suspense reaches resolution in the revelation that Rebecca was dying of cancer and goaded Maxim into shooting her. He gains reader sympathy by concluding, "It was her last practical joke, . . . the best of them all" (du Maurier, 374).

Modern suspense thrillers have changed little in the meting out of Gothic details preceding a simple disclosure or astonishing conclusion, such as the promised suicide in Marsha NORMAN's two-woman domestic play 'night, Mother (1982). Toni MORRISON's novel Song of Solomon (1977) follows Milkman, the protagonist, on an odyssey of self-discovery. By extending the quest to solve the mystery of a grandsire who left a gold stash in a cave, the author reprises much of the Reconstruction era horror faced by blacks fleeing the war-torn South. On his way southeast from Michigan to Hunters Cave in Danville, Pennsylvania, Milkman, like a modern Odysseus, encounters a kind, elderly minister, a bizarre midwife named Circe, and the loving arms of Sweet in the legendary community of Shalimar, home of Milkman's ancestors. Venturing on a bobcat hunt in Ryna's Gulch by creeping twilight, Milkman barely escapes Guitar, who stalks his old friend with garrotting wire and rifle. The suspenseful end produces an epiphany: "It did not matter which one of them would give up his ghost in the killing arms of his brother" (Morrison, 337).

Bibliography

du Maurier, Daphne. *Rebecca.* New York: Avon Books, 1971.

Morrison, Toni. *Song of Solomon.* New York: Plume, 1987.

Sage, Victor. *Horror Fiction in the Protestant Tradition.* New York: St. Martin's, 1988.

symbol

A symbol is a term, image, character, or action that has wider significance. Symbolism broadens the meaning of Gothic fiction from straightforward correspondence to one or more elevated meanings. Examples are manifold: the emerging villain AMBROSIO's dropping of his rosary in Matthew Gregory LEWIS's THE MONK (1796), the representation of the folkloric past as a vampire in Bram STOKER's DRACULA (1897), the FORESHADOWING of colonial racist evil in Joseph CONRAD's evocative title HEART OF DARKNESS (1902), and the folly of a glass church on a floating wood platform in Australian novelist Peter Carey's OSCAR AND LUCINDA (1988). Edgar Allan POE's "LIGEIA" (1838) displays a macabre male-female relationship that suggests a criticism of men married to intellectual wives. Further afield from the death-in-life scenario is an implication of the powers of intellect and creativity to transcend physical death. The reader has a choice: to accept the story as a SHORT GOTHIC FICTION; to interpret it as a psychological commentary on marriage; or, at an esoteric level, to revalue it as a philosophical representation of the endurance of art and thought.

As a literary device, symbolism allows the author to create concrete images that project abstract meanings, as with the broken cupid, a representation of a smashed romantic ideal in Daphne DU MAURIER's REBECCA (1938); the killing of the memory of a dead wife by chopping down a tree in "The Apple Tree" (1952), one of du Maurier's elegant SUPERNATURAL tales; and Arthur Miller's resetting of the McCarthy era in THE CRUCIBLE (1953), a title suggesting the testing of strength. The French novelist Honoré de Balzac issued an enduring shocker with *Le Peau de Chagrin* (*The Fatal Skin,* 1831), the story of a hellish antique shop where Raphael, the protagonist, receives a shrinking strip of shagreen (a green-dyed leather) that is empowered to grant his heart's desire. After attaining the normal joys of marriage and a settled life, he retreats into a drugged despair because he cannot stop the skin from shrinking. As the antique dealer indicated, the strength of yearning reduced the skin. Upon Raphael's reunion with his wife, he reaches for her and expires in her embrace. Balzac uses the skin as visible evidence of the reduction of energy from intense emotion, a concept crucial to the author's understanding of himself as an artist.

In GOTHIC CONVENTION, the standard ploy of the evil male VILLAIN confining the female NAIF in a DUNGEON or tower parallels the plight of women in a patriarchal society, where freedom of movement and expression is the option of males only. A dungeon can suggest the suffocation and CLAUSTROPHOBIA of immurement; a tower, according to Freudian interpretation, parallels the erect phallus as an implied threat or weapon. Thus, the plight of Emily ST. AUBERT in Ann RADCLIFFE's four-volume THE MYSTERIES OF UDOLPHO (1794) characterizes orphaned women who become the pawns or victims of male adventurers and scavengers seeking to satisfy or enrich themselves by manipulating, limiting, intimidating, torturing, or killing the weaker sex. To heighten the reader's sympathy for the victim in THE ITALIAN (1797), Radcliffe named her heroine Ellena Rosalba, literally "white rose," and the villain Montoni, a verbal link between his mountain castle and his intent to use the secluded setting for a nefarious purpose.

In American Gothic, symbolism performs a similar purpose of revealing layers of meaning. In the era's oft-quoted Gothic poem, "The Raven" (1844), Edgar Allan Poe dwells on an encounter with a talking bird as a token of the recurrent thoughts of grief, regret, and solitude that overwhelm a mourner. Nathaniel HAWTHORNE produces a proliferation of meanings for suffering in THE SCARLET LETTER (1850), guiding the reader to deplore the soulless, unhusbandly behavior of Roger Chillingworth and to redefine the blazing A on Hester Prynne's chest from being a symbol of adultery to a reward for angelic ministrations to the community. In Herman MELVILLE's dark romance Moby-Dick (1851), the white whale is an animate part of NATURE that obsesses Captain Ahab, who stalks the beast to wreak REVENGE for the loss of his leg in its jaws. Playwright August WILSON made good use of symbols in THE PIANO LESSON (1990), in which an heirloom piano embodies a black family's heritage as well as the ghost of a plantation slavemaster, who haunts the Charles apartment in their new setting in a Pittsburgh ghetto.

Bibliography

Karl, Frederick R. The Adversary Literature: The English Novel in the Eighteenth Century—A Study in Genre. New York: Farrar, Straus & Giroux, 1974.

Mighall, Robert. A Geography of Victorian Gothic Fiction: Mapping History's Nightmares. Oxford: Oxford University Press, 1999.

T

"The Tell-Tale Heart"
Edgar Allan Poe
(1843)

One of Edgar Allan POE's classic horror tales, "The Tell-Tale Heart" has been called a model of Gothic fiction. First printed in the January 1843 issue of the Boston *Pioneer*, it preceded "THE BLACK CAT" (1843), another psychological study of madness, STALKING, and murder. The author, battling depression over the failing health of his wife, Virginia Clemm Poe, organized the narrative of "The Tell-Tale Heart" around the protagonist's OBSESSION over the evil eye. The visual detail is so engrossing that it inflames the stalker to throttle an aged man and inter his corpse at the scene of the crime under planked flooring.

Poe approached the story as the monologue of an unidentified egocentric killer, whom critics have mused might be female. Cast as a psychotic and sadomasochist, the narrator tries to establish sanity by detailing the crime, step by step. The perpetrator admits his lethal sacrifice of a harmless old man and softens the act by smothering him. After concealing the corpse in the floor, the killer believes that no details remain to establish guilt. Poe enhances the beating of the killer's heart into an echoing conscience that causes the suspect to believe that investigators hear the rhythm. Driven to near hysteria, the killer divulges the deed.

Bibliography

Pritchard, Hollie. "Poe's 'The Tell-Tale Heart,'" *Explicator* 61, no. 3 (spring 2003): 144–147.

terror fiction

A broad term within the confines of Gothic literature, terror fiction is a subset of horrific possibilities. The genre includes the thriller, CONTES CRUELS (cruel tales), crime novel, *roman policier* (police novel), espionage novel and, to a lesser degree, the DETECTIVE STORY, GHOST STORY, and SUPERNATURAL tale. It also encompasses some adventure, soldier-of-fortune, and war fiction, for example, Jean-Paul Sartre's existential thriller "The Wall" (1939). The philosopher Edmund Burke explains in his essay "On the Sublime" (1757) that terror and pathos are essentials to emotional involvement in literature because they stimulate reader sympathies and imagination and allow the reader to identify with fictional characters. As a genre, terror fiction enables the reader to exercise a panoply of emotions that social mores leash and repress. As opposed to horror fiction, which freezes the victim in the face of inescapable doom, terror creates apprehension, heightens the senses, and frees the mind to plot modes of delay, self-defense, and escape.

The works of terror fiction depend on varying degrees of villainy and intimidation, crime, ATMOSPHERE, MYSTERY, FORESHADOWING, and SUSPENSE, all elements of Horace WALPOLE's prototypical Gothic novel *THE CASTLE OF OTRANTO* (1765), a romance built on MEDIEVALISM and the supernatural. Ann RADCLIFFE introduced the female response to terror with a Gothic masterwork, *THE MYSTERIES OF UDOLPHO* (1794), the literary touchstone of female emotion. The tale of imprisonment in a remote mountain setting introduces an orphaned protagonist, Emily ST. AUBERT, who falls into the clutches of a VILLAIN, Signor Montoni. A powerlessness common to dependent females, particularly virgins, generates in the young heiress a wide band of psychic imaginings that begins with fear of the dark and advances to fears of abandonment, mystery, the supernatural, rape, and death. Separated from her lover Valancourt, she projects on NATURE her feelings of isolation and dread.

The 19th century saw a demand for terror literature, which the American Gothic artist Edgar Allan POE published serially or in single issues of popular magazines. Contributing to the genre were Scottish novelist James HOGG's diabolic *The Memoirs and Confession of a Justified Sinner* (1824); Thomas De Quincey's *Klosterheim* (1832) and *The Avenger* (1838), two works that depict dread as opposed to actual violence; Wilkie COLLINS's detective thriller THE MOONSTONE (1868); and Sir Arthur Conan DOYLE's Sherlock HOLMES series, especially "The Adventure of the Speckled Band" (1892), which pictures a swamp adder, India's deadliest reptile, gripping a human head. In the 20th century, the voracious public promoted the terror genre and lionized Eric Ambler for *The Mask of Dimitrios* (1939), Dashiell Hammett for *The Maltese Falcon* (1930), Raymond Chandler for *The Big Sleep* (1939), and Frederick Forsyth for *The Day of the Jackal* (1971), which won the Mystery Writers of America Edgar Allan Poe award for orchestrating a suspenseful manhunt for a cold-blooded assassin. The 21st century saw the extenuation of terror literature with Dan Brown's best-seller THE DA VINCI CODE (2003), a thriller based on SECRECY, medieval lore, stalking, and the horrific murder of an elderly scholar found nude on the floor of the Louvre.

Bibliography

Heller, Terry. *The Delights of Terror: An Aesthetics of the Tale of Terror*. Urbana: University of Illinois Press, 1987.

Hume, Robert. "Gothic Versus Romantic: A Revaluation of the Gothic Novel," *Publication of the Modern Language Association* 84 (1969): 282–290.

"Thanatopsis"
William Cullen Bryant
(1817)

William Cullen BRYANT's earliest contribution to funeral poetry, "Thanatopsis" encompasses the conflict between Calvinism and pantheism. Like his Puritan forebears, the poet contemplated death from an American point of view rather than in the manner of the rhapsodic imaginings of Europe's GRAVEYARD POETS. He introduces dire reflections by calling on his supreme authority, NATURE, which heals his fears with compassion. That said, he plunges into the grim aspects of mortality, the morose pictures of pain, death, and preparation for burial "And breathless, darkness, and the narrow house, / Make thee to shudder, and grow sick at heart" (Bryant, 6). Less Gothic than his European predecessors, the poet avoids extremes of horror. He pictures the worst of death to be the loss of individuality and the absorption of a decaying human body into "that mysterious realm" (*ibid.*). For its maturity and dignity, the poem earned the praise of Christopher North, a reviewer for BLACKWOOD'S EDINBURGH MAGAZINE.

Less ebullient in his adult years, Bryant penned poems on the evanescence of flowers, a resonant farewell in "The Old Man's Funeral" (1824), and "Hymn to Death" (1825), a tight-lipped dirge marking the passing of his father. In the August 1876 issue of *Scribner's*, Bryant published "The Flood of Years," a mature reply to his youthful glimpse of humankind's march to the grave. Influenced by the nation's agonies during the Civil War, the poem pictures stark battlefield clashes marked by the flash of powder and the bloody foam on the dying breath of man and steed. The speaker turns away from the embrace of nature to the sounds of women wailing, but acknowledges once more that death is a natural event.

Bibliography

Bryant, William Cullen. *Thanatopsis*. Boston: Bibliophile Society, 1927.

Ruland, Richard, and Malcolm Bradbury. *From Puritanism to Postmodernism: A History of American Literature*. New York: Penguin, 1991.

"That Evening Sun"
William Faulkner
(1931)

One of William FAULKNER's most analyzed southern stories, "That Evening Sun" pictures the victimization of a lone woman in a female Gothic setting. The critic H. L. Mencken bowdlerized the sexually charged text before printing it in the *American Mercury;* it returned to Faulkner's original form in *These Thirteen* (1931). The story features the Compson family's black cook and laundress Nancy Mannigoe. A heavily nuanced STALKING tale, the action depicts her as doubly victimized—by the bank teller Stoval, the white man who impregnates her, and by her black husband, Jesus, who displays a "razor scar on his black face like a piece of dirty string" (Faulkner, 292). He seeks to repay Nancy for adultery with one stroke of the blade to her throat.

The story resets traditional European GOTHIC CONVENTIONs in the Jim Crow Mississippi of the 1930s, when black prostitutes like Nancy had little choice about how to support themselves and their children. A hopeless lone female sitting by the fireside, at the story's ambiguous conclusion Nancy can only await her fate at the hands of a patriarchal avenger. In the intervening time, she tries to swallow her coffee and emits an eerie sound born of terror and resignation to death. Enhancing the dread of the unseen stalker is a naive point of view limited to an UNRELIABLE NARRATOR, a white child who remembers the events as he observed them at age nine, when Nancy used him as a makeshift shield against Jesus.

Bibliography

Barger, James. *William Faulkner: Modern American Novelist and Novel Prize Winner.* Charlotteville, N.Y.: SamHar Press, 1989.

Faulkner, William. *Collected Stories of William Faulkner.* New York: Vintage Books, 1950.

Thornfield Hall

Charlotte BRONTË manipulates the chief setting of the gripping Victorian novel *JANE EYRE* (1847) as a reflection of the main characters' states of mind. After a 16-hour journey over the remote moors on a cold October day, the 19-year-old title character arrives at her new home but can discern through the mist only the gate, a drive, and a bow window. Indoors, she compares the oaken stairs, banisters, and gallery to church architecture. In keeping with GOTHIC CONVENTION, the dwelling is high-ceilinged, unappealing, and solitary, a FAIRY TALE setting similar in threat to the castle in the BLUEBEARD MYTH.

Brontë misleads the reader with the simple presentation of the 19th-century version of an obscure castle. By daylight on a fine autumn morning, Jane changes her initial opinion of Thornfield by surveying its three-story expanse. Seeing a masculine hand in its design, she calls it "a gentleman's manor-house, not a nobleman's seat" and comments on the gnarled old thorn trees that supplied an image for its naming (Brontë, 91). Contributing to the air of gentility is a library appointed with books, a spinet, an easel, and paired globes, one of the earth and the other of astral constellations. Jane questions the housekeeper about ghosts, but learns no scary traditions or rumors of hauntings. Fearless in her curiosity, Jane escapes the Gothic stereotype of the timorous maiden by exploring all the way to the attic trapdoor.

Brontë builds intrigue and mystery at Thornfield less from architecture than from habitation. She describes Jane's pacing agitatedly about the third floor and subjects her to late-night visits from a lurking lunatic, who shatters the stillness with a spine-chilling cackle. The author indicates that the disturbance issues from the room above Jane's quarters and echoes from one end of the hall to the other like an aural phantasm engulfing the manse. One night, after aiding her master, Edward ROCHESTER, in reviving a wounded guest, she joins Rochester at the door for some fresh air. He refutes her impression of Thornfield as a "splendid mansion" with his jaundiced view: "That the gilding is slime and the silk draperies cobwebs; that the marble is sordid slate, and the polished woods mere refuse chips and scaly bark" (*ibid.,* 203). In his embittered opinion, the manor takes on the hopelessness and decay of his secret marriage, which fell to ruin many years before he embarked from Jamaica with Bertha Mason, his crazed bride.

Brontë builds Jane's regard for Thornfield through contrast. On her return to the estate after a month at GATESHEAD HALL to sit with her dying aunt, Jane embraces the property like an old friend. Walking the last part of the way through ripe hayfields and rose hedges, she once more crosses a stile, the return of a SYMBOL of her passage to a new state of mind. As she approaches Rochester, she passes a blended image, a "tall brier, shooting leafy and flowery branches across the path," a suggestion of the thorny path to love and matrimony that lies ahead (ibid., 231). To his implication that she is a wraith or *ignis fatuus* emerging from the gloaming, she confides to Rochester that Thornfield is her home.

Brontë manipulates natural imagery as commentary on Jane's reclamation of Thornfield. In the emotional high that envelops her during summer days at the estate, she enjoys "a band of Italian days" when the manor sits among newly cut fields and fully leaved trees and hedges (ibid., 234). On Midsummer Eve, the beauty of the estate is at its height, the perfect time for Rochester's wooing. Like Eve straying past fruit-laden trees along the paths of Eden, Jane follows the scent of his cigar to the giant horse chestnut tree, but retreats into an ivied nook, a modest, self-effacing touch befitting a mere governess. On the stroke of midnight, Jane finds the housekeeper, like a shoreward sentinel, standing in silent disapproval of the couple's embraces.

The author elevates the MELODRAMA of the Edenic setting by introducing a summer storm and by blasting the tree with lightning, a startling Gothic touch and FORESHADOWING of a doomed union after Jane's coming to knowledge. On greeting Rochester the next morning, she experiences an intuitive warning "that smote and stunned," a portent of a lengthy trial far from Thornfield (ibid., 245). Brontë creates a pictorial turmoil of strong, searing wind that distorts tree limbs and produces a MELANCHOLY keening. The forbidding weather unsettles Jane during the prenuptial month, when she retreats to her chamber and experiences troubling DREAMS. After the wedding unravels in the revelation before witnesses of the true Mrs. Edward Rochester, the would-be groom compares his hated home to a "demons' vicinage" and vows to board up the hall and leave it to the madwoman in the third-floor room (ibid., 286).

Following Thornfield's destruction and Jane's return from the moors, Brontë presents the grand old hall in ruin as an emblem of the humbling of Edward Rochester. As before, Jane approaches through the stile, the recurring symbol of a life passage. Against an unpromising backdrop—a loud cawing from a dark rookery—Brontë interposes a romantic motif, the nightmarish tale of a lover anticipating a glance at his beloved and finding her "stone dead" (ibid., 406). The charred mansion in the distance is a shock, the remains of an apocalyptic fire. Jane first discerns the wasted grounds, then a sadly reduced exterior shell minus its roof, battlements, and chimneys. Like a defenseless outpost, Thornfield appears deathly quiet, alone, and returned to the wild. Jane's questions migrate from how the fire started to what victims may have died in the conflagration. Her mind shifts from thoughts of Rochester alive to a glance at the estate churchyard, where he might lie buried with his ancestors.

To make sense of Thornfield's desolation, the protagonist must ask questions. At the inn, Brontë jolts Jane with the waiter's comment that he once worked for the "late Mr. Rochester" (ibid., 407). After clarifying that he referred to Edward's father and not the current owner, the unnamed former butler offers limited details about the fire that consumed Thornfield at harvest time, a subdued moralistic symbol of end-of-life retribution for Rochester's DISSIPATIONS. Brontë employs pictorial Gothic—flames emerging in the dark of night, the work of a lunatic wife who kindled the governess's bed two months after Jane's departure. Thus, the wronged wife perverts the fires of passion into vengeance against a philandering husband and his imprisoning manse.

Bibliography

Brontë, Charlotte. *Jane Eyre*. New York: Bantam Books, 1981.

Gilbert, Sandra M., and Susan Gubar. *The Madwoman in the Attic*, 2nd ed. New Haven, Conn.: Yale University Press, 2000.

Hoeveler, Diane Long. *Gothic Feminism*. University Park: Pennsylvania State University Press, 1998.

Tieck, Johann Ludwig
(1773–1853)

The poet and novelist Johann Ludwig Tieck of Berlin was a major contributor to GERMAN GOTHIC horror fiction. He received a university education at Erlangen, Göttingen, and Halle before launching a writing career at age 21. From sensational stories and a novel, he turned to RO-MANTICISM and wrote plays, short stories, and dramatic FAIRY TALES, notably, *Ritter Blaubart (Bluebeard)* and *Der Gestiefelte Kater (Puss in Boots)*, the story of evil SHAPE-SHIFTING collected in *Volksmärchen (Folktales, 1797)* and later performed on a Berlin stage. Best known is a Gothic masterwork, "Wake Not the Dead" (1800), a tale of sorcery that begins with the bereaved Walter's keening over the grave of his beloved Brunhilda. Literary historians consider the story one of the first modern examples of VAMPIRISM.

While living at Jena, Tieck produced narrative verse and dramas. He translated Elizabethan plays and Miguel de Cervantes's *Don Quixote* (1615) and gave public readings. Tieck produced one of the initial female vampires in "The Bride of the Grave" (1817), in which a bride shape-shifts into a serpent and crushes the groom to death. In 1822, in the style of Johann Wolfgang von GOETHE, Tieck revived Teutonic myth and LEGEND by producing *Phantasus* (Apparition), a short fiction anthology that established his reputation for invention, particularly the symbolic fairy tale "Fortunat." The following year, Thomas Carlyle translated Tieck's short works into English as *German Romance* (1827). The text met the American demand for more European Gothic horror stories and pleased Edgar Allan POE, who admired the tales for their originality, especially "Die Elfen" (The elves) and "Das Pokal" (The goblet).

Bibliography

Blackall, Eric A. *The Novels of the German Romantics.* Ithaca, N.Y.: Cornell University Press, 1983.

Hadley, Michael. *The Undiscovered Genre: A Search for the German Gothic Novel.* Berne: Peter Lang, 1978.

Nickell, Joe. "Germany: Monsters, Myths, and Mysteries," *Skeptical Inquirer* 27, no. 2 (March–April 2003): 24–28.

tone

Like the tone of a storyteller's voice, literary tone projects the author's attitude toward the audience as well as toward the subject, MOOD, and moral stance of a work. Tone varies widely over a range of possibilities—from witty, casual, intimate, wistful, and playful, as with the tone of SAKI's wry cat story "Tobermory" (1911) and Oscar WILDE's light-hearted "The Canterville Ghost" (1889), to imploring, somber, suspicious, accusatory, ominous, and lethal. In Gothic literature, the projection of ambiguous, subtle, and indirect hints enhances MYSTERY and SUSPENSE, as with the somber ambivalence in Edgar Allan POE's ghoulish "ULALUME" (1847) and the affection and sympathy of William FAULKNER toward the protagonist in "A ROSE FOR EMILY" (1930) and of Katherine Anne Porter toward the title character in "The Jilting of Granny Weatherall" (1930), a last glimpse of an aggressive old woman who truly "weathered all," even desertion at the altar.

Tone controls the reader's sympathies, as with the reader's response to brooding resentment in William Styron's HISTORICAL NOVEL *The Confessions of Nat Turner* (1967), a SOUTHERN GOTHIC account of a murderous slave revolt on a Southampton, Virginia, plantation. Styron opens his four-part work with "Judgment Day," in which the speaker, a black slave shackled at the ankles, is rapt in a vision of mystery enshrouded by a gray dawn as he looks out to sea toward his homeland in West Africa. In neo-Gothic novels, tone misleads the reader from standard expectations, for example, with the symbiosis of police and werewolves in Whitley Strieber's *The Wolfen* (1978), a revival of the LYCANTHROPY novel, and the devil worship, alchemy, and loving relationship of the vampire Saint-Germain and the naive Madelaine de Montalia in Chelsea Quinn Yarbro's novel *Hotel Transylvania* (1978).

Bibliography

Heller, Terry. *The Delights of Terror: An Aesthetics of the Tale of Terror.* Urbana: University of Illinois Press, 1987.

Ruland, Richard, and Malcolm Bradbury. *From Puritanism to Postmodernism: A History of American Literature.* New York: Penguin, 1991.

translation

The shared strands of American, English, French, and German Gothic produced a Western canon of Gothic literature. Advancing the cross-fertilization of Gothic modes was the work of literary translators, professional wordsmiths who preserved the unique foreign flavor of imported texts. Among the writers who fleshed out their earnings from original writings with translations were Edward BULWER-LYTTON, Eliza PARSONS, Thomas Prescott PREST, Abbé PRÉVOST, Mary ROBINSON, Sir Walter SCOTT, Charlotte SMITH, Tobias SMOLLETT, and Johann Ludwig TIECK. The impact of translated texts preceded classic Gothic fiction with renderings of German dramatist and poet Andreas Gryphius's *Kirch-hof Gedanchen* (Graveyard thoughts, ca. 1650), which influenced the English and American graveyard poets. Contributing to ROMANTICISM was Antoine Galland's French translation of *The Arabian Nights* (1704–17), a major source of Oriental exotica.

The best of English Gothic fiction quickly found its way to the continent, including Clara REEVE's THE OLD ENGLISH BARON (1778), Matthew Gregory LEWIS's THE MONK (1796), Ann RADCLIFFE's THE ITALIAN (1797), and Charlotte DACRE's *The Libertine* (1807). English copies of European short fiction boosted sales of the *Strand* magazine; Sophia LEE's English versions of Baculard d'Arnaud's French novels did likewise for *Ladies' Magazine* in the 1780s. BLACKWOOD'S EDINBURGH MAGAZINE increased circulation by publishing English versions of stories by Johann von SCHILLER and E. T. A. HOFFMANN, whose *Die Elixiere des Teufels* (The Devil's Elixir, 1815–16) was a source for James HOGG's psychological thriller and murder MYSTERY *The Private Memoirs and Confessions of a Justified Sinner* (1824). A flurry of abridged plots and piracies also served the GOTHIC BLUEBOOK; Matthew Gregory Lewis's English renderings of the works of August Friedrich von Kotzebue, Schiller, and Heinrich Zschokke enlivened the English stage.

The Gothic novel proved to be a growth industry in Europe and North America. Mary Wollstonecraft SHELLEY's *FRANKENSTEIN* (1818) was a best-seller in English, French, German, Spanish, and Swedish. Charles Robert MATURIN intrigued a variety of readers with translations of MELMOTH THE WANDERER (1820); Victor Hugo was also a success with the forbidding *Notre-Dame de Paris* (*The Hunchback of Notre-Dame*, 1831) in multiple tongues. French and English versions of Vladimir Fyodorovich ODOEVSKY's *Russian Nights* (1844) carried Russian Gothic to new venues. Similarly, Théophile GAUTIER's erotic ghost story *La Morte Amoureuse* (The dead lover, 1836) flourished in English as "Clarimonde." His *Tales from Théophile Gautier* (1888) were rendered in English by Lafcadio HEARN, who also introduced English readers to the OTHERNESS of Chinese and JAPANESE GOTHIC. English adaptations of Jules-Gabriel JANIN's *frénétique* Gothic fiction in *L'Ane Mort et la Femme Guillotinée* (The dead donkey and the guillotined woman, 1829) were well received. The German version of Robert Montgomery BIRD's bloody mystery novel, NICK OF THE WOODS; or, The Jibbenainosay: A Tale of Kentucky (1837) carried FRONTIER GOTHIC to Europe. Two famous success stories are the French versions of Poe's poems and stories, translated by Charles BAUDELAIRE, and the demand for Wilkie COLLINS's GASLIGHT THRILLERs in French, German, and Russian.

Sophisticated English readers demanded access to the best in literature. Their cosmopolitan tastes called for adaptations of the Alsatian duo Émile ERCKMANN and Louis Alexandre CHATRIAN's *Contes Fantastiques* (Fantastic stories, 1847) and *Strange Stories* (1880) and Gaston LEROUX's THE PHANTOM OF THE OPERA (1910), which was available in English by 1911. S. Ansky's *Der Dybbuk* (The Dybbuk, 1916) became a world-famous Yiddish play after its publication in Bulgarian, English, French, German, Polish, Russian, Swedish, and Ukrainian. In more recent times, a market for world Gothic literature produced avid readers of French-Canadian author Anne Hébert's *Kamouraska* (1970), Hamada Kenji's translation of 18th-century Japanese Gothic stories as *Tales of Moonlight and Rain* (1971), Isabel ALLENDE's global best-seller THE HOUSE OF THE SPIRITS (1981), Laura Esquivel's Mexican FAIRY TALE *Like Water for Chocolate* (1989), and Charles Shiro Inouye's English translation of Izumi Kyoka's *Japanese Gothic Tales* (1996).

Bibliography

Horner, Avril, ed. *European Gothic: A Spirited Exchange, 1760–1960.* Manchester: Manchester University Press, 2002.

The Turn of the Screw
Henry James
(1898)

An ingenious subjectivity and inscrutable evil lie at the core Henry JAMES's *The Turn of the Screw,* a favorite American ghost thriller. It first appeared in print in *Collier's Weekly* before publication in *The Two Magics* (1898). Filled with OBSESSION, irony, macabre details, sustained tension, and the anticipation of VIOLENCE, the dramatic plot presents a psychological evaluation of an innocent woman in the grasp of an unidentified hazard. James sustains the ambiguity by depicting the unnamed governess's overworked imagination, a product of ROMANTICISM and neurosis. In the end, naiveté, poor judgment, and childish trust betray her, leaving unresolved the question of haunting at BLY HOUSE.

The evocative title offers multiple possibilities—the torment of the thumbscrew, a device common to the Spanish Inquisition and to slavers punishing runaways, and the eliciting of tension by heightening SUSPENSE. In the opening scenes, James creates a powerful SUBTEXT in the reading of the first-person ghost tale on December 28, the Feast of the Holy Innocents. He indicates that, by overlaying Gothic terror with childhood purity, the storyteller enhances chilling effects. A minor character seems to speak the author's delight by exclaiming, "Oh, how delicious!" (James, 8).

The children whom the governess supervises import from India the alien mystery of the English colonies, from which they have returned after the deaths of their parents in the field. In the final analysis, readers and critics debate the source of the narrator's visions of the spirits of former governess Miss Jessel and valet Peter Quint. Evidence leaves unspecified whether the apparitions are real glimpses or the hallucinations of an UNRELIABLE NARRATOR. In reference to his puzzling story, James gloated over his literary trickery, calling it "a piece of ingenuity pure and simple, of cold artistic calculation, an amusette to catch those not easily caught" (Stipe, 16).

Bibliography

James, Henry. *The Turn of the Screw and Daisy Miller.* New York: Laurel, 1954.

Ludwig, Sami. "Metaphors, Cognition and Behavior: The Reality of Sexual Puns in 'The Turn of the Screw,'" *Mosaic* 27, no. 1 (March 1994): 33–53.

Sawyer, Richard. "What's Your Title?—'The Turn of the Screw,'" *Studies in Short Fiction* 30, no. 1 (winter 1993): 53–61.

Stipe, Stormy. "The Ghosts of Henry James," *Biblio,* September 1998: 16.

Walker, Steven F. "James's 'The Turn of the Screw,'" *Explicator* 61, no. 2 (winter 2003): 94–96.

U

Udolpho

A fictitious castle in the Apennine Mountains of Italy, Udolpho is an ominous setting in Ann RADCLIFFE's lengthy terror romance THE MYSTERIES OF UDOLPHO (1794), the most successful novel of its day. The VILLAIN, Signor Montoni, transports his new wife and her niece, Emily ST. AUBERT, and the servant Annette from the Pyrenees to Venice and into the high country to Udolpho, an ancestral manse that serves as Emily's prison. Realizing the seriousness of her predicament, the heroine recognizes her uncle's intent to confine her in a tower of his secluded home, where he can "terrify her into obedience; or, that, should its gloomy and sequestered scenes fail of this effect, her forced marriage with the Count could there be solemnized with the secrecy, which was necessary to the honour of Montoni" (Radcliffe, 224). Thus, the retreat from society allows the villain to inflict evil on the NAIF without drawing the attention of potential rescuers and without sullying his reputation and noble standing.

Passing through vales and slopes, the heroine characterizes the setting as dark and horrible, but she keeps her options open for adventure. A PSYCHOLOGICAL INTERPRETATION equates her outlook as that of the virgin anticipating the transition from chastity to sexual awareness and deflowering. When she catches sight of the Gothic castle at sunset, she admires the grandeur of its ancient architecture, but shrinks from the moldering gray stone walls, purplish MELANCHOLY tint at evening, and dreary chambers. Inside the frowning castle, Emily gathers the courage to lift a black veil from a framed picture and instantly faints from the unidentified grimness that lies beneath. The symbolic response suggests the romantic ideal of the Middle Ages themselves—fascinating in their outsized proportions and external uplift, yet dim and fearful in their inner reaches. Much later in the narrative, the author returns to the veil and perceives that it covers a recess in which a corpse wrapped in winding sheet presents a worm-infested face to the heroine. The visage, which Emily misconstrues as real, is a wax model that suggests the foul duplicity of her captor.

Bibliography

Kozlowski, Lisa. "A Source for Ann Radcliffe's 'The Mysteries of Udolpho,'" Notes and Queries 44, no. 2 (June 1997). 228–230.

Radcliffe, Ann. The Mysteries of Udolpho. London: Oxford University Press, 1966.

"Ulalume"
Edgar Allan Poe
(1847)

One of the last four poems that Gothic verse master Edgar Allan POE published in the months before his death in 1849, "Ulalume" describes a lover's flight from sorrowful memories in the company of Psyche, his soul. The text, a despairing tomb pilgrimage that appeared in the December 1847 issue of the American Whig Review, is Poe's tribute to his dead wife, Virginia Clemm Poe, a 13-year-old cousin at the time of their secret marriage on September 22, 1835. The long narrative verse succeeds from extensive assonance with *oh* and *oo* sounds and the mounting effect of an ominous ATMOSPHERE. In the background, towering cypress trees shade a misty tarn as the seasons shift from late fall to winter on the anniversary of Ulalume's death.

As he does with Madeline USHER, Annabel Lee, Eulalie, Annie, and Marie Rogêt, Poe focuses on the title character for her delicacy, pathos, and youthful grace. Critics remark on his OBSESSION with frail but nubile damsels whose vulnerability mirrors the size and physique of the tubercular Virginia, who suffered a five-year decline before dying. Her demise on January 30, 1847, of a throat hemorrhage while cradling a cat to her bosom inflamed Poe's imagination, pushing him into depression, alcoholic excess, INSANITY, and suicidal urges some two years and nine months before a brain hemorrhage killed him. In the interim, he pushed his creative genius into dark corners for graphic representations of his dread of loss.

Bibliography

Pollin, Burton R. "Poe's 'Ulalume': Its Likely Source," *ANQ* 1, no. 1 (January 1988): 17–20.

unreliable narrator

The unreliable narrator looks at events and characters through deliberate falsehoods, the controlling factor in the Scottish novelist James HOGG's *The Private Memoirs and Confessions of a Justified Sinner* (1824), or from a childish, fallible, or skewed perspective that conflicts with fact, a common perspective of the NAIF and the peasant, as found in the commentary of Nelly Dean, the housekeeper in Emily BRONTË's *WUTHERING HEIGHTS* (1847) and the misunderstanding of a local prank in Ring Lardner's lethal FOOL TALE "Haircut" (1954). The reports of the questionable speaker may be biased, incomplete, deliberately fabricated, or, in the case of a naive or mentally impaired speaker, insufficient in understanding. The use of an unstable or questionable point of view is a Gothic romanticist's tool that enlarges the ambiguity of a ghost tale, as with the grief-deranged speaker in Edgar Allan POE's "LIGEIA"

(1838), the emotionally unstable Roderick USHER in Poe's classic horror story "THE FALL OF THE HOUSE OF USHER" (1839), and the maniac in denial of his psychosis in "THE TELL-TALE HEART" (1843). Guy de MAUPASSANT makes use of questionable logic in "La Horla" (Out There, 1887), a tale of haunting and madness. A fearful ambiguity wracks an estate owner, who burns his house and servants to rid himself of an apparition. Bram STOKER implies a shaky source in the speculative reportage of Jonathan HARKER, whose journal forms part of the narrative in *DRACULA* (1897). The fearful governess-narrator of Henry JAMES's *THE TURN OF THE SCREW* (1898) forces readers to separate reality from twisted reports and truth from lies.

Bibliography

Punter, David, ed. *The Literature of Terror*, vol. 1, 2nd ed. London: Longman, 1996.

Twitchell, James B. *The Living Dead: A Study of the Vampire in Romantic Literature*. Durham, N.C.: Duke University Press, 1981.

urban Gothic

As romanticism gave place to realism, Gothic fiction abandoned castle turrets and lapsed cloisters for the CLAUSTROPHOBIA, ABERRANT BEHAVIOR, and foreboding found in cityscapes. In place of encircling moats, stone-paved halls, and dungeons are the high-rise walls of modern cities, which house the MONSTERS of capitalism and shadow random crime and squalid living conditions in tenements and back alleys, such as the workers' house in wartime Detroit in Hariette Arnow's MELODRAMA *The Dollmaker* (1954). Upon arrival, the protagonist, Gertie Nevels, looks out on smokestacks, pipes, trains, and trucks belching steam and smoke. The author notes, "Here there seemed to be no people, even the cars with their rolled-up windows, frosted over like those of the cab, seemed empty of people, driving themselves through a world not meant for people" (Arnow, 168).

The growth of cities on both sides of the Atlantic fueled plots with the myriad headaches of living in close quarters. American urban Gothic got a head start with Charles Brockden BROWN's

ARTHUR MERVYN; or, Memoirs of the Year 1793 (1799), which dramatizes the terrors of Philadelphia's yellow fever epidemic. In England, Charles DICKENS exploited urban melodrama in OLIVER TWIST (1838), a novel picturing a sensitive orphan boy attempting to make his way in London amid rampant crime and want. Dickens pursued city blight in his ninth novel, BLEAK HOUSE (1853), which enlarges on Gothic scenarios attesting to a lack of charity for the poor and the failure of London families.

Unlike the classic Gothic writers William BECKFORD, Ann RADCLIFFE, and Matthew Gregory LEWIS, who reprised medieval terrors, urban Gothicists turned to police blotters for chilling stories of suicide, gang VIOLENCE, and the con artist's victimization of the weak and unsuspecting, a pervasive motif in the works of Flannery O'CONNOR. Short fiction writer George William Macarthur REYNOLDS expanded Gothic SENSATIONALISM into new territory with his GASLIGHT THRILLERs, which turned episodes of streetwalking, graverobbing, and sadistic crime into a literary phenomenon. Readers thrilled to his Mysteries of London (1844–48) and The Mysteries of the Court of London (1848–53), which developed muckraking headlines into disturbing voyeuristic fiction.

As the Atlantic seaboard sprouted metropolises, American Gothic writers found frontier and Wild West imagery giving place to the horrors of the concrete jungle. George Lippard produced a best-selling exposé in The Quaker City; or, The Monks of Monk Hall (1845), a seamy tale of ghosts, a men's club that seduces and rapes woman, and sex for sale in Philadelphia, where a doorman named Devil-Bug anticipates a cleansing apocalypse. Herman MELVILLE's "Bartleby the Scrivener" (1853) and "The Paradise of Bachelors and the Tartarus of Maids" (1855) note that apathy, the flip side of intimidation, carries its own terrors. Popular fiction concurred with Lippard and Melville and fostered the demand for sensationalism in the GOTHIC BLUEBOOK, the NEWGATE NOVEL, CONTES CRUELS (cruel tales), and serialized slasher crime and detective magazines. The French poet Charles BAUDELAIRE condensed city miseries in Les Fleurs du Mal (The Flowers of Evil, 1857), an influential body of decadent verse.

As a wave of citified Gothic battered the complacency of the Victorian Age, Gothic fiction ventured further into psychological miasmas and well-plotted mysteries that exploited the city dweller's unease. Wilkie COLLINS produced urban melodrama in The Woman in White (1860), an impetus to the detective fiction of Mary Elizabeth BRADDON. In the cultural mix of New Orleans, George Washington CABLE captured the displacement of the OUTSIDER in his Creole story "Jean-ah Poquelin" (1875) and depicted the moral decline of the aristocracy in Madame Delphine (1881). Bram STOKER played on urban anxiety with DRACULA (1897), which depicts the STALKING criminal and sexual deviate as a vampire, a suave monster symbolizing white citizens' fears of dark-skinned immigrants and threats to the English family.

The 20th century saw no letup in the threat to individuals in crowded cities where closeness to other people brought no assurance of safety or contentment. Joseph CONRAD developed the theme of the terrorist bomber in The Secret Agent (1907); Shirley JACKSON explored the illusion of democracy in "THE LOTTERY" (1949). Ray BRADBURY's "There Will Come Soft Rains" (1950) and H. P. LOVECRAFT's "The Rats in the Walls" (1924) shook the confidence of urbanites with images of aliens, demons, and technological terrors that thrive on big-city anonymity, isolation, and dependence on electronic security. Margaret Edson reset the MAD SCIENTIST motif in the Pulitzer Prize–winning play Wit (1999), which presents a woman in an end-stage of ovarian cancer depending on a cold, heartless physician for treatment and rescue from pain. The patient lives out her last days not in a Gothic castle but in the walled-off isolation cell of a modern hospital. August WILSON's suite of 10 plays, including Joe Turner's Come and Gone (1988), THE PIANO LESSON (1990), Seven Guitars (1995), and Gem of the Ocean (2003), depict the terrors of Pittsburgh's ghettos that blindside African Americans emigrating from the rural South.

Bibliography

Arnow, Harriette. The Dollmaker. New York: Avon Books, 1954.

Freedman, Samuel G. "August Wilson, Defining an Era," New York Times, (February 5, 2003): 1.

Goddu, Teresa A. *Gothic America: Narrative, History, and Nation.* New York: Columbia University Press, 1997.

Shannon, Sandra G. "Blues, History, and Dramaturgy," *African American Review* 27, no. 4 (winter 1993): 539–559.

Usher, Madeline

Like her hypersensitive twin, Roderick USHER, in Edgar Allan POE's classic horror story "THE FALL OF THE HOUSE OF USHER" (1839), the wraithlike Madeline Usher suffers a catatonic seizure, a twin of death that leaves her immobile and mute. The fatal trance that causes Roderick, a SYMBOL of consciousness, to inter his sister, a symbol of the unconscious state, in the family vault precipitates images of CLAUSTROPHOBIA and fear of PREMATURE BURIAL. Her revival after over a week of life-in-death entombment results in her startling reappearance just as her brother reads aloud to his unnamed guest a dragon-slaying hero tale, "The Mad Trist." Poe stresses the weakness of the Usher line by depicting Madeline as barely strong enough to claw her way out of the family crypt. Still shrouded in white burial robes stained with blood, she stands dreamlike and mute with only enough energy left to confront her twin before expiring from overexertion.

A feminist interpretation of Madeline's resurgence depicts her as the female counterpart to Ethelmed, the dragon-slayer in Roderick's story. As he reads aloud the death of a hapless hermit, Roderick himself is the victim of Madeline, who awakens from a deathlike rigor to avenge herself on the brother who has imprisoned and compromised her. Poe manipulates the reader's suspicions of evil by implying that Roderick sexually abuses his sister. By asserting herself, Madeline breaks free of the burial vault, a symbol of societal constraints on women, and assumes the qualities of the stereotypical male hero. Curiously, she remains mute, like women long silenced by exploitive males in perverse sexual alliances.

Bibliography

Benoit, Raymond. "Poe's 'The Fall of the House of Usher,'" *Explicator* 58, no. 2 (winter 2000): 79.

Hustis, Harriet. "'Reading Encrypted but Persistent': The Gothic of Reading and Poe's 'The Fall of the House of Usher,'" *Studies in American Fiction* 27, no. 1 (spring 1999): 3.

Usher, Roderick

The cadaverous, deranged host and raconteur in Edgar Allan POE's classic story "THE FALL OF THE HOUSE OF USHER" (1839), Roderick Usher, the twin brother of Madeline USHER, crumbles mentally as his ancestral home experiences a mystical dissolution and collapse from a sudden whirlwind. Pale and disheveled, he displays the symptoms of NEURASTHENIA, a family ailment marked by a disturbed psyche, introspection, OBSESSION, hyperexcitation, and heightened sensitivity to external stimulation from sound, texture, odor, and light. One of Poe's most dramatic Gothic narratives, the story implies that Roderick, by forcing incestuous relations with his twin and double, has brought ruin on himself and on the doomed House of Usher. Roderick, however, is a poor judge of his own situation. A classic depiction rendered through the device of an UNRELIABLE NARRATOR, the story emerges from an obscurity and ambiguity rooted in unspecified fears and terrors.

Critics interpret Roderick's bizarre morbidity as a model of profound mental collapse and an obsessive, paralyzing fear of death. A symbol of the conscious state, he lives alone on a large estate and regales a visiting friend with a lengthy narration of hypochondriacal ills and a terrifying dread that his family line is reaching its end. Usher's sudden death from a spirit overcharged with guilt and terror results after his sister, an alter ego and symbol of the unconscious state, breaks free of the family mausoleum and kills him as she collapses and expires on his body.

Bibliography

Dougherty, Stephen. "Foucault in the House of Usher: Some Historical Permutations in Poe's Gothic," *Papers on Language & Literature* 37, no. 1 (winter 2001): 3.

Hustis, Harriet. "'Reading Encrypted But Persistent': The Gothic of Reading and Poe's 'The Fall of the House of Usher,'" *Studies in American Fiction* 27, no. 1 (spring 1999): 3.

V

vampirism

A theme in HORROR NARRATIVES, vampirism was a Slavic belief in the vicious, self-serving acts of a hungering ghoul or predatory reanimated corpse. The concept was also the subject of folk tales and of Johann Wolfgang von GOETHE's ballad *Die Braut von Corinth* (*The Bride of Corinth*, 1797), an early version of Europe's female vampire that introduced eroticism and necrophilia as Gothic themes. According to the vampire motif, death traps in a decaying body a suffering soul, the dark twin of the BYRONIC HERO. Reanimation requires resuscitating meals of blood from normal humans. The vampire patiently schemes to obtain a coveted love object and drain away its life force. The fiend may extend its unspeakable meal by courting its prey like a lover or may overpower, seize, strangle, and gobble a serving of blood at one brief sitting. Critics compare the vampire's motivation as a fiendish parallel to passionate love or serial rape.

The wanderings of the parasitic vampire typically occur at night, a Gothic touch that links darkness with the SUPERNATURAL, SOMNAMBULISM, and mesmerism, a popular pseudoscience. Historically, dire images of the vampire's drained victims coincided with epidemic tuberculosis, which overwhelmed Europe in the 18th century, leaving patients depleted and pale. In fiction, these pathetic consumptives become vampires themselves and survive only from nightly attacks on additional victims. The concept of the vampire creating more vampires through a nonproductive sexuality paralleled an emerging understanding of microbial contagion.

During the protracted eastern European struggle between Christianity and advancing Islam, speculation about bloodsucking predators fueled European FOLKLORE and ALLEGORY in the peasant character Nosferatu, a Romanian vampire. One expert, Emily de Laszkowska Gerard, explained in detail in *The Land Beyond the Forest* (1888) how peasants conducted an exorcism of the vampire by shooting it with a pistol, decapitating the corpse, stuffing the mouth with garlic, burning the heart, and sprinkling the grave with the monster's ashes. The gruesome ritual intrigued romantic poets and Gothic novelists, particularly Matthew Gregory LEWIS, who includes a vampirish bleeding nun to foil two lovers' elopement in THE MONK (1796). Lord BYRON inserted a hellish description of vampirism in THE GIAOUR (1813); Samuel Taylor COLERIDGE dabbled in the theme in "CHRISTABEL" (1816), a ballad featuring the predatory Geraldine. Johann Ludwig TIECK followed with "The Bride of the Grave" (1817); Percy Bysshe SHELLEY, with the joy-devouring abstract figure in *Invocation to Misery* (1818); Dr. John POLIDORI, with "The Vampyre" (1819); and John KEATS, with "LA BELLE DAME SANS MERCI" (1819) and "LAMIA" (1819).

The image of the parasitic night stalker inflamed the curiosity of working-class readers of GOTHIC BLUEBOOKs, particularly VARNEY THE VAMPYRE; *or, The Feast of Blood* (1847), alternately attributed to Thomas Preskett PREST and James Malcolm Rymer. Campy in its clumsy handling of terror, the overlong story depicts the shrieking Flora with bulging eyes gazing from her bed at Sir

Francis Varney, who advances along the window ledge. In the light of a fire ignited by lightning, she recoils from long nails clawing at the glass and a fleshless hand reaching through a broken pane. The victim looks full into the face of a bloodless ghoul: "There was a tall, gaunt form—there was the faded ancient apparel—the lustrous metallic-looking eyes—its half-open mouth, exhibiting tusk-like teeth! It was—yes it was—the vampyre!" (*Varney*, Vol. 1, 30). The ravishment, a macabre rape scene, pictures her spasms in a parody of sexual orgasm that concludes with his hideous sucking from the puncture wounds in her neck.

Popular demand for the bloodsucking monster produced large audiences for a French MELODRAMA, Charles Nodier's *Le Vampire* (1820), source of the playwright James Robinson Planché's English stage version *The Vampire; or, The Bride of the Isles*, which opened in August 1820 in London at the English Opera House. Against the author's objections to a Scottish setting, the producer, Samuel Arnold, declared that he had already invested in costumes and music and argued that the audience would not care about the shift in locale. To heighten SENSATIONALISM, the stage manager built a trapdoor that allowed the vampire to make a sudden disappearance coincide with a clap of thunder, a viewer-pleasing ploy that boosted ticket sales. In Dublin, around 1820, Irish publisher J. Charles abridged the play into a sixpenny chapbook credited to Byron that featured a colored cover illustration, an unusual technological inducement to book buyers.

In the mid-19th century, the term *vampire* continued to crop up in less supernatural settings, including Alexey Konstantinovich Tolstoy's *Upyr* (*The Vampire*, 1841), the first vampire story by a Russian author. Notably, Emily BRONTË used the term to refer to the evil-tempered Gypsy schemer HEATHCLIFF in *WUTHERING HEIGHTS* (1847). As his ill temper mounts shortly before his death, the housekeeper, Nelly Dean, who has known and groomed him from childhood, asks herself, "Is he a ghoul, or a vampire?" (Brontë, 313). In answer to her own musing, she scolds herself vigorously: "What absurd nonsense it was to yield to that sense of horror" (*ibid.*).

The late Victorian era produced a variety of vampire characters, including Paul Féval's parody *La Ville-Vampire* (Vampire city, 1875), which flourished in an English translation. Writers expanded vampirism from male dominance to include a gendered mix of victims and practitioners. Gothic dramatist Sheridan LE FANU replaced male-on-female VIOLENCE with *Carmilla* (1872), a lesbian fiction about a woman who stalks only women. In 1893, dramatist Oscar WILDE's play *Salomé* further altered vampirism by giving it a biblical twist in casting the FEMME FATALE in the role of Herod's stepdaughter.

For a fuller understanding of vampirism, Bram STOKER's DRACULA (1897), a sexually perverse monster tale influenced by Le Fanu's ghoul, provides the reader with a rational intermediary, Dr. Abraham Van Helsing. In labored English, he expresses a healthy respect for the count's power and a clinician's interest in his victims' behaviors. At the novel's climax, he examines the remains of Lucy Westenra and summarizes to his fellow antivampire cavaliers, "In trance she died, and in trance she is Un-Dead, too. So it is that she differ from all other" (Stoker, 211). Her appearance puzzles him: "Usually when the Un-Dead sleep at home . . . their face show what they are, but this so sweet that was when she not Un-Dead she go back to the nothings of the common dead. There is no malign here" (*ibid.*). The UNRELIABLE NARRATOR Jonathan HARKER represents the perpetual skeptic in retreating from the necessary decapitation and staking of the corpse and musing to himself, "Is it possible that love is all subjective, or all objective?" (*ibid.*, 212).

The effect of vampire Gothic was so mesmerizing to the Western imagination that, according to James B. Twitchell, author of *The Living Dead: A Study of the Vampire in Romantic Literature* (1981), Dracula became an eponym for both the character and a metaphor for the monster type that subsists off OTHERNESS. According to Judith Halberstam, author of *Skin Shows* (1995), Stoker's vampire advances beyond Gothic horror: The count perpetuates a 19th-century religious connection with the vampire's physiognomy, which correlates feature for feature with the xenophobic, anti-Semitic stereotype of the Jew. The action also parallels Jew-haters' allegations that blood and money are integral to Judaic ritual. Halberstam concludes: "The vampire merges Jewishness and monstrosity and represents this hybrid monster as a threat to Englishness and English womanhood in particular" (Halberstam, 14).

Early 20th-century DECADENCE altered the parameters of classic vampirism. With the creation of Hanns Heinz EWERS's *Alraune* (The mandrakes, 1911), the story of a biological experiment that produces a voluptuous, but deadly female, vampirism degenerated into pure SADISM. Sir Arthur Conan DOYLE's publication of "The Adventure of the Sussex Vampire" (1924) in the *Strand* magazine injected into English crime fiction the possibility of alien behaviors in polite English society. Throughout the 20th century, vampire motifs colored some of the most successful Gothic fiction, notably, Djuna BARNES's prowling Robin Vote in *Nightwood* (1930), Stephen KING's infection of an entire New England town in *Salem's Lot* (1975), and Robert McCammon's twist on Los Angeles gang wars in *They Thirst* (1981). Annette Curtis Klause employed a gentle vampire, Simon, in the young adult classic *Silver Kiss* (1990), which preceded a teen craze for Yvonne Navarro's *Buffy the Vampire Slayer* books. Anne RICE succeeded with the wildly popular *INTERVIEW WITH THE VAMPIRE* (1976) and *The Vampire Lestat* (1985), which depicts the ghoul as a rock star. She continued the series in the 21st century with *Blood and Gold* (2001) and *Blood Canticle* (2003), another Lestat mystery that brings him into conflict with Memnoch the Devil.

Bibliography

Barber, Paul. *Vampires, Burial, and Death: Folklore and Reality*. New Haven, Conn.: Yale University Press, 1988.

Brontë, Emily. *Wuthering Heights*. New York: New American Library, 1959.

Goddu, Teresa A. "Vampire Gothic," *American Literary History* 11, no. 1 (1999): 125–141.

Hustis, Harriet. "Black and White and Read All Over: Performative Textuality in Bram Stoker's 'Dracula,'" *Studies in the Novel* 33, no. 1 (spring 2001): 18.

Ronay, Gabriel. *The Dracula Myth*. London: W. H. Allen, 1972.

Schmitt, Cannon. *Alien Nation: Nineteenth-Century Gothic Fictions and English Nationality*. Philadelphia: University of Pennsylvania Press, 1997.

Stoker, Bram. *Dracula*. New York: Bantam Books, 1981.

Varney the Vampire; or, The Feast of Blood. New York: Arno Press, 1970.

Wolf, Leonard. *A Dream of Dracula: In Search of the Living Dead*. New York: Popular Library, 1977.

Varney the Vampyre
James Malcolm Rymer
(1847)

England's first vampire novel, *Varney the Vampyre; or, The Feast of Blood* was one of Victorian England's most popular and most lucrative GOTHIC BLUEBOOKs, commonly dubbed "penny dreadfuls." The story, published anonymously, was most likely the work of the editor and author James Malcolm Rymer, although other sources name pulp writer Thomas Preskett (or Peckett) PREST or suggest a collaborative effort of several in-house authors employed by Edward Lloyd Enterprises. Published in 109 installments from 1845 to 1847, the 220 chapters tell of the long-lived ghoul Sir Francis Varney of Ratford Hall, Yorkshire, whose corpse a medical student retrieves from the gibbet and revives.

Like the WANDERING JEW, through cyclical acts of blood gluttony, Varney lives an extended lifespan that encompasses a chaotic era in the English monarchy during the successive rules of King Charles I, Oliver Cromwell, and King Charles II. The story opens on Varney's attack on a vulnerable young woman named Flora. When accidents threaten Varney's life, he revives instantly from beneficial moonrays, the source of his longevity. After ennui overcomes him, he tires of the game and relates his criminal history to a clergyman, the Reverend Mr. Bevan. Varney remarks on the insatiable urge to harm others: "My heart is burdened, and I have begun to plan to work mischief and misery and woe to all" (*Varney*, vol. 3, 847). Before relinquishing his life, he writes out his adventures for Bevan. After journeying to Naples, Varney follows a guide up the slope of Mount Vesuvius and leaps into the vortex.

The appeal of Varney to working-class buyers of penny dreadfuls derived from his immortality, clairvoyance, and freedom from the Victorian era's moral and religious strictures. The lengthy text, sold in eight-page installments for a penny each, meanders over a variety of episodes laced with MELODRAMA, VIOLENCE, and SUSPENSE. Varney's coffin, predatory lifestyle, his malevolent fangs, and his ability to defy gravity and walk up walls anticipate Bram STOKER's Transylvanian Count DRACULA, who was similarly gifted with SHAPE-SHIFTING and other unusual powers.

Bibliography

Barber, Paul. *Vampires, Burial, and Death: Folklore and Reality.* New Haven, Conn.: Yale University Press, 1988.

Gates, Barbara T. *Victorian Suicide: Mad Crimes and Sad Histories.* Princeton, N.J.: Princeton University Press, 1988.

Twitchell, James B. *The Living Dead: A Study of the Vampire in Romantic Literature.* Durham, N.C.: Duke University Press, 1981.

Vathek
William Beckford
(1782)

A model of anticlassical ORIENTAL ROMANCE, William BECKFORD's *Vathek: An Arabian Tale* is an ALLEGORY blended from fantasy, sensuality, DIABOLISM, black magic, and autobiography. Beckford appears to have drawn exotic images from William Jones's *The Seven Fountains: An Eastern Allegory* (1772). With the aid of the scholar Samuel Henley, Beckford completed his text in French while living in Paris. Against the author's orders, four years later, the text reached English readers in an unauthorized translation, *An Arabian Tale, from an Unpublished Manuscript* (1786), and in the original in France.

This tale of the grandson of the fabulously wealthy Harun ar-Rashid of Baghdad, the male protagonist of the *Arabian Nights,* describes how Caliph Vathek occupies his father's palace at Samarah, which he crams with art objects from around the globe. The self-indulgent protagonist lapses into sexual excess, gluttony for dainty foods, and drink from fountains flowing with wine and cordials. He falls under the power of a sorceress, his ambitious mother, Carathis, who summons Eblis, an Islamic Satan. The plot reaches romantic excess with a five-winged palace catering to the five senses and a power of retribution that can slay felons with a single blow.

Goading the caliph beyond endurance is a yearning to learn about the forbidden knowledge of the afterlife, a motivation dating to ancient astrologers and medieval alchemists. To acquire full understanding of heaven and hell, the foolhardy caliph defies his Islamic upbringing and employs the giaour, a wicked supernatural genie, to appease his greed for luxury and eroticism. In the standard Faustian plot, the demon prompts the caliph to greater daring, including pedophilia and the sacrifice of comely young boys, before leading him to utter damnation. At a high point of ESCAPISM from depression and ennui, Vathek commands, "Let the sun appear! let him illume my career! it matters not where it may end" (Beckford, 105).

By overemphasizing horrific criminality as well as sexual indulgence, vice, and sacrilege, Beckford anticipates a fascination with depravity that marked later Gothic fiction. Details range from strange to ARABESQUE to fantastic. Ruin hovers over the protagonist. In the demon's realm, Vathek enjoys a limited time to indulge himself and his mate Nouronihar in excess before surrendering to Eblis. To establish the excesses of violence and cruelty in the caliph, Beckford alternates episodes of brutality, VIOLENCE, and the GROTESQUE with glimpses of idylls and sense-satisfying beauty. Because of Vathek's protracted amorality, he lacks the credibility of a normal man enticed into a tragic debauchery of evil.

In the tale's falling action, Vathek retreats from an eternity of torment by summoning Carathis. As dizzied with power as Vathek and his mate, Carathis unveils a funereal scene, Beckford's version of hell: "Here, upon two beds of incorruptible cedar, lay recumbent the fleshless forms of the pre-adamite kings, who had been monarchs of the whole earth. They still possessed enough of life to be conscious of their deplorable condition" (*ibid.,* 112). Beckford heightens the scenario with Gothic emotion: "Their eyes retained a melancholy motion: they regarded one another with looks of the deepest rejection; each holding his right hand, motionless, on his heart" (*ibid.*) Carathis causes the destruction of Vathek and Nouronihar when their hearts ignite with eternal flame. Vathek, his soul "sullied . . . with a thousand crimes," plunges into the mass of souls in hell (*ibid.*, 120). The Dantean extremes of *Vathek* came back into fashion during the rise of late 19th-century DECADENCE, when poets Algernon Swinburne and Stéphane Mallarmé praised Beckford's vision for its artistry.

Bibliography

Beckford, William. *Vathek.* London: Oxford University Press, 1970.

Cope, Kevin L. "Moral Travel and the Pursuit of Nothing: *Vathek* and *Siris* as Philosophical Monologue," *Studies in Eighteenth-Century Culture* 18 (1988): 167–186.

Garrett, John. "'Ending in Infinity': William Beckford's Arabian Tale," *Eighteenth-Century Fiction* 5, no. 1 (1992): 15–34.

Knox-Shaw, Peter. "'Vathek' and 'The Seven Fountains' by Sir William Jones," *Notes and Queries* 42, no. 1 (March 1995): 75–76.

villain

In creating the classic GOTHIC NOVEL, originators realized the importance of pitting the cowering virgin or inexperienced youth against a blackhearted villain. The evildoer took on a variety of incarnations: the larger-than-life lying baron, foreign banditto, lustful monk or brutal abbess, sadistic inquisitor, callous relative, or the looming OUTSIDER. Authors made gleeful adjustments to the stereotype, as with the restless and cruel criminal-hero of Tobias SMOLLETT's *FERDINAND COUNT FATHOM* (1753); the intrusive corrupter Francis Carwin, the ventriloquist in Charles Brockden BROWN's *WIELAND* (1798); the implacable satanic nomad in Charles Robert MATURIN's *MELMOTH THE WANDERER* (1820); and the scheming Svengali, the demonic Jewish hypnotist of singer Trilby O'Ferrall in George du Maurier's sensational MELODRAMA *Trilby*, published serially from January through August 1894 in *Harper's Monthly*.

Friedrich von SCHILLER summarized the import of the villain to psychological fiction. In the introduction to his influential play *Die Räuber* (*The Robbers*, 1781), he defended a premise that studies of criminality must be dramatic to illustrate moral deficiency. He mused on the degree of vice in comparison to the intelligence of the perpetrator: "Perhaps the greatest villain is not farther removed from the most upright man than the petty offender; for the moral forces keep pace with the powers of the mind" (Dukore, 438).

Ann RADCLIFFE expanded on evil males by pairing them with predatory, power-mad, and usually sadistic and sexually depraved female coconspirators. Critic Diane Long Hoeveler, author of *Gothic Feminism* (1998), named the dire woman of FEMALE GOTHIC the "gothic antiheroine," beginning with Maria de Vellorno, the evil, libidinous stepmother in Radcliffe's *THE SICILIAN ROMANCE* (1790). The hard-hearted stepmothers like Maria experienced a long evolution, reaching back to the Cinderella myth, and followed their own pattern of OTHERNESS as the outsider lacking blood ties to the family. More perplexing is Madame Montoni, the compassionless aunt of Emily ST. AUBERT in Radcliffe's *THE MYSTERIES OF UDOLPHO* (1794), who negates her familial ties after marrying the Italian count Montoni, Emily's persecutor.

The prototype of the Gothic villain is the foreigner, a SYMBOL of xenophobic distrust, particularly of southern Mediterranean aristocrats. The classic example is the Sicilian marquis Mazzini in *The Sicilian Romance*, in which a father falsely convinces his daughter that her mother is dead. Radcliffe repeats the patterns with Montoni, the uncle-by-marriage who immures Emily in a grim Apennine castle. In the dismaying ATMOSPHERE, he escalates the passive menace of medieval architecture into an active threat. Radcliffe typifies his sinister nature less from physical intimidation than from his fierce glance: "The fire and keenness of his eyes, its proud exultation, its bold fierceness, its sullen watchfulness . . .; from the unusual expression of his countenance she had always shrunk" (Radcliffe, 157). Enslaved to crime, Montoni is the non-national, the alien loner who rejects the moderating influence of society, religion, and law. His exploitation of Emily is financial: Although he is depicted as a potential batterer, rapist, or killer, his weakness is gambling. By manipulating his niece, he can either control her potential on the marriage market or abscond with her inheritance.

Montoni became the prototype of dangerous imported villains to come, influencing Matthew

Gregory LEWIS's creation of the sexually depraved monk AMBROSIO in *THE MONK* (1796). The cleric is a countercultural threat whom the author mirrors with an aggressive female consort, the bewitching succubus Mathilda. By comparing the heroine Antonia's modesty with Mathilda's shameless sexuality, Ambrosio comes to value the NAIF over the siren and capitulates to perversity by fantasizing over rape of the timorous virgin. He aims his most violent acts toward assertive women by killing Elvira, Antonia's mother, for halting the rape. The act bears the SUBTEXT of society's devaluation of older women, who are more expendable than nubile maidens.

Radcliffe so disapproved of Lewis's extremes of sensuality and malevolence that she countered with the masterful monk SCHEDONI in *THE ITALIAN* (1797), a horror tale that approaches tragedy. Rather than depicting an outright criminal, she engineers a hero-villain whose fierce demeanor mirrors an ugly physiognomy. Crisscrossed with passions, his face displays an habitual severity from deep frown lines and glinting eyes that give the illusion of penetrating other people's hearts and secrets. In the denouement, she ends his predations, forcing him to swallow poison rather than face punishment for his crimes.

According to classic GOTHIC CONVENTION, the creation of the villain depended on HYPERBOLE and SENSATIONALISM. The pairing of a tender female with a baleful male required elevation of the wicked stalker's powers above those of the young hero. The resulting inequality sparked plotting, vengeance, drawn swords, and hand-to-hand grappling. This unbalanced triad (villain, hero, and female) appears in Schedoni's evil STALKING of Ellena Rosalba, the intended of the gentle, musically inclined Vivaldi, and in the corrosive charisma of Francis Carwin, an itinerant Irish ventriloquist and controller of a vulnerable brother and sister, Theodore and Clara WIELAND, in Charles Brockden Brown's *Wieland* (1798). Brown's evil meddler, whose deviance derives from study in Europe and a conversion to Catholicism in Spain, fabricates lies about the family that precipitate multiple tragedies. Like Shakespeare's Iago in *Othello* (ca. 1603), Carwin appears to harbor some inborn cruel streak that causes him to harm people, but he redeems himself via a last-minute diversion of Theodore from murdering Clara. The traditional out-of-kilter triad reached its explosive potential in Emily BRONTË's *WUTHERING HEIGHTS* (1847), in which HEATHCLIFF, a malcontent capable of violent emotions, characterizes the torture of his victims as an amusement. Like the black-cloaked evildoer of melodrama, he gloats over the corruptive nature of such villainy: "The tyrant grinds down his slaves and they don't turn against him; they crush those beneath them" (Brontë, 112).

Villainy takes on a discordant and paradoxical quality in the entrapment of the protagonist in nefarious deeds. Blurring the moral edges are depictions of the Gothic hero who is revealed as the good guy at the outset, as is the case with Maturin's Melmoth, or who displays qualities counter to villainy that cause the reader to both recoil from and sympathize with him, as with the status-conscious, womanizing soap manufacturer in Michel Faber's *THE CRIMSON PETAL AND THE WHITE* (2002). The evil, self-ennobling manipulator is a second type of paradoxical villain. In George du Maurier's *Trilby*, the user Svengali masters persuasion and plays his victim like a predator with a tasty morsel: "When he was playful, it was with a terrible playfulness, like that of a cat with a mouse—a weird ungainly cat, and most unclean; a sticky, haunting, long, lean, uncanny, black spider-cat, if there is such an animal outside a bad dream" (du Maurier, 108).

A third subtype, the satanic hero, is the hero-villain who intrigues and ameliorates villainy by a twisted equivocation of vice. Chief among these are the title figures in William BECKFORD's *VATHEK* (1782), John POLIDORI's "The Vampyre" (1819), and Bram STOKER's *DRACULA* (1897). In satanic fiction, the author applies a similar pairing of the powerless with the powerful, as with the vengeful herbalist Roger Chillingworth with the naive minister Arthur Dimmesdale in Nathaniel HAWTHORNE's *THE SCARLET LETTER* (1850). In the Scottish novelist James HOGG's *The Private Memoirs and Confessions of a Justified Sinner* (1824), the motif splits into dual levels after the demon Gil-Martin confers evil powers on his Calvinist nemesis, Robert Wringhim, a religious fanatic. As Gil-Martin manipulates his puppet, Wringhim becomes the self-righteous tormentor and punisher of supposed reprobates and heretics, violators of fanatic church doctrine. In contrast to the murder of Wringhim's brother George, Wringhim himself faces a far more terrifying demise at the hands of the implacable Gil-Martin, the grand villain.

Two other subclasses of villains illustrate the complexities of Gothic characterization. The Promethean hero-villain earns reader sympathy by rebelling against a power structure or overextending his strength, the situation with Mary Wollstonecraft SHELLEY's monster in FRANKENSTEIN (1818), who fails to exact justice from his negligent creator after months of stalking. The most enigmatic of villains, the BYRONIC HERO, is an ambiguous, quasi-demonic male figure whose aloofness and secretive, cynical behavior project sexual allure and a mystic renown, the qualities of the title character in Lord BYRON's closet drama MANFRED (1817), a suicidal prince wracked by guilt for causing a woman's death. As analyst Maurice Morgann explains in his "Essay on the Dramatic Character of Sir John Falstaff" (1777), moral ambiguity in such characters forces the reader to mediate between a rational understanding of overt actions and an intuitive sympathy for covert motivations.

Twentieth-century versions of the villain owe much to their originals. In *Le Fantôme de l'Opéra* (THE PHANTOM OF THE OPERA, 1910), author Gaston LEROUX evolves an enigmatic monster-man, Erik, the insane, yet pitiable stalker of an opera star. A jealous lover describes Erik, his ghastly rival, in terms little changed from villains of the previous century: "The man who hides behind that hideous mask of death! . . . The evil genius of the churchyard at Perros! . . . Red Death! . . . In a word, madam, your friend . . . your Angel of music!" (Leroux, 91). In 1935, the Argentinian writer Jorge Luis Borges contributed to crime and horror tales with *Historia Universal de la Infamia* (A Universal History of Infamy). Borges unearthed tales of obscure villains, scoundrels, pirates, gangsters, criminals, and slavers, all notorious historical figures. He produced a series on villains for a Buenos Aires newspaper depicting evil through bloody scenes resulting from duels, assault, and ambush. His collected tales—among them "The Wizard Postponed," "The Disinterested Killer Bill Harrigan," "The Masked Dyer, Hakim of Merv," "A The-

ologian in Death," and "Monk Eastman, Purveyor of Iniquities"—made a profound impact as a source for later Latin American literature.

Bibliography

Berman, Avis. "George du Maurier's 'Trilby' Whipped Up a Worldwide Storm," *Smithsonian* 24, no. 9 (December 1993): 110–116.

Brontë, Emily. *Wuthering Heights.* New York: New American Library, 1959.

Davison, Neil R. "The Jew as Homme/Femme-Fatale: Jewish (Art)ifice, Trilby, and Dreyfus," *Jewish Social Studies* (winter–spring 2002): 73–113.

Dukore, Bernard F., ed. *Dramatic Theory and Criticism.* Boston: Heinle, 1974.

du Maurier, George. *Trilby.* New York: Harper & Brothers, 1894.

Grossman, Jonathan H. "The Mythic Svengali: Anti-aestheticism in 'Trilby,'" *Studies in the Novel* 28, no. 4 (winter 1996): 525–543.

Leroux, Gaston. *The Phantom of the Opera.* Cutchogue, N.Y.: Buccaneer Books, 1976.

Radcliffe, Ann. *The Mysteries of Udolpho.* London: Oxford University Press, 1966.

Winter, Kari. "Sexual/Textual Politics of Terror," in *Misogyny in Literature: An Essay Collection.* New York: Garland, 1992: 89–101.

Villette
Charlotte Brontë
(1853)

Charlotte BRONTË's semiautobiographical *Villette*, the outgrowth of her months of study in Brussels, achieves Gothic intensity through a nested story of a punitive PREMATURE BURIAL. The novel dismays readers with its UNRELIABLE NARRATOR, Lucy Snowe, a Protestant NAIF enrolled in a Catholic convent in Belgium. Less robust than Brontë's Jane EYRE, the heroine is given to apathy and helplessness. Late in the evolution of Gothicism, the plot pictures her progress from innocence to maturity and sophistication. For ATMOSPHERE, the author creates a ghost that inhabits a garden, the REVENANT of a novice buried alive by monks for breaking her vows. Brontë inserts additional ANTI-CATHOLICISM in the grief of Monsieur Paul Emanuel, whose former love died after being coerced into a cloister. Gothic scenarios depict Lucy as terrified by visions of ghostly bedsheets, which the critic Diane Long Hoeveler, author of *Gothic Feminism* (1998), interprets as the paradox of the old maid's manless bed and the virgin's fear of deflowering.

Brontë relies on pictorial elements to dramatize an account of Snowe's rise to womanhood. Under duress, the heroine's unbridled imagination runs to extremes without the rein of reason developed from experience. Adding to the Gothic scenario is the gloomy home of Madame Walraven, with its shadowed arches and winding stair that put Lucy to flight from its overt intimidation. She puzzles over a disappearing letter and envisions a featureless phantom nun, a disembodied being dressed in black habit and veiled in white. In an evocative setting, the specter weighs on Lucy's imagination: "I own my heart quaked, my pulse leaped, when I suddenly heard breathing and rustling, and turning, saw in the deep shadow of the steps a deeper shadow still—a shape that moved and descended" (Brontë, 295).

In the falling action, Brontë eventually dispels all Gothic elements Radcliffean style with rational explanations. In full possession of self, Lucy survives to realize the dream of Jane Eyre, her own school where she can attain intellectual aims. The book won the admiration of a fellow female author, Mary Anne Evans, who later wrote as George Eliot.

Bibliography

Brontë, Charlotte. *Villette*. New York: Modern Library, 1997.

Forsyth, Beverly. "The Two Faces of Lucy Snowe: A Study in Deviant Behavior," *Studies in the Novel 29*, no. 1 (spring 1997): 17–25.

Hoeveler, Diane Long. *Gothic Feminism*. University Park: Pennsylvania State University Press, 1998.

Warhol, Robyn. "Double Gender, Double Genre in 'Jane Eyre' and 'Villette,'" *Studies in English Literature, 1500–1900* 36, no. 4 (autumn 1996): 857–875.

Villiers de L'Isle-Adam
(1838–1889)

A pioneer symbolist and master of the French *CONTES CRUELS* (cruel tales), Jean-Marie Mathias Philippe-Auguste, Comte de Villiers de L'Isle-Adam, wrote a profusion of dramas, novels, and taut Gothic fictions to the delight of European readers. From childhood, he was attracted to beauty, peculiarity, PRESCIENCE, and occultism. Mentored by the decadent symbolist poet Charles BAUDELAIRE and inspired by the GERMAN GOTHIC tales of E. T. A. HOFFMANN, Villiers devoted much of his youth to idealistic dreams of the perfect love. Like a French Lord BYRON, he lived the life of a romantic vagabond, followed mercurial whims, and satisfied a petulant wish to alarm with eccentric dress, strange writings, and shocking speech. His exhibitionism suited café society, which enjoyed his wit and rebellion against bourgeois morals and worshipped him like a cult hero.

Because the author was usually homeless, he scribbled his irreverent tales on crumpled napkins at wine bars and café tables. A strain of antireligious sentiment marked his more alarming stories, notably, the sin of the MAD SCIENTIST in "The Doctor's Heroism" (1883). Although fervidly Catholic, Villiers liked to shock readers with blasphemy as well as MYSTICISM, the GROTESQUE, weirdness, and terror of torment. These elements were the hallmarks of the satire *L'Eve Future* (The future Eve, 1886) and of the Gothic short fiction he collected in *Contes Cruels* (1883) and *Nouveaux Contes Cruels* (New cruel tales, 1888).

The response among young French readers to Villiers's macabre sensibilities boosted the author from ignominy to a giant of the symbolist movement, but hard living and privation ended his life at age 51. In June 1891, the *Strand* published an English translation of his most famous horror tale, "The Torture of Hope" (1883), the story of a rabbi tormented by the Spanish Inquisition and promised a death by fire extended for some three hours by the application of iced bandages. The short-short story concludes with the rabbi slipping out of the prison and easing into a garden only to find himself sneaking into the inner sanctum of the Grand Inquisitor himself. For such delicately told horrors, Villiers earned the admiration of the composer Richard Wagner, the short story writer Guy de MAUPASSANT, and the poets Stéphane Mallarmé, Paul Valéry, and William Butler Yeats.

Bibliography

Lathers, Marie. "'L'Eve Future' and the Hypnotic Feminine," *Romanic Review* 84, no. 1 (January 1993): 43–54.

Mikkonen, Kai. "Electric Lines of Desire: Narrative and the Woman's Body in Villiers de l'Isle-Adam's 'Future Eve,'" *Literature and Psychology* 44, nos. 1–2 (spring–summer 1998): 23–53.

violence

As an outgrowth of pagan vigor and Teutonic crudeness, violence surpassed mere threat in popular Gothic fiction. In England, the phenomena of the poke-and-gouge PUNCH AND JUDY glove-puppet show, GOTHIC BLUEBOOK, NEWGATE NOVEL, and penny ballad and broadside enticed into the literary marketplace a following drawn from the unrefined, largely uneducated working class. To sustain their interest, hack writers like Sarah WILKINSON pandered to the lowest common denominator with chapbook texts made lurid by a profusion of SADISM and sexual deviance, murder, rape, hangings, cannibalism, LYCANTHROPY, and VAMPIRISM. Francis LATHOM resorted to SADISM in the self-flagellation scenes of *The Midnight Bell: A German Story, Founded on Incidents in Real Life* (1798), a Gothic quest tale set at a ruined castle.

The Victorian era saw the bending of melodramatic violence to the ends of social betterment. Charles DICKENS, who came from a professional background in courtroom journalism, colored his child crime novel OLIVER TWIST (1838) with a sensational murder scene, the burglar Bill Sikes's attack on Nancy, his mistress. As she pleads for mercy, he frees himself from her grasp to seize a pistol: "The certainty of immediate detection if he fired, flashed across his mind even in the midst of his fury; and he beat it twice with all the force he could summon, upon the upturned face that almost touched his own" (Dickens, 787). The grisly scene concludes with Nancy staggering, eyes blinded with blood from a gash on her skull, and raising her folded hands in entreaty to her attacker. Sikes, in his most damning act, turns from sight of her to snatch a club and bludgeon her to death. The graphic episode became a popular outtake, *Sikes and Nancy*, which the author staged at his dramatic readings from January 1869 until the day preceding his death. A citation from *Tinsley's Magazine* quotes Dickens's response to the performance: "There was a fixed expression of horror of me, all over the theatre, which could not have been surpassed if I had been going to be hanged" (*ibid.*).

AMERICAN GOTHIC novels set in the New World wilderness stressed INSANITY, religious fanaticism, WITCHCRAFT, and racism as motivations for violent scenes. Charles Brockden BROWN, the father of the American Gothic novel, describes a berserk slayer of his wife and children in WIELAND (1798). In Robert Montgomery BIRD's NICK OF THE WOODS (1837), Sadism becomes the modus operandi of a serial killer of forest Indians who embellishes their corpses with crosses dug into the flesh. Perverse Puritanism, the cause of the Salem witch trials of 1692, colored Nathaniel HAWTHORNE's THE SCARLET LETTER (1850) and THE HOUSE OF THE SEVEN GABLES (1851). The latter opens with a legend of an innocent victim accused of sorcery and a grasping magnate choking on his own blood.

In short fiction, American master Edgar Allan POE presented the literary world with uniquely chilling forms of violence, including instances of throttling by an orangutan and PREMATURE BURIAL of a victim of catalepsy. In "The Mystery of Marie Rogêt" (1842), Poe embellishes death by reducing a delicate, womanly form to a GROTESQUE murder victim as described by the objective reporting on a police blotter. For maximum effect, the author heaps on details: a bloated and decomposing corpse, face mottled by dark blood, gore oozing from the mouth, and bruises on the throat in the shape of the killer's fingers.

During the 20th century, violence frequently overpowered Gothic works with excess, as with the Canadian prairie mayhem and family tyranny in Norwegian-American author Martha Ostenso's award-winning novel *Wild Geese* (1925), the strangling of a newborn in Pearl Buck's Pulitzer Prize–winning novel *The Good Earth* (1931), and the offhand shooting of Australian aborigines in Peter Carey's OSCAR AND LUCINDA (1988). Multiple details marked American Gothic scenes—for example, the ax murder, insanity, prophetic nightmare, and shotgun suicide in Katherine Anne Porter's story "Noon Wine" (1936). In 1959, the Argentinian Gothicist Julio Cortázar examined the horror of reliving another's dread in "Las Bagbas del Diablo" (The Devil's Spit), describing a photographer's realization that he has photographed a pedophile and his victim in the park. Jean RHYS's Caribbean verse "Our Gardener" (1977) describes from a small girl's point of view the cutlass slaying of her parents by Ken, the trusted family gardener. In the ghost novel BELOVED (1987), Toni MORRISON honored blacks murdered and worked to death during the plantation slave era. The story reveals the slow roasting of Six-o, a runaway slave, suspended by a rope from a plantation tree. At the crux of the novel, violence begets violence when Sethe, a runaway slave, frees her infant daughter from a life of misery by slitting her throat with a handsaw.

Bibliography

Deziel, Shanda. "Golden Harvest," *Maclean's,* March 5, 2001): 58.

Dickens, Charles. *Oliver Twist,* in vol. 1 of *The Annotated Dickens,* ed. by Edward Guiliano and Philip Collins. New York: Clarkson N. Potter, 1986.

Hollingsworth, Keith. *The Newgate Novel, 1830–1847.* Detroit: Wayne State University Press, 1963.

The Violent Bear It Away
Flannery O'Connor
(1960)

Flannery O'CONNOR reveals a SOUTHERN GOTHIC concept of prophecy with scenes of divine insight, arson, and homosexual VIOLENCE in *The Violent Bear It Away.* The novella depicts the confusion of the orphan Francis Marion Tarwater after his great uncle dies at the breakfast table. In flight from a relative intent on baptizing him, Tarwater drowns a retarded cousin, a mirror image of a religious rite exaggerated into murder. O'Connor inserts a note of VAMPIRISM with a stranger's rape of Tarwater, who is too drunk to defend himself. The text describes the opportunist's enjoyment of sex with an inert victim: "His delicate skin had acquired a faint pink tint as if he had refreshed himself on blood" (O'Connor, 261). In the last scene, Tarwater's vision of spiritual hunger propels him into a mystic mission. O'Connor's juxtaposition of ignorance with vision and the GROTESQUE with sanctity bemuses critics who grapple with her Gothic religious themes and motifs.

Bibliography

Passaro, Vince. "The Violent Bear It Away," *Harper's Magazine* 293, no. 1,756 (September 1996): 64–70.

Schaum, Melita. "'Erasing Angel': The Lucifer-Trickster Figure in Flannery O'Connor's Short Fiction," *Southern Literary Journal* 33, no. 1 (fall 2000): 1.

W

Walpole, Horace
(1717–1797)

An aristocrat, antiquarian, and art expert, Horace Walpole established the parameters of the GOTHIC NOVEL and elevated the adjectival meaning of *Gothic* from vilification to praise. He was born to privilege as the son of England's prime minister and attended the exclusive Eton school and King's College, Cambridge University. Before traveling France and Italy with the poet Thomas Gray, Walpole immersed himself in William Shakespeare's GROTESQUE characterizations. He later remarked in a letter to a friend, "Visions, you know, have always been my pasture," a metaphoric explanation for his delight in romance (Haining, 11).

At age 24, Walpole entered Parliament. He also dabbled in satire, writing "The Dear Witches" (1743), a political parody adapted from Shakespeare's *Macbeth* (ca. 1603) and published anonymously. As he grew bolder in the expression of creativity, he remodeled at Twickenham a pseudo-Gothic castle called Strawberry Hill, an impetus to England's Gothic revival in home design. Chronic gout soon limited his range of travel from home. In 1757, he set up his own printshop, which remained in operation for 32 years.

After enlarging his country manse with slender towers, crenellated battlements, and cloistered gardens, Walpole used his lonely bachelor's quarters as a setting for the inaugural Gothic romance, THE CASTLE OF OTRANTO (1765), an English application of the German SCHAUER-ROMANTIK and Shakespearean grotesque. During a period of personal exhaustion and disillusion with politics that demanded intellectual ESCAPISM, he completed the novel by interweaving ancient and modern strands of fiction. For composition, he allowed his fancy full range over an intriguing dream he experienced in June 1764. His method was AUTOMATIC WRITING, the issuance of episodes one by one immediately after they took shape in his mind. The impetus of subconscious desires and psychological projection turned his toy castle into a medieval setting enlarged to suit the plot, much as stagecraft develops the original story of a ballet or opera. The composition took only seven weeks of intense musing and nonstop writing daily from teatime until after one o'clock in the morning.

Walpole originated an enduring Gothic motif from the chivalric era of the haunted castle, trapdoors, feudal tyranny, and the manipulation of nature via the PATHETIC FALLACY. His tyrannic Manfred anticipated the heavy-visaged menace of the BYRONIC HERO. Walpole's creation of the chatty but intransigent servant and the exploitation of grotesqueness and bloody barbarities became so popular that *The Castle of Otranto* took on a life of its own, passing through 115 editions. An admirer, the critic and author Anna Laetitia BARBAULD, stated her delight in "the sportive effusion of a man of genius, who throws the reins loose upon the neck of his imagination" (Varma, 42).

Three years after writing his Gothic classic, Walpole produced a tragedy on the theme of incest, *The Mysterious Mother* (1768), an original GOTHIC DRAMA, and allowed fancy to generate grotesque exotica in *Hieroglyphic Tales* (1785), issued posthumously, as well as some historical musings on King Richard III. One of the stories, "Maddalena; or, The Fate of the Florentines," contains the horrific tale of Maddalena, who dies at the sight of her lover Borgiano being mangled by the wheel, a notorious bone breaker. In Walpole's lifetime, he saw the publication of his masterpiece in illustrated editions in Amsterdam, Berlin, Dublin, Paris, and Parma. At his death, he left Strawberry Hill as well as journals and letters that expressed his interests and friendships. His works had a lasting influence on Lord BYRON and Ann RADCLIFFE and intrigued Clara REEVE to attempt a less violent model of Gothicism for *The Champion of Virtue: A Gothic Story* (1777).

Bibliography

Alexander, Catherine M. S. "'The Dear Witches': Horace Walpole's 'Macbeth,'" *Review of English Studies* 49, no. 194 (May 1998): 131–144.

Barasch, Frances K. *The Grotesque.* Paris: Mouton, 1971.

Frank, Marcie. "Horace Walpole's Family Romances," *Modern Philology* 100, no. 3 (February 2003): 417–435.

Haining, Peter, ed. *Gothic Tales of Terror.* New York: Taplinger, 1972.

Varma, Devendra P. *The Gothic Flame.* New York: Russell & Russell, 1966.

wandering Jew

A popular motif of the doomed sinner in Christian FOLKLORE, the LEGEND of the wandering Jew influenced Gothic fiction, particularly the creation of such characters as AMBROSIO, the hero-VILLAIN in Matthew Gregory LEWIS's THE MONK (1796); the guilt-ridden wanderer in Samuel Taylor COLERIDGE's ballad THE RIME OF THE ANCIENT MARINER (1798); and Father Schemoli in Charles Robert MATURIN's *The Fatal Revenge; or, The Family of Montorio* (1807). The mythic Jewish pariah had his origin as a fictional straw man and repository of anti-Semitic hatreds. Identified as Joseph Cartaphilus, a porter to Pontius Pilate or an officer of the Sanhedrin, the wandering Jew supposedly mocked Jesus on the way to execution on Golgotha. Upon shouldering the cross, Jesus halted long enough to condemn Cartaphilus to an unending earthly journey until Judgment Day.

Based on a cryptic verse in Matthew 16:28 and substantiated by a curse on the Roman Malchus, who struck Jesus in John 18:20–22, the tale is a reverse of the FAUST LEGEND. While Faust bargained with Satan for a longer life, the long-lived wandering Jew was an undying protagonist who wished for death as an end to his unrelieved trekking throughout Europe, the British Isles, and Russia. The story first appeared in literature in *Flores Historiarum (The Flowers of History)*, which English monk Roger of Wendover, the chronicler of St. Albans Abbey, compiled in 1228. Historian Matthew of Paris enlarged on a supposed sighting of the Jew in Armenia in *Chronica Majora Anglorum* (Major history of the English, ca. 1258).

The legendary Jew made a peripatetic march through theological writings and pulpit sermons, in stage plays and ballads, as a subject for art and music, and as grist for chroniclers and folk-story tellers. In 1547, a new version identified the wanderer as Ahasverus (or Ahasuerus), a cobbler who refused to let Jesus rest on his way down the streets of Jerusalem to the crucifixion. Like an earthly demon, the aged scorner was the unwilling immortal, the supreme literary SYMBOL of alienation, OTHERNESS, and perpetual penitence. He was also a useful threat to naughty children and to parishioners, whom parsons chastened with reported sightings of the cursed Jew.

On a grander scale, the wanderer, yearning for redemption, justified hatred and persecution of all Jews throughout the Middle Ages, particularly during the Spanish Inquisition and the expulsion of Jews from Spain in the 1490s. The figure permeated much of German, French, and English romantic and Gothic literature—the title character in Christian Friedrich Schubart's *Der Ewige Jude: Eine Lyrische Rhapsodie* (The wandering Jew: A lyric rhapsody, 1783); a questing alchemist in William GODWIN's *St. Leon* (1799); a mysterious traveler in Charles Robert Maturin's MELMOTH THE WANDERER (1820); and the reviled protagonist in George Croly's *Salathiel, the Wandering Jew* (1828), which is set in Jerusalem during the repressive regimes of Nero and Titus. French novelist Eugène Sue's *Le Juif Errant (The Wandering Jew,*

1844) captures the pathos of the weary nomad: "Oh, that I might only finish my task!—'GO ON! GO ON!'—A single hour—only a single hour of repose—'GO ON!'—Alas! I leave those I love on the brink of the Abyss!—'GO ON! GO ON!'" (Haining, 740). Marked like Cain with a black cipher on his brow, he plods into a gale with his hands lifted in vain to heaven.

Among the romantic poets, Percy Bysshe SHELLEY made full use of pathetic, aimless figures in *The Wandering Jew; or, The Victim of the Eternal Avenger* (1810), which pictures Paulo marked by a cross on his forehead; in the sensational *St. Irvyne; or, The Rosicrucian* (1811); and for the unfinished short story "The Assassins" (1814). With "The Spectre Bride" (1822), William Harrison AINSWORTH produced a horrible vision of an evil wanderer gazing into the pit of hell where "the worm never dies and the fire is never quenched" (Haining, 327). In AMERICAN GOTHIC, the motif recurs in Nathaniel HAWTHORNE's "A Virtuoso's Collection" and "A Select Party" in *Mosses from an Old Manse* (1846) and in the MELANCHOLY figure in poet Edwin Arlington Robinson's "The Wandering Jew" (1921). The Czech playwright Karel ČAPEK reprised the wanderer as a long-lived female from 16th-century Crete in the DETECTIVE STORY "The Makropulos Case" (1922).

Bibliography

Anderson, George K. *The Legend of the Wandering Jew.* Providence, R.I.: Brown University Press, 1965.

Gardner, Martin. "The Wandering Jew and the Second Coming," *Free Inquiry* 15, no. 3 (summer 1995): 31–33.

Haining, Peter, ed. *Gothic Tales of Terror.* New York: Taplinger, 1972.

Waugh, Evelyn
(1903–1966)

The English satirical novelist Evelyn Arthur St. John Waugh combined Gothic touches with a cunning wit, capricious characters, and wickedly funny ironies. Waugh was a loner who preferred travel and quiet meditation to social engagements. Educated at Oxford University, he earned a living as a sometime teacher, journalist, and war correspondent, while writing novels. His works, sometimes compared to those of SAKI, are vignettes of the era's pretensions. In precise miniatures of human interaction, they express a consuming indignation at the decline of English society. Through his fiction, he protested a rush of modernism that infused his world with the clangor of jazz, the vulgarity of plastic furniture, and the garish abstractions of cubist art.

Gothic elements enhance Waugh's discomfiture with modernity. In *Decline and Fall* (1928), the story of an absurd antihero, Paul Pennyfeather, the author depicts fine old Tudor architecture threatened by low-cost, jerry-built replacements and the impropriety of a divinity major teaching at a boy's school under a cloud of alcohol abuse, pedophilia, and white slavery. A best-seller, *Vile Bodies* (1930), depicts a venal priest named Father Rothschild who travels with a fake beard in his valise. In *Black Mischief* (1932), filled with Abyssinian exotica, Waugh describes the generation of huge broods of deformed, GROTESQUE offspring and Basil Seal's unintentional cannibalism of Prudence, a former girlfriend, amid the drumming and debauchery of an African feast. Waugh reached farther into unusual situations for his short fiction. "Out of Depth" (1933) describes a vindictive magician who condemns an antagonist to time travel into the future.

Waugh won respect for the suspenseful short story "The Man Who Liked Dickens" (1933), a chapter of *A Handful of Dust* (1934) first published as a stand-alone tale in *Hearst's International Magazine*. The VILLAIN James Todd, an illiterate lover of sentimental Victorian fiction, imprisons Tony Last, who is lost in the jungles of Brazil. On arrival, "his feet were cut and grossly swollen; every exposed surface of skin was scarred by insect and bat bites; his eyes were wild with fever" (Waugh, 285). While administering a calabash of bitters to his guest, Todd speaks ominously of jungle simples, noting that plants cure, calm, kill, generate madness and fever, and rejuvenate the dead. In a miserable rainforest climate, Last is forced to read the novels of Dickens to a madman humorously modeled on Joseph CONRAD's Mr. Kurtz from *HEART OF DARKNESS* (1902). The sessions begin with *BLEAK HOUSE* (1853) and continue through five more titles.

World War II changed Waugh, increasing his insight into human psychology and his dark response toward human depravity. He reached his literary height with *Brideshead Revisited* (1945), a religious domestic novel in which DISSIPATION overcomes Sebastian Flyte and the modern world encroaches on the aristocratic Brideshead estate. After a visit to Forest Lawn Cemetery in Hollywood, Waugh produced a mordant vision of death in THE LOVED ONE (1948), an Anglo-American nightmare in cameo in which the mortician Dennis Barlow, an employee of the Happier Hunting Ground, a pet graveyard, romances funerary cosmetician Aimee Thanatogenos of Whispering Glades Memorial Park.

Bibliography

Allen, Bruce. "'World-Besotted Traveler': Evelyn Waugh's Savage Indignation," *World and I* 15, no. 5 (May 2000): 280.

Hitchens, Christopher. "Permanent Adolescent: His Vices Made Evelyn Waugh a King of Comedy and of Tragedy," *Atlantic Monthly* 291, no. 4 (May 2003): 107–112, 114–116.

Thompson, David. "The Anarchic Fantasies of Evelyn Waugh," *Biblio*, September 1998: 24.

Waugh, Evelyn. *A Handful of Dust*. Boston: Little, Brown & Co., 1962.

Wells, H. G.
(1866–1946)

George Herbert Wells holds a lofty place in science fiction, futurology, and utopian literature, but he also crafted numerous works in the horror, psychological fiction, and SUPERNATURAL modes. He gained insight into fantasy and prophecy from the novels of Jules Verne, which influenced his early short works published in the *Graphic*, the *Illustrated London News*, the *New Review, Pearson's*, and the *Strand*. Central to his interest in Gothic motifs and MYSTICISM was an examination of technology and its impact on human behaviors, the source of vampiric plants in "The Flowering of the Strange Orchid" (1894) and a terrifying death in "The Cone" (1895), in which Horrocks, a jealous husband, incinerates the adulterer Raut in Raut's ghastly industrial furnace.

Wells entertained and enlightened his fans with a variety of settings and characters. He showcased monstrous subterranean Morlocks in *The Time Machine* (1895) and the MAD SCIENTIST conducting vivisection and live animal experimentation in THE ISLAND OF DR. MOREAU (1896), which anticipates some of the more macabre aspects of cloning. He featured the stalker theme in *The Invisible Man* (1897), a classic cautionary tale about Griffin, who experiments with bleaching human blood and precipitates a spree of theft and murder. Wells incorporated numerous elements of Gothic literature in his short fiction, including MONSTERS in "The Sea Raiders" (1896), spectral experiences in a Gothic setting in "The Red Room" (1896), a delusion of a ghostly African skull terrorizing a Western businessman in "Pollock and the Porroh Man" (1897), astral projection in "The Stolen Body" (1903), and violent death in "The Country of the Blind" (1911). The story "In the Avu Observatory" (1894), describes how Woodhouse, an astronomer in Borneo, sights a Klaung-utang, a gray-brown flying beast that attacks with claws and beak. With a keen touch of wit, the story concludes: "On the whole, if the Borneo fauna is going to disgorge any more of its novelties upon me, I should prefer that it did so when I was not occupied in the observatory at night and alone" (Wells, 496).

In his speculative fiction, Wells tended to feature a single male experimenter or victim as suffering some outlandish physical or psychic mishap with chemicals and scientific paraphernalia, as in the terror tale "The Plattner Story" (1896), issued in *Thirty Strange Stories* (1897). The story describes a mysterious green powder that the protagonist lights with a match, causing the chemical to explode and send his body into space for nine days. Wells applies Orientalism and drollery to the inverted body of the comic antihero in "The Truth about Pyecraft" (1903), which describes a mystic recipe from India blending eggs, a pariah dog, and rattlesnake venom for a reducing elixir that causes Pyecraft to float about his library ceiling. In another, "The Inexperienced Ghost" (1903), Wells describes death that results from meddling in occultism. The protagonist Clayton tells his friends about an encounter with an ephemeral apparition at the Mermaid Club. In recreating the gestures of the ghost for fellow club members, Clayton falls dead, leaving them to conjecture whether he died of apoplexy or passed into the spiritual realm. Wells's deft stories inspired numerous followers—notably, the Argentinian short story writer Jorge Luis Borges and the expatriate Russian writer Vladimir Nabokov.

Bibliography

Achenbach, Joel. "The World According to Wells," *Smithsonian*, April 2001: 110.

Wells, H. G. *The War of the Worlds, with The Time Machine and Selected Short Stories*. New York: Platt & Munk, 1963.

Welty, Eudora
(1909–2001)

A revered literary stylist and model of imaginative SOUTHERN GOTHIC writing and STORYTELLING, the Pulitzer Prize–winning author Eudora Welty anchored her life and work in Jackson, Mississippi, her hometown. Confined to bed in childhood, she was reared in a loving household and was a well-read student and a keen observer of human interaction in the Jim Crow South. While working as a photographer and publicist during the Great Depression, she developed an eye for scenario and an ear for dialogue that served her as a fiction writer. Adding to her reputation for intriguing plots was a flair for dark absurdist humor displayed in the idiosyncrasies of Mississippi Delta residents, the source of her blend of rape with a playful tall tale in *The Robber Bridegroom* (1942), based on the GRIMM brothers' "Der Räuberbräutigam" (The Robber Bridegroom, 1857), and of family feuds and hurtful gossip in *Delta Wedding* (1946).

For the *Atlantic, Harper's*, the *Hudson Review, The New Yorker, Prairie Schooner*, and the *Sewanee Review*, Welty produced mildly GROTESQUE characters from the mindset and dialect of Southerners of varying social levels, as with the pathetic rain barrel suicide in "Clytie" (1941), the alienated OUTSIDER Miss Eckhart in "The Golden Apples" (1949), and the liberating ILLUSION nurtured by a girl imprisoned in a mismated union in "Livvie Is Back" (1943), winner of an O. Henry Memorial Contest Award. In a revered comic short story "Why I Live at the P.O.," anthologized in her first collection, *A Curtain of Green and Other Stories* (1941), Welty created the lovably paranoid sister of Stella-Rondo. An escapist classic, the story depicts Sister as fleeing from an inhospitable family home to the stuffy confinement of the post office on an ironic date, July 4—Independence Day.

Often compared to the fiction of Ambrose BIERCE, Nikolai GOGOL, Guy de MAUPASSANT, and Edgar Allan POE, Welty's most popular works range from the moderately terrifying to the truly strange, particularly "The Petrified Man," "Powerhouse," and "Death of a Traveling Salesman," all collected in *A Curtain of Green*. In "Lily Daw and the Three Ladies" (1941), Welty describes the casual decision of local meddlers to send a friend to the "Ellisville Institution for the Feeble-Minded of Mississippi" (Welty, 3). In "A Worn Path" (1941), set on the Old Natchez Trace, she describes the fearful trek of a black grandmother, Phoenix Jackson, for medicines to treat a grandson who swallowed lye. Along the way, Phoenix battles a ghostly scarecrow and eludes a barbed wire fence, armed white hunters, and a fierce black dog. The final descent from the medical office casts a pall of futility on Phoenix, whose frailty and age foreshadow a time when her grandson will have no one to fend for him.

Bibliography

Allen, Brooke. "A Universal Region: The Fiction of Eudora Welty," *New Criterion* 18, no. 2 (October 1999): 35.

Champion, Laurie. *The Critical Response to Eudora Welty's Fiction*. Westport, Conn.: Greenwood, 1994.

Marrs, Suzanne. *One Writer's Imagination: The Fiction of Eudora Welty*. Baton Rouge: Louisiana State University Press, 2002.

Owen, Jim. "Phoenix Jackson, William Wallace, and King MacLain: Welty's Mythic Travelers," *Southern Literary Journal* 34, no. 1 (fall 2001): 29–43.

Welty, Eudora. *The Collected Stories of Eudora Welty*. New York: Harcourt Brace Jovanovich, 1980.

werewolf

See LYCANTHROPY.

Wharton, Edith
(1862–1937)

The American social mannerist Edith Wharton employed a light touch and a masterful control of painful nuances in her Gothic fiction. Unlike the SENSATIONALISM that exploded from the horror tales of Ambrose BIERCE and Edgar Allan POE, her work displayed a debt to Poe in the genteel Gothic conventions of her verse—the poems "Botticelli's Madonna" (1891) and "The Tomb of Ilaria Giunigi" (1891), the sonnet series "Two Backgrounds" (1892) and "Chartres" (1893)—and in elegantly polished short fiction, notably MYSTERY and woman-centered EXOTICISM in the ghost tale "The Quicksand" (1902). She developed a series of forbidding mansions from Wyndclyffe, her Aunt Elizabeth's dour turreted house in Rhinebeck-on-the-Hudson, which Wharton visited one summer in her youth. She stored up Gothic behaviors, architecture, and decor for the ogreish Gus Trenor, would-be despoiler of the hapless Lily Bart in *The House of Mirth* (1905); SECRECY in the smoky confines of the library in *The Age of Innocence* (1910); and the suppressed passions amid a lamp-lit interior of the decrepit farmhouse with its creaking rocking chair in ETHAN FROME (1911), one of New England Gothic's chilling stories of unrequited love. Dominating the conclusion is the hellish atmosphere of the protagonist's home, where a resentful, witchy Zeena Frome tends the cranky invalid Mattie Silver.

Upon her venture into the GHOST STORY, Wharton celebrated the genre with a tribute to her mentor, Henry JAMES. In reflecting on early 20th-century Gothic trends, she commented in the introduction to her first collection of ghost stories, "I have made the depressing discovery that the faculty required for their enjoyment has become almost atrophied in modern man" (Wharton, 8). As a therapeutic venture, she wrote and compiled 11 of her SUPERNATURAL tales for publication. One of the most successful, "THE EYES" (1910), turns inward for a study of covert evil. Another, "The Lady's Maid's Bell" (1910), characterizes the demanding job of servant to the rich through the actions of a ghost maid for a demanding dowager, Mrs. Brympton. Some weeks before her death, Wharton submitted "All Souls," a terror story about a wealthy lady's servants who attend a witches' coven, published posthumously in *Ghosts* (1937), which she dedicated to the poet Walter DE LA MARE.

Bibliography
Fedorko, Kathy Anne. *Gender and Gothic in the Fiction of Edith Wharton.* Tuscaloosa: Alabama University Press, 1995.

Inness, Sherry. "'Loyal Saints or Devious Rascals': Domestic Servants in Edith Wharton's Stories 'The Lady's Maid's Bell' and 'All Souls,'" *Studies in Short Fiction* 36, no. 4 (fall 1999): 337–350.

Wharton, Edith. *The Ghost Stories of Edith Wharton.* New York: Scribner Paperback Fiction, 1973.

Wieland
Charles Brockden Brown
(1798)

The first important work by the first American Gothic writer, Charles Brockden BROWN, *Wieland; or, The Transformation: An American Tale* is an apparition tale that established America's national literature. Inspired by his pacifist Quaker upbringing and intrigued by a reading of a German *Schauerroman* (shudder novel), Cajetan Tschink's *Der Geisterseher* (The Ghost Seer, 1797), Brown set to work on America's first Gothic novel, an unrelenting terror narrative based on the evil influence of a learned Faustian VILLAIN and the VIOLENCE resulting from lunacy. For a plot, he chose from newspaper accounts a true psychological crime of family-killer James Yates, who blamed a hallucination—a vision of two angels—for inciting a mass murder that extended to his wife, children, and horses.

The novel abandoned European GOTHIC CONVENTIONs to tap the American consciousness. Symbolically, Brown sets Father Wieland on a journey from Germany to the New World, where urban deceptions and frontier perils await. Brown places the fictional version of the killings at Mittingen estate on the Schuylkill River in 1781. At the heart of the plot is America's conflicted response to religious frenzy, a subject that invests its early literature, sermons, and essays. Brown suffuses the account with MYSTERY, manic delusion, and a Puritanic paranoia, the outgrowth of New England zealotry and repression.

Beginning Brown's family saga is a sensational death—the transformation of Father Wieland, a morose but fervid evangelical, after erupting in a ball of fire. The author characterizes the elder Wieland as mournful, contemplative, and agitated by ecstasy and fear. In chapter 2, Wieland's wife is gazing out the window toward the family's private temple when her husband combusts with a flash of light and a loud explosion, leaving him naked and stricken with delirium. The old man dies within two hours, his body reduced to foul odor and putrefaction, a symbolic outflow of false ideals. From a startling beginning, Brown unfolds the fictional version of ritual murder through letters written by Clara Wieland, the persecuted heroine, a witness torn between rationality and terror at her brother Theodore's sacrifice of his wife Catherine and their four children to appease internal voices.

To enlarge on Gothic stereotypes, Brown expands the formulaic NAIF into a whole community of innocents living in a pastoral utopia, a flawed microcosm free of authoritarian control and devoid of public education. To inject danger into the setting, Brown depicts Wieland estate in CHIAROSCURO by night in interlacing shadows, a Gothic touch that James Fenimore Cooper emulated in his Leatherstocking series. Brown imposes evil on the Edenic locale with the seduction of Clara Wieland's maid by the charismatic Irishman Francis Carwin, a self-gratifying itinerant ventriloquist who convinces Theodore to kill his family as evidence of religious faith.

Brown stresses the psychological motivation of the murders. In the power of a progressive abnormality that sanctions no mercy for shrieking and contorted victims, the killer strangles his wife. He admits that a higher power commissioned the slayings and exults that he has successfully completed the deed, which he characterizes as a sacred sacrifice to God. When reason returns to Theodore, he stops short of murdering Clara. At her sorrowful admission that he is hopelessly insane, he plunges her knife into his neck, the only remedy for a destructive psychosis. The SUBTEXT implies an incestuous attraction between Clara and her brother that exonerates wife-killing, but will not allow him to slay his sister.

The novel's controlling theme is the growing materialism of a neophyte nation unsure of its ethos and spiritual direction. Against a canvas painted with a picturesque American idyll, Brown layers rustic and savage figures who, like serpents in Eden, threaten chaos in a frontier paradise. Symbolically, the deterioration of the Wieland compound reflects republican suspicions of experimental communes like Fruitlands, Amana, and Brook Farm that tried to govern themselves through piety, shared profits, and religious education. The skill with which Brown executes his novel earned the praise of the essayist and Gothic novelist William GODWIN and of the Quaker poet John Greenleaf Whittier, who compared the grievous family collapse to Greek tragedy and to Emily BRONTË's Gothic classic WUTHERING HEIGHTS (1847). The novel anticipates the lyric GROTESQUE and horror of Edgar Allan POE and the faith-driven barbarisms in the fiction of Nathaniel HAWTHORNE.

Bibliography

Fussell, Edwin Sill. "Wieland: A Literary and Historical Reading," Early American Literature 18, no. 2 (1983): 171–186.

Manning, Susan L. "Enlightenment's Dark Dreams: Two Fictions of Henry Mackenzie and Charles Brockden Brown," Eighteenth-Century Life 21, no. 3 (1997): 39–56.

Norwood, Liza West. "'I May Be a Stranger to the Grounds of Your Belief': Constructing Sense of Place in Wieland," Early American Literature 38, no. 1 (winter 2003): 89–123.

Rombes, Nicholas, Jr. "'All Was Lonely, Darksome, and Waste': 'Wieland' and the Construction of the New Republic," Studies in American Fiction 22, no. 2 (spring 1994): 37–46.

Verhoeven, W. M. "Gothic Logic: Charles Brockden Brown and the Science of Sensationalism," European Journal of American Culture 20, no. 2 (2001): 91–99.

Voloshin, Beverly R. "Wieland: Accounting for Appearances," New England Quarterly 59, no. 3 (1986): 341–357.

Wieland, Clara

The narrator in Charles Brockden BROWN's prototypical AMERICAN GOTHIC novel WIELAND; or, The

Transformation: An American Tale (1798), Clara Wieland is both NAIF and survivor of a gruesome tragedy. Following the bizarre death of her father, Theodore Wieland Sr., from spontaneous combustion, Clara and her brother, Theodore Jr., share the estate. Her brother and his family occupy the family manse. Clara, a single woman, lives in a cottage at the fringe of the property, a location suggesting a SUBTEXT of patriarchal belittlement of women. Brown orchestrates MYSTERY after a willful deceiver, ventriloquist Francis Carwin, arrives and upsets the serenity of the estate by issuing upsetting information, particularly a plot against Clara and a feigned statement from Clara concerning her affection for Carwin. Brown triangulates the characters of Clara with Henry Pleyel, her intended, and Carwin, who deliberately subverts an engagement.

Brown delineates Clara as a stout heroine who is sensible and resourceful enough to confront Carwin for his perverse intrusion into her life. Clara's physical illness resulting from her brother's murder of his family is an understandable emotional collapse from shock and grief. Restored to her former strength, she is equal to the job of facing down the conniving Carwin and to self-rescue from her brother, Theodore, who escapes from jail and, driven by a psychotic urge, threatens her life. In a twist on the DOPPELGÄNGER motif, the brother kills himself with the sister's approval and uses her knife to do the job. Brown carefully scripts the novel to show Clara the abler of the two Wieland siblings by rewarding her with marriage and a life in Europe, far from the horrors of the American frontier.

Bibliography

Heller, Terry. *The Delights of Terror: An Aesthetics of the Tale of Terror.* Urbana: University of Illinois Press, 1987.

Manly, William M. "The Importance of Point of View in Brockden Brown's 'Wieland,'" *American Literature* 35, no. 3 (1963): 311–312.

Wieland, Theodore

The pathological killer in Charles Brockden BROWN's landmark AMERICAN GOTHIC novel *WIELAND; or, The Transformation: An American Tale* (1798), Theodore Wieland Jr. represents the Old World notion of the member of the educated landed gentry who confronts the macabre challenges of the American frontier. Brown depicts him as tragically impaired by the religious evangelicalism of his father, the elder Theodore Wieland, who died after a sudden spontaneous combustion at the family's home temple. As though snatched from life by the forces of fanaticism, the father sets a pattern of odd human torments visited on a doomed lineage.

Like an American Iago, Francis Carwin is a perverse OUTSIDER. He replicates the Faustian obsessions of Ann RADCLIFFE's SCHEDONI and Matthew Gregory LEWIS's AMBROSIO, a diseased VILLAIN. Goaded by a demonic curiosity, Carwin corrupts Theodore through ventriloquism, producing mysterious voices and creating a rift between Theodore's sister Clara and her intended, Pleyel. When the instability of Theodore's faculties takes an unforeseen turn toward full-blown madness, at the novel's climax, he kills his wife and their four children and seriously undermines Clara's health. Driven by the Puritanic forces that undergird the settlement of New England, Theodore is the victim of the new nation's lack of moral direction. He becomes the Gothic stalker by escaping a jail cell and attempting to stab Clara. Brown elevates Theodore to a tragic figure by revealing his subversion by the evil Carwin and by precipitating Theodore's suicide. Significant to the falling action is his use of his sister's knife, a gesture that acknowledges her rationality and survivalism, two qualities that Theodore lacks in his confrontation with the American frontier.

Bibliography

Heller, Terry. *The Delights of Terror: An Aesthetics of the Tale of Terror.* Urbana: University of Illinois Press, 1987.

Manly, William M. "The Importance of Point of View in Brockden Brown's 'Wieland,'" *American Literature* 35, no. 3 (1963): 311–312.

Wilde, Oscar

(1856–1900)

A witty, mannered dramatist, lecturer, and fabulist, the Dublin-born Anglo-Irish writer Oscar Wilde extended his literary mastery over a number of genres and modes. Born at the height of Victorian hypocrisy and smugness, he flaunted rebellion through pursuit of the arts, outlandish foppery, and homosexual libertinism. While writing for the *Catholic Mirror, Irish Monthly, Kottobos, Pall Mall Gazette, Pan,* and *Woman's World,* he developed an interest in Gothicism. He was a literary supporter of author Mary Elizabeth BRADDON and an admirer of James HOGG's popular *The Private Memoirs and Confessions of a Justified Sinner* (1824) and the writings of Edgar Allan POE, particularly "The Oval Portrait" (1842), the macabre story of the power of art over a human soul. During Wilde's cover marriage to Constance Lloyd, he concealed his homosexuality in conservative domestic posing. For his sons Cyril and Vyvyan, he wrote instructive FAIRY TALEs, collected in *The Happy Prince and Other Tales* (1888), which incorporate beast lore, magic statues, a giant, a mystical flowering tree, and a martyred bird, the hero of "The Nightingale and the Rose." In the MELANCHOLY title story, Wilde depicts an Aragonese king mourning a wife who lies embalmed on a tapestried slab. At regular intervals, the king, muffled in a cloak, kneels at the site to cry, *"Mi reina! Mi reina!"* (My queen! My queen!) and to grasp her hands and kiss her face (Wilde, 247). In "The Birthday of the Infanta," included in *The House of Pomegranates* (1891), Wilde injects inspired fantasy with a mermaid, a star-child, and a dwarf whose sudden death from looking in a mirror destroys the innocence of a spoiled princess.

Between his two volumes of fairy tales, Wilde published "The Canterville Ghost" (1889), a frequently anthologized specter tale that places uninitiated American OUTSIDERs at a haunted English estate. Lighthearted in TONE and its depiction of disembodied skeletal hands and mystery noises, the story evades the terrors of the formulaic GHOST STORY to satirize the mistreatment of servants, women who enjoy chronic ill health, deathbed religious conversions, and misconceptions that the English maintain about American life and attitudes. Wilde pursues the usual strategies of Gothic STORYTELLING—the housekeeper dressed in black, bloodstains on the sitting-room floor, sliding panels in the staircase, and the obligatory stormy night—before revealing the ghost. The phantasm groans and exudes a greenish aura before taking into its confidence the NAIF, Virginia, who becomes his friend.

As an anti-Victorian lark, the author decks his comic Gothic story with a showy funeral procession that flaunts the Canterville coat of arms. As though on cue, the moon emerges from a cloud and a nightingale trills as the coffin sinks into the grave.

A charismatic social butterfly and insightful observer of human nature, Wilde completed the novel THE PICTURE OF DORIAN GRAY (1891), a dire analysis of duplicity and the murder of an artist and his art. He followed with SALOMÉ (1893), a stage play written in French that scandalized audiences for its portrayal of self-indulgent DISSIPATION in the dancer's choice of the head of Jokanaan (John the Baptist) as a stage prop. Wilde declined into ignominy after the marquis of Queensberry publicly reviled him for Wilde's protracted affair with the marquis's son, Lord Alfred "Bosie" Douglas. Wilde unsuccessfully sued Queensberry, and subsequently was tried for, and convicted of, illegal acts. After serving two years at hard labor in Wandsworth Prison, Wilde returned to freedom, but lost his mother, marriage, home, art collection, and sons, whom he never saw again. His legal, literary, and personal diminution influenced a friend and fellow Irishman, Bram STOKER, during the composition of DRACULA (1897).

In 1898, Wilde wrote a poetic protest of the arcane cruelties and Gothic torments of the treadmill at Pentonville Prison. Wilde's famous *The Ballad of Reading Gaol* (1898), issued in the *Daily Chronicle,* characterized souls in torment and the fly-blown corpse of a hanged inmate in a satanic realm conceived by the English penal system. Out of sympathy for the tortured protagonist in Charles Robert MATURIN's MELMOTH THE WANDERER (1820), Wilde called himself Sebastian Melmoth during his tour of France, Italy, and Sicily and his final months in a Paris hotel, where he remained in self-exile until his death from a mastoid infection. His influence on Gothic writers was substantial, including SAKI and Evelyn WAUGH.

Bibliography

Nassaar, Christopher S. "Wilde's 'The Ballad of Reading Gaol,'" *Explicator* 53, no. 3 (spring 1995): 158–161.

Schaffer, Talia. "A Wilde Desire Took Me: The Homoerotic History of Dracula," *English Literary History* 61, no. 1 (summer 1994): 381–435.

Wheatcroft, Geoffrey. "Not Green, Not Red, Not Pink: Oscar Wilde Cannot Be Simplified into an Irish Rebel, a Subversive Socialist, or a Gay Martyr," *Atlantic Monthly* 291, no. 4 (May 2003): 125–131.

Wilde, Oscar. *The Picture of Dorian Gray and Selected Stories.* New York: New American Library, 1983.

Wilkinson, Sarah
(?–ca. 1830)

A freelance writer of the GOTHIC BLUEBOOK for a quarter-century, Sarah Scudgell Wilkinson was one of the most-read authors of her day. She earned her living from publishers Dean & Munday and John Arliss by composing sensational fiction and condensing some 100 novels and GOTHIC DRAMAs, such as *The Sorcerer's Palace; or, The Princess of Sinadone* (1805), which features episodes in the life of an Arthurian knight of the Round Table. After publishing *The Thatched Cottage; or, Sorrows of Eugenia* (1806), she opened a subscription library. Her chief products were cheap thrillers, such as *The Spectre; or, The Ruins of Belfont Priory* (1806), in which a talking phantasm, the former Edward Gowen, conducts a man and woman to a burial vault to reveal his murder and the concealment of his remains. Wilkinson followed with *The Mysterious Novice; or, Convent of the Grey Penitents* (1809) and *The Convent of the Grey Penitents; or, The Apostate Nun* (1810), which overworked monastic settings. She built the texts around anti-Catholic plots, a lure to Protestant readers who were curious about celibacy and mystical rites.

For the Gothic market, Wilkinson diversified her writings. Her spectral subjects ran to apparitions and phantasms and her settings to medieval convents, castles, and caves, as in *The Subterraneous Passage; or, Gothic Cell* (1803), *Monkcliffe Abbey* (1805), and *Inkle and Yarico; or, Love in a Cave* (1805). She featured women in dire situations, as with the central figures in *The Mountain Cottager; or, The Deserted Bride* (1805), *The Fugitive Countess* (1807), *The Castle Spectre; or, Family Horrors* (1807), *The Child of Mystery* (1808), *The White Cottage of the Valley; or, The Mysterious Husband* (ca. 1810), and *The Castle of Montabino; or, The Orphan Sisters* (1810). Other of her undated MELODRAMAs include *The Castle of Oravilla, The Deformed Mendicant,* the intriguing Slavonic novel *Zittaw the Cruel; or The Woodsman's Daughter, A Polish Romance,* and *Ivy Castle; or, The Eve of St. Agnes,* which takes its subject from John KEATS's narrative poem.

While on the public dole after her husband's death and during her decline from breast cancer, Wilkinson augmented earnings from jobs as shop clerk and schoolmistress by abridging English and European fiction, writing songs, and authoring chapbooks. Her taste in Gothic novels was impeccable, encompassing the works of the Gothic specialist Matthew Gregory LEWIS and balladeer and historical novelist Sir Walter SCOTT. From history, she culled the plot of a villainous seduction novel, *The Tragical History of Jane Arnold, Commonly Called Crazy Jane; and Mr. Henry Percival; Giving an Account of Their Birth, Parentage, Courtship, and Melancholy End* (1817), one of Wilkinson's most reissued titles, and she also produced three volumes of short Gothic fiction in *New Tales* (1819). In *The Spectre of Lanmere Abbey* (1820), she emulated the GOTHIC CONVENTIONs created by Ann RADCLIFFE.

Bibliography

Haining, Peter, ed. *The Shilling Shockers.* New York: St. Martin's Press, 1978.

Wilkinson, Sarah Scudgell. *The Child of Mystery,* http://www.chawton.org/novels/child/index.html.

Williams, A. Susan, ed. *The Lifted Veil: The Book of Fantastic Literature by Women, 1800–World War II.* New York: Carroll & Graf, 1992.

Wilson, August
(1945–   )

American playwright Frederick August Wilson, winner of two Pulitzer Prizes, applied African STORYTELLING methods and Gothic techniques to a 10-play suite on African-American history that advances through each decade of the 20th century. By retrieving the horrors of bondage and segregation and their harm on 20th-century urban blacks, he educates playgoers about the corruption of materialism, bigotry, and the ill-gotten gains from slave labor. His humanistic plays enact commonplace events and themes amid strands of myth, folklore, ritual, and the suppressed aspirations of blacks displaced from spiritual wholeness by racism, slum life, crime, gambling, alcohol, drugs, and lust.

To make evils palpable, Wilson wields URBAN GOTHIC elements. *Ma Rainey's Black Bottom* (1985) describes an unforeseen stabbing death at a recording studio. In *Fences* (1985) and *Two Trains Running* (1991), death becomes a personified stalker and adversary of the innocent. The latter play contains a macabre self-mutilation by Clarissa "Risa" Turner, the waitress in Memphis Lee's cafe who discourages suitors by slicing her legs with a razor. The text also describes a 322-year-old mystic sage and visionary, Aunt Ester, a recurrent character who, like the WANDERING JEW, lives long beyond a normal lifespan. With the skills of an African juju priestess, she advises the seeker and consoles the mourner with the laying on of hands, an ancient method of conferring blessing. In *Gem of the Ocean* (2003), Ester gives Citizen Barlow a new aim for his misdirected life as a black emigré from the agrarian South trying to find his way in a Northern ghetto.

With *Joe Turner's Come and Gone* (1988), Wilson's Gothicism became more pronounced. He infused the humdrum life of a boarding house with SUPERSTITION—the mystic "shiny man" who directs the lost, an impromptu Afrocentric dance-and-shout, speaking in tongues, and animistic ritual. In his popular work *THE PIANO LESSON* (1990), he used the exorcism of a ghost to dramatize a family reevaluating its hopes as members shed Mississippi plantation mores and adapt to a rootless urban life in Pittsburgh. Wilson turns the goldenseal plant into a mystic healer in *Seven Guitars* (1995), a story of death and grief. One of the characters, Miss Sarah Degree, distributes root tea, a magic curative. The paranoid chicken slaughterer Hedley inserts an eerie FORESHADOWING of arbitrary slaying and dismemberment within a ritual circle, a suggestion of sorcery. A misguided visionary given to chaotic mutterings, he murders an unsuspecting musician with a lethal machete chop. Wilson speaks directly to paganism in *King Hedley II* (1999) with the naming of Ogun, a god from Yoruba myth who reunified himself after the winds dismembered him.

Bibliography

Ards, Angela. "The Diaspora Comes to Dartmouth," *American Theatre* 15, no. 5 (May–June 1998): 50–52.

Freedman, Samuel G. "August Wilson, Defining an Era," *New York Times*, February 5, 2003: 1.

Shannon, Sandra G. "Blues, History, and Dramaturgy," *African American Review* 27, no. 4 (winter 1993): 539–559.

Wolfe, Peter. *August Wilson.* New York: Twayne, 1999.

Wise Blood
Flannery O'Connor
(1952)

A multilayered allegory steeped in strangeness, Flannery O'CONNOR's *Wise Blood* centers on the lack-logic Hazel "Haze" MOTES, a Kafkaesque predator who operates his Church without Christ from an automobile. Only after striking himself blind does he obtain true insight into the human condition. In the falling action, Motes and his landlady, Mrs. Flood, carry on a long-running dialogue. She remarks about his peculiar manifestations of faith: "You must have been lying to me when you named your fine church. I wouldn't be surprised if you weren't some kind of an agent of the pope or got some connection with something funny" (O'Connor, 116). O'Connor's familiarity with Southern dialect and anti-Catholic suspicions rings true, casting the story in the direction of social criticism as well as spiritual symbolism.

For the reader's edification, O'Connor reaches a shocking apotheosis, a humanistic credo from the landlady, who contends, "If we don't help each other, Mr. Motes, there's nobody to help us. . . . Nobody. The world is an empty place" (*ibid.*, 118). A consummate fictional artist, the author was still finding her way within genius when she published the darkly comic novel, which received mixed reviews. However, she earned praise from several elite writers and critics, including Caroline Gordon, Robert Lowell, and John Crowe Ransom. When Gordon compared O'Connor to Kafka, critic J. F. Powers remarked, "Kafka? No, Kafka was much too young and tender to play in that league" (O'Connor, xv).

Bibliography

O'Connor, Flannery. *Three by Flannery O'Connor.* New York: Signet, 1983.

Sweeney, Gerald M. "O'Connor's 'Wise Blood,'" *Explicator* 56, no. 2 (winter 1998): 108–109.

witchcraft

Witchcraft is a frequent vehicle for FOLKLORE, LEGEND, ballad, and horror fiction, as found in Johann Wolfgang von GOETHE's enduring FAIRY TALE *Der Zauberlehrling* (*The Sorcerer's Apprentice*, 1797), the wind-riding sorceress in Nikolai GOGOL's "Viy" (1835), and SUPERNATURAL elements in Russian symbolist Valery Bryusov's *The Fiery Angel* (1908), which the composer Sergei Prokofiev used as the basis for an opera. As the critic Anne Williams explains in *Art of Darkness: A Poetics of Gothic* (1995), the MEDIEVALISM of Gothic fiction draws on a period when SUPERSTITION about witchcraft, LYCANTHROPY, SHAPE-SHIFTING, and ghosts was prevalent, as in the demonic *Walpurgisnacht* (witches' sabbath) spectacle in Goethe's *Faust* (1790–1832), and species-altering witchery in James HOGG's "The Witches of Traquair" (1828). Encouraging the English strain of sadistic sorcery tales was the 18th-century German *Schauerroman* (shudder novel), an impetus to horror fiction. In such Gothic witch scenarios, the protagonist, usually a decrepit crone or seductive succubus, could be diversified with additional identities and qualities—the wandering gypsy fortune-teller, the prostitute, the medium in touch with the dead, and the perverted cleric, as exemplified by the voluptuous witch of the alchemist's lab in William Child GREEN's "Secrets of Cabalism; or, Ravenstone and Alice of Huntingdon" (ca. 1819) and Mathilda, the beautiful, but corrupting she-monster in Matthew Gregory LEWIS's sensational novel THE MONK (1796). For background material, Lewis read Joseph Glanville's demonology text *Sadducismus Triumphatus; or, A Full and Plain Evidence Concerning Witches and Apparitions* (1681) and immersed his imagination in German horror tales.

Much of European Gothic witch lore bears an aura of fact, some provided by churchmen's sermons and tracts warning of the various shapes that Satan took to subvert Christianity. A forerunner and sensational example of the theme of black magic fueled George Brewer's two-volume shocker *The Witch of Ravensworth* (1808), the exposé of witch Ann Ramsey's infanticide, cannibalism, and blood drinking and her reliance on reptilian familiars. For consorting with Ann to rid himself of his wife and children, the Baron de la Braunch signs a pact with Askar, ruler of hell, a predictable motif of witch fiction. Hogg advanced the Scots view of sorcery in *The Witch of Fife* (1813), a romantic dialect ballad later set to music. In England, Lord BYRON added witchery to his closet drama MANFRED (1817); his former lover and imitator Lady Caroline LAMB applied sorcery to her Faustian pirate tale *Ada Reis* (1823). Charles Robert MATURIN's title VILLAIN manipulated reaction to the English Witchcraft Act of 1604 in MELMOTH THE WANDERER (1820), a multilayered Gothic classic.

A student of elements of witchcraft, Sir Walter SCOTT applied the fictional concept in his historical novel *Ivanhoe* (1819). The text depicts the condemnation of the saintly Rebecca to burn as a witch for training in Eastern pharmacopeia under mentorship of the healer Miriam. The maligning of Rebecca's character reveals an insidious anti-Semitism in courtiers who want to quell Ivanhoe's unnatural love for a Jew. Her accusers offer as evidence a box inscribed with Hebrew lettering. Beaumanoir deduced from the motto on the lid that Rebecca "can convert Scripture into blasphemy, mingling poison with our necessary food" (Scott, 348). In the novel's falling action, the author combines the drama of the courtroom and trial by combat. At a high point in chapter 43, he positions a black chair and stake ringed by sticks and chains along with a diabolical touch—four African slaves who appall an English audience "who gazed on them as on demons" (*ibid.*, 412). At the end of his career, Scott collected folk beliefs for his scholarly *Letters on Demonology and Witchcraft* (1830), which summarizes biblical texts that identify witches as poisoners and instruments of Satan.

German sorcery tales echoed Scott's interest in verisimilitude. In 1841, Wilhelm Meinhold began work on "Die Bernsteinhexe" (The Amber Witch, 1843), a SUSPENSE tale based on pre-Reformation persecution of German witches and composed with reference to actual court proceedings. It first appeared in print as a document composed by a minister at Coserow describing the arrest, judgment, and death sentence of Maria Schweidler, whom Wittich Appelmann, a malicious noble, charges with NECROMANCY. When the Prussian king Wilhelm IV expressed interest in the text, Meinhold had to admit that the story was fiction. Émile ERCKMANN and Louis Alexandre

CHATRIAN added to the strain of believable supernatural sorcery tales in their first anthology, *Contes Fantastiques* (Fantastic stories, 1847). William Harrison AINSWORTH produced *The Lancashire Witches: A Romance of Pendle Forest* (1849), the first depiction of England's historic witch trial in August 1612 by which King James I targeted a family of sorcerers called the Pendle witches.

In New World fiction, witchcraft made an impact on the Gothic mode by permeating the Central American lore of LA LLORONA, a wandering hag, and by fueling a subset of historical fiction about New England's horrific witch hunts. John Neal produced the first witch novel, *Rachel Dyer: A North American Story* (1828), an exposé of scapegoasting set during the witch trials in Salem, Massachusetts, in 1692. Nathaniel HAWTHORNE knew of the nation's sordid past from his family connection to a great-grandfather, Justice John Hathorne, who sent Salem's alleged witches to their deaths. Nearly a century and a half later, the novelist exploited Puritan superstitions and fear of the unknown in the short story "YOUNG GOODMAN BROWN" (1835), one of his most admired short works. Hawthorne expanded on Puritan legalism and female persecution with the novel THE SCARLET LETTER (1850), which contains brief mentions of the obscure dealings of Mistress Hibbins, a reputed witch.

Reaction to North America's persecution of female "witches" echoed through later Gothic writings. To the north, Canadian novelist Philippe-Aubert de Gaspé the Elder produced *Les Anciens Canadiens* (*The Canadians of Old*, 1863), one of Canada's enduring frontier works. Set in Quebec and based on New World lore, the story recounts accusations of sorcery and a hatchet murder. California author Gertrude ATHERTON created eerie effects for *The Christmas Witch*, a novella published in an 1893 issue of *Godey's Magazine*. Edith WHARTON triggered fears of complicity with the devil in "All Souls," an ambiguous terror story collected posthumously in *Ghosts* (1937). Angered by the 20th-century witch hunt during the McCarthy era, Arthur MILLER wrote an intriguing American GOTHIC DRAMA, THE CRUCIBLE (1953), a dramatization of the hysteria and misinformation that spawned an unforgettable community tragedy.

In late 20th-century writing, witchery recurred in the bicultural fiction of Rudolfo Alfonso Anaya, a Chicano writer from New Mexico, and of French-Canadian Gothicist Anne Hébert. In *Bless Me, Ultima* (1972), Anaya added to Southwestern American traditions the ambiguous professionalism of the *curandera,* a nurse-midwife who ministers to community needs with a mystic pharmacopoeia. Ultima, a gentle grandmother and herbal healer, comforts and strengthens her sensitive grandson Tony, a NAIF who suffers nightmares during his catechetical training. Safe in the company of "la Grande," he learns to respect the earth and Ultima's knowledge of NATURE.

Anaya depicts the powers of earth in Ultima's fight with the villain Tenorio, who stalks Tony and accuses his grandmother of being a *bruja* (witch). At a climactic face-off against evil, Ultima discloses her dependence on an owl as her familiar while redeeming Tony: "'—!Espíritu de mi alma! [Spirit of my soul]' I heard Ultima's command ring in the still night air, and a swirling of wings engulfed Tenorio" (Anaya, 245). The wings are those of an owl, which Tenorio shoots. Tony lapses into spiritual malaise after Tenorio fires the bullet that "shattered my childhood into a thousand fragments" (*ibid.*). As a gesture to the old lady's beneficent powers, the boy buries the owl at a forked juniper, a SYMBOL of the divergent path that the *curandera* walks.

In 1975, Anne Hébert complicated the idea of satanic possession and witchery in *Les Enfants du Sabbat* (*Children of the Black Sabbath*), a controversial novel depicting the moral corruption of the protagonist, Sister Julie of the Trinity, by a sorcerer near Quebec at the convent of the Sisters of the Precious Blood. The plot contains torture, emblematic markings on the flesh, and blood sacrifice and mimics scripture by describing a perverse virgin birth. In the end, the whole family of nuns yields to Satan's carnal glamour.

Bibliography

Anaya, Rudolfo A. *Bless Me, Ultima.* Berkeley, Calif.: Tonitiuh International, 1972.

Northey, Margot. *The Haunted Wilderness: The Gothic and Grotesque in Canadian Fiction.* Toronto: University of Toronto Press, 1976.

Pitcher, E. W. "On Authorship of Essay Serials in the European Magazine and The Lady's Monthly Museum: George Brewer and G. Bedingfield," *Notes and Queries* 44, no. 2 (June 1997): 238–239.

Scott, Sir Walter. *Ivanhoe.* New York: Bantam Books, 1988.

Wollstonecraft, Mary
(1759–1797)

A fair-minded feminist, Mary Wollstonecraft Godwin defied the twisted views of palpitating heroines and vindictive FEMME FATALEs served up in Gothic fiction. She left a miserable home life fraught with drunkenness and domestic violence to become a teacher and to compile *Thoughts on the Education of Daughters* (1786). As a critic for *Analytical Review,* she took a firm stand against romantic notions of happily-ever-after marriages, particularly those of Charlotte SMITH's wildly popular *Emmeline, the Orphan of the Castle* (1788). Wollstonecraft presented her own approach to romance in *Original Stories from Real Life* (1788) and *Mary, a Fiction* (1788), a fantasy diatribe against the sanctification of female virginity. The main character, who is married to a disgusting husband, wishes for death and a heaven where women are not forced into revolting marriages. In place of society's high expectations of domestic life, Wollstonecraft championed a broad-based education for women and a wholesome strength of mind and body, the themes of her essay *A Vindication of the Rights of Women* (1792), a social prospectus that Ann RADCLIFFE fictionalized in her Gothic novels.

Wollstonecraft was writing MARIA; OR, THE WRONGS OF WOMEN (1798) at the time of her death. Her husband, William GODWIN, published it posthumously. Literary historians have mused that her demise at age 38 from puerperal fever 10 days after giving birth may have inspired her daughter Mary Wollstonecraft SHELLEY to write FRANKENSTEIN (1818). Shelley appears to use the metaphors of laboratory work to create a monster to mirror her despair at her mother's death in childbirth.

Bibliography

Gamer, Michael. *Romanticism and the Gothic: Genre, Reception, and Canon Formation.* Cambridge: Cambridge University Press, 2000.

Hoeveler, Diane Long. *Gothic Feminism.* University Park: Pennsylvania State University Press, 1998.

Wood, Ellen
(1814–1887)

Ellen Price Wood, a writer of sensational fiction and ghost stories, was one of the most popular, prolific, and successful Gothic authors of the Victorian age. Like Carson MCCULLERS, Flannery O'CONNOR, and Mervyn PEAKE, she wrote her chilling stories from an invalid's chair. Impaired by a curved spine, she lived in France well into her 40s as the wife of Henry Wood, a financier and British legate. With the decline of his career, she began writing in earnest to support the family and, over a nine-year period, published short works in *Bentley's Miscellany* and *Colburn's New Monthly Magazine,* both owned by William Harrison AINSWORTH. Among the 100 pieces she submitted was a ghost story, "The Punishment of Gina Montani" (1852), which concludes with the dramatic disclosure of PREMATURE BURIAL—the corpse of Gina clad in nightdress and walled up in a secret passage. The Lord of Visinara attempts to exorcise her spirit, but his payments to monks for intercessory prayers prove futile.

Influenced by the detective novels and occultism of Edward BULWER-LYTTON, Wood made a major impact on the reading public by serializing a MELODRAMA, *East Lynne* (1861), the sensational story of murder, adultery, and scandal that went through four editions in the first half-year and appeared in numerous translations and stage adaptations. After completing two saga novels on crime and detective work, *Mrs. Halliburton's Troubles* (1862) and *The Channings* (1862), Wood began publishing *Argosy* magazine, for which she wrote autobiographical sketches and a large body of short fiction on hauntings, séances, telepathy, madness, and the SUPERNATURAL. She chose an eerie crypt as the setting for a Victorian ghost novel, *Shadow of Ahslydyat* (1862), the tale of an ancestral curse on the Godolphin family. The work earned her 1,000 guineas plus positive reviews in the *Athenaeum,* the *Court Journal,* and the *Spectator.* Admired for maintaining a respectable married life and upholding morality in Gothic fiction, she died a wealthy woman and left a substantial fortune to her son, Charles William Wood, who continued issuing new editions of her books.

Bibliography

Carnell, Jennifer. *The Literary Lives of Mary Elizabeth Braddon.* Hastings, Sussex: Sensation Press, 2000.

Wood, Charles W. "Mrs. Henry Wood: In Memoriam," *Argosy* 43 (1887): 251–270.

Wood, Ellen. "The Punishment of Gina Montani," *Colburn's New Monthly Magazine* 5, no. 2 (February 1852): 189–196.

Wuthering Heights
Emily Brontë
(1847)

A Gothic novel built on succeeding generations ruled by destructive passions, Emily BRONTË's WUTHERING HEIGHTS develops the story of an abused gypsy boy into a psychological study of sorrow, pride, and vengeful OBSESSION over an unobtainable love. The work went to press in secret from Brontë's overprotective father and immediately shocked Victorian readers. With a mystical intensity, the text showcased overt jealousies, hatreds, primal lusts, addictive love, and chaotic family confrontations. The text's SENSATIONALISM jolted Emily's sister, the novelist Charlotte BRONTË, who compared her reading of Emily's passages to inhaling lightning.

In the early Victorian era, fastidious authors avoided blatant sexuality in fiction. Nonetheless, Emily Brontë enhanced GOTHIC CONVENTION with details such as HEATHCLIFF's substitution of his own dark tress in Catherine EARNSHAW's locket for a lock of her husband's light-colored hair, physical union through the placement of Heathcliff's open casket adjacent to Catherine's, her self-starvation, and the scratching of the names of three Catherines on a window sill in view of the moors. These elements served as daring SYMBOLs of unresolved conflicts from childhood, blunted passion, and unrequited love emerging from a quasi-incestuous attraction between sister and foster brother.

To tell the story, Brontë channeled the successive narratives of Lockwood, Catherine, Nelly Dean, and Zillah through recollection, diary, and letter to produce a complex saga. The author establishes a mathematical proportion to motivations. As Hindley Earnshaw, the heir to WUTHERING HEIGHTS, increases his bold attacks on Heathcliff, a parallel growth of acceptance and friendship develops in his sister Catherine, who is the gypsy boy's constant companion. SUSPENSE builds with FORESHADOWINGs of a lethal clash, which the author delays until Hindley inherits the estate from his father. At Mr. Earnshaw's death, Heathcliff and Catherine mourn his passing in paired wails. By neglecting Catherine and allowing her to amuse herself in Heathcliff's company, Hindley encourages the disparate pair to share a peripatetic life on the moors. Idyllic days free from social restriction and home discipline come to an abrupt end after Skulker, the watchdog at neighboring Thrushcross Grange, bites Catherine's ankle. Borne indoors for care, she thrills to the grace of an ordered home.

In the unfolding story of Catherine Earnshaw's passion for the dark gypsy and her love for her refined dutiful husband Edgar, Brontë substitutes for carnal yearnings a rage and tumult in NATURE, which depicts outdoors the inner landscapes of conflicting desires and unrequited yearnings. From childhood, the lovers equate rambles on the moors with liberty, a symbolic release from the confines of social and sexual mores that Catherine embraces at Thrushcross Grange. When she succumbs to delirium, like Lady Macbeth she unburdens herself of anguish by talking in her sleep. Her lyric babblings presage an era of talk therapy by which patients rid themselves of mental torment.

In her only novel, Emily Brontë masters the Gothic powers of pessimism. The end of all constraint occurs in chapter 15 with the release of a fierce, consuming love that has grown from childhood into an outsized fixation. The exchange of overt brutalities drives Catherine and Heathcliff into abnormal compensation for the love they have denied. Both live for betrayal—Catherine's denial of her true nature and Heathcliff's deceitful trickery to destroy two families and gain control of their properties. The dominant reality of the text is the union of two lovers who choose to die together rather than live out unfulfilling relationships. Their unquiet souls haunt Wuthering Heights, expressing to dwellers of the moor the doom of lovers who die with carnal hungers unsatisfied.

Bibliography

Goodlett, Debra. "Love and Addiction in 'Wuthering Heights,'" *Midwest Quarterly* 37, no. 3 (spring 1996): 316–327.

Levy, Eric P. "The Psychology of Loneliness in 'Wuthering Heights,'" *Studies in the Novel* 28, no. 2 (summer 1996): 158–177.

Moers, Ellen. "Female Gothic: Monsters, Goblins, Freaks," *New York Review of Books* (April 4, 1974): 30–42.

Steinitz, Rebecca. "Diaries and Displacement in *Wuthering Heights,*" *Studies in the Novel* 32, no. 4 (winter 2000): 407.

Vine, Stephen. "The Wuther of the Other in 'Wuthering Heights,'" *Nineteenth-Century Literature* 49, no. 3 (December 1994): 339–359.

Wuthering Heights

The contrasting settings of Emily BRONTË's *WUTHERING HEIGHTS* (1847) amplify Catherine EARNSHAW's inner struggle with clashing values— risk-taking versus the settled life. The story opens at a forbidding Tudor-style estate in the wild, elusive Yorkshire landscape in north-central England, a barren setting that the author developed from the haunted houses mentioned in *BLACKWOOD'S EDINBURGH MAGAZINE.* Burdened with a disquieting ATMOSPHERE, the land is rugged and craggy, rising to uneven elevations from the open plateau. The distortion of vegetation foreshadows a blighting of human desires, which is the focus of the action.

Set on a hill, the isolated manse, with its impregnable stone walls and floor, rough beams, narrow windows, and fierce watchdogs, takes its name from the north wind and sweeping storms common to the sparsely populated English moorlands. The manse, sunk in disrepair, looks out on a mirror image of its desolation in the wind-distorted firs and gaunt thorns of an untamable landscape, where sheep innocently crop turf in the churchyard under the spring sky. Grass springs up between the flagstones; GROTESQUE carvings depict griffins and naughty children alongside the date *1500.* Like Catherine's conflicted nature, the setting symbolizes an untenable mix of tame with feral, antique with immediate, and welcoming with inhospitable. The expanse is the perfect habitat for the ramblings of two wild, tumultuous children, Catherine and HEATHCLIFF, whose innocent intimacy develops into an uncontrollable passion.

At Wuthering Heights, Catherine's unfettered spirit breathes free on the wild moors after languishing at Thrushcross Grange, the benign, overly refined home of her husband, with its latticed windows, SYMBOLs of confinement and emotional repression. In death, she continues to move beyond mortal barriers to scratch at the windows and whimper for Heathcliff, her lost love. Brontë reverses the forces with the second Catherine, who thrives in civilized settings, but cowers from the massy, vaguely threatening MEDIEVALISM of Wuthering Heights.

Bibliography

Heywood, Christopher. "Yorkshire Landscapes in 'Wuthering Heights,'" *Essays in Criticism* 48, no. 1 (January 1998): 13–33.

Smith, Lisa. "Landscape and Place in Wuthering Heights," *English Review* 11, no. 1 (September 2000): 22.

Y

Yearsley, Ann
(1753–1806)

The lyricist and playwright Ann Cromartie Yearsley, of Bristol, England, struggled from laboring-class ignorance to express her thoughts and imaginings. After teaching herself to spell and write grammatically, she read the poems of John Milton and the GRAVEYARD VERSE of Edward Young. She wrote under the pseudonym Lactilla, a reference to her work as a dairy maid. With the aid of a benefactor, author Hannah More, and a coterie of bluestockings, Yearsley began publishing in 1785. She produced the historical play *Earl Goodwin* (1791), which was performed at Bristol's Theatre Royal, and issued volumes of verse; among her poems was the MELANCHOLY abolitionist ode "Poem on the Inhumanity of the Slave Trade" (1788). With the proceeds of her writing and returns from a CIRCULATING LIBRARY at Bristol Hot Wells, she supported her family.

Yearsley published the four-volume Gothic MELODRAMA, *The Royal Captives* (1795), a work influenced by the novels of Horace WALPOLE and Ann RADCLIFFE. Yearsley subtitled the work "A Fragment of Secret History: Copied from an Old Manuscript," a double Gothic ploy incorporating both SECRECY and a hint of MEDIEVALISM. Popular in Europe and America, the story, set in France, is based on the legend of the Man in the Iron Mask, whom agents of King Louis XIV allegedly imprisoned in the Bastille in 1698. At a high point in the terror, protagonist Henry Capet enters the Hall of Execution and gazes on tortures: "the pincers, the dislocating wheel, the cord, the block, the axe, and the large goblet full of deadly poison!" (Yearsley, vol. 4, 13). Yearsley's version stressed the themes of political dissent and the confinement and suppression of women. Alexandre Dumas produced the political intrigue as a stage MYSTERY in 1846.

Bibliography

Kucich, Greg. "Women's Historiography and the (Dis)embodiment of Law: Ann Yearsley, Mary Hays, Elizabeth Benger," *Wordsworth Circle* 33, no. 1 (winter 2002): 3–7.

Markley, Robert. "Lactilla, Milkwoman of Clifton: The Life and Writings of Ann Yearsley, 1753–1806," *Studies in English Literature, 1500–1900* 37, no. 3 (summer 1997): 637–672.

Waldron, Mary. "Ann Yearsley: The Bristol Manuscript Revisited," *Triangle Journals* 3, no. 1 (1996).

Yearsley, Ann. *The Royal Captives*, 4 vols. New York: Garland, 1974.

"The Yellow Wallpaper"
Charlotte Perkins Gilman
(1892)

The feminist lecturer and writer Charlotte Perkins GILMAN created the classic AMERICAN GOTHIC tale of male-on-female domination and INSANITY in "The Yellow Wallpaper." A seminal work of FEMALE GOTHIC, it dramatizes the decline of a woman ostensibly killed by kindness. The text places John, a patronizing husband-doctor, in charge of his declining wife-patient. The ominous arrangement owes its ATMOSPHERE and TONE to the Gothic woman-controlling strategies created by writers such as Edgar Allan POE. The SUBTEXT warns the reader that institutionalization within four walls to punish sensitive, creative women for being themselves is a sure route to madness.

As a SYMBOL of claustrophobic oppression, the author's unnamed character, a new mother struggling for selfhood, passes through a hedge, locked gates, and an entranceway before languishing in total seclusion, like a scolded child returned to a suffocating womb. Significantly, she meets her fate in a child's room, the nursery of her family's summer home, a neglected country estate suggestive of the castles and ruins of classic Gothic fiction. Contrast spawns tension: inside the miserable lockup are "rings and things in the walls"; outside is a "delicious garden . . . large and shady" and inviting (Gilman, 714).

The unnamed speaker consents to the rest cure to end her unreasonable bouts of anger and hypersensitivity. For John's sake, she acts the part of subdued wife, "[taking] pains to control myself—before him, at least, and that makes me very tired" (ibid., 714). Forbidden even a pen for writing her thoughts, the patient nurses a dormant rage. To vent her fury, she redirects hatred toward the ARABESQUE wallpaper, a subject that Gilman, a former student at the Rhode Island School of Design, valued from an esthetic perspective.

The symbolism in the wall covering takes on domestic meaning as the patient weakens. She speaks indirectly of the insidious misery of marriage and hints at coercion and VIOLENCE in terms of the hideous wallpaper, which "has a kind of sub-pattern in a different shade, a particularly irritating one, for you can only see it in certain lights, and not clearly then" (ibid., 716). As the paper morphs into a monster, it takes on overt qualities of villainy through bulging eye shapes in the pattern that become unblinking watchers. Before her complete loss of control, the viewer witnesses a prophecy—the shape of an incarcerated woman in the decor, a DOPPELGÄNGER image of herself as a powerless, suppressed victim of patriarchy reduced to two dimensions and pasted to the wall. Gradually, horrific outlines appear in the design as the patient hallucinates and regresses to total collapse.

In redefining the home as an alien space, an extension of the Gothic dungeon, Gilman rails at arrogant males who exclude women from artistic and career opportunities and from all volition and decision making. In the estimation of the wallpaper-obsessed speaker, who reshapes her rage against coercion by making the pattern the "it" to be challenged: "You think you have mastered it, but just as you get well under way in following, it turns a back-somersault and there you are. It slaps you in the face, knocks you down, and tramples upon you. It is like a bad dream" (ibid., 719). In place of traditional hauntings, Gilman infects the irksome premises with a stench of decay that creeps through the walls, hovers, skulks, and lies in wait before leaping onto the speaker and saturating her hair. Subjected to barred windows and infantilized by a rigid medical environment, the speaker gradually loses her sense of self, crawls about the floor, rips the offending paper from the wall with nails and teeth, and barricades herself within her den.

Gilman's story resonates with MELODRAMA and with author sympathy for the victim, whose failed power struggle leaves her too sapped and undermined to cling to sanity. Like Edward ROCHESTER's view of Bertha Mason ROCHESTER, the "madwoman in the attic" in Charlotte BRONTË's JANE EYRE (1847), the husband-doctor's final view of the woman he dehumanized dismays and terrifies him, causing him to faint. Too late, he realizes that instead of restoring her to the role of wife and mother, the rest cure has destroyed her. Through the subtext, Gilman establishes that classic GOTHIC CONVENTIONs no longer applied to women's lives but that, by the 1890s, the sexist conditions that triggered Gothicism had not changed.

Bibliography

Bak, John S. "Escaping the Jaundiced Eye: Foucauldian Panopticism in Charlotte Perkins Gilman's 'The Yellow Wallpaper,'" *Studies in Short Fiction* 31, no. 1 (winter 1994): 39–46.

Gilman, Charlotte Perkins. "The Yellow Wallpaper," in *The Harper American Literature,* 2nd. ed. Donald McQuade, et al. New York: HarperCollins, 1994.

Hume, Beverly A. "Managing Madness in Gilman's 'The Yellow Wall-Paper,'" *Studies in American Fiction* 30, no. 1 (spring 2002): 3–30.

Lane, Ann J. *To Herland and Beyond.* New York: Meridian, 1991.

Roth, Marty. "Gilman's Arabesque Wallpaper," *Mosaic* 34, no. 4 (December 2001): 145–162.

Shawn, St. John. "An Updated Publication History of 'The Yellow Wall-Paper,'" *Studies in Short Fiction* 34, no. 2 (spring 1997): 237.

Weales, Gerald. "Perera: The Yellow Wallpaper," *Commonweal* 120, no. 3 (February 12, 1993): 16–17.

"Young Goodman Brown"
Nathaniel Hawthorne
(1835)

Nathaniel HAWTHORNE's "Young Goodman Brown," collected in *Mosses from an Old Manse* (1846), is an intimate ALLEGORY about a young married couple and their separate experiences with DIABOLISM. Much praised by Herman MELVILLE, the subdued dreamscape juggles two extremes light against dark and moral goodness against evil—in the mid-17th century, when belief in WITCHCRAFT was a given among New England's Puritans. In an ambiguous half-light, Faith bids farewell to her husband, but regrets his night-time journey "this night, dear husband, of all nights of the year," a reference to All Saints' Eve (Hawthorne, 1,033). Implications of a witches' sabbath deep in the forest contrast Faith's cap with a pink ribbon, a frail emblem of childlike innocence. In a nagging state of ambivalence, Goodman Brown clings to his wife's tender sensibilities and morality as he debates his entry into a witches' coven led by Satan, a wily shape-shifter.

Hawthorne stresses Brown's curiosity and boldness, two human failings that give meaning to the term *daredevil.* As he advances from the village of Salem, the story prickles with terrifying details: a staff that wriggles like a snake, the anointing of a broomstick with wolf's bane, and allusions to the burning of an Indian village, the lashing of a Quaker woman, illegitimacy and infanticide, and sexual congress with Satan. At the story's climax, Brown loses both his faith and Faith, his wife, whose pink ribbon flutters from a tree branch. The slender piece of evidence characterizes the small amount of contradiction that can drive the devout to deny God and embrace satanism.

Hawthorne is famous for the melodramatic pledge ritual amid blazing pines, which shed light on Puritan piety and the phantasms that blight the pious. In an ATMOSPHERE of perverted religion, Brown faces Faith before the unholy altar where a baptismal font appears to hold blood. The story stresses an imperfect understanding of Christianity and a single soul's struggle with temptation as Goodman Brown looks to heaven and resists corruption. Although he saves himself from perdition, his lost trust in Faith fills him with revulsion of her and other hypocritical pillars of goodness in the community whom he once admired. Because he has no moral landmarks to follow, a bleak solitude and paranoia escort him to the grave.

Bibliography

Hawthorne, Nathaniel. *The Complete Novels and Selected Tales of Nathaniel Hawthorne.* New York: Modern Library, 1937.

Keil, James C. "Hawthorne's 'Young Goodman Brown': Early Nineteenth-Century and Puritan Constructions of Gender," *New England Quarterly* 69 (March 1996): 33–55.

Z

Zastrozzi
Percy Bysshe Shelley
(1810)

At age 17, the romantic poet Percy Bysshe SHELLEY began writing *Zastrozzi: A Romance,* his first attempt at a diabolic MELODRAMA. Based on the sensational Gothic literature he had read while studying at Eton, the plot, setting, and style owe much to Ann RADCLIFFE's *THE ITALIAN* (1797), William GODWIN's *St. Leon* (1799), Matthew Gregory LEWIS's controversial *THE MONK* (1796) and *The Bravo of Venice* (1804), and Charlotte DACRE's *Zofloya; or, The Moor* (1806). At the core of a vengeful love triangle lie willful evil and VIOLENCE, two popular subjects among Gothicists. With the creation of his monstrous VILLAIN Zastrozzi, Shelley heightened the appeal of unimpeded self-indulgence, a theme suited to the writer's adolescence.

From traditional GOTHIC CONVENTIONs, Shelley carefully emulated the choice of dread castles crisscrossed with a maze of hallways obscured by CHIAROSCURO. He littered the scene with a satanic robber-chief, the bodies of a suicide and a murder victim, sexual libertines, and ghosts. A grappling melee between the villainess, Matilda La Contessa di Laurentini, and the innocent Julia concludes with multiple thrusts of a stiletto that pierce Julia's body even after she is obviously dead. As though betraying her gender in woman-on-woman rape, Matilda takes a fierce, phallic pleasure in plunging the blade up to the hilt in inert flesh.

In the resolution, Shelley reverts to a common Gothic ploy, the avenging arm of the Inquisition. At the tribunal, church officials reveal Julia's ghastly remains before leading in the towering atheist Zastrozzi. In the final scene, he lies on the rack, stretched and tortured while smiling his scorn and laughing convulsively. Though immature and derivative, the novel reveals Shelley's personal conflicts between morality and rebellion against religion. The Canadian playwright George F. Walker produced a satiric stage version, *Zastrozzi: The Master of Discipline* (1977), an operatic resetting that won critical acclaim for its retro version of blood and thunder.

Bibliography

Chesser, Eustace. *Shelley & Zastrozzi: Self-Revelation of a Neurotic.* London: Gregg/Archive, 1965.

Punter, David. *Gothic Pathologies: The Text, the Body and the Law.* New York: St. Martin's Press, 1998.

Whatley, John. "Romantic and Enlightened Eyes in the Gothic Novels of Percy Bysshe Shelley," *Gothic Studies* 1, no. 2 (1999): 201–221.

Zimansky, Curt R. "*Zastrozzi and The Bravo of Venice:* Another Shelley Borrowing," *Keats-Shelley Journal* 30 (1981): 15–17.

Abällino, der Grosse Bandit [Aballino, the great bandit] (1793), Heinrich Zschokke

The Abbey of Clunedale (1804), Nathan Drake

The Abbot (1820), Sir Walter Scott

The Abbot of Montserrat; or, The Pool of Blood (1826), William Child Green

The Abbot's Ghost (1867), Louisa May Alcott

Absalom, Absalom! (1936), William Faulkner

An Account of the Conduct and Proceedings of the Late John Gow, Captain of the Late Pirates Executed for Murther and Piracy (1725), anonymous

Account of the Trial of John Thurtell and Joseph Hunt (1824), Pierce Egan

"The Accursed Inhabitants of the House of Bly" (1992), Joyce Carol Oates

Ada Reis (1823), Caroline Lamb

Adelaide; or, The Countercharm (1813), Catherine Cuthbertson

"The Adventure of the Empty House" (1903), Sir Arthur Conan Doyle

"The Adventure of the Mazarin Stone" (1921), Sir Arthur Conan Doyle

"The Adventure of the Second Stain" (1904), Sir Arthur Conan Doyle

"The Adventure of the Speckled Band" (1892), Sir Arthur Conan Doyle

"The Adventure of the Sussex Vampire" (1924), Sir Arthur Conan Doyle

"The Adventures of a Breach-of-Promise Con Man" (1929), Karel Čapek

The Adventures of Hajji Baba of Ispahan (1824), James Morier

The Adventures of Sherlock Holmes (1894), Sir Arthur Conan Doyle

After Dark (1858), Dionysius Boucicault

"After Dark Vapors" (1817), John Keats

"Afterward" (1911), Edith Wharton

Against the Grain (1884), Joris-Karl Huysmans

The Age of Innocence (1920), Edith Wharton

Alan Fitz-Osborne (1786), Anne Fuller

Albertus (1833), Théophile Gautier

The Albert Victor Waltz (1890), Felix Burns

Alfonso, King of Castile (1801), Matthew Gregory Lewis

The Algerines; or, The Twins of Naples (1832), William Child Green

Alias Grace (1996), Margaret Atwood

Alice; or, The Mysteries (1838), Edward Bulwer-Lytton

"Alice's Godmother" (1925), Walter de la Mare

Aline and Valcour (1795), Marquis de Sade

"All Hallows" (1926), Walter de la Mare

"All Souls" (1937), Edith Wharton

"All Souls' Night" (1920), William Butler Yeats

Almoran and Hamet (1761), John Hawkesworth

"The Almshouse Window" (1847), Hans Christian Andersen

Alonzo the Brave and the Fair Imogene (1790), Matthew Gregory Lewis

Alraune (The mandrakes) (1911), Hanns Heinz Ewers

"The Anaconda" (1808), Matthew Gregory Lewis

Anastatius, or Memoirs of a Greek (1819), Thomas Hope

The Andromeda Strain (1969), Michael Crichton

Angels in America (1991, 1992), Tony Kushner

The Animated Skeleton (1798), anonymous

"Annabel Lee" (1849), Edgar Allan Poe

Anne Hereford (1867), Ellen Wood

Arabeski (Arabesques) (1835), Nikolai Gogol

"Arabesque: The Mouse" (1920), Alfred Edgar Coppard

"An Arabian Nightmare" (1851), Fitz-James O'Brien

The Arabian Nights (1704–17), Antoine Galland, trans.

Ardath: The Story of a Dead Self (1889), Marie Corelli

Around the World in Eighty Days (1873), Jules Verne

"Arria Marcella" (1852), Théophile Gautier

Arthur Mervyn (1799), Charles Brockden Brown

As I Lay Dying (1930), William Faulkner

"The Assassins" (1814), Percy Bysshe Shelley

Astonishment (1802), Francis Lathom

The Astrologer's Prediction; or, The Maniac's Fate (1826), anonymous

Auchindrane (1830), Sir Walter Scott

"Aura" (1962), Carlos Fuentes

Auriol; or, The Elixir of Life (1846), William Harrison Ainsworth

Aurora Floyd (1863), Mary Elizabeth Braddon

Avatar (1856), Théophile Gautier

The Avenger (1838), Thomas De Quincey

The Awful Disclosures of Maria Monk; or, The Hidden Secrets of a Nun's Life in a Convent (1836), T. B. Peterson

"Azathoth" (1922), H. P. Lovecraft

Babette's Feast (1959), Isak Dinesen

"A Ballad of François Villon" (1878), Algernon Swinburne

"The Ballad of Gregorio Cortez" (1901), anonymous

The Ballad of Reading Gaol (1898), Oscar Wilde

"The Ballad of the Dark Ladie" (1798), Samuel Taylor Coleridge

The Ballad of the Sad Café (1951), Carson McCullers

Balaoo (1912), Gaston Leroux

Barabbas: A Dream of the World's Tragedy (1893), Marie Corelli

"Barn Burning" (1939), William Faulkner

Barnaby Rudge (1841), Charles Dickens

Barry Lyndon (1844), William Makepeace Thackeray

"Bartleby the Scrivener" (1853), Herman Melville

"The Bascombe Valley Mystery" (1891), Sir Arthur Conan Doyle

The Bat (1920), Mary Roberts Rinehart

Bear (1977), Marian Engel

"The Bear" (1942), William Faulkner

"The Beast in the Cave" (1905), H. P. Lovecraft

"The Beast in the Jungle" (1903), Henry James

Beauty (1978), Robin McKinley

Beauty and the Barge (1905), W. W. Jacobs

"Beauty and the Beast" (1698), Charles Perrault

Beauty's Punishment (1984), Anne Rice

Beauty's Release (1985), Anne Rice

"The Beckoning Fair One" (1911), Oliver Onions

The Beetle (1897), Richard Marsh

The Beggar's Opera (1728), John Gay

Behind a Mask (1875), Louisa May Alcott

The Beleaguered City (1880), Margaret Oliphant

The Bell (1958), Iris Murdoch

"The Bell in the Fog" (1905), Gertrude Atherton

Bellefleur (1980), Joyce Carol Oates

"The Bells" (1848), Edgar Allan Poe

Beloved (1987), Toni Morrison

Benito Cereno (1855), Herman Melville

"Berenice" (1835), Edgar Allan Poe

Bertram; or, The Castle of Aldobrand (1816), Charles Robert Maturin

The Best of H. P. Lovecraft (1987), H. P. Lovecraft

"Between the Minute and the Hour" (1927), Alfred McLelland Burrage

"Between the World and Me" (1935), Richard Wright

"Big Claus and Little Claus" (1835), Hans Christian Andersen

Big Mama's Funeral (1962), Gabriel García Márquez

The Big Sleep (1939), Raymond Chandler

Billy Budd (1924), Herman Melville

"The Birds" (1952), Daphne du Maurier

Birdsong (1997), Sebastian Faulks

"The Birthday of the Infanta" (1888), Oscar Wilde

"The Birthmark" (1843), Nathaniel Hawthorne

The Black Band; or, The Mysteries of Midnight (1861), Mary Elizabeth Braddon

Black Bess; or, The Knight of the Road (1863–68), John Frederick Smith

"The Black Cat" (1843), Edgar Allan Poe

The Black Forest; or, the Cavern of Horrors (1802), anonymous

Black Mischief (1932), Evelyn Waugh

The Black Monk (1894), Anton Chekhov

The Black Monk; or, The Street of the Grey Turret (1844), Thomas Preskett Prest

Black Oxen (1923), Gertrude Atherton

The Black Prince (1973), Iris Murdoch

"The Black Spider" (ca. 1798), anonymous

Black-Eyed Susan (1829), Douglas William Jerrold

Blackwood Farm (2002), Anne Rice

Bleak House (1853), Charles Dickens

Bless Me, Ultima (1972), Rudolfo Anaya

The Blind Assassin (2001), Margaret Atwood

The Blithedale Romance (1852), Nathaniel Hawthorne

Blood and Gold (2001), Anne Rice

Blood Canticle (2003), Anne Rice

The Bloody Chamber (1979), Angela Carter

"The Blue Carbuncle" (1892), Sir Arthur Conan Doyle

The Bluest Eye (1969), Toni Morrison

"The Boar-Pig" (1914), Saki

The Body Snatcher (1881), Robert Louis Stevenson

"Bon-Bon" (1832), Edgar Allan Poe

"Botticelli's Madonna" (1891), Edith Wharton

"The Bottle Imp" (1888), Robert Louis Stevenson

"The Bottomless Grave" (1911), Ambrose Bierce

"Boule de Suif" (Butterball) (1880), Guy de Maupassant

"Bras Coupé" [1879], George Washington Cable

The Bravo of Venice: A Romance (1805), Matthew Gregory Lewis

"A Dream within a Dream" (1849), Edgar Allan Poe

Dreams of Terror and Death: The Dream Cycle of H. P. Lovecraft (1995), H. P. Lovecraft

Dr. Faustus (ca. 1588), Christopher Marlowe

Dr. Jekyll and Mr. Hyde (1886), Robert Louis Stevenson

"Dry September" (1931), William Faulkner

The Duchess of Malfi (ca. 1613), John Webster

Duke Christian of Luneberg; or, Traditions of the Harz (1824), Jane Porter

Duskouri Tales (2000), Byrd Roberts

Dvoynik [The Double] (1846), Fyodor Dostoevsky

"The Dying Indian" (1784), Philip Freneau

Earl Goodwin (1791), Ellen Wood

Earl Strongbow; or, The History of Richard de Clare and the Beautiful Geralda (1789), James White

East Lynne (1861), Ellen Wood

Ecarté; or, The Salons of Paris (1829), John Richardson

Edgar Huntly (1899), Charles Brockden Brown

Egmont (1787), Johann Wolfgang von Goethe

Ein Doppelgänger [A double-goer] (1887), Theodor Storm

Ein Golem (1851), Theodor Storm

Eleanor's Victory (1863), Mary Elizabeth Braddon

Elegy Written in a Country Churchyard (1751), Thomas Gray

Endymion (1818), John Keats

"England's Dead" (1826), Felicia Hemans

The English Patient (1996), Michael Ondaatje

Erlkönig [The elf king] (1782), Johann Wolfgang von Goethe

Ernest Maltravers (1837), Edward Bulwer-Lytton

"Esmé" (1911), Saki

The Eternal Smile (1920), Pär Fabian Lagerkvist

Ethan Frome (1911), Edith Wharton

Ethelinde; or, The Recluse of the Lake (1790), Charlotte Smith

Eugene Aram (1832), Edward Bulwer-Lytton

Eugene Onegin (1831), Alexander Pushkin

Eva Luna (1987), Isabel Allende

Evenings on a Farm near Dakanka (1831), Nikolai Gogol

The Eve of St. Agnes (1819), John Keats

The Exiles; or, Memories of Count de Cronstadt (1788), Clara Reeve

The Exorcist (1971), William Blatty

"An Expedition to Hell" (1836), James Hogg

"The Eyes" (1910), Edith Wharton

Fade (1988), Robert Cormier

Fahrenheit 451 (1953), Ray Bradbury

Falkland (1817), Edward Bulwer-Lytton

"The Fall of the House of Usher" (1839), Edgar Allan Poe

The Family Legend (1810), Joanna Baillie

The Family of Santraile; or, The Heir of Montault (1809), Harriet James

"Family" (1991), Joyce Carol Oates

Fashionable Mysteries (1829), Francis Lathom

Fatal Jealousy; or, Blood Will Have Blood! Containing the History of Count Almagro and Duke Alphonso (1807), anonymous

Fatal Revenge; or, The Family of Montorio (1807), Charles Robert Maturin

The Fatal Vow (1807), Francis Lathom

Faust (1790–1832), Johann Wolfgang von Goethe

Faust (1856), Ivan Turgenev

Faust: A Romance of the Secret Tribunals (1845–46), George Reynolds

"Fears in Solitude" (1798), Samuel Taylor Coleridge

Fences (1985), August Wilson

Ferdinand Count Fathom (1753), Tobias Smollett

"Fever 103°" (1965), Sylvia Plath

The Fiery Angel (1908), Valery Bryusov

"The Final Problem" (1893), Sir Arthur Conan Doyle

"The Finest Story in the World" (1893), Rudyard Kipling

Firebrand (2003), Marion Zimmer Bradley

Firestarter (1980), Stephen King

"The Fir Tree" (1845), Hans Christian Andersen

"The Fisherman and His Soul," (1891), Oscar Wilde

The Flag Station (1907), W. W. Jacobs

The Flame and the Flower (1974), Kathleen Woodiwiss

"Fleur" (1986), Louise Erdrich

"The Flowering of the Strange Orchid" (1894), H. G. Wells

The Foghorn (1934), Gertrude Atherton

The Forest House (1994), Marion Zimmer Bradley

"The Forsaken of God" (1849), William Mudford

Fortunio (1837), Théophile Gautier

The Fountainville Forest (1794), James Boaden

Four Years Voyages of Capt. George Roberts (1726), Daniel Defoe

"A Fragment: In the Manner of the Old Romances" (1793), Mary Hays

François de Bienville: Scenes of Seventeenth-Century Canadian Life (1870), Joseph Étienne Eugène Marmette

Frankenstein (1818), Mary Wollstonecraft Shelley

Frenchman's Creek (1941), Daphne du Maurier

"Friends of the Friends" (1896), Henry James

From a Buick 8 (2002), Stephen King

"Frost at Midnight" (1798), Samuel Taylor Coleridge

The Fugitive Countess; or, The Convent of St. Ursula (1807), Sarah Wilkinson

Further Disclosures of Maria Monk (1837), T. B. Peterson

"Gabriel-Ernest" (1909), Saki

"The Gambler Bobok" (1873), Vladimir Odoevsky

The Garden of Survival (1918), Algernon Blackwood

Gaston de Blondeville (1802), Ann Radcliffe

Gaywyck (2000), Vincent Virga

Gem of the Ocean (2003), August Wilson

A General History of the Robberies and Murders of the Most Notorious Pyrates (1724, 1728), Charles Johnson

The Gentle Shepherd (1790), Margaret Turner

George Geith of Fen Court (1864), Charlotte Cowan Riddell

Gerard; or, The World, the Flesh and the Devil (1891), Mary Elizabeth Braddon

Getting Out (1977), Marsha Norman

"The Ghost and the Bone-Setter" (1838), Sheridan Le Fanu

Ghost Book (1926), Cynthia Charteris Asquith

Ghost Kisses (1994), Gregory L. Norris

The Ghost of Jerry Bundler (1899), W. W. Jacobs

"Ghost Rental" (1874), Henry James

Ghosts (1937), Edith Wharton

Ghost Stories of an Antiquary (1904), M. R. James

Ghost Story (1979), Peter Straub

Giants in the Earth (1927), Ole Edvart Rölvaag

The Giaour (1813), Lord Byron

"Gimpel the Fool" (1957), Isaac Bashevis Singer

The Girl in a Swing (1980), Richard Adams

"Glenallan" (1826), Edward Bulwer-Lytton

Glenarvon (1816), Caroline Lamb

The Goblin Market (1862), Christina Rossetti

"The Gold Bug" (1843), Edgar Allan Poe

"The Golden Apples" (1949), Eudora Welty

The Golden Bowl (1904), Henry James

"The Golem" (1982), Isaac Bashevis Singer

The Good Apprentice (1985), Iris Murdoch

"Good Country People" (1955), Flannery O'Connor

The Good Earth (1931), Pearl Buck

"A Good Man Is Hard to Find" (1955), Flannery O'Connor

Gormenghast (1950), Mervyn Peake

Götz von Berlichingen [Goetz with the Iron Hand] (1773), Johann Wolfgang von Goethe

The Grandissimes: A Story of Creole Life (1879), George Washington Cable

The Grass Harp (1951), Truman Capote

"The Grave" (1743), Robert Blair

"Gray Wolf's Ha'nt" (1899), Charles Chesnutt

"The Great Cat's Tale" (1932), Karel Capek

Great Expectations (1861), Charles Dickens

Greater Trumps (1932), Charles Williams

The Great God Pan (1894), Arthur Machen

The Green Hand and Other Ghostly Tales from Around the World (1996), Joel Ben Izzy

The Green Knight (1993), Iris Murdoch

The Green Man (1969), Kingsley Amis

The Green Mile (1996), Stephen King

Grendel (1971), John Gardner

Grimms' Fairy Tales (1827), George Cruikshank

"The Grove of Ashtaroth" (1912), John Buchan

"Guests" (1923), Saki

Guilty; or Not Guilty; or, A Lesson for Husbands: A Tale (1822), Anne of Swansea

Guy Mannering (1815), Sir Walter Scott

"Haircut" (1954), W. Ring Lardner

Hamel, the Obeah Man (1827), anonymous

A Handful of Dust (1934), Evelyn Waugh

Han d'Islande (1823), Victor Hugo

The Handmaid's Tale (1985), Margaret Atwood

The Happy Prince and Other Tales (1888), Oscar Wilde

"The Harnt That Walks Chilhowee" (1884), Mary Noailles Murfree

Harvest Home (1973), Thomas Tryon

"The Hashish-Eater" (1922), Clark Ashton Smith

"The Haunted and the Haunters; or, The House and the Brain" (1857), Edward Bulwer-Lytton

"The Haunted Beach" (1800), Mary Robinson

The Haunted Cavern: A Caledonian Tale (1796), John Palmer

"The Haunted House" (1859), Charles Dickens

"The Haunted Subaltern" (1897), Rudyard Kipling

"The Haunted Valley" (1871), Ambrose Bierce

The Haunting of Hill House (1959), Shirley Jackson

"The Headless Hawk" (1949), Truman Capote

Heart and Science (1883), Wilkie Collins

The Heart Is a Lonely Hunter (1941), Carson McCullers

Heart of Darkness (1902), Joseph Conrad

"Henry Fitzowen—A Gothic Tale" (n.d.), Nathan Drake

Heroes and Villains (1969), Angela Carter

Hieroglyphic Tales (1785), Horace Walpole

The Highwayman (1907), Alfred Noyes

High Spirits (1982), Robertson Davies

Histoire de Cleveland [The story of Cleveland] (1731–39), Abbé Prévost

Histoires Grotesques et Sérieuses [Grotesque and serious tales] (1865), Charles Baudelaire

Historia Universal de la Infamia [A Universal History of Infamy] (1935), Jorge Luis Borges

Historia von Dr. Johan Fausten [The story of Dr. John Fausten] (1587), anonymous

The History of Charoba, Queen of Egypt (1785), Clara Reeve

The History of Nourjahad (1767), Frances Sheridan

The History of Rasselas, Prince of Abissinia (1759), Samuel Johnson

The History of the Remarkable Life of John Sheppard (1724), anonymous

The Hobbit (1937), J. R. R. Tolkien

"Hodmadod" (1933), Walter de la Mare

"The Hollow of the Three Hills" (1830), Nathaniel Hawthorne

"The Honeymoon of Mrs. Smith" (1997), Shirley Jackson

Horizon (1871), Augustin Daly

Horrid Mysteries (1757), Karl Grosse

Horrid Mysteries: A Story from the German of the Marquis of Grosse (1796), Peter Will

Hotel Transylvania (1978), Chelsea Quinn Yarbro

The Hound of Death (1933), Agatha Christie

The Hound of the Baskervilles (1902), Sir Arthur Conan Doyle

The House by the Churchyard (1861–62), Sheridan Le Fanu

House of Aspen (1799), Sir Walter Scott

The House of Mirth (1905), Edith Wharton

The House of Pomegranates (1891), Oscar Wilde

The House of the Seven Gables (1851), Nathaniel Hawthorne

The House of the Spirits (1981), Isabel Allende

The House on the Strand (1969), Daphne du Maurier

The Houses of Osma and Almeria; or, Convent of St. Ildefonso (1810), Regina Roche

"How Love Came to Professor Guildea" (1900), Robert Smythe Hichens

"Hughes, the Wehr-Wolf" (1838), Sutherland Menzies

The Human Chord (1910), Algernon Blackwood

"The Human Seasons" (1819), John Keats

The Hundred Secret Senses (1995), Amy Tan

I, Claudius (1934), Robert Graves

"The Idiot Boy" (1830), Margaret Northampton

"The Idiot" (1908), Joseph Conrad

Idlefonzo and Alberoni; or, Tales of Horror (1803), anonymous

I Heard the Owl Call My Name (1973), Margaret Craven

The Illustrated Man (1951), Ray Bradbury

The Impenetrable Secret (1805), Francis Lathom

"Imp of the Perverse" (1845), Edgar Allan Poe

In a Glass Darkly (1872), Sheridan Le Fanu

In Cold Blood (1966), Truman Capote

"Indian Woman's Death-Song" (1828), Felicia Hemans

"The Inexperienced Ghost" (1903), H. G. Wells

The Infernal Desire Machines of Doctor Hoffman (1972), Angela Carter

In Ghostly Japan (1899), Lafcadio Hearn

Inkle and Yarico; or, Love in a Cave (1805), Sarah Wilkinson

The Innocence of Father Brown (1911), Gilbert Keith Chesterton

Innocent Eréndira and Other Stories (1972), Gabriel García Márquez

Insomnia (1882), James Thomson

Interview with the Vampire (1976), Anne Rice

"In the Avu Observatory" (1894), H. G. Wells

Intruder in the Dust (1948), William Faulkner

"The Invisible Eye" (1849), Émile Erckmann and Louis Alexandre Chatrian

Invocation to Misery (1818), Percy Bysshe Shelley

"In Youth I Have Known One" (1827), Edgar Allan Poe

I, Robot (1950), Isaac Asimov

"The Iron Shroud" (1830), William Mudford

The Island of Dr. Moreau (1896), H. G. Wells

"Isle of Voices" (1893), Robert Louis Stevenson

The Italian (1797), Ann Radcliffe

The Italian Monk (1796), James Boaden

Italian Mysteries (1820), Francis Lathom

Ivanhoe (1819), Sir Walter Scott

Ivy Castle; or, The Eve of St. Agnes (n.d.), Sarah Wilkinson

Jack Sheppard (1839), William Harrison Ainsworth

Jackson's Dilemma (1995), Iris Murdoch

Jamaica Inn (1936), Daphne du Maurier

Jane Eyre (1847), Charlotte Brontë

Jane Eyre; or, The Secrets of Thornfield Hall (1849), John Courtney

"Jean-ah Poquelin" (1875), George Washington Cable

"Jerry Bundler" (1897), W. W. Jacobs

Jettature (1857), Théophile Gautier

The Jewel of Seven Stars (1904), Bram Stoker

"The Jewish Maiden" (1856), Hans Christian Andersen

"The Jilting of Granny Weatherall" (1930), Katherine Anne Porter

"Jiu-Roku-Zakura" (1904), Lafcadio Hearn

Joe Turner's Come and Gone (1988), August Wilson

John Marchmont's Legacy (1863), Mary Elizabeth Braddon

"The Jolly Corner" (1908), Henry James

Jonathan Wild (1743), Daniel Defoe

"Jordan's End" (1923), Ellen Glasgow

Julia of Louvain; or, Monkish Cruelty (1797), J. C. Cross

Juliette (1796), Marquis de Sade

Just an Ordinary Day (1996), Shirley Jackson

Justine (1801), Marquis de Sade

The Kadaitcha Sung (1990), Sam Watson

Kamouraska (1970), Anne Hébert

Karma (1918), Algernon Blackwood

Kidnapped (1886), Robert Louis Stevenson

Kincaid's Battery (1908), George Washington Cable

Kinder- und Hausmärchen [Children's and household tales] (1812, 1815, 1822), Grimm Brothers

Kindred (1979), Octavia Butler

King Hedley II (1999), August Wilson

"King Pest the First: A Tale Containing an Allegory" (1835), Edgar Allan Poe

Kirch-hof Gedanchen [Graveyard thoughts] (ca. 1650), Andreas Gryphius

Kirkland Revels (1962), Victoria Holt

The Kitchen God's Wife (1991), Amy Tan

Klosterheim (1832), Thomas De Quincey

Koenigsmark the Robber; or, The Terror of Bohemia (1801), H. J. Sarratt

Konjaku Monogatari [Tales of Times Now Past] (ca. 1130), anonymous

"Kruitzner, the German's Tale" (1797), Harriet Lee

"Kubla Khan" (1816), Samuel Taylor Coleridge

Kwaidan [Weird Tales] (1904), Lafcadio Hearn

"La Barbe Bleue" [Bluebeard] (1697), Charles Perrault

Là-Bas [Down There] (1891), Joris-Karl Huysmans

"La Belle Dame sans Merci" (1819), John Keats

"La Cafétière" [The coffee machine] (1831), Théophile Gautier

"La Chevelure" (The gold braid) (1884), Guy de Maupassant

La Comédie de la Mort [The comedy of death] (1838), Théophile Gautier

La Confession (1830), Jules Janin

Lady Audley's Secret (1862), Mary Elizabeth Braddon

"Lady Lazarus" (1963), Sylvia Plath

The Lady of Avalon (1997), Marion Zimmer Bradley

The Lady of the Shroud (1909), Bram Stoker

"The Lady's Maid's Bell" (1910), Edith Wharton

The Lady's Mile (1866), Mary Elizabeth Braddon

The Lair of the White Worm (1911), Bram Stoker

La Jeune Ameriquaine, et les Contes Marins [The young American and the sea stories] (1740), Gabrielle-Suzanne de Villeneuve

Lalla Rookh (1817), Thomas Moore

"La Llorona" (1987), Joe Hayes

"La Llorona" (1996), Yxta Maya Murray

La Llorona Legend (1984), Rudolfo A. Anaya

"La Main" [The hand] (1883), Guy de Maupassant

"La Main d'Ecorche" [The flayed hand] (1875), Guy de Maupassant

Lamia (1819), John Keats

"La Morte" [The Dead] (1887), Guy de Maupassant

La Morte Amoreuse [The dead lover] (1836), Théophile Gautier

The Lancashire Witches: A Romance of Pendle Forest (1849), William Harrison Ainsworth

The Land Beyond the Forest (1888), Emily de Laszkowska Gerard

L'Ane Mort et la Femme Guillotinée [The dead donkey and the guillotined woman] (1829), Jules Janin

"La Nuit" [The night] (1887), Guy de Maupassant

"Lara" (1814), Lord Byron

"Las Bagbas del Diablo" [The devil's spit] (1959), Julio Cortázar

Lasher (1994), Anne Rice

"The Last Judgment" (1929), Karel Čapek

The Last of the Lowries (1920), Paul Green

The Last of the Mohicans (1826), James Fenimore Cooper

"The Last of the Valerii" (1874), Henry James

La Ville-Vampire [Vampire city] (1875), Paul Féval

The Law and the Lady (1875), Wilkie Collins

The Lay of the Last Minstrel (1805), Sir Walter Scott

The Leaf Storm (1955), Gabriel García Márquez

Le Cimetière de la Madeleine [The graveyard of the Church of the Madeleine] (1800), J. F. Regnault-Warin

Le Comte de Comminges [The count of Comminges] (1764), François Baculard d'Arnaud

Le Crime d'Orcival [The Crime at Orcival] (1867), Émile Gaboriau

"Le Dernier Jour d'un Condamné" [The last day of a condemned man] (1829), Jules Janin

Le Diable Amoreux [The Devil in Love] (1772), Jacques Cazotte

"The Legend of Sleepy Hollow" (1820), Washington Irving

Legends of Terror! And Tales of the Wonderful and Wild (1840), G. Creed

"Le Horla, or Modern Ghosts" (1887), Guy de Maupassant

"Leixlip Castle: An Irish Family Legend" (1825), Charles Robert Maturin

Le Juif Errant [The Wandering Jew] (1844), Eugène Sue

Le Meneur des Loups [The Wolf-Leader] (1857), Alexandre Dumas père

Le Mystère de la Chambre Jaune [The Mystery of the Yellow Room] (1907), Gaston Leroux

"Lenore" (1831), Edgar Allan Poe

Le Parfum de la Dame en Noir [The fragrance of the lady in black] (1909), Gaston Leroux

Le Peau de Chagrin [The Fatal Skin] (1831), Honoré de Balzac

Les Anciens Canadiens [The Canadians of Old] (1863), Philippe-Aubert de Gaspé the Elder

Les Catacombes (1839), Jules Janin

Les Cenci (1935), Antonin Artaud

Les Crimes de l'Amour [The Crimes of Love] (1788), Marquis de Sade

Les Enfants du Sabbat [Children of the Black Sabbath] (1975), Anne Hébert

Les Esclaves de Paris [The keys of Paris] (1869), Émile Gaboriau

Les Fleurs du Mal [The Flowers of Evil] (1857), Charles Baudelaire

Maria Marten; or, The Murder in the Red Barn (1830), anonymous

Maria; or, The Wrongs of Women (1798), Mary Wollstonecraft

"Markheim" (1887), Robert Louis Stevenson

"The Mark of the Beast" (1891), Rudyard Kipling

Marmion, a Tale of Flodden Field (1807), Sir Walter Scott

"The Marsh King's Daughter" (1858), Hans Christian Andersen

"Mars Jeems's Nightmare" (1899), Charles Chesnutt

Mary Barton (1848), Elizabeth Gaskell

Mary, Maid of the Inn (1820), anonymous

The Mask of Dimitrios (1939), Eric Ambler

"The Masque of the Red Death" (1842), Edgar Allan Poe

The Master of Ballantrae (1889), Robert Louis Stevenson

Matrosengeschichten [Sailor stories] (1884), Karl Heinrich Ulrichs

Meditations among the Tombs (1745–47), James Hervey

Melmoth Reconcilié à l'Eglise [Melmoth reconciled to the church] (1892), Honoré de Balzac

Melmoth the Wanderer (1820), Charles Robert Maturin

Memnoch the Devil (1995), Anne Rice

Mémoires d'un Homme de Qualité [Memoirs of a man of quality] (1728–31), Abbé Prévost

Memoirs of Sherlock Holmes (1894), Sir Arthur Conan Doyle

Memoirs of Sir Roger de Clarendon (1793), Clara Reeve

Mephisto Waltz (1968), Fred Mustard Stewart

Merrick (2000), Anne Rice

"The Mesmeric Revelation" (1844), Edgar Allan Poe

The Messiah (1773), Friedrich Gottlieb Klopstock

"Metempsychosis" (1826), Robert Macnish

"Metzengerstein" (1832), Edgar Allan Poe

The Midnight Assassin; or, the Confessions of the Monk Rinaldi (1802), anonymous

The Midnight Bell: A German Story, Founded on Incidents in Real Life (1798), Francis Lathom

The Midnight Bell; or, The Abbey of St. Francis (1811), anonymous

The Milesian Chief (1812), Charles Robert Maturin

"Mimi-Nashi-Hoichi" (1904), Lafcadio Hearn

"The Minister's Black Veil" (1837), Nathaniel Hawthorne

Mirgorod (1835), Nikolai Gogol

Misery (1987), Stephen King

The Misfortunes of Elphin (1829), Thomas Love Peacock

The Missionary (1811), Sydney Owenson

"Miss Jemima" (1925), Walter de la Mare

Mistress of Mellyn (1960), Victoria Holt

The Mists of Avalon (1982), Marion Zimmer Bradley

"M. L." (1863), Louisa May Alcott

Moby Dick (1851), Herman Melville

A Modern Mephistopheles (1877), Louisa May Alcott

"Moiron" (1887), Guy de Maupassant

Moll Flanders (1722), Daniel Defoe

The Monastery (1820), Sir Walter Scott

Monastery of St. Colomb; or, The Atonement, a Novel (1813), Regina Roche

The Monk (1796), Matthew Gregory Lewis

The Monk and the Hangman's Daughter (1892), Ambrose Bierce

Monkcliffe Abbey (1805), Sarah Wilkinson

"The Monkey" (1934), Isak Dinesen

"The Monkey's Paw" (1902), W. W. Jacobs

The Monk Knight of St. John: A Tale of the Crusaders (1850), John Richardson

The Monk of Horror (1798), anonymous

"The Monks of St. Mark" (1804), Thomas Love Peacock

"Monos and Daimonos" (1830), Edward Bulwer-Lytton

Monsieur Lecoq (1869), Émile Gaboriau

"The Monster" (1898), Stephen Crane

Montalbert (1795), Charlotte Smith

"Montmorenci, a Fragment" (1798), Nathan Drake

"Morella" (1835), Edgar Allan Poe

"The Mortal Immortal, A Tale" (1833), Mary Wollstonecraft Shelley

The Moth and Other Stories (1995), Helena Maria Viramontes

The Mountain Cottager; or, The Deserted Bride (1805), Sarah Wilkinson

The Mousetrap (1952), Agatha Christie

Mrs. Halliburton's Troubles (1862), Ellen Wood

"MS. Found in a Bottle" (1833), Edgar Allan Poe

"The Mummy's Foot" (1863), Théophile Gautier

"The Murderer's Violin" (1876), Émile Erckmann and Louis Alexandre Chatrian

"My Contraband" (1863), Louisa May Alcott

"My Kinsman, Major Molineux" (1851), Nathaniel Hawthorne

"My Own True Ghost Story" (1888), Rudyard Kipling

"My Sister's Sleep" (1847), Dante Gabriel Rossetti

"My Soul Is Dark" (1815), Lord Byron

The Mysteries of London (1844–48), George Reynolds

The Mysteries of Paris (1842–43), Eugène Sue

The Mysteries of the Court of London (1848–53), George Reynolds

The Mysteries of Udolpho (1794), Ann Radcliffe

The Mysterious Bride; or, The Statue Spectre (ca. 1800), anonymous

The Mysterious Freebooter (1806), Francis Lathom

The Mysterious Marriage; or, The Heirship of Roselva (1798), Harriet Lee

The Mysterious Mother (1768), Horace Walpole

The Mysterious Novice; or, Convent of the Grey Penitents (1809), Sarah Wilkinson

The Mysterious Spaniard; or, The Ruins of St. Luke's Abbey (1807), anonymous

The Mysterious Stranger (1916), Mark Twain

The Mysterious Warning (1796), Eliza Parsons

Mystery (1800), Francis Lathom

The Mystery of Cloomber (1889), Sir Arthur Conan Doyle

The Mystery of Major Molineux (1881), Marcus Clarke

"The Mystery of Marie Rogêt" (1842), Edgar Allan Poe

"The Mystery of Sassassa Valley" (1879), Sir Arthur Conan Doyle

The Mystery of the Black Tower (1796), John Palmer

Mystic Events (1830), Francis Lathom

Nachtmahr [Nightmare] (1922), Hanns Heinz Ewers

Nachtstücke (Strange Stories) (1817), E. T. A. Hoffmann

The Name of the Rose (1980), Umberto Eco

The Narrative of All the Robberies, Escapes etc. of John Sheppard (1724), anonymous

The Narrative of Arthur Gordon Pym (1838), Edgar Allan Poe

The Natural (1952), Bernard Malamud

The Natural Daughter (1799), Mary Robinson

The Necromancer: A Romance (1851–52), George Reynolds

The Necromancer; or, The Tale of the Black Forest (1794), Peter Teuthold

Neue Volksmärchen der Deutschen [New German folk tales] (1789–93), Benedikte Naubert and Johann Mathias Müller

"Never Bet the Devil Your Head: A Tale with a Moral" (1841), Edgar Allan Poe

"The Nevsky Prospect" (1835), Nikolai Gogol

The New Arabian Nights (1882), Robert Louis Stevenson

The New Magdalen (1873), Wilkie Collins

"The New Melusina" (1826), Johann Wolfgang von Goethe

New Tales (1819), Sarah Wilkinson

New Tales of the Cthulhu Mythos (1980), John Ramsey Campbell

The New Terror (1926), Gaston Leroux

Nick of the Woods (1837), Robert Montgomery Bird

"Night and Morning" (1845), Edward Bulwer-Lytton

"The Nightingale and the Rose" (1888), Oscar Wilde

Nightmare Abbey (1818), Thomas Love Peacock

Nightmares & Dreamscapes (1993), Stephen King

'night, Mother (1982), Marsha Norman

The Night of the Hunter (1953), Davis Alexander Grubb

"A Night Piece on Death" (1721), Thomas Parnell

Nights at the Circus (1984), Angela Carter

"Night-Thoughts" (1742), Edward Young

Night Watches (1914), W. W. Jacobs

Nightwood (1930), Djuna Barnes

Nikolai Klimii Subterraneum [The subterranean voyage of Nicholas Klimm] (1741), Ludwig Holberg

"Nis and the Dame" (1868), Hans Christian Andersen

The Nocturnal Visit; or, The Mysterious Husband (ca. 1800), Regina Roche

"Noon Wine" (1936), Katherine Anne Porter

Northanger Abbey (1818), Jane Austen

"The Nose" (1835), Nikolai Gogol

Not After Midnight (1970), Daphne du Maurier

Notting Hill Mystery (1862–63), Charles Felix

Nouveaux Contes Cruels [New cruel tales] (1888), Villiers de L'Isle-Adam

Nouvelles Histoires Extraordinaires [New extraordinary tales] (1857), Charles Baudelaire

The Nun's Picture (1834), Regina Roche

Nussknacker und Mausekönig [Nutcracker and Mouseking] (1816), E. T. A. Hoffmann

Obake! Tales of Spirits Past and Present (1991), Brenda Wong Aoki

"An Occurrence at Owl Creek Bridge" (1891), Ambrose Bierce

The Octoroon, or Life in Louisiana (1859), Dionysius Boucicault

The Octoroon; or, The Lily of Louisiana (1861–62), Mary Elizabeth Braddon

"Ode to Evening" (1746), William Taylor Collins

"Ode to Fear" (1741), William Taylor Collins

Of Love and Shadows (1987), Isabel Allende

"Olalla" (1887), Robert Louis Stevenson

"Old Chevalier" (1934), Isak Dinesen

The Old English Baron (1778), Clara Reeve

"The Old Grave-Stone" (1852), Hans Christian Andersen

The Old Manor House (1793), Charlotte Smith

"The Old Nurse's Story" (1852), Elizabeth Gaskell

The Old Tower of Frankenstein (n.d.), anonymous

Omoo (1847), Herman Melville

"Omphale" (1834), Théophile Gautier

One Hundred Years of Solitude (1967), Gabriel García Márquez

The One-Pound Note and Other Tales (1820), Francis Lathom

"The One Who Saw" (1931), Alfred McLelland Burrage

"On the Pleasure Derived from Objects of Terror, with Sir Bertrand" (1773), Anna Laetitia Barbauld

"The Open Door" (1881), Margaret Oliphant

Ormond (1799), Charles Brockden Brown

Oroonoko (1688), Aphra Behn

Orphan of the Rhine: A Romance (1798), Eleanor Sleath

Orra: A Tragedy (1812), Joanna Baillie

Oscar and Lucinda (1988), Peter Carey

"Oshidori" (1904), Lafcadio Hearn
"The Ostler" (1855), Wilkie Collins
"O-Tei" (1904), Lafcadio Hearn
The Other Room (1896), Henry James
The Other Side of the Mirror (1961), Enrique Anderson Imbert
Other Voices, Other Rooms (1948), Truman Capote
"Our Gardener" (1977), Jean Rhys
"Out of Depth" (1933), Evelyn Waugh
"Out of the Deep" (1923), Walter de la Mare
"The Oval Portrait" (1842), Edgar Allan Poe
The Ox-Bow Incident (1940), Walter Van Tilburg Clark
"Palmyra" (1812), Thomas Love Peacock
"The Paradise of Bachelors and the Tartarus of Maids" (1855), Herman Melville
The Pardoner's Tale (ca. 1385), Geoffrey Chaucer
The Pastor's Fireside (1817), Jane Porter
The Pathfinder (1840), James Fenimore Cooper
Paul Clifford (1830), Edward Bulwer-Lytton
Paul Ferroll (1855), Caroline Clive
Pauline's Passion and Punishment (1862), Louisa May Alcott
Pauliska, ou La Perversité Moderne [Pauliska, or modern perversity] (1796), Reveroni Saint-Cyr
Pedro Páramo (1955), Juan Rulfo
Pelham (1828), Edward Bulwer-Lytton
The Periodic Table (1987), Primo Levi
The Persecution and Assassination of Marat as Performed by the Inmates of the Asylum of Charenton under the Direction of the Marquis de Sade (1964), Peter Weiss
"The Pestilence" (1793), Philip Freneau
"The Petrified Man" (1941), Eudora Welty
Pet Sematary (1988), Stephen King
Phantasiestücke in Callots Manier [Fantasy pieces in the style of Callot] (1815), E. T. A. Hoffmann
Phantasus [Apparition] (1822), Johann Ludwig Tieck
Phantom (1990), Susan Kay
The Phantom of the Opera (1910), Gaston Leroux
The Phantom of the Opera (1986), Andrew Lloyd Webber
"The Phantom Rickshaw" (1888), Rudyard Kipling
"Phantoms" (1864), Ivan Turgenev
Phantoms (1983), Dean Koontz
Phantoms of the Cloister; or, The Mysterious Manuscript (1795), anonymous
The Piano Lesson (1990), August Wilson
Pickwick Papers (1837), Charles Dickens
The Picture of Dorian Gray (1891), Oscar Wilde
The Picture of Palermo (1799), Mary Robinson
"The Pillar of Salt" (1949), Shirley Jackson
The Pirate (1822), Sir Walter Scott
The Place of the Lion (1931), Charles Williams
"The Plattner Story" (1896), H. G. Wells

"Poem on the Inhumanity of the Slave Trade" (1788), Ellen Wood
"Poison" (1953), Roald Dahl
The Polish Bandit (1824), Francis Lathom
The Polish Romance (n.d.), Sarah Wilkinson
"Pollock and the Porroh Man" (1897), H. G. Wells
"The Pomegranate Seed" (1912), Edith Wharton
The Poor Fool (1930), Erskine Caldwell
The Poor of New York (1857), Dionysius Boucicault
Pope Joan (1996), Donna Cross
"The Portrait" (1835), Nikolai Gogol
"The Portrait" (1847), Dante Gabriel Rossetti
The Portrait of a Lady (1881), Henry James
"Po' Sandy" (1899), Charles Chesnutt
"The Possessed One" (1831), anonymous
"The Pot of Tulips" (1855), Fitz-James O'Brien
Pour la Patrie [For My Country] (1895), Jules-Paul Tardivel
"Powerhouse" (1941), Eudora Welty
"Premonition" (1994), Joyce Carol Oates
The Priory of St. Bernard (1789), Martha Harley
"The Prisoner of Chillon" (1816), Lord Byron
"A Private Life" (1892), Henry James
The Private Memoirs and Confessions of a Justified Sinner (1824), James Hogg
"Prometheus" (1816), Lord Byron
The Prophecy of Duncannon; or, The Dwarf and the Seer (1824), William Child Green
Pudd'nhead Wilson (1894), Mark Twain
"Punch and Judy" (1938), Frederick Ignatius Cowles
"The Punishment of Gina Montani" (1852), Ellen Wood
"The Purloined Letter" (1844), Edgar Allan Poe
The Quaker City; or, The Monks of Monk Hall (1845), George Lippard
The Queen of Spades (1834), Alexander Pushkin
The Queen of the Cold-Blooded Tales (1993), Roberta Brown
Queen of the Damned (1988), Anne Rice
"Quicksand" (1902), Edith Wharton
Rachel Dyer (1828), John Neal
"Rappaccini's Daughter" (1844), Nathaniel Hawthorne
"Rapunzel" (1858), William Morris
"Rashomon" (1915), Ryunosuke Akutagawa
"The Rats in the Walls" (1924), H. P. Lovecraft
"The Raven" (1844), Edgar Allan Poe
Rayland Hall (ca. 1810), anonymous
Rebecca (1938), Daphne du Maurier
The Recess; or, A Tale of Other Times (1783–85), Sophia Lee
"The Recluse" (1930), Walter de la Mare
"The Recrudescence of Imray" (1891), Rudyard Kipling
"The Red Room" (1896), H. G. Wells
"The Red Shoes" (1845), Hans Christian Andersen

Sir Edward Seaward's Narrative of His Shipwreck (1831), Jane Porter

"Sis' Becky's Pickaninny" (1899), Charles Chesnutt

"The Skater of Ghost Lake" (1933), William Rose Benét

The Skeleton Clutch; or, The Goblet of Gore (1842), Thomas Preskett Prest

"Skin Crawlers" (1993), Roberta Brown

Smarra; or, The Demons of the Night (1821), Charles Nodier

"Smith: An Episode in a Lodging House" (1906), Algernon Blackwood

The Snake's Pass (1890), Bram Stoker

"Snow White" (1845), Hans Christian Andersen

Soifs [Thirsts] (1995), Marie-Claire Blais

Solyman and Almena (1762), John Langhorne

Some Chinese Ghosts (1887), Lafcadio Hearn

Someone Like You (1953), Roald Dahl

Something Wicked This Way Comes (1962), Ray Bradbury

"Some Words with a Mummy" (1845), Edgar Allan Poe

"Song" (1848), Christina Rossetti

Song of Solomon (1977), Toni Morrison

The Son of Ethelwolf (1789), Anne Fuller

Sora No Kaibutsu Aguii [Agwhee the sky monster] (1964), Kenzaburo Oe

The Sorcerer's Palace; or, The Princess of Sinadone (1805), Sarah Wilkinson

The Sorrows of Satan (1895), Marie Corelli

The Soul of Lilith (1892), Marie Corelli

"The Spectre Bride" (1822), William Harrison Ainsworth

"The Spectre Bridegroom" (1820), Washington Irving

The Spectre Mother; or, The Haunted Tower (1864), anonymous

The Spectre of Lanmere Abbey (1820), Sarah Wilkinson

The Spectre; or, The Ruins of Belfont Priory (1806), Sarah Wilkinson

Spirite (1866), Théophile Gautier

"The Spirit's Return" (1830), Felicia Hemans

The Spy (1821), James Fenimore Cooper

The Squatter's Ward (1919), Edward Sorensen

"Sredni Vashtar" (1911), Saki

St. Irvyne; or, The Rosicrucian (1811), Percy Bysshe Shelley

St. Leon (1799), William Godwin

St. Margaret's Cave; or, The Nun's Story (1801), Elizabeth Helme

"The Stolen Body" (1903), H. G. Wells

Stories of the Seen and Unseen (1885), Margaret Oliphant

"The Story of a Disappearance and an Appearance" (1919), M. R. James

"The Story of Hester Malpas" (1833), Letitia Elizabeth Landon

"The Story-Teller" (1914), Saki

The Storyteller (1981), Leslie Marmon Silko

The Strange Manuscript Found in a Copper Cylinder (1888), James de Mille

"The Strange Ride of Morrowbie Jukes" (1888), Rudyard Kipling

"Strangers Pilgrims" (1926), Walter de la Mare

Strange Stories (1880), Émile Erckmann and Louis Alexandre Chatrian

A Strange Story (1861), Edward Bulwer-Lytton

"The Striding Place" (1896), Gertrude Atherton

The String of Pearls (1846), Thomas Preskett Prest

The String of Pearls: The Fiend of Fleet Street (1847), George Dibdin Pitt

Studies in Love and Terror (1913), Marie Adelaide Belloc Lowndes

Studies of Death (1894), Stanislaus Eric Stenbock

The Subterraneous Passage; or, Gothic Cell (1803), Sarah Wilkinson

Suddenly Last Summer (1958), Tennessee Williams

Sula (1973), Toni Morrison

"The Supper at Elsinore" (1934), Isak Dinesen

Suspiria de Profundis [Sighs from the depths] (1845), Thomas De Quincey

Sweeney Todd (1979), Stephen Sondheim

Sweeney Todd, the Demon Barber of Fleet Street (1848), Thomas Preskett Prest

Sweet Savage Love (1974), Rosemary Rogers

The Swimming Pool (1952), Mary Roberts Rinehart

"The Sylph" (1837), Vladimir Odoevsky

"Sylvia's Death" (1965), Anne Sexton

"A Tale for a Chimney Corner" (1819), Leigh Hunt

The Tale of the Body Thief (1992), Anne Rice

"The Tale of the Mysterious Mirror" (1828), Sir Walter Scott

A Tale of Two Cities (1859), Charles Dickens

Tales of a Traveller (1824), Sir Walter Scott

Tales of Men and Ghosts (1911), Edith Wharton

Tales of Moonlight and Rain (1971), Ueda Akinari

Tales of Superstition (ca. 1820), anonymous

Tales of the Glauber Spa (1832), William Cullen Bryant

Tales of Wonder (1801), Matthew Gregory Lewis

The Talisman (1825), Sir Walter Scott

Taltos: Lives of the Mayfair Witches (1994), Anne Rice

"Taming a Tartar" (1988), Louisa May Alcott

"The Tapestried Chamber" (1828), Sir Walter Scott

Tawny Rachel; or, The Fortune Teller (ca. 1795), anonymous

"The Temple" (1996), Joyce Carol Oates

Tent Meeting (1987), Larry Larson, Levi Lee, and Rebecca Wackler

Thaddeus of Warsaw (1803), Jane Porter

"Thanatopsis" (1817), William Cullen Bryant

The Thatched Cottage; or, Sorrows of Eugenia (1806),
  Sarah Wilkinson
"That Evening Sun" (1931), William Faulkner
Their Eyes Were Watching God (1937), Zora Neale
  Hurston
"There Will Come Soft Rains" (1950), Ray Bradbury
"The Thesaurus of Horror; or, The Charnel House
  Explored!" (1819), John Snart
"They" (1905), Rudyard Kipling
They Thirst (1981), Robert McCammon
The Thin Man (1932), Dashiell Hammett
Thirty Strange Stories (1897), H. G. Wells
"This Lime-Tree Bower My Prison" (1800), Samuel
  Taylor Coleridge
"Thou Art the Man" (1844), Edgar Allan Poe
Thoughts in Prison (1777), William Dodd
"Thrawn Janet" (1887), Robert Louis Stevenson
The Three Impostors (1895), Arthur Machen
"The Three Sisters" (1914), W. W. Jacobs
Three Times Dead; or, The Secret of the Heath (1860),
  Mary Elizabeth Braddon
Thunder Heights (1960), Phyllis Whitney
"The Tiger Skin" (1924), Violet Hunt
"The Tiger's Skin" (1902), W. W. Jacobs
Ti-Jean and His Brothers (1970), Derek Walcott
The Time Machine (1895), H. G. Wells
The Time of Angels (1966), Iris Murdoch
"The Tinder-Box" (1835), Hans Christian Andersen
Tituba of Salem Village (1964), Ann Petry
Titus Alone (1959), Mervyn Peake
Titus Groan (1946), Mervyn Peake
"Tobermory" (1911), Saki
To Kill a Mockingbird (1960), Harper Lee
"The Toll House" (1909), W. W. Jacobs
"The Tombless Epitaph" (ca. 1809), Samuel Taylor
  Coleridge
"The Tomb of Ilaria Giunigi" (1891), Edith Wharton
"The Tooth" (1949), Shirley Jackson
"The Torture of Hope" (1883), Villiers de L'Isle-Adam
"To Sir Toby" (1792), Philip Freneau
To Wake the Dead (1980), John Ramsey Campbell
The Tower of London (1840), William Harrison Ainsworth
The Tower; or, The Romance of Ruthyne (1798), Sarah
  Lansdell
The Tradition of the Castle; or, Scenes in the Emerald Isle
  (1824), Regina Roche
*The Tragical History of Jane Arnold, Commonly Called
  Crazy Jane; and Mr. Henry Percival; Giving an
  Account of Their Birth, Parentage, Courtship, and
  Melancholy End* (1817), Sarah Wilkinson
The Tragic Comedy or Comical Tragedy of Punch and Judy
  (1828), Payne Collier and George Cruikshank

Treasure Island (1883), Robert Louis Stevenson
"The Trial for Murder" (1865), Charles Dickens
Trilby (1894), George du Maurier
A True and Genuine Account of the Late Jonathan Wild
  (1725), anonymous
A True Story of the Vampire (1894), Stanislaus Eric
  Stenbock
"The Truth about Pyecraft" (1903), H. G. Wells
The Turn of the Screw (1898), Henry James
2001: A Space Odyssey (1968), Arthur C. Clarke
Two Trains Running (1991), August Wilson
Typee (1846), Herman Melville
Ubu Roi [King Ubu] (1896), Alfred Jarry
"The Ugly Duckling" (1844), Hans Christian Andersen
Ugolino (1768), Heinrich Wilhelm von Gerstenberg
"Ulalume" (1847), Edgar Allan Poe
Uncle Silas (1864), Sheridan Le Fanu
Uncle Tom's Cabin (1851–52), Harriet Beecher Stowe
The Underdogs (1914), Mariano Azuela
Under the Gaslight (1867), Augustin Daly
Undine (1811), Friedrich de la Motte Fouqué
"Une Larme du Diable" [The devil's tear] (1839),
  Théophile Gautier
*Une Saison dans la Vie d'Emmanuel [A Season in the Life
  of Emmanuel]* (1965), Marie-Claire Blais
Une Saison en Enfer [A Season in Hell] (1873), Arthur
  Rimbaud
"The Unholy Compact Abjured" (1825), Charles
  Pigault-Lebrun
The Unicorn (1963), Iris Murdoch
The Unknown (1808), Francis Lathom
"Un Voyage à Cythère" [A voyage to Cythera] (1869),
  Charles Baudelaire
Vampir (1921), Hanns Heinz Ewers
The Vampire (1852), Dionysius Boucicault
"The Vampire" (2001), Joyce Carol Oates
The Vampire Armand (2000), Anne Rice
The Vampire Lestat (1985), Anne Rice
The Vampire; or, The Bride of the Isles (1820), James
  Robinson Planché
"The Vampyre" (1819), John Polidori
Vancenza; or, The Dangers of Credulity (1792), Mary
  Robinson
Varney the Vampyre, or, The Feast of Blood (1847),
  anonymous
Vathek (1782), William Beckford
"The Veldt" (1950), Ray Bradbury
Vendetta!; or, The Story of One Forgotten (1886), Marie
  Corelli
"The Vengeance of Nitocris" (1928), Tennessee
  Williams
Very Strange, But True (1803), Francis Lathom

The Victim of Seduction (1790), anonymous

Vile Bodies (1930), Evelyn Waugh

Villette (1853), Charlotte Brontë

The Violent Bear It Away (1960), Flannery O'Connor

The Violin (1997), Anne Rice

"The Virtuoso's Collection" (1846), Nathaniel Hawthorne

The Vision (1925), William Butler Yeats

The Vision of Mirza (1711), Joseph Addison

"Viy" (1835), Nikolai Gogol

The Vizard Mask (1994), Diana Norman

Volksmaerchen der Deutschen [German folk tales] (1782–87), Karl August Musäus

Volksmärchen [Folktales] (1797), Johann Ludwig Tieck

Wacousta; or, The Prophecy: A Tale of the Canadas (1832), John Richardson

Wagner the Wehr-Wolf (1847), George W. M. Reynolds

"Wake Not the Dead" (1800), Johann Ludwig Tieck

"The Wall" (1939), Jean-Paul Sartre

"The Wandering Jew" (1921), Edwin Arlington Robinson

The Wandering Jew; or, The Victim of the Eternal Avenger (1810), Percy Bysshe Shelley

The Wanderings of Warwick (1794), Charlotte Smith

The Wandering Spirit (1802), anonymous

Warbeck, a Pathetic Tale (1786), Sophia Lee

The War in Heaven (1930), Charles Williams

Watership Down (1972), Richard Adams

"The Water Spectre" (1809), Francis Lathom

The Wedding Dress (2002), Virginia Renfro Ellis

We Have Always Lived in the Castle (1962), Shirley Jackson

"Welcome Death!" (1743), Edward Young

"The Wendigo" (1910), Algernon Blackwood

"The Werewolf" (1995), Angela Carter

What Dreams May Come (1888), Gertrude Atherton

"What Dreams May Come" (1936), Walter de la Mare

"What Was It?" (1859), Fitz-James O'Brien

"When I Have Fears" (1818), John Keats

Where Are the Children? (1975), Mary Higgins Clark

"Where Are You Going, Where Have You Been?" (1970), Joyce Carol Oates

The Whitechapel Murders; or, On the Track of the Fiend (1898), Detective Warren

The White Cottage of the Valley; or, The Mysterious Husband (ca. 1810), Sarah Wilkinson

The White Morning (1918), Gertrude Atherton

"The White Wolf of the Hartz Mountains" (1839), Frederick Marryat

"Why I Live at the P.O." (1941), Eudora Welty

Why Paul Ferroll Killed His Wife (1860), Caroline Clive

Wide Sargasso Sea (1966), Jean Rhys

Wieland (1798), Charles Brockden Brown

Wild Geese (1925), Martha Ostenso

"William Wilson" (1839), Edgar Allan Poe

"The Willows" (1907), Algernon Blackwood

The Window at the White Cat (1910), Mary Roberts Rinehart

Windsor Castle (1848), William Harrison Ainsworth

The Winged Bull (1935), Dion Fortune

Wings of the Dove (1902), Henry James

Wise Blood (1952), Flannery O'Connor

Wit (1999), Margaret Edson

The Witches of Eastwick (1984), John Updike

"The Witches of Traquair" (1828), James Hogg

The Witching Hour (1990), Anne Rice

The Witch of Fife (1813), James Hogg

The Witch of Ravensworth (1808), George Brewey

"Without Benefit of Clergy" (1891), Rudyard Kipling

The Wolf and the Dove (1974), Kathleen Woodiwiss

Wolfen (1978), Whitley Strieber

Woman Hollering Creek and Other Stories (1991), Sandra Cisneros

The Woman in Black (1983), Susan Hill

The Woman in Black (1989), Stephen Mallatratt

The Woman in White (1860), Wilkie Collins

Woman on the Edge of Time (1979), Marge Piercy

The Woman Warrior (1975), Maxine Hong Kingston

"Wondersmith" (1859), Fitz-James O'Brien

"The Worn Path" (1941), Eudora Welty

Woven on the Loom of Time (1990), Enrique Anderson Imbert

Wuthering Heights (1847), Emily Brontë

Wylder's Hand (1864), Sheridan Le Fanu

"The Yellow Wallpaper" (1892), Charlotte Perkins Gilman

The Yemassee (1835), William Gilmore Simms

"You Are Now Entering the Human Heart" (1983), Janet Frame

"Young Goodman Brown" (1835), Nathaniel Hawthorne

"The Young Visitor" (1989), Mary Roberts Rinehart

Zanoni (1842), Edward Bulwer-Lytton

Zastrozzi: A Romance (1810), Percy Bysshe Shelley

Ziska: The Problem of a Wicked Soul (1897), Marie Corelli

Zittaw the Cruel; or The Woodsman's Daughter (n.d.), Sarah Wilkinson

Zofloya, or The Moor (1806), Charlotte Dacre

The Zombie (1995), Joyce Carol Oates

Major Authors of Gothic Literature and Their Works

RICHARD ADAMS
The Girl in a Swing (1980)
Watership Down (1972)

JOSEPH ADDISON
The Vision of Mirza (1711)

WILLIAM HARRISON AINSWORTH
Auriol; or, The Elixir of Life (1846)
Jack Sheppard (1839)
The Lancashire Witches: A Romance of Pendle Forest (1849)
Rookwood (1834)
"The Spectre Bride" (1822)
The Tower of London (1840)
Windsor Castle (1848)

UEDA AKINARI
Tales of Moonlight and Rain (1971)

RYUNOSUKE AKUTAGAWA
"Rashomon" (1915)

LOUISA MAY ALCOTT
Behind a Mask (1875)
The Long Fatal Love Chase (1866)
The Marble Woman (1865)
"M. L." (1863)
A Modern Mephistopheles (1877)
"My Contraband" (1863)
Pauline's Passion and Punishment (1862)
"Taming a Tartar" (1988)

ISABEL ALLENDE
Eva Luna (1987)
The House of the Spirits (1981)
Of Love and Shadows (1987)

ERIC AMBLER
The Mask of Dimitrios (1939)

KINGSLEY AMIS
The Green Man (1969)

RUDOLFO ANAYA
Bless Me, Ultima (1972)
La Llorona Legend (1984)

HANS CHRISTIAN ANDERSEN
"The Almshouse Window" (1847)
"Big Claus and Little Claus" (1835)
"The Cripple" (1872)
"The Fir Tree" (1845)
"The Jewish Maiden" (1856)
"The Little Match-Seller" (1846)
"The Little Mermaid" (1836)
"The Marsh King's Daughter" (1858)
"Nis and the Dame" (1868)
"The Old Grave-Stone" (1852)
"The Red Shoes" (1845)
"The Shadow" (1847)
"Snow White" (1845)
"The Tinder-Box" (1835)
"The Ugly Duckling" (1844)

ANNE OF SWANSEA
Chronicles of an Illustrious House (1816)
Deeds of Olden Times (1826)
Guilty; or Not Guilty; or, A Lesson for Husbands: A Tale (1822)

ANONYMOUS
An Account of the Conduct and Proceedings of the Late John Gow, Captain of the Late Pirates Executed for Murther and Piracy (1725)

The Animated Skeleton (1798)
The Astrologer's Prediction; or, The Maniac's Fate (1826)
"The Ballad of Gregorio Cortez" (1901)
The Black Forest; or, the Cavern of Horrors (1802)
"The Black Spider" (ca. 1798)
The Castle of St. Vallery (1792)
Chronicles of Crime and Criminals (ca. 1890)
"The Dance of the Dead" (ca. 1810)
"The Devil in the Belfry" (1839)
Fatal Jealousy; or, Blood Will Have Blood! Containing the History of Count Almagro and Duke Alphonso (1807)
Hamel, the Obeah Man (1827)
Historia von Dr. Johan Fausten [The story of Dr. John Fausten] (1587)
The History of the Remarkable Life of John Sheppard (1724)
Idlefonzo and Alberoni; or, Tales of Horror (1803)
Konjaku Monogatari [*Tales of Times Now Past*] (ca. 1130)
The Life and Exploits of Napoleon Bonaparte (ca. 1810)
The Life and Horrid Adventures of the Celebrated Dr. Faustus (1810)
The Lunatic and His Turkey: A Tale of Witchcraft (n.d.)
Maria Marten; or, The Murder in the Red Barn (1830)
Mary, Maid of the Inn (1820)
The Midnight Assassin; or, the Confessions of the Monk Rinaldi (1802)
The Midnight Bell; or, The Abbey of St. Francis (1811)
The Monk of Horror (1798)
The Mysterious Bride; or, The Statue Spectre (ca. 1800)
The Mysterious Spaniard; or, The Ruins of St. Luke's Abbey (1807)
The Narrative of All the Robberies, Escapes etc. of John Sheppard (1724)
The Old Tower of Frankenstein (n.d.)
Phantoms of the Cloister; or, The Mysterious Manuscript (1795)
"The Possessed One" (1831)
Rayland Hall (ca. 1810)
Robinson Crusoe (ca. 1830, Gothic bluebook)
The Round Tower; or, A Tale of Mystery (1803)
The Secret Tribunal; or, The Court of Wincelaus (1803)
The Severed Arm; or, The Wehr-Wolf of Limousin (ca. 1820)
The Sicilian Pirates; or, The Pillar of Mystery (ca. 1800)
The Spectre Mother; or, The Haunted Tower (1864)
Tales of Superstition (ca. 1820)
Tawny Rachel; or, The Fortune Teller (ca. 1795)
A True and Genuine Account of the Late Jonathan Wild (1725)
Varney the Vampyre, or, The Feast of Blood (1847)
The Victim of Seduction (1790)
The Wandering Spirit (1802)

S. ANSKY
Der Dybbuk (ca. 1916)

BRENDA WONG AOKI
Obake! Tales of Spirits Past and Present (1991)

HARRIETTE ARNOW
The Dollmaker (1954)

ANTONIN ARTAUD
Les Cenci (1935)

ISAAC ASIMOV
I, Robot (1950)

CYNTHIA CHARTERIS ASQUITH
Ghost Book (1926)

GERTRUDE ATHERTON
"The Bell in the Fog" (1905)
Black Oxen (1923)
The Christmas Witch (1893)
"The Dead and the Countess" (1905)
"Death and the Woman" (1892)
The Foghorn (1934)
"The Striding Place" (1896)
What Dreams May Come (1888)
The White Morning (1918)

MARGARET ATWOOD
Alias Grace (1996)
The Blind Assassin (2001)
Cat's Eye (1988)
The Handmaid's Tale (1985)
The Robber Bride (1993)

JANE AUSTEN
Northanger Abbey (1818)

MARIANO AZUELA
The Underdogs (1914)

JOANNA BAILLIE
De Montfort: A Tragedy on Hatred (1800)
The Family Legend (1810)
Orra: A Tragedy (1812)
A Series of Plays on the Passions (1798)

HONORÉ DE BALZAC
Le Peau de Chagrin [The Fatal Skin] (1831)
Melmoth Reconcilié à l'Eglise [Melmoth reconciled to the church] (1892)

ANNA LAETITIA BARBAULD
"On the Pleasure Derived from Objects of Terror, with Sir Bertrand" (1773)

DJUNA BARNES
Nightwood (1930)

C. F. BARRETT
"Douglas Castle; or, The Cell of Mystery, a Scottish Tale" (1803)

CHARLES BAUDELAIRE
Histoires Grotesques et Sérieuses [Grotesque and serious tales] (1865)
Les Fleurs du Mal [The Flowers of Evil] (1857)
Le Spleen de Paris (1869)
Nouvelles Histoires Extraordinaires [New extraordinary tales] (1857)
"Un Voyage à Cythère" [A Voyage to Cythera] (1869)

WILLIAM BECKFORD
Vathek (1782)

APHRA BEHN
Oroonoko (1688)

STEPHEN VINCENT BENÉT
"The Devil and Daniel Webster" (1939)

WILLIAM ROSE BENÉT
"The Skater of Ghost Lake" (1933)

AMBROSE BIERCE
"The Bottomless Grave" (1911)
Can Such Things Be? (1893)
"The Damned Thing" (1893)
"The Haunted Valley" (1871)
The Monk and the Hangman's Daughter (1892)
"An Occurrence at Owl Creek Bridge" (1891)
"The Secret of Macarger's Gulch" (1874)

ROBERT MONTGOMERY BIRD
Nick of the Woods (1837)
Sheppard Lee (1836)

ALGERNON BLACKWOOD
"The Camp of the Dog" (1908)
The Garden of Survival (1918)
The Human Chord (1910)
Karma (1918)
"The Listener" (1907)
"Secret Worship" (1908)
"Smith: An Episode in a Lodging House" (1906)
"The Wendigo" (1910)
"The Willows" (1907)

ROBERT BLAIR
"The Grave" (1743)

MARIE-CLAIRE BLAIS
Soifs [Thirsts] (1995)
Une Saison dans la Vie d'Emmanuel [A Season in the Life of Emmanuel] (1965)

WILLIAM BLATTY
The Exorcist (1971)

JAMES BOADEN
The Fountainville Forest (1794)
The Italian Monk (1796)

ELIZABETH BONHOTE
Bungay Castle (1796)

JORGE LUIS BORGES
Historia Universal de la Infamia [A Universal History of Infamy] (1935)

DIONYSIUS BOUCICAULT
After Dark (1858)
The Corsican Brothers (1852)
The Octoroon, or Life in Louisiana (1859)
The Poor of New York (1857)
Shaughraun (1875)
The Vampire (1852)

ELIZABETH BOWEN
"The Demon Lover" (1945)

RAY BRADBURY
Dandelion Wine (1957)
Fahrenheit 451 (1953)

The Illustrated Man (1951)
Something Wicked This Way Comes (1962)
"There Will Come Soft Rains" (1950)
"The Veldt" (1950)

MARY ELIZABETH BRADDON
Aurora Floyd (1863)
The Black Band; or, The Mysteries of Midnight (1861)
Dead Sea Fruit (1868)
The Doctor's Wife (1864)
Eleanor's Victory (1863)
Gerard; or, The World, the Flesh and the Devil (1891)
John Marchmont's Legacy (1863)
Lady Audley's Secret (1862)
The Lady's Mile (1866)
The Octoroon; or, The Lily of Louisiana (1861–62)
Three Times Dead; or, The Secret of the Heath (1860)

MARION ZIMMER BRADLEY
Firebrand (2003)
The Forest House (1994)
The Lady of Avalon (1997)
The Mists of Avalon (1982)
The Return to Avalon (1996)

GEORGE BREWEY
The Witch of Ravensworth (1808)

CHARLOTTE BRONTÉ
Jane Eyre (1847)
Villette (1853)

EMILY BRONTÉ
Wuthering Heights (1847)

CHARLES BROCKDEN BROWN
Arthur Mervyn (1799)
Edgar Huntly (1799)
Ormond (1799)
Wieland (1798)

DAN BROWN
The Da Vinci Code (2003)

ROBERTA BROWN
The Queen of the Cold-Blooded Tales (1993)
"Skin Crawlers" (1993)

WILLIAM CULLEN BRYANT
Tales of the Glauber Spa (1832)
"Thanatopsis" (1817)

VALERY BRYUSOV
The Fiery Angel (1908)

JOHN BUCHAN
"The Grove of Ashtaroth" (1912)

PEARL BUCK
The Good Earth (1931)

EDWARD BULWER-LYTTON
Alice; or, The Mysteries (1838)
The Coming Race (1871)
Ernest Maltravers (1837)
Eugene Aram (1832)
Falkland (1817)
"Glenallan" (1826)
"The Haunted and the Haunters; or, The House and the Brain" (1857)
Lucretia; or, The Children of the Night (1846)
"The Manuscript Found in a Mad-House" (1829)
"Monos and Daimonos" (1830)
"Night and Morning" (1845)
Paul Clifford (1830)
Pelham (1828)
A Strange Story (1861)
Zanoni (1842)

FELIX BURNS
The Albert Victor Waltz (1890)

ALFRED McLELLAND BURRAGE
"Between the Minute and the Hour" (1927)
"The One Who Saw" (1931)

PAUL BUSSON
The Man Who Was Born Again (1921)

OCTAVIA BUTLER
Kindred (1979)

LORD BYRON
The Bride of Abydos (1813)
The Corsair (1814)
"Darkness" (1816)

"The Destruction of Sennacherib" (1815)
The Giaour (1813)
"Lara" (1814)
"Lines Inscribed upon a Cup Formed from a Skull" (1808)
Manfred (1817)
"My Soul Is Dark" (1815)
"The Prisoner of Chillon" (1816)
"Prometheus" (1816)

GEORGE WASHINGTON CABLE
"Bras Coupé" (1879)
Cavalier (1901)
The Grandissimes: A Story of Creole Life (1879)
"Jean-ah Poquelin" (1875)
Kincaid's Battery (1908)
Madame Delphine (1881)

ERSKINE CALDWELL
The Poor Fool (1930)

JOHN RAMSEY CAMPBELL
New Tales of the Cthulhu Mythos (1980)
To Wake the Dead (1980)

KAREL ČAPEK
"The Adventures of a Breach-of-Promise Con Man"
    (1929)
"The Great Cat's Tale" (1932)
"The Last Judgment" (1929)
"The Makropulos Case" (1922)
R.U.R. (1921)

TRUMAN CAPOTE
"A Christmas Memory" (1956)
The Grass Harp (1951)
"The Headless Hawk" (1949)
In Cold Blood (1966)
Other Voices, Other Rooms (1948)
"Shut a Final Door" (1949)

PETER CAREY
Oscar and Lucinda (1988)

ANGELA CARTER
The Bloody Chamber (1979)
Heroes and Villains (1969)
The Infernal Desire Machines of Doctor Hoffman (1972)
The Magic Toyshop (1967)
Nights at the Circus (1984)

The Sadeian Woman and the Ideology of Pornography (1979)
The Shadow Dance (1966)
"The Werewolf" (1995)

JACQUES CAZOTTE
Le Diable Amoreux [The Devil in Love] (1772)

RAYMOND CHANDLER
The Big Sleep (1939)

FRED CHAPPELL
Dagon (1968)

MARY CHARLTON
Rosella, or Modern Occurrences (1799)

GEOFFREY CHAUCER
The Pardoner's Tale (ca. 1385)

ANTON CHEKHOV
The Black Monk (1894)

CHARLES CHESNUTT
"Gray Wolf's Ha'nt" (1899)
"Mars Jeems's Nightmare" (1899)
"Po' Sandy" (1899)
"Sis' Becky's Pickaninny" (1899)

GILBERT KEITH CHESTERTON
The Innocence of Father Brown (1911)

AGATHA CHRISTIE
The Hound of Death (1933)
The Mousetrap (1952)

SANDRA CISNEROS
Woman Hollering Creek and Other Stories (1991)

MARY HIGGINS CLARK
Where Are the Children? (1975)

WALTER VAN TILBURG CLARK
The Ox-Bow Incident (1940)

ARTHUR C. CLARKE
Childhood's End (1953)
2001: A Space Odyssey (1968)

MARCUS CLARKE
The Mystery of Major Molineux (1881)

LEONARD LANSON CLINE
The Dark Chamber (1927)

CAROLINE CLIVE
Paul Ferroll (1855)
Why Paul Ferroll Killed His Wife (1860)

SAMUEL TAYLOR COLERIDGE
"The Ballad of the Dark Ladie" (1798)
"Christabel" (1816)
"The Devil's Thoughts" (1799)
"Fears in Solitude" (1798)
"Frost at Midnight" (1798)
"Kubla Khan" (1816)
"Limbo" (1817)
The Rime of the Ancient Mariner (1798)
"This Lime-Tree Bower My Prison" (1800)
"The Tombless Epitaph" (ca. 1809)

PAYNE COLLIER AND GEORGE CRUIKSHANK
The Tragic Comedy or Comical Tragedy of Punch and Judy
(1828)

WILKIE COLLINS
"The Double-Bedded Room" (1859)
Heart and Science (1883)
The Law and the Lady (1875)
The New Magdalen (1873)
"The Ostler" (1855)
The Woman in White (1860)

WILLIAM TAYLOR COLLINS
"Ode to Evening" (1746)
"Ode to Fear" (1741)

JOSEPH CONRAD
Heart of Darkness (1902)
"The Idiot" (1908)
Lord Jim (1900)
The Secret Agent (1907)
"The Secret Sharer" (1912)

ROBIN COOK
Coma (1978)

JAMES FENIMORE COOPER
The Deerslayer (1841)
The Last of the Mohicans (1826)
The Pathfinder (1840)
The Spy (1821)

ALFRED EDGAR COPPARD
"Arabesque: The Mouse" (1920)

MARIE CORELLI
Ardath: The Story of a Dead Self (1889)
Barabbas: A Dream of the World's Tragedy (1893)
The Romance of Two Worlds (1886)
The Sorrows of Satan (1895)
The Soul of Lilith (1892)
Vendetta!; or, The Story of One Forgotten (1886)
Ziska: The Problem of a Wicked Soul (1897)

ROBERT CORMIER
Fade (1988)

JULIO CORTÁZAR
"Las Bagbas del Diablo" [The Devil's Spit] (1959)

JOHN COURTNEY
Jane Eyre; or, The Secrets of Thornfield Hall (1849)

FREDERICK IGNATIUS COWLES
"Punch and Judy" (1938)

STEPHEN CRANE
"The Monster" (1898)

MARGARET CRAVEN
I Heard the Owl Call My Name (1973)

G. CREED
Legends of Terror! And Tales of the Wonderful and Wild
(1840)

MICHAEL CRICHTON
The Andromeda Strain (1969)

GEORGE CROLY
Salathiel, the Wandering Jew (1828)

DONNA CROSS
Pope Joan (1996)

J. C. CROSS
Julia of Louvain; or, Monkish Cruelty (1797)

GEORGE CRUIKSHANK
Grimms' Fairy Tales (1827)

CATHERINE CUTHBERTSON
Adelaide; or, The Countercharm (1813)
Santo Sebastiano; or, The Young Protector (1806)

CHARLOTTE DACRE
The Confessions of the Nun of St. Omer (1805)
The Libertine (1807)
The School for Friends (ca. 1800)
Zofloya, or The Moor (1806)

ROALD DAHL
"Poison" (1953)
Someone Like You (1953)

AUGUSTIN DALY
Horizon (1871)
Under the Gaslight (1867)

GABRIELE D'ANNUNZIO
L'Innocente [The innocent] (1892)

FRANÇOIS BACULARD D'ARNAUD
Le Comte de Comminges [The count de Comminges] (1764)

ROBERTSON DAVIES
High Spirits (1982)

DANIEL DEFOE
Four Years Voyages of Capt. George Roberts (1726)
Jonathan Wild (1743)
The Life, Adventures, and Pyracies of the Famous Captain Singleton, Alias Smith (1720)
Moll Flanders (1722)

WALTER DE LA MARE
"Alice's Godmother" (1925)
"All Hallows" (1926)
"Broomsticks" (1925)

"Hodmadod" (1933)
"The Listeners" (1912)
"The Looking Glass" (1923)
"The Lost Track" (1926)
"Miss Jemima" (1925)
"Out of the Deep" (1923)
"The Recluse" (1930)
The Return (1910)
"The Scarecrow" (1945)
"Seaton's Aunt" (1923)
"Strangers Pilgrims" (1926)
"What Dreams May Come" (1936)

JAMES DE MILLE
The Strange Manuscript Found in a Copper Cylinder (1888)

THOMAS DE QUINCEY
The Avenger (1838)
Confessions of an English Opium Eater (1821)
"The Dice" (1823)
Klosterheim (1832)
Suspiria de Profundis [Sighs from the depths] (1845)

MARQUIS DE SADE
Aline and Valcour (1795)
Juliette (1796)
Justine (1801)
Les Crimes de l'Amour [The Crimes of Love] (1788)

CHARLES DICKENS
Barnaby Rudge (1841)
Bleak House (1853)
A Christmas Carol (1843)
Great Expectations (1861)
"The Haunted House" (1859)
Pickwick Papers (1837)
"The Signalman" (1866)
A Tale of Two Cities (1859)
"The Trial for Murder" (1865)

JAMES DICKEY
Deliverance (1970)

ISAK DINESEN
Babette's Feast (1959)
"The Dreamers" (1934)
"The Monkey" (1934)
"Old Chevalier" (1934)

Seven Gothic Tales (1934)
"The Supper at Elsinore" (1934)

WILLIAM DODD
Thoughts in Prison (1777)

FYODOR DOSTOEVSKY
Dvoynik [The Double] (1846)

SIR ARTHUR CONAN DOYLE
"The Adventure of the Empty House" (1903)
"The Adventure of the Mazarin Stone" (1921)
"The Adventure of the Second Stain" (1904)
"The Adventure of the Speckled Band" (1892)
"The Adventure of the Sussex Vampire" (1924)
The Adventures of Sherlock Holmes (1894)
"The Bascombe Valley Mystery" (1891)
"The Blue Carbuncle" (1892)
"Charles Augustus Milverton" (1905)
"The Final Problem" (1893)
The Hound of the Baskervilles (1902)
Memoirs of Sherlock Holmes (1894)
The Mystery of Cloomber (1889)
"The Mystery of Sassassa Valley" (1879)
"A Scandal in Bohemia" (1891)
"The Sign of the Four; or, The Problem of the Sholtos"
    (1890)

NATHAN DRAKE
The Abbey of Clunedale (1804)
The Abbot's Ghost (1867)
The Captive of the Banditti (n.d.)
"Henry Fitzowen—A Gothic Tale" (n.d.)
"Montmorenci, a Fragment" (1798)

ALEXANDRE DUMAS PÈRE
Le Meneur des Loups [The Wolf-Leader] (1857)

DAPHNE DU MAURIER
"The Birds" (1952)
"Don't Look Now" (1970)
Frenchman's Creek (1941)
The House on the Strand (1969)
Jamaica Inn (1936)
Not After Midnight (1970)
Rebecca (1938)

GEORGE DU MAURIER
Trilby (1894)

FRIEDRICH DÜRRENMATT
Der Besuch der Alten Dame [The Visit] (1956)

UMBERTO ECO
The Name of the Rose (1980)

MARGARET EDSON
Wit (1999)

PIERCE EGAN
Account of the Trial of John Thurtell and Joseph Hunt
    (1824)

GEORGE ELIOT
"The Lifted Veil" (1859)

KATE FERGUSON ELLIS
The Contested Castle (1989)

VIRGINIA RENFRO ELLIS
The Wedding Dress (2002)

MARIAN ENGEL
Bear (1977)

ÉMILE ERCKMANN AND LOUIS ALEXANDRE
    CHATRIAN
Contes Fantastiques [Fantastic stories] (1847)
"The Crab Spider" (1893)
"The Invisible Eye" (1849)
"The Man-Wolf" (1876)
"The Murderer's Violin" (1876)
Strange Stories (1880)

LOUISE ERDRICH
"Fleur" (1986)

LAURA ESQUIVEL
Like Water for Chocolate (1989)

HANNS HEINZ EWERS
Alraune [The Mandrakes] (1911)
Der Geisterseher [The ghost-seer] (1922)
Der Zauberlehrling Oder die Teufelsjäger [The sorcerer's
    apprentice; or, the devil hunter] (1907)
Nachtmahr [Nightmare] (1922)

Reiter in Deutscher Nacht [Rider of the night] (1932)
Vampir (1921)

MICHEL FABER
The Crimson Petal and the White (2002)

WILLIAM FAULKNER
Absalom, Absalom! (1936)
As I Lay Dying (1930)
"Barn Burning" (1939)
"The Bear" (1942)
"Dry September" (1931)
Intruder in the Dust (1948)
Light in August (1932)
"A Rose for Emily" (1930)
"The Rose of Lebanon" (1995)
Sanctuary (1931)
"That Evening Sun" (1931)

SEBASTIAN FAULKS
Birdsong (1997)

CHARLES FELIX
Notting Hill Mystery (1863)

EDNA FERBER
Cimarron (1929)

PAUL FÉVAL
La Ville-Vampire [Vampire city] (1875)

CHARLES GRANDISON FINNEY
The Circus of Dr. Lao (1935)

LAWRENCE FLAMMENBERG
Der Geisterbanner [The ghost banner] (1792)

FREDERICK FORSYTH
The Day of the Jackal (1971)

DION FORTUNE
The Winged Bull (1935)

FRIEDRICH DE LA MOTTE FOUQUÉ
Undine (1811)

JANET FRAME
"You Are Now Entering the Human Heart" (1983)

MARY E. WILKINS FREEMAN
The Long Arm (1895)

RICHARD AUSTIN FREEMAN
"The Case of Oscar Brodsky" (1912)

PHILIP FRENEAU
The British Prison-Ship (1781)
"The Dying Indian" (1784)
"Lines Occasioned by a Visit to an Old Indian Burying
     Ground" (1788)
"The Pestilence" (1793)
"To Sir Toby" (1792)

CARLOS FUENTES
"Aura" (1962)

ANNE FULLER
Alan Fitz-Osborne (1786)
The Son of Ethelwolf (1789)

ÉMILE GABORIAU
Monsieur Lecoq (1869)
Le Crime d'Orcival [The Crime at Orcival] (1867)
Les Esclaves de Paris [The keys of Paris] (1869)

ANTOINE GALLAND
The Arabian Nights (1704–17), trans.

GABRIEL GARCÍA MÁRQUEZ
Big Mama's Funeral (1962)
Chronicle of a Death Foretold (1982)
Innocent Eréndira and Other Stories (1972)
The Leaf Storm (1955)
Love in the Time of Cholera (1988)
One Hundred Years of Solitude (1967)

JOHN GARDNER
Grendel (1971)

ELIZABETH GASKELL
Mary Barton (1848)
"The Old Nurse's Story" (1852)

PHILIPPE-AUBERT DE GASPÉ THE ELDER
Les Anciens Canadiens [The Canadians of Old] (1863)

THÉOPHILE GAUTIER
Albertus (1833)
"Arria Marcella" (1852)
Avatar (1856)
Fortunio (1837)

Jettature (1857)
"La Cafétière" [The coffee machine] (1831)
La Comédie de la Mort [The comedy of death] (1838)
La Morte Amoreuse [The dead lover] (1836)
Les Grotesques (1844)
Mademoiselle de Maupin (1835)
"The Mummy's Foot" (1863)
"Omphale" (1834)
Spirite (1866)
"Une Larme du Diable" [The devil's tear] (1839)

JOHN GAY
The Beggar's Opera (1728)

EMILY DE LASZKOWSKA GERARD
The Land Beyond the Forest (1888)

HEINRICH WILHELM VON GERSTENBERG
Ugolino (1768)

CHARLOTTE PERKINS GILMAN
"The Yellow Wallpaper" (1892)

ELLEN GLASGOW
"Jordan's End" (1923)
"The Shadowy Third" (1916)

WILLIAM GODWIN
Caleb Williams (1794)
St. Leon (1799)

JOHANN WOLFGANG VON GOETHE
Claudine von Villa Bella (1775)
Der Zauberlehrling [The Sorcerer's Apprentice] (1797)
Die Braut von Corinth [The Bride of Corinth] (1797)
Egmont (1787)
Erlkönig [The Elf King] (1782)
Faust (1790–1832)
Götz von Berlichingen [Goetz with the Iron Hand] (1773)
"The New Melusina" (1826)
Reineke Fuchs [Reynard the Fox] (1794)

NIKOLAI GOGOL
Arabeski [Arabesques] (1835)
Dead Souls (1842)
"The Diary of a Madman" (1835)
Evenings on a Farm near Dakanka (1831)

Mirgorod (1835)
"The Nevsky Prospect" (1835)
"The Nose" (1835)
"The Portrait" (1835)
"Viy" (1835)

JEREMIAS GOTTHELF
Die Schwarze Spinne [The Black Spider] (1842)

ROBERT GRAVES
I, Claudius (1934)

THOMAS GRAY
Elegy Written in a Country Churchyard (1751)

PAUL GREEN
The Last of the Lowries (1920)

WILLIAM CHILD GREEN
The Abbot of Montserrat; or, The Pool of Blood (1826)
The Algerines; or, The Twins of Naples (1832)
The Maniac of the Desert (1821)
The Prophecy of Duncannon; or, The Dwarf and the Seer (1824)
"The Secrets of Cabalism; or, Ravenstone and Alice of Huntingdon" (ca. 1819)

ZANE GREY
Riders of the Purple Sage (1912)

GRIMM BROTHERS
"Der Räuberbräutigam" [The robber bridegroom] (1857)
Kinder- und Hausmärchen [Children's and household tales] (1812, 1815, 1822)

KARL GROSSE
Horrid Mysteries (1757)

DAVIS ALEXANDER GRUBB
The Night of the Hunter (1953)

ANDREAS GRYPHIUS
Kirch-hof Gedanchen [Graveyard thoughts] (ca. 1650)

DASHIELL HAMMETT
The Maltese Falcon (1930)
The Thin Man (1932)

MARTHA HARLEY
The Priory of St. Bernard (1789)

THOMAS HARRIS
Silence of the Lambs (1988)

JOHN HAWKESWORTH
Almoran and Hamet (1761)

NATHANIEL HAWTHORNE
"The Birthmark" (1843)
The Blithedale Romance (1852)
Doctor Grimshawe's Secret (1861)
"The Hollow of the Three Hills" (1830)
The House of the Seven Gables (1851)
The Marble Faun; or, The Romance of Monte Beni (1860)
"The Minister's Black Veil" (1837)
"My Kinsman, Major Molineux" (1851)
"Rappaccini's Daughter" (1844)
"Roger Malvin's Burial" (1832)
The Scarlet Letter (1850)
"A Select Party" (1846)
"The Virtuoso's Collection" (1846)
"Young Goodman Brown" (1835)

JOE HAYES
"La Llorona" (1987)

MARY HAYS
"A Fragment: In the Manner of the Old Romances" (1793)

LAFCADIO HEARN
"Clarimonde: A Supernatural Passion" (1888)
In Ghostly Japan (1899)
"Jiu-Roku-Zakura" (1904)
Kwaidan [Weird tales] (1904)
"Mimi-Nashi-Hoichi" (1904)
"Oshidori" (1904)
"O-Tei" (1904)
Some Chinese Ghosts (1887)

ANNE HÉBERT
Kamouraska (1970)
Les Enfants du Sabbat [Children of the Black Sabbath] (1975)

ELIZABETH HELME
St. Margaret's Cave; or, The Nun's Story (1801)

FELICIA HEMANS
"England's Dead" (1826)
"Indian Woman's Death-Song" (1828)
"The Spirit's Return" (1830)

BETH HENLEY
Crimes of the Heart (1979)
The Signature (1990)

JAMES HERVEY
Meditations among the Tombs (1745–47)

ROBERT SMYTHE HICHENS
"How Love Came to Professor Guildea" (1900)

SUSAN HILL
The Woman in Black (1983)

WILLIAM HOPE HODGSON
Carnacki the Ghost Finder (1913)

E. T. A. HOFFMANN
"Die Doppelgänger" [The double-goer] (1821)
Die Elixiere des Teufels [The Devil's Elixir] (1815 1816)
"Mademoiselle De Scudéry" (1819)
Nachtstücke [Strange Stories] (1817)
Nussknacker und Mausekönig [Nutcracker and Mouse-king] (1816)
Phantasiestücke in Callots Manier [Fantasy pieces in the style of Callot] (1814–15)
"The Sand-Man" (1817)

JAMES HOGG
"An Expedition to Hell" (1836)
The Private Memoirs and Confessions of a Justified Sinner (1824)
"The Witches of Traquair" (1828)
The Witch of Fife (1813)

LUDWIG HOLBERG
Nikolai Klimii Subterraneum [The subterranean voyage of Nicholas Klimm] (1741)

THOMAS HOLCROFT
The Child of Mystery (1801)

VICTORIA HOLT
Kirkland Revels (1962)
Mistress of Mellyn (1960)

THOMAS HOPE
Anastatius, or Memoirs of a Greek (1819)

VICTOR HUGO
Han d'Islande (1823)
Les Misérables (1862)

LEIGH HUNT
"A Tale for a Chimney Corner" (1819)

VIOLET HUNT
"The Tiger Skin" (1924)

ZORA NEALE HURSTON
Their Eyes Were Watching God (1937)

ALDOUS HUXLEY
The Devils of Loudun (1952)

JORIS-KARL HUYSMANS
Against the Grain (1884)
Là-Bas [Down There] (1891)

ENRIQUE ANDERSON IMBERT
The Other Side of the Mirror (1961)
Woven on the Loom of Time (1990)

WASHINGTON IRVING
"The Legend of Sleepy Hollow" (1820)
"The Spectre Bridegroom" (1820)

JOEL BEN IZZY
The Green Hand and Other Ghostly Tales from Around the World (1996)

SHIRLEY JACKSON
"The Bus" (1949)
"The Daemon Lover" (1949)
The Haunting of Hill House (1959)
"The Honeymoon of Mrs. Smith" (1997)
Just an Ordinary Day (1996)
"The Lottery" (1948)
"The Pillar of Salt" (1949)
"The Tooth" (1949)
We Have Always Lived in the Castle (1962)

W. W. JACOBS
Beauty and the Barge (1905)
"The Brown Man's Servant" (1897)

The Flag Station (1907)
The Ghost of Jerry Bundler (1899)
"Jerry Bundler" (1897)
"The Monkey's Paw" (1902)
Night Watches (1914)
"The Rival Beauties" (1896)
"The Three Sisters" (1914)
"The Tiger's Skin" (1902)
"The Toll House" (1909)

HARRIET JAMES
The Family of Santraile; or, The Heir of Montault (1809)

HENRY JAMES
"The Beast in the Jungle" (1903)
"De Grey" (1868)
"Friends of the Friends" (1896)
"Ghost Rental" (1874)
The Golden Bowl (1904)
"The Jolly Corner" (1908)
"The Last of the Valerii" (1874)
The Other Room (1896)
The Portrait of a Lady (1881)
"A Private Life" (1892)
A Sense of the Past (1900)
"Sir Dominick Ferrand" (1892)
The Turn of the Screw (1898)
Wings of the Dove (1902)

M[ONTAGUE] R[HODES] JAMES
"Canon Alberic's Scrap-Book" (1904)
"Casting the Runes" (1904)
Ghost Stories of an Antiquary (1904)
"The Story of a Disappearance and an Appearance" (1919)

JULES JANIN
Contes Fantastiques [Fantastic tales] (1832)
La Confession (1830)
L'Ane Mort et la Femme Guillotinée [The dead donkey and the guillotined woman] (1829)
"Le Dernier Jour d'un Condamné" [The last day of a condemned man] (1829)
Les Catacombes (1839)

ALFRED JARRY
Ubu Roi [King Ubu] (1896)

ROBERT JEPHSON
The Count of Narbonne (1781)

DOUGLAS WILLIAM JERROLD
Black-Eyed Susan (1829)

CHARLES JOHNSON
A General History of the Robberies and Murders of the
*   Most Notorious Pyrates* (1724, 1728)

SAMUEL JOHNSON
The History of Rasselas, Prince of Abissinia (1759)

WILLIAM JONES
The Seven Fountains: An Eastern Allegory (1772)

FRANZ KAFKA
"Die Verwandlung" *[The Metamorphosis]* (1912)

SUSAN KAY
Phantom (1990)

JOHN KEATS
"After Dark Vapors" (1817)
Endymion (1818)
The Eve of St. Agnes (1819)
"The Human Seasons" (1819)
"La Belle Dame sans Merci" (1819)
Lamia (1819)
"When I Have Fears" (1818)

STEPHEN KING
Carrie (1973)
Dolores Claiborne (1992)
Firestarter (1980)
From a Buick 8 (2002)
The Green Mile (1996)
Misery (1987)
Nightmares & Dreamscapes (1993)
Pet Sematary (1988)
'Salem's Lot (1975)
The Shining (1977)

MAXINE HONG KINGSTON
The Woman Warrior (1975)

RUDYARD KIPLING
"The City of Dreadful Night" (1891)
"The Finest Story in the World" (1893)
"The Haunted Subaltern" (1897)
Life's Handicap (1891)

"The Mark of the Beast" (1891)
"My Own True Ghost Story" (1888)
"The Phantom Rickshaw" (1888)
"The Recrudescence of Imray" (1891)
"The Strange Ride of Morrowbie Jukes" (1888)
"They" (1905)
"Without Benefit of Clergy" (1891)

WILLIAM KIRBY
Chien d'Or [The Golden Dog]: A Legend of Quebec (1859)

ANNETTE CURTIS KLAUSE
The Silver Kiss (1990)

FRIEDRICH GOTTLIEB KLOPSTOCK
The Messiah (1773)

DEAN KOONTZ
Phantoms (1983)

TONY KUSHNER
Angels in America (1991, 1992)

PÄR FABIAN LAGERKVIST
The Eternal Smile (1920)

CAROLINE LAMB
Ada Reis (1823)
Glenarvon (1816)

LETITIA ELIZABETH LANDON
"The Story of Hester Malpas" (1833)

JOHN LANGHORNE
Solyman and Almena (1762)

SARAH LANSDELL
The Tower; or, The Romance of Ruthyne (1798)

W. RING LARDNER
"Haircut" (1954)

LARRY LARSON, LEVI LEE, AND REBECCA
**   WACKLER**
Tent Meeting (1987)

FRANCIS LATHOM
Astonishment (1802)
The Castle of Ollada (1795)
Fashionable Mysteries (1829)
The Fatal Vow (1807)
The Impenetrable Secret (1805)
Italian Mysteries (1820)
The Midnight Bell: A German Story, Founded on Incidents in Real Life (1798)
The Mysterious Freebooter (1806)
Mystery (1800)
Mystic Events (1830)
The One-Pound Note and Other Tales (1820)
The Polish Bandit (1824)
The Unknown (1808)
Very Strange, But True (1803)
"The Water Spectre" (1809)

HARPER LEE
To Kill a Mockingbird (1960)

HARRIET LEE
"Kruitzner, the German's Tale" (1797)
The Mysterious Marriage; or, The Heirship of Roselva (1798)

HARRIET LEE AND SOPHIA LEE
The Canterbury Tales (1797–1805)

SOPHIA LEE
The Recess; or, A Tale of Other Times (1783–85)
Warbeck, a Pathetic Tale (1786)

SHERIDAN LE FANU
Carmilla (1872)
"The Ghost and the Bone-Setter" (1838)
The House by the Churchyard (1861–62)
In a Glass Darkly (1872)
The Rose and the Key (1871)
"Schalken the Painter" (1839)
Uncle Silas (1864)
Wylder's Hand (1864)

THOMAS LELAND
Longsword, Earl of Salisbury (1762)

MIKHAIL LERMONTOV
The Demon (1840)

GASTON LEROUX
Balaoo (1912)
Le Mystère de la Chambre Jaune [The Mystery of the Yellow Room] (1907)
Le Parfum de la Dame en Noir [The fragrance of the lady in black] (1909)
The Man Who Came Back from the Dead (1916)
The Man with the Black Feather (1912)
The New Terror (1926)
The Phantom of the Opera (1910)

PRIMO LEVI
The Periodic Table (1987)

IRA LEVIN
Rosemary's Baby (1967)

MATTHEW GREGORY LEWIS
Alfonso, King of Castile (1801)
Alonzo the Brave and the Fair Imogene (1790)
"The Anaconda" (1808)
The Bravo of Venice: A Romance (1805)
The Captive (1803)
The Castle Spectre (1798)
The Monk (1796)
Romantic Tales (1808)
Rugantino, the Bravo of Venice (1805)
Tales of Wonder (1801)

GEORGE LIPPARD
The Quaker City; or, The Monks of Monk Hall (1845)

H[OWARD] P[HILLIPS] LOVECRAFT
"Azathoth" (1922)
"The Beast in the Cave" (1905)
The Best of H. P. Lovecraft (1987)
"The Call of Cthulhu" (1928)
"The Descendent" (1926)
Dreams of Terror and Death: The Dream Cycle of H. P. Lovecraft (1995)
"The Rats in the Walls" (1924)

MARIE ADELAIDE BELLOC LOWNDES
The Lodger (1913)
Studies in Love and Terror (1913)

GEORGE LUCAS
The Castle of Saint Donats (1798)

THOMAS HENRY MACDERMOT
San Gloria (1920)

ARTHUR MACHEN [ARTHUR LLEWELLYN JONES]
The Great Pod Pan (1894)
The Three Impostors (1895)

ROBERT MACNISH
"Metempsychosis" (1826)

WILLIAM MAGINN
"The Man in the Bell" (1821)

BERNARD MALAMUD
The Natural (1952)

STÉPHANE MALLARMÉ
"Le Tombeau d'Edgar Poe" [Edgar Poe's tomb] (1876)

STEPHEN MALLATRATT
The Woman in Black (1989)

ROBERT MARASCO
Burnt Offerings (1973)

CHRISTOPHER MARLOWE
Dr. Faustus (ca. 1588)

JOSEPH ÉTIENNE EUGÈNE MARMETTE
François de Bienville: Scenes of Seventeenth-Century Canadian Life (1870)

FREDERICK MARRYAT
"The White Wolf of the Hartz Mountains" (1839)

RICHARD MARSH
The Beetle (1897)

CHARLES ROBERT MATURIN
Bertram; or, The Castle of Aldobrand (1816)
Fatal Revenge; or, The Family of Montorio (1807)
"Leixlip Castle: An Irish Family Legend" (1825)
Melmoth the Wanderer (1820)
The Milesian Chief (1812)

GUY DE MAUPASSANT
"Boule de Suif" [Butterball] (1880)
"La Chevelure" [The gold braid] (1884)
"La Main" [The hand] (1883)
"La Main d'Ecorche" [The flayed hand] (1875)
"La Morte" [The dead] (1887)
"La Nuit" [The night] (1887)
"Le Horla, or Modern Ghosts" (1887)
"Moiron" (1887)

ROBERT MCCAMMON
They Thirst (1981)

CARSON MCCULLERS
The Ballad of the Sad Café (1951)
The Heart Is a Lonely Hunter (1941)
Reflections in a Golden Eye (1941)

ROBIN MCKINLEY
Beauty (1978)

LARRY MCMURTRY
Lonesome Dove (1985)

HERMAN MELVILLE
"Bartleby the Scrivener" (1853)
Benito Cereno (1855)
Billy Budd (1924)
Moby-Dick (1851)
Omoo (1847)
"The Paradise of Bachelors and the Tartarus of Maids" (1855)
Typee (1846)

SUTHERLAND MENZIES
"Hughes, the Wehr-Wolf" (1838)

PROSPER MÉRIMÉE
"Lokis" (1869)

GUSTAV MEYRINK
Der Golem (1915)

ARTHUR MILLER
The Crucible (1953)

JOAQUIN MILLER
Danites of the Sierras (1876)

EDMUND MONTAGUE
The Demon of Sicily (1807)

JULIA MOORE
The Sentimental Song Book (1876)

THOMAS MOORE
Lalla Rookh (1817)

JAMES MORIER
The Adventures of Hajji Baba of Ispahan (1824)

WILLIAM MORRIS
"Rapunzel" (1858)
"Riding Together" (1856)

TONI MORRISON
Beloved (1987)
The Bluest Eye (1969)
Love (2003)
Song of Solomon (1977)
Sula (1973)

WILLIAM MUDFORD
"The Forsaken of God" (1849)
"The Iron Shroud" (1830)

IRIS MURDOCH
The Bell (1958)
The Black Prince (1973)
The Good Apprentice (1985)
The Green Knight (1993)
Jackson's Dilemma (1995)
The Sea, the Sea (1978)
The Time of Angels (1966)
The Unicorn (1963)

MARY NOAILLES MURFREE
"The Harnt That Walks Chilhowee" (1884)

YXTA MAYA MURRAY
"La Llorona" (1996)

KARL AUGUST MUSÄUS
Volksmaerchen der Deutschen [German folk tales]
    (1782–87)

BENEDIKTE NAUBERT AND JOHANN MATHIAS MÜLLER
Neue Volksmärchen der Deutschen [New German folk
    tales] (1789–93)

JOHN NEAL
Logan (1822)
Rachel Dyer (1828)

CHARLES NODIER
Le Vampire (1820)
Smarra; or, The Demons of the Night (1821)

DIANA NORMAN
The Vizard Mask (1994)

MARSHA NORMAN
Getting Out (1977)
'night, Mother (1982)

GREGORY L. NORRIS
Ghost Kisses (1994)

MARGARET NORTHAMPTON
"The Idiot Boy" (1830)

ALFRED NOYES
The Highwayman (1907)

JOYCE CAROL OATES
"The Accursed Inhabitants of the House of Bly" (1992)
Bellefleur (1980)
"Family" (1991)
"Lethal" (1992)
"Madison at Guignol" (2002)
"Premonition" (1994)
"Secret, Silent" (2001)
"The Temple" (1996)
"The Vampire" (2001)
"Where Are You Going, Where Have You Been?" (1970)
The Zombie (1995)

FITZ-JAMES O'BRIEN
"An Arabian Nightmare" (1851)
"The Diamond Lens" (1858)
"The Pot of Tulips" (1855)
"What Was It?" (1859)
"Wondersmith" (1859)

FLANNERY O'CONNOR
"The Displaced Person" (1953)
"Good Country People" (1955)
"A Good Man Is Hard to Find" (1955)
The Violent Bear It Away (1960)
Wise Blood (1952)

VLADIMIR ODOEVSKY
Cosmorama (1839)
"The Dream of Ridiculous Man" (1877)
"The Gambler Bobok" (1873)
Russkiye Notchi [Russian nights] (1844)
Salamander (1841)
"The Sylph" (1837)

KENZABURO OE
Sora No Kaibutsu Aguii [Agwhee the sky monster] (1964)

MARGARET OLIPHANT
The Beleaguered City (1880)
"The Library Window" (1896)
The Little Pilgrim of the Unseen (1882)
"The Open Door" (1881)
The Secret Chamber (1876)
Stories of the Seen and Unseen (1885)

MICHAEL ONDAATJE
The English Patient (1996)

OLIVER ONIONS
"The Beckoning Fair One" (1911)

MARTHA OSTENSO
Wild Geese (1925)

SYDNEY OWENSON
The Missionary (1811)

JOHN PALMER
The Haunted Cavern: A Caledonian Tale (1796)
The Mystery of the Black Tower (1796)

THOMAS PARNELL
"A Night Piece on Death" (1721)

ELIZA PARSONS
The Castle of Wolfenbach; or, The Horrid Machinations of the Count Berniti (1793)
The Mysterious Warning (1796)

THOMAS LOVE PEACOCK
Maid Marion (1818)
The Misfortunes of Elphin (1829)
"The Monks of St. Mark" (1804)
Nightmare Abbey (1818)
"Palmyra" (1812)

MERVYN PEAKE
Gormenghast (1950)
Titus Alone (1959)
Titus Groan (1946)

CHARLES PERRAULT
"Beauty and the Beast" (1698)
"La Barbe Bleue" [Bluebeard] (1697)

T. B. PETERSON
The Awful Disclosures of Maria Monk, or, The Hidden Secrets of a Nun's Life in a Convent (1836)
Further Disclosures of Maria Monk (1837)

ANN PETRY
Tituba of Salem Village (1964)

FELICE PICANO
Looking Glass Lives (1998)

MARGE PIERCY
Woman on the Edge of Time (1979)

CHARLES PIGAULT-LEBRUN
"The Unholy Compact Abjured" (1825)

GEORGE DIBDIN PITT
The String of Pearls: The Fiend of Fleet Street (1847)

GUILBERT DE PIXERÉCOURT
Coelina; ou, L'Enfant du Mystère [Coelina; or, the mysterious child] (1800)

JAMES ROBINSON PLANCHÉ
The Vampire; or, The Bride of the Isles (1820)

SYLVIA PLATH
"Fever 103°" (1965)
"Lady Lazarus" (1963)

EDGAR ALLAN POE
"Annabel Lee" (1849)
"The Bells" (1848)
"Berenice" (1835)
"The Black Cat" (1843)
"Bon-Bon" (1832)
"The Cask of Amontillado" (1846)
"A Descent into the Maelström" (1841)
"Dream-Land" (1844)
"A Dream within a Dream" (1849)
"The Fall of the House of Usher" (1839)
"The Gold Bug" (1843)
"Imp of the Perverse" (1845)
"In Youth I Have Known One" (1827)
"King Pest the First: A Tale Containing an Allegory"
    (1835)
"Lenore" (1831)
"Ligeia" (1838)
"The Masque of the Red Death" (1842)
"The Mesmeric Revelation" (1844)
"Metzengerstein" (1832)
"Morella" (1835)
"MS. Found in a Bottle" (1833)
"The Mystery of Marie Rogêt" (1842)
The Narrative of Arthur Gordon Pym (1838)
"Never Bet the Devil Your Head: A Tale with a Moral"
    (1841)
"The Oval Portrait" (1842)
"The Purloined Letter" (1844)
"The Raven" (1844)
"Silence—A Fable" (1838)
"Some Words with a Mummy" (1845)
"Thou Art the Man" (1844)
"Ulalume" (1847)
"William Wilson" (1839)

JOHN POLIDORI
"The Vampyre" (1819)

JANE PORTER
Duke Christian of Luneberg; or, Traditions of the Harz
    (1824)
The Pastor's Fireside (1817)
The Scottish Chiefs (1810)
Sir Edward Seaward's Narrative of His Shipwreck (1831)
Thaddeus of Warsaw (1803)

KATHERINE ANNE PORTER
"The Jilting of Granny Weatherall" (1930)
"Noon Wine" (1936)

JAN POTOCKI
The Manuscript Found in Saragossa (1815)

THOMAS PRESKETT PREST
The Black Monk; or, The Street of the Grey Turret (1844)
The Skeleton Clutch; or, The Goblet of Gore (1842)
The String of Pearls (1846)
Sweeney Todd, the Demon Barber of Fleet Street (1848)

ABBÉ PRÉVOST
Histoire de Cleveland [The story of Cleveland] (1731–39)
Manon Lescaut (1731)
Mémoires d'un Homme de Qualité [Memoirs of a man of
    quality] (1728–31)

ALEXANDER PUSHKIN
Eugene Onegin (1831)
The Queen of Spades (1834)

ANN RADCLIFFE
The Castles of Athlin and Dunbayne (1789)
Gaston de Blondeville (1802)
The Italian (1797)
The Mysteries of Udolpho (1794)
The Sicilian Romance (1790)

CLARA REEVE
The Exiles; or, Memories of Count de Cronstadt (1788)
The History of Charoba, Queen of Egypt (1785)
Memoirs of Sir Roger de Clarendon (1793)
The Old English Baron (1778)

J. F. REGNAULT-WARIN
Le Cimetière de la Madeleine [The graveyard of the
    Church of the Madeleine] (1800)

GEORGE REYNOLDS
Faust: A Romance of the Secret Tribunals (1845–46)
The Mysteries of London (1844–48)
The Mysteries of the Court of London (1848–53)
The Necromancer: A Romance (1851–52)
Wagner the Wehr-Wolf (1847)

JEAN RHYS
"Our Gardener" (1977)
Wide Sargasso Sea (1966)

ANNE RICE

Beauty's Punishment (1984)
Beauty's Release (1985)
Blackwood Farm (2002)
Blood and Gold (2001)
Blood Canticle (2003)
The Claiming of Sleeping Beauty (1983)
Interview with the Vampire (1976)
Lasher (1994)
Memnoch the Devil (1995)
Merrick (2000)
Queen of the Damned (1988)
The Servant of the Bones (1996)
The Tale of the Body Thief (1992)
Taltos: Lives of the Mayfair Witches (1994)
The Vampire Armand (2000)
The Vampire Lestat (1985)
The Violin (1997)
The Witching Hour (1990)

JOHN RICHARDSON

The Canadian Brothers; or, The Prophecy Fulfilled (1840)
Ecarté; or, The Salons of Paris (1829)
The Monk Knight of St. John: A Tale of the Crusaders (1850)
Wacousta; or, The Prophecy: A Tale of the Canadas (1832)

JEAN PAUL RICHTER

Siebenkäs (1796)

CHARLOTTE COWAN RIDDELL

George Geith of Fen Court (1864)

ARTHUR RIMBAUD

Une Saison en Enfer [A Season in Hell] (1873)

MARY ROBERTS RINEHART

The Bat (1920)
The Case of Jennie Brice (1913)
The Circular Staircase (1908)
The Man in Lower Ten (1906)
The Swimming Pool (1952)
The Window at the White Cat (1910)
"The Young Visitor" (1989)

BYRD ROBERTS

Duskouri Tales (2000)

EDWIN ARLINGTON ROBINSON

"The Wandering Jew" (1921)

MARY ROBINSON

"The Haunted Beach" (1800)
The Natural Daughter (1799)
The Picture of Palermo (1799)
Vancenza; or, The Dangers of Credulity (1792)

REGINA ROCHE

The Children of the Abbey: A Tale (1796)
Clermont (1798)
The Discarded Son; or, Haunt of the Banditti (1807)
The Houses of Osma and Almeria; or, Convent of St. Ilde-fonso (1810)
London Tales, or Reflective Portraits (1814)
The Maid of the Hamlet (1821)
Monastery of St. Colomb; or, The Atonement, a Novel (1813)
The Nocturnal Visit; or, The Mysterious Husband (ca. 1800)
The Nun's Picture (1834)
The Tradition of the Castle; or, Scenes in the Emerald Isle (1824)

ROSEMARY ROGERS

Sweet Savage Love (1974)

OLE EDVART RÖLVAAG

Giants in the Earth (1927)

YUDL ROSENBERG

The Maharal of Prague (1909)

CHRISTINA ROSSETTI

The Goblin Market (1862)
"Song" (1848)

DANTE GABRIEL ROSSETTI

"My Sister's Sleep" (1847)
"The Portrait" (1847)

JUAN RULFO

Pedro Páramo (1955)

SAKI [HECTOR HUGH MUNRO]

"The Boar-Pig" (1914)
"Esmé" (1911)
"Gabriel-Ernest" (1909)
"Guests" (1923)
"The She-Wolf" (1912)

"Sredni Vashtar" (1911)
"The Story-Teller" (1914)
"Tobermory" (1911)

REVERONI SAINT-CYR
Pauliska, ou La Perversité Moderne [Pauliska, or modern perversity] (1796)

MARI SANDOZ
Crazy Horse (1942)

H. J. SARRATT
Koenigsmark the Robber; or, The Terror of Bohemia (1801)

JEAN-PAUL SARTRE
"The Wall" (1939)

JACK WARNER SCHAEFER
Shane (1949)

FRIEDRICH VON SCHILLER
Der Geisterseher [The Ghost-Seer] (1786)
Die Räuber [The Robbers] (1781)

CHRISTIAN FRIEDRICH SCHUBART
Der Ewige Jude: Eine Lyrische Rhapsodie [The wandering Jew: A lyric rhapsody] (1783)

SIR WALTER SCOTT
The Abbot (1820)
Auchindrane (1830)
The Bride of Lammermoor (1819)
The Doom of Devorgoil (1830)
Guy Mannering (1815)
House of Aspen (1799)
Ivanhoe (1819)
The Lay of the Last Minstrel (1805)
Marmion, a Tale of Flodden Field (1807)
The Monastery (1820)
The Pirate (1822)
"The Tale of the Mysterious Mirror" (1828)
Tales of a Traveller (1824)
The Talisman (1825)
"The Tapestried Chamber" (1828)

ANNE SEXTON
"Sylvia's Death" (1963)

MARY WOLLSTONECRAFT SHELLEY
Frankenstein (1818)
"The Mortal Immortal, A Tale" (1833)

PERCY BYSSHE SHELLEY
"The Assassins" (1814)
Invocation to Misery (1818)
The Revolt of Islam (1817)
St. Irvyne; or, The Rosicrucian (1811)
The Wandering Jew; or, The Victim of the Eternal Avenger (1810)
Zastrozzi: A Romance (1810)

FRANCES SHERIDAN
The History of Nourjahad (1767)

LESLIE MARMON SILKO
The Storyteller (1981)

WILLIAM GILMORE SIMMS
The Yemassee (1835)

ISAAC BASHEVIS SINGER
"The Crown of Feathers" (1973)
Der Sotn in Gorey [Satan in Goray] (1935)
"The Destruction of Kreshev" (1942)
"Gimpel the Fool" (1957)
"The Golem" (1982)
The Magician of Lublin (1960)
"The Séance" (1968)

ELEANOR SLEATH
Orphan of the Rhine: A Romance (1798)

CHARLOTTE SMITH
Celestina (1791)
Ethelinde; or, The Recluse of the Lake (1790)
Letters of a Solitary Wanderer (1800–02)
Manon L'Escault; or, The Fatal Attachment (1785)
Montalbert (1795)
The Old Manor House (1793)
The Romance of Real Life (1787)
The Romance of the Forest (1791)
The Wanderings of Warwick (1794)

CLARK ASHTON SMITH
"The Hashish-Eater" (1922)

JOHN FREDERICK SMITH
Black Bess; or, The Knight of the Road (1863–68)

TOBIAS SMOLLETT
Ferdinand Count Fathom (1753)

JOHN SNART
"The Thesaurus of Horror; or, The Charnel House Explored!" (1819)

FYODOR SOLOGUB
The Little Demon (1907)

STEPHEN SONDHEIM
Sweeney Todd (1979)

EDWARD SORENSEN
The Squatter's Ward (1919)

FRÉDÉRIC SOULIÉ
Les Mémoires du Diable [The devil's memoirs] (1837–38)

HARRIET SPOFFORD
"Circumstance" (1863)

CHRISTINA STEAD
The Man Who Loved Children (1940)

STANISLAUS ERIC STENBOCK
Studies of Death (1894)
A True Story of the Vampire (1894)

ANNE SOPHIA STEPHENS
Malaeska: The Indian Wife of the White Hunter (1860)

ROBERT LOUIS STEVENSON
The Body Snatcher (1881)
"The Bottle Imp" (1888)
"The Devil and the Innkeeper" (1896)
Dr. Jekyll and Mr. Hyde (1886)
"Isle of Voices" (1893)
Kidnapped (1886)
"Markheim" (1887)
The Master of Ballantrae (1889)
The New Arabian Nights (1882)
"Olalla" (1887)
"Thrawn Janet" (1887)
Treasure Island (1883)

FRED MUSTARD STEWART
Mephisto Waltz (1968)

BRAM STOKER
Dracula (1897)
The Jewel of Seven Stars (1904)
The Lady of the Shroud (1909)
The Lair of the White Worm (1911)
The Snake's Pass (1890)

THEODOR STORM
Ein Doppelgänger [A double-goer] (1887)
Ein Golem (1851)

HARRIET BEECHER STOWE
Uncle Tom's Cabin (1851–52)

PETER STRAUB
Ghost Story (1979)

WHITLEY STRIEBER
Wolfen (1978)

WILLIAM STYRON
The Confessions of Nat Turner (1967)
Lie Down in Darkness (1951)

EUGÈNE SUE
Le Juif Errant (The Wandering Jew) (1844)
The Mysteries of Paris (1842–43)

ALGERNON SWINBURNE
"A Ballad of François Villon" (1878)

AMY TAN
The Hundred Secret Senses (1995)
The Kitchen God's Wife (1991)

JULES-PAUL TARDIVEL
Pour la Patrie [For My Country] (1895)

PETER TEUTHOLD
The Necromancer; or, The Tale of the Black Forest (1794)

WILLIAM MAKEPEACE THACKERAY
Barry Lyndon (1844)

JAMES THOMSON
The City of Dreadful Night (1874)
Insomnia (1882)

JOHANN LUDWIG TIECK
"The Bride of the Grave" (1817)
"Das Pokal" [The Goblet] (1827)
"Die Elfen" [The Elves] (1827)
Phantasus [Apparition] (1822)
Volksmärchen [Folktales] (1797)
"Wake Not the Dead" (1800)

J. R. R. TOLKIEN
The Hobbit (1937)
The Lord of the Rings (1954–55)

THOMAS TRYON
Harvest Home (1973)

CAJETAN TSCHINK
Der Geisterseher [The ghost seer] (1797)

IVAN TURGENEV
Faust (1856)
"Phantoms" (1864)

MARGARET TURNER
The Gentle Shepherd (1790)

MARK TWAIN
"The Man That Corrupted Hadleyburg" (1898)
The Mysterious Stranger (1916)
Pudd'nhead Wilson (1894)

KARL HEINRICH ULRICHS
Matrosengeschichten [Sailor stories] (1884)

JOHN UPDIKE
The Witches of Eastwick (1984)

JULES VERNE
Around the World in Eighty Days (1873)

GABRIELLE–SUZANNE DE VILLENEUVE
La Jeune Ameriquaine, et les Contes Marins [The young
    American and the sea stories] (1740)

VILLIERS DE L'ISLE-ADAM
Contes Cruels (1883)
"The Doctor's Heroism" (1883)
L'Eve Future [The future Eve] (1886)
Nouveaux Contes Cruels [New cruel tales] (1888)
"The Torture of Hope" (1883)

HELENA MARIA VIRAMONTES
The Moth and Other Stories (1995)

VINCENT VIRGA
Gaywyck (2000)

VOLTAIRE
Candide (1759)

CHRISTIAN AUGUST VULPIUS
Rinaldo Rinaldini (1798)

HEINRICH LEOPOLD WAGNER
The Child Murderess (1776)

DEREK WALCOTT
Ti-Jean and His Brothers (1970)

HORACE WALPOLE
The Castle of Otranto (1765)
"The Dear Witches" (1743)
Hieroglyphic Tales (1785)
The Mysterious Mother (1768)

DETECTIVE WARREN
The Whitechapel Murders; or, On the Track of the Fiend
    (1898)

SAM WATSON
The Kadaitcha Sung (1990)

EVELYN WAUGH
Black Mischief (1932)
Brideshead Revisited (1945)
Decline and Fall (1928)
A Handful of Dust (1934)
The Loved One (1948)
"The Man Who Liked Dickens" (1933)
"Out of Depth" (1933)
Vile Bodies (1930)

ANDREW LLOYD WEBBER

The Phantom of the Opera (1986)

JOHN WEBSTER

The Duchess of Malfi (ca. 1613)

PETER WEISS

The Persecution and Assassination of Marat as Performed by the Inmates of the Asylum of Charenton under the Direction of the Marquis de Sade (1964)

H. G. WELLS

"The Cone" (1895)
"The Country of the Blind" (1911)
"The Flowering of the Strange Orchid" (1894)
"The Inexperienced Ghost" (1903)
"In the Avu Observatory" (1894)
The Island of Dr. Moreau (1896)
"The Plattner Story" (1896)
"Pollock and the Porroh Man" (1897)
"The Red Room" (1896)
"The Sea Raiders" (1896)
"The Stolen Body" (1903)
Thirty Strange Stories (1897)
The Time Machine (1895)
"The Truth about Pyecraft" (1903)

EUDORA WELTY

"Clytie" (1941)
The Curtain of Green and Other Stories (1941)
"The Death of a Traveling Salesman" (1941)
Delta Wedding (1946)
"The Golden Apples" (1949)
"Lily Daw and the Three Ladies" (1941)
"Livvie Is Back" (1943)
"The Petrified Man" (1941)
"Powerhouse" (1941)
The Robber Bridegroom (1942)
"Why I Live at the P. O." (1941)
"The Worn Path" (1941)

EDITH WHARTON

"Afterward" (1911)
The Age of Innocence (1920)
"All Souls" (1937)
"Botticelli's Madonna" (1891)
Ethan Frome (1911)
"The Eyes" (1910)
Ghosts (1937)

The House of Mirth (1905)
"The Lady's Maid's Bell" (1910)
"The Pomegranate Seed" (1912)
"Quicksand" (1902)
Tales of Men and Ghosts (1911)
"The Tomb of Ilaria Giunigi" (1891)

JAMES WHITE

Earl Strongbow; or, The History of Richard de Clare and the Beautiful Geralda (1789)

PHYLLIS WHITNEY

Thunder Heights (1960)

OSCAR WILDE

The Ballad of Reading Gaol (1898)
"The Birthday of the Infanta" (1888)
"The Canterville Ghost" (1889)
"The Fisherman and His Soul" (1891)
The Happy Prince and Other Tales (1888)
The House of Pomegranates (1891)
"The Nightingale and the Rose" (1888)
The Picture of Dorian Gray (1891)
Salomé (1893)

SARAH WILKINSON

The Castle of Montabino; or, The Orphan Sisters (1810)
The Castle of Oravilla (n.d.)
The Castle Spectre; or, Family Horrors (1807)
The Child of Mystery (1808)
The Convent of the Grey Penitents; or, The Apostate Nun (1810)
The Deformed Mendicant (n.d.)
The Fugitive Countess; or, The Convent of St. Ursula (1807)
Inkle and Yarico; or, Love in a Cave (1805)
Ivy Castle; or, The Eve of St. Agnes (n.d.)
Monkcliffe Abbey (1805)
The Mountain Cottager; or, The Deserted Bride (1804)
The Mysterious Novice; or, Convent of the Grey Penitents (1809)
New Tales (1819)
The Polish Romance (n.d.)
The Sorcerer's Palace; or, The Princess of Sinadone (1805)
The Spectre of Lanmere Abbey (1820)
The Spectre; or, The Ruins of Belfont Priory (1806)
The Subterraneous Passage; or, Gothic Cell (1803)
The Thatched Cottage; or, Sorrows of Eugenia (1806)
The Tragical History of Jane Arnold, Commonly Called Crazy Jane; and Mr. Henry Percival; Giving an

Account of Their Birth, Parentage, Courtship, and Melancholy End (1817)
The White Cottage of the Valley; or, The Mysterious Husband (ca. 1810)
Zittaw the Cruel; or The Woodsman's Daughter (n.d.)

PETER WILL
Horrid Mysteries: A Story from the German of the Marquis of Grosse (1796)

CHARLES WILLIAMS
Greater Trumps (1932)
Many Dimensions (1931)
The Place of the Lion (1931)
War in Heaven (1930)

TENNESSEE WILLIAMS
Cat on a Hot Tin Roof (1955)
Suddenly Last Summer (1958)
"The Vengeance of Nitocris" (1928)

AUGUST WILSON
Fences (1985)
Gem of the Ocean (2003)
Joe Turner's Come and Gone (1988)
King Hedley II (1999)
Ma Rainey's Black Bottom (1985)
The Piano Lesson (1990)
Seven Guitars (1995)
Two Trains Running (1991)

MARY WOLLSTONECRAFT
Maria; or, The Wrongs of Women (1798)

ELLEN WOOD
Anne Hereford (1867)

The Channings (1862)
Earl Goodwin (1791)
East Lynne (1861)
Mrs. Halliburton's Troubles (1862)
"Poem on the Inhumanity of the Slave Trade" (1788)
"The Punishment of Gina Montani" (1852)
The Shadow of Ahslydyat (1862)

KATHLEEN WOODIWISS
The Flame and the Flower (1974)
The Wolf and the Dove (1974)

RICHARD WRIGHT
"Between the World and Me" (1935)

CHELSEA QUINN YARBRO
Hotel Transylvania (1978)

ANNE YEARSLEY
The Royal Captives (1795)

WILLIAM BUTLER YEATS
"All Souls' Night" (1920)
"The Magi" (1914)
"The Second Coming" (1921)
The Vision (1925)

EDWARD YOUNG
"Night-Thoughts" (1742)
"Welcome Death!" (1743)

HEINRICH ZSCHOKKE
Aböllino, der Grosse Bandit [Aballino, the great bandit] (1793)

A TIME LINE OF GOTHIC LITERATURE

Titles in **boldface** are significant contributions to the Gothic canon.

CA. 1130
Konjaku Monogatari [Tales of Times Now Past], anonymous

CA. 1385
The Pardoner's Tale, Geoffrey Chaucer

CA. 1587
Historia von Dr. Johan Fausten [The story of Dr. John Fausten], anonymous

CA. 1588
Dr. Faustus, Christopher Marlowe

CA. 1613
The Duchess of Malfi, John Webster

CA. 1650
Kirch-hof Gedanchen [Graveyard thoughts], Andreas Gryphius

1688
Oroonoko, Aphra Behn

1697
"La Barbe Bleue" [Bluebeard], Charles Perrault

1698
"Beauty and the Beast," Charles Perrault

1711
The Vision of Mirza, Joseph Addison

1717
The Arabian Nights, Antoine Galland, trans.

1720
The Life, Adventures, and Pyracies of the Famous Captain Singleton, Alias Smith, Daniel Defoe

1721
"A Night Piece on Death," Thomas Parnell

1722
Moll Flanders, Daniel Defoe

1724
The History of the Remarkable Life of John Sheppard, anonymous
The Narrative of All the Robberies, Escapes etc. of John Sheppard, anonymous

1725
A True and Genuine Account of the Late Jonathan Wild, anonymous

1725
An Account of the Conduct and Proceedings of the Late John Gow, Captain of the Late Pirates Executed for Murther and Piracy, anonymous

1726
Four Years Voyages of Capt. George Roberts, Daniel Defoe

1728
A General History of the Robberies and Murders of the Most Notorious Pyrates, Charles Johnson

1728
The Beggar's Opera, John Gay

1731
Manon Lescaut, Abbé Prévost
Mémoires d'un Homme de Qualité [Memoirs of a man of quality], Abbé Prévost

1739
Histoire de Cleveland [The story of Cleveland], Abbé Prévost

1740
La Jeune Ameriquaine, et les Contes Marins [The young American and the sea stories], Gabrielle-Suzanne de Villeneuve

1741
"Ode to Fear," William Taylor Collins
Nikolai Klimii Subterraneum [The subterranean voyage of Nicholas Klimm], Ludwig Holberg

1742
"Night-Thoughts," Edward Young

1743
Jonathan Wild, Daniel Defoe
"The Dear Witches," Horace Walpole
"The Grave," Robert Blair
"Welcome Death!" Edward Young

1746
"Ode to Evening," William Taylor Collins

1747
Meditations among the Tombs, James Hervey

1751
Elegy Written in a Country Churchyard, Thomas Gray

1753
Ferdinand Count Fathom, Tobias Smollett

1757
Horrid Mysteries, Karl Grosse

1759
Candide, Voltaire
The History of Rasselas, Prince of Abissinia, Samuel Johnson

1761
Almoran and Hamet, John Hawkesworth

1762
Longsword, Earl of Salisbury, Thomas Leland
Pauliska, ou La Perversité Moderne [Pauliska, or modern perversity], Reveroni Saint-Cyr
Solyman and Almena, John Langhorne

1765
The Castle of Otranto, Horace Walpole

1767
The History of Nourjahad, Frances Sheridan

1768
The Mysterious Mother, Horace Walpole
Ugolino, Heinrich Wilhelm von Gerstenberg

1772
Le Diable Amoreux [The Devil in Love], Jacques Cazotte
The Seven Fountains: An Eastern Allegory, William Jones

1773
Götz von Berlichingen [Goetz with the Iron Hand], Johann Wolfgang von Goethe
The Messiah, Friedrich Gottlieb Klopstock
"On the Pleasure Derived from Objects of Terror, with Sir Bertrand," Anna Laetitia Barbauld

1775
Claudine von Villa Bella, Johann Wolfgang von Goethe

1776
The Child Murderess, Heinrich Leopold Wagner

1777
Thoughts in Prison, William Dodd

1778
The Old English Baron, Clara Reeve

1781
The British Prison-Ship, Philip Freneau
The Count of Narbonne, Robert Jephson
Die Räuber [The Robbers], Friedrich von Schiller

1782
Erlkönig [The elf king], Johann Wolfgang von Goethe
Vathek, William Beckford

1783
Der Ewige Jude: Eine Lyrische Rhapsodie [The wandering
    Jew: A lyric rhapsody], Christian Friedrich
    Schubart

1784
"The Dying Indian," Philip Freneau

1785
Hieroglyphic Tales, Horace Walpole
The History of Charoba, Queen of Egypt, Clara Reeve
Manon L'Escaut; or, The Fatal Attachment, Charlotte
    Smith
The Recess; or, A Tale of Other Times, Sophia Lee

1786
Alan Fitz-Osborne, Anne Fuller
Der Geisterseher [The Ghost-Seer] (1786), Friedrich von
    Schiller
Warbeck, a Pathetic Tale, Sophia Lee

1787
Egmont, Johann Wolfgang von Goethe
The Romance of Real Life, Charlotte Smith
Volksmaerchen der Deutschen [German folk tales], Karl
    August Musäus

1788
The Exiles; or, Memories of Count de Cronstadt, Clara
    Reeve
Les Crimes de l'Amour [The Crimes of Love], Marquis
    de Sade
"Lines Occasioned by a Visit to an Old Indian Burying
    Ground," Philip Freneau
"Poem on the Inhumanity of the Slave Trade," Ellen
    Wood

1789
The Castles of Athlin and Dunbayne, Ann Radcliffe
*Earl Strongbow; or, The History of Richard de Clare and the
    Beautiful Geralda,* James White
The Priory of St. Bernard, Martha Harley
The Son of Ethelwolf, Anne Fuller

1790
Alonzo the Brave and the Fair Imogene, Matthew Gregory
    Lewis
Ethelinde; or, The Recluse of the Lake, Charlotte Smith
The Gentle Shepherd, Margaret Turner
The Sicilian Romance, Ann Radcliffe
The Victim of Seduction, anonymous

1791
Celestina, Charlotte Smith
Earl Goodwin, Ellen Wood
The Romance of the Forest, Charlotte Smith

1792
The Castle of St. Vallery, anonymous
Der Geisterbanner [The ghost banner], Lawrence
    Flammenberg
"To Sir Toby," Philip Freneau
Vancenza; or, The Dangers of Credulity, Mary Robinson

1793
Aballino, der Grosse Bandit [Aballino, the great bandit],
    Heinrich Zschokke
*The Castle of Wolfenbach; or, The Horrid Machinations of
    the Count Berniti,* Eliza Parsons
"A Fragment: In the Manner of the Old Romances,"
    Mary Hays
Memoirs of Sir Roger de Clarendon, Clara Reeve
Neue Volksmärchen der Deutschen [New German folk
    tales], Benedikte Naubert and Johann Mathias
    Müller
The Old Manor House, Charlotte Smith
"The Pestilence," Philip Freneau

1794
Caleb Williams, William Godwin
The Fountainville Forest, James Boaden
Le Comte de Comminges [The count de Comminges],
    François Baculard d'Arnaud
The Mysteries of Udolpho, Ann Radcliffe
The Necromancer; or, The Tale of the Black Forest, Peter
    Teuthold

Reineke Fuchs [Reynard the Fox], Johann Wolfgang von
    Goethe
The Wanderings of Warwick, Charlotte Smith

CA. 1795
Tawny Rachel; or, The Fortune Teller, anonymous

1795
Aline and Valcour, Marquis de Sade
The Castle of Ollada, Francis Lathom
Montalbert, Charlotte Smith
Phantoms of the Cloister; or, The Mysterious Manuscript,
    anonymous
The Royal Captives, Anne Yearsley

1796
Bungay Castle, Elizabeth Bonhote
The Children of the Abbey: A Tale, Regina Roche
The Haunted Cavern: A Caledonian Tale, John Palmer
*Horrid Mysteries: A Story from the German of the Marquis
    of Grosse,* Peter Will
The Italian Monk, James Boaden
Juliette, Marquis de Sade
The Monk, Matthew Gregory Lewis
The Mysterious Warning, Eliza Parsons
The Mystery of the Black Tower, John Palmer
Siebenkäs, Jean Paul Richter

1797
Der Geisterseher [The ghost-seer], Cajetan Tschink
Der Zauberlehrling [The sorcerer's apprentice], Johann
    Wolfgang von Goethe
Die Braut von Corinth [The Bride of Corinth], Johann
    Wolfgang von Goethe
The Italian, Ann Radcliffe
Julia of Louvain; or, Monkish Cruelty, J. C. Cross
"Kruitzner, the German's Tale," Harriet Lee
Volksmärchen [Folktales], Johann Ludwig Tieck

CA. 1798
"The Black Spider," anonymous

1798
The Animated Skeleton, anonymous
"The Ballad of the Dark Ladie," Samuel Taylor
    Coleridge
The Castle of Saint Donats, George Lucas
The Castle Spectre, Matthew Gregory Lewis
Clermont, Regina Roche
"Fears in Solitude," Samuel Taylor Coleridge

"Frost at Midnight," Samuel Taylor Coleridge
Maria; or, The Wrongs of Women, Mary Wollstonecraft
*The Midnight Bell: A German Story, Founded on Incidents
    in Real Life,* Francis Lathom
The Monk of Horror, anonymous
"Montmorenci, a Fragment," Nathan Drake
The Mysterious Marriage; or, The Heirship of Roselva,
    Harriet Lee
Orphan of the Rhine: A Romance, Eleanor Sleath
The Rime of the Ancient Mariner, Samuel Taylor
    Coleridge
Rinaldo Rinaldini, Christian August Vulpius
A Series of Plays on the Passions, Joanna Baillie
The Tower; or The Romance of Ruthyne, Sarah Lansdell
Wieland, Charles Brockden Brown

1799
Arthur Mervyn, Charles Brockden Brown
"The Devil's Thoughts," Samuel Taylor Coleridge
Edgar Huntly, Charles Brockden Brown
House of Aspen, Sir Walter Scott
The Natural Daughter, Mary Robinson
Ormond, Charles Brockden Brown
The Picture of Palermo, Mary Robinson
Rosella, or Modern Occurrences, Mary Charlton
St. Leon, William Godwin

CA. 1800
The Mysterious Bride; or, The Statue Spectre, anonymous
The Nocturnal Visit; or, The Mysterious Husband, Regina
    Roche
The School for Friends, Charlotte Dacre
The Sicilian Pirates; or, The Pillar of Mystery, anonymous

1800
Coelina; ou, L'Enfant du Mystère [Coelina; or, the
    mysterious child], Guilbert de Pixerécourt
De Montfort: A Tragedy on Hatred, Joanna Baillie
"The Haunted Beach," Mary Robinson
Le Cimetiere de la Madeleine [The graveyard of the
    Church of the Madeleine], J. F. Regnault-Warin
Mystery, Francis Lathom
"This Lime-Tree Bower My Prison," Samuel Taylor
    Coleridge
"Wake Not the Dead," Johann Ludwig Tieck

1801
Alfonso, King of Castile, Matthew Gregory Lewis
The Child of Mystery, Thomas Holcroft
Justine, Marquis de Sade

Koenigsmark the Robber; or, The Terror of Bohemia, H. J. Sarratt

St. Margaret's Cave; or, The Nun's Story, Elizabeth Helme

Tales of Wonder, Matthew Gregory Lewis

1802

Astonishment, Francis Lathom

The Black Forest; or, the Cavern of Horrors, anonymous

Gaston de Blondeville, Ann Radcliffe

Letters of a Solitary Wanderer, Charlotte Smith

The Midnight Assassin; or, the Confessions of the Monk Rinaldi, anonymous

The Wandering Spirit, anonymous

1803

The Captive, Matthew Gregory Lewis

"Douglas Castle; or, The Cell of Mystery, a Scottish Tale," C. F. Barrett

Idlefonzo and Alberoni; or, Tales of Horror, anonymous

The Round Tower; or, A Tale of Mystery, anonymous

The Secret Tribunal; or, The Court of Wincelaus, anonymous

The Subterraneous Passage; or, Gothic Cell, Sarah Wilkinson

Thaddeus of Warsaw, Jane Porter

Very Strange, But True, Francis Lathom

1804

The Abbey of Clunedale, Nathan Drake

"The Monks of St. Mark," Thomas Love Peacock

1805

The Bravo of Venice: A Romance, Matthew Gregory Lewis

The Canterbury Tales, Harriet Lee and Sophia Lee

The Confessions of the Nun of St. Omer, Charlotte Dacre

The Impenetrable Secret, Francis Lathom

Inkle and Yarico; or, Love in a Cave, Sarah Wilkinson

The Lay of the Last Minstrel, Sir Walter Scott

Monkcliffe Abbey, Sarah Wilkinson

Rugantino, the Bravo of Venice, Matthew Gregory Lewis

The Sorcerer's Palace; or, The Princess of Sinadone, Sarah Wilkinson

1806

The Mysterious Freebooter, Francis Lathom

Santo Sebastiano; or, The Young Protector, Catherine Cuthbertson

The Spectre; or, The Ruins of Belfont Priory, Sarah Wilkinson

The Thatched Cottage; or, Sorrows of Eugenia, Sarah Wilkinson

Zofloya, or The Moor, Charlotte Dacre

1807

The Castle Spectre; or, Family Horrors, Sarah Wilkinson

The Demon of Sicily, Edmund Montague

The Discarded Son; or, Haunt of the Banditti, Regina Roche

Fatal Jealousy; or, Blood Will Have Blood! Containing the History of Count Almagro and Duke Alphonso, anonymous

Fatal Revenge; or, The Family of Montorio, Charles Robert Maturin

The Fatal Vow, Francis Lathom

The Fugitive Countess; or, The Convent of St. Ursula, Sarah Wilkinson

The Libertine, Charlotte Dacre

Marmion, a Tale of Flodden Field, Sir Walter Scott

The Mysterious Spaniard; or, The Ruins of St. Luke's Abbey, anonymous

1808

"The Anaconda," Matthew Gregory Lewis

The Child of Mystery, Sarah Wilkinson

"Lines Inscribed upon a Cup Formed from a Skull," Lord Byron

Romantic Tales, Matthew Gregory Lewis

The Unknown, Francis Lathom

The Witch of Ravensworth, George Brewey

CA. 1809

"The Tombless Epitaph," Samuel Taylor Coleridge

1809

The Family of Santraile; or, The Heir of Montault, Harriet James

The Mysterious Novice; or, Convent of the Grey Penitents, Sarah Wilkinson

"The Water Spectre," Francis Lathom

CA. 1810

"The Dance of the Dead," anonymous

The Life and Exploits of Napoleon Bonaparte, anonymous

Rayland Hall, anonymous

The White Cottage of the Valley; or, The Mysterious Husband, Sarah Wilkinson

1810

The Castle of Montabino; or, The Orphan Sisters, Sarah Wilkinson

The Convent of the Grey Penitents; or, The Apostate Nun,
    Sarah Wilkinson
The Family Legend, Joanna Baillie
The Houses of Osma and Almeria; or, Convent of St.
    Ildefonso, Regina Roche
The Life and Horrid Adventures of the Celebrated Dr.
    Faustus, anonymous
The Scottish Chiefs, Jane Porter
The Wandering Jew; or, The Victim of the Eternal Avenger,
    Percy Bysshe Shelley
Zastrozzi: A Romance, Percy Bysshe Shelley

1811

The Midnight Bell; or, The Abbey of St. Francis, anonymous
The Missionary, Sydney Owenson
St. Irvyne; or, The Rosicrucian, Percy Bysshe Shelley
Undine, Friedrich de la Motte Fouqué

1812

The Milesian Chief, Charles Robert Maturin
Orra: A Tragedy, Joanna Baillie
"Palmyra," Thomas Love Peacock

1813

Adelaide; or, The Countercharm, Catherine Cuthbertson
The Bride of Abydos, Lord Byron
The Giaour, Lord Byron
Monastery of St. Colomb; or, The Atonement, a Novel,
    Regina Roche
The Witch of Fife, James Hogg

1814

"The Assassins," Percy Bysshe Shelley
The Corsair, Lord Byron
"La Chevelure" [The Gold Braid], Guy de Maupassant
"Lara," Lord Byron
London Tales, or Reflective Portraits, Regina Roche

1815

"The Destruction of Sennacherib," Lord Byron
Guy Mannering, Sir Walter Scott
The Manuscript Found in Saragossa, Jan Potocki
"My Soul Is Dark," Lord Byron
Phantasiestücke in Callots Manier [Fantasy pieces in the
    style of Callot], E. T. A. Hoffmann

1816

Bertram; or, The Castle of Aldobrand, Charles Robert
    Maturin

"**Christabel,**" Samuel Taylor Coleridge
Chronicles of an Illustrious House, Anne of Swansea
"Darkness," Lord Byron
Die Elixiere des Teufels [The Devil's Elixir], E. T. A.
    Hoffmann
Glenarvon, Caroline Lamb
"**Kubla Khan,**" Samuel Taylor Coleridge
Nussknacker und Mausekönig [Nutcracker and Mouse-
    king], E. T. A. Hoffmann
"**The Prisoner of Chillon,**" Lord Byron
"Prometheus," Lord Byron

1817

"After Dark Vapors," John Keats
"The Bride of the Grave," Johann Ludwig Tieck
Falkland, Edward Bulwer-Lytton
Lalla Rookh, Thomas Moore
"Limbo," Samuel Taylor Coleridge
Manfred, Lord Byron
The Pastor's Fireside, Jane Porter
The Revolt of Islam, Percy Bysshe Shelley
"The Sand-Man," E. T. A. Hoffmann
"**Thanatopsis,**" William Cullen Bryant
The Tragical History of Jane Arnold, Commonly Called
    Crazy Jane; and Mr. Henry Percival, Sarah Wilkinson

1818

Endymion, John Keats
Frankenstein, Mary Wollstonecraft Shelley
Invocation to Misery, Percy Bysshe Shelley
Maid Marion, Thomas Love Peacock
Nightmare Abbey, Thomas Love Peacock
Northanger Abbey, Jane Austen
"When I Have Fears," John Keats

CA. 1819

"The Secrets of Cabalism; or, Ravenstone and Alice of
    Huntingdon," William Child Green

1819

Anastatius, or Memoirs of a Greek, Thomas Hope
The Bride of Lammermoor, Sir Walter Scott
The Eve of St. Agnes, John Keats
"The Human Seasons," John Keats
Ivanhoe, Sir Walter Scott
"**La Belle Dame sans Merci,**" John Keats
Lamia (1819), John Keats
"Mademoiselle De Scudéry," E. T. A. Hoffmann
New Tales, Sarah Wilkinson
"A Tale for a Chimney Corner," Leigh Hunt

"The Thesaurus of Horror; or, The Charnel House Explored!" John Snart
"The Vampyre," John Polidori

CA. 1820
The Severed Arm; or, The Wehr-Wolf of Limousin, anonymous
Tales of Superstition, anonymous

1820
The Abbot, Sir Walter Scott
Italian Mysteries, Francis Lathom
"The Legend of Sleepy Hollow," Washington Irving
Le Vampire, Jean Charles Nodier
Mary, Maid of the Inn, anonymous
Melmoth the Wanderer, Charles Robert Maturin
The Monastery, Sir Walter Scott
The One-Pound Note and Other Tales, Francis Lathom
"The Spectre Bridegroom," Washington Irving
The Spectre of Lanmere Abbey, Sarah Wilkinson
The Vampire; or, The Bride of the Isles, James Robinson Planché

1821
Confessions of an English Opium Eater, Thomas De Quincey
"Die Doppelgänger" [The Double-Goer], E. T. A. Hoffmann
The Maid of the Hamlet, Regina Roche
The Maniac of the Desert, William Child Green
"The Man in the Bell," William Maginn
Smarra; or, The Demons of the Night, Charles Nodier
The Spy, James Fenimore Cooper

1822
"The Spectre Bride," William Harrison Ainsworth
Guilty; or Not Guilty; or, A Lesson for Husbands: A Tale, Anne of Swansea
Kinder- und Hausmärchen [Children's and household tales], Grimm Brothers
Logan, John Neal
Phantasus [Apparition], Johann Ludwig Tieck
The Pirate, Sir Walter Scott

1823
Ada Reis, Caroline Lamb
"The Dice," Thomas De Quincey
Han d'Islande, Victor Hugo

1824
Account of the Trial of John Thurtell and Joseph Hunt, Pierce Egan

The Adventures of Hajji Baba of Ispahan, James Morier
Duke Christian of Luneberg; or, Traditions of the Harz, Jane Porter
The Polish Bandit, Francis Lathom
The Private Memoirs and Confessions of a Justified Sinner, James Hogg
The Prophecy of Duncannon; or, The Dwarf and the Seer, William Child Green
Tales of a Traveller, Sir Walter Scott
The Tradition of the Castle; or, Scenes in the Emerald Isle, Regina Roche

1825
"Leixlip Castle: An Irish Family Legend," Charles Robert Maturin
The Talisman, Sir Walter Scott
"The Unholy Compact Abjured," Charles Pigault-Lebrun

1826
The Abbot of Montserrat; or, The Pool of Blood, William Child Green
The Astrologer's Prediction; or, The Maniac's Fate, anonymous
Deeds of Olden Times, Anne of Swansea
"England's Dead," Felicia Hemans
"Glenallan," Edward Bulwer-Lytton
The Last of the Mohicans, James Fenimore Cooper
"Metempsychosis," Robert Macnish
"The New Melusina," Johann Wolfgang von Goethe

1827
"Das Pokal" [The goblet], Johann Ludwig Tieck
"Die Elfen" [The elves], Johann Ludwig Tieck
Grimms' Fairy Tales, George Cruikshank
Hamel, the Obeah Man, anonymous
"In Youth I Have Known One," Edgar Allan Poe

1828
"Indian Woman's Death-Song," Felicia Hemans
Pelham, Edward Bulwer-Lytton
Rachel Dyer, John Neal
Salathiel, the Wandering Jew, George Croly
"The Tale of the Mysterious Mirror," Sir Walter Scott
"The Tapestried Chamber," Sir Walter Scott
The Tragic Comedy or Comical Tragedy of Punch and Judy, Payne Collier and George Cruikshank
"The Witches of Traquair," James Hogg

1829
Black-Eyed Susan, Douglas William Jerrold
Ecarté; or, The Salons of Paris, John Richardson

Fashionable Mysteries, Francis Lathom
L'Ane Mort et la Femme Guillotinée [The dead donkey and the guillotined woman], Jules Janin
"Le Dernier Jour d'un Condamné" [The last day of a condemned man], Jules Janin
"The Manuscript Found in a Mad-House," Edward Bulwer-Lytton
The Misfortunes of Elphin, Thomas Love Peacock

CA. 1830
Robinson Crusoe (Gothic bluebook), anonymous

1830
Auchindrane, Sir Walter Scott
The Doom of Devorgoil, Sir Walter Scott
"The Hollow of the Three Hills," Nathaniel Hawthorne
"The Idiot Boy," Margaret Northampton
"The Iron Shroud," William Mudford
La Confession, Jules Janin
Maria Marten; or, The Murder in the Red Barn, anonymous
"Monos and Daimonos," Edward Bulwer-Lytton
Mystic Events, Francis Lathom
Paul Clifford, Edward Bulwer-Lytton
"The Spirit's Return," Felicia Hemans

1831
Eugene Onegin, Alexander Pushkin
Evenings on a Farm near Dakanka, Nikolai Gogol
"La Cafétière" [The Coffee Machine], Théophile Gautier
"Lenore," Edgar Allan Poe
Le Peau de Chagrin [The Fatal Skin], Honoré de Balzac
"The Possessed One," anonymous
Sir Edward Seaward's Narrative of His Shipwreck, Jane Porter

1832
The Algerines; or, The Twins of Naples, William Child Green
"Bon-Bon," Edgar Allan Poe
Contes Fantastiques [Fantastic tales], Jules Janin
Eugene Aram, Edward Bulwer-Lytton
Faust, Johann Wolfgang von Goethe
Klosterheim, Thomas De Quincey
"Metzengerstein," Edgar Allan Poe
"Roger Malvin's Burial," Nathaniel Hawthorne
Tales of the Glauber Spa, William Cullen Bryant
Wacousta; or, The Prophecy: A Tale of the Canadas, John Richardson

1833
Albertus, Théophile Gautier
"MS. Found in a Bottle," Edgar Allan Poe
"The Mortal Immortal, A Tale," Mary Wollstonecraft Shelley
"The Story of Hester Malpas," Letitia Elizabeth Landon

1834
The Nun's Picture, Regina Roche
"Omphale," Théophile Gautier
The Queen of Spades, Alexander Pushkin
Rookwood, William Harrison Ainsworth

1835
Arabeski [Arabesques], Nikolai Gogol
"Berenice," Edgar Allan Poe
"Big Claus and Little Claus," Hans Christian Andersen
"The Diary of a Madman," Nikolai Gogol
"King Pest the First: A Tale Containing an Allegory," Edgar Allan Poe
Mademoiselle de Maupin, Théophile Gautier
Mirgorod, Nikolai Gogol
"Morella," Edgar Allan Poe
"The Nevsky Prospect," Nikolai Gogol
"The Nose," Nikolai Gogol
"The Portrait," Nikolai Gogol
"The Tinder-Box," Hans Christian Andersen
"Viy," Nikolai Gogol
The Yemassee, William Gilmore Simms
"Young Goodman Brown," Nathaniel Hawthorne

1836
The Awful Disclosures of Maria Monk; or, The Hidden Secrets of a Nun's Life in a Convent, T. B. Peterson
"An Expedition to Hell," James Hogg
La Morte Amoreuse [The dead lover], Théophile Gautier
"The Little Mermaid," Hans Christian Andersen
Sheppard Lee, Robert Montgomery Bird

1837
Ernest Maltravers, Edward Bulwer-Lytton
Fortunio, Théophile Gautier
Further Disclosures of Maria Monk, T. B. Peterson
"The Minister's Black Veil," Nathaniel Hawthorne
Nick of the Woods, Robert Montgomery Bird
Pickwick Papers, Charles Dickens
"The Sylph," Vladimir Odoevsky

1838
Alice; or, The Mysteries, Edward Bulwer-Lytton
The Avenger, Thomas De Quincey

"The Ghost and the Bone-Setter," Sheridan Le Fanu
La Comédie de la Mort [The comedy of death],
    Théophile Gautier
Les Mémoires du Diable [The devil's memoirs], Frédéric
    Soulié
"Ligeia," Edgar Allan Poe
The Narrative of Arthur Gordon Pym, Edgar Allan Poe
"Silence—A Fable," Edgar Allan Poe

1839

Cosmorama, Vladimir Odoevsky
"The Devil in the Belfry," anonymous
"The Fall of the House of Usher," Edgar Allan Poe
Jack Sheppard, William Harrison Ainsworth
Les Catacombes, Jules Janin
"Schalken the Painter," Sheridan Le Fanu
"Une Larme du Diable" [The Devil's Tear], Théophile
    Gautier
"The White Wolf of the Hartz Mountains," Frederick
    Marryat
"William Wilson," Edgar Allan Poe

1840

The Canadian Brothers; or, The Prophecy Fulfilled, John
    Richardson
The Demon, Mikhail Lermontov
Legends of Terror! And Tales of the Wonderful and Wild, G.
    Creed
The Pathfinder, James Fenimore Cooper
The Tower of London, William Harrison Ainsworth

1841

Barnaby Rudge, Charles Dickens
The Deerslayer, James Fenimore Cooper
"A Descent into the Maelström," Edgar Allan Poe
"Never Bet the Devil Your Head: A Tale with a Moral,"
    Edgar Allan Poe
Salamander, Vladimir Odoevsky

1842

Dead Souls, Nikolai Gogol
Die Schwarze Spinne [The Black Spider], Jeremias Gotthelf
"The Masque of the Red Death," Edgar Allan Poe
"The Mystery of Marie Rogêt," Edgar Allan Poe
"The Oval Portrait," Edgar Allan Poe
The Skeleton Clutch; or, The Goblet of Gore, Thomas
    Preskett Prest
Zanoni, Edward Bulwer-Lytton

1843

"The Birthmark," Nathaniel Hawthorne
"The Black Cat," Edgar Allan Poe

A Christmas Carol, Charles Dickens
"The Gold Bug," Edgar Allan Poe
The Mysteries of Paris, Eugène Sue

1844

Barry Lyndon, William Makepeace Thackeray
The Black Monk; or, The Street of the Grey Turret,
    Thomas Preskett Prest
"Dream-Land," Edgar Allan Poe
Le Juif Errant [The Wandering Jew], Eugène Sue
Les Grotesques, Théophile Gautier
"The Mesmeric Revelation," Edgar Allan Poe
"The Purloined Letter," Edgar Allan Poe
"Rappaccini's Daughter," Nathaniel Hawthorne
"The Raven," Edgar Allan Poe
Russkiye Notchi [Russian nights], Vladimir Odoevsky
"Thou Art the Man," Edgar Allan Poe
"The Ugly Duckling," Hans Christian Andersen

1845

"The Fir Tree," Hans Christian Andersen
"Imp of the Perverse," Edgar Allan Poe
"Night and Morning," Edward Bulwer-Lytton
"The Red Shoes," Hans Christian Andersen
"Snow White," Hans Christian Andersen
"Some Words with a Mummy," Edgar Allan Poe
The Quaker City; or, The Monks of Monk Hall, George
    Lippard
Suspiria de Profundis [Sighs from the depths], Thomas
    De Quincey

1846

"The Cask of Amontillado," Edgar Allan Poe
Dvoynik [The Double], Fyodor Dostoevsky
Faust: A Romance of the Secret Tribunals, George
    Reynolds
"The Little Match-Seller," Hans Christian Andersen
Lucretia; or, The Children of the Night (1846), Edward
    Bulwer-Lytton
"A Select Party," Nathaniel Hawthorne
The String of Pearls, Thomas Preskett Prest
Typee, Herman Melville
"The Virtuoso's Collection," Nathaniel Hawthorne

1847

"The Almshouse Window," Hans Christian Andersen
Contes Fantastiques [Fantastic tales], Émile Erckmann
    and Louis Alexandre Chatrian
Jane Eyre, Charlotte Brontë
"My Sister's Sleep," Dante Gabriel Rossetti

Omoo, Herman Melville
"The Portrait," Dante Gabriel Rossetti
"The Shadow," Hans Christian Andersen
The String of Pearls: The Fiend of Fleet Street, George
    Dibdin Pitt
"Ulalume," Edgar Allan Poe
Varney the Vampyre; or, The Feast of Blood, anonymous
Wagner the Wehr-Wolf, George Reynolds
Wuthering Heights, Emily Brontë

1848
"The Bells," Edgar Allan Poe
Mary Barton, Elizabeth Gaskell
The Mysteries of London, George Reynolds
"Song," Christina Rossetti
Sweeney Todd, the Demon Barber of Fleet Street, Thomas
    Preskett Prest
Windsor Castle, William Harrison Ainsworth

1849
"Annabel Lee," Edgar Allan Poe
Auriol; or, The Elixir of Life, William Harrison Ainsworth
"A Dream within a Dream," Edgar Allan Poe
"The Forsaken of God," William Mudford
"The Invisible Eye," Émile Erckmann and Louis
    Alexandre Chatrian
Jane Eyre; or, The Secrets of Thornfield Hall, John
    Courtney
The Lancashire Witches: A Romance of Pendle Forest,
    William Harrison Ainsworth

1850
The Monk Knight of St. John: A Tale of the Crusaders,
    John Richardson
The Scarlet Letter, Nathaniel Hawthorne

1851
"An Arabian Nightmare," Fitz-James O'Brien
Ein Golem, Theodor Storm
The House of the Seven Gables, Nathaniel Hawthorne
Moby-Dick, Herman Melville
"My Kinsman, Major Molineux," Nathaniel Hawthorne

1852
"Arria Marcella," Théophile Gautier
The Blithedale Romance, Nathaniel Hawthorne
The Corsican Brothers, Dionysius Boucicault
The Necromancer: A Romance, George Reynolds
"The Old Grave-Stone," Hans Christian Andersen
"The Old Nurse's Story," Elizabeth Gaskell

"The Punishment of Gina Montani," Ellen Wood
Uncle Tom's Cabin, Harriet Beecher Stowe
The Vampire, Dionysius Boucicault

1853
"Bartleby the Scrivener," Herman Melville
Bleak House, Charles Dickens
The Mysteries of the Court of London, George Reynolds
Villette, Charlotte Brontë

1855
Benito Cereno, Herman Melville
"The Ostler," Wilkie Collins
"The Paradise of Bachelors and the Tartarus of Maids,"
    Herman Melville
Paul Ferroll, Caroline Clive
"The Pot of Tulips," Fitz-James O'Brien

1856
Avatar, Théophile Gautier
Faust, Ivan Turgenev
"The Jewish Maiden," Hans Christian Andersen
"Riding Together," William Morris

1857
"Der Räuberbräutigam" [The Robber Bridegroom],
    Grimm brothers
"The Haunted and the Haunters; or, The House and the
    Brain," Edward Bulwer-Lytton
Jettature, Théophile Gautier
Le Meneur des Loups [The Wolf-Leader], Alexandre
    Dumas the Elder
Les Fleurs du Mal [The Flowers of Evil], Charles
    Baudelaire
Nouvelles Histoires Extraordinaires [New extraordinary
    tales], Charles Baudelaire
The Poor of New York, Dionysius Boucicault

1858
After Dark, Dionysius Boucicault
"The Diamond Lens," Fitz-James O'Brien
"The Marsh King's Daughter," Hans Christian Andersen
"Rapunzel," William Morris

1859
Chien d'Or [The Golden Dog]: A Legend of Quebec,
    William Kirby
"The Double-Bedded Room," Wilkie Collins
"The Haunted House," Charles Dickens
"The Lifted Veil," George Eliot

The Octoroon, or Life in Louisiana, Dionysius Boucicault
A Tale of Two Cities, Charles Dickens
"What Was It?" Fitz-James O'Brien
"Wondersmith," Fitz-James O'Brien

1860

Malaeska: The Indian Wife of the White Hunter, Anne
    Sophia Stephens
The Marble Faun; or, The Romance of Monte Beni,
    Nathaniel Hawthorne
Three Times Dead; or, The Secret of the Heath, Mary
    Elizabeth Braddon
Why Paul Ferroll Killed His Wife, Caroline Clive
The Woman in White, Wilkie Collins

1861

The Black Band; or, The Mysteries of Midnight, Mary
    Elizabeth Braddon
Doctor Grimshawe's Secret, Nathaniel Hawthorne
East Lynne, Ellen Wood
Great Expectations, Charles Dickens
A Strange Story, Edward Bulwer-Lytton

1862

The Channings, Ellen Wood
The Goblin Market, Christina Rossetti
The House by the Churchyard, Sheridan Le Fanu
Lady Audley's Secret, Mary Elizabeth Braddon
Les Misérables, Victor Hugo
Mrs. Halliburton's Troubles, Ellen Wood
The Octoroon; or, The Lily of Louisiana, Mary Elizabeth
    Braddon
Pauline's Passion and Punishment, Louisa May Alcott
The Shadow of Ahslydyat, Ellen Wood

1863

Aurora Floyd, Mary Elizabeth Braddon
"Circumstance," Harriet Spofford
Eleanor's Victory, Mary Elizabeth Braddon
John Marchmont's Legacy, Mary Elizabeth Braddon
Les Anciens Canadiens [The Canadians of Old], Philippe-
    Aubert de Gaspé the Elder
"M. L.," Louisa May Alcott
"The Mummy's Foot," Théophile Gautier
"My Contraband," Louisa May Alcott
Notting Hill Mystery, Charles Felix
The Unicorn, Iris Murdoch

1864

The Doctor's Wife, Mary Elizabeth Braddon
George Geith of Fen Court, Charlotte Cowan Riddell

"Phantoms," Ivan Turgenev
The Spectre Mother; or, The Haunted Tower, anonymous
Uncle Silas, Sheridan Le Fanu
Wylder's Hand, Sheridan Le Fanu

1865

Histoires Grotesques et Sérieuses [Grotesque and serious
    tales], Charles Baudelaire
The Marble Woman, Louisa May Alcott
"The Trial for Murder," Charles Dickens

1866

The Lady's Mile, Mary Elizabeth Braddon
The Long Fatal Love Chase, Louisa May Alcott
"The Signalman," Charles Dickens
Spirite, Théophile Gautier

1867

The Abbot's Ghost, Louisa May Alcott
Anne Hereford, Ellen Wood
Le Crime d'Orcival [The Crime at Orcival], Émile
    Gaboriau
Under the Gaslight, Augustin Daly

1868

Black Bess; or, The Knight of the Road, John Frederick
    Smith
Dead Sea Fruit, Mary Elizabeth Braddon
"De Grey," Henry James
"Nis and the Dame," Hans Christian Andersen

1869

Les Esclaves de Paris [The keys of Paris], Émile Gaboriau
Le Spleen de Paris, Charles Baudelaire
"Lokis," Prosper Mérimée
Monsieur Lecoq, Émile Gaboriau
"Un Voyage à Cythère" [A voyage to Cythera], Charles
    Baudelaire

1870

*François de Bienville: Scenes of Seventeenth-Century
    Canadian Life,* Joseph Étienne Eugène Marmette

1871

The Coming Race, Edward Bulwer-Lytton
"The Haunted Valley," Ambrose Bierce
Horizon, Augustin Daly
The Rose and the Key, Sheridan Le Fanu

1872
Carmilla, Sheridan Le Fanu
"The Cripple," Hans Christian Andersen
In a Glass Darkly, Sheridan Le Fanu

1873
Around the World in Eighty Days, Jules Verne
"The Gambler Bobok," Vladimir Odoevsky
The New Magdalen, Wilkie Collins
Une Saison en Enfer [A Season in Hell], Arthur Rimbaud

1874
The City of Dreadful Night, James Thomson
"Ghost Rental," Henry James
"The Last of the Valerii," Henry James
"The Secret of Macarger's Gulch," Ambrose Bierce

1875
Behind a Mask, Louisa May Alcott
"Jean-ah Poquelin," George Washington Cable
"La Main d'Ecorche" [The Flayed Hand], Guy de Maupassant
La Ville-Vampire [Vampire city], Paul Féval
The Law and the Lady, Wilkie Collins
Shaughraun, Dionysius Boucicault

1876
Danites of the Sierras, Joaquin Miller
"Le Tombeau d'Edgar Poe" [Edgar Poe's Tomb], Stéphane Mallarmé
"The Man-Wolf," Émile Erckmann and Louis Alexandre Chatrian
"The Murderer's Violin," Émile Erckmann and Louis Alexandre Chatrian
The Secret Chamber, Margaret Oliphant
The Sentimental Song Book, Julia Moore

1877
"The Dream of Ridiculous Man," Vladimir Odoevsky
A Modern Mephistopheles, Louisa May Alcott

1878
"A Ballad of François Villon," Algernon Swinburne

1879
"Bras Coupé" [Broken arm or Lopped arm], George Washington Cable
The Grandissimes: A Story of Creole Life, George Washington Cable

"The Mystery of Sassassa Valley," Sir Arthur Conan Doyle

1880
The Beleaguered City, Margaret Oliphant
"Boule de Suif" [Butterball], Guy de Maupassant
Strange Stories, Émile Erckmann and Louis Alexandre Chatrian

1881
The Body Snatcher, Robert Louis Stevenson
Madame Delphine, George Washington Cable
The Mystery of Major Molineux, Marcus Clarke
"The Open Door," Margaret Oliphant
The Portrait of a Lady, Henry James

1882
Insomnia, James Thomson
The Little Pilgrim of the Unseen, Margaret Oliphant
The New Arabian Nights, Robert Louis Stevenson

1883
Contes Cruels [Cruel Tales], Villiers de L'Isle-Adam
"The Doctor's Heroism," Villiers de L'Isle-Adam
Heart and Science, Wilkie Collins
"La Main" [The Hand], Guy de Maupassant
"The Torture of Hope," Villiers de L'Isle-Adam
Treasure Island, Robert Louis Stevenson

1884
Against the Grain, Joris-Karl Huysmans
"The Harnt That Walks Chilhowee," Mary Noailles Murfree
Matrosengeschichten [Sailor stories], Karl Heinrich Ulrichs

1885
Stories of the Seen and Unseen, Margaret Oliphant

1886
Dr. Jekyll and Mr. Hyde, Robert Louis Stevenson
Kidnapped (1886), Robert Louis Stevenson
L'Eve Future [The future Eve], Villiers de L'Isle-Adam
The Romance of Two Worlds, Marie Corelli
Vendetta!; or, The Story of One Forgotten, Marie Corelli

1887
Ein Doppelgänger [A double-goer], Theodor Storm
"La Morte" [The dead], Guy de Maupassant

"La Nuit" [The night], Guy de Maupassant
"Le Horla, or Modern Ghosts," Guy de Maupassant
"Markheim," Robert Louis Stevenson
"Moiron," Guy de Maupassant
"Olalla," Robert Louis Stevenson
Some Chinese Ghosts, Lafcadio Hearn
"Thrawn Janet," Robert Louis Stevenson

1888
"The Birthday of the Infanta," Oscar Wilde
"The Bottle Imp," Robert Louis Stevenson
"Clarimonde: A Supernatural Passion," Lafcadio Hearn
The Happy Prince and Other Tales, Oscar Wilde
The Land Beyond the Forest, Emily de Laszkowska Gerard
"My Own True Ghost Story," Rudyard Kipling
"The Nightingale and the Rose," Oscar Wilde
Nouveaux Contes Cruels [New cruel tales], Villiers de
    L'Isle-Adam
"The Phantom Rickshaw," Rudyard Kipling
The Strange Manuscript Found in a Copper Cylinder, James
    de Mille
"The Strange Ride of Morrowbie Jukes," Rudyard Kipling
What Dreams May Come, Gertrude Atherton

1889
Ardath: The Story of a Dead Self, Marie Corelli
"The Canterville Ghost," Oscar Wilde
"Friends of the Friends," Henry James
The Master of Ballantrae, Robert Louis Stevenson
The Mystery of Cloomber, Sir Arthur Conan Doyle

1890
The Albert Victor Waltz, Felix Burns
Chronicles of Crime and Criminals, anonymous
**"The Sign of the Four; or, The Problem of the
    Sholtos,"** Sir Arthur Conan Doyle
The Snake's Pass, Bram Stoker

1891
"The Bascombe Valley Mystery," Sir Arthur Conan
    Doyle
"Botticelli's Madonna," Edith Wharton
"The City of Dreadful Night," Rudyard Kipling
"The Fisherman and His Soul," Oscar Wilde
Gerard; or, The World, the Flesh and the Devil, Mary
    Elizabeth Braddon
The House of Pomegranates, Oscar Wilde
Là-Bas [Down there], Joris-Karl Huysmans
Life's Handicap, Rudyard Kipling
"The Mark of the Beast," Rudyard Kipling

"An Occurrence at Owl Creek Bridge," Ambrose
    Bierce
The Picture of Dorian Gray, Oscar Wilde
"The Recrudescence of Imray," Rudyard Kipling
"A Scandal in Bohemia," Sir Arthur Conan Doyle
"The Tomb of Ilaria Giunigi," Edith Wharton
"Without Benefit of Clergy," Rudyard Kipling

1892
"The Adventures of the Speckled Band," Sir Arthur
    Conan Doyle
"The Blue Carbuncle," Sir Arthur Conan Doyle
"Death and the Woman," Gertrude Atherton
L'Innocente [The innocent], Gabriele d'Annunzio
Melmoth Reconcilié à l'Eglise [Melmoth reconciled to the
    church], Honoré de Balzac
The Monk and the Hangman's Daughter, Ambrose Bierce
"A Private Life," Henry James
"Sir Dominick Ferrand," Henry James
The Soul of Lilith, Marie Corelli
"The Yellow Wallpaper," Charlotte Perkins Gilman

1893
Barabbas: A Dream of the World's Tragedy, Marie Corelli
Can Such Things Be?, Ambrose Bierce
The Christmas Witch, Gertrude Atherton
"The Crab Spider," Émile Erckmann and Louis
    Alexandre Chatrian
"The Damned Thing," Ambrose Bierce
"The Final Problem," Sir Arthur Conan Doyle
"The Finest Story in the World," Rudyard Kipling
"Isle of Voices," Robert Louis Stevenson
Salomé, Oscar Wilde

1894
The Adventures of Sherlock Holmes, Sir Arthur Conan
    Doyle
The Black Monk, Anton Chekhov
The Great God Pan, Arthur Machen
"In the Avu Observatory," H. G. Wells
"The Flowering of the Strange Orchid," H. G. Wells
Memoirs of Sherlock Holmes, Sir Arthur Conan Doyle
Pudd'nhead Wilson, Mark Twain
Studies of Death, Stanislaus Eric Stenbock
Trilby, George du Maurier
A True Story of the Vampire, Stanislaus Eric Stenbock

1895
"The Cone," H. G. Wells
The Long Arm, Mary E. Wilkins Freeman

Pour la Patrie [For My Country], Jules-Paul Tardivel
The Sorrows of Satan, Marie Corelli
The Time Machine, H. G. Wells
The Three Impostors, Arthur Machen

1896

"The Devil and the Innkeeper," Robert Louis Stevenson
The Island of Dr. Moreau, H. G. Wells
"The Library Window," Margaret Oliphant
The Other Room, Henry James
"The Plattner Story," H. G. Wells
"The Red Room," H. G. Wells
"The Rival Beauties," W. W. Jacobs
"The Sea Raiders," H. G. Wells
"The Striding Place," Gertrude Atherton
Ubu Roi [King Ubu], Alfred Jarry

1897

The Beetle, Richard Marsh
"The Brown Man's Servant," W. W. Jacobs
Dracula, Bram Stoker
"The Haunted Subaltern," Rudyard Kipling
"Jerry Bundler," W. W. Jacobs
"Pollock and the Porroh Man," H. G. Wells
Thirty Strange Stories, H. G. Wells
Ziska: The Problem of a Wicked Soul, Marie Corelli

1898

The Ballad of Reading Gaol, Oscar Wilde
"The Man That Corrupted Hadleyburg," Mark Twain
"The Monster," Stephen Crane
The Turn of the Screw, Henry James
The Whitechapel Murders; or, On the Track of the Fiend,
    Detective Warren

1899

The Ghost of Jerry Bundler, W. W. Jacobs
"Gray Wolf's Ha'nt," Charles Chesnutt
In Ghostly Japan, Lafcadio Hearn
"Mars Jeems's Nightmare," Charles Chesnutt
"Po' Sandy," Charles Chesnutt
"Sis' Becky's Pickaninny," Charles Chesnutt

1900

"How Love Came to Professor Guildea," Robert Smythe
    Hichens
Lord Jim, Joseph Conrad
A Sense of the Past, Henry James

1901

"The Ballad of Gregorio Cortez," anonymous
Cavalier, George Washington Cable

1902

Heart of Darkness, Joseph Conrad
The Hound of the Baskervilles, Sir Arthur Conan
    Doyle
The Little Demon, Fyodor Sologub
"The Monkey's Paw," W. W. Jacobs
"Quicksand," Edith Wharton
"The Tiger's Skin," W. W. Jacobs
Wings of the Dove, Henry James

1903

"The Adventure of the Empty House," Sir Arthur
    Conan Doyle
"The Beast in the Jungle," Henry James
"The Inexperienced Ghost," H. G. Wells
"The Stolen Body," H. G. Wells
"The Truth about Pyecraft," H. G. Wells

1904

"The Adventure of the Second Stain," Sir Arthur
    Conan Doyle
"Canon Alberic's Scrap-Book," M. R. James
"Casting the Runes," M. R. James
Ghost Stories of an Antiquary, M. R. James
The Golden Bowl, Henry James
The Jewel of Seven Stars, Bram Stoker
"Jiu-Roku-Zakura," Lafcadio Hearn
Kwaidan [Weird tales], Lafcadio Hearn
"Mimi-Nashi-Hoichi," Lafcadio Hearn
"Oshidori," Lafcadio Hearn
"O-Tei," Lafcadio Hearn

1905

"The Beast in the Cave," H. P. Lovecraft
Beauty and the Barge, W. W. Jacobs
"The Bell in the Fog," Gertrude Atherton
"Charles Augustus Milverton," Sir Arthur Conan
    Doyle
"The Dead and the Countess," Gertrude Atherton
The House of Mirth, Edith Wharton
"They," Rudyard Kipling

1906

The Man in Lower Ten, Mary Roberts Rinehart
"Smith: An Episode in a Lodging House," Algernon
    Blackwood

1907

Der Zauberlehrling Oder die Teufelsjäger [The sorcerer's
    apprentice; or, the devil hunter] (1907), Hanns
    Heinz Ewers
The Flag Station, W. W. Jacobs
The Highwayman, Alfred Noyes
*Le Mystère de la Chambre Jaune [The Mystery of the Yellow
    Room],* Gaston Leroux
"The Listener," Algernon Blackwood
The Secret Agent, Joseph Conrad
"The Willows," Algernon Blackwood

1908

"The Camp of the Dog," Algernon Blackwood
The Circular Staircase, Mary Roberts Rinehart
The Fiery Angel, Valery Bryusov
"The Idiot," Joseph Conrad
"The Jolly Corner," Henry James
Kincaid's Battery, George Washington Cable
"Secret Worship," Algernon Blackwood

1909

"Gabriel-Ernest," Saki
The Lady of the Shroud, Bram Stoker
Le Parfum de la Dame en Noir [The fragrance of the lady
    in black], Gaston Leroux
The Maharal of Prague, Yudl Rosenberg
"The Toll House," W. W. Jacobs

1910

"The Eyes," Edith Wharton
The Human Chord, Algernon Blackwood
"The Lady's Maid's Bell," Edith Wharton
The Phantom of the Opera, Gaston Leroux
The Return, Walter de la Mare
"The Wendigo," Algernon Blackwood
The Window at the White Cat, Mary Roberts Rinehart

1911

"Afterward," Edith Wharton
Alraune [The mandrakes], Hanns Heinz Ewers
"The Beckoning Fair One," Oliver Onions
"The Bottomless Grave," Ambrose Bierce
"The Country of the Blind," H. G. Wells
"Esmé," Saki
Ethan Frome, Edith Wharton
The Innocence of Father Brown, Gilbert Keith Chesterton
The Lair of the White Worm, Bram Stoker
"Sredni Vashtar," Saki
Tales of Men and Ghosts, Edith Wharton
"Tobermory," Saki

1912

Baloo, Gaston Leroux
"The Case of Oscar Brodsky," Richard Austin Freeman
"Die Verwandlung" [The Metamorphosis], Franz
    Kafka
"The Grove of Ashtaroth," John Buchan
"The Listeners," Walter de la Mare
The Man with the Black Feather, Gaston Leroux
"The Pomegranate Seed," Edith Wharton
Riders of the Purple Sage, Zane Grey
"The Secret Sharer," Joseph Conrad
"The She-Wolf," Saki

1913

Carnacki the Ghost Finder, William Hope Hodgson
The Case of Jennie Brice, Mary Roberts Rinehart
The Lodger, Marie Adelaide Belloc Lowndes
Studies in Love and Terror, Marie Adelaide Belloc
    Lowndes

1914

"The Boar-Pig," Saki
"The Magi," William Butler Yeats
Night Watches, W. W. Jacobs
"The Story-Teller," Saki
"The Three Sisters," W. W. Jacobs
The Underdogs, Mariano Azuela

1915

Der Golem, Gustav Meyrink
"Rashomon," Ryunosuke Akutagawa

CA. 1916

Der Dybbuk, S. Ansky

1916

The Man Who Came Back from the Dead, Gaston
    Leroux
The Mysterious Stranger, Mark Twain
"The Shadowy Third," Ellen Glasgow

1917

Nachtstücke [Strange Stories], E. T. A. Hoffmann

1918

The Garden of Survival, Algernon Blackwood
Karma, Algernon Blackwood
The White Morning, Gertrude Atherton

1919
The Squatter's Ward, Edward Sorensen
"The Story of a Disappearance and an Appearance,"
  M. R. James

1920
The Age of Innocence, Edith Wharton
"All Souls' Night," William Butler Yeats
"Arabesque: The Mouse," Alfred Edgar Coppard
The Bat, Mary Roberts Rinehart
The Eternal Smile, Pär Fabian Lagerkvist
The Last of the Lowries, Paul Green
San Gloria, Thomas Henry MacDermot

1921
"The Adventure of the Mazarin Stone," Sir Arthur
  Conan Doyle
The Man Who Was Born Again, Paul Busson
R. U. R., Karel Čapek
"The Second Coming," William Butler Yeats
Vampir, Hanns Heinz Ewers
"The Wandering Jew," Edwin Arlington Robinson

1922
"Azathoth," H. P. Lovecraft
Der Geisterseher [The Ghost-Seer], Hanns Heinz Ewers
"The Hashish-Eater," Clark Ashton Smith
"The Makropulos Case," Karel Čapek
Nachtmahr [Nightmare], Hanns Heinz Ewers

1923
Black Oxen, Gertrude Atherton
"Guests," Saki
"Jordan's End," Ellen Glasgow
"The Looking Glass," Walter de la Mare
"Out of the Deep," Walter de la Mare
"Seaton's Aunt," Walter de la Mare

1924
"The Adventure of the Sussex Vampire," Sir Arthur
  Conan Doyle
Billy Budd, Herman Melville
"The Rats in the Walls," H. P. Lovecraft
"The Tiger Skin," Violet Hunt

1925
"Alice's Godmother," Walter de la Mare
"Broomsticks," Walter de la Mare
"Miss Jemima," Walter de la Mare
The Vision, William Butler Yeats
Wild Geese, Martha Ostenso

1926
"All Hallows," Walter de la Mare
"The Descendent," H. P. Lovecraft
Ghost Book, Cynthia Charteris Asquith
"The Lost Track," Walter de la Mare
The New Terror, Gaston Leroux
"Strangers Pilgrims," Walter de la Mare

1927
"Between the Minute and the Hour," Alfred McLelland
  Burrage
The Dark Chamber, Leonard Lanson Cline
Giants in the Earth, Ole Edvart Rölvaag

1928
"The Call of Cthulhu," H. P. Lovecraft
Decline and Fall, Evelyn Waugh
"The Vengeance of Nitocris," Tennessee Williams

1929
"The Adventures of a Breach-of-Promise Con Man,"
  Karel Čapek
Cimarron, Edna Ferber
"The Last Judgment," Karel Čapek

1930
As I Lay Dying, William Faulkner
"The Jilting of Granny Weatherall," Katherine Anne
  Porter
The Maltese Falcon, Dashiell Hammett
Nightwood, Djuna Barnes
The Poor Fool, Erskine Caldwell
"The Recluse," Walter de la Mare
"A Rose for Emily," William Faulkner
Vile Bodies, Evelyn Waugh
The War in Heaven, Charles Williams

1931
"Dry September," William Faulkner
The Good Earth, Pearl Buck
Many Dimensions, Charles Williams
"The One Who Saw," Alfred McLelland Burrage
Sanctuary, William Faulkner
"That Evening Sun," William Faulkner

1932
Black Mischief, Evelyn Waugh
"The Great Cat's Tale," Karel Čapek
Greater Trumps, Charles Williams
Light in August, William Faulkner

Reiter in Deutscher Nacht [Rider of the Night], Hanns Heinz Ewers
The Thin Man, Dashiell Hammett

1933
"Hodmadod," Walter de la Mare
The Hound of Death, Agatha Christie
"The Man Who Liked Dickens," Evelyn Waugh
"Out of Depth," Evelyn Waugh
"The Skater of Ghost Lake," William Rose Benét

1934
"The Dreamers," Isak Dinesen
The Foghorn, Gertrude Atherton
A Handful of Dust, Evelyn Waugh
I, Claudius, Robert Graves
"The Monkey," Isak Dinesen
"Old Chevalier," Isak Dinesen
Seven Gothic Tales, Isak Dinesen
"The Supper at Elsinore," Isak Dinesen

1935
"Between the World and Me," Richard Wright
The Circus of Dr. Lao, Charles Grandison Finney
Der Sotn in Gorey [Satan in Goray], Isaac Bashevis Singer
Historia Universal de la Infamia *[A Universal History of Infamy],* Jorge Luis Borges
Les Cenci, Antonin Artaud
The Winged Bull, Dion Fortune

1936
Absalom, Absalom!, William Faulkner
Jamaica Inn, Daphne du Maurier
"Noon Wine," Katherine Anne Porter
"What Dreams May Come," Walter de la Mare

1937
"All Souls," Edith Wharton
Ghosts, Edith Wharton
The Hobbit, J. R. R. Tolkien
Their Eyes Were Watching God, Zora Neale Hurston

1938
"Punch and Judy," Frederick Ignatius Cowles
Rebecca, Daphne du Maurier

1939
"Barn Burning," William Faulkner
The Big Sleep, Raymond Chandler

"The Devil and Daniel Webster," Stephen Vincent Benét
"Hughes, the Wehr-Wolf," Sutherland Menzies
The Mask of Dimitrios, Eric Ambler
"The Wall," Jean-Paul Sartre

1940
The Man Who Loved Children, Christina Stead
The Ox-Bow Incident, Walter Van Tilburg Clark

1941
"Clytie," Eudora Welty
The Curtain of Green and Other Stories, Eudora Welty
"The Death of a Traveling Salesman," Eudora Welty
Frenchman's Creek, Daphne du Maurier
The Heart Is a Lonely Hunter, Carson McCullers
"Lily Daw and the Three Ladies," Eudora Welty
"The Petrified Man," Eudora Welty
"Powerhouse," Eudora Welty
Reflections in a Golden Eye, Carson McCullers
"Why I Live at the P. O.," Eudora Welty
"The Worn Path," Eudora Welty

1942
"The Bear," William Faulkner
Crazy Horse, Mari Sandoz
"The Destruction of Kreshev," Isaac Bashevis Singer
The Robber Bridegroom, Eudora Welty

1943
"Livvie Is Back," Eudora Welty

1945
Brideshead Revisited, Evelyn Waugh
"The Demon Lover," Elizabeth Bowen
"The Scarecrow," Walter de la Mare

1946
Delta Wedding, Eudora Welty
Titus Groan, Mervyn Peake

1948
"The Lottery," Shirley Jackson
Intruder in the Dust, William Faulkner
The Loved One, Evelyn Waugh
Other Voices, Other Rooms, Truman Capote

1949
"The Bus," Shirley Jackson
"The Daemon Lover," Shirley Jackson

"The Golden Apples," Eudora Welty
"The Headless Hawk," Truman Capote
"The Pillar of Salt," Shirley Jackson
Shane, Jack Warner Schaefer
"Shut a Final Door," Truman Capote
"The Tooth," Shirley Jackson

1950
Gormenghast, Mervyn Peake
I, Robot, Isaac Asimov
"There Will Come Soft Rains," Ray Bradbury
"The Veldt," Ray Bradbury

1951
The Ballad of the Sad Café, Carson McCullers
The Grass Harp, Truman Capote
The Illustrated Man, Ray Bradbury
Lie Down in Darkness, William Styron

1952
"The Birds," Daphne du Maurier
The Devils of Loudun, Aldous Huxley
The Mousetrap, Agatha Christie
The Natural, Bernard Malamud
The Swimming Pool, Mary Roberts Rinehart
Wise Blood, Flannery O'Connor

1953
Childhood's End, Arthur C. Clarke
The Crucible, Arthur Miller
"The Displaced Person," Flannery O'Connor
Fahrenheit 451, Ray Bradbury
The Night of the Hunter, Davis Alexander Grubb
"Poison," Roald Dahl
Someone Like You, Roald Dahl

1954
The Dollmaker, Harriette Arnow
"Haircut," W. Ring Lardner

1955
Cat on a Hot Tin Roof, Tennessee Williams
"Good Country People," Flannery O'Connor
"A Good Man Is Hard to Find," Flannery O'Connor
Pedro Páramo, Juan Rulfo
The Leaf Storm, Gabriel García Márquez
The Lord of the Rings, J. R. R. Tolkien

1956
"A Christmas Memory," Truman Capote
Der Besuch der Alten Dame [The Visit], Friedrich
    Dürrenmatt

1957
Dandelion Wine, Ray Bradbury
"Gimpel the Fool," Isaac Bashevis Singer

1958
The Bell, Iris Murdoch
Suddenly Last Summer, Tennessee Williams

1959
Babette's Feast, Isak Dinesen
The Haunting of Hill House, Shirley Jackson
"Las Bagbas del Diablo" [The devil's spit], Julio
    Cortázar
Titus Alone, Mervyn Peake

1960
The Magician of Lublin, Isaac Bashevis Singer
Mistress of Mellyn, Victoria Holt
Thunder Heights, Phyllis Whitney
To Kill a Mockingbird, Harper Lee
The Violent Bear It Away, Flannery O'Connor

1961
The Other Side of the Mirror, Enrique Anderson Imbert

1962
"Aura," Carlos Fuentes
Big Mama's Funeral, Gabriel García Márquez
Kirkland Revels, Victoria Holt
Something Wicked This Way Comes, Ray Bradbury
We Have Always Lived in the Castle, Shirley Jackson

1963
"Lady Lazarus," Sylvia Plath
"Sylvia's Death," Anne Sexton

1964
*The Persecution and Assassination of Marat as Performed
    by the Inmates of the Asylum of Charenton under the
    Direction of the Marquis de Sade,* Peter Weiss
Sora No Kaibutsu Aguii [Agwhee the sky monster],
    Kenzaburo Oe
Tituba of Salem Village, Ann Petry

1965
"Fever 103°," Sylvia Plath
*Une Saison dans la Vie d'Emmanuel [A Season in the Life
    of Emmanuel],* Marie-Claire Blais

1966
In Cold Blood, Truman Capote
The Shadow Dance, Angela Carter
The Time of Angels, Iris Murdoch
Wide Sargasso Sea, Jean Rhys

1967
The Confessions of Nat Turner, William Styron
The Magic Toyshop, Angela Carter
One Hundred Years of Solitude, Gabriel García Márquez
Rosemary's Baby, Ira Levin

1968
Dagon, Fred Chappell
Mephisto Waltz, Fred Mustard Stewart
"The Séance," Isaac Bashevis Singer
2001: A Space Odyssey, Arthur C. Clarke

1969
The Andromeda Strain, Michael Crichton
The Bluest Eye, Toni Morrison
The Green Man, Kingsley Amis
Heroes and Villains, Angela Carter
The House on the Strand, Daphne du Maurier

1970
Deliverance, James Dickey
"Don't Look Now," Daphne du Maurier
Kamouraska, Anne Hébert
Not After Midnight, Daphne du Maurier
Ti-Jean and His Brothers, Derek Walcott
"Where Are You Going, Where Have You Been?"
    Joyce Carol Oates

1971
The Day of the Jackal, Frederick Forsyth
The Exorcist, William Blatty
Tales of Moonlight and Rain, Ueda Akinari

1972
Bless Me, Ultima, Rudolfo Anaya
The Infernal Desire Machines of Doctor Hoffman, Angela
    Carter
Innocent Eréndira and Other Stories, Gabriel García
    Márquez
Watership Down, Richard Adams

1973
The Black Prince, Iris Murdoch
Burnt Offerings, Robert Marasco

Carrie, Stephen King
"The Crown of Feathers," Isaac Bashevis Singer
Harvest Home, Thomas Tryon
I Heard the Owl Call My Name, Margaret Craven
Sula, Toni Morrison

1974
Sweet Savage Love, Rosemary Rogers
The Flame and the Flower, Kathleen Woodiwiss
The Wolf and the Dove, Kathleen Woodiwiss

1975
Les Enfants du Sabbat [Children of the Black Sabbath],
    Anne Hébert
Salem's Lot, Stephen King
Where Are the Children? Mary Higgins Clark
The Woman Warrior, Maxine Hong Kingston

1976
Interview with the Vampire, Anne Rice

1977
Bear, Marian Engel
Getting Out, Marsha Norman
"Our Gardener," Jean Rhys
The Shining, Stephen King
Song of Solomon, Toni Morrison

1978
Beauty, Robin McKinley
Coma, Robin Cook
Hotel Transylvania, Chelsea Quinn Yarbro
The Sea, the Sea, Iris Murdoch
Wolfen, Whitley Strieber

1979
The Bloody Chamber, Angela Carter
Crimes of the Heart, Beth Henley
Ghost Story, Peter Straub
Grendel, John Gardner
Kindred, Octavia Butler
Sweeney Todd, Stephen Sondheim
Woman on the Edge of Time, Marge Piercy

1980
Bellefleur, Joyce Carol Oates
Firestarter, Stephen King
The Girl in a Swing, Richard Adams
The Name of the Rose, Umberto Eco

New Tales of the Cthulhu Mythos, John Ramsey Campbell
To Wake the Dead, John Ramsey Campbell

1981
The House of the Spirits, Isabel Allende
The Storyteller, Leslie Marmon Silko
They Thirst, Robert McCammon

1982
Chronicle of a Death Foretold, Gabriel García Márquez
"The Golem," Isaac Bashevis Singer
High Spirits, Robertson Davies
The Mists of Avalon, Marion Zimmer Bradley
'night, Mother, Marsha Norman

1983
The Claiming of Sleeping Beauty, Anne Rice
Phantoms, Dean Koontz
The Woman in Black, Susan Hill
"You Are Now Entering the Human Heart," Janet
  Frame

1984
Beauty's Punishment, Anne Rice
La Llorona Legend, Rudolfo A. Anaya
Nights at the Circus, Angela Carter
The Witches of Eastwick, John Updike

1985
Beauty's Release, Anne Rice
Fences, August Wilson
The Good Apprentice, Iris Murdoch
The Handmaid's Tale, Margaret Atwood
Lonesome Dove, Larry McMurtry
Ma Rainey's Black Bottom, August Wilson
The Vampire Lestat, Anne Rice

1986
"Fleur," Louise Erdrich
The Phantom of the Opera, Andrew Lloyd Webber

1987
Beloved, Toni Morrison
The Best of H. P. Lovecraft, H. P. Lovecraft
Eva Luna, Isabel Allende
"La Llorona," Joe Hayes
Misery, Stephen King
Of Love and Shadows, Isabel Allende
The Periodic Table, Primo Levi

Tent Meeting, Larry Larson, Levi Lee, and Rebecca
  Wackler

1988
Cat's Eye, Margaret Atwood
Fade, Robert Cormier
Joe Turner's Come and Gone, August Wilson
Love in the Time of Cholera, Gabriel García Márquez
Oscar and Lucinda, Peter Carey
Pet Sematary, Stephen King
Queen of the Damned, Anne Rice
Silence of the Lambs, Thomas Harris
"Taming a Tartar," Louisa May Alcott

1989
The Contested Castle, Kate Ferguson Ellis
Like Water for Chocolate, Laura Esquivel
The Woman in Black, Stephen Mallatratt
"The Young Visitor," Mary Roberts Rinehart

1990
The Kadaitcha Sung, Sam Watson
Phantom, Susan Kay
The Piano Lesson, August Wilson
The Signature, Beth Henley
The Silver Kiss, Annette Curtis Klause
The Witching Hour, Anne Rice
Woven on the Loom of Time, Enrique Anderson Imbert

1991
Angels in America, Part One, Tony Kushner
"Family," Joyce Carol Oates
The Kitchen God's Wife, Amy Tan
Obake! Tales of Spirits Past and Present, Brenda Wong
  Aoki
Two Trains Running, August Wilson
Woman Hollering Creek and Other Stories, Sandra
  Cisneros

1992
"The Accursed Inhabitants of the House of Bly,"
  Joyce Carol Oates
Angels in America, Part Two, Tony Kushner
Dolores Claiborne, Stephen King
"Lethal," Joyce Carol Oates
The Tale of the Body Thief, Anne Rice

1993
The Green Knight, Iris Murdoch
Nightmares & Dreamscapes, Stephen King

The Piano, Jane Campion
The Queen of the Cold-Blooded Tales, Roberta Brown
The Robber Bride, Margaret Atwood
"Skin Crawlers," Roberta Brown

1994

The Forest House, Marion Zimmer Bradley
Ghost Kisses, Gregory L. Norris
Lasher, Anne Rice
"Premonition," Joyce Carol Oates
Taltos: Lives of the Mayfair Witches, Anne Rice
The Vizard Mask, Diana Norman

1995

Dreams of Terror and Death: The Dream Cycle of H. P. Lovecraft, H. P. Lovecraft
The Hundred Secret Senses, Amy Tan
Jackson's Dilemma, Iris Murdoch
Memnoch the Devil, Anne Rice
The Moth and Other Stories, Helena Maria Viramontes
"The Rose of Lebanon," William Faulkner
Seven Guitars, August Wilson
Soifs [Thirsts], Marie-Claire Blais
"The Werewolf," Angela Carter
The Zombie, Joyce Carol Oates

1996

Alias Grace, Margaret Atwood
The English Patient, Michael Ondaatje
The Green Hand and Other Ghostly Tales from Around the World, Joel Ben Izzy
The Green Mile, Stephen King
"The Honeymoon of Mrs. Smith," Shirley Jackson
Just an Ordinary Day, Shirley Jackson
"La Llorona," Yxta Maya Murray
Pope Joan, Donna Cross
The Return to Avalon, Marion Zimmer Bradley
The Servant of the Bones, Anne Rice
"The Temple," Joyce Carol Oates

1997

Birdsong, Sebastian Faulks
The Lady of Avalon, Marion Zimmer Bradley
The Violin, Anne Rice

1998

Looking Glass Lives, Felice Picano

1999

King Hedley II, August Wilson
Wit, Margaret Edson

2000

Duskouri Tales, Byrd Roberts
Gaywyck, Vincent Virga
Merrick, Anne Rice
The Vampire Armand, Anne Rice

2001

The Blind Assassin, Margaret Atwood
Blood and Gold, Anne Rice
"Secret, Silent," Joyce Carol Oates
"The Vampire," Joyce Carol Oates

2002

Blackwood Farm, Anne Rice
The Crimson Petal and the White, Michel Faber
From a Buick 8, Stephen King
"Madison at Guignol," Joyce Carol Oates
The Wedding Dress, Virginia Renfro Ellis

2003

Blood Canticle, Anne Rice
The Da Vinci Code, Dan Brown
Firebrand, Marion Zimmer Bradley
Gem of the Ocean, August Wilson
Love, Toni Morrison

FILM NOIR AND CLASSIC GOTHIC WORKS AS CINEMA

Alraune, 1918, 1928, 1952
Always, 1989
Angels in America, 2003
Apocalypse Now, 1979
Around the World in Eighty Days, 1956
The Asphalt Jungle, 1950
Babette's Feast, 1987
The Ballad of the Sad Café, 1990
Beloved, 1998
The Big Sleep, 1946
The Birds, 1963
The Black Cat, 1934, 1941, 1981
Bleak House, 1959, 1985
Braveheart, 1995
Buried Alive, 1990
Burnt Offerings, 1976
Carrie, 1976
Cat on a Hot Tin Roof, 1958
Chinatown, 1974
A Christmas Memory, 1966
Cimarron, 1931, 1960
The City under the Sea, 1965
The Company of Wolves, 1984
The Conqueror Worm, 1968
Crimes of the Heart, 1986
The Crucible, 1957, 1996
Deliverance, 1972
Dolores Claiborne, 1995
Dr. Faustus, 1967
Dr. Jekyll and Mr. Hyde, 1921, 1931, 1941
The English Patient, 1996
Ethan Frome, 1993
The Exorcist, 1973, 1990
The Fall of the House of Usher, 1928
Fantasia, 1940
Firestarter, 1984
Frankenstein, 1931, 1958
Ghost, 1990

The Golem, 1914, 1920
The Good Earth, 1937
Gormenghast, 1999
The Grass Harp, 1996
Great Expectations, 1934, 1946, 1998
The Green Man, 1956
The Green Mile, 1999
Hans Christian Andersen, 1952
The Haunted Palace, 1963
The Haunting, 1963, 1999
The Heart Is a Lonely Hunter, 1968
Homunculus, 1916
The Hound of the Baskervilles, 1939, 1959, 1977
The House of the Spirits, 1994
The House of Usher, 1960
In Cold Blood, 1967
The Innocents, 1961
Intruder in the Dust, 1949
I, Robot, 2003
The Island of Dr. Moreau, 1977, 1996
The Island of Lost Souls, 1932
Jane Eyre, 1934, 1943, 1970, 1996
Kamouraska, 1973
The Killers, 1946
Kiss of Death, 1947
Kwaidan, 1965
La Chute de la Maison Usher [The Fall of the House of
    Usher], 1928
The Last of the Mohicans, 1936, 1992
Laura, 1944
Le Puits et le Pendule [The Pit and the Pendulum], 1910
Ligeia, 1965
The Lodger, 1926, 1932, 1944
Lonesome Dove, 1990
The Lottery, 1950
The Loved One, 1965
The Magic Toyshop, 1986
The Maltese Falcon, 1941

Mary Shelley's Frankenstein, 1994
The Masque of the Red Death, 1964
Midnight Cowboy, 1969
Mildred Pierce, 1945
Misery, 1990
The Mists of Avalon, 2001
Moby Dick, 1930, 1956
Mulan, 1998
The Murders in the Rue Morgue, 1971
The Naked City, 1948
The Name of the Rose, 1986
The Natural, 1984
'night, Mother, 1986
The Night of the Hunter, 1955
The Oblong Box, 1969
Oscar and Lucinda, 1997
The Ox-Bow Incident, 1943
Pet Sematary, 1989
The Phantom of the Opera, 1925, 1943, 1962, 1989
The Picture of Dorian Gray, 1945
The Pit and the Pendulum, 1961
The Postman Always Rings Twice, 1946
The Premature Burial, 1962
Rashomon, 1950

The Raven, 1963
The Red Shoes, 1948
Reflections in a Golden Eye, 1967
A Rose for Emily, 1982
Rosemary's Baby, 1968
Salem's Lot, 1979
Salomé, 1913, 1923, 1953, 1987
Sanctuary, 1960
The Shining, 1980, 1997
The Sign of Four, 1932
The Silence of the Lambs, 1990
Something Wicked This Way Comes, 1983
The Sound and the Fury, 1959
A Study in Scarlet, 1933
To Kill a Mockingbird, 1962
The Tomb of Ligeia, 1965
Touch of Evil, 1958
2001: A Space Odyssey, 1968
The Vij, 1960, 1967
Wide Sargasso Sea, 1992
The Witches of Eastwick, 1987
A Worn Path, 1994
Wuthering Heights, 1939, 1970, 1992
Young Frankenstein, 1974

BIBLIOGRAPHY OF PRIMARY SOURCES

Adams, Richard. *Watership Down*. New York: Avon, 1972.

Alcott, Louisa May. "Taming a Tartar." In *A Double Life: Newly Discovered Thrillers of Louisa May Alcott*, edited by Madeleine Stern. Boston: Little, Brown, 1988.

Allende, Isabel. *The House of the Spirits*. New York: Bantam Books, 1982.

———. *Eva Luna*. New York: Bantam Books, 1989.

Anaya, Rudolfo A. *Bless Me, Ultima*. Berkeley, Calif.: Tonitiuh International, 1972.

———. *The Legend of La Llorona: A Short Novel*. Berkeley, Calif.: Tonatiuh International, 1984.

Ansky, S. *The Dybbuk and Other Writings*. New York: Schocken Books, 1992.

Arnow, Harriette. *The Dollmaker*. New York: Avon Books, 1954.

Atherton, Gertrude. *What Dreams May Come*. Chicago: Belford, Clarke, 1888.

Atwood, Margaret. *The Blind Assassin*. New York: Anchor Books, 2001.

———. *The Robber Bride*. New York: Anchor Books, 1998.

———. *The Handmaid's Tale*. Toronto: O. W. Toad, 1986.

Austen, Jane. *Northanger Abbey*. New York: Modern Library, 1995.

Azuela, Mariano. *The Underdogs*. New York: Signet, 1962.

Baring-Gould, Sabine. *Myths of the Middle Ages*. London: Blandford, 1996.

Barnes, Djuna. *Nightwood: The Original Version and Related Drafts*. Normal, Ill.: Dalkey Archive, 1995.

———. *Ryder*. Normal, Ill.: Dalkey Archive, 1995.

Baudelaire, Charles. *The Poems and Prose Poems of Charles Baudelaire*. New York: Brentano's, 1919.

Beckford, William. *Dreams, Waking Thoughts and Incidents*. London: Ward, Lock, 1891.

———. *Vathek*. London: Oxford Univ. Press, 1970.

Berkeley, George. *George Berkeley's Principles and Dialogues*. Cambridge: Cambridge Univ. Press, 2000.

Bierce, Ambrose. *Civil War Stories*. New York: Dover, 1994.

———. *Ghost and Horror Stories of Ambrose Bierce*. New York: Dover, 1964.

———. *In the Midst of Life*. Mattituck, N.Y.: Amereon House, 1966.

———. *The Sardonic Humor of Ambrose Bierce*. New York: Dover, 1963.

Bird, Robert Montgomery. *Nick of the Woods; or, The Jibbenainosay*. New Haven, Conn.: College & University Press, 1967.

"Blackwood's Edinburgh Magazine," http://www-2.cs.cmu.edu/People/spok/serials/blackwoods.html. Accessed on April 28, 2004.

Blatty, William Peter. *The Exorcist*. New York: HarperCollins, 2000.

Borges, Jorge Luis. *A Universal History of Infamy*. London: Allen Lane, 1973.

Boucicault, Dion. *The Octoroon, or Life in Louisiana* in *Representative American Plays*. New York: D. Appleton-Century, 1938.

Bradbury, Ray. *Dandelion Wine*. New York: Bantam Books, 1959.

———. *Fahrenheit 451*. New York: Ballantine Books, 1954.

———. *The Illustrated Man*. New York: Bantam Books, 1951.

———. *Something Wicked This Way Comes*. New York: Bantam Books, 1962.

Braddon, M. E. *Lady Audley's Secret*. London: Tinsley Brothers, 1862.

Bradley, Marion Zimmer. *The Firebrand*. London: Roc, 2003.

———. *The Mists of Avalon*. New York: Del Rey, 1982.

Brontë, Charlotte. *Jane Eyre*. New York: Bantam Books, 1981.

———. *Villette*. New York: Modern Library, 1997.

Brontë, Emily. *Wuthering Heights*. New York: New American Library, 1959.

Brougham, John. *Jane Eyre* (play). New York: Samuel French, 1856.

Brown, Charles Brockden. *Arthur Mervyn or, Memoirs of the Year 1793*. Philadelphia: David McKay, 1889.

———. *Edgar Huntly; or, Memoirs of a Sleep-Walker*. New York: Penguin, 1988.

———. *Ormond; or, The Secret Witness*. New York: Broadview, 1999.

———. *Wieland; or, The Transformation*. New York: Harcourt Brace, 1926.

Brown, Dan. *The Da Vinci Code*. New York: Doubleday, 2003.

Bryant, William Cullen. *Thanatopsis*. Boston: Bibliophile Society, 1927.

Buck, Pearl. *The Good Earth*. New York: Pocket Books, 1975.

Bulwer-Lytton, Edward. *The Coming Race*. Santa Barbara, Calif.: Woodbridge, 1979.

Butler, Octavia. *Kindred*. Boston: Beacon, 1979.

Byron, Lord. *Byron's Poetry*. New York: W. W. Norton, 1980.

———. *Lord Byron, the Major Works*. Oxford: Oxford Univ. Press, 2000.

Cable, George Washington. *The Grandissimes: A Story of Creole Life*. New York: Sagamore Press, 1957.

Čapek, Karel. *R.U.R.* New York: Oxford Univ. Press, 1961.

Capote, Truman. *A Capote Reader*. New York: Random House, 1987.

———. *In Cold Blood: A True Account of a Multiple Murder and Its Consequences*. New York: New American Library, 1965.

Carey, Peter. *Oscar and Lucinda*. New York: Vintage Books, 1997.

Carter, Angela. *The Bloody Chamber and Other Stories*. New York: Penguin, 1990.

———. *Burning Your Boats: The Collected Short Stories*. New York: Henry Holt & Co., 1996.

———. *Fireworks: Nine Profane Pieces*. New York: Harper & Row, 1974.

———. *Nights at the Circus*. New York: Viking Press, 1986.

Chappell, Fred. *Dagon*. Baton Rouge: Louisiana State Univ. Press, 2002.

Chekhov, Anton. *The Black Monk and Other Stories*. New York: Hippocrene Books, 1990.

Cisneros, Sandra. *Woman Hollering Creek and Other Stories*. New York: Vintage Books, 1992.

Clarke, Arthur C. *2001: A Space Odyssey*. London: Roc, 2000.

Clive, Caroline. *Paul Ferroll*. Leipzig: Tauchnitz, 1856.

———. *Why Paul Ferroll Killed His Wife*. London: Saunders, Otley, 1860.

Coleridge, Samuel Taylor. *Samuel Taylor Coleridge: The Major Works*. Oxford: Oxford Univ. Press, 2000.

Collins, Wilkie. *Armadale*. Oxford: Oxford Univ. Press, 1999.

———. *The Black Robe*. New York: Indypublish, 2002.

———. *Heart and Science*. New York: AMS Press, 1970.

. *The Moonstone*. London: Penguin Books, 1998.

———. *Twelve Classic Ghost Stories*. New York: Dover, 1998.

———. *The Woman in White*. New York: Bantam Books, 1985.

Conrad, Joseph. *Heart of Darkness and The Secret Sharer*. New York: Signet, 1983.

Cook, Robin. *Coma*. New York: Signet, 2002.

Cooper, James Fenimore. *The Deerslayer*. New York: Signet, 1980.

———. *The Last of the Mohicans*. New York: Bantam Books, 1989.

Cormier, Robert. *Fade*. New York: Dell, 1988.

Cortázar, Julio. *Hopscotch*. New York: Pantheon, 1987.

Crane, Stephen. "The Monster," *Harper's Magazine* 97 (August 1898): 343–376.

Crichton, Michael. *The Andromeda Strain*. New York: Ballantine Books, 1993.

Croly, George. *Salathiel, the Wandering Jew*. New York: Funk & Wagnalls, 1901.

Cross, Donna. *Pope Joan*. New York: Ballantine Books, 1996.

Dahl, Roald. *Someone Like You*. London: Penguin, 1977.

de la Mare, Walter. *The Return*. New York: Dover, 1997.

———. *Short Stories 1895–1926*. London: Giles de la Mare, 1999.

De Quincey, Thomas. *Confessions of an English Opium Eater*. New York: Dover, 2001.

de Sade, Marquis. *The Crimes of Love*. New York: Bantam Books, 1964.

Dickens, Charles. *Bleak House*. Oxford: Oxford Univ. Press, 1996.

———. *A Christmas Carol*, vol. 1, *The Annotated Dickens*, ed. Edward Guiliano and Philip Collins. New York: Clarkson N. Potter, 1986.

———. *Great Expectations*, vol. 2, *The Annotated Dickens*, ed. Edward Guiliano and Philip Collins. New York: Clarkson N. Potter, 1986.

———. *Oliver Twist*, vol. 1, *The Annotated Dickens*, ed. Edward Guiliano and Philip Collins. New York: Clarkson N. Potter, 1986.

———. *A Tale of Two Cities*, vol. 2, *The Annotated Dickens*, ed. Edward Guiliano and Philip Collins. New York: Clarkson N. Potter, 1986.

Dickey, James. *Deliverance.* New York: Dell, 1970.

Dinesen, Isak. *Carnival: Entertainments and Posthumous Tales.* Chicago: University of Chicago Press, 1983.

———. *Seven Gothic Tales.* New York: Vintage Books, 1991.

———. *Winter's Tales.* New York: Vintage Books, 1993.

Doyle, Arthur Conan. *The Annotated Sherlock Holmes.* New York: Wings Books, 1967.

———, *The Crown Diamond*, http://www5a.biglobe.ne.jp/~gegebo/crown_en.htm. Accessed on April 28, 2004.

du Maurier, Daphne. *Classics of the Macabre.* Garden City, N.Y.: Doubleday, 1987.

———. *Rebecca.* New York: Avon Books, 1971.

———. *The Rebecca Notebook and Other Memories.* Garden City, N.Y.: Doubleday, 1980.

du Maurier, George. *Trilby.* New York: Harper & Brothers, 1894.

Eco, Umberto. *The Name of the Rose.* New York: Warner Books, 1983.

Edson, Margaret. *Wit.* New York: Faber & Faber, 1999.

Eliot, George. *The Lifted Veil; Brother Jacob.* New York: Oxford Univ. Press, 1999.

Ellis, Virginia Renfro. *The Wedding Dress.* New York: Ballantine Books, 2002.

Engel, Marian. *Bear.* New York: Atheneum, 1976.

Erckmann, Émile, and Alexandre Chatrian. *The Man-Wolf and Other Tales.* New York: Arno Press, 1976.

Erdrich, Louise. "Fleur." In *American Short Stories,* edited by Eugene Current-Garcia and Bert Hitchcock. New York: Longman, 2001.

Esquivel, Laura. *Like Water for Chocolate.* New York: Anchor Books, 1992.

Ewers, Hanns Heinz. "The Spider." In *Creeps by Night,* edited by Dashiell Hammett. New York: Belmont Books, 1961.

Faber, Michel. *The Crimson Petal and the White.* New York: Harcourt, 2002.

Faulkner, William. *Absalom, Absalom!* New York: Vintage International, 1990.

———. *As I Lay Dying.* New York: Vintage Books, 1964.

———. *Collected Stories of William Faulkner.* New York: Vintage Books, 1950.

———. *Intruder in the Dust.* New York: Vintage Books, 1948.

———. *The Portable Faulkner.* New York: Viking, 1966.

———. "Rose of Lebanon." In *New Stories from the South: The Year's Best of 1996,* ed. Shannon Ravenel. Chapel Hill, N.C.: Algonquin Books, 1996.

Faulks, Sebastian. *Birdsong: A Novel of Love and War.* New York: Vintage Books, 1997.

Feldman, Susan, ed. *The Storytelling Stone.* New York: Laurel, 1965.

Ferber, Edna. *Cimarron.* New York: Avenel, 1981.

Finney, Charles Grandison. *The Circus of Dr. Lao.* Lincoln: University of Nebraska Press, 2002.

Frame, Janet. *You Are Now Entering the Human Heart.* Wellington, N.Z.: Victoria Univ. Press, 1983.

Freneau, Philip. *The Last Poems of Philip Freneau.* New Brunswick, N.J.: Rutgers Univ. Press, 1945.

Gág, Wanda. *Tales from Grimm.* Eau Claire, Wis.: E. J. Hale, 1936.

García Márquez, Gabriel. *Chronicle of a Death Foretold.* New York: Ballantine Books, 1984.

Gardner, John. *Grendel.* New York: Ballantine Books, 1971.

Gaskell, Elizabeth. *Gothic Tales.* London: Penguin Books, 2001.

Gay, John. *The Beggar's Opera.* New York: Indypublish, 2002.

Gilman, Charlotte Perkins. "The Yellow Wallpaper," in *The Harper American Literature,* 2nd ed., ed. Donald McQuade, et al. New York: HarperCollins, 1994.

Godwin, William. *Caleb Williams.* London: Penguin, 1988.

Goethe, Johann Wolfgang von. *Poems and Ballads of Goethe.* New York: Holt and Williams, 1871.

———. *The Story of Reynard the Fox.* New York: Heritage, 1954.

Gogol, Nikolai. *Dead Souls.* New York: Vintage Books, 1997.

Green, William Child. *The Abbot of Montserrat or The Pool of Blood.* New York: Arno Press, 1977.

Grimm, the Brothers. *The Complete Grimms' Fairy Tales.* New York: Random House, 1972.

Haining, Peter, ed. *Gothic Tales of Terror.* New York: Taplinger, 1972.

Harris, Thomas. *Silence of the Lambs.* New York: St. Martin's Press, 1991.

"The Haunted Library: *Blackwood's Edinburgh Magazine,*" http://www2.widener.edu/Wolfgram-Memorial-Library/facultypages/gothic/journals.htm. Accessed on April 28, 2004.

Hawthorne, Nathaniel. *The Complete Novels and Selected Tales of Nathaniel Hawthorne.* New York: Modern Library, 1937.

———. *Doctor Grimshawe's Secret.* Cambridge, Mass.: Harvard Univ. Press, 1954.

Hayes, Joe. *La Llorona.* El Paso, Tex.: Cinco Puntos, 1987.

Hearn, Lafcadio. *Kwaidan.* Boston: Houghton Mifflin, 1904.

———. *Lafcadio Hearn's Japan.* New York: Charles E. Tuttle, 1997.

Hébert, Anne. *Children of the Black Sabbath.* New York: Crown, 1977.

Henley, Beth. *Crimes of the Heart.* New York: Penguin, 1981.

Hichens, Robert. *Tongues of Conscience.* London: Methuen, 1900.

Hoffmann, E. T. A. *The Golden Pot and Other Tales.* Oxford: Oxford University Press, 2000.

Hogg, James. *The Memoirs and Confession of a Justified Sinner.* New York: W. W. Norton, 1970.

Holt, Victoria. *Mistress of Mellyn.* New York: Fawcett, 1960.

Hugo, Victor. *Les Misérables.* New York: Fawcett, 1961.

Hunt, Leigh. *Essays by Leigh Hunt.* London: Walter Scott, 1900.

Hurston, Zora Neale. *Their Eyes Were Watching God.* Urbana: University of Illinois Press, 1978.

Irving, Washington. *The Legend of Sleepy Hollow.* New York: Tor, 1990.

Jackson, Shirley. *The Lottery; or, The Adventures of James Harris.* New York: Farrar, Straus, & Giroux, 1949.

———. *We Have Always Lived in the Castle.* New York: Viking, 1962.

Jacobs, W. W. *Selected Short Stories.* London: Bodley Head, 1975.

James, Henry. *The Short Stories of Henry James.* New York: Random House, 1945.

———. *The Turn of the Screw & Daisy Miller.* New York: Dell, 1954.

Janin, Jules. *The Dead Donkey and the Guillotined Woman.* Chislehurst, Kent: Gargoyle's Head Press, 1993.

Keats, John. *The Complete Poems of John Keats.* New York: Modern Library, 1994.

King, Stephen. *Danse Macabre.* New York: Everest House, 1981.

———. *Firestarter.* New York: Signet, 2001.

———. *From a Buick 8.* New York: Scribner, 2002.

———. *Nightmares & Dreamscapes.* New York: Viking, 1993.

Kingston, Maxine Hong. *The Woman Warrior.* New York: Vintage Books, 1976.

Kipling, Rudyard. *Kipling, a Selection of His Stories and Poems.* Garden City, N.Y.: Doubleday, 1956.

Kirby, William. *The Golden Dog.* Toronto: McClelland, 1984.

Kushner, Tony. *Angels in America.* New York: TCG, 1995.

Kyoka, Izumi. *Japanese Gothic Tales,* trans. by Charles Shiro Inouye. Honolulu: University of Hawaii Press, 1996.

Lagerkvist, Pär. *The Eternal Smile and Other Stories.* New York: Random House, 1956.

Langhorne, John. *Solyman and Almena.* London: C. Cooke, 1820.

Lardner, Ring W. *Haircut and Other Stories.* New York: Charles Scribner's Sons, 1954.

Larson, Larry, Levy Lee, and Rebecca Wackler. *Tent Meeting.* New York: Dramatists Play Service, 1987.

Lathom, Francis. *The Midnight Bell.* London: Skoob Books, 1989.

Lee, Harper. *To Kill a Mockingbird.* New York: Warner Books, 1960.

Le Fanu, Sheridan. *The Best Horror Stories.* London: Sphere, 1970.

———. *Uncle Silas.* London: Penguin, 2000.

Lermontov, Mikhail. *The Demon.* London: Richards Press. 1930.

Leroux, Gaston. *The Phantom of the Opera.* Cutchogue, N.Y.: Buccaneer Books, 1976.

Lewis, Matthew Gregory. *The Monk.* Oxford: Oxford University Press, 1998.

Lovecraft, H. P. *The Best of H. P. Lovecraft: Bloodcurdling Tales of Horror and the Macabre.* New York: Del Rey, 1987.

———. *Dreams of Terror and Death: The Dream Cycle of H. P. Lovecraft.* New York: Del Rey, 1995.

———. *The Dunwich Horror and Others.* Sauk City, Wis.: Arkham House, 1984.

———. *Tales of the Cthulhu Mythos.* New York: Del Rey, 1998.

———. *The Transition of H. P. Lovecraft: The Road to Madness.* New York: Del Rey, 1996.

Lowndes, Marie Belloc. *The Lodger.* New York: Avon, 1971.

MacDermot, Thomas. *San Gloria* in *The Penguin Book of Caribbean Verse in English.* Harmondsworth, Middlesex: Penguin, 1986.

Macpherson, James. *The Poems of Ossian and Related Works.* Edinburgh: Edinburgh University Press, 1996.

Malamud, Bernard. *The Natural.* New York: Avon Books, 1952.

Márquez, Gabriel García. *One Hundred Years of Solitude.* New York: Avon Books, 1970.

Marsh, Richard. *The Beetle.* New York: IndyPublish, 2003.

Matheson, Richard. *Nightmare at 20,000 Feet.* New York: St. Martin's Press, 2002.

Maturin, Charles Robert. *Melmoth the Wanderer.* Lincoln: University of Nebraska Press, 1961.

Maupassant, Guy de. *The Dark Side.* New York: Carroll & Graf, 1989.

McArthur, Mary. "La Llorona," *Midwest Quarterly* 42, no. 1 (autumn 2000): 42.

McCullers, Carson. *The Ballad of the Sad Café and Other Stories.* New York: Bantam, 1951.

McKinley, Robin. *Beauty.* New York: Pocket Books, 1978.

Melville, Herman. *Billy Budd and Other Stories.* New York: Penguin, 1986.

———. *Moby Dick, or The White Whale.* New York: New American Library, 1961.

———. *Typee.* New York: Signet, 1964.

Miller, Arthur. *The Crucible.* New York: Bantam Books, 1959.

Moore, Julia A. *The Sweet Singer of Michigan.* Chicago: Pascal Covici, 1928.

Morrison, Robert, and Chris Baldick, eds. *Tales of Terror from Blackwood's Magazine.* New York: Oxford Univ. Press, 1995.

Morrison, Toni. *Beloved.* New York: Plume, 1987.

———. *The Bluest Eye.* New York: Plume, 1994.

———. *Love.* New York: Alfred Knopf, 2003.

———. *Song of Solomon.* New York: Plume, 1987.

Munro, H. H. *Saki: The Complete Saki.* London: Penguin, 1998.

Murdoch, Iris. *The Black Prince.* New York: Viking 1973.

———. *The Green Knight.* New York: Viking, 1993.

———. *The Sea, the Sea.* New York: Viking, 1978.

———. *The Unicorn.* New York: Viking, 1987.

Murray, Yxta Maya. "La Llorona," *North American Review* 281, no. 6 (November–December 1996): 24–27.

Norman, Diana. *The Vizard Mask.* London: Penguin Books, 1994.

Norman, Marsha. *'night, Mother.* New York: Hill & Wang, 1983.

Norris, Gregory L. *Ghost Kisses.* San Francisco: Leyland, 1994.

Northampton, Lady Margaret Maclean Compton. *Irene: A Poem, In Six Cantos: Miscellaneous Poems.* London: Mills, Jowett, and Mills, 1833.

Oates, Joyce Carol. *American Gothic Tales.* New York: Plume, 1996.

———. *Beasts.* New York: Carroll & Graf, 2002.

———. *Haunted: Tales of the Grotesque.* New York: Dutton, 1994.

———. *Heat, and Other Stories.* New York: Dutton, 1991.

———. "Madison at Guignol," *Kenyon Review* 24, no. 1 (winter 2002): 43–50.

———. *The Seduction and Other Stories.* Los Angeles: Black Sparrow Press, 1975.

———. *Where Is Here?* New York: Ecco Press, 1992.

O'Connor, Flannery. *The Complete Stories of Flannery O'Connor.* New York: Farrar, Straus & Giroux, 1971.

———. *Three by Flannery O'Connor.* New York: Signet, 1983.

Odoevsky, V. F. *The Salamander and Other Gothic Tales.* London: Bristol Classical Press, 1992.

Oliphant, Carolina. *Life and Songs of the Baroness Nairne.* London: John Grant, 1905.

Peacock, Thomas Love. *The Novels of Thomas Love Peacock.* London: George Newnes, 1903.

Peake, Mervyn. *The Gormenghast Novels.* New York: Overlook Press, 1995.

Perrault, Charles. "Bluebeard" in *The Blue Fairy Book.* New York: Dover, 1965.

Picano, Felice. *Looking Glass Lives.* Los Angeles: Alyson, 1998.

Plath, Sylvia. *Collected Poems.* New York: Perennial, 1992.

Poe, Edgar Allan. *The Complete Stories.* New York: Alfred A. Knopf, 1992.

———. *Selected Stories and Poems.* New York: Airmont, 1962.

Polidori, John. *The Vampyre and Other Tales of the Macabre.* Oxford: Oxford University Press, 2001.

Porter, Jane. *The Scottish Chiefs.* New York: Athenaeum, 1991.

Prévost, Abbé. *Manon Lescaut* in *Great French Romances.* New York: Duell, Sloan and Pearce, 1946.

Pushkin, Alexander. *The Queen of Spades and Other Stories.* New York: Dover, 1994.

Radcliffe, Ann. *The Italian.* London: Oxford Univ. Press, 1968.

———. *The Mysteries of Udolpho.* London: Oxford University Press, 1966.

———. *A Sicilian Romance.* Oxford: Oxford Univ. Press, 1993.

Reynolds, George W. M. *Mysteries of London.* Edinburgh: Edinburgh Univ. Press, 1998.

Rhys, Jean. "Our Gardener" in *The Penguin Book of Caribbean Verse in English,* ed. Paula Burnett. Harmondsworth, Middlesex: Penguin, 1986.

———. *Wide Sargasso Sea.* New York: Norton, 1967.

Rice, Anne. *Interview with the Vampire.* New York: Ballantine Books, 1993.

Richardson, John. *Wacousta; or, The Prophecy.* Plattsburgh, N.Y.: McClelland & Stewart, 1996.

Rinehart, Mary Roberts. *The Case of Jennie Brice.* London: Kensington, 1997.

———. *The Circular Staircase.* New York: Dover, 1997.

———. "The Young Visitor" *Saturday Evening Post,* May–June 1989: 32–36.

Roberts, Byrd. *The Duskouri Tales.* San Francisco: GLB, 2000.

Rossetti, Christina, *The Goblin Market.* New York: Dover, 1994.

———. *Speaking Likenesses.* London: Macmillan, 1874.

Rulfo, Juan. *Pedro Páramo.* New York: Grove Press, 1994.

Scott, Sir Walter. *The Bride of Lammermoor.* Oxford: Oxford Univ. Press, 1998.

————. *Ivanhoe.* New York: Bantam Books, 1988.

————. *Letters on Demonology and Witchcraft,* 2nd ed. New York: George Routledge & Sons, 1885.

————. *Marmion, a Tale of Flodden Field.* New York: Macmillan, 1920.

Sexton, Anne. *The Complete Poems.* New York: Mariner, 1999.

Shelley, Mary. *Frankenstein.* New York: New American Library, 1963.

Shelley, Percy Bysshe. *Complete Poems of Percy Bysshe Shelley.* New York: Modern Library, 1994.

————. *Zastrozzi and St. Irvyne.* Oxford: Oxford Univ. Press, 1986.

Simms, William Gilmore. *The Yemassee.* New Haven, Conn.: College & Univ. Press, 1964.

Singer, Isaac Bashevis. *The Golem.* New York: Farrar, Straus, & Giroux, 1982.

————. *An Isaac Bashevis Singer Reader.* New York: Farrar, Straus & Giroux, 1960.

Smollett, Tobias. *The Adventures of Ferdinand Count Fathom.* Athens: University of Georgia Press, 1988.

Stevenson, Robert Louis. *Dr. Jekyll and Mr. Hyde.* New York: Bantam Books, 1981.

————. *Fables.* New York: Charles Scribner's Sons, 1905.

————. *The Master of Ballantrae.* New York: Modern Library, 2002.

Stoker, Bram. *The Annotated Dracula.* New York: Clarkson N. Potter, 1975.

————. *Dracula.* New York: Bantam Books, 1981.

————. *Lair of the White Worm.* Hanoi: Indypublish, 2002.

Stowe, Harriet Beecher. *Uncle Tom's Cabin; or, Life among the Lowly.* New York: Harper Classics, 1965.

Straub, Peter. *Ghost Story.* New York: Pocket Books, 1994.

Strieber, Whitley. *The Wolfen.* New York: Avon, 1988.

Styron, William. *The Confessions of Nat Turner.* New York: Vintage, 1993.

Swinburne, Algernon. *Works of Algernon Swinburne.* London: Wordsworth Editions, 1999.

Tan, Amy. *The Hundred Secret Senses.* New York: Ivy Books, 1996.

————. *The Kitchen God's Wife.* New York: Ivy Books, 1991.

Thomson, James. *The City of Dreadful Night and Other Poems.* London: Watts, 1934.

Turner, Margaret. *The Gentle Shepherd, a Scotch Pastoral.* London: T. Bensley, 1790.

Twain, Mark. *The Mysterious Stranger and Other Curious Tales.* New York: Random House, 1997.

————. *Pudd'nhead Wilson.* New York: New American Library, 1964.

Updike, John. *The Witches of Eastwick.* New York: Alfred A. Knopf, 1984.

Varney, the Vampire; or, The Feast of Blood, 3 vols. New York: Arno Press, 1970.

Verne, Jules. *Around the World in 80 Days.* New York: Laurel-Leaf, 1964.

Vidocq, Eugene Francois. *Memoirs of Vidocq.* London: Cassell, 1928.

Villiers de L'Isle-Adam. *Cruel Tales.* London: Oxford Univ. Press, 1963.

Viramontes, Helena Maria. *The Moth and Other Stories.* Houston, Tex.: Arte Publico, 1995.

Virga, Vincent. *Gaywyck.* Los Angeles: Alyson, 2000.

Voltaire. *Candide.* New York: Signet, 1961.

Walpole, Horace. *The Castle of Otranto.* London: Oxford Univ. Press, 1969.

Waugh, Evelyn. *A Handful of Dust.* Boston: Little, Brown, 1962.

————. *The Loved One.* Boston: Little, Brown, 1948.

Wells, H. G. *The Invisible Man.* New York: Airmont, 1964.

————. *The Island of Dr. Moreau.* New York: Modern Library, 1996.

————. *The Time Machine.* New York: Airmont, 1964.

————. *The War of the Worlds with The Time Machine and Selected Short Stories.* New York: Platt & Munk, 1963.

Welty, Eudora. *The Collected Stories of Eudora Welty.* New York: Harcourt Brace Jovanovich, 1980.

————. *The Robber Bridegroom.* Garden City, N.Y.: Doubleday, Doran, 1942.

Wharton, Edith. *Ethan Frome.* New York: Charles Scribner's Sons, 1970.

————. *The Ghost Stories of Edith Wharton.* New York: Scribner Paperback Fiction, 1973.

Wilde, Oscar. *The Importance of Being Earnest and Other Plays.* New York: Signet Classic, 1985.

————. *The Picture of Dorian Gray and Selected Stories.* New York: New American Library, 1983.

————. *Plays.* London: Penguin, 1954.

Wilkinson, Sarah Scudgell. *The Child of Mystery,* http://www.chawton.org/novels/child/index.html. Accessed on April 28, 2004.

Williams, A. Susan, ed. *The Lifted Veil: The Book of Fantastic Literature by Women, 1800–World War II.* New York: Carroll & Graf, 1992.

Williams, Charles. *War in Heaven.* Grand Rapids, Mich.: Wm. B. Eerdmans, 1981.

Williams, Tennessee. *Cat on a Hot Tin Roof.* New York: New American Library, 1989.

————. *Suddenly Last Summer.* New York: Dramatist's Play Service, 1998.

Wilson, August. *The Piano Lesson.* New York: Plume Books, 1990.

Wood, Ellen. "The Punishment of Gina Montani," *Colburn's New Monthly Magazine* 5, no. 2 (February 1852): 189–196.

Wright, Richard. "Between the World and Me," in *Black Voices.* New York: Mentor Books, 1968.

Yarbro, Chelsea Quinn. *Hotel Transylvania.* New York: Warner, 2002.

Yearsley, Ann. *The Royal Captives,* 4 vols. New York: Garland, 1974.

Yeats, William Butler. *The Collected Poems of W. B. Yeats.* New York: Macmillan, 1956.

Young, Edward. *Night Thoughts or the Complaint and the Consolation.* New York: Dover, 1996.

BIBLIOGRAPHY OF SECONDARY SOURCES

Abrams, Rebecca. "Review: *The Crimson Petal and the White*," *New Statesman* 131, no. 4,609 (October 14, 2002): 55.

Abu-Lughod, Lila. "Orientalism and Middle East Feminist Studies," *Feminist Studies* 27, no. 1 (spring 2001): 101–113.

Achenbach, Joel. "The World According to Wells," *Smithsonian* (April 2001): 110.

Adams, Jeffrey. "Orson Welles's 'The Trial': *Film Noir* and the Kafkaesque," *College Literature* 29, no. 3 (summer 2002): 140–157.

Alexander, Catherine M. S. "'The Dear Witches': Horace Walpole's 'Macbeth,'" *Review of English Studies* 49, no. 194 (May 1998): 131–144.

Alexander, Christine. "'That Kingdom of Gloom': Charlotte Brontë, the Annuals, and the Gothic," *Nineteenth-Century Literature* 47, no. 4 (March 1993): 409–436.

Allen, Brooke. "A Universal Region: The Fiction of Eudora Welty," *New Criterion* 18, no. 2 (October 1999). 35.

Allen, Bruce. "'World-Besotted Traveler': Evelyn Waugh's Savage Indignation," *World and I* 15, no. 5 (May 2000): 280.

Allende, Isabel. "Pinochet's Ghost," *New Perspectives Quarterly* 16, no. 3 (spring 1999): 22–26.

Allison, Dorothy. "The Future of Females: Octavia Butler's Mother Lode," in *Reading Black, Reading Feminist*. New York: Meridian, 1990.

Altink, Henrice. "Deviant and Dangerous: Pro-Slavery Representations of Slave Women's Sexuality," http://www.lea.univ-avignon.fr/slav/Altink.htm. Accessed on April 27, 2004.

Altschuler, Eric Lewin. "One of the Oldest Cases of Schizophrenia in Gogol's 'Diary of a Madman,'" *British Medical Journal* 323, no. 7,327 (December 22, 2001): 1,475–1,477.

Anderson, George K. *The Legend of the Wandering Jew.* Providence, R.I.: Brown University Press, 1965.

"Anna Laetitia Aiken (Later Barbauld)," http://www.english.upenn.edu/~mgamer/Etexts/barbauldessays.html#pleasure. Accessed on April 28, 2004.

"Ann Julia Hatton," *Sheffield Hallam University: Corvey Women Writers,* http://www2.shu.ac.uk/corvey/CW3/AuthorPage.cfm?Author=AJKH, 2000. Accessed on April 28, 2004.

Arata, Stephen D. "The Sedulous Ape: Atavism, Professionalism, and Stevenson's 'Jekyll and Hyde,'" *Criticism* 37, no. 2 (spring 1995): 233–259.

Ards, Angela. "The Diaspora Comes to Dartmouth," *American Theatre* 15, no. 5 (May–June 1998): 50–52.

Atwood, Margaret. "Cannibal Lecture: How Could a Culture So Apparently Boring As Ours Have Embraced the Flesh-devouring Wendigo?" *Saturday Night* 110, no. 9 (November 1995): 81–86.

———. "Ophelia Has a Lot to Answer For," http://www.web.net/owtoad/ophelia.html, 1997. Accessed on April 28, 2004.

———. *Second Words: Selected Critical Prose.* Toronto: Anansi, 1982.

———. *Strange Things: The Malevolent North in Canadian Literature.* Oxford: Clarendon Press, 1995.

———. *Survival: A Thematic Guide to Canadian Literature.* Toronto: Anansi, 1972.

Auchincloss, Louis. *Pioneers and Caretakers: A Study of Nine American Women Novelists.* Minneapolis: Univ. of Minnesota Press, 1965.

Auerbach, Nina. *Daphne du Maurier: Haunted Heiress.* Philadelphia: University of Pennsylvania Press, 1999.

———. *Our Vampires, Ourselves.* Chicago: Univ. of Chicago Press, 1995.

Babuts, Nicole. "Baudelaire: Les Fleurs du Mal," *Symposium* 49, no. 4 (winter 1996): 307–309.

Bak, John S. "Escaping the Jaundiced Eye: Foucauldian Panopticism in Charlotte Perkins Gilman's 'The Yellow Wallpaper,'" *Studies in Short Fiction* 31, no. 1 (winter 1994): 39–46.

Baker, Augusta, and Ellin Greene. *Storytelling: Art and Technique*. New York: R. R. Bowker, 1977.

Baker, Ray Palmer. *The History of English-Canadian Literature to the Confederation*. New York: Russell & Russell, 1968.

Ball, Stefan. "Coleridge's Ancestral Voices," *Contemporary Review* 278, no. 1,624 (May 2001): 298.

Barasch, Frances K. *The Grotesque*. Paris: Mouton, 1971.

Barber, Paul. *Vampires, Burial, and Death: Folklore and Reality*. New Haven, Conn.: Yale University Press, 1988.

Barger, James. *William Faulkner: Modern American Novelist and Nobel Prize Winner*. Charlotteville, N.Y.: SamHar Press, 1989.

Baring-Gould, Sabine. *Book of Were-Wolves*. London: Smith, Elder, 1865.

Baring-Gould, William S. and Ceil Baring-Gould. *The Annotated Mother Goose*. New York: Clarkson N. Potter, 1962.

Barrow, Susan M. "East/West: Appropriation of Aspects of the Orient in Maupassant's Bel-Ami," *Nineteenth-Century French Studies* (spring–summer 2002): 315–329.

Bartolomeo, Joseph F. "Subversion of Romance in 'The Old Manor House,'" *Studies in English Literature, 1500–1900* 33, no. 3 (summer 1993): 645–657.

Batchelor, John. "The Island of Dr. Moreau," *Review of English Studies* 47, no. 186 (May 1996): 286–288.

Bauer, Helen. *Rudyard Kipling: A Study of the Short Fiction*. New York: Twayne, 1994.

Bayley, John. *Elegy for Iris*. New York: St. Martin's, 2001.

Beattie, Valerie. "The Mystery at Thornfield: Representations of Madness in 'Jane Eyre,'" *Studies in the Novel* 28, no. 4 (winter 1996): 493–505.

Beaty, Frederick L. *The Ironic World of Evelyn Waugh*. Dekalb: Northern Illinois University Press, 1992.

Beetz, Kirk H. *Wilkie Collins: An Annotated Bibliography*. Metuchen, N.J.: Scarecrow, 1978.

Behrendt, Stephen C. "Felicia Hemans: Selected Poems, Letters, Reception Materials," *Criticism* 44, no. 2 (spring 2002): 217–222.

———. "Questioning the Romantic Novel," *Studies in the Novel* 26, no. 2 (summer 1994): 5–25.

Belford, Barbara. *Bram Stoker*. New York: Knopf, 1996.

Bellman, Samuel Irving. "Shirley Jackson: A Study of the Short Fiction," *Studies in Short Fiction* 31, no. 2 (spring 1994): 282–293.

Bennett, Rachel. "Oliver Twist," *Review of English Studies* 46, no. 181 (February 1995): 138–139.

Benoit, Raymond. "Irving's 'The Legend of Sleepy Hollow,'" *Explicator* 55, no. 1 (fall 1996): 15–17.

———. "Poe's 'The Fall of the House of Usher,'" *Explicator* 58, no. 2 (winter 2000): 79.

Bergland, Renee L. *The National Uncanny: Indian Ghosts and American Subjects*. Hanover, N.H.: Dartmouth College/University Press of New England, 2000.

Bering-Jensen, Helle. "California's Daughter: Gertrude Atherton and Her Times," *Smithsonian* 22, no. 12 (March 1992): 117–118.

Berman, Avis. "George du Maurier's 'Trilby' Whipped Up a Worldwide Storm," *Smithsonian* 24, no. 9 (December 1993): 110–116.

Bernbaum, Ernest, ed. *Anthology of Romanticism*. New York: Ronald, 1948.

Bernstein, Stephen. "Form and Ideology in the Gothic Novel," *Essays in Literature* 18 (fall 1991): 151–165.

Best, Debra E. "The Monster in the Family: A Reconsideration of Frankenstein's Domestic Relationships," *Women's Writing* 6, no. 3 (1999): 365.

Bidney, Martin. "Spirit-bird, Bowshot, Water-snake, Corpses, Cosmic Love: Reshaping the Coleridge Legacy in Dickey's 'Deliverance,'" *Papers on Language & Literature* 31, no. 4 (fall 1995): 389–405.

Bignell, Jonathan. "Lost Messages: The Handmaid's Tale, Novel and Film," *British Journal of Canadian Studies* 8, no. 1 (1993): 71–84.

Birden, Lorene M. "Saki's 'A Matter of Sentiment,'" *Explicator* 56, no. 3 (summer 1998): 201–204.

Birkerts, Sven. "The Name of the Rose," *New Republic* (September 5, 1983): 36–38.

Blackall, Eric A. *The Novels of the German Romantics*. Ithaca, N.Y.: Cornell Univ. Press, 1983.

Blais, Joline. "Qui est La?: Displaced Subjects in 'Wide Sargasso Sea' and 'Le Ravissement de Lol V. Stein,'" *College Literature* 20, no. 2 (June 1993): 98–118.

Blakemore, Steven. "Matthew Lewis's Black Mass: Sexual, Religious Inversion in 'The Monk,'" *Studies in the Novel* 30, no. 4 (winter 1998): 521.

Blakey, Dorothy. *The Minerva Press, 1790–1820*. London: Oxford Univ. Press, 1939.

Blankenship, Russell. *American Literature*. New York: Henry Holt, 1931.

Boan, Devon. "Call-and-Response: Parallel 'Slave Narrative' in August Wilson's 'The Piano Lesson,'" *African American Review* 32, no. 2 (summer 1998): 263–272.

Bonca, Cornel. "In Despair of the Old Adams: Angela Carter's 'The Infernal Desire Machines of Dr. Hoffman,'" *Review of Contemporary Fiction* 14, no. 3 (fall 1994): 56–62.

Boone, Troy. "'He Is English and Therefore Adventurous': Politics, Decadence, and 'Dracula,'" *Studies in the Novel* 25, no. 1 (spring 1993): 76–91.

Bordewich, Fergus M. "Wandering Ghost: The Odyssey of Lafcadio Hearn," *Smithsonian*, 22, no. 5 (August 1991): 120–122.

Boren, Mark. "Flannery O'Connor, Laughter, and the Word Made Flesh," *Studies in American Fiction* 26, no. 1 (spring 1998): 115–128.

Bradbury, John. *Renaissance in the South*. Chapel Hill: University of North Carolina Press, 1963.

Bradfield, Scott. "Remembering Angela Carter," *Review of Contemporary Fiction* 14, no. 3 (fall 1994): 90–93.

Brady, Valentini Papadopoulou. "'Manon Lescaut, C'est Lui': A Study of Point of View in Prévost's 'Manon Lescaut,'" *Intertexts* 5, no. 2 (fall 2001): 156–168.

Braun, William R. "Rekindling Miss Havisham's Fire," *Opera News* (June 2001): 30.

Brewer, Derek. *English Gothic Literature*. New York: Schocken Books, 1983.

Brickhouse, Anna. "'A Story of the Island of Cuba': William Cullen Bryant and the Hispanophone Americas," *Nineteenth-Century Literature* 56, no. 1 (June 2001): 1–22.

Brontë, Charlotte. *The Letters of Charlotte Brontë: With a Selection of Letters by Family and Friends. 1848 1851*. New York: Oxford Univ. Press, 2000.

Brooks, Peter. "Virtue and Terror: The Monk," *English Literary History* 40 (1973): 249–263.

Brown, Byron K. "John Snart's 'Thesaurus of Horror': An Indirect Source of Poe's 'The Premature Burial'?" *ANQ* 8, no. 3 (summer 1995): 11–14.

Brown, Ruth. "English Heritage and Australian Culture: The Church and Literature of England in *Oscar and Lucinda*," *Australian Literary Studies* 17, no. 2 (October 1995): 135–140.

Browne, Julius Henri. "A Few French Critics," *Harper's* 47 (June–November 1873).

Brustein, Robert. "'night, Mother," *New Republic* (May 2, 1983): 25–27.

———. "The Piano Lesson," *New Republic*, (May 21, 1990): 28–30.

Bucknell, Brad. "On 'Seeing' Salomé," *English Literary History* 60, no. 2 (summer 1993): 503–526.

Buckton, Oliver S. "Reanimating Stevenson's Corpus," *Nineteenth-Century Literature* 55, no. 1 (June 2000): 22.

Budick, E. Miller. "History and Other Spectres in *The Crucible*," *Modern Drama* 28, no. 4 (December 1985): 535–552.

Bullen, J. B. "An Anthology of Pre-Raphaelite Writings," *Notes and Queries* 45, no. 3 (September 1998): 399–400.

Bunge, Nancy. *Nathaniel Hawthorne*. New York: Twayne, 1993.

Burgess, Cheryl A., et al. "Facilitated Communication as an Ideomotor Response," *Psychological Science* 9, no. 1 (January 1998): 71–74.

Butterworth, Keen. "The Savage Mind: James Dickey's 'Deliverance,'" *Southern Literary Journal* 28, no. 2 (spring 1996): 69–78.

Butterworth, R. D. "A Christmas Carol and the Masque," *Studies in Short Fiction* 30, no. 1 (winter 1993): 63–69.

Bynum, Bill. "Neurasthenia," *Lancet* 361, no. 9,370 (May 17, 2003): 1,753.

Calder, Jenni. *Robert Louis Stevenson: A Critical Celebration*. New York: Barnes & Noble Imports, 1980.

Canaday, John. "The Rise and Fall and Rise Again of the Pre-Raphaelite Brotherhood," *Smithsonian* 14 (November 1983): 72–81.

Carbonell, Ana Maria. "From Llorona to Gritona: Coatlicue in Feminist Tales by Viramontes and Cisneros," *MELUS* 24, no. 2 (summer 1999): 53.

Carnell, Jennifer. *The Literary Lives of Mary Elizabeth Braddon*. Hastings, Sussex: Sensation Press, 2000.

Carroll, Noel. "Enjoying Horror Fictions: A Reply to Gaut," *British Journal of Aesthetics* 35, no. 1 (January 1995): 67–72.

Carso, Kerry Dean. "Diagnosing the 'Sir Walter Disease': American Architecture in the Age of Romantic Literature," *Mosaic* 35, no. 4 (December 2002): 121–142.

Cart, Michael. "What Walpole Wrought; or, The Horror! The Horror!" *Booklist* (October 15, 1997): 395.

Carver, Stephen. "Jack Sheppard," *The Literary Encyclopedia*, http://www.litencyc.com/php/sworks.php?rec=true&UID=4370. Accessed on April 28, 2004.

Casler, Jeanine. "The Primacy of the 'Rougher' Version: Neo-Conservative Editorial Practices and Clara Reeve's 'Old English Baron,'" *Papers on Language & Literature* 37, no. 4 (fall 2001): 404.

Castro, Joy. "Jean Rhys," *Review of Contemporary Fiction* 20, no. 1 (summer 2000): 8.

Cavalcanti, Ildney. "Utopias of/f Language in Contemporary Feminist Literary Dystopias," *Utopian Studies* 11, no. 2 (spring 2000): 152.

Cavendish, Richard. "Publication of 'The Hound of the Baskervilles': March 25th, 1902," *History Today* 52, no. 3 (March 2002): 57.

Cervo, Nathan. "Morris's 'Rapunzel,'" *Explicator* 51, no. 3 (spring 1993): 167–169.

Chaitkin, Gabriel. "'For He Was One of Us': Friedrich Schiller, the Poet of America," *American Almanac,* October 1996.

Chambers, E. K. *The Mediaeval Stage.* Mineola, N.Y.: Dover, 1996.

Champion, Laurie. *The Critical Response to Eudora Welty's Fiction.* Westport, Conn.: Greenwood, 1994.

Chandler, David. "'Psychic Torture' in 'Prometheus Unbound': An Idea from Italian Melodrama?" *Notes and Queries* 42, no. 2 (June 1995): 183–184.

Chandler, James. "Scott and the Scene of Explanation: Framing Contextuality in 'The Bride of Lammermoor,'" *Studies in the Novel* 26, no. 2 (summer 1994): 69–98.

Chase, Richard, and David Teasley. "Little Red Riding Hood: Werewolf and Prostitute," *Historian* 57, no. 4 (summer 1995): 769–776.

Cheaney, J. B. "Radical Orthodoxy—The Fiction of Flannery O'Connor," *World and I* 16, no. 5 (May 2001): 255.

Chen, Chih-Ping. "'Am I a Monster?': Jane Eyre among the Shadows of Freaks," *Studies in the Novel* 34, no. 4 (winter 2002): 367–384.

Chesser, Eustace. *Shelley & Zastrozzi: Self-Revelation of a Neurotic.* London: Gregg/Archive, 1965.

Chilton, Leslie A. "Not Quite Proven: Tobias Smollett's 'The Devil on Crutches,'" *Notes and Queries* 41, no. 2 (June 1994): 206–207.

Christensen, Allan C. "Bulwer, Bloch, Bussotti and the Filial Muse: Recalled and Foreseen Sources of Inspiration," *Mosaic* 26, no. 3 (summer 1993): 37–51.

Christophersen, Bill. *The Apparition in the Glass: Charles Brockden Brown's American Gothic.* Athens: Univ. of Georgia Press, 1993.

Church, Joseph. "In Black and White: The Reader's Part in Chesnutt's 'Gray Wolf's Ha'nt,'" *American Transcendental Quarterly* 13, no. 2 (June 1999): 121.

Clarke, Michael M. "Bronte's Jane Eyre and the Grimms' Cinderella," *Studies in English Literature, 1500–1900* 40, no. 4 (autumn 2000): 695.

Clery, E. J. *The Rise of Supernatural Fiction, 1762–1800.* Cambridge: Cambridge Univ. Press, 1995.

———. *Women's Gothic from Clara Reeve to Mary Shelley.* Tavistock, Devon: Northcote House, 2000.

Clements, Nicholaus. "Lovecraft's 'The Haunter of the Dark,'" *Explicator* 57, no. 2 (winter 1999): 98–100.

Coad, David. "Hymens, Lips and Masks: The Veil in Margaret Atwood's 'The Handmaid's Tale,'" *Literature and Psychology* (spring–summer 2001): 54.

Cochran, Peter. "A Note on Some Sources for the Feast in 'Don Juan' Canto III," *Notes and Queries* 40, no. 1 (March 1993): 43–45.

Coelsch-Foisner, Sabine. "Rossetti's 'Goblin Market,'" *Explicator* 61, no. 1 (fall 2002): 28–30.

Cohan, Steven. "Introduction" to *The Plays of James Boaden.* New York: Garland, 1980.

Cohen, Jeffrey Jerome, ed. *Monster Theory.* Minneapolis: University of Minnesota Press, 1996.

Colley, Mary. "Iris Murdoch—the 'Good Novelist,'" *Contemporary Review* 261, no. 1,523 (December 1992): 319–322.

Colon, Christine. "Christianity and Colonial Discourse in Joanna Baillie's 'The Bride,'" *Renascence: Essays on Values in Literature* 54, no. 3 (spring 2002): 162–177.

Colvin, Sarah. "Andreas Gryphius: A Modern Perspective," *Journal of European Studies* 24, no. 94 (June 1994): 191–192.

Cook, Richard M. *Carson McCullers.* New York: Frederick Unger, 1975.

Cook, William. "The Dog That Barked in the Night," *New Statesman* 130, no. 4,568 (December 17, 2001): 118–119.

Cope, Kevin L. "The Adventures of Ferdinand Count Fathom," *Studies in the Novel* 21, no. 4 (winter 1989): 442–444.

———. "Moral Travel and the Pursuit of Nothing: *Vathek* and *Siris* as Philosophical Monologue," *Studies in Eighteenth-Century Culture* 18 (1988): 167–186.

Corsbie, Ken. *Theatre in the Caribbean.* London: Hodder and Stoughton, 1984.

Cosslett, Tess. "Maria, or the Wrongs of Woman," *Notes and Queries* 42, no. 4 (December 1995): 502.

Coupe, Laurence. "The Hero's Journey," *English Review* 10, no. 3 (February 2000): 14.

Couzens, Gary. "Containing Multitudes: The Fiction of Joyce Carol Oates," *Third Alternative* no. 10 (spring 1996): 48–50.

Covey, William B. "More Than Night: *Film Noir* in its Contexts," *Film Criticism* 24, no. 2 (winter 1999): 66.

Coviello, Peter. "The American in Charity: 'Benito Cereno' and Gothic Anti-sentimentality," *Studies in American Fiction* 30, no. 2 (autumn 2002): 155–180.

Cox, Donna. "'I Have No Story to Tell!': Maternal Rage in Susan Hill's *The Woman in Black,*" *Intertexts* 4, no. 1 (spring 2000): 74–89.

Cox, Jeffrey N. "Introduction" to *Seven Gothic Dramas, 1789–1825.* Athens, Ohio: Ohio University Press, 1992.

Craig, Amanda. "On Charles Dickens's Great Expectations," *New Statesman* 131, no. 4,616 (December 2, 2002): 51–52.

Creighton, Joanne V. "Digging Deep into Familiar Ground," *Chicago Tribune* (November 17, 2002): 1.

———. *Joyce Carol Oates: Novels of the Middle Years.* New York: Twayne, 1992.

"The Crimson Petal and the White," *Kirkus Reviews,* (August 1, 2002): 1,059.

Croley, Laura Sagolla. "The Rhetoric of Reform in Stoker's *Dracula*: Depravity, Decline, and the Fin-de-siecle 'Residuum,'" *Criticism* 37, no. 1 (winter 1995): 85–108.

"Cruikshank Artwork at Princeton University Library." http://libweb5.princeton.edu/Visual_Materials/cruikshank/. Accessed on April 28, 2004.

Curren, Erik D. "Should Their Eyes Have Been Watching God?: Hurston's Use of Religious Experience and Gothic Horror," *African American Review* 29, no. 1 (spring 1995): 17–25.

D'Albertis, Deirdre. "The Domestic Drone: Margaret Oliphant and a Political History of the Novel," *Studies in English Literature, 1500–1900* 37, no. 4 (autumn 1997): 805–830.

Daniel, Anne Margaret. "Kipling's Use of Verse and Prose in 'Baa Baa, Black Sheep,'" *Studies in English Literature, 1500–1900* 37, no. 4 (autumn 1997): 857–876.

Daniel, George. *The Modern Dunciad. Virgil in London and Other Poems.* London: William Pickering, 1835.

David, Kathy S. "Beauty and the Beast: The 'Feminization' of Weyland in the Vampire Tapestry," *Extrapolation* 43, no. 1 (spring 2002): 62–80.

Davies, Damian Walford. "The Politics of Allusion: *Caleb Williams*, the *Iron Chest*, *Middlemarch*, and the *Armoire de Fer*," *Review of English Studies* 53, no. 212 (November 2002): 526–543.

Davison, Neil R. "The Jew as Homme/Femme-Fatale: Jewish (Art)ifice, *Trilby*, and Dreyfus," *Jewish Social Studies* (winter-spring 2002): 73–113.

Deiter, Kristen. "Cultural Expressions of the Victorian Age: The New Woman, *Jane Eyre,* and Interior Design," *Lamar Journal of the Humanities* 25, no. 2 (2000): 27–42.

Delcourt, Denyse. "Magie, Fiction, et Phantasme dans le 'Roman de Perceforest': Pour une Poetique de l'Illusion au Moyen Age," *Romanic Review* 85, no. 2 (March 1994): 167–178.

D'Eramso, Stacey. "Just an Ordinary Day," *Nation* (December 23, 1996): 25–26.

Derrickson, Teresa. "Race and the Gothic Monster: The Xenophobic Impulse of Louisa May Alcott's 'Taming a Tartar,'" *American Transcendental Quarterly* 15, no. 1 (March 2001): 43.

Derry, Stephen. "Mrs. Gaskell's Reference to Italian Punishment in 'Mary Barton,'" *Notes and Queries* 40, no. 4 (December 1993): 481–482.

de Sade, Marquis. *Idee sur les Romans.* Geneva: Slatkine, 1967.

Deziel, Shanda. "Golden Harvest," *Maclean's,* (March 5, 2001): 58.

"Dickens' London." http://www.fidnet.com/~dap1955/dickens/dickens_london_map.html. Accessed on April 28, 2004.

Diyen, H. "The Narrativity of Jonathan Wild in Defoe's Account of Jonathan Wild and Fielding's 'The Life of Jonathan Wild the Great,'" *Forum for Modern Language Studies* 34, no. 1 (January 1998): 16–28.

Dobrée, Bonamy. *Rudyard Kipling, Realist and Fabulist.* London: Oxford Univ. Pres, 1967.

Domecq, Alcina Lubitch. "La Llorona," *Literary Review* 43, no. 1 (fall 1999): 17.

Donaldson, Elizabeth J. "The Corpus of the Madwoman: Toward a Feminist Disability Studies Theory of Embodiment and Mental Illness," *NWSA Journal* 14, no. 3 (fall 2002): 99–119.

Donaldson, Susan V. "Making a Spectacle: Welty, Faulkner, and Southern Gothic," *Mississippi Quarterly* 50, no. 4 (fall 1997): 567–584.

Doody, Margaret Anne. "Deserts, Ruins, and Troubled Waters: Female Dreams in Fiction and the Development of the Gothic Novel," *Genre* 10 (1977): 529–573.

Dougherty, Stephen. "Foucault in the 'House of Usher': Some Historical Permutations in Poe's Gothic," *Papers on Language & Literature* 37, no. 1 (winter 2001): 3.

Dudley, David R. "Dead or Alive: The Booby-trapped Narrator of Poe's 'Masque of the Red Death,'" *Studies in Short Fiction* 30, no. 2 (spring 1993): 169–173.

Duffy, Dennis. "The Monk Knight of St. John," *American Review of Canadian Studies* 32, no. 4 (winter 2002): 722–724.

Dukes, Paul. "Fictory or Faction?" *History Today* 49, no. 9 (September 1999): 24.

Dukore, Bernard F., ed. *Dramatic Theory and Criticism.* Boston: Heinle & Heinle, 1974.

Dunn, James A. "Charlotte Dacre and the Feminization of Violence," *Nineteenth-Century Literature* 53, no. 3 (December 1998): 307.

Eads, Martha Greene. "Unwitting Redemption in Margaret Edson's 'Wit,'" *Christianity and Literature* 51, no. 2 (winter 2002): 241–255.

Eagleton, Terry. "Hard Times: False, Fragmented and Unfair, Dickens's 19th-century London Offers a

Grimly Prophetic Vision of the World Today," *New Statesman* 132, no. 4,632 (April 7, 2003): 40–41.

"East End Horror: Two More Women Murdered," *Woodford Times*, October 5, 1888.

Eckstein, Barbara. "Hawthorne's 'The Birthmark': Science and Romance as Belief," *Studies in Short Fiction* 26, no. 4 (fall 1989): 511–515.

Eco, Umberto, and Thomas A. Sebeok, eds. *The Sign of Three: Dupin, Holmes, Peirce*. Bloomington: Indiana Univ. Press, 1983.

Edgecombe, Rodney Stenning. "Keats's 'The Eve of St. Agnes,'" *Explicator* 52, no. 2 (winter 1994): 77–79.

Edmunds, Susan. "Through a Glass Darkly: Visions of Integrated Community in Flannery O'Connor's 'Wise Blood,'" *Contemporary Literature* 37, no. 4 (winter 1996): 559–584.

Eiselein, Gregory. "Humanitarianism and Uncertainty in 'Arthur Mervyn,'" *Essays in Literature* 22, no. 2 (fall 1995): 215–226.

Eisenger, Chester E., ed. *Fiction of the Forties*. Chicago: University of Chicago Press, 1963.

Elbert, Monika. "The Ligeia Syndrome, or, Many 'Happy Returns,' in Conrad's Gothic," *Conradiana* 33, no. 2 (summer 2001): 129–153.

Ellis, Kate Ferguson. *The Contested Castle: Gothic Novels and the Subversion of Domestic Ideology*. Urbana: Univ. of Illinois Press, 1989.

Endo, Paul. "Seeing Romantically in 'Lamia,'" *English Literary History* 66, no. 1 (spring 1999): 111.

Fedorko, Kathy Anne. *Gender and Gothic in the Fiction of Edith Wharton*. Tuscaloosa: Alabama University Press, 1995.

Fee, Margery. "Strange Things: The Malevolent North in Canadian Literature," *University of Toronto Quarterly* 67, no. 1 (winter 1997–98): 335–337.

Fenlon, Katherine Feeney. "John Gardner's 'The Ravages of Spring' as Re-creation of 'The Fall of the House of Usher,'" *Studies in Short Fiction* 31, no. 3 (summer 1994): 481–486.

Ferguson, Robert A. "Yellow Fever and Charles Brockden Brown: The Context of the Emerging Novelist," *Early American Literature* 14, no. 3 (1979–80): 293–305.

Fiedler, Leslie. *Love and Death in the American Novel*. Cleveland, Ohio: Meridian Books, 1962.

Finlayson, J. Caitlin. "Medieval Sources for Keatsian Creation in 'La Belle Dame sans Merci,'" *Philological Quarterly* 79, no. 2 (spring 2000): 225–247.

Fleenor, Juliann E., ed. *The Female Gothic*. Montreal: Eden, 1983.

Flora, Joseph M., and Lucinda H. MacKethan, eds. *The Companion to Southern Literature*. Baton Rouge: Louisiana State Univ. Press, 2002.

Forster, Margaret. *Daphne du Maurier*. New York: Doubleday, 1993.

Forsyth, Beverly. "The Two Faces of Lucy Snowe: A Study in Deviant Behavior," *Studies in the Novel* 29, no. 1 (spring 1997): 17–25.

Forward, Stephanie. "Idol of Suburbia: Marie Corelli and Late-Victorian Culture," *Critical Survey* 13, no. 2 (May 2001): 141–144.

Frank, Frederick S. *Gothic Fiction: A Master List of Twentieth-Century Criticism and Research*. Westport, Conn.: Meckler, 1988.

———. "Gothic Gold: The Sadleir-Black Collection of Gothic Fiction," *Studies in Eighteenth-Century Culture* 26 (1998): 287–312.

Frank, Marcie. "Horace Walpole's Family Romances," *Modern Philology* 100, no. 3 (February 2003): 417–435.

Franklin, J. Jeffrey. "The Merging of Spiritualities: Jane Eyre as Missionary of Love," *Nineteenth-Century Literature* 49, no. 4 (March 1995): 456–482.

Franklin, Rosemary. "Louisa May Alcott's Father(s) and 'The Marble Woman,'" *American Transcendental Quarterly* 13, no. 4 (December 1999): 253.

Fraser, Rebecca. *The Brontës: Charlotte Brontë and Her Family*. New York: Crown, 1988.

Freedman, Samuel G. "August Wilson, Defining an Era," *New York Times* (February 5, 2003): 1.

Freud, Sigmund. *"Das Unheimliche"* [The Uncanny], *Standard Edition*, vol. 17. London: Hogarth, 1955.

Frosch, Thomas. "Passive Resistance in Shelley: A Psychological View," *Journal of English and Germanic Philology* 98, no. 3 (July 1999): 373.

Frost, Adam. "A Hundred Years of Saki," *Contemporary Review* 275, no. 1,607 (December 1999): 302.

Frost, Robert. "The Fable of the Poor Orphan Child," *English Review* 10, no. 2 (November 1999): 10.

Frushell, Richard C. "Poe's Name 'Ligeia' and Milton," *ANQ* 11, no. 1 (winter 1998): 18–20.

Fry, Northrop. *Anatomy of Criticism*. Princeton, N.J.: Princeton Univ. Press, 1957.

Frye, Steven. "Constructing Indigeneity: Postcolonial Dynamics in Charles Brockden Brown's *Monthly Magazine and American Review*," *American Studies* 39, no. 3 (1998): 69–88.

Furbank, P. N., and W. R. Owen. "The Myth of Defoe as 'Applebee's Man,'" *Review of English Studies* 48, no. 190 (May 1997): 198–204.

Fusco, Richard. "Pensive Jester: The Literary Career of W. W. Jacobs," *Studies in Short Fiction* 35, no. 1 (winter 1998): 110.

Fussell, Edwin Sill. "*Wieland*: A Literary and Historical Reading," *Early American Literature* 18, no. 2 (1983): 171–186.

Gamer, Michael. "Authors in Effect: Lewis, Scott, and the Gothic Drama," *English Literary History* 66, no. 4 (winter 1999): 831–861.

———. *Romanticism and the Gothic: Genre, Reception, and Canon Formation.* Cambridge: Cambridge University Press, 2000.

Gamma. "History of a Critic," *Scribner's* 11, no. 6 (April 1876).

Gardner, Martin. "The Wandering Jew and the Second Coming," *Free Inquiry* 15, no. 3 (summer 1995): 31–33.

Garland, Henry and Mary. *The Oxford Companion to German Literature.* Oxford: Oxford University Press, 1997.

Garrett, John. "'Ending in Infinity': William Beckford's Arabian Tale," *Eighteenth-Century Fiction* 5, no. 1 (1992): 15–34.

Gates, Barbara T. *Victorian Suicide: Mad Crimes and Sad Histories.* Princeton, N.J.: Princeton Univ. Press, 1988.

Gaudet, Jodie R. "Wells's 'The Country of the Blind,'" *Explicator* 59, no. 4 (summer 2001): 195.

Gaut, Berys. "The Paradox of Horror," *British Journal of Aesthetics* 33, no. 4 (October 1993): 333–345.

Gemmett, Robert J. "The Caliph Vathek from England and the Continent to America," *American Book Collector* 18, no. 9 (May 1968): 12–19.

Gilbert, Sandra M., and Susan Gubar. *The Madwoman in the Attic,* 2nd ed. New Haven, Conn.: Yale University Press, 2000.

Gillan, Jennifer. "Focusing on the Wrong Front: Historical Displacement, the Maginot Line, and 'The Bluest Eye,'" *African American Review* 36, no. 2 (summer 2002): 283–298.

Glinert, Lewis. "Golem! the Making of a Modern Myth," *Symposium* 55, no. 2 (summer 2001): 78–91.

Glyn-Jones, William. "Beauty and the Beast: The Hellenic Culture Model as a Tool for Recovering the Original Human Blueprint," *Kindred Spirit* no. 61 (winter 2002): 45–47.

Goddu, Teresa A. "Blood Daggers and Lonesome Graveyards: The Gothic and Country Music," *South Atlantic Quarterly* 94, no. 1 (1995): 57–80.

———. *Gothic America: Narrative, History, and Nation.* New York: Columbia University Press, 1997.

———. "Vampire Gothic," *American Literary History* 11, no. 1 (spring 1999): 125–141.

Goldberg, Leonard S. "'This Gloom . . . Which Can Avail Thee Nothing': Cain and Skepticism," *Criticism* 41, no. 2 (spring 1999): 207.

Goldern, Catherine J. "George Cruikshank's Life, Times, and Art 2: 1835–1878," *Victorian Studies* 40, no. 4 (summer 1997): 680–682.

Goldner, Ellen J. "Other(ed) Ghosts: Gothicism and the Bonds of Reason in Melville, Chesnutt, and Morrison," *MELUS* 24, no. 1 (spring 1999): 59.

Golstein, Vladimir B. *Heroes of Their Times: Lermontov's Representation of the Heroic Self.* New Haven, Conn.: Yale University Press, 1992.

Goode, Okey. "Tobias Smollett: Novelist," *ANQ* 13, no. 3 (summer 2000): 61.

Goodlett, Debra. "Love and Addiction in 'Wuthering Heights,'" *Midwest Quarterly* 37, no. 3 (spring 1996): 316–327.

Gordon, Lyndall. *Charlotte Brontë: A Passionate Life.* New York: W. W. Norton, 1994.

Gordon, Mel, ed. *The Grand Guignol: Theatre of Fear and Terror.* New York: DaCapo, 1997.

Gorrara, Claire. *The Roman Noir in Post-War French Culture.* Oxford: Oxford University Press, 2003.

Gottschalk, Earl C. "Ray Bradbury Achieves His Own Fantasy," *Wall Street Journal* (October 28, 1985): 1.

Gould, Philip. "Race, Commerce, and the Literature of Yellow Fever in Early National Philadelphia," *Early American Literature* 35, no. 2 (2000): 157–186.

Govan, Sovan Y. "Connections, Links, and Extended Networks: Patterns in Octavia Butler's Science Fiction," *Black American Literature Forum* 18, no. 2 (1984): 82–87.

———. "Homage to Tradition: Octavia Butler Renovates the Historical Novel," *MELUS* 13, nos. 1–2 (1986): 79–96.

Graham, Ilse. *Goethe and Lessing: The Wellsprings of Creation.* New York: Harper & Row, 1973.

Grass, Sean C. "Nature's Perilous Variety in Rossetti's 'Goblin Market,'" *Nineteenth-Century Literature* 51, no. 3 (December 1996): 356–376.

Gray, John. "Draughtman's Contract," *New Statesman* 129, no. 4,173 (February 14, 2000): 51.

"Great Expectations," *Atlantic Monthly* 8, no. 47 (September 1861): 380–382.

Green, Andrew. "Location and the Journey in 'Frankenstein,'" *English Review* 11, no. 1 (November 2000): 20.

Greenwood, James. *The Wilds of London.* London: Chatto & Windus, 1874.

Greeson, Jennifer Rae. "The 'Mysteries and Miseries' of North Carolina: New York City, Urban Gothic Fiction, and *Incidents in the Life of a Slave Girl,*" *American Literature* 73, no. 2 (June 2001): 277–309.

Griffin, Amy A. "Jackson's 'The Lottery,'" *Explicator* 58, no. 1 (fall 1999): 44.

Griffin, Caroline. *Understanding Arthur Miller.* Columbia: University of South Carolina Press, 1996.

Griffin, Susan M. "'The Dark Stranger': Sensationalism and Anti-Catholicism in Sarah Josepha Hale's

Traits of American Life," Legacy 14, no. 1 (April 30, 1997): 13–24.

Gross, Robert F. "Consuming Hart: Sublimity and Gay Poetics in 'Suddenly Last Summer,'" *Theatre Journal* 47, no. 2 (May 1995): 229–251.

Grossman, Jonathan H. "The Mythic Svengali: Anti-aestheticism in 'Trilby,'" *Studies in the Novel* 28, no. 4 (winter 1996): 525–543.

Grove, Allen W. "To Make a Long Story Short: Gothic Fragments and the Gender Politics of Incompleteness," *Studies in Short Fiction* 34, no. 1 (1997): 1–10.

Groves, David. "'Confessions of an English Glutton': A (Probable) Source for James Hogg's 'Confessions,'" *Notes and Queries* 40, no. 1 (March 1993): 46–47.

Guest, Harry. "The Flowers of Evil: A New Translation of 'Les Fleurs du Mal,'" *Journal of European Studies* 24, no. 4 (December 1994): 413–417.

Guzlowski, John. "Isaac Bashevis Singer's 'Satan in Goray' and Bakhtin's Vision of the Carnivalesque," *CRITIQUE: Studies in Contemporary Fiction* 39, no. 2 (winter 1998): 167–175.

———. "Isaac Singer and the Threat of America," *Shofar* 20, no. 1 (fall 2001): 21.

Habibi, Don Asher. "The Experience of a Lifetime: Philosophical Reflections on a Narrative Device of Ambrose Bierce," *Studies in the Humanities* 29, no. 2 (December 2002): 83–109.

Hackmann, William Kent. "William Beckford: The Jamaican Connection," *Journal of Caribbean History* 32, no. 1–2 (1998): 23–45.

Hadley, Michael. *The Undiscovered Genre: A Search for the German Gothic Novel.* Berne: Peter Lang, 1978.

Hadlock, Philip G. "(Per)versions of Masculinity in Maupassant's 'La Mere aux Monstres,'" *French Forum* 27, no. 1 (winter 2002): 59–79.

Haining, Peter, ed. *The Shilling Shockers.* New York: St. Martin's, 1978.

Halberstam, Judith. "Technologies of Monstrosity: Bram Stoker's *Dracula,"* *Victorian Studies* 36, no. 3 (spring 1993): 333–354.

———. *Skin Shows: Gothic Horror and the Technology of Monsters.* Durham, N.C.: Duke University Press, 1995.

Hale, Dorothy J. "Profits of Altruism: *Caleb Williams* and *Arthur Mervyn,"* *Eighteenth-Century Studies* 22, no. 1 (1988): 47–69.

Hall, Joan Wylie. *Shirley Jackson: A Study of the Short Fiction.* New York: Twayne, 1993.

Hall, Patsy. "Building 'Bleak House,'" *English Review* 2001, no. 3 (February 2001): 24.

Hallissy, Margaret. "Reading the Plans: The Architectural Drawings in Umberto Eco's 'The Name of the Rose,'" *CRITIQUE: Studies in Contemporary Fiction* 42, no. 3 (spring 2001): 271.

Hamelman, Steve. "Rhapsodist in the Wilderness: Brown's Romantic Quest in 'Edgar Huntly,'" *Studies in American Fiction* 21, no. 2 (autumn 1993): 171–190.

Hamilton, Cynthia S. "Revisions, Rememories, and Exorcisms: Toni Morrison and the Slave Narrative," *Journal of American Studies* 30, no. 3 (1996): 30–32.

Hamlin, William M. "Casting Doubt in Marlowe's Doctor Faustus," *Studies in English Literature, 1500–1900* 41, no. 2 (spring 2001): 257.

Hammond, Alexander. "A Reconstruction of Poe's 1833 *Tales of the Folio Club,* Preliminary Notes," *Poe Studies* 5, no. 2 (December 1972): 25–32.

Hanson, Ellis. *Decadence and Catholicism.* Cambridge, Mass.: Harvard University Press, 1998.

Hardie, P. "The Speech of Pythagoras in Ovid, 'Metamorphoses' 15: Empedoclean Epos," *Classical Quarterly* 45, no. 1 (January–June 1995): 204.

Hargrove, Nancy D. "The Tragicomic Vision of Beth Henley's Drama," *Southern Quarterly* 22, no. 4 (summer 1984): 54–70.

Harries, Elizabeth W. "'Out in Left Field': Charlotte Smith's Prefaces, Bourdieu's Categories, and the Public Sphere," *Modern Language Quarterly* 58, no. 4 (December 1997): 457–473.

Hartman, D., et al. "Is There a Dissociative Process in Sleepwalking and Night Terrors?" *Postgraduate Medical Journal* 77, no. 906 (April 2001): 244.

Haslam, Richard. "Wilde's 'The Picture of Dorian Gray,'" *Explicator* 61, no. 2 (winter 2003): 96–98.

Haspel, Paul. "George Washington Cable and Bonaventure: A New Orleans Author's Literary Sojourn into Acadiana," *Southern Literary Journal* 35, no. 1 (fall 2002): 108–122.

Hawkins, Joan. "Gothic Revisited," *Review of Communication* 2, no. 3 (July 2002): 327–333.

Hecht, Anthony. "Walter de la Mare," *Wilson Quarterly* 21, no. 3 (summer 1997): 108–109.

Hedges, William L. "Charles Brockden Brown and the Culture of Contradictions," *Early American Literature* 9, no. 2 (1974): 107–142.

Heffern, Rich. "The Real Miracle: To Walk on Earth," *National Catholic Reporter* 38, no. 6 (December 7, 2001): 37–40.

Heller, Scott. "The Book That Created a Canon: 'Madwoman in the Attic' Turns 20," *Chronicle of Higher Education* 46, no. 17 (December 17, 1999): 20–21.

Heller, Terry. *The Delights of Terror: An Aesthetics of the Tale of Terror.* Urbana: University of Illinois Press, 1987.

Hempen, Daniela. "Bluebeard's Female Helper: The Ambiguous Role of the Strange Old Woman in the Grimms' 'Castle of Murder' and 'The Robber Bridegroom,'" *Folklore* 108 (1997): 45–48.

Hendershot, Cyndy. *The Animal Within: Masculinity and the Gothic.* Ann Arbor: University of Michigan Press, 1998.

Hennelly, Mark M. "Framing the Gothic: From Pillar to Post-Structuralism," *College Literature* 28, no. 3 (fall 2001): 68.

Hennessy, Brendan. *The Gothic Novel.* London: Longman, 1978.

Herdman, John. *The Double in Nineteenth-Century Fiction.* New York: Macmillan, 1990.

Heywood, Christopher. "Yorkshire Landscapes in 'Wuthering Heights,'" *Essays in Criticism* 48, no. 1 (January 1998): 13–33.

Hichens, Robert. *Tongues of Conscience.* London: Methuen, 1900.

Hildebrand, Dietrich von. *Fundamental Moral Attitudes.* New York: Longmans, Green, 1950.

Hiner, Susan. "Hand Writing: Dismembering and Remembering in Nodier, Nerval and Maupassant," *Nineteenth-Century French Studies* 30, nos. 3–4 (spring–summer 2002): 300–315.

Hitchens, Christopher. "Permanent Adolescent: His Vices Made Evelyn Waugh a King of Comedy and of Tragedy," *Atlantic Monthly* 291, no. 4 (May 2003): 107–112, 114–116.

Hodgson, John A., ed. *Sherlock Holmes: The Major Stories with Contemporary Critical Essays.* Boston: Bedford/St. Martin's, 1994.

Hodgson, Moira. "Die Räuber," *Nation* 243 (August 30, 1986): 155.

Hoeveler, Diane Long. "Gothic Drama as Nationalistic Catharsis," *Wordsworth Circle* 31, no. 3 (2000): 169–172.

———. *Gothic Feminism.* University Park: Pennsylvania State University Press, 1998.

———. "Postgothic Fiction: Joyce Carol Oates Turns the Screw on Henry James," *Studies in Short Fiction* 35, no. 4 (fall 1998): 355–372.

———. "Reading the Wound: Wollstonecraft's 'Wrongs of Women; or, Maria' and Trauma Theory," *Studies in the Novel* 31, no. 4 (winter 1999): 387.

Hoffman, Daniel. *Form and Fable in American Fiction.* New York: Oxford University Press, 1965.

Hoffman, Tod. "Dark Heart Beating: Conrad's Classic at 100," *Queen's Quarterly* 109, no. 1 (spring 2002): 73–84.

Hogsette, David S. "Margaret Atwood's Rhetorical Epilogue in 'The Handmaid's Tale': The Reader's Role in Empowering Offred's Speech Act," *Critique: Studies in Contemporary Fiction* 38, no. 4 (summer 1997): 262.

Hollingsworth, Keith. *The Newgate Novel, 1830–1847.* Detroit: Wayne State University Press, 1963.

Hopper, William. "A Werewolf of Our Own," *Maclean's* (October 28, 2002): 46.

Horner, Avril, ed. *European Gothic: A Spirited Exchange, 1760–1960.* Manchester: Manchester University Press, 2002.

Howard, Thomas. *The Novels of Charles Williams.* Fort Collins, Colo.: Ignatius Press, 1991.

Howe, Irving. "The Spell of Fagin—Reconsideration: 'Oliver Twist,'" *New Republic* 188 (June 20, 1983): 27–32.

———. *William Faulkner: A Critical Study.* New York: Vintage Books, 1962.

Howells, Carol Ann. *Margaret Atwood.* London: Macmillan, 1996.

Hudson, John. "Gothic, Romance and Satire in Northanger Abbey," *English Review* 12, no. 1 (September 2001): 21.

Hughes, Henry J. "Familiarity of the Strange: Japan's Gothic Tradition," *Criticism* 42, no. 1 (winter 2000): 59–89.

Hume, Beverly A. "Managing Madness in Gilman's 'The Yellow Wall-Paper,'" *Studies in American Fiction* 30, no. 1 (spring 2002): 3–30.

Hume, Robert. "Gothic Versus Romantic: A Revaluation of the Gothic Novel," *Publication of the Modern Language Association* 84 (1969): 282–290.

Hunt, Linda. "Charlotte Brontë and the Suffering Sisterhood," *Colby Library Quarterly* 19, no. 1 (1983): 7–17.

Hustis, Harriet. "Black and White and Read All Over: Performative Textuality in Bram Stoker's 'Dracula,'" *Studies in the Novel* 33, no. 1 (spring 2001): 18.

———. "'Reading Encrypted But Persistent': The Gothic of Reading and Poe's 'The Fall of the House of Usher,'" *Studies in American Fiction* 27, no. 1 (spring 1999): 3.

Hutchings, William. "On Writers and Writing," *World Literature Today* 68, no. 4 (autumn 1994): 819.

Ibsen, Kristine. *The Other Mirror: Women's Narrative in Mexico, 1980–1995.* Westport, Conn.: Greenwood, 1997.

Inness, Sherry. "'Loyal Saints or Devious Rascals': Domestic Servants in Edith Wharton's Stories 'The Lady's Maid's Bell' and 'All Souls,'" *Studies in Short Fiction* 36, no. 4 (fall 1999): 337–350.

"Irish Blood: Dracula," *Economist* 326, no. 7,796 (January 30, 1993): 85.

Isaac, Megan Lynn. "Sophia Lee and the Gothic of Female Community," *Studies in the Novel* 28, no. 2 (summer 1996): 200–217.

Isherwood, Charles. "The Woman in Black," *Variety* 383, no. 5 (June 18, 2001): 26.

Ivkovi, Milaca. "The Double as the 'Unseen' of Culture: Toward a Definition of *Doppelgänger,*" *Linguistics and Literature* 2, no. 7 (2000): 121–128.

Jackson, Trevor. "Demon Drink: George Cruikshank's 'The Worship of Bacchus' in Focus," *British Medical Journal* 322, no. 7,300 (June 16, 2001): 1,494.

James, Jamie. "The Caliph of Fonthill," *American Scholar* 72, no. 1 (winter 2003): 67–79.

Janson, H. W., and Anthony F. Janson. *History of Art,* 5th ed. rev. New York: Harry N. Abrams, 1997.

Jascoll, John. "Crowning a Literary Landmark," *Biblio* 4, no. 4 (April 1999): 36.

Jenkins, Ruth Y. "Authorizing Female Voice and Experience: Ghosts and Spirits in Kingston's 'The Woman Warrior' and Allende's 'The House of the Spirits,'" *MELUS* 19, no. 3 (fall 1994): 61–73.

Jerome, Jerome K. "Idle Idols," *Idler,* July 5, 1994.

Johannsen, Kristin L. "In Search of Lost Japan," *World and I* 17, no. 5 (May 2002): 106–113.

Johnson, Barbara E. "Allegory and Psychoanalysis," *Journal of African American History* 88, no. 1 (winter 2003): 66–70.

Johnson, George. "Algernon Blackwood," *English Literature in Transition, 1880–1920* 46, no. 2 (spring 2003): 195–199.

Johnson, Greg. "Blonde Ambition: An Interview with Joyce Carol Oates," *Prairie Schooner* 75, no. 3 (fall 2001): 15.

Kafer, Peter. "Charles Brockden Brown and Revolutionary Philadelphia: An Imagination in Context," *Pennsylvania Magazine of History and Biography* 116, no. 4 (1992): 467–498.

Kane, Paul. "Postcolonial/Postmodern Australian Literature and Peter Carey," *World Literature Today* 67, no. 3 (summer 1993): 519–522.

Kantrowitz, Barbara, et al. "The Bible's Lost Stories," *Newsweek* 142, no. 23 (December 8, 2003): 48–56.

Kaplan, Robert D. "Euphorias of Hatred: The Grim Lessons of a Novel by Gogol," *Atlantic Monthly* 291, no. 4 (May 2003): 44–45.

Karl, Frederick R. *The Adversary Literature: The English Novel in the Eighteenth Century: A Study in Genre.* New York: Farrar, Straus & Giroux, 1974.

Kauffmann, Stanley. "'night, Mother," *New Republic* 195 (October 13, 1986): 26.

———. Review of "The Birds," *New Republic* (April 13, 1963): 643.

Kayser, Wolfgang. *The Grotesque in Art and Literature.* Bloomington: Indiana University Press, 1963.

Keil, James C. "Hawthorne's 'Young Goodman Brown': Early Nineteenth-Century and Puritan Constructions of Gender," *New England Quarterly* 69 (March 1996): 33–55.

Kendrik, Robert. "Edward Rochester and the Margins of Masculinity in 'Jane Eyre' and 'Wide Sargasso Sea,'" *Papers on Language & Literature* 30, no. 3 (summer 1994): 235–256.

Ketchin, Susan. *The Christ-Haunted Landscape: Faith and Doubt in Southern Fiction.* Jackson: University Press of Mississippi, 1994.

Kidwai, A. R., and Vincent Newey. "The Burning Heart in Poe's 'Al Aaraaf': Another Possible Source," *Notes and Queries* 44, no. 3 (September 1997): 365–366.

Kincaid, James R. "*The Crimson Petal and the White:* The Victorian Nanny Diaries," *New York Times,* September 15, 2002: 14.

King, Richard H. *A Southern Renaissance: The Cultural Awakening of the American South, 1930–1955.* Oxford: Oxford University Press, 1980.

King, Stephen. *Danse Macabre.* New York: Berkley, 1997.

Kirby, Kathleen M. "Resurrection and Murder: An Analysis of Mourning," *American Imago* 50, no. 1 (spring 1993): 55–68.

Kirk, Connie Ann. *J. K. Rowling: A Biography.* Westport, Conn.: Greenwood Press, 2003.

Klimasmith, Betsy. "Slave, Master, Mistress, Slave: Genre and Interracial Desire in Louisa May Alcott's Fiction," *American Transcendental Quarterly* 11, no. 2 (1997): 115–135.

Klinghoffer, David. "Religious Fiction," *National Review* 55, no. 23 (December 8, 2003): 48–49.

Knight, Stephen. "The Case of the Great Detective," *Meanjin* 40, no. 2 (1981): 175–185.

Knox-Shaw, Peter. "'Vathek' and 'The Seven Fountains' by Sir William Jones," *Notes and Queries* 42, no. 1 (March 1995): 75–76.

Kohlschmidt, Werner. *A History of German Literature, 1760–1805.* New York: Holmes & Meier, 1975.

Kosenko, Peter. "A Marxist/Feminist Reading of Shirley Jackson's 'The Lottery,'" *New Orleans Review* 12, no. 1 (spring 1985): 27–32.

Koval, Ramona. "The Unexamined Life," *Meanjin* 46, no. 3/4 (1997): 666–672.

Koven, Mikel J. "'Have I Got a Monster for You!': Some Thoughts on the Golem, the X-Files, and the Jewish Horror Movie," *Folklore* 111, no. 2 (October 2000): 217.

Kozlowski, Lisa. "A Source for Ann Radcliffe's 'The Mysteries of Udolpho,'" *Notes and Queries* 44, no. 2 (June 1997): 228–229.

Kristeva, Julia. *Powers of Horror: An Essay on Abjection.* New York: Columbia University Press, 1982.

Kucich, Greg. "Women's Historiography and the (Dis)embodiment of Law: Ann Yearsley, Mary Hays, Elizabeth Benger," *Wordsworth Circle* 33, no. 1 (winter 2002): 3–7.

Kutchen, Larry. "The 'Vulgar Threat of the Canvas': Revolution and the Picturesque in Ann Eliza Bleecker, Crevecoeur, and Charles Brockden Brown," *Early American Literature* 36, no. 3 (2001): 395–425.

Labriola, Patrick. "Edgar Allan Poe and E. T. A. Hoffmann: The Double in 'William Wilson' and 'The Devil's Elixirs,'" *International Fiction Review* 29, nos. 1–2 (January 2002): 69–77.

LaChance, Charles. "Naive and Knowledgeable Nihilism in Byron's Gothic Verse," *Papers on Language & Literature* 32, no. 4 (fall 1996): 339–368.

Lagree, Michel. "De Veuillot a Tardivel, ou les Ambiguites de la Haine de la Modernité," *Historical Studies* (annual 2001): 251.

Lamb, Jonathan. "Recent Studies in the Restoration and Eighteenth Century," *Studies in English Literature, 1500–1900* 41 no. 3 (summer 2001): 623.

Lamonaca, Maria. "Jane's Crown of Thorns: Feminism and Christianity in Jane Eyre," *Studies in the Novel* 34, no. 3 (fall 2002): 245 263.

Lamonica, Drew. "Confounded Commas: Confusion in an Interpretation of Heathcliff," *Notes and Queries* 44, no. 3 (September 1997): 336.

Lane, Ann J. *To Herland and Beyond.* New York: Meridian, 1991.

Lane, Christopher. "Bulwer's Misanthropes and the Limits of Victorian Sympathy," *Victorian Studies* 44, no. 4 (summer 2002): 597–625.

Langer, Adam. "Italian Hero: Umberto Eco," *Book* (September–October 2002): 62–63.

Lathers, Marie. "'L'Eve Future' and the Hypnotic Feminine," *Romanic Review* 84, no. 1 (January 1993): 43–54.

Latta, Alan D. "Spinell and Connie: Joyce Carol Oates Re-Imagining Thomas Mann?" *Connotations* 9, no. 3 (1999/2000): 316–329.

Laughlin, Karen L. "Criminality, Desire, and Community: A Feminist Approach to Beth Henley's *Crimes of the Heart*," *Women and Performance* (1986): 35–51.

Leask, Nigel. "Irish Republicans and Gothic Eleutherarchs: Pacific Utopias in the Writings of Theobald Wolfe Tone and Charles Brockden Brown," *Huntington Library Quarterly* 63, no. 3 (2000): 347–367.

Leitch, Vincent B., gen. ed. *The Norton Anthology of Theory and Criticism.* New York: W. W. Norton, 2001.

Leiter, Samuel L. *Kabuki Encyclopedia: An English-Language Adaptation of Kabuki Jiten.* Westport, Conn.: Greenwood, 1979.

Lemasters, Carol. "Roles of a Lifetime," *Gay & Lesbian Review* 7, no. 3 (summer 2000): 48.

Levine, George, and U. C. Knoepflmacher, eds. *The Endurance of Frankenstein: Essays on Mary Shelley's Novel.* Berkeley: University of California Press, 1979.

Levine, Paul. "The American Novel Begins," *American Scholar* 35, no. 1 (1965): 134–148.

Levy, Eric P. "The Psychology of Loneliness in 'Wuthering Heights,'" *Studies in the Novel* 28, no. 2 (summer 1996): 158–177.

Lew, Joseph W. "The Deceptive Other: Mary Shelley's Critique of Orientalism in Frankenstein," *Studies in Romanticism* 30 (1991): 255–283.

———. "'Unprepared for Sudden Transformations': Identity and Politics in 'Melmoth the Wanderer,'" *Studies in the Novel* 26, no. 2 (summer 1994): 173–195.

Lewis, R. W. B. *Edith Wharton: A Biography.* New York: Fromm International, 1985.

Liggins, Emma. "The Medical Gaze and the Female Corpse: Looking at Bodies in Mary Shelley's 'Frankenstein,'" *Studies in the Novel* 32, no. 2 (summer 2000): 129.

Livesey, Margot. "The Double Life of Robert Louis Stevenson," *Atlantic Monthly* 274, no. 5 (November 1994): 140–146.

Lockhart, John Gibson. *The Life of Sir Walter Scott, Bart.* Edinburgh: Adam & Charles Black, 1884.

Lockwood, Robert P. "Maria Monk," *Catholic Heritage* (November/December 1996): 19–21.

Long, Richard W. "The England of Charles Dickens," *National Geographic* 145, no. 4 (April 1974): 443–481.

Longueil, Alfred. "The Word 'Gothic' in Eighteenth Century Criticism," *Modern Language Notes* 38, no. 8 (1923): 459–461.

Lovecraft, H. P. *The Annotated Supernatural Horror in Literature.* New York: Hippocampus, 2000.

Lovell-Smith, Rose. "Anti-housewives and Ogres' Housekeepers: The Roles of Bluebeard's Female Helper," *Folklore* 113, no. 2 (October 2002): 197–214.

Ludwig, Sami. "Metaphors, Cognition and Behavior: The Reality of Sexual Puns in 'The Turn of the Screw,'" *Mosaic* 27, no. 1 (March 1994): 33–53.

Lüth, Max. *European Folktale: Form and Nature*. Bloomington: Indiana University Press, 1982.

Lyall, Sarah. "A Writer's Tale Is Victorian; His Past, Gothic," *New York Times*, October 28, 2002: E1.

Mack, Robert L. *Thomas Gray: A Life*. New Haven, Conn.: Yale University Press, 2000.

Mackenthun, Gesa. "Captives and Sleepwalkers: The Ideological Revolutions of Post-Revolutionary Colonial Discourse," *European Review of Native American Studies* 11, no. 1 (1997): 19–26.

Mackenzie, Scott. "Ann Radcliffe's Gothic Narrative and the Readers at Home," *Studies in the Novel* 31, no. 4 (winter 1999): 409.

———. "Confessions of a Gentrified Sinner: Secrets in Scott and Hogg," *Studies in Romanticism* 41, no. 1 (spring 2002): 3–33.

MacNeil, Robert. *Eudora Welty: Seeing Black and White*. Jackson: University Press of Mississippi, 1990.

Madoff, Mark. "The Useful Myth of Gothic Ancestry," *Studies in Eighteenth-Century Culture* 8 (1979): 337–350.

"The Madwoman in the Attic: The Woman Writer and the 19th Century Literary Imagination," *Women and Language* 24, no. 1 (spring 2001): 39.

Maixner, Paul. *Robert Louis Stevenson: The Critical Heritage*. London: Routledge, Chapman & Hall, 1981.

Mangin, Edward. *An Essay on Light Reading*. London: Ridgway, 1805.

Mangione, Jerre. "Vampire," *New Republic* 81, no. 1,043 (November 28, 1934): 82–83.

Manly, William M. "The Importance of Point of View in Brockden Brown's 'Wieland,'" *American Literature* 35, no. 3 (1963): 311–312.

Manning, Susan L. "Enlightenment's Dark Dreams: Two Fictions of Henry Mackenzie and Charles Brockden Brown," *Eighteenth-Century Life* 21, no. 3 (1997): 39–56.

Manwaring, Randle. "Memories of Walter de la Mare," *Contemporary Review* 264, no. 1,538 (March 1994): 149–152.

Marcus, Steven. "Frankenstein: Myths of Scientific and Medical Knowledge and Stories of Human Relations," *Southern Review* 38, no. 1 (winter 2002): 188–202.

Markley, Robert. "Lactilla, Milkwoman of Clifton: The Life and Writings of Ann Yearsley, 1753–1806," *Studies in English Literature, 1500–1900* 37, no. 3 (summer 1997): 637–672.

Marling, William. *The American Roman Noir: Hammett, Cain, and Chandler*. Athens: University of Georgia Press, 1995.

Marrouchi, Mustapha. "Exile Runes," *College Literature* 28, no. 3 (fall 2001): 88.

Marrs, Suzanne. *One Writer's Imagination: The Fiction of Eudora Welty*. Baton Rouge: Louisiana State University Press, 2002.

Martens, Catherine. "Mother-Figures in *Surfacing* and *Lady Oracle*: An Interview with Margaret Atwood," *American Studies in Scandinavia* 16, no. 1 (1984): 45–54.

Martin, Sandra. Review of *The Robber Bride*, in *Quill & Quire* 59, no. 9 (September 1993).

Martin, Tony. "Transformations and Ambiguities in Keats's 'Lamia,'" *English Review* 13, no. 3 (February 2003): 6–9.

Martine, James J. *The Crucible: Politics, Property, and Pretense*. New York: Twayne, 1993.

Maus, Derek. "The Devils in the Details: The Role of Evil in the Short Fiction of Nikolai Vasilievich Gogol and Nathaniel Hawthorne," *Papers on Language & Literature* 38, no. 1 (winter 2002): 76.

May, Claire B. "'Christabel' and Abjection: Coleridge's Narrative in Process on Trial," *Studies in English Literature, 1500–1900* 37, no. 4 (autumn 1997): 699–723.

McCann, Andrew. "Colonial Gothic," *Australian Literary Studies* 19, no. 4 (October 2000): 399.

McCormick, Patrick. "Painted Out of the Picture," *U.S. Catholic* 68, no. 11 (November 2003): 36–38.

McGann, Jerome. "Mary Robinson and the Myth of Sappho," *Modern Language Quarterly* 56, no. 1 (March 1995): 55–76.

McGlathey, James M., ed. *The Brothers Grimm and Folktales*. Urbana: University of Illinois Press, 1992.

McIntyre, Clara Frances. *Ann Radcliffe in Relation to Her Time*. New Haven, Conn.: Yale Studies in English, 1970.

McMurray, Price. "Disabling Fictions: Race, History, and Ideology in Crane's 'The Monster,'" *Studies in American Fiction* 26, no. 1 (spring 1998): 51–72.

McMurtry, Jo. *Understanding Shakespeare's England*. Hamden, Conn.: Archon Books, 1989.

McNutt, Dan J. *The Eighteenth-Century Gothic Novel: An Annotated Bibliography of Criticism and Selected Texts*. New York: Garland, 1975.

McSweeney, Kerry. "'What's the Import?': Indefinitiveness of Meaning in Nineteenth-century Parabolic Poems," *Style* 36, no. 1 (spring 2002): 36–55.

Meadows, Susannah. "Who's Afraid of the Big Bad Werewolf?" *Newsweek*, August 26, 2002: 57.

Meigs, Cornelia, et al. *A Critical History of Children's Literature*. New York: Macmillan, 1953.

Melada, Ivan. "Oliver Twist: Whole Heart and Soul," *Studies in the Novel* 27, no. 2 (summer 1995): 218–230.

Messent, Peter B. *Literature of the Occult.* Englewood Cliffs, N.J.: Prentice-Hall, 1981.

Metzcher-Smith, Marilyn K. "James's 'The Beast in the Jungle,'" *Explicator* 53, no. 3 (spring 1995): 147–148.

Meyer, Michael J., ed. *Literature and the Grotesque.* Amsterdam: Rodopi, 1995.

Meyer, Susan. "Colonialism and the Figurative Strategy of *Jane Eyre,*" *Victorian Studies* 33, no. 2 (1990): 247–268.

Meyers, Jeffrey. *Joseph Conrad: A Biography.* New York: Cooper Square Press, 2001.

Meyers, Laura. "Fantasy Art Charms Collectors in the Art Market," *Art Business News* 29, no. 4 (April 2002): 48–50.

Michie, Elsie B. "Buying Brains: Trollope, Oliphant, and Vulgar Victorian Commerce," *Victorian Studies* 44, no. 1 (autumn 2001): 77–99.

Miesel, Sandra. "Dismantling *The Da Vinci Code,*" *Crisis,* September 1, 2003.

Mighall, Robert. *A Geography of Victorian Gothic Fiction: Mapping History's Nightmares.* Oxford: Oxford University Press, 1999.

Mikkonen, Kai. "Electric Lines of Desire: Narrative and the Woman's Body in Villiers de l'Isle-Adam's 'Future Eve,'" *Literature and Psychology* 44, nos. 1–2 (spring–summer 1998): 23–53.

Miller, Corki, and Mary Ellen Snodgrass. *Storytellers.* Jefferson, N.C.: McFarland, 1998.

Miller, Robin Feuer. "The Castle in the Gothic Novel," *Nineteenth Century* 9, nos. 1–2 (1984): 3–5, 48.

Mitchell, Angus. "New Light on the 'Heart of Darkness,'" *History Today* 49, no. 12 (December 1999): 20–27.

Moers, Ellen. "Female Gothic: Monsters, Goblins, Freaks," *New York Review of Books,* April 4, 1974: 30–42.

———. *Literary Women.* New York: Oxford University Press, 1977.

———. "The Monster's Mother," *New York Review of Books,* March 21, 1974: 24–33.

Mogen, David. *Ray Bradbury.* Boston: G. K. Hall, 1986.

Monahan, Kathleen Nolan. "Brown's 'Arthur Mervyn' and 'Ormond,'" *Explicator* 45, no. 3 (spring 1987): 18–20.

Monkman, Leslie G. "A World under Sentence: Richardson and the Interior," *University of Toronto Quarterly* 67, no. 1 (winter 1997–98): 244–245.

Moore, Gene M. "Art of Darkness," *Book,* May–June 2003: 22–23.

Morgentaler, Goldie. "Meditating on the Low: A Darwinian Reading of 'Great Expectations,'" *Studies in English Literature, 1500–1900* 38, no. 4 (autumn 1998): 707.

Morillo, John, and Wade Newhouse. "History, Romance, and the Sublime Sound of Truth in 'Ivanhoe,'" *Studies in the Novel* 32, no. 3 (fall 2000): 267.

Morley, Sheridan. "Dusting Off the Gaslight Thriller," *International Herald Tribune,* August 20, 1997: 10.

Motion, Andrew. *Keats.* Chicago: University of Chicago Press, 1999.

Mulvey-Roberts, Marie. "Fame, Notoriety and Madness: Edward Bulwer-Lytton Paying the Price of Greatness," *Critical Survey* 13, no. 2 (May 2001): 115–135.

Mulvihill, James. "A Periodical Source for Peacock's 'Headlong Hall,'" *Notes and Queries* 44, no. 3 (September 1997): 334–335.

Murdoch, H. Adlai. "Ghosts in the Mirror: Colonialism and Creole Indeterminacy in Brontë and Sand," *College Literature* 29, no. 1 (winter 2002): 1–31.

Murphy, John Patrick Michael. "An Early Advocate of Freedom of the Press," *Free Inquiry* 20, no. 3 (summer 2000): 54.

Mussari, Mark. "L'Heure Bleue," *Scandinavian Studies* 73, no. 1 (spring 2001): 43.

Mussell, Kay. *Women's Gothic and Romantic Fiction: A Reference Guide.* Westport, Conn.: Greenwood, 1981.

Nabokov, Vladimir. *Lectures on Russian Literature.* New York: Harcourt Brace, 1981.

Nadal, Marita. "Beyond the Gothic Sublime: Poe's Pym or the Journey of Equivocal (E)motion," *Mississippi Quarterly* 53, no. 3 (summer 2000): 373.

Napier, Elizabeth R. *The Failure of the Gothic.* Oxford: Oxford University Press, 1987.

Naremore, James. "American Film Noir: The History of an Idea," *Film Quarterly* 49, no. 2 (winter 1995): 12–28.

Nassaar, Christopher S. "Andersen's 'The Shadow' and Wilde's 'The Fisherman and His Soul': A Case of Influence," *Nineteenth-Century Literature* 50, no. 2 (September 1995): 217–224.

———. "Andersen's 'The Ugly Duckling' and Wilde's 'The Birthday of the Infanta,'" *Explicator* 55, no. 2 (winter 1997): 83–85.

———. "Wilde's 'The Ballad of Reading Gaol,'" *Explicator* 53, no. 3 (spring 1995): 158–161.

———, and Nataly Shaheen. "Wilde's 'Salomé,'" *Explicator* 59, no. 3 (spring 2001): 132.

Nattermann, Udo. "Dread and Desire: 'Europe' in Hawthorne's 'The Marble Faun,'" *Essays in Literature* 21, no. 1 (spring 1994): 54–66.

Neff, D. S. "'Manfred' and the Mac-Ivors," *ANQ* 10, no. 4 (fall 1997): 24–29.

Neill, Edward. "The Secret of 'Northanger Abbey,'" *Essays in Criticism* 47, no. 1 (January 1997): 13–32.

Nickell, Joe. "Exorcism! Driving Out the Nonsense," *Skeptical Inquirer* 25, no. 1 (January 2001): 20.

———. "Germany: Monsters, Myths, and Mysteries," *Skeptical Inquirer* 27, no. 2 (March–April 2003): 24–28.

Nickles, Thomas. "The Golem: What Everyone Should Know about Science," *British Journal for the Philosophy of Science* 46, no. 2 (June 1995): 261–266.

Nicoll, Allardyce. *A History of Early Nineteenth-Century Drama, 1800–1850.* Cambridge: Cambridge University Press, 1930.

Nigro, Kathleen Butterly. "Rebecca as Desdemona: 'A Maid That Paragons Description and Wild Fame,'" *College Literature* 27, no. 3 (fall 2000): 144.

Nixon, Nicola. "'Wide Sargasso Sea' and Jean Rhys's Interrogation of the 'Nature Wholly Alien' in 'Jane Eyre,'" *Essays in Literature* 21, no. 2 (fall 1994): 267–284.

Nordius, Janina. "A Tale of Other Places: Sophia Lee's 'The Recess' and Colonial Gothic," *Studies in the Novel* 34, no. 2 (summer 2002): 162–176.

"Northanger Canon," http://www.lib.virginia.edu/speccol/exhibits/gothic/north.html.

Northey, Margot. *The Haunted Wilderness: The Gothic and Grotesque in Canadian Fiction.* Toronto: University of Toronto Press, 1976.

Norton, Rictor, ed. *Gothic Readings: The First Wave, 1764–1840.* London: Leicester University Press, 2000.

———. *The Mistress of Udolpho.* London: Leicester University Press, 1999.

Norwood, Liza West. "'I May Be a Stranger to the Grounds of Your Belief': Constructing Sense of Place in Wieland," *Early American Literature* 38, no. 1 (winter 2003): 89–123.

Novak, Ralph. "The Vampire Lestat," *People Weekly* 24 (November 25, 1985): 21–22.

Nunokawa, Jeff. "The Importance of Being Bored: The Dividends of Ennui in 'The Picture of Dorian Gray,'" *Studies in the Novel* 28, no. 3 (fall 1996): 357–371.

Oates, Joyce Carol. "Madison at Guignol," *Kenyon Review* 24, no. 1 (winter 2002): 43–50.

———. "Romance and Anti-Romance: From Brontë's 'Jane Eyre' to Rhys's 'Wide Sargasso Sea,'" *Virginia Quarterly Review* 61, no. 6 (winter 1985): 44–58.

———. *Telling Stories.* New York: W. W. Norton, 1998.

———. *Where I've Been and Where I'm Going.* New York: Plume, 1999.

Ogier, Darryl. "Night Revels and Werewolfery in Calvinist Guernsey," *Folklore* 109 (1998): 53–62.

Okon, Christine M. "Dark City: The Lost World of *Film Noir*," *Journal of Popular Film and Television* 29, no. 4 (winter 2002): 190–191.

O'Mealy, Joseph H. "Rewriting Trollope and Yonge: Mrs. Oliphant's Phoebe Junior and the Realism Wars," *Texas Studies in Literature and Language* 39, no. 2 (summer 1997): 125–138.

O'Neill, John. "Freud and the Passions," *Canadian Journal of Sociology* 24, no. 1 (December–February 1998): 158–162.

Oost, Regina B. "'Servility and Command': Authorship in 'Melmoth the Wanderer,'" *Papers on Language & Literature* 31, no. 3 (summer 1995): 291–312.

"An Opera House Phantom," *New York Times,* February 19, 1911: 90.

Orel, Harold. *Critical Essays on Rudyard Kipling.* New York: G. K. Hall, 1989.

Orlans, Harold. "Canonizing the Marquis de Sade," *Change* 28, no. 4 (July–August 1996): 6–7.

Owen, Jim. "Phoenix Jackson, William Wallace, and King MacLain: Welty's Mythic Travelers," *Southern Literary Journal* 34, no. 1 (fall 2001): 29–43.

Ozolins, Aija. "Dreams and Doctrines: Dual Strands in Frankenstein," *Science-Fiction Studies* 2 (July 1975): 103–110.

Paffard, Mark. *Kipling's Indian Fiction.* New York: St. Martin's Press, 1989.

Paglia, Camille. *Sexual Personae.* New York: Vintage Books, 1990.

Pahl, Dennis. "The Gaze of History in 'Benito Cereno,'" *Studies in Short Fiction* 32, no. 2 (spring 1995): 171–183.

Paige, Linda Rohrer. "White Trash, Low Class, and No Class At All: Perverse Portraits of Phallic Power in Flannery O'Connor's 'Wise Blood,'" *Papers on Language & Literature* 33, no. 3 (summer 1997): 325–333.

Parkinson, Edward. "'That 'ere Ingian's One of Us!': Orality and Literacy in 'Wacousta,'" *Studies in the Novel* 29, no. 4 (winter 1997): 453–475.

Parks, Ward. "Prey Tell: How Heroes Perceive Monsters in Beowulf," *Journal of English and Germanic Philology* 92, no. 1 (January 1993): 1–16.

Parry, Susan. "Coleridge's 'Christabel,'" *Explicator* 58, no. 3 (spring 2000): 133.

———. "Keats's Lamia," *Explicator* 59, no. 4 (summer 2001): 178.

Passaro, Vince. "The Violent Bear It Away," *Harper's Magazine* 293, no. 1,756 (September 1996): 64–70.

Patey, Douglas Lane. *The Life of Evelyn Waugh: A Critical Biography.* Oxford: Blackwell, 1998.

Paulson, Ronald. "Gothic Fiction and the French Revolution," *English Literary History* 48 (1981): 532–553.

Payne, James Robert. "New South Narratives of Freedom: Rereading George Washington Cable's 'Tite

Poulette' and 'Madame Delphine,'" *MELUS* 27, no. 1 (spring 2002): 3–24.

Pearl, Nancy. "Gaslight Thrillers: The Original Victorians," *Library Journal* 126, no. 3, (February 15, 2001): 228.

Pearson, Jacqueline. "'These Tags of Literature': Some Uses of Allusion in the Early Novels of Angela Carter," *CRITIQUE: Studies in Contemporary Fiction* 40, no. 3 (spring 1999): 248.

Perkins, David. "The 'Ancient Mariner' and Its Interpreters: Some Versions of Coleridge," *Modern Language Quarterly* 57, no. 3 (September 1996): 425–448.

Perry, Seamus. "Reading 'The Eve of St. Agnes': The Multiples of Complex Literary Transaction," *Modern Philology* 100, no. 1 (August 2002): 130–133.

Petch, Simon. "The Business of the Barrister in 'A Tale of Two Cities,'" *Criticism* 44, no. 1 (winter 2002): 27–43.

Peters, John G. "Inside and Outside 'Jane Eyre' and Marginalization through Labeling," *Studies in the Novel* 28, no. 1 (spring 1996): 57–75.

Petersen, Kirsten Holst. "Gambling on Reality," *Australian Literary Studies* 15, no. 2 (1991): 107–116.

Petrie, Paul R. "Charles W. Chesnutt, 'The Conjure Woman,' and the Racial Limits of Literary Mediation," *Studies in American Fiction* 27, no. 2 (autumn 1999): 183.

Phillipson, Mark. "Byron's Revisited Haunts," *Studies in Romanticism* 39, no. 2 (summer 2000): 303.

Piacentino, Ed. "Poe's 'The Black Cat' as Psychobiography: Some Reflections on the Narratological Dynamics," *Studies in Short Fiction* 35, no. 2 (spring 1998): 153–168.

———. "'Sleepy Hollow' Comes South: Washington Irving's Influence on Old Southwestern Humor," *Southern Literary Journal* 30, no. 1 (fall 1997): 27–42.

Pitcher, E. W. "On Authorship of Essay Serials in the European Magazine and The Lady's Monthly Museum: George Brewer and G. Bedingfield," *Notes and Queries* 44, no. 2 (June 1997): 238–239.

Pittock, Murray G. H. "John Wilmot and Mr. Rochester," *Nineteenth-Century Literature* 41, no. 4 (1987): 462–469.

Pizzichini, Lillian. "The Blue House," *New Statesman* 132, no. 4,636 (May 5, 2003): 46–47.

Platzner, Robert L. "'Gothic versus Romantic': A Rejoinder," *Publication of the Modern Language Association* 86 (1971): 266–274.

Polet, Jeff. "A Blackened Sea: Religion and Crisis in the Work of Par Lagerkvist," *Renascence: Essays on Values in Literature* 54, no. 1 (fall 2001): 47–66.

Pollin, Burton R. "Poe's 'Ulalume': Its Likely Source," *ANQ* 1, no. 1 (January 1988): 17–20.

Poovey, Mary. "Ideology and the Mysteries of Udolpho," *Criticism: A Quarterly for Literature and the Arts* 21 (1979): 307–330.

Porter, David. "From Chinese to Goth: Walpole and the Gothic Repudiation of Chinoiserie," *Eighteenth-Century Life* 23, no. 1 (1999): 46–58.

Porter, Laurence M. "Poetiques de Baudelaire dans 'Les Fleurs du Mal': Rythme, Parfum, Lueur," *Romanic Review* 90, no. 2 (March 1999): 263.

"Premature Burial," *Journal of the American Medical Association* 279, no. 3, (January 21, 1998): 182.

Price, Robert M. "H. P. Lovecraft: Prophet of Humanism," *Humanist* 61, no. 4 (July 2001): 26.

Priestman, Martin. *Detective Fiction and Literature: The Figure on the Carpet.* London: Macmillan, 1990.

Pritchard, Hollie. "Poe's 'The Tell-Tale Heart,'" *Explicator* 61, no. 3 (spring 2003): 144–147.

Pugh, William White Tison. "Boundless Hearts in a Nightmare World: Queer Sentimentalism and Southern Gothicism in Truman Capote's 'Other Voices, Other Rooms,'" *Mississippi Quarterly* 51, no. 4 (fall 1998): 663.

Punter, David. *Gothic Pathologies: The Text, the Body and the Law.* New York: St. Martin's Press, 1998.

———. *The Literature of Terror,* vol. 1, 2nd ed. London: Longman, 1996.

Radin, Paul. *The Trickster: A Study in American Indian Mythology.* New York: Schocken Books, 1972.

Rafailovich, Pnina. "Tennessee Williams's South," *Southern Studies* 23, no. 2 (1984): 191–197.

Rajan, Tilottama. "Framing the Corpus: Godwin's 'Editing' of Wollstonecraft in 1798," *Studies in Romanticism* 39, no. 4 (winter 2000): 511.

Ramchand, Kenneth. *The West Indian Novel and Its Background.* New York: Barnes & Noble, 1970.

Ramsey, William M. "Family Matters in the Fiction of Charles W. Chesnutt," *Southern Literary Journal* 33, no. 2 (spring 2001): 30.

Ramsland, Katherine. "Eloquent Fantasies," *Biblio,* October 1998: 30.

———. *The Witches' Companion: The Official Guide to Anne Rice's Lives of the Mayfair Witches.* New York: Ballantine Books, 1996.

Rancour-Laferriere, Daniel. *Russian Nationalism from an Interdisciplinary Perspective: Imagining Russia.* Lewiston, N.Y.: Edwin Mellen Press, 2001.

Ranger, Paul. *Terror and Pity Reign in Every Breast: Gothic Drama in the London Patent Theatres, 1750–1820.* London: Society for Theatre Research, 1991.

Rappaport, Julian. "Community Narratives: Tales of Terror and Joy," *American Journal of Community Psychology* 28, no. 1 (February 2000): 1.

Rashkin, Esther. "Art as Symptom: A Portrait of Child Abuse in 'The Picture of Dorian Gray,'" *Modern Philology* 95, no. 1 (August 1997): 68–80.

Rayner, J. L., and G. T. Crook, eds. *The Complete Newgate Calendar.* London: Navarre Society Limited, 1926.

Reider, Noriko T. "The Emergence of Kaidan-shu: The Collection of Tales of the Strange and Mysterious in the Edo Period," *Asian Folklore Studies* 60, no. 1 (April 2001): 79.

Reidy, Maurice Timothy. "Breaking the Code," *Commonweal* 130, no. 15 (September 12, 2003): 46.

Reiss, John. "Hawthorne's 'The Scarlet Letter,'" *Explicator* 53, no. 4 (summer 1995): 200–201.

Review of *Caroline Lamb, This Infernal Woman,* by Susan Normington, *Contemporary Review* 279, no. 1,627 (August 2001): 126.

Review of *Nick of the Woods, Southern Literary Messenger* 3, no. 4 (April 1837): 254–257.

Rexroth, Kenneth. "Goethe," *Saturday Review,* April 19, 1969: 21.

Ribalow, M. Z. "Script Doctors," *The Sciences* 38, no. 6 (November–December 1998): 26–31.

Rice, Anne. "How I Write," *Writer* 114, no. 2 (February 2001): 66.

Rice, Thomas Jackson. "Death and Love in Iris Murdoch's 'The Time of the Angels,'" *CRITIQUE: Studies in Contemporary Fiction* 36, no. 2 (winter 1995): 130–144.

Richardson, John. *The Annals of London.* Berkeley: University of California Press, 2000.

Ringe, Donald A. "The Critical Response to Nathaniel Hawthorne's 'The Scarlet Letter,'" *ANQ* 7, no. 1 (January 1994): 61–62.

Rivers, Christopher. "Inintelligibles pour Une Femme Honnete: Sexuality, Textuality and Knowledge in Diderot's 'La Religieuse' and Gautier's 'Mademoiselle de Maupin,'" *Romanic Review* 86, no. 1 (January 1995): 1–29.

Roberts, Adam. "Dickens's Jarnydyce and Lytton's Gawtrey," *Notes and Queries* 43, no. 1 (March 1996): 45–46.

Roberts, Rex. "Sex and Death in Transylvania," *Insight on the News* 12, no. 21 (June 3, 1996): 32–33.

Robertson, Ritchie. "The Tale of Bluebeard in German Literature from the Eighteenth Century to the Present," *Journal of European Studies* 31, no. 2 (June 2001): 230–231.

Robinson, E. Arthur. "'New Approaches' in Poe Criticism," *Poe Studies* 4, no. 2 (December 1971): 48–50.

Rombes, Nicholas Jr. "'All Was Lonely, Darksome, and Waste': 'Wieland' and the Construction of the New Republic," *Studies in American Fiction* 22, no. 2 (spring 1994): 37–46.

Ronald, Ann. "Terror-Gothic: Nightmare and Dream," in *The Female Gothic.* Montreal: Eden Press, 1983: 176–186.

Ronay, Gabriel. *The Dracula Myth.* London: W. H. Allen, 1972.

Roof, Maria. "Maryse Conde and Isabel Allende: Family Saga Novels," *World Literature Today* 70, no. 2 (spring 1996): 283–288.

Rosen, Marjorie, and Nancy Matsumoto. "Lady of the Spirits," *People Weekly,* 41, no. 16 (May 2, 1994): 107–109.

Rosenberg, Samuel. *The Come As You Are Masquerade Party.* Englewood Cliffs, N.J.: Prentice-Hall, 1970.

Rosenman, Ellen Bayuk. "Spectacular Women: The Mysteries of London and the Female Body," *Victorian Studies* 40, no. 1 (autumn 1996): 31–64.

Roth, Marty. "Gilman's Arabesque Wallpaper," *Mosaic* 34, no. 4 (December 2001): 145–162.

Rout, Kathleen. "Who Do You Love? Anne Rice's Vampires and Their Moral Transition," *Journal of Popular Culture* 36, no. 3 (winter 2003): 473–479.

Rowan, Steven. "'Smoking Myriads of Houses': German-American Novelists View 1850s St. Louis," *Gateway Heritage* 20, no. 4 (2000): 30–41.

Rowell, Geoffrey. "Dickens and the Construction of Christmas," *History Today* 43, no. 17 (December 1993): 17–24.

Ruland, Richard, and Malcolm Bradbury. *From Puritanism to Postmodernism: A History of American Literature.* New York: Penguin, 1991.

Ruskin, John. *Modern Painters.* Boston: Dana Estes, 1873.

Sage, Victor. *Horror Fiction in the Protestant Tradition.* New York: St. Martin's, 1988.

Saglia, Diego. "Looking at the Other: Cultural Difference and the Traveller's Gaze in 'The Italian,'" *Studies in the Novel* 28, no. 1 (spring 1996): 12–37.

Said, Edward W. *Orientalism.* New York: Vintage, 1979.

Salvaggio, Ruth. "Octavia Butler and the Black Science-Fiction Heroine," *Black American Literature Forum* 18 (fall 1984): 78–81.

Sandiford, Keith A. "'Monk' Lewis and the Slavery Sublime: The Agon of Romantic Desire in the 'Journal,'" *Essays in Literature* 23, no. 1 (spring 1996): 84–98.

Sauvage, Leo. "Phantom of the Opera," *New Leader* 71, no. 3 (February 22, 1988): 21–22.

Sawyer, Richard. "What's Your Title?—'The Turn of the Screw,'" *Studies in Short Fiction* 30, no. 1 (winter 1993): 53–61.

Scandura, Jani. "Deadly Professions: Dracula, Undertakers, and the Embalmed Corpse," *Victorian Studies* 40, no. 1 (autumn 1996): 1–31.

Schaffer, Talia. "'A Wilde Desire Took Me': The Homoerotic History of Dracula," *English Literary History* 61, no. 1 (summer 1994): 381–435.

Schaum, Melita. "'Erasing Angel': The Lucifer-Trickster Figure in Flannery O'Connor's Short Fiction," *Southern Literary Journal* 33, no. 1 (fall 2000): 1.

Schimank, Uwe. "Daydreaming and Self-Assertion: The Life of Charlotte Brontë," *Bios* 14, no. 1 (2001): 3–25.

Schmitt, Cannon. *Alien Nation: Nineteenth-Century Gothic Fictions and English Nationality*. Philadelphia: University of Pennsylvania Press, 1997.

———. "Techniques of Terror, Technologies of Nationality: Ann Radcliffe's 'The Italian,'" *English Literary History* 61, no. 4 (winter 1994): 853–876.

Schneider, Steven Jay. "Thrice-told Tales: The Haunting, from Novel to Film . . . to Film," *Journal of Popular Film and Television* 30, no. 3 (fall 2002): 166–176.

Scholem, Gershom. *Kabbalah*. New York: Meridian Books, 1978.

———. *Origins of the Kabbalah*. Princeton, N.J.: Princeton University Press, 1987.

Schueller, Malini Johar. "Harems, Orientalist Subversions and the Crisis of Nationalism: The Case of Edgar Allan Poe and 'Ligeia,'" *Criticism* 37, no. 4 (fall 1995): 601–623.

Scott, John. "The Rise and Fall of Fonthill Abbey," *British History Illustrated* 2, no. 3 (1975): 2–11.

Seabury, Marcia Bundy. "The Monsters We Create: Woman on the Edge of Time and Frankenstein," *Critique: Studies in Contemporary Fiction* 42, no. 2 (winter 2001): 131–143.

Sedgwick, Eve Kosofsky. *Between Men: English Literature and Male Homosocial Desire*. New York: Columbia University Press, 1985.

———. "The Character in the Veil: Imagery of the Surface in the Gothic Novel," *Publication of the Modern Language Association* 96, no. 2 (1981): 255–270.

———. *Epistemology of the Closet*. Los Angeles: University of California Press, 1992.

Sen, Sambudha. "'Bleak House,' 'Vanity Fair,' and the Making of an Urban Aesthetic," *Nineteenth-Century Literature* 54, no. 4 (March 2000): 480.

Senf, Carol A. "Bram Stoker: History, Psychoanalysis and the Gothic," *Victorian Studies* 42, no. 4 (summer 2000): 675.

———. "Dracula: The Unseen Face in the Mirror," *Journal of Narrative Technique* 9 (1979): 170.

Serper, Zvika. "'Between Two Worlds': The Dybbuk and the Japanese Noh and Kabuki Ghost Plays," *Comparative Drama* 35, no. 3 (fall 2001): 345–376.

Setzer, Sharon. "Mary Robinson's Sylphid Self: The End of Feminine Self-fashioning," *Philological Quarterly* 75, no. 4 (fall 1996): 501–520.

———. "Romancing the Reign of Terror: Sexual Politics in Mary Robinson's 'Natural Daughter,'" *Criticism* 39, no. 4 (fall 1997): 531–550.

Shannon, Sandra G. "Blues, History, and Dramaturgy," *African American Review* 27, no. 4 (winter 1993): 539–559.

Shapiro, Laura. "Just an Ordinary Day," *Newsweek* 129, no. 2 (January 13, 1997): 70.

Sharp, Michele Turner. "Elegy unto Epitaph: Print Culture and Commemorative Practice in Gray's 'Elegy Written in a Country Churchyard,'" *Papers on Language & Literature* 38, no. 1 (winter 2002): 3.

Sharrett, Christopher. "The Endurance of *Film Noir*," *USA Today* 127, no. 2,638 (July 1998): 79.

Shaw, S. Bradley. "New England Gothic by the Light of Common Day: Lizzie Borden and Mary E. Wilkins Freeman's 'The Long Arm,'" *New England Quarterly* 70, no. 2 (1997): 211–236.

Shawn, St. John. "An Updated Publication History of 'The Yellow Wall-Paper,'" *Studies in Short Fiction* 34, no. 2 (spring 1997): 237.

Sherwin, Byron L. "The Golem, Zevi Ashkenazi, and Reproductive Biology," *Judaism: A Quarterly Journal of Jewish Life and Thought* 44, no. 3 (summer 1995): 314–322.

Signorotti, Elizabeth. "Repossessing the Body: Transgressive Desire in 'Carmilla' and 'Dracula,'" *Criticism* 38, no. 4 (fall 1996): 607–632.

Sikorska, Liliana. "Constructing the Middle Ages in Contemporary Literature and Culture: The Reading of Iris Murdoch's 'The Green Knight,'" *Studia Anglica Posnaniensia* (annual 2000): 259–271.

Simon, John. "The End of Immortality," *Opera News* 60, no. 9 (January 20, 1996): 12–16.

Smethurst, James. "Invented by Horror: The Gothic and African American Literary Ideology in *Native Son*," *African American Review* 35, no. 1 (2001): 29–40.

Smith, A. G. Lloyd. "Gothic Reception," *European Contributions to American Studies* 14, no. 1 (1988): 184–190.

Smith, Andrew. *Gothic Radicalism: Literature, Philosophy and Psychoanalysis in the Nineteenth Century*. New York: St. Martin's Press, 2000.

Smith, Greg. "The Literary Equivalent of a Big Mac and Fries?: Academics, Moralists, and the Stephen King Phenomenon," *Midwest Quarterly* 43, no. 4 (summer 2002): 329–346.

———. "Supernatural Ambiguity and Possibility in Irving's 'The Legend of Sleepy Hollow,'" *Midwest Quarterly* 42, no. 2 (winter 2001): 174.

Smith, Lisa. "Landscape and Place in Wuthering Heights," *English Review* 11, no. 1 (September 2000): 22.

Solomon, Irving D. "Latin American Women in Literature and Reality: García Márquez's 'One Hundred Years of Solitude,'" *Midwest Quarterly* 34, no. 2 (winter 1993): 192–205.

Southgate, M. Therese. "The Combat of the Giaour and Hassan," *JAMA* 285, no. 13 (April 4, 2001): 1,677.

Speaight, George. "The Origin of Punch and Judy: A New Clue?" *Theatre Research International* 20, no. 3 (autumn 1995): 200–206.

Spector, Judith Ann. "Marriage, Endings, and Art in Updike and Atwood," *Midwest Quarterly* 34, no. 4 (summer 1993): 426–445.

Spector, Robert Donald. *English Gothic: A Bibliographical Guide to Writers from Horace Walpole to Mary Shelley.* Westport, Conn.: Greenwood, 1984.

Spiller, Elizabeth A. "'Searching for the Route of Inventions': Retracing the Renaissance Discovery Narrative in Gabriel García Márquez," *CLIO* 28, no. 4 (summer 1999): 375.

Sringhall, John. "Horror Comics: The Nasties of the 1950s," *History Today* 44, no. 7 (July 1994): 10–13.

Starzyk, Lawrence J. "The Gallery of Memory: The Pictorial in 'Jane Eyre,'" *Papers on Language & Literature* 33, no. 3 (summer 1997): 288–309.

Steinitz, Rebecca. "Diaries and Displacement in *Wuthering Heights*," *Studies in the Novel* 32, no. 4 (winter 2000): 407.

Stephens, Robert O. *The Family Saga in the South: Generations and Destinies.* Baton Rouge: Louisiana State University Press, 1995.

Stevens, Carol. "Creatures for the Millennium," *Print* 50, no. 3 (May/June 1996): 36–45.

Stevens, David. *The Gothic Tradition.* Cambridge: Cambridge University Press, 2000.

Stewart, Charles. "Erotic Dreams and Nightmares from Antiquity to the Present," *Journal of the Royal Anthropological Institute* 8, no. 1 (June 2002): 1.

Stipe, Stormy. "The Ghosts of Henry James," *Biblio* (September 1998): 16.

Stoicheff, Peter. "'Something Uncanny': The Dream Structure in Ambrose Bierce's 'An Occurrence at Owl Creek Bridge,'" *Studies in Short Fiction* 30, no. 3 (summer 1993): 349–357.

Stoneman, Patsy. *Brontë Transformations: The Cultural Dissemination of "Wuthering Heights" and "Jane Eyre."* Upper Saddle River, N.J.: Prentice-Hall, 1996.

———. "Catherine Earnshaw's Journey to Her Home among the Dead: Fresh Thoughts on 'Wuthering Heights' and 'Epipsychidion,'" *Review of English Studies* 47, no. 188 (November 1996): 521–533.

Su, John J. "'Once I Would Have Gone Back . . . But Not Any Longer': Nostalgia and Narrative Ethics in 'Wide Sargasso Sea,'" *CRITIQUE: Studies in Contemporary Fiction* 44, no. 2 (winter 2003): 157–174.

Sullivan, Ceri. "Faustus and the Apple," *Review of English Studies* 47, no. 185 (February 1996): 47–50.

Sullivan, Jack. *Horror Literature: A Core Collection and Reference Guide.* New York: R. R. Bowker, 1981.

Sullivan, Rosemary. *The Red Shoes: Margaret Atwood Starting Out.* New York: HarperCollins, 1998.

Summers, Montague. *A Gothic Bibliography.* New York: Russell & Russell, 1964.

———. *The Gothic Quest: A History of the Gothic Novel.* London: Fortune Press, 1969.

Sundel, Al. "Heartaches and Limitations: Isaac Bashevis Singer," *Partisan Review* 69, no. 2 (spring 2002): 272–282.

Sweeney, Gerald M. "O'Connor's 'Wise Blood,'" *Explicator* 56, no. 2 (winter 1998): 108–109.

Symons, Julian. *The Tell-Tale Heart: The Life and Works of Edgar Allan Poe.* New York: Harper & Row, 1978.

Talese, Nan A. *Book Group Companion to Margaret Atwood's "The Robber Bride."* New York: Doubleday, 1993.

Tarr, Mary Muriel. *Catholicism in Gothic Fiction: A Study of the Nature and Function of Catholic Materials in Gothic Fiction in England, 1762–1820.* Washington, D.C.: Catholic University of America Press, 1946.

Tatar, Maria. *The Hard Facts of the Grimms' Fairy Tales.* Princeton, N.J.: Princeton University Press, 1987.

Tayko, Gail. "Teaching Isabel Allende's 'La Casa de los Espiritus,'" *College Literature* 19, no. 3 (October–February 1992): 228–232.

Taylor, Anya. "Coleridge and the Pleasures of Verse," *Studies in Romanticism* 40, no. 2 (winter 2001): 547–570.

———. "Coleridge's 'Christabel' and the Phantom Soul," *Studies in English Literature, 1500–1900* 42, no. 4 (autumn 2002): 707–731.

———. "Filling the Blanks: Coleridge and the Inscrutable Female Subject," *Wordsworth Circle* 33, no. 2 (spring 2002): 84–88.

Taylor, Susan B. "Stoker's 'Dracula,'" *Explicator* 55, no. 1 (fall 1996): 29–31.

Terry, Reginald. *Victorian Popular Fiction, 1860–80.* London: Macmillan, 1983.

Terwilliger, Thomas. *Root of Evil.* New York: Herald Tribune Books, 1929.

Thomas, David Wayne. "The 'Strange Music' of Salomé: Oscar Wilde's Rhetoric of Verbal Musicality," *Mosaic* 33, no. 1 (March 2000): 15.

Thompson, David. "The Anarchic Fantasies of Evelyn Waugh," *Biblio* (September 1998): 24.

Thompson, G. R. "The Face in the Pool: Reflections on the *Doppelgänger* Motif in 'The Fall of the House of Usher,'" *Poe Studies* 5, no. 1 (June 1972): 16–21.

Thompson, G. Richard, intro. *Romantic Gothic Tales, 1790–1840*. New York: Harper & Row, 1979.

Thompson, Stith. *The Folktale*. Berkeley: University of California Press, 1977.

Thompson, Terry W. "Conrad's 'Heart of Darkness,'" *Explicator* 60, no. 1 (fall 2001): 27–30.

———. "James's 'The Jolly Corner,'" *Explicator* 56, no. 3 (summer 1998): 192–195.

———. "Shelley's 'Frankenstein,'" *Explicator* 58, no. 4 (summer 2000): 191.

Thomson, Douglass H., et al., eds. *Gothic Writers: A Critical and Bibliographical Guide*. Westport, Conn.: Greenwood, 2001.

———. "Terror High and Low: The Aikins' 'On the Pleasure Derived From Objects of Terror; with Sir Bertrand, A Fragment,'" *Wordsworth Circle*, 29, no. 1 (1998): 72–75.

Thomson, Heidi. "Eavesdropping on 'The Eve of St. Agnes': Madeline's Sensual Ear and Porphyro's Ancient Ditty," *Journal of English and Germanic Philology* 97, no. 3 (July 1998): 337.

Thormahlen, Marianne. "The Lunatic and the Devil's Disciple: The 'Lovers' in 'Wuthering Heights,'" *Review of English Studies* 48, no. 190 (May 1997): 183–197.

Thum, Maureen. "Feminist or Anti-feminist? Gender-coded Role Models in the Tales Contributed by Dorothea Viehmann to the Grimm Brothers' 'Kinder- und Hausmärchen,'" *Germanic Review* 68, no. 1 (winter 1993): 11–31.

Thurman, Judith. *Isak Dinesen: The Life of a Storyteller*. New York: St. Martin's Press, 1982.

Todorov, Tsvetan. *The Fantastic*. Ithaca, N.Y.: Cornell University Press, 1975.

Tosi, Alessandra. "Vladimir Odoevsky and Romantic Poetics," *Journal of European Studies* 29, no. 2 (June 1999): 226.

Trott, Nicola. "A Life of Licence and Gothic Literature," *National Post* 2, 257 (August 19, 2000): B10.

Trousdale, Rachel. "Self-invention in Isak Dinesen's 'The Deluge at Norderney,' *Scandinavian Studies* 74, no. 2 (summer 2002): 205–222.

Tsang, Lori. "From Warrior to Poet," *Women's Review of Books* 19, nos. 10–11 (July 2002): 6.

Tuan, Yi-Fu. *Landscapes of Fear*. New York: Pantheon Books, 1979.

Tucker, Edward L. "A New Letter by William Cullen Bryant," *ANQ* 14, no. 2 (spring 2001): 24.

Tucker, Herbert F. "House Arrest: The Domestication of English Poetry in the 1820s," *New Literary History* 25, no. 3 (summer 1994): 521–548.

Turner, Alice K. *The History of Hell*. New York: Harcourt Brace, 1993.

Turner, Jack. "Iris Murdoch and the Good Psychoanalyst," *Twentieth Century Literature* 40, no. 3 (fall 1994): 300–317.

Twitchell, James B. *The Living Dead: A Study of the Vampire in Romantic Literature*. Durham, N.C.: Duke University Press, 1981.

Tytler, Graeme. "Dickens's 'The Signalman,'" *Explicator* 53, no. 1 (fall 1994): 26–29.

Uraizee, Joy. "'She Walked Away without Looking Back': Christophine and the Enigma of History in Jean Rhys' 'Wide Sargasso Sea,'" *CLIO* 38, no. 3 (spring 1999): 261.

Van Ghent, Dorothy. *The English Novel: Form and Function*. New York: Harper Torchbooks, 1953.

Varma, Devendra P. *The Gothic Flame*. New York: Russell & Russell, 1966.

Varnado, S. L. *Haunted Presence: The Numinous in Gothic Fiction*. Tuscaloosa: University of Alabama Press, 1987.

Vause, Mikel. "Frontier Gothic: Terror and Wonder at the Frontier in American Literature," *Weber Studies* 11, no. 2 (fall 1994): 141–142.

Verhoeven, W. M. "Gothic Logic: Charles Brockden Brown and the Science of Sensationalism," *European Journal of American Culture* 20, no. 2 (2001): 91–99.

Vickers, Anita. "Social Corruption and the Subversion of the American Success Story in *Arthur Mervyn*," *Prospects* 23 (1998): 129–145.

Vincent, Deirdre. "Images of Goethe through Schiller's 'Egmont,'" *University of Toronto Quarterly* 69, no. 1 (winter 1999–2000).

Vine, Stephen. "The Wuther of the Other in 'Wuthering Heights,'" *Nineteenth-Century Literature* 49, no. 3 (December 1994): 339–359.

Viswanathan, Guari. "The Ordinary Business of Occultism," *Critical Inquiry* 27, no. 1 (autumn 2000): 1.

Voloshin, Beverly R. "*Wieland*: Accounting for Appearances," *New England Quarterly* 59, no. 3 (1986): 341–357.

Von Mucke, Dorothea. "The Imaginary Materiality of Writing in Poe's 'Ligeia,'" *Differences: A Journal of Feminist Cultural Studies* 11, no. 2 (summer 1999): 53.

Wain, Marianne. "The Double in Romantic Narrative: A Preliminary Study," *Germanic Review* 36, no. 4 (December 1961): 257–268.

Waldron, Mary. "Ann Yearsley: The Bristol Manuscript Revisited," *Triangle Journals* 3, no. 1 (1996).

Walker, Steven F. "James's 'The Turn of the Screw,'" *Explicator* 61, no. 2 (winter 2003): 94–96.

Walsh, Susan. "Bodies of Capital: 'Great Expectations' and the Climacteric Economy," *Victorian Studies* 37, no. 1 (autumn 1993): 73–98.

Warhol, Robyn. "Double Gender, Double Genre in 'Jane Eyre' and 'Villette,'" *Studies in English Literature, 1500–1900* 36, no. 4 (autumn 1996): 857–875.

Weales, Gerald. "Perera: The Yellow Wallpaper," *Commonweal* 120, no. 3 (February 12, 1993): 16–17.

Webber, Andrew J. *The Doppelgänger: Double Visions in German Literature.* Oxford: Clarendon Press, 1997.

Weinert, Laurent. "Angela Carter's 'The Bloody Chamber' at the Metal Shed at the Toy Factory," *Back Stage West* 10, no. 4 (January 23, 2003): 19.

Welch, Dennis M. "'Christabel,' 'King Lear,' and the Cinderella Folktale," *Papers on Language & Literature* 32, no. 3 (summer 1996): 291–313.

Welsch, Tricia. "Yoked Together by Violence," *Film Criticism* 22, no. 1 (fall 1997): 62–73.

Wesley, Marilyn C. *Refusal and Transgression in Joyce Carol Oates' Fiction.* Westport, Conn.: Greenwood, 1993.

———. "Reverence, Rape, Resistance: Joyce Carol Oates and Feminist Film Theory," *Mosaic* 32, no. 3 (September 1999): 75.

Whatley, John. "Romantic and Enlightened Eyes in the Gothic Novels of Percy Bysshe Shelley," *Gothic Studies* 1, no. 2 (1999): 201–221.

Wheatcroft, Geoffrey. "Not Green, Not Red, Not Pink: Oscar Wilde Cannot Be Simplified into an Irish Rebel, a Subversive Socialist, or a Gay Martyr," *Atlantic Monthly* 291, no. 4 (May 2003): 125–131.

White, Jeannette S. "Baring Slavery's Darkest Secrets: Charles Chesnutt's Conjure Tales as Masks of Truth," *Southern Literary Journal* 27, no. 1 (fall 1994): 85–103.

White, Pamela C. "Two Vampires of 1828," *Opera Quarterly* 5, no. 1 (spring 1987): 22–57.

White, Terry. "Allegorical Evil, Existentialist Choice in O'Connor, Oates and Styron," *Midwest Quarterly* 34, no. 4 (summer 1993): 383–397.

Whitt, Jan. *Allegory and the Modern Southern Novel.* Macon, Ga.: Mercer University Press, 1994.

Whyte, William. "An Architect of Promise: George Gilbert Scott (1839–1897) and the Late Gothic Revival," *English Historical Review* 118, no. 476 (April 2003): 542–543.

Wiesenthal, Christine. "Regarding Christina Rossetti's 'Reflection,'" *Victorian Poetry* 39, no. 3 (fall 2001): 389–407.

Wildgen, Katherine E. "Making the Shadow Conscious: The Enduring Legacy of Gaston Leroux," *Symposium* 55, no. 3 (fall 2001): 155–167.

Williams, Andrew P. "The Silent Threat: A (Re)viewing of the 'Sexual Other' in 'The Phantom of the Opera' and 'Nosferatu,'" *Midwest Quarterly* 38, no. 1 (autumn 1996): 90–101.

Williams, Anne. *Art of Darkness: A Poetics of Gothic.* Chicago: University of Chicago Press, 1995.

Williams, A. Susan, ed. *The Lifted Veil: The Book of Fantastic Literature by Women, 1800–World War II.* New York: Carroll & Graf, 1992.

Willingham-Sirmans, Karen, and Mary Lowe-Evans. "Jackson's 'The Tooth,'" *Explicator* 55, no. 2 (winter 1997): 96–98.

Willis, Chris. "The Female Sherlock: 'Lady Detectives' in Victorian and Edwardian Fiction," http://www.chriswillis.freeserve.co.uk/femsherlock.htm.

———. "Mary Elizabeth Braddon and the Literary Marketplace: A Study in Commercial Authorship," http://www.chriswillis.freeserve.co.uk/meb2.html.

Wilson, Colin. "Starlight Man: The Extraordinary Life of Algernon Blackwood," *Spectator* 287, no. 9,043 (December 1, 2001): 46–47.

Wilt, Judith. *Ghosts of the Gothic.* Princeton: Princeton University Press, 1980.

Windschuttle. Keith. "Edward Said's 'Orientalism' Revisited," *New Criterion* 17, no. 5 (January 1999): 30.

Winter, Douglas E. "The Man Who Invented American Gothic," *Insight on the News* 15, no. 2 (January 11, 1999): 36.

Winter, Kari. "Sexual/Textual Politics of Terror" in *Misogyny in Literature: An Essay Collection.* New York: Garland, 1992: 89–101.

Wohleber, Curt. "The Man Who Can Scare Stephen King," *American Heritage,* 46, no. 8 (December 1995): 82–90.

Wolf, Leonard. *Bluebeard: The Life and Crimes of Gilles de Rais.* New York: Clarkson N. Potter, 1980.

———. *A Dream of Dracula: In Search of the Living Dead.* New York: Popular Library, 1977.

Wolfe, Peter. *August Wilson.* New York: Twayne, 1999.

Wolff, Cynthia. "The Radcliffean Gothic Model," in *The Female Gothic.* Montreal: Eden Press, 1983: 207–223.

Wood, Charles W. "Mrs. Henry Wood: In Memoriam," *Argosy* 43 (1887): 251–270.

Wood, Ellen. "The Punishment of Gina Montani," *Colburn's New Monthly Magazine* 5, no. 2 (February 1852): 189–196.

Worth, George J. *William Harrison Ainsworth*. New York: Twayne, 1972.

Wright, Daniel L. "'The Prisonhouse of My Disposition': A Study of the Psychology of Addiction in 'Dr. Jekyll and Mr. Hyde,'" *Studies in the Novel* 26, no. 3 (fall 1994): 254–267.

Wright, Julia M. "Lewis's 'Anaconda': Gothic Homonyms and Sympathetic Distinctions," *Gothic Studies* 3, no. 3 (2001): 262–378.

Wyatt, Petronella. "Gothic Tales," *Spectator* 292, no. 9,119 (May 17, 2003): 85.

Wylie, Joan. *Shirley Jackson: A Study of the Short Fiction*. New York: Twayne, 1994.

Yarbrough, Scott. "The Dark Lady: Temple Drake as Femme Fatale," *Southern Literary Journal* 31, no. 2 (spring 1999): 50.

Young, Philip. "Born Decadent: The American Novel and Charles Brockden Brown," *Southern Review* 17, no. 3 (1981): 501–519.

Yousef, Nancy. "The Monster in a Dark Room: Frankenstein, Feminism, and Philosophy," *Modern Language Quarterly* 63, no. 2 (June 2002): 197–226.

Yuan Shu. "Cultural Politics and Chinese-American Female Subjectivity: Rethinking Kingston's 'Woman Warrior,'" *MELUS* 26, no. 2 (summer 2001): 199–224.

Zabus, Chantal. "Soifs," *World Literature Today* 71, no. 4 (autumn 1997): 745–746.

Zimansky, Curt R. "*Zastrozzi* and *The Bravo of Venice*: Another Shelley Borrowing," *Keats-Shelley Journal* 30 (1981): 15–17.

INDEX

Note: **Boldface** page numbers indicate main entries.

A

The Abbess (Ireland) 11
The Abbey of Clunedale (Drake) **1**
The Abbot of Montserrat; or, The Pool of Blood (Green) 115, 165
aberrant behavior **1–2.** *See also* obsession
  allegory and 4–5
  in *The Giaour* (Byron) 142–143
  Gogol, Nikolai, and 146–147
  in *Great Expectations* (Dickens) 170
  melodrama and 231
  in *The Narrative of Arthur Gordon Pym* (Poe) 248
  in *Nick of the Woods* (Bird) 254
  Oates, Joyce Carol, and 257
  in *Oscar and Lucinda* (Carey) 267
  possession and 278
  revenge as 291
  urban Gothic and 342
Absalom, Absalom (Faulkner) **3**, 4
Ada Reis (Lamb) 207
Addison, Joseph 157–158
"The Adventure of the Speckled Band" (Doyle) 85
"The Adventure of the Sussex Vampire" (Doyle) 347
"The Adventures of a Breach-of-Promise Con Man" (Capek) 48
The Adventures of Caleb Williams; or, Things As They Are (Godwin) **47–48**, 145, 324
The Adventures of Ferdinand Count Fathom (Smollett) 121, 321
Ainsworth, William Harrison **3–4**, 77, 253, 357
Alcott, Louisa May **7–8**, 91, 269
alienation. *See* outsiders
allegory **4–5**
  in "The Birthmark" (Hawthorne) 29
  in *Bleak House* (Dickens) 32–33
  in *Dracula* (Stoker) 87
  in *Frankenstein* (Shelley) 316
  García Márquez, Gabriel, and 134
  in "The Masque of the Red Death" (Poe) 222

in *The Red Shoes* (Andersen) 278
in *The Rime of the Ancient Mariner* (Coleridge) 294
in *The Scarlet Letter* (Hawthorne) 305–306
in *Something Wicked This Way Comes* (Bradbury) 321–322
vampire motif and 345
in *Vathek* (Beckford) 348
in "Young Goodman Brown" (Hawthorne) 373
Allende, Isabel **5–6**, 54, 62, 184–185, 259, 264
Alleyne, Ellen 302
Alraune (The mandrakes, Ewers) 106–107, 347
Ambrosio **6**, 76, 81, 92, 188, 350
American Gothic **6–9**
  aberrant behavior in 2
  anti-Catholicism in 12
  Atherton, Gertrude, and 14–15
  Benito Cereno (Melville) **26–27**
  Bierce, Ambrose, and 27
  Brown, Charles Brockden, and 41, 266, 360
  The Crucible (Miller) **66–67**
  diabolism in 76
  doppelgänger motif in 84
  German Gothic and 140
  Gothic convention and 154
  Illuminati novels and 187–188
  illusion in 188–189
  Nick of the Woods (Bird) 254
  settings 159
  shape-shifting in 315
  symbolism in 333
  terror fiction 335
  translation and 339–340
  urban Gothic in 343
  violence in 353–354
  wandering Jew motif in 357
  "The Yellow Wallpaper" (Gilman) 371–372
American Gothic Tales 257
American graveyard movement 162

"The Anaconda" (Lewis) **9**, 212
Anatomy of Criticism (Fry) 230
The Anatomy of Melancholy (Burton) 227
Anaya, Rudolfo 123, 249, 367
Andersen, Hans Christian **9–10**, 278
Anderson, Sherwood 167
"And of Clay Are We Created" (Allende) 5
Angels in America (Kushner) 246, 269
"Annabel Lee" (Poe) 275
Anne (Ann) of Swansea 10
Ansky, S. 54, 98–99
anti-Catholicism **11–12**
  in *The Da Vinci Code* (Brown) 70
  in *Der Geisterseher* (*The Ghost-Seer*, Schiller) 72
  female victims and 119
  in *The Italian* (Radcliffe) 192, 310
  in *The Letters of a Solitary Wanderer* (Smith) 320
  in *Melmoth the Wanderer* (Maturin) 223, 224, 229
  in *The Midnight Bell* (Lathom) 208
  in *The Monk* (Lewis) 6, 11, 53, 211–212, 235–236
  Roche, Regina, and 296
  in *Villette* (Brontë) 351–352
  Wilkinson, Sarah, and 364
anti-Semitism 356
Aphrodite, a Memoir of the Senses (Allende) 5
Applebee, John 252
arabesque **12–13**
architecture. *See* Gothic architecture and art
Ardath: The Story of a Dead Self (Corelli) 64
Armadale (Collins) 61
Arnow, Harriette 342
Around the World in 80 Days (Verne) 107
art. *See* Gothic architecture and art
Arthur Mervyn (Brown) **13–14**
Art of Darkness: A Poetics of Gothic (Williams) 158–159
As I Lay Dying (Faulkner) 167